THE TRAVELLER'S HANDBOOK

THE TRAVELLER'S HANDBOOK

Edited by
MELISSA SHALES

in association with
MARION RONKE
and RICHARD HARRINGTON

Published by
HEINEMANN : LONDON
and
WEXAS Ltd

William Heinemann Ltd
10 Upper Grosvenor Street, London W1X 9PA
LONDON MELBOURNE TORONTO
JOHANNESBURG AUCKLAND

This completely revised and enlarged edition first published 1985

434 14828 8

Printed in Great Britain at The Pitman Press, Bath

Contents

GETTING THERE BY:

YOUR SPECIAL NEEDS

PAPERS, RESERVATIONS, ETC.

MONEY, TAXES, ETC.

PREPARING YOUR THINGS

A BASIC GUIDE TO HEALTH

A PLACE TO STAY

DEALING WITH PEOPLE

WHEN THINGS GO WRONG

KEEPING TRACK

MAPS

DIRECTORIES

Rules and Regulations

Introduction

Travel has been endowed by the modern world with all the glamour and magical mystery lacking in the humdrum routine of our daily lives. Devotees come from every age and walk of life, from school children to old age pensioners, beauty queens to philosophers, and every one of them has a different, if exotic, inner vision of 'foreign climes'. Some dream of standing far above the world on Everest's peak; some of lying on golden beaches while lissom girls in overgrown daisy chains serve endless long cool drinks; some, fired by the romance of history, follow faithfully in the steps of Livingstone or Marco Polo. Yet to them all, travel is seen as an escape to an ideal world where problems and boredom are at an end, where they are heroes, where the scenery and way of life are enough to send you into raptures and where no one *ever* catches a cold.

Amongst the rapidly growing numbers leaving the Western world in search of their personal paradise, some, no doubt, find it. Others come up against mosquitos, draining heat, poor food and flat tyres; not to mention bureaucrats and bed bugs and hour upon hour of endless, empty, unchanging flatness, so bare of entertainment that the sight of a tree can bring delight. And many of them return home ill, much poorer, and with all sense of romance and adventure shattered.

Travel is not an automatic paradise – anything but. Most travellers do not last too long before they start fantasising about comfortable beds and thinking with affection of commuter trains and traffic jams. However those who know just what they will be up against and something of how to cope with it have a far greater chance of being able to take the horrors in their stride and really enjoy themselves along the way. If you have the right medicines, the ubiquitous traveller's tummy is a minor irritant for a couple of days; without them it can lay you out for weeks. So, as the Boy Scouts say, be prepared!

'Next time, I'll know better,' is a common cry amongst returning travellers. With good advice before you go, you can get it right first time. What *The Traveller's Handbook* is trying to do is to prepare the traveller for the worst (and, of course, the best), teaching everyone from the trans-Atlantic businessman to the 'round-the-world-on-$1-a-day' traveller how to look after themselves with minimum stress and maximum security. Few brochures are prepared to be realistic about the problems you will face; problems are bad publicity. We have tried to fill that gap, with tried and tested advice from experts, many of whom have learned over the years in an agonising process of trial and error.

Although early editions of *The Traveller's Handbook* went under other names, this is the fourth in a line of ever-expanding books, as we fill gaps in the information it contains, cover new situations arising from the changing face of travel, and hopefully, give more help to more people. The original book was aimed very precisely at the off-beat traveller and while each subsequent edition widened its scope, this is the first to cover all types of travel and all price ranges. The emphasis, of course, is still with the independent traveller who will be in far more need of advice than the package tourist with a courier to do his worrying. And while we have now included Europe, we are still concentrating on the Third World, about which far less is known and which provides a great many more problems. We have also included more information for Australians, New Zealanders and Canadians. As any traveller will tell you, there are a great many citizens of these countries slowly making their way around the world, often taking years to do so.

As before, the book is divided into two sections: the first, a series of chapters offering advice and information on a wide range of subjects from how to buy an air ticket or trace lost luggage to survival techniques should you be stranded away from civilization; the second consists of instant reference material for use both while planning a trip and when abroad. This is now listed in sections by subject with, for instance, *Publications* offering not only a comprehensive list of further reading, but also information on where to get hold of it.

Every attempt has been made to ensure accuracy, but it should be realized that things will obviously change during the lifespan of the book. We ask you to forgive inaccuracies caused by circumstances totally beyond our control. Inclusion of the name of a firm or association should not be taken to signify the testimony or approval of the editor or publishers. Nor are the views expressed or statements made by the text contributors anything but their own, and any instances of disagreement or contradiction between two authors should be laid at the door of human variability and not at that of the editor. Thanks are due to all the many organizations and individuals who responded to our requests for information. We should like to ask all readers to keep us up to date with any changes or new information suitable for publication in the next edition.

I should like to offer particular thanks to Marion Ronke, Ginny Lunn, Lorna Lloyd and Sally Harris, all of whom have spent endless hours at typewriters and telephones checking facts and compiling lists.

Melissa Shales
Editor

Notes on Contributors

Major Sir Crispin Agnew of Lochnaw, Bt., Royal Highland Fusiliers, was born in 1944 and began his career in exploration 22 years later as a member of the Royal Navy Expedition to East Greenland. He has since led Services Expeditions to East Greenland and Chile and been a member of expeditions to Elephant Island, Nuptse – where he reached about 7,925m – and Everest. He has climbed in the UK and the Alps since 1960. He is also Chief of the Clan.

Sarah Anderson grew up in London. After leaving school, she worked in a bookshop and then spent two years in the United States, travelling and working. After this she travelled extensively in Asia. On returning to England she took a degree in Chinese which was followed by further spells in bookshops. In 1980, she opened London's first travel bookshop selling both old and new books – thus combining her two main interests of travel and books.

Guy Arnold is an author and lecturer who has travelled widely in Africa. A contributor to many journals on African affairs, his books include *Kenyatta and the Politics of Africa*, *Modern Nigeria*, *Strategic Highways of Africa* (with Ruth Weiss) and *Aid in Africa*.

Martin Ayres has had a life-long interest in cycling, and was a track racing cyclist himself. For seven years he was Production Controller of Carlton Cycles (the lightweight division of Raleigh), and for the last few years he has been Editor of *Cycling* magazine.

Maurice and Maralyn Bailey were born in 1932 and 1941 respectively. They have been sailing for many years and in 1968 started to live aboard their boat. They are best remembered for their epic 118 day ordeal in the Pacific Ocean after they had been cast adrift in a liferaft when a wounded sperm whale attacked and sank their yacht *Auralyn*. Since their rescue they have built *Auralyn II* and completed a 32,000km circumnavigation of South America.

Betty Barnes first started travelling in her late teens with a cycle tour of Europe in 1950. She joined the Metropolitan Police later that year and was seconded to Nigeria from 1959 to 1961 to run the women's police force there. During her time in Africa she visited most West African countries from Cameroon to Sierra Leone, and over the next few years visited North Africa and the Near East. After her retirement from the police force in 1975, she travelled from Canada to southern Argentina and back, and then around the world. She now lives on Vancouver Island, British Columbia.

Since 1963, **Greg Brooks** (born 1944) has interspersed three periods of full-time study with teaching in France, Kenya, England and Northern Ireland. He has travelled widely in Eastern and Central Africa and in Western and Southern Europe.

Tony Bush is Editor of the international trade and finance magazine *Export Direction*, which he joined in 1977 from Fleet Street. He is also author of the *Business Travel Planner* (pub. Oyez), an updatable book which aims to help travellers arrange trips and avoid pitfalls.

John Carlton is a keen walker and rucksack traveller. He has been a member of the YHA for over 25 years and has also worked in the travel trade for the same time. After a long period of service on voluntary committees of the Association, he decided to bring both interests together and may currently be found behind the counter of YHA Travel in London. He has visited most countries in Western and Eastern Europe, Morocco, Canada and the USA.

David Chapelle has been a freelance journalist, marketing consultant and playwright for some twenty years now. Previously he was Marketing

Manager of Godfrey Davis and then Europcar UK.

Roger Chapman, MBE, BA, FRGS was commissioned into the Green Howards after completing a Geography degree at Oxford and a spell at Sandhurst. He has been involved in a great many expeditions – down the Blue Nile and Zaire Rivers, to East Greenland with the British Schools Exploration Society, and Papua New Guinea with Operation Drake amongst them. A novelist, and white water expert, he is currently National Selection Co-ordinator of Operation Raleigh.

Michael Colbourne, OBE, MB, ChBEd. 1942, FRCPEd. 1970, M. 1962, FFCM 1974, DPh University of London 1951 used to be Editor of *The Tropical Doctor* magazine. He is currently a part-time lecturer at the Ross Institute, London and a member of the World Health Organization's expert panel on Malaria, as well as being a Councillor of the Royal Society of Tropical Medicine and Hygiene.

Ingrid Cranfield edited three previous editions of this book: *Off the Beaten Track* (1977), *The Independent Traveller's Handbook* (1980) and *The Traveller's Handbook* (1982). She is a freelance writer and journalist, a translator, consultant and broadcaster. Her first book was *The Challengers: British and Commonwealth Adventure Since 1945* (1976) and her latest *Skiing Down Everest and Other Crazy Adventures* (Severn House, 1983). She is a Fellow of the Royal Geographical Society and a Member of Council of Endeavour Training Ltd.

Sheila Critchley is a Canadian journalist now based in London. She is currently running an airline in-flight magazine – perfect therapy for her (now cured) fear of flying.

René Dee was born in Switzerland in 1946 and educated in Britain, where he became a regular soldier in the Intelligence Corps, serving in Singapore and Malaysia. In 1967, after leaving the army, he travelled overland to India and Nepal and in 1969 led a series of three week adventure holidays to Morocco, from which stemmed his love of desert travel. By 1972 he had formed his own company specializing in treks by camel and mule. This ceased to trade in 1975, owing to economic hardships, and he went on to work for Twickenham Travel.

John Douglas, author and photographer, is a former Army officer who has travelled solo and with expeditions throughout Southern and South-East Asia, and through much of Africa and the Arctic. His most recent book is *Creative Techniques in Travel Photography*. He is a director of Geoslides Photo Library and advises a number of Third World countries on tourist development.

Doris Dow became a single expatriate in Central Africa, married, and spent 24 years there before returning to the UK. She is by profession a secretary and teacher of commercial subjects, but after active involvement with the Women's Corona Society in London on the information and briefing services, she is now Director of this department. She is also Editor-in-Chief of the Society's series of *Notes For Newcomers*.

Peggy Drage is a sociologist, painter and grandmother of seven. She has travelled widely in Europe and India, Sri Lanka and Nepal. On retirement, she and her husband did a six-month journey through the Americas following the Andes-Rockies chain, as well as visiting the Amazon Basin and the Galapagos Islands. She has returned several times since to Mexico, which has greatly influenced her painting, and had an exhibition in 1981 at the Anglo-Hispanic Institute in London.

Dr John Frankland is a General Practitioner who has been a caver for over 30 years and Medical Officer to the Cave Rescue Organization for more then fifteen. He has advised many British caving expeditions and explored caves in Europe and North and South America.

Michael Furnell has been involved with property journalism for more than three decades; he has edited *Homefinder* magazine since 1953 and in 1965 he founded *Homes Overseas*, the monthly specialist periodical devoted to the needs of people wishing to purchase a holiday or retirement home in the sun. He also started the quarterly magazine *Time-Sharing Homes and Holidays* three years ago and is a broadcaster on overseas property matters.

Jon Gardey grew up in California and has lived in Alaska, Switzerland and England. He is the author of a book on Alaska and his writing and photography have appeared in most of the major magazines in the world. He travels regularly to the remote parts of the globe. His latest involvement is with 'experimental travel' – a scheme to teach people to get the most from any trips they take.

Dr Bob Gibbons is an ecologist and photographer who has travelled widely in Asia and Europe on various expeditions. At present he works in nature conservation, but in his spare time he runs a slide library specializing in travel and natural history photographs.

Jan Glen, born in Australia, has travelled independently in West Africa, the Sahara, Europe and through Asia. She is joint author, with her husband, of *The Sahara Handbook*.

Simon Glen is an Australian who has lived and worked in Central and West Africa for over twenty years. He is a teacher by profession and has travelled by van through Africa, Asia and throughout Australia and New Zealand. With years of experience and an intimate knowledge of desert travel, he has compiled, with his wife, *The Sahara Handbook*.

Robin Hanbury-Tenison, OBE, is a well-known explorer, author and broadcaster. He has taken part in over a dozen major expeditions in South America, Africa and the Far East, is a Vice-President of the Royal Geographical Society and in 1977/8, led their largest scientific expedition ever to the Gunung Mulu National Park in Borneo. He has written a book about this expedition called *Mulu – The Rain Forest* and has also written several other books, his latest being an autobiography *Worlds Apart*. He is currently President of Survival International, the organization that seeks to prevent the extinction of the world's remaining tribal groups.

Geoff Hann was born in 1937 and began travelling extensively in 1969 after a period in industry. He founded Hann Overland in 1972, after travelling overland to Kathmandu, and has operated overland tours and adventure holidays since then, leading many of them personally.

Nick Hanna is a freelance journalist specializing in student and youth travel. He is presently Travel Editor of *National Student* and he also contributes regularly to other publications. He has travelled widely, particularly in Europe, Africa and Asia.

Bryan Hanson is an executive member of The Globetrotters Club and editor of the *Globetrotter's Handbook* as well as being a guest editor of the Globetrotters' magazine. He has worked as a driver and courier for the Overland Company, has lived in Africa and travelled extensively.

Richard Harrington is a widely travelled freelance travel writer.

Chris Hawkesworth has made over 40 films since 1967 for television, including two of expeditions in the Himalayas. He now works in the professional medium of 16mm and also broadcasts videotapes. His main interests are white-water river canoeing and sailing. He also runs an outdoor film hire distribution and wild water expedition equipment company.

Dagmar Hingston is presently employed as an electricity board saleslady. Her experience with disabled travellers began after her husband was diagnosed as suffering from multiple sclerosis – together they have travelled to many countries and are determined to keep doing so.

John Hoban is Director of Publicity for the BBC External Services.

David Hodgson, AIIP, was senior staff photojournalist and later picture editor with Features International. He has travelled throughout the world on assignments and his work has appeared in many magazines including *Life*, *Match*, and *Stern*. He is the author of eight books on photography.

Robert Holmes has travelled extensively to remote places throughout the world. He is an experienced mountaineer and has taken part in many expeditions. He is widely known and acknowledged as one of Britain's most accomplished wilderness photographers – his work has appeared in numerous books and magazines. He is presently living in California where, in between his travels, he continues to photograph, write and teach. He is contributing editor to *Darkroom Photography* magazine and teaches wilderness photography at the California Academy of Sciences. He has already been elected to membership of the prestigious American Society of Magazine Photographers.

Graham Holt has travelled extensively in Eastern and Western Europe, Southern Africa, South-East Asia and Taiwan privately as a railway enthusiast, amassing a personal collection of some 30,000 photographs and colour transparencies. In 1979, he married a sugar factory chemist he met while gathering information for a proposed book on Philippine Sugar Railways.

Malcolm Irvine is presently a registered Insurance broker. He has spent the last four years in insurance for adventure and overland travellers.

Jack Jackson is an experienced expedition leader and overland traveller, explorer, mountaineer, and driver. He is co-author with Ellen Crampton of *The Asian Highway* (Angus and Robertson, London 1979) and author of *The Four Wheel Drive Book* (Gentry, London, 1982), detailed and authoritative manuals for the overlander.

Diane Johnson joined the YHA at fourteen. Her travels have taken her overland to India, on the Trans-Siberian railway to Japan, to Iceland, Morocco, Kenya, Tanzania, Southern Africa, Israel and North America. She stays at Hostels wherever possible and works as YHA Education Liaison Officer in London.

Peter Lane is a Veterinary Surgeon currently practising in Surrey, England.

Ian Lyon reports regularly on overseas countries for BBC TV and radio, He presents 'Travel Choice' on BBC TV's *Pebble Mill at One*. He has travelled widely in Europe, America, the Caribbean, the Pacific and Africa. Formerly he was Editor of *The Illustrated London News* and Managing Editor with the Consumer Association, publishers of *Which?*

Colin McElduff is a Fellow of the Royal Geographical Society, the Royal Anthropological Institute and the Society of Antiquaries (Scotland). He served in the Royal West African Frontier Force in India, Burma and Africa during World War II. On leaving the Army he joined the Colonial Police Service, serving in Malaya, Cyprus, Nigeria and Borneo. He gained invaluable experience as a commander of special forces in Malaya and Cyprus and as a Staff Officer Operations during two national emergencies, co-ordinating police and military operations. In 1965 he returned to the UK and has settled down in Surrey. He is the author of several books on long-distance motoring and currently works for the Royal Automobile Club.

Eddie McGee, a former paratrooper and Sergeant Major in the regular Army, qualified diver, self-defence teacher and top Army survival expert, now runs his own Survival Centre at Pateley Bridge, Yorkshire. He has travelled the world as an explorer and professional survival adviser on many expeditions including the Zaïre River Expedition and Operation Drake. His books include *No Need to Die* (Crompton), *Stay Alive with Eddie McGee* (Corgi, based on the ITV series), *Fighting Back: A Woman's Guide to Self-Defence* (Sphere) and *Go Camping with Eddie McGee* (Corgi).

Alex McWhirter, born in 1948, has worked in the travel industry since he left school; with a large tour operator in Toronto, Canada in the early days; and later, back in the UK, with all kinds of travel outlets from sleepy suburban offices to the travel departments of multinational oil and chemical companies. He joined *Business Traveller* magazine as their Travel Adviser in 1979 and is now responsible for editing much of the magazine. He has travelled widely, especially in Europe, the Middle East and the Far East.

Alastair Matheson is a Kenyan journalist who has travelled widely in Africa as correspondent for *The Observer* and *Time* magazine. He also worked for some years with the United Nations, including the Children's Fund (UNICEF) and the Environmental Programme (UNEP). He is currently Editor of the wildlife magazine *Africana*, published in Nairobi.

Sylvia Matheson has spent most of her adult life in the East and now lives with her husband in Abu Dhabi (UAE). Author, broadcaster and lecturer, her books include *Persia: An Archaeological Guide*, *Time Off to Dig* (on archaeology in Afghanistan) and *The Tigers of Baluchistan* (life with a Baluch tribe). She has contributed articles to leading international publications, studied archaeology at London University, and worked on digs in Afghanistan, Pakistan, Burma and Iran. She now accompanies specialized groups as a guest lecturer on tours to Asian countries.

Dr Mark Milburn first visited Africa aged twenty. After some years in the Army, where his last uniform was that of the SAS, he undertook further travel in the Middle East and the Sahara. His published findings are extensive in journals of learned societies and he has written English language books on a Saharan journey, Tuareg origins, and the Saharan megaliths and stone structures.

Wendy Myers was born in Sheffield, England in 1941 and left home at the age of eighteen to see the world. Seven years later she returned home. The story of her hitchhiking, living and working experiences abroad is recounted in her book *Seven League Boots* (Hodder and Stoughton, 1969). She is a SRN, a State Certified Midwife, a Health Visitor and has studied at the Hospital for Tropical Diseases, London. She has done medical work in the Solomon Islands, Nepal and Burkina Faso (Upper Volta) and is currently employed by the Save the Children Fund.

Bob Nance is an Australian who took up sailing in 1963, when he was 24. He has since cruised nearly 160,000km, including three passages round Cape Horn. For five years he worked on tugs delivering fuel along the northwest coast of British Columbia.

David Orchard is a tour leader for Guerba Expeditions of Devizes, Wiltshire, and consequently spends most of his time in Africa. He writes about his travels from time to time for women's magazines.

Chris Parrott was born in 1946 in Aldershot, England, and has lived in France, Singapore, Spain and Brazil, as well as travelling extensively in Europe, the Middle East and the Americas. Until July 1977 he was Head of Geography and Physical Education in the British School, Rio de Janeiro. He occasionally leads overland trips to Peru and Bolivia. He edits *Trailfinder* magazine and has written a geography text book on South America.

E. G. Peacock, MBE, worked overseas as a Customs Officer for 27 years. From 1947 to 1962 he was Serving Officer in the Customs and Excise of Malaya. In 1964, he moved to Malawi, where, in 1969, he was promoted to Deputy Controller of Customs and Excise.

Tony Pearson is one of few people in Britain to have made a serious study of outdoor equipment, studying it at an academic level. He followed this by working for several years for Field and Trek (Equipment) Ltd and, while there, wrote a regular equipment column 'Gear Up' for *The Traveller*.

Christopher Portway has been a freelance travel writer for the best part of a decade, is the author of several books, Travel Editor of a women's magazine, and is a member of the Guild of Travel Writers.

Paul Pratt has been a ship's radio officer in the British Merchant Navy and an electronics engineer in Britain and Scandinavia. His interest in motorcycles began with cross country sporting trials and now he claims the longest continuous journey in motorcycle history which, between 1966 and 1979, took him through 48 countries, a distance of nearly 165,000km. He gives illustrated lectures, and his book *World Understanding on Two Wheels* is now in its second edition.

After graduating from Durhan University with a degree in geography, **Rowena Quantrill** married and has since lived in Belgium, Cuba, the Philippines, Nigeria, and Venezuela. She and her husband have four children, with whom they have travelled widely, including an overland bus trip from Kathmandu to London.

Philip Ray has been a journalist for the whole of his career and has specialized in writing about the airline and travel businesses for the past fifteen years. He was Deputy Editor of *Travel News*, the weekly UK travel trade newspaper from 1969 to 1978, when he switched to freelance writing and market research consultancy. He has travelled widely throughout the world on business but his favourite holiday pursuit is walking in the Alps, the Lake District or the Scottish Highlands.

Ray Reece is a tall (1.9m) electronics consultant who, at the age of 41, set a world record for the fastest cycle circumnavigation of the world: 20,800 road km in 143 days between June and November 1971. He was educated in Malta and the UK, speaks Arabic fluently and is also a water polo international. He sings, plays a guitar and drums and writes music.

Beth Roberts was born in Caernarvon, North Wales, and qualified as a science teacher in Wrexham in 1967. Travel became a consuming passion after she had travelled overland to Jordan for a three-month visit to her parents there. Since then she has spent every summer in southern Europe, the Middle East or North America. In 1980 she returned from a year spent travelling around the world visiting twenty countries.

Marion Ronke, born in 1960, is Dutch by birth, but grew up abroad living in Canada, Kenya, Italy and, for six years, India. She has travelled widely throughout Europe and overland to India. Now in England, she has a BA Hons. in Modern Languages and works as a travel consultant with WEXAS International.

David Ruddell is an Irishman who has lived and worked in West Africa for ten years, and still visits the region at least twice a year. He is a journalist and author, and is also involved in the travel trade. He writes regularly for the weekly magazine *West Africa* as well as various other publications, both in the UK and in West Africa.

Dave Saunders taught English and Geography in secondary schools for three years – one in

England and two in Jamaica. He then worked for two years as a feature writer and technical reporter on *Amateur Photographer* magazine. In 1979 he went freelance and now contributes regular articles to the photographic press in Britain, USA and Australia. He has written on photography, travel and adventure sports for a wide variety of magazines and newspapers. He has been Travel Editor of *Adventure Sports and Travel* and has edited *Sportscope* magazine. He is the author of two books, one on life in Jamaica, the other about West Indians in Britain. His colour/black and white picture library covers the Caribbean, North and South America, Europe, Australia, India and Nepal.

Mary Schantz is a freelance writer who contributes to *Mother Earth News* and writes a regular column on cookery for *Wilderness Camping* magazine. She also teaches 'Trek Out', a YMCA-sponsored camping and wilderness survival programme. She has done most of her camping in Alaska and in the Northern Appalachians.

Gilbert Schwartz, a teacher and veteran traveller, spent over a year researching and compiling his book, *The Climate Advisor* (Climate Guide Publications, New York), which has met with considerable success and is now in its second printing.

Melissa Shales, born in 1958, was brought up in Zimbabwe, but returned to Britain to do a degree in History and Archaeology at Exeter University. Since graduating, she has been a journalist, taking over as Editor of *The Traveller* in 1982. She has travelled widely in Africa and Europe and is a Fellow of the Royal Geographical Society.

Tim Sharman has worked as an engineer, a record producer, and a radio features writer, travelling abroad often, especially in Europe. In 1980, he spent five months walking across Eastern Europe from the Baltic to Istanbul, a journey which produced a great fund of stories, pictures and a book. He now heads the European Geographic Survey and hopes, by bringing back information and photographs that illuminate European events, projects and ways of life, to change people's 'mental map' of the region.

Anne Sharpley joined the Evening Standard in 1954 and for a number of years covered world events, starting with the Cyprus Emergency and Suez. She has won awards as Woman Journalist of the Year and Descriptive Writer of the Year. She has now 'retired' to travel writing and appears regularly on the travel page of the *New Standard*.

Ted Simon rode a Triumph 500cc motorcycle round the world, starting in 1973 and returning in 1977. He travelled extensively in Africa, Latin America, Australia and Asia and his articles appeared in the *Sunday Times*. His book on the journey is called *Jupiter's Travels* (Hamish Hamilton, UK, and Doubleday, USA).

Anthony Smith is a Zoologist by training and a writer, broadcaster, and presenter of television programmes, including the *Wilderness* series on BBC Television. His first expedition was to Iran with an Oxford University team in 1950. Since then he has ridden a motorcycle the length of Africa, written an account of the Royal Geographical Society/Royal Society Mato Grosso Expedition of 1967, and built and flown hydrogen-filled balloons and airships. He was co-founder of the British Balloon and Airship Club and sits on the RGS Expeditions Committee.

Richard Snailham was born in 1930. He read Modern History at Oxford and was a school teacher until, in 1965, he became a Senior Lecturer at the Royal Military Academy, Sandhurst. He has been on expeditions to the Middle East, Ethiopia, Zaïre, Jamaica, Ecuador, Honduras and Nepal and recently led parties of tourists to Ethiopia and China. He was co-founder and first Honorary Secretary of the Scientific Exploration Society, is the author of three expedition books and lectures widely on his travel experiences. He is Secretary for the council of the Young Explorers' Trust and President of the Globetrotters Club.

Victoria Southwell was educated in West Africa and Singapore before studying Photography at Manchester Polytechnic. She has worked as a stills photographer both in this country and overseas. During the autumn and winter of 1981/2 she was the photographer for the 'British Archaeological Project to Iraq' and in 1983 she was photographer to the Kora Research Project, a joint Royal Geographical Society and National Museums of Kenya multi-disciplinary expedition. She now works part-time for a photo-library while freelancing as a photographer and journalist and writing a book about a Victorian lady explorer.

Julie Batchelor is a teacher who travelled extensively during school and university vacations.

Her husband **John Batchelor** is a Fellow of the Royal Geographical Society and current chairman of the Globetrotters Club. He has travelled extensively in Africa including a one-year trans-Africa expedition and a trip through Africa on a motorcycle. In 1973, John and Julie travelled across the Sahara in a 20-year-old ex-RAF ambulance; in 1974 they made the first descent of the Zaïre River by kayak; and in 1976 and 1978 they took expeditions to Irian Jaya and Gabon.

Peter Boxhall started his career as an Arabist with Army Intelligence. Since then, he has worked and travelled in most of the major Arab countries, as Personal Secretary to the Sultan of Oman and for the Save the Children Fund in North Africa. He is currently curator of a new Armed Forces Museum in Muscat, Oman.

Hilary Bradt was once an occupational therapist but now divides her time between leading trips in South America for an American adventure travel company, and writing and publishing guide books for independent travellers.

Dr Peter Steele was born in 1935 and qualified as a doctor in 1960. He has climbed in Britain, the Pyrenees, the Alps, North Africa, Mexico, Nepal and the Cordillera Vilcacamba. He has worked at a mission hospital in Kathmandu and with the Grenfell Flying Doctor Service in northern Labrador, where he travelled the coast by dog team and boat. With his wife, Sarah, he has driven overland to India, and with his family, comprising two children under the age of four, travelled on mule-back across the Himalayan Kingdom of Bhutan. In 1972, he hitchhiked around South America with his ten-year-old son. He was physician to the International Expedition to Mount Everest in 1971. Author of several books on exploration and exploration medicine, he is now in practice in Whitehorse, Yukon Territory, Canada.

Harry Stevens is Austrian by birth but has spent most of his adult life in Britain, where he owns and runs an engineering and electronics firm. His business travels frequently take him out of the country, particularly to Europe and the Far East.

Rick Strange, FRGS, LRPS, is a professional freelance travel photographer specializing in travel brochures. He has also sold pictures throughout the world for encyclopedias, advertisements, calendars, feature articles, text books and many other uses. He studied at the German School of Photography in New York where he obtained eight diplomas and the only Bronze Medal Award for Outstanding Colour Photography to be awarded there in five years. An ex-director of the J. Allen Cash Worldwide Photo-Library, he is now associated with Feature-Pix Colour Photo-Library and has a personal photo collection of over 35,000 colour transparencies from 60 countries.

Ludmilla Tüting is a journalist, writer and publisher, and an experienced traveller. Her travels centre on Nepal and she has written many books about it. She lives in Berlin and is a television personality in Germany. She founded and runs the *Deutsche Zentrale für Globetrotter*, a club for independent travellers.

Penny Watts-Russell was born in 1948, obtained a degree in Social Anthropology and Swahili at the London School of Oriental and African Studies and became the first Editor of the WEXAS magazine, then called *Expedition.* Since leaving this post, she has been Sub-Editor on *The Illustrated London News* and Assistant Editor of *Arts and Adventure* and *Executive World.* Currently she is a freelance editor and researcher.

Elizabeth Whitten is Reference Librarian at the National Broadcasting Commission of Papua New Guinea. A New Zealander by birth, she has travelled widely both outside and within Papua New Guinea, where she has lived for over 25 years. She is a keen blue water yachtswoman and has written travel articles for *Pacific Islands Monthly*.

P. J. Whyte is a SRN/RMN nurse who has recently returned from working in medical clinics in Gabon, Angola and the Congo.

Brian Williams is a Welshman who spent ten years teaching Maths in Wales, Australia and Brazil. Having travelled extensively around South America, he returned to the UK where he became involved in the adventure travel business and now, through his own company, Journey Latin America, operates tours exclusively to that part of the world.

Peter Fairney Williams is a physical education specialist serving in the Royal Air Force with the rank of Wing Commander. He is the author of seven books on outdoor activities which cover canoeing, hillwalking and all aspects of camping.

Anne Wilson was born in 1952 in Birmingham. Armed with a BA Hons. in Social Psychology from Sussex University, she came to London where she quickly joined the Consumers' Association. Three years working on *Which?* magazine were followed by another four exploring the globe and writing reports for *Holiday Which?*, a job which embraced anything from Motorway Service Areas in Britain to the Indian pyramids in Mexico. Since 1981, she has worked freelance, contributing to *Time Out, What Holiday?* and various women's magazines.

Shane Winser is Information Officer of the Royal Geographical Society and its Expedition Advisory Centre. She studied Zoology and Information Science at university in London, before helping her husband to organize scientific expeditions to Sarawak, Pakistan, and Kenya. She is currently writing *The Guiness Book of Expeditions* and provides the answers for The Traveller Replies column of *The Traveller*.

Nigel Winser is the Expedition Officer of the Royal Geographical Society and their Expedition Advisory Centre. He is currently Projects Director for the Wahibah Sands Project, an expedition to Oman in 1985/86. He has been responsible for the field logistics and support for the last three projects put into the field by the RGS including Mulu (Sarawak), Karakoram (Pakistan) and Kora (Kenya).

David Woolley was born in 1934. After some experience as a pilot and air traffic controller, he worked for several aviation magazines. From 1973 to 1983, he was Editor of *Airports International*, and in April 1983, he joined *Interavia*, the Swiss-based aerospace monthly, as its air transport editor. He is married and lives in the depths of the Sussex countryside.

Carol Wright has been a travel writer for 20 years. At present she is Travel Editor of *House and Garden* and Chairperson of the Guild of Travel Writers. She has written 28 books including *The Travel Survival Guide*.

Where and When

Places in Vogue

by Richard Harrington and Melissa Shales

The sociology of the holiday is a strange affair. It is as easy to tell what a person is like from where they went last summer as by looking at their bookshelves. The holiday brackets one mentally (the nearest art gallery or the knobbly knees competition), physically (lie on a beach or climb a mountain), and financially (Camber Sands or the Himalayas). They also involve a great deal of one-upmanship. The Joneses went to Scotland, so the Smiths must go to Greece, and because the Smiths are going to Greece, Miss Williams down the road sets off with a smirk for Nepal. Soon, not to be outdone, the Smiths and the Joneses will also end up in Nepal. In such a way does mass tourism grow.

Of course, there are genuine travellers, and a great many of them, but mass tourism is a product of advertising, financial incentives and peer pressure. The destinations popular with independent travellers today are destined to be the big resorts of ten years hence. Bali, for instance, was big with certain travellers in the 1930s – with the *cognoscenti* of the times, but it was not until the 1970s that it started to feature in the glossy tour brochures. And by now there is a travelling clique that has pronounced Bali 'quite ruined' and has gone off in search of a less developed piece of paradise.

The true independent travellers – horrified as they may be to admit it – act as trailblazers, both opening the eyes of the local inhabitants to the financial incentives of tourism, and those of the operators to a new area for development. Greece, in the 1960s, was a hippy hang-out.

The chain starts with airports, or more precisely, runways – runways that can take 707s, DC-8s and 747s. A classic example is the Seychelles, which blossomed in the early 1970s after the opening of an airport built to accommodate the big jets.

With the airports come the hotels, mostly of the same plastic American kind that has become the mark of resort hotels everywhere. And with the hotels comes a proliferation of other effects – good and bad – radiating out in circles to influence the rest of the country concerned.

Yet tourism is a fickle commodity, dependent on all manner of external factors from the state of the economy in richer nations – holidays are the first thing to go when the standard of living falls – to fluctuations in the world currency market; from revolutions to the whims of fashion. More easily than any other industry, tourism is threatened by disaster. The Seychelles, whose economy is 95 per cent dependent on tourism, was poised on the brink of financial disaster after their recent coup; the effects of the fighting in Grenada were felt throughout the Caribbean, even on islands several thousand miles away. And it is an industry that is constantly on the move, seeking out new experience; that can ruin a beach or country, only to discard it in favour of somewhere new.

Changing Fashions

The popular resorts of the 1970s are easy to name. In the Caribbean, Jamaica and the Bahamas faded, while Barbados and St. Lucia came into vogue. In black Africa, it was Kenya that won all the prizes for attracting cash-loaded tourists – in the process of which they turned Malindi into a giant German-speaking brothel. Further north, Egypt came, went, and came again, according to the vagaries of the war with Israel. The Tunisians implemented the Italian marketing plan they had commissioned in the 1960s and turned tourism into a massive foreign exchange earner, compensation for being an oil-less country flanked by oil-rich Algeria and Libya.

The late 1970s brought into fashion countries that had previously been out of reach of the Western masses. French and German tourists flocked to the Maldives, Nepal, India, Thailand and Sri Lanka. The beautiful state of Ladakh, once the remote home of a gentle Tibetan people, is now flooded each summer around the capital of Leh with souvenir-hunting tourists from Europe. Priceless artefacts have been sold for a pittance. Tough, money-hungry Kashmiri traders have moved in to monopolize most commercial activities. And all this because the Indian government opened a new air link to Leh a few years ago.

Not far away, in Nepal, the highland peoples' traditional ways of life are increasingly affected by tourists. There are still beautiful treks to be made in Nepal, but the one to be avoided is one few can resist – to Everest Base Camp.

Thousands now take the traditional route from Lukla airstrip or further afield, and the main hazards of the trip are human pollution and hepatitis.

The Encroaching Masses

The hippy trails of the East have given way to mass tourism; the brothels of Bangkok, the ripoffs of Pataya Beach, the Australian hordes on Bali's Kuta Beach – they all add up to a pathetic picture of mass tourism at its worst.

For the rich, China was the fashionable destination of 1979. Trips were made, not just to Beijing, but further afield to Urumchi, where New York's Linblad Travel beat London's Thomas Cook by two weeks in the race to bring the first Western tour group since before the war. Since then, China has become the 'in' destination for independent travellers, although it hasn't yet been taken up in any large way by the mass tour operators.

Linblad, which caters for the ultra-rich and exclusive, is now offering luxury cruises to the Antarctic.

The last couple of years have seen some major changes in long-haul travel as the Nile Route has become far less certain politically; and the final nail has been put in the coffin of the tottering route overland to Asia, with Iran dubious, Afghanistan impossible, and the area around the India/Pakistan border unsettled.

The Caribbean has been left almost entirely to the jet set and the package tourists. India and Nepal are getting so crowded they are becoming positively commonplace. Traffic between Europe and the United States is at an all time high with the new round of cut-price Atlantic travel led by Virgin and People Express.

Cheap round-the-world air tickets are opening up a great many gateway cities such as Singapore, Hong Kong and Los Angeles, and bringing even Australia and the South Pacific within more people's budgets. Interest in Australia and New Zealand as holiday destinations is growing, where previously travel here was confined to the so-called VFR (Visiting Friends and Relatives) market.

Tropical islands that look like sets for *South Pacific* have already suffered from American and Australasian tourism. But as the European hordes arrive, spearheaded as ever by the Germans (who are, on average, a good ten years ahead of the British), places like Tahiti will get even worse – which is saying a lot, for Polynesia already combines all that is worst in colonial snobbery with all that is worst in the manners of the metropolitan French.

South America stands out as the last part of the world to succumb *en masse*, yet even here, things are now changing and the trail to Machu Picchu is getting crowded.

A Tidal Effect

If it all sounds awful, mostly it is. But in the inevitable process, some money is getting through to the people of the countries concerned. It hasn't made the people of Barbados any nicer over the last ten years, but now at least they are better fed and clothed and educated.

During the 1970s, people got used to going abroad, whether to Ibiza or Yugoslavia; the 1980s are seeing them now becoming more adventurous, prepared to fly further, and less inclined to just sit on a beach once they get there.

In the meantime, all over the world, a small number of Westerners are sitting on empty tropical beaches, buying genuine artefacts for next to nothing, being invited into the homes of locals, exchanging smiles with people along the road, sharing their food with children who do not ask for money. They are the forerunners by some ten years of the hordes who will follow when Third World governments conspire with big business to put in hotels and airports. These pioneers are of course not all good, and neither necessarily is the small impact they make as they go. What is certain, however, is that these visitors are lucky. There will soon be a time when there are no such places left to visit.

Countries at War

by Ingrid Cranfield

People, especially politicians, on both sides of the nuclear divide, like to congratulate themselves that 'we have had forty years of world peace'. Are we really so inured to violence that we don't any more notice wars going on before our eyes? True, modern war is a difficult activity to define. Prior to 1945, wars were usually formally declared. This has not happened since.

Istvan Kende, an expert on conflict, has defined war as any armed conflict in which all the following elements exist:

1. Fighting by regular armed forces (including military police forces and other armed services) on at least one side – that is, the presence and engagement of the armed forces of the government in power.
2. A certain degree of organization and organized fighting on both opposing sides, even if this organization extends only to organized defence.
3. A certain continuity between the armed clashes, however sporadic.
4. Centrally organized guerrilla forces are also regarded as making war, insofar as their activities extend over a considerable part of the country concerned.

By this definition, the battle for the Falklands was strictly not a war but a campaign.

Nevertheless, this particular rose by whatever name still smells as foul and the idea that we have had years of unbroken peace is a wierd and ghastly self-delusion. In the period 1945–79, there were at least 140 wars, with a new war beginning somewhere in the world every three months. Most of these wars were fought in the Third World. The total duration of these conflicts exceeded 380 years; the territory of 75 countries and the armed forces of 85 states were involved. Since September 1945 there was not a single day on which one or several wars were not being fought somewhere in the world. On an 'average' day, about twelve wars were fought and the number of people killed in wars since World War II exceeds 30 million.

About 85 per cent of the wars in that period were civil wars, aimed at overthrowing the ruling régime or fought for tribal, religious, minority or similar reasons. Between 1962 and 1975 alone there were 105 military coups in various parts of the world and in 1975 alone, 25 per cent of all member states of the United Nations were ruled by military governments.

The United Kingdom has been fighting a guerrilla war in Northern Ireland since 1969. This is the only war currently being fought in a 'modern', developed country.

The average length of wars between 1945 and 1979 was just over three years, although about half lasted for less than a year. Some 20 per cent went on for longer than six years. One of the most enduring conflicts is that between Eritrean forces of the Eritrean Liberation Front Revolutionary Council, fighting for autonomy for two and a half million Muslims, and the Ethiopian army. This war has been going on since the Council was founded in 1958.

Some conflicts are complex as well as lengthy. The Kurds, four million strong in Iran alone, have long been demanding regional autonomy for Kurdistan and the preservation of their language and culture. Kurdish guerrillas are fighting government forces in Iran, Iraq, and Turkey, adopting hit and run tactics and often crossing borders to strike at strategic targets.

Modern wars are not always fought

by modern means. The uprising in Vanuatu, then the New Hebrides, in 1980, pitted the British and French governments, condominium rulers of 92 years' standing against an island chief and a handful of men armed with bows and arrows.

The Middle East

The volatile Middle East continues to suffer bloodshed and devastation which stops just short of all-out war. The Israeli invasion of Lebanon in 1982 precipitated a reorganization of the leadership of the Palestine Liberation Organization, splintering the movement into rival factions. Meanwhile, the people whom the PLO supposedly represents, the Palestinian refugees, became a trial to the Arab nations which had long harboured but failed to assimilate or care for them. Once again the Palestinians were displaced by conflicts between their own fighters and other Arabs. Syria, which originally entered Lebanon as a peace-keeping force, has been loth to leave and has helped hasten the departure from that territory of foreign troops other than its own. Syria is backed by the Soviet Union, which has replaced the fighter planes and tanks it lost in the Lebanon conflict of 1982 and supplied it with long-range anti-aircraft missiles. In addition to tanks facing the Golan Heights and in the Bekaa Valley of Lebanon, Syria has surface-to-surface missiles which, if deployed, could reach targets in Lebanon, Israel and the United States' Sixth Fleet in the Mediterranean. These SS-21 missiles carry nuclear warheads or high explosives and have never before been deployed outside the Warsaw Pact nations. Lebanon's populace remains highly fragmented and partition of the country seems the most likely outcome of the disturbances.

From the traveller's point of view, the regions to avoid are the so-called 'North Bank' of Israel, the coastal area of Lebanon between Sidon and Acre, and the eastern half of Syria within reach of the Iraqi border. The régimes of Syria and Iraq are on the worst possible terms and it may be impossible or inadvisable to travel directly between the two capitals; Amman is the obvious link. By and large, Jordan, Turkey and the whole of the Arabian Peninsula are safe enough for travellers.

Iran–Iraq

Iran and Iraq have been locked in battle since September 1980 and there is constant danger that the conflict will escalate. The original engagement stemmed largely from reciprocal accusations of interference in domestic affairs. Both countries have oil-based economies which have been severely disrupted by the conflict.

Iran's oil exports, flowing mainly from the Kharg Island oil terminal in the Gulf, total 2,000,000 barrels of oil a day, bringing in an annual revenue of $25,000 million. Kharg Island has come in for frequent bomb attacks by Iraq, which is also attempting to weaken the Iranian economy by firing direct at civilian targets. By the same token, Iran has blocked sea traffic from the southern Iraqi town of Basrah and has destroyed two Iraqi oil-loading terminals in the Gulf. Both sides attribute loss of shipping to the other. When, in late 1983, Iran tried to destroy Iraq's oil export pipeline through Turkey, Iran retaliated with attacks on cities and towns, using long-range artillery and surface-to-surface missiles, causing 200 deaths.

Of particular concern is the Iran–Japan Petrochemical Company's project at Bandar Khomeini, also on the Persian Gulf, which has already been bombed several times and is now closely protected by Iranian forces, including anti-aircraft missiles and war planes stationed nearby. Japan purchases some 500,000 barrels of oil a day from Iran and depends on this source more heavily than on any other. Japan also does business with Iraq, but on a smaller scale.

At the time of writing, Iraq owns Exocet missiles carried by five Super-Etendards bought from France, but has not used them in the fighting against Iran. Iraq also buys Soviet equipment and arms from Egypt to the tune of US$1,000 million per year. The worst fears for the region are that Iraq may completely destroy the Kharg Island installations and Iran may retaliate by preventing Iraqi shipping from using the Straits of Hormuz, which control the entrance to the Gulf. With a quarter of their petroleum supplies thus blocked, the Western powers would have to intervene. Meanwhile, the concern is that Iraq could inflict such damage on Iran's economy that its government could fall, leaving a power vacuum.

Until 1980, overland journeys through Asia were usually routed through central Iran and Afghanistan. Tour operators were then obliged to seek alternative routes, e.g. from Isfahan, Iran to Quetta, Pakistan via Baluchistan, or to overfly the trouble spots, linking Istanbul, Damascus or Amman with Karachi. Late in 1982, certain overland tour operators reverted tentatively to the practice of traversing Iran, keeping open their option of overflying in case of difficulty.

Afghanistan

In Afghanistan, the government of Babrak Karmal was installed by a Soviet-executed coup on 27 December 1979. Internal and external opposition to the invasion was widespread. The Western powers pressed for Afghanistan to be declared neutral and non-aligned. Inside the country, Muslim rebels, the *Mujaheddin*, called for a holy war to repel the invaders and joined forces with deserters from the regular Afghan army to mount guerrilla attacks on the Soviet troops. There is no sign of an end to the Soviet occupation of Afghanistan, which the Russians may intend to incorporate into the Union as another Soviet Socialist Republic. Soviet air power has been built up to the point where bases in Afghanistan could provide Soviet naval forces in the Indian Ocean with air cover. Troops are established in considerable strength on the eastern border of Iran. The foothold in Afghanistan offers the Soviets the opportunity to intervene in the internal politics of Iran and Pakistan. It is estimated (late 1983) that there are between 110,000 and 120,000 Soviet troops stationed in Afghanistan, on a six-month tour of duty, with perhaps an additional 20,000 to 40,000 troops during periods of overlap. Afghanistan watchers predict however that there will be no let-up in internal resistance to the occupying forces: the Afghanis are known for their fierce independence.

Southeast Asia

Khmer Rouge activists continue to make incursions into northern Kampuchea in an attempt to unseat the Vietnamese-installed régime in Phnom Penh. Reasonable law and order have been re-established in Vietnam itself and in Laos, other than in the areas of the Kampuchean border, and in military-ruled Thailand away from the northern border country. Local difficulties make life difficult in Portuguese Timor, West Irian and northern Burma (the latter being little problem to tourists who are normally permitted to stay no longer than one week in the country). The activities of the Indonesian security forces can prove a burden to travellers, especially in Sumatra and outlying islands. In the Philippines, the main dangers to the visitor are civilian crime and police repression, particularly outside Manila.

South and West Asia

Dhofar in Oman is temporarily quiet, since an understanding has been reached between South Yemen and Oman. Discontent rumbles in Jammu and Kashmir, without flaring up; however Assam and the northeastern parts of India, which have recently seen fierce and massive rioting, are areas to steer clear of. At the time of writing, there is a state of emergency in the Punjab, and the world waits to see whether India can survive Mrs Gandhi's assassination without mass violence.

China

While certain areas, such as western Tibet, remain closed or virtually so, China is nowadays very welcoming to travellers and may soon open the border between Sinkiang and the USSR, a region whose monasteries and other cultural riches would attract many visitors.

Northern and Western Africa

Conflicts in this region are fuelled by many factors, not least of them fuel itself. Morocco and Mauritania vie with one another for control of the uranium deposits which lie under the Sahara. Libya has achieved a recent rapprochement with Morocco through an arrangement to exchange its oil for Moroccan resources; but Libya's military engagement in Chad is a heavy drain on its oil wealth. Morocco is in serious debt for various reasons, including a decline in phosphate prices and its involvement in the war in the western Sahara. Whether or not a referendum resolves the nearly ten-year conflict between Morocco and the Polisario rebels defending their unilaterally declared Saharan Arab Democratic Republic, the area will remain uncomfortable for some time to come. Meanwhile, antique disputes continue to rumble, such as the quarrel between Burkina Faso (Upper Volta) and Mali over boundaries, the legacy of nineteenth century French rule. Sudan's régime has lately become more repressive with the adoption of the ancient harsh and repressive Arab laws for the maintenance of law, order and morality as they interpret it. The Ethiopian government remains locked in combat with the forces for Eritrean liberation. Somalia and the Horn of Africa harbour one of the world's greatest concentrations of refugees.

Any change of régime in the region gives rise to immediate difficulties and travellers are advised to keep a sharp eye on the short term.

Eastern and Southern Africa

South Africa seems unable to quell the activities of the outlawed African National Congress and other nationalist movements, which infiltrate trained terrorists into South Africa and attack selected key targets. South Africa lost its mandate over Namibia (South West Africa) in 1966 and its administration of the area since is not recognized by the United Nations. Swapo, the nationalist movement, aims to establish a government in Namibia, a prospect viewed by Pretoria as a sell-out of whites and a submission to Soviet Communism. Insurgency continues in northern Mozambique and Angola. Uganda remains a problem but Zaire's economic stringencies are forcing the government to adopt a more positive attitude towards tourism.

Central and South America

Cuban, and ultimately Soviet-backed, revolts continue in El Salvador, Nicaragua and Guatemala, peasants organizing guerrilla raids in the countryside to wrest back traditional lands, and urban terrorists working directly against civilian and military régimes. In Guatemala, Colombia and Bolivia, right-wing 'death squads' of the government security forces are accused of torturing and killing many hundreds of suspects and detainees. Bolivia has in the past been very unstable politically, experiencing no fewer than six coups between 1958 and 1963. Chile's government has had to extend emergency powers in response to continuing demonstrations against the President by the Democratic Alliance, but the 'Beagle Island' conflict with Argentina is at a low ebb.

The Outlook

It should go without saying that travellers, unless they are war correspondents, are well advised to keep out of war zones, even assuming they could gain entry in the first place. The risks are obvious. Any Westerner in Kabul today could easily be taken for a Russian. Tourists react quickly to news of war and internal conflict. Once the troubles are over it may take years for some semblance of normality to return – and the tourists with it. A few travellers, in the right place at the right time, have noticed that the post-conflict period can be an ideal one for travel, with the whole country virtually theirs alone.

Conflict will almost certainly continue to increase in the Third World. Any one of the many present or future wars could escalate to a war involving the Superpowers and thence to a world war, whether nuclear or not. Third World wars are, therefore, of crucial concern to us all.

Note: The author would like to acknowledge the help given her in preparing this article by Major S. Robert Elliot, Information Officer at The International Institute for Strategic Studies. Interpretations and judgements are, however, hers alone. The reader will appreciate that the picture of international politics is constantly changing and that events occur at a much faster rate than the revision of published texts.

Climate and its Relevance to Travel

by Gilbert Schwartz

Prospective travellers may prepare for their trip carefully, consulting guidebooks, choosing the most desirable accommodation, designing an appropriate itinerary and making thorough preparations in general. But the traveller frequently fails to investigate the most important ingredient affecting the failure or success of the trip: the weather.

Well, maybe there isn't much you can do to guarantee good weather but you can do some things to help minimize disappointment.

Be sure to do your homework. Look up reference books on the subject and use them to help select the most favourable times and travel locations. Remember, when interpreting climate information, some statistics are necessary but they could sometimes be misleading. Look for comparisons. Especially compare the prospective location with an area at home or with which you are familiar. For example, San Francisco, California, has a temperature range for July from a maximum average of 18°C to a minimum of 12°C with no precipitation. This becomes more meaningful when it is compared to New York City which has a range of 29°C to 20°C and, on average, eleven days during the month have rain of 0.25cm or more.

So, in spite of the fact that California has a reputation for being warm and sunny, if you're planning a trip to San Francisco in the summer, don't forget to take a sweater! The average temperatures are cold and the winds are a brisk 17.5kmph, windier even than Chicago, the 'windy city'.

Sources

Up-to-date weather conditions and forecasts may be obtained from various sources. A current weather map, which is based on information furnished by government as well as private weather services, is the main way of getting a general picture of weather patterns over a large area. These weather maps show conditions around the country at ground level. Elements which are of particular interest to travellers and may be shown on the map include temperatures, pressure change, wind speed and direction, cloud type, current weather, and precipitation.

Of course, the weather information and projected forecasts must be interpreted. You may do well to alter your itinerary and stay clear of areas that project undesirable or threatening weather conditions. Especially keep alert for severe weather conditions such as storms, heavy rains, etc. For example, you should remember when travelling in mountainous regions that flash floods can strike with little or no warning. Distant rain may be channelled into gullies and ravines, turning a quiet streamside campsite into a rampaging torrent within minutes.

Incidentally, there is excellent literature available through the US Government Printing Office prepared by the National Weather Service. For example, information on safety during lightning, flash floods, hurricanes and tornadoes, as well as publications containing summaries and other data pertaining to weather and climate are available. Write to Superintendent of Documents, US Government Printing Office, Washington DC 20420, for a list of publications. In Britain, information on overseas climate and weather is obtainable from the Overseas Enquiry Bureau, Meteorological Office, Bracknell, Berkshire (Tel: (0344) 420242 ext. 2267).

Basic Elements

After you have had an opportunity to review reference materials on climate and sources for weather forecasts you should become acquainted with the meaning of some basic weather elements and learn how they may affect your travel preparations.

Perhaps the most important weather element is temperature. Temperature is important because it is a good indicator of body comfort. The ideal air temperature is around 27°C.

Temperatures generally decrease at higher latitudes and at higher elevations, on average by around 1.7°C for every 300m increase in elevation up to 9,000m.

Wind, which is air in motion, is another important weather element. Winds are caused by pressure gradients, the difference in pressure between two locations. Air moves from an area of high pressure toward an area of low pressure. The greater the pressure gradient, the faster the wind. Sea breezes form when cool high pressure air flows from the water onshore to the low pressure area created by warm air over the land. On a clear, hot summer day, the sea breeze will begin mid-morning and can blow inland as far as 16km at wind speeds of 16–24kmph. In the evening, the process is reversed. An offshore land breeze blows at a more gentle speed, usually about half the speed of the daytime onshore wind.

A somewhat similar situation occurs in the mountains and valleys. During the daytime, the valley floor and sides and the air above them warm up considerably. This air is less dense than the colder air higher up so it rises along the slopes, creating a 'valley wind'. In the summer, the southern slopes receive more sun and heat up more, which results in valley winds that are stronger than their north slope cousins. At night, the process is reversed and downslope 'mountain winds' result from the cold air above the mountain tops draining down into the valley.

Winds are also affected by such factors as synoptic (large area) pressure differences and by day-night effects. The sun produces maximum wind speeds while at night winds near the ground are usually weak or absent. Wind speed is also influenced by how rough the ground is. Over smooth water surfaces, the wind speed increases very rapidly with increasing altitude and reaches a peak speed at a height of about 180m. Over rough terrain, the wind speed increases more gradually with increasing altitude and does not reach its peak until about 450m.

Comfort

As we well know, wind, temperature and humidity have a bearing on our comfort. To indicate how combinations of these elements affect the weather we experience, two indices should be understood; wind chill factor and temperature/humidity comfort index (THI).

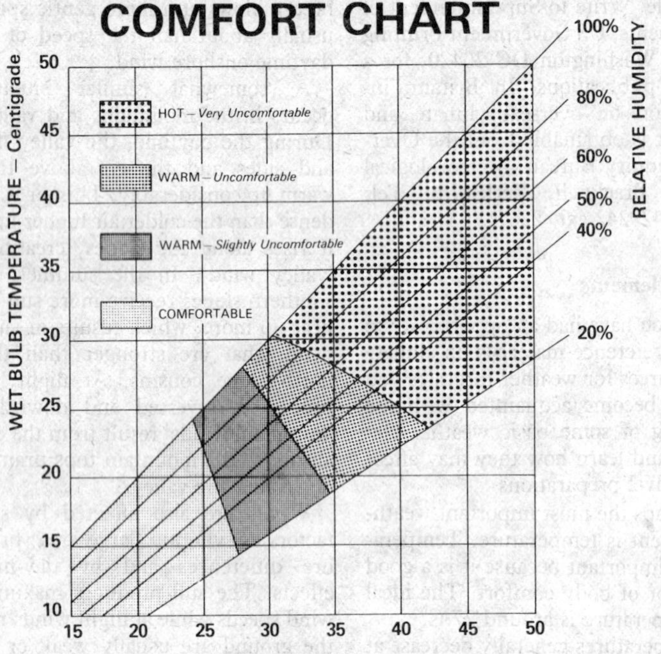

To use the comfort chart, start by locating the vertical line that corresponds to the air temperature. Next, find the sloping line that corresponds to the relative humidity. The intersection of these two lines will put you into one of four comfort categories: (1) hot and very uncomfortable, (2) warm and uncomfortable, (3) warm and slightly uncomfortable, and (4) comfortable.

Wind Chill Factor

The wind chill factor is the cooling effect on the body of any combination of wind and temperature. It accounts for the rate at which our exposed skin loses heat under differing wind-temperature conditions. In a wind of 32kmph, −4°C will feel like −19°C. This effect is called 'wind chill', the measure of cold one feels regardless of the temperature. Chill increases as the temperature drops and winds get stronger, up to about 72kmph, beyond which there is little increase. Thus at −12°C, increasing the wind from 0 to 8kmph reduces temperature by only two degrees, but a change in wind speed from 64–72kmph reduces it only 0.5°C.

The wind may not always be naturally caused. For example, someone skiing into the wind may receive quite a chill. If one is moving into the wind, the speed of travel is added to the wind speed; thus if the wind is blowing at 16kmph and one's speed is 24kmph into the wind, the actual air movement against the body is 40kmph. At −9°C this air speed gives a wind chill equivalent to −30°C.

This is easily cold enough for exposed parts of the body to sustain frostbite.

A combination of warm temperatures and humidity have a significant bearing on our comfort, particularly in warmer climates when the higher the relative humidity, the less comfortable we are. This is a result of the corresponding decrease in the rate at which moisture can evaporate from the skin's surface. Since the cooling of the air next to the skin by the evaporation of perspiration is what causes a cooling sensation, a day with 70 per cent relative humidity and 27°C temperature is far less comfortable than one with 25 per cent humidity and 43°C temperature. The THI was developed in order to measure this relative comfort. But remember, where there is low humidity and a high temperature, your comfort can mislead you, for though you feel safe, you may be in danger of burning.

WIND CHILL CHART

Estimated Wind Speed in kmph	Actual Thermometer Reading (C)											
	10	4.5	−1	−6.5	−12	−17.5	−23	−28.5	−34	−39.5	−45	−50.5
	Equivalent Temperature (C)											
calm	10	4.5	−1	−6.5	−12	−17.5	−23	−28.5	−34	−39.5	−45	−50.5
8	9	3	−3	−9	−14.5	−20.5	−26	−32	−38	−44	−49.5	−55.5
16	4.5	−2	−9	−15.5	−23	−29.5	−36	−43.5	−50	−56.5	−64	−70.5
24	2	−5.5	−13	−20.5	−22	−38	−43	−50	−58	−65	−73	−80
32	0	−8	−15.5	−23 5	−31.5	−39.5	−47	−55	−63.5	−71	−79	−86.5
40	−1	−9	−18	−26	−34	−42	−50.5	−59	−66.5	−75.5	−83.5	−91.5
48	−2	−10.5	−19	−22	−36	−44.5	−53	−61.5	−70	−78.5	−87	−95.5
56	−3	−11.5	−20	−28.5	−37	−45	−55	−63.5	−72	−80.5	−89.5	−98.5
64	−3.5	−12	−21	−29.5	−38.5	−47	−56	−65	−73.5	−82	−91	−100
(wind speeds greater than 64 kmph have little additional effect)	**LITTLE DANGER** for properly clothed persons				**INCREASING DANGER**			**GREAT DANGER**				
					Danger from freezing of exposed flesh							

Layman's Forecast

Lacking the sophisticated instruments and sources for weather data, you may still be able to project your own forecasts. Become familiar with basic weather elements such as pressure signs, clouds, wind changes, etc. Learn how these indicators change before the weather does.

A layman should beware of the climate statistics he sees in many tourist brochures. The climate will almost always be more severe than is evident from the quoted rainfall, temperature and sunshine figures. All-important humidity figures are usually not given (Bali might be empty of tourists half the year if they were), and temperature figures may be averages over day and night, and well below (or above) actual normal maximum (or minimum) temperatures. Or they may represent averages recorded at 0600 or 1800 hours, because these figures will look most attractive to visitors.

Something else you will not find easily is water temperature. Winter sun holidays are now extremely popular. A lot of people do not realize however that although the daytime air temperatures may be in the low 20°sC, water temperatures may only be about 5–15°C and swimming without a wetsuit impossible.

The sea takes longer to warm up than the land each summer. Conversely it takes longer to cool down in the autumn. Reckon on a lag between sea and land temperatures of about one and a half months. In Tunisia, the sea is a lot cooler in March than in October. On the other hand, by March air and land temperatures are already rising with the beginning of summer. They will reach their highest point in June/July, but the sea will take until August/September to be fully warmed up.

In winter, comfortably warm water is almost a certainty in the tropics; more doubtful in the subtropics, for which you should find and study year-round water temperatures. You may just decide to go in summer instead, even though it will probably cost more. In short, warm air and warm water don't always go together.

Familiarity with climate information, whether you rely on primary or secondary sources, will go a long way towards permitting you to get the most out of your next trip.

Seasonal Travel

by Richard Harrington

An inexperienced traveller may not think too much about seasons of the year before he sets off. He knows it's always hot in Indonesia and cold in the Arctic. The seasoned traveller, on the other hand, plans his trip very carefully around certain times of the year.

Airlines, hotels and tour operators have off-peak seasons, when they adjust their prices downwards. These prices are governed by demand rather than by climatic seasons – most Mediterranean countries are at their most idyllic in May, when charter flights are at their lowest. However, a great deal of Mediterranean tourism is governed by school holidays, so the demand is comparatively low during the term. And sometimes one-way traffic distorts the fare structure, e.g. westbound fares across the Atlantic are at their lowest when the climate is at its best in many of the destination countries, but are governed by the amount of traffic travelling in the other direction.

Climate – rainfall, humidity, temperature – produces the most obvious type of season. Climates that are no trial to local people may have devastating effects on those ill-adapted souls arriving from more temperate regions.

Hurricanes Hardly Happen?

For reasons still little understood, certain tropical regions of the globe are subject to seasonal monsoon rains, cyclones, hurricanes and tornadoes. For most people, these are non-travel seasons. On the other hand, travel deals may be so attractive in these periods that you may decide to make the trip because you know you could never afford it at any other time. A surfer may choose to travel in the stormiest seasons of the year, knowing that these are usually the times for the biggest and best waves.

There are other types of season too. Big game and birdlife may be more spectacular in certain months. Endemic diseases may be caught more easily at certain times of year. In Arctic Canada and Alaska there are two great torments: an icy wind in winter and mosquitoes in summer. The blessing is that you never get both at the same time.

The going may be physically impossible, or almost so, in certain months. Few have dared to move on the Arctic ice cap during the continuous night of freezing winter. Yachtsmen crossing the Atlantic from west to east avoid a winter crossing on the northern route, and those sailing on the Pacific circuit from North America to Hawaii, Tahiti and New Zealand try to complete the last leg of the voyage before the summer cyclones begin. In the jungles of the African west coast and of 'Africa's armpit' – Cameroon, the Congo, Zaïre etc. – the going is very rough and extremely unpleasant during the rainy season from May to August. The best time to start a trans-Africa crossing from London would be September/October when the height of the Saharan summer and the rainy season further south have both passed. Autumn and, better still, spring are the best times for a Sahara crossing.

Trekking in Nepal has become so popular that it's worth knowing the best times for it. The best visibility, lowest precipitation, brightest weather, and most tolerable night time temperatures occur between the end of September and the end of May, and within this period the best 'subseason' is the autumn, from October to mid-December. January and February are very cold, with snow above 3,000m but visibility is good and trekking is still possible. Spring arrives around late February or early March. The monsoon, with its poor visibility, mud and leeches, has its onset about the end of March.

A little-known fact is that since hot air is thinner than cold and hot air rises, the air at altitude will be even thinner than when cold. While the heat itself, in high altitude cities like Mexico City, La Paz, Addis Ababa or Nairobi, is unlikely to be overwhelming, the rarified air may leave you exhausted for several days if you don't take it easy when you get there. If you are susceptible to altitude, then winter is probably the best time to go. The heat is also likely to be less overpowering then.

Man, Maker of All Seasons

Man too creates seasons which can affect the traveller, and the Westerner will sometimes find them hard to predict. The festivals of the Orthodox Church do not often coincide with those of the Western churches. The Islamic religious calendar is based upon the lunar month and is therefore always out of step with our own progression of months and years. The Kandy Perahera festival in Sri Lanka is one of a number of events whose exact dates are settled by astrologers at inconveniently short notice. So, for instance, if you plan to visit a Muslim country during Ramadan, the month of fasting, bear in mind that the local people will do without food from sunup to sundown. Various services will be disrupted or unavailable. Meals will be hard to obtain outside the tourist areas. And you may be woken by whole families noisily eating a meal before dawn puts an end to the revelry. However a meal shared with an Arab family during Ramadan is a treat to be remembered. In the Haj season, when Muslims from West Africa to Indonesia flock to Mecca on pilgrimage, air services along the necessary routes are totally disrupted for ordinary travellers.

Come and Join the Dance

In the West Indies, Guyana and Brazil, Carnival is a time of the year when normally poor people are given the chance to forget their worries and feel rich. Cities like Port of Spain in Trinidad and Rio de Janeiro in Brazil have become magnets for tourists, but are to be avoided at that time if you have business to do there and are not interested in the Carnival itself.

Major festivals in Europe and elsewhere always attract culture seekers. The centres concerned become impossibly crowded; hotels fill up; airline passengers get 'bumped' off overbooked aircraft; and visitors pay over the odds for everything because all prices in town have been doubled for the duration. So, for certain countries, especially in Central and South America, a look at the festivals calendar should be part of your planning.

If you decide to beat the crowds and travel to a well-touristed area out of season, there is one more thing to watch out for. The weather could still be glorious, the swimming perfect, but from one day to the next, everything can close down and you could find yourself without transport, entertainment and even food. There is little benefit to be gained from avoiding the crowds if all museums and places of interest are closed, and you have a choice of one place to eat for your entire visit.

Before you go anywhere, look closely at the climate, and read a *geography* book about the place you will visit. You may learn things that the tourist brochures and propaganda guidebooks won't tell you for fear of discouraging you.

Checking the seasons will affect your choice of clothes for the trip, the amount of money you take, possibly the choice of film for your camera.

But even knowing all this, the experienced traveller – or the inexperienced traveller with a taste for adventure – will often seek consciously to avoid the 'best' time. Climates and seasons present their own challenge. Who can claim really to know India who has not felt the crashing force of the monsoon rains? Or to be acquainted with Islamic culture without experiencing the tension of the month of Ramadan?

A Guide to Seasonal Travel

by Paul Pratt and Melissa Shales

Africa

North – the climate here varies widely from the warm and pleasant greenery of a Mediterranean climate in the coastal regions to the arid heat of the deep Sahara.

Rains on the coast usually fall between September and May and are heavy, but not prolonged. It can get cool enough for snow to settle in the mountainous areas, but temperatures will not usually fall below freezing, even in winter. In summer, temperatures are high (up to around 40°C) but bearable.

The Sahara, on the other hand, is

extreme, with maximum summer temperatures of around 50°C and minimum winter temperatures of around −3°C. The temperature can fall extremely rapidly, with freezing nights following blisteringly hot days. What little, if any, rain there is can fall at any time of year. The desert is also prone to strong winds and dust storms.

West – at no time is the climate in West Africa likely to be comfortable, although some areas and times of the year are worse than others. The coastal areas are extremely wet and humid, with up to 2,500mm of rain falling in two rainy seasons – in May and June and then again in October. In the north, there is considerably less rain, with only one wet period between June and September. However, the humidity is still high, only lessened by the arrival of the *harmattan*, a hot, dry, dusty, north-easterly wind blowing from the Sahara. Temperatures remain high and relatively even throughout the year.

East – although much of this area is on or near the equator, little of it has an 'equatorial' climate. The lowlands of Eritrea, Somalia and Djibouti in the extreme east have a very low, uncertain rainfall, creating near desert conditions plagued by severe droughts. Further down the coast, the high lowland temperatures are moderated by constant sea breezes. The temperatures inland are brought down by high altitude plateaux and mountain ranges to about the level found in Britain at the height of summer. They are reasonably stable all year round although the Kenya highlands have a cooler, cloudy 'winter' from June to September. There are two rains in most areas in April and May and for a couple of months between July and November, depending on the latitude.

South – the whole area from Angola, Zambia and Malawi southwards tends to be fairly pleasant and healthy, although there are major variations from the Mediterranean climate of the Cape Province with its mild winters and warm, sunny summers to the semi-desert sprawl of the Kalahari and the relatively wet areas of Swaziland, inland Mozambique and the Zimbabwe highlands in the east. In the more northern areas, there is a definite summer rainy season from December to March, while the temperatures are highest. On the south coast, there is some rain all year round. The west coast, with few rains, has cloud and fog due to the cold Benguela current, which also helps keep down the temperature. The best times of the year to visit are April/May and September when the weather is fine, but not too hot or humid.

North America

Almost half of Canada and most of Alaska in the north is beyond the Arctic Circle and suffers from the desperately harsh weather associated with this latitude. The ground is tundra and rarely melts for more than a couple of feet and even though summer temperatures are often surprisingly high, the summers are short-lived. Snow and frost are possible at any time of the year, while the northern areas have permanent snow cover. The coast is ice-bound for most of the year.

The whole centre of the continent is prone to severe and very changeable weather, as the lowlying land of the Great Plains or the Canadian Prairies offers no resistance to sweeping winds that tear across the continent both from the Gulf and the Arctic. The east is fairly wet, but the west has very little rain, resulting in desert and semi-desert country in the south. Winter temperatures in the north can go as low as −40°C, and can be very low even in the south, with strong winds and blizzards. In the north, winter is long-lived. Summers are sunny and often scorchingly hot.

In general, the coastal areas of North America are far kinder than the centre of the continent. The Pacific coast is blocked by the Rockies from the sweeping winds, and in the Vancouver area, the climate is similar to that of Great Britain. Sea breezes keep it cool further south.

Seasons change fairly gradually on the east coast, but the northerly areas still suffer from the extremes of temperature which give New York its fabled humid heatwaves and winter blizzards. New York, in spite of being far further north, is often much hotter than San Francisco. The Newfoundland area has heavy fog and icebergs for shipping to contend with. Florida and the Gulf States to the south have a tropical climate, with warm weather all year round, winter sun and summer thunderstorms. This is the area most likely to be affected by hurricanes and tornadoes, although cyclones are possible throughout the country.

Mexico and Central America

The best time to visit this area is during the dry season (winter) from November to April. However, the mountains and plains facing the Caribbean have heavy rainfall throughout the year, which is usually worst from September to February. The mountains and plains facing the Pacific have negligible rainfall from December to April.

Central and North Mexico tend to have a longer dry season and the wet season is seldom troublesome to the traveller as it usually rains only between 1600 and 1700 hours. The temperature is affected by the altitude. The unpleasant combination of excessive heat and humidity at the height of the wet season should be avoided, if possible, at the lower altitudes.

South America

The climatic conditions of the South American continent are determined to a great extent by the trade winds which, if they originate in high pressure areas, are not necessarily carriers of moisture. With four regional exceptions, rain in South America is confined to the summer months, both north and south of the equator. The exceptions are (i) South Brazil and the eastern coast of Argentina and Uruguay; (ii) the Amazonian region; (iii) the southern Chilean coastal winter rainfall region; (iv) the coastal area of north-east Brazil. The highest rainfall in South America is recorded in the Amazon basin, the coastlands of Guyana and Suriname, the coastlands of Colombia, Ecuador and south-west Chile. Altitude determines temperature, especially in the Andean countries near to the equator:

hot – up to 1,000m; temperate – 1,000 to 2,000m; cold – above 2,000m.

Ecuador
Dry season: June to October. The coast is very hot and wet, especially during the period December to May. The mountain roads can be very dangerous during the wet season owing to landslides.

Peru
During the colder months, June to November, little rainfall but damp on the coast, high humidity and fog. From December to May, travel through the mountains can be hazardous owing to heavy rain which may result in landslides, causing road blockage and long delays.

Bolivia
Heavy rainfall on the high western plateau from May to November. Rains in all seasons in the eastern part of the country.

Chile
Just over the border from Bolivia, one of the driest deserts in the world faces the Pacific coast.

Argentina
The winter months, June to October are the best time for visiting Argentina. Buenos Aires can be oppressively hot and humid from mid-December to the end of February. Climate ranges from the sub-tropical north to sub-Antarctic in Tierra del Fuego.

Paraguay
The best time for a visit is from May to October when it is relatively dry. The heaviest rainfall is from December to March, at which time it is most likely to be oppressively hot and humid.

Brazil
The dry season occurs from May to October apart from in the Amazon basin and the Recife area which has a tropical rainy season from April to July.

The Far East and South-East Asia

Japan
Japan lies in the north temperate zone. Spring and autumn are the best times for a visit. With the exception of Hokkaido, the large cities are extremely hot in summer. Hokkaido is very cold in winter. Seasonal vacational periods, especially school holidays, should be avoided if one is going to enjoy visiting temples, palaces and the like in relative comfort.

Korea
Korea is located in the north temperate zone, with spring and autumn the best times for touring. The deep blue skies of late September/October and early November, along with the warm sunny days and cool evenings, are among Korea's most beautiful natural assets. Though it tends to be rather windy, spring is also a very pleasant time for a Korean visit. There is a short but pronounced wet season starting towards the end of June and lasting into early August: at this time, over 50 per cent of the year's rain falls and it is usually very hot and humid.

Hong Kong
Subtropical climate: hot, humid and wet summer with a cool, but generally dry winter. Typhoon season is usually from July to August. The autumn, which lasts from late September to early December, is the best time for visiting, as the temperature and

humidity will have fallen and there are many clear, sunny days.

Macao
Macao has a similar climate but the summers are a little more bearable on account of the greater exposure to the breezes and there is also an abundance of trees for shelter during the hot summer.

Thailand
Hot, tropical climate with high humidity. Best time for touring is from November to February. March to May is extremely hot and the wet season arrives with the South West Monsoon during June and lasts until October.

Malaysia
There are no marked wet or dry seasons in Malaysia. October to January is the wettest period on the east coast, October/November on the west coast. Sabah has an equable tropical climate; October and April/May are usually the best times for a visit. Sarawak is seldom uncomfortably hot but is apt to be extremely wet. Typhoons are almost unknown in East Malaysia.

Singapore
Like Malaysia, Singapore has no pronounced wet or dry season. The even, constant heat is mitigated by sea breezes. The frequent rain showers have a negligible cooling effect.

Philippines
The Philippines have a similar climate to Thailand. The best time to travel in the islands is during the dry season, November to March. March to May is usually dry and extremely hot. The South West Monsoon brings the rain from May to November; also the islands north of Samar through Luzon are prone to be affected by typhoons during the period July to September.

The Visayas islands, Mindanao and Palawan, are affected to a lesser degree by the South West Monsoon and it is still possible to travel comfortably during the wet season south of Samar island, as long sunny periods are usually interspersed with heavy rain showers.

The Indian Subcontinent

Sri Lanka
The South West Monsoon brings rain from May to August at Colombo and in the south-west generally and the North East Monsoon determines the rainy season from November to February in the north-east. The most popular time for a visit is during the northern hemisphere's winter.

India
The climate of South India is similar to that of South-East Asia, warm and humid. The South West Monsoon brings the rainy season to most parts of India, starting in the south-west and spreading north and east from mid-May through June. Assam has an extremely heavy rainfall during monsoon seasons. Generally speaking, the period from November to April is the best time to visit. From April until the start of the South West Monsoon, the northern Indian plains are extremely hot though the northern hill stations provide a pleasant alternative until the start of the monsoon rains. These places usually have a severe winter.

Nepal
March is pleasant, when all the rhododendrons are in bloom. The monsoon rains begin in April.

Middle East

A large proportion of this area is desert – flat, low-lying land with virtually no rain and some of the hottest temperatures on earth. Humidity is high along the coast and travellers should beware of heat exhaustion and even heat stroke. What little rain there is falls between November and March. To the north, in Iran and Iraq, the desert gives way to the great steppelands, prone to extremes of heat and cold, with rain in winter and spring. Melting snow from the surrounding mountains causes spectacular floods from March to May.

The climate is considerably more pleasant in the Mediterranean areas with long, hot, sunny summers and mild, wet winters. The coast is humid, but even this is tempered by steady sea breezes. The only really unpleasant aspect of the climate here is the hot, dry, dusty desert wind which blows at the beginning and end of summer.

Europe

Only in the far north and those areas a long way from the sea does the climate in Europe get to be extreme. In northern Scandinavia and some of the inland eastern bloc countries such as Bulgaria, there are long, bitterly cold winters with heavy snow and, at times, arctic temperatures.

In western Europe, the snow tends to settle only for a few days at a time; in Britain, the Benelux countries and Germany, winter is characterized chiefly by continuous cloud cover, with rain or sleet. In the Alps, heavy snow showers tend to alternate with brilliant sunshine, offering ideal conditions for winter sports. There are four distinct seasons, and while good weather cannot be guaranteed during any of them, all are worth seeing. Summer is generally short, and the temperature varies widely from one year to the next, climbing at times to match that on the Mediterranean.

For sun worshippers, the Mediterranean is probably the ideal location, hot for much of the year, but rarely too hot or humid to be bearable. Rain falls in short, sharp bursts, unlike the continuous drizzle to be found further north. Winter is mild and snow rare.

Australasia

Australia
For such a vast land mass, there are few variations in the weather here. A crescent-shaped rain belt follows the coast to provide a habitable stretch around the enormous semi-desert 'outback'. The only mountains – the Snowy Mountains in the east – do, as their name suggests, have significant snowfalls, although even here it does not lie long. The east is the wettest part of the country owing to trade winds which blow off the Pacific. The rainfall pattern varies throughout the country: the north and north-east have definite summer rains between November and April; the south and west have winter rains; while in the east and south-east the rains fall year-round. Tropical cyclones with high winds and torrential rain occur fairly frequently in the north-east and north-west.

Tasmania, further south and more mountainous, has a temperate climate similar to Britain's.

New Zealand

Although at a different latitude, the great expanse of water around New Zealand gives it a maritime climate similar to Britain's. The far north has a sub-tropical climate with mild winters and warm, humid summers. There are year-round snow fields in the south, and snow fall on most areas in winter. Although the weather is changeable, there is a surprising amount of sunshine, making this country ideal for most outdoor activities. The best time to visit is from December to March, at the height of summer.

Papua New Guinea

The climate here is a fairly standard tropical one – hot and wet all year, although the time and amount of the rains are greatly influenced by the high mountains that run the length of the country. The rains are heavy, but not continuous. While the coast tends to be humid, the highlands are pleasant.

Finding Out More

Choosing Maps

by Ingrid Cranfield

A few years ago, an explorer, who had better be nameless, travelled a vast distance through South America, relying for his route-finding on a linear list of place-names he could expect to encounter en route and a rudimentary sketch map with his projected route inked in – both items prepared for him by someone else. It was a bit like orienteering on a giant scale – to reach Brazil, turn right at Santiago – except that compass bearings were virtually ignored in the master plan because the use of a compass was also beyond our explorer's ken. To make progress, he had first to find out where he was and then ask the way to the next place on the list. That he got anywhere at all speaks volumes for the power of the spoken word and the generosity of the local people.

Needless to say, our explorer was not much of a hand with maps. And, of course, he is not alone. Thousands of motorists lurch along to their destination by following signposts or asking directions, ignorant perhaps of the fact that a map would be a better source of the necessary information. Fundamentally, people use maps for three different purposes: to locate a feature in a known or partly known context; to gain an overall impression of some facts or data – with a view to comparison with other information on a different area – for example, population distribution or geology; or to select information directly relevant to the map user's intentions, such as to plan a route or navigate a river. In the third case, the user will doubtless consign some of the new information to memory, but he will also want to keep the map by him in order to verify his movements.

As a wide-ranging international traveller, your use of maps will mainly be in the third category, albeit on a more ambitious level than finding a scenic route from Lowestoft to Looe. Whatever American Express may say, it is maps you cannot afford to leave home without. You may protest that, like the explorer mentioned above, you're inexperienced and a bit nervous about the whole business. No need. Grasp a few basics and the rewards will outweigh the effort.

Elements of a Map

The first thing to think about is scale, which is the measure that relates distances on the map to corresponding distances on the ground. A small scale map gives a broad overview of a sizeable area, while a large scale map shows a limited area in greater detail. One source of confusion about scale is the phrase 'on a large scale', which, in common parlance, means extensive: yet to show a 'large scale' feature on a map may require a *small* scale. One way of remembering the difference between small and large scale maps, therefore, is to note that features on a small scale map *appear* small, those on a large scale map, large. For most practical purposes, maps at a scale of about 1:1,000,000 or smaller are generally considered small scale; those of, say, between 1:20,000 and 1:1,000,000 large scale. Scales larger than 1:20,000 are used on town plans, maps of individual properties or installations and the like.

Map readers may find it useful to make a mental note of one scale and the measure it represents; all other scales can then be compared with it. Thus a scale of 1:100,000 means that a centimetre on the map represents 100,000cms, or one kilometre, on the ground. Metrication in mapping has meant a transition from scales representing round distances in miles (1:63,360 = 1 inch to 1 mile) to scales using multiples of ten (1:50,000, 1:250,000 and so on). The official body that produces maps of the United Kingdom is the Ordnance Survey, which in the last fifteen years or so has been phasing out its maps based on the mile and replacing them with metric maps.

The choice of scale in a map naturally depends on the purpose for which the map is intended. A motorist planning a route cross-country will probably find a map at 1:500,000 quite satisfactory. A rambler, eager to note smallish features in the fields, be they tumuli or pubs, will be well advised to acquire a map, or more frequently, several adjoining map sheets, drawn on 1:50,000 or 1:25,000. Many official mapping authorities base their map series on a national grid, a network of lines which divide the country into small units and represent the edges of individual map sheets. An index for the series (available for consultation at the map retail outlet or in some cases printed on the back of each sheet in the series) shows which map sheets are needed to cover the area of the purchaser's interest.

Another basic distinction to note is that between topographic and thematic maps. Topographic maps (which include most OS maps) show the general nature of the country: the lie of the land, the location and extent of land use and land cover (forests, marshes, farmland), the courses of roads, railways and other lines of communication, the presence of waterways and any other salient features, whether natural (e.g. mountains, sea-cliffs) or man-made (e.g. airports, quarries).

A thematic map focuses instead on a particular aspect of the region: relief (the configuration of the land), communications, climate, land use, population distribution, industry, agriculture. Thus a road map gives – or should give – detailed information on the road network and associated features and amenities (e.g. petrol stations, motorway exit points, mileages between towns); but it may give little or no indication of relief, built-up areas or features of interest to travellers. Similarly a 'tourist' map will show attractions for the sightseer – castles, museums, lakes, archaeological sites, parks – but will probably skimp on information on the exact road pattern, sizes of towns and other features of, presumably, peripheral interest to the tourist. For travel, as opposed to adventure or exploration, you will normally need a general map – although, if you're going somewhere really remote you may be limited by what you can find, and that may be a historical map of caravan routes or a map showing the retreat of glaciers.

All maps employ symbols and it is a good policy to familiarize oneself with the symbols used before taking a map into the field. Some mapmakers use representational symbols, i.e. simplified drawings of features; others use abstract or geometric symbols, e.g. triangles of different colours, to represent different products at industrial sites. The representation of relief is the subject of much variation: methods include hill-shading, which simulates the appearance of the terrain as it might look from the air; spot heights; and contours (lines joining points which are the same height above sea level).

Since maps are two-dimensional representations of a three-dimensional world, some aspects of the truth are necessarily compromised. The way in which the globe, or part of it, is transferred graphically onto paper is called a map projection. There are many types of projection and the type used is nearly always specified on a map. You need not worry too much about which map projection you have in front of you: the larger scale of map the less the projection matters anyway, since the flat sheet of paper more nearly represents a small area of ground, which is nearly flat, than the whole globe, which is spherical. But be a little wary of using a map in a way for which it was not designed: on an equal area projection, for example, you will go astray if you try to extract accurate bearings from it.

What to Look For

Apart from scale and content, what should you look for in selecting a map? Legibility is one criterion. A balance should exist between the provision of information, especially of place names, and the prevention of a cluttered look; and a clear type face and size are, of course, most important. The map's main features should make a strong and unequivocal impact, e.g. colours should be graded logically to convey the correct impression of a variation in altitude, concentration or any other scale or continuum. Language and place name variants may have a bearing on the map's usefulness in some circumstances. Poor physical design in a map – the ease with which it folds, whether or not it is waterproof, the presence or absence of a folder or cover – may cause disproportionate inconvenience in the field.

Map Producers

Who produces maps? Britain's Overseas Surveys Directorate provides back-up mapping services for various countries and still publishes probably the best available maps of such other nations as Nepal, Cameroon, Niger, Maldive Islands, Bolivia and Chad. Certain of the former French possessions, e.g. Algeria and other countries in north and west Africa, are covered by a series published by the *Institut Géographique National* in Paris. The IGN is represented in the UK by:

McCarta Ltd
122 Kings Cross Road

London WC1X 9DS
Tel: 01-278 0896/7

Official map-making by governments and national agencies – usually a civilian (often called geological) and a military survey – has made great strides in the last decade, so that detailed maps of most countries are now produced by the countries themselves. A national series worth singling out is the 1:25,000 (formerly 1:24,000) map of the USA, a series which numbers many thousands of sheets.

For larger scales, consider using sheets of the following international series:

1. The Operational Navigation Chart (ONC) at 1:1,000,000, produced by various publishers, e.g. the Civil Aviation Authority (UK) and the USAF. The series is constantly updated and some sheets are now into their tenth edition.
2. The World Aeronautical Chart (WAC) at 1:1,000,000, produced for aviators. These are available in the UK from Edward Stanford (address below) or from International Air Radio, which stocks these maps for airlines. Tel: 01-574 2411 ext. 414.
3. The International Map of the World (IMW) at 1:1,000,000, an older series, still used by Australia, India, Pakistan, and by France in mapping former French Africa, but generally being phased out and replaced for practical purposes by the above two series.
4. The Tactical Pilotage Chart (TPC) at 1:500,000, which gives topographical data although made especially for air navigation. Less of the world is covered currently by the TPCs than by the ONCs. The TPCs show magnetic variation.
5. The Map of the World at 1:250,000, an international project which has fallen largely into disuse and is being replaced by:
6. The Joint Operations Graphic (JOG) at 1:250,000, sheets of which are produced by the nation in question, some of whom release the maps to the general public (e.g. Canada, Norway) and some of whom do not (e.g. UK). The JOG comes in two editions – air and land.

Although some of these series are produced for specialists, they can also be useful to route planners; and for some remote – or politically inaccessible – areas they are simply the most detailed maps available in the West. Be sure to ask for the most up-to-date edition of any map sheet you buy.

The publications of commercial map producers may sometimes rival those of the national authority in quality. In Britain there are a number of fine map publishers such as George Philip and Son, Geographia, and John Bartholomew. In the USA, the National Geographic Society has a prolific cartographic output; NGS maps always carry a profusion of place-names. Map publication is not of course the exclusive province of specialists. Road, tourist and other maps are put out for the purposes of promotion or information by, for instance, petrol companies and tourist offices. In Western countries, petrol companies' maps are usually given away free and are of a high standard; in the Third World, they are generally less reliable, despite the fact that the user has to pay to get one. Automobile clubs usually produce maps of their own and neighbouring countries, though these are often only available to members. The Australian and the American Automobile Associations produce excellent maps of their areas; in Britain the Automobile Association and the Royal Automobile Club sell maps of all Europe, Asia and Africa. The road maps of the Argentine Automobile Club are said to be exceptionally good. Motoring organizations in Europe can often supply detailed maps of the Sahara routes.

The Michelin Tyre Company has a reputation for excellent route maps, and produces a justly famous series covering Africa at 1:4,000,000. One authority on the Sahara noted, however, that even these maps contain some quite serious errors. Michelin maps of Mali show main routes incorrectly, track classifications out of date and emphasis on the wrong place names. As a safeguard, travellers should always carry large scale maps as well. Michelin are, of course, not the only company guilty of perpetrating cartographic errors. Mapmakers often take the easy way out by referring to existing sources rather than surveying the ground and so mistakes in reading, copying, interpreting, printing and even in wishful thinking are perpetuated. Why, for example, is Nome in Alaska so called? Because someone misread 'Name' scrawled on a map.

If you want to know what maps are available to cover your field of interest, visit (in Britain) the public map room at the Royal Geographical Society or the British Library. Here you may consult maps, discover where to buy them, make your own notes and photocopies from maps held in the library's collection, or arrange for them to be photocopied for your own private use. (Note: the laws of copyright generally prevent maps from being photocopied for reproduction. Also note: if a photocopy is a different size from the original, it is also a different scale.) Maps may be purchased from specialist outlets (e.g. Stanfords, 12–14 Long Acre, London WC2E 9LP) or from other stockists (e.g. Harrods). Best of all for the international traveller, is Geo Center Internationales Landkartenhaus, Postfach 80 05 07, D-7000 Stuttgart 80. Tel: (07 11) 73 30 29. Geo Center is probably the world's largest stockist of all kinds of maps and is well worth contacting, if not actually visiting.

With the now commonplace use of aerial and satellite photography as aids in mapmaking, nearly all of the world has been surveyed and charted, if not actually trodden. You must not expect to find any more virgin territory. Console yourself: you may not be the first, but you could (with the right maps) be the best equipped.

For further information see registers of map publishers and retailers from page 560.

Background Reading

by Hilary Bradt

With all the fuss involved in preparing for a trip, background reading often stays in the background or is neglected altogether. Yet the proper choice of a travel guide can make all the difference between a relaxed, enjoyable trip and one fraught with anxiety and disappointment, and a good travel book can heighten enjoyment by lending familiarity to the places visited.

Of course, your reading requirements depend on the type of trip you are planning. There's little point in buying a book on the archaeology of Tunisia if all you plan to do in North Africa is lie on a beach; or in buying one of those *$25 a Day* books on how to enjoy cities cheaply if you plan to spend as short a time as possible in them.

Broadly speaking, guidebooks are designed to inform you on necessary preparations for your trip, and to guide you on your travels, while travel books are out to entertain, providing useful information in passing. For most people, background reading involves the use of libraries, both local reference libraries and specialist ones such as those at the Royal Geographical Society, the Natural History Museum, and universities. It is much easier to read up on a specific subject than a general one, and those seeking specialist information will have little trouble. It is the first time traveller who finds the wealth of information on his chosen country or continent bewildering and is likely to be overwhelmed by choice. He is advised to begin by reading an informative and interesting travel book which gives the general feel of the place. Such a book will probably have an annotated bibliography directing the reader to other recommended books.

The *National Geographic* magazine is an excellent source of background material (although reality is often a little disappointing after those marvellous photos). Large libraries bind the magazine in six-month batches, plus a separate index, which makes it a simple matter to look up your special interest. Articles from other magazines, such as *The Traveller*, and newspapers are particularly useful for busy people with a thirst for knowledge, and have the added advantage that they can be cut out and taken on the trip. A list of the contents of past issues can often be had on request, especially if accompanied by a s.a.e. Articles which appeared only mildly interesting when read at home become quite riveting once you're in the country described. The same applies to books. Holiday reading matter should be carefully selected, however, and in no sense should it be heavy, or it will be left at the hotel while you sit on the beach guiltily reading *Time* magazine.

Overland travellers with unlimited time will prefer to do much of their reading en route, when they have had the chance to decide which aspects of a country most interest them. The British Council libraries in capital cities are often useful (although the emphasis is on British culture) and national libraries sometimes have books in English, as do universities. English language bookshops will also have a better selection of titles on that country than can be found at home.

The proper selection of a guidebook is as important to the traveller as the choice of luggage or footwear. It should advise and inform, be evocative yet objective, and help you plan your trip and make maximum use of your travel time. The price of books has risen so sharply in recent years that travellers are often reluctant to buy them. Yet most guidebooks cost only as much as a meal in a restaurant and, in contrast, can be thoroughly sampled before buying. Surely books are still among the best bargains available!

A Guide to Guides

by Christopher Portway, with additions by Melissa Shales

There are guidebooks and there are guidebooks. By which profound statement I mean that there are those guides that are an absolute depository of information and facts though deadly serious about it; those, like the *Michelin Green Guides* that are best read, book in hand, as you roam the villages of, say, Brittany; and there are those guides most advantageously perused both before and after a journey. Of course most guides should be read twice anyway; first as a chore before departure and again upon return when it becomes a much pleasanter exercise as you read about subjects with which you are familiar.

In this ever-changing age, guidebooks become out of date as the printer's ink dries, but there are some which are reprinted at regular intervals thus retaining their topicality. Such indomitable works as the *South American Handbook* (Travel and Trade Publications), the *Penguin Travel Guides*, covering, to date, *Europe*, *United States*, *Canada*, *South America* and the *Caribbean*, *Bermuda and the Bahamas*, and the *Michelin Red Guides*, in English, on *France* and *Great Britain* remain with us year after year.

The guidebook author these days embraces not only continents, countries and regions but delves, in ever more detail, into the particular activities they offer and the transport systems within them. Even Michelin, for so long exclusive to the regions of France, has branched out, not only into *Austria*, *Canada*, *Germany*, *Italy*, *London*, *Portugal*, *Spain* and the *USA*, but also into *Camping and Caravanning in France*.

Camping

Even in this last, somewhat narrow category, there are other titles aimed at the caravanner such as *The Caravan Book* by Christine Fagg (Exley), a useful how-to-do-it guide, *The Campground and Trailer Park Guide* (to the USA) (Rand McNally) and the regularly produced *Deneway Guide* (PO Box 286, Rottingdean, Brighton) detailing sites and parks.

Climbing, backpacking and walking have, by their increased popularity, encouraged into being a whole library of guides. I have before me John Cleare's beautifully illustrated *Mountains and Mountaineering* (Collins) which tells the reader a great deal about the mountain ranges of the world from the Himalayas down to the lovely but insignificant hills of the English Lake District, and, by the same author, *Mountaineering* (Blandford), a useful introduction to the pastime, again superbly illustrated by a master of alpine photography.

Backpacking experts are two-a-penny with Hilary and George Bradt's *Backpacking and Trekking in . . .* paperbacks leading a field of titles such as *The Backpacker's Handbook* by Derek Booth (Letts), *The Complete Guide to Hiking and Backpacking* (Winchester Press, USA), *Weekend*

Walking by Rob Hunter (Oxford Illustrated Press), *Britain at Your Feet* by David Wickers and Art Pedersen (Hamlyn), *Winter Skills* by Rob Hunter (Constable) plus the small but concise *Spur Books of Backpacking, Hill Trekking* and *Walking* to name but a few in this useful set.

Even hitch-hiking has a champion in Simon Calder and his *Hitch-hiker's Manual* as well as *Europe – A Manual for Hitch-hikers* (Vacation Work).

Transport

Nor are railways ignored. Though not exactly a guide book, Sphere's *Great Railway Journeys of the World* together with Lutterworth's *Railways for Pleasure* by Kenneth Westcott Jones which is, will set readers on the right rails for long-distance train journeys as well as preserved railways in Britain. And in the sphere of world train travel, dare I mention my own latest title, *The Great Railway Adventure* (Oxford Illustrated Press).

Touring by car is a popular pastime and this, of course, really opens the floodgates to a whole range of regional guides. France and her byways inspired Arthur Eperon to produce *Traveller's France* followed by *Encore Traveller's France* (Pan Books) that television brought to the attention of those wanting suggestions for a leisurely route through that fair country instead of simply blinding south on expensive and savage motorways. A somewhat similar format is produced by Richard Binns under his own publishing label of Chilton House, a brave effort that brought his *French Leave*, *France à la Carte*, and *Hidden France* almost as much kudos as Arthur Eperon's creations.

Other guidebooks that will find a ready readership in the general field of touring could be those of the Batsford label which include *Cornwall*, *Corfu*, *Burgundy*, *Athens*, *Egypt*, *West Germany* and elsewhere while the invariably excellent *Blue Guides* (Benn) – of which there are dozens – and *Red Guides* (Ward Lock) on *Northumbria* and other British counties are extremely comprehensive and packed full of information.

It is of course the *Michelin Green Guides* again that come into their own for touring France but there are others that have a particular appeal such as the *Guide de Relais Routier* for those looking for restaurants along the way. And while on the subject of France, I must mention Keith Spence's delightful and beautifully written *Britanny and the Bretons* (Gollancz) – hardly a guide perhaps but it will teach you much about Brittany – and the *Shell Guide to France* (Michael Joseph), a gazetteer of French towns plus some useful and well-presented facts about France and the French.

Touring America is a popular pastime these days and, of course, there are guidebooks to match. A good general introduction to the subject can be found with *A Visitor's Travel Guide to the United States* (Rand McNally and EP Publishing) and the *Mobil Travel Guides* (Rand McNally) to various quite large areas. I found the *Rand McNally Guide to California* and *Florida* extremely useful when I was last visiting these states and there are other titles available or in preparation. *West Coast USA* by Ine van Dam (Murray) is another regional guide I recommend, this one on the subject of the three states bordering the Pacific. For those on a limited budget,

Michael van Haag's *Moneywise Guides to* . . . are also worth looking at.

Further Afield

So to the world at large and two new titles that fill a need – for they look at the economical way of living in the regions they cover – are *A Rough Guide to Spain* and *A Rough Guide to Greece* (Routledge and Kegan Paul). And talking of Greece, anyone finding themselves in the wild north-western corner of that country would do well to invest in *Epirus* by Arthur Foss (Faber), a very readable tome. Collins are producing an ever-increasing number of small, inexpensive, superficial but useful pocket editions called *Welcome Guides to ...*, covering Europe, North Africa and North America. For those who wish to remain comfortable in spite of a limited budget, Arthur Frommer's series . . . *on $25 a Day* would be hard to beat. And in Crete I found *The Traveller's Guide to Crete* by John Bowman (Cape) to be an intelligently composed member of a family of such guides.

To tackle China only a year or two after its still restricted opening is a daunting project, so all praise to Elizabeth Morrell for her *Visitor's Guide to China* (Joseph) and Brian Schwartz for *China Off The Beaten Track* (Harvill Press). The best of the burgeoning guides to India is *India: a Travel Survival Kit*, one of a rapidly growing series from Lonely Planet Publications that already covers much of the Far East and is now expanding into the Americas. *The Trekker's Guide to the Himalaya and Karakoram* by Hugh Swift (Hodder and Stoughton) is a very useful practical guide to this popular holiday area.

Travelling hopefully is something of an art and there are guides to help attain it. The best, in my opinion, covering general holiday travel is *The Travel Survival Guide* by Carol Wright (David and Charles) which even tells you how to be a stowaway. The amateur expeditioner on the other hand might prefer Richard Harrington's *500 Inside Tips for the Long Haul Traveller* (WEXAS) or the more comprehensive *Traveller's Handbook* you are now reading. John Hatt's *The Tropical Traveller* (Pan) is another book full of practical advice well worth heeding.

Which leaves me with just two recommendations. Before you leave for foreign fields, don't forget to put the dog or cat out. *The Good Kennel and Cattery Guide* by Monica Hart (Collins) will tell you where and how much it will cost. And when you come back? If you can raise £20-odd from all the money you've saved by reading and acting upon the advice given by a good guidebook, then invest in Peter Yapp's *Travellers' Dictionary of Quotations* (Routledge and Kegan Paul) which, placed by your armchair, will keep you amused when there's nothing on the telly.

Good travelling, and may you know what you're seeing and doing.

Highlights and Hassles

Western Europe

by Melissa Shales

There is a danger that, as people look further afield in search of excitement and adventure, they will forget Europe – 'tame', 'on-the-doorstep' Europe. Yet Western Europe is, in many ways, the ideal place to travel, particularly if you are restricted in the amount of time that you can take off. It contains many of the world's greatest cities, much of the world's great art and architecture, and a wide variety of cultures and lifestyles. Outside the cities there are also endless things to see. And the distance between them is never too far.

This small continent is littered with major (and minor) airports, excellent road and rail systems. Packages and charter flights and a dazzling array of discounts and cheap deals bring potentially high fares down to a reasonable level, as long as you are prepared to travel outside peak hours. Tickets such as Inter-Rail for the under 26s can take you all round Europe for a month for little over £100. It may be an unforgettable experience to travel for a week third class on Indian Railways, but if you have only two weeks off from a crowded work schedule, it is a relief to get to your destination in relative comfort and at a reasonable speed. In Europe, we might all complain like mad about inefficiency, but the transport network is, on the whole, positively luxurious.

Hitchhiking is generally easy, although France doesn't have too good a reputation, but is banned on motorways, *autobahns* etc. However, these trunk roads usually have numerous service stations where hitching is not only legal but extremely successful.

There is rarely any real problem in making yourself understood. On a recent trip to Switzerland, I armed myself with a phrasebook and dictionary and practised waving my arms, only to find that these scientific preparations were almost totally unnecessary as everyone spoke pretty good English. It was easy, but disappointing. The European languages are the universal ones and the general standard of education is high. In smaller countries, such as the Scandinavian ones and the Netherlands, it seems common for children to learn four languages at school – and English is always one of them.

Space

Europe's main fault is its size in relation to its population, a situation worsened by the vast number of tourists that descend each year – some 100 million around the Mediterranean. It is certainly not the place for those who, above all else, crave wide open spaces devoid of any human activity.

You will have to accept that where you go, so go thousands of others – by the coach load. Sightseeing has to be done at the crack of dawn, before the tour parties arrive, or out of season. And while you may be prepared to put up with rain, wind and sleet, you will find that many historic sites, museums, hotels, restaurants, etc. shut for the winter.

I personally find that the best time to travel is either just before Easter, as the season is slowly grinding into action, or at the end of September, when it is tottering to a close. Although the weather is very uncertain in spring, it will normally be kind to you in late autumn, and the Mediterranean is still quite warm enough for swimming and sunbathing.

Another point, in this overcrowded place, is that it is worth avoiding the school holidays if possible – crowds magically double and the noise level triples about three days after the end of term. Holidaying out of season also has the advantage of costing considerably less.

If you are heading for the major cities of Europe, it may even be worth travelling in December. The cities are rarely affected badly by the weather, and while sunshine is pleasant, it is not essential if you are spending so much time under cover. The Christmas shops are magnificent, and this time of year often sees the best of the year's theatre.

Accommodation

There is an abundance of choice in accommodation from five star hotels with world famous names, such as the Ritz or the George Cinq, to modern chains, from *pensions* to pubs, hostels or campsites. The price range is similarly wide – a night at the Ritz would probably pay for a two-week camping holiday – but a general rule of thumb is that things are considerably more expensive than their Third World counterparts, with the exceptions of the big chains such as Holiday Inns, which are expensive everywhere. On the whole, Europe is not vastly expensive – and the advent of fast food has meant that you can eat relatively healthily on a low budget.

Food, of course, varies wildly in quality, but there are few places in Europe where it is impossible to find the sort of food which we normally only dream about – at a cost. The French and the Italians, in particular, are very jealous of the reputation of their food, and meals play a leading role in the day's activities. Other countries are perhaps not so vehement in the defence of their local dishes, but awareness is growing, and the caff is giving way to the bistro all over the continent.

I, personally, would not choose Europe for a beach holiday if I could afford to go elsewhere, with overcrowding, concrete beachfronts, and a growing danger of disease from pollution, but there are still places around the Mediterranean where it is possible to be relatively isolated, and where the coast has not been wrecked by tourist development. The lack of a tide, sharks and dangerous currents make the swimming far safer than on many more picturesque beaches.

A Sense of Time

What makes Europe unique is not its beaches, or even its scenery, lovely as much of this may be, but the long, visible history and sense of tradition that are built into the culture. Europeans tend to take for granted the fact that their churches are 900 years old, that their cities are living museums, and that they inhabit houses built centuries ago. It is easy for a Londoner to walk past Westminster Abbey without even noticing it, but it is an education to watch Americans trying to absorb the concept of such a lengthy heritage.

To travel away from home in Europe gives us all a renewed sense of the past, and a new eye for beauty jaded by close proximity. It is an unforgettable experience to sit in Venice and watch St Mark's turn to gold in the evening sun, or in Notre Dame while organ music fills the air so richly that even the stone hums in response. You can wander round the living stone of Pompeii with Pliny's vivid account of the day Vesuvius erupted in your mind. The history is so real you can share an anguish two thousand years old. And through it all, you can see the continent still changing, building on the past. Nature has not been so cruel as to obliterate former civilizations as she has often done in the jungles and the deserts. She has left a wealth of inspiration that will always ensure that Europe is alive, and unafraid to innovate and experiment.

Outside the towns you can watch the fishing boats coming in, dusty donkeys moving through the tortured olive trees, sleek cows in fields of technicolour green, hills covered by winding vines, patterned green and gold of feudal fields. You can walk through lush woodland, and dramatic snow-capped peaks, or on the stark open spaces of moor and marsh. Compare them with the Prairies or the Himalayas and they are small, but they are also beautiful.

People-Watching

There are parts of Europe where 'people-watching' is still worthwhile, but they are becoming few and far between – at least, that is, if you want quaint peasantry in local dress. Lifestyles tend, on the whole, to be sophisticated, with televisions, pop and rock, denim and leather universal amongst the young. Occasionally you see someone wearing *lederhosen* or clogs, but nine times out of ten, they will turn out to be tourists. In Latin countries, all the widows still wear black, and national costumes everywhere still get dusted off for highdays and holidays, but they are no longer central to the culture. Where once you might have found Little Bo Peep, you will now probably find Mohican haircuts and steel studs.

In general, people are so used to tourism that you won't ever find annoying curiosity about strangers, but neither will you find the friendliness that allows you to be taken, as a stranger, into someone's home. In Europe, if they invite you to eat, it will be in a restaurant, until such time as you are well-known and trusted. You are more likely to be exploited by the few who depend on tourism for their livelihood and ignored, as far as possible, by the rest of the population. It takes more than a smile to win friends in this cynical society.

You won't find peace, or freedom, or innocence in Europe, but you will find a stunning artistic heritage, a sense of pride in tradition and an exciting, pulsating way of life.

Eastern Europe

by Tim Sharman

If ever there is a region which gives good value in exchange for prejudice, this is it, for, whatever you may have heard or whatever you may believe, there are many more highlights than hassles to be had when travelling in Eastern Europe. My introduction was a walk from the Baltic coast to Poland south and east to Istanbul and – unless you are crossing the Gobi desert – this must be the best way to meet a country. A day spent walking is rich with detail and the face to face contact is available no other way. You may travel as you wish, for visas are easily obtainable for all countries except Albania.

Poland – to start at the 'top' of the map – may appear flat and uninteresting, but on the ground you will find a unique mood and scenes that are positively medieval. With most agriculture in private ownership, there has been little development in the rural areas where the horse and cart are still seen in every cobbled country lane and old and young alike can be met on a summer's evening walking the cow down the road to graze on the verges. Friendly and curious people they are, too. A chain of glacial lakes stretches across the northern plain, providing the perfect environment for mosquitoes and kayaks, both of which are found in great number. I slept in orchards and fields, old cottages and modern apartments, but the best surprise in Poland is the Youth Hostel at Schroniska, which serves as a school, except in the summer. Some hostels have dormitories, others private rooms with radio and television; all are very cheap.

Trains are also remarkably cheap, but free travel is encouraged with an official hitchhiking scheme whereby you wave a card and drivers score points for giving lifts to members. Details are available in most towns. The low cost of everything can be a problem, for most visitors have to exchange a fixed amount of currency each day, US$15 at the time of writing – an amount almost impossible to spend, short of buying new boots every afternoon. No doubt drivers will use a lot on fuel, if they can find it; fuel stations are few and far between. In spite of the present situation in Poland, visitors are still welcome, but check first.

In the south of Poland and extending through eastern Czechoslovakia are the Tatra and Mala Tatra mountains which provide good climbing and in winter many opportunities for off-*piste* skiing. Facilities are good with mountain huts and, in Slovakia, luxurious low-level camping sites which allow small tents to be pitched in the deeply rutted spaces ignored by the car campers. The beer is good and the food plentiful. The long wooded ridges form a barrier between the northern plain and the Danube basin; and the mood changes dramatically when you drop down on to the great flat land that forms so much of the modern state of Hungary. This was once the bottom of a great inland sea and the small portion of this that is left, Lake Balaton, is a major tourist centre and best avoided by all except windsurfers and sociologists. The flat, sandy plain has great tracts of moving dunes, millions of acres of sunflowers, some of the most relaxed and friendly people you will meet in Europe, generally a high standard of living, and hot, dry summers. Again there are good camping sites and a system of Youth Hostels similar to Poland's although less widespread.

Bicycle, Cart and Tractor

Here the bicycle reigns supreme except, that is, far away from the main routes, for in many places the smaller roads are nothing but deep dry sand tracks and locally the horse and cart and tractor are the favoured means of transport. To make the effort of walking out onto one of the vast stretches of open grassland, such as the Hortobágy in the east or the Bugac in the south, near Kecskemét, is to experience a very special sense of space. There are no problems in Hungary, no fixed amounts of money to change, but good food, good wine, interesting old towns such as Eger against the hills in the north and Pécs with its dozen or so museums in the south; and through it all slides the sluggish Danube. South of this watercourse the plain runs on to the dry hills of Yugoslavia; complex, forested, often rugged and containing some of the biggest tracts of wilderness on the continent.

Romania has a great deal going for it but it is worth mentioning a couple of points of relevance to those of us who cannot afford to travel but insist on doing so. It is illegal to stay overnight in a private house without police permission. Any repercussions will be felt by the host more than the visitor, so do not compromise these kind people. Secondly, do not expect to be able to book into a friendly-looking third category hotel without a problem for, if there is a soulless concrete first category hotel anywhere near, all tourists will be directed to it to be charged $25 a night for a bed, even in a small, featureless town. And the campsites, too, are variable, ranging from the excellent to a sandpit full of dead beach huts. Do not be put off, however, by these drawbacks for this is probably the most fascinating and attractive country in this region. The great curve of the Carpathian watershed provides adventure and discovery for a lifetime, with great rounded domes of forest and high grassland in the east, rocky crags in the south and, lying within these containing hills, Transylvania, until this century a part of the Hungarian empire and still retaining in many places its Magyar culture and character.

As you travel here, in one village you will be addressed in Romanian, the next in Hungarian and quite possibly German in the one after that. This is confusing when you have been trudging along all day practising a few phrases in Romanian, the easiest language for the non-linguist to comprehend, looking as it does like a mixture of French, Spanish and Italian. Here also are the Romany gypsies, still wandering around the hills, asleep in their horsedrawn covered wagons or begging in the larger towns. And do not ignore Moldavia, that strip of land between the mountains and the Soviet border, for it is a fragment of the great Russian steppe and the clothing of the many shepherds will confirm this connection. However, the magnet of the eastern marches must be the delta of the Danube where life, land, and water merge into a unique composition.

The Danube Divide

The rich southern plains lead once again to the inevitable Danube but once across – and there is only one bridge – you will feel an immediate physical and cultural change. The most obvious aspect is that the written word is in Cyrillic script. Signposts too – so make sure your map is bilingual, otherwise you can be instantly lost. The sound of the language is familiar, however, if you have a smattering of some Slavic tongue, and an attempt to communicate is worthwhile because the Bulgarians are, in my experience, particularly hospitable and generous. One notable day, I stopped in a village for a drink and I was still there a week later.

In the central plain around the river Maritsa there are many modern and rapidly expanding towns, but mostly the country is mountainous, the southern Rhodope range having many peaks over 2,900m and much for the lover of wildlife who may even run across the odd brown bear or wolf pack.

What of problems general to the region as a whole? Obviously, be sensible with your camera, keep it in its case at railway stations, airports and when passing factories and military camps. I had an embarrassing hour or two in Poland after snapping a narrow gauge steam locomotive in a small country town; whilst in a mountain village in Czechoslovakia police destroyed my film after I was seen photographing a gypsy camp. Often action is at the whim of a local officer, so if questioned smile a lot, shake hands with everyone and tell them what a great country it is! With regard to the famous black market in money, resist temptation because you never know with whom you are dealing and deportation is very humiliating. Most prices are reasonable enough at the official rate. Finally, tee-totallers beware, for this is drinking country: little old men with silver teeth will produce unlabelled bottles of firewater at the nod of a head and since to refuse is to insult you will need to be prepared for some powerful home brews.

The Middle East

by Beth Roberts

Owing to the numerous and complex political differences in the Middle East, this is not perhaps the easiest area of the world in which to travel. Religious and social differences too can cause embarrassment and misunderstandings for the unprepared Western traveller. Especially when going to a Muslim country, it is well worth swotting up on the etiquette beforehand (*see How to Be In with Islam, page 409*).

Of the nine main countries in the Middle East, there are only four which are likely to welcome foreign visitors. These are Turkey, Egypt, Israel and Jordan. The political position in Iraq makes travel impossible, and while Syria is still perfectly accessible, it seems unwise until their involvement with the Lebanon is at an end. The Lebanon, once the jewel of the Middle East, is now a shattered ruin that is likely to be closed to travellers for the foreseeable future.

Turkey

The cheapest way into Turkey from the West is overland to Istanbul, by train, bus or car. Please remember, if travelling this way, that a transit visa is required for Bulgaria. It is also possible to get a ferry from Venice or Brindisi to Ismir. Hospitality is a cornerstone of the Turkish way of life. Accept it as graciously as possible, as a refusal could cause offence.

Turkey is largely an Islamic country. When visiting a mosque, you are required to remove your shoes before entering and wash your feet at the water taps outside. The floors of the larger mosques, such as the Blue Mosque in Istanbul, are covered with layers of rugs. The great mosques of Istanbul are some of the most beautiful in the world.

A visit to the covered bazaar in Istanbul is a must: leather work of all kinds can be bought at low prices, but haggle and shop around for the best bargains. A famous 'hangout' in Istanbul is the Pudding Shop, where you can find a hitchhiking partner of the opposite sex, which is essential, especially for women who, travelling alone, would almost certainly be molested. Males alone too would have little luck with rides. In mixed company however, the worst that could happen would be that the man could be offered money for 'his' woman.

Travel around the urban areas of Turkey is most convenient by *dolmus* – shared taxis, recognizable by the black and yellow chequered band around the car. Make sure of the charge before entering to avoid argument at the end of your journey. The coffee shops and fish restaurants under the Galata Bridge, which crosses the Golden Horn in Istanbul, are a fascinating glimpse of the real Turkey – not a 'put-up job' for the gullible tourist.

Turkey can be reached by ferry from several of the Greek islands in the Aegean, but this can prove very expensive, as relations between the two countries are less than cordial; to discourage travellers from crossing to mainland Turkey, the Greek authorities levy an exit tax.

If you propose to travel through Turkey to visit the other Middle Eastern countries, there are two main routes; the direct one, following the E5 through Ankara and Adana to Antioch (Antakya); or the more scenic route, via the Dardanelles, Troy, Izmir, Ephesus and around the Mediterranean coast to Adana. The crossing of the Bosphorus at Istanbul is a simple matter since the opening of the huge suspension bridge.

Syria and Jordan

Syria has little to offer (bar some splendid Crusader castles) that is outstanding or worth a detour from the main route through to Jordan, via Homs or Damascus. Damascus is renowned for its silk and the downtown market is interesting. From here you can reach Jordan by train, bus, shared taxi (in Jordan it's called a service taxi) or hitchhike.

Of all the Arab countries, Jordan is the friendliest. Poor in comparison to their oil rich neighbours, the Jordanians have half a million Palestinian refugees in their midst. There are many fascinating places to visit. On the road from Damascus to Amman, there is Jerash – the Pompeii of the Middle East – where the tracks of the chariot wheels can still be seen in the paving stones of the main street. This second century Gaeco-Roman city was simply abandoned, and the topsoil of years covered it, preserving the ancient stonework.

In order to cross to the West Bank and hence into Israel, one must have a 'West Bank' permit, which can be obtained only from the Ministry of the Interior in King Hussein Street. A bus or service taxi will take you from Amman to King Hussein Bridge, where you cross the River Jordan to the West Bank.

No visit to Jordan is complete without a dip in the Dead Sea and a visit to Petra, 'the rose red city half as old as time', hidden away in the encircling rocky mountains south of the Dead Sea. This ancient city was literally carved out of the solid rock two thousand years ago by the Nabataeans. In order to see all of Petra, it is wise to stay overnight. If you are hardy you can sleep in one of the Nabataean caves; if not, in the government rest house. For a really splendid experience, get up before dawn to watch the sun come up over the city.

The long, white beaches, as yet largely undeveloped, along the Red Sea coast of Jordan, abound with tropical fish and fabulous underwater coral reefs. Aqaba is ringed by mountains, so is very sheltered, thus providing all-year-round bathing and sun-bathing. Service taxis run regularly out of Amman to Aqaba, Petra, Jerash, etc.

Camp David Country

Visitors to Israel who intend to return to an Arab country within the life of their passport should ensure that the entry and exit stamps are not recorded in their passports. On request, the Israeli authorities will put the stamps on a separate piece of paper. From the border you can get a service taxi to Damascus Gate, the entrance to the old city of Jerusalem.

Since inflation is daily higher in Israel, you should change money from day to day. It is as well to have small denomination cash for this reason. Hitchhiking is an accepted practice in Israel, but can be slow if there are soldiers about, as they always get priority. Since food and hostel accommodation are expensive, travellers do sleep on the beach. If you do the same, beware of thieves. The buses are crowded and you must reserve a seat.

Eilat is hot and dirty, very 'touristy' and not to be recommended, especially if you have been to Aqaba.

Israel is, of course, well known for its kibbutz system. If you are interested in working and staying on a kibbutz, information can be obtained from the Israeli Government Tourist Office, or from various kibbutz representatives of which there are some in London as well as Tel Aviv. You should be prepared to stay for at least two months. Working holidays in Israel can prove expensive as you have to pay, at least initially, to go and put in hours of back breaking hard labour, whether on a kibbutz or an archaeological dig.

Since the agreement between Egypt and Israel, a very popular route to Cairo is from Jerusalem via El Arish in the Sinai. It is important to get your visa for Egypt before you reach the border post, otherwise you are likely to be required to change a large amount of money into Egyptian pounds at the official rate. Other routes into Egypt are by boat, from Greece or Cyprus to Alexandria, or by air from Istanbul (good prices are to be had on shopping around). A local bus runs from Cairo airport to Tahrir Square, near the River Nile.

As soon as possible after arriving in Egypt, within seven days at the latest, you must register with the passport office. The main office is in Tahrir Square. You are not told about this on arrival in the country, though the stamp in your passport may be an indication, for those who read Arabic.

Food in Egypt tends to be a great problem, meat especially being expensive and meagre.

The pyramids and the Sphinx at Giza are just a short bus ride away from Tahrir Square. Go early to arrive before the heat of the day and the coachloads of tourists. You can get to Alexandria by bus from Tahrir Square, or by train, if you can manage to find the right queue for tickets! Buying train tickets for Luxor or Aswan also tends to be a problem; you need to spend several hours at the station, some days before you wish to go.

Arabia and Beyond

Those wishing to go to Saudi Arabia may be able to get a three-day visa, extendable in Jeddah for a further three days. This is definitely not a country for the single female to visit as Islamic law on women is very repressive here. From Jeddah it is possible to go to Sana'a, Yemen, where the beaches are said to be good and where many expatriates living in Saudi Arabia go on holiday. For the foreseeable future travelling in Iran is likely to be unwise, although it is still possible to transit through the south of the country from Pakistan, so that buses from Nepal and India are getting through.

The USSR

by Christopher Portway

The only economic method of visiting the USSR is by way of a package tour. It is the same, I suppose, with most countries of the world but it's more than just economics so far as Mother Russia is concerned. With her there's the question of control and surveillance of visitors and it's so much easier to ensure that a group of people look upon what's good for them than to attempt to blinker an inquisitive individual traveller. The Soviet Union yearns for the hard Western currency of tourism but makes little effort to hide a revulsion for tourists.

Here, more than in any other Communist country, I was to discover this depressing fact. My journeying in the USSR has only been of the individual variety so my related findings concern the non-packaged visitor. And let me say right now that it is a most interesting country to visit in either capacity, so don't allow my acid comments to deflect you from going.

My entry into the Soviet Union has always been via Brest-Litovsk on the main railway line between Warsaw and Moscow. This line is on the classic invasion route through ByeloRussia. Napoleon's armies passed that way. So did the Germans and Poles in World War I, and again, the Germans in World War II. Maybe this is the reason for the savage border controls here. They don't always search your luggage but make a great fuss about Bibles and 'unprogressive' literature. Invariably I leave Brest with my tail between my legs, so my advice is to arrive in the country by air. I'm told that officials actually smile at the Sheremetyevo Airport, though they didn't the one time I came through in transit on an Air India flight from Delhi.

Moscow

I can't in all honesty recommend Moscow's Bucharest Hotel to which you may be assigned. It is a tourist class hotel, not de luxe, in which class – to use an Imperialist word – most packaged visitors are housed. And let me say at this point that the visitor to Mother Russia has little say in the selection of a hotel. There is just the choice of grades and the money you pay. Intourist do the rest. Every town and resort open to foreigners – there are about 100, which is precious few in a vast country like Russia – has one or more hotels run by the state tourist department and it is into one of these you go.

On my last visit to Moscow, the porter watched me struggling with my bags but made no effort to help. At the reception desk began a process that, with occasional variations, was to be repeated at every establishment I was to stay in over the length and breadth of the Soviet Union. Joining a queue, I inched towards a bespectacled woman of severe countenance. To her I submitted my passport – which she retained – and my sheaf of accommodation vouchers obtained previously in London. (As with all Socialist countries, the issue and validity of a visa is dependent upon the number of days you are staying in the country, but in Russia your itinery is also predestined.) In exchange, I was given an accommodation coupon (there is a subtle difference but it escaped me) and, carefully clipped into a little blue folder, my breakfast coupons. There followed an interval for ledger and form filling and, though the Soviet Union may be lavishly equipped with IBMs, it doesn't seem to have got around to carbon paper.

Subsequent to this and sundry interruptions, I was directed to another room optimistically entitled 'Service Bureau'. Here I was supposed to finalize arrangements for my already scheduled onwar journey, for you can book into no Russian hotel until it knows when it can get rid of you. I found the 'Service Bureau' to be crammed with a seething, frustrated swarm of guests all talking at the top of their voices in a babble of tongues but with nobody listening. So I tried to short-circuit the system and was promptly given a reprimand, full attention and my onward rail ticket. Also the instructions that a taxi would be awaiting two days hence to take me to the Yaroslavski Railway Station at 0800 and 'you will present yourself at it at that time'. My informant didn't actually add 'or else'.

For two days Moscow was all mine. Lenin's Tomb is a 'must' – particularly since a foreign visitor is pushed up to the front of the eternal queue – but don't try taking photos as I did! The Moscow Metro is also worth a ride or two if only to see the stations, which are highly decorative. The cost is only a few kopeks. Money changers will pounce on you from out of the shadows and make attractive financial propositions, but ignore them unless you want to experience the inside of Lubyanka. Jeans and jazzy shirts are in great demand too but one can't very well do a striptease in front of the Kremlin. The GUM Department Store is another Moscow 'sight' but to buy anything there – as if you'd want to – means a bigger hassle than booking into the Bucharest Hotel. A purchase involves a simple procedure made complicated. Following selection of goods, payment has to be made at a desk. Queue No. 1. Return to goods counter to exchange receipt for goods. Queue No. 2. Should goods need wrapping there is a special department carrying out the service. Queue No. 3. But there is a short cut here – bring your own wrapping paper. Soviet newspapers sell like hot cakes, possibly for that very reason.

Inadequate Lifts and Plumbing

Back at the Bucharest I found only one of the four lifts working. This is about the average ratio of working lifts throughout the Soviet Union. Banish any ideas you may have of getting away with any tomfoolery like bedroom visitors. That exclusively Russian institution, the Keeper of the Floor, a woman of massive proportions behind a massive desk – both specially constructed for the job – will see that you and you alone can pass. She has eyes like a hawk, very definite ideas on morals and she never sleeps. If she accepts you as a fit subject to grace her domain you are handed your bedroom key.

My room was old-fashioned and full of inadequate plumbing. There was a telephone and a radio tuned to a fixed station. There was a washbasin with no plug. At four in the morning the radio boomed out the Soviet National Anthem and at 4.30 came the first of three early calls I'd never ordered. On my last day my own early call woke somebody, I suppose, for it never came through to me.

Rail Travel

I have travelled over most of the USSR on its railways. To me they are the best thing in the country. They keep perfect time; the coaches are roomy (because of the wide gauge) and are a window, both outwards on Russia and inwards, on the Russians. A train is the only place you can really talk to a canny but hospitable people. In a compartment without the eyes of authority on them, they reveal all; politics and popsies, especially after a few luke-warm beers and vodkas in the restaurant car or the home-made variety in their briefcases. Tea is available from the ever-operating samovar at a few kopeks per tumbler. These, together with rock-hard Cuban sugar lumps form part of the compartment furniture. Your coach attendant will bring the tea, vacuum clean the carpet, bring your bedding at night (but not make your bed). She will also scream for official intervention should you try leaving the train at a stop that holds 'no facilities' for tourists, i.e. is forbidden to foreigners. You will travel soft class, i.e. first class, since hard class – second class – is for peasants only. I managed to travel hard class all the way to Vladivostok (no facilities) on Train No. 2 – the Trans-Siberian Express – but that's another story.

Air Travel

Air travel in the Soviet Union, like everywhere else, is dull. But it is made duller by there being fewer titbits in flight. The taking of photographs over the Motherland is strictly *verboten*. If you want to liven things up, try it. When an aircraft lands at an unscheduled airport – with or without facilities – and everyone is delayed for hours with no explanation, you're not expected to ask why.

Individual Travellers

An individual traveller is afforded individual attention. At each destination an Intourist guide will meet you off the train or plane. No use trying to dodge him or her (usually a her), as I did, for it only makes them stroppy. For your money you get a lengthy lecture on the local factory production figures, a drive round the town and instructions as to where you go next. You may walk around on your own in permitted towns, but try to leave and you'll come a cropper at the control points that ring every urban centre.

A camera is looked upon with grave suspicion in Russia, but is not forbidden. There is a long list of taboo subjects including all the obvious items and many others like bridges, stations, policemen and soldiers. You may take pictures of railway trains – but not the track they run on. Soviet authority is touchy as hell near the Chinese border.

There are 'hard currency' shops where you can buy objects that Russians can't. Segregation is a recurring theme anywhere. They try to separate you from the locals at every turn but I don't like being separated, so continuously resist it. Eventually one wins the day because authority dare not make too much of a fuss since Communism has a lot to do with the proletariat, doesn't it? And an individual traveller has quite a job to keep hotel managements from mistaking him for a group visitor, although this can be an advantage. 'What group do you belong to?' you're asked time and time again, and each time you explain you're a loner. 'But you *must* be with a group' they insist and eventually you find yourself with a Bulgarian, a Polish or an East German party. They're always nice people so you go along with it. Then comes the time to pay for the beers and vodkas and extras – and sometimes whole meals if you're not on a prepaid jaunt – but you're told '*Niet*, payment is made by the group leader on a communal basis', so you argue a bit and shrug your shoulders. Thus many of my bills were paid by the Bulgarian, Polish and East German economies, which suited me fine.

So enjoy your visit to Mother Russia, but do remember to take with you a plug and a sense of humour.

Southern Asia

by Sylvia Matheson

Whatever anyone says, the joys of travelling anywhere east of Suez by far outweigh any tribulations for me: the refreshingly delicious green tea, lifesaving after a hot and dusty journey; the unaffected friendliness of folk at the wayside *chai khanas*; the patient and spontaneous helpfulness of truck drivers in their gaudily decorated behemoths; the inexpensive, but clean and simple accommodation at dak bungalows and station restrooms in India, Pakistan and Bangladesh; leisurely journeys on river steamers from Dacca to Khulna and the Sunderbans, tropical forest home of the Royal Bengal Tiger and other increasingly rare wildlife; mouthwatering meals aboard of fresh-caught Hilsa fish, baked to perfection, a Bangladesh speciality; the haunting songs of the fishermen; the fantastically fine muslins woven here; the jute and bamboo souvenirs.

Assam has dense jungles dripping with orchids, breathtaking views of the Himalayas towering above the Kaziranga Game Reserve with its rare white rhinos and charming guest house on stilts; near-naked Naga hillmen politely requesting discarded tin cans; and wild elephants blocking the main road!

You can take sybaritic holidays in luxuriously furnished houseboats on Kashmir's Dal Lake, with well-trained servants to wait on you and colourful *shikaras* paddled up to your verandah offering fresh flowers, groceries, the mail or suede coats made to measure overnight. And on the mainland, the famous Suffering Moses Emporium and handsome Persian carpets from the Government factory, handwoven by craftsmen whose ancestors came here from Iran centuries ago.

If you take local buses almost anywhere on the subcontinent, you not only see more of the country, with frequent stops for folk haring across the desert or down a mountain track bearing squawking chickens and mysterious, bulging bundles, but you soon make friends with fellow passengers eager to share their provender and invite you to their homes. Even if you don't think you'll need them, take biscuits, sweets, fruits or such to return their hospitality.

Of course, there are also nuisances, not least of which are revolutions and *coups d'états*. At the time of going to press, the overland route to India is extremely difficult, with a very uncertain atmosphere in Iran, the route through Afghanistan shut and likely to remain so, and the current uneasy situation in the Punjab.

Three Cardinal Rules

Wherever you go in Asia, and for that matter, the Middle East too, three things are of the utmost importance. First, make sure all your documents are in order and to be on the safe side, carry at least ten spare passport photos with you; I have even found a photocopy of my birth certificate has helped, God knows why. In addition, any kind of official-looking pass with your photograph on it, preferably stamped and covered with signatures, can be immensely useful, especially at little-used frontiers or when dealing with petty officials who are often illitrate or, at best, unable to read English. An official-looking piece of paper is usually all that the guardian of a shrine, for instance, may require to allow you to photograph – plus, perhaps, a discreetly offered *baksheesh*, a fact I learnt to my cost after I was stopped from even walking around a remote archaeological site on the borders of eastern Iran, and this despite previous assurances from the highest officials that no special permits were required. I never did manage to return.

Secondly, your appearance: no matter how rugged your journey has been, when you reach a frontier make sure you look respectable, i.e. shaven, unless you have a full beard, hair cut to a reasonable length, combed and clean; shirts with long sleeves that can be rolled up once away from the crowds, and above all, no shorts please! You may get away with wearing them, but the impression you leave will not be favourable; if tourists understood the contemptuous, scandalized comments made, they would surely take a little more care. And in strictly Muslim countries, girls, please don't wear those see-through dresses or sleeveless, backless sun tops – at least, not at the frontiers. Keep them for the pool or the seaside. I know of several instances where quite respectable girls with bare arms and legs have been abducted and raped, sometimes to disappear for good, and their menfolk assassinated.

The third essential is patience and you must have plenty of this in all situations. However provoked, never lose your temper. Be prepared for a thorough – and I mean thorough – search of your vehicle and baggage. You may have been told that no cholera inoculations are needed but if you're stopped by the roadside twice in half an hour, and ordered to take a couple of capsules with a mug of dubious-looking water, don't argue. Do it!

Smile and Sip

If you take the trouble to learn even a few words of the language of the country – Farsi helps in Iran, the odd Pushtu phrase and Urdu in Pakistan, and Hindi (the spoken language is virtually the same as Urdu) in India – you'll find tremendous response and friendliness. Actually, as I've found out, one can carry on a conversation for hours without really knowing a word of each other's language, gestures and expression being wonderful interpreters. Of course, in India, Pakistan, Sri Lanka and Bangladesh, you'll usually find someone who speaks English of a kind, even in remote areas; old ex-Servicemen, schoolteachers, and students rush to help the stranger.

Inevitably military guards appear along highways leading to frontiers; obey any orders to stop immediately as many are trigger-happy. Smile – and show all your papers without fuss. And never bring out your camera at bridges, railway stations, airfields or frontiers without making sure photography is permitted. (Of course you might camouflage yourself among the camels and sneak a picture, but is it worth it?)

The Sub-Continent

Places like Sikkim, Swat, Bhutan and Nepal usually require special permits. Bhutan, for instance, requires applications two and a half months in advance and firmly refuses permits to mountaineers or those involved in publicity or research.

Most travellers from Great Britain will feel at home in both Pakistan and India, not only from the language point of view, but because, despite their eagerness to get rid of their Imperialist rulers, they now welcome Britons both as residents and travellers and it's almost impossible not to make friends among all but the most orthodox families. But bear in mind that in both countries there are communities, no matter how Western-educated, which observe strict taboos. Among the strict Muslims, women are still secluded from all but close male relatives; high caste Brahmins will entertain you lavishly, but excuse themselves from eating or drinking with you. Don't take it personally, just accept the situation.

Bombay airport has been rated the worst in the world after Tokyo and Lagos – avoid it if you possibly can. If you can't, well, try more patience! Pinpoint a senior official and put your case to him calmly but firmly, blaming lack of communication or your own ignorance rather than stupidity or cussedness on the part of the staff.

Sri Lanka, in spite of the recent upheavals, is a delightfully relaxed island, again very pro-British, and apt to produce less official hassle than either India or Pakistan. Being predominantly Buddhist it is also more tolerant in many ways. However, as in India and Pakistan, currency regulations are fairly strict, and a strict record of your dealings should be kept. Sometimes on busy days you may find it overlooked but why court trouble?

There are also strict regulations in all countries regarding the export of antiques and in Sri Lanka particularly, regarding gems, the blue sapphires, rubies and, one of the island's great buys, cat's eyes. There are many good fakes around and the safest bet is to buy through the State Gem Corporation which not only guarantees its own sales but will test all your outside purchases free of charge. Keep your receipts, as they will be handy for customs at home as well.

Men and women should cover their heads in a mosque, women should do so in a Hindu temple, but bare heads are *de rigueur* in Buddhist shrines, and bare feet in all. However, many temple courtyards are of marble, sizzling in the sun; sacred paths can be stony, thorny and covered with the debris from sacred pigeons; airline socklets or ordinary socks are usually acceptable.

Many Orientals enjoy rock-hard pillows, while local transport often involves broken springs and knife-like corners. A couple of small airline-type pillows can mitigate these discomforts considerably, while handbag flasks of water or a soft drink, coupled with a miniature of something more stimulating, can ease the most wearisome journey without giving offence, if handled discreetly.

China

by Richard Snailham

China is one of today's most popular travel destinations and rightly so, for it is a country of great natural and man-made splendours and infinite interest. It also has the merit of being new, since although China opened her doors to group travel in late 1977, it is only the last couple of years that independent travel has been possible, with some 280 cities open to foreigners at the time of writing. Most travellers will be met at the point of entry by guides from the China International Travel Service who will often gather around them a motley group of independent travellers and chaperone them throughout until the moment of exit.

Sometimes it is possible, with a good deal of bureaucratic hassle, to get transit visas if you intend to enter China on the Trans-Siberian Railway via Ulan Ude and Ulan Bator (Mongolia), but as yet, it is still not possible to travel overland from Nepal via Tibet. Permits are needed, incidentally, by Chinese and foreigner alike before they may leave the perimeter of any city.

Foreign Friends

Even within organized tours, which are still the easiest way to get around, there is scope for independent action. The two Lüxingshe guides who normally accompany a group of fifteen to twenty 'foreign friends' are not especially leech-like, and indeed exhibit a refreshing degree of flexibility in the choice of places to be visited and the order in which they are taken. The guides I met showed a great capacity for inventiveness and surprise, great good humour, and were eminently teasable.

Visitors who sign up for a tour are asked what they want to see several weeks before departure. Now, it is of little use to put down 'The Lop Nor Nuclear Weapon Testing Site' or even a humble PLA barracks. But judicious study of a guide book will give an idea of what there is in each locality.

Foreign Friends who feel, during the visit itself, that they are not getting their whack of education, or are missing out on the keenly anticipated look at acupuncture in action, will find that guides, given a day or two's notice, will arrange something without much difficulty (which is perhaps most of all possible in an essentially unfree, authoritarian society, where no vice chairman of school revolutionary committee dare say no). Hospitals and even operating theatres were once open to visits by members of groups. This is no longer the case unless the group is made up of trained medical personnel. The only hospital on the tourist track that is easy to visit is the one at Zhengzhou on the Yellow River. But you can still visit health centres in communes where acupuncture can actually be experienced.

I had once imagined that we would be dragged groaning around one ball-bearing factory after another, but my group's three-week programme only included one such glimpse of industry – at the remarkable The East is Red tractor plant at Loyang. Everything is very sensibly balanced and due note is taken of individual requests. If you are an ancient music freak, just ask and you will be pointed in the direction of an ancient music shop. No part of the programme is compulsory and personal idiosyncrasies can be indulged at any time. The guides, of course, like to know, but at the same time can be very helpful to the independent. There is no concern shown at guests leaping on buses or taking taxis wherever they wish to go.

If you want to see the Great Wall, the Summer Palace, the Temple of Heaven, and so on, *and* still want to be independent, then you must have stamina. Chinese cities come to life at about 5.30am and there is much to be seen and photographed in the early morning before the 8am breakfast: squads of serious-looking senior citizens under the trees on the Chang'an Avenue in Beijing exercising every last muscle in the slow motion of *tai-chi-chuen*; phalanxes of bicycles carrying droves of Mao-suited workers weaving their way alongside the big, articulated buses, down the immense broad avenue, to the peril of any jay-walker. Escape from the hotel is also possible after lunch – Chinese guides are great ones for their siesta – or in the evening after supper, if strength will permit: dark streets – entirely safe, milling crowds, some stores still open, excellent ice cream available.

Permits and Packages

Entry to China is achieved, as *Time* magazine once said 'with a minimum of immigration fuzzbuzz'. What permits are needed? Well, a visa is about the only prerequisite. If you come from South Africa, South Korea, Israel or the Vatican City you may have problems – China does not even have postal communications with these states. All visitors, on arrival, have to fill in a Baggage Declaration form for Customs, stating what jewellery or other precious metals or stones you are carrying and listing watches, radios, cameras, calculators, recorders and typewriters. A Customs official then marks with a triangle those items which must be taken out of the country on departure, and keeps a duplicate copy of the declaration. At the exit point the visitor may have to produce this form, together with the 'triangulated' articles.

Foreign Friends are enjoined to keep all certificates from banks when exchanging traveller's cheques for examination by Customs officials on departure, but in my experience, this is a pretty cursory inspection (except when one tries to change Chinese money back). There is no evidence yet of a black market in China and the official exchange rate is quite realistic. Nor do the Chinese operate the wretched 'minimum expenditure per person' system found in some other developing countries. Once you have paid your tour fee you can be as canny as you like.

The Chinese, at present, love Foreign Friends, with their funny eyes and bridged noses and hair of varying colours and styles – because we spend plenty of *yuan* and, for the most part, share their apprehensions of the Soviet Union. They are often frankly curious, and particularly in the remoter areas, you will often find yourself surrounded by a crowd. So go to China, wear what you like, and even if you decide to take the easy option and travel within the constraints of the Lüxingshe system, you will find you can still be pretty independent.

Japan, Hong Kong, Korea and Taiwan

by Beth Roberts

For the non-linguist, Japan, Korea and Taiwan are difficult parts of the world in which to travel, not only because Japanese, Chinese and Korean are difficult to pronounce but because the written word is only rarely put into Roman type. It is therefore difficult to recognize landmarks, know what street you are in, etc. However, the local people in these countries are most helpful and will often go miles out of their way to guide you back to where you are staying, to the railway station or wherever you need to go. It is amazing how much you can convey with the use of your hands, making 'chuff chuff' noises to indicate the railway, and so on. In Japan, English is widely taught in the secondary schools, but the emphasis is on the written word and not the spoken. Consequently, English spoken by a Japanese is often very difficult to understand because of its strange, flat pronunciation. Many exporting businesses are very aware of this problem, and a lucrative living can be made teaching spoken English to the business executives of various companies. A work permit is, however, not simple to get. There is a fairly numerous band of people illegally teaching English in Japan. To renew their visas, they go across periodically to Korea.

Japan

Japan consists of four main islands. Honshu is the largest, containing the cities of Tokyo, Osaka and Kyoto. There are more than 3,000 smaller islands.

Tokyo, the capital, has a population of over ten million people. The city grew from a small fishing village in the sixteenth century, and is therefore rather haphazard, and with no real centre. The Ginza–Marunouchi areas have most of the things normally found in a city centre.

There are two international airports into Tokyo. The old one, called Haneda, is nineteen kilometres south of the city and a monorail from the departure area can take you downtown in about quarter of an hour. From the new airport, Narita, 59km north of Tokyo, it is more complicated and involves several changes to get to the city centre.

The Japanese National Tourist Organization (JNTO) has desks at the airports and produces a number of useful publications in English. Don't leave the airport without looking them up. An underground guide and a map of Tokyo are essential for finding your way around the city. A better entry point to Japan is perhaps Osaka International Airport, from which there is a bus into town taking about half an hour or to Kyoto, taking about one and a half hours.

Japanese food is similar to Chinese, but includes a lot of raw fish, not instantly regarded by the Westerner as edible! Chopsticks are the usual tools for eating, although a knife and fork can sometimes be obtained upon request. Japanese chopsticks are smaller and have a narrower point than the Chinese ones, and so prove easier to use.

Hitchhiking is the cheapest and often the easiest way to get around Japan, though in the main cities, the underground systems offer a good alternative. For those with more money, there is an excellent network of high speed 'bullet' trains. It is essential to get maps and information in Tokyo or Kyoto on all places you wish to visit, as little information in English is available elsewhere. You must always carry your Alien's Registration Card or passport, otherwise you could be liable to arrest if you are unable to produce it.

Korea

In Korea, as in Japan, the people value courtesy on a personal level and are sometimes embarrassingly respectful to foreigners. There is a great shortage of quality goods such as cameras, tape recorders, radios, etc., and also some types of clothing.

Bringing certain goods into Hong Kong (not drugs or other illegal imports) may secure for you in exchange a free trip to Seoul or rather better hotel accommodation than you could have expected. If you buy a camera in Hong Kong, you will be able to sell it in Korea – though not the most expensive models. Film is very expensive in Korea, so buy in Hong Kong, in the duty-free shops, if possible.

The best way to get to Korea is by a flight from Hong Kong or the ferry from Shimonoseki, in the south of the main island of Honshu, to Pusan, on the south-east point of the Korean coast. Fairly good deals can be found on air tickets for a round trip from Hong Kong to Seoul, Tokyo, Taipei, Manila and back to Hong Kong. Hitchhiking is again good in Korea if you keep to the main routes. Trains are fairly cheap, but not as well organized as in Japan. Buses are the main form of transport: there is a good cross-country network, although some of the roads are pretty rough. The bus does however give you an invaluable introduction to the 'real Korea' and its people. There is a Korean Tourist Association with an office in the Korean Airline Building in Seoul, which could prove helpful.

Theft is a problem in Korea, although the locals do not look for trouble with foreigners without provocation. Still, keep a good eye on any valuables and papers at all times. Accommodation is cheap and not hard to find, usually around the railway stations. The Korean name for an inn is *yeo-kwan*. As in Japan, it is customary to sit and sleep on the floor. Meals are sometimes included in the price, even if you do not eat there – so ask!

Taiwan

The first problem in planning to visit Taiwan is to find out where to get a visa. Since the recognition of Communist China, the status of Taiwan has been affected. In many countries there is no embassy and no Taiwan listing under directory information about embassies and consulates. Visas are often handled by a travel company or a trade mission. The quickest route to the appropriate office is via any travel agent in Manila, Hong Kong or wherever you are.

Upon arrival in Taipei, see the Taiwan Visitors' Association desk at the airport. They will give you maps and other information, printed in English. They can also give you the cards of the various hostels in Taipei, and with the help of the small map you can ask for the correct bus stop. This can be quite a problem if you do not find anyone who speaks a little English.

Also in the airport terminal is a desk where you can purchase a bus ticket into town; ask for the red ticket, for the non-air conditioned bus (half the price of the air conditioned bus).

Giving blood is a very good way to raise money in Taiwan. At the Veterans' Hospital (No. 224 bus from Chungshan Road), 600cc of blood can earn you enough to live on for a couple of weeks! Importing goods is also worthwhile: whisky and cigarettes can be sold at a profit e.g. in a barber's shop.

The food in Taiwan is excellent and very cheap – good news for all who enjoy Chinese cooking. The language barrier is easily overcome, since food is displayed on a hot plate and customers simply point at what they fancy. However it is best to eat fairly early as the food is then more plentiful; later in the evening, only the more expensive dishes will be left. The local rice wine is very cheap, but needs to be diluted with apple juice or orange, as it is very potent and not very pleasant on its own. On the table in each restaurant is a saucer of small red cone-shaped things. Try one at your peril! – they are chillies and extremely hot. Avoid them chopped up in dishes too.

Taiwan is an oval-shaped island, the main centres of population being around the coast. Across the middle of the island is a road which should definitely not be missed. It is the most spectacular road that I have ever travelled on, making the roads across the Alps appear mundane by comparison. I understand that it took six years to build and cost the lives of forty-three workers. The train runs often from Taipei to Keelung and there is a bus station just outside the railway station. The train is again the better bet for travel south to Hualen, but a bus can be caught just outside the railway station into town. Every day at 9am a bus runs to Teinshang, through Taroko Gorge. From there onwards it is simple to hitchhike towards the west coast and back to Taipei.

Hong Kong and Macao

Hong Kong is a fascinating place, full of food halls, street markets and duty-free shops, among many other things. Some very helpful information is available from the Hong Kong Tourist Association desk in the terminal building at the airport. In particular, ask for the *Official Guidebook* which really has everything in it a traveller may want to know about Hong Kong. Kowloon is the cheaper area to stay as all the large hotels are on Hong Kong Island. A ferry runs to the island from the Star Ferry terminal at the end of Nathan Road. The terminal for ferries to other surrounding islands and Macao is located to the left of Star Ferry on the Hong Kong Island side. The Peak, the highest point on Hong Kong Island, offers a spectacular view over most of the harbour. A funicular railway takes passengers to a lookout point at nearly 600 metres above sea level – not to be missed on a clear day.

If you plan to buy a camera, radio and any of the other goods found in this duty-free port, beware: the guarantee offered is applicable only for Hong Kong in most cases. So if your purchase proves faulty once you are out of the colony, there is nothing you can do about it. However, if you need a new pair of glasses, opticians' prices in Hong Kong are extremely favourable.

An excursion to Macao, the small Portuguese colony 65km due west of Hong Kong, is another must. There is no airport in Macao; the only way to reach the colony is by ferry, hydrofoil or jetfoil from Connaught Road, Hong Kong Island. The three-hour ferry ride is the cheapest way. For a short trip (which saves you the expense of accommodation) you could catch the ferry from Hong Kong at 2.30am, spend the day and evening there – Macao offers gaming and many other lively forms of night life – and leave again at 4.30am! A visa is needed for Macao, but can be obtained on arrival. Don't go to Macao at the weekend if you can avoid it, as the accommodation prices often double and rooms become hard to find. Information can be obtained at the very efficient Macao Tourist Information Bureau in Star House, next to the Star Ferry, Kowloon side.

South East Asia and ASEAN

by Graham Holt

Since I first set foot in Singapore at three o'clock one very humid morning in 1972, South-East Asia has been the part of the world in which I have most enjoyed travelling. Bureaucratic hassles, the challenge associated with public transport and accommodation, the variety of peoples, food, places and things to see all add to the lure of the area.

Fortunately, English-speaking people have little difficulty in communicating. Even way off the beaten track, someone can usually be found with a desire to use some knowledge of the language. The presence of British and American colonialists before World War II, followed by subsequent military actions and the advent of television, brought the English language to the area. Most countries seem to have had more than their fair share of military personnel on R & R. Whether in the jungle, on a plantation, in a village market or a city street the almost universal cry is 'Hi, Joe!' 'Do you eat rice? or bananas? or coconuts?' are just as common as variations on the theme 'Hey, Mister! You want taxi? girl?'

If you want to try the local languages, Malay and Indonesian are similar to each other and relatively simple, compared with Siamese, which has eighteen vowels and a script based on a combination of Sanskrit and Pali. The Philippine islands, with 87 different dialects, are particularly daunting.

Tagalog (Filipino) is the national, but by no means the universal one. My wife comes from Negros where they speak Ilongo and Cebuano in adjacent areas. The use of similar words with opposite meanings can be embarrassing to the local inhabitants, so stick to English.

Slow Boat from China

Having decided which countries you will visit, then book your tickets. Most countries insist on that annoying 'ticket-out' before issuing a visa. Buying bargain basement tickets is not recommended if there is a chance that you may later want to get a refund and travel on one of the 'cattle' boats plying between Malaysia, Singapore, Sumatra, Java and Borneo. The back door method of entering or leaving the Philippines via Zamboanga on a slow unscheduled flight linking Tarakan in Indonesian Borneo is not recommended. Depending on the level of terrorist activity in Mindanao foreigners may be escorted to the first plane out for their own safety. Use Manila or Cebu when international flights are operating. In Asia, always make confirmation of your return flight as soon after arrival as possible. Sometimes westbound flights on some carriers are fully booked for weeks and they are not too fussy about who gets crossed off the list.

Visas are readily obtainable for most countries, but border officials are very hot on length of hair and 'respectability' of dress. Men should cut their hair reasonably short, and everyone should dress conventionally for borders or risk an enforced stay in a transit lounge.

Singapore, in particular, is obsessed with 'long haired youths' and if the hair is 'over the eyes, over the ears or over the collar' you cannot even buy a stamp for a postcard home in any post office let alone get a seven day visa. With luck you may be allowed to stay twenty-four hours if you are also carrying a fat wad of traveller's cheques.

Visa extensions may be granted to personal applicants at immigration offices in capital cities, assuming you have sufficient funds for your stay. Extra long stays may require registration as an alien, a process involving form filling, photographing, finger printing and fees. If asked to register, check if it will entail court clearance and permission to 'emigrate' before you can then leave. It could be cheaper and easier to fly out to a neighbouring country and return on a new visa.

Whenever dealing with government departments in Asia you will come across what Westerners call bribery and corruption. The Indonesians have the word *corrupsi* for it – too strong a word really for what is just tipping for services rendered. Sometimes there is even a self-employed person available to work your papers for you for a small fee. Since he knows the system, he will manage in one hour what could take you two days to accomplish.

Bring a Bottle

'Gifts' to officials are common practice, so be prepared. The tourist arriving at an airport will have to fill in a highly detailed declaration regarding alcohol, cigarettes, electrical goods, jewellery and foreign currencies brought into the country. The visitor or leader of any party is then apt to be invited to a private room where it is made clear that irregularities with passports, visas, etc. will be found unless bottles of spirits, cigarettes and cash change hands. Customs having had their whack, it then becomes the turn of the immigration officers to do the same. Visitors are expected to be equally generous when they leave the country: if they have no alcohol left, they may be told to go and buy some at the Duty-Free Shop. Frequent travellers therefore take several bottles of a less expensive whisky with them, prepared to pass over small amounts and make sure that they only declare modest sums of currency. Of course, some visitors may be lucky and encounter no difficulties, but it does no harm to be prepared.

Changing money becomes increasingly difficult with distance from the capital. Realization that the US dollar is not the only foreign currency worth having is slowly getting through to Asians, but it is still the most readily exchanged. Surprisingly, Swiss francs are among the most difficult. Thomas Cook and American Express traveller's cheques are well known and easy to cash in Asia, so ask your bank for these in preference to their own name ones which take hours or days for clearance. The old Asian black market has diminished considerably, but you can often get a few per cent extra with little risk of being flung behind bars. Licensed money changers and importers pay extra to get the foreign exchange, but beware of pickpockets who hang around outside their premises.

Some countries insist that excess must be converted to dollars before you leave. If not, better hang onto it and try asking around in Singapore, where very favourable rates can usually be had for any currency.

Customs do not present problems unless dope smuggling is your scene. If so, your reward could be the firing squad, or, if the authorities are more lenient, life imprisonment. Malaysia has an automatic death penalty even for possession.

When the customs officer makes a thorough search of your baggage, seizes that little plastic bag of white powder and calls for assistance, don't panic! This happened to me once. Much to their surprise and disappointment, all the officials had found was soap powder. Security checks are very thorough, particularly at Manila, where there have been hijackings and bombings. My pocket knife once travelled with the Captain from Manila to Bangkok but I was allowed to retain a much more lethal pair of scissors – possibly to cut my hair during the flight?

Public and Private Transport

Travelling by public transport can be very frustrating, strenuous and enjoyable at the same time. Non-existent timetables, late running and vehicles designed for people averaging about one and a half metres tall add to the discomfort. How do you sleep with your legs or head over the end of those deck 'cots' on the inter-island ferries in the Philippines? The ubiquitous Philippine 'Jeepneys' seem to be all sharp hooks and bolts protruding where smaller people don't make contact. Doorways on trains tend to be low and seats in buses, tricycles and trishaws are small and cramped. However, I can recommend taking a long journey along dusty roads on one of those windowless buses constructed on truck chassis. You may have to share your seat with an assortment of parcels while fighting cocks peck your ankles, chickens cluck in baskets on the roof and piglets or goats occupy the baggage lockers, but this is a good way to meet the local inhabitants.

Even in Thailand you can tell where you are as most place names are repeated in Western script. A surprising exception is the Kwai River Bridge, to which it is more interesting and substantially cheaper to travel by train than by tourist coach. Trains in Thailand are fairly punctual but other countries can have very erratic services. It is not unknown for Indonesian branch trains to be cancelled several hours after departure time owing to locomotive failure or lack of fuel.

The availability of self-drive cars is very patchy but your hotel porter or taxi driver will find someone who will drive you. This is cheaper than renting. These local drivers know the route and the conditions, so don't be surprised if they take several extra spare wheels because of the rough roads. Rented cars are often supplied without even any tools.

Hotels, Prices, Dishes

Hotels are very sparse away from the tourist spots as the only people likely to use them are commercial travellers, who are usually accommodated by their customers. A bed for the night can be one of your least worries if you are prepared to accept whatever is offered. A mattress and single sheet with a margarine can to get water from the gold fish tank for a shower one night could be followed by a five star hotel the next. Hotels and eating places tend to charge fair prices, so there is no need to haggle as you do when buying souvenirs. Large stores have expensive fixed prices. You get better value at the market stalls, where you are expected to haggle. Never tried it? Well, as a rule, decide what you are prepared to pay. If they quote more than twice this figure, look at something else. If they quote less than twice, try offering about 25 per cent of their figure and after a bit of a wrangle, you will probably get the item for about 50 to 60 per cent of the first price. That is often as little as 30 per cent of the store price.

Food variety is fantastic, many of the local dishes being very tasty, but others (in my view) quite revolting. There is an endless selection of fish and fruits to sample. Don't be put off by smells, since some of the most foul odours accompany the fruits most delectable to the palate. The kitchen may be one place where very little English is spoken, so in small eating places go to see what they have and point to what you want cooked for you.

Desecration of their statues and monuments is one way to upset the easygoing Asians. As you respect your freedom and traditions, so do they. Travel agents' brochures may depict models draped over national monuments or sitting on the lap of a Buddha statue, but don't emulate them. Similarly, refrain from patting children on the head in Buddhist countries, since this can be taken as a sign of disrespect and may lead to a breach of the peace. Both misdemeanours could put you behind bars for the night at least. As everywhere, you will enjoy yourself if you tread sensitively and with awareness.

The Pacific

by Betty Barnes

Scattered between the tropics of Cancer and Capricorn lie thousands of islands peopled by Polynesians, Melanesians and Micronesians. They comprise low-lying coral or high volcanic islands. One thing is certain: to explore this fascinating region of the world the traveller requires plenty of time and patience.

There is something here to suit every taste – from the Hawaiian Islands geared to the tourist who enjoys his creature comforts, even on vacation, to the remote, unique Easter Island where most visitors are accommodated in the homes of the islanders.

To reach the Pacific from Europe can be expensive. There are four principle points of entry. One is Hong Kong from where you fly southeast or, with luck, sail on one of the hundreds of cargo ships plying out of Kowloon. Or you could enter the area by air from Los Angeles to Hawaii and the South. If you have been travelling in South America you could fly from Santiago, Chile, due west to Easter Island and from there to Tahiti. But perhaps your preference would be to leave from Sydney, Australia, flying to Lord Howe and Norfolk Islands before heading north into the central Pacific. There are frequent cruise ships departing Sydney throughout most of the year, on which it is possible to take a passage for a few days in order to reach one of the South Pacific islands.

Fiji

A good centre for exploration is Fiji. This one country alone comprises some three hundred islands: I managed to visit sixteen of them. Viti Levu, the largest, is developing into a tourist attraction with several new hotels along the south coast and in Suva, the capital. To see the island and meet its people, I hired a guide and together we walked from Tavua Bay in the central north of the island to Sigatoka in the south. During the week's journey we stayed overnight in villages en route, usually in the chief's *bura*, where the food was simple but recognizable. The small but charming island of Ovalau can be reached by ferry boat to Levuka, the one-time capital on Fiji. The Royal Hotel is comfortable, as is the Ovalau Guest House where I stayed at very low cost. The Yasawa Islands to the northwest of Viti Levu are very beautiful: one can take a three-day cruise out of Lautoka (fairly expensive) or with luck get a ride on one of the Yasawa boats calling at Lautoka to pick up provisions – but first make sure you will be allowed to land once you arrive. The best way to explore the islands is undoubtedly by cargo ship. Most of the vessels in Suva harbour display a notice stating their next destination and expected date of departure, so by direct approach to the Captain a passage can be secured. There is a government cargo ship, the *SS Yumbula* and on this I visited Makongai, the old leper colony; Koro; the second largest island, Vanua Levu, where, near the main town of Lambasa, much of the land is given over to growing sugar cane; and finally Taveuni, Fiji's third largest island. This is the home of the *Tangimauthia*, perhaps one of the world's rarest flowers. The plant attaches itself to the trees that grow around the rim of an extinct volcano and it was in full bloom in December. In Suva can be found the offices of two shipping lines and with the William and Gosling's *MV Kaunitoni* I sailed to the southern Lau islands.

This group is nearer Tonga than Fiji and consequently the people are a mixture of Melanesian and Polynesian. Between December and March sudden ocean storms can blow up so it helps to be a good sailor. The Lau islands are the least touched by outside visitors, the people here unspoilt and charming in their natural dignity. The wooden bowls from which the traditional drink of *yongona* is served are carved on the island of Kambara. Lakemba, home of one of Fiji's political leaders, is the only island served by air.

Standing Stones

From here you may be able to board a Tongan cargo ship; failing that it's a two hour flight from Suva to Nuku'alofa, capital of the Kingdom of Tonga, situated on Tongatabu, the most southerly of the three main Tongan groups. The island has quite a lot to offer, from the 800-year-old

Stonehenge-like structure to the trees around Kolovai village, the habitat of thousands of fruit bats. Make a visit to the desiccated-coconut factory.

A daily service serves Eua, a small island but ideal for those who enjoy walking in the forest. Boats to the two northern groups are infrequent, but a 20-seater aircraft flies low enough to make the flight interesting – over coral reefs and active volcanic craters. Have your camera ready! Ha'apai, unlike the other groups, comprises many low coral islands. The only place to stay is the Government Rest House at Pangai, basic and self-catering. The Tongans are devout Christians, the Sabbath being truly a day of rest for everyone. Even with the increase in visitors it is still considered indecent for women to be seen in shorts or bikinis. The Vava'u group in the north is perhaps the most beautiful, best approached by sailing into Neiafu's land-locked harbour. Swimming is excellent from white sand beaches. There is one modern hotel but more attractive is Stowaway Village where I learnt to plait palm fronds for roofing and baskets.

Five hundred kilometres to the north, across the International Date Line, lies Samoa, considered the heart of Polynesia. Western Samoa is an independent state with Apia its capital. Hire a motor cycle to explore Upolu island. A must here is Vailima, home of R. L. Stevenson, now the residence of the Head of State (who at the time of my visit was on tour, so I was able to go inside the house). Above this is Mount Vaea, at the summit of which is Stevenson's tomb. The view is worth the rough, hot climb.

There is a motor launch that will take passengers to Savai'i, the only accommodation being one or two guesthouses. Much of the island is a moon landscape of lava fields. The American way of life has filtered into the islands of America Samoa, where many US citizens have built retirement homes near Pago Pago. Under a similar cultural influence are the islands around Guam; over the centuries the Spanish, Germans and Japanese have all left their mark. A cheap way of travelling round this group is by the Field Trip Vessels, though departure dates are uncertain and priority space goes to those on official business.

A knowledge of French is an advantage in both New Caledonia and the New Hebrides. With French and English you should have few problems of communication during your travels in the Pacific.

Papua New Guinea

by Elizabeth Whitten

Papua New Guinea, a land of rugged, primaeval beauty which has much to offer the adventurous traveller, lies halfway between the northern and southern hemisphere at the north-eastern tip of Australia. Nowhere else will you find so many cultures blended in one nation. With a population of just over three million, there are 700 cultural groups, each unique in language and tradition.

Of the two main tourist attractions, one is the Highlands Show, held on alternate years either at Mt Hagen or Goroko. Although the shows have shrunk since the great days when they were fostered by expatriates to attract tourists, they continue to be of interest to the world. Here, hundreds of tribesmen walk or come by truck to wear their magnificent traditional finery consisting of high headdresses of Bird of Paradise plumes, their pearl shell ornaments and grass skirts, and to perform the age-old songs.

The second is a tour of the mighty Sepik river. One can fly into the area or take a houseboat tour along it. Here are some of the finest examples of primitive art. Rich in tradition, the Sepik fosters a style of art and architecture unique even in PNG. Nowhere else are seen the *hau Tambarans* or spirit houses soaring hundreds of feet from the ground and richly decorated with brilliant murals. The houses are used in initiation and other rites still practised today. Here also you have the opportunity to purchase artefacts which are highly prized in museums and private collections throughout the world.

Year-Round Attractions

All provinces have some sort of annual festival, to help the people retain some of their ancient customs and traditions. The way of life is expressed in their art, carvings, masks, figures, stone axes and basketware.

For those who like it warm, the climate is a joy, cooled by the steady South East Trade Winds for most of the year. Swimming, sailing, windsurfing, flying, fishing, skindiving, golf and indeed most sports can be enjoyed all year through. Clubs exist for most sports and visitors are welcome.

The people are warmhearted and generous and visitors usually receive a friendly welcome. However, it is wise to take care where matters of tradition are concerned. This is still a somewhat raw country and ranging far alone is not recommended.

Papua New Guinea is easier and cheaper than ever before to visit. Air Niu Gini with its fleet of Boeing and Fokker jets operates weekly flights between Hawaii, Singapore, Manila, Hong Kong and the Solomon Islands plus almost daily flights to and from Australia through Sydney, Brisbane or Cairns.

English is one of the three official languages and is readily understood. Of the other two – Hiri Motu and Pidgin English – Pidgin can be easily understood and spoken with the aid of a phrasebook available at newsagents.

Papua New Guinea is one of the last places on earth where the rare and beautiful Bird of Paradise still survives. The country also has fifty-one varieties of pigeons, the richest collection of kingfishers in the world, a staggering variety of small and large parrots, and a wealth of other birds.

Limitations

But there are nuisances awaiting the traveller to Papua New Guinea, including the inevitable ones about visas, etc. At present PNG is on no scheduled passenger liner route: a few cruise ships call in each year, but these allow limited opportunity to see anything but the port of call.

Since independence in 1975 some well-appointed air-conditioned hotels have been erected and more are scheduled, but they are expensive, and it is hard to get bookings, especially during the period May to August. If you have a booking double-check it; then take the confirmation along with you. In most centres accommodation is basic – but usually still expensive. The Tourist Board is promoting a scheme of lower cost, clean, comfortable, village-style guest houses run by nationals, but few as yet exist.

A high range of mountains, with peaks rising to 4,000 metres and above, runs almost the entire distance through the middle of the island. This makes internal travel difficult. Few road networks connect the provinces because of the mountainous terrain. A Highland Highway links Lae with the interior, but the capital, Port Moresby, has no road links with the nineteen provinces. Where roads exist there is a system of PMVs (Public Motor Vehicles) – licensed and controlled vehicles, usually light blue buses or covered trucks, which can be hailed anywhere outside the towns and at frequent bus shelters within. For a small sum, you can cover a considerable distance. Otherwise, all internal travel is by aircraft. Air Niu Gini services the main centre and third level operators serve the hundreds of smaller strips in more remote areas. All airlines operate with a small fleet; in case your flight should be cancelled with little or no notice, fly early. PNG is very air-minded. Flying is expensive, but a stand-by fare scheme operates between main centres.

A last word about the climate: the midday sun at the equator can be diabolical. Take a hat – take two hats – and an umbrella and plenty of suncream.

Australia and New Zealand

by Beth Roberts and Simon Glen

Australia is some seven and three-quarter million square kilometres in area, and the most urbanized country in the world, with 80–85 per cent of the population living in cities of over 100,000. Australians tend to be heavily reliant upon urban amenities and have relatively little experience of outback life, with a tendency to believe that outback motoring requires a four-wheel-drive vehicle. Correspondingly few know how to handle a two-wheel-drive vehicle in off-road conditions.

The centre of Australia is mostly desert. Although not to be underestimated as a lethal trap for the unwary and foolhardy, the deserts are not so arid as deserts elsewhere. In Australian deserts, one is never out of sight of natural vegetation.

Because of the very large distances between towns, travel is expensive and time-consuming unless you can afford to fly. It is however possible to hitchhike on the main routes; and apparently it is possible to get a ride on a goods train from the Goods Depot in Adelaide to Perth. (Take food and, especially, water for the three-day journey.) There is a stretch of Highway 1, called the Gold Coast Highway, between Brisbane and the NSW border, where hitchhiking is not advised. Many unsuspecting travellers have disappeared without trace! The Cunningham and New England Highways south from Brisbane towards Sydney are safe; moreover this is the route taken by the heavy transport vehicles.

The beaches of Queensland are largely unspoilt, the weather is good, but beware of the bluebottle – a small jellyfish with a possibly fatal sting. If you are the outdoor activity type, keen on camping, canoeing, riding, etc., the Brisbane Adventurers Club (address in the local phone book) is worth joining. They have a club hostel in Brisbane where you can stay, and organize various trips and activities. The tropical northern cities experience extremely high humidity in the rainy season, which makes them seem hotter than Sydney, Adelaide, Melbourne and Brisbane, where summer temperatures are actually higher.

Roads and Rains

Northern Australia is likely to be humid and uncomfortable, but not unbearable, during the rainy season from December to March. Travel along main roads, asphalt or gravel, may be delayed by heavy rains or swollen rivers for up to a fortnight. Waiting for the floods to recede is the only answer. The police may place road barriers after heavy downpours to prevent foolhardy people from getting into trouble, but more importantly to prevent long distance trucks from churning up the gravel roads into muddy quagmires and getting bogged. Often roads will have to be rebuilt after trucks have carved them up. However, away from the main routes, such as to the Cape York Peninsula and into Arnhemland, roads are invariably impassable for months until the dry season returns. The route between Perth and Darwin is often closed for one reason or another.

An Aussiepass, which gives unlimited coach travel for the period of its validity, is useful. Unfortunately, unlike Greyhound in the States, you cannot always be guaranteed a seat. Because of the great distances between stops, it is usually not economical to put an extra bus on the route.

In both Australia and New Zealand, driving is on the left, but there are some rules which may seem strange to visiting motorists. One should not, for example, park facing oncoming traffic. In Australia, overtaking on the left is permitted where there is more than one lane in each direction. Motorists must, however, give way to *all* traffic on the right unless signs indicate otherwise. Thus many Australians habitually drive straight out of a tiny side street into a multilane highway, forcing all traffic on their left to come to an abrupt halt – the origin of many an accident.

The Social Scene

If you are looking for work of a casual nature to boost your flagging finances, an office in Sydney called Industrial Overload can perhaps help you, although, as Australia is a very male-orientated country, there is not a lot of work considered suitable for a woman. Fruit picking is possible in the south: enquire at Melbourne Youth Hostel.

Australians prefer casual dress, particularly outside the big city centres, but are wary of people who look 'different', except in a few rural communities where alternative lifestyles have been accepted.

It is also a sad fact, and one of which dark-complexioned visitors should be aware, that there is some sub-surface racism especially in northern Queensland and in many outback towns. Occasionally there are *de facto* colour bars at pubs and the squatter settlements on the outskirts of some northern rural towns (in old car bodies, tents and 'humpies') attest to the gulf between Aboriginal and white Australians.

Visitors to remoter areas require a permit to enter or travel through each of the Aboriginal or Islander communities, which often cover vast areas. These permits are usually obtainable from state and federal government departments responsible for Aboriginal Affairs, in Alice Springs, Darwin, Perth, Brisbane, Townsville and Cairns. Sometimes permits are available on arrival, such as at Bamaga, the main centre for the Torres Strait Islander communities.

Beer and No Skittles

At Australian pubs the beer, which is strong lager, is served ice cold, sometimes in a refrigerated glass. In Australian slang, a 'tube' is a beer can and a 'stubby' a small beer bottle. Draught is also available. Pubs offer excellent lunches (with T-bone steak) very cheaply. There are several clubs with gaming machines which offer a free buffet at lunchtime in Sydney. Women are not always welcome in pubs in Australia and New Zealand. If in doubt, go to the 'Lounge Bar'.

Especially outside of Sydney and Melbourne there is a latent 'wowserism' (puritanism) throughout Australia and New Zealand. There are few major sporting events in New Zealand on Sundays and most shops and many restaurants close from Friday night to Monday morning. It is an 'early to bed, early to rise' country. Until 1968, all public bars in New Zealand closed at 6.00pm and to this day most pubs in both countries are closed on Sundays. In Queensland it is illegal to walk in the street carrying any bottle of beer, wine or other alcohol which is not wrapped in a plain brown paper bag. Yet Aussies and Kiwis are far from being teetotal, as the thousands of empty beer cans that litter country roads will attest. There are only three breweries in New Zealand, of which DB make the best beer (much weaker than the Australian variety). Food there is bland and uninteresting; sauces are unheard of; and if you wear jeans and/or flip-flops you will be refused service in many places.

Luckily for the traveller with paperbacks for the journey, there are many secondhand bookshops in both countries which not only sell but also buy used books.

In Australia, patients have to pay for all medical services and then, if members, claim refunds from a medical insurance fund or company, except in Queensland where all government public hospitals and outpatients services are free. In New Zealand, hospital treatment is free and visits to doctors are heavily subsidized. A government-run accident insurance scheme automatically covers everyone in New Zealand, even visitors, from the moment they step out of their aircraft. Thus it is impossible to sue in the courts for damages in cases of injury or death in New Zealand.

Time Machine

New Zealand is one of the few countries with negative population growth. Young Kiwis leave with every departing flight. To go to New Zealand is like travelling in a time machine back fifty years. There is an abundance of greenery; there are twenty sheep for every person; spectacular scenery from the boiling mud pools of Rotorua to the clear and unpolluted waters of Haast Pass, Mount Cook and Arthur's Pass in the Southern Alps.

The best way to see New Zealand is to fly to Auckland, travel south and leave from Christchurch.

Imports attract a very high tax and Customs duty and, as New Zealand is too lightly populated to support its own car industry, all cars are twice as expensive as in Australia or Britain. New cars are to be seen, of course, but twenty- or even fifty-year-old vehicles are common as well.

New Zealand's products are few, so there is very little choice in the shops between different brands. Meat and dairy products are fairly cheap, but a lot of young people seem to be vegetarians. Rock oysters are a free food delicacy to be found among the rocks on the shores of the North Island. A screwdriver and a rock can remove them.

Besides Maoris, thousands of Samoans, Tongans, Cook Islanders, Fijians and Indians live permanently in New Zealand. The Maoris are very friendly and if you get a chance to go to a *hungi*, don't miss it. The food is cooked in a hole in the ground covered with leaves and soil. It takes a long time, but the result is mouth-watering!

Hitchhiking is relatively safe in New Zealand. There is a network of airports throughout the country, but tickets bought in New Zealand are liable to a tax which makes them very expensive. It is advisable to have an onward or return ticket purchased outside New Zealand. A Tourist Pass is available, giving unlimited travel on bus, train and inter-island ferries over a specified time.

Both New Zealand and Australia offer tremendous opportunities for rugged outdoor holidays. If while roughing it, you are overdue, someone will organize a search party. If, through illness, injury, loneliness, boredom or fear, you long for the trappings of organized Western society, you are never very far away from fresh milk, clean water, fuel supplies, a chance to wash, the Flying Doctor or a pub. Moreover, you have no borders to cross, no authoritarian régimes to endure, and everyone speaks English! New Zealand, a frustrating country for the ordinary visitor, is especially attractive to the hunting, fishing and climbing enthusiast.

Both Australians and New Zealanders are partial to superlatives. They make exaggerated claims about themselves ('world's greatest consumers of beer') and call something 'internationally known' when in fact it is known only to a local resident's American relative who was taken to see it a few years ago! But there are indeed some splendours in both countries.

North America

by Hilary Bradt

The joys of travel in North America? There are so many! A random list gives us such marvels as the Bell telephone system, cheap Xerox copies, Amtrak, motels with colour TV and vibrating beds, 'Have a nice day!' at six in the morning and eleven at night, and the scenery: the canyons of the southwest, the Canadian Rockies, Route 1 down the west coast, New England's forests in the autumn, New England's villages at any time, and the national parks anywhere. Add the joys of hiking in the High Sierras, lying on the beach in California, eating lobster in Maine, going to a midnight movie in Chicago or Shakespeare in the Park in New York, and you have the formula for a pretty good holiday.

A practical joy is the ease with which you can get things done. Businesses usually open at 8.30am and people are actually anxious to help you at that hour. You can be served a meal or drink at any time in most places, and even travelling with children can be a joy in North America where there is a much higher tolerance of 'self-expression' than we allow ourselves. Many restaurants serve 'kiddie portions' (food-stuffed adults, alas, may not order these despite the attractively small helpings and prices) and provide high chairs for tots who can scream and dribble to indulgent smiles at the next table.

Another undoubted joy is the sheer niceness of most Americans and their embarrassing Anglophilia. If you're British, it's rare to meet someone who doesn't love your accent, your actors, your countryside and your history, and want to tell you so. Fewer love your country's politicians but they don't allow this to stand in the way of friendship. Canadians are less vociferously pro-British; politics and the flood of British immigrants have seen to this.

Train Your Sights

There are aspects of the American scene which fall into the category of Gloriously Vulgar or Sociologically Fascinating, though some travellers would put them firmly in the Nuisance Section. These include the frightful Quaint Villages which have been permitted to mushroom on the outskirts of National Parks, and the derelicts or weirdos who hang out at Greyhound bus terminals.

Travel itself falls somewhere in between joy and nuisance. The efficiency and speed with which travel arrangements can be made are certainly wonderful (unless you are stuck in one of those endless queues at a Greyhound bus ticket counter), and the cheap travel bargains are equally joy-making. (Never simply buy a ticket to a destination, but check for special deals. For instance, a family of two or more people can travel at greatly reduced rates on Amtrak, and if you travel mid-week by plane or train you can usually get a reduction.) But it's hard to raise much enthusiasm for the actual experience of sitting in a car, bus, train, or plane.

The glorious North American scenery is mostly by-passed by the superhighways. Trains take by far the prettiest routes, but are slow. (Apart from a short stretch served by the Metroliner, there are no high speed trains of Britain's standard.) There's an awful lot of the Prairies or Mid-West to be crossed before you reach interesting mountainous scenery. Since the maximum speed limit in the USA and Canada is 88kmph, it also takes a long time to get anywhere by car or bus. Tourists should try to take minor roads where the human impact on the landscape is always interesting, even if the scenery itself isn't.

One of the best travel bargains in the US is Driveaway cars. If you have a valid driving licence, are over 21, and can give the names and addresses of two or three references in the town you're starting from and one at your destination, you can deliver a car to any large town in the USA free of charge and with the first tank of petrol paid for. You may only drive the direct route (although some meandering is acceptable) and the time allowed is not overly generous, but this is a popular method of travelling and in the summer the demand for cars exceeds the supply of drivers. Off season, however, you have a very good chance of finding a car going to the right place at the right time. All cities have this service; look up Automobiles-Driveaway in the telephone directory yellow pages, and ask if they have a car going to your planned destination.

Joking Aside

It's difficult to think of the black side of American travel as a nuisance. It's either unpleasant or dangerous, but forewarned is forearmed, and sometimes it's just a question of understanding the language. And if you think you speak the same language, try telling someone 'I'm going to the post', or, more entertainingly, 'I'll knock you up in the morning'. There is an American/English dictionary on the market to help solve this problem. You're less likely to run into verbal misunderstandings, however, than to fail to see the American sense of humour which is often based on what the British would call rudeness. It's not, it's just Americans being American. So if an official at Kennedy Airport is insulting (and they're hand-picked for this quality), try joking with him (or her). (Better, smile to show it *is* a joke.) It's rather fun and it often works.

Travellers in North America often pay insufficient attention to border formalities. Most people now know that the US requires you to have a tourist visa and that it may take several weeks to get, but may forget Canada's border requirements when making a spur of the moment decision to visit, say, Vancouver from Seattle. I have frequently travelled by bus from the US to Canada when an arguing or tearful tourist has been dumped at the border to tramp the long road back to town because he or she did not have 'sufficient funds' and a return or onward ticket out of Canada. Border regulations between the two countries are zealously followed. Luggage is searched (I know a hiker who was delayed three hours while some dried parsley flakes found in his backpack were analysed in the lab and questions asked). So whichever direction you travel in, comply with the regulations. Other rules to be watched out for, which vary from state to state, are the so-called 'blue laws' restricting sales of alcoholic beverages.

Bugs and Thugs

Much more disastrous than border problems are medical costs, and the importance of medical insurance cannot be overemphasized. Even a visit to a doctor can use up a sizeable chunk of your travel budget.

Most people equate America with violence, and it is certainly an aspect of that country that must be lived with – as over 200 million Americans do. The chance of falling victim to motiveless violence is very small and there's nothing you can do about it anyway. But you can take precautions against robbery: if you want to, or have to, visit ghettos or wander around late at night, leave money and valuables in the hotel safe. Lock your room when you are in it; you should really ask to see identification before you let anyone into the room, although many people would prefer to take a risk than bring paranoia to these lengths. In fact, it's really much more enjoyable to trust people. Let your European naïvété carry you through, as so many of your predecessors have. Don't be afraid to hitch-hike or walk through Central Park or talk with strangers, and bear in mind a story I heard recently of a British couple visiting Chicago. As they stepped from their car near the hotel, three armed men approached and demanded money. 'Don't be ridiculous, we're British!' said the wife. The men put away their guns and walked away.

Central America

by Betty Barnes

The majority of travellers enter Central America from the north, by way of Mexico. There are no good roads into Belize; the only one that even comes near the description is that from Belize, the capital, to Cayo. Buses are few and in poor condition and most of the local people use the rivers as highways. Much of the country is swamp or tropical jungle, a paradise for the naturalist.

The Pan American Highway 190 is the principal route connecting Mexico with Guatemala. Be prepared for delays and the financial demands of every type of border official. It may be less of a nuisance to cross at Highway 200, on which route the border town of Tapachula has a resident Guatemalan Consul who will issue documents. Throughout the region, avoid Sunday crossings.

These descendants of the Mayans show little of the greatness of the ancestors; however their ancient cities at Tikal and Huehuetenango remain to delight the visitor. This is a region of severe earthquakes and as you journey throughout Central America you will see plenty of evidence of past devastation. Bear the possibility in mind when you select your campsite.

When you shop in any of the many markets, Chichicastenango being one of the better known, be prepared to barter for food and souvenirs. Few of the Indians speak Spanish, but those in the business of selling acquire a basic knowledge. Lake Atitlán is one of the loveliest in the country, set in a ring of mountains, though the approach road to Panajachel is very steep. Upon leaving Guatemala, you will likely find that you are asked for more money. There is little you can do if the return of your documents can only be secured with a bribe.

In El Salvador, I found the officials who issued me with a tourist card refreshingly helpful. (This, of course, predated the war!) Recently, one has to be extremely wary, as the tourist officials seem to do their level best to ignore the fighting. You should take much of what they say and many of their excursions with a pinch of salt if you value your hide. El Salvador is the most highly populated country in Central America, as is apparent from the fact that every bit of shoreline around beautiful Lake Coatepeque is privately owned. Even by the smaller Lake Ilopango it is difficult to find a place to camp. The old town of San Vicente has a good fruit market. San Miguel is the last town of any size at which you will find a bank prior to reaching the border with Honduras.

Throughout Central America banks will be found in sizeable towns only and many of these are unfamiliar with traveller's cheques issued by United Kingdom banks. Better to use American Express cheques as these are acknowledged. Should you be unfortunate enough to lose them, then at least they can be replaced.

When you enter Honduras on the Pan American Highway in your own vehicle, you will find that this will be fumigated (whether you wish it or not) and that, moreover, you will have to pay for the privilege.

Most visitors are issued free of charge with a 48-hour transit permit, which gives one the impression that visitors are not encouraged. The only macadamized road in the whole country is the 150km stretch in the southern tip that links it with its neighbours. In the shadow of the ultra-modern skyscrapers of Tegucigalpa is the shanty town where live the rural families who have moved in for a better life. They still do their laundry in the river. To the north, there is a considerable railway system – its main purpose, however, is to transport bananas.

Earthquake Country

Nicaragua, largest of the Central American countries, with its heaviest population concentration within fifty miles of the Pacific Ocean, offers more to the visitor than the countries so far mentioned. The centre of the country is mountainous and sparsely populated. Dozens of fishing villages are strung along the swampy lagoon-indented Caribbean shoreline, best explored from the sea. León is an attractive town with an interesting cathedral. From here, there is a fairly good road, the N14, and a bus service to the coastal village of Poneloya, where there is an excellent beach for swimming. On one side of the main square there is an inexpensive hotel, and here too are some holiday homes owned by the minority white population. Managua, the capital, set on the shores of the lake of the same name was virtually wiped out in 1972 by a severe earthquake. Little has been done toward reconstruction. In the village of Masaya nearby there is a thriving cottage industry for the tourist, producing such things as straw hats and carved rocking chairs. About 40km from the capital, in Diriamba, during the third week of January, occurs one of the country's principal religious festivals. Dating back some four hundred years, it has authentic ancient Indian features.

One of the principal roads follows the west shore of Lake Nicaragua – more like an inland sea – which was possibly once part of the Pacific, as both shark and swordfish are to be found in its waters. The 1,500-metre-high volcanoes on the island of Ometepe can be seen from the shore.

Costa Rica does not impose any

entry fee, but if you have a vehicle, there is a compulsory insurance cover. It is soon apparent that you are now in a more prosperous country, with education free and obligatory, and a thriving middle class. For the first 150km there are many cattle ranches, beef being one of the main exports. The coffee here is some of the best I have ever tasted. Costa Rica is famous for its painted carts which are built and decorated by hand in small factories around Sarchi Norte.

There is a railway that spans the country from coast to coast. San José is a pleasant city, with a cathedral and National Theatre of interest. Not far away is Cartago where the basilica is a place of pilgrimage; inside are thousands of tiny replicas in gold and silver of various parts of the human anatomy said to have been offered by cured pilgrims. The walls of the old church, destroyed by an earthquake in 1910, remain standing.

To the north lies the 3,200 metre Mt Irazú, an active volcano that occasionally covers the surrounding area with ash. The road to the top is very rough, the only public transport being by taxi. Given a clear day it is possible to see the ocean on either side of the country. The scenery through the Cordillera de Talamanca with its high mountains and tropical jungle is some of the best in Central America; here one can find many wild orchids and beautiful birds. The road then follows the Rio Grande de Térraba almost all the way to the border.

Panama and the Canal

In Panama, the police carry screwdrivers, apparently to remove the numberplates from the vehicles of offending motorists. Scenically, Panama is less impressive than its neighbours. Outwardly the inhabitants are more resentful of the Americans, a feeling encouraged by external leftist influence; however I found the people friendly and helpful. Santa Clara provides excellent swimming and it is possible to camp there. The story goes that in the forest near El Valle there are trees with square trunks, though it took me a long hot search to find one, and that was in poor shape. The main highway into Panama City crosses a bridge aptly signposted 'Gateway to the Americas'. The US dollar is acceptable throughout the country.

The Panama Canal splits the country geographically as well as strategically. A strip five miles wide known as the Canal Zone stretches along either side of the waterway. This is governed by the USA and two American cities have been established within the area: Cristobal adjoining Colón and Balboa.

Many shops and restaurants in Panama City are owned by Indians and Orientals. Generally I found the city dirty – certainly in direct contrast with Balboa. Strictly speaking, unless you are part of the US population of the Canal Zone, the comforts and amenities of that area are denied to you. However, if one is discreet one can enjoy the YMCA cafeteria and similarly the Yacht Club facilities at Balboa, which are first rate. Many oceangoing yachts call here and for anyone with a good knowledge of sailing there is sometimes an opportunity to crew on one of these boats, perhaps bound for the Caribbean islands. Visit the old city of Panama, sacked by Captain Morgan, the pirate, in 1671.

Beyond Panama City the road continues for only about 80kms; then the country reverts to jungle and swamp. One day the Pan American Highway will be pushed through to Colombia at an astronomical cost. In the meantime, it is possible to walk through the Darien Gap. But not alone: hire the services of guides, each one of whom will take you along an 80km stretch. And take a hammock and mosquito net.

Alternately, it may be possible to get passage on one of the many ships passing through the Canal from Colón to Barranquilla in Colombia if it is your intention to carry on south.

Some knowledge of Spanish can be an asset, if only to minimize the chance of your being deceived. And keep the safety of your possessions in mind at all times.

This entire region is in a permanent atmosphere of political turmoil and this has turned into violence and civil war in many areas. There seems to be no simple solution, so for the foreseeable future, all travellers in Central America should be extremely careful of where and how they travel and get expert advice before setting out. However much you wish to see a place, it is not worth endangering your life.

The Caribbean

by Ian Lyon

From the bulletin board of a hotel in St. Lucia: 'Don't sit under a coconut tree. The velocity of a falling nut is 50 feet per second. A tree is 90 feet high, the acceleration is 32 feet per second. Don't walk around barefoot and don't bathe for any period of time in streams.'

So much for those notions of 'paradise' invoked by many of the glossy brochures. The Caribbean is a complex area of pride, intense political pressures, poverty and a volatile tourist industry located in luxurious coastal hotels.

Many visitors remain oblivious to the poverty; many local residents are often sceptical of dependence on the fickle whims of tourists who tend to vanish at the slightest sign of ordinary conflicts among the islands; political disturbance, party strife, labour resentments, nationalist movements. There are some connoisseurs for whom these are the precise times to visit the area, aware that the main herd of sunbathers and cocktail sippers will have left.

Another larger band of devotees has discovered the bargain time: usually from mid-April till mid-June with hotel prices virtually halved. Prices are still low from July to November but then the warmth is blighted by sticky humidity and the season for hurricanes is usually August to October. At these times the main crowds of North American visitors have gone; many US cities spend their summer sweltering in sticky clammy heat, so the Caribbean presents such US citizens with no real product difference.

Bargain Time

The bargain time of mid-April to June usually means plenty of sunny days, quieter beaches, more chance to explore. The possible hazards of such a period include water shortages at your hotel, polio, typhoid, tetanus – and bilharzia, on St. Lucia, at any rate. Here it is wise to avoid bathing in streams and pools, however romantic the setting. Avoid the temptation to pick small, green 'crab apples' on the poisonous manchineel trees: don't pick their leaves and avoid standing under them during any downpour.

The prime quality demanded of the traveller in the Caribbean is patience. Many tourists arriving on huge, wide-bodied jets, hell-bent on discovering instant paradise, are shocked by dingy airports and often tedious delays in getting on further flights to the smaller islands. For this sort of impatient traveller, who cannot bear to see precious vacation time slip by on sweltering airport benches, the best bets are probably the islands of Antigua or St. Lucia, served directly by jets. Antigua boasts a wide selection of beaches – over 300 of them – which is just as well, for those beside your hotel can be very narrow strips of sand due to tidal movements in the summer months. The landscape of Antigua is generally flat, dull scrub, dilapidated sugar mills and rusting wrecks of cars. It is a fine place for swimming and snorkelling, scenically uninspiring, yet with high hopes of boosting its tourist industry through more hotels and a £4 million airport terminal to ease passengers' travails.

St. Lucia does not have as many beaches as Antigua, but it does have that mix of golden sands, luxuriant green valleys, thick forest and steep roads which have resisted the creeping incursions of commercialism. The best golden expanses of beaches are Réduit, La Choc, Vigie, and Saline Point. Those on the east, windward coast are dangerous while the black sand beaches are in the south, near the town of Soufrière.

Another island on the direct jet routes is Barbados – at first sight the least adventurous choice in all the Caribbean. According to the menu in the airport café, virtually everything comes 'with chips'. There is Kensington Oval, consecrated to cricket. And villages bear names like Worthing, Windsor or Hastings. It lacks the lush forests of St. Lucia – and is correspondingly easier to tour. The independent-minded, who feel imprisoned by the set timetables of most hotels will find the south coast, between Bridgetown and Oistins a good place to rent apartments, which are hard to find on the other islands. Despite the island's popularity with generations of US and UK tourists, the local cuisine has not disappeared; there are spiced pork (*souse*), a baked blend of coconut and cassava known as *cassava pone* and succulent grapefruit (shaddocks). To sample the local product lovingly prepared, the best time is Sunday buffet lunch at leading hotels. To get away from the developed resort complexes, head for the northerly 'parish' of St. Lucy and North Point.

Island Retreats

But the greatest joys (and frustrations) of a Caribbean trip lie in making for the smaller islands off the main international airline routes. It can prove difficult. I was flying from Grenada to Antigua. Suddenly we were informed that we would be landing at

Barbados where another plane would take us on to Antigua. It did and I just made the connection with my BA plane to London. Moral: allow plenty of time for such rerouting and leave your remoter haven with twenty-four hours to spare.

Among such retreats are the following:

For rugged beauty, tangled forests, rare parrots, bastard mahogany, hercules beetles and few beaches for swimming: Dominica.

As a base for sailing among the Grenadine islands, where the local volcano's last eruption was in 1974: St. Vincent, within easy reach of the isles of Bequia and Carriacou.

For superb sands, lush vegetation, secure harbour and the most dignified of the islands' capitals: Grenada, still free from the ravages of tourism despite having one of the biggest yacht marinas in the Caribbean. The recent trouble here seems to have caused no lasting damage, physically or emotionally, to the island and there should be no second thoughts about going here on this account.

The Caribbean has its own standards, pride and etiquette. Much of the hotel food is imported and deep frozen – from the USA. The spindly cattle of Antigua are not a reliable source of prime cuts. Service is often slower than in Europe: some impervious company directors should remember they are on holiday, not at war. Many residents bitterly resent photographs being taken of them. And one doesn't drive down Whitehall in a swimsuit and Minimoke. The Caribbean (not, please, the West Indies) expects a similar care and consideration in its capitals.

South America

by Brian Williams

It's probably true to say that the joys of South America reflect the dreams you have had about it; dreams fed on stories from childhood, or vignettes from television, and occasionally a picture in a brochure. The joys are in finding that the descendants of the Incas still dress and live in much the same way as they did half a millennium ago; that Bolivian women wear bowler hats and countless layers of skirts, just as the brochures say; that the vendors sit by the railway and sell chickens and llama wool and sweet corn, just as they did in the film about Butch Cassidy.

There are some disappointments, of course: the Amazon is far too wide – it takes oceangoing liners as far as Iquitos in Peru! – to appreciate or photograph, and one is left with the option of a compromise excursion on a smaller, more evocative river, or a roll full of pictures of muddy water with a strip of green in the far distance. This is not the Amazon that two generations of Colonel Fawcett stories have evoked.

And the Bolivian Altiplano is just that. Mile upon mile of flat, semi-arid, infertile plain with a hint of mountain in the distance. Is this the impassable terrain that those bold *conquistadores* trudged?

But there are also surprises. The Iguaçu Falls far surpass as a spectacle both the better known Niagara and Victoria Falls; picking your way through the ruined cells of Devil's Island, you relive the lives of the prisoners there far more intensely than watching any Steve McQueen movie; and the icy splendour of the Southern Andes rivals anything the Himalayas have to offer.

The Size of Your Wallet

Tribulations there are many, especially in those countries where the standard of living is low. Whereas many parts of the world welcome the visitor who comes on a limited budget more warmly than the well-heeled tourist, South America is different, or at least it is in the well-visited areas. Here the treatment you receive is in direct relationship to the size of your wallet, and nowhere is this truer than in Cuzco. Much of the energy of the local population is directed towards relieving you of your hard-earned hard currency. Little boys offer to clean your shoes for what you understand in sign language to be 10 *soles* (about 2p) but which turns out to be 10 *libras* (about 20p) or even *wan dora* (one dollar). Cheap, even at those rates, but you end up with the feeling that you've been ripped off.

But then it's not surprising that the locals should resent the limited budget traveller. As a rule this traveller is young and is carrying more money in his money belt than the man in the Cuzco street earns in a year. And he tries to beat him down a few miserable pence for a slightly cheaper poncho. I am probably guilty too in this respect, but if you stand back a moment and watch a well-fed European in his early twenties bargain with a man who has lived forty or fifty years in the harsh realities of the Altiplano, you can begin to understand why all is not sweetness and smiles.

And yet go a few kilometres beyond the major tourist centres and your impression will be a completely different one. The impassive sullenness of the Andean Indians and Mestizos is still a characteristic, but you know it's directed at life in general, and not at you.

Language, Lunch and Latins

A knowledge of Spanish is going to be a help, of course. Misunderstandings don't get out of hand if both parties can more or less follow what the other is saying. English is not widely understood, even in the main cities, and though it's possible to travel right around South America without a word of Spanish (or, in Brazil, Portuguese) you'll find it a real advantage if you master the basics before you go. American Spanish is not so very different from Peninsular Spanish.

Your first encounter with the written language will probably be the menu. If you're adventurous, just plough in and worry later about the lungs and so on you've just eaten. Otherwise try a restaurant where you'll be able to relate something on the menu to what you can see around you. Incidentally, one thing you'll find rather unnerving is the way the same dish varies from one restaurant to the next, and how it may be entirely different in the next country.

Frontiers can sometimes be a problem. First, land frontier crossing points are not always open. Lunchtime will invariably find doors locked and traffic barriers down, and, of course, if time zones change, there will be absolutely no coordination between the two sides. Both posts will close at 1pm on the dot, for an hour. Unfortunately, in Bolivia, when the post reopens, it's just 1pm in Peru and their post has just closed.

I once saw an Italian try to bribe his way around this problem ('We Latins understand how things are done') and sure enough he marched triumphantly through the door which had miraculously opened for him, and not for the thirty or so people in front of him in the queue. He did not re-emerge to join his two companions. When the post reopened, on time, it transpired that his insistence on the urgency of his journey had earned him two hours locked in the broom cupboard. The man who stamps the passport had a glint in his normally impassive Andean eye.

Security

The biggest by far of all nuisances in Latin America is security. Thieves can slice a hole in your shoulder bag and make off with your camera before you know it's happened. Put your bag down for a second to take a photo, or try on a sweater, and that's the last you'll see of it. For this reason, I always advise travellers in South America to carry all valuables in a money belt and on their person at all times.

You can never be completely secure, but you may as well make the task as difficult as possible for the thief. Surprisingly enough, luggage checked onto buses, or into a hotel room is usually safer than that you keep with you. Thieves know that you keep your valuables close at hand. Danger points are: bus stations, trains, airports, markets, crowded restaurants, hotel foyers. Particularly watch out for those few moments before a train pulls into a station. Danger cities are: Lima, Cuzco, Puno, Arequipa, La Paz (Bolivia), Guayaquil, Bogotá (and all of Colombia), Caracas, Rio. Remember, thieves make a very good living from tourists because they are *very good* at their job.

One thing that does seem to upset travellers in South America, needlessly in my opinion, is the frequent stopping to show passports at all manner of internal control posts. It's time-consuming, of course, but then time means very little to the man who's filling out the details of your passport in a grubby exercise book. Name: Colwyn Bay; Nationality: Northern Ireland; Occupation: Civil Status; Father's Name . . . and so on. Don't tell him he's got it wrong. Accuracy isn't important. It's enough that he takes the time to do it. The locals accept it with resignation, why shouldn't we?

Consolations

If you've read this far you're probably beginning to wonder why you should even consider going to Latin America in the first place. There are consolations. Peru, Ecuador and Bolivia are very cheap, and even a good quality hotel is only £5 a night (I'm not talking of the Sheratons of this world).

Machu Picchu is every bit as evocative as it's cracked up to be, with the mist rolling across the ruins and the snowcapped mountains in the distance. Stumble across an Indian wedding and watch the flashing eyes of the young girls as they dance, their skirts swirling like a carousel around them. Sit in a bar in Brazil's Ouro Preto, looking out onto the floodlit square and the beautifully preserved colonial buildings. Go window shopping down Calle Florida in Buenos Aires. Watch the *garotas de Ipanema* slink adolescently across the sand to meet the peroxide blonde *surfistas* on Rio's Arpoador Beach. Or get stuck in an Andean village miles from anywhere, way off a bus route, where there's no hotel or restaurant and nothing recognizable to eat or drink anyway.

Spend three weeks or three months in South America and you spend the rest of your life wanting to go back.

North Africa

by Mark Milburn

To many people, 'North Africa' means the zone bordering the Mediterranean. Travel here is comfortable, with food and lodging readily available in many areas. People touring here may well qualify as the sort of visitors preferred by most authorities; hiring cars, eating in restaurants, buying souvenirs and generally contributing towards the national economy. Local thieves and 'guides' may also get some of the pickings.

Not so those venturing further afield, into the Sahara or even across the greatest desert on earth, falling into the category of travellers in Northern Africa as a whole. They will not be nearly so welcome to those whose duty it is to pass them along towards the next checkpoint. They tend to come in their own vehicles, carrying most of their own food and sometimes much fuel from a neighbouring land. They will rarely stay in the few hotels available nor, barring some mishap to themselves or to their means of locomotion, will they leave much cash behind them.

Worse still, their vehicles may be unfit for the rigours of a desert journey, in which case there are several courses of action open to those who control movement in the territory concerned: to forbid departure of the party, to try and induce it to use another route, or even insist on travel in convoy with other vehicles, occupied by tourists or nationals. If these latter be tourists, then the equilibrium of both groups can be upset, since their reasons for the journey may well differ. A final option is to allow the vehicle to continue, always assuming that its occupants will not be in mortal danger should it break down. If it does, and has to be abandoned, then the human vultures will appear from nowhere to pick it clean, while the occupants can hope to be evacuated by some lorry driver, who will probably charge something for his services.

About the worst that can happen, from the police or army point of view, is that a tourist vehicle unwittingly leaves its planned route before breaking down, causing a great deal of trouble to those who must organize and effect a search. If rescued, the tourists may well prove unable to pay for such a costly operation. However, it can also happen that nobody worries about a lost vehicle, since the departure point authorities omit to inform those farther along the line that it has even set off: communications are often extremely lax in a frontier zone. Hence the importance of using at least two cars, if going off the beaten track.

The difficulties of obtaining reliable information about the other traffic on certain routes can be enormous, as I found out once in the far south of Mauritania, where only a festive season caused rather more movement than usual. In retrospect, breakdown could have proved fatal.

There is another growing problem in dealing with desert authorities, less beneficial to the traveller – that of a constant need for bribery. One recent party in the Western Sahara reported that they were being stopped every ten miles or so, and bribes of up to £15 a head were necessary before they were allowed to continue. Unscrupulous officials out in the middle of nowhere have it sewn up tightly – you dance to their tune, or stay put.

More Trouble Than You Are Worth

The desert traveller is, then, considered to be rather more trouble than he is worth. If he acts in a way that causes trouble to the police or army, whether through irresponsibility or not, he runs the risk of getting his route banned to future tourists, with all the frustration that this can entail. A group arriving in Niger to undertake, for instance, a specific 200km journey in a zone famed for its scenic beauty will not appreciate being told, on arrival, that it has been closed since last week, owing to someone else's lack of thought.

Much of the hazard, or anyway the anguish, of desert travel is occasioned by the slackness of manufacturers on whose products you may be forced to rely. If the 'service' is respect of a given product is appalling in Europe, then beware of taking it to Africa. Imagine, for example, that a motor agent says he has effected a major service, and that after only 1,000km third gear is hard to shift, causing eventual abandonment of the trip. Or that after 2,000km, much wear is evident on the front tyres and the tie-rods prove to be bent. When taxed with these anomalies, the British representative in Madrid answers that 'no one has ever complained before'. No matter who is at fault, your trip is wrecked.

A second case could involve a crashed vehicle, delivered to a Moroccan agent for repair, who gives it to an outside coachbuilder whose incompetence is almost total. Complaints to the manufacturer produce a friendly letter from apparently British principals, who invite the owner to bring his car to Casablanca where they will endeavour to put things right. When the owner calls to collect, the coachwork has not even been touched or the oil changed, since they 'do not know which brand you use.' A further approach now elicits the astounding reply that the apparently British principals can put no actual pressure on their associates. Does one try again? Or does one leave the coachwork as it is, a permanent advertisement for the manufacturer's 'service'?

Bush Telegraph

The security of the régime, though not perforce that of tourists, is of paramount importance in Africa. Thus a scientific enquiry aimed at bettering the lot of women in the Sahel is something to be undertaken only after careful preparation. Bush telegraph operates like wildfire and assuming that even one of you speaks the local language, the cat will be out of the bag in no time, unless you are able, for instance, to disguise your activities as an investigation of native music. In zones where few northerners ever penetrate, you will stick out like a sore thumb. The police or army may even try to help you: some will be just as foreign as you are and will welcome any diversion that brightens up a boring existence. They also have an uncanny affinity with any liquor you may be carrying.

Girls are another fatal attraction, though females who get bothered could bear in mind that the same cop or corporal has probably met others who genuinely wanted a 'bit of bother': it takes at least two to make love. As for local women, Africans in the last century were amazed at the ability of Europeans to travel without female company. Some rules written long ago advised European men working amongst them to avoid them like the plague. Though the women may not appreciate such forebearance, it was argued, their menfolk certainly will. If one just cannot be good, then it pays to be very, very careful.

For would-be camel riders in the remote regions, it is worth remembering not only the severe limitations imposed by pasture, water availability, time and physical fitness (*see Travel by Camel on page 213*), but also the different mentality of the locals with whom you will have to live and work. Imperfect knowledge of their language can be a huge problem, as I learned to my cost in Arabia. Some Saharan authorities have also cunningly spread the word that anyone who takes off into the blue with unauthorized tourists risks a spell in jail – as a Targui friend of mine found out too late. Anyone who thinks that a camel journey does not involve many hours daily spent pulling the brute along on a string should read Theodore Monod's *Meharees* (1937). And lastly, beware of dry wells.

Above It All

A reasonable substitute, depending only on the precise requirements of your journey, would be to drive into a mountainous zone, then to make long walks around your parked vehicle, moving it as and when necessary. Often it will be safe to lock the car and leave it. Or one member may enjoy pottering around the camp to keep an eye on things. Many rewards are to be reaped by moving into areas where a vehicle cannot go. Apart from getting 'up above it all', with a good chance of spotting animals or birds whose presence you never suspected, the exercise will work physical wonders. Much rock art, both painted and carved, is only to be reached on foot. And because of the passion of a Munich mountaineer and mapmaker for getting as high as possible and then checking that all visible peaks were where they should be, I have some entrancing photographs of little-known regions, plus more of Ahaggar summits seen from most unusual angles.

Scorpions and snakes are not supposed to molest tourists in the winter months, though fitness and acclimatization are prerequisites to safe desert walking: he who tours alone does so at his own peril. Imagine being immobilized and having to await the inevitable attentions of jackals and hyenas, which prey on weakening creatures. Adequate food, clothing and water are always carried, plus navigational and emergency bivouac gear. Healthy and nourishing food may itself deter illnesses which can inconvenience the whole party and even prejudice the accomplishment of an aim.

West Africa

by David Ruddell

West Africa is often considered the most 'African' part of Africa. Throughout the colonial period white settlement was forbidden (except briefly on the Ivory Coast). This was no great show of selfless altruism on the part of the British and French colonizers, for this was the hot, humid 'white man's grave'. Unfamiliar diseases had struck down many an early colonial trader within months of arrival. The net result is a positive one for today's European traveller: this part of Africa is remarkably free of the racial bitterness and antagonism that casts a shadow over travel in some parts of this exciting continent.

If West Africa means 'jungle' (a European term – the Africans call it forest), it also means desert. These two extremes make up almost half of the area. But for the most part the region is covered in open grassland and scrub – the vast, sweeping savannah that stretches across the middle belt from Senegal to Chad, separating the rainy coastal forests from the parched fringes of the Sahara.

As a traveller to West Africa you follow in a long and impressive tradition. The great Arab scholar Ibn Battuta chronicled his travels there as early as the fourteenth century; the Portuguese were already regular visitors to Benin a hundred years later, and in the late 1700s Mungo Park sought to travel the length of the River Niger. They all found what today's traveller will still find – an area of great physical, historical and cultural differences, but with a common thread of 'African-ness' (Senghor called it 'negritude') running through it.

History

It is important to understand a little of the history of the region, even if you have never considered yourself a history buff. For history has a marked effect on travel in West Africa, even today. Before the Europeans arrived, West Africa was made up of communities ranging from great nation states (such as Songhai, Mali, Benin, etc) to small village-scale groups. The European 'scramble for Africa' divided the region into a patchwork of colonies. The British and the French took little account of existing nations when they drew lines on maps and created their colonial borders. Those borders stuck, and the colonies eventually became independent modern states, a sort of overlay on the map of traditional West Africa. So today, the Ewe people straddle the border between Togo and Ghana and the Hausa are found in Nigeria, Niger and Benin, and this pattern is repeated elsewhere.

The colonies (and today's successor nations) varied in size and shape from the tiny Gambia to the massive Nigeria. Each colony was 'developed' as little or as much as was worthwhile in terms of colonial exploitation. So some countries have fairly good road and rail systems, while others have little or nothing. As there was very little contact between the British and the French, each system developed separately. This means that today travel within individual countries can be easy enough, but travel between them can often be difficult and frustrating.

Travel

Distances are great (over 1,000 miles from Lagos to Lake Chad, both within Nigeria). And even short distances, like the 280 miles from Lagos to Accra, can take a long time because of formalities at the three international borders to be crossed. The ideal way of travelling is with your own (fairly robust) vehicle. Short of this, the choice is between air, road and rail. There are air links between most countries, and several have a fairly wide network of domestic services, though times are often somewhat erratic and not always as per the printed timetable. Fares are not cheap, but in a few cases (such as getting from Guinea to The Gambia) air travel is the only practical method.

Hitch-hiking, in the 'no-charge' sense that we know it in Europe, is not part of the West African scene. That is not to say drivers will not stop and pick people up. They sometimes will, but will often expect to be paid the normal fare for the journey. Your visitor status might occasionally get you a free ride, but don't bank on it.

In many cases where there appears to be a choice between rail and road, the choice may not be real. Ordinary trains are often slow, serving every small town along the line. You will share tightly packed, slatted wooden seats with masses of others, and with every type of agricultural produce, much of it alive and squawking! Express trains can be OK, and in a few cases may actually be the best way to travel – especially if you can afford first or second class. Use the train where possible in Togo, Burkina Faso (Upper Volta) and the Ivory Coast. Nigerian trains have a bad reputation but have improved enormously over the last few years, and now offer a serious alternative to road travel on the long North–South routes. The train is also a practical way of moving between Senegal and Mali.

Mammy-wagons

Road transport ranges from 'proper' coaches and shared taxies to so-called 'mammy-wagons' – large wooden lorries with removable bench seats, which double as goods and passenger transport. Do not expect comfort: if you get it consider it a bonus. Travel can be a hot and dirty business in West Africa, so be prepared: make sure you do not go too long without access to a good bed and shower. Several countries, like Ghana and Sierra Leone, have a state-owned transport system, offering a good network of coach routes. But tickets are often at a premium and may have to be booked a day in advance. Check at local offices, and do not always take no for an answer – paying a pound or two over the odds may get you a ticket on the 'full' coach.

Shared long-distance taxis are universal. They are usually Peugeot estate cars converted to take up to eight passengers. Often considered a posh way to travel, they usually cost 10 to 20 per cent more than a sardine-packed minibus or mammy-wagon. They also travel faster, and leave more frequently. Passenger transport normally leaves only when all seats are occupied – and a few more! So the smaller the vehicle, the shorter the wait for a full payload. Apart from the coaches, which have their own stations, all the other vehicles normally leave from the 'lorry station' ('motor park' in Nigeria) or the *gare de louage* or *gare de* whatever your destination in the French-speaking areas.

The roads themselves vary. In some of the wealthier countries, paved roads abound, while in others like Burkina Faso (Upper Volta), Niger and Guinea-Bissau they are few and far between. But they all suffer badly in the rainy season. Potholes and bad stretches are the norm rather than the exception.

Tourism

Apart from The Gambia and to a much more limited extent Ivory Coast, Senegal and Sierra Leone, the tourism boom has not hit West Africa yet. Indeed there is so little real grasp of the idea of travelling for the sheer hell of it that you are sure to meet some suspicion, especially out of the main cities. But urban Africans are used to 'mad, rich Europeans' who spend money on going places with no real purpose other than going there.

Accommodation ranges from the Hilton-style glass palaces of Lagos, Abidjan and most other capital cities to very cheap, and often squalid places with the minimum of facilities. You will find something between the two in most cities, but many smaller towns lack any sort of hotel. However there are sometimes some government rest houses that are basic, cheap and good. 'Hotel' can also mean drinking place, so do not imagine that everywhere described as a hotel actually has accommodation. In some towns and cities, some small hotels may actually be brothels where rooms are rented by the hour – check that out first, and save untold embarrassment!

Eating is generally easier in the French-speaking countries, where French cultural imperialism imposed French tastes in a way that is not paralleled in the former British colonies. So it is much easier to get a good, cheap vaguely French meal that you recognize. Staple West African foods are often pounded, and are meant to be swallowed without chewing – a difficult feat for the European palate. But rice is also universal, and a basic rice and 'stew' meal (rice, meat and sauce – but beware the pepper) is available at roadside and market eating places, widely known as 'chop-bars'. If you visit Kano you must try the local '*suya*' (kebab) and in Freetown you can gorge yourself on the cheapest, most delicious prawn meals imaginable.

Cold lager beer is excellent, but be careful – it is much stronger than most European beers. There are local corn beers, like '*pito*' in Ghana or '*burukutu*' in Nigeria. But as with pubs in Britain, you would be missing a major part of a people's culture if you never visited a traditional drinking house.

Automatic Wealth

If you are planning to work your way around West Africa, forget it. Unemployment is high, and wages can be abysmally low. However poor you think you are, you are rich. Anyone who can afford to travel across continents is rich, and if you are white this will confirm your relative wealth. This can affect the prices you are asked in market-places where bargaining is expected, and to a certain extent the correct price is the price the customer can afford. This does not apply to meals, minor items such as cigarettes and roadside snacks, and fares on public transport other than taxis (generally unmetred – a fare should be agreed before boarding).

Most West Africans are open, friendly, welcoming people. Off the beaten track a white person may attract the attention of small children who call out *Baturi*, *Oboroni* or whatever the local word for white person is. If you are black, you will almost certainly be assumed to be American. Some visitors find Nigeria, by far the largest and most dynamic country in the region, with a population of over 100 million, less attractive than other places. People are often forward, not particularly interested in Europeans and they will certainly not kow-tow to them. But if you are going to West Africa to find primitive bliss and colonial servility, best stay at home.

West Africa is not exactly a feminist stronghold, though women have traditionally held, and continue to hold, far more responsible positions than has been usual in the western world. Women travellers should expect sexism and come-ons, especially if they wear shorts or even go to bars. Much of the region is Muslim, so women save themselves a lot of hassle if they follow a dress code that is suitably 'moral'. Men too would do well to have a look at what the average town-dweller is wearing and follow suit. Shorts can be much less comfortable than trousers (yes!) and are not widely worn. Scruffy dress can often be interpreted as an insult to your hosts, the local people.

Volatile Politics

West Africa is a politically volatile area, but this need not worry the traveller in terms of physical danger. This writer has lived through four *coups d'état* in the region with no problems. But it is important to keep up-to-date with events, because a coup will often mean borders are closed, communications cut, and a curfew imposed for anything from a few days to several weeks. Disagreements between neighbouring countries can also result in border closures; the Togo–Ghana and the Liberia–Sierra Leone frontiers have been closed at various times in the last year. A portable short-wave radio will supplement local enquiries and it is well worth listening to local stations as well as the BBC World Service. Few countries are so oppressive as to be uncomfortable for visitors, though it is perhaps not such a good idea to head for Equatorial Guinea, and Chad is still dangerous. The recent coup in Nigeria is popular, and has made things easier for most people. However, it is still not a good idea to walk the streets of Lagos late at night – stories of armed bandits, though exaggerated, are essentially true. Guinea's new military government promises that the country will now be more accessible to outsiders. Keep within the law, be civil and courteous even in the face of provocation, do not make unreasonable demands or expect deference, and all will be well.

West Africa's immediate political problems often stem from the region's position in the world system. The landlocked countries are very poor – Mali, Burkina Faso (Upper Volta) and Niger rank among the very poorest in the world. Since the oil crisis of the early 70s, several economies have gone steadily downhill. Ghana is beset by multiple problems: there was very little food last year. The drought, combined with lack of foreign currency to import food, made life almost unbearable. Many countries are plagued by regular shortages of petrol, bringing movement to a near standstill. Electricity supplies are often erratic, due to a combination of low water levels in hydro-electric dams, and shortage of spare parts for generators. But life goes on, and these hassles, except in the most extreme cases, should not deter the traveller. A visit to West Africa will be a rewarding and memorable experience for anyone who is not looking for an all mod cons, Costa Blanca style holiday.

East Africa

by Alastair Matheson and Victoria Southwell

Just because the countries of East Africa straddle the Equator, do not imagine that everywhere is as hot and humid as the coastal belt. Large parts of the area have a temperate climate all year round, the result of the high altitudes of the interior. In fact, there is so little variation in temperature through the year that locals never use the expressions 'summer' or 'winter': to do so at once gives away the foreign visitor, for seasons here are distinguished by being 'wet' or 'dry'. There are two wet seasons a year through much of East Africa.

When they come, the rains are heavy with dramatic thunderstorms. After many months of living in a parched landscape swept by searing hot winds, people tend to become edgy as the rainy season nears, emotional tensions often matching those of the stormladen atmosphere. People rarely venture out of doors during the storms unless it is imperative – and then a stout golfing umbrella is about the only effective protection.

But it is pure joy to wake up in the tea-growing country of Kericho, or look out on Mount Elgon from Kitale, in the crisp, clear atmosphere after a good night's rain has settled the dust and washed out the haze, so that everything is crystal clear and you can see for miles over a green countryside. The clarity of the high altitude air enhances the scene and the fluffy white cumulus clouds look as if they are cardboard cut-outs pinned to the brilliant blue sky.

Another major problem found during the dry months is dust. Allergy apart, it is seldom a serious health hazard and only the discomfort and possible damage to fragile clothing are a nuisance. Dust can damage cameras, films and delicate equipment such as exposure metres and tape recorders. When travelling in the African bush it is advisable to keep such items in plastic bags which can be sealed up or tightly fastened. (When you hear your camera lens grating as if it has scouring powder in it, you know it's too late!)

Bureaucracy

For the traveller in East Africa, the first major nuisance comes on arrival at the airport. Officials tend to look on all tourists as gullible, only too ready to part with cash at the slightest hint of a problem. The secret is to stand one's ground when challenged by greedy functionaries looking for a quick bribe; adopt an air of authority and a 'been-through-all-this-before' attitude and eventually you'll be waved through the health, customs, or immigration check – so long as you are carrying nothing that you really *need* to hide!

Never carry firearms on tour in Africa. Even if you are honest and declare them, the red tape and bureaucracy can be mind-boggling and too time-consuming to be worth it, unless you are a fanatic hunter with a brace of elephant guns – in which case it is up to your safari operator to handle the problem. At worst, if a nervous roadblock finds a gun it can lead to accusations of spying, mercenary activities and suchlike, and even to a very uncomfortable stay in prison.

Out and About

Kenya, Tanzania and Uganda all have extensive road networks, and most of the main trunk roads are tarred, although not always in the best condition, especially in Uganda after its years of trouble. Travel is quite easy on the major roads, but a good map is essential, as are the basic spares. Only the more experienced or ambitious traveller should venture off the tarred roads in an ordinary saloon car, especially in the rainy season. During the rains, what looks on the map like a well-used road can degenerate into a boulder-strewn track, churned up by deep ditches which only a moon buggy could negotiate successfully.

Well off the beaten track, one of the great joys is being able to pitch a tent for the night just where you fancy. You will rarely be disturbed. Obviously, you don't camp just anywhere in a game park or reserve, but usually you will find designated campsites which are perfectly safe, even supplied with water, although this is not always safe for drinking. Along the coast, private property must be respected and the risk of theft considered. In Kenya's far north, however, camping almost anywhere is perfectly safe and usually the only nuisance is being stared at by a bevy of children – and their elders – who have probably not had more than a fleeting glimpse of a white skin before.

Rest houses, when vacant, are available for visitors' use for a small fee. Some of the most delightful are in Western Uganda and others grace the hilltops in Rwanda and neighbouring Burundi; they are a vital facility when there are no other hotels or lodgings for hundreds of kilometres. Of course, one has to be self-sufficient, as the rest house (*gîte* in Rwanda) only provides shelter, and maybe beds, tables and chairs.

The Coast

The East African coast may be divided into two geographic regions; the

Somali coast to the north and the Swahili coast to the south. The Somali coast is arid and lined with sand dunes, inhabited by nomads. The Swahili coast, on the other hand, enjoys good rainfall, is fringed by coral reefs, and has mangrove forests which provide timber for building and export. The area is peopled by a mix of Arabs and Bantu-speaking Africans, and has been strongly Islamic since the ninth century. With the '*nyika*' behind, the coastal people have, for centuries, looked east, trading with Arabia and India. The sophistication of this culture and European colonization make the coast very different from the rest of black Africa.

Wide, white sandy beaches, whispering palms, an azure sea, coral gardens, a carefree lifestyle and friendly people typify Kenya's coast. There are four main centres with interconnecting flights from Nairobi to Mombasa, Malindi and Lamu. There are fine hotels, self-catering chalets and campsites while a protective reef near Mombasa makes inshore waters safe for every beach lover.

In Mombasa itself is the massive sixteenth century Fort Jesus and the streets of the old town are worth exploring. Try and find the perfume shops down near the *dhow* harbour. Further north, near Watamu, is Gedi, the remains of a thirteenth-century Arab state. Watamu and Malindi are deep sea fishing centres with shark, marlin and sail fish the most sought after catches. Lamu is a little island paradise. Free of Zanzibar's political tarnish, it survives as a living example of the medieval Arab culture.

In Tanzania, Dar-es-Salaam (which means 'haven of peace') nestles in one of the prettiest harbours in the world. Most of its streets are narrow and winding with low buildings, many dating back to the Arab period. There are reliable and efficient air services by Air Tanzania to all main towns, a train service offering first, second and third class, and a good network of roads. Self-drive car hire, however, is extremely expensive.

Just outside Dar-es-Salaam, there is a string of beach hotels which guarantee rest on the beautifully white and unspoilt beaches. The Tanzanian government has recently given tourism its full support, but its hotels and lodges are expensive to maintain. Zanzibar may have lost a coat of paint but its hotels remain comfortable. This island of spices is best explored on foot and the government tours are recommended. All visitors must conform to the strict Muslim rules on dress – long skirts for women, no shorts or tight-fitting trousers for men. Men must also wear their hair short or they will get a 'free haircut'.

Inland

Inland, East Africa has been made famous by the lyrical descriptions of nineteenth century explorers and their successors: Mounts Kenya and Kilimanjaro, the wildlife of Serengetti and the Ngorongoro Crater, Lake Victoria – 'the jewel of Africa', the Ruwenzoris – Mountains of the Moon. For the wildlife enthusiast, or even for those who love the wide open spaces that typify Africa, East Africa has it all.

Travelling in East Africa can be a pleasure if one is not pressed for time, so that if the unexpected happens and an air connection is missed or cancelled, schedules further along the route are not seriously disrupted. The Swahili equivalent of Spain's *mañana* is *bado kidogo*, which translated literally means 'a little later' – and that could well be the motto for this part of the world.

Southern Africa

by Guy Arnold and Melissa Shales

The range of travel possibilities in southern Africa is not simply one of choice – between countries, game parks, scenery, beaches, or whatever the fancy of the traveller may be – but also one of size and that should be a factor in all planning. Malawi looks small enough on the map of Africa, yet it is the size of England; the entire British Isles would fit three times into Zambia. Travel plans, therefore must take account of distances which can sometimes be both daunting and wearying.

Africa, moreover, has generally been the continent hardest hit by the increases in oil prices, so that those who hire a car must expect a large part of their expenses to go in hire charges and petrol.

South Africa

South Africa has made great efforts to attract tourists: it has both the facilities and the scenery to make holidays worthwhile and exciting. But there are drawbacks. Access is easy by air to Jan Smuts Airport (Johannesburg) and thence by numerous connections to other parts of the country; by sea; by road or rail from Mozambique, Botswana or Zimbabwe. Visas are usually required. There are excellent hotels running through five stars – for whites – and a range of restaurants and eating places at a variety of prices catering for the average tourist as well as the wealthy. Black travellers, however, have to make special arrangements about accommodation unless they can afford to stay at international class hotels all the time: these can now take people of any race. Car hire is readily possible and roads are good; there are many organized coach tours.

The problems are those of attitudes. White South Africans, despite an appearance of being cosmopolitan, are deeply affected by isolation and their views and consequent reaction to outsiders result from being 'cocooned'. Even mild dissent from established authority can be equated with Communism and they are so defensive as to be deeply suspicious of the critical outsider. Thus normal politics should be avoided. Race politics are even more explosive. A visitor should not take political books or magazines or anything even mildly pornographic – there is a huge list of banned publications. Sex across race is strictly taboo. It is an offence to stay in another 'group' or race area; and though much has been made of the ending of petty apartheid, the real problem in South Africa for any enlightened visitor is that he will find himself in a country where racial mixing and political discussion of the kind found automatically in Britain are simply alien. Just about everything closes on Sundays and travel into the homeland areas requires permits. Some beaches are strictly segregated. If all these drawbacks and inhibitions are taken into account,

South Africa has much to offer in scenery, beaches, games parks, and comfortable facilities – for whites.

Zimbabwe

In Zimbabwe, on the other hand, there is no longer any legal segregation, although it will probably be some time before all the country's inhabitants mingle freely. There is still a great deal of uneasiness on the part of both blacks and whites after so many years of racial prejudice and violence. The white population is still shrinking steadily, but this should not affect the traveller.

The government is doing all it can to promote tourism – an uphill struggle against continuous bad publicity in the foreign press. Zimbabwe has advantages over many African countries in its spectacular attractions, and also in that its tourist infrastructure has already been laid, with a large number of hotels in existence, although not all of them are currently open. At the top end of the market, the hotels are extremely luxurious.

Scenically, the country is well worth visiting, with such magnificent sights as the Victoria Falls and the Zimbabwe Ruins. The landscape varies greatly from the semi-desert savannah of the Botswana border to the lush green of the Eastern Highlands. Public transport is poor, and a car is really needed.

The east of the country seems to be safe, but continuing violence in the west has virtually closed off a good third of the country to tourists, including the Matopos hills, where Cecil Rhodes is buried. There seems little hope of any solution in the near future.

The Smaller Countries

Resources in the smaller countries vary widely. Lesotho, which offers remarkable scenery, still has a long way to go though it is developing its tourist facilities remarkably well and at speed. In the towns, accommodation and other facilities are, on the whole, of a high standard.

Mozambique, with its fairy-tale beaches, used to have a thriving tourist industry, although facilities never quite reached the standard one would expect from the numbers that used them. During the civil war this all came to a halt, as game parks were shot out for food, and the closed border with Zimbabwe cut off the country's main source of tourist revenue. The government is now beginning to try and attract back some of the South African trade, but in a country hit by famine and desperate poverty, it seems unlikely that the industry will flourish for some time to come.

Transkei and Bophutatswana are both taking advantage of South Africa's strict moral code to provide those things for South Africans which their own government will not – wine, women and gambling. Sun City and other similar developments do overwhelming business as South Africans pour across the border for 'racial mixing' (which means sex) and betting.

Swaziland and Malawi are both relying still on their spectacular scenery for the little tourism they have. Both are peaceful, stable countries with enormous amounts to offer those prepared to wander from the established track.

Little is known about these small countries, overshadowed as they are by the political upheavals in their larger neighbours, yet untroubled by violence (except in Mozambique), they could pave the way to a far more secure form of tourism in Southern Africa.

Game Parks

Those who seek big game should be careful about how they choose their game parks. Some, as in Kenya, have easy access from the cities and Land Rovers at the lodges to take visitors through the parks. In Botswana, however, game parks are far more remote and inaccessible, and to visit them requires a four-wheel-drive vehicle, a guide and *time*. For this reason, Botswana's policy is to attract principally the wealthier tourist who intends to make his visit into something of a safari.

Kruger National Park in South Africa is probably the most developed of the parks in southern Africa – and for that reason, my least favourite. It has well laid out and comfortable camps, some tarred roads and a railway running through part of it. Yet it has lost something of the bush atmosphere and is too tame, too like a zoo to be true to the spirit of Africa.

Hwange, in Zimbabwe, covers a vast area of several thousand square miles, although not all of it is open to tourists. It is dusty and dirty, but the camps are quite comfortable and the animal population high.

The Luangwa Valley in Zambia is much less developed. But it is possible to go on walking tours here and it is surprising to discover quite how much of a barrier a car's windows can be.

The Right Side of the Law

Everywhere in Africa the politics are fast-moving and it is always wise to know what is going on in a country so as not to talk out of turn. Tourists can easily get into trouble or be mistaken for spies if they become involved, quite innocently, in political discussions, so they should steer clear of them.

It is important to obey signs precisely: if, on the approach to a bridge, it says drive at 5mph, this means 5mph and not just slowly. Irate soldiers in Zambia, for example, have turned visitors back at the end of a bridge and made them return to the other side and then cross again at the correct speed. In Swaziland, the police are fond of laying speed traps on the main road into Mbabane (from South Africa) and fine drivers who have exceeded the limit on the spot.

Every country has its particular quirks, and it is as well to know about them. The local people are, on the whole, extremely friendly and generous – provided you don't touch sticky subjects – and will happily offer advice. Take it, even if you don't like it. They have years of experience and the tragedies amongst tourists in the past have all been amongst people who ignored local warnings. There is political uncertainty and there is violence, but with common sense, it need never affect you.

Great Journeys Overland

Down and Around Africa

by David Orchard and Melissa Shales

Crossing Africa is still one of the major overland journeys of the world, and no easy undertaking. There is an immense variety of climates, terrain, peoples and history, all of which add together with an extremely 'fluid' political situation to make it a true challenge in all terms.

Across the Sahara

Crossing the Sahara is still quite an expedition, beginning either at Tangiers (through the High Atlas and into Algeria), Alger (via the old Roman city of Constantine), or Tunis (past the huge Roman Amphitheatre at El Djem and across the Chott El Djerid).

From here there are three major trans Sahara routes: the eastern, the central (the trade route) via Gardaia along the tar-sealed road to Tamanrasset, and the western route along the Libyan border to Djanet, crossing the Fadnoun Plateau, with an optional trek into the Tassil N Ajjer to see the 3,000-year-old rock paintings. From Djanet, travellers are advised to go west past the Hermitage of P. de Foucauld at Assekrem and on to Tamanrasset. From Tam, the route heads due south past Assamarka, the isolated Foreign Legion fortress (no photos permitted) that is the border with Niger, past the salt workings at Tegguiddan Tessoum, where salt caravans, camels laden with tablets of salt, plod their way south and into Agadèz, with its silversmiths still making crosses by a molten wax method as their forefathers did.

As one heads south to Kano or south-west to Niamey, the vegetation thickens, and there are more people and more cattle. This is Fulani country – ornately bejewelled people congregating around wells with goats, camels and cattle. The western route goes from Béchar across the Tanezrouft down to Goa (remember to make an excursion to Tombouctou) and into Niamey.

From Kano or Niamey it is a simple run south on good roads into the thickening forests to Accra, Lomé or Lagos.

These routes all remain open to travellers who have made the proper preparations, although the Algerian authorities are becoming extremely reluctant to let anyone through whom they feel they might have to rescue later. So be warned, you will be unlikely to be allowed to undertake the journey in a clapped-out *Deux Chevaux*.

Recent reports coming back to Britain indicate that bribery is on a sharp upward curve and it is proving extremely expensive to satisfy all the outstretched hands in this section of the Sahara.

Trans-Africa (West to East)

From the coastal highway at Accra, Lomé or Lagos, the route follows the tar-sealed road down to Douala (a short, unsealed section near the border), past Mount Cameroon to Yaoundé, the very French capital in the highlands of the Cameroons. Further east past Boali Falls is Bangui, capital of the Central African Republic. Here the traveller has a choice of routes, through Zaïre to Kisingani, or north-east, through the eastern CAR and on to Juba. Either way the roads are bad, supplies are unobtainable, and there are few fuel stations, yet the people are friendly and a ball-point pen can still be bartered for two dozen oranges. From Juba the route joins the Cario/Nairobi route south via Lake Turkana. From Kisingani the traveller can go east through the Virunga National Park to Kampala and on to Nairobi, or south-east through Rwanda, the 'Switzerland of Africa', and the Volcano National Park where the traveller may be lucky enough to catch a glimpse of the mountain gorillas. The route continues through Kigali into Tanzania, south around Lake Victoria or via Mount Kilimanjaro to Dar es Salaam.

Uganda seems, at the time of writing, to be relatively stable, and a number of very favourable reports have been received about the behaviour of the police and army. However, there are still bandits around and you should be cautious. The Ugandans are not terribly keen on giving out visas to tourists, so you are unlikely to be able to get there for a while unless you can give them a good reason.

Cairo to Nairobi

Egypt has been a Mecca for travellers for many years with its pyramids, the ancient temples of Luxor and Karnak and the valleys of the Kings and Queens. Only recently have foreign-registered vehicles been allowed into the country, but a tar-sealed road stretches from Alexandria to Aswan. From Wadi Halfa, the track leaves the Nile and takes a straight route across the Nubian Desert to Abu Hamed, from where the route follows the Nile all the way to Juba. From Khartoum, where Blue Nile meets White Nile, African meets Arab, one goes south via Sennar, Kosti to Malakal and the beginning of the Sudd, that vast area of marsh and moorland, the size of the UK, where herds of a hundred giraffe are commonplace, where the Dinka, the tall noble savage, strides the plains with nothing but a spear, and life has changed little in a thousand years.

On to Juba, the capital of the south, not a hustling, bustling city, where excitement can be stirred up by a rogue hippo in the Nile or the arrival of supplies on the steamer from the north. From Juba, the route takes the traveller through the narrow corridor to Lokichokio and on to Lake Turkana (the Jade Sea of Hillaby fame). South of Lodwar the road separates, west via Kitale for banks, beers and supplies, or east to Lakes Baringo and Beroria for flamingoes by the thousand. The roads join at Nakuru for the tar-sealed road to Nairobi.

This route has often been described as 'Africa the old and new': the tomb of Tutankhamun, the temple of Queen Hatshepsut, and the cites of Cairo and Nairobi are the old and new elements linked vaguely by the Nile.

Nairobi to Cape Town

To everybody's relief, including the two countries concerned, the border between Kenya and Tanzania has recently reopened, once again allowing free traffic to the overlanders. The best route south is through the game reserves of Masai Mara and Serengeti, by the Ngorongoro crater to Arusha, a climb up Kilimanjaro (5,963m), an extinct, snow-capped volcano and the highest point in Africa, and on to Dar es Salaam. The road west to Lusaka follows the line of the TanZam railway and is an easy section of the journey. It is not on the main route south, but it may be worth considering a small detour to Malawi. This beautiful country is all but neglected by tourists, but is one of the most beautiful spots in southern Africa. Further south, another worthwhile detour is into Swaziland, again rarely visited in the rush to fall off Africa at Cape Point.

From Lusaka, passing through Zambia's copper belt, the traveller has a choice of routes, south-east into Zimbabwe, past Lake Kariba and through the Hwange National Park, or south-west, past the Victoria Falls and the wildlife park on the Okavango Delta on the edge of the Kalahari desert in Botswana and then on to the Republic of South Africa. However, while it is worth trying to see Kariba, the Victoria Falls and Hwange, the rest of western Zimbabwe is not currently safe for overland travel, except under armed escort. Either cross into Botswana as fast as possible or swing east to Harare, and go south to Mutare on the Mozambique border, through the mountain ranges of the Eastern Highlands, then down past the Great Zimbabwe ruins and cross into South Africa via Beit Bridge.

Once in South Africa, the route goes through the gold city of Johannesburg, through the Orange Free State, across the Karoo (a wonderful sight in spring when the desert is covered by sheets of flowers) to Cape Town and Table Mountain: a dramatic end to a dramatic continent.

A four-wheel-drive vehicle is not necessary for most of these routes providing one travels in the dry season. The west/east section is probably the most difficult with little available in the way of fuel and supplies. High ground clearance, such as on a VW Campervan, is essential. The problems that will arise will be primarily political: closed borders, visa difficulties, military takeovers or outright wars. But with a clear head and luck, it is still the journey of a lifetime.

Around South America

by Chris Parrott

The Gringo Trail (not to be confused with the Inca Trail) is what everyone calls the most frequently travelled route through and around South America. *Gringo* is derived either from 'Green go home' in the days when the US Army used to wear green uniforms, or from *Griego*, the

Spanish word for Greek. Despite assurances in the guide-books that the term is so widely used to refer to anyone with a pale complexion that it has lost its unfriendly connotations, it is definitely not a complimentary form of address. If you need confirmation, watch how a blond Argentine reacts to being called *Gringo*.

The Trail begins in whichever gateway happens to be the cheapest to fly into from Europe or the USA. Let's start in the north, in Colombia. The coast here boasts beautiful golden beaches, clear water and crystal streams cascading down from the 5,800 metre summits of the Sierra Nevada. To the south is the big industrial port of Barranquilla and then Cartagena, an impressively fortified town dating from 1533, through which, for nearly three hundred years, gold and treasures were chanelled from throughout the Spanish colonies. Passing through the hot swampland and then inland up the attractive forested slopes of the Cordillera Occidental, the traveller emerges on a high plateau where Bogotá is sited, at 2,620 metres. The Gold Museum has over 10,000 examples of pre-Colombian artefacts. An hour away are the salt mines of Zipaquira, inside which the workers carved an amazing 23 metre high cathedral.

South from Bogotá are the Tequendama Falls, the splendid valley of the Magdalena River and, high up on the Magdalena Gorge, the village of San Agustin. Here hundreds of primitive stone statues, representing gods of a little known ancient Indian culture, guard the entrances to tombs. The road then loops back over high moorland to Popayan, a fine city with monasteries and cloisters in the Spanish style. The tortured landscape near here has been said to resemble 'violently crumpled bedclothes'; tilled fields on the opposite mountain faces 'look nearly vertical'.

So the road crosses into Ecuador. Just north of Quito, the equator, *La Mitad Del Mundo*, cuts the road, a few hundred metres from the grand stone monument built to mark the meridian. Quito itself is at 2,700 metres, ringed by peaks, amongst them the volcanoes of Pinchincha. It has much fine colonial architecture including, according to *The South American Handbook*, eighty-six churches, many of them gleaming with gold.

The Andes

Travellers then cross the Andes, passing from near-Arctic semi-tundra, through temperate forest, equatorial jungle and down to the hot total desert of the Peruvian coast, punctuated by oases of agricultural land where irrigation has distributed the melt-waters from the Andes over the littoral. Here too the ancient empires of the Chavin, Mochica, Nazca and Chimu people flourished. Ruined Chan-Chan, near Trujillo, was the Chimu capital; nearby Sechin has a large square temple, 3,500 years old, incised with carvings of victorious leaders and dismembered foes.

A popular detour here is to turn inland at the fishing port of Chimbote and head for the Callejon de Huaylas. The route passes through the spectacular Cañón del Pato, where the road is literally drilled through the rock wall of the canyon, with 'windows' down to the roaring maelstrom of the Santa river below. The Callejon de Huaylas valley runs along the foot of the Cordillera Blanca; here the 1970 earthquake buried the town of Yungay under an avalanche of mud. The towns of Caraz and Huaraz make good centres for walking and trekking in the Cordillera, and the road south across the mountains has spectacular views of the snowcapped Cordillera Blanca.

The coast near Lima is picturesque and rich in fish and birdlife, owing to the Humboldt Current. Lima itself has both shanty towns (*barrios*) and affluent suburbs, parks and fine beaches. Well worth seeing are the National Museum of Anthropology and Archaeology, the Gold Museum at Monterrico on the outskirts of town, and the Amano private museum.

South from Lima

From Lima, there are two routes south. One branches into the mountains – the pass reaches 4,800 metres – through the zinc smelting town of La Oroya, to Huancayo. The road continues through Ayacucho and Abancay to Cuzco, and though Lima/Cuzco looks a relatively short distance on the map, it actually represents about fifty hours of continuous travel overland. The other route follows the fast coast road through the desert past the wine centre of Ica to Nazca with its vast and little understood lines, on to Arequipa. There are several cut-off routes – from Pisco, or Nazca, for example, or you can take the train from Arequipa in a grand circle, to get to Cuzco.

One thing that is certain: any route in Peru that crosses the Andes is tortuous, time-consuming, and stunningly spectacular.

Cuzco sits in a sheltered hollow at 3,500 metres. This was the capital of the Inca Empire. Inca stonework forms the base of many of the Spanish buildings and the ancient city layout survives to this day. Overlooking Cuzco's red roofs is the ruined fortress of Sacsahuaman. Nearby too are the ruins of Pisac and Ollantaitambo and, reached by train only, down the valley of the Urubamba (further upstream, this is called the Vilcanota), the 'Lost City of the Incas', Machu Picchu. This magnificent ruined city sited nearly 500 metres above the river was overgrown with jungle until its discovery in 1911. There are several legends which add to the mystery of the lost city. One states that after the sacking of Cuzco, the Virgins of the Sun fled to this city, whose existence was unknown to the Spanish. Others say that the Incas themselves had erased all mention of the city from their oral histories, retribution for some now forever-censored local uprising long before Pizarro and his men set foot in Peru.

From Cuzco, the road crosses the watershed of the Andes to the dry and dusty Altiplano, a high treeless plateau stretching from here across much of the Bolivan upland. Here lies Lake Titicaca, at 3,810 metres the world's highest navigable lake, blazing a deep blue because of ultra-violet rays. On the floating reed islands of the lake live the Uru-Aymará Indians. Across the border in Bolivia are the ruins of Tiahuanaco, relic of an ancient race; the main feature is the carved 'Gate of the Sun'.

La Paz lies in a valley just below the

rim of the Altiplano, the city centre lying at approximately 3,500 metres.

La Paz and Beyond

From La Paz, there are three possible routes, depending on the size of the circuit that you intend making.

1. Eastwards through the relatively low-lying city of Cochabamba to Santa Cruz, then on by rail to Corumba on the Brazilian border, from where you can head for São Paulo or the Iguaçu Falls. The road from Santa Cruz to Corumba and any of those from Bolivia to Paraguay are suitable for four-wheel-drive only.
2. Southwards via Cochabamba to Sucre and the mining town of Potosi to Villazón on the Argentine border and points south. NB: Since April 1982, British passport holders have required a visa to enter Argentina. At the time of going to press, visas issued in London take several months to process; it helps to have a sponsor (friend or relative, etc.) oiling the wheels at the other end. Visas are handled by the Brazilian Embassy (Argentine Interests Section) at 111 Cadogan Gardens SW3. Tel: 01-730 7997. Holders of Irish passports do not need visas.
3. Southwards to Arica in northern Chile. The roads gradually peter out over the salt pans and quicksands that stretch over this region – a region that should only be traversed in the dry season (May to November) and then with very great care. The road passes through the very beautiful Lauca National Park, and then continues (for the most part tar-sealed) through the Atacama desert, the farmlands and vineyards of central Chile to the so-called 'Little Switzerland' of mountainous southern Chile.

There is no road in Chile south of Puerto Montt, and the most usual point of crossing the border south of Santiago is that near Osorno to reach Bariloche, now a fashionable ski resort in Argentina. This route may not be passable in winter (June to October). The road from Santiago to Mendoza via Uspallata is kept open all year round – though in winter the road uses the railway tunnel and does not pass the famous Christ of the Andes statue. Travel south from Bariloche takes you over often unmade roads in the foothills of the Andes through the beautiful Argentine lake district to Viedma and Calafate. Here the lakes are fed by meltwaters from the Patagonian icecap, and 'arms' of the lakes are sometimes blocked by tongues of glacial ice. The scenery around Lago Argentino, for example, is some of the most spectacular anywhere in the world. Roads here are passable at most times of year, though from June to October, four-wheel-drive is advisable.

The South

It is possible to reach South America's southernmost tip, Tierra del Fuego, by ferry from near Rio Gallegos, or from Punta Arenas across the border in Chile.

In winter it's impossible to cross the mountains by road to reach the small town of Ushuaia on Tierra del

Fuego's south coast, but there are regular flights throughout the year from nearby Gallegos and Rio Grande.

A worthwhile excursion from Punta Arenas (Chile) is to Puerto Natales and the famous Torres del Paine National Park: a must for mountaineers, and an unforgettable experience for anyone who thinks that those etchings by early explorers always made mountains look ridiculously precipitous.

The fast straight east coast road through temperate scrubland takes you north again via Comodoro Rivadavia, Puerto Madryn with its Welsh-speaking colony, to Bahia Blanca and Buenos Aires. This cosmopolitan city of nearly ten million inhabitants lies on the estuary of the River Plate, a few hours by ferry from Montevideo in Uruguay.

Most travellers tend to bypass the rolling cattle-grazed plains of Uruguay in favour of the roads northwards, either through Santa Fe and Resistencia to Asunción, or direct to Iguaçu via Posadas and the Misiones province. Though there are several ferries, there are only three bridging points across the Paraná River between Buenos Aires and Asunción. The first and newest is at Zarate; the second is the tunnel from Santa Fe to Rosario; and the third is the bridge between Resistencia and Corrientes.

There is a good fast road from Asunción to Foz do Iguaçu (in Brazil) where the frontier is crossed by bridge. Car and passenger ferries from Foz do Iguaçu (Pôrto Meira) in Brazil to Puerto Iguaçu (or Iguassu) in Argentina, make it possible to visit these spectacular falls from both sides of the river.

Plantations of Brazil

The dense forest that once spread across Brazil from Iguaçu to Rio and beyond is gradually making way for coffee and soya bean plantations, though there is a particularly special stretch of road between Curitiba and São Paulo, since the new road follows the Serra do Mar coastal range. Carriageways are often separated by several kilometres as east-bound traffic goes around one side of a jungle-clad mountain, while west-bound takes the high road.

From São Paulo there are two routes to Rio – one through Santos and Angra dos Reis along a beautiful coast road; the other the fast motorway, along the ridge of the mountains via the steel town of Volta Redonda.

Rio is a focus: from here routes divide once more.

1. The north-east coast road through Salvador, Recife and Fortaleza to Belém at the mouth of the Amazon. Many travellers feel that this route, passing through the regions first settled by Portugal and her slaves four centuries ago, is the real Brazil.
2. Northwest via Belo Horizonte and the old mining towns of Minas Gerais province, such as Ouro Preto, Congonhas, Tiradentes and Mariana. This route leads to that oasis of modernity, that ultimate in planned cities, Brasilia.

There are several routes up to the Amazon basin from Brasilia; the fastest and easiest is direct to Belém via Anapolis. On this road there is a cut-off at Estreito, along the Transamazónica Highway to Altamira and Santarém.

Alternatively you can follow the newer road west to Cuiabá, and then take the Transamazónica north to Santarém. At both Belém and Santarém there are river steamers to Manaus though, for anyone with their own vehicle to ship, car ferries are few and far between. A more practical route in this instance is that to the west, to Cuiabá and Pôrto Velho, and then north along the new road via Humaitá to Careiro on the south bank of the Amazon opposite Manaus. From here there are three ferries daily across to Manaus.

In the days when Brazil held a monopoly of rubber supplies, Manaus built a splendid (and recently restored) opera house for the best mezzo-sopranos in the world; and the rubber barons lit their cigars with 1,000 *milreis* notes. Most of that glitter has faded, though edifices built of stone imported from Britain are still to be seen.

From here, riverboats ply the Rio Negro and the Rio Branco, tributaries of the Amazon, and they provide a break from overlanding and a convenient, if primitive, way of visiting remote villages. North from Manaus the authorities have 'subdued' the Indians who, for years, threatened white lives on the road to Boa Vista, and the route is now passable in safety.

Angel Falls

The road between Boa Vista and the gold mining town of El Dorado (Venezuela) winds through spectacularly beautiful country passing the sheer-sided 'Lost World' of Mount Roraima at the junction of the three countries. Side trips can be taken to the world's highest waterfall, Angel Falls (979 metres), either from El Dorado or from Puerto Ordaz (shortly to become part of the new city of Ciudad Guayana).

After crossing the Orinoco, you'll soon reach Caracas, having completed almost a full circle of the continent. If you've still not seen enough, there's a route eastwards that is definitely not on the Gringo Trail. It is not possible, owing to border disputes, to cross the frontier from Venezuela to Guyana. From Boa Vista (Brazil) however, there is a road of sorts to the frontier and a fordable river into Lethem. In the dry season, it's possible to drive all the way to Georgetown, and from there along the coast to the Corentyne River. Getting across that and into Nieuw Nickerie in Surinam will cause problems for those with their own vehicles, though there is an infrequent ferry. In fact, it's possible to drive all the way to Cayenne in French Guiana, though the road is little more than a sand track in places, and there are a number of rivers that have to be crossed by ferry.

Saint Laurent lies just over the river from Suriname, in French Guiana, and the remnants of both this penal colony and the better-known one of the Isles de Salut are beginning to prove something of a tourist attraction. Devil's Island is part of the Isles de Salut Group, but is hard to reach.

At Cayenne, the road ends, though it is possible to fly either direct to Belém at the mouth of the Amazon or to Saint Georges, just across the river from the Brazilian river port of Oiapoque, from where a road runs all the way to Macapá. There are ferries to Belém from there, and that puts you back on the route southwards to Rio either along the north-east coast, or south to Brasilia. In fact, you could just keep circling and recircling the continent in ever decreasing circles, clockwise and anticlockwise. It's a very dizzying part of the world in every respect!

Overland Through Asia

by Geoff Hann

Several factors have combined to disrupt the traditional overland route to Asia of late, notably internal turmoil and changes of government within Iran and Afghanistan, together with the invasion of Afghanistan by Russia, the Iran/Iraq war, which is beginning to spill into the other Gulf states, and even ripples from the civil war in Lebanon. Bureaucracy too has increased in many of the Asian countries. Pre-departure documentation has become all important. Woe betide the traveller who arrives on the border of India without a *carnet de passages* for his vehicle, correct in every detail. Flexibility of attitude and mind is as important now as it was to the early Victorian traveller.

In some circumstances, overflights of extremely troubled areas have to be considered. The route through Iran is still theoretically open, although there may be a difficulty in getting visas, but travellers are being advised in the strongest possible terms not to drive through until the situation both within the country and with Iraq has been resolved. Afghanistan is very definitely closed to tourists and is likely to remain so for the foreseeable future.

The most used overland route begins in London, crosses the Channel by ferry to either Ostend or Zeebrugge and connects with the E5 road for a rapid transit through Belgium, Germany, Austria, Yugoslavia and Bulgaria to Turkey. There are, of course, minor variations. But whether one travels at a leisurely pace or a gallop, the first major halt is Istanbul, introduction to the East, a noisy melting-pot of nationalities and full of historical interest. A place too to gather your breath, rest, repair vehicles, and pick up news of the road ahead from fellow travellers.

Istanbul Connections

From Istanbul there is a choice of route. The shortest one is through the north of Turkey onto the great Anatolian Plateau. The road travels via Ankara, the modern capital of Turkey, and passes through Sivas, Erzurum and Ağri to the border with Iran. Doğubayazit is the last Turkish town and is overlooked by Mount Ararat, the traditional seat of Noah's Ark. This border crossing, known universally as Bazargan, is now the main crossing for all traffic. Many of the other crossings such as Serou, just south of Lake Van, are subject to local conflicts. Make careful local enquiries before attempting to use them. But Turkey has so much to offer that most travellers will want to travel more slowly. The most effective way to do so is to backtrack slightly from Istanbul to the Dardanelles. The Çannakale crossing is the usual way and the road follows the coastline very closely. Troy, Bergama (Pergamon), modern Izmir and ancient Ephesus are just some of the places to visit. From Ephesus, the road loops inland before coming back to the coast at Antalya. Another long scenic drive directly by the sea passes by and through Alanya, Silifke, Mersin and Adana. For those intending to cross into Iran by the Bazargan border, an ideal route is north from Mersin onto the Central Turkish Plateau via the volcanic tufa area around Nevşehir and Kayseri. The small towns of Urgup and the villages such as Göreme are world famous for the early Christian churches and tombs carved out of the rock. The underground city of Derinkuyu also should not be missed.

It is only a few hours from this area to resume the northern route at Sivas. Those intent on seeing something of eastern Turkey should follow the road to Malatya, Elâziğ, Bingol, and Lake Van – beautiful scenery and a Kurdish area. At Van, the border crossing of Serou is close by, as is a road leading north to Bazargan.

The Middle East Route

At the time of writing, this route is closed by the war in Iran/Iraq, but should it reopen, it is well worth considering with a great deal of interest to see on the way.

It begins at Adana, where one turns south and follows the path used by many invaders, through the Syrian Gates to Antakya, ancient Antioch. It is a short distance to the border and Baba El Hawa, the Syrian entry post. Business takes a while here and travellers should be patient.

Syria is much underrated by travellers, suffering a bad press as it does because of its political stance. But it offers unbounded Arab hospitality and contains a staggering quantity of historical remains. Many of the sites have romantic settings, such as Palmyra, Rosafya, crumpled remains out in the desert and great Crusader castles set on mountain peaks. Halab (Aleppo) is the first introduction to the Arab world, noisy, but full of interesting people, ruined sites and good food. Travelling on southwards through Hamah, with its great eighteenth-century water wheels, and Homs, one reaches Damascus, the capital. Here are the beautiful Ommayad mosque, Saladin's tomb and the biblical 'Street called Straight', together with a huge *souk* or market.

Continuing south, cross the border at Deraa into Jordan, a country with a Western approach, where tourism is a major source of income. But nothing can detract from Petra, Jordan's pre-eminent attraction. This fabulous hidden valley lined with rock tombs is approximately 280km south of Amman off the Desert Highway. A natural continuation of this diversion would be a further trip south, to the beaches of Aqaba, before returning to Amman, Jordan's capital.

God-given Relief

From Amman, the overland route turns east, heading straight into the stony desert to Iraq and Baghdad ('gift of God' in Arabic) as a welcome relief at the end. The city is a large, sprawling one. Babylon is nearby, as are the holy cities of An Najaf and Karbala, important centres for the Shi'ite Muslim faith. For the overlander, the usual route is to Al Basran (Basra), another long desert journey. This city is the most southerly in Iraq, famous for its date groves and as the birthplace of Sinbad the Sailor. Normally a ferry crossing and a drive of twelve kilometres into Iran towards Abadan would have sufficed for the next section. However, Basra is currently at the very heart of the fighting, with all the land around bitterly disputed. So the traveller must turn around further north and head back to Turkey.

Back in Turkey, he must return to Bazargan, refuelling before he crosses the border, since fuel may become very difficult to obtain for some distance. Mākū and Tabriz are the main cities with a Turkish flavour. The countryside is delightful – winding valleys lined with poplar trees through low hills – until one comes to the flat plain that stretches to Tehran. Tehran is one of the fastest-growing cities in the world: its hideous traffic and pollution are striking. Travellers will need to guard their language in present circumstances, as people are sensitive. Travellers used then to go through to Afghanistan, but this is obviously now no longer possible, and it seems unlikely that the route will open again, so there is no choice but to travel south, bypassing Qom, the theological centre, to Esfahan, known for its mosques and handicrafts. Further south is Persepolis, ancient palace and religious city of the Persians, burnt by Alexander the Great when he conquered the Empire. Close by is the garden city of Shirāz, tree-lined and populated by courteous people.

Wild Country

But to resume the overland route, return to Esfahan and turn south-east to Yazd, home of the Fire Worshippers and the Towers of Silence. Skirting the Dasht-e-Lut desert, the road travels via Kermān and the oasis of Bam to Zāhedān. Motorists should pay particular attention to their vehicles before leaving Esfehan for this stretch of their journey. Conditions can be difficult and spare parts are not readily available.

From Zāhedān, the next section is rough and very remote from civilisation as we know it. The province of Baluchistan is quite removed from the rest of Pakistan, a wild country of wild people, with extremes of temperature. Dalbandin is the first major town along this route, some 160km into the country beyond the Customs post. Next comes Quetta, capital of the province, an interesting town in which to relax after the strenuous journey from Esfahan. Thence the road travels the Bolan Pass – famous from the great days of the British Army – on to Sukkur and Multan and then to Lahore. The North West Frontier and Khyber Pass, which would have formed part of the route from Afghanistan, have recently been closed to travellers in an attempt to try to clear up the drug-trafficking in the area.

Lahore is modern and bustling but with a red fort and many Moghul remains and gardens; many good restaurants and a fine museum too. It is also an excellent place for motor repairs and spare parts.

India

Now comes a short journey to the Wagha border with India – and much red tape. Amritsar is also only a short distance down the road and the first stop within India. In the old part of the town is the Golden Temple, heart of the Sikh religion. At the time of writing, the Punjab area is closed due to fighting between the Sikhs and Hindus, and has been officially declared to be in a state of emergency.

From Amritsar, the traveller can divert north to Kashmir, a two- or three-day journey up a scenic mountain road to Srinagar. Here houseboats on Dal Lake offer every luxury. High in the mountains are Leh and Zanskar.

But from Amritsar the Grand Trunk Road carries on through the prosperous Punjab to Delhi – for many travellers, journey's end, and a place to luxuriate in modern hotels, buy handicrafts and sightsee. Others go on to Nepal, either to trek in the Himalayas or to fly on to Bangkok and south-east Asia.

One leaves Delhi slightly south-west on a very good road for Jaipur, city of pink sandstone and centre of the precious-stone trade. Jaipur to Agra is another day's travel. Here one passes Fatehpur Sikri, the deserted sixteenth-century city, and Agra, home of the incomparable Taj Mahal, as also of the Red Fort, Little Taj and Great Mosque.

From Agra the road leads south to cross the Chambal river and through Gwalior to Khajuraho, with its amazing temples set in the midst of scrub jungle.

In another day, the traveller can be in Varanasi (Benares), situated on the holy Ganges, a place of pilgrimage for Hindus and of insight into the Hindu faith and therefore India itself for the traveller. A few kilometres from the city is Sarnath, scene of the Buddha's first sermon.

Magical Moment

As one leaves by the north and passes through Gorakhpur one approaches the foothills of the Himalayas. It is a magical moment when the great mountain peaks first come into view. The India/Nepal border is a very Asian affair and is best left to the morning if possible.

The route to Pokhara, up through the mountains, is the easier of the two routes into Nepal and also gives the opportunity of seeing more of the country. A complete day is required to reach the Pokhara valley but to arrive at sunset and glimpse the slopes of the Annapurna mountain range turn pink in the evening light is to witness one of the earth's most splendid sights. Pokhara is something of a Shangri-La and is a good trekking centre.

A journey of between seven and ten hours takes one to Kathmandu, once a mysterious city, now a thriving tourist centre. Kathmandu and its valley are worth many days' exploration – nice people, good food, a magnificent backcloth of the world's highest mountains, art treasures in every street. What traveller could ask for more?

Great Train Journeys

by Christopher Portway

A famous express can never die. Witness the appeals of the *Direct Orient Express* that ran from Paris to Istanbul which, in substance if not wholly in route, has been resurrected by private enterprise and, in spite of exorbitant fares, is booked solid for months ahead. There are many travellers who obtain their kicks from riding those famed expresses of the world, crossing countries or continents in a manner no other machine can offer, whether it flies, floats or rolls.

For its last decade and more the *Direct Orient* was, alas, the dullest, slowest and most inefficient of trains with all its former glory lost to the caprices of politics and the whims of individual nations along the route. The through express may have passed into history but the line remains inviolate – even if one does have to change at Belgrade. And in case you didn't know – and few do – there *is* still a real Orient Express which runs daily between Paris and Bucharest via Strasbourg, Munich, Vienna and Budapest.

Europe

Let's take a look at some famous names – and possibly a few not so famous – in the railway express train game and consider their offerings and delights.

We'll start in Britain – and the names that come immediately to mind are *The Flying Scotsman* and *The Royal Scott*. Neither quite looks as it used to as they streak between London and Edinburgh and Glasgow in five hours or so headed by their unromantic diesel or electric units. But efficient they are, whatever opinions you may hold of British Rail in other realms.

The continent of Europe is a treasure trove of titled expresses. Most bear names that are not only evocative-sounding but also indicate their route either directly – like the *Venezia Express* (between Venice and Athens via Belgrade) – or indirectly, such as the *Chopin* (between Vienna and Moscow via Warsaw) or the *Wiener Walzer* on which I remember trotting happily but not particularly efficiently from Basel, via Graz, Vienna and Budapest to Bucharest some years ago. Even if you're not a wizard with a compass the *Nord-West Express* between London, Hook, Hamburg, and Copenhagen, the *Ost-West Express* between London, Brussels, Cologne, Berlin, Warsaw and Moscow (plus a Paris section), the *Nord Express* (same route as the *Nord-West*) and the *Sud Express* (Paris-Lisbon) indicate their direction of travel. Only the *Remus* (Vienna, Venice, Milan, Rome), the *Romulus* (ditto), the *Lusitania* (Madrid-Lisbon) and *Britannia* (London, Cologne, Munich) might not make their intentions clear.

For interest and incident, I suggest either the *Ost-West Express* or the *Hook of Holland-Moscow*, which follow the classic invasion route across central and eastern Europe. What with traversing the territory of two Germanies, two Berlins, Poland and European USSR, not only do you experience some entertaining frontier controls (they used to be particularly vicious at Brest Litovsk) but you pass over the blood-soaked battlegrounds resulting from the crazed ambitions of Napoleon and Hitler.

The above are all international expresses, but there are many named and sometimes very much glossier and faster Trans-Europ, TGV and Inter-City services such as run by the *Cisalpin* (Paris-Milan), *Rembrandt* (Amsterdam-Stuttgart), *Le Capitole* (Paris-Toulouse) and the famous

Train Bleu (Paris, Marseilles, Ventimiglia) between destinations in often no more than one or two countries, particularly France, which knows a thing or two about fast, smooth-running trains. I have not yet sampled the new *Citalia* between London and Rimini and Rome which serves only clients of CIT, the Italian Tourist Organisation.

North America

Our cousins across the Atlantic have some notions of train namings very different from those of Europe. First, it must be pointed out that only the trains of the United States East Coast can, on the basis of speed, be looked on as expresses at all. This said, let me recommend with enthusiasm a journey across that great country in the hands of Amtrak, the United States rail passenger handling corporation, who run slow, but impressive long-distance trains bearing the most striking names of all. Except, again on the East Coast, train services are thin on the ground but what they lose out on in speed and frequency is made up by comfort and sense of occasion. Transcontinental trains offer observation domes, cocktail lounges, restaurants and sleeping cars – including roomettes – and cinema shows interspersed with Bingo. Some of the most well-known of these 'expresses' are the *San Francisco Zephyr* (Chicago-Oakland), the *Montrealer* (Montreal-Washington DC), *Silver Meteor* and *Silver Star* (New York-Miami), *Broadway Limited* (New York - Washington DC - Chicago), *Coast Starlight* (Seattle - Los Angeles), *Empire Builder* (Chicago - Portland) and *The Crescent* (New York - New Orleans). A host of exciting names, including the famed *Metroliner*, serve the New York-Philadelphia-Washington DC lines, many at high speed.

Canada too has brought its competing private companies to heel and put its passenger-carrying services under a centralized handling authority, this one called VIA. The most famous express – although again more in substance than in speed, is the *Canadian*, making the three-day journey between Montreal, Toronto and Vancouver a delight and offering similar facilities as supplied by Amtrak. I once made the run in the cab of the locomotive, arriving at Calgary an hour and a half late because the driver kept saying 'I'll go slow round the next bend as there's a good view for you to photograph'!

Asia

An even vaster land mass covered by a rail network is the USSR and the one express name that trips off the tongue without much bidding is the *Trans-Siberian Express* though the name of the train is actually the *Russia*. I spent nine days on it some years ago grinding – again at no more than 30 mph – the 6000 miles from Moscow to Vladivostock, stopping at all 98 stations in between. Soviet trains, with their wide gauge track, are spacious and quite comfortable. Tea is endlessly supplied in half-pint glasses by the lady coach attendant who draws it from the ever-operating samovar. And in the restaurant car, at least a few of the dishes of the dozens listed in the menu are available and, occasionally, it includes caviar – if you're quick enough. Otherwise it's Borsch, Borsch and more Borsch. A Western visitor may only travel soft class (first class in Imperialistic terms) but has to make up his/her own bed, while a strange contradiction to the usual prim and proper Russian attitude is that, as likely as not, you'll be expected to share a 'bedroom' with a member of the opposite sex. Only three cities along the way are open to the likes of you and me – Novosibirsk, Irkutsk, and Khabarovsk. Don't try and alight at Omsk as I did – it doesn't work – and Vladivostock is emphatically out of bounds (though you can reach Nahodka if you are in transit to Japan).

Asia can raise some interesting and quite well-known expresses which are more fun than efficient. From Istanbul to Baghdad runs the *Taurus Express*, which takes three days for the journey and is invariably hours late. Leaving from Istanbul's Haydarpasa Station, it passes through Turkey, Syria and Iraq, so be ready for trouble, but you do meet some priceless characters within its smoke-begrimed coaches.

A return to the balmy Victorian era of elegant train travel can be experienced on some of the long distance but nameless expresses of Chinese Railways. On the Hong Kong to Canton, Shanghai, Peking express or that from Peking to Datong, I not only had revolutionary opera interwoven with travel instructions on the TV, but lace curtains and silk lampshades à la Brighton Belle and a thermos of jasmin tea in my compartment.

India, of course, is the very epitome of railway heritage and it produces some fine and famous expresses to match. Two that will be recognized are the *Frontier Mail* (Amritsar-Delhi-Bombay) and the *Taj Express* (Delhi-Agra). On the former, I spent many uncomfortable hours – that ran into days – squeezed, standing up, in a then third-class compartment containing 39 bodies. But by travelling air-conditioned or first class at ludicrously low prices, you can move around India in almost super-luxury. And you'll never go hungry on an Indian train. Actually, the best place to eat on the sub-continent is the railway station where there are often not only different classes of restaurants, but those catering for Indian, vegetarian and European tastes. On similar, but better value lines to the *Venice-Simplon Orient Express* is a tourist train called the *Palace on Wheels* that makes a seven-day circuit of Rajasthan, giving the passenger a taste of train travel as it was understood by the maharajas. Even its golden coaches were ex-maharajan owned while Rajasthan itself is full of magic maharajan castles, forts and palaces. But more down-to-earth expresses of Indian Railways include the *Rajdhani Express* (Delhi-Calcutta), *Gitanjali Express* (Calcutta-Bombay) and the *Howrah-Kalka Mail* (Calcutta-Delhi-Kalka) which connects with a delightful narrow-gauge railcar that zigzags up the hill to Simla.

Still to Sample

There are, as yet, a number of express trains that, alas, I have not yet managed to ride. South Africa – a name synonymous with great trains – has its ultra-famous *Blue Train* upon which I have my sights. It runs between Pretoria and Cape Town via Johannesburg and Kimberley from March until the end of August about three times weekly and is the last word in luxury with even staterooms available for those who can afford them.

In Australia, the old *Ghan Express* is no more, but a less romantic but probably more efficient train runs the long hot desert miles between Adelaide, Port Pirie and Alice Springs. However it is a route, rather than a particular train, that is, perhaps, most famous; the Transcontinental Railway from Sydney to Perth – the 'long straight' as it is sometimes called, all 2,230 miles of it. And while at this end of the world one shouldn't overlook New Zealand's *Northerner* running daily between Auckland and Wellington.

Japan, of course, is famous for its bullet trains or super expresses out of Tokyo, but, soullessly, they are given no names.

Nor does Thailand go in for fancy titles though the 500 mile route between Bangkok and Chiang Mai is covered by a train sometimes known as the *Northern Express* which makes a delightful ride through the jungle and paddy fields of that steamy country.

I managed to ride the East African Railways before the split-up of the federation, but Kenya Railway's Mombasa-Nairobi-Malaba service is worthy of the term 'famous express' with its superb views of the Great Rift Valley and the wild animals that take the passing trains for granted.

When is an express not an express? With railways, it's not just a matter of speed but of prestige, route and the pure joy of travel they offer.

Getting There by: Air, Vehicles, Other

Air

In Control of Aviation

by Philip Ray

The world of air travel is littered with the initials of the official bodies which appear on the face of it to control virtually every aspect of flying – ICAO, IATA, FAA, CAB, CAA etc.

It could well be asked why this particular branch of economic activity should be singled out for special treatment by governments. The international shipping industry, after all, is not subject to nearly the same constraints as aviation and a virtually free market exists. But when the governments of the world met in Chicago in 1944 to prepare the way for the post-war pattern of civil aviation, they agreed the fundamental principle which is now enshrined in international law, that each nation has sovereignty over its own airspace. This means that any government has the power to grant or refuse permission for the airline of another country to overfly its territory, to make a technical stop – to refuel, for instance – or to pick up and set down fare-paying passengers. By extension of this principle, governments also lay down the conditions under which foreign airlines may pick up traffic – for instance, by agreeing the routes which can be served, by imposing restrictions on capacity or by approval of the fares that can be charged. In practice, all these questions are resolved between governments on a bilateral basis in what are called air service agreements.

Regulation

But almost every government in the world exercises regulatory control over its own domestic airline industry as well to a greater or lesser extent. Perhaps the strongest argument in favour of some form of domestic regulation is the uncontroversial need to supervise safety standards: otherwise, it is argued, airlines might cut corners in order to save costs. The main area of current debate and controversy is the extent to which regulatory bodies should exercise economic control over the airlines in terms of the allocation of routes, the entry of new carriers into the market and fares charged.

Alone in the world, the USA has gone for complete deregulation domestically, so that airlines are free to open up new routes or move into markets already served by other carriers without having to seek approval. Elsewhere in the world, competition is tightly controlled. In France, for instance, the two national carriers, Air France and UTA, have their designated operating areas and there appears to be no provision in the

French system for the two carriers to compete with each other. Every other European country has only one major international flag carrier airline to operate scheduled services – Germany with Lufthansa, the Netherlands with KLM, the Scandinavian countries with SAS, and so on. Perhaps the most liberal attitude outside the USA has been adopted by the United Kingdom, whose Civil Aviation Authority has authorized competition between the two major international airlines, British Airways and British Caledonian, on certain routes and has also licensed smaller airlines like British Midland Airways and now Virgin Atlantic to operate trans-Atlantic routes.

At the crux of the argument on deregulation is the balance that has to be drawn between the need to give the traveller the better deal which competition often provides and the desirability of maintaining a financially strong airline industry.

A more detailed look at some of the leading regulatory bodies in world aviation may provide some pointers as to how the present system works in practice.

ICAO (International Civil Aviation Organization)

ICAO is not exactly a household name, and its activities are rarely publicized in the lay press, but it plays an important behind-the-scenes role in laying down standards and controlling the legal framework for international civil aviation.

It is based in Montreal and was set up following the Chicago Convention of 1944 which laid the foundations of the international air transport system as we know it today. It is made up of representatives of some 150 governments and its controlling bodies are the Assembly, which normally meets every three years, and the Council, which controls the day-to-day activities of the organization.

The organization also lays down international standards for air navigation, air traffic control, technical requirements and safety and security procedures and was responsible for concluding international agreements on the action needed to deter aircraft hijackings. ICAO works closely with the United Nations and controls assistance development programmes in Third World countries under the UN Development Programme.

ICAO came into the headlines when it investigated the shooting down of the Korean Airlines Boeing 747 in September 1983. Its report was inconclusive but it led to the calling of an extraordinary meeting of the Assembly in spring 1984 to consider new international procedures and possible amendments to the Chicago Convention which would mean that such a tragic incident need never recur.

On the economic front, ICAO monitors the finances and traffic patterns of the world's airlines and issues research reports from time to time.

IATA (International Air Transport Association)

IATA is a much more controversial body than ICAO because, as the trade association for more than a hundred of the world's international scheduled airlines, it is often criticized by consumer interests as being a fare-fixing cartel. This has always been contested by IATA, which points out that a true cartel would not just fix prices but would also share out capacity and market quotas among its members. It could also be argued that if IATA is a cartel, it is a remarkably unsuccessful one, given the appalling financial results of the world's airlines over the past few years.

IATA's fare-fixing role is one which has, effectively, been thrust upon it. The world's governments agreed in the Chicago Convention that they would retain ultimate control of the fares to be charged by airlines picking up or setting down traffic in their countries but in practice they delegated this task to the airlines. To this day, fare agreements by airlines are normally rubber-stamped by governments. But most governments do use their reserve powers to direct their airlines to charge special fares for certain routes or for certain categories of travellers – seamen on duty, for instance. Even here, though, the 'directives' are often inspired by the airlines themselves because they have not been able to secure agreement for a particular fare within IATA. Sometimes, too, the importance of IATA's fare-fixing role can be exaggerated. It frequently happens that the airlines serving a particular region cannot agree on a new fares package, but this rarely spells disaster. Fares between the various countries are simply agreed bilaterally by the respective national airlines and are then approved by governments.

Agreement of tariffs is only one of IATA's functions, albeit the best known. In fact, there is now a move towards a much more liberal approach to fares: between Europe and the USA, for instance, the IATA airlines agree only a 'zone of reasonableness' for fares and the carriers can then make adjustments up or down within this band without having to go back to the conference table.

Many of IATA's activities are less publicized. While ICAO has been agreeing standards at an international level on technical matters like air safety procedures, meteorological services, engineering and so on, it has had to lean heavily on the advice of the airlines via IATA. From the passenger's point of view, the greatest benefit has come from agreements between IATA members on a standard form of airline ticket which enables the passenger to travel round the world on one ticket with, say, six different airlines, and make only one payment which is then apportioned between the carriers by the IATA Clearing House. It is also IATA which lays down the consumer-protection standards for the travel agencies which it appoints to sell international air tickets.

The association has also been active in campaigning against government-imposed increases in user charges – which are ultimately reflected in higher fares – and in fighting for the elimination of airport red tape by encouraging Customs and Immigration authorities to improve the traveller's lot with innovations like the red/green channel system.

CAB (US Civil Aeronautics Board)

Until 1978 the CAB was the world's most powerful and best-known air regulatory body. It exercised strict control over virtually all US airlines (except those operating solely within the boundaries of their own state) and was also responsible for granting permits for foreign airlines to operate to and from the USA. Surprisingly for a free-enterprise country like the USA, the CAB was a fairly conservative body, although its membership changed from time to time, depending on the politics of the President. The CAB took a fairly cautious line on authorizing competition from a new airline on an existing route and its attitude towards charter flights was much more restrictive than that which has applied in Europe for the past twenty years.

But all that changed in 1978 when President Carter pushed through the Airline Deregulation Act, which created a free market for domestic services within the US and spelt the beginning of the end of the CAB. US airlines can now operate on any domestic route they choose and they can set their own fares without having to obtain CAB approval. This liberalization has enabled dynamic new carriers like People Express and Muse Air to emerge and make a remarkable impact on the US airline scene.

For the time being the CAB retains its anti-trust role of ensuring that airlines do not reach any restrictive agreements behind the scenes, and its Bureau of International Aviation assists the State Department in negotiating air-service agreements with other countries. But by January 1, 1985, the CAB is due to be disbanded completely and most of its remaining functions will be transferred to the Federal Department of Transportation. The Transportation Department will also co-operate with the State Department on the negotiation of bilateral air-service agreements and other international aviation matters while the Department of Justice will probably take over the anti-trust role.

FAA (Federal Aviation Administration)

Not affected by the demise of the CAB, the FAA deals mostly with airport management, air traffic control, air safety and technical matters. Despite their complete economic freedom, all US airlines still have to conform with FAA safety standards.

CAA (UK Civil Aviation Authority)

Airline regulatory bodies are usually an integral part of a government ministry, but the CAA is unusual in being only an agency of government which operates very much at arm's length from whichever government is in power.

It functions under guidelines laid down by Parliament in the Civil Aviation Acts, but this is a fairly loose framework which gives it considerable freedom to develop its own policies without Ministers breathing down its neck all the time. At the same time, the Authority is an important source of advice to the government on aviation matters, including airport policy.

Broadly, the CAA's role combines those of the CAB and the FAA in the States. It has a particularly important function in the monitoring of safety standards, notably in the licensing of airports and aircrew and in the approval and inspection of airlines' operational procedures (although investigation of air accidents remains the responsibility of the Department of Transport). Most of the publicity about the CAA's activities, though, concerns its economic-regulation functions in approving fares and granting licences for new routes. It has the job of monitoring the financial integrity of the UK's airlines and also of the leading package-tour operators which use air services. The UK airline scene is particularly dynamic, so the Authority often has the difficult task of choosing between two or three applicants for a particular route. The CAA's powers do not extend to foreign airlines, which come under the control of the Department of Transport, but the Authority is usually represented in bilateral negotiations on air routes with foreign governments.

The CAA has consistently adopted a more liberal approach than some of its counterparts – its original licensing of Laker's Skytrain would have been unthinkable anywhere else in Europe – but in January 1984, the Authority launched a wide-ranging review of its licensing policies which could lead to an even more liberal approach, particularly on domestic routes.

The Traveller's Protection

by Philip Ray

More people probably suffer financial loss through dealing with shady second-hand car dealers than through booking a holiday with a company that goes bust. But the buyer of a package holiday undoubtedly enjoys a higher level of financial protection than applies in any other product or service industry.

Some economic pundits might question whether such a high level of protection is really necessary. Surely, they would argue, there is no reason why the rule 'let the buyer beware' should not apply to the purchase of a holiday as much as to anything else. But a holiday is different from most other commodities. If you buy a car or a television set and it doesn't work, you have a claim against the dealer and, in any case, you can inspect the goods before you buy them. With a holiday, however, you are buying a dream and you are parting with your money months in advance on the strength of that dream. And the temptation of this little pot of cash-flow has been too much to resist for some dubious entrepreneurs in the past.

The financial failure of a tour company also has implications in terms of diplomatic relations with other countries. It is certainly embarrassing for the Government if hundreds or thousands of holidaymakers are stranded on some foreign shore with their hotel bills unpaid by a bankrupt tour company.

Need For Protection

It was the travel trade itself which saw the need to offer better protection for the public way back in 1964 when a company called Fiesta Tours collapsed. But it took until 1970 for a proper scheme to emerge when members of the Tour Operators' Study Group (TOSG), which accounts for about three-quarters of all package tour sales, agreed that they would each provide a bond to cover consumers against financial failure. Two years later a similar scheme was drawn up for all other tour operators belonging to the Association of British Travel Agents (ABTA).

At the same time, the Civil Aviation Authority was given statutory powers to license tour-operating companies which organized package tours based on charter flights and, again, provision of a bond was made a condition of being granted an air travel organizer's licence (ATOL for short).

Everyone thought at the time that there would be little danger of a consumer losing money in future through the failure of a tour company. But in August 1974, the Court Line group of companies collapsed at the height of the holiday season when cash flow should theoretically have been at its strongest and it looked as if customers of its tour companies, Clarksons and Halcyon, might collectively lose millions of pounds.

So the Government stepped in and set up a new statutory organization, the Air Travel Reserve Fund Agency, which repaid the Court Line holidaymakers out of a Treasury loan which was repaid through a levy on holidays over the next two or three years.

Present Position

That remains the basic structure of consumer protection to this day: the CAA requires all tour operators selling package tours based on charter flights to provide a bond equivalent to fifteen per cent of their anticipated turnover (which can be reduced to ten per cent, depending on an operator's finances). Member tour operators of ABTA are bonded by the CAA for a lower level of turnover – ten per cent, which can be reduced to seven per cent – because of the 'mutual aid' service which is made available to repatriate stranded holidaymakers when a company collapses.

If an operator fails, the bond is drawn on to recompense disappointed holidaymakers and when the fund is exhausted – and only then – the Air Travel Reserve Fund can be called on, as it was in 1982 when Laker Airways' tour-operating subsidiaries were dragged down by the collapse of their parent company.

But protection on the so-called 'licensable' holidays is only part of the story, because there is a tremendous variety of holidays (almost one-third of the total) which do not need to be licensed by the CAA – those based on many scheduled flights or on rail, coach or sea travel, for example. The CAA and Air Travel Reserve Fund have no involvement in these holidays and it is left to ABTA and the Bus and Coach Council to offer voluntary protection.

ABTA insists on bonds to the tune of ten per cent of anticipated turnover for all its member operators for the whole of their 'non-licensable' turnover and this is backed up by a new insurance scheme which provides cover to the tune of £3 million to serve as a second line of defence in the same way that the ATRF does for licensable holidays.

The seventeen members of TOSG have gone a stage further by bonding non-licensable business at twenty per cent of anticipated turnover and also by providing a £2.5 million back-up insurance cover.

ABTA also protects consumers against the financial failure of any of its 5,000 High Street retail travel agents. All new members have to provide a bond of up to £10,000 and there is also an indemnity insurance scheme which protects customers against the failure of any retail agent to the tune of £75,000 per outlet. As a final line of defence, ABTA has a retailers' fund which currently stands at close on £200,000.

ABTA's consumer-protection machinery is underpinned by an agreement known as Stabilizer, under which member travel agents may not sell non-ABTA tour operators' inclusive tours, while ABTA tour operators may not trade through non-member travel agents, although some dispensations from this rule are granted. This Stabilizer system was approved by the Restrictive Practices Court in 1982 as being in the public interest and the judge cited the importance of the protection offered by ABTA on 'non-licensable' holidays.

Loopholes

The holiday purchaser does now appear, on the face of it, to be adequately protected against a tour operator's failure by virtue of the CAA/ATRF/ABTA machinery, although the chairman of the Reserve Fund feels that the £16.5 million currently in the kitty would not be sufficient to handle a major collapse in the peak season.

And there are other gaps in the consumer protection network. There is no formalized system to guard consumers against the failure of a scheduled airline – witness the successive collapses of Laker Airways and Braniff International within two months in 1982, when thousands of travellers lost their money. Most of the customers who booked package tours with one of Laker's holiday companies eventually got their money back, but those who had booked seats on the Sky train scheduled service have still not been refunded and are simply creditors in the Laker liquidation. This problem must eventually be solved in one way or the other. Airline failures are not too common, but over the past couple of years, two or three American carriers have followed Laker and Braniff into oblivion.

Another grey area of consumer protection in the UK that has to be tackled involves package holidays based on scheduled flights. In some cases – broadly, those where a tour operator makes an advance financial commitment for a block of seats on a scheduled flight – a CAA license is required. But there are many other cases where even the CAA and tour operators are uncertain whether a licence is needed or not and the matter may eventually have to be resolved in the courts.

This is no mere academic point: ATRF has refused to make payments to Laker customers who had booked inclusive holidays in North America based on scheduled Skytrain services because it regards them as having been 'non-licensable', but a number of tour operators still confuse clients by suggesting in their brochures that all their holidays are covered by the ATRF when, in fact, they may not be.

The ideal solution in the long term would be for all air-based package tours to require a CAA licence, irrespective of whether they are based on scheduled or charter flights.

Understanding Air Fares

by Philip Ray and Alex McWhirter

The world of airline tariffs is an incredibly complex one, but given the help of a well-trained airline reservations clerk or travel agent you can make some substantial savings on your travel by using the various loopholes and legitimate discounts which the system provides.

There are so many permutations of possible fares that, as any travel agent handling complicated itineraries for business executives will tell you, six different airlines will quote six different fares for a particular trip.

To generalize, full-rate first-class and business-class fares have shown a steady increase over the years but the cost of some promotional discounted fares has been held down, if not actually reduced. And quite apart from the vast range of 'official' fares there are also the special deals offered through the 'bucket-shops' (see also page 114).

On major international routes like London–New York, some 30 different fares are available depending on the airline you fly with, the time of the year and even, in some cases, the day of the week.

On other routes to the US – for instance, London–Los Angeles – it can sometimes be cheaper to take an indirect flight and change at a US airport like Chicago. Within the US, domestic fares are changing so rapidly that many airlines have given up publishing fare tables and update the information every day on the computer systems used by their travel agents and reservations staff.

Here are the main types of fare available:

First Class
Completely flexible fares; reservations can be changed to alternative departure date or to another airline. No cancellation charges. Valid one year; stopovers permitted; when travelling between two points IATA regulations allow a 20 per cent mileage deviation at no extra cost. For example, if paying full-fare London–Cairo you could travel out via Paris, Zurich and Athens and return via Beirut, Rome and Amsterdam at no extra cost. On a long journey such as London–Sydney, you could fly via Hong Kong at no extra cost or via the USA or Japan at only a small surcharge. You can exceed this 20 per cent mileage allowance by up to 25 per cent by paying a surcharge. This comes in increments of 5 per cent; for example, a journey London–Frankfurt–Zurich would incur a 5 per cent surcharge, whereas London–Brussels–Zurich would be included in the mileage allowance. When using this extra mileage allowance, back-tracking is not permitted. Should the 25 per cent allowance be exceeded you must pay the cost of each individual sector: for instance London–Brussels, Brussels–Paris, Paris–London. Concorde fares are based on the normal first-class fare plus a supplement, which averages about 20 per cent.

Business Class/Full Economy Class
Completely flexible fare with same concessions for mileage deviations as first-class (see above). Business-class usually offers an enhanced standard of service and more comfortable seating but sometimes involves a premium of between 5 per cent and 20 per cent on the normal economy fare.

Point-to-Point Economy
Applies mainly to travel between the UK and US and, as the name implies, is valid only for travel between the two points shown on the ticket. This means that no mileage deviation is

permitted, nor can the ticket be used for connecting flights with another airline. The ticket has to be booked and paid for in one transaction and there is a charge if you cancel your flight. A similar fare within Europe is known as Eurobudget, which is available at a discount on the full fare but is subject to a 50 per cent cancellation charge.

Apex/Super Apex
Stands for Advance Purchase Excursion. It has become the airlines' main method of official discounting and is normally available only on a round-trip basis, except to the Far East and Australia where one-way Apex fares are available. Must be booked and paid for some time in advance, ranging from two weeks to one month depending on destination, and usually a minimum stay abroad is required. No stopovers are permitted and there are cancellation and amendment fees which vary with the destination. Reductions on some long-haul routes can be as high as 60 per cent off the normal full fare.

Pex/Super Pex
Stands for 'Public Excursion' fare and is similar to Apex, except that there is no restrictive advance-purchase requirement. Applies only in Europe and stay must normally include a Saturday night at the destination. There is a 50 per cent penalty for cancellation.

Excursion Fares
Available on many long-haul routes, with restrictions on minimum and maximum length of stay. Normally for round-trip travel only but fewer restrictions than Apex or Pex – flights can be changed, for example. Typical saving on the full economy fare is between 25 per cent and 30 per cent.

Spouse Fares
Apply on routes throughout Europe. If one partner pays the full business-class or Club-class fare, the other partner can travel at a 50 per cent discount. Tickets have a maximum validity of five days. No stopovers are permitted and husband and wife must travel together on both the outbound and inbound journeys. Airlines will, however, generally make an exception when company regulations or insurance policies stipulate that a couple must always travel separately.

ITX Fares
Now an almost extinct category, ITX fares are used by travel agents to construct tailor-made inclusive packages. Now that new low fares like Apex and Pex are available, the demand for ITX fares has diminished and they are now available only on flights to Germany and the USSR.

Children's and Infants' Fares
An infant under two years of age accompanied by an adult and not occupying a separate seat is carried at 10 per cent of the adult fare. Any additional infants under two years of age occupying a separate seat and accompanying the same adult, and children aged 2–11 inclusive, are carried at half the adult fare. Some fares do not carry these reductions – for example many Apex fares allow only a one-third discount for children – and certain standby fares allow no reduction at all.

Student Fares
Provided the necessary forms are completed, bona fide students are entitled to a reduction of 25 per cent off the normal fare. Student fares are not available on the North Atlantic routes and are becoming less widely used elsewhere because so many other fares like Apex offer bigger reductions.

Youth Fares
Available for travel on many routes inside Europe for young people between the ages of 12 and 21. The reduction is 25 per cent off the normal fare but, again, a cheaper fare like Apex or Pex is usually available. For routes to the Middle East the upper age limit is 23, or up to 27 for *bona fide* students.

Standby Fares
Generally available only on routes to the USA, and even then only in the July-September peak season. Available only on day of departure. Standby tickets are also available on some UK domestic routes. Akin to the standby fare is the late-booking fare offered by British Airways to Athens, Malta and Gibraltar. This can be bought up to three months in advance but seat availability is not confirmed until the day before departure.

Round the World (RTW) Fares
An ingenious method of keeping down your travel costs is the Round the World (RTW) fare offered by a number of airlines or combinations of airlines – for example, British Airways with Air New Zealand or British Caledonian with Northwest. The first sector of your itinerary usually has to be booked about three weeks in advance, but after that you can book your flights as you go along. You usually have to make a minimum number of stopovers and you are not allowed to 'backtrack'. You can even buy a first-class RTW ticket with some airlines which actually undercuts the normal economy fare.

Charters
Advance-booking charters (ABCs) still flourish across the Atlantic, mainly during the peak summer season, and the rules are similar to those governing the scheduled airlines' Apex fares. You have to book at least 21 days in advance and you must be away at least seven days. On flights to the US, charters provide some quite substantial savings on the normal scheduled fares but to Canada charter fares are usually at or about the Apex level. Charter services operate from a number of provincial points, which makes them more convenient than scheduled flights for many people.

Within Europe, there is a well-organized network of charter flights which can give savings of 70 per cent off the normal IATA fare. These flights operate not only to the Mediterranean sunspots but also to cites like Geneva and Munich and, for legal reasons, are ranked technically as package tours, so the fare will probably include £1 to cover nominal accommodation. Charters can be booked up to the time of departure but return dates may not be so flexible as on scheduled flights. For instance, you may be able to return only seven days or 14 days after the outward journey.

Scheduled Consolidation Fares
These are charter-priced seats sold for travel on scheduled flights. They are usually intended to be the basis of inclusive packages but often end up as flight-only tickets sold through bucket-shops.

Airpasses
Special Airpasses are available in a number of countries which enable you to make big savings on domestic travel.

Some of the best value is to be had in the US, where all the major airlines offer Airpass deals giving virtually unlimited travel on their networks, although you are frequently allowed to make only one stopover per city and there is a ceiling on the number of stopovers you can make. You may be restricted from flying at busy periods. Airpasses usually have to be bought before arrival in the US.

To qualify for some of the best deals you have to travel to the US on a particular airline's trans-Atlantic services. The best plan is to find out which airline has the network which conforms most closely to your preferred itinerary.

A number of other countries with well-developed air services, including Australia, Brazil, India and New Zealand, also offer Airpass schemes.

How to Read an Airline Ticket

by Philip Ray and Alex McWhirter

An airline ticket is really a legal contract which specifies and restricts the services that passengers may expect and when they may expect them. On each ticket, the duties and liabilities of both passenger and airline are clearly stated – whether it is a scheduled or a charter flight – and each passenger must be in possession of a ticket for the journey to be undertaken. An agreement known as the Warsaw Convention limits the liability of most airlines in cases of injury or death involving a passenger and also for baggage loss or damage. This agreement is usually explained on the inside cover of the ticket or a summary is inserted in a loose-leaf form.

The format of IATA issued tickets in the UK is being changed during 1984 to pave the way for the introduction of the so-called Bank Settlement Plan (BSP) on January 1, 1985. Instead of having to keep a stock of tickets for each airline with which they deal, travel agents will have one common stock of 'neutral' tickets, but a special plate will be slotted into the ticket validator at the time of issue to indicate whose services are being used. The whole BSP operation is essentially an exercise to simplify accounting procedures for both travel agents and airlines.

The flight coupons themselves will not show many differences after the introduction of BSP. On the top right-hand side is the fare construction box which, on a multi-sector itinerary, indicates how the fare is to be apportioned among the different carriers. Cities are denoted by their three-letter codes, e.g. LHR is London Heathrow, ROM is Rome, CPH is Copenhagen, LAX is Los Angeles and so on. The fare construction may be shown in FCUs (Fare Construction Units), a universal 'currency' in which fares are frequently expressed. The amount in FCUs is converted into the currency of the country of issue which is shown in the fare box in the left-hand corner. The British pound sterling is shown as UKL so as to distinguish it from other sterling currencies. Where local taxes are to be paid these are also shown and the final amount to be paid is shown in the total box.

At the bottom of the right-hand side is the 'Form of Payment' box. If you pay for the ticket by cash, it will either be left blank or the word 'cash' will be written in. If it is paid by cheque, the word 'cheque' or abbreviation 'chq' will be used. If the ticket is bought with a credit card, the letters 'CC' will be written, followed by the name of the issuing company, the card number and its expiry date. If you have an account with the travel agent the clerk will write 'Non ref', which means that no refund can be obtained except through the issuing office.

In the 'Baggage' section of the ticket, only the 'Allow.' column is completed by the agent; this shows the free baggage allowance to which you are entitled. The number of pieces, checked and unchecked weights are completed when the passenger checks in. 'PC' indicates that the piece concept is in operation, as it is on more and more routes. There are validity boxes immediately above the cities on your itinerary. These 'not valid before' and 'not valid after' entries relate to promotional fares with minimum/maximum stay requirements and the relevant dates will be shown here. If you have a full-fare ticket where there is no minimum-stay requirement and the maximum is one year, these boxes are frequently left blank.

Immediately to the right of the itinerary there is a column headed 'Fare/Class basis'. The letters most commonly inserted are 'F' for First Class or 'Y' for Economy Class. The 'Y' will often be followed by other letters to describe the fare, especially if it is a promotional type. For example, 'YH' would mean a high-season fare; 'YZ' a youth fare; 'YLAP' a low-season Apex; 'YE' Excursion etc.

To the right of the fare/allow. box is the space for the two-letter code of the carrier, e.g. LH for Lufthansa, BR for British Caledonian, BA for British Airways or AZ for Alitalia. However, the airline industry has now run out of possible combinations of two-letter codes and three-letter codes are gradually being introduced. Next follows the flight number and class of travel on that particular flight. Most international flight numbers consist of three figures but for UK domestic flights four figures are frequently used. The date is written as, for example, 04 JUN and not as 4th June, while the time is shown on the basis of the 24 hour clock, e.g. 14.30 hrs is written instead of 2.30pm (The twelve hour clock is still used for domestic travel within the USA). In the 'Status' box the letters 'OK' must be written if you have a confirmed flight, 'RQ' if the flight has been requested but not yet confirmed and 'WL' if the flight has been wait-listed. If you haven't decided when you want to travel, the word 'OPEN' is written, spread out across the flight number, date, time and status boxes. Infants, who travel for a ten per cent fare on international journeys, are not entitled to a seat or baggage allowance so that the reservations entry will be marked 'No seat' and the allowance marked 'nil'. Your ticket is valid for travel only when date-stamped with a travel agency or airline validator which is completed with the clerk's signature or initials.

Choosing an Airline

by Alex McWhirter and Philip Ray

Airlines spend huge amounts on advertising to tell us all about their exotic in-flight cuisine, their glamorous stewardesses or their swish new aircraft. But surveys conducted regularly among frequent travellers – particularly those who have to fly on business – tell us that all these 'service' factors are not terribly important when it comes to choosing an airline. The typical traveller will choose the airline that offers a schedule which conforms most closely to his planned itinerary. The frequency of service is the next most important factor, followed a long way behind by the attractiveness of the stewardesses. So a lot of airline advertising probably does no more than reinforce a choice which the consumer has already made.

Most people will want to choose a flight which involves as few changes en route as possible. For departures from London this means, as often as not, that there is a choice between only two or three carriers: British Airways, British Caledonian and the flag-carrier of the destination country. There are a few exceptions like the routes from London to New York and to Los Angeles, on each of which there are two British and two American airlines, or the London–Hong Kong route, on which there is extremely tough competition between BA, BCal, and Cathay Pacific, Hong Kong's own airline.

A close examination of the ABC World Airways Guide – which lists every scheduled service worldwide – does reveal a few exceptions, though. Between London and Paris, for example, there are services by no less than twelve airlines, and between London and Frankfurt there are thirteen. Many of these services are 'tail-end' sectors of long haul flights originating in the Far East or North America and are frequently the source of some interesting discount fare deals. But they are usually operated at a low frequency and are of little interest to the traveller in a hurry.

One word or warning: don't always assume that what appears to be a through flight is necessarily so. Some American airlines, in particular, are fond of operating what are called 'change-of-guage' services which are shown as a through service with the same flight number but in fact involve a change of aircraft en route. This is a misleading practice which the regulatory authorities would be well advised to stamp out.

London's two airports, Heathrow and Gatwick, have direct flights to such a tremendous range of destinations that there is generally no need to fly to a continental airport and change flights there. But passengers living away from the South-East often have the choice of flying either to London or the continent to pick up their connection. Amsterdam's Schipol Airport and KLM, the national carrier of the Netherlands, have been extremely active in trying to persuade more Britons to fly via Amsterdam, which now has feeder-airline connections from most provincial UK points. It is always worth checking to see if there is a convenient connection via a continental gateway, but in general, there is usually a wider range of destinations and a higher frequency via London.

Fly Me, Fly Me Not

Ultimately, how you fly is governed by the fare you pay, which in turn will be determined by your class of travel and by which carrier you fly with. There are generally four classes of air travel: Supersonic, First, Business and Economy (or Tourist). (*See sections on Business, Luxury and Budget travel on pages 246, 242 and 222*).

When choosing an airline for a long haul flight, the general rule is to choose the carrier with the fewest stops, not only to avoid fatigue, but also to reduce the chance of incurring delays while on the ground.

If you are not in a desperate hurry to reach your destination on a really long-haul route like UK–Australia, a stopover en route is recommended because it will help to mitigate some of the worst effects of jetlag (see page 133). The flight from London to New Zealand via Los Angeles is one of the longest in the world, but London–LA is a tiring enough flight as it is and a stopover for a night or two is a good idea.

Some passengers have doubts about flying with airlines of the Third World countries. In a few cases these fears may be justified – some domestic airlines in South America, for instance, have pretty poor safety records – but in fact they are often represented by progressive and efficient carriers like Singapore Airlines and Air-India.

The standards of on-board service offered by carriers from the Far East are probably the highest in the world – service is not a dirty word in Asia – but to generalize it is probably true to say that the most efficient in terms of punctuality and operational integrity are those of Europe and North America. British Airways, for instance, has had a lot of criticism over the years but it is generally regarded as a world leader in setting high operational and technical standards. Now that its punctuality has been vastly improved, it will be a force to be reckoned with. Other highly regarded airlines include British Caledonian, Swissair, SAS, Lufthansa, KLM and Japan Air Lines.

Unless price is your main consideration, avoid flying with Aeroflot, the Soviet Union's national carrier, which dumps seats on to the market at massively discounted prices to raise hard currency. Some of the deals it offers involve a stopover at an airport transit hotel in Moscow, which by all accounts is not a particularly enjoyable experience.

Some Third World airlines which excel in in-flight service may not be so good on the ground. When travelling in Third World countries, never attempt to make your reservation by phone, but visit the airline's office and get them to validate your ticket in front of you. Always check and double-check your reservation, as most airlines in out of the way parts of the world do not have computerized reservation systems and mistakes are frequently made.

Charters

The network of charter flights both inside and outside Europe is wider than many people imagine. On international routes within Europe, charters account for more than half the market in terms of passenger-kilometres. Most charter flights within Europe carry passengers going on conventional package tours but more and more flights are taking passengers on a 'seat only' basis, albeit with nominal accommodation provided to conform with government regulations.

Many charter flights still operate across the North Atlantic during the summer despite competition from cheap Super-Apex fares offered by the scheduled airlines. The popularity of charters between Europe and North America tends to go in cycles: when the dollar is strong, charters do well because North Americans realize that they can buy a cheap holiday in Europe. Equally, when the dollar is weak there is a downturn in the charter market. Even when the dollar is strong, European passengers can still find attractive deals on American-originating charters because blocks of seats are often made available to tour operators at knockdown rates. All these North Atlantic charters operate under the ABC (Advance Booking Charter) rules, which mean you have to book at least 21 days before departure.

A big advantage of ABC flights is that in summer, when most people want to travel, a wide choice of UK departure points is offered, including provincial points like Cardiff, Newcastle, Manchester and Prestwick.

Extras and Specials

For many scheduled flights it's possible to request certain special meals such as kosher or vegetarian and to put in seat requests – for example, window, aisle, smoking or non-smoking etc. If travelling on a long-haul flight, it's a good idea to advise the airline of your contact phone number, so that you can be informed on the day of your departure if there is a major delay.

VIP treatment can take the form of better handling on the ground. An airline representative will smooth you through all the hassles of check-in and will escort you to the airline's own VIP lounge. The cabin crew will be informed of your presence and will make every effort to ensure that your flight is a comfortable and enjoyable one. Airlines normally grant VIP treatment to senior government officials and commercially important customers. Some airlines will allow you to use their VIP lounges if you have paid the first-class or full economy-class fare and your travel agent has cleared this facility with the airline's sales department beforehand. Other airlines insist that you must be a member of their executive club or 'frequent traveller' club before they grant you admittance, while some carriers merely charge an annual membership fee which allows you to use their executive lounge whether or not you're actually flying with them. But don't expect VIP treatment if you're travelling at a discount rate.

Human Cargo

In really off-beat parts of the world, cargo aircraft may offer cheap travel, although creature comforts are largely ignored and safety even more so. Remote airstrips are the most likely places to find such services, but cargo aircraft do fly all over the world, even into larger terminals. Approach the captain at the airport or the office of the cargo company to find out whether there are any flights available and if they will take passengers. You will have to be ready to go at short notice and keep in frequent touch with the office as there may be no timetable to speak of and the pilot will simply take off when he and the load are ready.

It is sometimes possible to get free flights on military aircraft, especially in Latin America. Travellers should investigate this option on the spot and should also take account of any political considerations.

Airports and How to Get the Most Out of Them

by Philip Ray and David Woolley

You just can't generalize about airports. An airport can be a teeming, sprawling terminal like London's Heathrow, or New York's John F. Kennedy, or it might be a concrete strip in the African desert or the Australian outback. Or it could be a grass field with a tin shed on the Orkney island of Westray, where the sheep have to be cleared off the 'runway' before the aeroplane takes off on the world's shortest flight to the neighbouring island of Papa Westray.

All experienced travellers will have their favourite and not-so-favourite airports, but the problem is that we don't always have a choice. If, for example, you want to fly from London to Johannesburg, you will have to go from Heathrow, even if you can't stand the place. But if you are travelling from the centre of London to Manhattan, you do have a choice. You can either fly from Heathrow to JFK – the world's Blue Riband air route – or you can use two less congested airports in the shape of Gatwick and Newark.

It's worth listening to airport horror stories recounted by friends and acquaintances because they can provide some pointers in planning your journey and help you avoid some of the world's air-travel black-spots.

In the past, airports like New York's JFK, Los Angeles International and Miami International acquired a bad name because of their congested terminals and the long delays in processing jumbo-loads of passengers through Customs and Immigration. Wise travellers, in particular those making US domestic connections, have got into the habit of routing themselves via a less congested airport like Boston's Logan International rather than JFK. Others have discovered that they can reach Los Angeles just as quickly by changing flights and clearing Customs in, say, Dallas, Fort Worth, which has fewer international flights and, hence, less congestion at the processing points. To be fair, though, the airport authorities in both New York and Los Angeles have been making determined efforts to improve conditions for their passengers and the next two or three years will show how successful they have been.

Basic Requirements

The basic requirement of an airport for any traveller is that it should be easy to reach and that it should have all the facilities to make the journey as smooth and hassle-free as possible. This means, ideally, that it should not be too congested; it should be well signposted; and there should be moving walkways or rapid-transit systems to eliminate those long route marches which are so notorious at some airports. Bussing should not be necessary to reach one's flight and, for arriving passengers, baggage delivery should be as speedy as possible (although this is frequently the responsibility of the airline rather than of the airport authority).

Allow plenty of time to get to the airport. It is always best to assume that you are going to be delayed by late-running buses or trains or by traffic congestion if you are driving. Not so long ago, airlines started trimming their minimum check-in times, but now the trend has gone in the reverse direction because of the regrettable need to allow time for security checking. Two or three years ago, flights at one UK airport were badly delayed during the summer peak because there were just not enough X-ray machines to cope with the number of passengers.

Of course, these days, the airport authorities actually want you to check in early because they reckon you will have time on your hands and money to spend in the restaurants and in those tempting duty-free shops. Shopping is now big business for the airport authorities, particularly in Europe where most passengers are travelling on international services. In 1982–3, the British Airports Authority notched up a trading profit of £63 million from its commercial activities, which also included car-parking concessions. It actually lost money on the fees which it charged the airlines, so if it had not been for the commercial income, user charges would have gone up, pushing up air fares in turn.

The BAA is currently mounting an even more aggressive marketing campaign for its duty-free shops and claims to be making higher profits from retailing than the giant Tesco supermarket chain. And the popularity of Amsterdam's Schipol Airport has been built up largely on the bargain-basement shopping facilities which it provides. The level of prices in the duty-free shops is sometimes criticized on the basis that the profit margins are allegedly excessive, but the fact remains that they are usually well below High Street prices on items like liquor and tobacco which attract a high rate of duty. The criticisms are frequently more valid on items like cameras or electronic goods where the price savings are often insignificant.

One nasty shock which you may encounter at some airports, particularly outside Europe and North America, is a demand for payment of an airport tax when you check in. In some countries the amount may be purely nominal, but in Hong Kong it is almost £10. Airport taxes exist within Europe but almost invariably they are built into the air fare. It would be a great boon to air travellers if the same practice was adopted worldwide.

Some Major Airports

London Heathrow

It's fashionable to knock Heathrow, but in reality, it is a remarkably efficient operation and it remains the world's busiest international airport, both in terms of the number of passengers handled and the number of destinations served. In fact, you can reach almost any destination in the world from Heathrow with no more than one or two changes in aircraft. The main point to watch is to double-check which of the three terminals your flight departs from. To complicate matters, a fourth terminal is being opened in 1985 and then you will have to be doubly careful as it will be served by a separate Tube station.

London Gatwick

Undoubtedly Britain's biggest airport success story, Gatwick has continued its rapid expansion during the recession and is now the world's fifth busiest international airport. It has the best communications of any UK airport with its direct rail and motorway links and in fact, it is now quicker to get from central London to Gatwick by mainline rail than it is by Tube to Heathrow. Gatwick's pride and joy is its circular satellite pier, opened in 1983, which is linked to the main terminal by an automated rapid-transit system running on an overhead guideway. Gatwick is fast approaching its theoretical capacity and a second terminal is being built to cater for continued growth from 1987 onwards.

Amsterdam (Schipol)

To borrow computer jargon, Schipol is a user-friendly airport. The airport authority has deliberately provided more space in the passenger terminal than it really needs, with the result that the building is rarely overcrowded. The duty-free shopping area is one of the best and cheapest; it occupies one side of the main airside concourse and has practically everything from a bottle of scent to a gold-plated Pentax. Schipol has its own railway station, with good connections to the south (The Hague and Rotterdam). The new line has not reached Amsterdam city centre, but a short ride to the RAI station puts you on the edge of the city near the exhibition centre and connections with the local tram service.

Frankfurt

Frankfurt's single passenger terminal is very large, often very crowded and not that well signed. Be prepared for quite long walking distances and leave time for the duty-free shop, which you will find tucked away up a staircase at your departure gate. In the bowels of the earth below the terminal is a railway station with an excellent service not only to Frankfurt but also to neighbouring areas. Also in the basement is a vast supermarket; buy your wine here, not in the duty-free shop. For those with the inclination and the time, Dr Miller's sex shop and cinema are also to be found below stairs. When catching an early morning flight, eat before you get to the airport. Breakfast in the airside restaurant is a scrum and everywhere else is closed.

Paris (Charles de Gaulle)

Also known as Roissy, the main Paris airport has two terminals, one (No. 1) mainly for foreign airlines and the other (No. 2) mainly for Air France and Air Inter. No. 1 is a circular concrete monolith, something of a showpiece when opened about ten years ago but now showing signs of wear and tear. Circular buildings are notoriously confusing, so watch the signs to avoid extra walking. The duty-free shopping area is cramped and not among Europe's cheapest. No. 2 terminal is altogether more modern and more convenient. Trains take you to and from Paris but the station is inconveniently placed a shuttle-bus ride away from the two terminals; a good alternative is the Air France bus service into town.

Zurich
Switzerland's main gateway airport is large, modern and convenient and rarely seems to be overcrowded. Little touches like the ability to check in at any desk for any flight add to the favourable impression. If you need to talk to Customs on leaving the country, you can call up a Customs officer on closed-circuit television. On the way in, the Immigration officers work with admirable speed, but still your baggage is often waiting for you when you get to the claim area. Trains from the airport railway station serve not just Zurich but the whole of Switzerland, and when you return, you can check your baggage for the flight at many railway stations.

New York (John F. Kennedy)
As usual at major US airports, there is a terminal at Kennedy for each of the major airlines, plus an international terminal. Unusually for the USA, a foreign carrier – British Airways – also has its own terminal. The problem with this arrangement is that a change of airline means a change of terminal, and congestion on the service roads used by the shuttle buses has for years been a major source of complaint. Now the Port Authority has done much to alleviate the problem and has speeded up bus transfer by abolishing the fare. For those in a hurry, Kennedy is linked to downtown Manhattan by helicopter.

Atlanta (Hartsfield International)
Atlanta boasts the world's second busiest airport, but between half and three-quarters of the travellers using it are merely changing flights and not visiting the city at all. The single passenger terminal, designed with this fact in mind, is vast, but easy to get around in. It has its own underground trains to whisk you from one airline's patch to another or to the international terminal or the exit. The trains are fully automatic, even to the extent that a recorded voice will rebuke you if you obstruct the doors. There are plenty of bars, but not many places to eat, and for such a large airport, surprisingly poor shopping facilities. An excellent place to change flights in a hurry, but no place to linger in.

Los Angeles International
Known to Americans as LAX, from its official code-name, Los Angeles International used to be a byword among international travellers for wasted hours spent queuing in Customs and Immigration. The road circling the several terminals used to harbour an eternal traffic jam, so that even changing from one airline to another was a problem. All that is changing now thanks to a massive reconstruction programme, ostensibly to cater for the Olympic Games, although it would have been necessary anyway. A long struggle to get better Customs procedures – such as the red/green channel system, long used in other countries – now seems about to pay off.

Singapore (Changi)
The amazing success of Singapore Airlines has taken its tiny home country to tenth place in the world league by size of airline industry. To cope with its expanding traffic, and that of the many foreign airlines serving Singapore, a brand-new airport, much of it on reclaimed land, was opened in 1981. The single, H-shaped passenger terminal was designed by Singaporeans who first studied the successes and failures of airport designers all over the world. They seem to have avoided the pitfalls and have produced a terminal that is efficiently run and pleasant and easy to use. Not the least of its attractions is the availability of duty-free shops on arrival as well as departure.

Tokyo (Narita)
Airlines hate Narita because the landing charges are among the world's highest. When it opened a few years back it was an armed encampment with police everywhere because of the activities of local protest groups. All that has subsided, leaving an efficient airport handling an enormous throughput of passengers fairly effortlessly. Narita's main trouble begins when you try to get there from downtown: the airport is forty miles out, and the traffic has to be seen to be believed. Leave plenty of time and then some more.

Making Claims Against Airlines

by Philip Ray and Alex McWhirter

You have only to read the correspondence columns in the specialist business travel magazines each month to see what a fashionable occupation it is to complain about airline services. Some people seem to enjoy writing letters of complaint so much that they make a profession of it. They complain at the slightest hiccup and write long letters detailing every flaw, claiming huge sums in compensation and threatening legal action if it is not forthcoming by return.

But the fact is that no matter how much their inefficiency costs you in time, trouble, missed meetings, lost deals and overnight hotel bills, the airlines in many cases are not obliged to pay you anything. They are covered for most eventualities in their Conditions of Carriage which are printed on the inside cover of the ticket. However, this is not to say that, in the increasingly competitive environment, the more enlightened airlines do not take customer attitudes seriously. Some airline chief executives take a personal interest in passenger complaints and have frequent 'purges' when they insist on seeing every letter of complaint that comes in on a particular day.

If you have a complaint against an airline which you cannot resolve satisfactorily it is worth contacting the Air Transport Users' Committee (129 Kingsway, London WC2B 6NN). The committee is funded and appointed by the Civil Aviation Authority but operates completely independently and, indeed, has frequently been known to criticize some of the Authority's decisions. The committee has only a small secretariat and is not really geared up to handle a large volume of complaints, but it has had some success in securing *ex gratia* payments for passengers who have been inconvenienced in some way. All the same, the committee likes to receive passenger complaints because it is a useful way of bringing to light some serious problems which can lead to high-level pressure being brought to bear on the airline or airlines involved. Some of the subjects dealt with by the committee in 1983 included baggage labelling, the carriage of disabled passengers, communications with Heathrow and domestic fares.

Procedure

Here are some tips which may make complaining to an airline more effective:

1. The first person to write to is the customer relations manager. You can write to the chairman if it makes you feel better but it makes little difference – unless that happens to be the day that the chairman decides to have his 'purge'. If you've made your booking through a travel agent, send him a copy of the letter and if the agent does a fair amount of business with that carrier (especially if it is a foreign airline) it's a good idea to ask the agent to take up the complaint for you.
2. Keep your letter brief, simple, calm and to the point. Remember also to give the date, flight number, location and route where the incident took place. All these details seem obvious but it's amazing how many people omit them.
3. Keep all ticket stubs, baggage claims and anything else you may have from the flight involved. You may have to produce them if the airline requires substantiation of your complaint.
4. If you have no success after all this, write to the Air Transport Users' Committee. Send it copies of all the correspondence you've had with the airline and let it take the matter from there.

Lost Luggage

Most frequent travellers will at some time have experienced that sinking feeling when the carousel stops going round and their baggage is not on it. The first thing to do if your luggage does not appear is to check with an airline official in the baggage-claim area. It could be that your baggage is of a non-standard shape – a heavy rucksack, for example – which cannot be handled easily on the conveyor belt and it will then be brought to the claim area by hand. But if your baggage really has not arrived on the same flight as yourself you will have to complete a Property Irregularity Report (PIR), which will give a description of the baggage, a list of its contents and the address to which it should be forwarded.

It is sometimes worth hanging around at the airport for an hour or two because there is always the chance that your baggage may arrive on the next flight. This sometimes happens if you have had to make a tight flight connection and your baggage hasn't quite made it. But if there is only one flight a day there is no point in waiting and the airline will forward the baggage to you at its expense. In this case, ask the airline for an allowance to enable you to buy the basic necessities for an overnight stay – nightwear, toiletries, and underwear for example.

If your baggage never arrives at all, you should make a claim against the airline within 21 days. Airlines' liability for lost luggage is limited by international agreement and the level of compensation is based on the weight of your baggage, which explains why it is filled in on your ticket by the check-in clerk. The maximum rate of compensation at present is US$20 per kilo for checked baggage and US$400 per passenger for unchecked baggage.

The same procedure applies to baggage which you find to be damaged when you claim it. The damage should be reported immediately to an airline official and, again, you will have to fill in a PIR form which you should follow up with a formal claim against the airline.

Overbooking

Losing one's baggage may be the ultimate nightmare in air travel but the phenomenon of 'bumping' must run it a close second. 'Bumping' occurs when you arrive at the airport with a confirmed ticket, only to be told that there is no seat for you because the flight is overbooked.

Most airlines overbook their flights deliberately because they know that there will always be a few passengers who make a booking and then don't turn up ('no shows' in airline jargon). On some busy routes like Brussels–London on a Friday evening, some business travellers book themselves on four or five different flights, so that there is a horrendous 'no-show' problem and the airlines can, perhaps, be forgiven for overbooking.

The use of computers has enabled airlines to work out their overbooking factors quite scientifically, but just occasionally things don't quite work out and a few confirmed passengers have to be 'bumped'.

If you are unlucky enough to be 'bumped', you may be entitled to compensation under a scheme drawn up by the major European airlines. You are entitled to a 50% refund of the one-way fare for the sector involved – subject to a ceiling of £100 – if you are transferred to a flight which is due to arrive at your destination more than four hours after the scheduled time of your originally-planned flight. Efforts by the Air Transport Users' Committee to increase this ceiling to £200 have so far been unsuccessful.

Injury or Death

Airlines' liabilities to their passengers were originally laid down by an agreement called the Warsaw Convention which was signed in 1929. The basic principle was that the infant airline industry could have been crippled if it had been forced by the courts to pay massive amounts of compensation to passengers or their relatives for death or injury in the event of an accident.

The trade-off was that the airlines undertook to pay compensation up to a set ceiling irrespective of whether negligence on their part was proved. The limit of compensation was set at 250,000 French gold francs, an obsolete currency which is nevertheless still used to this day as the official unit of compensation and converted into local currencies. In the UK, for instance, the sterling equivalent is currently laid down by statute as £11,799, which is generally accepted to be a hopelessly inadequate level of compensation.

The parties to the Warsaw Convention met in Montreal in 1975 and signed four protocols which would have substituted for the gold franc the Special Drawing Right (SDR), the international unit of account devised by the International Monetary Fund. But these protocols have not yet been ratified and the gold franc remains the official unit of compensation worldwide. The UK government has now decided to ratify the Montreal protocols, but it points out that thirty states must ratify each protocol before it can come into force. If insufficient countries ratify the protocols, they say, it would review its adherence to the system of compensation provided for under the Warsaw Convention and its protocols.

In a number of countries, the airlines now offer a higher level of compensation than the Warsaw limits, either voluntarily or as a result of government directives. In the UK, it is a condition of all British airlines' licences that they should set their liability limit at 100,000 SDRs (equivalent to about £74,000), the same figure which would apply under the Montreal protocols. But the Air Transport Users' Committee recently reported that there were more than a dozen different limits in force, ranging from 40,000 to 100,000 SDRs, equivalent to £29,600 to £74,000. This means that if passengers want to know the extent of their cover they need to enquire from each airline that they will be using.

Even if international agreement to ratify the Montreal protocols cannot be reached, there seems a strong case for making it a condition that every airline flying into the UK should adopt the 100,000 SDR limit.

It is worth noting that an airline's liability is unlimited if gross negligence or wilful misconduct can be proved.

The Ticket Out

by Ingrid Cranfield

Many countries require a traveller to show a ticket out of the country before he is issued with a visa or allowed over the border into the country. This onward ticket is normally expected to be a plane ticket, though sufficient evidence of the traveller's respectability and solvency can ensure that a ticket for some other means of transport will be accepted.

Onward tickets are no problem for travellers who wish to use them, but many people, especially overlanders, want to enter a country, but have no intention of flying out. For them, it will be desirable to try and get a refund.

Some countries require that the onward ticket be shown on application for a visa, but not thereafter. The purchaser can get a visa and then cash in his ticket before he actually leaves home. If you do this, it is best to buy the ticket on credit, so that no cash need change hands either on purchase or on refund.

However, countries with this precondition for a visa will nearly always want to see the onward ticket at the point of immigration. If the buyer does not intend to use it, he will have to obtain a refund either in the country or after he has left. For many reasons, it is best, therefore, to buy direct from a large carrier with many offices in convenient places and not through a travel agency, and to pay in cash or traveller's cheques.

Buying outside the region for travel to the Third World, you should use a hard currency which will be foreign to your destination. In many countries you will not be allowed to purchase in any but a hard currency. If you buy in one soft currency, you cannot expect to be refunded in another, and this could prove inconvenient. Some Third World authorities are anxious to prevent export of their currency and will prefer refunds to be given in hard currency. Elsewhere, refunds will be given in the local currency, which will generally be a soft one. But if your purchase was in a hard currency, you are, at least, in a stronger position when requesting the same in exchange.

Buying in the region is usually cheaper, especially if the black market rate is favourable, except where ticket taxes are very high. To avoid paying such taxes, buy elsewhere, or get a friend to buy you a ticket in another country and post it to you (suitably disguised).

The rules on refunding tickets vary from one place and one carrier, sometimes even one office, to another. Tickets are sometimes stamped 'nonrefundable' (and the ink is sometimes eradicated by unscrupulous travellers!), but such tickets are, in any case, usually transferable. Refunds in the form of MCOs (Miscellaneous Charges Orders) should be accepted, as these can be used to buy any airline ticket or service. An MCO can even serve as an altered ticket and, like a ticket, can be cashed in separately.

Finally, make a note of the ticket number in case of loss; buy yourself a return or onward ticket to avoid being stranded if you're visiting a really remote destination; and do, for the airline's sake, cancel any reservation you don't intend to use.

Flying in Comfort

by Richard Harrington

Flying is physically a lot more stressing than a lot of people realize. And there's more to the problem than time zones. Modern jet aircraft are artificially pressurized at an altitude pressure of around 1,500–2,000m. That means that when you're flying at an altitude of, say, 12,000m in a Boeing 747, the cabin pressure inside is what it would be if you were outside at a height of 1,500–2,000m above sea level. Most people live a lot closer to sea level than this and to be rocketed almost instantly to a height of 2,000m (so far as their body is concerned) takes a considerable amount of adjustment. Fortunately, the human body is a remarkably adaptable organism, and for most individuals this experience is stressful, but not fatal.

Although it might seem more practical to pressurize the cabin to sea level pressure, this is currently impossible. A modern jet with sea level cabin pressure would have to have extremely strong (and therefore heavy) outside walls to prevent the difference between inside and outside pressure from causing the aircraft walls to rupture in mid-flight. At present, no economically viable lightweight material is available that is strong enough to do the job. Another problem is that if there were a rupture at, say, 14,000m in an aircraft with an interior pressure equal to that at sea level, there would be no chance for the oxygen masks to drop in the huge sucking process that would occur as the air inside emptied through the hole in the aircraft. A 2,000m equivalent pressure at least gives passengers and oxygen masks a chance if this occurs.

Inside the cabin, humidifiers and fragrance disguise all the odours of large numbers of people in a confined space. On a long flight you're breathing polluted air.

Surviving the Onslaught

What can you do to help your body survive the onslaught? First you can loosen your clothing. The body swells in the thinner air of the cabin, so take off your shoes, undo your belt, tilt your seat right back, put a couple of pillows in the lumbar region of your back and one behind your neck, and whether you're trying to sleep or simply rest, cover your eyes with a pair of air travel blinkers (ask the stewardess for a pair if you haven't brought any with you). Temperatures rise and fall notoriously inside an aircraft, so have a blanket ready over your knees in case you nod off and wake up later to find that you're freezing.

When I look at all that space wasted over passengers' heads in a Boeing 747, and all those half empty hand baggage lockers, I often wonder why aircraft manufacturers don't arrange things so that comfortable hammocks can be slung over our heads for those who want to sleep – or better still, small *couchettes* in tiers like those found in modern submarines. Personally, I'd prefer such comfort, whatever it might do to the tidiness of the cabin interior.

Circulation, Consumption and Comfort

It's tempting, on a long flight, to feel you're not getting your money's worth if you don't eat and drink everything that's going. Stop and resist the temptation, even if you're in First Class and all that food and drink seems to be what most of the extra cost is all about. Most people find it best to eat lightly before leaving home and little or nothing during the flight. Foods that are too rich or spicy and foods that you're unaccustomed to will do little to make you feel good in flight. Neither will alcohol. Some people claim that they travel better if they drink fizzy drinks in flight, although if inclined to indigestion, the gas can cause discomfort as it is affected by the lower pressure in the cabin. Tea and coffee are diuretics (increase urine output) and so have the undesirable effect of further dehydrating the drinker who is already in the very dry atmosphere of the cabin. Fruit juices and plain water are best.

Smoking raises the level of carbon monoxide in the blood – and incidentally in the atmosphere, so that non-smokers can also suffer the ill effects if seated close to smokers – and reduces the smoker's tolerance to altitude. A smoker is already effectively at 1,500–2,000m before he leaves the ground. He is more inclined to breathlessness and excessive dryness than the non-smoker.

Walk up and down as frequently as possible during a flight to keep your circulation in shape, and don't resist the urge to go to the toilet (avoid the queues by going before meals). The time will pass more quickly, and you'll feel better for it, if you get well into an unputdownable novel before leaving home and try to finish it during the flight. This trick always works better than half-heartedly flicking through an in-flight magazine.

You may try to find out how full a plane is before you book, or choose to fly in the low season to increase your chance of getting empty seats to stretch out on for a good sleep. If you've got a choice of seats on a stretched DC-8, for example, remember that there's more leg room by the emergency exit over the wings. On the other hand, stewardesses tend to gather at the tail of the plane on most airlines, so they try not to give seats there away unless asked. That means you may have more chance of ending up with empty seats next to you if you go for the back two rows (also statistically the safest place in a crash). Seats in the middle compartment over the forward part of the wing are said to give the smoothest ride; the front area of the plane is however quietest.

You might travel with your own pillow, which will be a useful supplement to the postage-stamp sized pillows supplied by most airlines.

Finally, if you're going to sleep in flight, put a 'DO NOT DISTURB' notice by your seat and pass the chance of another free drink or face towel every time your friendly neighbourhood stewardess comes round.

You probably won't arrive at the other end raring to go, but if you've planned it wisely to arrive just before nightfall, and if you take a brisk walk before going to bed, you might just get lucky and go straight to sleep without waking up on home time two hours later.

Jetlag

by Melissa Shales

Every year, as the holiday season swings into action, millions of people join that bleary-eyed band of professional travellers who stumble their way around the world muttering sourly about jetlag. For holiday-makers, jetlag is an irritating waste of precious time away from the office, but for the many businessmen, politicians, air crew and public figures for whom travelling is unavoidable, it can be an expensive disaster. Scientific research is now proving that jetlag can lower mental and physical efficiency by up to twenty per cent. And that means that many vital decisions are being taken while considerably below par. Former US Secretary of State John Foster Dulles publicly admitted responsibility for the Suez Crisis, claiming that his hasty and poorly thought decisions were the result of chronic jetlag.

Causes and Symptoms

Initial symptoms include extreme fatigue, which can affect concentration, memory and performance. Other effects can be constipation or diarrhoea, insomnia, loss of appetite, headache, impaired night vision and peripheral vision. On a flight half way round the world, total readjustment can take up to a fortnight.

Since the 1940s, it has been known that the human body functions through a complicated series of cyclical rhythms governing every natural process from ageing and reproduction to breathing and swallowing. This 'circadian' rhythm is governed by the five senses of sight, sound, touch, taste and smell, as well as three less physically obvious senses. The sense of place is similar to the more highly developed instinct that causes birds to migrate within a particular pattern and area, or whales to cross the earth to calve; the sense of time has a natural cycle of around 25 hours, which is adjusted by external factors, such as light and dark, to regulate our daily living – the 'internal clock' that wakes you just before the alarm goes off and tells you when it is time for a meal; and the sense of well-being is dependent on the synchronization of the other senses to make our bodies function efficiently – when you live an erratic life you use far more nervous energy just trying to cope with the day to day demands of living. If any of these senses is disrupted, the disorientation is physical as well as mental as the body's chemistry adapts to the new rhythms caused by major displacement in both time and space. This disruption, caused by rapid movement to a totally different time cycle, is what is known as jetlag.

Effects

The effects of jetlag normally only become serious if the time difference is over three hours, so many north-south flights, although they will result in travel fatigue, will not actually cause much jetlag. A rough guideline suggests that 24 hours recovery time is required for every two hours time difference, although this will obviously vary according to each individual. Some organizations, such as the International Civil Aviation Organization (ICAO) are now building a recovery formula into travel schedules and time is allowed for recuperation before any work is done. One firm of management consultants in the USA has ruled that no major financial decision should be taken by its executives during the recovery period.

The effects of jetlag can be altered by personal attributes and habits. Generally, the younger you are, the less it will affect you, to the point where small babies, who almost sleep the clock round, are totally unaffected. A person with rigid habits will suffer more if they are disrupted, while people who are either very early risers or night owls can make their habit work for them, dependent upon the direction they are travelling in.

Prevention

The effects of jetlag cannot be avoided, but there are ways of lessening their impact. Dr Charles Ehret of the Argonne National Laboratory in the USA has devised a dietary programme designed to minimize the effects of jetlag by adjusting the body over a four-day period prior to flight. It was originally used by the US Army Rapid Deployment Force, but is now available to the public through a book which Dr Ehret has written in conjunction with Lynne Waller Scanlon – *Overcoming Jetlag* (Berkeley Books, $4.95). During the pre-flight period, you alternately 'feast' and 'fast', swopping meals of either high protein value to stimulate activity and high carbohydrate to induce sleep, or fasting, to 'deplete the liver's store of carbohydrates and prepare the body's clock for resetting'. It seems to help, but requires willpower which, when even tea and coffee are severely regulated, few possess.

In a more general book, *The Jetlag Book* (Crown Publishers, $4.95), writer Don Kowet offers a wide selection of ways to help relieve the misery caused by long-haul flying. As well as the causes and effects of jetlag, he discusses in some depth why the actual flight is so tiring and offers many solutions, many of which are pure common sense if we thought them out for ourselves. For instance, although the cabin is pressurized, the oxygen is still rarified (at about the level found at 7,000 feet above sea level) and the humidity level is around two per cent (instead of an average 30 per cent on the ground). Space is confined, restricting even the most gentle exercise. His advice includes sets of exercises which can be performed in your seat, ways of passing the time to prevent you getting bored or uptight, suggestions on eating, and a warning not to smoke or drink during the flight as the effect of both is heightened by the rarified atmosphere.

Jetlag is an inconvenience that is here to stay and has to be faced by an ever-growing population of air travellers, but with some commonsense and willpower, the effects can be minimized to the point where you might no longer need to spend half your stay abroad recovering from the journey.

Fear of Flying

by Sheila Critchley

More people fly today than ever before, yet many – experienced air travellers as well as novices – suffer anguish and apprehension at the mere thought of flying. A survey by the Boeing aircraft company in the USA suggested that as many as one out of seven people experience anxiety when flying and that women outnumber men two to one in these feelings of uneasiness. The crews know them as 'the white-knuckle brigade'.

A certain amount of concern is perhaps inevitable. The sheer size of modern jet aircraft, which appear awkward and unwieldy on the ground, makes one wonder how they will manage to get into the air – and stay there. Most of these fears are irrational and are perhaps based on the certain knowledge that once in the aircraft, we, as passengers, are powerless to control our fate, which depends solely on the skill and training of the crew. There is little comfort for these people in the numerous statistical compilations which show that modern air transport is many times safer than transport by car or rail. According to Lloyds of London, it is 25 times safer to travel by air than by car. A spokesman for Lloyd's Aviation Underwriting said that if you consider all the world's airlines, there are some 600 to 1,000 people killed every year. This figure compares to an annual toll on the roads of some 55,000 in the United States, 12,000 in France and 5,000 in the United Kingdom. One sardonic pilot used to announce on landing, 'You've now completed the safest part of your journey. Drive carefully.'

Anxiety

Most people's fear remains just that – anxiety which gives rise to signs of stress but on a manageable scale. For others, however, the anxiety can become an unmanageable fear, known as *aviophobia* or fear of flying. Symptoms include feelings of panic, sweating, palpitations, depression, sleeplessness, weeping spells, and sometimes temporary paralysis. Phobias are deep seated and often require therapy to search out the root cause. Psychologists studying *aviophobia* suggest that in serious cases, there may be an overlap with *claustrophobia* (fear of confined places) and *aerophobia* (fear of heights). Professional help can be obtained from specialists in behavioural psychotherapy. Unlike other phobias, though, which may impair a person's ability to function in society, those suffering from *aviophobia* may simply adopt avoidance of air travel as a means of coping. Only those whose jobs necessitate a great deal of foreign travel are forced into finding a solution.

One source of many people's fear of flying is simply a lack of knowledge about how an aircraft works and about which sounds are usual and to be expected. Visiting airports and observing planes taking off and landing can help overcome this problem. Reading about flying can also help (though air disaster fiction can hardly be recommended). Talking to other people who fly regularly can be reassuring. Frequent air travellers are familiar with the sequence of sounds which indicates everything is proceeding normally: the dull 'thonk' when the landing gear retracts on take-off; the seeming deceleration of the engine speed to cruising velocity; the resonance of the engines at certain speeds among other things. Since most people are familiar with the sounds in their cars and listen almost subconsciously to the changed 'tones' that indicate mechanical difficulties, people who are unsure about flying often feel a certain disquiet when they can't identify 'normal' from 'abnormal' sounds in an aircraft.

Air turbulence can also be upsetting. Most modern aircraft fly above areas of severe winds (such as during thunderstorms) and pilots receive constant reports on upcoming weather conditions from monitoring towers. Nonetheless, air currents up to 20,000 feet may buffet aircraft and the 'cobblestoning' effect can be frightening even to experienced air travellers. Flight crews are aware of this problem and usually make an announcement to allay undue worries.

If you are afraid to fly, tell the stewardess when you board so that the crew can keep an eye on you. Hyperventilation is a common symptom of anxiety; the cure is to breathe slowly and deeply into a paper bag. Remember that all aircraft crew are professionals; their training is far more rigorous than, say, that required to obtain a driving licence.

Emergencies

It is probably worth mentioning that the cabin crew's main responsibility is not dispensing food and drink to passengers but rather the safety of everyone on board. There is usually a minimum of one flight attendant for every fifty passengers. The briefings on emergency procedures which are given at the beginning of every flight are not routine matters: they can mean the difference between life and death and should be taken seriously. Each type of aeroplane has different positions for emergency exits, oxygen supplies, and design and positioning of life jackets. The demonstrations by air crew of emergency procedures are for the benefit of everyone on board and should be watched and listened to attentively. In an emergency situation, action needs to occur in the first fifteen seconds – there is no time to discover that you don't know where the emergency exits are situated. Learning about what to do in an emergency should reduce fear, not increase it.

Relaxation

One way of coping with fear of flying (at least in the short term) is to learn how to relax. In fact, in-flight alcohol, movies, reading material and taped music are all conducive to relaxation. Some airlines have conducted programmes for those they call 'fearful flyers'. These seminars consist of recorded tapes offering advice on relaxation techniques, statistical information on how safe it really is, group discussions where everyone is encouraged to discuss their fears and recorded simulations of the sounds to be expected in flight. Familiarization is the key concept behind all of these behaviourist therapy programmes; instruction in rhythmic deep breathing and sometimes even hypnosis can assist the person in learning to control his or her physical signs of anxiety. A graduate of one of these programmes confirmed its beneficial effects: 'I enjoyed the course, especially sharing my misgivings with other people and discovering I wasn't alone with my fears. At the end of the course, we actually went up on a one-hour flight and I was able to apply all the techniques I had learned. In fact, I actually managed to enjoy the flight – something I would not have ever believed I could do.'

A certain amount of anxiety about flying is to be expected. For most people, a long distance flight is not something one does every day. On the qther hand, there is always a first time for everyone, even those who have chosen to make flying their career. The more you fly, the more likely you are to come to terms with your fears. Some anxiety is inevitable, but in the case of flying, the statistics are on your side.

Vehicles

Overland by Truck or Van

by Simon Glen

Travelling overland in your own vehicle gives you independence, freedom to go where you like and when you like, and a familiar bolthole away from the milling crowds and the alienation one invariably feels in a different culture. The vehicle may seem expensive to start with, but when one takes into consideration the cost of transport and accommodation, it begins to become more realistic, particularly if you can escape the bed bugs and filth that often seem to accompany the cheapest accommodation.

Which Vehicle?

The choice of a vehicle is often a problem, because every type has its limitations. The final choice depends much on what is to be compromised. A Range Rover is superb in the sands of the Sahara's Bilma Erg, a place one would not normally take a fully equipped Volkswagen campervan. But after a while one longs for the convenience and comfort of the Volkswagen Kombi, for it is impossible to sleep full length in a Range Rover without the tailgate open and all the stores, fuel and water removed. Moreover, a Range Rover is very fond of petrol (a real problem when it comes to endless fuelless stretches such as through central Africa). Renault 4 and Citroen 2CV panel vans are even more cramped than a Range Rover but they are far more economical to buy, run and repair, even though they are not usually suitable for the Bilma Erg. Thus, for a protracted transcontinental or round-the-world journey, the vehicle chosen must be very carefully considered, bearing in mind, first, the sacrifices one has to make in order to benefit from the advantages of more cramped vehicles; second, the length of time one expects to be on the road; and third, the degree of home comforts one wants along the way.

Avoid big American-style conversions, and other British and German variants. They have lots of space and other home comforts, like showers, toilets, microwave ovens, and loads of storage; but their fuel consumption, weight, low clearance, poor traction, very small front and rear approach and departure angles, and sheer size make them most unsuitable for a journey off the beaten track. If you feel you need the extra space of a big vehicle, then a Mercedes Unimog, or even a big M.A.N. four-wheel-drive truck with living quarters built onto the back would be much more suitable for the Sahara's sands and Zaïre's mud. However, the costs involved in buying, running and shipping these vehicles would deter all but the exceptionally wealthy.

Generally, the small Mercedes 207 and 208 vans and the Volkswagen LT vans are also too big and cumbersome, causing their owners untold hard work and anxiety, even on simple journeys like the two main trans-Saharan routes. The optimum size would seem to be that of the aircooled Volkswagen Type 2 Kombi and the Ford Transit (though the latter has problems with a very low front axle and inferior traction). This size is big enough to live in and to carry food, water, spares, stove, fridge, beds, clothes, extra fuel, sand ladders and two people in comfort, yet remains economical to run, small enough to negotiate narrow bush tracks and light enough to make debogging less frequent and easier.

A high-roofed van is good to stand up in and provides extra storage, but is more expensive on ferries and ships. It also offers increased wind resistance, thus pushing up fuel consumption and making the engine work harder and hotter, shortening its life and increasing the risk of mechanical failure.

Conversions

An elevating roof or fibreglass 'pop-top' campervan conversion has several advantages over a fixed roof van. Not only is it lower, but it can sleep extra people upstairs (e.g. children), provide extra headroom while camped, and insulate well in tropical heat. Some well-designed fibre-glass pop-tops do not collect condensation even when you cook inside them when the roof is laden with snow. Some of the disadvantages are that they can, in extreme cases, be easier to break into; they look more conspicuous and more inviting to thieves than a plain top; and they have to be retracted before a driver, disturbed in the night, can depart in a hurry.

In some vans, the hole cut in the roof has actually weakened the structure of the vehicle. The ordeal of driving through Africa, especially, will cause structural failures and cracks in the body and chassis – failures that would normally not occur if the car spent its life in Europe. As an example, all elevating roof VW conversions should have the 'VW Option M073' built into the vehicle when the conversion job is being done – two roof-mounted plates that give torsional support to the chassis. The same sorts of precautions should be taken with other vans like the Toyota Hiace, Ford Transit, and Bedford CF. The roof is not an integral part of the structure of a Land Rover and cutting a hole in it does not affect the chassis.

Four-wheel-drive is not necessary to travel the length and breadth of Africa, Australia or South America. The Darien Gap is for expeditions and not independent travellers. Two-wheel-drive vehicles have successfully taken their occupants through such difficult areas as the parallel sand ridges of the Sahara's Bilma Erg and Australia's Simpson Desert. Nevertheless, these trips have invariably been completed by people with considerable experience and expertise.

A demountable caravan fitted to four-wheel-drive pick-ups like the Land Rover, Toyota Land Cruiser and Toyota Hi-Lux could provide a lot more room and comfort, but demountables are not generally robust enough to stand up to the off-road conditions of an overland journey through Africa. They also add considerably to the height and width of the vehicle and are altogether more expensive than a proper conversion. Moreover, you cannot walk through from the cab to the living compartment.

In deserts, if one doesn't have a campervan, sleeping on a roof-rack can be a most pleasant way of keeping cool and avoiding spiders and scorpions. 'Air Camper' folding roof-rack tents offer these advantages, but they can be miserably cold in some climates and make one vulnerable to thieves and other ill-intentioned people.

Furnishings and Fittings

Preferably camper conversions should have furniture made of marine plywood rather than particle board, as it is stronger, more durable, lighter and not prone to disintegration if wet.

If your vehicle is finally destined for the US it must satisfy US Department of Transport and State regulations for the basic vehicle and the conversion. The same applies to campervans destined permanently for Australia where equally strict Australian Design Rules apply to both the car and the conversion.

Most water filtration systems (e.g. Katadyn) are portable, though Safari (Water Treatments) Ltd produce a wall-mounted model which can be fitted to a campervan. On many campervans the water tank and even a gas bottle are mounted beneath the floor where they are most vulnerable away from made-up roads.

Front-opening quarter vents in the front doors are sometimes most appreciated in warm climates, as are a pair of fans built into the through-flow ventilation system. However, front quarter vents can be attractive to thieves. Fresh air is essential when sleeping inside a vehicle in tropical lands and a roof vent is just not enough to create an adequate draught. Louvred windows provide the answer. Equip them also with mosquito gauze and, because they are louvred, they can be left wide open even in heavy rain allowing a draught of cool air without admitting either mosquitoes or thieves.

Radios, Roof-Racks and Refrigerators

Having up-to-date information along the route can be a big help, forewarning you of riots, floods, cyclones, earthquakes, revolutions, strikes, currency problems and fuel shortages. A dashboard-mounted car radio will enable you to listen to the excellent shortwave services of the BBC, Voice of America, Radio Moscow, Deutsche Welle and Radio Australia.

Though it will increase fuel consumption considerably, a roof-rack is fine for Europe or North America. Generally, one should carry heavy objects like full jerry cans inside the vehicle, preferably in a central location between the axles. The roof-rack should be reserved for a few relatively light but large and cumbersome items like sand ladders, a shovel and perhaps an empty jerry can or two.

On a long transcontinental journey, one will normally have to do without a fridge. (It is often preferable to use the space and weight for more fundamental items like jerry cans or spare parts.) However, for a large quantity of films and some medicines, one could consider one of the new dry operating thermoelectric 'Peltier Effect' fridges (Koolatron Industries). A product of American aerospace technology, this tiny lightweight fridge has recently revolutionized camping refrigeration.

Finally, whatever type of vehicle you take, and however you equip it, you should aim to be as self-sufficient as possible. You should have food to last for weeks not days, clothing to suit the changing climatic and social conditions, and the tools, spare parts and personal ability to maintain your vehicle and keep it going. Without these, and in spite of the occasional genuine kind person, you will be conned, jilted and exploited to the extent that the journey will be a major ordeal. With adequate care and preparation your overland journey will be one of the most pleasurable experiences of a lifetime.

The Expedition Vehicle

by Jack Jackson

All expeditions have to make a compromise between what they can afford, what can best handle the terrain to be encountered and whether all spares and fuel need to be carried or are available en route.

Unless they are heavily sponsored, few expeditions can afford to buy new four-wheel-drive vehicles larger than one tonne. So used ex-military vehicles are the norm. When buying these, it is best to ignore the so-called 'rebuilt' vehicles and to buy the vehicle and plenty of spares. Then strip and rebuild it yourself; this way you know it is done properly, learn the likely weaknesses and will know how to fix things again if they go wrong in the field. Many military vehicles and smaller Japanese diesel four-wheel-drives have 24 volt electrics, so unless you convert these to 12 volt, you will need to carry all spares for these.

What's Needed?

If you do not plan to encounter soft sand, mud or snow but intend to stay on hard tracks in the dry season and your payload is mostly people who, when necessary, can get out and push, then you really only need a two-wheel-drive vehicle; so long as it is of the truck type with enough strength and ground clearance. Such vehicles, fitted with larger tyres and sometimes a lower axle ratio, are very successful all over Africa south of the Sahara as local 'Souk buses'.

Where tracks are narrow, overhung and subject to landslides, such as in outlying mountainous areas like the Karakoram, then the only useable vehicles are the smallest lightweight four-wheel-drives, such as soft-topped Land Rover 88s and Jeep CJ5s. These vehicles also give the best performance when traversing soft sand and steep sand dunes, but their small payload and fuel carrying capacity restrict them to short journeys.

If costs were no problem and all spares were to be carried, the ideal four-wheel-drive expedition vehicle would have a payload of one ton, evenly distributed between all four wheels, short wheelbase, forward control, high ground clearance, large wheels and tyres, good power to weight ratio and reasonable fuel consumption. The vehicles best fitting this specification are the Mercedes Unimogs, the Fiat PC65 and PC75 models and the Land Rover Military 101″ one tonne. All these are specialist vehicles for best cross-country performance and are soft-topped to keep the centre of gravity low.

For the overlander or smaller expedition, taking into account price, availability of spares and working life, the most commonly used vehicles are the long wheelbased Land Rover, the smaller Mercedes Unimogs and the four ton Bedford M type trucks.

Which Vehicle?

The Land Rover is the most comfortable and the hard top version gives protection against the elements and thieves. There are plenty of spare parts available worldwide; they are easy to work on because everything bolts on and the aluminium alloy body does not rust, so the inevitable bent body panel can be hammered back into rough shape and then forgotten; you do not need to be Hercules to change a wheel and can easily resell the vehicle at the end of the expedition.

Where heavier payloads are envisaged, especially nowadays in Africa, where many countries are desperately short of fuel and one has to carry large amounts along with you, the most popular four-wheel-drive vehicles are Bedford M type trucks and Mercedes Unimogs. Bedford trucks are cheap, simple and in some parts crude. They have good cross country performance when handled sensibly and slowly, but are too heavy for soft sand. They go wrong often, but repairs can usually be improvised. The 550 engine is more reliable than the 330 engine but the clutch can be a weak point. Fuel tank straps tend to break, but the tanks can be held on with strong nylon rope until repairs can be arranged. Spares need to be taken out from the UK, but some are also available in Nairobi.

Ex-NATO Mercedes Unimogs are the nearest to the ideal expedition vehicle that the average expedition is likely to be able to afford. Their cross-country performance is exceptional, their portal axles give them extra ground clearance, though this also makes them easier to turn over. It is almost impossible to get them stuck in sand, though they will stick in mud. Ex-NATO Unimogs usually have relatively small petrol engines, so you need to use the gearbox well, but fuel consumption is good. The standard six-speed, one-range gearbox can be altered to a four-speed, two-range gearbox, which is useful in sand. Four-wheel-drive can be engaged at any speed without declutching. Diff locks are standard. The chassis is cleverly arranged to give good weight distribution over all four wheels at almost any angle, but gives a bad ride over corrugations.

Mechanically, the Unimog is overcomplicated; it does not go wrong often, but when it does it is difficult to work on and needs many special tools. Later models have the clutch set to one side of the transmission, instead of in line with it, making it much easier to change.

Unimogs are best bought from NATO forces in Germany; spares must be carried with you. Diesel Unimogs are usually ex-Agriculture or Building Contractor and are therefore less well maintained than forces vehicles.

Whichever vehicle you choose, keep things simple, avoid power steering, automatic transmissions and air conditioning, all of which sap engine power, have poor reliability and contribute to overheating. Also avoid freewheeling hubs.

Maintenance

By using several identical vehicles travelling in convoy, you can minimize the weight of spares and tyres to be carried. The idea of using one large vehicle to carry fuel etc., accompanying several smaller, more agile vehicles, does not work out well in practice. The larger vehicles will often be heavily bogged down and the smaller vehicles will have difficulty in towing it out, often damaging their own drive train in the process. Also the vast difference in overall journey speed plus the extra spares needed causes many problems, unless you are to have a static base camp.

Overloading is the largest single cause of broken-down vehicles and the easiest to avoid. Calculate your payload against the maker's recommendation for the vehicle. Water is ten pounds per gallon, fuel roughly eight pounds a gallon, plus the container. Concentrate on the essentials and cut back on the luxuries. If could make all the difference between success and failure.

For rough terrain, trailers are not advisable. They get stuck in sand, slip into ditches and overturn on bad tracks. Even powered trailers have been known to overturn the prime vehicle. On corrugated tracks, trailer contents soon become unrecognisable. Trailers are impossible to manhandle in sand or mud and make life difficult if you have to turn around in an awkward situation.

If you must take a trailer, make sure that it has the same wheels and tyres as the towing vehicle, that the hitch is the strong NATO type and that the wiring loom is well fixed along the chassis where it will be protected from bushes and stones.

Petrol Versus Diesel

Weight for weight, petrol engines have more power than diesel engines, but for expeditions they have several disadvantages. In hot countries there is a considerable risk of fire and the constant problem of vapour lock, which is at its worst on steep climbs, or long climbs at altitude. Dust, which often contains iron, gets into and shorts out the distributor. High tension leads break down and if much river crossing has to be accomplished, water in the electrics causes you more trouble. A further problem is that high-octane fuel is not usually available and low-octane fuel will soon damage a sophisticated engine. However, petrol engines are more easily repaired by the less experienced mechanic.

Diesel fuel does not have the fire risk of petrol and is usually about one third of the price of petrol, outside Europe. It also tends to be more readily available, as it is used by trucks and tractors.

Diesel engines are heavier and more expensive to buy, but are generally more reliable and need less maintenance, though a more knowledgeable mechanic is required if they do go wrong. An advantage to expeditions is the extra torque available at low engine revolutions: this allows a higher gear in the rough, which improves fuel consumption, which means less weight of fuel needs to be carried for a long section without fuel supplies – and this improves fuel consumption still further.

A second filter in the fuel line is essential to protect the pump from bad fuel in the Third World. A water sedimentor is useful, but needs to be well protected from stones and knocks.

Tyres

Long-distance travellers usually have to cover several different types of terrain, which makes it difficult to choose just one type of tyre to cover the whole route. Unless you expect to spend most of your time in mud or snow, you should avoid the aggressive tread, so-called cross-country or all-terrain tyres. These have a large open cleated tread which is excellent in mud or snow, but on sand they tear away the firmer surface crust, putting the vehicle into the softer sand underneath. These open treads also tear up quickly on mixed ground with sharp stones and rocks.

If you expect to spend a lot of time in soft sand, then you will need high flotation tyres with little tread pattern which tend to compress the sand causing least disturbance to the firmer surface crust. Today's standard for such work is the Michelin XS, which has just enough tread pattern to be also useable on dry roads. These are, however, dangerous on wet roads or ice. The XS is a soft flexible radial tyre, ideal for low pressure sand use, but easily cut up on sharp stones.

Most expeditions cover mixed ground, needing a general truck type tyre. These have a closed tread with enough tyre width and lugs in the outside of the tread, to be good mixed country tyres, although obviously not as good in mud or soft sand. Such tyres, when fitted with snow chains are as good as any all-terrain tyre for snow or mud use and, if of radial construction, can be run soft to improve their flotation on sand. The best tyre in this category is the Michelin XZY series.

Radial or Cross Ply?

Radial tyres are more flexible and have less heat build up when run soft in sand than cross ply tyres. They also have less rolling resistance, thus improving fuel consumption. For heavy expedition work, Michelin steel braced radials are preferable. With radial tyres you must have the correct inner tubes, preferably by the same manufacturer. Radial and cross ply tyres should not be mixed.

Radial tyres 'set' in use, so when changed around to even out tyre wear, they should preferably be kept on the same side of the vehicle. A further advantage of radials is that they are easier to remove from the wheel rim with tyre levers, when you get punctures in the field.

Radial tyres have soft side walls which are easily torn on sharp stones, so if you have to drive over such stones, try to use the centre of the tyre, where the tread is thickest.

For soft sand use, radial tyres can be run at 40 per cent pressure at speeds below ten miles per hour and 75 per cent pressure for mixed terrain below twenty miles per hour. Remember to reflate to full pressure as soon as you return to firm ground.

Tubeless tyres are totally impracticable for expedition work, so use tubed tyres and carry several spare inner tubes.

A vehicle travelling alone in bad terrain should carry at least one extra tyre besides the one on the spare wheel. Several vehicles travelling together should all have the same type of tyres for full inter-changeability.

Land Rovers

by Jack Jackson

Despite some weaknesses, Land Rovers are the most durable and reliable four-wheel-drive small vehicles for expeditions and overland use. Their spartan comforts are their main attributes: most of their recent challengers are too softly sprung and have too many car-type comforts to have any real reliability in hard, cross-country terrain. Some models are somewhat underpowered, but their low fuel consumption and the general availability of spare parts around the world make them a popular choice.

No vehicle will remain in mint condition after cross-country use but, in the UK at least, Land Rovers can currently be resold after a year's hard work for a thoroughly respectable proportion of the original price. Having driven some fifty different Land Rovers over the last ten years in difficult terrain in Africa and Asia, as well as almost every other four-wheel-drive vehicle, I still find the Land Rover hard to beat.

Which Model?

The short wheelbase is usually avoided because of its small loadcarrying capacity but remember that in off-the-road use, particularly on sand dunes, a short wheelbase is a distinct advantage. Hard-top models are best for protection against thieves. When considering long wheelbase models, it is best to avoid the six-cylinder models, including the one ton and the forward control. All of these cost more to buy, give more than the normal amount of trouble, are harder to find spares for and recoup less on resale. The six-cylinder engine uses more fuel and more engine oil than the four-cylinder engine and the carburettor does not like dust or dirty fuel, often needing to be stripped and cleaned twice a day in very dusty areas. The electrical fuel pump always gives trouble. The forward control, which is now discontinued except in Spain, turns over very easily and, as with the six-cylinder, Series I and Series IIA Land Rovers, rear half shafts break very easily if the driver is at all heavy footed.

The 1-tonne and the Series III six-cylinder models with their stronger Salisbury rear differentials wear the drive plates instead of the half shafts and these are much easier to replace. But you can never find spare parts for the 1-tonne EMV front differential outside the UK. Both the 1-tonne and forward control models go through rear prop shaft universal joints and their balloon tyres very quickly. It is generally agreed that the four-cylinder models are underpowered but the increased power of the six-cylinder model does not compensate for its disadvantages.

The V8 Land Rover has continuous four-wheel-drive and differential lock, which on tests in Africa have proved to reduce petrol consumption in sand and to save wear and tear on suspension over corrugations, owing to improved pace. Sand tyres to match the increased engine size can make easier work on difficult traction conditions. There is only one major drawback: there is no room to fit jerry can brackets in the front, and rear brackets tend to put undue stress on the back panels.

The new Land Rover 110s are designed for speed, economy and comfort on the newer, improved roads in Africa and Asia. Built on a strengthened Range Rover type chassis and suspension with permanent four-wheel-drive and centre differential lock, stronger gearbox, disc brakes on the front and better doors all around, the vehicle is a vast improvement.

For lightweight safari or personnel carrier use it will be ideal, but for heavy expedition work, the difficulty in uprating coil springs easily may be a major drawback.

Military Land Rovers will continue to be of the leaf spring Series III types, so spares for these will be more widely available worldwide.

The high capacity 109s and 110s will be good starting chassis for conversions and heavier loads.

The current Range Rover is not spacious enough nor has it the load carrying capacity for true expedition use.

Any hard top or station wagon Land Rover will suit you if you do not intend to go off the road much when heavily loaded. If you buy a new Land Rover, run it for a few months before setting off on your trip. This allows the wet weather to get at the hundreds of nuts and bolts keeping the body together. If bolts rust in a bit, it will save you a lot of time later on. If you take a brand new Land Rover into a hot climate, you will regularly have to spend hours tightening nuts and bolts that have come loose, particularly those around the roof and windscreen.

Series IIA and Series III Comparisons

Series IIA Land Rovers had stronger bodywork and chassis than Series III models and their only serious weakness was the rear differential but this was fully interchangeable with the front differential and the job does not require any special tools. Series IIA gearboxes did not have syncromesh on the first two gears. Heavy footed drivers often broke rear half shafts.

The differential on the 109″ Series III models is bigger and stronger, but it is not interchangeable with the front one if things go wrong and requires a differential case spreader to get them out. I have never known a half shaft to go on this new differential. Instead the drive plate on the road wheel end goes. This is much simpler to replace as long as all the little metal shavings that spread out into the bearing are washed out. Also these differentials, unlike those of the 11A model, are not fitted with a recessed drain plug. This is a very simple and not very costly point, but when driving on rough roads the stones thrown up constantly strike the differentials and quickly batter the drain plug to a shape which no spanner or even Stillson wrench will fit. Even worse, the drain plug can become unscrewed and all the oil run out before you become aware of it.

Series III gearboxes have a poor reputation, the new five-speed gearbox, available as an option, is a great improvement. Series III gearboxes constantly blow the oil seal between the main gearbox and the transfer box. The rear output oil seal on the transfer box often then fails from the increased oil pressure and level whilst the main gearbox needs constant topping up.

The alternator fitted as standard to later models is not as reliable as it should be and its fragile diodes cannot be repaired in the field. It is best to get an exchange unit after 60,000km or before any big trip and also carry a spare slip ring and bushes.

The Series III windscreen frame is much weaker than that on the Series IIA. It usually has to be reinforced at all four corners if much travel on bad roads is envisaged. The bracket where the windscreen hinge fits to the bulkhead is also very weak and the inner windscreen tie bolts break regularly, so some spares should be carried. The oil filler cap tends to vibrate off and disappear, so carry a spare. The same cap also fits the radiator.

The Series IIIs and 110s have nylon inerts on the bonnet hinges which regularly vibrate out and disappear, so carry spares. Since the catch which holds the bonnet closed will also break, especially if the spare wheel is carried on the bonnet, add some webbing or, better still, spring metal bonnet catches.

Rebuilt ex-military Land Rovers are quite a good buy and there are still a few Series I Land Rovers around, but they are very basic and spares for them are easier to find in scrapyards abroad than in the UK.

Diesel Options

Early Land Rover diesel engines were not renowned for their reliability; the new five-bearing crankshaft diesel engines are better but still underpowered. Land Rover Ltd still refuse to believe that the Third World requires a large, trouble-free diesel engine. Leyland in Australia have got tired of waiting and now fit an Isuzu 3.9 litre diesel engine as an option in their 109s, 110s and Range Rovers. In the UK, independent companies will fit Perkins 4,203 and 4,154 or Ford York diesel engines to Land Rovers or the Perkins 200 series 4,182 diesel engine to replace the V8 petrol engine in the 109″ V8, 110″ V8 and Range Rover. Various turbo-charged diesel engines are also available but are not sensible for off-road work. Land Rover Ltd, together with Perkins, are working on a turbo-charged V8 diesel based on the V8 petrol engine, but I cannot imagine this being of any use at all for hard cross-country use.

Roof-racks

These need to be strong to be of any use. Many on the market are very flimsy and will soon break up on badly corrugated piste. Weight for weight, tubular section is always stronger than box section and it should be heavily galvanized.

To extend a roof-rack or to put jerrycans of water or petrol over or even beyond the windscreen is absolute lunacy. The long wheelbase Land Rover is designed so that most of the weight is carried over the rear wheels. The maximum extra weight allowed for in front is the spare tyre and a winch. It does not take much more than this to break the front springs or even bend the axle. In any case, forward visibility is impossible when going downhill with such an extended roof-rack. A full length roof-rack can be safely fitted but it must be carefully loaded, remembering that Land Rover recommend a total roof weight of not more than 90 kg and that a good roof-rack (full-length) weighs almost 90 kg itself! Expect damage to the body-work and reinforce likely points of stress. A good roof-rack design will also have its supports positioned to be in line with the main body supports. It will also have fittings along the back of the vehicle to prevent it from juddering forward on corrugated roads. Without these fittings, holes will be worn in the aluminium roof.

Nylon or terylene rope is best for tying baggage down as hemp rope doesn't last too well in the sun. Hemp is also hard on the hands from all the absorbed dust and grit. Rubber roof-rack straps are useful, but those sold in Europe soon crack up in the sun. You can use circular strips from old inner tubes and add metal hooks to make your own straps: these will stand up to the constant sunlight without breaking.

Tall drivers will find more room in a standard hard-top Land Rover than in a station wagon, because the back seat can fall back further on the standard model. On the station wagon you can solve this by moving the top handrail behind the front seats back by 5cm with 32mm steel plate from the door pillar to the handrail mounting holes. The seat can then fall the maximum amount, held correctly by the stops at its base.

Other extras

Stone-guards for lights are very useful, but you need a design which allows you to clean the mud off the lights without removing them (water hoses do not usually exist off the beaten track) and such a design is hard to find. Air horns must be fitted in such a location that the horns do not fill with mud, e.g. on the roof or within the body. Horns can be operated by a floor-mounted dipswitch. An isolator may be located on the dashboard to prevent accidental operation of the horn.

A heavily loaded vehicle will need 1-tonne springs fitted onto the rear and diesel springs or stronger fitted to the front. It is perfectly possible to fit 1-tonne springs to Series IIA and Series III Land Rovers, though you may come across mechanics who tell you it is impossible. When you do this, of course, you must keep a careful eye on the spring hangers, shackle pins and bushes. Generally the bushes go and you will have to replace them most often. Since I began to fit one-ton springs I have found that I have rarely had to replace one. So instead of carrying many complete spare rear springs, I carry the main leaves only as spares in case of emergency.

Sump guards are unlikely to be required because the chassis and the front axle take most of the knocks. The petrol tank at the rear is more likely to be clouted.

A good, powerful spotlight fitted on the rear of the roof-rack will be invaluable when reversing and will provide enough light for pitching a tent.

Normal reversing lights will be of no use.

The steering lock on any Land Rover used in a dusty area will jam regularly. If you don't remove the steering lock be sure to carry spare keys. If it gets very sticky with dust it is better to leave the key in the lock and never remove it. Do not oil steering locks, but use special dry graphite lock lubricant.

Volkswagen Kombis

by Simon Glen

The Volkswagen Kombi, Bus or Type 2, can be seen in use in almost every country outside the Soviet bloc and China. Anyone who has travelled overland through Africa, Asia, the Americas or around Australia will have to agree that VW Kombis are, without doubt, the most popular independent traveller's overland vehicle. The VW's ability to survive misuse (up to a point), carry heavy loads over rough terrain economically, and at the same time provide the privacy of a mobile home are some of the factors which make it so popular. Moreover, it is one of the few forward control vans in the world which passes strict US Department of Transport crash tests in which the driver and front seat passenger can expect to survive in a 52kmph head-on collision if seat-belted.

The Kombi has a one-tonne load capacity and far more living space in it than a long wheelbase Land Rover or Land Cruiser. It lacks the four-wheel-drive capability but partly makes up for it with its robust independent suspension, high ground clearance and engine weight over the driven wheels. With experience and astute driving a Kombi can be taken to places that will amaze some four-wheel-drive pundits. The notorious 25km 'sea of sand' between In Guezzam and Assamaka in the Sahara has ensnared many a Land Rover or Land Cruiser driver for hours while Kombis have stormed through unscathed in minutes.

The Kombi suspension and chassis are very strong and have a reputation equal to that of the Land Rover, Land Cruiser, Peugot 404 and 504, and Citroen 2CV for taking a punishment in rough conditions as well as for surviving protracted owner neglect and abuse. The alloy engines are similarly reliable and resistant to neglect. Being air-cooled they have no radiators, hoses, and water pumps to corrode or water passageways to freeze or clog up with mineral deposits. They are low-stressed engines that are simple to understand and easy to maintain. If in trouble, local knowledge in the ways of VW motors can be found in almost every corner of the globe. Spare parts and expert service are available in almost every city in the world (except in the Soviet bloc, China, and some Indian cities).

Size, Cost and Power

A Kombi is considerably cheaper to run than petrol-driven Land Rovers and Land Cruisers and probably the only reasonably sized four-wheel-drive vehicles able to match its fuel consumption are the four cylinder Land Rovers and Toyota diesels. However, for the price of a basic new four-cylinder long wheelbase Land Rover without any extra equipment or conversion, one could have a new 1600 Kombi fully converted as a pop-top camper van with jerrycans, sand ladders, spare parts, etc.

Very occasionally, when bogged down in the Sahara's sand or Zaïre's mud, the Kombi overlander will wish he had four-wheel-drive, but with a little patience, sweat, a shovel, a tyre gauge, and sand ladders or chains, he will get through. Moreover, for the rest of the journey, he will be far more comfortable in the security and homeliness of his Kombi. Larger four-wheel-drives like the Steyr Pinzgauer, Mercedes Unimog and Volvo C303 do have the space of the Kombi but, at nearly three times the cost and more than double the fuel consumption, they are vehicles for the very affluent independent traveller.

Other two-wheel-drive van type vehicles of the Kombi's size are commonly used by overland travellers: the Ford Transit, Toyota Hiace, Datsun E20, Leyland Sherpa, Bedford CF and the Commer/Dodge 2000. They all lack the VW's traction, four-wheel independent suspension, high ground clearance, access to worldwide parts and expertise, off-road ability, durability and strength. Larger vans like the Volkswagen LT series, Mercedes 207 and 208, and Fiat 242 have the same disadvantages as well as being just too big and cumbersome to consider seriously off the beaten track.

A prerequisite to understanding and maintaining a Kombi is a decent workshop manual. Official VW workshop manuals come in fifteen volumes and are not publicly available but other good one-volume manuals are published by J. H. Haynes & Co. Ltd (Yeovil, Somerset, UK) and by Volkswagen of America Inc. (Englewood Cliffs, New Jersey). Available from Volkswagen AG of Wolfsburg, West Germany is a pamphlet entitled *Group Z4: Instructions for Operating Passenger Cars and Transporters in Tropical Climates*. Not only does this give useful advice, but it also lists all the options available for VWs.

There are basically two types of air-cooled engine available for the Kombi. The larger and more modern design is the Type 4 engine in 1,700cm^3, 1,800cm^3 and 2,000cm^3 form with either carburettors or fuel injection. Because of its complexity and the fact that it has only been marketed in sophisticated countries like Britain, Germany, USA, South Africa and Australia, it should not be taken to less developed countries even though it is more powerful, runs cooler and is as reliable as the older engine design. The smaller 1,600cm^3 engine available is the Beetle engine with a basic design originating from Hitler's pre-war people's car. Detailed design improvements have taken place continuously since then to the extent that if it is serviced and maintained properly it will survive over 160,000km (as the author's has) through deserts and snow across several continents without needing any overhaul. This motor will not drop a valve, crack a cylinder, or hole a piston if it has been well maintained.

Care and Maintenance

Nevertheless, there are four areas that are vital to a Kombi's well-being on a protracted overland journey:

(1) If driven fast on asphalt roads or if just driven in extremely hot

conditions, oil temperatures will approach 127°C, the permitted maximum. Slow down and allow the engine to cool. Do not stop and immediately switch off if the oil temperature is high, as the temperature will actually increase when the cooling fan is not operating and there is a danger of cracking a cylinder head. Instead, allow the engine to idle for ten to fifteen minutes until the temperature descends to about 105°C. The best safeguard against overheating is to fit a VDO oil temperature gauge. The sensor replaces the dipstick.

(2) Tappet or valve clearances should be checked every 2–3,000km. Not only will this minimize the chances of burning valves but it could also let you know when a valve stem is stretching and likely to drop.

(3) In dusty conditions, inspection of the air-cleaner every day is vital. A rear-engined vehicle is exceptionally vulnerable to dust and the standard air-cleaner fitted to European, US and Australian VWs is inadequate, to say the least. 1,600cm^3 Kombis should have oil-bath air-cleaners or the optional air-cleaner with the clear plastic 'cyclone' separator stage. Bigger Type 4-engined Kombis should have either the 1972 model flat oil-bath air-cleaner or a two-stage cleaner.

If the air cleaner is neglected, dust will enter the combustion chamber causing very rapid valve and piston-ring failure and finally bearing seizure through abrasion or lack of oil.

(4) Ensure that timing and dwell angle (contact point gap) are correct, otherwise overheating will result, with cracked cylinder heads, blocked distortion and valve failure.

If these four maintenance points are adhered to rigorously and frequently, your Kombi should not let you down, provided that the motor is in good condition before departure.

Old engines should not be trusted. Previous owners may have done terrible things to them which will not show up until you have to climb a long steep Andean pass or cross 50km of soft Saharan *feche feche*. When buying a used Kombi, it would be sound policy to have an expert dismantle and rebuild your engine to ensure its reliability, your financial security in foreign lands, and your safety in deserts and jungles.

Suspension, brakes and electrics will look after themselves with normal maintenance, but do not overload the front of the Kombi as this will lead to premature torsion bar and coil spring breakages and then further suspension damage. The petrol tank is safely located well away from damage. A protector plate for the front of the gearbox and a grille to protect the bottom of the engine block are highly recommended, as is the removal of the front anti-roll bar (except on coil spring models) at the beginning of a journey off the beaten track as otherwise it will soon become bent and therefore totally useless.

Preventing and Repairing Damage

If a VW Kombi (1968–1971 models) has broken its engine carrier, the whole transmission and power unit will drag on the ground (not possible with later or earlier models). Drill or knock two holes in the floor above the engine compartment and use your steel tow rope to wire up the motor into its normal position. You can continue for thousands of kilometres like this.

If you have an oil temperature gauge and feel that the engine is getting too hot, stop and allow it to cool down by idling. If it is too late and it is showing signs of seizure like loss of power and knocking, switch off immediately to prevent further damage. If there is a partial seizure, remember that a flat air-cooled VW engine will run on three cylinders. To isolate a cylinder, remove the con rod and piston and disconnect the spark plug, close the valves by removing the pushrods or rocker arms. You must seal the disconnected cylinder and, to avoid a disastrous explosion, you must *not* allow the plug to operate.

You are travelling along at a brisk pace. The motor is hot. There is a loud explosion from the engine. Switch off immediately. Chances are that your motor has 'dropped' a valve (usually through overheating, incorrect tappet settings, or worn valve guides.) You must switch off immediately to minimize further damage to the combustion chamber, piston and remaining valves. When dismantling the engine, remove both cylinder heads as the force of the explosion when the valve dropped will have sent bits and pieces of valve through the inlet manifold to the opposite cylinder.

If your Kombi motor has developed a major and rapid oil leak, and, upon inspection, you find it to be a split oil cooler, this is usually a sign that one or both of the oil pressure relief valves has jammed closed. A new oil cooler has to be fitted, although binding the damaged one with wire and copious Araldite will work for a while. However, the jammed oil pressure relief valves must be dislodged and a 10mm tap has to be used to extract these thimble-like pieces of metal. Either new valves should be fitted or the old ones cleaned up with sand paper before being installed. Remember, too, that the problem of jammed oil pressure relief valves is usually caused by wear or distortion through overheating or a combination of both.

If your Kombi has a damaged or leaking pushrod tube (caused by hitting large rocks or dried mud in ruts or *ornières*), it may be easily remedied by fitting a concertina pushrod tube (available from most non-agency but specialist VW shops and garages). Jack up the car on the damaged side to avoid further oil loss. When the engine is cool enough to work on, remove the tappet cover and unscrew the two rocker shaft retaining nuts simultaneously. Remove the rocker shaft and pull out the pushrod from the damaged tube. Bend out the damaged tube and replace it with the emergency concertina type. This can be a permanent fixture. Do up the shaft nuts to the correct torque setting, top up with oil and drive off. Check the tappets the following morning.

If you have a bent track rod, remove it (preferably with the correct ball-joint extractor tool) and hammer it straight on a rock. If you leave it bent, not only will you have accelerated abnormal tyre wear, but in deep sand it will cause you to roll your vehicle.

Never trust other people's work on

your car, no matter whether it is a 'bush mechanic' in Agadez or a large main dealer in Britain or Germany. Always inspect the work done on your car afterwards. A major breakdown could be financially disastrous in Colombia or even the cause of your death in the Sahara, but this won't affect the mechanic who was careless in London or Frankfurt. Sometimes a 'bush mechanic' doesn't mind if the customer looks over his shoulder, 'advising', especially if he helps the process along with the occasional cigarette or can of soft drink.

Taboos

With Kombis there are a number of taboos:

(1) Don't drive with the engine lid open. Far from cooling the motor, this allows hot air expelled from the cooling ducts and hot exhaust gases to be sucked in.
(2) Don't overload the front. This compresses the springs and in rough conditions one needs to maximize suspension travel in order to absorb shocks and gain most traction. Load the centre of the vehicle with heavy jerry cans, etc. first. Preferably do not carry heavy objects on a roof-rack as this raises the centre of gravity and in rough overland conditions will cause the roof-rack to break up.
(3) Don't fit a special extractor exhaust system. Invariably, these decrease ground clearance, and impede access to the tappet covers; and, most importantly, they do not provide sufficient back pressure to the exhaust valves resulting in burned and leaking valves (a telltale sign is backfiring).
(4) Do not fit wide wheels as they rarely provide extra traction, are a problem for puncture repairs and, in the longterm, can unduly stress wheel bearings and suspension components.
(5) Do not fit air-adjustable or gas-filled shock absorbers. The former are an unnecessary complexity that may go wrong and the latter can become too stiff or hard on corrugations causing undue stress on the other parts of the suspension.
(6) Avoid mounting a bull bar, roof bar or crash bar. Not only will it interfere with the designed progressive crumple rate of the front of the vehicle, but it will make panel-beating more difficult and can add unwarranted extra weight to the front suspension, especially if a spare wheel is fitted to it.
(7) Don't hope a strange noise will go away. Stop, locate and fix it. Similarly, do not neglect an oil leak. Constantly check the rear door and engine lid for signs of oil spots. These are blown up onto the back of the vehicle by the suction created at the rear as it travels along. They indicate a serious oil leak.
(8) Do not fit a water tank under the floor. It will soon get smashed to pieces in rough conditions.
(9) Do not 'hot up' the engine with high performance equipment like special carburettors, high-lift camshaft, roller bearings, extractor exhaust, big-bore barrels, etc. They may be good for drag races from the traffic lights but they overstress an engine designed for low stress re-

liability. As such, they are a recipe for disaster. A VW goes better overland in stock standard form.

Buying and Modifying

When buying a new Kombi for overland travel, bear in mind the market where you may eventually sell it. There are many complex and expensive modifications needed to satisfy US specifications (especially for California) or the Australian Design Rules (especially NSW). When ordering, this is also the time to have a variety of other useful optional extras fitted by the factory on the assembly line. Some of these are:

- M 103 Heavy duty shock absorbers
- M 156 Large oil-bath air-cleaner
- M 240 Low compression engine (recessed piston crowns)
- M 089 Laminated windscreen
- M 220 Limited slip differential
- M 513 Protection plate for front of transmission
- M 509 Additional engine compartment dust sealing
- M 203 Ebersbacher auxiliary heater

It would be wise to fit a good set of air horns which you will have to use constantly in countries like India and Pakistan.

It is essential that a second battery be fitted. It does not need to be linked in series with the original battery. Just change batteries around every week or so. Make sure the second battery is securely mounted.

And obviously, select your tyres carefully, and take a good range of spare parts and tools. You will often find that your sanity, if not your life, depends on your ability to get yourself out of trouble.

Off Road Driving

by Jack Jackson

Off road driving techniques vary with the ability and weight of the vehicle, as well as with the driver. Some vehicles have greater capabilities than many drivers can handle and there may often be more than one way of solving a particular problem. So pre-expedition driver training is often worthwhile as a means of educating newcomers to both their own and the vehicle's capabilities.

Alert but restrained driving is essential. A light foot and low gears in four-wheel-drive will usually get one through soft or difficult ground situations. Sometimes sheer speed may be better, but if you lose control at speed you could suffer severe damage or injury. Remember that careful driving in the first instance can save you time, money and effort. Broken chassis, springs and half shafts and burnt out clutches are caused by the driver, not the vehicle.

Before you do any off-road driving, look under your vehicle and note the position of its lowest points; springs, axles, differentials and gearbox. These will often be lower than you think and the differentials are usually off centre. Remember their clearance and position when traversing obstacles which you cannot get around. Do not hook your thumbs around the steering wheel, the sudden twist of the wheel when a front wheel hits a stone or rut can easily break them. If you have a vehicle with non-syncromesh gears, then practice double declutching techniques, so that you can change gear smoothly.

Scouting Ahead

Always travel at a sensible speed, keeping your eyes some twenty yards ahead, watching for difficulties. If you are on a track where it is possible that another vehicle may come the other way, have a passenger keep a look out further ahead whilst you concentrate on negotiating the awkward areas. Travel only at speeds which allow you to stop comfortably within the limit of clear vision. Always travel slowly to the brow of a hump or a sharp bend, there may be a large boulder, hole or sheer drop into a river bed beyond it.

Apart from soft sand, most situations where four-wheel-drive is needed also require low range, which gives you better traction, torque and control. They will normally also require you to stop and inspect the route on foot first, so you will therefore engage low range before starting off again, but on soft sand it is useful to be able to engage low range on the move. On some vehicles this requires plenty of practice of double declutching and the ensuing confidence in being able to achieve this smoothly will usually save you from getting stuck. For most situations, first gear low range is too low, and you might spin the wheels; use second or third gear, except over bad rocks.

When going downhill on a loose surface, it is essential to use four-wheel-drive low range with engine braking. Never touch the brakes or you will lose control.

With full-time four-wheel-drive systems, remember to engage lock before entering difficult situations.

If you have been in four-wheel-drive on a hard surface, when you change back into two-wheel-drive or, in the case of permanent four-wheel-drive systems, you unlock the centre differential lock, you might find this change and the steering difficult. This is due to wind up between the axles, which will scrub tyres and damage the drive train. If you are lightly loaded, you can free this wind up by driving backwards for about ten yards, whilst swinging the steering wheel from side to side. If, on the other hand, you are heavily loaded, you will have to free it by jacking up one front wheel clear of the ground.

Make use of the rhythm of the suspension, touch the brakes lightly as you approach the crest of a hump and release them as you pass over it; this will stop you from flying. When you come to a sharp dip or rut, cross it at an angle, so that only one wheel at a time drops into it. Steer the wheel towards and over the terrain's high points to maintain maximum ground clearance. If you cannot avoid a large or sharp boulder, drive the wheels on one side directly over it rather than trying to straddle it. Do not drive on the outside edge of tracks with a steep drop, they may be undermined by water and collapse under the weight. If you have to travel along deep ruts, try to straddle one of the ruts rather than being in both with your transmission dragging the ground in the centre. Cross narrow river beds at an angle so that you do not get stuck in a dip at 90 degrees with no room left for manoeuvre.

Ground Inspection

When on sand, watch out for any changes in colour. If the surface you are driving on is firm and the colour of the surface remains the same, then the going is likely to be the same. If, however, there is a change in colour you should be prepared for possible softer sand. Moving sand dunes and dry river beds produce the most difficult soft sand.

Keep an eye on previous vehicle tracks, they will give you an indication of trouble spots which you might be able to avoid.

All difficult sections should be inspected on foot first. This can save you a lot of hard work getting unstuck later. If you are not sure of being able to see the route or obstacles clearly from the driving seat, get a passenger to stand in a safe place where he can see the problem clearly and direct you; arrange a clear system of hand signal directions with the person beforehand, as vocal directions can be drowned by engine noise.

Sometimes you might have to build up a route, putting stones or sand ladders across drainage ditches, or weak bridges, or chipping away high corners or levering aside large boulders. If you have to rebuild a track or fill in a hole completely, do so from above, rolling boulders down instead of wasting energy lifting them from below. Where possible bind them together by mixing with tree branches or bushes.

In Third World countries, always inspect local bridges before using them; if there are signs that local vehicles cross the river instead of the bridge, then that is the safest way to go.

Stuck Fast

If you are stuck in a rut on firm ground, try rocking out by quickly shifting from first to reverse gear, but do not try this on sand or mud, as you will only dig in deeper. If you cannot rock out, then jack up the offending wheel and fill up the rut with stones or logs. A high lift jack makes this much easier and can, with care, also be used to shunt the vehicle sideways out of the rut.

If a rock suddenly appears and you cannot stop in time, then hit it square on with a tyre, which is more resilient and more easily repaired than your undercarriage. To traverse large boulders, use first gear low range and crawl over, using the engine for both drive and braking. Avoid slipping the clutch or touching the brakes or you will lose control.

On loose surfaces, do not change gear whilst going up or downhill or you can lose traction. Always change to a lower gear before you reach the problem to remain in control. If you lose traction going up such a hill, try swinging the steering wheel from side to side – you may get a fresh bite and make the top. If you fail going up a steep hill, make a fast change into reverse, make sure you are in four-wheel-drive with the centre differential locked if you have one and use the engine as a brake to back down the same way you came up. Do not try to turn round or go down on the brakes.

Always be prepared to stop quickly on the top of a steep hill or sand dune, the way down the other side may be at a completely different angle. Descend steep hills in low range four-wheel-drive second or third gear, using the engine as a brake. Do not tackle steep hills diagonally; if you lose traction and slip sideways, you may turn over or roll to the bottom. Only cross slopes if absolutely necessary. If you must do so, take the least possible angle and make any turns quickly.

Crossing Water

Before crossing water, stop and inspect it first, if possible by wading through. Is the bottom solid or moving? Are there an large holes caused by previously stuck vehicles, which must be filled in or driven round? Is there a sensible angle into it and out on the other side? Is there a current fast enough to necessitate your aiming upstream to get straight across? How deep it is? Will it come above the exhaust, cooling fan or vehicle floor? Four-wheel-drive vehicles should have poppet valves on the axle breathers, which will keep out water whilst the oils are hot and there is good pressure within, but if you get stuck under water for several hours, the axle oils will need to be changed. Some vehicles have a plug which should be screwed into the clutch housing when much work is done in water, but this should be removed as soon as possible afterwards.

If the water comes above the fan, then the fan belt should be disconnected. If the water comes above the floor, then you should move any articles which could be damaged by it. Petrol engines should have plenty of ignition sealant around the coil, ignition leads and distributor.

Difficult or deep water should be crossed in low range four-wheel-drive, keeping the engine speed high. This keeps enough pressure in the exhaust to stop the back pressure of the water from stalling the engine, whilst the forward speed is not high enough to create a bow wave and spray water over the electrics. Diesel engines are a great advantage here. If you stall in the water, remove the spark plugs or injectors and try driving out in bottom gear on the the starter motor. This works over short distances.

On easy crossings, keep the brakes dry by keeping the left foot lightly on the brake pedal. Once out of any water, dry out the brakes by driving a couple of miles this way. Disc brakes are self-cleaning, but drum brakes fill up with water and sediment, so should be cleaned regularly. Don't forget the transmission brakes on some vehicles.

A vehicle stuck in glacier melt water or sea water for more than a couple of hours will need very thorough washing and several oil changes to get rid of salt and silt. With salt water, electrical connections can be permanently damaged.

Sand

Sandy beaches are usually firm enough for a vehicle between high tide mark and four yards from the sea itself, where there is likely to be an undertow. Beware of the incoming tide, which is often faster than you envisaged and can cut you off from your point of exit. Where there are large puddles or streaming water on a sea beach, beware of quicksand.

The key to soft sand is flotation and steady momentum; any abrupt changes in speed or direction can break through the firmer surface crust, putting the wheels into the softer sand below. Use as high a gear as is possible, so that you do not induce wheelspin. If you do not have special sand tyres, speed up as you approach a soft section and try to maintain an even speed and a straight line as you cross it. If you find yourself sticking, press down gently on the accelerator; if you have to change down, you must do it very smoothly to avoid wheelspin. In large soft sand areas, use flotation tyres and/or reduced tyre pressure (*see section on Tyres in Expedition Vehicles, page 141*) and drive slowly in four-wheel-drive.

Do not travel in other people's tracks, the crust has already been broken and your vehicle's undercarriage will be that much lower, and therefore nearer to sticking to start with. Keeping your eye on other people's tracks will warn you of soft sections, but do not follow them for navigation, as they may be 50 years old.

In general, flat sand with pebbles or grass on its surface, or obvious wind-blown corrugations, will support a vehicle. If in doubt, get out and walk the section first. Stamp your feet; if you get a firm footprint then it should support your vehicle, but if you get a vague oval, then it is too soft. If the soft section is short, you can make a track with sand ladders, but if it is long, then low tyre pressures and low range four-wheel-drive will be needed. Bedford four ton trucks will not handle soft sand without the assistance of sand mats and lots of human pushing power.

Dry river beds can be very soft and difficult to get out of. Drift sand will always be soft. If you wish to stop voluntarily on soft sand, find a place on top of a rise, preferably pointing downhill and roll to a stop instead of using the brakes and breaking the crust.

Many vehicles have too much weight on the rear wheels when loaded and these wheels often break through and dig in, leaving the front wheels spinning uselessly on the surface. A couple of passengers sitting on the bonnet can help for short bad sections, but you must not overload the front continuously or you will damage the front axle.

Sand dunes need proper high flotation sand tyres; you need speed to get up a dune, but must be able to stop on the top, as there may be a sheer drop on the other side. Dunes are best climbed where the angle is least, so known routes, in opposing directions are usually many miles apart, to make use of the easiest angles. In the late afternoon, when the sun is low, it is difficult to spot sudden changes in dune strata and many accidents occur with vehicles flying off the end of steep drops, so do not travel at this time of day. Most deserts freeze overnight in the winter months, making the surface crust much firmer. Even if they do not freeze, there is always some dew in the surface crust, making it firmest around dawn, so this is the time to tackle the softest sections. Local drivers often travel at night, but unless you know the route really well this will be too dangerous, so start at dawn and then camp around mid-afternoon before the light gets too difficult and the sand is at its softest.

In large sand dune areas when travelling longitudinally stay as high up the dunes as possible, then if you feel your vehicle begin to stick, you can gain momentum by aiming downhill and try again. The bottom of the well between the dunes usually has the softest sand.

Getting Unstuck in Sand

Once you are stuck in sand, do not spin the wheels or try to rock out as you will only go in deeper and may damage the transmission. First unload the passengers and with them pushing try to reverse out in low range. The torque on the propellor shafts tends to tilt the front and rear axles in opposite directions relative to the chassis. So, if you have not dug in too deep, when you engage reverse, you tend to tilt the axles in the opposite direction, thus getting traction on the wheels that lost it before. If you stopped soon enough in the first place, then this technique will get you out; if it does not, then the only answer is to start digging and use sand ladders. It is tempting to do only half of the digging required, but this usually fails and you end up working twice as hard in the end. Self recovery with a winch does not work well either. Sand deserts do not abound with trees and burying the spare wheel or a stake deep enough to winch you out is as hard as digging the vehicle out in the first place. A second vehicle on firm ground with a winch or tow rope can help, but you will have to dig out the stuck vehicle first, so get down to it and dig.

Long handled shovels are best – you have to get right under the diffs and small shovels and folding tools are useless. Recce the area and decide whether the vehicle must come out forwards or backwards. Dig the sand clear of all points which are touching it, dig the wheels clear and then dig a sloping ramp from all wheels to the surface in the intended direction of travel. Lay down sand ladders in the ramp's back wheels only if things are not too bad, all four wheels if things are very bad. Push the ends of the ladders under the wheels as far as possible so that they do not shoot out. A high lift jack can help here. If you are using sand ladders as opposed to perforated steel plates, then mark their position in the sand with upright shovels as they often disappear in use and can be hard to find later. Then with only the driver in the vehicle and all passengers pushing, the vehicle should come out using low range. If the passengers are very fit, they can dig up the sand ladders quickly and keep placing them under the wheels of the moving vehicle. Sometimes, when a ladder is not properly under a wheel when the vehicle first mounts it, it can pop up and damage a body panel or exhaust pipe, so an agile person has to keep a foot on the free end to keep it down. Remember to move very quickly once things are safe, though, or you'll get run over!

Bringing the vehicle out backwards is usually the shortest way to reach firm ground, but you still have to get across or around the bad section. Once out, the driver should not stop again until he has reached firm ground, so the passengers may have a long, hot walk carrying the sand ladders and shovels. With a large convoy, a ramp of several ladders can be made up on bad sections and all hands should help.

Vehicles of one ton or under need only carry lightweight sand ladders. They should be just long enough to fit comfortably between the wheel base. One vehicle alone needs to carry four, but vehicles in convoy need only carry two each, as they can help each other out. Heavier vehicles need to carry heavy perforated steel plate. It is silly to weigh down lightweight vehicles with this, as one often sees in Africa.

Sand ladders and perforated steel plate bend in use, so when you have finished all the soft sand sections, lay them on hard ground with the ends on the ground and the bend in the air and drive over them to straighten them out.

Salt Flats (*Sebkhas, Chotts*) are like quick sand, you sink fast and if you cannot be towed out quickly, it can be permanent. In areas known for their salt flats, stick to the track and preferably convoy with another four-wheel-drive vehicle. If you are unlucky enough to hit one, try to drive back to firm ground in a wide arc. Do not stop and try to reverse.

Dirt Roads

On dirt roads, watch out for stones thrown up by other vehicles (and in some countries, small boys), which break your windscreen. Do not overtake when you cannot see through the dust of the vehicle ahead, there may be something coming the other way. Use the horn to warn vehicles that you are about to overtake. If you cannot overtake, drop back clear of the other vehicle's dust. On dirt roads, culverts do not always extend to the full width of the road, so watch out for these when overtaking and be especially careful of this in snow.

Avoid driving at night; potholes, culverts, broken down trucks, bullock carts and people are hard to see and many trucks drive at speed without lights and then blind you with full beam on spotting you. In many countries, there are unlit chains and logs across the roads at night as checkpoints.

Corrugations are parallel ridges across ungraded roads caused by the return spring rates of heavy traffic and, in really bad conditions, can be up to ten inches deep. They give an effect similar to sitting on a pneumatic drill to both the vehicle and its occupants. Heavy vehicles have no choice but to travel slowly, but lightweight vehicles often 'iron' out the bumps by finding the right speed to skim over the top of the ruts. This is usually 30–40mph, any faster can be dangerous. Going fast over corrugations increases tyre temperatures, thus causing more punctures. Softly sprung vehicles such as the Range Rover, Toyota Land Cruiser and American four-wheel-drives can go faster more comfortably on corrugations, often blowing tyres and, as a consequence, turning over under these conditions, usually with fatal consequences. Short wheel base (i.e. less than 100 inches) vehicles are very unstable on corrugations and often spin and turn over. The only sensible answer is to travel at a reasonable speed, make regular stops to ease your growing frustration and be extra vigilant for punctures. One is often tempted to try travelling beside the corrugations, but remember that thousands of other vehicles have tried that before and given up – hence the corrugations. So take it steady and try to be patient.

Third World ferries should be embarked and disembarked in four-wheel-drive.

Mud

Momentum is also the key to getting through mud, but there are likely to be more unseen problems underneath the mud, than in sand. If it is not too deep, the wheels might find traction on firm ground beneath, so if there are existing tracks and they are not deep enough to ground your transmission in the centre, then such tracks are worth using. Otherwise, slog through in as high a gear as possible, as you would with sand, avoiding any sudden changes of speed or direction.

If the mud is heavy with clay, even aggressive tread tyres will soon clog up, so unless you are using self-cleaning mud tyres such as dumper tyres, or terra tyres, then you will gain a lot by fitting chains.

Muddy areas are likely to be near trees, one of the few areas where a winch is useful.

If you stick badly, digging out can be very heavy work. It is best to jack up the vehicle and fill in the holes under the wheels with stones, logs or bushes; a high lift jack can make things much easier here, but be careful of it slipping. if there is a lot of water, dig a channel to drain it away. Perforated steel plate can be useful in mud, but sand ladders become too slippery.

When you get back on the paved road, clear as much mud as possible off the wheels and propeller shafts, or the extra weight will put them out of balance and cause damage. Drive steadily for several miles to clear the tyre treads or you could skid.

If you are unlucky, you might get the centre of the vehicle's undercarriage stuck on rocks or a tree stump. The answer to this is to jack up one side of the vehicle and build a ramp under the wheels. If you cannot go forwards or backwards, unload the vehicle and use a high lift jack to lever the front and rear ends sideways, one end at a time. This is done by jacking up the vehicle at the centre of the front or rear bumper or chassis and then pushing it sideways off the jack. Beware of injury to yourself and check that the vehicle will not land in an even worse position before you do it.

Snow and Ice

Snow is the most deceptive surface to drive on because it does not always conform with the terrain it covers. If there is a road or track, stay in the middle of it to avoid sliding into ditches or culverts at the side. Drive slowly in four-wheel-drive, in as high a gear as is possible and avoid any sudden changes in speed or direction. Use the engine for braking. If you have to use the brakes, give several short pumps to avoid the wheels locking.

Snow chains are better than studded tyres for off road use and should be either on all four wheels, or on the rear wheels only. Having chains on the front wheels will only put you into a spin if you touch the brakes going downhill. If the vehicle is empty, put a couple of hundredweight sacks of sand over the rear axle. Chains on all four wheels are the only sensible answer to large areas of ice.

If you drive into a drift, you will have to dig out and it is easiest to come out backwards. Off road driving in snow will be easier at night, or in the early morning, when the snow is firmest and the mud below it frozen. As with sand, high flotation tyres are an advantage. If they are fitted with chains, they should be at the correct pressures, not at low pressure or the chains will damage them. Carry a good sleeping bag in case you get stuck and have a long wait for help. Use only the strongest heavyweight chains; having to mend broken chains in freezing conditions is not a pleasant experience. If you start to spin, do not touch the brakes; depress the clutch, then, with all four wheels rolling free, you will regain the steering.

In very cold conditions, if you have a diesel engine, dilute the diesel fuel with one part petrol to fifteen parts diesel to stop it freezing up (use one to ten for arctic temperatures).

Convoy Driving

When travelling in convoy, it is best for the vehicles to be well spread out so that each has room to manoeuvre, does not get into other vehicles' dust, and has room to stop on firm ground should one or more vehicles get stuck. It is good to use a system where any vehicle which gets stuck, or needs help, switches its headlights onto mainbeam. This is particularly important in desert situations. All drivers should keep an eye out for headlights in their mirrors, as these can usually be seen when the vehicle cannot. If the vehicle ahead of you is stuck, you will see when you catch it up anyway. Thus if someone is stuck, other vehicles stop where possible and return to help; on foot, if necessary, in soft sand. In a convoy situation, the rear vehicle should have a good mechanic and a good spare wheel and tyre, in case of breakdown.

Drivers should keep to the allotted convoy order to avoid confusion and unnecessary searches. In difficult terrain, the convoy leader should make stops at regular intervals to check that all is well with the other vehicles.

Running Repairs

by Jack Jackson

Before you go, use your vehicle for several months to run in any new parts properly, enable you to find any weaknesses and become acquainted with its handling and maintenance. Give it a thorough overhaul before leaving. If you fit any extras, make sure that they are as strong as the original vehicle. For accurate navigation, you should know how accurate your odometer is for the tyres fitted. Larger tyres, e.g. sand tyres, will have a longer rolling circumference.

Once in the field, check the chassis, springs, spring shackles and bushes, steering, bodywork, exhaust and tyres every evening when you stop for the day. Every morning when it is cool, check engine oil, battery electrolyte, tyre pressures, cooling water and fill the fuel tank. Check transmission oils and hydraulic fluids at least every third day. In dusty areas, keep breather vents clear on the axle and gearbox. Keep an eye on electrical cables for worn insulation, which could lead to a fire. Make sure that you carry and use the correct oils and fluids in all cases. Deionizing water crystals are easier to carry than distilled water for the battery. Remember to oil door hinges, door locks, padlocks etc. and remember that in many deserts you need antifreeze in the engine for night temperatures. Brush all parts clear of sand or dust before working on them. Have a tarpaulin to lie on and keep things clean when working under the vehicle. Clear goggles will keep the dirt out of your eyes. A small vice fitted to a strong part of the vehicle will aid many repairs. In scrub or insect country you will need to brush down the radiation mesh regularly.

Overturned Vehicles

Short wheel base vehicles have a habit of breaking away or spinning on bends and corrugations, often turning over in the process, so drive these vehicles with extra care. Given the nature of the terrain they cover, overturned vehicles are not unusual on expeditions. Usually it happens at such a slow speed that no one is injured nor even windows broken. First make sure the engine is stopped and battery disconnected. Check for human injury, then completely unload the vehicle. Once unloaded, vehicles can usually be uprighted easily using manpower, though a second vehicle and/or winch can make things easier in the right conditions. Once the vehicle is righted, check for damage, sort out all oil levels and spilt battery acid and then turn the engine over several times without the plugs or injectors in to clear the bores, before running the engine again.

Punctures

Punctures are the most common problem in off road travel. Rear wheel punctures often destroy the inner tube, so several spare inner tubes should be carried. Wherever possible, I prefer to repair punctures with a known good tube and get the punctured one vulcanized properly when I next visit a larger town, but you should always carry a repair kit in case you use up all your inner tubes. Hot patch repair kits do not work well enough on truck inner tubes. Michelin radial tyres have the advantage that their beads almost fall off the wheel rim when flat. If you cannot break a bead, try driving over it or using a jack and the weight of the vehicle. If the wheel has the rim on one side wider than the other, only attempt to remove the tyre over the narrowest side, starting with both beads in the well of the wheel; narrow tyre levers are more efficient than wide ones. Sweep out all sand and grit, file off any sharp burrs on the wheel and put everything back together on a ground sheet to stop any sand or grit getting in to cause further punctures.

When refitting the tyre, use liquid soap and water or bead lubricant and a Schrader valve tool to hold the inner tube valve in place. Pump the tyre up enough to refit the bead on the rim, then let it down again to release any twists in the inner tube. Then pump the tyre up again to full rear tyre pressure. If the wheel has to be fitted on the front at a later date, it is easy to let some air out.

Foot pumps have a short life in sand and are hard work. If your vehicle does not already have a compressor, then use a spark plug fitting pump if you have a petrol engine, or an electric pump if you have a diesel engine. Keep all pumps clear of sand. When using electric pumps, keep the engine running at charging speed.

Damaged steel braced radial tyres often have a sharp end of wire internally, causing further punctures. These should be cut down as short as is possible and the tyre then gaitered, using thicker truck inner tubes. The edges of the gaiter need to be bevelled and the tyre must be at full pressure to stop the gaiter from moving about. On paved road, gaitered tyres behave like a buckled wheel, so they are dangerous. Most truck tyres, including Michelin XZY, can be legally recut when worn, and the re-cuts are useful to use on sharp stones where tyres cut up easily.

Wheelbraces get overworked in off-road use, so have a good socket or ring spanner available, to fit the wheel nuts.

In soft sand, use a strong one-foot-square metal or wooden plate under the jack, when jacking up the vehicle. Two jacks, preferably including a high lift jack, are often necessary in off road conditions.

With a hot wheel after a puncture, you may need an extension tube on the wheel brace to undo the wheel nuts, but do not retighten them this way or you will cause damage.

Fuel Problems

Bad fuel is common; extra fuel filters are useful for everyone and essential for diesel engines. The main problems are water and sediment. When things get bad, it is quicker in the long run to drain the fuel tank, decant the fuel and clean it out. Alway keep the wire mesh filter in the fuel filler in place. Do not let the fuel tank level fall too low as this will produce water and sediment in the fuel lines. With a diesel engine, you may then have to bleed the system. If fuelling up from 40 gallon drums, give them time to settle and leave the bottom inch, which will often be water and grit. If you have petrol in jerry cans in a hot, dry country, always earth them to discharge any static electricity, before opening. Fuel starvation is often caused by dust blocking the breather hole in the fuel tank filler cap. Electric fuel pumps are very unreliable; carry a complete spare. For mechanical fuel pumps, carry a reconditioning kit. In hot countries or in low gear at altitude, mechanical fuel pumps on petrol engines often get hot and cause vapour lock. Wrap the pump in bandages and pour water on it to cool it down. If this is a constant problem, fit a plastic pipe from the windscreen washer system to the bandaged fuel pump and squirt it regularly.

Low pressure fuel pipes can be repaired using epoxy resin glues, bound by self-vulcanizing rubber tape. High-pressure injector pipes need to be braised or completely replaced. Carry spares of these and spare injectors. Diesel engine problems are usually fuel or water, and you should know how to bleed the system correctly. If this fails to correct the problem, check all pipes and joints, fuel pump and filter seals for leaks. Hair line cracks in the high pressure injector pipes are hardest to find. Fuel tank leaks repair best with glass reinforced fibre kits.

Electrical Problems

These are another constant problem. With petrol engines, it is well worth changing the ignition system to electronic systems without contacts. Carry a spare distributor cap, rotor arm, plugs, points, condenser and coil – all tend to break up or short out in hot countries. Replace modern high-tension leads with the older copper wire type and carry a spare set. Keep a constant check on plugs and points. If you are losing power, first check the gap and wear on the points. Spray all ignition parts with sealer to keep out dust and water. Keep battery connections tight, clean and greased. Replace the battery slip-on connections with the older clamp-on type. Keep battery plates covered with electrolyte, top up only with distilled water or deionized water. Batteries are best checked with a battery hydrometer. There are special instruments for checking the modern sealed-for-life batteries.

Alternators and batteries should be disconnected before any arc welding is done on the vehicle. Never run the engine with the alternator or battery disconnected. Alternators are not as reliable as they should be; if the diodes are separate, carry spares, if not carry a complete spare alternator. Always carry a spare voltage regulator. On some vehicles the red charging warning light on the dash board is part of the circuit, so carry spare bulbs for all lights. Make sure you carry spare fuses and fan belts.

Arctic temperatures are a very specialist situation. Vehicles are stored overnight in heated hangars. When in the field, engines are either left running or else have an electric engine heater, which is plugged into a mains power supply. Oils are either specialist or diluted to the makers' recommendations. Petrol is the preferred fuel for lighter vehicles, but for heavier uses, diesel vehicles have heaters built into the fuel tank and the fuel is diluted with petrol. All fuel is scrupulously inspected for water before being used. Batteries must be in tip-top condition, as they lose efficiency when cold.

General Problems and Improvisations

Steering locks are best removed; if not leave the key in them permanently in dusty areas. A spare set of keys should be hidden safely somewhere under the body or the chassis.

When replacing wheel hub bearing oil seals, it pays to replace the metal mating piece also.

Wire hose clips are best replaced with flat metal Jubilee type clips; carry spare hoses. Hoses can be repaired in an emergency with self-vulcanizing rubber tape. Heater hoses can be blocked with a spark plug.

Bad radiator leaks can be sealed with epoxy resin or glass reinforced fibre. For small leaks, add some Rad-weld, porridge or raw egg to the radiator water. Always use a torque wrench on aluminium cylinder heads or other aluminium components.

In sand, always work on a ground sheet and don't put parts down in the sand. In sand storm areas, make a protected working area around the vehicle using tarpaulins.

Clean the threads of nuts and bolts with a wire brush before trying to remove them.

If you get wheel shimmy on returning to paved roads, first check for mud, buckled wheels, gaitered tyres and loose wheel bearings. If it is none of these, check the swivel pins, which can usually be dampened by removing shims. Carry any spare parts containing rubber well away from heat.

If you cannot get into gear, first check for stones caught up in the linkage.

If you use jerry cans, carry spare rubber seals. Always carry water in light-proof cans to stop the growth of algae.

Lengths of strong chain with long bolts plus wood, or tyre levers can be used as splints on broken chassis parts, axles or leaf springs.

If you do not have a differential lock, and need one in an emergency, you can lock the spinning wheel by tightening up the brake adjuster cam, but only use this system for a few yards at a time.

For emergency fuel tanks, use a jerry can on the roof, with a hose connected to the fuel lift pump. Drive slowly and never let the can get lower than half full.

If one vehicle in a convoy has a defunct charging system, swap that vehicle's battery every 100 kilometres.

For repair work at night, or camp illumination, small fluorescent lights have the least drain on the battery.

If the engine is overheating, it will cool down quickest going downhill in gear using the running engine as a brake. If you stop with a hot engine then, unless it is showing signs of seizure, keep the engine ticking over fast; this will cool it down quicker and more evenly than if you stop it.

With oil bath type air cleaners, make sure that there are not any pin holes in the rubber connecting hose between the air cleaner and the engine inlet manifold.

Roof-mounted air inlet pipes are best avoided as they tend to break if on corrugations.

If you have a partially seized engine, a six-cylinder engine can be run on four cylinders and a four-cylinder engine on three in a real emergency. To isolate a cylinder, remove the piston and connecting rod, disconnect the spark plug and high tension lead (or the injector if diesel). Close the valves by removing the push rods or rocker arms if overhead cam. If diesel, feed the fuel from the disconnected fuel injector pipe to a safe place away from the heat of the engine. Drive slowly. If you have a hole in the block, seal it with any sheet metal plus glass reinforced plastic and self-tapping screws, to keep out dust or sand.

In an emergency, you can run a diesel engine on kerosene (paraffin) or domestic heating oil, by adding one part of engine oil to 100 parts of the fuel, to lubricate the injector pump. In hot climates, diesel engine oils are good for use in petrol engines, but petrol engine oils should not be used for diesel engines.

Bent track rods should be hammered back as straight as possible to minimize tyre scrubbing and the possibility of a roll.

If you break a rear half shaft, you can continue in two-wheel-drive by removing both rear half shafts and putting the vehicle into four-wheel-drive. If the rear differential is broken, remove both rear half shafts and the rear propeller shaft and engage four-wheel-drive. If a permanent four-wheel-drive jams in the centre differential lock position, remove the front propeller shaft and drive on slowly.

Temporary drain or filler plugs can be whittled from wood and sealed in with epoxy resin.

Silicon RTV compound can be used for most gaskets, other than cylinder head gaskets. Silicone RTV compound or PTFE tape are useful when putting together leaking fuel line connections.

Paper gaskets can be reused if covered in grease.

If you develop a hydraulic brake fluid leak and do not have spare, travel on slowly, using the engine as a brake. If the leak is really bad, you can disconnect a metal pipe upstream of the leak, bend it over and hammer the end flat, or fit an old pipe to which this has already been done. Rubber hoses can be clamped, using a round bar to minimize damage. If you have a dual system, then the brakes will still work as normal, but if not, you will have uneven braking on only three wheels. When replacing brake pipes, copper ones are more easy to work with.

If you lose your clutch you can still change gear, by adjusting the engine speed, as with double declutching. It is best to start the engine with it already in second gear.

Four-wheel-drive vehicles are high off the ground and it is often easier to work on the engine if you put the spare wheel on the ground and stand on it. If your bonnet can be hinged right back, tie it back so that the wind does not drop it on your head.

Steering relays which do not have a filler point can be topped up by removing two opposite top cover bolts and filling through one till oil comes out of the other.

If you burst an oil gauge pressure pipe, remove the T piece, remove the electric pressure sender from it and screw this back into the block. You will then still have the electric low pressure warning light.

Motor Manufacturers' Concessionaires and Agents

by Colin McElduff

Motor manufacturers have concessionaires and agents throughout the world who are responsible for the importation of vehicles, availability of services and spares etc. Once you decided on the vehicle to use you should, therefore, approach its manufacturer for a list of concessionaires and agents in the countries you are visting, so that you are able to evaluate its spares potential.

Today, motor manufacturers are constantly reviewing their viability in terms of production and sales. The effect on universal availability of spares is, however, long term, so the transcontinental motorist derives little immediate benefit. Nevertheless, there is the possibility that the spares of one manufacturer's vehicle will be suitable for another and a careful study of the subject is always worthwhile.

Whatever you do, choose a vehicle with a good spares potential, for it is inevitable that you will be faced with a breakdown at some stage of your journey. Be prepared by finding out your vehicle's weak points and use this as a basis for the spares to be taken, for you must not rely too much on being able to obtain them en route. When it comes to the crunch, the factors concerning spares availability may be divided into three – the assumed, the known and the unknown.

It is therefore unwise to assume, because you have a list of the vehicle's concessionaires and agents that the spares you require will be readily available. They never are, for some of the countries you are visiting may have broken off old ties and now no longer enjoy the expertise and use of equipment so provided in the past. This is often the case in Third World countries. Sometimes the cause of shortages may be the country's balance of payments problem, at other times, just downright political instability.

A great deal is known. To reiterate, check out the manufacturer of your vehicle and obtain a family tree of its affiliations, so that you will have some idea where to direct your search should the need arise. For example, vehicles produced by Vauxhall and Opel have parts common to each other, as also do Ford (UK) and Taunus (Germany) together with Saab, whose V4 engine is used in some Ford models. British Leyland and Innocenti (Italy) also have an affiliation and Honda have joined them to produce certain models. Talbot (UK) and Talbot/Simca (France) are similarly affiliated. Polski Fiat and Lada produce models based on the Fiat design. Because of the intricate spider's web representing connections between manufacturers, it would be confusing to expand on this here, but look into it for your own vehicle.

As always, the unknown is legion, but when in doubt, apply logic. Ask yourself how a local would approach your situation where, for instance, there is little hope of obtaining that urgently needed spare part? The answer? He will cannibalise, and is an expert in doing so. The 'bush mechanic' exists by virtue of his resourcefulness and his ability to adapt under any conditions. He may not know what a concessionaire is, but he does know, as John Steele Gordon puts it in *Overlanding*, how to make the 'radiator hose of a 1953 Chevrolet serve as an exhaust pipe for a 1973 Volkswagen and vice versa'.

Motorists' Checklist

by Jack Jackson

If you are an experienced off-road motorist and vehicle camper, you are, without doubt, the best person to decide exactly what you need to do and take for your trip. Still, even extensive experience doesn't guarantee perfect recall and everyone might find it useful to jog their memories by consulting other people's lists.

These lists do assume some experience – for without some mechanical expertise, for example, an immaculately stocked toolbox is of limited use. It is also assumed that the motorist in question will spend at least some time driving off-road, most probably in a four-wheel-drive vehicle.

Vehicle Spares and Tools

Petrol Engines

3 fan belts
1 complete set of gaskets
4 oil filters (change every 5,000km)
2 tubes of Silicone RTV gasket compound
1 complete set of radiator hoses
2 metres of spare heater hose
2 metres of spare fuel pipe hose
½ metre of spare distributor vacuum pipe hose
2 exhaust valves
1 inlet valve
1 valve spring
Fine and coarse valve grinding paste and valve grinding tool
1 valve spring compressor
1 fuel pump repair kit (if electric type, take a complete spare pump)
1 water pump repair kit

1 carburettor overhaul kit
2 sets of spark plugs
1 timing light or 12 volt bulb and holder with leads
3 sets of contact breaker points (preferably with hard fibre cam follower because plastic types wear fast and close up in the heat)
2 rotor arms
1 condenser
1 spark plug spanner
1 distributor cap
1 set of high tension leads (older wire type)
1 ignition coil
Slip ring and brushes for alternator or complete spare alternator
If you have a dynamo, carry spare brushes
2 cans of spray type ignition sealer for dusty and wet conditions
2 spare air intake filters if you do not have the oil-bath type

Extras for Diesel Engines

Delete spark plugs, contact breaker points, rotor arms, distributor cap, high tension leads and coil from the above and substitute:

1 spare set of injectors plus cleaning kit
1 complete set of injector pipes
1 set injector seating washers
1 set injector return pipe washers
1 metre plastic fuel pipe plus spare nuts and ferrules
A second in-line fuel filter
4 fuel filter elements
3 spare heater plugs if fitted

Brakes and Clutch

2 wheel cylinder kits (one right and one left)
1 flexible brake hose
1 brake bleeding kit (or fit automatic valves)
1 brake master cylinder seals kit
1 clutch master cylinder seals kit
1 clutch slave cylinder kit
(It is important to keep all these kits away from heat)
1 clutch plate
If you have an automatic gearbox, make sure you have plenty of the special fluid for this and and a spare starter motor.
If you have power steering, carry the correct fluid and spare hoses.

General Spares

2 warning triangles (compulsory in most countries)
1 good workshop manual (not the car handbook)
1 good torch or, better still, fluorescent light with leads to work from vehicle battery, plus spare bulbs or tubes
1 extra tyre in addition to the spare wheel, making two spares in all
One spare wheel only will be necessary if two identical vehicles are travelling together
3 extra inner tubes
1 large inner tube repair kit
1 Schrader spark plug fitting tyre pump if you have a petrol engine or 1 Schrader model 202 12 volt electric tyre pump if you have a diesel engine
Plenty of good quality engine oil plus
2 litres of distilled water or 1 bottle of water deionizing crystals
12 volt soldering iron and solder
Hand drill and drills
16 metres of nylon or terylene tow rope strong enough to upright an overturned vehicle
1 set of tyre levers and 1kg sledge hammer for tyres
5 spare inner tube valve cores and 2 valve core tools

1 good jack and wheel brace (if hydraulic, carry spare fluid)
1 (at least) metal fuel can e.g. jerry can
1 grease gun and a tin of multipurpose grease
1 gallon (4.5 litres) of correct differential and gearbox oil
1 large fire extinguisher suitable for petrol and electrical fires
4 inner tube valve dust caps (metal type)
1 reel of self-amalgamating rubber tape for leaking hoses
1 pair heavy duty electric jump leads at least 3 metres long
10 push fit electrical connectors (or type to suit vehicle)
2 universal joints for prop shafts
½ litre can of brake and clutch fluid
1 small can of general light oil for hinges, door locks, etc.
1 large can WD40
1 starting handle, if available
2 complete sets of spare keys kept in different places
1 small Isopon or fibre glass kit for repairing fuel tank and body holes
2 kits of general adhesive, e.g. Bostik or Araldite Rapid
1 tin of hand cleaner (washing up liquid will do in an emergency)
Spare fuses and bulbs for all lights including those on the dash panel which are often part of the charging circuit
1 radiator cap
Antifreeze if route passes through cold areas
Spare windscreen wipers for use on return journey (keep away from heat)
Inner and outer wheel bearings
A good tool kit containing:
Wire brush to clean dirty threads plus large and small flat and round files
Socket set
Torque wrench
Ring and open ended spanners
Hacksaw and spare blades
Selection of spare nuts, bolts and washers of type and thread to fit vehicle
30cm Stillson pipe wrench
1 box spanner for large wheel bearing lock nuts
Hammer
Large and small cold chisels for large and stubborn nuts
Self-grip wrench
Broad and thin nosed pliers
Circlip pliers
Insulating tape
3 metres electrical wire (vehicle type not mains)
1 set of feeler gauges
Small adjustable wrench
Tube of gasket cement, e.g. Red Hermetite
Tube Loctite thread sealer
Large and small slot head and Phillips head screwdrivers
Accurate tyre pressure gauge
Hardwood or steel plate to support the jack on soft ground

Extra for off-road use
1 pair of 1½ metre sand ladders
3 wheel bearing hub oil seals
1 rear gearbox oil seal
1 rear differential oil seal
1 rear spring main leaf complete with bushes
1 front spring main leaf complete with bushes
4 spare spring bushes
4 spring centre bolts
1 set (=4) of spring shackle plates
1 set (=4) of spring shackle pins
If you have coil springs, carry one spare, plus 2 spare mountings and 4 bushes

1 set of shock absorber mounting rubbers
2 spare engine mountings
1 spare gearbox mounting
2 door hinge pins
1 screw jack (to use on its side when changing springs and/or bushes)
2 metre length of strong chain and bolts to fit it for splinting broken chassis axle or spring parts
Snow chains for rear wheels if you expect a lot of mud or snow
5cm paint brush to dust off the engine so that you can work on it
Large groundsheet for lying on when working under the vehicle or repairing tyres, so as to prevent sand from getting between the inner tube and the tyre
1 high lift jack in case of bogging
2 small shovels for digging out
2 stearing ball joints
2 rear axle U bolts
1 front axle U bolt
2 spare padlocks
Radiator stop leak compound (porridge will do in emergency)

Specific to Series IIA Land Rovers
1 set rear axle half shafts – heavy duty

Specific to Series III Land Rovers
1 complete gear change lever if you have welded bush type (or replace with groove and rubber ring type)
4 nylon bonnet hinge inserts (or 2 homemade aluminium ones)
2 windscreen outer hinge bolts (No. 346984)
2 windscreen inner tie bolts
2 rear differential drain plugs
1 set big end nuts
1 rear axle drive plate
2 radiator caps

Maintenance Check Before Departure

1. Change oil and oil filter
2. Clean air filter and change oil bath
3. Lube driveshafts, winch, speedometer cable
4. Lube all locks with dry graphite; adjust and lube all doors
5. Clean or replace all fuel filters
6. Inspect undercarriage for fluid leaks, loose bolts etc.
7. Rotate all five tyres inspecting for cuts and wear
8. Adjust brakes if needed
9. Check adjustment of carburettor
10. Check fanbelts and accessory belts
11. Check sparkplugs. Clean and regap if needed (replace as necessary)
12. Check ignition timing
13. Check and top up:
    front and rear differentials
    swivel-pin housings
    transmission
    transfer case
    overdrive (if applicable)
    steering box
    battery
    battery and clutch fluid
    cooling system
    crankcase
14. Check that there are no rattles
15. Inspect radiator and heater hoses
16. Check breather vents on both axles
17. Check all lights
18. Check wheel balance and front end alignment and always do so with new tyres and wheels

Some Useful Tips

Here are some ideas for off-road driving, whether for weekenders or for long haul expeditioners in remote regions:

1. If you're trying to attract the attention of rescuers and have no flares, try setting fire to the spare tyre with petrol. But remember that unless a friend is expecting you, no one is likely to come looking for you in the middle of nowhere. So always make sure that there's someone who'll come to look for you if you haven't reported by a certain date. Do not leave the immediate area of the vehicle.
2. Air conditioning causes radiator water temperature to rise. One way to create the opposite effect if radiator temperature is getting too high is to turn on the heating – not very pleasant in tropical heat, but it may save your engine from blowing.
3. If you deflate the tyres for off-road driving, remember to reflate them again when you return to the highway. Don't deflate tyres too much off-road if the vehicle is heavy.
4. You should know the maximum weight supportable by each wheel at maximum tyre pressure. You should inflate the tyres below the maximum tyre pressure unless GVW is close to tyre maximum. The tyre manufacturer should supply a chart showing optimum pressure for different loads on different terrains (usually limited to on/off road).
5. Never drive a deflated tyre over sharp rocks.
6. To get the correct tyre pressure, measure pressure when the tyres are cold before use.
7. Remember that the weight of one imperial gallon of petrol is around 4kg and the weight of one imperial gallon of water is around 4.5kg. These figures are extremely important on a long trip when it comes to calculating GVW without the help of a truck weighing scale. An imperial gallon is about 25 per cent greater in volume than a US gallon.
8. If your radiator is gathering a lot of insects, you'll help cooling by cleaning them off from time to time. You'll help keep temperature down by not mounting spare tyres, jerry cans and other pieces of equpment in front of the radiator grille.
9. Don't mix two different types of engine oil if you can help it.
10. When filling up with engine oil, bring the level up to halfway between the high and low marks on the dip-stick and no further.
11. Rotate your five tyres every 6,500km (8,000km for radials, which should only be changed front to rear and vice versa on the same side).
12. For accurate positioning, always take compass readings well away from the vehicle to avoid distortion by the vehicle's magnetic field.
13. Try to get clearly written guarantees with everything you buy for your travel needs and return warranty card to the manufacturers for registration.

Quenching Your Vehicle's Thirst

Some Notes on Petrol and Diesel

1. The Land Rover has been available for many years in petrol and diesel versions.

2. In the USA, they are developing more and more diesel vehicles.
3. Diesel is usually easier to come by than petrol since all trucks and tractors use it.
4. In some areas, e.g. the Sahara, supply difficulties can cause shortages of both diesel and petrol, though petrol supply often suffers less.
5. The main advantages of diesel are: lower fire risk (very important), no electrical ignition to malfunction where there is a lot of dust or water, better torque at low revolutions, and it is more economical. Since diesel gives more km to the litre than petrol you need to carry less and so there is also a weight saving. Diesel fuel is usually cheaper than petrol: in the Third World, it only costs one third as much as petrol.
6. Diesel makes for a noisy engine – bad for morale on a long, tiring trip.
7. In countries where fuel is imported, costs of petrol and oil are usually higher than in countries that have their own and are oil exporters.
8. Petrol is most expensive in Europe. In Asia, costs are lower, partly because some Asian countries are self-sufficient in petroleum. In the oil-producing countries of North and West Africa, prices are quite low; elsewhere in Africa, they are somewhat higher, about on a par with Asian prices i.e. 50–80 per cent of European prices. In Latin America, petrol costs roughly half as much as in Europe.
9. In certain European and North African countries (consulates or tourist offices will advise which), heavy taxes are imposed on fuel in order to restrict domestic consumption. At the same time, the governments wish to encourage tourism. So tourists are offered petrol coupons to be used instead of or as well as money in paying for petrol.

Below Deck: Shipping a Vehicle

by Simon Glen, with contributions on motorcycles from Paul Pratt

On protracted around-the-world overland journeys, the biggest single expense and headache is likely to be the shipment of your vehicle.

The astronomical costs are the most daunting part. However, the alternative of selling your vehicle at the end of one transcontinental section and buying another at the start of the next could be far more expensive and fraught with even more problems: shipping your personal effects, the sale of your vehicle and buying another one, *carnet* rules, and fitting out a new vehicle in a strange country. Sometimes this policy may pay, especially where camperized vehicles are common, such as in the USA or Australia, but it would be most difficult in India or Colombia. There is a lot to be said for paying extra for shipping a vehicle that you know and can rely upon, especially in order to travel in Third World countries.

Shipping costs rise almost monthly. The only truly reliable prices are those obtained from shipping agents at your port of embarkation. Moreover, in these days of freight rates controlled by governments and conferences, do not expect to find a tramp steamer that will take your car for a pittance. Such bargains are rare and most unlikely to be found in developed countries. Nevertheless, it still pays to shop around. Occasionally bargains are available.

Most shipping lines charge by volume, but some by weight, length, or even area. The size of the vehicle can make a very considerable difference to the costs involved. Over short sea-crossings, it is always worth looking for a drive-on/drive-off car ferry – they are more numerous than might be thought and cost considerably less than orthodox freighting.

Containers

Usually, the most expensive method of shipping is by container as one has to pay for the ridiculously high 'unpacking' fees and often the 'shortfall' or space in the container that the vehicle does not occupy. However, it is possibly the most protected method, eliminating shipboard pilferage, loading damage, and corrosion. You can also ship your car fully laden whereas at many ports this may not be possible because of union and port authority regulations, necessitating the extra hassle and expense of unloading and shipping your personal effects separately.

If you should need to send a motorcycle ahead of you unaccompanied, the shipping agent will probably request that the machine be crated. In this case, the cost of having a crate made can be more than the actual freight charge. A good plan is to obtain an old crate from a motorcycle dealer or, if possible, to make a crate yourself.

Occasionally there are shipwrecks or fires at sea and marine insurance could be a worthwhile additional expense (usually two per cent of the car's value plus seafreight). However, most damage and theft is likely to occur on the ground where marine insurance is not applicable. Your vehicle is most vulnerable while it sits at the wharf. This is where the damage usually takes place: being sideswiped by a passing fork-lift truck or having paint dropped on it; but far worse is the theft and pilferage that take place. Stay with your vehicle as long as you can and, if possible, camp in it at the wharf or in the shed and refuse to leave it. You can do this in some ports, especially in Third World countries where waterside workers and port officials may actually prefer your presence in order to prevent theft and minimize damage. In some ports, wharf workers are grateful for your assistance with loading or unloading by driving the car to or from the crane, and parking it on deck or in the ship's hold. In these circumstances, it certainly helps to establish good rapport with dock workers.

Vehicle Preparation

Generally, it pays not to disconnect the battery if at all possible, though you could ensure that power consumption components like the oil temperature gauge and clock are disconnected in order to minimize battery power loss. If the vehicle is hard to move there is a danger that a fork-life truck will be used to move it with consequent damage to the chassis, gear box and propeller shaft. Ideally, if it has to be left unattended for some time, then all access to the living compartment should be locked with keys that are different from those for the cab and ignition, which are usually given to the agent or a ship's official such as head checker or purser. If necessary, a temporary partition should be erected to separate the cab from the rest of the interior. Ensure that all interior cupboards at least look heavily and securely padlocked. Check that all curtains are drawn and all windows closed. Remove all food that may go off during the voyage and take with you anything you may need while the car is at sea, unless you are accompanying it and can be given access to it on the ship.

Draining the fuel tank is usually difficult and never insisted upon; and it could also cause problems with moving the car. However, do not ship the vehicle with full jerry cans in it and check that full gas bottles are not likely to leak. Fires at sea are invariably disastrous.

With a motorcycle, it is very likely that in the absence of a drive-on/drive-off facility, you will be expected to direct the loading and offloading yourself. Of first importance then, unless there is a wide level gangway in place, is to resist any attempts that may be made, in the interests of saving time and effort, to load the machine with the luggage still attached and/or using a plank between the dockside and the ship.

The safest method of loading is to attach the motorcycle to the hook of the ship's derrick or the dock's crane with a couple of slings, first removing the luggage and windshield fairing or any other accessory that might get damaged. If you plan to make a large number of sea passages, from island to island, for example, it could be worthwhile carrying your own tailor-made rope slings. All ships do have slings on board for their own use, however. The design of the motorcycle will determine the correct position of the slings. In most cases, one can be passed under the steering head and the other through the frame just in front of the rear shock absorber mountings. If the slings are approximately the same length they should reach the crane hook over the bike's centre of gravity, with the machine almost level, all set to make a good two point landing. This method is equally good if used in loading a bike from a small boat to a large tanker or cargo ship which cannot go alongside.

It is best to quote your vehicle's dimensions or weights from a printed manufacturer's leaflet or handbook, ignoring extraneous attachments and only innocently remembering the roof-rack, tow-bar or externally mounted spare wheel if actually challenged on the wharf (rarely is a vehicle actually measured). By this time it is usually too much hassle for officials to bother recalculating your car's volume or area or revising the different categories of charges. However, an uncooperative official at this stage can cause considerable problems, especially if shipping has to be paid for in foreign currency and banks have already closed for the long weekend.

Deck Cargo

If the vehicle is to be shipped as deck cargo, it is advisable to have the entire exterior and underneath sprayed with diesolene as protection against sea air, salt spray and waves, for even on a large vessel, a storm will result in waves breaking over the deck – and the car. Diesolene is easily washed off with detergent after the voyage. Coating the car like this can also make thieves reluctant to pilfer from such a dirty vehicle. It would also be worthwhile spraying the interior of your vehicle with a residual insecticide like Baygon because it is so easy for your car to collect a crop of the inevitable ship's cockroaches.

A bike also needs to be stowed away from the ravages of salt water spray. On a cargo ship one of the best places is above or alongside the engine room. If there is no shelter available and the motorcycle must remain on deck, then be sure to cover it with tarpaulin and a thick coating of grease.

Processing

Generally, one should not commit oneself financially months in advance to a particular sailing date, as overland travel is by nature unpredictable and usually takes longer than one plans. In certain cases where bookings have been known to be heavy (e.g. Madras–Penang and Singapore–Fremantle) or where one has time- and finance-related concerns, then, of course, advance bookings are an asset. One might regret having to wait months for the next sailing.

Always allow several days for your car to be processed for shipment or for unloading and release. Patience, perseverance, and civility are essential as you trudge from one bureaucrat to another and to another and back again, each of them at different ends of the port or different parts of the town and each with their own forms and fees. Never get angry, in spite of arrogance, incompetence, and the heat, as this will inevitably make your departure that much more difficult. Take along at least three sheets of carbon paper for the many forms to be filled in and have your vehicle's numbers, dimensions and other details as well as your own passport and documentation details written out in advance on a handy piece of cardboard for constant reference. Dressing 'respectably' can be quite a help. Don't forget to ensure that your *carnet* is processed correctly. Processing your car can take only a few hours or it may take a week: one hour at San Francisco, a morning at Madras, and a full four days at Fremantle in Australia. It might even take months at Lagos or at some of the Persian Gulf ports where congestion can be phenomenal.

Wherever possible, handle the documentation and clear your vehicle yourself. This cuts out the middleman's fees and may even shorten the time taken. It also allows you to make personal contact with port officials and workers and can help ensure that they take care of your home on wheels. At times, in Third World countries, after you have assessed the situation, small gifts or tips may be in order.

After Unloading

Usually, after unloading, you are not allowed to drive out of the port area unless you show evidence of road insurance. However, the strictness varies considerably. When landing a car in most European countries, a Green Card insurance cover note is all that is necessary. At Piraeus in Greece, the car's details are also entered on your passport. At Vancouver insurance may be difficult, though not impossible, to obtain without actually registering the car with British Columbian licence plates. At Fremantle, one is compelled to have it tested and if your vehicle's annual registration, tax or licence have expired, then it has to be issued with Western Australian number plates. This last Australian example contrasts sharply with the treatment at the port of Townsville in the same country where, after customs clearance, one is free to take the car and go. However, at most Australian and New Zealand ports you will be required to have your car steam-cleaned after customs and before the roadworthiness test. Taking a right-hand-drive car to Egypt can cause hassles: one is forced to leave it in Alexandria and travel by train to Cairo to get special permission for temporary importation of a car with the steering on the 'wrong' side. Similarly, all left-hand steering vehicles temporarily brought into Australia have to have a large notice placed on the rear warning other vehicles. Brazilian ports should be avoided as *carnets* are rarely acceptable at sea frontiers and the customs guarantees therefore needed could be ruinous. With such varied treatment around the world it pays to keep one's vehicle licence or tax valid throughout the trip as a temporarily imported car with up-to-date registration is (with the possible exception of Egypt) invariably acceptable.

Permanently importing a car to a foreign country can sometimes be most hazardous. In many cases, the import duty will be astronomic, especially if you have not owned the car for long. For some countries, like the USA and Australia, cars manufactured during the 1970s and later have to conform to progressively more stringent safety and exhaust emission regulations. Importing such vehicles can be relatively simple, in spite of the high duty, but licencing them for road use by traffic authorities may be prohibitively expensive because of the extensive modifications to the car that are required. Only in very limited circumstances, such as for older vehicles and for temporary visitor importation, is one permitted to have a left-hand-drive car registered in Australia for road use.

For advice on particular ports, the most reliable is that from other overlanders who have just come through the place to which you are going. Even so, on arrival you may find the situation very different and you may have to sift the truth from exaggeration and bravado.

Which Route?

Shipping by freighter or passenger shipping for yourself and your car is relatively easy to obtain from Europe to the Americas, Africa and even to Australasia. So is North America to Latin America, the Far East, Australasia and Africa, though hard work and perseverance may be needed to track it down. By contrast, shipping between Australia and Africa is not only rare, but often more expensive than to Europe. Even more difficult to find is shipping between Latin America and Australasia. On rare occasions, cruise liners cross these oceans, so positioning themselves for the southern summer cruise season and they will take passengers' cars. However, it is usually to be expected that when you find shipping for your vehicle on these routes, you will have to fly separately and wait several weeks at either end.

Generally, a check through the latest *ABC Shipping Guide* (published monthly) will reveal quite a number of passenger carrying freighters on the less difficult routes. These are, however, very popular with people wishing to cruise in a leisurely but unorganized way. Consequently, one may have to book even years ahead for a passage which is often more expensive than first class air travel. Nevertheless, there are often cancellations and the extra costs may still be cheaper than the combination of air fares and accommodation at the other end while you wait for your car to arrive.

It may prove impossible to ship your motorcycle, in which case you will have to resort to sending it by air. The machine is most likely to be transported lying on its side and loading/unloading will be carried out by hand. For this operation, two good crashbars are invaluable for handholds and, even more important, to locate the motor and prevent damage while in transit.

Although vehicle shipping is very expensive, often hard to find, and fraught with hassles, it does allow you the pleasure and security of travelling in a distant continent totally independently. In the long term it can be cheaper than relying on public transport and hotel, hostel or rented accommodation, and being independent of these gives you an unprecedented freedom to go where you please. So, next time you see a VW Kombi in London with Queensland number plates, please remember that the owner is not crazy!

Selling a Car Abroad

Selling a car is legal in some countries, illegal in others. Most often, if you enter a country with a car, you are not permitted to leave without it. In countries which require a *carnet*, the car will almost certainly be recorded in your passport. This makes leaving without the vehicle trickier, unless of course you have a passport with a pasted-in page ready to receive the stamp for the car, and you are not above tearing the page out before you leave. Even for a broken down car, people have sometimes had to pay the entire value of the vehicle to the tax authorities just to abandon it.

Another fairly common variant is that you can take the car in to the country without paying duty if you have owned the car for some time (usually a year) and that you continue to own it for at least two years before selling. Unless you are planning to stay in the country, this is of little value to the overlander who has arrived at the edge of a continent and wants to dispose of his vehicle and fly home.

Laws can, of course, be bent or dodged. You can, for example, sell a car 'legally' in the zone between two international borders, or to someone (diplomat, foreign resident) who is not bound by the law. In legal vehicle sales, it is usually the buyer who pays the tax.

Laws and regulations of the relevant countries pertaining to the sale of a foreign vehicle should be studied before any transaction is embarked upon. Ask the AA, or the Customs Office of the country concerned what the position is before you leave. Otherwise, unless you have time to drive it home again, you may find yourself having to pay enormous amounts to have the vehicle shipped.

Renting a Car

by David Chapelle

The late afternoon heat and the smell of the tropics hit me immediately the aircraft door was opened. Dishevelled and disoriented I crossed the tarmac to the terminal building. Habit made me hurry, heat and humidity slowed me down. In the crowded arrival hall I was a civilization and a continent away from Gatwick's chaotic bustle: little was familiar until I spotted the familiar yellow and black of the Hertz man. He led me to the car – a recent model European – and drove me into town to complete the formalities. En route I had my first taste of tropical traffic – ancient, over-loaded vehicles hurling themselves at us like missiles on what passed for the main road, to say nothing of the aimless amble of beast or human right into our path.

Renting a car in some Third World countries – those which the Third World Foundation defines as the 120 non-aligned countries – creates a distinct echo of the pioneering days of the American West, except for horses, read cars. The forerunner of the car-hire depot was the livery stable where you rented or changed horses and from it has grown the sophisticated multi-million dollar industry we know today as car rental, geared to jet travel, instant reservation systems, rent-it-here/leave-it-there, credit cards, etc. And for the traveller seeking to open new markets, explore new territories or just to recapture some of that pioneering spirit by breaking new ground on holiday in farther-away places, the major international companies (Hertz, Europcar, and Avis in particular) are pushing the frontiers back by developing their networks throughout the underdeveloped world.

In fact, car rental in the Third World is almost entirely in the hands of the major international operators, except for a few local companies here and there with a small self-drive fleet, and of course, the ubiquitous taxi – very often ancient, ill-maintained and expensive. In fact, the majors are aiming to establish the same standard of service expected by the experienced traveller and frequent car hirer from Europe or North America – although it can be difficult to maintain this with the inevitable restraints of climate, local legislation and economy, let alone temperament.

Hertz, who are represented in 33 countries in Africa alone – which constitutes a quarter of their total worldwide network of representation in 120 countries – considers this market to be a very important one for the future and are spending considerable time and effort in opening new franchises as well as making sure that existing operations conform to their worldwide standards. The market is growing steadily, but business is tiny by Western standards and since fleets are relatively small, the broad recommendation would seem to be that clients should always make advance reservations, ideally a few days ahead of arrival. All other services are available, e.g. credit facilities, rent-it-here/leave-it-there within countries and rental staff are normally bi-lingual in at least English or French, depending on the country concerned.

The Europcar/National worldwide system is represented in 45 of the non-aligned Third-World countries and is growing steadily and consistently in line with services, facilities and standards maintained elsewhere in the network. The latest jewel in their crown is the National Car Rental operation in China (a first in the major rental company league); although you cannot drive by yourself there, a chauffeur is obligatory, the details of rental and conditions make interesting reading in their directory.

Europcar claims to be the largest international operator in the Middle East, although Avis are also very strong there with 75 rental locations in the Arab world and a fleet of more than 2,000 vehicles. All three of the major operators are constantly looking for opportunities to push the frontiers back by opening more locations – and here and there one can also find Budget and Interrent represented.

Endless Trouble

The difficulties these companies face can be almost insurmountable in providing not only a car rental facility but also a service, cars and staff at a standard commensurate with those elsewhere, and as such they are the pioneers in opening up new countries in the Third World for the traveller who otherwise would have a much more difficult task on his own. The problems reflect this.

First, there's the local political scene – some countries are in a state of almost constant war, either civil or with their neighbours. Some are openly unfriendly to Western (as opposed to Eastern bloc) visitors. Currency problems for the government can make it difficult to pay for cars outside the country – and none are manufactured locally. Few people locally own cars, so service and repair facilities are few and far between and of poor standard: so incidentally are petrol stations. There is no local car rental industry, and there are not many taxis that aren't ancient and probably unsafe.

Roads – outside the towns – are poor and often impassable for part of the year and driving 100 miles can often present more road hazards and potentially dangerous situations than even Hollywood could dream up. Sign-posts, road directions – and often maps too – can be non-existent, while although in some areas English, French or even German is understood, there are vast tracts where a pidgin version might or might not get you by, leaving just sign-language: a difficult problem when you want to explain that your differential is not functioning or the ignition/carburretion system has developed terminal vehicular asthma.

In the affluent Arab world, it is possible to find a relatively sophisticated car rental facility, but even where splendid dual carriageways connect some cities, the wandering driver can go back a hundred years just by taking a wrong turn. Within Africa, the simple business of moving between two places that we take for granted in Europe has to be seen in a totally different light, and planning is essential. One-way rentals – rent-it-here/leave-it-there – are usually available within one's country's boundaries, except in a few cases (Avis offer such a facility between Burkina Faso

(Upper Volta) and Abidjan in the Ivory Coast). Very often, though, the only way to travel between towns and countries is by air and then to rent again locally. In the relevant areas, safari-type vehicles are becoming more available, and of course short trips to game reserves etc. can be arranged. Very often renting a car will also include the services of a driver – who can be very valuable (not of course to be confused with what we understand as chauffeur-driven).

To sum up then, if you're considering a visit to a Third-World country and possibly renting a car, first do your homework and consult one of the major companies: it's likely they've already established a facility there. If not, and there are many countries where no facility is available or even envisaged, you're on your own to bargain with the natives when you get there. And there's a good reason for Hertz, Avis *et al.* not to be there – they've already tried. You won't find car rental – as we know it – in, for instance, Libya, Somalia, Equatorial Guinea or Algeria – and many more countries yet.

If there is a facility offered by one of the major companies, reserve your vehicle a few days in advance. When you arrive, be a little more patient with the staff, and of course with the people you meet: they don't meet or handle that many Europeans and don't understand our pace and attitudes. Anyhow, it's their country so adjust to their pace – it's difficult not to do so.

Local Advice

Above all, take advice and use their local knowledge: accept their recommendations on insurance and take the maximum: hire a chauffeur if they say so (he can be very valuable in getting an elephant to pull you out of a swamp) and don't expect good roads: you won't find that the equivalent of the Kingston by-pass goes very far – normally just to the edge of town.

Observe the local climate (roads can become impassable in the rainy season), customs (in more ways than one: don't try to smuggle gold out of Dubai in your rented car, it's been done too often) and regulations (you must have at least two people occupying a taxi to go into the centre of Singapore at certain times, and it's not worth renting self-drive, try a chauffeur-driven deal). And above all, keep your eyes open for the unexpected: even in a safari park, keep your windows rolled up. We lose more drivers that way . . .

Other

River Travel

by John and Julie Batchelor

Wherever you want to go in the world, the chances are that you can get there by river. Indeed, the more remote your destination, the more likely it will be that the only way of getting there, without taking to the air, will be by river. This is particularly true of tropical regions where, throughout the history of exploration, rivers have been the key that has opened the door to the interior. It is still the case that for those who really want to penetrate deep into a country, to learn about the place and its peoples through direct contact, the best way to do so is by water.

River travel splits neatly into three categories: public transport, private hire and your own transport.

Public Transport

Wherever there is a large navigable river, whether it be in Africa, South America, Asia or even Europe, you will find some form of river transport. This can range from a luxury floating hotel on the Nile to a dug-out canoe in the forests of Africa and South America. And between these extremes, all over the world there can be found the basic work-a-day ferries which ply between villages and towns carrying every conceivable type of commodity and quite often an unbelievably large number of people.

Let's start by examining travel on an everyday ferry. First you must buy your ticket. The usual method is to turn up at the water front, find out which boat is going in your direction and then locate the the agent's office. With luck, this will be a simple matter, but on occasion even finding out where to purchase your ticket can be an endless problem. Don't be put off. Just turn up at your boat, go on board and find someone, preferably someone in authority, to take your money. You'll have no difficulty in doing this, so long as you do not embarrass people by asking for receipts.

Board the boat as early as possible. It is probable that it will be extremely crowded, so if you are a deck passenger you will need to stake out your corner of the deck and defend it against all comers. Make sure of your sleeping arrangements immediately. In South America this will mean getting your hammock in place, in Africa and the Far East making sure you have enough space to spread out your sleeping mat. Take care about your positioning. If you are on a trip lasting a number of days do not place yourself near the one and only toilet on board. By the end of the journey the location of this facility will be obvious to anyone with a sense of smell. Keep away from the air outlet from the engine room unless you have a particular liking for being asphyxiated by diesel fumes. If rain is expected, make sure you are under cover. On most boats a tarpaulin shelter is rigged up over the central area. Try to get a spot near the middle as those at the edges tend to get wet. Even if rain is unlikely it is still a good idea to find shade from the sun. For those unused to it, sitting in the tropical sun all day can be unpleasant and dangerous.

Go equipped. There may be some facilities for food and drink on board, but in practice this will probably only mean warm beer and unidentified local specialities which you might prefer not to have to live on. Assume there will be nothing. Take everthing you need for the whole journey, plus a couple of days just in case. On the Zaïre river, for instance, it is quite common for boats to get stuck on sand banks, sometimes for days on end. Just be prepared. And don't forget the insects. The lights of the boat are sure to attract an interesting collection of wildlife during the tropical night, so take a mosquito net.

Occasionally, for those with money, there may be cabins available on the larger river boats, but don't expect too much of these. If there is supposed to be water, it will only be intermittent at best, and there certainly won't be a plug. The facilities will be very basic and you are almost certain to have the company of hordes of cockroaches who will take particular delight in sampling your food and exploring your belongings. Occupying a cabin on a multi-class boat also marks you out as 'rich' and thus subject to attention from the less desirable of your fellow passengers. Lock you cabin door and do not leave your window open at night. In order to lock the cabin you will also have to go equipped with a length of chain and padlock. On most boats the advantages of a cabin are minimal.

Longer journeys, especially on African rivers, tend to be one long party. Huge quantities of beer are drunk and very loud music plays throughout the night. It is quite likely that you will be looked on as a guest and expected to take an active part in the festivities. It's a good way of making friends, but don't expect a restful time.

Given these few commonsense precautions and preparations, you will have a rewarding trip. By the time you reach your destination you will have many new friends, have learnt a few essential words of the local language and have offers of accommodation, all of which will make your stay pleasanter and the next stage of your journey easier.

Private Hire

In order to progress further up the river from the section navigable by larger boats, you will have to look around for transport to hire. This may be a small motor boat, but is more likely to be a dug-out canoe with an outboard motor. When negotiating for this sort of transport, local knowledge is everything: who's reliable and owns a reliable boat or canoe. With luck, your new-found friends from the first stage of your journey will advise you and take care of the negotiations over price. This is by far the best option. Failing that, it is a question of your own judgement. What you are looking for is a well-equipped boat with a well-serviced motor and a teetotal crew. In all probability such an ideal combination doesn't exist – at least we have never found it. So we are back to common sense. Do look at the boat before coming to any agreement. If possible try to have a test run just to make sure the motor works. Try to establish that the boatman knows the area you want to go to. If he already smells of drink at ten in the morning, he may not be the most reliable man around. This last point could be important. If you are returning the same way you will need to arrange for your boatman to pick you up again at a particular time and place. The chances of this happening if he is likely to disappear on an extended drunken binge once he has your money is remote in the extreme. Take your time over the return arrangements. Make sure that everyone knows and understands the place, the day and the time that they are required to meet you. Don't forget that not everyone can read or tell the time. If you have friends in the place, get them to check that the boatman leaves when planned. Agree on the price to be paid before you go and do not pay anything until you arrive at the destination. If the part of the deal is that you provide the fuel, buy it yourself and hand it over only when everyone and everything is ready for departure. Establish clearly what the food and drink arrangements are as you may be expected to feed the crew.

Once you are on your way, it is a question again of common sense. Take ready-prepared food. Protect yourself from the sun and your equipment from rain and spray. If you are travelling by dug-out canoe, it will be a long uncomfortable trip with little opportunity for stretching your legs. Make sure you have something to sit on, preferably something soft, but don't forget that the bottom of the canoe will soon be full of water.

Once you have arrived at your destination, make sure that you are in the right place before letting the boat go! If the boatman is coming back for you go over all the arrangements one more time. Do not pay in advance for the return if you can possibly avoid it. If the boatman has the money, there is little incentive for him to keep his part of the bargain. If absolutely necessary, give just enough to cover the cost of the fuel.

Own Transport

After exhausting the possibilities of public transport and hire, you must make your own way to the remote headwaters of your river. You may have brought your own equipment, which will probably be an inflatable with outboard motor or a canoe. If you have got this far, we can assume that you know all about the requirements of your own equipment. Both inflatables and rigid kayaks are bulky items to transport over thousands of miles so you might consider a collapsible canoe which you assemble once you have reached this part of your trip. We have not used them personally but have heard very good reports on them in use under very rigorous conditions.

Your chances of finding fuel for the outboard motor on the remote headwaters of almost any river in the world are negligible. Take all you need with you. Your chances of finding food and hospitality will depend on the part of the world you are exploring. In South America, you are unlikely to find any villages and the only people you may meet are nomadic Indians who, given present circumstances, could be hostile. You will have to be totally self-sufficient. In Africa the situation is quite different. Virtually anywhere that you can reach with your boat will have a village or fishing encampment of some description. The villagers will show you hospitality and in all probability you will be able to buy fresh vegetables, fruit and fish from the people. Take basic supplies and enough for emergencies but expect to be able to supplement this with local produce.

Another alternative could be to buy a local canoe, although this option is fraught with dangers. Buying a second-hand canoe is as tricky as buying a second-hand car without knowing anything about mechanics. You can easily be fobbed off with a dud. We know of a number of people who have paddled off proudly in their new canoe only to sink steadily below the surface as water seeped in through cracks and patches. This is usually a fairly slow process so that by the time you realize your error you are too far away from the village to do anything about it. A word or two about dug-out canoes: these are simply hollowed-out tree trunks and come in all sizes. The stability of the canoe depends on the expertise of the man who made it. They are usually heavy, difficult to propel in a straight line, prone to capsize, uncomfortable and extremely hard work! The larger ones can weigh over a ton which makes it almost impossible for a small group to take one out of the water for repairs. Paddling dug-outs is best left to the experts. Only if you are desperate – and going downstream – should you entertain the idea.

Travel Etiquette

When travelling in remote areas anywhere in the world, it should always be remembered that you are the guest. You are the one who must adjust to local circumstances and take great pains not to offend the customs and traditions of the people you are visiting. To refuse hospitality will almost always cause offence. Remember that you are the odd one out and that is natural for your hosts to be inquisitive and fascinated by everything you do. However tired or irritable you may be, you have chosen to put yourself in this position and it is your job to accept close examination with a good grace. Before travelling, do take the trouble to research both the area you intend to visit and its people. Try to have some idea of what is expected of you before you go to a village. If you are offered food and accommodation accept it. Do not be squeamish about eating what is offered. After all, the local people have survived on whatever it is, so it is unlikely to do you very much damage.

No two trips are ever the same, thank goodness! The advice we have tried to give is nothing more than common sense. If you apply this to whatever you are doing, you will not go far wrong. Just remember that what may be impossible today can be achieved tomorrow . . . or perhaps the next day . . . or the next. Don't be in a hurry. There is so much to be enjoyed. Take your time . . . and good luck!

Overland by Public Transport

by Chris Parrott

It's not everyone who has the resources to plan, equip, and insure a full-scale Range Rover expedition across one of the less developed continents, though it's the sort of thing we all dream about. One possible answer is to travel with an overland company, but here the drawback is that you cannot choose your travelling companions or your itinerary. You can, however, do it all more cheaply on your own, by public transport. Generally speaking, wherever overland companies take their trucks, there public transport goes too. And often public transport goes where overland companies cannot – over the snow-bound Andes to Ushuaia in Tierra del Fuego, across Siberia to the Pacific.

Of course, Damascus to Aleppo is not quite the same as getting on a coach to Washington DC at the New York Greyhound Terminal, nor does 'First Class' imply in Bolivia quite what it does on the 18.43 from Paddington to Reading.

A Schedule of Surprises

The Damascus to Aleppo bus is an ancient Mercedes welded together from the remains of past generations of Damascus/Aleppo buses, and propelled in equal proportions by a fuming diesel engine, the Will of Allah, and the passengers (from behind). It makes unscheduled stops while the driver visits his grandmother in Homs, when the driver's friend visits the Post Office in the middle of nowhere, and when the whole bus answers the call of nature – the women squatting on the left, and the men standing on the right (the French normally display more cool at moments like this).

First Class in Bolivia means hard, upright seats, already full of people and chickens spilling over from Second Class; whimpering children; no heating, even in high passes at night in winter; passageways blocked by shapeless bundles and festering cheeses; impromptu customs searches at 4am; and toilets negotiable only by those equipped with Wellingtons and a farmyard upbringing. Trains rarely arrive or depart on time, and the author has experienced a delay of twenty-six hours on a journey (ostensibly) of eight hours. But these trains are nothing if not interesting.

The secret of the cheapness of this means of travelling lies in the fact that it is *public* – and therefore the principal means by which the public of a country moves from place to place. It follows that if the standard of living of the majority of people is low, so will the cost of public transport be low. A twenty hour bus ride from Lima to Arequipa in southern Peru can cost as little as $10; a twenty hour bus ride in Brazil from Rio de Janeiro to the Paraguayan border costs about $20; whilst a twenty hour bus ride through France or Germany would cost $40 or more. It all depends on the ability of the local population to pay.

Of course there are disadvantages to travel by public transport:

1. Photography is difficult at 70mph, and though most drivers will stop occasionally, they have their schedules to keep to.
2. You may find that all transport over a certain route is fully booked

for the week ahead, or there is a transport strike.
3. You may find that your seat has been sold twice. In circumstances like this, tempers fray and people begin to speak too quickly for your few words of the local language to be of much use.

Efficiency of reservation arrangements varies from one part of the world to the next. The following may serve as a general guide to travelling in the undeveloped parts of the world.

Booking

Whenever you arrive in a place, try and find out about transport and how far ahead it is booked up. It may be, for example, that you want to stay in Ankara for three days, and that it's usually necessary to book a passage four days in advance to get to Iskenderun. If you book on the day you arrive, you have only one day to kill; if you book on the day you intended leaving, you have four days to kill. This is a basic rule and applies to all methods of transport.

Routing

Try to be as flexible as possible about your routing and means of transport. There are at least six ways to get from La Paz in Bolivia to Rio de Janeiro in Brazil. Check all possible routes before making a final decision.

Timing

Don't try and plan your itinerary down to the nearest day – nothing is ever that reliable in the less developed world (or the developed world for that matter.) You should allow a ten to twenty per cent delay factor if, for example, you have to be at a certain point at a certain time to catch your plane home.

Possessions

Baggage is often snatched at terminals. Be sure, if you are not travelling within sight of your bags, that they have the correct destination clearly marked, and that they do actually get loaded. Breakfast in New York, dinner in London, baggage in Tokyo happens all too often. Arriving or leaving early in the morning or late at night you are particularly vulnerable to thieves; this is the time when you must be most on your guard. Never leave anything valuable on a bus while you have a quick drink, not even if the driver says the bus door will be locked.

Borders

Prices rise dramatically whenever a journey is made during the course of which a national frontier is crossed. Usually it's cheaper to take a bus as far as the frontier, walk across and then continue your journey by the local transport in the new country. 'International' services are always more expensive, whether airlines, buses, trains or boats. (The author recalls that a donkey ride to the Mexican frontier cost him 20 *pesos* but to have crossed the international bridge as far as the Belize Immigration Office, an extra 40 metres, would have increased the cost to 40 *pesos*.)

Fare and Medium

Each particular medium of transport has its own special features.

Trains are generally slower than buses, and the seats may be of wood. There is often no restriction on the number of seats sold, and delays are long and frequent. However, slow trains make photography easier, and the journeys are usually more pleasant than on buses if not too crowded. It's often worth going to the station a couple of days before you're due to leave and watching to see what happens. It will tell you whether you need to turn up two hours early to be sure of a seat.

Buses reflect the sort of terrain they cross; if the roads are paved and well maintained, the buses are usually modern and in fair condition. If the journey involves unmade mountain roads, your bus and journey are not going to be very comfortable.

If you are travelling through bandit country – or a country where political stability conforms to the Third World stereotype – it may be a consolation when the whole bus is stopped and robbed by bandits or searched by transit police (robbed too, some say). If you're in your own vehicle or hitch-hiking, it is somehow far more demoralizing. You probably lose the same things, or have your Tampax broken in half by over-zealous soldiers in search of drugs, but it affects you less if you're just part of a coach load.

Urban transport. One of London's biggest failures has been its inability to provide a cheap mass transit system within the city. Other Western industrialized capitals seem to have managed it to a greater or lesser extent, but the Third World has really got the problem licked – for the locals at least. Most urban dwellers in the Third World own no car; they have to travel by public transport – bus, train, rickshaw, underground and so on. The networks are labyrinthine in the complexity, the services frequent and the fares cheap. Everyone uses the system; which generates which, I do not know, but it works. The problem is that there is rarely any information on the extent of the network available for the tourist or traveller. He's meant to go by taxi or limousine. Buy yourself a city map, jump on a bus and explore. It's a great way of seeing the city cheaply with no censorship; getting your bearings; and spending next to nothing in the process.

Boats. This, if you're lucky, could mean an oceangoing yacht that takes passengers as crew between, say, St. Lucia and Barbados, or a cement boat from Rhodes to Turkey or an Amazon river steamer. With a little help from your wallet, most captains can be persuaded to accept passengers. A good rule is to take your own food supply for the duration of the trip and a hammock if there is no official accommodation.

Cargo boats ply the rivers Amazon, the Congo and Ubangi in Zaïre, the Niger in Mali, the White Nile in the Sudan, the river Gambia and Ecuador's river Guaya, where an all-night crossing costs about 13 *sucres* (30p).

Planes. In areas where planes are the only means of communication, they are often very cheap or even free. Flying across the Gulf of Aden to Djibouti, for example, costs as little as sailing. A good trick is to enquire about privately owned planes at mission schools (in Africa) or at aero-clubs. Someone who is going 'up country' may be only too pleased to have your company. Similarly, in parts of South America, the Air Forces of several countries have cheap scheduled flights to less accessible areas, though, of course, one must be prepared for canvas seats and grass runways.

Hitchhiking

by Wendy Myers

For the person who likes conversing with strangers, relishes using newly acquired languages and yet enjoys being (often suddenly) quite alone, far off the beaten track, hitchhiking must be hard to beat as a principal way of getting about. I say 'principal' because, in my opinion, nobody should set off on a journey intending to be completely reliant on other people's goodwill. Those who set out on foot, hoping for a lift, but feeling happy to walk, will be pleasantly relieved when one comes, whereas the type of attitude that feels it to be the duty of total strangers to transport one from A to B free of charge whenever one wishes could mean a long series of disappointments.

One April morning, I left England to 'walk around the world'. Seven years and over a hundred countries later, I returned home with enough interesting material to fill the equivalent of eight books and enormous experience of hitchhiking, which had been my main method of travelling.

Firstly, even for a long trip, the amount of luggage you can take is extremely limited when hitchhiking. Only take as much as can be carried comfortably while walking. My own rucksack, which I carried with reasonable ease, weighed 16kg. As a guide to clothing, I suggest strong shirts, shorts and trousers, plus a sweater for cold weather. T-shirts worn next to the skin will both decrease the pressure of the rucksack straps and mop up perspiration. Strong comfortable shoes are a must, while sandals and 'flip-flops' come in handy for hot climates or if one has blisters. Swimming gear, toilet articles, a set of 'smart' clothes and some light 'all over' garment to relax in should all find a space. A small first aid kit is a sensible acquisition and should include water purifiers, and anti-malarial pills. Finally three 'musts' – sunhat, water bottle and diary . . .

Rules of Thumb

People give lifts for a number of acceptable reasons and, if these can be discovered as soon as possible and complied with, a pleasant journey should ensue. It could be that, facing a long tedious road ahead, a driver wants to ensure against falling asleep, or maybe he wishes to practise his English, or just 'likes foreigners'. Perhaps help with driving is hoped for . . . I had a wonderful tour around New Zealand's North Island with a holidaying resident who had been ill and was on the look-out for a possible co-driver. On another occasion I rode with an illiterate Australian cattle drover for whom I had to read the names on the signposts. Drivers also sometimes find hitchhikers, who are foreigners like themselves, useful sources of information on places to stay, the local territory and other potential passengers.

In Third World countries, it is not only foreigners who hitchhike but the locals themselves, who are usually either young middle-class students, poor people or military personnel going home on leave. The first group are the most fruitful contacts for a driver as they prove, on the whole, to be well-informed and hospitable.

Conduct will make or mar the future for hitchhikers: those who snore for hours in the back seat or eat whatever food they find are hardly a good advertisement.

In my experience, it is very rare actually to have to 'thumb down' a vehicle – and waving an outstretched arm in front of moving traffic is downright dangerous. Upon seeing a hiker, drivers will stop – if they want to. Waving a flattened palm is the most appropriate gesture if one is needed. If in doubt, ask other hitchhikers what they do.

Lifts are given most readily to mixed couples. Women are safer travelling in pairs. Three or more hitchhikers may prove too many and could do better if they split up for a while. Too little luggage can be taken as the mark of a 'bum'; too much is a hindrance. A girl with no luggage, thumbing a lift, will often stop a car, but if a boyfriend suddenly emerges from hiding with two large rucksacks, the driver of a small vehicle will be understandably infuriated. The politest way of requesting a lift was one I discovered in Fairbanks, Alaska. 'If you want to get a ride from here, phone the radio people', I was told. 'Your message will be broadcast immediately. This is a remote town so we all try to help each other.' I did just that and somebody phoned to offer me a lift the same day.

In order to get a lift in the more conventional way, it is advisable to look as 'straight' and as clean as possible. Avoid wearing sunglasses (which prevent eye-to-eye contact with the driver) and wear light coloured clothes so that you are more visible. Stand where traffic is slow, where you can be easily seen, and where drivers are able to stop. Petrol stations, border posts and police checkpoints, ferry terminal exits, roadside restaurants, traffic lights and road intersections can all be good places. At night, make sure the spot you choose is lit. If there are two of you, one should wait by the road while the other speaks to drivers who have already stopped to use whatever facility or comply with whatever regulation there is at that place. The unwritten rule in hitchhiking is that more recent arrivals move further down the road.

Hikers bound eastwards for the Middle East stand a good chance of getting their first long distance lift at the German–Austrian border near Salzburg, probably in a lorry. Lorries nearly always have to stop at borders and in places may not pass at all on a Sunday. This is a good opportunity for the hiker to talk to the drivers and find himself an offer. If you are in a town, you could telephone trucking companies to ask if there are any vehicles about to go your way.

Being helpful and courteous to people along the road is always a good policy; it can also get you lifts. Stopping to help the owner of a broken-down vehicle may earn you gratitude in the form of something to help you on your way.

Sign Here

A sign indicating your desired destination is useful. Make the destination fairly local so that neither you nor the driver is committed in advance to a very long journey together. If you find you are congenial, you can always discuss further stages of the journey later. The sign must bear a name written in the local language and script, and even here, courtesy pays: some people have had success with a sign reading simply 'please'. Deliberately making an obvious bad mistake on the sign can work well too. Write 'East' on the sign and then stand on the side of the road where the traffic flows west and some drivers will stop to point out your mistake. You feign confusion and soon you're away with one of these benevolent drivers – headed westwards, which is where you wanted to go in the first place.

Keep an eye on vehicle registration numbers. They are useful for gaining an idea of where any vehicle has come from or may be heading, and for tracking down the owner in case of theft or trouble.

Before you accept a lift, size up the car's occupants. Don't get into a car with drunks or maniacs. If you do and find out too late, ask to be put down. Saying you have to relieve yourself usually does the trick. When a mixed couple are travelling together, it is customary for the man to sit next to the driver, at least until everyone's confidence is assured. In some countries, unmarked cars are in fact taxis; and lorry drivers expect to earn something from their passengers. If in doubt, ask if there will be a charge. Except in an emergency, never let a driver set you down in the middle of nowhere; you may be stuck there for hours, or even days. And if you're set down in a town, make it the far side and not the near, so that you're not thrown back on public transport or walking.

Hikers should be prepared to give something in exchange for a ride such as interesting conversation, help with map reading or an English lesson. If they join the vehicle for a longish time, say more than a day, they should offer to pay their share of petrol, and tolls, and of course, pay for their own food and lodging. And they should remember they are guests on someone else's property. That means no requests for adjustments to windows, heating etc. unless prompted by the driver. When wet and muddy, it is considerate to wait and see whether one's host wishes to protect the car seat or floor before one enters. The hiker should be prepared to leave a vehicle when asked to. Drivers may require time to themselves for the last lap of a journey and they should certainly not be made to feel guilty if their destination falls several kilometres short of one's own. On the whole, people who give lifts are kind and unselfish.

Around the World

All over Europe, Australia and New Zealand, drivers are 'geared' to hitchhikers, but elsewhere it can be a different matter. In many Far Eastern countries, car travel is popular now and hikers will readily be offered lifts through Sri Lanka, Thailand, Malaysia, Singapore and Japan. In rural India, cars are less common, but there drivers go out of their way to aid a traveller – which may not only involve transport but board and lodging as well. In Laos, Vietnam and the Philippines, hitchhiking on trucks is relatively easy, but not always advisable for girls. The same applies for South America, along whose roads *camiones* with cheerful drivers (often ex-cowboys) rumble for days and nights on end.

Through most of East, West and South Africa, there is considerable traffic. In Central African countries, where long distances over inhospitable terrain must be covered, trucks are the commonest vehicles to be found, and the same applies to the Sahara. To cross the Desert the two most popular routes northwards run from Gao and Agadez. The latter is the longer, more varied route and that is the one I chose. An Algerian driver smuggling Nigerian sheep took me all the way across the Sahara to his home in El Golea. With this hospitable desert Arab and his companions, I spent bitterly cold nights beneath a canvas spread on the sand, got chased by police between In Salah and Ragane, cheered when we escaped and kept the pre-Ramadan fast.

In jungle-covered lands such as Zaïre, and the Gambia, roads are less frequented than rivers. The same applies to the Amazon region of Brazil and parts of Laos. Thus one's transport may vary – from the pillion of a motor-bike to enormous trucks with 34 wheels on the ground. When one gets right off the beaten track, it is not uncommon to find people who own little boats or private planes. Two of the occasions on which such free lifts were offered to me involved a boat journey along the Mekong river from Vientiane to Savannakhet in Laos and a flight between St Louis (Senegal) and Nouakchott (Mauritania). At times one may cover vast distances in the same vehicle, such as when a new car is being delivered from one country to another.

Here I should mention one exception to walking on for miles between lifts, and that is through the vast stretches of sparsely populated territory, where it is either very hot or very cold. It has been known for hikers to perish in such conditions, for most are either unequipped with adequate warm gear for the one or enough water for the other. One such place is Australia's Nullarbor Plain. The traveller who enters it on foot must beware. The temperature can soar to 45°C in the shade and in many places it has not rained for years. At a place called Karalee stands the only hotel between Coolgardie and Southern Cross. Right on the railway line, it is the only place within 185km that can supply one with a drink. Villages shown on the map become increasingly smaller on the ground as one penetrates the desert, diminishing to one house in the scrub with a sign up saying 'No petrol here'.

Rivers too can foil the hitchhiker. In the same country, the road between Wyndham and Darwin may suddenly become impassable from mid-November when the rivers begin to run.

Between Lifts

The traveller off the beaten track will encounter a great variety of types of lodging, from free sleeping places such as railway stations, barns and beaches, to paid accommodation. Invitations to stay with people should never be expected, but it would be a rare hiker who returned home without having enjoyed the thrill of living as 'one of the family' with hosts of other lands.

One soon discovers that there are situations where both hiking and hitchhiking would be either unwise or impossible. Then one must investigate the possibility of paid transport, which can range in price from the hundreds of dollars charged for visiting the Pacific Islands on a liner to a matter of pence to rent a bicycle in Sarawak for 24 hours.

When funds run low, they can be boosted by temporary jobs – such as fruit picking, teaching English, or even donating blood.

Problems

There are many potential problems to be faced by the hitchhiker, starting with language. Most people who offer lifts speak English or another 'international' tongue such as French, Spanish or German. And if not, a friendly smile and the use of sign language are universally accepted methods of communication. Hitchhiking, on the whole, can be considered dangerous only in Western countries.

There are the obvious hazards faced by a girl travelling alone. As one who knows, I can confidently assure readers that if a girl is modestly attired and makes clear her reason for hitchhiking, problems should be minimal. My only really frightening experiences resulted from travelling with drivers who, unpredictably, were to get themselves intoxicated with drugs (such as from chewing *coca* leaves) or alcohol. A direct 'Will you come to bed with me?' type of approach from a normal male can invariably be rebuffed by laughing it off, discussing his family, expressing great anxiety at such a proposal, or by pleading sudden sickness and leaving the vehicle rapidly . . .

Finally, it is sad but true that many a journey through otherwise unspoiled lands is hindered by political disputes and sometimes violence. Such was my experience in Ethiopia, Sudan and war-smitten North and South Vietnam.

My rule here would simply be 'obey the rules' and 'never interfere'. A politely worded, sensible-sounding request to continue one's journey is generally granted, as long as one remains courteous and carries travel documents which are in impeccable order.

Here then are some tips gleaned from my personal experience. Prices and politics have altered since my own journey in the 1960s; so have place names. But people themselves won't have changed, and he who travels as a worthy ambassador of his own nation will win many hearts overseas.

So, good luck to you on your travels and, should lifts at times be few and far between, remember these words of a Chinese philosopher: 'The journey of a thousand miles begins with one step.'

Motorcycling

by Ted Simon

It seems pointless to argue the merits of motorcycles as against other kinds of vehicles. Everyone knows more or less what the motorcycle can do, and attitudes to it generally are quite sharply defined. The majority is against it, and so much the better for those of us who recognize its advantages. Who wants to be part of a herd? Let me just say that I am writing here for people who think of travelling through the broad open spaces of Africa and Latin America, or across the great Asian land mass. Riding in Europe or North America is straightforward, and even the problems posed in Australia are relatively clear cut. As for those fanatics whose notion of travelling is to set the fastest time between Berlin and Singapore, I am all for abandoning them where they fall, under the stones and knives of angry Muslim villagers.

Here then are some points in favour of the motorcycle, for the few who care to consider them. In my view, it is the most versatile vehicle there is for moving through strange countries at a reasonable pace, experiencing changing conditions and meeting with people in remote places. It can cover immense distances, and will take you where cars can hardly go. It is easily and cheaply freighted across lakes and oceans, and it can usually be trucked out of trouble without much difficulty, where a car might anchor you to the spot for weeks. If you choose a good bike for your purpose, it will be economical and easy to repair, and it can be made to carry quite astonishing amounts of stuff if your systems are right.

Sit Up and Take Notice

In return the bike demands the highest level of awareness from its rider. You need not be an expert, but you must be enthusiastic and keep all your wits about you. It is an unforgiving vehicle which does not suffer fools at all. As well as the more obvious hazards of potholes, maniacal truck drivers and stray animals, there are the less tangible perils like dehydration, hypothermia and plain mental fatigue to recognize and avoid.

The bike, then, poses a real challenge to its rider, and it may seem to verge on masochism to accept it, but my argument is that by choosing to travel in a way that demands top physical and mental performance you equip yourself to benefit a thousand times more from what comes your way, enabling you quite soon to brush aside the discomforts that plague lazier travellers.

You absolutely must sit up and take notice to survive at all. The weather and temperature are critical factors; the moods and customs of the people affect you vitally; you are vulnerable and sensitive to everything around you; and you learn fast. You build up resistances faster too, your instincts are sharper and truer, and you adjust more readily to changes in the climate, both physical and social.

Here endeth the eulogy upon the bike.

After all these generalizations, it is difficult to be particular. There is no one bike for all seasons, nor one for all riders. The BMW is a splendid machine with a splendid reputation for touring, but it is *not* infallible, and it *is* expensive. British bikes need a lot of maintenance but they are ruggedly engineered and easily repaired, given the parts or a Punjabi workshop to make them up. Japanese bikes have a shorter useful life, but they work very well, and their dealer networks are incomparable. They are hard to beat as a practical proposition provided you go for models with a tried record of reliability.

On the whole, I would aim for an engine capacity of between 500cc and 750cc. Lightness is a great plus factor. Too much power is an embarrassment, but a small engine will do fine if you don't mean to hump a lot of stuff over the Andes, or carry another person as well.

One's Company

I travelled alone almost all the way around the world, but most people prefer to travel in company. As a machine the motorcycle is obviously at its best used by one person, and it is my opinion that you learn faster and get the maximum feedback on your own, but I know that for many such loneliness would be unthinkable. Even so, you need to be very clear about your reasons for choosing to travel in company. If it is only for security then my advice is to forget it. Groups of nervous travellers chattering to each other in some outlandish tongue spread waves of paranoia much faster than a single weary rider struggling to make contact in the local language. A motorcycle will attract attention in most places. The problem is to turn that interest to good account. In some countries (Brazil, for example) a motorcycle is a symbol of playboy wealth, and an invitation to thieves. In parts of Africa and the Andes, it is still an unfamiliar and disturbing object. Whether the attention it attracts works for the rider or against him depends on his own awareness of others and the positive energy he can generate towards his environment.

It is very important in poor countries not to flaunt wealth and superiority. All machinery has this effect anyway, but it can be much reduced by a suitable layer of dirt and a muted exhaust system. I avoided having too much glittering chrome and electric paintwork, and I regarded most modern leathers and motorcycle gear as a real handicap. I wore an open face helmet for four years and never regretted it, and when I stopped among people, I always took it off to make sure they saw me as a real person. My ideal was always to get as far away as possible from the advertised image of the smart motorcyclist, and to talk to people spontaneously in a relaxed manner. If one can teach oneself to drop shyness with strangers, the rewards are dramatic. Silence is usually interpreted as stand-offishness, and is almost as much a barrier as a foreign language.

Care and Repair

Obviously you should know your bike and be prepared to look after it. Carry as many tools as you can use, and all the small spares you can afford. Fit a capacitor so that you don't need a battery to start. Weld a disc on the swing stand to hold the bike in soft dirt. Take two chains and use one to draw the other off its sprockets. This makes frequent chain-cleaning less painful, something that should be done in desert conditions. Take a tin of Swarfega or Palmit; it's very useful where water is at a premium and for easing off rims. Buy good patches and take them (I like 'Tip-Top'); you won't get them there. The Schrader pump, which screws into a cylinder in place of the spark plug, is a fine gadget, and one of the best reasons for running on two cylinders. Aerosol repair canisters, unfortunately, do not always work. The quickly detachable wheel arrangement on the Triumph saved me a lot of irritation too.

Change oil every 2,500km and don't buy it loose if you can avoid it. Make *certain* your air filter is good enough. Some production models will not keep out fine desert grit, and the consequences are not good. Equally important are low compression pistons to take the strain off and to accept lousy fuel.

I ran on Avon tyres and used a rear tread on the front wheel, which worked well. A set of tyres gave me 19,000km or more. The hardest country for tyres was India, because of the constant braking for oxcarts on tarmac roads. It was the only place where the front tyre wore out before the rear one because, of course, it's the front brakes that do most of the stopping.

Insurance is a problem that worries many people. Get it as you go along. I was uninsured everywhere except when the authorities made it impossible for me to enter without buying it. This was most definitely illegal and I do not recommend it: if you get clobbered you have only yourself to blame. (*See Insurance on page 281 and Driving Requirements on page 684*.)

Other things I found essential were: a stove, a good, all-purpose knife, some primitive cooking equipment and a store of staples like rice and beans. Naturally you need to carry water too, up to four or five litres, if possible. I found the ability to feed myself when I felt like it was a great protection against sickness, as well as an incentive to wander even further off the beaten track. In the end I finished with quite a complex kitchen in one of my boxes, but of course that's just a matter of taste.

Don't . . .

Finally a few things I learned not to do:

Don't ride without arms, knees and eyes covered and watch out for bee swarms, unless you use a screen, which I did not.

Do not carry a gun or any offensive weapon unless you want to invite violence.

Do not allow yourself to be hustled into starting off anywhere until you're ready; something is bound to go wrong or get lost.

Do not let helpful people entice you into following their cars at ridiculous speeds over dirt roads and potholes. They have no idea what bikes can do. Always set your own pace and get used to the pleasures of easy riding.

Resist the habit of thinking that you must get to the next big city before nightfall. You miss everything that's good along the way and, in any case, the cities are the least interesting places.

Don't expect things to go to plan, and don't worry when they don't. Perhaps the hardest truth to appreciate when starting a long journey is that the mishaps and unexpected problems always lead to the best discoveries and the most memorable experiences. And if things insist on going too smoothly, you can always try running out of petrol on purpose.

bove Deck: Complimentary or Vorking Ocean Passages

y Paul Pratt

n these days of universal air travel, ew globetrotters have to make the hoice between travelling by ship or y plane. But the overlander with his wn vehicle has to consider the merits f ocean transport. And while the nerits are pretty clear, there are still roblems.

It's true that drive-on/drive-off ehicle ferries are the rule in Europe, nd that some other parts of the vorld have adequate inter-island assenger/cargo boats which can car-y a motorcycle, or even a car, on leck. But to secure a sea passage vhile accompanying a vehicle, though ighly desirable, is difficult because of he present shortage of passenger/argo ships on intercontinental outes. The romantic days when you ould simply board a tramp steamer nd work a passage to some distant hore are nearly over, the scene now eing all but destroyed by a complex ureaucracy involving many organiza-ions such as port authorities, im-nigration, shipping unions and the ike.

Nevertheless a person who is not in egular employment while travelling nd is therefore unable to save the equired fare quickly can, by using a ittle resourcefulness, some time and nlimited patience, make alternative rrangements.

One possibility if you have any xperience, although it is virtually mpossible to take a vehicle with you, s to arrange to crew on a private acht, of which a surprisingly large umber flit between the glamour spots of the world. Notice boards in marinas, the yachting magazines and personal contact in sailing communities can all help find berths.

A Working Passage

Many travellers have extreme ideas about the possibility of obtaining a complimentary passage by ship or plane or working one's ship passage as a 'workaway' or supernumerary crew member. They think that because they are on a trip and far away from home, it should be easy. Others consider the whole prospect downright hopeless from the start. My own experience indicates that the truth lies somewhere between these two extremes.

In the case of a complimentary or reduced fare, it is necessary to offer the shipping company or airline a worthwhile and valuable service in return. For myself, I would customarily carry out a complete PR programme for the company concerned. This could take several forms: circulating press releases which gave an account of my travels to date and how I came to join the ship, directed particularly at the media in ports of call on the vessel's regular trade route; articles and photographs supplied for the company's house journal; lectures illustrated with coloured slides, delivered at sea to the crew and passengers; or an agreement to mention the company in my publications and lectures during and after the completion of the journey.

The working passage is a rather different situation and, for the most part, consists of convincing the ship's captain and crew that you can be of service on the ship and then obtaining the cooperation of the shipping agent and/or shipowners. I was successful in obtaining working or concessionary passages in every case during my twelve and a half years travel with the sole exception of the first passage (Liverpool to New Orleans, 1966) and, of course, a few short distance ferries and inter-island boats.

Approaches

How do you go about it, and what happens when you do? In the first instance, the traveller usually approaches a shipping agent to enquire about working a passage to his required destination. Lacking a direct introduction to the General Manager, he is directed to a junior clerk who will most likely give a negative and discouraging answer. There is no need to be disheartened by this. The shipping agent has no reason to be interested in helping a traveller obtain a working passage since the agency stands to earn no money in this way, will become involved in extra paperwork on your account, and has to accept some unwanted responsibility if things fail to work out to everybody's satisfaction.

After your enquiry has been forcefully turned down, you then ask whether they would object to your visiting a suitable ship and speaking to the captain. They can hardly raise any real objections, and once this request is granted, you are over the first hurdle. You now have *approved* access to the docks, which means that you can, almost certainly, visit any other ships which happen to be in port at that time.

The next step is to visit the ship as soon as possible after arrival and meet the captain, bringing all available re
ferences concerning your qualifica
tions and character along with an
press releases concerning your jour
ney. Then just hope for the best.
person with qualifications which ca
be utilized on board ship, e.g. cater
ing or engineering, will have a bette
chance of success than most. Best c
all is to have worked on ships before
In my own case, I was able to mak
use of my formal training in servicin
electronic equipment and assisted th
ship's electrician on general electrica
maintenance.

Even after obtaining the agreemen
of the captain it may be necessary t
cable the ship's owners for forma
approval. This can take valuable time
I once missed a ship in San Francisc
because the owner's confirmation wa
received after the ship had sailed!

Flexible Arrangements

Given the right circumstances, th
best possible procedure is to write
letter to the ship at the previous por
of call. This will give the captain tim
to consider the matter and discuss i
with other crew members. Ships ofte
spend only a short period of time i
port. Before docking the captain ma
have been up all night supervisin
coastal navigation, the preparation o
documents, etc., and after dealin
with port bureaucracy, will hav
minimum interest in receiving unex
pected visitors.

As a general rule, Scandinavia
ships are the best bet, usually bein
efficiently run, clean, safe, and merci
fully free of the labour union prob
lems which plague other ships (fron
the USA, for example), making flexi
ble arrangements difficult.

Arranging a working passage may sound like a drawn out and complicated procedure, but if you are instead to accompany your vehicle as a paying passenger, you are certain to encounter just as much unavoidable bureaucracy and unreliable information on shipping dates, as well as having to meet the very heavy shipping and loading/unloading charges.

Once you are established on the ship as a 'workaway' then, as a crew member, you are accepted as part of the scene. The crew will care for your property as their own and you can suggest a location for the storage of your vehicle as far as possible under cover, safe from the destructive salt spray and accessible for maintenance during the voyage. While working my passage, I have had the use of the best equipped workshops of the whole journey – on board ship! The crew usually supervise the loading and offloading of the vehicle and so minimize the risk of damage and theft. Since thieves are always active on any dock, constant vigilance is necessary. The only dockside theft I ever experienced, however, was in Liverpool where, acting on the advice of the agent, I left my tool box in a 'safe lockup' on the dock, only to have it broken open.

Sailing: The Rough and the Smooth

by Bob Nance

For most of us, voyaging by yacht has romantic connotations. The reality is that it is a time-consuming and costly business. A good ground rule to apply is to estimate the time and cost involved, double both and then add a little more.

In fitting out a yacht it is wise to use the best quality equipment. Regard each item as a long-term investment and it will pay off in safety and lower maintenance costs. Cut costs, if necessary, in some other area so as to be able to purchase valuable items of equipment.

There are always differences of opinion amongst sailors about the quantity and type of electronic equipment suitable for a yacht. The large yachts may have radar, Loran or Omega systems, which are of great value for navigation, but they are expensive and require a power source. Away from Europe and North America, maintenance and replacement of parts could be the cause of delays. Many smaller yachts, including my own, *Tzu Hang*, carry no electronic equipment other than a small radio direction finder and radio receiver. There have been many instances where lives have been saved by the use of a radio transmitter. By choice I do not carry one: I prefer to rely on my own resources should we strike trouble and always make the crew aware of this fact. The trickiest part of using a radio transmitter is to know which crystals for which frequencies should be used in different parts of the world (*see Radio Communication on page 418*).

A radio direction finder can be of great value when making landfalls or cruising along coastal areas in most parts of the world; and it is desirable also to have a good depth sounder.

Provisioning

When provisioning for a voyage to remote parts, it is usually better and cheaper to stock up on bulk foods such as rice and flour and on canned foods before leaving Europe or North America. Though bulk foods vary little in price throughout the world, their quality in Africa or South or Central America tends to be inferior. Canned foods last for a long time. I have carried cans aboard *Tzu Hang* for up to four years and found the contents still in good condition. Meat needs to be bought bottled or canned, but fruit, vegetables and some other provisions can be bought fresh at local markets. Buying fresh foods where possible is preferable and generally cheaper. Fresh food keeps well at sea, even without refrigeration. We have cruised for over two months in the Patagonian canals of Chile without being able to purchase fresh supplies and without refrigeration. Remember that high islands will normally have some fresh fruit available, while low islands and atolls are unreliable for all fresh provisions, including water.

Fresh supplies can be supplemented by fish, for those skilled enough to catch them, but it is worth noting that some reef fish in the tropics are poisonous. Shellfish are usually abundant in colder areas, but it often takes a diver equipped with a wet suit to catch them.

A last word on provisions: freeze-dried foods are excellent, but the large quantities of water required to make them up may prohibit their use on a yacht.

Corruption and Catastrophe

In selecting crew, beware of overcrowding, which is a major source of trouble. A skipper should avoid being dependent on a large crew: at worst, he may be held to ransom by a mutinous crew, aware that he cannot proceed without them.

We all tend to think we are free of officialdom once on a yacht, but there are still plenty of formalities to be observed. In planning a cruise, apply for visas and permits ahead of time. The consulate or embassy of the countries concerned will advise you what papers are required for entry and exit. Knowing what is in store is the best way to avoid irritations, fines and restrictions.

It is proper, and avoids creating friction with officials, to fly the quarantine flag and the flag of the country you are entering as a courtesy. Whether you arrive at night, at a remote spot or in a harbour, always seek out officials as soon as possible, if necessary making your way to an official entry point or town. Most countries have quite a lot of paperwork to enter a yacht, which can entail seeing several officials and, in some cases, checking in and out of each port. In many countries, a patrol boat coming across your yacht anchored and yourself perhaps ashore without papers for entry will have you promptly arrested and your boat towed under guard to the nearest police or military station. In Australia, the United States, Canada and New Zealand, to name but a few countries, your boat will most likely be confiscated if you enter without going through Customs. In these countries, and in the Pacific and the Caribbean islands, officials generally process incoming yachts quickly and efficiently. But it is always as well to allow plenty of time for this processing and essential to conform to the regulations.

It is acceptable to anchor in a remote bay or anchorage in many countries provided you fly the quarantine flag and do not go ashore. In case of emergency, the captain can go ashore alone to make contact with officials.

Occasionally you may encounter corrupt officialdom and be asked for illegal payments. Start by refusing to pay and request to see the head of the department concerned. If the official does not retract and the amount is small, it is probably better to show discretion and pay up.

Don't set out on a voyage without leaving behind you a reasonable bank balance that can be drawn upon in emergencies. As everywhere else, so too at sea, money is a necessary part of living. Your reserve fund need not, however, be enormous. Nobody can plan for catastrophic expenses. It is still possible to work your way around the world to meet your travel expenses, but to rely on this means of support nowadays is risky, as each year there are more and more restrictions and greater numbers of people travelling.

Shipshape and Safe

Maintenance of the yacht will be of prime importance and as much spare equipment should be carried as possible. Paints vary in quality, but can be obtained everywhere, though bottom paint is frequently not available and usually exorbitantly expensive. Again it is best to carry a good supply with you. When hauling a yacht or getting the work done at yards and yacht clubs, remember always to make sure of the costs and have them written down. Verbal agreements sometimes lead to misunderstandings.

In some areas, notably in the Caribbean, where drug-smuggling is a major problem, sailors have recently claimed to have been boarded, chased, threatened, or even fired on, and people and vessels have disappeared. The authorities claim that most violent incidents occur when an innocent party stumbles across smugglers making a transfer. There is little the ordinary sailor can do about this kind of trouble except to be aware of it and thus perhaps avoid it. If you think you've encountered something illegal, tell the police – from a safe distance – but don't get involved yourself at any cost.

Travel With a Pack Animal

by Roger Chapman

The donkey is the most desirable beast of burden for the novice and remains the favourite of the more experienced camper . . . if only because the donkey carries all his equipment, leaving him free to enjoy the countryside unburdened. Although small and gentle, the donkey is strong and dependable; no pack animal excels him for surefootedness or matches his character. He makes the ideal companion for children old enough to travel into the mountains or hills and for the adult who prefers to travel at a pace slow enough to appreciate the scenery, wildlife and wilderness that no vehicle can reach.

Rock climber, hunter, fisherman, scientist or artist who has too much gear to carry into the mountains may prefer to take the larger and faster mule, but if he is sensible, he will practice first on the smaller and more patient donkey. The principles of pack animal management are the same, but the mule is stronger, more likely to kick or bite if provoked, and requires firmer handling than the donkey. The advantage of a mule is obvious: whereas a donkey can only carry about 50kg (100lb), the mule, if expertly packed, can carry a payload of 100kg (200lb). Although both are good for fifteen miles a day on reasonable trails, the donkeys will have to be led on foot, whereas mules, which can travel at a good speed, require everyone to be mounted; unless their handlers are fast hikers.

Planning

To determine the number of animals needed before an expedition or holiday the approximate pack load must be calculated. The stock requirement for a ten-day trip can be calculated by dividing the number of people by two, but taking the higher whole number if the split does not work evenly. Thus, a family of five would take three donkeys. It is difficult to control more than ten donkeys on the trail, so don't use them with a party of twenty or more unless certain individuals are prepared to carry large packs to reduce the number of animals. Mules are usually led by a single hiker or are tied in groups of not more than five animals led by a man on horseback. This is the 'string' of mules often mentioned in Westerns; each lead rope passes through the left hand breeching ring of preceding animal's harness and is then tied around the animal's neck with a bowline. One or more horses are usually sent out with pack mules because mules respect and stick close to these 'chaperones'.

Whichever method you decide to use, don't prepare a detailed itinerary before your journey; wait and see how you get on during the first few days when you should attempt no more than 8–10 miles (12–16km) a day. Later you will be able to average 12–15 miles (20–24km), but you should not count on doing more than 15 miles (24km) a day although it is possible, with early starts and a lighter load, if you really have to.

Campers who use pack animals seldom restrict themselves to the equipment list of a backpacker. There is no need to do so, but before preparing elaborate menus and extensive wardrobes, you would do well to consider the price of hiring a pack animal. The more elaborate, heavy equipment, the more donkeys or mules there are to hire, load, unload, groom and find pasture for. In selecting your personal equipment you have more freedom ... perhaps a blow up mattress instead of a 'Karrimat', or a larger tent instead of the small 'basha' ... but it should not exceed 12kg (24lb) and should be packed into several of those small cylindrical soft bags or a seaman's kitbag. You can take your sleeping bag as a separate bundle and take a small knapsack for those personal items such as spare sweaters, camera, first aid kit and snacks required during the day. But there are some special items you will require if you are not hiring an efficient guide and handler: repair kit for broken pack saddles and extra straps for mending harness. An essential item is a 100lb spring scale for balancing the sacks or panniers before you load them on the pack animals in the morning. Remember too that each donkey/mule will be hired out with a halter, lead rope, two 'sacks', a pack cover and a thirty-foot pack rope. In addition, there will be pickets and shackle straps, curry combs, froghooks, canvas buckets, tools and possibly ointment or powders to heal saddle sores.

Animal Handling

The art of handling pack animals is not a difficult one, but, unfortunately, you cannot learn it entirely from a book. With surprisingly little experience in the field, the novice soon becomes an expert packer, confident that he can handle any situation which may arise on the trail and, above all, that he has learnt that uncertain science of getting the pack animal to do what he wants it to do. The donkey is more responsive than the mule and is quick to return friendship, especially if he knows he is being well packed, well fed and well rested. The mule tends to be more truculent, angry and resentful until he knows who is in charge. Therefore, an attitude of firmness and consideration towards the animal is paramount.

Perhaps the easiest way to learn the techniques of handling pack animals is to look at a typical day and consider the problems as they arise.

Collecting in the Morning

Pack animals can either be let loose, hobbled or picketed during the night. The latter is preferable, as even a mule which has its front legs hobbled can wander for miles during the night searching for suitable grass. If the animal is picketed, unloosen the strap around the fetlock which is attached to the picket rope and lead him back to the campsite by the halter. If the animals are loose, you may have to allow a good half hour or so to catch them. Collect the gentle ones first, returning later for the recalcitrant animals. Approach each cautiously, talking to him and offering a palmful of oats before grabbing the halter.

Tying Up and Grooming

Even the gentlest pack animal will need to be tied up to a tree or post before packing. The rope should be tied with a clove hitch at about waist height. Keep the rope short, otherwise the animal will walk round and round the tree as you follow with the saddle. It also prevents him stepping on or tripping over the rope. It is advisable to keep the animals well apart, but not too far from your pile of packed sacks or panniers.

Often donkeys, in particular, will have a roll during the night, so they require a good work-over with the brush or curry comb to remove dust or caked mud. Most animals enjoy this, but you mustn't forget that one end can bite and the other end can give a mighty kick. Personally, I always spend some time stroking the animal around the head and ears, talking to him before I attempt to groom him. Ears are very good indicators of mood. If the ears are upright, he is alert and apprehensive, so a few words and strokes will give him confidence; soon the ears will relax and lie back, but if the ears turn and stretch right back along his neck, then there is a good chance you are in for trouble. The first time he nips, thump him in the ribs and swear at him. He will soon learn that you do not appreciate this kind of gesture.

Your main reason for grooming is to remove caked dirt which may cause sores once the animal is loaded. Remove this dirt with a brush and clean rag, and if there is an open wound, apply one of the many animal antiseptic ointments or sprinkle on boric acid powder which will help to dry it up. Finally, check each hoof quickly to see that no stone or twig has lodged in the soft pad. Lean against the animal, then warn him by tapping the leg all the way down the flank, past the knee to the fetlock, before lifting the hoof; otherwise you will never succeed. If there is a stone lodged between the shoe and the hoof, prise it out with a frog hook.

Saddling and Loading

Animals are used to being loaded from the left or near side. First you fold the saddle blanket, place it far forward then slide it back into position along the animal's back so that the hair lies smooth. Check that it hangs evenly on both sides, sufficient to protect the flanks from the loaded sacks. Stand behind the mule or donkey – but not too close – and check it before you proceed further. Pick up the pack saddle – two moulded pieces of wood jointed by two cross-trees – and place it on the saddle blanket so it fits in the hollows behind the withers. Tie up the breast strap and rear strap before tying the girth tight. Two people will be required to load the equipment in the soft canvas sacks onto the saddle pack, but it is essential to weigh the sacks before you place them on the cross-trees; they should be within 2kg of each other. If the saddle is straight, but one sack is lower than the other, correct the length of the ear loops.

On the Trail

Morning is the best time to travel, so you must hit the trail early, preferably before seven am. At a steady 2km an hour, you will be able to cover the majority of the day's journey by the time the sun is at its hottest. This will allow you to spend a good three hours rest-halt at midday before setting off once more for a final couple of hours before searching for a campsite. Avoid late camps, so start looking by four pm.

During the first few days you may have some trouble getting your donkeys or mules to move close together and at a steady pace. One man should walk behind each animal if they are being led and if there are any hold ups, he can apply a few swipes of a willow switch to the hind-quarters. It is a waste of time to shout at the animals or threaten them constantly as it only makes them distrustful and skittish. The notorious stubbornness of the mule or donkey is usually the result of bad handling in the past. Sometimes, it is a result of fear or fatigue, but less so of sheer cussedness or an attempt to see how much he can get away with. The only occasion when I could not get a mule moving was travelling across some snow patches in the mountains of Kashmir. Eventually, after losing my temper and lashing him with a switch, I persuaded him to move forward slowly across the snow, only for him to fall through the icy surface and disappear into a snow hole. It took my companion and me three hours to unload him, pull him out and calm him down before we could repack. I learned a good lesson from my lack of awareness of the innate intelligence of the mule.

Understanding

There is no problem with unpacking; it can be done quickly and efficiently. Just remember to place all the equipment neatly together so it is not mixed up. Keep individual saddles, sacks and harnesses close enough together to cover with the waterproof cover in case of rain. Once unloaded, the donkeys or mules can be groomed, watered and led off to the pasture area where they are to be picketed for the night.

Recently, I took my wife and two young daughters on a 120-mile journey across the Cévennes mountains in south-east France. We followed Robert Louis Stevenson's route which he described in his charming little book *Travels With a Donkey*. We took three donkeys – two as pack animals and one for the children to take turns in riding – on a trail which had not changed much over the past hundred years. It made an ideal holiday, and we returned tanned, fitter, enchanted by the French countryside and aware that it was the character of our brave little donkeys which had made our enjoyment complete.

The speed with which the children mastered the technique of pack animal management was encouraging because it allowed us to complete our self-imposed task with enough time to explore the wilder parts of the mountains and enjoy the countryside at the leisurely pace of our four-footed companions. We also took a hundred flies from one side of the Cévennes to the other, but that is another story.

The Train Now Standing . . .

by Christopher Portway

Trains. A word spelling the daily grind to and from work for many, the gateway to new worlds for some, a vehicle to adventure for a few. Somewhere in between comes the category of person who loves trains simply for the railway's sake and there are just a few eccentrics like me who find in world train travel something of the elixir of life.

Planning a long distance train journey is part of the attraction. The Thomas Cook International Timetables are the bibles of the likes of me; their snippets of information unearthed from a morass of footnotes spelling out the shape of wanderings still to come. I donated one such footnote, which I find a source of great pride, and I also donated the Ibarra–San Lorenzo train timings as nobody else could prize them out of the Ecuadorian State Railway Headquarters. This notwithstanding, what is still not made quite clear by Mr Cook is that first class travel on this amazing line means riding a converted British Leyland *bus* while lesser breeds in second class have to make do with the back of a British Leyland *lorry*. Both types of vehicle have a habit of running out of petrol in tunnels, and passengers – first and second class – are expected to dig their way out of the frequent landslides to which the line is prone.

Cook's Turkish Railway section also contains some gems of understatement only appreciated by those who have sweated out the journey between Istanbul and Baghdad. 'Passengers in direct transit by rail should allow at least eight hours for connections between trains' reads a footnote, from which it can be deduced that some Turkish trains do not stick too laboriously to their published timetable. If they did, I can assure you that nobody would catch them. When I was last on such a train it won my accolade for being the slowest in the world and there was the kind of rapport between driver and passengers that allowed for walking beside the train picking flowers and fruit en route. The cooking of meat on charcoal burners on the carriage floor was another original activity and if you weren't asphyxiated by smoke coming in the window while the train was in tunnels then you were by that coming from within your compartment.

For a final word on the Thomas Cook tomes and what they do and do not tell you in their cryptic fashion, take Table 5942 of Pakistan Railways as an example. The Quetta–Kahedan (southern Iran) line is one to be avoided: even I found it hard going. The intense heat of the Baluchistan Desert frequently buckles the rails; anti-government tribes have a penchant for venting their wrath on the the trains; progress across the shifting sands that cover the tracks is dead slow; and, with only two trains in each direction a week, overcrowding is rife. Again passengers are expected to help repair track when necessary.

Standards of Comfort

One thing about travelling such trains in Asia is that you will never want for food. At every stop vendors fall over themselves to serve you titbits of cooked meat and cake. Select what you eat with care or you risk a variety of tummy upsets.

The general comfort of train travel will, of course, vary from country to country and from railway to railway. All over Western Europe, the trains are luxurious, efficient and expensive. In Eastern Europe too the trains are generally good. The one exception might be Albanian Rail, but since I'm one of the few Westerners to have risked the wrath of the totalitarian Albanian People's Republic by commuting between Tirana, Durres and Elbasan on crackpot trains that are forbidden to foreigners, this is of little interest to most travellers. Soviet trains are paragons of plain comfort and timekeeping. In Cuba, in spite of a personal application made to Dr Castro, I was allowed nowhere near a train.

In the United States, the railway is very thin on the ground and train travel is looked upon by Americans as no more than a once-in-a-lifetime fun way to cross the country.

The railways of South America are less efficient and less comfortable but cheaper to travel and, most importantly, offer their passengers a window onto the countryside.

You are also amongst the local people, which is a major attraction of travelling on such trains. The cheaper seats are intolerably hard and the carriage windows have a tendency to remain immovably open or closed, but one's fellow travellers are the more colourful. In Peru is the Central Railway from Lima to Oroya on to Huancayo and Hauncavelica which is one of the wonders of Latin America. The line reaches its maximum altitude of 4,782m to make it the highest passenger-carrying railway in the world. White-coated medical staff flit about the corridors equipped with oxygen apparatus for the use of altitude-stricken passengers.

Arrangements

You can, if you prefer, leave all the arranging of a multi-country journey to a travel agent but these gentry usually have little imagination or knowledge where trains are concerned and simply book you seats on the more reliable expresses or deflect you to the airlines. However, always be prepared for the unexpected when you come to put your rail itinerary to the test. Trains may come and trains may go, but not always the way you thought.

With the ever-spiralling cost of petrol, it is cheaper to travel by train – even in Britain where rail transportation is looked upon as expensive – than it is by car, though, of course, this depends on numbers carried in the car. Very many of the railway-orientated nations give the intending rail traveller a variety of special offers that, in numerous circumstances, reduce fares dramatically. In Britain it has become almost as complex a business to sort them out as is the selection of best-buy fares across the Atlantic.

British Rail ties in with several rail systems on the continent to arrange inclusive rail holidays or tours while youngsters under 26 can obtain Inter-Rail passes covering a month's unlimited travel in Europe for, currently, around £100. (*See the Budget Traveller, page 222.*) And once there, a maze of rail travel offers are on tap. To find out more about them it is an idea to write in advance to the London tourist office of the country concerned. France, in particular, has many fine rail travel bargains in the shop window.

One big advantage of train riding over coach travel and flying is that there is space to move around and better opportunities for meeting fellow-passengers. You can eat on a train, sleep on a train, and it is certainly a more restful method of covering distance than any other mechanical means of propulsion. On some railways you can buy tickets in advance; on some you can't, but the train invariably gets there more or less on time. Board it in the right frame of mind and it's fun too.

Travel by Freighter

by Ingrid Cranfield

The International Conventions and Conferences on Marine Safety have defined a freighter (or cargo liner, which is the same thing) as 'a vessel principally engaged in transporting goods, which is licensed to carry a maximum of twelve passengers.' 'Vessels principally engaged' in goods traffic, yet carrying *more* than twelve passengers, are called combination cargo-passenger ships. In common parlance there are cargo freighters and passenger freighters, the cargo freighters (curiously enough) being the ones that carry more passengers, perhaps up to 100. Nowadays the average freighter carries from two to twelve passengers. In the United States, there remains just one freighter line which carries up to 100 passengers (and has a doctor on board).

The slow boat to China still exists, but passengers are less likely to be able to board it than ever before. In recent years many lines have discontinued taking passengers; on those that still do, space is extremely limited and preference is given to people taking a round trip. The average freighter passenger these days is not a traveller merely taking the leisurely route from A to B but a holidaymaker with perhaps fifty or sixty days free in which to roam the oceans before returning to home port. Freighters being primarily cargo carriers, they give precedence to cargo and people accordingly fall into second place.

Cargo Comes First

There's another reason for the decline in vacancies for passengers, which has to do with the animate nature of people and the inanimate nature of cargo. Passengers require food and attention, comfortable accommodation and service. Passengers make demands and complaints. Goods just lie there quietly and behave themselves.

Many sailings are booked up a year or more in advance. To make sure of a passage, it is often worthwhile to ask the shipping line if you can be put on a waiting list if no booking is immediately available. This usually pays off, as there is normally no charge and cancellations often occur. Most freighter voyages begin in the USA, very few in Europe. Bookings have, with few exceptions, to be made locally: an agent in the USA could control space available for East or West Coast sailings but not for European ones. Since departure dates are variable, notification to embark would be most difficult, and anyway, preference is shown to those taking a round trip from the United States.

Perhaps the biggest attraction of freighter travel, for the person with few pressing time commitments who savours the unexpected, is the flexibility of departure dates and itinerary common to cargo ships. The initial date of departure may vary by a few days; a port may be added to the itinerary or deleted from it; arrival times may be brought forward or put back. If the duration of the passage is longer than anticipated, the passenger pays no additional charge. There is no existing legislation that requires performance bonds for ships with fewer than fifty passengers. You should therefore enquire what is likely to happen with regard to refunds or alternative arrangements in the event of a cancellation or delay.

Freighters visit off-beat ports not usually serviced by cruise liners and stay longer in each port than do such passenger ships. However, with the increase in containerization, cargo liners can load and unload more quickly than they once did and consequently spend less time in port. Passengers who wish to have more time ashore should choose bulk-loading ships since their cargo takes longer to move. On a container vessel cabins overlooking the bow of the ship have the poorest view since this area is always filled with containers.

While freighters do not dock at passenger terminals, where tourist information is usually to be found, and no formal arrangements are made for passenger shore excursions, plenty of advice on sights to see will be forthcoming from the crew or, in advance, from the shipping line or its agents, and from the tourist offices in ports on the itinerary. Still on the subject of ports, one should caution that not all freighters disembark passengers at the same port at which they embarked. However, a passenger is normally guaranteed a passage back to his home country. It is advisable to take along on the voyage a few extra passport photographs in case of calls to unscheduled ports where visas may be required.

Life Afloat

Most of the freighters currently in operation are of postwar construction, with cruising speeds of 16–23 knots. They usually offer well-appointed and spacious accommodation amidships (where there is little vibration from propellers). Common rooms are frequently air-conditioned and many vessels have not only a lounge but also a games room and a library. No shipboard entertainments are provided, as a rule, except perhaps for film shows two or three times a week.

Passengers mix freely with the crew and take meals with the officers, which affords ample opportunity for the passengers to quiz their hosts about life at sea and ports of call to be visited along the way. Meals are served – at one sitting – on the early side: breakfast around 7.30–8.30am, lunch 11.30–12.30pm, tea – 3.00pm, cocktails – 5.00pm and dinner at about 6.00pm. Special diets cannot usually be catered for.

Casual wear is the order of the day – and usually of the evening as well.

For comparable accommodation and meals, the freighter passenger normally pays considerably less than the passenger on a cruise liner, and small extras, such as between-meal snacks, are often included in the overall price.

If fully laden, a freighter can give a smoother ride than a cruise ship, as most of the ship's weight is carried below the water level. The vessel therefore lies low in the water, much of it out of reach of the wind and surface swell. Additionally, the weight of the cargo acts as a stabilizer; and the wide beam of the vessel counteracts any tendency to roll.

Many freighter passengers are retired people over the age of sixty. Older people particularly should note that most freighters carry no doctor on board. The shipping companies require would-be passengers over sixty-five to submit a letter from a GP stating they are fit to travel. Medical supplies are however always carried on board and all officers are trained in first aid. In the event of serious illness or emergency, a doctor on another ship or from a shore station can be called for advice or summoned to the freighter, or the patient is put ashore or transferred to another ship.

Children are not accepted as passengers on freighters.

Some lines offer single occupancies as well as doubles, so that solo passengers are well catered for; elsewhere single people would, of course, have to be prepared to share a double cabin.

Tips

A few tips for freighter travellers:

1. Consult the shipping line concerned for information; often better still, ask your travel agent to advise on competitive sailings and other connections for onward travel. The

cost of tickets bought from an agent is no more than from the shipping company itself. Ask the company for a pass to visit the freighter on which you are considering a voyage before you make a reservation.

2. Plan and make your reservation as far ahead as possible, as certain popular routes and sailing times fill up rapidly.

3. Ask about special permits that may be required. Passengers embarking in the USA who are not themselves US citizens may need an Income Tax Clearance Certificate (Sailing Permit). This is obtainable on application in person from an office of the US Department of Internal Revenue.

4. Insure your baggage fully, as the liability of the shipping company is severely limited. Valuables may be placed in the ship's safe, but the risks are assumed by the owner.

5. Consult the company or travel agent about the shipping of vehicles, furniture or household effects or if you wish pets to accompany you on your voyage. Mail can be sent to passengers care of the port agent; letters should be marked with the name, sailing date and destination of the vessel.

6. The Purser, Ship's Steward and other officers are at your disposal on board. Discuss with them any problems you may encounter with shipboard life, especially such minor matters as tipping. The waiter and room steward will expect a tip: five per cent of the total fare split between them is a good guide.

7. Pack a pair of low-heeled, rubber-soled shoes: they are a must for safety when your vessels hits rough seas. And take plenty of reading material in case the sea, the company and the activities begin to pall.

Useful address for British readers: Pitt and Scott Travel Ltd., 3 Cathedral Place, London EC4M 7DT (Tel: 01-248 6474) produce an annual brochure containing details of voyages by freighter. Destinations include the Caribbean, Canada, the USA, South America, Africa, the Far East, Australia and New Zealand, Poland and Finland.

Backpacking

by Hilary Bradt

The word 'backpacking' has been recently imported from America, along with some of the lightweight equipment which made feasible the whole concept of walking for days carrying the necessary food and shelter. 'Backpacking' is often rather loosely used to cover hitchhiking and rough overland travel, but here we take it in its narrower sense, meaning to explore and enjoy the undeveloped parts of the world in the best way possible as an independent traveller – on foot. If you have only hiked in Britain you'll have little concept of wilderness in the American sense where you can walk for several days without passing human habitation. The Third World offers a different possibility – that of seeing the country, its rural life and natural history by hiking along paths worn smooth by the feet of countless peasants who habitually walk long distances from village to town, or hut to pasture.

Planning and Preparation

Equipment and provisions should be chosen with care, but only after you've researched the climate and terrain of your chosen region. Remember that high altitudes mean cold or freezing nights, and burning sun in the day; that tropical vegetation at low altitudes means humidity and mosquitoes; that equatorial countries have a rainy and dry season, rather than summer and winter, and that you'll be walking along mostly good paths in the Third World but on rougher terrain in the more developed countries where trails may be poorly maintained. Essential equipment includes a tent (this needn't weigh more than 2–3kg), sleeping bag (down filled if you're hiking in dry areas, artificial fill if heavy rain is expected), stove, and some dried food (which can be supplemented with the ubiquitous package soup). Bear in mind that if your pack weighs more than one quarter of your body weight you're not going to enjoy walking with it. If you are new to backpacking, get expert advice before buying your equipment. A good sports shop should help you, and there are many books on the subject.

Obviously you must be reasonably fit before setting out on a backpacking trip, but don't be overly concerned about it. After all, you can stop for the night more or less when and where you want, so there's no excuse for marathon daily mileage. I always start gently doing about eleven kilometres a day until I'm adjusted to the terrain and properly acclimatized.

Health

Backpacking is an excellent cure for the usual traveller's maladies – by preparing your own food and collecting your own water (purifying it if necessary), any stomach problems you started with will soon disappear. But remember that should you become sick or injured, help may be days away. So be prepared and bring such essentials as antibiotics, surgical tape and dressings in your medical kit. If you are hiking in low-lying areas in Africa or South America, anti-malarial drugs should be taken.

Perhaps the biggest health hazard facing backpackers is altitude sickness. The two most serious forms, pulmonary oedema and cerebral oedema, are often fatal. Acclimatize properly by climbing as slowly as possible, and spending several days at a high altitude before starting your hike. (*See section on Health on page 342.*)

Finding Your Way

If you are planning to backpack in the national parks or protected areas of the developed world, you'll have no trouble finding books and maps to guide you along every mile of your chosen route. There are few books describing hikes in the Third World, however, but here it's more exciting to discover your own route. What you do need is some sort of map, even if it's only a good road map, and a compass. Providing the area you've selected is populated by indigenous people, there'll be plenty of paths. Quite good topographical maps are available in most countries (*see article on Choosing Maps on page 24*). Ex-British colonies usually have excellent ones, though they may be a little out of date. Local mountaineering clubs are often good sources of information.

Although you may lose your way from time to time, don't confuse it with being lost. After all, the whole point of backpacking is to see interesting wildlife and people, so who cares if your destination changes during the course of your hike? As long as you keep to inhabited areas, there'll always be people to advise you. It's when you venture into real wilderness that you may find yourself in trouble. Above the treeline, the lack of paths presents no particular problem, providing you have a compass, but lower down it is dangerous and stupid to continue if the path has petered out. And you must remember that that scant high altitude vegetation turns into dense, unfriendly jungle as you lose height. Believe me, once you've tried forcing your way through spiny, stinging shrubs while rotting logs collapse under your feet and vines catch on your pack, you'll never again be too proud to retrace your steps.

Guides

Most people exploring unknown country rely on guides, and if you have a specific goal, such as some ruins hidden in the jungle or a distant mountain peak, it is obviously sensible to take a local person along to show you the way. Mere backpackers, however, will usually enjoy themselves more without the incessant chatter or blackmail which is unfortunately a frequent accompaniment. Guides often get lost, too. As you can see, I'm prejudiced against guides because the few times I've been obliged to use them, they've been inefficient or downright crooked, and spoiled the feeling of adventure. To me, nothing in travel comes close to the exhilaration of approaching a pass and having no idea what you'll see from the top, or what is round the next corner. This is the essence of backpacking.

Minimum Impact

Wherever you hike you have a responsibility to leave the place unchanged by your passing. This consciousness of your impact on the environment can vary from keeping to the path and designated campsites in heavily used areas such as some American National Parks, to respecting the customs and traditions of 'primitive' indigenous people. It goes without saying that you should leave no litter, or evidence of your campsite, but fewer travellers realize the harm that may be done to a fragile culture by the indiscriminate handing out of gifts or money.

Conclusion

There are few truly wild places left in the world for the traveller to explore. Many are accessible only on foot and the adventurous backpacker will see scenery, people and wildlife denied to the car-bound explorer. And if, from time to time, he indulges in more conventional forms of travel, he can take comfort in the knowledge that he carries food and shelter on his back which will tide him over any emergency.

Travel by Camel

by René Dee

In this mechanized and industrial epoch, the camel does not seem to be an obvious choice of travelling companion when sophisticated cross-country vehicles exist for the toughest of terrains. Add to this the stockpile of derisory and mocking myths, truths and sayings about the camel and one is forced to ask the question: why use camels at all?

Purely as a means of getting from A to B when time is the most important factor, the camel should not even be considered. As a means of transport for scientific groups who wish to carry out useful research in the field, the camel is limiting. It can be awkward and risky transporting delicate equipment and specimens. However, for the individual, small group and expedition wishing to see the desert as it should be seen, the camel is an unrivalled means of transport.

Go Safely in the Desert

From my own personal point of view, the primary reason must be that, unlike any motorized vehicle, camels allow you to integrate completely with the desert and the people within it – something which is impossible to do at 80kmph enclosed in a 'tin can'. A vehicle in the desert can be like a prison cell and the constant noise of the engine tends to blur all sense of solitude, vastness and deafening quiet which are an integral part of the desert.

Travel by camel allows the entire pace of life to slow down from a racy 80kmph to a steady 6.5kmph, enabling you to unwind, take in and visually appreciate the overall magnificence and individual details of the desert.

Secondly, camels do, of course, have the ability to reach certain areas inaccessible to vehicles, especially through rocky and narrow mountain passes, although camels are not always happy on this terrain and extreme care has to be taken to ensure they do not slip or twist a leg. They are as sensitive as they appear insensitive.

Thirdly, in practical terms they cause far fewer problems where maintenance, breakdown and repairs are concerned. No bulky spares are needed nor expensive mechanical equipment to carry out repairs. Camels do not need a great deal of fuel and can exist adequately (given that they are not burdened with excessively heavy loads) for five to ten days without water. Camels go on and on and on and on until they die; and then one has the option of eating them, altogether far better tasting than a Michelin tyre.

Lastly, camels *must* be far more cost effective if you compare directly with vehicles; although this depends on whether your intended expedition/journey already includes a motorized section. If you fly direct to your departure point, or as near as possible to it, you will incur none of the heavy costs related to transporting a vehicle, not to mention the cost of buying it. If the camel trek is to be an integral portion of a motorized journey, then the cost saving will not apply, as, of course, hire fees for camels and guides will be additional.

In many ways, combining these two forms of travel is ideal and a very good way of highlighting my primary point in favour of transport by camel. If you do decide on this combination, make sure you schedule the camel journey for the very end of your expedition and that the return leg by vehicle is either minimal or purely functional, as I can guarantee that after a period of ten days or more travelling slowly and gently through the desert by camel, your vehicle will take on the characteristics of a rocket ship and all sense of freedom, enquiry and interest will be dulled to the extreme. An overwhelming sense of disillusion and disinterest will prevail. Previously exciting sights, desert towns and Arab civilization, will pall after such intense involvement with the desert, its people and its lifestyle.

First Steps

For the individual or group organizer wanting to get off the beaten track by camel his first real problem is to find them, and to gather every bit of information possible about who owns them, whether or not they are for hire, for how much, what equipment/stores/provisions are included, if at all, and lastly, what the guides/owners are capable of and whether they are willing to accompany you. It is not much good arriving at Tamanrasset, Timbouctou or Tindouf without knowing some, if not all, of the answers to these questions. Good predeparture research is vital but the problem is that 90 per cent of the information won't be found in any tourist office, embassy, library or travel agent. Particularly if you're considering a major journey exclusively by camel, you'll more than likely have to undertake a preliminary fact-finding recce to your proposed departure point to establish contacts among camel owners and guides. It may well be that camels and/or reliable guides do not exist in the area where you wish to carry out your expedition.

I would suggest, therefore, that you start first with a reliable source of information such as the Royal Geographical Society, which has expedition reports and advice which can be used as a primary source of reference, including names and addresses to write to for up-to-date information about the area that interests you. Up-to-date information is without doubt the key to it all. Very often this can be gleaned from the commercial overland companies whose drivers are passing your area of interest regularly and may even have had personal experience of the journey you intend to make. Equally important is the fact that in the course of their travels, they build up an impressive collection of contacts who could well help in the final goal of finding suitable guides, smoothing over formalities and getting introductions to local officials, etc. Most overland travel companies are very approachable so long as you appreciate that their time is restricted and that their business is selling travel and not running an advisory service.

In all the best Red Indian stories, the guide is the all-knowing, all-seeing person in whom all faith is put. However, as various people have discovered to their cost, this is not always so. Many so-called guides know very little of the desert and its ways. How then to find someone who really does know the route/area, has a sense of desert lore and who preferably owns his own camel? I can only reiterate that the best way to do so is through personal recommendation. Having found him, put your faith in him, let him choose your camels and make sure that your relationship remains as amicable as possible. You will be living together for many days in conditions which are familiar to him but alien to you, and you need his support. Arrogance does not fit into desert travel, especially from a *nasrani*. Mutual respect and a good rapport are essential.

Pack Up Your Troubles

Once you've managed to establish all this and you're actually out there, what are the do's and don'ts and logistics of travel by camel? Most individuals and expeditions (scientifically oriented or not) will want, I imagine, to incorporate a camel trek within an existing vehicle-led expedition, so I am really talking only of short-range treks of around ten to fifteen days' duration, up to 400km. If this is so, you will need relatively little equipment/stores and it is essential that this is kept to a minimum. Remember that the more equipment you take, the more camels you will need, which will require more guides, which means more cost, more pasture and water, longer delays in loading, unloading, cooking and setting up camp and a longer wait in the morning while the camels are being rounded up after a night of pasturing.

Be prepared also for a very swift deterioration of equipment. In a vehicle, you can at least keep possessions clean and safe to a degree, but packing kit onto a camel denies any form of protection – especially since it is not unknown for camels to stumble and fall or to roll you over suddenly and ignominiously if something is not to their liking, such as a slipped load or uncomfortable saddle. My advice is to pack all your belongings in a seaman's kitbag which can be roped on to the camel's side easily, is pliable, hardwearing and, because it is soft and not angular, doesn't threaten to rub a hole in the camel's side or backbone. (I have seen a badly placed baggage saddle wear a hole the size of a man's fist into the back of a camel.) If rectangular aluminium boxes containing cameras or other delicate equipment are being carried, make sure that they are well roped on the top of the camel and that there is sufficient padding underneath so as not to cause friction. Moreover, you'll always have to take your shoes off while riding because over a period of hours, let alone days, you could wear out the protective hair on the camel's neck and eventually cause open sores.

Water should be carried in goatskin *guerbas* and 20 litre round metal *bidons* which can again be roped up easily and hung either side of the baggage camel under protective covers. Take plenty of rope for tying on equipment, saddles etc. and keep one length of fiteen metres intact for using at wells where there may be no facilities for hauling up water. Don't take any cooking stoves – the open fire is adequate and far less likely to break down. Don't take any sophisticated tents either; they will probably be ruined within days and anyway are just not necessary. I have always used a piece of cotton cloth approximately six metres square which, with two poles for support front and rear and with sand or boulders at the sides and corner, makes a very good overnight shelter for half a dozen people. Night in the desert can be extremely cold, particularly of course in the winter, but the makeshift 'tent' has a more important role during the day when it provides shelter for the essential two hour lunch stop and rest.

The Day's Schedule

Your daily itinerary and schedule should be geared to the practical implications of travelling by camel. That is to say that each night's stop will, where possible, be in an area where pasture is to be found for the camels to graze. Although one can take along grain and dried dates for camels to eat, normal grazing is also vital. The camels are unloaded and hobbled (two front legs are tied closely together), but you will find they can wander as much as three or four kilometres overnight and there is only one way to fetch them – on foot. Binoculars are extremely useful as spotting camels over such a distance can be a nightmare. They may be hidden behind dunes and not come into view for some time.

Other useful equipment includes goggles for protection in sandstorms, a prescription-suited pair of sunglasses and, of course, sun cream. Above all, take comfortable and hardwearing footwear for it is almost certain that you will walk at least half the way once you have become fully acclimatized. I would suggest that you take Spanish fell boots or something similar, which are cheap, very light, give ankle support over uneven terrain, are durable and very comfortable. The one disadvantage of boots by day is that your feet will get very hot, but it's a far better choice than battered, blistered and lacerated feet when one has to keep up with the camels' steady 6.5kmph. Nomads wear sandals, but if you take a close look at a nomad's foot, you will see that it is not dissimilar to the sandal itself, i.e. as hard and tough as leather. Yours resembles a baby's bottom by comparison – so it is essential that you get some heavy walking practice in beforehand with the boots/shoes/sandals you intend to wear. (If your journey is likely to be a long one, then you could possibly try sandals, as there will be time for the inevitable wearing-in process with blisters, as well as stubbed toes and feet spiked by the lethal acacia thorn).

For clothing, I personally wear a local, free-flowing robe like the *gandoura*, local pantaloons and a *chèche* – a three metre length of cotton cloth which can be tied round the head and/or face and neck for protection against the sun. You can also use it as a rope, fly whisk and face protector in sandstorms. In the bitter cold nights and early mornings of winter desert travel, go to bed with it wrapped around your neck, face and head to keep warm. If local clothing embarrasses and inhibits you, stick to loose cotton shirts and trousers. Forget your tight jeans and bring loose fitting cotton underwear. Anything nylon and tight fitting next to the skin will result in chafing and sores. Do, however, also take some warm clothing and blankets, including socks and jumpers. As soon as the sun sets in the desert, the temperature drops dramatically. Catching cold in the desert is unbearable. Colds are extremely common and spread like wildfire. Take a good down sleeping bag and a groundsheet. Your sleeping bag and blankets can also serve as padding for certain types of camel saddle. In the

Western Sahara you will find the Mauritanian butterfly variety, which envelopes you on four sides. You're liable to slide back and forth uncomfortably and get blisters unless you pad the saddle. The Tuareg saddle is commonly used in the Algerian Sahara. This is a more traditional saddle with a fierce looking forward pommel which threatens man's very manhood should you be thrown forward against it. In Saudi Arabia, female camels are ridden and seating positions are taken up behind the dromedary's single hump rather than on or forward of it.

Culture Shock

Never travel alone in the desert, without even a guide. Ideal group size would be seven group members, one group leader, three guides, eleven riding camels and three baggage camels. The individual traveller should take at least one guide with him and three or four camels.

Be prepared for a mind-blowing sequence of mental experience, especially if you are not accustomed to the alien environment, company and pace, which can lead to introspection, uncertainty and even paranoia. Travel by camel with nomad guides is the complete reversal of our normal lifestyle. Therefore it is as important to be mentally prepared for this culture shock as it is to be physically prepared. Make no mistake, travel by camel is hard, physically uncompromising and mentally torturing at times. But a *méharée* satisfactorily accomplished will alter your concept of life and its overall values, and the desert's hold over you will never loosen.

The Two-Wheeled Traveller

by Ray Reece and Martin Ayres

Cycling offers a hard and sometimes painful way of having a good time away from it all. But no matter where you travel on a bicycle, you can be sure of having an experience that no money can buy.

Home touring or transcontinental touring? There is quite a difference, both in approach and equipment. Whichever you are doing you do so under your own steam. Playing it tough or cool may look good at first, but one day you'll be saying a little prayer for anything you can do to make life a little easier on the way. In long-distance touring, one just must not leave things to chance, for the friendly cycle-dealer or drugstore you hope will put everything right in the next town usually doesn't exist.

The Machine

Old or new? If it's a once in a lifetime big tour, there is a temptation, if you're loaded (not many 'bikies' are), to treat yourself to a brand new machine, but the chances are your old one, especially if you are aiming at more than 5,000km, will be more trustworthy, particularly the frame. It is however worth renewing all the rotating parts. The frame size should be approximately 25cm less than your inside leg measurement, and of the best quality tube, or else you'll be spending more time in the welding shops than out, if travelling in Asia! Frame angles should be between 71° and 73° only.

The wheels *must* receive special attention, for they are going to carry more load and get more punishment than you ever thought possible. The rims must be steel, for in the event of a disaster, they can still be hammered, welded or even kicked back into a rideable shape. As for size, some controversy exists, for 68.5cm high pressure wheels are not only as rare as gold dust in many parts of the world, but are also somewhat lacking in reliability and comfort. In my experience, however, they are still the best choice. In an emergency, a 66cm tyre, of the type English tourists traditionally prefer can be fitted into a 68.5cm frame, but not usually the other way round. You have to carry spares anyway, and the 68.5cm tyres are lighter, less bulky, roll better, and provide an extra turn of speed which can often get you out of trouble. You can cover more ground when conditions are good and the smoother tread is much less likely to pick up grit and punctures on even the roughest dirt track, especially if you keep the pressure about ten per cent below average. Beware, though, of ruts and potholes.

Reckon on about 5,000km for a rear tyre and about 10,000km for the front. Wide flange hubs are the best choice, but not the quick release type, which are too easily stolen. The spokes must be top – repeat top – quality, using a gauge thicker than normal (e.g. twelve gauge double butted) at least on the rear wheel, and built to only a moderate tension, *not* tied and soldered.

The real hassle, if you weigh around 90kg, is spoke breakage on the gear side. Normally this means carrying a sprocket remover, but depending on the ratios and the type of freewheel, a spoke can be pushed through, sometimes by slightly enlarging the sprocket lightening holes beforehand and fitted without any dismantling.

Recent design innovations have produced freewheels that can be removed by a simple tool, rather than an extractor which is really a workshop tool and of little use for roadside repairs.

All bearings are best packed with grease (Molygrease) which will keep the dirt and water out. Spend some time getting each adjustment really 'neat' and you'll have no problems. Buy the best quality brakes you can afford, 'cheapies' will need constant adjustment and, because they are made from inferior materials, will feel spongy. Use wet weather blocks, the combination of soft composition blocks on wet steel rims is lethal. Pedals must be of good quality. They are exposed to the wet and grit from the road and are vulnerable to damage if the bike topples over, as it inevitably will. Toe clips and straps are strongly recommended, especially for struggling up mountains. Gear change mechanisms must be metal as they straighten more easily. Ten speed 'derailleurs' are fine and can be repaired or patched more easily than hub gears. Ratios should be 85–200cm. You'll be glad of mudguards, for even in the hottest country, it always manages to bucket down sooner or later. Handlebars are a personal thing, but with drops you have a choice of position, and it can sure take a load off your butt!

Which brings us to the saddle – another item of personal taste. The traditional leather saddle is unrivalled for comfort, but you will need to treat it with dressing or linseed oil until supple and ready to be 'broken in' to your shape. The newer plastic saddles need no breaking in, are light in weight, impervious to wet, and if covered in suede or leather 'breathe' in the same way as the traditional designs.

Rear panniers are best for luggage. Don't carry too much on the front of the bike, it makes the steering sluggish. However, a handlebar-mounted bag is useful for maps, camera, food, gloves, etc., and most are easily detached and have a shoulder strap for off-the-bike use. Don't carry anything at all on your back.

Keep your tool kit light. Chunky nuts and bolts are increasingly being replaced by Allen screws, saving weight on the bike and needing only a lightweight key in the tool kit. Otherwise you will need at least a combination spanner that will fit every nut on the cycle, a screwdriver, spoke key, chain rivet extractor, puncture kit, small flat file, scissors, two-tube epoxy glue, a small brush for chain and gear cleaning, PUC tape, spare brake blocks, and front and rear wheel nuts, pump connection and spare inner tube. Don't forget a pen knife and a piece of string.

Your cycle is your lifeline, but everywhere you go, even in the most civilized countries, someone will think he needs it more than you. So use a good cycle lock always. The 'indestructible' hardened steel ones are best. They're expensive, heavy and cumbersome, but they are the only locks capable of standing up to a determined thief with a pair of bolt cutters.

Typical advice when camping in Turkey: 'Tie it to a sensitive part of your body' (and they don't mean your big toe!). Wherever possible, keep it in sight or, better still, take it with you, meeting the raised eyebrow and protests with a smile; people will usually understand.

Routes, Rules and Ruses

Which way to go? Don't just get a route map and play it by ear. Every bit of planning will pay off. On a cycle, you've got to be more particular, but your reward will be that you really get something out of it, instead of giving it everything you've got just to make it through. Check out contours, temperatures, rainfall and unusual happenings like floods, monsoons, snow at altitude, sandstorm seasons, drought, etc.

Visas and inoculations are every bit as important for cyclists as for other travellers. Sometimes people are turned back at a border on a technicality – and on a bicycle, that can be disastrous. One poor fellow I met had to backtrack 650km each way just to get a yellow fever jab. Don't ever try dodging the formalities; get all the required passport stamps. Some countries will also want to stamp the cycle frame number in your passport, so make sure it is visible. What you take in you must take out, or you will be charged duty, on the assumption that the bike has been sold.

One very good tip is to keep all your documents – passport, bills, traveller's cheques and medical tickets – in a small zippered bag around your neck at all times. Money belts are, in my experience, too obvious, uncomfortable, and not safe. Remember that in some countries a passport is worth more on the black market than everything else you have put together!

Those who want to skip some of the

distance by other transport, *beware*. Supervise handling and stowage yourself. In many countries cycles are carried in separate trains from passengers and get lost. Cycles carried on roof-racks of buses get swiped off at low bridges. On ships, ask a crewman for some rope and tie the bike down securely. Fortunately, on aircraft, there is seldom a problem, but don't dismantle your machine unless requested to do so.

Training is a tough problem. First decide what weekly mileage you hope to achieve. 450km is comfortable, or if you are very fit, 550–700km. 1,000km a week is possible, but this is strictly for the 'superman' category. Aim at doing at least half of your scheduled weekly mileage each week for about four or five weeks before you leave, until the week before you take off; then forget the bike and recharge your batteries!

On the Road

In Europe, particularly the East, watch out for big trucks. In Italy, everyone is a Grand Prix driver! In Turkey, beware of flying buses with pilots instead of drivers. In many Third World countries watch out for everyone – they drive on both sides of the road – or straight down the middle. In India and Pakistan, mind the bullock carts, though the main hazard is what they leave behind. The most dangerous threat to a cyclist is a rabid dog. With the exception of the UK and a few small islands, this threat is everywhere. Don't ever take a gamble: consider getting vaccinated before you go and after any contact with a suspect animal go straight to the nearest hospital. Any other course of action may be fatal (*see article on Rabies on page 362*).

Accommodation is an area you can play by ear, often to great advantage. While it may be great to curl up in a comfortable hotel occasionally, don't miss the ultimate experience of cycle-touring with its total freedom of choice and contact with the common man. Beggar or millionaire, you will learn from everyone you meet.

When off the beaten track, always try to camp near another group or habitation. Ask permission if necessary. When completely alone, or in hostile regions, don't make camp until just on dusk. Be sure you haven't been watched and stay out of sight, particularly of the road and its car headlamps. Never ride at night. Women should not travel without some muscle in the party if venturing beyond Western Europe and the States.

Some advice once given to a traveller in New York was 'Keep a smile on your face and your hands in your pockets.' Well, this goes for riders abroad too, but be sure to keep one hand on your bike as well. Treat others as you would have them treat you, even if you can't speak the lingo, and in any tricky situation just offer a handshake – it will usually be accepted. If not, make mileage. And always remember; watch out for those motorists!

What Type of Travel?

The Budget Traveller

By Land

by Nick Hanna and Greg Brookes

There are a number of travel discount schemes that are not dependent upon student status, although most of these are nevertheless youth schemes, for which you cease to be eligible once you reach between 24 and 26. *The Federation of International Youth Travel Organizations* is made up of 125 organizations throughout the world which specialize in youth travel. A membership card entitles you to a range of concessions similar, although not identical to those given by ISIC (*see Student Traveller, page 249*). It is available to everyone under the age of 26, and is issued with a handbook listing all the concession entitlements. Youth Hostels and the YM (or W) CA (*see Hostels, page 378*) are now open to everyone, regardless of age, offering a good network of cheap, clean if spartan accommodation around the world.

There are two alternatives for cheap train travel. The first is an Inter-Rail card, which gives you unlimited free travel for one month in nineteen countries in Europe and North Africa, and costs £115. The card also allows you half price (but not free) travel on British Rail, and there are reductions on many shipping lines. It is available without condition to everyone who is under 26 and a national of UK or Ireland or a country whose railways do not participate in the scheme. If nationals of these countries can prove they live in UK or Ireland, they are also eligible.

The second option is a BIGE ticket, which like the Inter-Rail card is open to anyone under 26. These give you half price fares to over 2,000 European destinations and are valid for two months. The main specialists are Transalpino and Eurotrain.

Travelling round Britain there are worthwhile savings to be made. An absolute must is a Young Person's Railcard – for those under 24 – which costs £12, is valid for a year, and entitles you to half price British Rail tickets. It can be used on most journeys except where there are restrictions like minimum fares at peak hours. At the other end of the age scale, there are similar rail cards for old age pensioners, who can also travel extremely cheaply on National Express coaches at certain times, and can travel free by London Transport.

A half price youth rail card is also available in West Germany from GSTS. *The Deutsche Bundesbahn Junior Pass* allows half price rail travel for everyone under the age of 23.

By Air
by Philip Ray

It was at a travel industry conference in the early 1970s that the phrase 'bucket shop' was first used to denote an outlet specializing in the sale of air tickets at an 'illegal' discount. Such is the power of the media that the term – which was derived from shady activities in the nineteenth century US stock market – is now universally understood, even by those who have never flown in their lives.

Back in the early 1970s, the world of bucket shops was a pretty sleazy one, based on back rooms in Chinese supermarkets, or in flyblown first-floor offices in Soho. One or two of the early entrepreneurs actually ended up in prison and some of the cheap tickets which found their way on to the market place had, in fact, been stolen. One bucket shop which collapsed in 1977 traded as a 'reunion club' and ended up owing more than £620,000 to thousands of people who had been saving up to visit relatives abroad, not to mention another £614,000 owed to the airlines.

The owner of this club was eventually jailed for trading with intent to defraud; he knew that the 'club' could not meet its liabilities and yet he continued to trade for almost a year.

Failures still do occur – in 1983, an Aberdeen firm collapsed and customers lost their money – but it is noticeable that the bucket shop is beginning to 'come out'. Outlets are being opened in the high streets of provincial cities by respected companies with long experience of the travel business, and even some of the household names in retail travel are now able to supply discounted tickets.

It is worth taking a closer look at the discounting phenomenon and at what makes it 'illegal', if indeed it is. It is an economic fact of life that, on average, the world's scheduled airlines fill only two-thirds of their seats, so there is a very powerful inducement to fill the remaining one-third by any means possible. Assuming that overheads have been covered by the two-thirds paying 'normal' fares (although this is not necessarily a valid assumption), anything earned from one extra passenger means a bigger profit or, more likely, a smaller loss – provided that it covers the cost of in-flight meals and the notional cost of the extra fuel needed.

There are also plenty of third-world and eastern-bloc airlines which do not particularly care what rates they charge provided that they can earn some valuable hard currency.

The 'illegality' of discounting stems from the internationally agreed convention that governments can approve or disapprove the fares charged by the airlines using their airspace, and most countries have provision in their legislation which makes the sale of tickets illegal at other than the officially-approved rates. In the UK the legal position is not quite so clear-cut. British airlines are regulated by the Civil Aviation Authority and there is specific legislation which lays down heavy penalties against discounting. Foreign airlines, however, are separately controlled by the Department of Transport and, depending on whether there is a specific provision on tariffs in their permits, they may or may not be liable to be brought before the courts for discounting. There is a third class of airliner – the so-called offline carriers – which do not actually operate services into the UK but which maintain sales offices here. These airlines can, quite legally, do whatever they want in terms of discounting, because there is no law that can catch them.

All this is somewhat academic in the real world because no British government has ever tried to enforce the law, which suggests that perhaps it is time for it to be repealed.

What is happening in the UK marketplace at present is that the airlines themselves are attempting to stamp out discounting through a series of what are euphemistically called Yield Improvement Programmes. All the major carriers in a particular market – the UK-Australia route, for example – sign an undertaking that they will maintain the agreed tariffs and this agreement is then policed by inspectors who make test purchases of tickets in bucket shops. The tickets are bought at the discounted rate and are then presented to the airlines for refund at the officially approved fare, the difference representing a 'fine' for non-complicance with the agreement.

Taking the UK-Australia route again, experience of the first six months after the YIP became effective in July 1983 showed that the agreement seemed to be holding and the discounts which had once been widely available in the market could no longer be obtained. This was probably because Asian carriers like Malaysian Airline System and Thai International were allowed to sell tickets to Australia at a six per cent discount off the 'official' rate. But the irony was that some of the airlines operating through to Australia did not improve their yields. They continued supplying their consolidators – the bucket shops' wholesalers – with tickets at the pre-YIP net race, but insisted that the minimum YIP fare should still apply in the marketplace. The result has simply been that the bucket shops have been able to improve their profit margin substantially or to make special offers like a free stopover in the Far East.

The Passenger's Viewpoint

The consumer's dilemma has always been that an element of risk is still attached to the bucket shop market because it is perceived as operating at the fringe of the law. The passenger, it must be stressed, does not commit any offence in buying a bucket shop ticket and, to confuse matters still further, a high proportion of tickets sold in bucket shops are perfectly legitimate anyway – for example, the many round-the-world scheduled fares or low-cost European charter flights.

The risk element can be exaggerated. Only a tiny proportion of bucket shop clients suffer financial loss in any year, and there are plenty of satisfied customers who have managed to make substantial savings on their trip. Perhaps word-of-mouth recommendation from a friend is a good way to find a reliable outlet for a discount fare deal.

It is a good sign if a bucket shop has been established for some time in good premises with a street-level office. If possible you should make a personal visit to assess the knowledge of the staff rather than just relying on a telephone call. Ask as many questions as possible and find out any likely snags – like a protracted stopover en route in an unattractive part of the world – and make sure which airline you're flying with.

It is a good indication of a bucket shop's reliability if it holds an Access or Visa appointment because the card firms check the financial integrity of their appointed outlets very thoroughly. Use of a credit card does give you added security because, under the Consumer Credit Act, the card company becomes liable for provision of the service you have bought in the event of the retailer's failure.

It is also a good sign if the office is a member of the Association of British Travel Agents (look for the ABTA sticker on the door) because you are then protected by the association's financial safeguards (*see page 113*).

And readers of this Handbook will not need reminding that WEXAS is a long-established and reliable source of discounted tickets to all parts of the world, backed up by the guarantees which come through membership of IATA and ABTA.

The Packaged Traveller

by Hilary Bradt

In 1841 Thomas Cook advertised that he had arranged a special train to take a group of temperance workers from Leicester to Loughborough for a meeting some ten miles away. From this humble beginning has grown a giant tourist industry which has helped the balance of payments in countries all over the world as well as enabling almost anyone to have a taste of 'abroad'. Experienced travellers often scorn package holidays as appealing to the 'If it's Tuesday, this must be Belgium' mentality, without realizing how much time and money can be saved, and how many worthwhile places seen, by joining a tour. And now that package tours have expanded into activity holidays a new world, often impenetrable by all but the most determined individual, has opened up for the adventurous person in search of the safely exotic.

The most convenient way of booking any sort of package tour is through a travel agent. Although you can usually deal directly with the company offering the trip, a good travel agent will save you hours of time and hassle. Not everyone realizes that travel agents earn their income from commissions on sales and not from any charge levied on the customer, so you pay nothing for their services. If your travel agent is a member of ABTA or has the Air Tour Operator's Licence (*see The Traveller's Protection, page 112*) you are less likely to become the victim of overbooking or other travel malpractice, and if something does go wrong and it's the company's fault, you do have some recourse.

Do your preparatory brochure reading carefully. If you choose a trip to Greece in mid-summer and can't stand the heat, that's not your travel agent's fault, nor can they be held responsible for the inefficiencies that are inherent in Third World travel. An honest guide book will warn you of the negative aspects of the countries you are interested in, and likewise, a brochure is more likely to be taken seriously if the picture painted is not too rosy. Beware of advertising jargonese that could be fluffing over the fact that your half-built hotel is a couple of miles from the sea, which can just be glimpsed tantalisingly from one room on the top floor.

Short Haul

Under this heading we can include a two-week holiday in Turkey, a 'weekend break' in Majorca, or a day's sightseeing in some foreign city. Prices are generally low, as it is this category which covers the vast bulk of package holidays, but there are also plenty of bargains to be had, especially off season, as a glance at any travel agent's window or the holiday section of the newspapers will show you. Just be careful to check the credentials of any company offering unbelievably cheap trips.

Going on a package tour does not necessarily mean travelling in a group. Often the 'package' consists of air tickets and accommodation only, and you are free to explore during the day. And you don't *have* to stay in the allocated hotel; sometimes the savings on the airfare are such that you can afford to use the hotel for a couple of nights then head off on your own and do some travelling.

Even brief sightseeing tours are often well worth while for independent travellers. Some of the world's most fascinating places are virtually impossible to get to on your own, and even if easily accessible, sightseeing can be tiring or uninformative without transport or a guide. Tours are easily arranged. Your hotels should be able to recommend a reliable agency, you can look in the yellow pages of the phone book, or simply walk down the main street until you find one. When setting up your tour it helps to have some information on the site or sights you want to visit. Try to meet your guide the day before to make sure he/she is knowledgeable and speaks good English, and if you enjoy walking, make it clear that a tour on foot would be preferable to spending all day on a bus.

Long Haul

Overland journeys lasting several months are the most popular form of package tour for young people, pensioners and others for whom time is no object. And for those with less time to spare, plenty of companies offer two- or three-week tours which still use the converted trucks which are the hallmark of long overland trips. Dodge three-ton trucks, completely stripped and rebuilt to suit the needs of each company, are the vehicles preferred, being rugged enough to cope with the varied terrain and conditions found on a trans-continental journey. Nights are spent in tents or simple rest houses, and most overlanders cook their own meals on a rota system and eat occasionally in local restaurants.

Most long haul trips involve journeys through Africa, Asia, South America and, to a lesser extent, Australia. The most popular routes are London to Kathmandu, which is open again despite problems in the Middle East, and Africa, which offers various possibilities such as the Nile route from Egypt through Sudan to Kenya, the Sahara from Morocco to French West Africa, Nairobi down to South Africa, or even North Africa all the way to Cape Town. South America is nearly as popular, with a variety of routes.

These are rugged trips, and a great test of psychological fortitude as well as physical endurance. Being with the same group of people for several months in often trying conditions can be a strain on even the most sociable traveller, so if you suspect your patience may snap after a few weeks, don't try it. A long overland trip is a bargain in terms of daily expenditure. Eighteen weeks through Africa costs about £1,700, or £13 per day.

Choose your overland company with care. Some have temptingly low prices but unscrupulous employees like the driver I met in Africa. After dropping his group to do some sightseeing, he drove away and sold the truck. No doubt a rare occurrence, but you are safer if you use a reputable company or go through WEXAS (45 Brompton Road, London SW3 1DE) who have long experience of dealing with overland companies.

Special Interest

Holiday makers are no longer content just to lie in the sun, but are looking for something more active. Several companies now specialize in activity holidays or adventure travel, which is the fastest-growing area of the travel business, and their brochures show a wide range of trips, from hang-gliding in Nepal to weaving in Ecuador, trekking in Africa or taking part in conservation projects or archaeological digs (*see About Joining a Project Overseas, page 228*). Activity holidays appeal most to professional people in their 30s and 40s, probably because they are the most expensive form of package tour (three weeks trekking in the Himalayas can cost around £1,000, excluding the air fare, for one example), and the most demanding mentally and physically. Most trips are graded to indicate the degree of fitness required, but the companies point out that even the lowest graded tours are designed for active people and the fitter you are, the more you'll enjoy the trip.

These tours often involve an impressive amount of organization; providing transport to remote areas, porters or pack animals to carry the luggage, doctors to attend the sick, instructors, interpreters, guides and experts of all sorts. No wonder they are expensive. Carefully planned to give the feeling of adventure without the danger, they enable people to see and experience aspects of a country or culture they could not experience on their own, or take part in an activity or sport impossible in their own country.

Before selecting an activity holiday, you will want to send for as many brochures and catalogues as possible. A good travel agent specializing in this sort of tour will advise you and newspapers and magazines generally carry numerous small ads for these companies. Don't make price the main consideration when comparing brochures. If this is going to be the trip of your life, an extra £100 is not going to make much difference. Check that the price quoted includes the airfare; in Britain it usually does, but American companies usually quote the land costs only. Don't hesitate to contact the company and ask for names and phone numbers of clients who've been on the trip you're interested in. A successful company will have no qualms about putting you in touch with such people.

Once you have signed up and paid your deposit, the company should send you an equipment list, reading list, medical information and so on. If you are dealing with a travel agency rather than the company running the tour, make sure you receive these. It is inconvenient and often impossible to shop for special items once you arrive.

Joining a Project Overseas

by Ingrid Cranfield with Nigel and Shane Winser

There are many operators in Britain and abroad offering adventurous holidays and 'expeditions', which can be ideal for somebody who wants an unusual trip. Naturally you pay to join one of these, but the preparations and responsibilities are correspondingly few. The WEXAS Discoverers brochure lists a number of such trips; others are advertised in the outdoor magazines. There are also two useful books: *Adventure Holidays* published by Vacation Work Publications Ltd which lists holidays by the type of sport or activity, and *Adventure and Discovery* published by the Central Bureau for Educational Visits and Exchanges which gives its listings by country.

There are also many informal groups which set out on adventurous trips which are not expeditions – the main difference being that an expedition aims to prove, alter or discover something and to bring back results, while a holiday does not. Magazines like *Private Eye* or *Time Out* and the travel magazines are useful for finding out about these. However, you should beware that the informal group you team up with are not just trying to pay for a holiday for themselves. However tempting the trip sounds, don't join up if you don't like or trust the people you are going to have to travel with (*see Selecting a Travelling Companion on page 254*).

Joining a genuine expedition demands considerable preparation, commitment and teamwork. Expedition organizers and leaders nowadays demand that a participant have some special skill or expertise, without which he will be of little use.

In Britain, the Royal Geographical Society is in the mainstream of serious research expeditions or study projects abroad. Nearly all major expeditions with a geographical content mounted from this country march by under its gaze, hoping to attract its approval and/or its support. There is, however, no way in which an interested individual can join an RGS-supported expedition through the offices of the Society itself since the Society does not officially oversee the formation of expedition groups. Ready-made parties apply annually (by late January) for the Society's nod of approval or a grant.

Expedition organizers, members or originators still in search of a group or any kind of expedition advice should go direct to the Expedition Advisory Centre, set up by the RGS and the Young Explorers' Trust and housed in the RGS building at 1 Kensington Gore, London SW7 2AR (Tel: 01-581 2057). The EAC exists to help those planning overseas expeditions and provides a number of services including a register of forthcoming expeditions to help leaders find personnel and funding and help qualified people to find suitable places on expeditions. Particularly valuable are its publications, *The Expedition Planner's Handbook and Directory*, a series of notes on specific aspects of expedition organizations, and a booklet entitled *Joining an Expedition* which lists most of the organizing bodies of 'pure' expeditions, for young people.

Other expeditionary bodies include the Brathay Exploration Group, Brathay Hall, Ambleside, Cumbria LA22 0HP (Tel: (09663) 3042) which sends out some twenty expeditions each year for young people aged between 16 and 22, both in the UK and abroad. All provide experience of living in a remote region and many of the overseas projects also have a significant scientific content. The British Schools Exploring Society, 1 Kensington Gore, London SW7 2AR (Tel: 01-584 0710) organizes one major expedition each summer for sixteen to nineteen year olds.

For budding archaeologists, Archaeology Abroad, 31–34 Gordon Square, London WC1H 0PY (Tel: 01-387 6052) is an organization which helps directors of overseas excavations to find suitable personnel through its bulletins.

Between 1984 and 1988, one of the largest expeditions ever to leave the UK will be taking 4,000 young people from many nations on a round-the-world voyage to undertake a series of scientific and community tasks. The Operation Raleigh Selection Committee, The Warehouse, 52 St Catherine's Way, London E1 9LB will be dispersing application forms at regular intervals throughout this time to choose young people aged between 17 and 24 years old to take part in each of the three-month phases.

For those with more time available, there are a number of US-based organizations whose functions are to help or staff expeditions. One is Earthwatch, 10 Juniper Road, Box 127, Belmont, MA 02178, USA (Tel: (617) 489 3030), a private, non profit-making body which identifies qualified volunteers to staff and finance research expeditions. It was founded in 1971 to serve as a bridge between the public and the scientific community, and has since fielded over 7,000 people on research expeditions in 57 countries. Volunteers do not need to have any special skills to join expeditions and anyone aged 16–75 may apply. In 1984, Earthwatch organized 300 teams worldwide. Funds are raised from the participants and other private sources. For two- to three-week expeditions, costs range from $500 to over $2,000, which covers all field expenses. Work on an expedition may qualify participants for academic credit. Membership, which costs $20 a year or $35 for two years, makes one eligible to join expeditions and secures a magazine, published three times a year, giving updates and advance notices of research projects. Working in conjunction with Earthwatch is the Center for Field Research – at the same address – which arranges financial support for research investigators whose projects can constructively utilize non-specialists in the field. Projects approved by the Center are recommended to Earthwatch for support. There are field offices in Australia, California, East Africa and the UK at 31 Hyde Park Gate, London SW 7 (Tel: 01-589 9316).

The University Research Expeditions Program (UREP), University of California, Berkeley, CA 94720, USA (Tel: (415) 642 6586) mounts expeditions to conduct scientific fieldwork in various disciplines and geographical locations, providing opportunities for interested donor-participants to become members of the field team and receive instructional materials and in-field training. Again, no special academic or field experience is necessary and the age limits are 16-75. Members contribute equal shares to the cost of the expedition and a limited number of partial scholarships are available to students and teachers. Academic credit may be granted for participation in certain projects.

It is possible to travel in a group and never make contact with the people of the countries you pass through. The Commonwealth Youth Exchange Council promotes contact between groups of young people of the Commonwealth by funding visits by groups from Britain to an overseas Commonwealth country or vice versa. The programme, to attract CYEC funding, must be useful in its own right and involve contact between visitors and hosts, preferably including joint activities. The aim is 'to provide meaningful contact and better understanding between Commonwealth young people' and if possible should lead to a continuing two-way link. Visits must be arranged through an established organization and led by a responsible person. Two-thirds of each group must consist of people aged between 15 and 25 years. Further information is available from the Executive Secretary, Mr R. F. Grey, CYEC, 18 Fleet Street, London EC4Y 1AA (Tel: 01-353 3901).

People wishing to work or study abroad without necessarily joining an expedition should consult the Central Bureau for Educational Visits and Exchanges, Seymour Mews House, Seymour Mews (off Wigmore Street), London W1 (Tel: 01-486 5101). Its publications are extremely useful. The Bureau, which also has offices in Edinburgh and Belfast, has details of jobs, study opportunities, youth organizations and holidays in some sixty countries.

A Year Off (previously known as *Time Between*), published by CRAC Publications, Hobsons Press (Cambridge) Ltd, Bateman Street, Cambridge, CB2 1LZ (Tel: (0223) 354551) provides information about voluntary service, work camps and summer projects, paid work, *au pair* work, study courses and scholarships and travel, adventure and expeditions. Aimed at people with time to spare between school and higher education, it discusses the pros and cons of using that year in this special way, giving the views of both students and career experts. The 1983 paperback edition costs £1.85.

Study Abroad, published by UNESCO, 7 Place de Fontenoy, Paris 75007, France and available from HMSO, PO Box 276, London SW8 5DT, describes some 2,600 opportunities for post-secondary study in all academic and professional fields and details of scholarships, assistant-ships, travel grants and other forms of financial assistance available. The 24th edition, 1983–86, costs £8.25.

Vacation Work Publications, of 9 Park End Street, Oxford OX1 1HJ, publish many guides and directories for those seeking permanent jobs or summer jobs abroad, unusual travel opportunities, voluntary work and working travel. Their most recent publication is Susan Griffith's *Work Your Way Around the World*.

Often travel for its own sake seems insufficient for those who wish to provide practical help for those who live in the country they are to visit. The Brandt report has made those of us who live in industrial Europe (the West) more aware of the acute differences between 'North' and 'South'. If you feel that you have both the time and the specialist skills needed to be a volunteer you should probably start by reading two very helpful directories: *Volunteer Work Abroad* from the CBEVE and/or *The International Directory of Voluntary Work* by Gillian Nineham and David Woodworth, published by Vacation Work. Both books give an outline of the organizations who are willing and able to accept volunteer workers on overseas projects and the skill and commitment required of the volunteer.

At this stage you should be aware that the majority of host countries who welcome volunteers usually require skilled personnel such as nurses, teachers, agronomists and civil engineers. They may be unable to pay even your air fares although many provide board and lodging, and you may be expected to help for at least a year or two. Remember that during that time you probably won't be travelling but will be based in a poor urban community or remote rural village.

If you feel that you are suitably qualified and have the emotional maturity to be a volunteer you may like to discuss your hopes and ambitions to serve with someone who has already been one. You can contact an ex-volunteer through their own organization: Returned Volunteer Action, 1c Cambridge Terrace, Regents Park, London NW1 4JL (Tel: 01-935 9447), which maintains a register of volunteers who have served on many projects in many different areas of the world. They may even be able to direct you personally to an organization which is appropriate to both your and their needs. Their publication *Thinking About Volunteering* is very frank about some of the problems you may face before or after you have been a volunteer.

Finding the right organization for you takes time, so don't expect to leave next week. The four main agencies who send out volunteers from the UK as part of the British Government's Overseas Aid Programme are: The Catholic Institute for International Relations (CIIR), International Voluntary Service (IVS), United Nations Association International Service (UNA) and Voluntary Service Overseas (VSO). These are co-ordinated through the British Volunteer Programme (BVP), 2 Cambridge Terrace, London NW1 4JL (Tel: 01-486 4980). Over 400 volunteers go abroad each year through these organizations, all are over 21 with professional work experience. BVP produce a number of introductory booklets and will supply you with the standard application form that you will need to complete before you can be selected to join CIIR, IVS, UNA or VSO.

If you wish to apply to work for an international aid organization then the International Recruitment Unit of the Overseas Development Administration, Abercrombie House, Eaglesham Road, East Kilbridge, Glasgow G75

8EA (Tel: (035 52) 41199) will be able to advise you through its booklets *Why Not Serve Overseas?* and *Opportunities Overseas with International Organizations*.

Timeshare and Home Exchange

by Michael Furnell

The majority of people believe that timesharing is something new which has only developed over the past decade or so, but in fact it is not really a new concept because as far back as the last century villagers were time-sharing water in Cyprus where there was no piped supply.

Property timeshare is believed to have been initiated in the 1960s when certain French developers of ski apartments experienced difficulty in selling their leisure accommodation outright, and decided to offer for sale the ownership of weekly or fortnightly segments at the same time each year for ever.

The idea spread to other parts of Europe including Spain. On the Costa Blanca coast a British company, who was building apartments in Calpe, offered co-ownership of two-bedroom flats in the main shopping street, near the sea. Prices were as little as £250 per week's usage in the summer in perpetuity. Winter periods were even cheaper at £180 for a month and easy terms were available on the payment of a £50 deposit with the balance payable at £4.50 per month over three years.

The Americans soon recognized this form of holiday home ownership, and in the early stages converted condominiums, motels and hotels which were not viable in their original form into time-share units. Often these had rather basic facilities and it is only in recent years that developers in Florida and elsewhere have realized that top-quality homes with luxury facilities are the key to successful multi-ownership.

It was not until 1976 that timesharing was launched in Britain. The very first site was in a beautiful loch side location at Kinloch Rannoch in the Highlands of Scotland. The final phase is now complete and altogether there are eighty-five units. The on-site facilites include a dry ski slope, indoor swimming pool with jacuzzi, two squash courts, marina, tennis court, boating, curling rink, conference centre and a school of adventure. Prices of the remaining periods start at about £5,000 per week.

The aim of timesharing is to provide luxury quality holiday homes for which a once only capital sum is paid at today's prices, so that future holidays are secure whatever happens, for no hotel bills or holiday rents need to be paid in the coming years, just a reasonable annual sum to cover maintenance expenses.

With the initial costs being shared among a number of owners the standard of accommodation and the luxury specification can be much higher than normal and often the furnishings and equipment are better than in most permanent homes.

Timesharing is sold by several different methods at prices from as little as £500 to nearly £10,000 for a week. When a freehold is purchased the period of time which you buy is yours to use 'forever', and you may let, sell, assign or leave the property to your heirs in your will. In England and Wales the law only permits ownership for a maximum of 80 years but in Scotland and Wales and many other parts of the world, ownership in perpetuity is possible.

Membership of a club which grants a right to use a specified property for a stated number of years is an alternative scheme. Here the assets of the club, i.e. buildings, land and facilities are generally held by a trustee which is often a Bank or Insurance company. A transferable membership certificate is normally issued to each purchaser.

The formation of a public limited company with the issue of ordinary shares which vary in price according to the time of year chosen for occupancy has also been used as a vehicle for marketing timeshare. Each share provides one week's occupancy for a set number of years, usually 20 or 25 years. The properties are then sold in the open market and the proceeds divided among the shareholders.

The Hapimag concept uses capital contributed by members to purchase land and build holiday homes, in various parts of Europe. Each member is entitled to holiday points which can be used for a vacation of a week or more in a chosen Hapimag development at any time of year.

The Holiday Property Bond introduced by Villa Owners Club Ltd provides for the funds contributed by participants to be divided between the acquisition of timeshare property and the purchase of gilt-edge certificates. The income from the latter pays for management and maintenance fees. Holiday points are issued to bond holders according to the amount invested and these are used to select the use of one of the properties owned by the Club. The properties are valued on a points per week basis depending on the size, location and season chosen. Investors are permitted to encash their bonds at any time after two years.

New Trends

Recent trends have been towards group ownership where each property is sold to a small number of owners. In the 'Ten Keys' scheme, shareholders are allocated three fortnightly periods every 61 weeks to allow them to enjoy use of the property at different times of year for an expenditure of between £4,700 and £7,700. In order to help each group of owners to get to know each other, meetings are held in the UK to discuss matters relating to the joint venture.

The Four Owners method pioneered by housebuilders Comben for their sites on Portugal's Algarve, involves the purchase of the title for a quarter of each year, and each owner is allotted two weeks use at the height of summer, one month in either spring or autumn plus six weeks during the remainder of the year. Occupation dates revolve annually to give each owner the opportunity of holidays at each season. Capital outlay is of course greater but still enables a family to enjoy part ownership of a superb villa in a very pleasant location for around £12,500.

To ensure adequate maintenance and administration of the properties, a management company is established on each scheme; this may be part of the developer's organization or a nominee employed by them. After a scheme has been completed, the individual owners may join together to establish their own management organization. The cost of management is recovered from an annual fee payable by all owners and should cover insurance, staffing, renovation, heat and light, gardening and the care of all communal facilities. Fees vary between about £40 and £120 per annum and are sometimes linked to the cost of living index.

Golden Rules

The Golden Rules to be remembered when buying a timeshare home are:

1. Purchase from a well established developer or selling agent who already has a reputation for fair dealing and offering really successful schemes.
2. The location of the property is vital, so be sure to select a well situated development with adequate facilities and a quality atmosphere. Be sure that it appeals to the family as well as yourself to ensure that you are all able to enjoy regular visits. If you are likely to want to resell in the future, the location could be even more important.
3. Check carefully the annual maintenance costs and be sure you know what they cover. Part of the yearly charges should be accumulated by the management to cover replacements, new furnishings and regular major redecorations.
4. If all the amenities promised by the sales staff are not already in existence, get a written commitment from the vendors that they will be completed.
5. Ascertain the rights of owners if the builder or management company gets into financial difficulties, and ascertain if it is possible for the owners to appoint a new management company if they are not satisfied with the service of the original one.
6. Before signing any documents which commit you to purchasing time, and also management contracts, have the wording checked by a solicitor. It is better to pay a fee for legal advice than to be committed to an unsatisfactory transaction.
7. Talk to an existing owner wherever possible before purchasing.
8. Find out if the vendor owns the property, and if they do not, discover who holds the freehold and if there is any mortagage on the property.
9. The experts believe that any timeshare scheme should have a minimum of ten units to be viable. If it is too small, amenities may be lacking and each owner's share of management costs may be excessive.
10. Are payments held in trust pending the issue of title documents, or a licence to use, and has a trustee been appointed to hold the master title deeds?

Investment

Timesharing is not a conventional money making investment in property, although some owners who purchased time in the earliest schemes have enjoyed substantial capital appreciation over the past seven years. Essentially you are investing in leisure and pleasure but you cannot expect inflation-proof holidays. What you are buying is vacation accommodation at today's prices, but expenditure on travel, food and entertainment is likely to rise in future years according to the rate of inflation.

Exchange Facilities

It was recognized long ago that after a few years, many timeshare owners may want a change of scene for annual holidays, and as a result, organizations were established to arrange exchange facilities for timeshare owners. There are exciting possibilities for owners to swap their seaside apartment in say, England's west country, for a contemporary style bungalow in, perhaps, Florida or an Andalucian type *pueblo* in Spain. Today there are three major exchange organizations operating in the UK and between them they offer an immense variety of timeshare accommodation in many holiday destinations. All had their origins in America, and now have their offices in England.

Resort Condominiums International (RCI) was formed by Jan and Cristel De Haan ten years ago, and is the largest established exchange organization, Headquarters are in Indianapolis, USA, the European HQ is in London and there are regional offices in Monaco, Johannesburg, Mexico, Sydney, Florida, California and Naguya. Over 350,000 subscribers in 36 countries are offered 700 holiday locations in Europe, Africa, the continent of America, Australia and Japan.

Interval International, whose world headquarters are in Miami, has a European office in London, branches in California and Buffalo, New York, and a representative in Mexico. Started in 1976 Interval International now has over 150,000 member families who are offered the choice of 400 resorts in 30 countries. A full service travel agency serves members, transportation needs, and savings are offered on air fares, car rentals etc.

Exchange Network from Encinitas, California, a subsidiary of the Southmark Corporation, a Dallas based land development company, has just established a European headquarters at Ascot, Berkshire. Over 320 resorts and developments are available for exchanges by UK timeshare owners. Those in Europe include locations in France, Spain, Portugal, West Germany, Switzerland, Austria, Italy, Greece and Scandinavia.

There is an annual membership fee payable by each participant in the RCI and II schemes and the developer usually pays this for each owner in the first two or three years. In addition, a modest fee is due when an exchange is successfully organized.

Exchange Network makes no annual membership charge and accepts applications from any owner even if the development in which they own property is not affiliated to the E.N. A directory of timeshare resorts is published costing £25 and this has to be purchased by participants who are also charged a fee for each exchange arranged.

Orderly Growth

The British Property Timeshare Association was formed in 1981 to try and ensure the orderly growth of the industry, and membership now includes the majority of the best known developers. A consumer protection committee, comprising independent advisers from various professional organizations, has been set up and a code of ethics is imposed on members in their dealings with UK domiciled timeshare purchasers. An insurance bonding scheme for members is being processed and information providing surveys among owners are being conducted.

An encouraging aspect for the future well-being of the timeshare industry is the active participation of well known building firms such as Barratt, Wimpey, Comben and Hunting Gate, who all have their own developments in the UK, Spain or Portugal. A number of other commercial firms such as Grandmet and the Kenning group are also involved, and this must help to ensure that the public will realize that timesharing is a viable proposition and has a real future.

Homeswop

Many British home owners fancy the idea of exchanging their home with another family in Europe or elsewhere for a fortnight or a month, in order to enjoy a 'free' holiday – apart from transport costs. Although the idea is attractive, there are many problems to be overcome unless you arrange the swop with friends. A number of relatively small organizations have been established to arrange holiday home exchanges, but few of them have been successful.

Now Pan-Am is supporting a new programme known as 'The Great Exchange' which aims to take all the work and worry out of exchanging homes in the UK and USA. The organization undertakes to make extensive cross-checks to match exchanging families' needs and lifestyles. Trained representatives personally visit every exchange home to guarantee accuracy of descriptions and comprehensive free insurance cover on homes and contents is provided. Great Exchange arranges flights by Pan-Am at varying fare levels for both families and can also fix up car, caravan or boat swopping. To qualify for membership, which costs £15, the property in Britain should be in the Greater London area and a further sum of £25 is due for the personal inspection.

The locations of the American properties are in Florida, Los Angeles, San Francisco and New York.

The Expatriate Traveller

by Doris Dow

Nowadays, governments, large organizations and big companies all compete for the expertise and skills they require. More and more people leave their own country to live and work abroad. These expatriates go off with high hopes and expectations; in spite of increased earning power, some are disappointed and frustrated and return home for good. Others adapt well to the challenge of a new life and continue in the expatriate scene for many years, and find it difficult to repatriate. 'Expatriates' should not be confused with 'settlers' – people who originated (years or generations back) from other countries but have a permanent commitment to their adopted country.

Contracts

It is important that the terms of the contract are understood, and signed both by the employer and the employee; if it is in another language, a reliable translation should be obtained before signing on the dotted line. Contracts should set out the terms and conditions of employment, including minimum length of contract, working hours and overtime, remuneration, allowances for/provision of accommodation, car, education, medical and dental cover, leave and terminal gratuities/bonuses, dismissal clauses and compassionate leave arrangements. Many jobs abroad offer what seem to be on paper very large salaries, but the attitudes of employers, their willingness to accept responsibility and to offer support when necessary, are often worth more than extra money.

Documentation

Before departure, visas, work permits, driving licences, health regulations and other documentation must be attended to. Acquiring the necessary visas from embassies can entail many visits and long waits, but the first lessons of an aspiring expatriate are quickly learned – of acquiring tolerance, patience, perseverance and good humour. For those working for a large company or international organization, the documentation is usually done for them.

Preparations for the Move

Find out what inoculations are required or advisable and arrange to have them as soon as possible. If prophylactics are necessary, one's family doctor, the Hospital for Tropical Diseases or well-known travel agents will advise on which type and dosage is suitable.

Time spent doing some 'homework' on the country you are going to, its lifestyle, traditions and customs is very worthwhile. Mental preparation is just as important as the practical plans, as working and living in a country is quite a different experience from a holiday there. Search libraries and bookshops for travel books and up-to-date guides. For Commonwealth countries, there are excellent permanent exhibitions at the Commonwealth Institute, Kensington High Street, London. Embassies should also be helpful on specific information on currency, import regulations, etc. – also what *not* to import.

Other valuable sources of information are: The Women's Corona Society, 501 Eland House, Stag Place, London SW1E 5DH (Tel: 01-828 1652/3) whose *Notes for Newcomers* series for over a hundred countries (£2 per set) give practical details of what to take, what will be found there, education, health, leisure activities, etc.; and The Royal Commonwealth Society, Northumberland Avenue, London WC2N 5BJ (Tel: 01-930 6733) which also produces good fact sheets (£3 per set). (*For other publications, see book list and list of periodicals in the reference section*).

Finance

Arrangements should be made to continue National Health Insurance contributions, as this is an extremely good investment. All financial aspects of the move should be studied and arranged *before* departure – tax clearance, financial regulations and exchange controls in your country of destination, investments, etc. There are firms and consultancies specializing in this field, e.g. Wilfred T. Fry Ltd, 31 Queen Street, Exeter, Devon EX4 3SR (also London and Worthing) and The Expatriate Consultancy Ltd, 32 Trumpington Street, Cambridge CB2 1QY.

Despatch and Arrival of Effects

There are many international firms who specialize in overseas removals; for those who have to make their own arrangements, it is advisable to approach more than one firm for an estimate.

When travelling by air, include as many basic essentials as possible in accompanied baggage in order to be self-sufficient for the first few days, including several paperbacks to get through lengthy waits and sleepless nights due to jet lag. Always ensure that personal luggage is locked and insured.

Many people find air freight the quickest, easiest and safest way of consigning goods; lists of all contents should be available for customs clearance, shipping agents, insurance, etc. and two copies of these lists should always be retained. Baggage allowances are usually generous and first entry into a country generally permits duty-free import of personal and household effects. In many countries there is a ready sale for secondhand effects at the end of a contract, often at advantageous prices, so it is worthwhile making full use of the allowance. There are only a few instances where what is imported must be taken away again in its entirety.

Sea freight for heavier items should be crated and listed – translation into the appropriate language can often hasten customs clearance. Hiring a good local agent who knows the ropes can often be a good investment. Realistic insurance of all effects is essential.

Arrival at Destination

If possible, arrange to be met at the airport, and/or have a contact telephone number. Make sure that hotel accommodation has been booked, and keep all receipts for later reimbursement. Salary may be delayed; try to have some traveller's cheques to cover this eventuality.

A long journey and the shock of new climatic conditions can be depressing until acclimatization is achieved – so use your commonsense and allow yourself time to adjust. Be prepared for long delays at Customs and Immigration – patience and good humour will pay dividends and don't judge the country by its officialdom. *Do not* exchange money, except through official channels.

Housing

It is likely that permanent accommodation will not be available immediately, necessitating a few days or even weeks stay in a hotel. Make use of this freedom to get acquainted with local sources of supply, etc.

To many expatriates, disappointment can begin with housing and furniture, which often does not match up to expectations. Reserve judgement at the beginning, because what may seem a drawback can turn out to be an advantage. There is a big difference in standards between local and expatriate employers, and there is no firm basis for comparison. In oil-rich states, it may well be that expatriate housing is much humbler than that of the nationals. On the other hand, accommodation may be very luxurious and spacious. The less fortunate expatriate should refrain from envious comparisons and, with careful thought and inexpensive ingenuity, make the best of what comes along. Work camps/compounds and high rise flats are all very real challenges to the good homemaker.

Medical Care

Primary medical care is sometimes much better than one might expect, easily contacted and near at hand. Further care may be available, but if not, serious cases are flown out for emergency or specialist treatment. Large organizations often have their own hospitals, clinics and doctors. Government contracts usually provide free medical facilities. It is always wise to have a good dental check-up before departure from home; anybody needing medication on a regular basis should take a good supply to last until an alternative source is established.

Education

Very young children are often well catered for by play groups and nursery schools. Later, there are international schools, company schools, and private or state schools. These vary considerably, but given a good school and parents who take advantage of all there is to offer in the locality, a child will have made a good start. There is often a waiting list and information about schools should be obtained and an early approach made for enrolment, well ahead of departure. For those going to outlying areas, it may be necessary to consider correspondence courses, e.g. World Wide Education Service, Strode House 44–50 Osnaburgh Street, London NW1 3NN (Ages 5–15).

Many contracts provide for boarding school in the UK and regular holiday visits to parents. As the older child might well lack stimulation and local schooling might be inadequate, early consideration should be given to choosing a boarding school. An Educational Trust will assist. It is a hard decision to take, but the partings at the end of the holidays are compensated for by the pleasure with which children look forward to travelling out to their parents at the end of term. In most places, special events are laid on for them, they feel special having a home overseas and travelling experience makes them more responsible, confident and resourceful. The Women's Corona Society also provides an escort service from airport to school trains etc.

Children are often used as an excuse for the wife to return home, but for children at boarding school, it is often more important for them to feel that they have a solid family base than to have Mum on the doorstep.

Marriage

The move should be talked over very carefully as it can have a profound effect on a marriage. For busy working parents and weary commuters, expatriate life can be an opportunity to spend more time together as a family, and if both partners are keen, the novelty of the strange environment can be a rewarding experience. I would advise against married men taking single person's contracts or splitting the partnership for long periods of time, as it places too great a strain on communication. Starting again could help rebuild a shaky marriage, but it could also split it apart completely if an unwilling person is ripped away from everything familiar. So think before you move!

Single Men and Women

Single (or unaccompanied) men often live in camps which are isolated. They have frequent short leaves and money to spend. A special interest – sport or hobby – gives them the chance to form stable friendships and does away with propping up the bar for company in their spare time.

A single woman usually has to establish a home as well as tackling the job. However, the job, with a real and worthwhile challenge, gives her an advantage over many wives who often find themselves at sea with nothing to do but keep house. A single woman is generally in great demand in a lively social whirl, but this needs to be handled with great care. She is often an object of great interest to the local population who find it difficult to understand that she has no man to tell her what to do, and may receive many offers of marriage because of this!

Wives

While women are generally expected to be supportive of their husbands as they come to terms with a new job, it should also be remembered that they too need support and encouragement as they establish a new home, meet new people and adapt to a different lifestyle.

At all times the rules and regulations and laws of a country must be obeyed. Western women often find the new cultures and traditions difficult to embrace and inhibiting, e.g. in a Muslim country, and it is essential to prepare for this. *Living Overseas* one day courses for men and women are designed by the Women's Corona Society to counsel on adaptation to a new lifestyle and provide an opportunity to meet someone with current knowledge of their country. These courses are held at regular intervals, or at special request, and cost £20 per person.

Many women give up careers or interesting part-time jobs to accompany their husbands overseas, and in a number of places, there is no opportunity for them to get a job. Work permits can often be obtained in the teaching or medical professions but not always where her husband is posted. If your husband is with a big company, it might be worth asking them about jobs, or otherwise consider the possibilities of working on your own, or doing voluntary work.

Careful planning and preparation for the use of leisure time, whether it is because of no outside employment or greater freedom from household duties because of servants, is essential to counteract boredom and initial loneliness. There are many hobbies and interests to be resurrected or embarked upon. Join groups with local knowledge e.g. archaeological, historical, wildlife, photographic, amateur dramatics etc. Involvement in the local scene through clubs and organizations helps understanding and leads to more tolerant attitudes of cultural differences. Learning the language, a correspondence course to gain new qualifications or just for pleasure – the possibilities are many and varied for the wife determined to make the most of her stay in another country. There may be a lack of facilities (she may have to cut the family's hair!), she may have to put up with a number of uncongenial conditions, but there are so many other rewards to supply the icing for the cake.

Expatriates are on the whole friendlier and less inhibited than in their home environment. The sun, outdoor pursuits, less clothing, often make people appear more attractive and relaxed. Social life is important for, except in the big cities, self-entertainment is necessary. This often provides scope for great ingenuity and many find latent and surprising talents hitherto undeveloped. In what is often a male-orientated society, it is important for the wife to cultivate her own interests, making sure of an independent identity, rather than identifying too much with her husband's job and position. And with servants, there is more time to experiment, as she is no longer saddled with the day to day chores involved in running the house.

Servants

The availability of domestic help brings an easier lifestyle and is recommended for hot and humid climates where the energy gets sapped. Many people are diffident about employing servants and don't know how to cope with them. With an initial trial period and the advice of someone who speaks the language and has kept a servant for some time, it is possible for a good relationship to be formed. Settle for a few qualities or skills suitable for the family's needs and be tolerant about other shortcomings. Establish what is wanted and agree time off. A servant who is respected becomes part of an extended family.

Lifestyle

Respect the local customs and laws about behaviour and dress, etiquette and the Highway Code, etc., and be aware of local sensitivities so that you don't offend them. Be prepared for what might appear odd or rude behaviour. Cultural differences can lead to all sorts of misunderstandings. Reserve judgement, take advice from happily established residents and concentrate first on personal relations. Forget efficiency and don't expect things to happen in a hurry. Polite conversation and courtesy are priorities – sincere interest, tolerance and a joke work wonders. Beware of criticising before you've attempted to understand a situation.

Security

Security can be a problem, but commonsense measures, security guards and alarm systems are used in greater or lesser degree according to local hazards. Wilful violence is rare. It is possible for the expatriate to get caught up in political reprisals, but this is fortunately very rare indeed. It is wise to register with the Consular Section of your Embassy or High Commission on first arrival, so they know where to find you in cases of emergency – don't wait until trouble arises as communications can be difficult.

Summary

The expatriate's life can suffer considerable privation through lack of consumer goods and a low standard of living, or can be extremely rewarding with higher standards of housing and a hectic social life as well as a worthwhile job.

The challenge of helping a country to develop can be very stimulating and addictive – whatever the conditions encountered – which is the reason why so many expatriates return overseas again and again. Friendships made abroad are often more binding and congenial, through shared experiences, than those made at home. Valuable experience in a job often leads to promotion. The tolerance and understanding of other races and cultures learned through the expatriate experience of shorter or longer duration, means that life will forever afterwards be enriched.

In the Lap of Luxury

by Carol Wright

A dictionary definition of 'luxury' is 'anything not necessary but used for personal gratification'. This applies particularly to travel since many have a dream goal; a vision of real pampering on the move on Concorde or *QE2* or in five-star hotels. Hotel maids in New York have saved all their lives to board the *QE2*'s world cruise. One widow gradually sold her treasures, eventually even her home, to make that voyage each year.

In most luxury travel dreams, there is much looking back in nostalgia to a time of slower pace, innumerable porters and servants; no need to manhandle luggage on wheels, take self-service meals or fight for space round a pool. Then, social hostesses took banana boats to Jamaica to escape winter and recover from the rigours of the season. Pre war it was said on transatlantic liners that 'only snobs drank a *second* bottle of champagne before breakfast'.

Cruising

Alas, champagne breakfasts have almost disappeared according to the restaurant manager of *QE2*'s top grill room, and security has ended the magnificent sailing day parties. But cruising is probably considered the nearest we still have to old-time luxury. It's a pricy indulgence with fuel prices pushing up touring by sea. The cheapest berth on *QE2*'s 1984 eighty-three day round the world cruise including flight from Britain to New York by Concorde is £7,810. *Sea Princess*, P & O's liner, charges from £7,380 to £13,590 for her ninety day earth-girdling from Southampton. *QE2*'s top price is £39,700 per person in the top-grade suite with their own private sundeck over the bridge, split level living room with stereo centre, silver drinks service, special porcelain service for breakfast and afternoon tea, gold plated taps in the two bathrooms and specially designed bed linen.

Top ships with a luxury tag include *QE2*, with her new covered deck buffet areas, free Californian spa courses, and title of the world's top cavier consumer; *Sea Princess* with largish cabins, many with fridge and sitting area, and thoughtful luggage-handling on Mediterranean cruises so the passenger at the end does not have to bother from cabin to Gatwick carousel and there's no unseemly shoving you off the moment the final port is reached, you can use the ship and its food till your plane departs: *Vistafjord* and *Sagafjord*, recently bought by Cunard, are beautifully designed and get the US top ships ratings each year; and the Royal Viking ships are also sleek and cleanly Scandinavian in decor, but rather distant in crew relations; the company has one of the glossiest and most readable of cruising brochures. P & O's Princess Line, based on the US West Coast, have a fine reputation for food (Italian chefs and serving staff), clean lines, comfort and, rarely found on cruise ships, good Hollywood orchestrated entertainment. These cruises are now being marketed with inclusive air fare and overnight hotel in port from Britain for the first time. In October 1984, *Royal Princess* was added to the fleet, a sleekly modern superliner with all outside cabins.

Concorde

QE2 links one-way Concorde flights on transatlantic trips. Concorde scores with speed, alleviating jet lag, swollen ankles and the boredom of overnight Atlantic flights; it's just three hours back from New York. But it is somewhat cramped in seating space; the curved earth scenes looking like sixteenth-century maps and purpling upper atmosphere are stunning, but service, because of lack of space, is trimmed to simpler-than-other-first-class affairs, though the champagne flows and the food, like other British Airways food, is designed by top international chefs like the Roux brothers.

First class plane travel is certainly a luxury, not a necessity; the back end, and hopefully the luggage, will all arrive at the same time. However, for any journey over five hours, if one can afford the extra, first class travel is definitely worthwhile. The copious food and champagne is pleasant, but space, toilet access when wanted and the pampered élitist feeling are more satisfying. Sleeperette chairs on most international lines prevent the tray on your knees and prodding in the behind cramps of economy class. With foot rest and good recline angle and, on British Airways, adjustable head rest and seat contoured by a Guy's Hospital back expert, one can lie on one's side and sleep. Air Canada have the most capacious wool blankets, not those static-filled, lacy, string-like shawls of most airlines and have recently improved their service to among the best in the air.

Philippine Airlines, as well as good food and good service, has the most luxurious relaxer, called Cloud 9. Here, for a small supplement on the first class fare, one can book a full-length bed with sheets, blankets and pillows. One has the normal seat downstairs for meal and movie times. Upstairs, the lights are kept dim throughout the trip and with a seat belt over the stomach, the traveller can sleep through landings, stopovers and takeoffs. One-upping PAL on sky-high sleep (unless, like Mrs Thatcher on her return from Williamsberg, you buy the upper first class section of British Airways jumbos and have a bed installed) is Regent Air's service between Los Angeles and New York. On their 727 jets, there is a maximum of 36 passengers (compared to the normal 130) carried amid art deco surroundings with champagne, caviar and fresh lobster all the way and a choice of four private compartments with queen-sized beds. The fare is almost a thousand dollars more than the regular first class at $539 (economy is $199).

For short flights to European and UK destinations, it is not a costly luxury to hire your own plane if there are four or more passengers. Often the joy of having your own plane where and when you want it is cheaper than the sum of the scheduled return fares. Details can be obtained from the Air Taxi Operators Association, Hamilton House, 39 King's Road, Haselmere, Surrey GU27 2QA.

Rail

Top trains, like South Africa's Blue Train, Canadian Viarail, Italy's Setter Bello, the Grande Vitesse in France, and even the new airconditioned quieter Mark III sleepers on British Rail overnight Inter-City (now to Scotland and Penzance) give a touch of style to travel. Trains in India like the Rajasthan Express have become popular with tourists and the revival of the Venice-Simplon Orient Express shows a yearning for older style luxury. Though overrated and overpriced, it is an experience to rattle on these ancient coaches on modern rails, lurching to the dining car over slicing plates of steel linking carriages, that makes one realize the advance the Inter-City 125 has made in rail comfort. Putting together the ultimates in what we consider luxury today is Excalibur Travel, John Plank World Travel Ltd, Concorde/Orient Express Division, 61 Seamoor Road, Westbourne, Bournemouth, BH4 9AE who link Concorde, Orient Express and a stay in Venice at the Cipriani for a memorable long weekend costing around £1,069.

A collection of old maharajahs' coaches has become the Palace on Wheels in India, with a week of intensive daily sightseeing of Rajasthan's moghul might and travelling by night. Luxurious is an overrated adjective but it is preferable to touring by air, and each eight-bedded carriage (with two washrooms with showers) has two attendants to cope with snacks, drink bearing and laundry. The food is good, with a choice of Indian or Continental.

Road

Coach travel hasn't much panache as a luxury form of transport, but marketed through Custom Tours, 14 Queen Anne Terrace, Plymouth PL4 8EG there is a deluxe coach tour through Western USA on lounge cruiser coaches containing 20 (compared with a customary 46 seats), swivel armchairs for wide window views with overnight stays at first class hotels and all meals included. In Asia, chauffeur driven car holidays, when pace and place can be decided by the traveller, are available from Coromandel Tours from around £878.

A Villa in Jamaica

In the lordly days when all hotels seemed to be called Westminster or Bristol, it was smart to have a private yacht or villa for the season. Rent of both is still possible though flotilla sailing and egg-box Costa apartments are not luxurious modern answers. Camper and Nicholsons, 16 Regency Street, London SW1P 4DD rent out big and beautiful yachts and power cruisers of every size and shape in the Mediterranean and Carribean; basic rental costs per week are anything from $5,000 upwards for five or more passengers.

Hiring villas can be grand as in Jamaica or Southern Portugal where servants come in the package and there is usually a pool or garden in the property. In Portugal, Meon Travel have graded their villas on a star system so renters can easily tell which has the best amenities. OSL produce a brochure called 'Luxury Villas' that includes superb properties like Bears House in Barbados from £460 per person per week with a staff of butler, cook, laundress, maid and gardener, with four bedrooms with *en suite* bathrooms and huge private pool. In Barbados one can also combine the amenities of hotel (with free water sports facilities) and a large, self-contained apartment well furnished at Glitter Bay (the old Cunard holiday home) or Cobblers Cove around an old plantation house.

But at the end of the travel day however luxurious, a pampered perch is essential for the night. Manor house hotels in Britain such as those belonging to the Prestige or Pride of Britain marketing groups and well serviced Far Eastern hotels like the Mandarin and Peninsula groups are the tops. There are glossy hotels like the Manila, with its crystal glass trees in the Champagne dining room where background music is supplied by a section of the National Philharmonic; the Four Seasons hotels with their good service and well-designed, spacious rooms; L'Ermitage in Beverly Hills where lengthy white cadillacs are provided to take you shopping; the Nova Park in Paris with its open plan bathroom/bedroom/bar which you divide yourself with curtains, its purple erotic decor, 24 hour video film library and restaurant and entertainment in the hotel complete with 20 resident musicians; and the Cipriani in Venice with private garden patios for side rooms with TV's that rise from chrome coffee table at the touch of a button and some of the world's best pasta in the dining room.

But the ultimate for me is a Givenchy suite at Singapore's Hilton Hotel. The spacious rooms with big garden terraces are on a separate floor serviced by Chinese butlers dressed in pin stripe, who fix appointments, take breakfast orders, deliver parcels and messages. On arrival, a maid brings a glass of champagne and unpacks for you, taking away soiled or crumpled clothes to be returned next day fresh and pressed; and each day all laundry is done free. While she works, you can nibble a handmade chocolate from a salver decorated with orchids and, like the massive mound of tropical fruit, kept topped up each day, or sip a drink from the array of cut glass decanters filled with spirits, read papers or magazines, watch TV or write a note at a desk well supplied with personalized notepaper. To unwind from the flight or sightseeing, the bathroom has its own turkish steam cabinet and bath with gold-plated taps and jacuzzi whirlpool which billows the free Givenchy bath foam into candy floss clouds as you soak it out and decide whether to take Chinese food on the roof top, *nouvelle cuisine* based on what was fresh in the market that morning in the downstairs restaurant, or full afternoon tea in the music room – an area which changes pace all day until it ends as a sophisticated late night disco with music tuned so only the dancers get its full benefit, not the talkers around the floor.

The Business Traveller

by Philip Ray

The business traveller is being courted more assiduously than ever by the world's airlines, hotel groups, car-rental companies, railways and travel agents. Business travel has never shown the dramatic growth that has characterized the holiday market but it is coveted by companies in the travel business because it is good, steady year-round traffic, and traditionally more profitable because, on average, the business traveller is reckoned to spend more than the holidaymaker.

But it is no longer possible to make the once-fashionable generalization that the business traveller will pay whatever price is demanded on the basis that the firm is paying anyway. Experience during the recession has shown that companies have been taking advantage of every opportunity to cut down on their travel costs by using discounted air fares as well as special offers by hotel groups and even normal package holidays which happen to be based in a business destination.

This 'trading down' has had a beneficial effect in the long term because it has meant that the airlines, in particular, have been re-examining and upgrading the quality of the service they give business travellers. As a result, the executive travelling at full fare now enjoys a better deal than ever before.

The traditional complaint by business travellers was that they paid a high fare but had to sit in the same cabin as, say, a group of inebriated seamen flying home on leave or families with screaming small children who had probably paid only half the amount but had exactly the same on-board food and service. This was an understandable complaint but the economic fact of life was that the high fare had nothing to do with the quality of the food or the travelling companions, but with the fact that it was completely flexible and allowed the business traveller to change or cancel flights as often as he or she wanted without having to pay any financial penalty. The cheap fare traveller, on the other hand, was probably using an inflexible ticket and would have had to pay a hefty penalty for cancellation or change of itinerary.

But the business fare was perceived as offering poor value for money and the airlines had to reverse this impression by providing a service for business travellers which was demonstrably better value and yet still provided the intangible factor of complete flexibility.

Business Class

On scheduled services within Europe, most airlines responded to the demand for a better deal for business travellers by abolishing the little-used first-class and concentrating their efforts instead on a new business class, which parades under different marketing names like British Airways' Club Class or Scandinavian Airlines' Euroclass. Two notable exceptions have been Swissair and Lufthansa which both insisted on retaining first-class service within Europe and provided no extra facilities for full-fare business travellers in economy class. But early in 1984, Swissair announced that it would be offering three classes (first, business and economy) on all its routes worldwide.

Most European business class services offer special check-in facilities, executive lounges at some airports, free drinks on board and an improved standard of meal service. Not all airlines have a dedicated cabin for business travellers; some have adopted the so-called 'flexible divider' technique, which consists simply of stringing a curtain across the cabin to separate the business traveller from the common herd in economy.

On intercontinental routes, the new business class services have been steadily upgraded and have now reached the point where first class may no longer be a viable proposition for the airlines. The 'flexible divider' system, while just about acceptable within Europe, met with a good deal of passenger resistance when it was introduced on long-haul routes because business travellers still had to endure the same generally cramped seats as those used in economy class.

So, starting on the important North Atlantic routes, the airlines abandoned the nine-abreast seating in business class on their Boeing 747s and, instead, fitted six-abreast seats in three blocks of two, as well as providing more leg room. This standard of comfort is now becoming the norm worldwide and BA, for instance, upgraded from Club Class to Super Club on all its long-haul services as from May 1984. In addition to the basic business-class perks which are standard within Europe, long-haul travellers also receive little extras like free headsets, toiletry kits and slipperettes, and sometimes, additional perks like a free helicopter transfer from New York's John F. Kennedy International Airport to downtown Manhatten.

With all these inducements for the business traveller paying only the full economy fare – or at least with only a small premium on top of the normal fare – the airlines have had to consider how they can continue to provide an attractive first class service. In most cases, the solution has been to make sleeper or 'Sleeperette' type seats a standard fitment in first class, while Philippine Air Lines is one of the few carriers to install real beds which the safety authorities have certificated for use even during takeoff or landing. (*See Lap of Luxury, page 242*.)

Cost cutting

But most cost-conscious business travellers can still save quite a lot of money – provided they don't mind travelling at the back of the aircraft with the masses. If you are planning to attend a conference, the date of which you know a long time in advance, you can frequently buy an advance-purchase excursion fare (Apex) at anything up to half the cost of the full fare. Remember, however, that there are heavy penalties if you want to cancel or change your flight. It is often worth looking around for a package trip, like those offered by specialist tour operators to tie in with a trade fair. Some travel agencies and tour operators also offer attractive packages to long-haul destinations like Tokyo which provide not only the air fare but also hotel accommodation for a total price which is often less that the full business class fare. But, once again, this type of deal does not offer the flexibility of the full fare ticket and you will probably not be able to change your flight if your business schedule overruns.

If you are planning an extensive tour within the USA, it is well worth investigating the many 'Airpasses' issued by American domestic airlines which offer unlimited travel over their networks for a given period, although there are usually some restrictions on routing.

There are also countless deals on fares to be made through both high street travel agents and bucket shops (*see The Budget Traveller, page 222*). Some of the best deals are to be found in the round-the-world fares offered by a number of airlines which can enable you to plan a complicated business itinerary at a knockdown rate.

Hotels

It is one of life's paradoxes that business travellers who have found it fashionable to criticize the high level of international air fares have not batted an eyelid at paying some of the exorbitant prices charged by international hotels.

But in the same way that airlines were forced to come to terms with the trading-down by the recession, the hotels have likewise had to offer the business traveller a better deal. For clients paying the full room rate – or even a premium rate in some cases – many of the world's major hotel groups have come up with ideas like Executive Clubs and Gold Cards which offer a variety of added-value benefits. Some provide entire floors of superior-standard rooms with a full-time manager to look after their special requests and possibly valet and butler service as well. Pre-registration, late check-out and free use of health clubs are other typical facilities which are frequently offered.

At the same time, most major hotel groups are prepared to offer discounts or 'corporate rates' to business organizations which are prepared to give them a reasonable amount of business. With careful planning by your company's business travel manager – if you have one – it is possible to negotiate discounts of up to 20 per cent with many leading hotel chains. Even if you are not a regular customer, it is always worth asking for a discount and seeing what happens.

Each group has its own scheme for corporate discounts, frequently involving a guarantee of so many room-nights or so much business in a given period. The schemes are constantly being changed but at the time of writing, Trusthouse Forte was offering a Gold Card giving discounts of up to eight per cent to companies providing more than £10,000 worth of business annually, while Crest Hotels had a Business Club with ten per cent discounts open to companies booking 250 rooms a year. Gold Card Corporate membership of WEXAS includes discounts at Sheraton Hotels worldwide as well as discounts at several other London hotels.

If you use a specialist travel agency to handle your business travel, the chances are that it will have access to a number of corporate-rate deals because of its big buying power. Thomas Cook, for instance, has agreements with a number of major chains, including Hilton and Sheraton, providing for discounts of up to 15 per cent. American Express, with its international connections, says that it can arrange discounts of up to 30 per cent at more than 2,000 hotels worldwide.

Within the UK, it is often worth

checking the brochures of the many mini-break tour operators, because some of them offer packages to important business centres, with or without rail travel, at prices which offer huge reductions over the normal hotel rate.

Rail Travel

The importance of the rail network for the business traveller within Britain and on the Continent is sometimes overlooked, but the various national railways are just as keen as the airlines to get their hands on this potentially lucrative section of the market.

British Rail, in spite of constant criticism, must run one of the best services in Europe from a business traveller's point of view, with fast trains and high frequency. And in 1983, BR relaunched its Inter-City service with the introduction of a number of 'Executive' trains offering special facilities like improved meal service and free newspapers. A 'Travel Key' charge card has also been introduced which gives discounts on rail travel, restaurant-car meals, hotels and car rental, as well as special inducements like a free weekend in Amsterdam for heavy rail spenders.

France does not always measure up to Britain in terms of train frequency, but it has won the prize for high speed with the introduction of the TGV (*Train a Grande Vitesse*) which operates at up to 270km/hour (169mph) from Paris to Lyon, Marseille and Geneva. Germany, Switzerland and the Netherlands also have notably efficient rail services which operate at frequent and regular intervals and are often competitive with the airlines in terms of timing.

Travel Agents

Competition to secure commercial accounts among the leading multiple travel agencies is extremely intense so you are definitely in a buyer's market if you are looking for an agency to look after your company's travel arrangements. All the multiples are desperate to secure more revenue if they are to meet the targets set by the airlines and other principals and so earn bonus commission. And to secure the account, they may well be willing to offer a discount on your business as well as extended credit in some cases. If your expenditure on travel is sufficiently high, the agency may even be willing to install a staff member in your office to work exclusively on your account.

But the level of discount that you may be offered is not so important as the quality of service you will receive. A skilled and knowledgeable agent may well be able to save you more on your air fares than anything you might get in the way of 'kickbacks' simply by knowing what is available on the market. The really switched-on agency will also be able to provide you with a 24 hour service, personal delivery of tickets when necessary and will also be able to look after your requirements for conferences, exhibitions or incentive travel.

The Student Traveller

by Nick Hanna and Greg Brookes

Student travellers can take advantage of a comprehensive range of special discounts both at home and abroad which enable you to go almost anywhere in the world on the cheap.

To qualify for reduced rates to most destinations, you need an *International Student Identity Card* (ISIC) which is obtainable from local student travel offices or by post from ISIC, PO Box 90, London WC1. Holders of NUS full-time cards simply need to pay £3 to get the ISIC portion validated. All full-time students are eligible; applications should include proof of students status, a passport photo, full name, date of birth, nationality and the £3 fee. Postal applicants should also include an SAE.

The ISIC card is issued by the Geneva-based International Student Travel Conference, who, in conjunction with the NUS, publish a booklet called *The International Student Travel Guide* which tells you exactly what discounts students are eligible for. The ISIC card is recognized all over the world and allows holders reduced rates at many art galleries and other places of cultural and educational interest, as well as reductions on local transport.

The ISIC card is not, however, officially recognized in Eastern Europe where they have their own equivalent, the International Union of Students Card. These are difficult to obtain in Britain, although it is worth asking your local student travel office, and you will probably have to apply to the student authorities once you get into Eastern Europe.

The Council of Europe Cultural Identity Card is available free to postgraduate (not undergraduate) students, teachers, and a few other groups. It gives reduced or free admission to places of cultural interest in all member countries of the Council of Europe, and the Vatican; but not in the country of issue and only when produced with a passport. The card may not be used by those travelling for commercial reasons. For information and the application forms, write to the CBEVE (*see page 222*).

Accommodation

A useful booklet published by ISTC is *Low Cost Accommodation: Europe* which is available from student travel offices for £1. It lists over 1,200 places to stay divided into four price categories (budget, inexpensive, moderate or expensive) and a system of symbols indicates whether the hotel is near the station, airport or beach and what percentage discount they give to students.

For cheap accommodation in the USA students can get a '*Where to Stay USA*' card which costs £3.50 for ISIC holders. It entitles you to a 25 per cent discount on hotels and motels listed in their 48-page directory.

In West Germany students can use university catering facilities (Mensas) which are decent, reasonably priced and open all year round. Student accommodation is available, though usually only during local university vacations.

Travel

Cheap rail travel is now dependent chiefly upon age, and is generally open to everyone under the age of 26 but student discounts are available on coaches. It pays to compare prices carefully between coach and rail because although coaches are normally considerably cheaper, sometimes the difference can be as little as £5, and trains are obviously preferable in terms of speed and comfort. Apart from these exceptions, coaches are generally at least £20 cheaper than trains, and both Euroways Coaches and Supabus offer discounts to ICIS holders on most (but not all routes). Some examples (figures in brackets indicate normal adult fares, all prices are return): Turin £75 (£102), Florence £83 (£114), Bologna £79 (£107), Lyons £39 (£54), Cordoba £107 (£120).

Ferries also offer student discounts. On Irish Sea Ferries, it is 25 per cent, crossing the North Sea 20 per cent, and on DFDS Ferries to Germany, 50 per cent. Student fares are also available on some cross-channel and Mediterranean ferries.

Within Britain, National Express gives students a 30 per cent reduction on all standard fares (but not Rapide services) on production of an ISIC card.

Air

Valuable discounts are available for air travel. Student charters are operated by the major student travel organizations under the umbrella of the Student Air Travel Association. Most of the flights are in the long summer vacation, and are generally open to ISIC card holders under 30 (some are only open to those under 28) and their spouses and dependent children as long as they are travelling on the same flight.

Students travelling between their home and place of study abroad are also eligible for 25 per cent off standard fares if they arrange beforehand to get a Student Certificate from the airline (apply well in advance). Because these reductions only apply to standard fares, you might be better off with a discount ticket from elsewhere. Local student travel offices often have preferential arrangements with particular airlines and so are able to offer special bargains.

Travel offices

Student travel offices are a good source of information about every kind of discount; there are nearly sixty of them in Britian, one for every campus or university town. They are coordinated by the National Association of Student Travel Offices (NASTO). Staff are often themselves seasoned travellers and can be a mine of information on budget travel in foreign countries. But check out the high street travel agent as well and compare prices before making a final decision.

Another source of information on student discounts is *The Student Travel Manual* produced annually by STA Travel (to obtain a free copy contact STA Travel, 74 Old Brompton Road, London SW7. Tel: 01-581 1022). Although they started out life as Student Travel Australia, the services offered by STA now cover both hemispheres, making them Britain's biggest and most influential student travel operator. They have three offices in London and others throughout Australia, South East Asia, the Far East and the USA.

Another major operator is Worldwide Student Travel (for a free brochure contact them at 37 Store Street, London WC1E 7BZ. Tel: 01-580 7733). Also worth checking out is London Student Travel (Head Office:

Victoria Travel Centre, 52 Grosvenor Gardens, London SW1W 0AG. Tel: 01-730 8111) who have three offices in London, and others in Liverpool, Manchester and Oxford.

Working and Studying Abroad

There are several very good references for students who wish to work abroad such as *Working Holidays* published by the Central Bureau for Educational Visits and Exchanges, and a very useful series of books from Vacation Work Publications. (*See Joining a Project Overseas, on page 228, and booklist on page* 577).

North America is a favourite destination for students who want a working holiday. The British Universities North America Club (BUNAC) is a non profit-making organization that exists to give students the chance to get to the States. They've got six programmes in the USA and Canada, offering a wide choice of jobs and locations, and for all of them, BUNAC gets you that vital work permit.

The general work and travel programme, Work America, allows you a visa so that you can take virtually any summer job you find yourself; the air fare has to be paid in advance – they suggest that bank managers will usually oblige with a loan. Places are limited, so it's vital that the lengthy application process is started early. Hundreds of opportunities can be found in BUNAC's *Job Directory*.

If you enjoy the company of children, then they have a BUNACAMP programme which places students in summer camps as counsellors. The round trip ticket is paid for, and you get full board and lodging plus pocket money. Students with specialist skills (music, sports, arts or sciences) are preferred, but more importantly, you must be able to deal with children.

Another deal that provides you with air fares, full board and lodging and a job is KAMP, the kitchen and maintenance programme. Contact BUNAC at 58/60 Berners Street, London W1P 3AE. Tel: 01-637 7686.

Camp America provides similar facilities with a free flight, free board and work permit all as part of the package. The placement procedure likewise takes a long time, so apply early. They are at 37 Queens Gate, London SW7 5HR. Tel: 01-589 3223.

To study abroad, you must first be sure you can cope adequately with the local language. Organizations such as the CBEVE, and the British Council should be able to help, as should the Cultural Attaché at the relevant embassy. If possible, ask someone who has just returned for more details about local conditions and lifestyle.

Grants

Ask your university/polytechnic/higher education department/local authority if it has any special trust funds for student travel. If it has, it won't be much, but every little helps. Two handbooks on grants are *The Directory of Grant Making Trusts* and *The Grants Register*. Both are expensive, but should be in your student library. The library noticeboard is also a good place to look for details of bursaries, or exchange scholarships which could well lead to a year's studying or travelling upon graduation.

Your Special Needs

Selecting Travelling Companions

by Nigel Winser

> 'I would say that this matter of relationships between members . . . can be more important than the achievement of the stated objective, be it crossing a desert or an ocean, the exploration of a jungle or the ascent of a mountain peak.'
> – John Hunt

'Bill always takes his boots off inside the tent and Ben has yet to cook a decent meal . . . yackety yack, moan, moan.' A familiar and typical hue and cry, triggered by lack of privacy and repetitive food. Add to the melting-pot such problems as financial mismanagement, change of itinerary, ill health and a stolen rucksack, and you may realize that you have not given as much thought to the choice of your travelling companion as you should. While the fire remains hot there is little you can do about it, so it is worth thinking about before you depart.

All travelling groups will have storms, so don't kid yourself that they won't happen to you. But perhaps you can weather them without breaking up the party.

I am not concerned here with choosing specialist members of a team, which is up to the leader of the group. The more specialized the positions the more specific the qualifications required.

Leaders are fortunate to be able to draw on the experiences of many past expeditions as well as long-term projects in Antarctica where all nations have studied personnel selection and interview techniques in detail. It is lucky we don't all have to go through such interviews because you and I probably wouldn't make it.

Common Sense

In theory, choosing your companions is common sense. You are looking for good-humoured individuals who, by their understanding and agreement of the objectives, form a close bond and so create a functional and cohesive team. It also helps if you like each other.

People go on journeys to satisfy ambitions, however disparate. The more you understand everyone else's ambitions, the better you will be at assessing the strength of the bonds that maintain the group. But it is not that easy. A common problem arises when for instance en route you require someone to do a job such as repair a vehicle. Suddenly your good friend has to be moulded into a mechanic, a role for which he may or may not be fit. The other solution is to have in your party a mechanic whom you have never met but who has to be moulded into a 'good friend'. There are no black-and-white guidelines here. If any virtues were to be singled out to aid your decision, high tolerance and adaptability would be two.

So, with no fixed guidelines, how can you begin to choose your companions? The single factor most likely to upset the group on a journey will be that an individual does not satisfy his or her own reasons for going. Fellow members of the party will be directly or indirectly blamed for preventing such satisfaction. Travelling itself acts as a catalyst to any dispute and provocations and pressures may build up to intolerable levels. Any bonds that have formed will be stretched to the limit, as individuals continually reassess their expectations.

It is assumed that differing personality traits are to blame here. While there are, of course, exceptions, I do not believe that personality clashes are sufficient to account for groups breaking up. I see them as symptoms of disorder within the group, and a lack of cohesion within the group owing to ill-matched objectives to be the original cause. It is worth mentioning here that the 'organization' of the trip will come under fire whenever difficulties arise; and while no one wants to lose the freedom of individual travel, the machinery of group travel (shared kitty, agreed itinerary, overall responsibility) should be well oiled.

Practical Tips

From a practical point of view, you may like to consider the following tips, which apply as much to two hitchhikers as to a full-blown expedition:

1. Get to know one another before you go. If necessary, go to the pub together and get slightly pickled and see if you can get on just as well in the morning.
2. Discuss openly with all members of the group the overall objectives of the trip and see how many of the group disagree. Are all members of the group going to be satisfied with the plans as they stand?
3. Discuss openly the leader's (or the main organizer's, if there is one) motivation in wanting to undertake this particular journey. Is he or she using the trip to further selfish ambitions? If these are made clear beforehand so much the better, particularly if the others are not connected with the hidden objective.
4. Discuss and plan to solve the problems which will certainly crop up. The regular ones are poor health, stolen goods, accidents, insurance, itinerary. If everyone knows where he stands before the chips are down, the chance of remaining a group improves.
5. If possible, have the team working together before departure, particularly if there has been allocation of duties. To know where you fit in is important.
6. If there is to be any form of hierarchy, it must be established before leaving and not enforced en route. If everyone can be made to feel that he or she is an integral part of the group and the group's interdependence, you will all stay

together throughout the journey and have a rewarding and enjoyable experience.

The Woman Traveller

by Ludmilla Tüting

Strict moral codes make the life of female travellers all over the world more difficult. If you want to avoid trouble you must listen to some unwritten rules.

'You can judge a man by the cut of his suit' – I don't like that saying. For me, it reflects the whole mendacity and dual morality of our society. Whenever I have to pack my rucksack to travel to Asia my trouble with clothes begins. Each time the same thing: shall I take some of my good stuff with me? A nice little skirt would open doors much faster and would afford me more respect. Things can be made much easier in Muslim countries. The more I play up to being a lady or the more determined and authoritarian my appearance becomes, the less I'll be regarded as a plaything. But that whole façade is so repugnant to me that until now I've unpacked my 'good' stuff again.

Western women are, in fact, regarded in most of the underdeveloped countries, and even in Southern Europe, as nothing better than loose women. Even the company of a man doesn't help much in Muslim countries. For instance, Iranians are especially prone to touching our breasts or grasping us between the legs in the bazaars or on the streets. As I was propositioned frequently in non-Muslim countries although accompanied by a male, I began to think about the situation. But it took me years to realize my mistake: mainly I just didn't behave in a feminine way.

Stay in Stereotype

Clichés which are used to stereotype the role of women can be expected and found mainly in the orthodox countries. I have never played this role. On the contrary, I always started discussions about the contrast between East and West, or about the fact that daughters and sons go through with arranged marriages not having seen each other before. I talked enthusiastically about how beautiful it is to travel alone, how you are more open to experience and its many other advantages. Apart from that, I liked to look people straight in the face, but I should not have done this with men. My most chaste dress was in vain if I looked deep into their eyes. They usually took it as an invitation. These men are not used to it; their women avoid eye contact. I try to do so too, but it is difficult. I do not feel obliged to live a lie, but the stiff moral concepts applicable to women leave me with no choice. I find I have to accept other countries as they are, otherwise I had better stay at home. So:

- If I travel with a 'constant' partner, we act as a married couple and tell people we have at least two sons, daughters being worthless.
- If I travel alone, I carry with me a photo of 'my husband and our sons' and show it when necessary. The photo should never show wealthy surroundings; as a background, nature is the best of all.

- On principle I wear a real wedding ring, none of the cheap ones. Wearing the ring on the left hand in these countries means that you are married. Ten years ago, the same stupid trick was even sometimes necessary at home.
- I now avoid eye contact with men. In strong Muslim countries it is a good idea to wear sunglasses with opaque mirror lenses.
- The most successful method of warding off molestation is to learn defensive replies in the native tongue of those countries which are renowned for this problem.
- I only give obvious reasons for why I travel on my own: because of my profession, my studies, or because I want to visit friends or relations.
- I only wear small T-shirts with a bra underneath and a waistcoat on top. I always cover my shoulders, upper arms, and, of course, my legs. Nearly everywhere naked legs are considered disrespectful to the customs of the country, particularly in places like temples. Having bare legs is as bad as wearing nothing at all.
- It is only when I have known people for a long time that I am willing to discuss controversial topics.
- I try to avoid everything which could possibly give the impression that I am 'game'. Whether in Asia or Latin America, it is a matter of prestige for many men to go to bed with a European or white woman. Accordingly, if they scent a chance, they will use all their charm and tricks to gain their objective. A few times I have been very disappointed and very angry when they tried to use force, although I was a guest of the whole family. Especially in Latin America, as you may know, the macho cult demands that a man has a mistress as well as a wife and this state of affairs is generally accepted. The Koran allows a man to take four women as long as he can ensure that he will provide each of them with similar material conditions.

- The Western-oriented men in the cities are the most dangerous. Television has a great deal to do with this. In under-developed countries you will notice that many low-cost American trash programmes make up a large part of the station's schedule. And from these, many men get the impression that Western women are only to be regarded as objects of sexual amusement, and frequently the victims of direct violent acts.
- If you find yourself in the position when you are actually about to be raped, there is only one thing to do: keep cool! Panic only angers the perpetrator. As bad as it is, normally the woman will not die and after a few minutes, it's all over. It is important that you don't become paranoid about being attacked and even if it should happen to you, don't become a psychological wreck. Therefore here are three tips which you may find useful:
  - ⋆ Try to start a conversation with your attacker. Possibly warn him that you have venereal disease.
  - ⋆ Beat or bite his testicles so that he is forced to let you go because he is in pain.
  - ⋆ Simulate excitement so that he feels secure and the possibility of killing you does not enter his mind.

I have recovered from several attempted rapes. The first time it happened to me was in a little village hospital in Pakistan, when I naively went for a medical examination because of acute appendicitis. Three doctors immediately made passes at me. And even though I was in agony because of the pain they merely offered me whisky and howled 'Let's have a party!'

Peculiarly, the setting of another attempt was in a heavily-guarded building in Brazil: that is, in the German Consulate in Rio, where marksmen stood on guard to protect a visiting ambassador from abduction. However, in the corridor, a messenger, already stripped down to his underpants, was waiting for me.

In India, there is a pocket-book against hippies which created a sensation in 1974 and encouraged the opinion that every tourist who doesn't wear elegant clothes and stay at the Sheraton must be a hippy. This book is a collection of all imaginable prejudices against young Western people but was sold as an 'analysis'. The author, an officer, came to the conclusion that hippies are only involved in sex and drugs. They come to India, distribute themselves, stink and leave behind a heap of rubbish.

It is also important to know that in most countries, exchange of tenderness in public is scorned. One is only allowed to express tender feelings within one's own four walls. For example, when a couple meet again at an airport in Delhi, the women at best fling themselves into the dust to kiss their husband's feet. An embrace is impossible, but on the contrary it is usual to see men holding hands when going for a stroll and it doesn't automatically mean they are homosexual!

Morals, Traditions and Taboos

The strict moral codes, made by men to protect women, begin on our own doorsteps, with the Italians. In Italy, as late as 1981, a law was abolished which allowed extenuating circumstances to men who murdered their wife, daughter or sister for having immoral sex, just to rescue their honour.

In Muslim society, a similarly peculiar interpretation of honour exists (male honour of course; female honour doesn't exist). If an unmarried female member of the family loses her virginity, the honour of the man is in danger; he loses face. He himself can be the worst lecher but that will not matter. In Berlin, among the migrant workers, Turkish gynaecologists replace young Turkish girls' hymens, otherwise they wouldn't be able to find a husband.

Where false upbringing and the acceptance of foolish role-playing attitudes can lead, we know only too well from our own countries. However, over here I have the right to criticize. Nevertheless, if I mention that women in menstruation are, in many countries, regarded as unclean, I still say it with unbelievable astonishment. A woman should therefore be quiet about her period or she could, for instance, be refused admission to temples, and she may not touch certain foods and men.

The worst violation, in my opinion, is the circumcision of young women in the Northern part of Africa from Egypt to Senegal, where the clitoris is cut out and the vulva are stitched together, leaving only a minute opening. I always shiver when I think how the procedure takes place under primitive, unhygienic conditions. For procreation, the vulva are temporarily separated. The moral: your wife remains clean, the man finds sexual satisfaction elsewhere.

Muslims like to emphasize the advantages the Koran brought to their women, which is also true. They finally acquired material security during the marriage – but that was in the seventh century. They still have few rights and, if not married, none at all.

It is a question of interpretation of the Koran when Muslim men maintain the tradition that their women wear veils. Even in Europe, the orthodox Muslim adheres more to tradition than Mohammed because Mohammed wrote that face, hands and feet may stay exposed. What is important about that? The hair should be covered, which is why a scarf worn by tourist women in strict regions can only be an advantage. An Arab once said to a friend: 'A woman who shows her hair might as well present herself naked.' The veil in the Middle East is called the Hidschaab or Tschador and on the Indian subcontinent, Pardah, Under the veil, which in Afghanistan completely covers the face, the women wear the latest cosmetics. If a woman walks through the streets with her legs bared and unaccompanied, she should not wonder if she is looked upon as a whore. By walking through a bazaar, she further risks running the gauntlet. More than a few women tourists do this even on purpose, but do so to the detriment of other women. Just as scorned are those on the border separating Colombia and Venezuela who acquire the coveted visas from immigration officers by going to bed with them. So much more is the anger of the women who won't submit and have to travel the 500 kilometres back.

Something to be aware of when striking up friendships while abroad is that you could only be the means to an end. A marriage contract is often the only way of entering a Western country and a romance with a local man could, in fact, just be his ticket out. However, it would be absurd to avoid all relationships while travelling, on whatever basis they are formed.

For contraception on long journeys, the coil is supposed to be most suitable, but it should be tested long before setting out for compatibility. Those who wish to take the pill should take an ample supply, and be careful on long flights with time differences and in cases of diarrhoea. Condoms are highly recommended for use while travelling as they are obtainable everywhere and also give protection against venereal disease.

Sex aside, a few years ago, one noticed that few women travelled alone. Today there are many, often travelling in pairs. Many had bad experiences before the journey started while looking for male partners – only frisky young girls are sought as travelling companions. From whichever angle I look at it, I always seem to arrive back at the same theme. Perhaps it is time more women travellers spoke out in favour of a little respect.

This article has been reprinted from the Globetrotters Handbook, whom we would like to thank for permission to use it.

The Elderly Traveller

by Peggy Drage

In terms of the traveller, 'elderly' would seem to mean not so much advancing years as diminishing physical endurance. I hope to show that, given a little time and forethought, the elderly can still manage to travel independently and enjoy it.

Of course, there is the attitude of others to take into account. For instance, some freighter companies, car hire firms, and even adventure holiday companies will not accept clients beyond the age of 65 or 70 and it is wise for people of this age to look closely at the small print of any travel insurance they may wish to take out. On the other hand, some countries have 'bonuses' for the retired, such as the *Carte Vermeil* in France which allows retired people of any nationality to travel by rail at reduced fares. We have found, too, that immigration and customs officials tend to be less suspicious these days, assuming perhaps that 'oldies' are less likely to be involved in drug rackets or looking for jobs.

Time on Your Side

One of the advantages of being retired is that, paradoxically, time is on your side. You are no longer obliged to rush back to family or job and can travel in a more leisurely manner. So it is possible to break up journeys into smaller, more manageable, portions and allow for rest periods when necessary. This is particularly true when driving. We have just completed a long drive through Mexico where, although the roads are fairly good, you have to contend with their narrowness, the dazzling light, other people's often reckless driving and also a great many extra-long vehicles and buses, all of which add up to hard driving conditions. We found that, by limiting our daily mileage, starting early in the morning and sometimes staying not one night in a place, but two or three, the whole trip was made much easier. There are benefits in this: you arrive reasonably fresh for the hassle of finding accommodation in a strange town and any sightseeing can be done in a leisurely manner. Moreover, an unhurried meal and a chat with a 'local' can be far more rewarding than trying to rush around and see the sights. Another small tip for the driver who may have back trouble (and this is apt to hit people of all ages) is to place a thick guidebook between the seat back and the bottom of your spine – a small thing, but a real help and also an excuse to bring that heavy book!

Similarly, a long haul flight can be broken up for an overnight – or longer – stay without necessarily incurring extra expense: for instance, many US airlines give reduced fares for inland travel if you buy your ticket before leaving Europe. This means that you can get a cheap and comparatively short transatlantic flight and, after an overnight stop, carry on the next day. This way you can see another city and, after all, one has to sleep somewhere! This can also be a help with jetlag. Off-peak travel is good value if time is not of the essence. Also worth looking into are the round-the-world tickets being offered by several airlines. These are very cheap, last a long time, if you are not in a hurry, and allow you a large number of stopovers within the original fare, as long as you keep going in the same direction.

Health

Two of the most unpleasant and disrupting hazards of travel are traveller's diarrhoea and altitude sickness. These can hit both young and old: I have seen a busload of schoolchildren completely laid out by *soroche* on the top of Popocatapetl in Mexico, but to older people they can be more dangerous than mere temporary symptoms. Any elderly traveller thinking of going to the Andes, Himalayas, or any other high spots of the world should be a little wary. Competent medical advice and a check-up should be sought before deciding on the trip. Some holiday companies sensibly ask for a fitness certificate before selling their more strenuous trips, and if you are travelling independently, there is even more reason to follow the same precautions as there will be no one there to help should you get ill.

On arrival at high altitude, get plenty of rest, even if you feel quite well and however tempting it is to rush out and 'see'. Above all, the altitude should not be varied more than necessary. Spending a few days at a high altitude, coming down for a 'rest' and then going on somewhere else just as high can be disastrous. I did this, mistakenly, in the Andes and blithely dismissed the consequences, feeling that a stiff upper lip was indicated. The result was that I suffered permanent heart damage which has prevented full enjoyment of subsequent journeys in Nepal and Mexico. Altitude and extremes of heat and cold should be treated with respect.

If you are going to use your retirement to catch up on all the travelling you haven't done before, it is vitally important, particularly if wandering off the beaten track, to know your own physical limitations. If you get ill, or break a limb when elderly, it will take a lot longer to heal and it is often doubtful as to whether you will fully recover your strength. Even ordinary exhaustion, something common to most eager travellers, can be far more debilitating than in a younger person. Get as fit as possible before you go, and deprive yourself of as few comforts as possible on your journeys.

Double Your Money

In these days of few or no porters in the more affluent countries and long walks at airports, the old adage about planning your money and your luggage and then doubling the former and halving the latter is more applicable than ever. Try to travel in your heaviest clothes rather than pack them and remember that an anorak is better than a coat anywhere – that is, unless you are going to attend formal gatherings en route, when a good-looking raincoat is lightweight and useful. Instead of taking guidebooks, make notes beforehand. It is surprising what reading matter can be found or swapped with fellow travellers in different parts of the world.

Above all, hand luggage should be limited to a minimum and there should not be too much indulgence in the Duty Free shop.

Provided sufficient care is taken to match partners, home exchange works very well (*see article on page 232*). The exchange does not even need to be simultaneous: some people live in caravans or stay with relatives or have a country hide-away they use while the exchangers are in their home and in this way, the best of all worlds is available – you can go away in winter and allow the exchangers to come in summer, and everyone is happy.

Camping and trailer parks are another way of life for people with plenty of time. Thousands of retired people in the USA and Canada spend their winter trailing south as far as Mexico, living largely on the fish and game they catch, and return home in the spring. They are known as 'snowbirds' and almost literally drive south in flocks, not always to the delight of residents or other motorized travellers.

One more bonus of the mature is that they have had time to acquire more experience, knowledge and perhaps a language or two to widen and enrich the pleasures of travel. To travel not in order to arrive but to enjoy should perhaps be our motto.

Travelling With (and Before) Children

by Rowena Quantrill

Many people believe that once they have children, travel must be restricted to the safe and conventional, at least until the children have reached their teens. This need not be so. Children are remarkably adaptable and with forethought and planning can be taken almost anywhere. We have travelled extensively and happily, even when our children were very small. Our four children look back on the overland journey which, when aged between six and twelve, they made with us, as one of the best experiences of their lives.

There are, however, two important facts to remember when travelling with children. First, it will be harder work than travelling alone, and second, children can usually only put up with a limited amount of sightseeing or shopping. If you want to visit the bazaar or the nearest temple in the morning, find somewhere to swim or scramble on rocks in the afternoon, or vice versa.

There are also other advantages and disadvantages. On the plus side, children learn responsibility and practical information; the unfamiliarity of the outside world tends to knit a family more closely together; and discounts in travel and accommodation are often such that it is cheaper to bring children with you than to leave them behind, where you will have to pay to have them cared for or send them on an alternative holiday, e.g. to camp, and worry about them into the bargain. Drawbacks include the need, especially for a woman travelling alone with children, to find sitters from time to time along the way; and the fact that children often miss their friends and complain bitterly about it. Parents looking for babysitters abroad will find that local student organizations often offer such a service; hotels too may provide supervised nurseries and playgrounds and an evening sitting service.

Travel Light

Most people going to more remote areas have, of necessity, to travel light. The easiest thing to cut down on with children is clothes. So long as what you take is easy to wash and dries quickly (polyester/cotton mixes are good) you can get away with two outfits. Remember to take along a sewing kit and some spare buttons for on-the-spot repairs. Do make sure that you have something waterproof for them and a warm sweater, as it can turn cold even in the tropics. Children generally tolerate heat better than adults but feel the cold more and a cold child is a miserable one.

It is usually worth carrying a small supply of emergency food, e.g. peanut butter, cheese, cans of baked beans, etc. If your child is a fairly adventurous eater, this will probably be enough, but if he's fussy, it may be worth taking along a lightweight stove, packets of soup, etc., so you can cook the occasional meal. (This is supposing you aren't camping and cooking all your meals anyway.) If you give the children vitamin pills or drops every day you will worry less about their getting a balanced diet. When travelling in a hot country, it is vital to carry sufficient water containers with you as thirsty children complain endlessly and an adequate fluid intake is important for good health.

Make sure that they have all the necessary vaccinations before they go (*see section on Inoculations on page 342*) and consult your doctor about the contents of the medicine chest.

Keeping Them Amused

What games and amusements you take will depend very much on your children, but don't overdo it. I would recommend: as many favourite books as you can manage, plenty of paper, colouring books, pens and pencils, a pack of cards, and, for older children, a game such as chess or Scrabble which can be played while travelling. Word games and games built around the moving scenery outside the car (or bus or train) window – counting things, identifying things – have the added advantage of requiring no equipment. If children want to bring a soft toy, let them, as this will provide security in the various strange and different places they have to sleep. Do, however, make sure it is a reasonable choice – my daughter is very attached to a stuffed hippopotamus!

If you are travelling in a group it is very important that your children behave in a reasonably polite and considerate manner and if they do, you may well find other people will do a good deal of the amusing for you. With younger children it is important to keep up routines like reading a bedtime story and do be prepared to read to them at other times too, even if all you really want to do is look at the view.

It pays to find out as much as you can beforehand about places you are visiting and pass on the more striking facts to the children: they will be far more interested if they know that something is the largest in the world; was once the crater of a giant volcano; or is the home of a living goddess the same age as themselves, or whatever. Older children will appreciate being given clearly written guidebooks to read beforehand or route maps to study. They also usually respond well to being given responsibility for a particular aspect of a journey, e.g. learning Arabic numerals so that you will know what the coins are worth.

The Under Threes

What I have said so far applies mainly to children of about three years and upwards. The problems of younger children are somewhat different. If you want to travel with a small baby, do try to breastfeed; it cuts out about half the difficulties in one go. If travelling in a vehicle with a bottlefed baby, get one of those food warming devices that plugs into the cigarette lighter on the dashboard.

Obviously you will need to carry more with you. Disposable nappies are bulky but more suitable when you are likely to have problems with the washing and drying of cloth nappies. However, a lot depends on where you are going. In hot, dry climates, e.g. in the Middle East and the Indian subcontinent, disposing of so-called disposable nappies can be difficult. Here, four or five cloth nappies would suffice instead, for they dry very quickly hung like curtains round the car windows (this cools the car too) or pinned on the back of the papoose.

A papoose is undoubtedly the easiest way of carrying a baby around and heshe will probably remain contented for hours travelling in this manner. For hot climates, prickly heat powder may prove useful.

Flying with a baby can be a trial. Hold the baby on your lap during takeoff and landing and whenever the 'Fasten Seat Belts' sign comes on. The change in air pressure may come as a shock to a baby and cause him to cry, but his discomfort will be quickly relieved by a few sips of water. Make sure that you keep the nappy-changing operation quite separate from the eating and serving of food (yours and other people's).

The toddler stage is possibly the most difficult of all and it is probably best to try and avoid long journeys with children of this age.

In one way, the children themselves can be a positive asset to their parents. In the Catholic countries especially, where small children are venerated, your child may be the point of introduction to other children and thence their parents. Between small children of different nationalities and colour there are no barriers. Where real contact with local people may otherwise be impossible, it often happens easily through the spontaneity and natural friendliness of children. From your children you will gain a new perspective on travel for you will be seeing things through their eyes.

They, on the other hand, though they may miss out on schooling and more conventional experiences, will more than make up for this by gaining some knowledge of different environments, cultures and landscapes and by sharing your love of travel.

Travel in Pregnancy

Pregnancy is, of course, not in itself an illness, but certain precautions against its becoming one need to be taken. Pregnant women should avoid very long journeys especially in the first three and last two months, during which there is a risk of miscarriage or prematurity, caused by tiredness or the mother's altered posture, which can also lead to thrombosis. After eight months, most airlines ask pregnant passengers to present a doctor's certificate attesting that there is no special danger of premature birth or complications. Flying itself seems to pose some risk: airline stewardesses have more miscarriages than other women. This is possibly because of oxygen deficiency in aircraft cabins where the pressure during flight is equivalent to that prevailing at an altitude of 1,500–2,000 metres. For the same reason, even experienced mountaineers should avoid going to high altitudes whilst pregnant.

Most reasonable exercise is recommended during pregnancy, but overexertion is certainly not advised. Nor is any activity which takes place far from the opportunity to call for medical assistance, e.g. sailing. Walking is especially good for circulation and for toning the leg muscles, but long hikes come under the heading of 'overdoing it'. Cycling and swimming, in moderation, are fine. Women who are accustomed to having saunas may continue to do so during pregnancy, so long as the heat is not too fierce; those who are new to the experience should defer it, since saunas tend to be rather dehydrating. There is no evidence that there is any risk of inducing premature birth or of damaging the foetus by sexual intercourse, even during the last weeks of pregnancy.

Most women will know by now that it is most unwise to smoke during pregnancy and that alcohol should be taken in moderation. Pregnant women should not have smallpox or yellow fever vaccinations. Malaria prophylaxes should only be taken under a doctor's supervision.

The Lone Male

by Bryan Hanson with the assistance of Steve Bartlett and Andy Pappas

Much has been written on this subject for the 'fairer sex', but how many dire spots or awkward situations can the lonely male avoid if he is given a bit of advice? The lone traveller depends more on the locals than the accompanied. Taking a female along has its advantages, depending both on the relationship and the female. One often has to spend time and energy defending them from the odd amorous male along the way, but hitch-hiking is often easier, beds warmer and social gatherings that much more congenial, to say nothing of the companionship. Predatory females and males are kept at bay and the odd fevered brow can be soothed. But we digress, you are alone. You are that much more vulnerable. Ripping-off (which now seems part of the travel jargon) is that much easier for the unscrupulous, and a team with this intent can work that much better on one person.

Safety

Avoid placing yourself in a position to be mugged and even killed without trace. In some poor countries, people are desperate and, however poor you feel, to them you will be the picture of Western affluence. Places like Eastern Turkey, parts of South America and Africa are notorious for gangs who work in a violent way. Don't venture into 'no-go' areas out of curiosity or bravado, especially at night. Try to overcome a vulnerability which stems from your natural wish to trust everyone.

About muggings: don't fight back unless the odds are very much on your side, you may get yourself killed. Best to carry a smallish amount of money which can be surrendered on such occasions, while your main store stays safe. I have heard of travellers who have been knifed for resisting – and don't forget the karate expert who was shot on Kata beach in Thailand.

Try not to make the most valuable part of your luggage obvious. Clutching at a shiny camera bag or small holdall will usually mean it will get nicked! Keep cameras in tatty bags and packs and remember that memories are in the brain and not on film.

Meeting people along the way is one of the joys of travel, but again be careful about showing where you keep your valuables. Sharing a room is cheap, but not if you wake up alone and penniless. A digital padlock is a good idea if sharing as no keys are involved. Sleeping in railway stations is an experience, but remember that the toilets are usually the meeting place for gays. In Third World countries, two men travelling together gain respect if they let it be known they are brothers, or have some family connection.

If you have to walk in dangerous areas at night, you can pretend to be mad; hop, pull on a forelock and twitch and yelp regularly and you will be left alone. If you must wear valuables, keep them well out of sight, especially your watch. As with a vehicle, you will have fewer worries without it – or baggage. A good idea is to take all your old clothes and instead of washing them, give them away until you have none and probably by that time you will be able to buy replacements for next to nothing.

Examine cheap rooms for windows which can be opened from outside. Most people put money under pillows; don't. A rubber door wedge is not too cumbersome to carry and can be useful. I have heard of places where hotel owners, thieves and police are working together (this mostly happens in much used places on well trodden routes). In situations where you feel in the right but are given the run around, insist on speaking to the highest official available and be firm with him. Always take names, especially in Iron Curtain countries, and you will have more chance of meeting an official who can take a decision and not be bound by rule books written for morons. You may need help from a British representative abroad. Some can be helpful, but they are very rare. Most don't want to rock the local boat and have a keen and skilled way of passing you on. Insist on help; it is your right. Point out, if necessary, that they are living in a style to which they are normally unaccustomed on your taxes, and if you are helpless to make them move in Ruritania, just wait until you get home to your uncle in the Foreign Office!

No matter how scruffy you have become, it really pays to look your best to officials of all kinds, however old fashioned it may seem. This also applies to hitch-hiking. In my student days, I always got superior lifts with an umbrella!

There have been one or two reports of people on public transport or offering lifts in South America using drugged sweets; sounds phony but it isn't. A recent report from Israel tells of sleeping gas being used on campers. Never underestimate thieves. In Nigeria it is common for them to be naked and covered with grease and use long poles studded with razor blades. In India, lots of people are robbed on trains by boys who travel on the roof and come down through the windows at night. If you want to be sophisticated, there is an electronic device which sounds an alarm if your luggage is removed a small distance from you. Locks on cases, even soft ones, at least let you know they have been tampered with.

After Your Body

No doubt everyone has to develop their own ways of coping with predatory males or females. Some are only after your charms or body, but most are after your wallet. The number of pretty seventeen year old girls who genuinely go for middle-aged men are few. A firm, positive, eye-to-eye refusal will usually quell the males, although in some areas it could be 'playing hard to get'. Females can be much more difficult and embarrassing, especially if staying in a home with the husband present. You could bring out your portable door wedge, make a few references to social diseases or, if desperate obviously scratch the lower regions! Most times, such liaisons are a lot more trouble than they're worth.

Partaking of commercial horizontal refreshment can also be hazardous. In the Far East there are strains of VD which are incurable and one should at least use a condom. In Manila and Bangkok there is a sad, but growing, trade in child sex, both boys and girls. It is more than anti-social to encourage this. Reformers are rendered helpless by the large amounts of money to be made. The *International Herald Tribune* tells of nuns who say they cannot expect children to work for an honest living for a hundredth of the money.

In nightclubs the girls will flock. Tell them you are broke, you have no money, you are only there for the beer. Don't waste their time, they have a living to make. In Kenya a policeman was heard to advise sticking to the town for pleasure as there is so much VD in the bush. This may follow in similar countries, as in Nigeria, where I never met one person who had visited a harlot (the local word) and did not end up at the clinic. Keep a very high standard of hygiene at all times.

It is often a good thing to strike up a relationship with a local girl while travelling. If she is making the same journey, she can save a lot of money by obtaining things for you at local prices and it also helps you get into the local culture. But remember not to offend. If she is a business girl or married, separated or divorced, there should be little trouble. But single girls are very tempting and respectable. Their innocence makes them easy to fall in love with, but you may have ruined their lives. You move on, they have to stay and face local prejudices. No local will consider them even if the relationship has been platonic. In many cases, she may even end up in prostitution. This is particularly true of Thailand where, although there is a lot of vice, the moral code of the average Thai is very high and conservative.

Dress

In dress, follow the local, but do not offend. I don't mean wear *dhotis*, *jalabas* or grass skirts. But if they have developed loose, cooling rig-outs, it must be for a well tried reason. In some instances, Western garments are tolerated, but not really acceptable; scanty shorts for example, especially without underwear, or tight trousers which endeavour to tell your religion.

Solitude and Friendship

Of course, you will strike up friendships on the way, and this is a particularly good idea for the more dangerous parts of your trip. You can continue or split up by agreement. If you stay alone you are probably self-sufficient by nature, adventurous to a degree or maybe a nut! Be wary of planning long trips with an advertisement link-up and spend some time together before the trip. Try to talk to someone who has travelled with him/her before and, to be fair, offer to let them do the same. None see us as others. Should you be travelling alone and signs of psychological depression appear, seek companionship and help at once. Do not wait until you are a screaming nut who will be avoided by everyone. This is most important.

We have met many travellers who have been alone for a long time, and they develop certain characteristics which make them anti-social and boring. Watch out for them in yourself and try to correct them. They are people who look at places and hosts from a selfish angle 'how much can I exploit them before I have to leave?'; people who ask advice but don't listen, who talk endlessly, who change socks rather than wash them because they have become used to degrees of cleanliness. If a host mentions a bath or shower, he is usually trying to pluck up the courage to tell you something.

If you want to leave a good taste in the mouth of your host, here are a few dos and don'ts which have plagued us in London, having offered a multitude of travellers rest:

1. Use *poste restante*, so the host does not have to forward letters after you.
2. Always use the public phone. Charges in each country differ and this way you make sure your host doesn't foot the bill for your calls.
3. Do not overstay your welcome. Try to fix the length of your visit when you arrive or before you are invited.
4. Send money well ahead to an international bank. Try to keep your host out of the inevitable hassle.
5. Do not ask the host to mail things home for you after you've left. Do it yourself.
6. Try to make some recompense, like an invitation out to a meal. A few nights lodging saves you a lot of money. Don't be mean.

This article was first published in the Globetrotter's Handbook by whose kind permission it appears here.

The Disabled Traveller

by Dagmar Hingston

Perhaps the most daunting task that faces the disabled traveller is ensuring that the holiday remains free from disaster. With common sense, modern technology, willpower and the help of friends, virtually anything is possible, and disability should no longer be a bar to travel. Over the years I have not encountered any problems, simply because I have found that people are only too willing to lend a hand, and provided advance warning is given to everybody concerned, everything will go smoothly.

As a sufferer from multiple sclerosis, diagnosed nine years ago, my husband has travelled to many countries, with my help and his doctor's blessing. As anyone who suffers from this disease of the central nervous system knows, the symptoms occur in various different ways, so that it is difficult to lay down any hard and fast rules concerning travel abroad. Bearing this in mind, the handicapped traveller and their helper will be able to judge the type of journey they can undertake.

British Rail

British Rail have published a very useful leaflet entitled *British Rail and Disabled Travellers*. It is free of charge and can be obtained at any railway station. It is a self-explanatory leaflet which can be used as a general guideline. However, facilities may differ from area to area and it is advisable to telephone the station manager if there are any specific problems you wish to discuss.

Having given advance warning to the railway staff about the time of arrival and the disabled traveller's needs, arrangements will be made for you to be met at the station entrance. In most stations, the disabled traveller can be wheeled into the luggage lift and onto the appropriate platform, and, if necessary, British Rail will supply a wheelchair.

Once on board, the wheel chair can be positioned close to the seat while its user is helped into a normal seat. In the latest second class coaches, a table has been omitted from one group of seats nearest the entrance and next to the toilet. Consultation with one's own G.P. will enable him to advise about incontinence aids to be taken on a journey. Toilet facilities are not suitable for wheelchairs as the doors are too narrow. Truly wheelchair bound passengers will also find it difficult to enter the restaurant car for a meal, but drinks and refreshments may be brought to passengers in their seat. Radiopaging ahead ensures that the disabled passenger and helper will be met by railway staff at connecting stations.

Of course, conditions abroad will vary widely, although most Western countries have facilities as good as, or better than, those found in Britain. In the Third World, it is probably more sensible to hire a car rather than rely on the generally erratic and uncomfortable public transport.

At the Airport

It is the responsibility of the traveller and/or any able-bodied people travelling with him to make sure that all arrangements will go smoothly on arrival at the airport. Again, advance warning is essential; a week before the holiday commences, a telephone call will confirm that all is well.

From the time you have checked in with an airline, until the end of the journey, the airline provide any help needed. When a booking is made through a travel agent, ask him to explain to the airline staff the nature of the disability and whether a wheel chair will be required.

Each airline has its own handling agent who will arrange for someone to help when you arrive at the airport, provided they know in advance how and when you are travelling, and the time of your flight. Direct line telephones to the handling agent are available at the set-down and pick-up points. Seating, reserved for disabled people, has also been provided at these areas. Special facilities are indicated by signs displaying the wheelchair symbol. Unisex toilets, conforming to the latest standards, are also indicated by this sign.

A disabled person is always boarded first on an aircraft and is taken by a member of staff past all the necessary formalities, via ramps and lifts, to the departure lounge. *Who Looks After You?* leaflets can be obtained by writing to the publications department of any main airport.

Each airline makes its own arrangements for assisting handicapped travellers. British Caledonian, British Airways and other major airlines will wheel the disabled passenger from the departure lounge, through the tunnelled entrance to the aircraft. If the disabled person cannot walk to the seat, a small carrying chair will be made available. These seats carry all the latest equipment conforming to safety standards. On most flights, if empty seats are available, airline staff will invite the disabled passenger to make use of two or three seats to stretch out and enjoy a well-earned sleep. A useful booklet, *Care in the Air*, is obtainable from the Airline Users' Committee, Space House, 43–59 Kingsway, London WC2B 6TL. Also available from the same address is *Flight Plan – Hints for Airline Passengers*.

If your journey involves connections with different airlines, be sure to inform each airline individually, and don't rely on the message being passed down the line. And if your final destination is not an international airport, check beforehand on the facilities available for disabled travellers. They may consist of a couple of strong men who will carry you off the plane and leave you in a corner until such time as your own wheelchair is found.

The disabled passenger is usually the last to leave the airport and once again, carrying seats will be used to carry the handicapped person either to a wheelchair or a motorized vehicle. The larger American airports have a delightful vehicle which transports passengers to the terminal building. The tailgate lift eases the wheelchair passenger into a special compartment whilst other passengers use an upper level.

North America

Travelling throughout the United States and Canada is indeed a most pleasurable experience. There are a number of domestic airlines operating flights between all major centres in the United States, although at some of the smaller airports a disabled passenger will usually be carried bodily into the smaller aircraft.

The wide four-lane freeways leading out of most major cities make for effortless driving and several major hire firms are able to offer cars with hand controls. The Greyhound Bus network, which spans the United States, offers a range of tourist tickets which make touring inexpensive and folding wheelchairs and crutches are not charged as excess baggage. There are many access guides to different regions and towns all over the United States. These are available from the Travel Survey Department, Rehabilitation International USA, 1123 Broadway, New York, NY 10010, USA. Another useful publication is *The Wheelchair Traveller* by Douglas Innand, Ball Hill Road, Milford, New Hampshire 03055, USA.

Even some years ago, American hotels and public buildings were fully equipped to look after disabled travellers' needs: ramped pavements everywhere; disabled rooms for the handicapped, consisting of large, wide-spaced doorways, call buttons, showers with seats, levered handles instead of awkward taps on washbasins and baths, and raised toilet seats. All the public buildings have unisex toilet facilities, ramped entrances, telephones at waist level and special entrances into banks make life a great deal easier for the disabled traveller.

Coach Travel

There are, as yet, very few coaches in Britain which are, in any way, adapted to take disabled people, although many social services departments and voluntary organizations own adapted vehicles which are always fully utilized. However, some local coach operators, although they do not own specially adapted vehicles, will hire coaches to groups of disabled people and helpers. One such firm in the West Country is Trathens, based in Plymouth. They also have offices in London, Bristol, and Exeter. Although a few seats may sometimes be removed to allow more space for wheelchair users, it remains necessary for disabled people to be lifted up the coach steps. On some of these trips, the helpfulness of staff can more than make up for the lack of carrying chairs and luxury coaches have all the necessary facilities on board including a drinks machine, video recorder and TV screen to enjoy a film show and toilet facilities reached by a few steps. On the older type of coach these are situated at the back and on the level. Air conditioning and fully reclining seats add to the passenger's comfort. On the many stops throughout the journey, the drivers will ensure that restaurant and toilet facilities are within reach of a wheelchair passenger.

More and more hotels are offering facilities for the disabled traveller and access guides are available for most countries. In my experience, I have found that many hotels will gladly send details and illustrations of their premises and the surrounding countryside. Public transport drivers in many countries are extremely helpful – we found them particularly so in Yugoslavia. Even if there are, as yet, no specific access guides for the disabled in a particular area and it seems at first glance to be sensible to keep to the hotel area, there are usually many excursions available to surrounding places of interest and the courier will be able to advise on their suitability. Two excellent books are *Directory for the Disabled* compiled by Ann Darnbrough and Derek Kinnade and *Holidays for the Handicapped*, a publication of the Royal Association for Disability and Rehabilitation, price £1.50.

Finally, it is most advisable to take out a holiday insurance policy. Disabled people might find that they encounter a problem here since insurance companies might, in their policies, exclude pre-existing medical conditions. Your tour operator or travel agent can advise on the best type of cover, and it is essential to check the small print to make sure that your disability does not figure as one of the policy exclusions. Two insurance brokers I can recommend are C. R. Toogood and Co Ltd, Duncombe House, Ockham Road North, East Horsley, Leatherhead, Surrey KT24 6NX and The Insurance Programme for the Disabled, Greenway Insurance Brokers (UK) Ltd, First Floor, Peek House, 20 Eastcheap, London EC3M 1DR.

(*For further information, please see Disabled section of the booklist on page 592, and the Disabled Associations list on page 612.*)

Papers, Reservations, Etc.

Visas

by Jack Jackson

The queue at the Libyan embassy visa section stretched all the way around the room, out of the door and down the steps. But the traveller wasn't too worried. He'd been warned that the Libyans and the Nigerians were slower than anyone else in issuing visas.

He's also been tipped off about getting translators to fill out his form in Arabic and this had been done, except – as he discovered about two hours later when he slipped his documents across the counter – for one thing. The year that his passport expired was not in Arabic script.

The error was pointed out. The traveller responded with a friendly nod and a wink. Perhaps the clerk could simply correct it. But no, that couldn't be done.

So, biting his tongue, the traveller collected up his bits and pieces and shot around the corner to his translator, who was fortunately nearby because of the number of Arab embassies in the area.

The correction was made and the traveller joined the queue again. Another hour or so passed and he was back at the counter. But no – he was still not going to get a visa. Why? The explanation was absurdly simple. The form couldn't be accepted because it had a crossing out on it where the Arabic script replaced the old figures.

Why hadn't this been pointed out the previous time around? The clerk looked impassive: the question hadn't been asked . . .

So, beware! On the face of it, getting a visa doesn't look too difficult. You are told to produce your passport, fill out a form, provide two or three passport-sized photographs and, perhaps, a letter of guarantee from an employer if you are going on company business. That done, it should then just be a case of handing over your money (cash or postal order; cheques aren't accepted) and, in return, receiving a slip of paper or a stamp in your passport.

But if it was that easy visa clerks wouldn't have any fun, human nature would have changed and the world would be a better place to live in.

Tourists Not Wanted

The first thing to remember is that many of the most interesting countries just don't want tourists – or visitors of any kind, come to that, beyond the bare minimum necessary to keep the wheels of commerce and diplomacy turning. Libya is one such country. On both religious and ideological grounds, its rulers regard it as desirable to keep out the godless, capitalistic, lascivious Western hordes. Furthermore, the country has vast oil revenues and has no need of the foreign exchange that tourists might bring in. It is therefore a seller's market where visas are concerned. It can afford to pick and choose.

Fanatical Muslim countries are hard on women travellers. Libya will not give visas to unmarried women under 33 years of age or to men under 26 years of age. Saudi Arabia will not give visas to unmarried women at all and even married women find it almost impossible to get one. For transit visa use only, girls travelling with men can 'obtain' Muslim marriage licences in Amman (Jordan).

Nigeria and Gabon, though not as rich as Libya, are equally difficult to penetrate. Once again, the presence of oil has meant that neither has felt the need to set up a tourist industry or to make it easy for independent travellers to get in. Those who enter generally do so in spite of the visa section of the relevant embassy, not because of it. The Gabonese embassy in London is a citadel. It is difficult to get through to it on the phone and it is difficult to persuade anyone to answer the front door when you turn up in person. Once inside, you find that all visa applications must be referred to Libreville for 'clearance' (the kiss of death). You are required to send the telex requesting your visa at your own expense and that, generally, is the last you hear of it since no one in Libreville seems inclined to reply.

The Nigerian system is, if anything, even more frustrating and obscure. Tourist visas are impossible and business visas are not issued unless supported by a comprehensive series of testimonials validated by the Federal Immigration Authority in Lagos.

Passing the Buck

The same syndrome is particularly prevalent in Africa, but also quite widespread elsewhere. More and more embassies seem to be appreciating the subtle merits of passing the buck on visas by referring all applications 'home' to be vetted. Somali embassies throughout the world have been on to this super dodge for years creating an almost foolproof system whereby only people who have visited the country before and can produce cast-iron local references on demand are able to get in.

Oman, South Yemen and Cuba also come into this category. The oddity of the practice in Somalia's case, however, is that the government itself is actively promoting tourism and would like to see the number of tourist arrivals increase. Individual embassies deliberately frustrate this objective, it would seem, partly to skip all that troublesome paperwork and partly to avoid taking the blame if any tourist misbehaves himself in Mogadishu.

The general point to be made from all this is that visa officers from most countries that are not well established tourist destinations operate on the single principle of 'if in doubt, don't'. They have absolute power over your application and neither the time nor the inclination to engage in individual rulings. It therefore pays to be polite and to persevere with dignity. Fill in all forms accurately and without quibble and don't get irritated if you have to sit around for a long while.

Be Prepared

A tip to remember is that the embassy at home of the country you wish to visit may behave differently from embassies of the same country overseas. If you want to visit, say, Sierra Leone, don't worry too much if you find it difficult to pick up a visa here. Wait until you are out in West Africa and put in your application at the Sierra Leone High Commission in Banjul (The Gambia) or in any other country where there is a Sierra Leone mission. Chances are your visa will be granted without a quibble. It follows that it is good sense on any extended trip over a number of borders, to carry at least twenty technically perfect passport photos of yourself and also some sheets of carbon paper to speed up the business of filling in forms in triplicate.

Whatever precautions you take, however, and wherever in the world you take them, several countries have odd quirks that can temporarily defeat an otherwise perfect application. Carbon copies of forms may not be enough, for instance. The work-to-rule bloodymindedness of some officials can lead them to demand that all forms be filled out painstakingly and individually by hand. It is also worth remembering that a number of countries now refuse to accept visa applications in red or green ink – on the grounds that ink is 'blue'.

Cash on Delivery

There are other, more serious, pitfalls to watch out for than the colour of your pen. Ghanaian embassies and high commissions will not issue your visa until you have purchased minimum daily expenditure vouchers in the local currency to cover the duration of your trip. The visa clerk will require you to pay for these in cash and will not accept a cheque – a nuisance, if you are in a hurry, as the Ghanaian embassy in London is some distance from any bank. The going rate for vouchers at the moment is 140 *cedis* for the first day (about £25) and 70 *cedis* for each day after. The ostensible reason for this is that the authorities wish to make certain that you do not go broke on Ghanaian soil. In fact it is done to ensure that at least some of your expenditure as a tourist passes through the official banking system rather than through the roaring black market. Since Ghana is a genuinely nice country presently going through troubled times, it seems only fair to comply with this rule to the letter (the way round it is to take a visa for two days and extend it on arrival). If you do buy *cedi* vouchers to cover your whole trip, however, don't assume they will be anything like sufficient to your needs. Local food prices (imported foods are almost unobtainable) are relatively high, so you may be tempted to try the black market – at three times the official rate – at your own risk.

Pariah Visas

Certain visas on your passport may not, in themselves, be difficult to get, but can exclude you from travelling to other countries. Anyone with an Israeli stamp will be refused entry by every country in the Arab league. Similarly, don't try to go to China if you have evidence on your passport of a visit to Taiwan, or to visit much of black Africa if you have a South African visa. The British authorities will generally issue two passports, to anyone needing to travel in these contentious areas. However, there are signs that this loophole may no longer be wide enough. Nigerian diplomats, for instance, will not put a visa on a new passport until they have vetted the applicant's old one for South African stamps.

At the time of going to press, Iraq was not issuing tourist visas. When it does issue them, it requires a baptismal certificate as proof that the bearer is Christian and not Jewish.

The bureacratic wrangles described, it is worth adding, are not just something inflicted on hapless British travellers by 'them out there'. Britain itself is often an extremely difficult country for anyone from the Third World to visit. Our stringent entry regulations are wielded like so many blunt axes by the churlish, aggressive and sometimes vulgar immigration officers at Heathrow and other airports. Before commenting too disparagingly on the motes in others' eyes, we should try to remove our own particular beam.

Guidelines

Here are some of the bare facts about visas and some points to note when obtaining them:

– Allow plenty of time for obtaining visas; for most Asian countries in London you need three to five days, for African countries, it will often be a lot longer. Some African countries do not have representation in London and visas must be obtained in Paris or Rome. If applying by post, allow up to three weeks, but check with individual embassies before posting your passport. Very often your vaccination certificate is required along with proof of purchase of airline tickets for onward travel.

– Some countries, e.g. Nepal, Sudan, Egypt, require proof of available funds when you apply for a visa in Europe, or a letter from a known operator if you are travelling on an organized tour, and may even require you to change a certain amount of hard currency into local currency at the official bank rate. This problem can often be avoided when a visa is obtained in a bordering country, e.g. Sudan for Egypt, India for Nepal, but such situations can never be guaranteed and may change at short notice. In most cases, it is easiest to get a visa in your country of origin, one notable exception being that German nationals cannot obtain a Sudanese visa in Germany, but can do so in the UK.

– Some countries, e.g. Ethiopia, require a letter of introduction from your embassy if you apply for a visa in a country other than your country of origin. This takes time and costs money.

– Algeria at present requires such a large amount of money to be changed into local currency before entry that no traveller who is not making full use of local hotels would consider it worthwhile. Many Eastern European countries operate the same system.

– During periods of unrest some countries will only issue business visas.

– If you are travelling on, or overland, many countries will not issue a visa unless you already have a visa for the next country en route, so get all your visas in the reverse of the order in which you will use them. This is especially true for travel through Africa. However, many visas are valid for three months from the date of issue, so for lengthy overland journeys visas must be obtained en route.

– Visas often state specifically the port of entry into the country, so overlanders should make sure they stick to their proposed route.

– Visas obtained in your country of residence will be full tourist visas (different types of visa are issued to people on business or working in a country). Do not rely on obtaining visas on, or just before the border. This was once possible but, with tightening restrictions, visas can usually be obtained in capital cities only, e.g. Nepalese visas are easily obtainable in Delhi and Burmese in Kathmandu.

– In London, some consulates, e.g. Sudan and Yemen Arab Republic, will only accept payment in postal orders, even if you attend personally.

– If your passport gets filled up and you still have a valid visa in it, a new passport can be tied to the old one with a seal, thus retaining the use of that visa. British nationals who renew their passports abroad should ensure that the new passport has written into it that 'the owner has the right of abode in the United Kingdom' otherwise they can be refused entry on their return.

– Most countries will extend a full tourist visa two or three times for a fee but only when the present visa has almost expired and normally only in the capital city. Once you have had a tourist visa extended, you will normally also need an exit visa before you can leave and will also have to provide definite proof of onward travel. This takes two or three days to get, so apply early. Some countries require an exit visa anyway, e.g. Yemen Arab Republic. Do not overstay a tourist visa without renewing it: this can involve a heavy fine, an appearance in court (Iran) or, in times of political unrest, a spell in prison.

– Finally watch out for the duration of visas. If you have a long stay in any country, however relaxed its entry regulations may appear to be, get your visa before you go. Thailand is a good example of this. You are allowed to enter for up to fifteen days without any visa at all, provided you have money and a ticket to get out. You simply get a stamp in your passport as you arrive at the airport showing the date by which you must leave the country. The problem is that if you do not leave by then you will end up wasting at least a day in custody explaining yourself to an immigration officer and paying a fine. The alternative is a visa issued in London or elsewhere by a Thai embassy or consulate. This visa is valid for up to sixty days. It can be extended while in Thailand but – and this is an absolutely immovable constraint – the fifteen-day entry permit cannot be extended under any circumstances.

Permits, Registration and Restricted Areas

by Jack Jackson

Ten or twelve years ago, travel in the Third World was, for a Westerner, relatively easy, with few restrictions and little in the way of police checks, paperwork or permissions to hold the traveller back. Europe, in those days, offered more barriers with frequent customs and police enquiries. Nowadays, the position is reversed. In most Third World countries the hindrances to free travel grow yearly in number and variety.

Ambiguous taxes are demanded at borders and airports. The legality of these may be questionable, but the man behind the desk is all-powerful, so the traveller does not have any choice.

Many countries with unstable monetary systems and flourishing black markets now require the traveller to complete on entry a currency declaration, detailing all monies, jewellery, cameras, tape recorders etc. This is checked on departure against bank receipts for any money changed. Algerian authorities are very thorough in their searches of departing travellers. Other countries with the same regulations include India, Nepal, Tanzania, Kenya, Sudan and Ethiopia (*See Money Problems – the Illegal Side, page 300*). With groups, border officials naturally try to cut down massive form filling by completing just one form for the group leader. This can make life very difficult later if one person in a group wishes to change money at a bank and does not have his own individual form, and cannot immediately produce the group form, or the leader to vouch for him. Individual forms should be obtained if possible.

Deliberate Delays

Some countries purposely delay the issue of permits. The Nepalese authorities keep travellers waiting in Kathmandu for their trekking permits so that they will spend more money there. As most trekkers are limited for time, a straightforward Tourist Tax would be more acceptable.

In many places, the law requires that you register with the police within twenty-four hours of arrival. Often a fee is even charged for this. If you are staying at a hotel, they will normally take care of your registration and the costs are included in your room charges, but if you are in a very small hotel, camping or staying with friends, you will either have to do it yourself or pay someone to do it for you. As this often entails fighting through a queue of several hundred people at the Immigration Office – with the chance you have picked the wrong queue anyway – *baksheesh* to a hotel employee to do it for you is a good investment. Most of these countries require you to register with the police in each town you stop in, and in some cases, e.g. Southern Sudan, you have to report to the police in every town or village through which you pass. In smaller places, registration is usually much easier.

Permission from central government may be necessary to travel outside the major cities. This is so in the Yemen Arab Republic, the Sudan, Ethiopia and Nepal among others. Usually you go to the Ministry of the Interior for this permission, but if a Tourist Office exists, it is wise to go there first. Any expedition or trekking party will have to do this anyway; only Nepal has a separate office for trekking permits.

Restricted Areas

Most countries have restricted or forbidden areas somewhere. To visit Sikkim, Nagaland or Bhutan you must apply to the central government in Delhi. In some other restricted areas, permission remains with the local officials, e.g. Tamanrasset or Djanet for the Algerian Sahara; Agadez for the Niger Sahara; the District Commissioner in Chitral for Kafiristan; Juba for Southern Sudan.

Much of Asia and Africa has large areas of desert or semi-desert. Restrictions on travel in these areas are formulated by the government for travellers' safety and take account of such obvious things as ensuring that the travellers have good strong vehicles carrying plenty of drinking water and fuel and they will be spending the nights in safe places. Unfortunately, officials in these out-of-the-way areas tend to be the bad boys of their profession. Forced to live in inhospitable places they are usually very bored and often turn to drink and drugs. Hence when a party of Westerners turns up they see this as a chance to show their power, get their own back for the old colonial injustices, hold the travellers up for a day or more, charge them *baksheesh*, turn on a tape recorder and insist on a dance with each of the girls and suggest they go to bed with them and if there is a hotel locally, hold them overnight so as to exact a percentage from the hotel keeper. Unfortunately your permit from the central government means nothing here. These people are a law unto themselves.

Some have been known to insist on a visa from nationals of a country who do not require one, which often involves returning to the nearest capital city where incredulous officials may or may not be able to sort things out.

The police in Djanet (Algerian Sahara) really have it tied up: you cannot get fuel to leave without their permission and to get that you have to spend a lot of money with the local tourist organization and hotel as well as fork out *baksheesh* to the police themselves.

Local officials also have a habit of taking from you your government permit and then 'losing' it. This makes life difficult both there and also with local officials later on in other areas. It is therefore best to carry ten or so photostats of the original government permission (photocopiers are always available in capital cities) and never hand over the original. Let officials see the original, but always give them a photostat instead.

If you are travelling as a group, all officials will want a group list from you, so carry a dozen or more copies of a list of names, passport numbers, nationalities, dates of issue, numbers of visas and occupations.

Photography Permits

Some countries, e.g. Sudan, Mali, Cameroon, require that you get a photography permit. These are usually available in the capital only, so overland travellers will have problems until they can get to the capital and obtain one. As with currency declarations, officials obviously like to save work by giving one permit per group, but it is best to get one per person. I have known several instances where big-headed students have made citizens' arrests of people taking photographs – who then had to spend a couple of hours at the police station waiting for their leader with the photo permit to be located.

Photo permits for the Sudan are

now available through the tourist office in London as well as the tourist office in Khartoum, but they do not cover Southern Sudan, for which permits are only available with difficulty in Juba. Possession of a photo permit does not necessarily mean that you can take photographs. It is usually best to enquire with the local police first.

In theory you should be able to find out about documents and permit requirements from the consulate in your country of origin, but in the Third World this can never be relied on as local officials make their own rules. Information from source books such as this one and recent travellers are your best guide.

Do as much as you can before you leave home, but carry plenty of passport-sized photographs and be prepared for delays, harassment, palms held out and large doses of the unexpected.

Travel Insurance

by Malcolm Irvine

One of the most important aspects of planning a major trip abroad is insurance, but we frequently find that it has been overlooked until the last minute or has not been costed accurately into the budget.

Personal

The first and most important thing is to determine that you are purchasing the correct insurance for your particular activities and involvements. It is much better to deal with a professional insurance broker who has knowledge of such matters, than make the mistake of buying a mundane travel insurance policy from your local high street travel agent. A policy that is designed for a few weeks in the sun on the Costa Brava is of no help to you if you find yourself as a stretcher case in deepest Africa in need of immediate air evacuation. Don't be afraid to ask for an explanation of the insurance policy that you are purchasing or written confirmation that it is suitable for your purposes. It might be interesting for readers to know that in terms of monies paid in claims settlement, the list is topped by cancellation claims, followed closely by baggage and personal effects claims. Medical expenses are beginning to feature more widely now owing to escalating costs, and then come the claims for other less important sections of cover.

It is most common nowadays to purchase an inclusive policy where the sums insured for the various sections of cover have been tailored to suit 99 per cent of travellers. A breakdown of such an inclusive policy into its various sections would be as follows:

Medical Expenses. Although medical insurance may not rank the highest in terms of monies paid in claims, it must surely be considered the most important – one can replace lost belongings, but one cannot replace one's health or body. Over the last few years, inflation and the more general availability of expert medical attention has resulted in a large increase in the cost of medical care, and the need to have adequate cover is therefore essential. At the time of writing in 1983, we would recommend a minimum sum insured of £25,000 and for peace of mind, would strongly suggest a sum insured of £50,000. Make sure that your cover is total rather than giving specified maximum amounts for any individual section such as ambulances, hospital beds, surgery etc. A high sum insured is of no help to you if you can only spend a limited part of it on any one aspect of your treatment.

If you are in a remote area, then suitable treatment may not be available locally and in such cases, it might be necessary to incur ambulance charges, air fares or air ambulance charges in order to obtain treatment. In exceptional circumstances, this might even involve repatriation. A personal air ambulance can obviously be very expensive, but even if you are able to use scheduled flights, as a stretcher case you would need to have four seats on a plane, plus another seat for a nurse or companion to accompany you, as airlines will not accept stretcher cases on their own.

Bear in mind that in such a case, you will not have the opportunity to shop around for a cheap ticket – you will have to travel as a scheduled passenger and pay the full fare for all of the seats or spaces that are needed.

Air evacuation from remote areas would be covered by medical insurance if it were necessary because of an accident or illness. However, be careful as 'search and rescue expenses' would not be covered unless you had specified them and paid an additional premium.

Most policies will include a twenty-four-hour emergency service in respect of medical or accident claims. This will entail your making contact with the UK; and do bear in mind, it can only be put into operation if you are able to request help. In most cases, the emergency service will provide financial guarantees so that treatment or transport arrangements can be made. Although air ambulances are used within Europe for repatriating sick or injured persons, it is extremely rare for an air ambulance to be used on intercontinental flights.

Be wary of relying on an everyday private health insurance policy that might already be in existence. Although it may operate outside your normal country of residence, there are bound to be gaps in the cover and almost certainly will be limited with regard to the amount that can be spent on any single aspect of medical attention.

Personal Accident Insurance. Most comprehensive policies would automatically include personal accident insurance, normally for an amount of £5,000. This is payable in the event of death, loss of a limb or an eye or total disablement by an accident. Whilst it is reassuring to know that this cover is in force, it is not generally considered to be important, since any person who is concerned about such matters will most probably have a policy operative on a regular basis. Unless the activities that you are going to be involved in are particularly hazardous, there is no more reason to think you will have an accident overseas than in your normal country of residence.

Cancellation or Curtailment. This covers irrecoverable deposits or payments made in advance where a journey has to be cancelled or curtailed for some good reason such as the insured's own ill health or that of a relative back home, or even a travelling companion. The sum insured obviously has to relate to the type of prepayments that are being made – as a general rule £1,000 tends to be the figure. If one is involved with air tickets alone, the cancellation charges, and consequently the amount that might be lost, are sometimes quite low, but look at it from the worst possible point of view. An airline may make just a 10 per cent cancellation charge if you notify them that you cannot use the seat and they consequently resell it, but what would happen if you were to become ill two hours before departure and, in airline jargon, become a 'no show'? In such circumstances, the value of your ticket might be lost altogether.

Personal liability. This gives protection for compensation payable for injury, loss or damage to other people or to property. However, this excludes risks which should be more properly covered by a separate insurance such as third party motor insurance. A domestic policy may include this cover, but if not, it is included within most travel policies without cost.

Strike and delay. This section was only introduced a few years ago and relates to industrial action, breakdown or adverse weather conditions, which cause a delay on the first outward or first return leg of the journey. As a rule, compensation of £20 per day is payable for a maximum of three days, but only after an initial twelve-hour delay. Alternatively, for the outward journey only total abandonment is possible, in which case a refund of the cancellation charges imposed by the tour operator or airline would be made. This section of cover tends to be included within most comprehensive policies or is available on payment of a small additional premium.

Travel Trade Indemnity. This is a totally new type of cover which has only recently been introduced and effects your outlay in the event of financial failure of an airline, transporation company or travel agent. It was introduced following the collapse of some airlines in the early 1980s and will either be included within the cost of some comprehensive policies or may be available upon payment of an extra premium.

Baggage and Personal Money

There can sometimes be difficulties in obtaining this cover for overland journeys, although most long-distance independent travellers tend to take with them little of great value other than photographic equipment. Such items should already be insured on what is known as an 'all risks' basis, and this cover often operates worldwide for a limited period of time, which it is quite easy to extend.

Most policies will be subject to a limit for valuable items and it is not usually possible to extend these limits. Travel insurance is meant to cover those risks which are not already insured in your home country. If you have valuables which you have been using uninsured in the UK, then you might as well continue on the same basis while travelling overseas.

If your journey is part of an expedition and you have supplies and scientific equipment with you, there should be no difficulty in obtaining insurance cover, since the risk for a properly organized party is much less than for independent travellers. Do check that the insurance includes items which you might be sending in advance as freight and for certain areas, check whether you need *Carnet de Passage* documents.

As far as money is concerned, one is effectively referring to actual cash, although cover also relates to traveller's cheques, documents etc. If the loss of traveller's cheques is reported in the correct manner, there is no monetary loss and it is often a condition of the insurance that such action is taken. Most policies will cover the additional expenses involved – perhaps telex charges to notify a bank or additional accommodation expenses whilst waiting for replacement funds to be sent.

Within the money section, most insurances will also include air tickets, and whereas money cover is normally limited to £200, on the more specialized policies for long-haul travellers, air tickets are insured for a much higher amount. Some airlines will provide replacement tickets without any difficulty, but there are a few that will insist on full payment being made for replacements, with a refund unavailable for as long as eighteen months afterwards. Whilst it is almost unheard of for a thief to try and use an air ticket, there are these few airlines who insist on waiting a long time before accepting the position.

Vehicle Insurance

Once outside of the European area, vehicle insurance does present certain difficulties and it is certainly not possible to arrange a single comprehensive insurance policy as we know it in this country. This is due to the varying legislation in different parts of the world on liability or third-part[y] insurance. Vehicle insurance can b[e] understood by the following equation

Third party liability +
Accidental damage, fire and theft
= Comprehensive

Within the European 'Green Car[d] area' a single comprehensive insurance policy can be arranged – either a[s] a one off policy on a short period basi[s] or as an extension of an existing British policy. At the time of writing, th[e] Green Card area includes all o[f] Europe plus Morocco, Tunisia, Turkey and Iran. However, not all insurers are prepared to give cover in th[e] more outlying parts of Europe. W[e] are therefore referring to areas wher[e] a UK policy is not available.

Third Party Liability. This sectio[n] of cover will need to be arrange[d] locally at each border, which in itsel[f] can present problems. In some part[s] of the world, such as Algeria, insurance is nationalized and there is [a] reasonably efficient method of sellin[g] the insurance to travellers. The cost i[s] reasonably low – approximately £2[0] for one month, but the cover given b[y] such insurance is also low by European standards. It is not unusual t[o] hear of liability limits as low a[s] £5,000, whereas in Europe, liabilit[y] limits are generally from £250,00[0] upwards.

Theoretically, third-party insurance is a legal requirement in virtuall[y] every country in the world, but ther[e] are several who are totally indifferen[t] as to whether travellers have insurance or not. If this insurance is no[t] automatically offered at the border, i[t] is strongly recommended that yo[u] seek it out. However limited, it doe[s] at least give some measure of protec tion and the cost will certainly be low by our standards.

Warning

1. Cover is not readily available at some borders and in many areas covers bodily injury claims only, which means you may have to pay the cost of damage to other people's property yourself.
2. Liability limits can be absurdly low by European standards, but unfortunately there is no other means of arranging this cover.
3. It is not uncommon to hear of relatively large amounts being demanded for local certificates (one can only guess as to whether or not the premium is passed on to the insurance company).
4. We have also heard of people arriving at a border late on a Friday evening and having to wait until Monday morning before being able to arrange insurance and pass on their way.

Accidental Damage, Fire and Theft. As you will see from the equation earlier, this is the other half of a comprehensive insurance policy and simply covers damage caused to one's own vehicle as the result of an accident or fire or theft. It is in no way connected with liability risks and consequently, this cover is available from Lloyds of London on a worldwide basis. Unfortunately, this cover is expensive, since in nearly all claims Lloyds underwriters have to pay out for repairs and have very little chance of recovering their outlay, even if you were not at fault. Irrespective of the circumstances of a vehicle accident, it is surprising how many witnesses will suddenly appear to claim that the local driver was blameless and the visitor totally at fault!

This insurance is very strongly recommended on valuable vehicles. In the event of an accident occurring, one would need to make contact with the local Lloyds agent. Repairs would then be completed by the most suitable repairer or in many cases, temporary repairs are completed at the time and full repairs are left until the vehicle is back in the UK. As a general rule, repairs are authorized very quickly, since the insurers are aware of the inconvenience that any delay might cause and because the insurers are responsible for the repairs, irrespective of liability in the accident.

Carnet Indemnity Insurance. This is arranged in conjunction with *Carnet de Passage* documents issued by the British Automobile Association. Before issuing the *Carnet*, the AA will require a financial guarantee equal to the highest possible duties that could be payable on the vehicle in the countries it is intended to visit. Generally, this figure is approximately twice the UK value of the vehicle, although for India and certain South American countries, the figure is much higher. The insurance premium is then calculated at $3\frac{1}{2}$ per cent of that figure for Africa or South America and 5 per cent for Asia, but the premium is on a sliding scale, and for very large amounts reduces down as low as 1 per cent. In addition, the AA will require a service charge of about £20 and a refundable deposit of £100.

Life Assurance

As a general rule, life assurance cover is not taken out specifically for overseas travel, since most people who have family responsibilities will already have a policy in force. Although life assurance policies are not normally subject to exclusions, if your journey is of a hazardous nature, it would be as well to give written details to the life office concerned and ask for their written confirmation that they accept the position. Sometimes they may impose an additional premium just for the period whilst you are away, but the amount involved is generally quite low and it is well worth the peace of mind that it gives to know that your cover is fully operative.

Arranging Insurance and Claims

As I've said before, I would recommend the advice of an experienced, professional insurance broker for anything other than the totally standard European holiday. Be sure to outline your proposed activities, and if you are buying a standard policy, don't be afraid to ask for written confirmation that it is suitable for your needs.

If you are booking through one of the specialist travel agencies that deals with overland or long distance travel, then they will almost certainly have a tailor-made policy available. However, do be wary if you are dealing with a normal High Street agency since it is quite possible that the counter clerk will have no real knowledge of the suitability of the insurance that they might offer you.

As far as vehicle insurance is concerned, a proposal form will need to be completed and you must disclose all material facts relating to both your own driving experience and that of any other person who might be using the vehicle. It is much better to spend some time giving all information about yourself and your requirements to the insurer before taking out the cover, than finding after an accident that there is a gap in the insurance. This also relates to personal medical insurance, although as a rule, readers of this article will not be excluded from cover due to age or existing illnesses or disabilities.

As far as claims are concerned, do be patient and bear in mind that contrary to popular belief, insurers do like paying claims. However, they do require certain information and if it is not available, there are going to be inevitable delays in dealing with paperwork. Any expenditure will need to be supported by receipts and any loss will need to be supported by a written statement from the local police authorities, airline or government agency.

If possible, claims should be left until you return to the UK and under no circumstances should you send original documentation by post from overseas, since it can go astray so easily. Unless you have incurred large expenditure for which you require reimbursement while you are still away, it is much better to leave things until you return, when you can collate all of your paperwork and present your claim in a concise manner. Most claims can be dealt with in a period of two weeks, but if you happen to lose a valuable item, don't be surprised if the insurers insist on seeing a receipt, valuation or some other documentation relating to the original purchase.

Most claims will be subject to an excess – this is normally £15 for personal claims and is imposed by insurers simply because the cost of dealing with small claims can sometimes be more than the value of the claim itself. Vehicle insurance claims will generally be subject to a much higher excess, which is imposed in order to keep the premiums to a reasonable level and to cut out claims for the inevitable minor scratches or dents that will occur on any long journey.

US Passports and Medical Requirements

Application for a new passport must be made in person to:

1. A postal employee designated by the postmaster at selected post offices.
2. A passport agent at one of the Passport Agencies, located in Boston, Chicago, Honolulu, Los Angeles, Miami, New Orleans, New York, Philadelphia, San Francisco, Seattle, and Washington DC (see below for addresses).
3. A clerk of any federal court.
4. A clerk of any state court of record.
5. A judge or clerk of selected probate courts.
6. A US embassy in a foreign country.

The applicant must present:

1. Proof of US citizenship i.e.
   (i) a certified copy of his birth certificate under the seal of the official registrar; or
   (ii) a naturalization certificate; or
   (iii) a consular report of birth or certification of birth; or
   (iv) his previous passport.
2. Two recent identical photographs that are good likenesses (Note 1).
3. Identification, e.g. a valid driving licence with a signature and containing a photograph or physical description.

The application:

1. is usually processed in ten days or less.
2. costs $42.00 for Adults over 18; $27.00 under 18.

The passport:

1. is valid for ten years from the date of issue for adults over 18; five years for persons under 18.
2. comes in two sizes, the standard 24 page size and the 48 page size (Note 2).
3. can be supplied with extension pages (Note 3).

Application for passport renewal by a passport holder can be made in person at any of the places listed above, or in certain circumstances by mail, together with a complete form DSP-82 '*Application for Passport by Mail*', (available from tourist agencies and the places listed above), the previous passport, two new photographs and $35 (Note 4).

Note 1: Photographs need not be taken professionally as long as they are clear and show the applicant full-face and with no hat against a plain white or light coloured background. Photographs must measure 2in × 2in. Since photographs are often required for visa applications and other formalities, it is advisable to have quite a number printed. Colour photographs are permitted on US passports but since other countries often insist on black and white photographs for visas, etc., it is best to have these. Machine photographs are not acceptable.

Note 2: Travellers intending to visit Third World and other countries where visas are required and copious entry and exit stamps are entered into passports should ask specifically for the 48 page passport.

Note 3: An accordion sheet of extra pages can also be issued to provide additional space in a valid passport, by any consulate or passport office abroad.

Note 4: When a passport expires, so too do all the visas and permits contained therein. These must be reapplied for after obtaining the new passport. The same is true if a passport is lost or replaced.

For convenience: print the holder's name and the passport number on a label and stick this to the front cover of the passport to ensure instant identification and save time at borders.

For safety: keep the passport with you at all times, if possible in a leather or cloth pouch strung around your neck. Apart from customs officials, police, passport agents, consular officials and, in many European countries, hotel clerks and train conductors, very few people are authorized to handle or inspect passports. Do not give your passport to any unauthorized person. It may be a good idea to take a xerox copy of your passport abroad with you, especially if you intend to visit Eastern Europe, where an official may casually borrow your passport and disappear while he stamps your visa in it.

Visas and Tourist Cards

A visa is an official permit to enter a country, granted by the government of that country. Visas are usually stamped in the passport and are valid for a particular purpose and stated time. Visas can be obtained from the country's consulates either in the USA or abroad. Ordinarily they should be obtained in advance; certain countries even require that the applicant obtain his visa from the consulate nearest to his place of residence. Some countries require a tourist card instead of a visa; these are available from consulates in the USA, from some travel agencies and airlines, or at the border.

Visa and tourist card requirements change frequently, according to the vagaries of political circumstance. To check the current situation, consult form M-264 *Visa Requirements of Foreign Governments*, available at any passport agency.

For the address of the nearest consulate or consular agent, consult the *Congressional Directory*, available in most libraries.

US Passport Agencies

Boston Room E, 123 John F. Kennedy Building, Government Center, Boston, MA 02203. Tel: (617) 223-3831.

Chicago Room 331, Federal Office Building, 230 South Dearborn Street, Chicago, IL 60604. Tel: (312) 353–7155.

Honolulu Federal Building, 335 Merchant Street, Honolulu, HI 96813. Tel: (808) 546–2130.

Los Angeles	Hawthorne Federal Building, Room 2W16, 1500 Aviation Boulevard, Lawndale, Los Angeles, CA 90261, Tel: (213) 536-6503.
Miami	Room 804, Federal Office Building, 51 Southwest First Avenue, Miami, FL 33130. Tel: (305) 350-4681.
New Orleans	Room 400, International Trade Mart, 2 Canal Street, New Orleans, LA 70130. Tel: (504) 589-6161.
New York	Room 270, Rockefeller Center, 630 Fifth Avenue, New York, NY 10020. Tel: (212) 541-7710.
Philadelphia	Room 4426, Federal Building, 600 Arch Street, Philadelphia, PA 19106. Tel: (215) 597-7480.
San Francisco	Room 1405, Federal Building, 450 Golden Gate Avenue, San Francisco, CA 94102. Tel: (415) 556-2630.
Seattle	Room 906, Federal Building, 915 Second Avenue, Seattle, WA 98174. Tel: (206) 442-7945.
Washington	Passport Office, 1425 K Street, NW, Washington DC, 20524. Tel: (202) 783-8170.

Medical Requirements for US Travellers

The US Public Health Service (USPHS) is the main source of information for the traveller on medical requirements. There are two centres: The USPHS, National Communicable Disease Center, Atlanta, GA 30333, deals with health requirements and animal and plant quarantine regulations for the US and other countries and publishes a small booklet *Health Information for International Travel*, which is available on request. The USPHS, 330 Independence Avenue, SW, Washington DC 20201, provides information on vaccinations and other immunizations required for visitors to foreign countries and in some cases will also administer the necessary shots.

UK Passports and Medical Requirements

A UK passport is valid for five to ten years and is obtainable from regional passport offices:

Passport Office Addresses:

London Passport Office
Clive House
70–78 Petty France
London SW1H 9HD
Tel: (01) 213-3344/7272/6161/3434

Liverpool Passport Office
5th Floor
India Buildings
Water Street
Liverpool L2 0QZ
Tel: (051) 237-3010

Newport Passport Office
Olympia House
Upper Dock Street
Newport
Gwent NPT 1XA
Tel: (0633) 56292

Peterborough Passport Office
55 Westfield Road
Peterborough
Cambs PE3 6GT
Tel: (0733) 895555

Glasgow Passport Office
1st Floor
Empire House
131 West Nile Street
Glasgow G1 2RY
Tel: (041) 332-0271

Belfast Passport Office
Hampton House
47–53 High Street
Belfast BT1 2AS
Tel: (0232) 232371

British nationals must apply for a

passport on a special form obtainable from travel agents, passport offices or any main post office. The application must be countersigned by a bank manager, solicitor, barrister, doctor, clergyman or someone of equal standing who knows the applicant personally. The application should be sent to the passport office for the applicant's area of residence. Two full face photographs must accompany the application. The fee is £15 for a 30 page passport or £30 for one of 94 pages. Four weeks should be allowed for the application to be processed.

For travel within Western Europe (excluding the German Democratic Republic and East Berlin), you can travel on a British Visitor's Passport. This costs half as much as a full passport, but is valid for twelve months only. British Visitor's Passports and application forms for them are available from any main post office from Monday to Friday. The British Visitors Passport is not available from passport offices, other than in Belfast, and is only available to British citizens, British Dependent Territories citizens or British Overseas citizens for holiday purposes of up to three months. It is not renewable.

If you lose your passport, tell the local police first. Then contact the nearest British Embassy or Consulate by telephone or telegram. The telegraphic address of any British Embassy is PRODROME, of a High Commission UK REP and of a British Consulate BRITAIN followed by the name of the town.

Normally the Consul will issue a new passport, valid for up to twelve months, as soon as possible after checking with the issuing office in the UK. For this reason, it is highly advisable to keep a separate note of your passport number and its date and place of issue. The new passport is valid in all the countries in which the original was valid and costs the same. On expiry, it can be extended to a full ten year passport when you return to the UK, at no extra charge if your original passport has not been found.

In case of emergency or great urgency, the Consul can issue instead a Single Journey Emergency Passport, which enables the holder to return to the UK but will be confiscated on his return. Or the consul may issue a passport that is valid for, say, a month – without checking with the issuing officer – and this permits the holder to return to the UK via several other countries.

Medical Requirements for UK Travellers

The Department of Health and Social Security, Alexander Fleming House, Elephant and Castle, London SE1 publishes a leaflet *Protect Your Health Abroad* (SA 35) which contains up-to-date inoculation requirements for travellers. This may be obtained by telephoning the DHSS on 01-407 5522 ext. 6711. The main offices from which the leaflet may be obtained in Wales, Northern Ireland and Scotland are, respectively:

Welsh Office
17th Floor
Pearl Assurance House
Greyfriars Road
Cardiff CF1 3RT

DHSS
Dundonald House
Upper Newtownards Road
Belfast BT4 3SF

Scottish Home and Health Department
St Andrew's House
Edinburgh EH1 3DE

The Health Control Unit, Terminal 3 Arrivals, Heathrow Airport, Hounslow, Middlesex TW6 1NB (Tel: (01) 759-7208) gives similar information.

Sources of advice on the prevention of tropical diseases are:

The London School of Hygiene and Tropical Medicine
Keppel Street
(Gower Street)
London WC1E 7HT
Tel: (01) 636-8636

The Hospital for Tropical Diseases
4 St Pancras Way
London NW1 0PE
Tel: (01) 387-4411

The Liverpool School of Tropical Medicine
Pembroke Place
Liverpool L3 5QA
Tel: (051) 708-9393

British Airways Medical Department
75 Regent Street
London W1
Tel: (01) 439-9584

Documentation for the International Motorist

by Colin McElduff

The following advice is directed towards United Kingdom motorists and should be used as a general guide only, for each and every case produces its own requirements dependent upon the countries concerned and the circumstances and regulations prevailing at the time. As many travellers neglect documentation – some of which should be obtained well in advance of departure – list all that is known to be relevant to your trip and make enquiries as to the remainder. In any case, on most overland trips you will need the following:

1. Driving Licence
2. Insurance – Health
3. Insurance – Third Party and/or
4. International Motor Insurance Certificate (Green Card)
5. International Registration Distinguishing Sign (GB etc)
6. Passport
7. Vehicle Registration Certificate

Depending on your country of departure and those through which you will be travelling, you may additionally need your birth certificate, extra passport photographs and:

8. *Acquits à Caution*
9. Bail Bond
10. *Carnet* ATA
11. *Carnet Camping*
12. *Carnet de Passages en Douane*
13. Certificate of Authority for Borrowed or Hired Vehicle
14. International Certificate for Motor Vehicles
15. International Driving Permit (IDP)
16. International Student Identity Card or International Scholar Identity Card
17. International Certificate of Vaccination (Yellow Card)
18. Motoring Organization Membership Card
19. Petrol Coupons

20. Visa/Entry Permits
21. Work Permits
22. Photographic Permits

1. *Driving Licence* In Italy, a translation of the visitor's National Driving Licence is required. This may be obtained from the motoring organizations. Motorists in possession of an IDP do not require a translation.

2. *Health Insurance* Due to the high cost of medical care outside Britain, insurance is essential. (*See Travel Insurance on page 281.*)

3. *Third Party Insurance* This is essential to cover claims relating to bodily injury to or death of third parties as a result of the vehicle's use. When travelling in countries outside the scope of the 'Green Card' – which is generally outside Europe – third party insurance should be taken out at the first opportunity on entering the country.

4. *International Motor Insurance Certificate (Green Card)* Whilst a Green Card is technically no longer necessary in EEC countries, it is extremely unwise to visit these countries without it, as it remains as readily acceptable evidence of insurance to enable a driver to benefit from international claims-handling facilities. In any case, a Green Card is required in all European countries outside the EEC. It should be obtained from the insurance company that is currently insuring your vehicle.

5. *International Registration Distinguishing Sign* This sign is mandatory and should be of the country in which your vehicle is registered, thus identifying your registration plates.

6. *Passport* Ensure that this is up to date and will still be valid during your entire trip. Also make sure that none of the countries already recorded in it is anathema to those you will visit on your journey.

7. *Vehicle Registration Certificate* This is an essential document to take. However, further proof of ownership or authority to use the vehicle may sometimes be required.

8. *Acquits à Caution* This is a French customs document, guaranteed by the Automobile Club France and in turn by the motoring organization issuing it. The document permits entry into France of spare parts for the repair of a temporarily imported vehicle without payment of customs duties or taxes. The spare parts may be imported at the same time as the vehicle or on their own.

9. *Bail Bond* If you are visiting Spain, it is a wise precaution to obtain a Spanish Bail Bond from a motoring organization. A driver involved in an accident may be required to lodge a deposit with the local Spanish court both for civil liability and criminal responsibility. Failure to meet this demand may result in imprisonment for the driver and detention of the vehicle until funds are available.

10. *Carnet ATA* This is a customs document, valid for twelve months, which facilitates the entry without payment of customs, duties, etc. of professional equipment, goods for international exhibition and commercial samples, temporarily imported into certain countries, a list of which may be obtained from the London Chamber of Commerce and Industry, 69 Cannon Street, London EC4 (Tel: (01) 248 4444) or through one of their many offices throughout the UK.

11. *Carnet Camping* An international document jointly produced by the three international organizations

dealing with camping and caravanning – the *Fédération Internationale de l'Automobile, the Fédération Internationale de Camping and Caravaning* and the *Alliance Internationale de Tourisme*. It serves as an identity document and facilitates entry to sites under the wing of the mentioned organizations, sometimes at reduced rates. In addition, the document provides personal accident cover up to a specified sum for those names in it. You should approach a motoring organization for this document.

12. *Carnet de Passages en Douane* This is an internationally recognized customs document. If acceptable to a country, it will entitle the holder to import temporarily a vehicle, caravan, trailer, boat etc, without the need to deposit the appropriate customs duties and taxes.

The issuing authority of the *carnet* is made directly responsible for payment of customs duties and taxes if the *carnet* is not discharged correctly, i.e. if the owner violates another country's customs regulations, e.g. by selling the vehicle illegally. Consequently, any substantial payment will be recovered from the *carnet* holder under the terms of the signed issuing agreement.

Motoring organizations are issuing authorities and will provide details and issue documents upon receipt of a bank guarantee, cash deposit or an insurance indemnity from an agreed firm of brokers, to cover any potential liability. The sum required is determined by the motoring organization taking into consideration the countries the vehicle will enter, which will naturally have to be declared when application for the *carnet* is made.

Normally the amount of the bond required as security for the *carnet* is related to the maximum import duty on motor vehicles required at the country or countries into which one's car will be temporarily imported. Thus, if one is to travel through India, where import duty on cars can be as high as 300/400 per cent, the bond required on a car worth £5,000 would be £15,000/£20,000.

In the case of a bank guarantee, you need to have collateral with the issuing bank or funds sufficient to cover the amount required to be guaranteed. These funds cannot be withdrawn until the bank's guarantee is surrendered by the motoring organization. This is done when the *carnet* is returned correctly discharged. The procedure is for the bank manager to provide a letter of indemnity to the motoring association.

When the applicant has insufficient funds or security to cover the bond, he may pay a premium to an insurance company (the AA and the RAC have their own nominated insurance companies with which they have *carnet* indemnity agreements) and the company will act as his guarantor, providing a letter of indemnity to the AA or RAC. The premium varies from about 3 to 10 per cent of the total bond required. Only in special circumstances is this premium partially refundable. A broker can also arrange for an indemnity letter.

There are certain points to watch, however. The car must usually be registered in the country where the *carnet* is issued. In some cases, at the discretion of the issuing club or association, being a citizen of the country where the *carnet* is issued is an alternative, even though the car has been registered elsewhere. In all cases, membership of the issuing club is a requirement.

A *carnet* is required for most long transcontinental journeys and should be obtained regardless of the fact that some of the countries on the itinerary do not require it; for example, Nigeria. To be without one where one *is* required usually means being turned back if you have insufficient funds to cover the customs deposit for entry.

A *carnet de passages en douane* is valid for twelve months from the date of issue and may be extended beyond the expiry date by applying to the motoring organization in the country in which the holder is at the time. The name of the motoring organization is shown on the front cover of the *carnet*. An extension should be noted on every page and not just the inside cover in order to avoid difficulties at border checks. When a new *carnet* is required, the application must be made to the original issuing authority. *Carnets* are issued with five, eleven or twenty-five pages, depending on the number of countries to be visited, and a nominal fee is charged accordingly to cover administration.

Each page contains an entry voucher (*volet d'entrée*), exit voucher (*volet de sortie*) and a counterfoil (*souche*). When the vehicle, etc., leaves the country, the customs officer endorses the exit part of the counterfoil and detaches the appropriate exit voucher, thus discharging the *carnet*. If you have not taken care to have this done, the validity of the carnet may be suspended until it is rectified.

13. *Certificate of Authority for Borrowed or Hired Vehicle* This is required when a vehicle is borrowed or hired and should bear the signature of the owner. This must be the same as on the Registration Certificate which must also be taken. A motoring organization will provide a 'Vehicle on Hire/Loan' certificate.

14. *International Certificate for Motor Vehicles* In countries where the British Vehicle Registration Certificate is not accepted, this document is required, and is issued by a motoring organization.

15. *International Driving Permit* An IDP is required by the driver of a vehicle in countries that do not accept the national Driving Licence of the visiting motorist. It is issued on request by motoring organizations for a small fee and is valid for twelve months from the date of issue. An IDP can only be issued in the country of the applicant's national Driving Licence.

16. *Student Identity Cards* Student cards are extremely useful not only for the many discounts they obtain, but as a means of identification, and should be taken if you are entitled to one. (*See The Student Traveller, on page 249.*)

17. *International Certificate of Vaccination* This document is essential if you are travelling to countries that require evidence of mandatory prescribed vaccinations. Available from your local health authority, together with advice on vaccinations recommended.

18. *Motoring Organization Membership Card* Most countries have a motoring organization which is a member of the *Alliance Internationale de Tourisme* (AIT) or the *Fédération Internationale de l'Automobile* (FIA) and provides certain reciprocal membership privileges to members of other motoring organizations.

19. *Petrol Coupons* These are

issued to visiting motorists in some countries either to promote tourism or where there are restrictions on the residents' use of petrol. Motoring organizations can advise which countries issue petrol coupons.

20. *Visa Entry Permits* Required to visit/enter/travel through some countries, regions or districts, e.g. The Sudan, some regions in the Algerian Sahara, and districts in northern India, etc. Consult government representatives of the relevant countries before you leave home.

21. *Work Permits* Employment permits are required in most countries, even for casual labour. You should consult the nearest representative of the country/countries in which you intend to work.

22. *Photographic Permits* Many countries, especially in the Third World, insist that a permit must be obtained before any photograph can be taken. It is essential to ensure that you obtain the necessary permit or permits for the countries you are about to visit. If you don't and are caught taking photos when one is needed, you may be fined, imprisoned, have your equipment confiscated or be inflicted with a combination of the aforementioned.

Money, Taxes, Etc.

Money Problems – The Legal Side

by Harry Stevens with additions by Melissa Shales

I belong to that generation whose first real experience of foreign travel was courtesy of HMG – when European towns were teeming with black marketeers trying to prove to every young serviceman that 200 British cigarettes were really worth 200, or even 300DM. Traveller's cheques and banks hardly existed and credit cards, like ballpoint pens, had not yet been invented. So my trust in ready cash as the essential ingredient for trouble-free travelling is no doubt due to this early conditioning.

Cash is, of course, intrinsically less safe to carry than traveller's cheques, especially when these are fully refundable when lost – but not all of them are, particularly when a 'finder' has cashed them in before the loss has been reported.

Nowadays, I carry all three: traveller's cheques, credit cards and cash; but only a slim book of traveller's cheques, which I hold in reserve in case I *do* run out of cash – and for use in countries which do not allow one to bring in banknotes of their own currency. If travelling in Europe, it is also worth applying for a Eurocheque Card which allows you to use a British cheque book on the continent. Particularly on short trips, this could mean that you don't have to go to the trouble of getting foreign exchange before departure. However, the cash I carry always includes a few low denomination dollar bills useful for 'emergency' tips, or taxi fares almost anywhere.

There are a number of cogent reasons for equipping yourself with the currency of the country you are about to visit before you get there.

1. Even on the plane you may find you can make agreeable savings by paying in some currency other than sterling.
2. Immediately on arrival it may be difficult, or even impossible, to change your money and in any case, you may be doubtful as to whether you are being offered a good rate of exchange.
3. Yes, the immediate problem of tipping a porter, making a phone call and paying for a taxi or airport bus must be solved long before reaching your hotel. And when you do, this does not necessarily solve your problem as not all hotels exchange traveller's cheques for cash

(and not necessarily at any time of day or night) and if they do, the vexed question of the rate of exchange arises once more.

Having one's pocket picked is a particular travel risk, especially in hot climates, where one's garments will have fewer, if any, concealed pockets. With this in mind I developed a special defensive mechanism, born of experience: in immediate postwar Italy, I was warned never to carry my wallet in a hip pocket as thieves, armed with a razor blade set into a stick, were apparently able to slit open a man's hip pocket without the wearer's noticing until much later. So I acquired an American money clip which is strong enough to clasp my slim book of traveller's cheques, two or three credit cards, my few 'fall back' dollar bills and the currency of the country I am about to visit. All this, neatly folded in half, I carry in one of my two inside trouser pockets. For women travellers I would recommend a pouch or money belt or the zip pocket of a loose jacket, in preference to the easily snatched handbag . . . The same tips apply to all those, of either sex, who prefer to travel in jeans! For extra safety I sometimes split my cash float and follow both the above procedures.

To avoid theft, it is always sensible to take further precautions: for example, when making casual purchases, do not allow strangers to see where you carry your money (nor indeed how much!) In cities like New York, it may also be a good idea to carry a special decoy wallet containing a small sum of money (say, between $20 and $50), which is said to satisfy most would-be attackers – from whom one would dearly like to keep the fact that one is carrying a great deal more . . .

Many countries do not allow unrestricted import or export of their currency – and in a number of countries for 'unrestricted' read 'nil'! So one *has* to exchange traveller's cheques or hard cash on arrival (and there is usually a small advantage in favour of the cheques). In addition, if several countries are to be visited, it is usually best not to keep bank notes of a currency no longer required on that journey (although I do hold on to small change and some low denomination notes, if there is a likelihood of a next time). Every such exchange results in a loss but the sums involved are usually not large and one can console oneself with the thought that the next taxi ride will help to recoup it. Remember to keep a record of all financial transactions, particularly in financially sensitive countries, as you may well be asked to account for everything before you are allowed to leave the country.

If you are planning to be away for a long time, and possibly travel through many countries, there is one other way to ensure that you don't have to carry too much with you and risk losing it all in some remote village. Before you leave home, set up a number of accounts along the way through the London branches of national banks and arrange for money to be wired over to you at regular intervals. Ask the foreign section of your own bank to advise you the best way of doing this, and be careful not to wire more money than you will need into countries with tight export restrictions. No one will mind the sterling coming in, but they may well object to it leaving again, and if not careful you could find yourself with a nest egg gathering dust in a country you are never likely to visit again.

Money Problems – The Illegal Side

by Jack Jackson

Ten years ago, it used to be common for dealers on black markets in Third World countries to offer money at two or three times the official rate. Nowadays, however, most countries, acting on the advice of the International Monetary Fund or the World Bank, have altered their currency exchange regulations so that in most cases black market rates are only ten to twenty per cent higher than the normal bank rate. Buyers should always weigh up the risks before dealing, remembering that in black market operations the traveller, just as easily as the dealer, can end up in prison.

In countries recently ravaged by war or *coups d'état* black markets usually continue to thrive at good rates. In Uganda, for example, the black market rate is nearly five times the official rate for US dollars.

Dollar-mania

Black markets usually operate best in ports where it is easy to ship money out and goods back in and where, with the help of a little *baksheesh* to customs officers, nobody in government pay need know or admit knowing. However, a new quasi black market has been growing in the last ten years, operated by European or American technicians working in oil fields or on international aid or construction programmes. These people are usually paid an allowance in local currency which is more than they need to live on and are often keen to get rid of some of it in exchange for dollars, at a good rate to the buyer. In much of Islamic Africa and the poorer Middle Eastern countries, you will also find Egyptian, Syrian or Palestinian teachers employed in smaller villages who are very keen to convert their salary into US dollars.

Another method of dealing, common in Islamic Africa, Kenya and Uganda, is for a local businessman or hotel owner to 'lend' you funds locally, which you repay in hard currency into his own, or a relative's, bank account in the UK. Those who travel regularly often arrange this in the UK before leaving, but local businessmen will also take a risk on an unfamiliar traveller if he is reasonably dressed and staying in recognized (though smaller) hotels, because their own currency is worthless to them. Even in large, top quality hotels, the cashiers will often take payment in hard currency at black market rates, if the customer pays them outside the manager's normal working hours. Many of the same methods are found in South America, although travellers should particularly avoid street trading there, as they are more likely to be robbed.

On-the-spot black market deals are always for cash and nearly always for US dollars. A few countries with strong links and trade with the UK or Germany will trade in pounds sterling or deutschmarks, but no other currencies, even strong ones such as the Swiss franc, will find black market buyers. Deutschmarks go down well in Turkey and Iran; pounds sterling in Pakistan, India and Nepal. Elsewhere, the US dollar is the prime requirement.

Normally, larger denomination notes fetch a higher rate as they are easier to smuggle out. However, since a recent spate of forgeries, many dealers no longer like to accept $100 bills. Avoid the older $100 bills which do not have 'In God We Trust' written on them; even though they may not be forgeries, most dealers will not touch them. Also avoid English £50 and £20 notes which may be unknown to smaller dealers. There is no longer any problem attached to taking money out of the UK, so it is best to buy dollars there before you leave. The old tricks with sterling traveller's cheques are no longer needed.

Declaration Forms

Many countries with black market problems insist on a declaration of all money and valuables on entry and check this against bank receipts on exit. Remember that you may be searched both on entry and exit and any excess funds will be confiscated. If you want to take in some undeclared money for use in the black market, you should understand the risks. Obviously you must change a reasonable amount of money legally at a bank and keep receipts so that you will be able to explain what you have lived on during your stay. You will also need these receipts if you are going to try and change local currency back into hard currency when you leave. It is most inadvisable to try, since most countries make it very difficult for you to do this, despite their literature claiming that you may. The local officials – who probably don't read the literature – like to remove your excess local money and keep it for themselves. The bank clerk who tells you he cannot change your money back is in on the act; he informs the custom officials how much money you have and they, acting on his tip-off, search you as you try to leave.

Currency declaration forms are taken very seriously in Ethiopia and Algeria and you must have an explanation for any discrepancy. If, for instance, any money which is entered on your form is stolen, get a letter about it from the police or you may have trouble when you come to leave the country.

Some countries, e.g. Sudan and Ethiopia get around some of the black market by making you pay for hotels in hard currency at the legal business rate which is often lower than the official tourist rate and much lower than the black market rate.

International airline tickets will always be charged the same way plus a premium ordered by IATA to cover currency fluctuations. Hence, such tickets are much cheaper if bought in Europe. Internal air tickets can usually be bought with black money but you may have to pay a local ticketing agent to do it in his name.

Beware of black market currency quotations by normally acceptable press, such as upmarket Sunday papers, Newsweek and the BBC as they quote local correspondents who have to be careful what they say for fear of deportation. During the Haj of 1983 these sources quoted 1.78 Sudanese pounds to the US dollar, when in fact the true black market rate was 2.18. The official business rate at that time was only 1.28.

Street Trading

Black market dealers are usually found where budget travellers are most likely to be, e.g. in smaller hotels, bars, shops selling tourist items; in very small towns try the pharmacy. In the main streets of a city or port, street traders will chase you and, assuming you don't know the correct rate of exchange, will start with a very low rate. It is usually worth bargaining to see how high you can go – and then approach safer places such as small hotels to check the real rate. Street trading is very risky: you should never show that you have a lot of money, as there is a high risk that you will be short-changed, have money stolen from the bundle by sleight of hand, see all your money grabbed and run off with, or meet one of those dealers who has a crooked, profit-sharing partnership with the police. In general, show only the amount of money you want to exchange and keep all other money out of sight beneath your clothes.

One part of the world in which to be particularly wary is Eastern Europe, where there is a great demand for hard currency that can be exchanged for exorbitant rates if a person has the right contacts. Here the money-changer and his client are in more danger than anywhere else because of particularly close surveillance by the authorities, who crack down hard on black money transactions. It's also believed that the authorities use their own people as a plant, so the unsuspecting 'client' could find himself negotiating with a state official. It's advisable not even to ask what the rate is.

Refuse any approaches to buy your passport or traveller's cheques. This kind of trading is becoming so common that many embassies delay issuing fresh passports to travellers who may or may not have genuinely lost their own. Getting traveller's cheques replaced in the Third World can take months.

Black market rates fluctuate with both inflation and availability. Rates will increase dramatically in the Islamic world when the time for the annual pilgrimage to Mecca (the Haj) approaches and decreases rapidly when a lot of upmarket travellers are in town, or a cruise ship or fleet ship is in port. Dealing out of season commands a better rate.

Central London banks often carry an excess of Arab currency and one of their branches may be happy to offload a weak currency at a good rate. It is always worth checking whether this is so before you buy.

In very remote areas the local people do not handle money and like instead to be paid in kind: preferred items are T-shirts, jeans and shoes and, in some parts of Eastern Europe, good clothing, records and tapes.

Wherever you are, always check that you have not been shortchanged. Bank cashiers try this regularly in the Third World. Many people end up changing money on the black market just because it can take up to two hours to go through legal channels.

Begging

Begging is probably the world's second oldest profession. In the Muslim and Hindu world giving a percentage of one's income to the poor is considered a legal form of paying tax. However, with the increase of mass upmarket tourism, begging is becoming an increasingly popular way of living, not only amongst the obviously poor people of the Third World, but also amongst Western hippies and confidence tricksters who claim to be refugees.

In some countries, beggars are terribly persistent, knowing full well that wearing you down produces results. Mere persistence may not be too hard for you to repel, but worst of all are the young children, often blind or with deformed limbs, who are guaranteed to arouse your pity. What you may not realize however, is that the child may have been intentionally deformed or blinded by his parents in order to make a successful beggar of him. The child is almost certainly encouraged by his family to beg and may be their chief source of income, since the child beggar can perhaps earn more in a day than his father working in the fields or factories. Remember also that a child who is out begging is necessarily missing school, which he should be attending. An adult with no education or experience other than begging tends to be less successful than a child. What are his options? Crime, if he is fit, destitution if crippled. Begging is obviously easier than work, but to give money is to contribute to a vicious circle. By withholding money you may help to eradicate these appalling practices.

Hard and Soft Currencies

by Christopher Portway

The subject of international currency is one of vast proportions but it only needs to be touched on here insofar as its ramifications are felt by the traveller abroad.

We have all heard of hard and soft currencies, yet do we all know exactly what the terms mean? Basically the term 'hard currency' is another phrase for *strong* currency: in other words, a currency that is in demand (and therefore useful) because everyone has faith in it. 'Soft currency' is the direct opposite, but what makes things somewhat blurred at the edges are the ever-changing degrees of hardness and softness. Classed as hard currencies at present are those of the Western European nations together with the American and Canadian dollars and the Japanese *yen* – though, even here, some are harder than others. Soft currency areas include many of the Third World countries and the Communist bloc – though again with fluctuating degrees of 'softness'; the Yugoslav *dinar*, for instance, being more in demand – and therefore stronger – than the Russian *rouble*.

Thus when the traveller goes abroad, he or she will obviously choose hard currency cash or traveller's cheques to take since they will be acceptable – even welcomed – in varying degrees all over the world. A traveller, in fact, will have little choice, since soft currency is virtually unobtainable in most of the hard currency territories, while currencies like the Yugoslav *dinar* and the Egyptian pound – somewhere between hard and soft – are only obtainable in small quantities while their countries of origin additionally impose severe restrictions on re-exportation.

Financial Advantages

What are the *financial* advantages of

taking either one's own currency, foreign currency purchased locally, or traveller's cheques? When making a brief visit to most countries I usually take sterling notes since it avoids the hassles and dilatoriness of some foreign banking systems and their sometimes erratic opening and closing times. But for the traveller seeking economy rather than convenience a better bet would be to make use of the 'retail' facilities for a bank transfer – which is what traveller's cheques are all about. These cheques are normally made out in the currency of the country of the issuing bank – though they need not be: dollar traveller's cheques are issued by banks all over the world nowadays. While the British traveller carries, for example, Midland Bank sterling traveller's cheques, he is not yet 'in' foreign currency – he is merely carrying a negotiable claim on his bank which a foreign bank will normally accept. When the traveller exchanges this sterling claim in, say, France, the French bank pays out francs and will mail the traveller's cheque back to the Midland. When the Midland receives it, it, in turn, will credit the sterling to the London account of the French bank – which the French bank will have to sell at the prevailing sterling–franc rate if it wants to regain its original francs.

Thus a traveller's cheque involves the foreign bank in a degree of foreign exchange risk for the time it takes for the traveller's cheque to clear. Because of this, and also the relatively expensive collection process, rates on traveller's cheques, while normally more favourable for the traveller than those obtainable by buying foreign notes, are still significantly less favourable than the rates a traveller may see quoted in the financial pages of the newspapers.

Local Currency

There are variations on this theme introduced by individual banks to make the purchase of goods, services and local currency that much simpler – but at a not inconsiderable handling charge. Most of the big banks are keen to involve a holidaymaker or traveller in Europe and the Mediterranean countries in their Eurocheque scheme wherein one's personal cheques or supplied special cheques, up to certain limit, are negotiable when supported by a Eurocheque Encashment Card. This way you can pay an account in the local currency without the trouble of having to work out the sterling equivalent prior to settlement by traveller's cheque or cash sterling.

However, the choice of carrying banknotes, traveller's cheques or whatever may also be affected by the possibilities of a change in currency values. Because the traveller gets 'in' to foreign exchange earlier when he buys foreign notes at his own bank, this may be to the traveller's advantage should the 'home' currency fall suddenly against the foreign currency. Alternatively, if the traveller fears devaluation by the destination country, he or she she will be better off staying in sterling either in the form of cash or cheques as long as possible, buying foreign currency on arrival in small amounts as the need arises.

This all may sound complicated and worrying, but it has no need to be so. While we happily bet our shirts on horses, dogs, Ernie and even the stock market, and take an active interest in doing so, why not the involuntray act of money exchange? It's all part of the game called 'travel'.

Travel Now, Pay Later: Travel Finance Schemes

by Roger Balsom and Ingrid Cranfield

To read about exotic destinations and yet be unable to travel because of financial restraints is both tantalizing and frustrating. Perhaps a few hints on where to raise that necessary and apparently elusive cash will inspire you to take the plunge and travel now.

If you don't have the money to hand, you may wonder what the hurry is. Why travel at all in the short term? The answer is that if you delay, you may well see your objective changed out of sight or its frontiers closed to visitors – an all too frequent occurrence these days. A young man once asked desert traveller Wilfred Thesiger: 'Can I expect to travel as you have done?' The answer was a simple 'No'. Thesiger was not being deliberately discouraging, but merely stating the fact that the world and its people change so rapidly that sometimes it is not possible to recapture things seen and achieved only a few years previously, let alone to retrace routes travelled by explorers 30 or 40 years ago.

The message is: travel now and pay later, if necessary.

Figure It Out

In general terms, it is easier to get finance against a recognized package holiday (where discount is sometimes available on prepayment), be it overland in Africa or Asia or a cultural experience in China. If all you want is to purchase isolated elements of a journey, you may find that you can only get an advance against airfares ex-UK. The ground arrangements will then have to be purchased locally, and for these you will need a cash loan. Some banks and schemes give cash that will cover all travel finance (see below). Borrowing money from other than a recognized source is not to be recommended.

How much will it cost? Figures will vary and should be checked with your bank, but the following may serve as an example (November 1983):

> To borrow £2,000 you will pay another £570 over 36 months; thus £2,000 at current rate of interest – 9½% per annum – in 36 equal monthly payments of £71.39 equals a total of £2,570 at an APR of 18.4%.

Security to cover the loan may be required. You can calculate varying rates of interest as the APR changes.

Credit Sources

Travel Agents and Associations. Some travel agents are familiar with travel credit, but the majority (with the exception of those below) will give you a strange look and a nod towards the exit. Most will, however, accept major British credit cards and some American ones, but usually only after reference to airlines – who may accept the credit card when the agent may not.

1. W. H. Smith Travel

Here regular monthly payments allow

you credit against a holiday or travel services purchased through the company. For example: £10 per month gives you £200 credit, on a sliding scale up to £250 per month which yields £5,000 credit. Interest is paid on your savings at a rate of one per cent below finance house base rate and is credited monthly. Any debit is calculated at (APR) 28.3 per cent. The scheme is arranged through Mercantile Credit. A leaflet is available.

2. AA Travel Services (Members' Holiday Loan Plan)
Sums from £200 to £2,000 are available, with repayments over 12, 18 or 24 months. Available for travel services, the scheme is organized through Mercantile Credit. A leaflet is available.

3. RAC Members' Finance
Up to £5,000 can be spread over between twelve and 60 monthly repayments. Special low rates of interest are applied to these loans, which are arranged through Lombard Finance. Leaflet available.

4. Thomas Cook Budget Account
Up to £3,000 can be borrowed (i.e. up to fifteen times the amount you can afford to pay back monthly). £1,005 can be instantly confirmed if you have a bank current account and you agree to pay by standing order. You also need a bank card and proof of your address. Interest is charged at prevailing APR on any outstanding balance.

If you enter the scheme before you travel, interest will also be paid on your savings. Finance is arranged through Forward Trust Ltd and a leaflet is available.

Credit and Charge Cards. Credit and charge cards may be used not only to purchase air tickets etc., but also while travelling, to pay bills and, in some instances, for cash advance. Check with the issuers of your card before you travel as to whether it is valid for your route.

1. Visa
A card is issued free with a set credit limit. No interest is charged on outstanding amounts if paid within the time limit. Interest on outstanding balance: 23.1% per annum. The card is widely accepted internationally. Several banks and institutions issue credit cards. The originator of the Visa card was Barclays Bank, and to the bank's account holders, it also doubles as a cheque guarantee card.

2. Access
The card is issued free with a set credit limit. No interest is charged on the outstanding amount if paid within the time limit. Interest on outstanding balance: 23.1% per annum. The card is widely accepted internationally and is interchangeable with the Mastercharge card in the USA or the Eurocard in Europe.

3. American Express
Green Card: £17.50 annual subscription (with a £17.50 initial enrolment fee). No interest is charged on credit but repayment is expected in full immediately upon receipt of the monthly statement. There is normally no specific pre-set spending limit. The card gives access to over 1,000 American Express offices throughout the world, where English speaking staff not only give travel advice but will cash personal cheques up to £500 (subject to local regulations). Added to this is the

benefit of £35,000 worth of travel accident insurance and *poste restante* facilities. Gold Card: £40 per annum subscription (plus £20 enrolment fee – waived if the applicant is already the holder of a Green Card). Credit and payment arrangements are the same as for the Green Card. Possession of the Gold Card, however, gives the holder £7,500 unsecured overdraft facilities at Lloyds Bank and up to £1,000 in cash or travellers' cheques through a personal cheque cashed at American Express offices worldwide. The deposit for car hire is waived for holders of the Gold Card, which also carries £150,000 of travel accident insurance and qualifies for access to a 24-hour emergency telephone service.

Both Green and Gold charge cards are well worth having, but to qualify for a Green Card you must be earning around £8,500 per annum and for a Gold Card £20,000 per annum. American Express is not linked to the Eurocheque system. Local rules concerning the use of American Express cards vary considerably, so it is best to get the leaflet and check with reference to specific time, place and circumstances.

4. Diners Club International

The annual subscription is £17.50 (with an initial enrolment fee of £10). No interest is charged on credit but the debit balance has to be paid in full, monthly. There is no spending limit and the card is widely accepted by airlines, car hire firms etc. To qualify for a card, your yearly earnings must be at least £8,000.

5. British Airways – Air Travel Card

(International or North America)

This card is issued on payment of a US $425 cash deposit. This is not a limit to its use. The card is used both by individuals and by businesses to purchase air tickets to and from major cities everywhere in the world. No service charge is made on unlimited credit for air travel.

6. Car Rental Credit Cards

These too can be useful for defraying costs, as settlement is expected monthly. No charge is made for the card, which in some instances – not all – carries a discount and a waiver of deposits.

7. British Telecom International Telephone Credit Card

This card may be used for calls to the UK from abroad and is useful as a way of keeping a supply of cash for other travel expenses and of avoiding the surcharges often imposed by hotels for the use of the telephone.

8. Company cards

Airlines, hotel groups and other companies provide credit or offer discount cards to regular users. Ask around.

Banks. Major banks operate personal loan schemes. Credit varies from £1,000 to £5,000. Leaflets are available from Midland, Barclays and National Westminster, all of whom promote such schemes. Alternatively, approach your bank manager for an individual arrangement.

MCO (*Miscellaneous Charge Order*). Obtained through a travel agent or airline, this document (which looks like an air ticket) may be used to purchase air tickets or pay for other air travel facilities such as excess baggage charges. Its cost, which varies according to your requirements, may be reclaimed if it is not used, but only at the purchasing source. An MCO is accepted by all IATA airlines. Your travel agent will tell you if it is valid for your area of travel. An MCO adds flexibility to your journey, but it is no substitute for a confirmed air ticket. However, it does mean that you can purchase at home something that will help you in the field. It could be useful to include some MCOs in your loan scheme.

Mortgage. If you own a house, you could consider a second mortgage. It all depends on how much importance you attach to travelling.

International Travel Card Æ(USA). Of the various types of travel credit available in the USA, note in particular the International Travel Card, which costs $35 for a year or $49.50 for two years. Members may obtain a free second night's accommodation at many hotels and motels in the USA and in 28 other countries, provided that the traveller pays the hotel's 'regular published rate' for the first night. Other member benefits include directories of hotels and motels throughout the world, $10,000 free travel insurance, the facility to purchase unlimited American Express foreign traveller's cheques by mail, free currency exchange by mail or at any Mutual of Omaha counter at US or Canadian airports, car hire discounts of 20–30 per cent, and a free pocket road atlas. The card is available from: International Travel Card, PO Box 5080, Des Plaines, IL60018, USA. Tel. numbers in mainland USA (credit card orders) toll free: (800) 874 4400 ext. 208 or in Florida (800) 453 8777; enquiries to (904) 399 8300.

Shop around as schemes change and new ones develop. The pointers we have given may at least stimulate your ideas and give you access to money for a journey you have dreamed about but not previously contemplated actually making.

Preparing Your Things

Luggage: How to Choose It, Keep It, Find It and Pack It

by Hilary Bradt

The original meaning of 'luggage' is 'what has to be lugged about'. Lightweight materials have made lugging obsolete for sensible travellers these days, but there is a bewildering choice of containers for all your portable possessions.

What you buy in the way of luggage and what you put in it obviously depends on how and where you are travelling. If your journey is in one conveyance and you are staying put once you arrive, you can be as eccentric as the Durrell family who travelled to Corfu with 'two trunks of books and a briefcase containing his clothes' (Lawrence) and 'four books on natural history, a butterfly net, a dog and a jam jar full of caterpillars all in imminent danger of turning into chrysalids' (Gerald, author of *My Family and Other Animals*, from which the quotations come).

If, however, you will be constantly on the move and rarely spend more than one night in any place, your luggage must be easy to pack, transport and carry.

What to Bring

There are two important considerations to bear in mind when choosing luggage. First, weight is less of a problem than bulk. Travel light if you can, but if you can't, travel small. Second, bring whatever you need to keep you happy. It's a help to know yourself. If you can travel, like Laurie Lee, with a tent, a change of clothes, a blanket and a violin, or like Rick Berg, author of *The Art and Adventure of Travelling Cheaply* who took only a small rucksack (day pack) for his six-year sojourn, you will indeed be free. Most people, however, are too dependent on their customary possessions and diversions suddenly to abandon them, and must pack accordingly.

Suitcase, Backpack or . . .?

Your choice of luggage is of the utmost importance and will probably involve making a purchase. Making do with granny's old suitcase or Uncle John's scouting rucksack may spoil your trip.

Most young overland travellers carry a standard external frame backpack despite its unsuitability for this type of travel. Anyone who's had to stand in a crowded Third World bus or the London underground in rush hour wearing one of these things will know the problem. You take up three times as much room as normal, and the possessions strapped to the outside of your pack may be out of your sight, but will certainly not be out of the minds of your fellow passengers – or out of their eyes, laps and air space. No wonder backpackers have a bad name. And because they do, many Third World countries are prejudiced to the extent of banning them. On arriving at the Paraguay border some years ago I was forced to wrap my pack in a sheet sleeping bag and carry it as luggage in the most literal sense.

That aluminium frame is fragile, as you will discover when someone stands on it. And of course since you carry the backpack behind you, you're particularly vulnerable to thieves, who don't even have to be very expert to unzip and rob those handy external pockets. And have you ever hitchhiked in a Mini carrying your pack in your lap? Can you honestly say you were comfortable? Finally, some airlines refuse to carry this type of pack unless it's packed in a box.

So leave the frame packs to the genuine backpackers they were designed for. Hitchhikers and travellers who expect to walk a fair bit during their travels should still carry a backpack, but one with an internal frame. This small variation in design makes all the difference – the pack can be carried comfortable on your lap, it need be no wider than your body, and everything can be fitted inside. It can be checked onto a plane with no trouble, and carried on a porter's head or mule's back.

For the average overland traveller, the ideal solution is the combination bag and backpack. This type of luggage has become justly popular in recent years; basically it is a sturdy bag with padded shoulder straps that can be hidden in a special zip compartment when approaching a sensitive border or when travelling by plane.

If you are joining an organized group or do not expect to carry your own luggage, you will find a duffel bag the most practical solution. Or two duffel bags since you have two hands. These soft zipped bags are strong and light and can fit into awkward spaces that preclude rigid suitcases. They fit snugly into the bottom of a canoe or back of a bus and are easily carried by porters or pack animals. In the Third World, small boys with the strength of Hercules throng bus stations in the hope of earning your small tip for carrying luggage.

When selecting a duffel bag, choose one made from strong material with a stout zip that can be padlocked to the side or otherwise secured against thieves. Avoid those khaki army sausage bags with the opening at one end. The article you need at any given time will invariably be at the bottom.

Suppose you're a regular air traveller, what will be the best type of luggage for you? Probably the conventional suitcase, and in that case, you will be well advised – as with most travel purchases – to get the best you can afford, unless you want to replace your 'bargain' luggage after virtually every flight. Cheap materials do not stand up to airline handling. Now that some flights have eliminated the weight allowance in favour of a limit of two pieces, neither of which must measure more than 67 inches (that's height by length by width), it's as well to buy luggage that conforms to that size. Suitcases with built-in wheels are a great advantage in the many airports which do not supply trolleys.

If you are using soft-sided luggage, choose items made from a strong material, e.g. nylon. Leather items should be scrutinized for cracking around the expanded areas: the leather should be of a uniform thickness throughout the item. Check the zip, which should not only be strong but also unobtrusive so as not to catch on clothing etc., and the stitching, which should be even and secure with no gaps or loose threads. If you have the choice, get a bag with one handle only: porters tend to toss luggage around by one handle and this can play havoc with a bag designed to be carried by two. Conveyor belts have a nasty habit of smearing luggage: darker colours stand up to this treatment more happily. Before walking away with your purchase, remember to ask about its care, especially which cleaning materials you should use.

Carry-on luggage should be used for anything you can't do without for a few days, whether it's photos of your children, your own special sleeping tablets or the address of the friend you're going straight from the airport to visit. Not to mention 'uninsurables' such as sums of money or vital papers. To fit under an aeroplane seat, a carry-on bag must measure no more than 450 × 350 × 150mm (18 × 14 × 6ins).

As well as a carry-on bag, you are allowed the following free items: a handbag (women only – sorry men; as this is in addition to the carry-on luggage, better take as big a handbag as possible to make the most of your luck), an overcoat, an umbrella or walking stick, a small camera, a pair of binoculars, infant's food for the flight, a carrying basket, an invalid's fully collapsible wheelchair, a pair of crutches, reading material in reasonable quantities, and any duty-free goods you have acquired since checking-in.

Some thought should be given to accessory bags. Everyone ends up with more luggage than they started with because of presents, local crafts, maps, etc. collected on the way, and a light foldable bag is very useful. Canvas and straw have their followers. I'm devoted to plastic bags myself and carry a good supply, even though the bottom usually falls out or the handles tear.

Security

Choose a bag or backpack with security in mind. Your possessions are at risk in two ways: your bag may be opened and some items removed, or the whole bag may be stolen. Most travellers have been robbed at some time or other, the most frequent occurrence being that small items simply disappeared from their luggage. Make sure that your luggage can be locked. With duffel bags this is no problem – a small padlock will secure the zip to the ring at the base of the handle. Adapt the bag yourself if necessary. Combination locks are more effective than standard padlocks as they are rarely seen in the Third World and so thieves have not learned how to pick them. They also protect the clients of those manufacturers whose products are all fitted with the same key! It is harder to lock a backpack; use your ingenuity. One effective method is to make a strong pack cover with metal rings round the edges, through which can be passed a cable lock to secure the cover round the pack. Luggage may also be slashed, but this treatment is usually reserved for handbags. Apart from buying reinforced steel cases there is little you can do about it. A strong leather strap around a suitcase may help keep your luggage safe and, anyway, does no harm.

For easy identification of your luggage, try coloured tape or some other personal markings on the outside. Stick-on labels are safer than the dangling kind, as they cannot be ripped off so easily. You may not care if you lose the label itself, but such items are useful guides to thieves as to who is going where – and who, by deduction, is not at home.

During my travels, I've been robbed of five small bags. I finally learned never to carry something that is easily run off with unless it is firmly secured to my person. If you keep your most valuable possessions in the centre of a locked heavy pack or bag they're pretty safe. If you can barely carry your luggage, a thief will have the same problem.

Allowances for Air Travel

On international flights, the IATA Tourist and Economy Class allowance is normally 20kg (44lbs), that for First Class 30kg (66lbs). For transatlantic flights and some others (e.g. USA to South America), however, you can take far more luggage since the weight system has been cancelled and the only restriction is to two pieces of luggage no larger than 67 inches. Before you fly, always check with the airline on luggage allowances and ask if the same applies to the home journey. For instance, if you fly Ecuatoriana from Miami to Quito, you will fly down on the two piece system, but will be restricted to 20kg for your return – a nasty shock for the present-laden tourist.

What to do if you have excess baggage? You could of course just pay the charges, but we assume that you'll want to do something more interesting than that. Well, if you know in advance that your baggage will exceed the free allowance, you could take some of it to the airport a few days before you yourself fly and have it sent on ahead . . . by cargo/freight, which is much cheaper than the normal accompanied baggage rate. However, this is inadvisable in the Third World, where retrieving your luggage from customs can take several days. There are ways of getting extra bags on board; on departure you can wait around by the check-in desk until you spot another amiable-looking passenger who has a spare baggage allowance. If he permits it and the airline clerk permits it (they usually do), you can pool your luggage together. If this doesn't work, don't worry, airlines will usually let slightly overweight luggage through and anyway, an ingenious traveller can usually manage to find a way round the problem. My record is five bags weighing a total of 70kg transported from South America to Miami (weight limit 20kg) and on to London (piece limit – two) without paying excess charges.

Packing

Joan Bakewell, in *The Complete Traveller*, suggests thinking of what to take under the following headings: toiletries and overnight, unders, overs, accessories, paperwork and extras. Whilst it is true to say that everything can be classified under these headings, campers and caravanners and others who must take the appurtenances of home with them will almost certainly find that the 'extras' section expands dramatically over the normal few extras required by, say, airline passengers.

The latter should be warned that aerosols and the ink in fountain pens tend to leak in the pressurized atmosphere of an aeroplane – such items should not be packed in your suitcases but may be safe enough in your hand luggage where you can keep an eye on them; lighter fuel is not permitted on an aircraft; photographic film can be damaged by X-rays used at security checks – you may be allowed to hand your film around the checkpoint instead of passing it through.

When packing, put irregular-shaped items such as shoes at the bottom (and don't forget to fill up the shoes with soft or small items such as underwear or jewellery), topped by clothes in layers separated by sheets of plastic or tissue paper. Trousers, skirts and dresses, still on their hangers or folded with tissue paper between layers, go towards the top, but the topmost stratum in your case should be occupied by T-shirts, blouses and shirts, small items of clothing, and then some enveloping piece such as a dressing-gown or shawl over everything. Some travellers like to keep their toilet items in different groups, which makes sense when you consider that you don't wash your hair with the same frequency as you wash your face or go out in strong sun.

Do not overpack: if you have to force the lid of your suitcase to close, you may bend the luggage frame or break the hinges, with the obvious ensuing risk to the contents. Underpacking, especially in soft-sided luggage, is also undesirable, since the cases need to be padded out to resist tears to the outer covering.

Travel Clothing

by Jan Glen

Method of travel can be a big deciding factor in your choice of suitable clothing. The amount of storage space available is the ultimate restriction for backpackers, a major one for motorcyclists, less so for motorists who can pack clothes for every climate and other eventuality. Choosing which clothing to pack initially is often a matter of trial and error. Clothes that prove unnecessary can, of course, be posted home and additional clothing bought along the way if routes and climates change. However, prices and quality en route may not be to your liking.

Climate has to enter into one's calculations. If several different climatic zones are to be crossed, then the problem is compounded. If, for example, one travels from Britain to the Sahara by road in mid-winter, warm winter clothing has to be packed for the European leg of the journey. However, the Sahara at this time of year is cold during the night only and some warm clothing could become redundant.

Travelling in deserts really causes few problems, provided all clothing is wrapped in plastic to protect it from the fine penetrating dust. Cotton clothing is best for both men and women and a wide-brimmed hat is a good idea if you intend walking in the sun. Flip-flops or thonged sandals suffice for footwear in most places, except in Sahel regions where scorpions and large lethal thorns are hazards.

Rain forest, with its tropical heat and clammy humidity, is a different story. Humidity can be very exhausting and may make the actual temperature seem much higher than it really is. For walking one must keep in mind the hazards of this environment. Muddy and slippery leech-infested tracks make sandals or flip-flops less suitable than closed-in leather or rubber shoes or boots. Cottons are again more comfortable than synthetics, and in both desert and rain forest environments cotton underwear can minimize discomfort.

For colder climates and in mountainous areas, you need to take a great deal of care in choosing suitable clothing. Warm, windproof and waterproof clothing should be chosen on the layer principle. (*See Recent Developments in Outdoor Equipment on page 324*.)

Custom and Status

Social custom is also a very important consideration. When in someone else's country, the last thing one wishes to do is offend. Yet this is often done unintentionally and local people are frequently too polite to complain. If you are able to swim where you are travelling, remember that local custom may find bikinis and men's brief trunks quite offensive. It is always safer to have modest wear: one-piece costumes for women and well-covering trunks or shorts for men. Careful observation of how local people dress when and if they swim can set your standard. Avoid swimming where dishes or clothes are washed or drinking water is collected, as this may also offend.

Because a Western woman's status is quite superior to that of her counterparts in other societies, she should be especially cautious in her dress. Some countries, Malawi for example, have been very concerned since the 1960s about the dress of their Western visitors. Dresses above the knee, shorts and trousers for women are actually illegal in that country. In the Saharan oasis town of Tamanrasset a Western girl, wearing only a tight pair of shorts and a bikini top, and with bare feet, was physically thrown out of a bar. In Algeria, Morocco, Tunisia, Libya, Iran and many other Muslim countries, the sort of dress which would arouse least hostility towards a Western woman would include both a headscarf and a long, dark-coloured skirt. Iran, especially since the revolution, is even stricter than some other Islamic states. In many Islamic countries, women are rarely seen, seldom heard, and when they are seen they are covered up from head to toe. Let the local standard be your guide even if allowances are made for Westerners.

Even Mediterranean countries can be a problem for women if the customs of modesty are not observed. Many are the stories of women being approached and having their bottoms pinched, or worse, in Greece and Italy. Bikinis and shorts in these places should be reserved strictly for resorts where they have become acceptable for foreigners. In Athens, a seemingly cosmopolitan city, I have been harassed when dressed in conservative jeans and accompanied constantly by my husband.

Papua New Guinea has long been a home for expatriates, chiefly Australians, who are renowned for casual dress and an 'anything goes' attitude. However, attitudes have been modified to conform to local custom. Bikinis and shorts are generally out and although a long skirt is not at all necessary in Port Moresby it would be wise to be careful in outlying regions.

When visiting India, dress conservatively out or respect for that country's large Muslim population. Hindu women also wear long saris, are very modest and often have an inferior social status. If visiting a Sikh temple, it is also customary to wear a hat or some form of head covering.

Although, as stated above, nothing is frowned upon in Australia, girls hitchhiking there and in New Zealand in very provocative shorts or bikinis are really offering to pay for their ride in a sometimes violent way they may not have anticipated.

Men's Wear

A man's position is quite different when travelling in male-dominated societies. Because of the significant difference between formal and informal dress for men, they should carry both types. In isolated hot regions where no local people will be encountered, men can comfortably wear shorts and flip-flops and go about shirtless. In towns and at borders, however, the traveller's appearance should be much more formal. Long, straight-legged trousers, a clean, conservative shirt, shoes, and tidy hair will give a look of affluence and respectability. Even a tie may be handy at times. The impression this dress creates will promote a more gracious attitude from shopkeepers and businessmen and could well moderate the zealousness of authoritarian border officials.

In Australia, New Zealand, and southern Africa, shorts are the accepted daily dress even for businessmen. However, even in cosmopolitan London they attract curious glances. Therefore, shorts are best reserved for the out of the way places.

Long hair and untidy beards on men are a bone of contention in many countries. In Singapore a man's hair must be well above the collar and not touch the ears or eyebrows. Malawi forbids entry to men with long hair and flared trousers. Morocco's entry requirements empower border officials to refuse entry to men with long hair or 'hippy appearance' despite their having valid travel documents. Even where this disapproval is not specified by law, it often exists in practice. Officials may discriminate against travellers of 'unsuitable' appearance by considerably delaying their entry. Incidentally, men with greying hairs are often well respected in less developed countries.

Blend In

Dress is far more important for the independent traveller than for the regular tourist on the more beaten track, who has the protection of tour guides or companies and the safety of numbers. Offending the local people can have unpleasant consequences for the individual alone and away from civilization.

Adopting local dress because of a desire to 'go ethnic' is suitable when actually travelling and living as the locals do. One example of this would be as a member of a camel caravan, where it would not only be justified but sensible to adopt the *tagoulmoust* to protect your face from the dust and dryness. On a camel you would also be more comfortable wearing a *sarouel* (baggy trousers) and loose shirt. However, in many circumstances, no matter how practical the local dress may be it is wise to wear it with discretion. Imagine how ridiculous a Western tourist would look on the streets of Port Moresby wearing nothing but some 'arsegrass' strung around his waist. You surely don't wish to offend the local people, but neither do you want to become a laughing stock to them. A good idea is to aim to blend in rather than stand out as a foreign visitor. As a foreigner you are at times already at a disadvantage but you can try to minimize this by, for example, avoiding pretentousness. Wearing a ten gallon hat, pith helmet or slouch hat tends to attract unwanted attention.

It is strictly illegal for tourists to wear military clothing in the Niger and, however cheap army surplus may be, it is best avoided in many other countries too, where it can have unwanted connotations. This is especially so in 'white mercenary' sensitive Africa. 'Obvious' jewellery is also best avoided by travellers because its style will be unusual and it is regarded as a sign of wealth. Displaying it invites theft. Moreover, worn by men, together with shorts, it has other meanings. An example is the attractive young man, shirtless, with shorts, silver bangles and neck chains, in a Saharan oasis hotel, who was most put out because he had been approached and propositioned by several local men. Homosexuality occurs internationally and advances are made to willing-looking men in the same way as they are made to women in the heterosexual sense. The author's husband, always a conservative dresser, did once forget this in Beirut and wore standard Australian businessmen's shorts and long socks. The resultant cat calls and wolf whistles from young men sent him fleeing back to his hotel to change into long trousers.

A pair of overalls or very tatty old clothes are most useful for working on the vehicle en route, allowing you to protect other clothes from grease and dirt.

If you run out of small change or presents to reward local people who have been very helpful, especially in less developed countries, secondhand Western clothing is often prestigious and it can suit everybody if you give away some clothes as you travel. Jeans are a popular example.

By urging conservative and demure dress in Third World countries, one is not being prudish. Rather, by dressing sensitively, one can travel unharassed in almost any area. In places still relatively untouched by Western influence, the impression one creates can ensure that travellers who follow are welcome visitors.

Lightweight Equipment

by Peter F. Williams

The main items of lightweight equipment required for a venture off the beaten track are a tent, a sleeping bag, stove, cooking and eating utensils, plus a rucksack or pack frame and sack. Added to your load will be food, spare clothing and personal gear. Whether you are a hill trekker, hitch-hiker or are just planning a backpacking holiday by road/air, then on foot, you will have one thing in common – at some time or most of the time you will have to provide the motive power for whatever equipment is to be carried. You therefore need to consider very carefully what gear is to be taken, how to carry it and the best methods of packing to employ. Take note that if your journey is planned across difficult terrain then the weight of your load should not exceed one third of your body weight; for young people 14kg is the maximum weight advised. These limitations are necessary as the energy required to cover such ground can equal that used in heavy manual work, so you cannot afford to carry non-essential gear.

Lightweight Tents

A well-designed lightweight tent should normally have sufficient room for two people to sleep in and adequate space to cook in if weather conditions are bad. When selecting your tent, such factors as expected weather conditions, altitude, temperature and any requirement for fine weight limitation should be taken into account. Here are a few points to note:

1. Select a design made by a reputable manufacturer and carefully read the maker's specification for the tent including the work it is designed for, e.g. base camp use, mountaineering, a low level bivouac, etc.
2. If you intend to operate in wet conditions note that some modern tents are designed so that the flysheet is erected first. The inner tent can then be erected under and protected by the flysheet. When you strike camp, the procedure is reversed and the inner tent packed first.
3. Consider the weight of the tent in relation to the all-up weight of the rest of your gear. It may be feasible to split the weight of the tent with a companion, one person carrying the main tent, the other the flysheet and poles.
4. A down-to-earth flysheet will, in bad weather, give maximum protection to the inner tent and make the tent warmer in cold conditions. It will also help to keep it cool when the weather is very hot.
5. A built-in groundsheet that extends about 8cm up the side, front and back walls will eliminate the draughts that would otherwise blow in under the walls. It will give insulation from damp ground and if the area does get very wet, the groundsheet will keep the inside of the tent dry.
6. Note that some mountain tents are designed for dry conditions and are not suited for prolonged use in very wet weather.
7. Fine netting should cover all vents to keep out mosquitoes and gnats.

Your tent may be your home for days, perhaps even weeks. It is therefore important that the design, weight, size and degree of protection it offers suit your purpose and give the comfort you require.

Sleeping Bags

The degree of insulation afforded by sleeping bags is dependent not only on the type and amount of the filling, but also its arrangement within the sleeping bag's walls. The filling has to be contained so that it does not slip or move within the walls and produce cold areas. This is done by dividing the walls into squares, sections or tubes. In some bags, the outer wall is drawn by the quilting stitches to the inner wall. In the region of the lines of stitches cold spots form because of the lack of thickness and insulation. This type of quilting is unsuitable for use in colder conditions unless you are prepared to wear additional gear when you go to bed, such as woollen tights or a wool shirt and socks. However, where two layers of simple quilting are used to make a double wall effect, the insulation is excellent. Boxed or walled sleeping bags are normally more expensive than the single walled quilted bag but are a much better purchase as the walls are kept completely separate from one another. The filling is contained in areas or boxes by fabric compartment walls stitched between the outer and inner covers. These boxes allow for the full expansion or 'loft' of the filling when it is warmed by the body and therefore give a continuous uniform layer of filling to insulate the sleeper. To permit this, choose a sleeping bag large enough to let you wrap yourself in a blanket *inside* the bag.

A sleeping bag fitted with a draw-cord is preferable for a bag will afford maximum warmth only if it can seal in the heat generated by the body. When the cord is pulled, your body, from the shoulders down, should be as snug as the quality of the bag can make you. Expensive sub-zero bags are often mummy-shaped with a built-in hood to cover the head and neck. Such designs have a drawstring that will close the hood to leave only a small space for breathing.

Here are a few points to note when selecting a sleeping bag:

1. Select a design made by a reputable manufacturer and carefully read the maker's specification for the bag and the conditions in which the bag is suitable for use. e.g. light summer use, cold weather, Arctic conditions.
2. A down-filled bag is best; the weight of the filling will indicate the thermal properties of the bag. 1.4kg of goose or duck down will make a very snug bag suitable for use in very cold weather. 0.9kg of similar filling makes a good, warm general purpose bag. 0.5kg of down will provide the warmth for use in summer conditions only.
3. The presence of a few feathers in a goose down bag helps to keep the bag lofted up and warm when wet. Wool and artificial fibres retain their insulating properties when wet, down does not.
4. Make sure that the length of the bag is adequate. Adult sizes normally range from about 2m to 2.3m.
5. Shapes of bags can vary; some are rectangular, others tapered or mummy-shaped. Mummy-shaped bags are normally more suited for low temperatures and tapered designs used for moderate conditions. Rectangular bags are normally best suited for low level summer conditions.

6. A waterproof nylon carrying or stuff bag is necessary to keep the bag clean and dry.
7. If you do not intend to use a tent, but sleep rough, purchase a sleeping bag cover made with a strong waterproof base and a top that will give extra protection from cold and damp.
8. A wool or brushed cotton inner sheet will give extra warmth and help to keep the bag clean, for otherwise body moisture can be absorbed by the filling.
9. If travelling light, use an air mattress.

Remember, you will spend six to eight hours daily in your sleeping bag, in bad weather perhaps much longer. The comfort it gives you is therefore very important, so buy the best that you can afford.

Stoves

There are various types of lightweight stoves on the market including those fuelled by solid fuel, methylated spirit, paraffin, petrol or gas. However, several factors need to be considered before purchasing a stove and these include weight, price, size and the availability and cost of fuel. Information on the fuel capacity, boiling time and the one charge burning time will also give an indication of a stove's overall efficiency.

The most popular solid fuel stove on the British market is the design that, when folded, resembles a small, flat, light steel box which measures a little larger than a pack of cards and encloses the solid fuel blocks. When erected, the stove comprises a pot stand with supporting legs and a burner on which the fuel blocks are placed. The fuel blocks will light even when partially damp and partially used blocks can be put out and retained for use later. Heat control is effected by adding or reducing the amount of fuel on the burner plate. The best cooking results are obtained if lightweight aluminium cooking utensils are used as the stove cannot generate pressure like a gas or petrol stove. The solid fuel stove has no working parts that can malfunction.

The methylated fuel picnic stove is the cheapest and one of the simplest types of lightweight stove available. The Express type weighs 224gm and measures 11cm in diameter by 7.5cm high. The stove has no working parts but comprises a hollow steel cup with a perforated rim. This stands inside the combined pot stand and wind shield. Meths is poured into the cup to a set level indicated and then a match applied to the centre of the cup ensures a flickering flame that soon settles down to form a very effective gas-like ring of fire emitted from the perforated rim. The disadvantage with the methylated fuel picnic stove is that it is not possible to control the heat output and it uses a fair amount of fuel. A 56gm charge of fuel will burn for 29 minutes in calm conditions at 22°C, long enough to heat several dishes; 0.3 litres of water will boil in five minutes.

The Trangia Storm Cooker 25 is a more advanced design comprising an aluminium cook set with two large frying pans, saucepan and pot lifter. The stove will boil a litre of water in eight minutes. The Storm Cooker measures 11 × 23cm and weighs one kg.

The Primus type of paraffin pressure stove is a Swedish invention well known throughout the world. It is cheap to run and will give a long burning time. The stove has a high heat output but it is also possible to control the pressure from very low to quite intense heat. The paraffin pressure stove works on the principle of vaporizing paraffin by compressing air. The burner of the stove is first heated by a priming of meths or solid fuel set on fire in the cup specially designed for this purpose and located midway up the stem of the stove. A few pumps are then given to the main reservoir and a match applied to the burner enables the paraffin vapour to catch. The stove will then start to roar so that the spreader ring glows red hot. However, you cannot afford to neglect a pressure stove. The jet requires cleaning from time to time and after much use, the pressure washer may need to be renewed.

There are various excellent petrol-fuelled pressure stoves on the British market such as the 0.6 litre capacity Optimus 11B which weighs just over 1.8kg or the smaller one-third capacity Optimus 8R which only weighs 0.3kg. It will burn for about 45 minutes on a single filling of fuel that weighs 84gm.

The well-known American camping firm Coleman retails a number of excellent lightweight petrol stoves. They also produce their own fuel for gasoline camping appliances that is sold widely in the States, even in one store towns. It burns clean, prevents clogging or gumming up and has a rust and corrosion inhibitor. Remember that petrol gives off toxic fumes when burnt and should not be used in a confined space. It is also extremely important that the manufacturer's instructions are read carefully so that you know exactly how to use and service your petrol stove. Also take note that stoves sold in Great Britain are normally intended for use with unleaded petrol.

Generally speaking, lightweight gas stoves are not expensive to buy but cost more to run than liquid fuelled paraffin or petrol stoves. The advantage of gas is that it is clean and requires no priming, and the pressure can be finely controlled. A gas cartridge with a capacity of 170–225gm will normally give over two hours of burning time. However, unlike in other types of lightweight stove, as the fuel commences to run out, the pressure will drop considerably for quite some time and delay cooking. Take note that when butane gas is used at low temperatures, difficulty can be experienced in lighting the stove, and the stove may then burn with little pressure. Propane gas however will burn well in cold conditions.

Utensils

At the absolute minimum, two vessels are needed for cooking: a frying pan and a pot. There are numerous good lightweight canteens on the market that compromise both cooking and eating utensils. When purchasing such equipment, make sure that the items are also compact and the utensils will fit neatly inside one another, for a rucksack has little spare room for bulky gear. A two-man canteen need not add up to more than 0.7kg in weight. Cooking pots should be seamless to avoid possible leaks and a wide base makes for quicker cooking and less fuel used. When considering lightweight frying pans, check for stability on the stove, particularly those types which have long folding handles. If the weight of the handle outweighs that of the pan and its contents, it will be unstable and could be dangerous unless the handle is held continuously throughout the whole cooking operation. Utensils that incorporate the paint pot type of handle are not designed for the handle to stay upright away from the heat. You will therefore need a grip handle that weighs only 42gm with which it is possible to handle these and any other hot utensils in safety.

Load Carrying

There are three types of load carrying equipment to consider – the traditional rucksack, the frame rucksack and the pack frame and sack.

The Rucksack: The rucksack is basically a container bag that has no supporting frame and lies directly on the back of the walker supported by two shoulder straps. Rucksacks are often made of 420gm proofed close weave cotton canvas or 200–280gm proofed nylon. They weigh about one to two kg yet can have a capacity of about 40 litres or even more. Some modern designs are contoured to shape the back. Large external pockets are useful, particularly if lined with additional proofing such as oil cloth, for the stove and liquid fuel can then be carried separately with no possibility of contamination of food or clothes in the main bag. A pull-out plastic sleeve fitted with a draw cord at the top of the sack makes for security and the extra protection of contents in bad weather. A large lid with long straps will ensure that the tent, which is a comparatively heavy item, can be carried in a waterproof cover on top of the sack, held securely by the tightened lid straps.

The rucksack needs to be packed carefully to ensure that the weight is distributed evenly and that no sharp item can dig into your back. It has the disadvantage that it will cause the back to sweat as there is no circulation of air between the canvas and the body. However, it is normally lighter and cheaper than the frame rucksack or pack frame and sack. When empty it can be used as a mattress to lie on at night and give insulation from dampness and cold striking up through the ground.

Frame Rucksacks: Modern frame rucksacks comprise a steel or aluminium frame onto which the sack is built. The frame rucksack distributes the load well and allows adequate ventilation of the back which is not possible with frameless models. The Norwegian Meis design is popular both in the USA and Europe and has a capacious canvas sack built onto a light aluminium frame that incorporates a waist support. Before purchasing a frame rucksack, check that the frame fits the back well and if a waist support is incorporated, that it fits around and does not dig into your back. The frame rucksack should be comfortable to wear, be carried high on the back and have the capacity to take all the gear you need.

Pack Frames: The pack frame is capable of supporting large or heavy loads. Most frames weigh only about 0.7–0.9kg and are made of strong alloy tubing, either welded together or linked by plastic joints. Strengthened V bars are often fitted to resist distortion from heavy loads. However, Coleman of Wichita, Kansas, have introduced a new concept frame construction and produced a moulded frame made from high impact material called Ram-Flex. The material is durable at all temperatures and gives controlled flexibility to move with your body. It has numerous moulded slots that allow considerable adjustments to the supporting straps. The slots can also be used to tie on extra gear. Custom designed sacks are normally attached to frames by pin mountings or by straps but it is possible to carry any reasonable load from the large duffel-type sailor sack to a self-designed canvas sack, provided it is strapped securely to the frame and is not unwieldy in shape.

It is important that the frame fits properly and some frames are adjustable. The frame should contour the body. The distance between the top harness attachment point and the bottom of the cross band on the frame should equal the distance between the highest prominent neck bone and the hip bone. When the loaded frame is carried, it will then lie with the cross band resting on the hips. A padded waist belt will help take the weight off the shoulders and give extra support.

Packing the Load

When you walk the body is balanced so that the line of gravity runs down the spine through the legs to the ground. Any weight carried on the back also has its line of gravity that runs parallel to that of the walker. The closer together these two lines can be kept, the easier it is to carry a load and walk upright. It is therefore important that the centre of gravity of your load should be kept both as high and as far forward as possible. This can be achieved by dividing the pack into three vertical zones. Into Zone A, which is the area close to your back, place the objects which have the greatest density with the heavier items highest. The tent should be packed at the top of the sack, either held in place by the lid or strapped to the poles of the pack frame. In the middle, Zone B, pack items of medium density, and in Zone C, furthest away from your centre of gravity, pack the lightest items. If high density items should be packed in Zone C, the excess weight will tend to pull you backwards and you are forced to lean forward from the waist.

In addition to the general principles of zoning your gear, there are other factors that need to be considered. Emergency items, such as the cagoule and overtrousers that will be needed in the event of sudden bad weather, and emergency rations, should be packed near the top of the sack. If you use a rucksack, avoid sharp objects against the back. Last wanted items such as night gear or reserve food should go in the bottom half of the sack. Where the arrangement of items in the sack is not so critical, such as when short distances are to be covered or when hitchhiking, then you may prefer to divide the sack into a night side and a day side with the sleeping bag, sleeping gear, toilet kit, torch and towel neatly packed on one side and day items such as food, stove, and reserve clothing on the other side. The general principle of heavier items on top will still apply. It is good practice to keep spare clothing and the sleeping bag in light polythene bags for driving rain can penetrate the smallest flaw in the canvas. Of course, if the sleeping bag is carried externally, it should be rolled neatly, placed in a waterproof container and tied below the sack to the pack frame. Above all, keep the load as compact as possible so that if you initially travel by train or coach your movements are not hindered by a load that is too wide or has protruding items tied externally that can snag on doors or handles. Such a load will present the same difficulty in the field when moving through brushwood or along overgrown paths.

Once you have satisfied yourself that you have achieved the best way of storing your gear in the sack, take note of the actual position of items and always pack them in the same order. In this way your equipment is easy to find – even in the dark.

Recent Developments in Outdoor Equipment

by Tony Pearson

The pace of development in outdoor equipment has accelerated enormously in recent years. The reasons for this growth are numerous and are obviously closely linked with the general growth of interest in outdoor activities. However, one common thread seems to run almost uninterrupted through development trends, linking the design progress of different types of gear – synthetic materials in all their complexity and variety. With the exception of stoves (where there seems to have been a marked lack of development) most of the main product groups; boots, sleeping bags, tents, and clothing have all been changed fantastically by their influence.

It probably started with the introduction of nylon for tents and waterproofs, but the scene changed rapidly as other materials were developed. Nylon has been joined by Cordura, Polyester, Gore-Tex, Entrant, Hollofill, Thinsulate and many, many more branded synthetic fabrics and fillings. Taking the different products in turn, it can be seen how the use of synthetics is at the heart of current design.

Boots

In 1983, boots were to the outdoor trade what videos were to home entertainment. The changes were so prolific that they have dominated two successive annual trade fairs, overshadowing all other product news. Having recovered from the first wave of synthetic fabric lightweights the market was turned on its head almost as quickly with secondary developments. But by early 1984, things began to calm down and four distinct and unique groups of boots are left to provide for your every possible need!

At the lightweight end of the scale are the fabric/suede constructions inspired largely by the Karrimor KSB3s (destined to become the most popular and shortest-lived boot of the '80s). These models combine natural and synthetic materials to create a very comfortable boot, but they offer only minimal water resistance and will rarely stand up to the harsh treatment inevitable on a trek or expedition. Some models have a waterproof but air permeable Gore-Tex liner, but in most cases this is stitched in place which creates leak points. At best it helps the boots to breath in warm weather and speeds up drying if they do get wet.

The successes and failures of these boots were quickly analysed and led to the introduction of new leather boots with many of the advantages developed on the original lightweight. The synthetic link is maintained by the successful inclusion of moulded nylon through soles which can be created with controlled flex properties and graded according to the size of boot. This is important since it means that a boot designed to give above average support on rough ground will do so no matter what size it is.

Most manufacturers, having learnt a great deal, are now returning to using leather and the new leather lightweights are generally well suited to light or rough walking in spring to autumn conditions. Their limitations are found when it is necessary to use crampons, since only the heaviest models are suitable.

The third group is formed by the traditional medium to heavy leather boots suitable for both walking and scrambling and winter crampon use with the exception of hard climbing. These have changed little and therefore do not fall under the heading of this article.

High mountain boots are the last group and here is one of the greatest successes of synthetics over natural fabrics. Plastic shelled models like the Koflach Ultra and Vivas have almost replaced the fully stiffened leather boot. They have the advantage of not absorbing water and consequently they don't freeze up. They are also lighter to start with than their leather equivalent. Don't be tempted by these boots however if your main interest is walking, their inherent stiffness will make them uncomfortable.

I couldn't leave the subject of boots without special mention of two products which are particularly impressive. The first is the Brasher boot designed by Chris Brasher of Olympic and Marathon fame. The significant qualities of this model are lightweight suppleness and surprising water resistance for such a light boot. They answer my prayers for soft but durable boots which can be worn for a long day in the hills, giving adequate security without the normal restriction I feel from heavier boots. I've even inadvertently driven home in them, having forgotten to change into lighter footwear! The second major boot development comes from Berghaus and combines a boot and gaiter to form a system which boasts the advantages of both a good boot and a Wellington. The system is called Trionic and the secret lies in a groove around the sole of the boot which is compatible with a bead on the inside edge of the separate gaiter's rubber round. The effect is superb, giving excellent flexibility of use for the relatively lightweight Trionic boot.

Rucksacks

In terms of synthetic fabrics, Cordura and other brands of texturized nylon are the order of the day for rucksacks. Cordura itself is an offshoot of bullet proof vest development. It is basically nylon but the fibres have been engineered to give them a coarse texture. The result is a woven fabric not unlike cotton canvas but it has better abrasion resistance, can be proofed like any other nylon and absorbs virtually no water – in short, it is the ideal rucksack fabric. Other changes in rucksack design tend to be concerned mainly with the carrying harness where adjustability is the current feature on designers' mind. All the major manufacturers now offer models which can be tailored to the individual after purchase. This concept tends to rely increasingly on moulded nylon components, maintaining the common thread of synthetics.

There is no doubt that modern rucksacks are exceptionally comfortable, but the obsession with adding extra features and, dare I say, gimmicks, is pushing up weight to ridiculous levels where the advantage of lightweight synthetic fabrics is lost. There is also a tendency to push out new models before all the teething problems have been ironed out, so do beware of 'totally new concepts'.

If you consider pack/frame systems to be more flexible for your purposes, then my advice is to buy immediately as they simply won't be around for much longer. Unfortunately, they don't fit into the modern rucksack 'image'. Whichever system takes your fancy, check the weight, check the fancy components and make sure that you're not unknowingly testing out a new concept at the expense of reliability.

Clothing

The totally synthetic clothing system for general backpacking or trekking is almost upon us, with the exception of a small cotton content in one or two garments and wollen socks. Consider, for example, this layered clothing system which has become my own personal choice within the last few years.

It starts with polypropelene underwear, Lifa by Helly Hansen, in warm weather and heavier warmer top and long johns by Mountain Equipment in the winter. This layer is topped by an all-nylon fibre-pile jacket, again Helly Hansen, and a pair of either polyester/cotton breeches (Rohan) or nylon/cotton trousers by Mountain Equipment. A polyester/cotton double jacket (Rohan) acts as windproof and multi-pocketed storage system and the whole assembly is then covered in really foul weather by a Gore-Tex nylon suit from Brasher. Add to this lot a pair of nylon outer/synthetic pile inner mitts and a Thermofleece synthetic balaclava and we're almost there. Socks are still basically wool, though with nylon added to increase their durability. Finally, my boots are currently leather, but their water resistance owes a great deal more to the skills of the chemist than to nature.

The advantages of this synthetic personal environment I create are largely connected with drying times, which are conveniently short, and weights, which are kept to a minimum. The disadvantages are the static buildup (which can be spectacular when undressing!) and the much quicker rate at which synthetic underwear becomes unsavoury. No doubt many people will leap to the defence of wool and cotton on reading this, but all tastes are subjective and my choice is based on experience of both natural and synthetic fabric clothing, and for me at least, technology wins hands down.

Look out in the shops for an absolute profusion of garments made from a fabric called fleece (the Americans call it bunting). This is destined to take over from fibre-pile as the number one fabric for what I call intermediate warmwear, that is, the layers between underwear and windproofs. Fleece is all-synthetic and has a rather tighter weave than fibre-pile, making it marginally more wind resistant. But don't be misled by talk of 'windproofing qualities' as this is gross exaggeration. It certainly has an attractive look and feel to it with its exceptionally soft texture and it wears a little like wool, going 'agreeably shaggy' in the words of Mountain Equipment. As to whether it is warmer than fibre-pile, the laboratories say it certainly is, my experience in the hills says that it isn't and so the argument will go on.

Sleeping Bags

To the casual observer, it would appear that very little is happening to the design of sleeping bags. They are still the same basic shape and the principle behind their function, of surrounding the sleeper with still, insulative air, remains unchanged. The changes that are occurring do so on the inside, between the fabric layers where they can't be seen, and that's a marketing department's dream, so watch out! Advertisements for sleeping bags are increasingly accompanied by graphs, laboratory test results, microscopic photography and all manner of mind boggling data. It's all geared to explaining the merits of whatever filling lies between the thin layers of fabric.

Superloft from ICI and Quallofil from Du Pont are the latest synthetic wonders and no doubt the graphs illustrate that they give marginally better insulation than their predecessors. The problem with synthetic sleeping bags – and this is where my pro-synthetic feelings change – is that they are still a long, long way from simulating the properties of down and feathers. They do admittedly have the advantages of easy cleaning, the ability to perform well in damp conditions and reduced intitial cost, but these plus points must be balanced against their extra weight and bulk and considerably shorter life span, qualities which I feel let them down badly for serious regular use or expedition work. Also, down-filled bags are increasingly available with waterproof Gore-Tex shell coverings which don't create condensation problems. This is an excellent example of combining natural and synthetic materials to the best advantage.

Tents

If synthetic is the key word relating to developments in outdoor equipment generally, 'flexible loops' are the pertinent words concerning tent design.

The availability of good quality and reliable flexible alloy poles has given tent designers a new incentive in the 1980s. Hoops, domes, tunnels and even 'Dunnels', dominate the tent catalogues with their excellent space to weight ratios. Inner walls rising almost vertically from the ground sheet curve gracefully to flattish roofs creating a much more usable living space than in ridge tents.

However the penalty for all this space is vulnerability in really wild weather. The flexible poles tend to distort uncomfortably in gusty winds, which is not conducive to sleep, and in extreme conditions, breakups are not uncommon. The Geodesic systems such as are employed by some Wintergear and Phoenix models show much more resistance to this movement but the cost is extra pole footage and consequently, extra weight.

Another innovation in tents is the use of Gore-Tex fabric. The fabric is waterproof but its millions of tiny pores can allow water molecules (vapour) to pass through, reducing problems of condensation. In practice, some condensation may still form and under very humid conditions, combined with relatively low temperatures, it can increase to unacceptable levels. Despite this, the single skin Gore-Tex models currently available are exceptionally light and very quick to pitch, factors which will obviously appeal to many people. Prices for these tents are high but durability is equal to any conventional nylon model.

Heavier base tents for expedition use do not seem to attract innovative design and the twin 'A' pole ridge design is still the one to recommend. The famous Vango Force Ten range remains practically unchanged and is still the firm favourite for most long term and group use.

If dome tents look more attractive because of the space they offer it is worth bearing in mind that their poles are definitely more vulnerable in bad weather and also more difficult to repair in an emergency. There are also fewer models available made from heavier fabrics for greater durability.

Stoves

Little progress seems to have been made in this area of equipment, largely because of prohibitively high initial production costs for new models. Optimus have settled for modifying their famous paraffin and petrol stoves by the addition of a triple fuel burner on several models. The benefits of using petrol, paraffin or even methylated spirits as available are obvious, but initial tests would suggest that performance is lost over the original single fuel models.

Probably the most significant development has been in the fuel rather than stoves. Epi Gas now produce their small resealable cartridges in a Butane/Propane mixture which will burn at much colder temperatures than conventional cartridges. This facility was previously only available by special arrangement with the manufacturers, but the move by Epi Gas should promote similar action by other cartridge suppliers in the future, making gas a suitable choice for cold weather expeditions.

General development trends in equipment are definitely towards higher technology and more sophisticated products and the rate of development is increasing. The whole outdoor equipment trade seems to be moving into a higher gear in response to the increase in leisure activity, with things changing so quickly that even retailers are finding it hard to keep pace. My advice to anyone purchasing new equipment today would be to go to a specialist supplier for sound advice and be cautious of frills and gimmicks – they have no useful place. Look for sound logical development based on proven equipment rather than totally new concepts which have a habit of showing their inadequacies at the most inconvenient times.

Survival Kits

by Eddie McGee

Survival: fighting to live when all help has gone.
A survivor: one who lives when others die.

I am fortunate enough to have travelled to almost every part of the world, both in a military capacity and as an explorer, and, more times than I care to remember, I have had to rely on my survival skills and techniques.

The best memories are of the times when I used the support of my improvised 'mini' survival kit: an assorted collection of bits and pieces stuffed into nothing larger than an everyday matchbox. The items mentioned are, of course, my own personal preference. It is important for *you* to be sure that you are capable of getting maximum use from each item in your kit, so choose carefully. If possible, pack things which can be used in more than one situation.

The Improvised 'Mini' Survival Kit

Before describing what should go into the kit, let me make a few general points about survival. And before you begin stuffing everything into the box, ask yourself the following questions:

How would I stand up to finding myself lost, cut off from civilization, with no one to talk to and no one to help me?

Would I be able to organize myself and keep myself alive until help arrived?

If help did not come, would I be able to improvise, catch food, take care of myself medically, travel and find directions safely?

The answers to these questions are very important. For example, catching food. You may think that this is easy, but it isn't. Rabbits don't simply walk into your cooking pot! First, they have to be caught, and trapping is a great skill. The best of traps and snares are ineffective if they have not been properly set and sited. And once caught, animals have to be skinned, cleaned and cooked. Do *you* know how to do these things correctly?

Basically there are two types of survival situation. One is when, for reasons beyond your control, you are suddenly stranded. The other is when, like many thousands of travellers and explorers, you put yourself into that situation to test your own ability. The latter is somewhat artificial in that if you feel it is getting beyond your limits you can walk away from it. It is a very different story if you are stranded against your will. At some point, it is almost certain that you will find yourself under pressure, and pressure in the unknown often leads to panic and fear. This happens to everyone who has had to endure survival stress, but if you can get your fear under control, there is no reason why you should become another statistic . . .

So – what is a survival kit? It is the means of helping you stay alive under extreme conditions, no matter where you are. Here are the contents of my own kit. The container is, as I have said, nothing more than a matchbox.

There are two types of box: cardboard and plastic (the type that hotels and nightclubs often have made for promotional purposes). The plastic one is better (as it is stronger), but whichever one you use, the contents remain the same.

The first thing to do with either type of box is waterproof the matches. This is simple. Hold a lighted candle over the part of the box where the matches go and melt a covering of wax into it; place the matches in the wax (head to toe) and cover them with another layer of wax. (The wax itself could come in handy later on.) While the wax is hot, seal in some more of your survival aids: half a dozen assorted fish hooks, needles and pins, at least two safety razor blades.

Now cut yourself two lengths of hacksaw blade; sharpen one on one side and grind the other to a point. These will slip easily down the side of the box and, clipped together, they make a superb pair of tweezers or skinning knives.

Get hold of a couple of sausage shaped (rather than round) balloons, or better still, rubber contraceptives, which are ten times more durable than balloons but equally light and compact. Either will, if filled correctly, hold water (a balloon takes a gallon very easily); it can make a good fire lighter if necessary; and it will, at a push, substitute as a torniquet, a fishing rod, or a bandage. Before you pack these, wrap lengths of fishing line and cotton around them.

A couple of Aspirins or Codeine can also be added now (leave them in their protective foil wrappers), along with a couple of Elastoplasts.

A snare wire is a very valuable piece of your survival kit. Choose the type that is made up of half a dozen strands of wire, available at most hardware stores, rather than the single strand type. Pack it with care.

Include a small piece of magnet. This can be used to make a simple survival compass if you don't have one of the very many small 'button' compasses on the market.

There should also be room for a plastic bag, about 15cm square, and a 15cm square of tin foil. A small reflector glass could also be added. Include a couple of carbide pills, the ones used by potholers: put into headlamps with a very small amount of water, the pills give off a very strong, inflammable gas which ignites when it comes into contact with a flame. On a cold, wet windy day, these can be invaluable for lighting a fire. Lastly, add a couple of birthday cake candles and a spare striker pad (from another matchbox) to your kit.

The box should now be full. Wrap some waterproof tape around the box to seal in all the items and to keep it dry.

You may find it hard to believe that all these things can be fitted into such a small space but they *will* if you pack them carefully. This is, after all, a very *basic* survival pack: it won't cover *all* your needs but it is small enough to carry around with you at all times. Keep it safely – some day it may save your life!

In a larger survival pack you can include many other items, e.g. torch, compass, whistle (see below).

Car Survival Pack

Putting together a car survival pack is not nearly as difficult as the matchbox kit. First, you have the luxury of somewhere to stow the pack and are no longer restricted by weight and bulk. Second, you have a much wider range of articles to choose from.

Food and Drink

Where possible, the food should be the sort that requires very little, if any, preparation. Dehydrated foods are fine but remember that more often than not, they require preparation and cooking and this can pose a problem if water is scarce. Also, many of the dehydrated foods, especially soups, tend to be a little salty and, if you are short of water, the last thing you want is a raging thirst.

Bars of chocolate, Mars Bars, glucose sweets – even fudge and toffee – are always good stand-bys. Pack at least six Oxo cubes and a dozen tea bags and coffee bags. If you have a sweet tooth, include some dried milk powder and a packet of saccharin. If you're going to make yourself a cup of tea or coffee, then do it in style!

If you are stranded, you must make every effort to find water as soon as possible; not only for drinking and cooking, but also for hygiene purposes and for your morale in general. Include in your pack a couple of good strong plastic bags which you can use as water containers.

To cook any dehydrated food, you will need some form of container (like a biscuit tin). This can also hold the rest of the survival pack.

You will need matches to start a fire but they must be of the windproof/waterproof type. Just in case, take along a spare cigarette lighter and a good quality magnifying glass. A fire at any time is a terrific morale booster.

Take a good supply of fishing gear, including assorted hooks, a couple of floats and plenty of line. If space is still available, stow an old fishing rod somewhere in the boot of your car.

Medicine and Hygiene

Keeping yourself clean and fresh is an important morale booster in a survival situation. So pack a spare packet of safety razor blades, a bar of soap, toothbrush, toothpaste and a brush or comb. And for drying, bandaging etc., a baby's nappy (an old soldier's trick, this): compact, easy to stow, soft and dry. Don't forget a packet of safety pins, a needle and cotton, a small pair of folding scissors and a pair of tweezers. None of these items should take up too much room if packed properly.

You will need enough medical supplies to get you through any *minor* ailment or injury. (*See section on Health, on page 342.*)

Safety and Rescue

Pack a torch with spare batteries and bulbs, a good solid whistle, a compass and a strong knife. The knife is of paramount importance. I prefer the rigid blade to the folding type, which tends to rust very easily and soon weakens and breaks. It can also be difficult and dangerous to use in very harsh conditions, especially when your hands are numb with cold! The rigid type is far more versatile and longer lasting.

My own knife is an ex-Army one. The blade is 30cms long, 5cms wide, and from blade to cutting edge tapers to 0.5cm thick. In my opinion, this is the minimum thickness for safety. If the knife is to be used as an axe, it is most important that the blade continues right through the handle. I have removed the manufacturer's handle from my knife and replaced it with string and cloth binding. This eliminates all shock through the handle when chopping hard woods. At one section on the back blade, I have added some saw cutting grooves as this makes the cutting of vines and rope much easier. The sheath is made of canvas, which is strong, durable, and easy to repair.

Small folding axes can make excellent aids to survival and can be used in place of the knife for some jobs. A folding shovel and pick can also be very useful. These are very light, robust and easily obtainable from any ex-Army store. Try to take along at least one hacksaw blade, even though you may already have a couple in your standard car tool kit.

Worth having is a device on the market called a 'screecher', an anti-mugging aid. It is a small aerosol canister which, when pressed, gives off a loud, piercing scream. The noise will chase off most wild animals and, of course, will let other people know where you are.

Take along some tough outer clothing, wrapped in a couple of plastic bags. Squeeze the air out and put two or three strong elastic bands around the tops of the bags. Stuff them well away inside the boot, where they will stay dry and reasonably fit for use.

I have talked so far about a survival pack to put *into* your car. But remember – the car itself is a mobile survival aid, protecting you from the weather and serving, to all intents and purposes, as your home if you are stranded. Keep the car out in the open where possible so that rescuers can identify its shape and colour. In hot regions, the car's shadow can offer shelter from the heat of the sun. It is not *always* advisable to remain inside the car for protection. If, for instance, the temperature drops well below zero at night, it may be safer and warmer to spend the night in a snow hole or Igloo (which is where your protective clothing comes in).

Basic Rules

First, stay with your car as long as you can. Second, stay calm, think logically, and above all, try not to panic. Arrange your thoughts under these headings: inspection (yourself and equipment), protection (shelter), location (where you think you are), signals (warning signs to help rescuers). If you think help is coming, try to imagine what the rescuers are looking for. Help them all you can. Call out, wave, make a noise. (Marker panels, fluorescent strips of cloth used to attract rescuers, can be placed on the ground, draped over a bush or your car.) If you use a fire to attract attention, remember: black smoke for snow conditions (use rubber hoses, old shoes, Wellingtons, etc.), white smoke for forest or moors (use bracken, leaves, grass, etc.). Have the fire ready to light. During the night, try to reflect the fire's glow in the direction from which you think help may be coming. Consider the following when setting up your markers: shape, shine, shadows, silhouette, space, movement, noise and smells.

Apart from the tools and clothing, there is no reason why all of the items I have listed should not pack away into a box no larger than an average-sized shoe box. Just before you close the lid, remember to include some toilet paper, writing paper and a pencil.

Food and Water: Better Safe than Sorry

by Ingrid Cranfield

The following notes are for travellers who intend to get their supplies along the way, from shops, hotels or restaurants. Wilderness backpackers who buy food in advance and carry with them much of what they need for the duration of their trip should turn to *Food on the Move* on page 335.

Canned, powdered and dried foods are usually safe to eat, although, because they are often imported, they are more expensive than at home, especially so outside the major cities. Staples such as flour and cooking oils are nearly always safe.

Fresh Foods

Meat, poultry, fish and shellfish should look and smell fresh and be thoroughly cooked, though not overcooked, as soon as possible after purchase. They should be eaten while still hot or kept continuously refrigerated after preparation. Clean fish yourself if possible. Eggs are safe enough if reasonably fresh. Milk may harbour disease-producing organisms (tuberculosis, brucellosis). The 'pasteurised' label in underdeveloped countries should not be depended upon. For safety, if not ideal taste, boil the milk before drinking. (Canned or powdered milk may generally be used without boiling for drinking or in cooking). Butter and margarine are safe unless obviously rancid. Margarine's keeping qualities are better than those of butter. Cheese, especially hard and semi-hard varieties and aged cheeses with a rind, is normally quite safe; soft cheese is not so reliable.

Vegetables for cooking are safe if boiled for a short time. See that on vegetables for peeling and fruits with a peel, the peel is intact. Wash them thoroughly and peel them yourself if you plan to eat them raw.

Moist or creamy pastries should not be eaten unless they have been continuously refrigerated. Dry baked goods, such as bread and cakes, are usually safe even without refrigeration.

Always look for food that is as fresh as possible. If you can watch livestock being killed and cooked or any other food being prepared before you eat it, so much the better. Don't be deceived by plush surroundings and glib assurances. Often the large restaurant with its questionable standards of hygiene and practice of cooking food ahead of time is a less safe bet than the wayside vendor from whom you can take food cooked on an open fire, without giving flies or another person the chance to recontaminate it. Before preparing bought food, always wash your hands in water that has been chlorinated or otherwise purified (see below).

In restaurants, well-cooked meat, fish, poultry, vegetables and eggs, cheese, unpeeled raw fruit, coffee, tea and bread are nearly always safe; so are fruit drinks if the fruit is pressed in front of you.

In the tropics, avoid steak tartare and other raw meats which carry a risk of tapeworm.

Protect freshly bought meat from flies and insects with a muslin cover. Meat that is just 'on the turn' can sometimes be saved by washing it in strong salty water. If this removes the glistening appearance and sickly sweet smell, the meat is probably then safe to eat.

Cold foods, especially those that can't be peeled, such as salads, are a risk, as are any foods that have been left standing for some time after cooking, when they will be a breeding ground for microbes. Ice cream especially is to be avoided in underdeveloped countries. There too, preservatives may have been added to rice and other grains and pulses, and need to be removed by thorough washing as they are indigestible.

Water

Assume all water is unsafe for drinking unless you are perfectly sure it is otherwise. You have no natural immunity to local diseases carried in tap water: dysentery, typhoid and cholera among them. Hotels, and restaurants, and even foreign airlines almost all use ordinary local water which could be contaminated, however much the owners and staff tell you otherwise. If it is hot enough to make you withdraw your hand, it is *probably* safe.

Water from streams, lakes and other untreated sources should be assumed unfit to drink except in high mountain areas where there is no habitation upstream – but then glacial mud or mica in alpine rivers is especially irritating to the gut.

In desert and semi-arid areas, you may commonly find sulphurous streams which have water which is unpleasant to taste but not harmful, and rarely find arsenical springs, which are the reverse! Sea water is undrinkable unless distilled, but perfectly all right for cooking. Be careful of sea water near very built-up or industrial areas, however, as sewage and industrial pollution are creating real danger of poisoning.

You can purify water for drinking by boiling it vigorously for at least ten minutes or by using water purification tablets, solutions or filters. Boiling kills most organisms, including amoeba cysts and infectious hepatitis virus. Chemical treatment can be less effective than boiling, takes longer and leaves an aftertaste, but in hot climates where a high fluid intake is mandatory, purifying tablets may be the only practical way of treating water while on the move. Take an adequate supply.

Pharmacists can usually supply tablets that purify with chlorine such as Puritabs (UK) or Halazone (USA), or those that release iodine, such as Potable-Aqua (UK), or Globaline (USA).

Tincture of iodine is just as effective as iodine tablets, though troublesome to use. Add one drop to a glass of water, swill the mixture around to wet all surfaces you may touch with your lips and leave it to stand for twenty minutes, and this will render the water safe for drinking. (Strain first and double the dosage for cloudy water.) For very long term use, or if pregnant, avoid iodine which can cause a temporary, if harmless, enlargement of the thyroid gland.

Another method is to add two drops per quart of ordinary bleach

(5.25 per cent solution of hypochlorite) to clear water (twice as much for cloudy water), agitate and leave it to stand for 30 minutes.

Recent rapid advances in technology have produced water purifying devices which have carbon filters to get rid of suspended organic matter and a chemical filter for the viruses. Devices such as the Katadyn Pocket Filter and the Survival Straw are well worth investigating (*see list in Equipment section on page 631*).

Tea and coffee made from boiled water are fine. Alcohol does not sterilize water for drinking, though undiluted alcoholic beverages such as wine and beer are normally safe.

Water in the form of carbonated bottled drinks is usually safe, if bottled, diluted or transferred to other containers in large reliable plants. Open them yourself or have them opened in front of you. Even this isn't a foolproof guarantee, because unscrupulous vendors have been known to water such drinks as Coca-Cola and sell them in resealed bottles. If this story makes you nervous . . . don't even buy carbonated drinks in a Third World country. Uncarbonated drinks can be dangerous, as the sugar content permits rapid multiplication of bacteria. Don't buy drinks from a jug.

Ice is no safer than the water from which it is made. Do not boil mineralized water as the taste is unpleasant and the process may only concentrate dangerous minerals. Once purified, water remains safe indefinitely as long as there is no chance for recontamination from the outside.

For brushing your teeth, use water that has been made safe or some carbonated drink. For washing and bathing, tap water is usually sufficiently safe.

Hookworms, leeches and snail-borne parasites picked up from water or moist ground may cause a variety of other ills from the mild to the rather serious (*see section on Health on page 342*). Leeches can be removed by touching them with a lighted cigarette or match. Don't pull them off, as this will only increase the likelihood of infection.

Last word: Take reasonable care, but don't get hysterical about precautions with food and water. Expecting to stay healthy is half the battle: and your vaccinations will make strong allies.

Food on the Move

by Mary Schantz

'Good food even makes up for rain and hard beds. Good fellowship is at its best around good meals.' Whoever said this so aptly really said a mouthful. Wholesome, mouthwatering food and plenty of it, can make even the worst camping conditions more bearable. But no matter how fantastic the scenery, soft the beds or fine the weather, the enjoyment of any outing wanes quickly when the food is lousy. The problem is: How do you insure you'll have good food on your trip off the beaten track?

There is no one 'right' menu for a camping trip. We all have slightly different tastes in food. Besides, there is an almost endless number of menu possibilities, the choice is yours. So, what should you pack? Here are a few points you'll want to consider when choosing the right foods for you: *weight, bulk, cost per kg*. Obviously, water-weighted, tinplated canned foods are out. So are most perishables. Especially if you are going to be lugging your pantry on your back, you'll want only lightweight, longlasting, compact foods. Some of the lightest, of course, are the freeze-drieds. You can buy complete freeze-dried meals – just add boiling water and wait five minutes. Most are that easy to prepare. They have their drawbacks, however. First, they're mighty expensive. Second, even if you like these pre-packaged offerings, and many people don't, you can get tired of them very quickly. I find that a much more exciting and economical alternative is to buy dry or dehydrated foods at the supermarket and combine them to create your own imaginative dinners. Dried beans, cereals, instant potato, meat bars, crackers, dry soup mixes, cocoa, pudding, gingerbread and instant cheesecake mixes are just a few of the possibilities, But don't forget to pack a few spices to make your creations possible – chilli, curry, garlic and onion powder, Italian seasoning, cinnamon, salt, pepper and whatever else you fancy.

Nutritional Value

Because hiking, biking, canoeing and wilderness camping are pretty strenuous activities, you'll need to fuel yourself with plenty of high energy foods (around 3,000 calories/day in summer and more in winter).

Fat contains more than twice as much energy per kg as proteins and carbohydrates do. So include plenty of hard cheese and margarine (both of which will last for weeks if kept out of the sun), and foods like nuts and peanut butter that stick to your ribs. Powdered milk and eggs are great lightweight sources of complete protein that can be added to almost anything you make and will help balance any meal. Dried fruits, pasta, rice and flour are good high carbohydrate fuel foods, as are the quick energy fruit drinks and sugar snacks. If you're worried about vitamins and minerals, pack vitamin pills. And drink high-in-C fruit drinks.

Quantity

Most people tend to work up a big appetite outdoors. About 0.9 to 1.2kg of food per person per day is average. How much of which foods will make up that weight is up to you. You can guess pretty accurately about how much macaroni or cheese or how many pudding mixes you are likely to need.

Unless you are a fantastic angler, don't count on fish to supplement your diet. And unless you're well versed in an area's flora, don't count on eating nature's salads. Except for the common berries or easily identifiable greens, why risk stomach aches, indigestion, or the effects of more serious poisoning?

Palatability

Last but not least, what do you like? If you don't care for instant butterscotch pudding or freeze-dried stew, don't take it along. You'll probably like it even less after two days on the trail. And if you've never tried something before, don't take the chance. Do your experimenting beforehand. Don't shock your digestive system with a lot of strange or different new foods. Stick as closely as possible to what you're used to in order to avoid stomach upsets and indigestion. And make sure you pack a wide enough variety of foods to ensure that you won't be subjected to five oatmeal breakfasts in a row or be locked into an inflexible menu plan.

Packaging Your Food

After purchasing your food, the next step is to repackage it. Except for freeze-dried meals or other specially sealed foods, it's a good idea to store supplies and spices in small plastic freezer bags. Just pour in your pancake mix, salt or gingerbread mix, drop an identifying label in if you want to take all the guesswork (and fun) out of it, and tie a loose knot. Double-bag when in doubt.

Taking plastic into the wilderness may offend one's inner sensibilities but, believe me, it works well. On a month-long expedition recently into the rainy south-east of Alaska, I learned just how handy these lightweight, flexible, recyclable, *moistureproof* bags really are.

Preparing Great Meals

Although cooking over an open fire is great fun, many areas don't allow and can't support campfires. So don't head off without a stove. When choosing the stove that's right for your needs, keep in mind that size, weight and *reliability* become more of a concern, the further off the beaten track track you go.

Aside from a stove, you'll also need plenty of matches, a collapsible water jug, purification tablets, a nesting set of aluminium pots, a non-stick frying pan with cover, a few knives, pot grips or holders, a scrubbing pad, and a heavy bag in which to store your soot-bottomed pans. You'll also need individual eating utensils: spoon, cup and bowl will do.

Also take a few recipes with you, or learn them before you leave. You can even have such luxuries as fresh-baked bread if you are prepared to make the effort.

Some things I've learned about camp cooking – the hard way:

1. Cook on low heat to avoid scorching.
2. Taste before salting – bouillon cubes and powdered bases, often added to camp casseroles, are very salty. Don't overdo it by adding more!
3. Add rice, pasta, etc. to boiling water – not to cold – to avoid sticky or slimy texture.
4. Add freeze-dried or dehydrated foods (onion flakes, freeze-dried corn etc.) early on in your recipes to allow time for rehydration.
5. Add powdered milk and eggs, cheese and thickeners (flour, wheat germ etc.) to recipes last when heating.
6. When melting snow for water, don't let the bottom of the pan go dry or it will scorch. Keep packing the snow down to the bottom.
7. Add extra water at high altitudes when boiling. Water evaporates more rapidly as the boiling point drops.

Cleaning Up

Soap residue can make you sick. Most seasoned campers, after one experience with 'soap sickness of the stomach', recommend using only a scouring pad and water when it comes time for the clean-up. Boiling water can be used to sterilize and is good for removing the remains of your glued-on pasta or cheese dinners. Soak and then scrub.

Use those recyclable pastic bags to store leftovers and to carry out any litter. Leave the wilderness kitchen clean – and ready for your next feat of mealtime magic!

Shopping List

Here's a sample list of lightweight, inexpensive, versatile, easily packable, mostly non-perishable foods to feed four or five for two weeks off the beaten track:

Food, in kg:

1.8 macaroni
1.4 noodles
1 rice
1 spaghetti
0.5 pearl barley
0.5 navy beans
0.5 split peas
0.25 wheatgerm
2.25 whole grain flour
1 cornmeal
1 potato flakes
0.5 green beans (freeze-dried)
0.5 onion flakes
0.25 corn (freeze-dried)
0.25 peas (freeze-dried)
0.25 carrots (freeze-dried)
2.25 raisins
1 prunes
0.5 apricots (dried)
0.5 apple (dried)
0.5 mixed fruit (dried)
1 tomato base powder
0.25 beef base powder
1.8 soup mixes
0.5 bacon bits (vegetable protein)
2.25 meat bars
2.25 peanut butter
2.25 peanuts
0.5 sunflower seeds
1 walnuts
0.25 coconut
0.25 popcorn
4.5 margarine
2.25 powdered milk
0.5 powdered eggs
4.5 hard cheddar cheese
2.25 cheese or plain crackers
3.6 brown sugar
2.25 cocoa
2.25 honey
0.25 tea
0.5 instant coffee
2.25 fruit drink crystals
0.5 jelly mix
0.5 pudding mix
0.75 gingerbread mix
0.5 instant cheesecake mix
1 chocolate slabs or drops

Spices, in grams:

450 salt
60 pepper
30 oregano
30 onion powder
30 garlic powder
15 curry powder
15 chilli powder
15 dry mustard
7 basil
100 cinnamon
7 ginger
7 nutmeg
100 baking powder
60 baking soda
60 vanilla
7 yeast

This list is a suggestion. If you choose to use it, be sure to tailor it to your tastes. In other words, if you want powdered scrambled eggs and bacon bits for breakfast every morning, you're going to need more of both. And less oatmeal!

A Basic Guide to Health

Getting Organized

by Drs Peter Steele and John Frankland

The unprepared and the unwary are those for whom expeditions abroad can end in misery and expense. You are off on the trip of a lifetime. If you are a wise traveller you prepare documents, check equipment and carry spares in case of emergency. It is logical to take as much care of your health for if this lets you down you may be throwing away a great experience and risking huge costs. At least one member of the party and preferably all would profit from a formal course in first aid as organized by the St John Ambulance or Red Cross. Much of this can be forgotten again but the basic principles are essential, as is the ability to improvise, since accidents never happen in close proximity to your first aid supplies.

Preparations

Beside your travel documents, do not forget:

1. Form E.111 or your medical insurance policy. If you are taking any medicines or drugs regularly, take an adequate supply with the dosage and *pharmacological* name marked on the bottle since proprietary names vary from country to country. If you have any current or past significant illness, get medical advice on how sensible an undertaking your trip represents. Advice on how any relapses or complications might be handled and whether any particular drugs are available for these should also be sought.
2. Personal medical information which can be imprinted on a bracelet or medallion; blood group, allergies, diabetic or steroid treatment dosage, recurring illnesses and continuous medication. This is safer than a card carried in the pocket and may be life-saving in an emergency.
3. A doctor's letter setting out any special medical problems, with translations into appropriate languages. If you are taking large amounts of medication with you, this should also be mentioned, so that it can be shown at customs if necessary.
4. Spare spectacles and your lens prescription.

Tooth fillings tend to loosen in the cold, so a dental check-up may save agony later. If you suspect piles, seek an examination. Feet should be in good shape as much may be expected of them.

If you are not in the peak of condition, build up your fitness with regular graded activity over some months before departure and seek medical advice if this brings on any health problems.

Insurance – British Travellers

Falling ill abroad can be very expensive. The European Economic Community will allow eligible citizens of any member country to get *urgent* treatment free, or at a reduced cost, during temporary stays. Continuing treatment for a pre-existing illness, e.g. asthma, high blood pressure, etc. may not fall within the definition of 'urgent' treatment and may not attract these benefits. Also these arrangements do not apply if you are working or living in another EEC country. In these circumstances you should write to the DHSS Overseas Branch at Newcastle-upon-Tyne, NE98 1YX, seeking information on your rights to health care in the other country.

Not all are eligible for urgent treatment, this being determined by your current or previous National Insurance contribution status. The self-employed and the unemployed may find themselves ineligible. The current position is that somebody who is insured as self-employed, if he *has been employed* at some time, is eligible and will continue to be so after retirement. Any person who has been self-employed for the whole of his working life is ineligible, even though every due National Insurance contribution may have been paid. Discriminatory, but true. Students also beware.

Even in some EEC countries (e.g. France, Belgium and Luxembourg) you will be covered for approximately 70 per cent of treatment only and the remainder may be costly. You may also have to pay the full cost initially and then claim back the 70 per cent share. For these reasons, travellers should consider taking out private insurance to cover the part of the cost they may have to meet themselves. See the DHSS leaflet SA.36, *How to Get Treatment in Other EEC Countries*.

Outside the EEC, some countries offer emergency care either free or for a part fee only. This concession may apply only in public hospitals and not in private clinics and it is often necessary to show your National Health Service medical card as well as your UK passport. The following countries offer reduced rate or free medical care (subject to certain provisos) for UK citizens: Austria, Bulgaria, Channel Islands, Czechoslovakia, Finland, East Germany, Hungary, Malta, New Zealand, Norway, Poland, Portugal, Romania, Sweden, USSR and Yugoslavia.

To get full details, obtain leaflet SA.28/30, *Medical Treatment During Visits Abroad* at your local DHSS office. If you are then travelling through EEC countries, complete form CM1 at the back of this leaflet and return it to your local DHSS office as soon as you know the dates of your visit, but not more than six months before you plan to leave. You will be sent form E.111 which you must then carry with your passport to be eligible for benefit in all EEC countries (except Denmark, Gibraltar, and the Irish Republic which do not require form E.111).

Elsewhere the cost of consultation, medicines, treatment and hospital care must be paid by the patient. As this could be financially crippling, full health insurance is a wise precaution (*see Travel Insurance on page 281*). In America, if you are taken gravely ill or appreciably injured, the final medical account may seem astronomic – American doctors really earn big money. Discuss with your travel agent the adequacy of your cover should high technology care be needed.

If you incur medical expenses, present your policy to the doctor and ask him to send the bill direct to your insurance company. Many doctors will demand cash and the level of their fees may alarm you. Keep a reserve of traveller's cheques for this purpose, insist on a receipt and the insurance company will reimburse you on return.

Do not expect the medical standards of your home country in your wanderings. Some practitioners include expensive drugs routinely for the simplest of conditions and multivitamin therapy, intravenous injections and the inevitable suppositories may be given unnecessarily to run up a bigger bill. Be prepared to barter diplomatically about this, to offer those drugs you are carrying for treatment if appropriate and even to shop around for medical advice.

Insurance – American Travellers

Travel protection plans offered by travel agencies or insurance companies do not normally include sickness insurance in the States. On the other hand, domestic group or individual health policies uually cover the holder outside the United States.

Blue Cross and Blue Shield plans give some protection to travellers in the form of reimbursement on their return to the USA, though medical expenses must be met initially as they arise. Medicare does not give coverage outside the USA and its possessions, but people who are eligible for it may take advantage of a special extra programme offered by Blue Cross and Blue Shield which *does* cover them outside the country.

Travel health insurance policies do not typically cover previously existing illnesses which arose within a given prior period of time (sometimes as much as a year) nor such conditions as pregnancy, childbirth, miscarriage, abortion, nervous or mental disorders, dental treatment or cosmetic surgery.

Even with adequate health insurance, the traveller is very likely to have to pay for any treatment received abroad at the time and direct to the institution or practitioner involved. Occasionally, a foreign hospital may permit a traveller to pay on his return home. Travellers must keep receipts for presentation to the insurance company which is to reimburse them.

In some countries, American visitors are eligible for free or reduced rate treatment. In the UK, Denmark and New Zealand, where there are free health or accident programmes, Americans are entitled to the same benefits as citizens of those countries. Elsewhere, e.g. in Yugoslavia, health care may be free to its citizens but not to American tourists. In the USSR, a doctor's visit is free, but patients must pay for any medication or hospital treatment. In other countries, e.g. the Netherlands, people with insufficient funds may be excused payment.

Immunization

Immunization can protect you from certain infectious diseases that are common in countries abroad but rare at home. Your local District Community Physician's Department (UK) or Public Health Service Office (USA) will advise you on the inoculations necessary for a particular country you may wish to visit and how to obtain them, either at a clinic or through your family doctor. Do not leave it to the last moment as a full course can take up to three months.

Immunization is not obligatory in Europe or North America, but it is wise to be protected as follows:

1. Typhoid, paratyphoid A & B and tetanus (TABT). Two injections are given one month apart. An unpleasant reaction, with a sore arm and headache, is not uncommon, and you must avoid alcohol for 24 hours. After a wound from a dirty object or an animal bite, you should obtain a booster dose of tetanus toxoid. Full protection against tetanus is essential to anyone roughing it in the tropics where this nasty illness is more prevalent.

2. Cholera, yellow fever and smallpox. World Health Organization certificates of vaccination against these three diseases exist and you may need to show them to gain access to certain countries. No documentary evidence of other immunizations is needed, but this does not mean they should be ignored.

In 1979, the World Health Organization declared the world free of *smallpox* after two years had elapsed since the last reported case despite meticulous surveillance. Since then the only need for smallpox vaccinations has been to satisfy frontier bureaucrats in developing countries, who have been subject to pressures to withdraw this requirement. In fact, there are now very few countries who still require the vaccination, but check with the embassy before you go.

Cholera certificates are still definitely needed to cross many frontiers – two injections a minimum of ten days apart. This injection can be combined with TAB (TAB Chol). The certificate is valid for six months only, so on a long journey have the injections just before you go.

Yellow fever immunization is needed for Central and South America and Central Africa and for travellers in other countries who have journeyed through or come from these areas. In the UK this can be given only in designated centres (address from your local Community Physician); all other immunizations can be done by your General Practitioner. A single injection is necessary. There are no reactions and the certificate is valid for a period of ten years.

If a smallpox vaccination is also needed, get the yellow fever injection first and the smallpox can be given a week later – if you do it the other way round there has to be a three-week interval between the two.

Most people will have had childhood immunization against *diphtheria, polio* and *tuberculosis* (BCG). However, these last two can be real hazards in developing countries, especially off the tourist track, so check your immunization status and consider a poliomyelitis booster dose. Most countries do not make immunization an entry requirement.

The polio vaccine is given by mouth. Even in parts of Europe and around the Mediterranean, polio cases are not infrequent. Protection is very well worth having, as polio can kill or paralyse and is irreversible.

Three months should be allowed for a full course of immunization, but in an emergency, a 'crash course' of smallpox, TABT, yellow fever (and cholera) can be given in fifteen days.

(*For information on protection against malaria, see article on page 359.*)

3. Infectious hepatitis (jaundice) is a real hazard to travellers through areas without or with primitive sewage systems. Perhaps more return with this ailment that with all the exotic diseases. An injection of 750mgm of human gamma globulin gives reasonably effective passive immunity for six months against the commonest strain and is highly recommended. In the UK this has been available free on the NHS to all at-risk travellers since 1976.

Where vaccines are contra-indicated for a particular patient, this should be noted on his International Certificate and he would be wise to secure written permission to enter a country without the relevant vaccination, from its consulate.

For any further information on mandatory and recommended vaccinations, consult leaflet SA.35, (*Health Protection*) from the DHSS and some travel agents. This also lists cities with vaccination centres.

On Your Return

On returning from a long trip most travellers will experience some euphoria and elation as family reunions occur and interested friends want to hear all about their adventures. After this, as relaxation and perhaps jet lag set in, a period of apathy, exhaustion and weariness can follow. Recognize this and allow a few quiet days if it is feasible. There are usually many pressures at this stage especially if equipment is to be unpacked and sorted out, photographs processed, sponsors need thanking. Another pressure, for most people, is the none too welcome thought of returning to the mundane chores involved in earning one's daily bread.

If your travels have been challenging, then a couple of recovery days will probably make you work more efficiently thereafter and cope more expeditiously with the thousand tasks which seem to need urgent attention.

After a time of excitement and adventure, some will go through a period of being restless and bored with the simple routine of home and work. They may not be aware of this temporary change in personality but their families certainly will be. Having pointed out this problem, we cannot suggest any way of overcoming it except perhaps to recommend that everyone concerned try to recognize it and be a little more tolerant than normal. This may not be a sensible time to take major decisions affecting career, family and business.

Some people will be relieved to arrive in their hygienic home after wandering in areas containing some of the world's nastiest diseases. Unfortunately, the risk of ill health is not altogether gone, for you may still be incubating an illness acquired abroad – perhaps for a few months e.g. hepatitis, or, at the extreme, for a few years with rabies.

After your return any medical symptoms or even just a feeling of debility or chronic ill health must not be ignored – medical help should be sought. Tell your physician carefully where you have travelled, even including brief aeroplane stopovers. It may be that you are carrying some illness outside the spectrum that he normally has to consider. Sadly this has been known to cause mistaken diagnoses so that malaria has been labelled as influenza with occasionally fatal consequences. Tropical worms and other parasites, enteric fevers, typhus, histoplasmosis (a fungus disease breathed in on guano, so cavers are especially at risk), tuberculosis, tropical virus diseases, amoebic dysentry and hepatitis may all need to be excluded and for this to be done efficiently, many patients will need the special expertise of a Tropical Diseases Unit. Some doctors may not consider this referral but if you feel appreciably ill and a clear diagnosis is not rapidly forthcoming, then it is sensible to request diplomatically that your doctor refer you to a unit with experience in tropical diseases.

Human nature being as it is, some will arrive home with venereal disease, which is much more prevalent in some developing countries than in the UK. If you have been at risk of acquiring this, a visit to the Special Clinic (VD Clinic) at any hospital is sensible. No appointment or referral from a general practitioner is necessary.

After leaving malarial areas, many will feel less motivated to continue their anti-malarial drugs. It is strongly recommended that these be taken for a full 28 days after leaving the endemic area. Failing to do this has caused many, much to their surprise, to develop malaria some weeks after they thought they were totally safe. This is more than a nuisance – it has occasionally caused deaths.

Fortunately the majority of travellers return home with nothing other than pleasant memories of an enjoyable interlude in the lives.

Travel Stress

by Hilary Bradt

The scene is familiar; a crowded bus station in some third world country; passengers push and shove excitedly. An angry discordant voice rings out: 'But I've got a reserved seat! Look, it says number 18, but there's someone sitting there!' The foreigner may or may not win this battle, but ultimately he will lose the war between 'what should be' (his expectations) and 'what is' (their culture), and become yet another victim of stress.

It is ironic that this complaint, so fashionable among businessmen, should be such a problem for many travellers who thought they had escaped such pressures when they left their home country. But by travelling rough, they are immediately immersing themselves in a different culture and thus subjecting themselves to a new set of psychological stresses.

The physical deprivations that are inherent in budget travel are not usually a problem: most travellers adjust well enough to having a shower every two months, eating beans and rice every day and sleeping in dirty, lumpy beds in company with the local insect life. These are part of the certainties of this mode of travel. It's the uncertainties that wear people down; the buses that double-book their seats, usually leave an hour or so late, but occasionally slip away early; the landslide that blocks the road to the coast on the one day of the month that a boat leaves for Paradise Island; the inevitable *mañana* response; the struggle with a foreign language and foreign attitudes.

Culture Shock

It's this 'foreignness' which often comes as an unexpected shock. The people are different, their customs are different, and so are their basic values and moralities. Irritatingly, these differences are most frequently exhibited by those who amble down the Third World Corridors of Power, controlling the fate of travellers, but ordinary people are different too. Believers in Universal Brotherhood often find this hard to accept, as do women travelling alone. Many travellers escape back to their own culture periodically by mixing with the upper classes of the countries in which they are travelling – people who were educated in Europe or America and are westernized in their outlook. Come to think of it, maybe this is why hitch-hikers show so few signs of travel stress – they meet wealthier car owners and can often lapse into a childlike dependence on their hosts.

Fear and Anxiety

At least hitch-hikers can alternate between blissful relaxation and sheer terror, as can other adventurous travellers. Fear, in small doses, never did anyone harm. It seems a necessary ingredient to everyday life; consciously or unconsciously, most people seek out danger. If they don't go rock climbing or parachute jumping, they drive too fast, refuse to give up smoking, or resign from their safe jobs to travel the world. The stab of fear that travellers experience as they traverse a glacier, eye a gun-toting soldier or approach a 'difficult' border is followed by a feeling of exhilaration once the perceived danger has passed. A rush of adrenalin is OK; the hazard is the prolonged state of tension or stress, to which the body reacts in a variety of ways: irritability, headaches, inability to sleep at night and a continuous feeling of anxiety.

The budget traveller is particularly at risk because shortage of money provokes so many additional anxieties to the cultural stresses mentioned earlier. The day-to-day worry of running out of money is an obvious one, but there is also the fear of being robbed (no money to replace stolen items) and of becoming ill. Many travellers worry about their health anyway, but those who can't afford a doctor, let alone a stay in hospital, can become quite obsessional. Yet these are the people who travel in a manner most likely to jeopardize their health. Since their plan is often 'to travel until the money runs out', those diseases with a long incubation period, such as hepatitis, will manifest themselves during the trip. Chronic illnesses like amoebic dysentery undermine the health and well-being of many budget travellers, leaving them far more susceptible to psychological pressures.

Even the open-endedness of their journey may cause anxiety.

Tranquillizers

Now I've convinced you that half the world's travellers are heading for a nervous breakdown rather than the nearest beach, let's see what can be done to ease the situation (apart from bringing more money).

There are tranquillizers. This is how most doctors treat the symptoms of stress since they assume that the problems causing the anxiety are an unavoidable part of everyday life. Travellers should not rule them out (I've met people who consume Valium and marijuana – another effective tranquillizer – until they scarcely know who they are), but since they have chosen to be in their situation, it should be possible to eliminate some of the reasons.

They can begin by asking themselves why they decided to travel in the first place. If it was 'to get away from it all' then journeying for long distances seems a bit pointless; better to hole up in a small village or island and begin the lotus-eating life. If the motive for travel is a keen interest in natural history, archaeology or people, then the problems inherent in getting to their destination are usually overridden in the excitement of arriving. However, those who find the lets and hindrances that stand between them and their goal too nerve-wracking – and the more enthusiastic they are, the more frustrated they'll become – should consider relaxing their budget in favour of spending more money on transportation etc., even if it does mean a shorter trip.

The average overlander, however, considers the journey the object. He will probably find that time on the road will gradually eliminate his anxieties. Like a young man I met in Ecuador. He was forever thinking about his money situation, but when I met him again in Bolivia, he was a changed man, relaxed and happy.

'Well,' he said, in answer to my question, 'You remember I was always worrying about running out of money? Now I have, so I have nothing to worry about!'

If a traveller can learn the language and appreciate the differences between the countries he visits and his own, he will come a long way towards understanding and finally accepting them. Then his tensions and frustrations will finally disappear.

But travellers should not expect too much of themselves. You are what you are, and a few months of travel are not going to undo the conditioning of your formative years. Know yourself, your strengths and weaknesses, and plan your trip accordingly. And if you don't know yourself at the start of a long journey, you will by the end.

Sun and Snow: Illness and the Elements

by Drs Peter Steele and John Frankland

For travellers from temperate countries, one of the greatest problems they have to face is the dramatic difference in climatic conditions. No matter how often you tell yourself it is going to be hot, nothing can prepare you for the way it will hit you in the Sahara or the equatorial jungle.

Sun

The sun can be a stealthy enemy. Sunlight reflects strongly off snow and light coloured rocks; its rays penetrate hazy cloud and are more powerful the higher you climb. Until you have a good tan, protect yourself with clothing and a hat. An ultraviolet barrier cream screens the skin, but with excessive sun it merely acts as fat in the frying process. Rationing sunlight is cheaper and more effective.

If you are planning to travel in hot weather, train for it by exercising in the heat beforehand and/or spending a few sessions in a sauna bath. This way your body will learn to perspire at lower temperatures and the network of capillaries in the skin will increase so that more blood can travel to the skin. Enzymes in the body will also change, allowing you to make more physical effort while producing less heat. On the trail, stop frequently to rest, drink and eat before you need to so as to replace all the salts necessary to prevent cramps and weakness. Salt tablets, part of the White Raj in a pith helmet image, are needed less than most imagine. In the tropics most people will produce almost salt-free perspiration after acclimatization, especially if conditioning is gone through, and generous salt supplements on food will keep a satisfactory salt level in the blood. In the first week of exertion in the heat it may be reasonable to offer them, but after this it is generally not necessary. However, some will feel better if they take them and it is perhaps unfair to deny them this probably placebo response.

Sunburn: Calamine soothes shrimp-pink prickly-hot skin; if you turn bright lobster you are severely burnt and should obtain a steroid cream.

Heat exhaustion and heatstroke ('sunstroke'): If you develop a high temperature and feel ill after being in strong sun, cool yourself with cold water sponging or ice packs, take ample fluid, drink slowly, and take Aspirin to lower your temperature and relieve headache. This, together with salt and rest, is the treatment for heat exhaustion, which is a fairly common condition that can occur in or out of the sun, e.g. after heavy work in shaded, but hot and humid conditions. Heat exhaustion can be due to a) simple faints precipitated by heat, b) water loss, c) salt deprivation or d) psychological factors.

Rarely, a more serious condition occurs, mainly in elderly or ailing people. On a humid day, an overheated body may attempt to cool by a massive sweating, with little effect, for it is the evaporation of the sweat that cools, not the sweating alone. Excessive water loss will eventually cause the body's heat regulating mechanism to break down and inhibit any further sweating. The patient's temperature may rise to 40.5°C or more. Collapse from heatstroke warrants urgent medical help, as there is a danger of damage to internal organs and the brain and a 25–30 per cent death rate. Meanwhile keep the patient cool, by immersion in cold water if possible or in a well-ventilated place. Try to reduce his temperature and keep it from rising again above 38°C.

Snowblindness: is caused by an ultraviolet burn on the cornea, resulting in intense pain and swelling of the eyes.

It can be prevented by wearing dark glasses or goggles; horizontal slits cut in a piece of cardboard will do in an emergency. Amethocaine drops will ease the pain enough to reach help. Then put Homatropine drops and chloromycetin ointment in the eyes and wear dark glasses or cover with eyepads and a bandage if the pain is severe.

Exposure/Exhaustion Syndrome

Hypothermia occurs when the temperature of the central core of the body falls below about 35°C owing to the combined effect of wind, wet and cold. Exhaustion and low morale worsen it. If someone behaves in an uncharacteristic manner – apathetic, stumbling, swearing, uncontrolled shivering – be on your guard. He may suddenly collapse and die.

First priorities are to stop and shelter the victim in a tent, lean-to or polythene bag, and to re-warm him by skin-to-skin contact, by dressing him in dry clothing and by putting him in a sleeping bag, in close contact with someone else, if possible. Then give him hot drinks, but no alcohol. If his condition does not improve, you may have to call help and evacuate him by stretcher.

Those travelling in areas where exposure is likely should read up the features and treatment of this very real hazard.

High Altitude Ills

Up to 3,500m you have little to fear – no more than on an ordinary mountain walking holiday. If you are not shaping up too well, reconsider the wisdom of climbing higher for you are entering the realm of the high, thin, cold, dry air. Slow ascent is the secret of easy acclimatization to altitude. Breathing and heartbeat speed up; a thumping headache and nausea make you feel miserable. At night, sleep is elusive. You may notice a peculiar irregularity in the pattern of breathing (Cheyne Stokes respiration) when, for a short period, breathing appears to have stopped and then gradually increases in stepwise fashion until if eventually falls off again. The normal output of urine may be diminished and very dilute.

The unpleasant symptoms of acclimatization usually pass off in a few days, but they may develop into Acute Mountain Sickness. This rarely starts below 4,500m so is unlikely in the Alps, but may occur in Africa, the Andes or the Himalayas.

If you begin to feel more ill than you would expect for your own degree of fitness and acclimatization, go down quickly and stay down rather than battle on for glory – and end up under a pile of stones on the glacier. Acute Mountain Sickness can quickly develop into High Altitude Pulmonary (lung) Oedema, or Cerebral (brain) Oedema (known in the USA as HAPE – High Altitude Pulmonary Edema, and HACE – High Altitude Cerebral Edema). This is swelling due to abnormal water retention. Women are more susceptible in the days before their periods. This is a potentially lethal disease, the cause of which is not understood, but it can affect all ages, the fit and the unfit, those who have risen quickly and those who have not.

If someone suddenly feels, and looks, puffy in the face, goes blue round the lips, has bubbly breathing and even pink frothy sputum, evacuate him urgently to a lower altitude. Oxygen (if available) and a diuretic drug Frusemide (*Lasix*) may help to clear water from the lungs, but they are no substitute for rapid descent which has a miraculous effect. Those who have suffered once are likely to do so again, and should therefore beware.

Thrombosis: Persistent deep calf tenderness and slight fever and pain – more than muscular ache – may indicate a vein thrombosis. Women on the pill are especially at risk. You should rest, preferably with the legs bandaged and elevated, and start an antibiotic. This is a serious illness, so descend and seek medical advice.

Piles, which commonly trouble people at high altitude, are probably due to raising the pressure inside the abdomen by overbreathing while carrying heavy loads. A haemorrhoidal suppository (*Anusol*) gives temporary relief.

Dry cough is eased by inhaling steam. Codeine Phosphate 15mgm dampens it. In a bout of violent coughing, you can fracture a rib. The agony may make you think you have had a heart attack but the chances are slim.

Frostbite should not occur if you are clothed properly and take commonsense precautions. If you get very cold, rewarm the part quickly against warm flesh (someone else's if possible). *Do not* rub it or you will damage the skin and cause further wounding which may become infected. Drugs, which dilate the blood vessels (vasodilators) have no specific action against frostbite although they make you feel a warm glow inside. This can be very dangerous as you are losing heat from the rest of your body and you may be tipped into exposure.

If a foot is frozen, it is better to walk on it back to a low camp where you can rapidly rewarm it in water of 42–44°C. Therafter the victim must be carried.

Dehydration

The sedentary dweller from a moderate climate may well find that tropical temperatures plus the need for a high work rate will cause weakness and suboptimal performance due to dehydration, despite an increased fluid intake. In deserts, in small boats and also at high altitude dehydration can be a real risk.

Owing to immobility from any cause, particularly if fever or diarrhoea are present, the fluid intake may fall to a level where dehydration can develop. In a temperate climate around 1500ml (2.6 pints) of fluids daily are adequate but working hard in the tropics may cause this volume of perspiration in just one and a half hours.

Dehydration is best expressed as a percentage loss of body weight, one to five per cent causing thirst and vague discomfort, six to ten per cent causing headache and inability to walk and ten to twenty per cent delirium leading to coma and death. Drinking sea water or urine in survival situations only causes a more rapid deterioration.

To estimate fluid requirements, assume that an average unacclimatized man working out of doors in extreme hot/wet or hot/dry conditions will drink seven to nine litres (twelve to sixteen pints) of fluids per day. 'Voluntary dehydration', symp-

:omless initially, is common if drinking fluids are not within easy reach and palatable.

In temperate climates the average diet contains an excess of salt which is excreted in sweat and urine. Over two to three days in the tropics adaptation reduces the amount of salt in sweat and urine to negligible levels. During the first two weeks dehydration may be accompanied by salt depletion so that supplements are of value. Generally the treatment is simply rest and an increased fluid intake until the urine volume is adequate (around one litre or one and a half pints a day) and visibly normal or pale in colour.

In early days of heat exposure a definite self-discipline in achieving a sufficiently high fluid intake is necessary. Those treating ill patients must watch and encourage this aspect of their treatment. The most obvious features of marked dehydration are sunken eyes and a looseness of the pinched skin. If these cannot be corrected by oral fluids a serious situation is developing and medical aid should be sought as intravenous fluids are likely to be needed.

Immersion in Water

Prolonged immersion in all but tropical waters carries a life-threatening hazard of hypothermia which is probably a bigger risk than drowning. The amount of subcutaneous fat will affect survival time considerably but a naked man of average build will be helpless from hypothermia after 20–30 minutes in water at 5°C and one and a half to two hours in water at 15°C.

If thick clothing is worn these intervals will be increased to 40–60 minutes at 5°C and four to five hours at 15°C. Thus, if a ship is to be abandoned or a small boat is threatened, warm clothing should be donned with a waterproof outer suit if one is available. Cold can cause dilation of blood vessels in the hands and feet and thus increase heat loss so that mitts and footwear are also desirable as is protection for the head and neck.

Some flotation aid such as a life-jacket, wreckage, an upturned bucket or even air trapped in a waterproof coat should be sought. When in the water, float quietly instead of swimming. With the stress of cold water combined with a threatening situation swimming is a normal reaction but, because of its stirring effect on the surrounding water, and despite the heat it generates, swimming will merely accelerate loss of body heat. Swim only if no flotation aid is available, if threatened by a sinking ship or if rescue by others is not possible and land is within reach. Whilst waiting for rescue, float quietly as all exercise will accelerate cooling.

Nature's Annoyances

by Drs Peter Steele and John Frankland

From flies and mosquitoes, bees, wasps, ants and hornets; from fleas, lice and bed bugs; from sea urchins and jellyfish; and from a host of other creepy-crawlies we pray deliverance. Repellent sprays and creams (usually based on Dimethylphthalate) last only a few hours but are essential for those prone to a severe reaction to insect bites; they will generally already be aware of this. Though everyone will be bitten, fierce reactions and distress will be caused only in a few. Remove any stings. Calamine cream or lotion or *Anthisan* (Mepyramine Maleate) cream will help. If distress remains, antihistamine tablets e.g. *Piriton* (Chlorpheniramine) 4mgm three times daily, with Aspirin as a pain killing adjunct, should be used. Good hygiene is necessary to prevent large reactions to multiple bites from becoming infected. If this happens, rest, antihistamine tablets, antibiotics and clean dressings will usually effect a cure.

Anthropods: Lice, fleas and bed bugs are kept at bay by ICI Louse and Insect Powder.

Worms: Worms are common in tropical countries. They cause an itchy bottom and can often be seen in stools. Take one Peperazine (*Pripsen*) sachet.

Mosquitoes are usually only a bother at lower altitudes. A net makes sleeping more comfortable but does not guarantee protection from malaria (*see article on page 358*).

Chiggers are larval mites which carry scrub typhus, in eastern and southern Asia and the islands of the southern and western Pacific. Hikers in grassy areas are most likely to contract the disease, which can be cured by the use of a Tetracycline or Chloramphenicol.

Snakes: Clean the area of the bite (not by urinating on it). Try to identify the snake: if possible, kill it and take it to the hospital with you for identification. In the USA, where rattlesnake and cottonmouth snakes prevail, sucking the wound is favoured in a victim who is well covered in fat. To prepare for this, sterilize a knife in a flame, make a cut into each fang mark about half a centimetre long and half a centimetre deep. Suck the wound, spitting out the venom, for about fifteen minutes. If more than half an hour has passed since the victim was bitten, do not suck or cut the wound, as this may do more harm than good. In South America, Africa and Asia, sucking is, in any case, useless, since cobra venom is the main hazard and this is not easily removed by suction.

Keep the victim quiet, do not move the affected part, e.g. in the case of a bite on the foot, do not allow him to walk even one step. In any case, the victim should be carried to hospital, if possible, instead of walking. Meanwhile apply a cloth or elastic bandage between the wound and the heart to slow the circulation of the venom; loosen the bandage for a minute or two in every fifteen. Give no stimulants, e.g. alcohol, as this dilates the blood vessels and accelerates circulation of the poison, but give a sedative.

Local hospitals probably carry a serum against the bites of common local snakes. Polyvalent antivenin is available but it is expensive, difficult to get hold of and itself very hazardous because of the risk of inducing shock. If given it should be injected, but not more than three hours after the bite and *never* unless the features of poisoning develop – despite assurances from some quarters that its use is mandatory. Watch the patient for signs of allergic shock: shivering, rapid heartbeat, low pulse. If ice is available, wrap it in a cloth and pack it around the affected part. In case of infection, give antibiotics. Consider also giving painkilling medication and antihistamine. If the patient survives the first 24 hours after being bitten, he will probably recover, though some deaths do occur after this interval. It is worth mentioning, however, that only 30 per cent of victims of venomous snakes die.

Dogs: Rabies exists in most countries with a few fortunate exceptions such as Britain and Australia. To help limit the spread of this awful disease, abide strictly by the anti-rabies regulations and never smuggle animals home from abroad. The new human Diploid cell 'Merriaux' anti-rabies vaccine has completely superseded the old painful multi-injection Duck Embryo vaccine but will probably not be available in primitive countries and may not be available in the USA either. Anyone handling bats, small mammals etc. should have this before departure. The British should cease to be dog lovers abroad and should leave well alone any animal displaying abnormal behaviour. A bite from a dog or any other mammal always warrants a doctor's advice on the prevalence of rabies in the district and the advisability of vaccination for a victim not already so protected. At the very least, an anti-tetanus booster is recommended. If at all possible, capture the animal so that it can be tested for rabies.

Wash the wound as soon as possible with soap and water and follow this with a three per cent solution of hydrogen peroxide. In the absence of water or hydrogen peroxide, wash with any sterile liquid – beer, cold tea or coffee or any carbonated drink will do.

(*For further information, see article on Rabies on page 362.*)

Scorpions: Only a few species have a severely poisonous sting. As with snakes, prevention is better than cure. Carry a stout stick to test the nature of anything you can't identify. Wear thick boots and watch where you put your feet. Before donning clothes and boots in the morning in scorpion territory, i.e. dry country, shake them out.

If bitten, the treatment is rest, analgesics, antihistamines and probably a course of antibiotics. Tarantula-type spider bites come into this category. Whip scorpions are harmless.

Leeches are most troublesome during and shortly after the monsoon in the tropics. You do not feel them bite and may only notice a bootful of blood at the end of the day. Open sandals let you see them early and insect repellent discourages them – a lighted cigarette or salt makes the leech drop off.

Wasp stings – vinegar. *Bee stings* – antihistamine ointment.

Bilharzia is widespread in many tropical areas, so avoid swimming in slow-flowing rivers and lakes where the flukes breed.

(*For further information, see separate article on Bilharzia on page 357.*)

Poisoning: Try to make the person sick by sticking fingers down his throat. Under ideal conditions, the treatment of choice in children is syrup (not fluid extract) of ipecacuanha when there is a risk of toxicity, provided that treatment is given under medical supervision within four hours of ingestion and that the poison is not corrosive, a petroleum distillate or an antiemetic. For adults, support of vital functions should be the primary concern of those administering first aid, followed by a stomach washout. Though giving a salt solution is no longer the preferred treatment, it will be the best available under most expedition or trip conditions.

Bilharzia

by P. J. Whyte

Though improved sanitation and general hygiene measures have gone some way to eradicating bilharzia on a global basis, it still ranks as one of the most important, and least heeded diseases in the tropics and sub-tropical regions. It is particularly prevalent in North African countries, most especially in the Nile Delta; but most other African countries are affected as far south as South Africa, while different strains of a limited nature occur in many parts of the Far East and Brazil.

It is also referred to as *Schistosomiasis*, or 'blood fluke disease' because the schistosoma, which enters the blood, is a trematode worm or 'fluke'.

Infection

These parasites are dependent on aquatic snails, man and water contaminated with the faeces and urine of infected persons. Thus, wherever there are humans, there is a chance of the disease. The larvae of the worms develop in the snail and are then discharged into the fresh water. As the snails prefer a warm stagnant habitat, these are the areas of which to be particularly careful. Confident statements by the locals that their particular river is too high, too cold, or too fast-flowing should, however, be treated with scepticism. Try and avoid *all* natural, untreated water in potentially infected areas. Man is usually affected when bathing, or drinking, but it is easily as common for him to be affected while simply crossing a river where there is no bridge.

The mode of entry is through the skin or, if the water is drunk, the larvae (now called cercariae) burrow through the lining of the mouth and throat. They need man to mature and the cercariae waste no time in entering the bloodstream, and then graduating to a base in the liver. Here a development process occurs, the adult parasites forming, and then migrating to attack either the bowel or the bladder.

Symptoms

While there can often be no signs of having contracted the disease, some species of cercariae will leave an irritating rash at the point of entry through the skin. This will normally appear about 24 hours after infection and will disappear again after about 48 hours. For the disease to mature (the first eggs to form) and other symptoms to start can take 25 to 28 days with one form and anything from 50 to 80 days with the others. At this point, the sufferer may develop a general body pruritus, accompanied by a severe fever, marked by a very high temperature and annoying agitation. Where the parasitic adults form illustrates the subsequent symptoms that appear. If in the bowel, there is bloody diarrhoea, abdominal pain, anorexia, loss of weight, and a general feeling of mental apathy. The bladder presents signs of cystitis and blood in the urine. This 'haematuria' can last for several months, while in the chronic stage stones may form in the bladder.

Anaemia is common to all with such obvious blood loss, and this in turn leads to further paleness, breathlessness, palpitations and particular fatigue.

Treatment

Anyone who has been in contact with natural water in the tropics would be well advised to have a diagnostic test on their return home, so that if they have contracted the disease, it can be caught and treated in the early stages. There is, as yet, no vaccine, and while work continues on trying to develop one, it seems unlikely that the position will change for some time. The disease can, however, be treated with a wide range of drugs, Meridizol being the most common of them.

If the disease is allowed to progress too far before treatment, the patient can be too weak to tolerate the rigours of the drug therapy, in which case bed rest plays a major part.

Prevention

Most emphasis needs to be placed on the prevention methods necessary to combat the disease. Awareness of bilharzia's existence, and the conditions in which one is likely to catch it go a long way towards helping avoid contact. Those who do know have a duty to 'educate' others in its dangers and prevention. One should not urinate or defaecate in the vicinity of water, or bathe in fresh water channels and streams, a remark also applicable to washing clothes. All wells should be protected, and while proper sanitation would go a long way towards preventing the spread of the disease, it will be a long time before this is universal.

The vast progress that has seen massive irrigation schemes to increase crops has also increased the areas that the snails can thrive in. These intermediate hosts favour quiet streams close to living communities, but must also have plant life to survive. If the snails themselves cannot be eradicated, attempts should be made to kill off the plant life. But even private swimming pools are not exempt, particularly if the water comes from a local stream, though isolation methods greatly reduce this hazard.

The traveller may consider personal physical protection as a starting point: always wear shoes in pools and bathing streams, and cover the ankles and feet when wading through water. Try to avoid the inland waters, and to use the bridges however inconvenient they may appear. I would recommend cotton wool ear plugs if you have to submerge your head.

Unless actually filtered, all water for drinking should be boiled or treated with chlorine tablets, and products such as Dettol added to water used for bathing.

An added precaution could be to apply a barrier repellant lotion to the exposed areas of the body, except the eyes. With all these creams, the degree of protection depends on the individual, sweat loss, temperature of the water, and the potency of the creatures. Nevertheless, they can assist, but if you are unfortunate enough to suffer an accidental contact, immediately rub the skin dry with clean, unaffected cloths, being extremely careful to make sure you have left no area out.

There are many who consider that the complete eradication of the snail and worms is nigh-on impossible, and instead iron supplements are freely given to combat the anaemia, which is the main presenting illness. But the determined traveller must not ignore his own education or his moral duty in preventing any further spread of bilharzia.

Malaria

by Michael Colbourne

Malaria remains one of the most prevalent of tropical diseases, causing sickness and death to those living in malarious countries and posing a threat to the traveller.

Malaria is an infection caused by a parasite that develops in the red blood corpuscles which it eventually destroys, causing fever, headache and anaemia. There are two main types of malaria. The malignant Plasmodium, *falciparum*, is the more severe as the infected corpuscles 'stick' in the internal organs. If this occurs in the brain it may lead to coma and even death if the infection is not treated. Falciparum malaria is commoner where the temperature is high; untreated it may last for up to two years.

The second type is 'benign (*vivax*) malaria which causes the same headache, fever and anaemia but rarely the life-threatening complications associated with falciparum malaria. Vivax malaria has a greater tendency to relapse, even after treatment and attacks may occur up to four years after the original infection. It is common in tropical countries, except in West and Central Africa, but its distribution is wider both to the north and the south than that of falciparum malaria. In the summer it is found in many non-tropical areas. Before it was eliminated after the Second World War, it was common in many parts of Europe.

Infection

The way malaria passes from person to person is peculiar. Most of the organisms which cause infection, such as influenza or tuberculosis, pass from person to person through the air. Malaria is transmitted by the bite of a female mosquito. Mosquitoes, when they bite someone suffering from malaria, may suck up blood containing malaria parasites which develop within the mosquito. After about ten days, the mosquito may pass on the parasites to her next victim. The parasite will only develop in certain species of anopheline mosquitoes; in any other species, the parasite will die within the mosquito.

Most people know that there is a connection between mosquitoes and malaria. Not so many know that the mosquito merely transfers the disease carrying malaria parasites from one person to another. The anopheline mosquito responsible usually comes unobtrusively in the night; the common 'nuisance' mosquitoes are seldom malaria carriers. Exact knowledge of the habits of these mosquitoes helps us understand and control the disease, but it is the malaria parasite that causes the disease and is our more immediate enemy.

Distribution

It is generally known that malaria is commoner in tropical countries (*see map on page 360*) but there is less understanding of the widely different risk of getting malaria in different places. The risk can be measured by considering the chance of being bitten by a mosquito carrying malaria parasites. In the lightly stippled areas on the map, the chance is less than 1:2,000 per year of exposure; in the more heavily shaded areas, it varies from this low risk to more than 100 infected bites a year. The very dangerous areas are tropical Africa and coastal New Guinea. This variation means that for many travellers, taking preventive measures is a sensible precaution like wearing a seat belt; for those visiting really dangerous places, neglect of these precautions is like crossing a busy road with your eyes shut. You may 'make it' once or twice, but it will not be long before you succumb – and the malaria found in tropical Africa is usually the more malignant type that is often fatal.

These facts are important, otherwise people who have avoided malaria without taking precaution in areas with little malaria, such as Morocco, will think they will be equally safe if they take their family on a holiday to the Kenya coast and neglect to protect themselves.

Another misconception is that malaria was practically eliminated from the world in the '60s. Some people think that after its virtual elimination, it is back again and even worse than before. There is some truth in these views, but the position is rather more complicated. Many countries that were originally malarious are now free of the disease – usually, but not entirely, the more temperate – Europe, North America, Australia, much of North East Asia; but also most of the Caribbean Islands, Taiwan, Hong Kong and Singapore are free of the disease. Good progress is still being made in South America, in parts of the Middle East and in some countries in Asia.

Protection

In the most malarious areas, especially tropical Africa, in spite of considerable research into methods of controlling the disease, little has been achieved either in reducing the burden of malaria on residents or in making these countries safer for the visitor.

Protecting the traveller from malaria depends on avoiding mosquito bites, especially at night, and the use of antimalarial drugs to destroy the parasite should infection take place.

The best way to avoid dangerous mosquito bites is to sleep in a mosquito proof bedroom or, if that is not possible, under a mosquito net. It is important to get rid of any mosquitoes in the room by using a 'knock-down' insecticide before retiring. Between sunset and going to bed, bites can be reduced by wearing clothes that restrict the biteable area of skin – long sleeves and protection for the ankles which are so loved by mosquitoes.

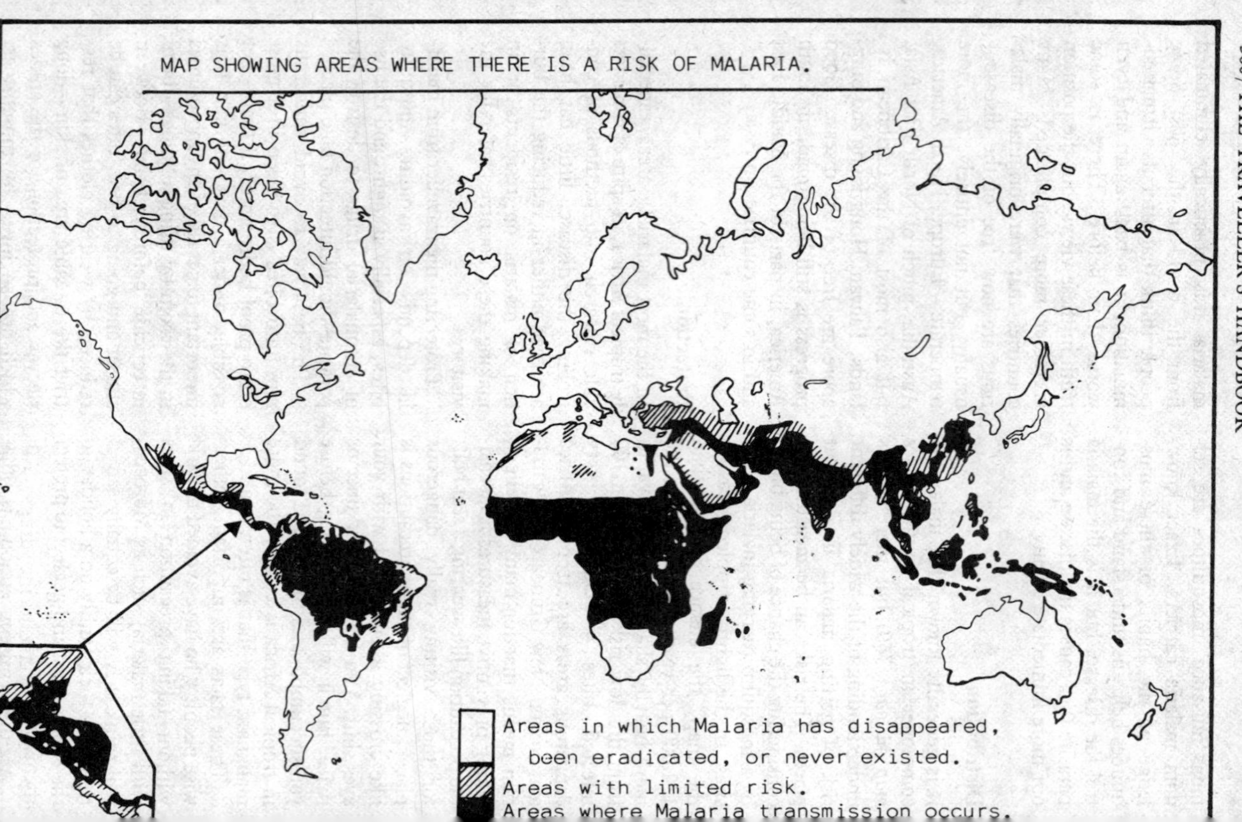
MAP SHOWING AREAS WHERE THERE IS A RISK OF MALARIA.
Areas in which Malaria has disappeared, been eradicated, or never existed.
Areas with limited risk.
Areas where Malaria transmission occurs.

Some temporary protection can be obtained by the use of repellants. There are many commercial brands; those containing diethyltoluamide or dimethylphthalata are recommended. Burning mosquito coils will keep a restricted area mosquito free.

Protection against bites is clearly important, but it can seldom be relied on completely. Unfortunately the selection of the most suitable anti-malarial drug has now become more complicated and the position changes even from month to month. For many years it has been known that some of the antimalarials were becoming less effective as the parasites become less sensitive to them. Recently the problem has become really serious as the effectiveness of chloroquine – one of the safest and most useful antimalarial drugs – has become ineffective against *Plasmodium falciparum*.

Advice has to be based on first principles – is the area to be visited malarious? What are the species of malaria parasite to be found in that area? Which antimalarial drugs are effective in these circumstances? Is the possible toxicity of the drug greater than the risk of malaria? Are there any special circumstances which may influence the choice of drug – such as pregnancy (or possible pregnancy) or the extreme youth of the traveller?

Some travellers are uncertain exactly which places they are going to visit and may change their itinerary at short notice; these need special advice. It is very difficult to give simple advice. The adviser with no doubts is likely to be incompletely informed or may be unwilling to balance the risk of malaria against possible toxic effects of the drugs. All travellers would be well advised to seek up-to-date information from specialist sources before leaving home (*see list on page 638*).

There are two approaches to obtaining the most appropriate advice: first, make a study of the sources of information and make your own decision; the second, ask your adviser what precautions he would take himself if he were making the same trip. It will be clear that with so many variables, sources of advice are likely to disagree on details, but no one will disagree that some form of prophylaxis is to be recommended when visiting the malarious areas and that it is absolutely essential when going to tropical Africa. Another unpleasant fact is that none of the anti-malarial drugs is completely effective and that a few unlucky travellers will get malaria, even if they have followed exactly the best advice available.

Symptoms

It is therefore advisable for the traveller to know what sort of symptoms may occur. There are many excellent descriptions of malarial attacks in medical textbooks – the cold, shivering stage, the hot stage and the stage of profuse sweats as the temperature falls. This cycle takes about 24 hours and is repeated every other day. It is a valid description of *Plasmodium Vivax* malaria in those who have had several attacks but is not typical of the first attack of malaria in the non-immune travellers. Malaria can mimic many diseases but it usually starts as a 'flu-like' condition with fever and headache; but vomiting and even diarrhoea may be the more obvious symptoms. It is essential to remember that any illness, even one that occurs several months after a visit to an endemic area may possibly be malaria and your doctor should be informed of the details of the trip. This is especially important after visits to tropical Africa, where symptoms may change from mild to serious with unpleasant speed.

Rabies

by Peter Lane

The tragic death from rabies some time ago of an English woman who had visited India and developed symptoms several months after returning home, must have given many a traveller pause to think. Rabies or, as it is sometimes known, hydrophobia, is one of the most terrible of diseases and the victim suffers dreadfully over a prolonged period before finally dying.

What then are the risks to the traveller, especially in the more exotic parts of the world where disease in animals is not controlled as closely as in Europe? Should one worry and take precautions, or disregard it as a risk to be suffered along with all the other hazards of foreign travel?

Rabies is one of the oldest diseases of man, who invariably contracts it from animals. It was certainly known to the people of ancient Egypt, Greece and Rome, who ascribed it to evil spirits when ordinary docile and friendly animals became suddenly aggressive and vicious.

Virus

In fact, rabies is caused by a virus which is excreted in large amounts in the saliva of affected animals. The disease is passed on from one individual to another when a healthy animal or human is bitten by an affected animal. It is not even necessary for a bite to occur, as the disease can also be transmitted when an affected animal merely licks a slightly scratched hand or, for instance, the saliva of a spitting cat sprays into the eye.

Once the virus has gained entry by these means, it passes into the nearest small nerves and migrates along them to the bigger nerves. It moves gradually along these until it reaches the brain. At the same time, it multiplies and appears in the saliva. This means that it will take longer to reach the brain if the bite is on the hand or foot than if it is on the face or neck, simply because it has further to travel. Thus it can often happen that many months elapse before the disease manifests itself and the victim may not even remember the occurrence that led to his dreadful plight.

In man, the first symptoms are those of fever, lack of appetite, headache, lethargy, nausea and sore throat. Sometimes there are tingling sensations around the area where the infection first entered the body. After a few days, the victim becomes extremely sensitive to light and sound and excessive salivation develops. As it progresses, spasms of the throat muscles begin and swallowing becomes impossible. These spasms can be brought on by the mere sight of water, hence the alternative name, hydrophobia – fear of water. In addition, there are periods when the victim loses all rational behaviour and throws fits. The patient invariably dies after days of suffering.

Recognising Rabies

There must surely be nothing worse than being bitten or licked by a strange looking animal and then waiting for months to see if rabies symptoms begin to develop. However, there is much that you can do to protect yourself. Remember that, outside Britain, you are, with few exceptions, almost certainly entering a land where the disease is endemic in the wild animal population. This reservoir of infection also ensures that domestic animals will also contract it. The disease is even prevalent within mainland Europe – particularly in France and Germany.

The best precaution of all is to completely disregard all animals when abroad. Resist the urge to stroke or fondle any dogs or cats. Remember that all warm-blooded animals can develop rabies and pass it on to humans.

This will cut the risk but not eliminate it entirely. When animals develop rabies, they frequently change their behaviour, and any animal behaving uncharateristically should be treated with extreme caution. Normally aggressive animals might first become excessively friendly and vice versa. Dogs will sometimes change the tone of their voice and develop a howling type of bark. At a later stage of the disease, infected animals might show signs of terror, become vicious or run madly around with their jaws paralysed in the open position, drooling saliva. If they develop the furious form of the disease, they will travel over many miles during the course of a few days and will attack any other animal or human they encounter. Wild animals, such as foxes, can lose their natural fear of man and will enter dwellings to attack anyone inside. In Central and South America, there exist vampire bats, which bite their victims to suck blood. Even birds are susceptible.

It is unlikely that anyone would contract rabies from a carcass unless the animal had recently died and they were to examine the mouth region with their hands. Nevertheless all dead animals should be given a wide berth if only because of other diseases which they might transmit.

Vaccination

The second precaution that you can take is to be vaccinated before you set off on your travels. In the old days, a course of rabies vaccination was a series of very painful injections given into the abdomen over a period of days. Nowadays, the procedure is much pleasanter and is simply the normal type of injection given into the arm and repeated two weeks later.

It is probably only necessary to be vaccinated if you are intending to enter a geographical area of high risk or if your journey will bring you into close contact with animals. If you decide upon being vaccinated, see your doctor at least two months before the start of your journey. The vaccine is not normally kept in stock and it can take some time to obtain it. You will also want to ensure that the vaccine has time to stimulate the development of immunity in the body before you leave. The vaccination must, unfortunately, be paid for.

If you are bitten or licked by an animal of which you are suspicious, immediately wash the wound vigorously with soap and water ensuring, in the process, that all dirt is removed. Rinse all the soap away with copious amounts of water. This procedure will often mechanically remove the virus from the tissues before it has a chance to take hold. Then seek out a local qualified doctor and submit to his treatment. But don't rely solely on this and immediately consult your own doctor on your return. If you have any reason to be dissatisfied with the treatment given by the local doctor, change your travel arrangements and obtain professional medical help in a more reliable area. Even if you were not vaccinated before you left home, it still need not be too late to be treated with serum and vaccine after the event.

Most importantly, do not allow fear of rabies to spoil enjoyment of your travels. It can only be contracted in the manner which I have described and you will be quite safe if you follow the general procedures outlined above.

Delhi Belly to Dysentery

by Drs Peter Steele and John Frankland

The following advice aims to help you avoid illnesses commonly met abroad, most of which can be treated by yourself in the first instance. If, however, the condition doesn't improve, or even rapidly worsens after the first 24–48 hours, you should seek medical help. In some areas the most highly trained person around will be the local pharmacist who will both dispense medication and perform medical treatments. Your consulate or embassy or the nearest office of the Peace Corps will usually have a doctor. In the remotest places sponsored mission hospitals may offer an excellent and devoted service, probably with English speaking staff. When your trip is over, if you do not wish to ship home drugs and dressings, they will be more than glad to accept them.

Travel Sickness

If you suspect travel sickness could upset you, take antihistamine tablets starting one hour before the journey. All of these can make some people drowsy, so if you need to be alert, e.g. to drive, find one in which you are safe. *Piriton* (Chlorpheniramine) 4mgm three times daily is usually as good as any.

Travel sickness is caused by the conflict of messages received by the brain from the eyes, inner ear and sensors in the muscles and joints. *Stugeron*, long prescribed in maladies involving dizziness or loss of balance, has begun to emerge as a remedy for seasickness. The manufacturers, Janssen Pharmaceutical Ltd., claim that *Stugeron* (Cinnarizine) in 15mgm doses, does not cause undue drowsiness.

Traveller's Diarrhoea

Gippy Tummy, Delhi Belly, Kathmandu Quickstep – traveller's diarrhoea has as many names as patent remedies. It strikes most travellers at some stage in their journey, making more trouble than all the other illnesses put together. The causes are usually untraceable but may include gluttony, change in climate and an upset in the bacteria that are normal and necessary in the bowel. Infection with disease-causing organisms carried in water and food is less common.

Much of the pleasure of travelling abroad comes from eating local food and drinking wine; it is hardly worth going all that way for beer, fish and chips. But be moderate to prevent the tummy upset that will spoil your trip.

Prevention: Food and especially water warrant the utmost care. (*See Food and Water; Advice for the Long Distance Traveller on page 333*.)

Hygiene: Lavatories abroad are often dirty. You may have to squat and keep your balance by holding onto the walls. Wash your hands carefully with soap as soon as possible afterwards. Take your own toilet paper as newsprint is rough and fragile. At campsites, dig a latrine hole well away from the tents and your water supply. If, in cramped surroundings, any member of a group gets diarrhoea, all the others should become more fastidious in personal hygiene, particularly with hand washing after visiting the toilet and before preparing food or eating.

Cholera: 1973 saw a worldwide epidemic, notably in parts of Italy, and cases have been reported from several Mediterranean countries recently, as well as in more obvious places. The cholera organisms come only from the human intestine and are spread by faecally contaminated water, not by direct contact or inhalation. Raw shellfish collect the bug and so are particularly dangerous. A sudden onset of profuse watery diarrhoea in an epidemic area calls for immediate attention. Unfortunately, the immunizations against this disease are not too effective. Tourists should be particularly careful as the rapidly worsening pollution problem around major resort areas is paving the way for cholera outbreaks of epidemic proportions if precautions are not taken.

Treatment: The illness usually clears up on its own in two to three days. You may also vomit and, because a lot of body water is lost, you may feel groggy. Go to bed and drink unlimited fluids (at least half a litre an hour). Avoid eating – except dried toast and peeled, grated apple gone brown (pectin).

For the vast majority of travellers with diarrhoea, by far the most effective remedy is to take nothing at all by mouth except fluids. This will achieve a cure more rapidly than a normal diet combined with any medication in the world. Certainly an unaccustomed, probably more exotic, diet and any form of therapy are likely to mean a more prolonged period of bowel disturbance and thereby perhaps acute distress. Simply resting your disturbed alimentary tract by not giving it solid food which will be speedily evacuated is the basis of the effective cure.

Many find this advice hard to accept and particularly under expedition circumstances, sufferers may have to go on working and thus may choose to continue eating. In this case, antidiarrhoeal tablets will be of value.

Lomotil (four tabs initially and then two tabs four times daily as required) or Codeine Phosphate tablets 30mg – two tabs four times daily are required – are probably as effective and compact a medication as any.

Antibiotics, though fashionable, should not be used blindly since they kill normal bacteria, which are protective, as well as poison-producing ones. They also contribute to the development of antibiotic-resistant strains of the organisms.

Lomotoil, a narcotic analogue, provides symptomatic relief only. It is not recommended for children, pregnant women, or in cases of acute bacillary dysentry or diarrhoea complicated by other symptoms e.g. the existence of gross blood or pus in the stool.

Enterovioform, once a popular remedy, is of doubtful therapeutic or prophylactic value and has even been implicated in neurological disease. At present this drug is not licensed in the USA.

An antimicrobial drug, *Vibramycin*, has shown good results in some cases but is only recommended for people who are especially susceptible or at high risk and then only for short periods, because of the difficulties encountered with antibiotics mentioned above. Incidentally, advancing age is associated with a lower incidence of traveller's diarrhoea.

Recuperation can be hastened when the time is right by appropriate fluid intake – not water or bottled sodas, which lack potassium and other vital ingredients. The WHO has recommended the following solution for rehydration in severe attacks of diarrhoea: Potassium chloride, ¼ tspn; Sodium bicarbonate, ½ tspn; Sodium chloride (table salt) ½ tspn; Glucose 2 tspn; or Sucrose 4 tspn; added to one litre or one quart of water. Or the following two solutions – less accurate, but more readily obtainable – can be made up and drunk alternately;

1. Orange or other fruit juice, 225gm; table salt, one pinch; honey or corn syrup, ½ tspn; or table sugar one tspn; and
2. Pure water, 225gm; and baking soda (sodium bicarbonate), ¼ tspn.

Other liquid should be taken freely, but preferably not milk, coffee, strong tea, cocoa or soft drinks containing caffeine.

Dysentery

If diarrhoea does not stop within 24 hours of this treatment, or if blood appears in the stools, consult a doctor as you may be suffering from dysentery. If you cannot find help, the best drug to start with is Cotrimoxazole (*Septrin, Bactrim*). Bacillary dysentery starts suddenly with acute diarrhoea, fever and malaise. Amoebic dysentery causes slimy mucus and blood and warrants laboratory investigation and treatment. Its severity builds up slowly over several days.

Indigestion

Any antacid will ease gutrot, indigestion, and perhaps a hangover. Tablets are more portable than mixtures and are just as effective. Magnesium trisilicate acts as a laxative and, as some diarrhoea often coexists, aluminium hydroxide (*Aludrox*) tablets may be more suitable. Everyone will need them on most journeys even if only to cure indiscreet eating and drinking. *Maxalon* (Metaclopramide) tablets four times daily will help suppress vomiting.

Constipation

Drink plenty and eat fruit. If this fails, take two laxative tablets.

NB: Beware the person who feels sick, has no appetite, a dirty, coated tongue and pain in the belly. If the abdomen is tender, particularly in the lower right quarter, suspect appendicitis and visit a doctor. If no doctor is available, rest the patient, give fluids only with antibiotics and pain killers. Evacuation must then be considered.

Other Ailments and Injuries

by Drs Peter Steele and John Frankland

Antibiotics must not be eaten indiscriminately, but if you develop an infection with a high fever and rapid pulse when you are away in the wilds on your own, blind therapy with a broad spectrum bug-killing drug may be justified. Cotrimoxazole (*Septrin*, *Bactrim*) or Amoxycillin (*Amoxyl*) should be taken for a full five-day course. In malarial areas, treatment must also be considered even if regular prophylaxis has been taken; a three day treatment should abort most attacks. If it does not, then seek medical advice. If there is fever, supportive measures such as rest, shade, frequent sponging with cool water, two Aspirin tablets every four to six hours and an adequate intake of fluids are essential.

Waterworks

Urinary infection is more common in women, and begins as frequent passing of urine with burning pain. Drink a pint of water hourly with a tablespoon of bicarbonate of soda and take an antibiotic if it does not improve in a day.

Women travellers have the extra burden of coping with menstrual problems en route. If on the pill it is totally safe to start the new pack immediately after finishing the current pack without the usual six or seven day interval. This will avoid menstrual loss or certainly minimise it, saving quite a nuisance. If, however, a woman on the pill in a mixed party gets diarrhoea for more than one day, the pill may not be absorbed and she should assume she is not protected for that cycle. An unwanted pregnancy in a remote spot will cause much distress!

To complicate the issue the menstrual cycle of both non-takers and takers of the pill may become irregular or stop temporarily while travelling and adventuring. This is harmless and needs no medical intervention. Women on the pill are more at risk from thrombosis and thrush.

Sexually Transmitted Diseases

Gonorrhoea ('clap') and syphilis have been spread worldwide by the increase in air travel. Some forms of gonorrhoea are resistant to penicillin, and recent increases in such well-publicised diseases as herpes and aids also prove difficult to cure, but most are treatable if caught early enough. Diagnosis can be difficult, especially in women, and prevention is better than cure. Avoidance of casual sexual contacts is helpful; and a sheath gives some measure of protection.

Local Infections

Eyes: If the eyes are pink and feel gritty, wear dark glasses and put in chloromycetin ointment. A few drops of Amethocaine will anaesthetize the cornea so you can dig out a foreign body. Homatropine dilates the pupil and relieves spasm but will temporarily blur the vision.

Ears: Keep dry with a light plug of cotton wool but don't poke matches in. If there is discharge and pain, take an antibiotic.

Sinusitis: gives a headache (felt worse on stooping), 'toothache' in the upper jaw, and often a thick, snotty discharge from the nose. Inhale steam in Tinct. Benz. or sniff a tea brew with a towel over your head to help drainage. Decongestant drops may clear the nose if it is mildly bunged up, but true sinusitis needs an antibiotic.

Throat: Cold dry air irritates the throat and makes it sore. Gargle with a couple of Aspirins or table salt dissolved in warm water; or suck antiseptic lozenges.

Teeth: When it is difficult to brush your teeth, chew gum. If a filling comes out, a plug of cotton wool soaked in oil of cloves eases the pain; gutta percha, softened in boiling water, is easily plastered into the hole as a temporary filling. Hot salt mouthwashes encourage pus to discharge from a dental abcess but an antibiotic will be needed.

Feet take a hammering so boots must fit and be comfortable. Climbing boots are rarely necessary on the approach march to a mountain; gym shoes are useful. At the first sign of rubbing put on a plaster.

Blisters: Burst with a sterile blade or needle (boiled for three minutes or hold in a flame until red hot). Remove dead skin, spray with Tinct. Benz. Cover the raw area with zinc oxide plaster and leave in place for several days to allow new skin to form.

Athlete's Foot can become very florid in the tropics so treat this problem before departure. The newer antifungal creams e.g. *Canestin*, are very effective and supersede antifungal dusting powders but do not eliminate the need for sensible foot hygiene. In very moist conditions, e.g. in the rain forest, on cave explorations or in small boats, macerated feet can become a real and incapacitating problem. A silicone-based barrier cream in adequate supply is essential under these conditions.

Skin sepsis: In muddy or wet conditions most travellers will get some skin sepsis on small wounds. Without sensible hygiene these can be disabling, especially in jungle conditions. Cuts and grazes should be washed thoroughly with soap and water or an antiseptic solution; five per cent Mercurochrome Aq. dabbed on cuts and grazes is an excellent antiseptic as the skin remains dry (creams will leave it greasy and attract dirt). Other suitable antiseptics are potassium permanganate and gentian violet. Large abrasions should be covered with a vaseline gauze e.g. Jelonet or Sofratulle, then a dry gauze, and kept covered until a dry scab forms, after which they can be treated daily with Mercurochrome solution and left exposed. Anchor dressings are useful for awkward places e.g. fingers, heels. If a cut is clean and gaping, bring the edges together with Steristrips in place of stitches.

Unconsciousness

The causes range from drowning to head injury, diabetes to epilepsy. Untrained laymen should merely attempt to place the victim in the coma position – lying on his side with the head lower than the chest to allow secretions, blood or vomit to drain away from the lungs. Hold the chin forward to prevent the tongue falling back and obstructing the airway. Don't try any fancy manoeuvres unless you are practised, as you may do more harm than good.

All unconscious patients from any cause, particularly after trauma, should be placed in the coma position until they recover. This takes priority over any other first aid manoeuvre.

Fainting: Lay the unconscious person down and raise the legs to return extra blood to the brain.

Injury

Nature is a wonderful healer if given adequate encouragement.

Superficial wounds: see above.

Deep wounds: Firm pressure on a wound dressing will stop most bleeding. If blood seeps through, put more dressings on top, secured with absorbent crepe bandages and keep up the pressure. Elevate the part if possible.

On trips to remote spots at least one member of the party should learn to put in simple sutures. This is not difficult – a friendly doctor or casualty sister can teach the essentials in ten minutes. People have practised on a piece of dog meat and on several occasions this has been put to good use. Pulling the wound edges together is all that is necessary; a neat cosmetic result is not usually important.

Burns: Superficial burns are simply skin wounds. Leave open to the air to form a dry crust under which healing goes on. If this is not possible cover with *Melolin* dressings. Burn creams offer no magic. Deep burns must be kept scrupulously clean and treated urgently by a doctor. Give drinks freely to replace lost fluids.

Sprains: A sprained ankle ligament, usually on the outside of the joint, is a common and likely injury. With broad Elastoplast 'stirrup strapping', walking may still be possible. Put two or three long lengths from mid-calf on the non-injured side under the foot and, with tension applied and the ankle twisted towards the injured side, attach along the calf on the injured side. Follow this with circular strapping from toes to mid-calf overlapping by half on each turn. First aid treatment of sprains and bruises is immobilization (I), cold, e.g. cold compresses (C) and elevation (E); remember ICE.

If painful movement and swelling persist, suspect a fracture.

Fractures: immobilize the part by splinting to a rigid structure; the arm can be strapped to the chest, both legs can be tied together. Temporary splints can be made from a rolled newspaper, an ice-axe or a branch. Pain may be agonizing and is due to movement of broken bone ends on each other; full doses of strong pain killers are needed.

The aim of splinting fractures is to reduce pain and bleeding at the fracture site and thereby reduce shock. Comfort is the best criterion of efficiency of a splint but remember that to immobilise a fracture when the victim is being carried, splints may need to be tighter than seems necessary for comfort when he is at rest, particularly over rough ground. Wounds at a fracture site or visible bones must be covered immediately with sterile or the cleanest material available and if this happens start antibiotic treatment at once. Pneumatic splints provide excellent support but may be inadequate when a victim with a broken leg has a difficult stretcher ride across rough ground. They are of no value for fractured femurs (thigh bones). If you decide to take them get the Athletic Long Leg splint which fits over a climbing boot where the Standard Long Leg splint does not.

Pain: Pain killers fall into three strengths for different grades of pain:

MILD: Aspirin (lowers the temperature but can irritate the stomach). Dose: Up to four 300mg tablets initially, then repeat two tablets at four hourly intervals as necessary. Paracetamol is a useful alternative. Dose: Up to four 500mg tablets, then repeat two tablets four hourly as necessary.

MODERATE: Pentazocine. *Fortral* is probably the best for parties without a doctor who do not wish to impinge on scheduled drug regulations. Dose: Up to four 25mg tablets or two 50mg capsules four hourly as necessary.

STRONG: Pethidine. Morphine – available on special prescription only and there is a risk of trouble with the law if you are caught with these drugs in your possession. Further, they are potentially hazardous (e.g. they may depress breathing) and *should be used only by those with previous special instruction in their use.*

A Suggested Medical Kit

by Drs Peter Steele and John Frankland

For British travellers our normally generous National Health Service does not supply medication for trips abroad (other than for a pre-existing medical condition), and all drugs needed for this purpose have to be purchased – usually at a considerably greater expense than anticipated. Friendly doctors, usually General Practitioners, may, if feeling generous, defray this expense by donating drug 'samples'. Travellers should otherwise ask their doctor to sign the entire list as a private prescription.

American travellers should also obtain drugs on prescription; in some cases it is illegal to buy or possess them without prescription. Take with you the drug prescriptions supplied with the drugs or photocopies of their descriptions (with indications, recommended dosage, etc) . In the USA all drugs are listed in *The Physician's Desk Reference*, published annually. American travellers within easy reach of Mexico may consider buying drugs there: many more drugs are available without prescription than in the USA and they are considerably cheaper.

Store your medical kit in a waterproof and dustproof container that is lockable and kept locked. Transfer liquids and tablets to plastic bottles and attach labels with Sellotape as stuck-on labels can come off in wet heat. Certain items can be stored in plastic pouches with zips. If storing the kit in a vehicle, keep it away from the floor, which is likely to be too hot, and keep it easily accessible at all times. At least one person should be thoroughly familiar with the contents of the kit, knowing instantly the exact location and application of each item. The kit therefore needs to be kept permanently in impeccable order. Where possible one person should issue supplies, as open house will encourage rooting about, the opening of new supplies when part used ones are available, and general chaos. The same person should oversee stocks of drugs and dressings in case more need to be obtained.

For 4–6 persons for 2 months

Basic

Dressings	1 Elastoplast dressing strip 91cm
	50 assorted size Elastoplast dressings
	1 Zinc Oxide strapping plaster 2.5cm × 4.5m
	2 Elastoplast strapping 7.5cm × 4.5m
	1 pack Steristrip 0.6cm × 10cm – to hold small wounds together
	1 Bandage Crepe 7.5cm
	1 Bandage Cotton 5cm
	1 Bandage Triangular
	12 Gauze squares plain
	16 *Melolin* dressings 10 × 10cm – place next to dry wounds
	4 Jelonet or Sofratulle Dressings 10 × 10cm – place next to moist wounds
	1 small cotton wool pack (compressed)
	1 wound dressing No. 15
	1 Netelast Dressing (Head size) – to retain dressings
Cleansing	1 bar soap
	50ml Dettol or TCP solution – to wash wounds
Instruments	1 pr. each Scissors blunt/sharp
	1 Forceps – blunt end
	1 Scalpel blade (sterile)
	4 Safety pins
	2 Thermometers (1 'sub-normal' if low temperature likely)
	Disposable syringes and needles if injectable drugs included
	Paper and ballpoint pen to note drugs given
	2 × 3.0 chromic catgut sutures

Medicines

Pain Killers (mild) see text	100 tabs Soluble Aspirin 300mgs
	50 tabs Paracetamol 500mgs
(moderate) see text	20 Caps *Fortral* 50mgs (Pentazocine)
(strong)	10 tabs Pethidine 50mgs
	or 4 Inj. Pethidine 100 mgs – See warning in text
Antibiotic	40 Cotrimoxazole (*Septrin*, *Bactrim*) – 2 tablets night and morning for five days
	2 ampoules Triplopen
	2 ampoules sterile water – 1 injection i.m. Triplopen and sterile water to patient with an infection who can't swallow
Antihistamine	40 tabs Promethazine (*Phenergan*) 25mgs. – 1 at night
	50 tabs Chlorpheniramine (*Piriton*) 4mgs – 13 × daily as needed
Sleeping	20 tabs Nitrazepam
	(*Mogadon*) 5mgs – 1 or 2 at night
Sedation	20 tabs Diazepam (*Valium*) 2mgs – 1 3 × daily as needed
Diarrhoea	225g Kaolin powder – 2 teaspoonsful in water as necessary
	40 tabs Codeine Phosphate 30mgs – 2 4 × daily as needed
	100 tabs *Lomotil* (Diphenoxylate) – 4 immediately then 2 4 × daily as needed

Constipation	10 tabs *Senokot* – 1–4 at night as needed
Indigestion	30 tabs *Aludrox* or Magnesium Trisilicate – 1 or 2 anytime
	10 tabs *Maxalon* – 1 up to four times daily as necessary for vomiting
Salt	20 tabs *Slow Na.* (Slow sodium) 1-3 daily for 2 days
Anti-worm	4 sachets *Pripsen* (Piperazine) – 1 sachet, repeat in 10 days
Eyes and Ears	5ml *Neo-cortef* eye/ear drops – apply four times daily as necessary
	2 minims Amethocaine – to anaesthetize the eyes
	2 minims Homatropine – to rest an inflamed eye
Teeth	Oil of cloves – apply to aching tooth
	1 gutta percha temporary filling
Skin: Sun	2 tubes *Uvistat* 1 *Lipsyl* 1 tube Calamine cream – apply when necessary
Insects	3 tubes *Flypel* or equivalent
	3 tubes *Anthisan* cream – apply 3 × daily
Fungal infections	1 tube *Canestin* ointment – apply 3 × daily
Barrier cream	1 60g *Conotrane* ointment – apply when necessary
Bruises and sprains	1 × 14g *Lasonil* ointment – apply 3 × daily
Antiseptic	1 10ml 5% Mercurochrome Aq. – apply daily
Infestations	1 ICI Louse and Insect powder – dust with this daily as necessary
Haemorrhoids	10 *Anusol* suppositories – use twice daily
Diuretic (high altitude only)	20 tabs *Lasix* (Frusemide) 40mgs – 2 tabs 4 hourly
Anti-Malarials Preventative	tabs *Paludrine* (Proguanil) – 1 daily
or	tabs *Maloprim* or *Fansidar* (Pyrimethamine) – 1 weekly
	from entering malarial area until 28 days after leaving the area.
Treatment	40 tabs Chloroquine Phosphate – 4 immediately, 2 in six hours then one twice daily for 2 more days
Directory	IAMAT OR INTERMEDIC or other directory of English-speaking doctors.

Individual Kit

Dressings	1 Plaster strip 30 × 6cm
	1 Zinc oxide 2.5cm × 3m 4 *Melolin* 5 × 5cm 1 Crepe bandage 7.5cm 1 Razor blade Paper and ballpoint pen 10 *Fortral* 20 *Phenergan* (25mg)
Diarrhoea	60 *Lomotil*
Sun	1 tube *Uvistat* 1 *Lipsyl*
Throat/Skin/Eyes/Ears	12 Aspirin 1 tube (4gm) *Neo-cortef* eye/ear drops 100 Water purifying tablets If travelling in remote areas for a long period, add appropriate quantities of antibiotics, Chloroquine Phosphate, and *Paludrine*, *Maloprim* or *Fansidar*

Personal drugs sufficient for the whole trip or a list of sources from which they can be obtained in the countries to be visited

Drugs Referred to – Alternative Names Used in Other Countries

The person in charge of the medical kit should understand the appropriate usage and dosage of all the drugs carried. It also helps if brief notes on this are on the labels of all drug containers.

Pharmaceutical Name	*Commonest UK Brand Name*	*Commonest Brand Names in other countries*
Aluminium Hydroxide	Aludrox	Maalox (USA) Actal (Various countries)
Chloroquine Phosphate	Avlaclor	Aralen Hydrochloride (USA)
Chlorpheniramine	Piriton	Allertab, Chlormine, Histadur, Telmin (USA) Chlortrone (Canada)
Chlorimazole 1%	Canestin Cream	Lomotrin (USA)
Codeine Phosphate	Codeine Phosphate	Paveral (Canada)
Cotrimoxazole & Sulpha	Septrin or Bactrim	Septra (USA)
Diazepam	Valium	E-Pam, Serenach, Vival (Canada)
Dimethicone & Hydrargaphen	Conotrane Oint.	Versotrane (Canada)
Diphenoxylate & Atropine	Lomotil	Diarsed (France)
Frusemide	Lasix	Lasiix (France)
Heparinoid & Hyaluronidase	Lasonil Oint.	Hyazine (USA) Wydase (Canada)
Mepyramine Maleate	Anthisan Cream	Antical Cream (USA) Statomin Cream (USA)
Mercurochrome Aq 5%	Mercurochrome Aq 5%	Mercurescein (Canada)
Metoclopramide	Maxolon	Maxeran (Canada) Reglan (USA)
Mexenone	Uvistat Oint.	Uvicone (Australia)
Neomycin & Hydrocortisone	Neo-Cortef Eye/Ear Drops	Neobiotic (USA) Herisan Antibiotic (Canada)
Nitrazepam	Mogadon	Remmnos (Various countries)
Parcetamol	Paracetamol	Capitol, Dolanex, Febrigesic, Nebs (USA) Tempra (Canada)
Pencillins (Mixture of 3)	Triplopen Inj.	Benapen (S. Africa)
Pentazocine	Fortral	Talwin (Canada & USA) Sosenyl (Various countries)
Pethidine	Pethidine	Demeral (USA & Canada) Physadon (Canada)
Piperazine	Pripsen	Antepar (USA) Piperzinal (Canada)
Proguanil	Paludrine	Paludrinal (Canada)
Promethazine	Phenergan	Promethopar (USA) Zipan (USA) Histantil (Canada)
Pyrimethamine	Daraprim or Fansidar	Fansidar, Maloprim (Various countries) Falcidar (Colombia & Venezuela)
Slow release sodium chloride	Slow Na	Neutrasil (Canada) Trisomin (USA)
Standardized Senna Extract	Senokot	Colonorm (Germany)
Vaseline Gauze	Jelonet Gauze or Sofratulle Gauze	Petroleum Gauze (USA)

Diseases

Name of Disease	*Type of Disease*	*How acquired*	*Characteristics*	*Where found*	*Vaccine*
Smallpox (Variola)	Virus	By contact with infected person, articles handled by infected person, flies or by inhalation of polluted air.	Acute infectious fever with headache, vomiting, backache, rigor, temperature of 39.5°C and spots which turn to blisters, then pustules, then crusts. High mortality rate.		yes
Diphtheria	Bacterium	By close contact with infected person, articles handled by infected person.	Toxins absorbed by body, causing systemic poisoning, with sore throat, fever and extreme difficulty in breathing. Sometimes fatal.		yes. Immunity conferred by attack is short-lived.
Polio	Virus	From food, droplets, from an infected person or a carrier. Enters body through intestinal tract.	Affects nerve roots, with headache, vomiting, muscular pains, fever, sometimes convulsions. Severe paralysis and death are not uncommon.		Salk and Sabin vaccines.
Whooping Cough (Pertussis)	Bacterium	By droplet infection.	Fever, running nose, explosive cough followed by long drawn-out crowing inspiration, perhaps vomiting.		yes – lessens severity of attack.
Mumps	Virus	From infected person.	Affects salivary glands and in males may lead to orchitis, inflammation of the testes.		yes – gives protection for up to 2 years.
Tetanus	Bacterium	Through wound or open sore.	Intense and extremely painful muscle spasms.		yes
Measles	Virus	Through respiratory tract, from infected person.	Rather like acute cold at first, then sensitive eyes, cough, sore throat, rash, maybe headache and temperature of 39°C or more.		yes
German Measles (Rubella)	Virus	From infected person.	Rash, mild fever and cold-like symptoms.		yes – may be recommended for women of child-bearing age who have not had the disease.

Chickenpox (Varicella)	Virus	From infected person – child with chickenpox or adult with shingles.	Rash beginning on trunk and spreading outwards, spots turning to blisters, then scabs. Complications rare.		no. One attack confers immunity for life.
Malaria	Plasmodium	Bite of Anopheles mosquito.	Alternating hot, cold and sweating stages with high fever and aches. Disease recurs.	Low-lying marshy land, hot and humid, tropics and sub-tropics, esp. India and parts of America and Africa.	no – but prophylactics are available, e.g. Chloroquine, Paludrine.
Plague	Bacterium	Flies that live on rats; and droplet infection from another person.	Fever, swollen glands. High mortality rate.	Endemic in southern Asia and Africa.	yes – gives partial protection only. Modern treatment is to give sulpha drugs combined with Streptomycin where outbreaks occur.
Yellow Fever	Virus	Bite of Aëdes aegypti mosquito.	Attacks liver and other organs, with fever, rigor, vomiting, jaundice and partial or total suppression of urine. May be fatal.	Moist tropical areas of East and West Africa, Central and South America	yes – given by clinics only, as vaccine is easily damaged or contaminated.
Cholera	Bacterium	From the human intestine, spread by faecally contaminated food or water.	Intestinal infection, with fever, cramps, vomiting, extremely severe diarrhoea, loss of body water and salts.	Endemic in southern Asia, outbreaks occur elsewhere, esp. in war or famine.	yes – effective 6 months only; lessens severity.
Typhoid Fever	Bacterium of salmonella family	Carriers or infected persons, contaminated food or water.	Generalized fever, headache, often acute diarrhoea, nosebleeds, pink rash on abdomen and chest; delirium and temporary loss of memory common.	Endemic in underdeveloped areas, both temperate and tropical, esp. India.	yes – gives protection for a year or more lessens severity.
Typhus Fever	Rickettsial organism (intermediate between bacterium and virus)	Bite of skin parasites, e.g. lice, fleas, ticks, mites.	High fever, headache, rash, clots, pains in back and limbs, rigors; great prostration and delirium.	Endemic in Third World, esp. in uplands of East Africa, Latin America and Asia.	yes

Name of Disease	*Type of Disease*	*How acquired*	*Characteristics*	*Where found*	*Vaccine*
Infective Epidemic Hepatitis	Virus	Droplets or close contact with infected person; contaminated food and water.	Acute inflammation of liver; similar to intestinal influenza, followed by swollen, very tender liver, jaundice.		no*
Serum Hepatitis	Virus	Contaminated hypodermic needles or other medical instruments.	Virus extremely tough, even survives boiling water for a time. Disease similar to but more severe than Infective Hepatitis.		no**
Rabies (Hydrophobia)	Virus	Bite of infected animal (mammals only).	Painful muscle spasms, esp. those brought on by breathing and swallowing; mania, paralysis and death from heart failure. Death almost inevitable after symptoms have manifested themselves.		yes – can be given if appropriate, on doctor's advice.
VD		Sexual contact with infected person.	Syphilis: painless sores at point of sexual contact. Gonorrhoea & urethritis: in men, discharge and pain on passing water; in women, usually no symptoms initially, later pain and infertility.		no – but treatment after infection is always successful to a degree.
Bilharzia		From bathing in water infected by flukes.	Bladder variety: blood in urine. Bowel variety: fever and diarrhoea.	Africa.	no

*Ghamma globulin, an extract of blood serum, gives temporary passive immunity, for 4–6 months, to this and various other viral diseases, including German Measles. It is given by intramuscular injection. It gives complete protection against some diseases and attenuates others. Against Serum Hepatitis there is no evidence that Gamma globulin is effective, except perhaps in very large doses.

**As a preventive measure, disposable syringes or other instruments may be used where there is a risk of infection from instruments inadequately sterilized. Travellers may wish to carry a supply of disposable syringes in their medical kit.

A Place to Stay

Hostelling

by John Carlton and Diane Johnson

Youth Hostels are ideal for the budget traveller, offering an extensive network of accommodation around the world of a reasonable standard and at very affordable prices. They are designed primarily for young people, but there is no age limit (except in Bavaria, Germany) and they are used by the 'young at heart' of all ages.

Youth Hostel facilities are provided by a club run not for profit, but to help young people to travel, to know and love the countryside and appreciate other cultures, thereby promoting international friendship. Each country runs its own hostels independently (usually by committees from within its membership) and the national Youth Hostel Associations of each country are linked through the International Youth Hostel Federation. The Federation (a United Nations style organization) lays down basic standards for its members, but each National Association interprets these in the light of its own local culture.

Theoretically, membership of an Association is necessary for all travellers wishing to use the facilities, but this rule is lax in some countries outside Europe. However, membership is worthwhile, even as a precautionary measure. In England and Wales, the annual subscription is currently £5 for those over 21 or £3 for those between 16 and 21. A similar small fee is the norm elsewhere. It is possible to obtain YHA membership at an Association office (and sometimes at a hostel) outside one's country of residence, but one then pays a much higher fee.

Facilities

Once a member you can stay in any of about 5,000 hostels in 50 countries throughout the world. Basically, a Youth Hostel will provide a bed in a dormitory of varying size. A hostel will have anything from four to 100 beds. There are toilet and washing facilities and a communal room where members can meet, all at a cost of the local equivalent of from £1 to £3 for the night. In most countries, members will find facilities to cook their own food. Cooking utensils and crockery are provided, but not always cutlery. In some countries, cheap meals, cooked by the warden or staff in charge, are on offer.

One familiar feature of Youth Hostel life is the sheet sleeping bag – a sheet sewn into a bag with a space for a pillow. Any traveller intending to use the hostels should have one, although at some hostels there are sheets which may, or indeed, must be hired to protect the mattresses. Most hostels provide blankets and consider that these are adequately protected by the traveller's own sheet sleeping bag. In this respect, as in others, Youth Hostel customs vary from country to country.

A full list of the world's Youth Hostels can be obtained from information centres. Ask for the *International Handbook* – Vol. 1, Europe and the Mediterranean, and Volume 2, The Rest of the World. Each volume costs £2.25 including postage. As well as listing the addresses and facilities of each hostel, the handbook summarizes the local regulations for each country, including prices, lower age limits, facilities for families, etc. However, all the information given is subject to correction as circumstances change during the year and, of course, prices will inevitably rise in time.

Europe

Europe (including many countries in Eastern Europe, but not Russia) is well covered by hostels and the wide variation in their characteristics reflects the local culture of each country. Hostels in the British Isles are perhaps now unique in expecting a small domestic duty from members before departure, but this does help to emphasize to members that they are part of a self-helping club. This idea is less apparent in some countries where the Youth Hostel is often run, with the agreement of the National Association concerned, by the local municipality as a service, and relations between members and staff are strictly commercial. The club atmosphere is stronger also in France, Holland, and Greece. For hostel atmosphere, try Cassis, situated in an isolated position on the hills overlooking the *calanques* of Marseilles, 30km from the city. In West Germany, where the Youth Hostel movement started in 1909, Youth Hostels are plentiful – mostly large, well-appointed buildings, but lacking members' cooking facilities. They are largely devoted to school parties. Scandinavian hostels are also usually well appointed, many having family rooms, and there is therefore more emphasis on family hostelling. Iceland has seven simple hostels.

Africa

In North Africa, there are hostels in Morocco, Tunisia, Libya, Egypt and the Sudan. These too reflect the local culture. Try calling at Asni, a hostel in a Moroccan village 65km south of Marrakesh on the edge of the High Atlas mountains. Here the warden has three wives and will talk to you with great charm in French.

The Kenyan YHA has nine hostels, two of which are on the coast. One is at Malindi and the other at Kanami, about 25km north of Mombasa, in an idyllic setting amongst the coconut palms a few yards from a deserted white sandy beach. The Nairobi hostel is a meeting place for international travellers and at Nanyuki the hostel is close to one of the routes up Mount Kenya. Kitale hostel, near the Ugandan border, is part of a farm with accommodation for eight people and the one room serves as dormitory, dining and common room.

The rest of Africa is devoid of

hostels until one reaches the south. Lesotho has one hostel, Mazeru, which is well worth a visit. Local young Basutos use the hostel as a youth centre, so travellers have a chance to meet them. There is a South African YHA but, because of the country's apartheid policy, it cannot be a member of the International Federation. The membership cards of white members of the Associations within the Federation will, however, be accepted in South Africa. The hostel at Camps Bay, Cape Town, is in a beautiful situation, looking out across the Atlantic Ocean with Table Mountain almost immediately behind it. Unfortunately, Port Elizabeth Hostel, a lovely old Victorian house, is very scruffy by South African standards, but it's in a good position near Kings Beach.

Zimbabwe has two hostels.

Asia

Israel's YHA consists of some 30 hostels, the smallest, in the heart of the old city of Jerusalem, having 70 beds. All provide meals, and many have family rooms, but the members' kitchens are poor. Orphira hostel in southern Sinai is fairly new, with superb snorkelling and diving close at hand. Syrian hostels are small and reasonably equipped. Many hostellers travelling to or from India meet in Damascus. There are fifteen very well-equipped hostels in Saudi Arabia, but only one or two are as yet open to women.

There is a good network in Pakistan, mostly well kept, and there are also a number of Government rest houses open to hostellers, as are some schools in certain areas during school holidays. Indian hostels tend to be mainly in schools and colleges and are therefore only open for short periods of the year, although there is a large new permanent hostel in Delhi. Some hostels do not provide any kind of bedding, even mattresses. Sri Lanka has several hostels including one in Kandy and one in Colombo; here, too, Government rest houses and dak bungalows provide alternative accommodation at a reasonable price. There is a hostel at Kathmandu in Nepal.

The Philippines, South Korea, Malaysia and Thailand all have some hostels of which the Malaysian ones are particularly well organized. In Thailand, some hostels listed in the *International Handbook* appear not to exist. The Bangkok hostel, however, certainly does. None of the five Hong Kong hostels is in the city itself.

Three hostels have recently been opened in New Caledonia under the auspices of the French Association.

Japan has the most extensive network of hostels outside Europe, numbering some 600. There are two kinds – Western style with the usual bunk beds and the Japanese style with a mattress rolled out on the floor. Television is a common feature. Several hostels are on the smaller islands of the country such as Awaji, an island in the Inland Sea. Japanese food is served in most hostels – a bowl of rice, probably served with raw egg, fish and seaweed and eaten with chopsticks.

Australasia and America

Australia has over 100 hostels, mostly in New South Wales, Queensland and Western Australia. Distances between them are great. The smaller, more remote ones, do not have a resident warden and the key has to be collected from a neighbour.

New Zealand has hostels throughout the country. They are fairly small and simple, with no meals provided, but have adequate cooking facilities. Many are in beautiful country, such as the hostel near Mount Cook.

The Canadians still give preference to those arriving on foot or by bike over motorists. They also run a number of temporary city hostels in the summer. There are not many hostels in North American, considering the size of the continent. There are a few hostels in some of the biggest cities. (In the USA, a city hostel will often turn out to be a YMCA offering rooms to YHA members at reduced rates.) Most are in isolated areas of scenic interest not always accessible by public transport. There are, however, chains of hostels in New England, Colorado and the Canadian Rockies. A feature of the United States is the 'Home Hostel' where accommodation is offered to members in private houses.

In Central and South America, Youth Hostelling has not yet caught on seriously, although there are a few hostels in Mexico, Argentina, Chile, Uruguay and Colombia.

Although in the poorer countries of the world you can obtain other accommodation as cheaply as in the local Youth Hostel, members have the advantage of being able to look up an address in advance at points all over the world. They can then stay at the local branch of their own 'club' finding (albeit minimal) common standards of accommodation and be sure of meeting and exchanging experiences with fellow travellers.

Information from:

England and Wales
YHA,
Trevelyan House
8 St. Stephen's Hill
St. Albans
Herts AL1 2DY
Tel: (0727) 55215

YHA Services Ltd
14 Southampton Street
London WC2E 7HY

Scotland
YHA,
7 Glebe Crescent,
Stirling FK8 2JA

Northern Ireland
YHA,
56 Bradbury Place
Belfast BT2 1RU

United States
American Youth Hostels Inc
National Administration Offices
1332 I Street North-West
8th Floor
Washington DC 20005
Tel: (202) 783161

Canada
Canadian Hostelling Association
National Sport and Recreation Centre
333 River Road
Vanier City
Ottowa
Ontario K1L 8B9
Tel: (613) 746 0060

Australia
Youth Hostel Association
60 Mary Street
Surry Hill
New South Wales 2010
Tel: (02) 212 1151

New Zealand
YHA of New Zealand Inc
PO Box 436
Christchurch C1
Tel: 799 970

Non-federated associations

South Africa
YHA
PO Box 4402
Cape Town

Zimbabwe
YHA
PO Box 8521
Causeway
Harare

Camping

I. Do You Really Need it?

by Anthony Smith

The first real camping I ever did was on a student expedition to Persia. There I learned the principle of inessential necessities. We were travelling by truck and could therefore pile everything on board, taking everything we could possibly think of that we might need. The truck could transport it all and we only had the problem of sorting through the excess of gear whenever we wished for something. Later this expedition travelled by donkey as this was the most practical method of visiting the outlying districts in our study area. Miraculously, the number of necessities diminished as we realized the indisputable truth that donkeys carry less than trucks. Later still the expedition travelled on foot, this being the only practical method of prolonging our journey after the donkey drivers had failed to coerce higher rates of pay from very empty student pockets.

Amazingly, the number of necessities decreased yet again as a bunch of humans realized they could carry far less than donkeys and much, much less than trucks. The important lesson learned was that happiness, welfare and ability to work did not lessen one iota as the wherewithal for camping decreased in quantity. In fact it could even have been argued that these three blessings increased as less time was spent in making and breaking camp.

This lesson had to be learned several times over. Sometimes later I was about to travel from Cape Town to England by motorbike. As I wished to sleep out, provide my own meals and experience a road network that was largely corrugated dirt, I found no difficulty in compiling a considerable list of necessities. We must have all made these lists – of corkscrews, tin openers, self-heating soup – and they are great fun, with a momentum that is hard to resist. 'Why not a spare tin opener?' 'And more medicine and another inner tube?' 'Isn't it wise to take more shirts and stave off prickly heat?' Fortunately the garage that sold me the bike put a stop to such idiot thinking. I had just strapped on a sack containing the real essentials – like passport, documents, maps, money and address book – when a passing mechanic told me that any more weight would break the bike's back. (It was a modest machine.) Thus it was that I proceeded up the length of Africa without a sleeping bag, tent, groundsheet, spare petrol, oil, tools, food or even water, and never had cause for regret concerning this lack of wealth. Indeed I blessed the freedom it gave me. I could arrive anywhere, remove my one essential sack and know that nothing, save the bike itself, could be stolen. To have possessions is to be in danger of losing them. Better by far to save the robbers their trouble and start with nothing.

Kippered Hammock

A sound tip is to do what the locals do. If they sleep out with nothing more than a blanket it is probable that your frame can do likewise. If they can get by with a handful of dates at sunset it is quite likely that you too can dispense with half a hundredweight of dried egg, cocoa, vitamin tablets, corned beef, chocolate – and self-heating soup. To follow local practice, then try to improve upon it, can, however, prove disastrous. Having learned the knack of sleeping in a Brazilian hammock, so that my body was as horizontal as if it were in bed, I decided one thunderous night to bring modern technology to my aid. I covered myself with one of those metallic space blankets to keep out the inevitable downpour. Unfortunately, while I was asleep, the wretched thing slipped round beneath me and I awoke to find my body afloat in the pool of water it had collected. Being the first man to drown in a hammock is a poor way of achieving immortality. I looked over at my Indian travelling companion. Instead of fooling around with sub-lethal blankets, he had built a fire longitudinally beneath his hammock. Doubtless kippered by the smoke, but certainly dry, he slept the whole night through.

Planning and Adventure

One trouble with our camping notions is that we are confused by a lingering memory of childhood expeditions. I camp with my children every year and half the fun is not quite getting it right. As all adventure is said to be bad planning, so is a memorable camping holiday in which the guys act as trip wires, the air mattress farts into nothingness and even the tent itself falls victim to the first wind above a breeze. Adults are therefore imbued with an expectation that camping is a slightly comic caper, rich with potential mishap. Those who camp a lot, such as wildlife photographers, have got over this teething stage. They expect camping to be (almost) as smooth and straightforward a business as living in a house. They do their best to make cooking, eating, washing and sleeping no more time-consuming than it is back home. The joy of finding grass in the soup or ants in the pants wears off for them on about the second day. It is only the temporary camper, knowing he will be back in a hotel (thank God) within a week, who does not bother to set things up properly in camp.

I like the camping set-up to be as modest as possible. I have noticed though that others disagree, welcoming every kind of extra. If it is not going to rain, and is not cold, for example, I see little need for a covering. This may be laziness on my part, but it is no Spartan longing to suffer. A night spent beneath the stars that finishes with the first bright shafts of dawn is hardly punishment – but some seem to think it so, and concentrate on removing the natural environment as much as possible.

Surviving Natural Hazards

I remember a valley in the Zagros mountains where I had to stay with some colleagues. I had thought a sleeping bag would be sufficient and placed mine in a dried-up stream, which had piled up sand for additional comfort. Certain others of the party erected large tents with yet larger flysheets (however improbable rain was at that time of year). They also started up a considerable generator which bathed the area in sound and light. As electricity was not a predominant feature of those wild regions considerable numbers of moths and other insects, idling their way between the Persian Gulf and the Caspian Sea, were astonished at such a quantity of illumination and flew down to investigate. To counter their invasion, one camper set fire to several of those insect repellent coils and the whole campsite was shrouded in noxious effluent. Over in the dried-up stream I and two fellow spirits were amazed at the camping travesty down the way. We were even more astonished when, after a peaceful night, we awoke to hear complaints that a strong wind had so flapped at the flies that no one inside a tent had achieved a wink of sleep.

The most civilized camping I have ever experienced was in the Himalayas. The season was spring and tents are then most necessary both at the lower altitudes (where it rains a lot) and at the higher ones (where it freezes quite considerably). Major refreshment is also necessary because walking in those mountains is exhausting work, being always up, as the local saying puts it, except when its down. We slept inside sleeping bags on foam rubber within thick tents. We ate hot meals three times a day. We did very well – but then we did not carry a thing. For the six of us there were 36 porters at the outset, the number being reduced as we ate into the provisions these men were carrying. I laboured up and down mighty valleys, longing for the next refreshment point and always delighted to see the already-erected tents at each night's stopping place. Personally I was burdened with one camera, the smallest of notebooks and nothing more. The living conditions, as I have said, were excellent, but what would they have become if I had been asked to carry everything I needed myself? It is at that point, when neither trucks, nor donkeys, nor incredibly hardy mountain men are available, that the camper's true necessities are clarified. For myself, I am happy even to dispense with the toothbrush if I have to carry the thing all day long. Just a blanket will do if that is what the locals use. My body may not be like theirs in the early days, but, given encouragement, it can become half as good as the weeks go by.

II. Yes, You Really Need It

by Jack Jackson

This advice applies to campers for whom weight of equipment is not of the first importance.

Tents

Large groups planning to have a fixed camp for some time will find it very useful to have a large mess tent where the party can all congregate for meals and during bad weather.

Inflatable tents have obvious drawbacks. Dust, grit, thorns and sunlight destroy the rubber, and if blown up in the cool of the day, these tents have a habit of bursting when sunlight warms up the air in them too much.

On the hard, sunbaked ground in hot countries the pegs normally supplied with tents are of little use, so have some good, thick, strong pegs made for you from 60mm iron, or else use 15cm nails. As wooden mallets will not drive pegs in, carry a normal claw hammer and you can also use the claw to pull the pegs out again. In loosely compacted snow, standard metal pegs do not have much holding power, so it is useful to make some with a larger surface area from 2.5-cm angle alloy. Even this does not solve all the problems because any warmth during the day will make the pegs warm up, melt the snow around them, and pull out – so the tent falls down. The answer is to use very big pegs or ice axes for the two main guys fore and aft and then, for all the other guys, dig a hole about 25cm deep, put the pegs in horizontally with the guy line around its centre and compress fresh snow down hard with your boots on it to fill the hole.

Vango now offer a special 'tent anchor' for snow and soft sand; it is not any better in snow than the method describe above, but is good in soft sand. Four of these would normally be all you would carry per tent.

If you sleep without a tent, you will need a mosquito net in some areas. There are several types on the market, but they are not usually big enough to tuck in properly, so get the ex-army ones which have the extra advantage of needing only one point of suspension: your camera tripod or ice axe will do for this if there is not a vehicle or tent nearby.

Since tents take heavy wear, carry some strong thread and a sailmaker's needle for repairs plus some spare groundsheet material and adhesive. Tents which are to be carried by porters, on donkeys, or on a vehicle roof rack are best kept in a strong kit bag or they will soon be torn.

When you are staying in a sunny area for several days and have no need to get up early, pitch your tent in a shaded spot (remember that the sun rises in the east!), or the heat will drive you out soon after sunrise. If it is not a windy area, a 'space blanket' covering the reflecting side of the tent will help keep the tent cool during the day.

Mattresses

In cold places, you should not sleep directly on the ground so use some form of insulation. Air beds have disadvantages: inflating them is hard work when you are tired; sharp stones, thorns and sunlight all work against them; you will certainly spend a lot of time patching them up. If you decide to use one, be sure it is rubber not plastic, and then only pump it halfway. If you pump it any higher, you will roll around and probably fall off. Even on cold nights you will wake up in a puddle of condensed perspiration unless you have put a blanket or woollen jumper between yourself and the mattress. An air mattress is useful if one needs to travel light. Camp beds tend to be narrow, collapse frequently, tear holes in the groundsheet and soon break up altogether. Worst of all, cold air circulates underneath the bed. Since your body weight compresses the bedding, only several layers of blankets will give you the insulation you need.

The best mattress for cold weather camping is made of polythene or rubber foam. Unfortunately, the majority of those on the market are cheap and not dense enough. Even the best name brands such as Dunlop are not adequate. However, one brand stands out above all others in density and thickness. This is made by P. T. C. Langdon and is called Spatzmola. Spatzmola foams are not easy to find and may have to be ordered. In the UK you can usually get them at Pindisports or order them from other camping suppliers. Though they cost twice the price of the others, they are by far the most comfortable and are highly recommended.

All foams tend to tear very easily but if you make a washable cotton cover which fully encloses them, they will last for several years. Foams, being bulky, are best wrapped in strong waterproof covers during transport. Personally, I use only half a Spatzmola, enough for hips to shoulder and use a climber's closed-cell foam insulating mat called Karrimat, known in the USA as insulite, for my legs and feet. This cuts down on bulk. One advantage of foam mattresses is that the perspiration that collects in them evaporates very quickly when aired so they are easy to keep fresh and dry. Remember to give the foam an airing every second day. Karrimat make mats of any size to order. Karrimat also comes in a 3-mm thickness suitable for putting under a groundsheet for protection against sharp stones or on ice, where otherwise the tent groundsheet could stick to the ice and be torn while trying to get it free.

On a long overland trip, you can combat changing conditions with a combination of two sleeping bags. First get a medium-quality nylon-covered down-filled sleeping bag and, if you are tall, make sure it is long enough for you. This bag will be the one you use most often for medium cold nights. Secondly, get a cheap all-synthetic bag, i.e. one filled with artificial fibre. These cheap, easily washable bags are best for use along on warmer nights and outside the down bag for very cold nights. Make sure the synthetic bag is big enough to go outside the down bag without compressing it when fully lofted up.

In polar and high mountain areas, the golden rule when travelling is never to be parted from your own sleeping bag, in case a blizzard or accident breaks up the party.

Furniture and Utensils

The aluminium chairs on the market today are covered with light cotton. This rots quickly in intense sunlight. Look around for nylon or terylene-covered furniture or replace the cotton coverings with your own. Full-size ammunition boxes are good for protecting kitchenware and also make good seats.

When buying utensils, go for the dull-grey aluminium ones. Shiny-type aluminium pans tend to crack and split with repeated knocks and vibration. Billies, pots and pans, plates, mugs, cutlery, etc., should be firmly packed inside boxes or they will rub against each other and end up as a mass of metal filings. A pressure cooker guarantees sterile food and can double as a large billy, so if you have room it is a very good investment.

Kettles with lids are preferable to whistling kettles, which are difficult to fill from cans or streams. For melting snow and ice it is best to use billies. Big strong aluminium billies are best bought at Army and Navy auctions or surplus stores.

A wide range of non-breakable cups and plates is available, but you will find that soft plastic ones leave a bad aftertaste so it is better to pay a little more and get melamine. Stick to large mugs with firm wide bases that will not tip over easily. Insulated mugs soon become smelly and unhygienic because dirt and water get between the two layers and cannot be cleaned out.

Many people like metal mugs but if you like your drinks hot you may find the handle too hot to touch or burn your lips on the metal. Melamine mugs soon get stained with tea or coffee but there are cleaners available, or Steradent is a perfectly adequate and much cheaper substitute. Heavyweight stainless steel cutlery is much more durable than aluminium for a long expedition.

For carrying water, ex-military plastic jerry cans are best, as they are lightproof and therefore algae will not grow inside them as it does with normal plastic watercans.

Stoves and Gas

Liquid petroleum gas is usually referred to as Calor Gas or butane gas in the UK and by various oil company names worldwide, such as Shellgas or Essogas. Though available worldwide there are different fittings on the bottles in different countries and these are not interchangeable.

Various smaller non-refillable gas cartridges exist for smaller camping stoves under various trade marks and fittings, the most common of these being Camping Gaz which is available in Europe, some African and Arabian countries, South East Asia and Australia. For high-altitude and cold-weather use, Camping Gaz can be ordered as propane in Europe. Refillable Camping Gaz bottles as supplied in Europe are meant to be factory refilled, but in some countries, e.g., Algeria, Morocco, Yemen Arab Republic, they are available with an overfill release so that you can fill them yourself from a larger domestic butane gas supply.

Gas bottles are very heavy and refilling can be a major nuisance as connectors and regulations vary from country to country. Neither butane nor propane is readily found in Asia. Enterprising campsite managers in Turkey and Iran have discovered ways of filling gas bottles from their own supply. Stand well clear while they do it as the process involves pushing down the ball valve with a nail or small stone and then overfilling from a bottled supply of higher pressure. This can cause flare-up problems when the bottle is used with standard cooking equipment so if you use this source of supply, it is advisable to release some of the pressure by opening up the valve for a couple of minutes well away from any open flame before hooking it up. The refillable Camping Gaz containers with a side overfill valve are available in France to special order.

The 2.7kg gas cartridge or the 4.5kg gas cylinder are the best sizes to carry. Gas is, without doubt, the easiest and cleanest fuel to use for cooking. Where you use a pressure reduction valve on a low-pressure appliance, there will always be a rubber tube connection. Make sure that you carry some spares of the correct-size rubber tubing.

Lighting stoves is always a problem in cold climates or at altitude. Local matches and Russian matches never work unless you strike three together, so take a supply of Bryant and May. The best answer seems to be a butane cigarette lighter kept in your trouser pocket, where it will be warm. Remember to carry plenty of refills.

Space Blankets

Space blankets, very much advertised by their manufacturers, are, on the evidence, not much better than a polythene sheet or bag. Body perspiration tends to condense on the inside of them, making the sleeping bag wet so that the person inside gets cold. In hot or desert areas, however, used in reverse to reflect the sun, they are very good during the heat of the day to keep a tent or vehicle cool. If necessary, a plastic sheet or space blanket can be spread over a ring of boulders to make an effective bath.

Buying

When buying equipment, be especially wary of any shop that calls itself an expedition supplier but does not stock the better brands of equipment. All the top-class equipment suppliers will give trade discounts to genuine expeditions or group buyers such as clubs or educational establishments and some, such as Pindisports and Field and Trek, have special contract departments for this service.

Camping Checklist

by Jack Jackson

For a party or family of four which doesn't have to worry about travelling light:

Good compass, maps and guidebooks
Selection of plastic bags for waste disposal, etc.
Clingfilm and aluminium foil for food and cooking
Large bowl for washing up and washing
4 × 20 litre water jerry cans – strong ex-military-type
Fire extinguisher
Large supply of paper towels, toilet paper, Scotchbrites, plus dishcloths, e.g. J-cloths and tea-towels
Large supply of good matches in waterproof box and/or disposable lighters
Washing up liquid for dishes (also good for greasy hands)
Frying pan
Pressure cooker
Selection of strong saucepans or billies
Kettle with lid (not whistling type which is difficult to fill from cans or streams)
Tin opener – good heavyweight or wall type
Stainless steel cutlery
Plastic screw-top jars for sugar, salt,

coffee, tea, etc.
1 large sharp bread knife
2 small sharp vegetable knives
1 large serving spoon and soup ladle
Good twin burner for your gas supply, otherwise petrol or kerosene twin burner cooker
Good sleeping bag or sleeping bag combination for the climate expected, plus mattress of your choice
Combined mosquito and insect repellent spray
Battery-powered fluorescent light
4 lightweight folding chairs
Plates and/or bowls for eating
Wide-bottomed mugs which do not tip over easily
Large supply of paper plates if you have room
Short-handled hand-axe
Thin nylon line to use as clothesline, plus clothes pegs
6 plastic or wire lightweight clothes hangers
Washing powder for clothes
6 metres of plastic tubing to fill water tank or jerry cans
2 tubes of universal glue/sealant, e.g. Bostik
Chamois leather
Sponges
6 heavy rubber 'tie downs'
Water-purification filters plus tablets or iodine as backup
Phrase books/dictionaries
2 torches plus spare batteries
Kitchen scissors
Ordinary scissors
Small plastic dustpan and brush
Soap, shampoo, toothpaste, towels
Medical first-aid kit plus multivitamins
Elastic bands
Sewing kit and safety pins
Cassette player and selection of cassettes
Selection of reading material
Hidden strong-box or money belt

Many other things to be taken along, but most of these are personal belongings. They include:

dental floss, waterproof watch, Kleenex and handkerchiefs (good for many other reasons than blowing your nose), clothing and underwear, socks, trousers, shirts, tie (for the formal invitation that may crop up; store the tie rolled up in a jar with a lid), dress (for that same occasion), jackets, coats, raincoats, gloves, bathing suits, shoes, jumpers, belts, parkas with hoods, moisturising cream, toothbrushes, comb, pocket-knife, camera, film, photographic accessories, anti-malarial tablets and salt tablets where required, sun barrier cream, sunglasses, medicaments, spare spectacles if worn, passports, visas, traveller's cheques, inoculation certificates, car papers, insurance papers, money, airmail writing paper, envelopes and pens.

On a Limited Budget

by Christopher Portway

There is a military saying that 'any bloody fool can be uncomfortable' which has a lot going for it. For the traveller it is equally pertinent. However, while the soldier's degree of comfort is governed by strategic circumstances and disciplinary attitudes of the higher echelons, that of the traveller is usually governed by cost and security with comfort itself being the best on offer between the two.

This is not to say that even a

traveller – as opposed to tourist – has to slum it all the time. I myself don't really go much for luxury hotels, although as a travel writer, I'm not always able to escape the multiple star attention at their hands. The trouble is that most quality establishments have a depressing sameness about them. Not that I don't sometimes appreciate their comforts and gastronomic excesses after weeks in the African bush or Asian jungle.

Oddly enough, it's the reverse of the coin that lingers in my memory. Long after the Bournemouth Carlton or Nairobi Norfolk's expensive attractions are no more than a hole in the bank balance, the recollection of a night of exquisite horror in an Afghan dosshouse takes on the allure of fond evocation.

Thus it can be said that the cheaper you go, the more interesting are the people you're likely to meet and, basically, the more satisfaction the traveller is wont to attain. We usually visit a strange country to see how it ticks and you won't learn anything from an air-conditioned, chromium-plated emporium whether it's in Bangkok or Bali. Yet, having said this, let me revert to my opinion that an occasional encroachment into millionaire's row does wonders for morale as well as the state of one's cleanliness.

Vehicle and/or tent camping is one method of keeping accommodation costs down, but both have their limitations so far as comfort and security are concerned. Even the most basic hotel, hostel, pension or guest house can usually rise to a shower (if only a cold one) and many will rustle up a meal which can make a nice change from eternal self-catering. Leave your luggage somewhere before arriving at the hotel, so as to avoid giving the impression that you are desperate to accept the first room offered. *Always* ask to see the room before deciding to sleep in it and check the price – not forgetting the government taxes and other additions. In many Third World countries, a vital consideration is security, so it is important to make sure your bedroom door has a lock that works.

Bed and Breakfast

In some countries of the world there are government-run, or state-owned accommodations that are well worth considering on all counts. The *pousadas* of Portugal are a case in point; good value, but not cheap. And, of course, the internationally known and respected Youth Hostel Association has a reputation to uphold. And in Europe too, there are in France, the *gîtes*, a home from home – or at least someone else's home – where you can stay for periods long or short. But they are not normally bookable for periods of less than one week, reckoned from Saturday to Saturday.

The British institution of Bed and Breakfast is spreading – you'll frequently see *zimmer* and *chambre* in German and French windows and they are fine so far as the room with a bed is concerned, but breakfast is usually extra or not at all and France, in particular, does so short-change one with breakfast. But in the United States, they have the right idea with a bed and breakfast where a stack of pancakes covered in syrup is added to a mammoth British-style fry-up. The concept has not yet completely conquered North America, but give it time; they still can't quite get rid of their down-at-heel motel image. However, you can, even now, book ahead with one of the B&B 'chains' prior to arrival in the United States and so have your accommodation fixed all along your proposed route. (Travel Associates Ltd, 1 Morden Lane, London SE13.)

Throughout Africa and Asia, good and inexpensive board and lodging is provided by 'resthouses'. Those in India I know particularly well. Each varies in character, amenities offered, comfort and – vital to some – the availability of water for washing. In the Himalayas, those built by the forest administration under former British rule were constructed in high, commanding positions far above villages and roads. Here they are built of stone and timber in what might be described as Victorian railway station style, each with two or three bedrooms, plainly furnished, with a bathroom and storeroom at the rear. The wooden veranda at the front is the trademark of all such resthouses, while respectfully at a distance are the staff quarters and kitchen. In the more remote areas, all signs of the minor luxuries a traveller could expect during the time of the British Raj have vanished, but nearer towns, I found treats in store: freshly painted bungalows valiantly clinging to the remnants of their former glory. Resthouses can also be found in Iran, sporting the added luxury of Persian carpets, while Indian Dak bungalows are also available extremely cheaply on a first come, first served basis.

The Communist Countries

In the Communist countries, one is more constrained. China insists you go into a tourist hotel whether you like it or not, and most are enormous barrack-like places, perfectly adequate for comfort though far from luxurious and lacking the slightest individuality or character. No need for security here as violent crime and theft are rare. It was only at Turfan, in Sinkiang that I came across a charming lodge – a foreign visitor's guesthouse they called it – with a grapevine-roofed forecourt and old-fashioned waterjug and bowls for washing. In Inner Mongolia they offered me a tourist *yurt* which was clean and comfortable, and not at all like the real thing. In Russia, nothing ever worked in the tourist hotels I stayed in: lifts inoperative, telephones that trilled unasked for early morning calls, baths and basins with no plugs, and taps that produced rusty water or none. The East European states, as well as Russia, sometimes make entry conditional upon the purchase of accommodation in advance because of their anxiety to get their hands on our hard currency. But once you are in, a number of People's Republics – but not the Soviet Union – offer a choice of graded hotels, hostels or private house accommodation at a fixed and inexpensive price. Your private house hosts will almost certainly be selected not only for linguistic ability but also for political reliability but, nevertheless, this is a very worthwhile form of board and lodging. I have stayed thus in Bulgaria and Romania and in both countries I was given meals that formed no part of the transaction though I managed to return the compliment by sending my hosts some English books they were unable to obtain locally.

Desperation

I've never yet had to bribe my way into a hotel though the practice is said to be widespread in Third World countries. I have, however, arrived in towns where hotels could not or would not accept me. This happened in Libya. Just try getting a room, however modest, in its capital, Tripoli! Making a reservation won't help either for they'll deny having received your instructions – even if you've got their booking confirmation to wave in their faces. My solution was to lay out my sleeping bag in the lush gardens of the city's central square and prepare for a perfectly satisfactory night under the stars. Within minutes, along came a jeep-load of armed police demanding that I sleep in a hotel. 'Find one for me and I will,' I replied. And, you know, they did.

In countries like China – including Tibet, which is now opening its expensive but evocative doors – a visitor can, in normal circumstances, travel only in a group with prearranged accommodation, so hotel booking problems don't arise. It was the same when I went to Cuba a few years back; there, whatever the calibre of the hotel, there was no air-conditioning, which meant that summer nights were one long sweat. In these conditions, it's best to escape to the beach or swimming pool – or even the shower, if it works. Another group-minded country is Albania where its foreign tourists-only hotels leave much to be desired. Even in Tirana's showpiece Dajti, I flushed the downstairs toilet and sent a river of water through the foyer. At the Adriatik in the port and resort of Durres, water came on only at night, between two and three a.m. The more pernickety of us adjusted our lives accordingly though I undertook my ablutions in the sea and used the quite undrinkable ersatz coffee for shaving.

Worse than no air-conditioning is too much air-conditioning and the United States is the chief culprit here. I stayed once in the second-best hotel in Dallas; a whole suite of rooms they gave me, but I spent most of my night unscrewing the bolted-up window.

Desert Lodgings

The desert, of course, produces another kind of lodging that comes under the heading of hospitality. A traveller in the Sahara or the Gobi will never lack for food and shelter, for among the great sand seas and stony plains, all men are equal. A Bedouin tent is filthy, full of vermin and dirty sheep, goats and children, while the sand-gritted food offerings are best not too closely observed. But here is to be found the true brotherhood of man: so never abuse such offerings, for the deserts of this world have a way of dealing with the foolish and the selfish.

If you are travelling in Arabia or Yemen, you will come across the *fondouk*, a kind of dormitory where everyone sleeps happily on mattresses on the floor. Many of these community sleeping rooms are multi-storey houses more like medieval forts, and some will supply a simple but satisfying meal. Conveniences and amenities are of the roughest and with no electric light a torch becomes a prime possession if you have to find the loo at night. A problem here is security of one's belongings and the best solution I can offer is to take what you can to bed with you. In a land where hotel accommodation is viciously expensive, the *fondouk* has its points.

Turkey, Iran, Afghanistan, Pakistan, India – the route to the East – can produce some real nightmares of accommodation that you will remember with delight back at home (I speak now of days gone by and – God, war and revolution willing – days to come). The Majestic – no more than a doss-house – in Jelalabad shines the darkest in my personal tableau of sheer horror. We slept in rows along a kind of sleeping gallery. My neighbours were bearded, leering Afghan tribesmen engulfed in colourful robes and powerful smells, and they went to bed not only with their baggy trousers on but also their daggers, swords and assorted musketry. Trapped in the middle of this snoring mob I lay feeling the rats scurrying over my blanket and, in the early hours, watched the most bulbous spider in history slowly descending towards me from a bug-infested ceiling.

There are no rules for worldwide hotel sojourning, but one important accoutrement for the traveller is an ability to accept life as it comes and appreciate the culture – or lack of it – of the country concerned. Accommodation can, if you let it, tell you a lot about people, particularly in those lodgings to be had at the lower end of the scale. They'll cost you little but the experience will be immense.

Palaces of the People

by Carol Wright

Hotels are one of the world's oldest professions, and travellers have been consoled by their variability since the days when Mary and Joseph found there was no room at the inn. In certain African countries and in large cities where hotel construction has not kept up with visitor demand, overbooking still exists and the traveller must expect a little tipping, in West Africa in particular, to smooth his path to bed. In other places, it's best to remain unmoved on somewhat slim rights of confirmed vouchers and booking slip and threaten to sleep in the lobby if not accommodated. If one exists, the local tourist board is likely to be the most sympathetic to complaints and will try and find accommodation if possible.

Booking

Booking through a London hotel agency such as HRI, who have represented de luxe hotels since 1927, or part of an international chain gets free direct and confirmed bookings by telex. The French Government Tourist Office issues a helpful calendar showing when Paris hotels are likely to be at their fullest.

It's worth checking too with a leading convention firm or magazine if there is a convention on at your chosen destination. Delhi, last March, summarily closed all its five-star hotels, removed booked-in clients, and filled them with delegates for the non-aligned conference. In any case, there is nothing worse than being the single traveller among hearty name-labelled hordes. I once stayed at the 1,407-bedroomed Grand Hyatt in New York along with 1,300 lady masons. It took a half-hour supervized queue to get to an elevator. Service, whether in room or restaurant, disappears when a convention is on.

As a general hotel principle, small is beautiful. In anything under 50 rooms, more attention and character are to be expected. The big international chains like Hilton, Sheraton, THF and Hyatt have realized that the businessman and regular, educated traveller does not like the impersonal attitude of the big hotels. For the businessman, many Far Eastern hotels include a Business Corner with office-style facilities and the Gatwick Hilton has dial secretarial help from the rooms. The London Hilton provides bleepers for in-hotel phone messages. But the big chains are taking a leaf out of the airlines' book, with the executive class-section and splitting off a floor of their property and turning this into a club-like area for a small extra charge. These floors have separate access, usually a hostess, club room for free breakfast, bar service, magazines and games and separate fast checkout. Now non-smokers can have separate facilities in an increasing number of hotels like the Four Seasons group and Manila Hilton.

Speedy checkout is needed by anyone at a hotel, and in the UK and the States, the larger hotels are helping to facilitate this by taking a credit card impression on arrival so bills can be sent on after departure. In cities where hotel construction has exceeded customer demand such as Hong Kong (currently), Manila and Bangkok, one can often get good rates with a little reception desk bargaining and showing of business cards. Off-season bargains can be sought and being in a business hotel at weekends often earns a discount. Holiday Inns in Britain, for example, encourage family weekends with the inclusion of special children's hostesses and programme of activities.

Entertainment

To keep clients fit and amused, leading groups are increasingly providing sports and health club amenities. It may be as simple as the loan of jogging gear and a map as at the Four Seasons hotels, or jogging tracks round the hotel as at Rome's Sheraton and Toronto's Castle Harbour (which is heated in winter) and the health club provision is increasing even in our own Post Houses. In Sweden, compulsory fallout shelters often double as a gym for guests. Holiday Inns go for indoor pools and many in Britain also have sun bed/solarium areas. Tennis is a Marriott thing and massage in the Far East can often be summoned on room service. The Carlton Hotel in Bournemouth has its own branch of Champneys health farm and in the States, Hilton Inns have a special book on exercises to be done in the rooms and diet recipes are served in the restaurants.

The more costly hotels can provide more service such as the Swiss Burgenstock hotel where, if you can find a nice picnic spot, the hotel will send out hampers for a *fête champêtre*. Service can be providing spectacles to read the menu, a yachtsman's weather centre as at Stanwell House in Lymington, a house astrologer as at Agra's Sheraton, or just cleaning shoes overnight. Service is more forthcoming in countries where labour is cheap; the Philippines, India and Hong Kong have excellently serviced hotels. In Third World countries where women still stay at home and room service is done by boys, the standard is not always as high.

Caring for the soul rather than the body of a visitor is rare apart from bibles in the bedside drawer, but the Hyatt Galindo in Mexico, Manila Hilton, Jameson in Harare and Burgenstock all have their own chapels. Many Japanese hotels have special wedding rooms.

Self Service

While top American hotels are putting more continental-style service into their glossiest properties, the cutting back on services is one way of keeping hotel prices down. The New Airliner Hotel at Miami Airport is one of three such self-service hotels in Florida and Scandinavian countries are trying variations of this. At Miami, while saving about a third off local prices, one collects towels, soap and plastic glasses from the reception on arrival and carries one's luggage to the room where the bed is made up for the only time during the stay. Fresh sheets can be exchanged for used as required at reception and a vacuum cleaner borrowed for self-housekeeping.

The Japanese, with high land costs, have gone for cheap (around £7 a night) capsule hotels in which one sleeps in something resembling a tiered inside of a washing machine; body-sized, with inset radio, TV, alarm and radio and a pull-down blind. Bathrooms are on separate floors and in some there are areas for ladies.

The future in hotels, predicts Holiday Inns' president, is a computer terminal in each room, from which dining table, menu and wines can be selected and ordered by remote control and hotel services detailed on the screen. Bathrooms will all contain whirlpool and steam baths in addition to a shower and tub and hotel rooms will be linked to airline seats and luggage transferred automatically to rooms from the plane (some hope here).

Women Alone

Women travelling alone get less than welcoming reactions from some hotel areas, particularly in Japan where they refuse to believe you travel alone and in Britain, where you are often thought to be someone 'not quite nice'. American hotels often site women near the elevator; noisy, but it saves long night walks along dim corridors. Best Western did a survey and found women want good lighting, mirrors and security; lockable doors rather than the hairdriers, magazines and flowers which Hilton provide in the States. The Bristol in London has a special club floor for women and the lovely ability to have hair and beauty treatments in your own room. The New Otani in Japan has a separate floor for mothers with small children with special baby foods and nursery. THF detail their Family Holiday Hotels with special facilities for children and provide children's menus at their establishments.

Dogs do well at the Imperial in Torquay where they will provide a special dog's dinner and at Henllys Hall on Anglesey where the last weekend of every month is offered as a luxury weekend for dogs; two nights' bed and breakfast is £40 per dog, £20 per adult; the dog also gets a small-version, four-poster bed.

Palace Hotels

Best value hotels are where governments are keen to encourage visitors to spread out and see more of their country. The demise of the maharajahs helped India have a set of uniquely sumptuous palace hotels. Sri Lanka has kept up the old raj rest house system for tourists and in Spain and Portugal old manor houses, palaces, castles and convents have been turned into paradors and pousadas, beautiful, characterful stop-over places at low prices with local food. Details can be obtained for the tourist boards and they are essentially usable for motor touring. In Greece, the national Xenia group of simple, but quite adequate hotels provided good basic accommodation before private hotels sprang up.

Airport hotels are, on the whole, places to be avoided, drawing to themselves the dreariness and characterless practicality of airports; the most dull of nightly international human filing cabinets. The Sheraton Skyline at Heathrow is an exception with superb end-of-lobby tropical plants, a garden surrounding a big indoor pool with café tables – and here they have comfortable rooms. The same company's River House two minutes from Miami's terminals is a hotel where you could contemplate a vacation overlooking a championship golf course and river with boats for hire, swimming pool, tennis courts and live nightly music and good restaurants. The Gatwick Hilton has in-room flight departure displays on TV screens, its own health club, pool, and is fifteen minutes flat from room to check-in counter. The Rome Sheraton has Alitalia check-in and baggage carriage from the lobby and the Bombay airport's Centaur has Air India check-in and a delightful circular pool area.

The traveller does not often want a bed overnight. Late evening or middle of the night plane or train departure necessitates a rest and wash during the day. Hotels have enough problems getting one lot of guests out before another arrives, but do not always make enough of day-room possibilities. Airport areas are better bets and often quote a reasonable day figure, such as £20 for half a day at the Berkeley Arms, Cranford. This is worth considering faced with long departure delays as one can relax, doze, watch TV, bathe and order food or room service and return to the terminal on the free hotel bus; much better than sitting it out in dirty, crowded lounges. In Italy, the Alberghi diurnale at the railway stations are boons for day rest and bath facilities.

Security

Hotels can be as varied as up a tree (in Kenya and Zimbabwe game parks); down a hole, or Roman well, as at Matmata in Tunisia's Sahara fringe for coolness; in a floating museum as on the *Queen Mary* at Long Beach; in castles or converted cow sheds. But with all, for casual arrivals, one should ask to see the room and check its price before agreeing to stay. Valuables should be put in the hotel safe; get a detailed receipt for them and remember that hotels have very low limits in law on what they will pay out if anything is stolen from their safe nd will often not inform the police in ase the hotel gets a bad name. A ifco hang-on-the-door-handle alarm elps against sneak thieves. Be wary f hotels that don't cover key boards ehind reception. The London hotel olice squad (one of only two in existnce, along with New York) says otel theft is reduced when key oards are not visible and thieves an't tell who is in or out. The Hilton roup is introducing Uniquey computer numbered cards that open doors nd are destroyed after each guest aves. Luggage should be put on rrival in special hotel luggage rooms, ot left in piles in the lobby. Hotels, articularly in the Middle East, rob heir clients when they use the phone. possible use a public phone or elephone credit card to cut big surharges.

dditions to Comfort

ther extras to take to hotels, however glossy, are an alarm clock; eyeshades – few hotel curtains fit properly and light pours in under the doors – wax ear plugs against the inevitable room by the lift shaft, over the kitchen or disco; a plastic hanger to drip-dry clothes when thief-proof fixed hangers are the only ones in the room and a small torch in case of power failure, fire and a need to find the bathroom in a hurry at night – the Lai Lai in Taipei does provide a rechargeable torch fixed by the bedside. Check out fire exits and instructions; many US hotels now provide booklets and TV programmes on what to do. The future, it is said, will have plastic bags with fire safety masks hung behind the door. Meanwhile, the nervous can take a light S-cape hood made for the National Coal Board with vision visor and filtered breathing. And remember the hurricane season in the Caribbean is at its peak in August and September; the Jamaica Hilton records winds of 135mph and has its own wind emergency regulations.

Dealing with People

Learning a Language

Adapted from an article in Holiday Which? with the kind permission of the Consumers' Association, and updated by Anne Wilson.

Can you tell a *tarte* from a *torte*, or even a *tortilla*? Or is your contact with the locals confined to schoolroom French, gesticulating hands or English pronounced slowly and clearly at the top of your voice?

Adult education classes in holiday languages are booming, and in every newspaper or bookshop you can see claims for 'almost instant packaged language learning' using the 'latest wonder method'. So how do you start?

We've looked at the main ways used to learn a language – local education authority (LEA) classes and teach-yourself methods – and at the main advantages and disadvantages of each.

Learning methods

The main ways of learning are:

Group classes – lots available, run by LEAs, private language schools or cultural institutes – such as the *Alliance Français* or *Goethe-Institut*. They can involve anything from one evening a week to intensive courses all day for several weeks. Ask your local education authority, local library, the cultural section of an embassy, or look up 'Schools – Language' in the Yellow Pages. Cost: LEA courses are usually cheapest, from about £8 for a term; private schools charge widely varying prices for their courses, anything from around £30 to well over £1,000 (for an intensive course of several weeks).

Private tuition – private language schools and some LEAs have private classes. The Institute of Linguists, 24a Highbury Grove, London N5 2EA (Tel: 01-359 7445) or regional branches of teachers' associations such as the Modern Language Association (head office at the same address as the Institute of Linguists (Tel: 01-359 7953)) can give details of private tutors or where to find out about them; also look under 'Tutoring' in the Yellow Pages or the small ads in, for example, the LEA guides to courses. Cost: from £5 to £15 per hour. Intensive courses can be pretty pricy. For instance, one week's Total Immersion Course at a Berlitz Language School – branches in London, Birmingham, Leeds, Manchester and Edinburgh – might set you back as much as £1,400.

Correspondence courses – offered by some colleges, listed by the Council for the Accreditation of Correspond ence Colleges (CACC), 27 Marylebone Road, London NW1 5JS. Tel: 01-935 5391. Cost: from about £40 to £80 – intensive or advanced courses can cost a lot more.

Teach yourself – using books, or a combination of books, cassette tapes, records, radio and television; you might be able to borrow these from libraries. Cost from nothing if you borrow a book to around £400 for a full programme of cassettes and learning books.

Language laboratory courses – offered by LEAs, particularly in larger polytechnics or technical colleges, and by private language schools. They may be flexible 'use the lab when you want' schemes or fixed classes, or supplementary to other, mainly group, courses. They vary from simple tape records with headphones to computer-controlled systems, with individual booths connected to a master console. In some laboratories, students can work at their own pace, recording and then listening to their own voices. In others, pace is controlled by the teacher, so a student can't play them back. In all language laboratory work, a lot depends on how much supervision the teacher is able to give, and how good the course material is. Repeated drills can quickly become boring.

Residential short courses – details in a calendar (around £1 inc. postage) published by the National Institute of Adult Education, 19B De Montfort Street, Leicester. Tel: (0533) 551451. Cost: from about £30 for a weekend and from £80 for two weeks.

Full information on these ways of learning and details of how to find out about them can be obtained from the Centre for Information on Language Teaching and Research (CILT), 20 Carlton House Terrace, London SW1Y 5AP (Tel: 01-839 2626), in particular from their *Information Guide 8, Part time and intensive language study: a guide for adult learners* (£1.20 plus 45p postage, or look at it for free in their library). CILT's Publications Catalogue (a free booklet) contains many other guides and books you might find useful. Their library has lots of helpful information, including directories and lists of courses. They publish bibliographies of course materials, and will give advice on the type of course to suit you, and where you can get it. Write to them, giving them as many details of yourself and your needs as you can.

Which Method?

Every method has advantages and disadvantages. Which you choose may depend on things like how much time you have, whether you can get to a language centre, whether you can do day or evening classes, what LEA facilities are like, and what you are prepared to spend.

Many people seem to find a combination of several ways of learning a language best and most enjoyable – such as group classes which use audio-visual aids and/or a language laboratory, group classes plus a BBC TV or radio course, or a teach-yourself system with individual tuition or perhaps a short residential summer course. However, it sometimes takes quite a bit of extra effort.

Even within one method of learning, systems of teaching may vary. For example, many courses use 'direct method' teaching – which means that English is banned, and grammar is not taught formally. You are immersed in the new language and learn to repeat and imitate. While this is a popular method for learning holiday words and phrases, it may have drawbacks in that you can only learn a language superficially without grammar – although it might hold your interest better in the early stages.

There are many local education authority courses, with differing levels, aims and approaches, such as 'conversation', 'refresher', 'intensive', 'audio-visual', 'examination' and even some special short or holiday courses. There are day and evening classes, usually for one or two hours, once or twice a week, running from ten to thirty weeks with breaks during school holidays. You're more likely to find the exact class to suit your needs, particularly past the beginner's stage, if you live in or near a large town. In some areas, you have to join an exam course, such as one for GCE O-level. If the language you want to learn isn't offered, try to make up a group yourself. LEAs will usually try to find a teacher if there are about fifteen people wishing to study a subject.

A large proportion of LEA courses use audio-visual aids such as TV, videotape, radio, slides and cassettes or records. Some classes use only the foreign language, others a lot of English. Some are conversational, others concentrate on grammar. Some students find their classes excellent for learning vocabulary, others are disappointed. Quite a few classes use BBC material.

The level of ability in classes varies greatly, particularly in those other than for beginners, in less-populated districts, or for less popular languages. Too wide a range of ability can make for uneven or slow progress especially when pace is determined by the slowest members of the class.

The standard of teaching also varies, as does the amount of individual help given. In a two-hour session there is not much time for individual help. LEA enthusiasm for using native teachers, often proudly proclaimed, is not always matched by their ability to select a competent one. 'We were taught by a French woman whose English was difficult to understand' and 'Teachers were Spaniards rather than teachers' are typical complaints.

The fall-out rate in LEA courses is high, a fact that some students find to their advantage, since teaching becomes more personal. However, classes can be closed if they fall below a certain size (usually eight or nine – sometimes as many as fourteen). Cost courses range from £8 to £100, and vary according to length and type of course, the number of hours per week, and the LEA area. At larger centres, such as Polytechnics and Colleges of Art, they usually cost more from £20 to £30 for one class a week to £50 for two – they may include language laboratory facilities and NUS membership. OAPs, under-18s and those doing more than one evening class pay less; as does anyone registered unemployed – for instance those living in Inner London pay just £1 (for any number of courses), and the concessionary rate in Birmingham is £4.50.

Overall, students enjoy their courses very much and classes can even become social occasions. How well you do depends on how much work you put in. There is a difficulty in achieving any real competence in the language in only one lesson a week, and it is highly advisable to supplement this method with as many short intensive courses as possible. Two or three days' concentrated practice can bring quite surprising progress.

On Your Own

No one teach-yourself method seems to stand out as better than others for all things. The main problems are:

1. The self-discipline needed. You need to set aside regular study periods and resist the temptation to skip over boring bits of grammar or those aspects which give you trouble.
2. Pronunciation can be a problem. When there is no one to hear and correct you, mistakes – in pronunciation, grammar, and vocabulary – may go unnoticed and so be learnt and repeated.
3. There is no one to answer your questions or check your work and progress. More simply, there is no one with whom to converse. Taking a correspondence course is one way of learning on your own at home which can avoid some of these problems, since you have the advantage of professional guidance.

The main advantages are:

1. You can work at your own pace.
2. After the course is finished, you can always start again, or just repeat certain parts of it.
3. You can listen to records and cassettes while doing other things.

Teach-yourself Techniques

There are many methods available, including books, cassettes and tapes, radio and television courses. A combination of two or more methods can be the most helpful way of covering different aspects of learning a language, so you pay attention to pronunciation as well as reading and writing.

Books and tapes – Living French by T. W. Knight, £2.25 and *Beginners' Italian* by Ottario Negro, about £2, are useful for gaining a practical grounding in the language, especially with the accompanying cassettes, about £10 for two. These books are part of a series available in other languages (also with cassettes) published by Hodder and Stoughton, who also publish the *Teach Yourself* series in lots of languages, from £1.50 to £4.50. The cassettes are available from Tutor Tape Co. Ltd, 100 Great Russell Street, London WC1B 3LE (Tel: 01-580 7552). Tutor Tape offer many other books and tapes, including the *Talking* series by Sofroniou and Phillips, with conversational phrases, book 50p, cassette about £5. Reel-to-reel tapes are slightly more expensive; prices include postage and packing.

Hugo's Simplified System, a series in several languages titled . . . *In Three Months*, costs about £25 for the full course of four cassettes or records and book (which costs from £1.50 to £2.50 on its own). They also have a conversational course, *Speak French/German/Spanish/Italian Today*, about £5 for a booklet and a cassette. The *Made Simple* series, published by William Heinemann, cost about £3; cassettes to go with the books, £15 for two (inc. p&p), are available in some languages from Students Recordings Ltd, 88 Queen Street, Newton Abbot, Devon (Tel: (0626) 67026). Berlitz publish phrase books in lots of languages, with a cassette, about £8. Collins' phrase books cost £1.50.

Audio systems – Linguaphone have different systems: from Sonodisc (with cassettes in French, German and Spanish) at £35, to systems at about £118 (records or cassettes in many languages) and £135 (records or cassettes in French, German, Spanish and Italian). Their Minilab costs £235, including a portable language lab (cassettes in French, German, Spanish, Italian, Russian, Swedish and Arabic); there is also an Executive Minilab costing about £490, mainly aimed at business travellers. Linguaphone provide a postal advisory service, offering guidance and help with problems. Their Travel Pack includes a cassette and captioned picture cards covering emergency holiday situations, in French, German, Spanish and Italian, and costs about £10. They also have a French course on video at £145.

The Stillitron cassette system, in French, German, Spanish, Italian and Arabic, includes a 'visual feedback' device which corrects multiple choice questions and a multiple choice exam service. The system can be used at home and costs about £400.

World of Learning's PILL cassette system in French, German, Spanish, Italian, Russian and Afrikaans costs about £85, as does their French conversation course. They also offer portable language labs at about £140.

Berlitz have a cassette system in French, German, Spanish and Italian, costing about £35 for the basic course and about £70 for the comprehensive course.

BBC courses – Television or radio courses usually start at the beginning of October, you can find out about these from the September *Radio Times* supplement, *Look, Listen, Learn*, your local library, or Educational Broadcasting Information, Continuing Education (30/CE), BBC, Broadcasting House, London W1AA. Tel: 01-580 4468. There is a variety of courses including combined radio and television courses and short 'crash' courses. You can get past BBC programmes in the form of cassettes and records, as well as accompanying textbooks from BBC Publications, 35 Marylebone High Street, London W1A 1AA (also by mail order from BBC Publications, PO Box 234, London SE1 3TH), or from your local bookseller. Costs range from 60p to about £20; not all courses have cassettes. For example, there are six short, intensive courses designed to give travellers a basic grounding in vocabulary and conversation, called *Get by in* French, German, Spanish, Italian, Greek or Portuguese, costing from £7.60 to £9.95 for a book and two cassettes. There are many other beginners' courses and more advanced courses for those who already have some knowledge of the language. The BBC also produce a German Kit, based on their *Kontakte* series, which is a complete, self-contained language course for beginners to teach themselves in their own time, costing about £60 for eight cassettes and two books. A similar French Kit costs about £100.

How Long Does It Take?

Experts reckon that an adult can expect to learn 1,000 to 3,000 words during the first year. One student who went on holiday to Leningrad after two terms of weekly group classes (plus four hours of homework a week) said: 'I obviously didn't know very much, but was able to read the names of shops, goods and so on, exchange common courtesies, ask the way and do shopping; it added an extra dimension to my holiday. It was great to be able to read the Cyrillic script. It meant one could confidently go around Leningrad on one's own; one didn't have to stay with the group for fear of getting lost.'

How long *you* will need before you could cope as well depends on many things: the skill of your teacher, your motivation, how much time you have, and your ability to learn, and knowledge of other languages.

A few points which might help you:

1. Have a goal at the end of the course, such as a planned trip to the country where the language is spoken.
2. Group classes can be a stimulation, particularly if you are encouraged to chat to your fellow pupils in the language.
3. Lively teaching makes a lot of difference.
4. Audio-visual aids help, particularly when combined with other methods.
5. You need to study regularly (CILT recommends you do homework for double the time you spend in classes each week).

In the end it all depends on your commitment. Nothing compensates for laziness and nothing replaces steady daily practice.

Unusual Languages

You need to approach the learning of an unusual language with rather more care and consideration than the more familiar European ones. Mastering a language like Japanese or Arabic, for example, is quite different to brushing up on rusty school French or picking up a closely related language like Spanish or Italian. It still helps if you have already learnt a foreign language, however, as you will have some idea of the basic principles of grammar. You need to be highly motivated to embark on the daunting task of learning a language which has a different alphabet and difficult pronunciation. I would recommend attending a course initially; you will find it much easier than studying on your own.

The opportunities for learning unusual languages are obviously not as wide as for the 'big four' – French, German, Spanish and Italian. It's worth exploring all possible avenues. The Centres for Information on Language Teaching (CILT) publish a series of very useful *Language and Culture Guides* (costing about £2 each) on languages less commonly taught in Britain – from Arabic to Chinese, Japanese, Swedish, Serbo-Croat, Swahili and about 25 others. The guides include lists of courses available, recommended books, and sources of further information. The choice of methods available to you depends on where you live. Your chances of finding a LEA or language school course are much greater in a major town, especially where there is a high concentration of ethnic minorities. In London, for example, ILEA offer courses covering nearly 50 different languages – including tongues as different and distant as Armenian, Afrikaans, Gaelic, Gujarati, Malayan, Mandarin, Persian, Punjabi and Yoruba. If you could interest enough people in learning a particular language for which there is no course available, the LEA will generally try to arrange classes if there is a suitable teacher.

Not only is it advisable to have some professional guidance, but the standard of teaching is even more crucial than with more familiar languages. It can make a world of difference to how easily you are able to grasp the fundamentals. Individual tuition can be very helpful, especially when you start, or if levels of ability differ widely in a group class. The Institute of Linguists offers advice and information; they also set exams in many unusual languages, which can provide a useful goal to work towards. There are few correspondence courses available for less popular languages, but the degree of self-discipline required and difficult pronunciation present particular problems that make this method less satisfactory in this instance.

The more 'foreign' a language is, the more difficult it is to get to grips with. So time spent on intensive learning is valuable in becoming familiar with the new letters, sounds and constructions. If possible, professional tuition should be accompanied by as much study on your own as possible. There is a variety of books and tapes available to help with home study – including some of those mentioned in the teach-yourself section above – information and sources are given in the CILT guides. For example, the Hodder and Stoughton *Teach Yourself* series covers 60 languages, including such unusual ones as Czech, Catalan, Cantonese, Icelandic, Indonesian, Samoan, Sanskrit, and so on. The Linguaphone audio system (costing £118) comes in 28 languages. There are BBC publications and courses in Arabic, Chinese, Gaelic, Russian, Greek and Portuguese.

Communicating: Breaking the Barriers

by Jon Gardey

Barriers to communication off the beaten track exist just because of who you are: a visitor from another civilisation. It is necessary to show the local people that underneath the surface impression of strange clothes and foreign manners is another human being like them.

The first step is to approach local inhabitants as if you are their guest. You are. It is their country, their village, their hut, their lifestyle. You are a welcome, or perhaps an unwelcome, intruder into their familiar daily routine. Always be aware that they may see very few faces other than those of their family or the other families in the village. Their initial impression of you is likely to be one of unease and wariness. Be reassuring. Move slowly. If possible, learn a few words of local greeting and repeat them to everyone you meet in the village. It is very important to keep smiling, carry an open and friendly face, even if you feel exactly the opposite. Hold out your hand, open, in a gesture that says to them that you want to be with them, a gesture that includes them in your experience. Hold your body in a relaxed, non-aggressive manner. Try to take out of the first encounter anything that might anger them, or turn to shyness their initial approaches to you. If they offer a hand, take it firmly, even if it is encrusted with what you might consider filth. Be as close as possible, don't hold back or be distant, either in attitude or voice. Coming on strong in an effort to get something from a local person will only build unncessary barriers to communication.

Words and Pictures

Begin with words. If you are asking for directions repeat the name of the place several times, but *do not point* in the direction you think it is, or suggest possible directions by voice. Usually the local person, in an effort to please his visitor, will nod helpfully in the direction you are pointing, or agree with you that, yes, Namdrung *is* that way, if you say so. It may be in the opposite direction.

Merely say Namdrung and throw up your hands in a gesture that indicates a total lack of knowledge. Most local people are delighted to help someone genuinely in need, and, after a conference with their friends, will come up with a solution to your problem. When *they* point, repeat the name of the place several times more, varying the pronunciation, to check if it is the same place you want to go. It is also a good idea to repeat this whole procedure with someone else in another part of the village and frequently along the way to check for consistency.

In most areas it is highly likely that none of the local people will speak any language you are familiar with. Communicating with them then becomes a problem in demonstration: you must *show* them what you want, or perform your message.

If you are asking for information more difficult than directions, use your hands to build a picture of what you need in the air. Pictures, in the air, on sand, on a piece of paper, are the only ways to communicate sometimes, and frequently they are the clearest. Use these symbols when you receive blank stares in answer to your questions. Use sound: noises with your voice, or objects that you have in your possession that are similar, or of which you would like more.

Giving and Getting

Not all of your contact with local people will be to get something from them. Don't forget that you have a unique opportunity to bring them something from your own culture. Try to make it something that will enrich theirs; try to give them an *experience* of your culture. Again, show them what it looks like: postcards, magazines. Let them experience its tools. If you have a camera let the local people, especially the children, look through the viewfinder. Put on a telephoto so they can get a new look at their own countryside. Take along an instant print camera, photograph them, and give them the print (just be careful, or this can get out of hand). Most important: become involved. Carry Aspirin to cure headaches, real or imagined, that you find out about. If someone in the village seems to need help, say in lifting a log, offer a hand. Contribute yourself as an expression of your culture.

If you want to take photographs, be patient. Don't bring out your camera until you have established a rapport, and be as unobtrusive as possible. If anyone objects, stop. A bribe for a photograph or payment for information is justified only if the situation is unusual. A simple request for directions is no reason for a gift. If the local people do something out of the ordinary for you, reward them as you would a friend at home. The best gift you can give them is your friendship and openness. They are not performers doing an act, but ordinary people living out their lives in circumstances that seem strange to us.

I have found myself using gifts as a means of *avoiding* contact with remote people, especially children; as a way of pacifying them. I think it is better to enter and leave their lives with as much warmth as I can give, and now I leave the sweets at home. If you are camped near a village, invite some of the local people over to share your food, and try to have them sit among your party.

On some of the more travelled routes, such as Morocco, or the main trekking trails of Nepal, the local children, used to being given sweets by passing trekkers, will swarm around for more. I suggest that you smile (always) and refuse them. Show them pictures, your favourite juggling act. Then give them something creative, such as pencils.

If a local event is in progress stand back, try to get into a shadow, and watch from a distance. You will be seen and noticed, no matter what you do, but it helps to minimize your presence. If you want to get closer, edge forward slowly, observing the participants, especially the older people, for signs that you are not wanted. If they frown, retire. Respect their attempts to keep their culture and its customs as free as possible from outside influence.

The people in the remote places are still in an age before machines and live their lives close to the earth in comfortable routine. Where you and I come from is sophisticated, hard and alien to them. We must come into their lives as gently as possible, and, when we go, leave no marks.

Officialdom

In less remote areas where the local people have had more experience of travellers, you must still observe the rules of patience, openmindedness and respect for the lifestyle of others. But you will encounter people with more preconceived notions about foreigners – and most of those notions will be unfavourable.

In these circumstances – and indeed anywhere your safety or comfort may depend on your approach – avoid seeming to put any local person, especially a minor official, in the wrong. Appeal to his emotions, enlist his magnanimous aid, save his face at all costs. Your own calmness can calm others. If you are delayed or detained, try 'giving up', reading a book, smiling. Should you be accused of some misdemeanour, such as 'jumping' a control point, far better to admit your 'mistake' than to be accused of spying – though even this is fairly standard practice in the Third World and shouldn't flap you unduly.

Wherever you go in the Third World, tones and pitches of voice will vary; 'personal distance' between people conversing may be less than you are used to; attitudes and priorities will differ from your own. Accept people as they are and you can hope that with time and a gentle approach, they will accept you also.

Language

Where you have the opportunity of learning or using a smattering of the local language, try to make things easier for yourself by asking questions that limit responses to what you understand; by asking questions the replies to which will add – helpfully and manageably – to your vocabulary. Make it clear to your listeners that your command of the language is limited. Note down what you learn and try constantly to build on what you know.

Always familiarize yourself with the cultural limitations that may restrict topics of conversation or choice of conversation partner.

Keep Your Hands to Yourself

Gestures can be a danger area. The British thumbs-up sign is an obscenity in some countries, such as Sardinia and parts of the Middle East, where it means roughly 'sit on this' or 'up yours'. In such places – and anywhere, if in doubt – the way to hitch a ride is to wave limply with a flattened hand.

The ring sign made with thumb and forefinger is also obscene in Turkey and elsewhere. And in France it can mean 'zero', i.e., 'worthless' – the exact opposite of the meaning 'OK' or 'excellent' for which the British and Americans use it.

By contrast, our own obscene insult gesture, the two-finger sign, is used interchangeably in Italy with the Churchillian V-sign. Which way round you hold your fingers makes no difference – it's still understood as a friendly gesture meaning 'victory' or 'peace'.

In Greece, as Desmond Morris tells us in Robert Morley's *Book of Bricks* (London, Wiedenfeld, 1978), there is another problem to do with a gesture called the *moutza*. In this, the hand is raised flat, 'palm towards the victim and pushed towards him as if about to thrust an invisible custard pie in his face'. To us it means simply 'go back, go back', but to a Greek it is a hideous insult. It dates from Byzantine times, when chained prisoners were paraded through the streets and abused by having handfuls of filth from the gutter picked up by onlookers and thrust into their faces. Though naturally the brutal practice has long since ceased, the evil meaning of the *moutza* has not been forgotten.

How to be in with Islam

by Peter Boxhall

Like any nation with an important history, the Arab people are proud of their past. Not only because of an empire which once stretched from the far reaches of China to the gates of France, or their many great philosophers, scientists, seafarers, soldiers and traders; but because they are one people, sharing a common language and culture, following the same religion which has become an integral part of their lives and behaviour.

Language

Arabic is a difficult language for us to learn, but it is a beautiful, expressive language which, in the early days of Islam, came to incorporate all the permissible culture, literature and poetry of Arab society. Small West African children, sitting under *cola* trees write their Koranic lessons on wooden boards; infant Yemenis learn and chant in unison *Surahs* of the Holy Book; school competitions are held perenially in the Kingdom of Saudi Arabia and elsewhere, to judge the students' memory and knowledge of their written religion.

So, as in any foreign environment, the traveller would do well to try and learn some Arabic. For without the greetings, the enquiries, the pleasantries of everyday conversation and the ability to purchase one's requirements, many of the benefits and pleasures of travel are forgone. Best, too, to learn classical (Koranic) Arabic which is understood throughout the Arabic speaking world (although the farther one is away from the Arabian Peninsula in, for example, the Magribian countries of Morocco, Tunisia, and Algeria, the more difficult it is to comprehend the dialectical replies one receives).

Not long ago, before the advent of oil, when one travelled in the harsh environment of the Arabian Desert, the warlike, nomadic bedu tribes would, if they saw you came in peace, greet you with *salaam alaikum* and afford you the hospitality of their tents. If 'bread and salt' were offered to you, you were 'on their face': inviolate, protected, a welcome guest for as long as you wished to stay. *Baiti Baitak* (my house is your house) was the sentiment expressed. This generous, hospitable principle still prevails throughout the Arab world.

Bureaucracy

Although they are subordinates to the overall sense of Arabness, each of the Arab kingdoms, emirates, sultanates and republics has its own national characteristics. In those far-off medieval days of the Arab Empire, there were no frontiers to cross, no need for passports, there was a common currency, a purer language. Today it is different: there is bureaucracy abroad in the Arab world – mostly, it can be said, a legacy of former colonial administrations. So be patient, tolerant, and good humoured about passports, visas, immunization, currency controls, customs. Many of the Arab countries emerged only recently to their present independent status and it has taken us, in the West, some hundreds of years to evolve our systems of public administration and bureaucratic procedure.

One has to remember that generally the Arab does not have the same pressing (obsessional?) sense of urgency that we do. No discourtesy is meant. Does it really matter? Tomorrow is another day and the sun will rise again and set.

Neither in his bureaucratic or even everyday dealings with you does the Arab take much notice of your status, official or induced. When I was Personal Secretary to the Governor of

Jeddah, important corporation chiefs and industrialists used to visit him in his *majlis*. They were received courteously and served the traditional *qahwa*. The Arab, however, is a great democrat and even these important people had, often to their annoyance, to wait their turn. Yet on one occasion, a comparatively poor *shaiba* came in from the streets, went straight up to His Excellency, kissed him on the shoulder and extracting a scroll from the voluminous folds of his *thobe* (the uniform dress worn by all Saudis), proceeded to read its full, eulogistic length in a high-pitched quavering voice.

To the Arab, it is of little importance to know who or what you represent; he is more interested in who you are. If he likes you, you will soon be aware of it. The sense of touch is to the Arabs a means of communication. Westerners, from colder climates, should not therefore be too reticent, distant or aloof.

Watch and listen, for example, to how the Yemenis greet each other: the long repetitious enquiries as to each other's state of health; the handshake; the finger that will sometimes curl towards the mouth, to indicate they are merely on speaking terms, casual acquaintances; sometimes to the heart, to indicate that they are intimate friends. The embrace, the kiss on both cheeks, which are mainly customary in the Near East and Magribian countries . . .. If you allow the Arab to take you as a friend in his way, he may even invite you to his house.

Social Conventions

Baiti Baitak is the greatest courtesy. Do not, though, be critical, admiring or admonitory towards the furniture in the house. If you admire the material things, your hospitable host may feel impelled to give you the object of your admiration. Conversely, remember that if your taste in furnishing does not correspond with that of your host, the Arab is not much interested in the possession of beautiful material goods.

If it is an old-style house, you must always take your shoes off, and may be expected to sit on the floor supported by cushions. Then all manner of unfamiliar, exotic dishes may be served to you. If it is painful to plunge your fingers into a steaming mound of rice, and difficult to eat what are locally considered to be the choice pieces of meat, forget your inhibitions and thin skin, eat everything you are offered with your right hand and at least appear to enjoy it. Remember . . . your host is probably offering the best, sometimes the last remaining, provisions in his house.

Once, in the Jordan desert, I was entertained by an important tribal *sheikh* in his black, goat-hair tent. An enormous platter, supported by four tribal retainers, was brought in and put in our midst. On the platter, surmounted by a mound of rice, was a whole baby camel, within that camel a sheep, within that sheep, pigeons . . . Bedu scarcely talk at all at a meal; it is too important, too infrequent an occasion. So we ate quickly, belching often from indigestion, with many an appreciative *Al Hamdulillah*, for it is natural to do so. When replete, rosewater was brought round for us to wash our hands and we men moved out to the cooling evening sands to drink coffee and converse, and listen to stories of tribal life, while the tribal ladies, who had cooked the meal, entered the tent from the rear, with the children to complete the feast.

In some Arab countries, alcoholic drink is permitted. In others, it is definitely not. From my two years' experience in Saudi Arabia and three in Libya, I know it is actually possible to obtain whisky, for example, but it is at a price – perhaps £50 a bottle, which, for me at least – is too expensive an indulgence, even if it were not for the penalties if caught.

Coffee and tea are the habitual refreshments: in Saudi Arabia, as was the custom in my municipal office, the small handleless cups of *qishr* are poured from the straw-filled beak of a brass coffee pot. 'Arabian coffee' is also famous: almost half coffee powder, half sugar. One should only drink half or two-thirds though and if you are served a glass of cold water with it, remember that an Arab will normally drink the water first, to quench his thirst, then the coffee, so the taste of this valued beverage may continue to linger in the mouth.

In North Africa tea is a more customary drink. Tea *nuss wa nuss* with milk, in Sudan, for example; tea in small glasses with mint, in the Magrib; tea even with nuts, in Libya. Whoever was it said that the English are the world's greatest tea drinkers? Visiting the Sanussi tribe in Libya, in Cyrenaica, I once had to drink 32 glasses of tea in the course of a morning. The tea maker, as with the Arabian coffee maker, is greatly respected for his art.

Dress

In most of the Arab world, normal European-type dress is appropriate, but it should be modest in appearance. Again, if, as we should do, we take notice of Arab custom, which is based in history on sound common sense, we might do well to remember that in hot, dusty conditions, the Bedu put *on* clothes to protect themselves against the elements, not, as we Westerners tend to do, take them *off*.

As to whether one should adopt the local dress in the particularly hot, arid countries of the Arab world is probably a matter of personal preference. The *thobe* is universally worn in Saudi Arabia, the *futah* in the Yemens and South Arabia. I personally used to wear the *futah*, but in Saudi Arabia, although the Governor suggested I should wear the *thobe* I felt inhibited from doing so, as none of the other expatriates appeared to adopt it.

Religion

The final, and perhaps most important, piece of advice I can offer to the traveller is to repeat the need to respect Islam. Not all Arabs are Muslim, but nearly all are, and Islam represents their religion and their way of life, as well as their guidance for moral and social behaviour.

In the same sense that Muslims are exhorted (in the Koran) to be compassionate towards the non-believer (and to widows, orphans and the sick), so too should we respect the 'Faithful'. Sometimes one may meet religious fanatics, openly hostile, but it is rare to do so and I can only recall, in my many years in Arab countries, one such occasion. Some schoolboys in south Algeria enquired why, if I spoke Arabic, I was not a Muslim, and on hearing my answer responded: '*inta timshi fi'n nar*' ('You will walk in he fires (of Hell?)').

In some countries, you can go into mosques when prayers are not in progress, in others, one cannot. Always ask for permission to photograph mosques, and in the stricter countries, women, old men and children.

Respect, too, the various religious occasions and that all-important month-long fast of Ramadan. My Yemeni doctors and nurses all observed Ramadan, so one year I joined them, to see exactly what an ordeal it was for them. Thereafter, my admiration for them, and for others who keep the fast, was unbounded, and I certainly do not think we should exacerbate the situation in this difficult period by smoking, eating or drinking in public.

Ahlan wa sahlan: welcome! You will hear the expression often in the Arab world, and it will be sincerely meant.

Porter, Sir? Guide?

by Richard Snailham

Porters, guides, interpreters and their ilk can be a great nuisance – it is difficult to feel at ease at the Pyramids surrounded by droves of importunate Arabs, all called Mahmoud or Ahmed, and all claiming to be the only and indispensable authority on Cheops, Thutmose, etc. – but they can just as often be invaluable, as when one is about to venture into wild, badly mapped country. I would not recommend venturing far from the Pan-American Highway into the remoter corners of the Ecuadorean Andes, for instance, without local guides.

Faced with the first situation, I find it best to appear indifferent, to affect disdain, flourish a guidebook and make it clear that I can get myself around without Mahmoud's unwelcome attentions. Generally, some persistent boy will tag along regardless and begin telling me the story whether I like it or not. Not only may he turn out to be a tolerable compromise but might prove, as often I found to be the case in the Ethiopian Highlands, an engaging companion whose *pourboire* is thoroughly deserved. It is not difficult to find a guide in well-visited tourist spots; they seem to emerge out of the stones.

At some famous sites a guide is obligatory, as we find it is in places closer to home; one would not expect to go round a French *château*, for example, without a practised, often multi-lingual cicerone.

Fixing a Price

If a journey is involved, or any form of transport, or any great length of time, it is as well to discover the fee in advance, as one might on engaging a gondola in Venice – if only to allow the shock of the often inordinate sum asked. Some sort of bargaining may be possible, depending on the circumstances: one could haggle with a Tanzanian hire-car driver for a two-day trip to Ngorongoro, but probably not with a Hong Kong Chinese girl courier operating a hotel-to-hotel, all-in bus trip to Repulse Bay and back.

It is also worth being extremely careful about who you choose, and how much you pay, if you are going to be dependent for your safety on your guide or porter. There have been several stories in recent years of guides taking travellers into remote regions then refusing to bring them back without a hefty extra payment. The practice seems to be particularly prevalent in the Himalayas.

Guides quite often get lost. In open country it is as well to maintain your navigation by dead reckoning and repeatedly ask the names of prominent features. Never pose questions like 'Is it far?' because guides rarely have any communicable concept of distance, nor 'Will we get there tonight?' because they tend to wish to please and will give you the answer they know you want to hear. Porterage has its various aspects too: an often unpleasant but necessary part of travel between airport and hotel: French railway stations with their *prix fixé* per item of baggage (fixed pretty high, too); and at the other extreme there is the uncharted problem-ridden business of arranging for porters off the beaten track.

Hiring porters amid the clamour of airport or railway station has few rules: follow your gear carefully, have your mind tuned to the local units of currency and the exchange rate, follow the local rules if there are any and don't overtip. I still shudder when I recall watching some of my quite elderly flock walk with their suitcases into a dense mass of grubby bodies outside Karachi airport, the air loud with suppliant screeches and thin, brown fingers clutching urgently at the Gucci handles.

Porterage in the Wilds

Out in the *ulu* there are other, different considerations to keep in mind. Porterage often involves animal transport. Porters and their animals have to be fed and perhaps sheltered. If they are to be away from home for many days some kind of advance payment may be necessary. If you are moving across their country you have to consider how they will get back to their homes.

In all negotiations of this sort, it is best to involve a local middleman. If you have an indigenous student or scientist or an attached police officer or soldier with your party he will be best at overcoming language barriers and agreeing what will seem to him to be a fair rate for the job. Otherwise, porters or guides are best hired through a local chief or landowner. This is essential in most wild parts of Africa or South America where tribal or semi-feudal societies prevail.

Sometimes local men will not wish to come forward as porters whatever the inducements. Even though we could offer marvellous goodies like planks of wood, rope, slightly dented but serviceable jerry cans (to a tribe still using gourds), the proud Shankilla of the lower Blue Nile would not carry for us because it would have shamed them: carrying loads is women's work. Blashford-Snell nearly asked them to send their women along, but, since that might have been misunderstood, employed the village boys instead. Other tribesmen, like the Bakongo on the banks of the Zaïre River, where porterage since the advent of Stanley in 1877 has been a minor industry, have no such compunction. Some of the best porters we have ever had were Angolan FNLA refugees in Bas-Zaïre, who, with their broad smiles and outlandish hats helped us re-launch our giant inflatables in 1975.

Bonuses

With large numbers of men it is best to deal with a single head porter and pay him for his pains. But pay each man personally, a portion of his cash at the outset, if you wish, but keep the bulk until arrival at your destination. It is an added kindness and a mark of gratitude if there is something in your stores – plastic bags, wire, spare clothing, cigarettes, even empty tins and other containers – which you can distribute as a bonus.

Porters are generally honest, but it is as well to keep your baggage train in the centre of the column in case the odd load should slip off into the bush. And with this arrangement it is easier to see and act promptly when a porter who is fatigued or taken ill needs to be relieved.

I am in favour of taking porters and guides into wild country rather than trying to struggle along without them. They may be difficult, like the Shankilla; they may abandon you precipitately, as ours did on the slopes of Mount Sangay, but they do add a colourful extra dimension to the journey, and they can be a form of security in hostile, lawless country. And when you pay them, be sure to tell the rest of your party you have done so, so that they don't, as happened once in Ecuador, get paid twice.

Anything to Declare?

by E. G. Peacock

When the expedition leaders of the first Younghusband expeditionary force set off, after months of preparation in India, to subdue Tibet and take the forbidden city of Lhasa, they had barely reached the frontier when they were halted by a British officer of the China customs post. The experience was perhaps as irritating for Younghusband as it can be today for the traveller. It was probably quite disturbing too for that officer, after months, perhaps years, of surveying the empty snows for the odd package tour, suddenly one day to see the endless columns of laden men and pack mules toiling up the passes. History does not record if he ever recovered from the shock.

Misunderstandings

If there is one certainty in cross-frontier travel today it is that customs posts are a universal phenomenon and will be encountered even in the most unlikely places. The problems that frequently arise are often the result of misunderstanding on one or both sides, and not, as many harassed travellers feel, deliberate malice.

The average traveller, even the seasoned one, tends to approach a customs checkpoint with a degree of apprehension. This commonly manifests itself in suspiciously nervous behaviour or, with another type of person, in a kind of defensive arrogance. The customs officer, on the other hand, also feels some disquiet, especially if he is inexperienced in passenger examination. The nature of the transaction between traveller and customs officer seems to engender a special sort of hostility. The bad feelings on both sides of the counter are, however, quite unhelpful and generally unnecessary – unless, of course, the traveller is knowingly breaking the law, in which case he has good reason to regard the customs officer as an adversary.

The majority of countries place considerable importance upon their tourist trade, and with good reason. And most governments concerned with promoting tourism are also aware that the visitor's first and last contact with the country is almost always with the customs officials: generally they try to instil in the latter the need to ensure that the impressions so given are favourable. But also, and somewhat paradoxically, they expect customs officers to display a conscientious diligence in the enforcement of import and export laws.

Remember, therefore, that nine times out of ten you are dealing with an official torn between two apparently conflicting sets of instructions, who is psychologically poised to behave in any one of several quite different ways and who may well take his cue from you. Too great a degree of suspiciously nervous behaviour and he can be forgiven for a more than usually thorough examination – even if it is in the middle of a sandstorm. Too overbearing an attitude and he can likewise be pardoned if he stands on his small authority and unreels the red tape.

Tugs, Barges and Cigarette Lighters

One complaint read only too often is of stupidity on the part of a customs officer. How often do we read the 'amusing' anecdote in travel books about the almost incredible obtuseness of a remote border official who delays an intelligent and law-abiding traveller for hours while going through an incomprehensible pantomime of official nonsense.

True, it happens, and, incidentally, creates some useful 'copy' for journalists. But it must be understood that the innumerable laws and regulations required to be administered by customs have grown more complex with the months that pass. The traveller that descends in a Land Rover upon an isolated border post, that has perhaps seen a couple of small camel caravans in the last month, and produces for clearance a bewildering array of vehicle parts, camera equipment and the latest drugs for every known ailment must expect to bump into a mental block of considerable proportions.

Inevitably, too, some quaint examples of tariff classifications will arise, especially if the customs officer has spent the better part of his life in a rural or village environment without much exposure to modern gadgetry. Certainly, he will have been trained, but it is not easy for such training to cope with every eventuality. How, for example, do you explain the fact that a Ronson cigarette lighter does not come under the heading of 'tugs, barges and lighters', or that logarithm tables are not furniture?

Travellers have a right to expect a high degree of competence when passing the frontier of a sophisticated country. But those with a reasonable amount of human understanding will make allowances in other circumstances and, I guarantee, will almost invariably be met halfway. On the odd occasion when they are not, I would be prepared to wager that they have had the misfortune to arrive at the border ten minutes after an irascible but intrepid travelling salesman blazing new trails with a sample case of microchips.

Horses for Courses

It should go without saying, although it doesn't, that different places have different regulations. While it is generally recognized that such items such as dangerous drugs and pornography are undesirable imports (although what constitutes these varies wildly from country to country), almost every country has, in addition, its own large range of apparently illogical prohibitions and restrictions. Malawi, for instance, bans goods bearing the national emblems as a trade mark; the cockerel and the rising sun are both national emblems. However strange regulations like this may seem to travellers, it makes sense to find out about them in advance. Tourist brochures will not normally give the details, so make a point of asking either at the tourist office or the embassy. And also ask about dress regulations or you could find yourself in the undignified position of being given a compulsory haircut at the border post.

Almost everywhere there are particular items which should never be found in your luggage. In some parts of the world you may wish to carry a gun for protection against marauding bandits. Unless you have all the necessary permits in advance, don't do it. Even then, the red tape, the suspicion and the potential for trouble are such that it is probably not worth it. The authorities can often be more dangerous than any bandits you are likely to meet and may view the possession of weapons (particularly if unlicensed) as tantamount to armed insurrection. Other countries verge on paranoia when it comes to currency and have stringent regulations governing its import and export. And remember it isn't the customs who make the laws or prescribe the penalties, so it will do no good arguing with them.

Commonsense Precautions

What can one do when travelling the remote byways to avoid trouble on the frontiers? It is obviously not possible to guard against everything that can happen, but some general tips are well worth observing.

Arrive at border posts at a reasonable time, and in daylight where possible. Avoid local feastdays and holidays.

Be relaxed in manner and smile often. Do not appear overanxious or impatient. Remain polite and friendly whatever the provocation and never make threats of complaint to higher authority even if you intend to do so.

Do not expect the officer to unload, open, unpack or repack luggage but give the impression that you are more than willing to do so.

Do not carry firearms and ammunition unless these are fully covered by local permits. If you have these, produce the items and the permits before being asked. On no account wait until they are discovered.

Do not carry alcoholic beverages into Islamic countries unless you know that they are permitted.

Do not carry or wear items of military-looking clothing such as camouflage jackets.

Carry only normal drugs and remedies and then keep them in properly labelled containers. If they are for your regular use, carry a letter to that effect.

Do not carry literature that could

be considered even remotely objectionable on either moral or political grounds.

Declare all currency, traveller's cheques and gold.

Declare any item about which you have doubts. Failing to do so is in itself an offence and declaration is at least an indication of honest intent.

Advance Planning

It is always a good idea, before leaving on a trip, to call at the nearest office of the overseas representative of any country you intend to visit to find out what special regulations you should observe. This is particularly advisable if you are travelling by vehicle as quite complicated rules of temporary importation, payment of duty on deposit, acceptances of triptiques, etc., often apply and these may be beyond the powers of the officers at a small border post. Bear in mind that there is no guarantee that you will receive reliable information from embassies, high commissions, or consulates. Diplomats are not always *au fait* with their own customs formalities. If time permits, it is better to write to the Director or Controller of Customs in the country of destination asking specific questions. You can then take his reply with you for production at the border. It will carry a lot of weight.

When I worked as a customs officer in both Africa and the Far East, I never failed to be amazed by the number of expeditions which neglected to arrange customs clearance prior to arrival. Months of preparation were often devoted to getting approval from various ministries (the ones concerned with the particular sphere of interest of the expedition). The story was always the same. The Minister of Health, of Mines, of Forestry, of Wildlife or whatever had given his blessing and then forgotten he had done so. Often, too, an interested local benefactor had arranged accommodation and itineraries, entertainment and hospitality. Everything in fact had been organized to a split-second schedule. Full of confidence, the expedition then flew or trucked in, with specialized equipment ranging from cases of pemmican to litres of the latest experimental fertility drug. At this point the unfeeling and obstructive customs officer entered from stage left and brought the whole show to a grinding halt. The expedition leader would then rush about, tearing his hair, while sheaves of lists were gone through with an exasperating slowness. The letters on ministry notepaper wishing the project well and promising every cooperation invariably failed to make an impression. At the close of play, abuse was heaped on the customs for fettering academic endeavour with red tape. And only because it did not occur to anyone to consult them in advance.

The customs officer everywhere is a normal human being who has a complicated and unpleasant task to perform. He will react favourably to a friendly and cooperative approach. The barrier across the road is only symbolic after all.

Over the Airwaves

by John Hoban and Melissa Shales

Most people going abroad, whatever the reason, like to keep in touch with what is going on at home and in the world at large. If travelling in politically unstable countries, it is also advisable to keep in touch with what is happening within the country. Finding news – particularly in an understandable language – is not always easy. English language newspapers may not be available, and local radio services, if not actually unintelligible, may be less than reliable. So take a radio.

Two-way Radio

For travellers to very remote or dangerous areas, it may even be worth taking a two-way radio or, at the very least, a search and rescue beacon. Chances are that you would never need anything more than a CB-style set-up, so that if you break down, you are able to alert someone, whether the authorities or just a passing driver, and request help. If you are planning a large expedition that will be in the field for some months, it is worth considering taking a larger field radio. It can be an easy way of arranging re-supply or helping with navigation, or summoning aid in an emergency. You can keep sponsors and the media in close contact with the progress of the expedition, and it could prove to be a major boost to the morale of expedition members who are away from home and families for a very long time.

The selection of which type of radio to take is a complicated business, depending on many factors from the conditions in which it will be used (weather conditions and terrain), the type of transport to be taken and what use the radio will be put to. It is an extremely specialist subject and expert advice and training should be sought before you take any decision. A dead radio, or one in the hands of an incompetent operator, is worse than useless. The Expedition Advisory Centre at the Royal Geographical Society, 1 Kensington Gore, London SW7 2AR (Tel: 01-581 2057) publishes a set of notes on *Radio Communications for Expeditions* which offer an introduction to the subject with a good list of suggested further reading.

London Calling

For the rest of us, however, our only contact over the airwaves will be through a transistor radio. Make sure you take a set that can pick up BBC World Service. For general convenience, you will want a set which has a tuning scale for Medium Wave, Long Wave and VHF. Don't get one which has only one tuning scale for Short Wave; the stations will be crammed so closely together as to make selection difficult. So look for a set with at least three Short Wave tuning scales, and the more the better. Make sure too that it covers at least 49 to 16 metres (6–17 MegaHertz). It should take widely available batteries (and take plenty of spares). These receivers all have a built-in aerial for Medium Wave and a telescopic one for Short Wave and VHF, but not all sets have provision for an external wire aerial and earth. Look for these as, in difficult listening conditions, an external aerial and an earth can be very helpful.

News is the backbone of the BBC World Service with bulletins of World News on the hour for 17 out of the 24, and more detailed half-hour news reports regularly. Programmes about

Britain include *News about Britain*, *British Press Review*, *Radio Newsreel* as well as daily *Financial News* and *Stock Market Reports* and a weekly *Financial Review*. The time between is filled with anything from pop music to test cricket or drama. If you have been away from home for a long time, there is something incredibly reassuring about the cool calm Britishness of the presenters. It'll make you homesick, but it also acts as a sort of 'security blanket' when surrounded by undiluted 'foreigness'.

Wandering Frequencies

Only in a few parts of the world can you listen to the World Service on Medium Wave, so it usually has to be Short Wave. Unlike Medium Wave, Short Wave frequencies have to change according to the time of day and the time of year. This is not as complicated as it first seems, and if you are in one place you will quickly find out which frequencies are most satisfactory at which times. But if you are moving constantly, you will have to battle with a new set of frequencies for each place you stop.

The times of broadcasts and the frequencies for different parts of the world are too extensive to set out here, and anyway they change every few months. Though the World Service is on the air 24 hours a day, it is not designed to be heard everywhere all that time. The aim is to provide signal at peak listening times of early morning and evening, although some parts of the world get much more than this. The full times and frequencies for different parts of the world can be obtained from the BBC. The World Service publishes its own monthly programme journal – *London Calling*, which is available on subscription if you want a regular copy sent to you personally. It can also be picked up free from most British Embassies, High Commissions and Consulates as well as offices of the British Council.

If you want full details, write to BBC External Services Publicity, Bush House, PO Box 76, Strand, London WC2B 4PH, saying where and when you are going. They will then send you the appropriate programme and frequency information for the area together with some useful guidance on how to tune in.

Post and Telecommunications

by Penny Watts-Russell

A crude form of long-distance communication, smoke signals by day and fires by night, used by ancient Egyptians, Assyrians and Greeks, proved effective in its time, as one homecoming traveller as far back as 1084 BC found out to its cost. Beacon fires established on line of sight locations communicated to the faithless Clytemnestra, at her palace of Argos in ancient Greece, the news of the fall of Troy some 800km distant and the imminent return of her husband, Agamemnon – and so enabled her, forewarned, to plan his murder with her lover.

In more recent times – up until about two hundred years ago – the quickest way of communicating home took weeks, even months, mail being transported by messenger, mail coach and sailing ship. In 1798, it took two months for news of Nelson's victory on the Nile to reach London.

It was the invention of the electric telegraph in the mid-nineteenth century – enabling messages to be sent at the speed of light – that produced a major revolution in communications and heralded *tele-* (i.e. far off, covering a distance) communications. In our own day these include the use of telegraphy, telephone, radio, television and satellite to transmit messages. The telegrams, telex and telephone that make use of a world-wide telecommunications network are the most relevant in the context of the traveller contacting home while abroad; in addition, of course, to postal facilities.

Post

It is best to send all letters air mail. Those from Europe automatically go by air, but further afield you also have the choice of surface mail which, as in the pre-jet age, can take weeks to arrive.

Telegrams

Telegrams are traditionally the speediest way of sending unwordy messages home, though in recent years in business communications they are losing ground to telexes. Three main classes of international telegram are often available: *urgent* rate for priority; *ordinary*; and letter (deferred delivery service) designed for lengthy and less urgent messages. In some Commonwealth countries there is also a special greetings letter telegram at a special reduced rate for non-commercial personal messages. To speed up delivery you can address your telegram to your correspondent's telephone or telex number or Registered Telegraphic Address (a unique word providing his name, address and delivery instructions), the last two usually applying to business connections.

Telegraphic facilities are to be found in post and telegraph offices and in some hotels (as in Moscow). For the majority of leisure travellers, telegraphy is likely to be the most convenient method for despatching messages home quickly.

Telex

Telex – acronym for Teletypewriter Exchange Service – is a telegraphic system using telephone lines through which are sent direct current pulses representing characters typed onto a typewriter keyboard. Telexing has the advantage over telegrams in that your messages are not affected by time differences and can be received and recorded even if your correspondent's office is shut. With the expansion of the international telex network, which encompasses almost two hundred countries, it is therefore understandable that business travellers whose firms are subscribers, should turn to telex. Public telex booths and services are located at main post offices and telegraph offices, and in many international hotels.

Credit Card

Cable and Wireless Ltd encourages the business traveller 'to communicate around the world on credit'. Holders of their transferred account telegraphic card reap the benefits of being able to file international telegrams and to send international telex messages from public call offices without prepayment of charges. Show your card and the cost of your communications (not telephone) can be charged to your company's account for later payment in your home country. You also receive a miniature international directory of telecommunications centres.

Credit cards and information regarding the scheme can be obtained from International Credit Card Service, Cable and Wireless Ltd, Mercury House, Theobalds Road, London WC1X 8RX. Tel: 01-242 4433, ext 4345/8.

The Telephone

The telephone can provide the most immediate and personal means of communication, made easier and quicker through the international direct dialling (IDD) system that – provided you know the dialling codes – enables you to dial direct to the UK from most European countries and many others throughout the world without going through the operator.

The IDD network does not yet fully interlock, which means that you cannot automatically phone any country within the grid from any other, and there are still some countries that have not been linked in. In these cases, calls will have to be placed through the operator. But where it is possible, you will have to dial a sequence of four numbers: the international access code; the country code of the country you are phoning; the area code within that country; and the personal number.

Hints

Just a few other words of advice. Write down the number in full before you dial, so that each digit is dialled carefully and without long pauses; and be prepared to wait up to a minute before you are connected, because IDD calls have to travel long distances. Remember too to check, before leaving for overseas, the STD numbers (area codes within your home country) you are likely to call: dialling the international access code and country code would be to no avail without the area code. Lastly, there is likely to be a time difference between the two countries, so remember to check that you won't be phoning at three o'clock in the morning.

Publications

British Telecom International Telecommunications produce a series of leaflets called *Phoning and Writing Home*, which includes most European countries plus Japan; and *International Direct Dialling country code leaflets* covering all countries within the IDD system, which are helpful for area codes of their major towns. These can be obtained free by dialling 100 during normal office hours and asking for Freefone 2013.

Also available from most post offices in the UK is a leaflet *How to contact home when you're abroad*.

(*For further information see Getting in touch with Home on page 758.*)

When Things Go Wrong

Avoidable Hassles

by Tony Bush and Richard Harrington

A traveller's best friend is experience – and it can take dozens of trips to build this up the hard way. But, fortunately, there are some tips that can be passed on to help the unwary before they even step on a plane.

Most people have the good sense to work out their journey time to the airport and then add a 'little extra' for unforeseen delays. But is that little extra enough should something major go wrong – if the car breaks down, for instance, or there are traffic tailbacks due to roadworks or an accident?

Remember too, to try and avoid travelling at peak periods such as Christmas, Easter and July and August, when families are taking their holidays. This applies particularly to weekends, especially Saturdays.

Taxis and Taxes

Most travellers would agree that the task of dealing with taxi drivers could just about be elevated to a science. In some parts of the world overcharging alone would be a blessing. What is really disconcerting is the driver who cannons through red lights or uses part of the pavement to overtake on the inside.

And what about the fare? Without a meter, the obvious foreigner will almost certainly be overcharged. But even the sight of a rank full of taxis with meters should not raise too much hope. Meters often 'break' just as you are getting in.

Two good tips for dealing with the drivers of unmetered taxis are:

1. Know a little of the local language – at least enough to be able to say 'hello', 'please take me to . . .', and 'how much?' and 'thank you'. This throws the driver a little. After all, the driver's aim is only to try and make an extra pound or two. He does not want to get involved in a major row at the risk of being reported to the authorities.
2. Try and get the correct amount to hand over. It prevents the driver pleading that he has not got sufficient change – a ruse that often succeeds – particularly when the fare is in a hurry and it prevents 'misunderstandings'.

A typical misunderstanding might go like this: the traveller hands over a note worth, say, 100 blanks for a trip that he believed was going to cost him 20 blanks. However, the driver, with the note safely tucked into his pocket, tells him he was wrong; he misheard or was misinformed. In fact, the journey cost 30 blanks and 70 blanks is handed over. This leaves the passenger in an invidious position. He cannot snatch his note back and instead, is faced with the indignity of having to argue about an amount that may be just over a pound or so (very rarely would a driver attempt to cheat on too large a scale).

In most cases, the traveller will shrug his shoulders, walk away and put his loss down to experience. And this is what the driver is relying on. That is the reason he is not too greedy. He knows that even the most prosperous looking passenger would baulk at too big a reduction in his change.

The traveller should find out before or during his trip whether he will be required to pay an airport tax on departure, and if so, how much. This is normally only a token sum, but it would be frustrating to have to change a £20 or £50 traveller's cheque in order to pay it. Departure taxes are almost always payable in local currency. Occasionally an equivalent sum in US dollars will be accepted. The ideal arrangement is to work out roughly how much transport to the airport will cost, add on the airport tax, if any, and then throw in a little extra for incidentals.

Tea Oils the Wheels

If you must spread around a little 'dash' to oil the palms that facilitate your progress, do so carefully, after checking how to do it properly with someone who knows the ropes. You may be able, for instance, to avoid a few days in a Mexican jail for a mythical driving offence. On the other hand, you could end up in jail for trying to bribe an officer of the law – and then you might have to hand out a great deal more to get out rather than rot for a few months while waiting for a trial. The $1 or $5 bill tucked in the passport is the safest approach if you to decide on bribery, as you can always claim that you keep your money there for safety. But it may only be an invitation to officials to search you more thoroughly – and since all officials ask for identity papers, you could go through a lot of dollars in this way. When you think a bribe is called for, there's no need for excessive discretion. Ask how much the 'fine' is or whether there is any way of obtaining faster service . . .

Bribes, by the way, go under an entertaining assortment of different names. *Dash* is the term in West Africa, except in Liberia, where the euphemistic expression is *cool water*. *Mattabiche* – which means 'tip', 'corruption' or 'graft' – oils the wheels in Zaïre. In East Africa, the Swahili word for tea, *chai*, serves the same function. *Baksheesh* is probably the best known name for the phenomenon and is widely used in the Middle East. It is a Persian word, found also in Turkish and Arabic, that originally meant a tip or gratuity, but took on the connotation of bribe when it was used of money paid by a new Sultan to his troops. *El soborno* is 'payoff' in Spanish-speaking countries, except Mexico, where the word for 'bite' – *la mordida* – is used. In India you have the *backhander*, in Japan *wairo* or, when referring more generally to corruption, *kuori kiri*, which translates lyrically as 'black mist'. The French refer to the 'jug of wine' or *pot-de-vin*, the Italians to a 'little envelope', a *bustarella*. Germans have an honestly distasteful term for a distasteful thing: *Schmiergeld*, which means 'lubricating money'. Even here, however, exporters gloss over the matter by simply using the abbreviation *N.A. Nutzliche Abgabe* which means 'useful contribution'.

Smiling Strangers

Beware of the Smiling Stranger when abroad. It is here that experience really counts as it is often extremely difficult to separate the con man from a genuinely friendly person.

A favourite ploy is for him to offer his services as a guide. If he asks for cash, don't say you would like to help, but all your money is tied up in traveller's cheques. The Smiling Stranger has heard that one before and will offer to accompany you to your hotel and wait while a cheque is cashed.

The warning about confidence tricksters also applies to some extent to street traders. Not the man who operates from a well set-up stand, but the fellow who wanders about with his arms full of bracelets or wooden carvings. He may give the souvenir hunter a good deal, but prices on the stands or in the shops should be checked first. Sometimes they will be cheaper in the latter, when, frankly, they should not even compare. After all, the wanderer does not have any overheads.

Real Dangers

Some remoter parts of the world are dangerous, and the traveller used to comparatively safe and familiar Europe, finds it hard to take warnings seriously. You should.

Avoid countries where there is a violent revolution or other civil disturbance taking place – an obvious point, but one surprisingly often ignored. Your own embassy or consulate will almost certainly advise against visiting areas of dubious safety as it will be their responsibilty to help extricate you if you get into difficulties. On the other hand the embassy of the country concerned will usually play down the degree of disturbance. The most reliable reports on a situation are to be had from fellow travellers and local newspapers. If a disturbance develops while you are in a foreign country, report to your embassy for advice and to register your whereabouts, in case you should be advised to leave.

There are, of course, many Third World countries which can never be considered entirely safe, but thousands of travellers still go there each year without any trouble. Having done your homework, it is up to you to decide whether, for you personally, the risks outweigh your desire to go there. And if you do, *always* listen to what the locals say and follow their advice.

Local Courtesies

One of the biggest minefields for the unsuspecting traveller is local courtesies and customs and most of us have our pet stories about how we unwittingly infringed them.

It is worth knowing that you should not insult a Brazilian by talking to him in Spanish. The Brazilians are proud of the fact that they are the only nation in South America to speak Portuguese.

It's also important to understand that the Chinese, Japanese and Koreans believe in formalities before friendship and that they all gobble up business cards. Everyone should certainly realise that they must not ask a Muslim for his *Christian* name. And it is of passing interest that Hungarians like to do a lot of handshaking.

It is easy to become neurotic about the importance of local customs, but many Third World people today, at least in major towns, have some understanding of Western ways and, although they do not want to see their own traditions trampled on or insulted, they don't expect all travellers to look like Lawrence of Arabia or behave like a character from *The Mikado*.

Civility, politeness, warmth and straight dealing transcend any language and cultural barriers.

The Model Visitor

Ideally you should always wear glasses (not dark ones, which are the prerogative of the police and the refuge of terrorists), a dark suit, white shirt, a dark tie and carry an umbrella. In practice, this is not much fun when the temperature is 45°C in the shade, the humidity is 100 per cent and your luggage weighs 35kg. Nevertheless, try to keep your clothes clean, use a suitcase instead of a rucksack if not backpacking, shave and get your hair cut as close to a crewcut as possible without looking like an astronaut. A moustache is better than a beard, but avoid both if possible.

Do not try smuggling anything through customs, especially drugs. Hash and grass may be common in the countries you visit, but be careful if you buy any. A local dealer may be a police informer. Prosecutions are becoming more common and penalties increasingly severe – from ten years' hard labour to death for trafficking in 'hard' drugs, and sentences hardly more lenient in some countries for mere possession. There's no excuse for failing to research the countries you intend to visit. Talk to people who have lived in or visited them and find out what problems you are likely to encounter. If you go prepared and adopt a sympathetic, understanding frame of mind you should be able to manage without trouble.

How to Survive Without Money

by Bryan Hanson

Obviously one of the most important things to keep in mind while travelling is the safety of your possessions. Do your best to minimise the chances of theft and you will run far less of a risk of being left destitute in a foreign country. Try and separate your funds, both in your luggage and on your person so as to frustrate thieves and reduce losses. And before you leave home, make arrangements with a reliable person whom you can contact for help in an emergency.

American Express probably issue the most reliable and easily negotiable traveller's cheques, have the most refund points in the world and possibly hold the record for the speediest reimbursements. In remote spots, lesser-known cheques and even sterling notes may be refused; the dollar is, if not in too large a denomination, acceptable. Smaller value notes are less worth forging and are therefore more readily exchanged.

Play for Sympathy

Avoiding robbery is the best course. If you come face to face with your thieves then use all the skills in communication you have picked up on your travels. Try humour, at least try and get their sympathy, and always ask them to leave items which will be of no immediate value to them, but are inconvenient for you to replace.

They are usually after cash and valuables which are easily converted into cash. Try to get the rest back and risk asking for enough money for a bus or taxi fare if you feel the situation is not too tense. Acting mad can help, as can asking the thieves for help or advice.

Consider what action you can take if you find yourself penniless in a foreign land. Report thefts to the police and obtain the necessary form for insurance purposes. You may have to insist on this and even sit down and write it out for them to sign. Whatever it takes, you mustn't leave without it; it may be essential to you for onward travel.

Local custom may play a part in your success. In Lima, for instance, the police will only accept statements on paper with a special mark sold only by one lady on the steps of an obscure church found with the help of a guide. They have a way of sharing in your misfortune – or sharing it out!

If there is an embassy or consulate, report to them for help. In a remote spot, you are more likely to get help from the latter. You may have to interrupt a few bridge parties, but insist, it is your right to be helped. In cases of proven hardship, they will pay your fare home by (in their opinion) the most expedient route in exchange for your passport and the issue of travel papers. If your appearance suits they may also let you phone your family or bank for funds. If they do, proceed with thought.

Have the money sent either to the embassy via the Foreign Office or to the bank's local representative with a covering letter or cable sent to you under separate cover. This will give you proof that the money has been sent when you turn up at the bank. I have met many starving people on the shiny steps of banks being denied money which is sitting there in the care of a lazy or corrupt clerk, or in the wrong file. Other countries do not always use our order of filing and letters could be filed under 'M' or 'J' for Mr John Smith. Have your communications addressed to your family name followed by initials (and titles if you feel the need).

Quite an effective, proven way of moving onto a more sophisticated place or getting home, is to phone your contact at home and ask him to telex air tickets for a flight out. They pay at home and the airline is much more efficient than the bank. This has the additional advantage of circumventing the mickey mouse currency regulations which various countries impose. Algeria is a perfect example. The country insists that air fares are paid in 'hard' currency, but that money transferred into the country is automatically changed into Algerian as it arrives. One then has to apply to the central bank for permission to change it back (at a loss) in order to buy your air ticket. A telexed ticket can have you airborne in a couple of hours (I've done it).

Local Generosity

In desperate situations, help can be obtained from people locally. These fall into two main groups. Expatriates, who live unusually well, are not too keen on the image that young travellers seriously trying to meet the local scene create, but once you have pierced the inevitable armour they have put up from experience, they are able to help.

They often have telex facilities at their disposal, business connections within or out of the country and friends amongst the local officialdom. Their help and experience is usually well worth having.

Next the missionaries. From experience I would suggest you try the Roman Catholics first as the priests come from the working classes and a certain empathy with empty pockets. The other denominations tend to live better, but put up more resistance to helping. (I came across an American/Norwegian group in the Cameroons suffering from a crisis because the last plane had left no maple syrup.) Swallow your principles or keep quiet and repay the hospitality when you can, they often need their faith in human nature boosted from time to time.

You will receive kindness from other temples, mosques and chapels and can go there if you are starving. Again do not abuse assistance and repay it when you can.

Real desperation may bring you to selling blood, and selling branded clothes in which you have thoughtfully chosen to travel, in exchange for cheap local goods. But local religious communities are the best bet and usually turn up an intelligent person who can give advice.

In Third World countries being poor and going without is no big deal – you may be in the same boat as some 90 per cent of the population. A camaraderie will exist, so you will probably be able to share what little is available. It would be wrong to abuse the customs of hospitality, but on the other hand, be very careful of your hygiene, so as not to give yourself even more problems through illness. However, I recently heard that vomiting over the check-in clerk may get you three seats together so you can sleep on the plane.

Happy travelling!

In Trouble With the Law

by Bryan Hanson

Ignorance is no more of an excuse abroad than it is here for having broken the law. Consideration is usually given to the traveller but this is often in direct proportion to the funds available.

Always keep calm, to show anger is often regarded as loss of face. Be humble and do not rant and rave unless it is the last resort and you are amongst your own kind who understand. Try to insist on seeing the highest official possible. Take the names of all others you come across on the way up – this tends to lead you to someone who is high or intelligent enough to make a decision away from the book of rules. Also, in totalitarian régimes 'having your name took' is postively threatening.

Pay the Fine

If you are guilty and the offence is trivial, admit it. Do not get involved with lawyers unless you really have to. The fine will most probably be less painful on your funds than their fees.

On the other hand, do not misinterpret the subtleties of the local system. In Nigeria, I pleaded guilty to a trivial offence without a lawyer and found myself facing the maximum sentence. If I had used one, an 'agreement fee' would have been shared with the magistrate and the case dismissed on a technicality. If we had paid the small bribe initially demanded by the police, we would not have gone to court!

More serious situations bring more difficulties and you should make every effort to contact your local national representative. The cover is thinning out – for instance, 'our man in Dakar' has to cover most of West Africa. A lawyer is next on the list to contact, probably followed by a priest.

It is a good idea to carry lists of government representatives in all the countries through which you intend to travel – especially if you are leaving the beaten track. Remember they work short office hours (I once had a long and very fruitless conversation with a Serbo-Croat cleaner because I expected someone to be there before ten and after noon!). There should be a duty officer available at weekends.

Keep in Contact

Regular messages home are a good practice. Even if they are only postcards saying 'Clapham Common was never like this', they narrow down the area of search should one go missing. If doubtful of the area you are travelling in, also keep in regular contact with the embassy, and give them your proposed itinerary, so that if you don't show up by a certain time, they know to start looking.

The tradition of bribery is a fact of life in many countries and reaches much further down the ladder than it does here. I find the practice distasteful and have avoided it on many occasions, only to find myself paying eventually in other ways. In retrospect, I am not sure if 'interfering with these local customs' is wise. But how to go about it when all else has failed? It is the most delicate of operations, but here are a couple of suggestions. It is almost always a mistake to make a straight offer, unless one has been asked. 'Face' is as important to the lowly official as it is to a prince in his palace. One possible approach is 'Officer, I have not had a chance to change enough money since I arrived in your beautiful country, can you please help me?' Another is to place some money in your passport or among your other documents; when they are examined, it can be taken or ignored, and no one need be upset.

In Detention

Once you've been locked up and all attempts to contact officials have been denied, a more subtle approach is needed. One can only depend on locals leaving the place with messages, or more probably rely on a religious representative who may be prepared to take the risk. Sometimes it is possible to use a local lad and send him C.O.D. to the nearest embassy or consulate, even if it's over a border, with a suitable written plea.

Third World detention premises are usually primitive and provide the minimum of filthy food. You may even have to pay to feed yourself. Time has little significance, so make your means spin out. Even though money talks the world over, try not to declare your resources or you may not get any satisfaction until the last penny has been shared out among the locals.

A practice which could help is to change your status to that of incognito official or journalist. But be careful! You must sound the situation out carefully before embarking on this course as it could result in your plight being considerably worsened. And if you are found out, you could put a lot of genuine journalists at risk.

Humour and a willingness on your part to lose face can often defuse a tense and potentially awkward moment. Travelling gives you life-skills in judging people and an instinctive knowledge of how to act. Use your experience to your advantage and don't let daunting lists of advice keep you quivering at home.

If you have the gall it is often a good idea to learn the names of a few high-ranking officials and name drop blatantly. How far you carry this is up to you, but when I married off my cousin to the Minister of Justice in Turkey, he didn't mind a bit.

Arms, Violence and Espionage

by Christopher Portway

Being something of an inquisitive journalist with a penchant for visiting those countries normal people don't, I have, over the years, developed a new hobby. Some of us collect stamps, cigarette cards, matchboxes. I collect interrogations. And the preliminary to interrogation is, of course, arrest and detention, which makes me, perhaps, a suitable person to dwell for a few moments on some of the activities that can land the innocent traveller in stir as well as the best way of handling matters arising therefrom.

There are no set rules governing what are and are not crimes in some countries, and when simple interest becomes espionage. Different régimes have different ways of playing the game and it's not just cut-and-dried crimes like robbing a bank or even dealing on the black market that can put you behind bars. Perhaps a brief résumé of some of my own experiences will give you the general idea and suggest means of extracting oneself from the clutches of warped authority.

Violence: Don't Resist; Do Avoid

The crime of violence for the object of robbery is, of course, much more likely to be directed at you and, in this unhappy eventuality, my advice is to offer no resistance. It is virtually certain that those who inflict their hostile attentions upon you know what they are doing and have taken into account any possible acts of self-defence on the part of their intended victim. It may hurt your pride, but you live to tell the tale this way and, after all, if you're insured, the material losses will be made good by your insurance company following submission of a copy of the police report of the incident.

In many poorer countries, it is advisable not to hold or wear anything that is too obviously expensive, especially at night. The two continents where it is important to be particuly wary are Africa and South America.

The most important robbery-with-violence-prone city I know is Bogotá, Colombia, where in certain streets you can be 99 per cent certain of being attacked. Having had most of my worldly goods lifted off me – but not violently, in neighbouring Ecuador, I made sure I lost nothing else by walking Bogotá's treacherous streets with a naked machete in my hand.

The British Exporter robbed three times – once at gunpoint – in as many days in basically friendly Rio spent his remaining week there avoiding *favelas* (shanty towns on the outskirts of the city where many thieves live) and making sure that he was in a taxi after nightfall – when local drivers start to shoot the lights for fear of being mugged if they stop. Sometimes rolled-up newspapers are thrust through quarter-lights and drivers find themselves looking at the end of a revolver or the tip of a sheathknife.

One of the worst cities in Africa for theft is Dar Es Salaam where locals tell stories of Harlem-style car strippings. Drivers return to where they parked to find their car wheels have been stolen. The Tanzanian capital is also one of several African cities that can be dangerous at night, especially on the outskirts, where the streets are unlit. Another danger spot is the road between the railway station and the town of Oakland, California – especially after dark – but such attacks can take place in many other cities and, indeed, in some rural areas. In 1977 I walked right through Peru not knowing that the region was infested with cattle rustlers reputed to kill without mercy if they thought they'd been seen. Occasionally, ignorance can indeed be bliss.

Basically the best advice in places like this is to stay in the city centre at night. If it is imperative to move away from the lights, go by taxi and try not to go alone. And don't forget to press the door locks down when you get in. There are some countries – Egypt is a prime example – where other people just jump in if the car has to stop for any reason. Naturally, they're generally just an extra fare, but you can never be certain.

If, by mischance, you do find yourself walking along an unlit and remote road at night, at least walk in the middle of it. This will lessen the chance of being surprised by someone concealed in the shadows. And when you have to move over for a passing car, use its headlights as your 'searchlight' over the next ten or twenty metres.

Another good tip when in more rugged parts of the world is to avoid stray dogs. One businessman visiting Sana'a in the Yemen Arab Republic found packs of wild dogs roaming the streets – and there was no shortage of rabies among them.

Protecting yourself from attack by carrying a firearm is not recommended. Even in those countries that do permit it the necessary papers are difficult to come by. But that's not the point. The idea that a pistol under the car seat or one's belt is protection is usually nonsense. In many countries a gun is a prize in itself to a violent thief who will make every effort to procure one. And in countries with strict gun laws, being found with an unauthorised weapon can bring severe penalties.

Espionage: a Multitude of Sins

It is that nasty word 'espionage' that becomes a stock accusation beloved by perverted authority. Spying covers a multitude of sins and is a most conveniently vague charge for laying against anyone who sees more than is good for him (or her). It is the Communist countries of Europe and elsewhere in which you have to be most careful but some states in black Africa, Central America and the Middle East are picking up the idea fast. Spying, of a sort, can be directed against you too. In my time I have been followed by minions of the secret police in Prague and Vladivostok for hours on end. Personally, I quite enjoyed the experience and led a merry dance through a series of department stores in a vain effort to shake them off. If nothing else, I gave them blisters.

In World War II, to go back a bit, I escaped from my POW camp in Poland by the unwitting courtesy of the German State Railway. The journey came to an abrupt end at Gestapo HQ in Cracow. In post-war years the then Orient Express carred me visa-less, into Stalin-controlled Communist Czechoslavkia. That journey put me inside as a compulsory guest of the STB, the Czech secret police. I have met minor inconveniences of a similar nature in countries like Russia, Albania, Yugoslavia and several in the Middle East but it was only much more recently that I bumped into real trouble again. In Idi Amin's Uganda.

Interrogations James Bond Style

The venues of all my interrogations have been depressingly similar. That in Kampala, for instance, consisted of a bare concrete-walled office containing a cheap desk, a hard-backed chair or two, a filing cabinet, a telephone and an askew photograph of Idi Amin. This consistency fitted Cracow, Prague and Kishinev, except that in Nazi days nobody would dream of an askew Führer. Prague boasted an anglepoise lamp but then Communist methods of extracting information always did border on the James Bond.

Methods of arrest or apprehension obviously vary with the circumstances. For the record, in World War II, I was handed over to the Gestapo in Cracow by a bunch of Bavarian squaddies who could find no excuse for my lobbing a brick through the window of a bakery after curfew. In Czechoslavakia I was caught crossing a railway bridge in a frontier zone and, with five burp-guns aligned to one's navel, heroics are hard to come by. In the Soviet Union it was simply a case of my being caught with my trousers down in a 'soft class' toilet and with an out-of-date visa valid only for a place where I was not. And in Uganda there was no reason at all beyond an edict from Idi that stipulated a policy of let's-be-beastly-to-the-British!

Keep Your Answers Simple

But the latter's line of questioning was different. It wasn't so much why had I come, but why had I come for so brief a period? That and the young Ugandan law student arrested with me. Being in close confinement in a railway carriage for 24 hours we had become travelling companions which, coupled with my suspiciously brief stay, spelt 'dirty work at the cross-roads' to Ugandan authority. And rummaging about in our wallets and pockets, they found bits of paper on which we had scribbled our exchanged addresses. It had been the student's idea and a pretty harmless one but, abruptly, I was made aware how small inconsistencies can be blown up into a balloon of deepest suspicion. All along I maintained I hardly knew the guy. Which reminds me that the Gestapo too had an irksome habit of looking for a scapegoat amongst the local populace.

Then we came to the next hurdle. 'How is it your passport indicates you are a company director and this card shows you are a journalist?' To explain that I was once a company director and had retained the title in my passport in preference to the sometimes provocative 'journalist' would have only complicated matters. So I offered the white lie that I was still a company director and only a journalist in my spare time. It didn't help much.

And, you know, there comes a moment when you actually begin to believe that you are a spy or whatever it is they are trying to suggest you might be. It creeps up on you when they catch you out on some harmless answer to a question. In Kampala I felt the symptoms and resolved to keep my answers simple and remember them the second time round.

For instance: 'What school did you attend?' I gave the one I was at the longest. There was no need to mention the other two.

My regimental association membership card came up for scrutiny. 'What rank were you?' I was asked.

'Corporal' I replied, giving the lowest rank I had held. Pride alone prevented me from saying 'Private'.

'Which army?' came the further enquiry. I had to admit that it was British.

Every now and again I would get in a bleat about having a train to catch more as a cornerstone of normality than pious hope of catching it. And there comes a point in most interrogations when there is a lull in proceedings during which one can mount a counter-attack. The 'Why-the-hell-am-I-here? What-crime-am-I-supposed-to-have-committed?' sort of thing which at least raises the morale if not the roof.

Of course, in Nazi Germany such outbursts helped little for, in declared wartime, one's rights are minimal and the Gestapo had such disgusting methods of upholding theirs. But in the grey world of a cold war the borderline of bloodymindedness is ill-defined. At Kishinev the KGB had the impertinence to charge me a fiver a day for my incarceration in a filthy room in a frontier unit's barracks. I voiced my indignation loud and clear and eventually won a refund. In Czechoslovakia my outburst had a different effect. The interrogator was so bewildered that he raised his eyes to the ceiling long enough for me to pinch one of his pencils. And in the cell that became my home for months, a pencil was a real treasure. Now let it be said, in general, that the one demand you have the right to make is that you be put in touch with your embassy or consulate. I once wasn't and it caused an international incident.

In another of Kampala's Police HQ interrogation rooms all my proffered answers had to be repeated at dicta-ion speed. It was partly a ruse, of ourse, to see if the second set matched the first and I was going to be damn sure it did.

I suppose one lesson I ought to have earnt from all this is to take no incriminating evidence like press cards, association membership cards, other travellers' addresses and the like. But a few red herrings do so add to the entertainment.

Fill the Bath – It Looks Like Civil War

by Anne Sharpley

Don't take it too personally when the shooting starts. They're almost certainly not shooting at you – and if they are, it's even safer since the level of marksmanship is so low, at least in all street-shooting I've been caught up in that you're almost invulnerable. Hollywood never comes to your aid at such moments. You'd have thought that the rigorous early training we all get at the movies in both armed and unarmed fighting would have got into our reflexes. But it's all so much more muddled when it happens. Far from knowing when and where to duck I could never make out where the fighting was coming from or which side of the wall or handy car to duck behind.

As for hand-to-hand fighting, far from the balletic, clearly defined movements of cinematic bouts, everyone gets puffed, or sick, or falls over in a shambles of misunderstood intentions. Nor is there that crack on the jaw to let you know who's being hit when. So it's even poor for spectator interest.

As a reporter it is usually my actual work to be there and see what's happening. This means I can't follow my own best advice, which is to get out. Sticking around is the easy bit.

It is the next stage of events that sets in during and after the street fighting that is always the real difficulty. The paraphernalia of street blocks, cordons, summary arrests and general paralysis as order is imposed on a troubled area presents the visitor with his worst problems.

Communications with the outside world cease, public utilities go wrong and airports close.

It is this sort of scene you can guarantee will take over. So forget the bullet proof vest you wish you'd thought of and get on with the practicalities. The first and best rule is worth observing before you leave home – never pack more than you can run with. Always include a smaller, lighter bag such as an airline overnight bag because if things gets really nasty you need something handy with a shoulder strap to pick up and clear out with in a hurry.

Essentials

If you're in a situation in which something is likely to happen, it is worth keeping this bag packed with essentials. Don't run about with suitcases, it can't be done for long.

Always bring in your duty-free allowance if you know things are likely to get tough. Even if you're a non-smoking teetotaller who hates scent, they're the stuff of which bribes and rewards for favours are made. And as banks close or the money exchange goes berserk they may end up as your only bargaining resource. And remember that drink is a useful stimulant, as well as solace. If I have to stay up all night I do it on regular small nips of whisky.

The next bit of advice will seem absurd at first, but you'll regret having laughed if you ever get into one of those long-standing semi-siege situations that sometimes happen when you're stuck in a hotel that either can't or won't provide for you. Take on of those little aluminium pans with a solid fuel burner – so small it will slip into your pocket. You can boil water at the rate of quarter of a pint to one solid fuel stick, which is about the size of a cigarette. You can get the whole thing from camping shops for only a few pounds.

If you take a few tea bags or a small jar of instant coffee, this will not only help if you're an addict of these things, but again wins friends and allies in an hour of need. Serve up in tooth mug, but don't forget to put in a spoon before you pour in boiling water or you'll crack the glass.

As the water either goes off completely, or turns a threatening colour, it is just as well to have a means of making water sterile. And at the very least it provides a shave.

If things look ugly it is a good idea to fill the bath. You can keep filling it if supplies continue, but you can't get water at all if they really stop. Not only have you a means of keeping the loo in a less revolting state, but you can wash yourself and keep away thirst (boil the water first, of course). I always like to carry a small box of biscuits, although this isn't anything more than a psychological trick to reinforce a feeling to self-sufficiency.

If things are really popping nobody in a hotel wants to know about you, but they get rather interested in your property. It's a great time for getting everything nicked. I came back from Prague in 1968 with scarcely a thing left. What's yours suddenly becomes theirs. So remember that overnight bag and carry it with you everywhere.

Whether you should try to look less conspicuously foreign is a moot point. War correspondents usually get themselves kitted out in a sort of quasi-military set of clothes and where there are women soldiers, as in Israel, I have too. If nothing else, it meant I could fill my taxi with girl soldiers and let them get me past the road blocks with their papers. But when I found myself in action before I had time to change, I was told later by a captured sniper that it had only been my pretty pink blouse that had saved me. He'd had me in his sights and liked the colour so he couldn't bring himself to shoot me!

However, you're much more likely to be holed up in your hotel. If things are exploding, it's as well to get whatever glass is removable down on the floor, draw curtains and blinds against window glass and drape mirrors you can't take down with blankets and towels. Glass is the biggest danger you face. Locate the fire escape and if it's remote get yourself somewhere else to stay either in the same hotel or elsewhere.

Identity in a Crisis

It's always worth trying to pretend you're from a country they're not having a row with, although local knowledge of nationalities is always limited, so don't try Finnish or Papuan. This is for occasional use when they're running around looking for someone to duff up. Hit the right nationality and you're so popular they won't put you down. Crowds are very emotional and the least thing sends them one way or the other. In Algeria, I found I had a winning ticket by saying I was British, or English to be more precise. I became the object of gallant attention from a group of youths who decided to accompany me as a sort of bodyguard. All very honourable and very sweet.

Women are still quite often chivalrously treated in the Middle East. I found that to get through road blocks in Algeria I could simply say I was an 'English Miss' without having to hand over my passport with the damning word 'journalist' in it. What echoes it evoked, why they were so responsive, I never quite found out but I like to think that I'd modestly linked up with those amazing bossy Englishwomen from Hester Stanhope on who'd been in the Middle East.

Certainly I found that Muslim sentries were unable to challenge me. I always walked straight through, looking determined.

Another useful tip for visiting women in tricky situations in Muslim countries is to apply to visit the chief wife of whoever is in power. There's always a go-between who will arrange it for a sum, escort you there, and help generally. As women in harems are bored out of their minds, they're usually delighted to see another woman from the outside world. If they like you – which you must make sure of (that's where the duty-free scent or your best blouse or scarf come in) – they'll do a great deal to help. They always have more power than is generally believed.

Keep Calling

While ordinary communications often stop altogether it is a good idea to tell your family or company to keep on telephoning you from outside. So often, I've found it impossible to get calls out while incoming calls made it.

You can always try the journalists' old trick of getting out to the airport and picking a friendly face about to board whatever aircraft is leaving and get them to take a message.

One belief I've always had, which may not necessarily work, but always has for me, is that befriending a taxi driver can be extremely useful. They're a much maligned lot. What you do is practise your basic physiognomy – a derided skill, but it's all you've got – and pick a driver you think you could trust. Then use him all the time, paying him over the odds, of course. Take an interest in him and his family, and you will find a friend.

A taxi driver not only knows where everything is and what's going on, but can also act as interpreter and spare hand.

Explain what you're trying to do and they soon enter into the spirit of things. There was one taxi driver in Cyprus who virtually did my job for me. He was not only fearless, he was accurate too! And we're still friends.

Not that these sorts of happening are confined to abroad anymore. Imagine my rage when relaxing at home one Sunday evening I hear the all too familiar sound of shots a few yards away. I happen to live in Balcombe Street.

This article first appeared in Business Traveller magazine, June 1980, by whose kind permissions it is reproduced here. – Ed.

Mishaps, Major and Minor: What to Do

Loss or Theft

	To Avoid:	*Notify:*	*Provide:*	*Expect:*
Passport	Keep a note of the passport number, separate from the passport itself.	Police and nearest consulate or embassy.	Passport number, details or your travel plans and dates, photos of yourself.	To be issued with an exit visa, an emergency travel document or emergency passport (for which there is usually a small charge).
Traveller's cheques	Ask for printed advice from issuing bank or authority; follow advice and keep it with you. Keep a note of the serial numbers of the cheques, separate from the cheques themselves.	Police and issuing bank, or agent thereof; *or* Thomas Cook or Wagon Lits office if issued by Cooks; *or* nearest branch of American Express if issued by Amex.	Details of issuing authority, and if possible, serial numbers of cheques.	From Amex, during working hours, a rapid refund: *or* from Avis, at weekends and in an emergency, an immediate loan of up to US$100 for Amex cheques, *or* with some delay, replacement cheques from any other issuing body.
Credit cards	Keep a note of card numbers and of the issuing company's address, separate from the cards themselves.	Police and bank or issuing company (telephone, telex or cable from post office, large hotel, etc.)		Old card to be cancelled to avoid fraudulent use; eventual replacement issued.
Vehicle	Don't leave vehicle unlocked!	Police and insurance company.	All possible methods of identification such as registration, engine, and chassis numbers.	To be issued with a note of confirmation by the police.

	To Avoid:	*Notify:*	*Provide:*	*Expect:*
Money	Do not carry all your money in the same place; a small, obvious amount will often satisfy thieves.	Police and nearest embassy or consulate; and telex bank asking them to authorise a local bank to issue money to you.		Loan from consulate or embassy in an emergency (a small charge is made for this service, payable later) and your passport to be surrendered as security. Money cabled out to a Third World country takes at least two weeks and persistent enquiry at the receiving bank.
Luggage and Valuables	Take a copy of your insurance certificate. Air travel: take out extra insurance, available from travel agents, as the carrier's liabilty is limited. Watch to ensure luggage goes on conveyor belt. Keep receipts.	Police and manager of hotel, campsite, etc. Airline personnel within four hours of arrival. Ensure that they fill in a 'loss or damage' form.	Copy of your insurance certificate	Carrier to find luggage within three days; or to pay compensation which, on international flights, is based on weight, not value.
Vehicle Documents	Keep a full set of photocopies of driving license, insurance documentation (green card or equivalent), registration book, bail bond and other documents separately from original. One option: get an International Driving Permit and use this *instead* of your licence.	Police	Details of driving licence; photocopies of relevant documents.	To be issued with a note of confirmation by police; in some countries, a temporary replacement of your driving licence to be issued by the national automobile club on provision of details of your licence.

If:

you have a road accident – notify the police and fill in details on the form supplied with your insurance card or, if you don't have one, take down names and addresses of people involved and of witnesses; a photographic record of the incident will also come in useful.

you are stopped for committing a traffic offence – do not remonstrate, pay any fine demanded, but insist on being issued with an official receipt. (This helps to ensure that you are being charged at the correct rate for the offence.)

you witness a crime or accident – you are required in some countries to stay on the scene and render assistance. This does not apply to a civil disturbance or commotion, when it is best to keep clear in order to avoid a false arrest or charge.

you get into trouble with the police for a suspected crime – insist on speaking to your consulate or embassy, if the police fail to inform them as a matter of course.

you are the victim of a crime – inform the police and your consulate or embassy.

you need a lawyer – consult your consulate or embassy, who will advise you on legal aid and procedures and be able to refer you to English-speaking lawyers and interpreters.

you need to make a telephone call home from a Third World country – the most effective, if expensive, way may be to forgo using a post office or the services of a cheap hotel and actually book into a Hilton or the nearest equivalent so as to use its telephone system. Even this takes time – one traveller reported a fifteen hour wait for a call from the Hilton in Rabat, Morocco.

you fall ill – you will usually be required to pay for some or all of the treatment, even if you can subsequently reclaim expenses. This is possible for British travellers in some countries, provided that they keep receipts for medical attention received and medicament supplied and send them to the Dept of Health and Social Security, Overseas Group, Newcastle-upon-Tyne, UK NE98 1YX.

a member of your party dies – consider having the body cremated locally, which may be less distressing and is usually cheaper than have the body transported back home. The ashes can be flown home for internment. Inform the police and nearest consulate or embassy, who will provide valuable advice and support.

Editor's note:
This article draws on material in a feature entitled 'What should you do if . . .' published in the *Sunday Times*.

Survival in the Cold

by Sir Crispin Agnew of Lochnaw, Bt.

Some of the most wonderful areas in the world have cold environments and living in them poses a constant challenge. Survival becomes a continual battle against exposure or, as it is sometimes called, hypothermia. Exposure occurs when the body loses its heat faster than its mechanism can replace the heat loss. Man needs a constant body temperature of about 36.9°C. If it falls too much below this level, death will occur. In outline, at 33.9°C, the muscles cease to work and the victim becomes immobile; at 32.8°C he becomes confused; at 31°C (a drop of only six degrees from normal body temperature) he becomes unconscious and at 28°C he will die.

People who survive longest in the wild are those who never get into difficulties. Prevention is better than cure, so prepare well. Study the environment and carry appropriate and adequate shelter and clothing, with sufficient food for the whole trip including a survival reserve. An emergency food pack should contain simple sugars which are easy to digest and provide immediate heat generation. If it is possible to carry a cooker and provide cooked food, so much the better. The route must be within your capabilities and you should note possible shelter and escape routes along the way.

Caught Out

Now let us consider what must be done if despite all the preparations you are caught out in a survival situation. Three things cause exposure and are therefore the greatest danger to survival. The colder it is, the greater the danger, but linked to temperature are two other factors – wind and wetness. Wind carries away body heat by convection and this then has to replaced by burning more body energy. Scientists have shown a direct correlation between wind and temperature which is called the wind-chill factor. The temperature and wind together combine to produce an apparent temperature considerably lower than the real one (*see Climate and its Relevance to Travel on page 10*).

The third factor in the equation is the wet. Water is a good conductor which destroys the insulation of clothing, for when it evaporates, it extracts heat from the surrounding area and thus lowers body temperature. Physiologists have defined the insulation factor of clothing in 'Clo's'. For normal winter trekking you wear about '2 Clo's' of insulation, but if the clothing becomes wet, then the 'Clo' factor falls from '2 Clo's' to '.75 Clo's'. Wet clothing increases the speed at which you lose body heat and this is greatly increased if it is windy. Stay dry at all costs and avoid the often fatal downward cold-wet spiral.

Clothing

Recent technological advances have brought a multitude of new synthetics onto the market, many of which are expressly designed to cope with the stressful conditions imposed by outdoor activities, whether they are just more hardwearing, or waterproofed, extra warm or half the weight of their natural counterpart. Vapour-barrier insulation retains heat by preventing evaporative cooling of the body vapour in circumstances where the user is inactive and producing little liquid perspiration. It is therefore an excellent material for sleeping bag liners and such. Polypropylene encourages evaporation but draws perspiration away from the body. Normally, evaporation on the skin has a cooling effect. When the evaporation takes place in a zone that is not in direct contact with the skin, the body suffers less cooling. Polypropylene is therefore a suitable material for clothing for strenous activity in cold weather conditions, e.g. ski touring. Other increasingly popular materials are Dunova, viloft/polyester and fibre-pile, which are all used for underwear and Gore-Tex, an excellent outer layer, which allows perspiration to escape while still being completely waterproof. But even this is only a small number of what is now available, and it is well worth consulting a specialist about your particular needs before you set off.

You may think that being physically fit will increase your chances of survival if hypothermia sets in. True, it will help a little, but the amount of fat you are carrying is far more important. Body fat reduces the heat loss and provides fuel to keep the blood temperature raised. Women have a layer of subcutaneous fat and will often survive longer than men as a result.

Good clothing is vital. Even if you have tents and other camping equipment, if your clothing is not good and fitted to the environment then you will be unable to move. Woollens or nylon pile are much to be preferred to cottons or straight nylons because wools and pile retain their warmth much better, particularly when wet. Several layers of clothing are better than one thick layer because they trap the warm air and also give great flexibility in changing temperatures. A suitable combination of clothing for a cold temperature is: (for the top half) a vest, a woollen shirt, a lightweight woollen pullover, a pile jacket, with a windproof anorak and a waterproof cagoule for the outer covering; (for the lower half) good boots and gaiters, woollen socks, long woollen underwear, woollen breeches or trousers and waterproof trousers on top. The body loses a lot of heat through the head which should be covered by a woollen hat. Ensure that there is no gap at the stomach where the body's temperature is generated and maintained. Down clothing, sleeping bags etc. should be considered, but their weight must be balanced against probable use. If you do decide to take down, make sure it has a waterproof outer skin as wet feathers can be extremely difficult to dry.

In a survival situation you must maintain the body's core temperature as near normal as possible. When the air temperature drops, the body shuts off blood from the extremities (such as the fingers and toes) in order to shorten the circuit and maintain the core body temperature, which is essentially in the stomach area. There is also shivering, which burns up sugar in the muscles and generates heat. You must try to prevent frostbite by keeping the extremities warm – in your armpits or your crotch – but it is better to lose fingers than to die. It is essential to seek shelter from the wind. At its most basic this might be the lee of a rock or slope but this should be improved upon wherever possible. Above the snow line it may be possible to dig a snow hole or build an igloo, but if these are not available, tree or rock shelters can be built. A very simple shelter is provided by a two metre polythene bag, which keeps out wind and rain.

Body Fuels

You should have fed well before setting off in the morning and continued to eat small snacks at regular intervals during the day to maintain the blood sugar level. If you have done this, you will meet any crisis well-nourished. A regular intake of food during the survival period refuels the body and helps it to generate heat. Liquid intake is also important because without fluid the body finds it difficult to digest food. Outdoor winter activity requires an intake of at least two litres of water a day to prevent exhaustion, kidney strain and dehydration. Dehydration is one of those factors which lower your body's resistance to the elements. Great care must be taken to keep survival packs as light as possible. Nothing will exhaust a party more than carrying heavy packs, for they may well then be forced to bivouac before reaching their destination. Fats and starches are the most important foods for cold weather activity; sugars are also valuable.

In the cold, wind and wet you must anticipate and learn to recognize the symptoms of exposure and once they appear, take immediate action to prevent the situation from getting worse. The symptoms of exposure can be summed up as 'acting drunk'. A person suffering from exposure may begin to stagger, appear tired or listless, display unreasonable behaviour or have sudden uncontrollable shivering fits. You will notice that he begins to slow down or stumble and he may complain of disturbance or failure of his vision.

If your party is getting exhausted and liable to exposure, stop early, because it is easier to take the necessary action while you still have spare energy. Seek shelter from the elements. Once in your shelter, put on all your spare clothing, have something to eat and make every effort to maintain your core temperature. Huddle together for extra warmth and keep your hands and feet warm by placing them in each other's armpits. There is a great temptation when feeling cold to try and generate heat through violent excercise; resist it, because you will merely disperse heat by convection and send warm blood to the cold extremities, which will then return to the core at a lower temperature. Vital reserves of energy will then be used to regenerate the heat. Likewise, do not take alcohol as it creates a false illusion of warmth, sending blood to the cold extremities and lowering the body temperature overall.

The Will to Live

Understanding the problem and taking steps to solve it are half the battle for survival, but however good your equipment, shelter and clothing, you will not survive unless your mental attitude is right. The will to live is vital. We have many examples in the annals of exploration: Shackleton's party surviving for many months on Elephant Island in the Antarctic; Walter Bonatti surviving on Mont Blanc for over five days while some members of his party died on the first day in the same conditions. If you do not have the will to live then you will not begin to take the most elementary necessary precautions. Cultivate determination and it will enhance your survival chances.

Nobody can guarantee you comfort in a really cold environment, but with proper practical and mental preparation, you will probably never be engaged in a real life and death struggle.

Safety and Survival at Sea

by Maurice and Maralyn Bailey

Survival is as old as the world, but, because of the manner of our modern way of living, where we specialize and employ specialists for the necessities of life, relatively few people have to live an utterly basic existence with all the shrouds of 'progressive' materialism and comforts stripped away. Intellectually naked and with only a vestige of civilized living left, survivors discover, or more correctly rediscover, other codes of behaviour to comply with a primitive lifestyle reminiscent of remote millennia. Armed with our basic animal instincts we are all capable of enduring, to a greater or lesser degree, conditions of acute hardship; and sailors have long taken more than a passing interest in the consequences of shipwreck.

Our requirements for safety and survival at sea can be summarised under four headings: The Boat; Safety; Damage Control, and Survival.

The Boat

For us safety at sea begins with the boat. A soundly constructed watertight hull with no vulnerable stress points is the first priority. Then must come the security of the mast and rigging, of the rudder and its fastenings. After this, meticulous attention to maintenance will form the basis of safe cruising. If the mast fittings and rigging are oversize they will add appreciably to the crew's peace of mind. The best available ground tackle is a cheap insurance and long distance voyagers will be well advised to carry more than two anchors with ample cable of above average weight. Since the sails will, for the long distance sailor, be the main source of power, a second suit of working sails is well worth considering, especially when one contemplates the rapid deterioration of Dacron in ultraviolet light. Even on a sailboat everything mechanical and electrical should be thoroughly overhauled annually or before the start of a long passage and ample spare parts and tools should be carried.

Safety

Almost everything in this world that comes under the heading of adventure has its moments of danger and all seafarers must realize this. They must become self-reliant without dependence upon any outside assistance when things start going wrong.

It is impossible to compile a list of safety equipment in any order of priority since it is all, to our minds, necessary to a boat being prepared for a long voyage or, in truth, any cruise. There will be many things which have apparently been overlooked and it could be argued, for example, that adequate up-to-date charts are items of safety equipment. We would suggest that another, though less evident, aid to safety would be a self-steering device, electronic or wind-activated, which relieves the crew of the exhausting business of steering and allows them to give their full attention to lookout tasks. No excuse can be found for economy with pyrotechnics and every boat should be liberally endowed with up-to-date flares. It is absolutely essential to have rocket-type flares on board, and if they go off with a bang, so much the better. White hand flares should be kept handy at all times to warn approaching ships of your presence. The argument for fitting an octahedral radar reflector permanently to the mast in such a way as to present many surfaces to the projected beam is very sound.

Some considerable thought must be

given to the various safety harness systems available to ensure the harness will be comfortable to get into, quick to adjust and, just as important, easy to get out of in an emergency. Every crew member should have a harness and no one should leave the security of the cabin or cockpit in heavy weather or at night without being hooked on. Whether the crew are equipped with buoyancy aids or life-jackets is a matter of individual preference. We prefer the lifejacket because, in its deflated state, it is less of an encumbrance to the wearer.

Lifebuoys should be equipped with automatically activated strobe lights and dan buoys. Lifebuoys come in two versions, horseshoe and circular, of which we prefer the latter. Ample fire extinguishers and a gas detection device must be added to the list.

The important contribution made by the health of the crew towards safety cannot be overlooked. Nothing can upset the efficiency or morale of a crew more than to be constantly beset by worries over the health of one of their number. We cannot warn too strongly of the consequences which follow the inability of the crew to live amicably together within the restricting confines of a small boat. A trained and rested crew, physically fit and mentally compatible, and following a fair and acceptable routine should be able to cope with any emergency.

Damage Control

The one really frightening aspect of damage to a small boat at sea is that a fairly small and potentially repairable leak in the hull may rapidly exceed the capacity of the pumps and sink the boat. When a leak is discovered, through collision or stress of weather, shock may easily give way to panic and the crew's uncoordinated actions may impede any concerted effort to implement correct damage control.

Any discussion of damage control must include the advantages or disadvantages of installing some emergency buoyancy into the boat itself. Watertight bulkheads with firm sealing doors are an obvious way to contain damage and maintain buoyancy but it is very difficult to use these in small boats without encroaching on the living space. The installation of permanent built-in buoyancy by using materials such as expanded polystyrene foam in the bow and stern sections is another possibility. Another, but expensive, method is to install a series of buoyancy bags stowed deflated over 'wasted' space and connected to a remote CO_2 gas cylinder.

With a ruptured hull the one real hope of saving the boat is the use of a quick and effective collision mat or plug to cover the hole. Any damage control procedure must be set in motion promptly, on the understanding, however, that once one is committed to one course of action it will probably be too late to attempt an alternative if the first fails. A sail or canopy lowered over the bows and dragged aft to cover the hole, secured firmly on either side of the boat, can be effective. There are available patented collision mats including pneumatic cushion affairs and an umbrella-type device. We carry two of the latter types in addition to a collision mat of our own design. This consists of two pieces of heavy canvas cut as equilateral triangles with one metre sides sewn together with a piece of carpet sandwiched in between. The edges are roped and heavy thimbles in the corners have ropes spliced on. The ropes are long enough to wrap around the hull.

After a ruptured hull, the biggest worry facing the ocean voyager in a sailboat has always been the possibilty of being dismasted. From the start it is important to have a clear practical plan for rigging a jury mast and sail. The ship's jury equipment should include tools necessary to clear away damage, prepared patching and shoring implements and copious spares for everything. An emergency steering system must also be worked out before setting sail.

Survival

The best time to learn about survival techniques is before the event. Learning must include a study of past cases and of alternative equipment specifications. Literally, survival starts as soon as a boat fails to function in the way it was meant to: in other words, when a boat is dismasted, or a power boat develops engine trouble, or the hull has sustained some damage which impedes its performance.

After the decision to abandon ship the castaways must be clear in their minds what priority is to be given when salvaging items from the wreck. The quicker everyone is off the boat the better, but the essential items for survival must be ready to hand and not encumbered by an accumulation of non-essential articles.

There has been a lot of intelligent argument about the merits of using a dinghy instead of a life raft. The dinghy's main advantage lies in its capacity for propulsion by oar or by sail, which would enable survivors to reach safety, especially in coastal waters. However, when compared to a liferaft, it will provide less room for each man, is less stable and it lacks, to start with anyway, the essential canopy to protect the survivors from the sun and from heat loss. Liferafts are a static means of survival and do not lend themselves well to manoeuvrability which is, of course, all to the good if a search for the survivors has been mounted. For ourselves, the liferaft would be the main instrument of survival, but we would make every effort to take the dinghy as well.

Talk of safety and survival must always include the subject of radios. While a good receiving apparatus is a necessary piece of the yacht's navigational equipment, a transmitter is often an expensive luxury for a small boat voyager. A fixed transmitter cannot be taken into the liferaft and must be operated *in situ* and its use is dependent upon the time and the personnel available to operate it in the emergency. The cost of fitting an automatic distress device is justified but even this will take a little time to activate. Small compact radio telephones suitable for the limited space available on board yachts, especially line-of-sight VHF, have too short a range which makes their benefit doubtful in mid-ocean. In addition, transmitters are susceptible to poor earthing. However, every yacht would be well advised to carry a small portable transmitter for broadcasting on the emergency frequencies despite its high cost.

Every yacht should be equipped with a survival pack or 'panic bag' and we think it should contain supplies to sustain a crew for a minimum of four days. The following list would be the *minimum* for four people:

10 × 450ml cans of water
6 × 500gm packs of compressed glucose and vitaminized survival biscuits (total 14,000 cals)
100 vitamin tablets
simple first aid kit
lanoline-based cream for sunburn
20 anti-seasickness tablets
electric torch
heliograph
4 red rocket flares
4 red hand flares
4 smoke flares
2 × fluorescine dye
fishing kit
solar still
2 knives
pocket compass
2 sponges

Ideally the items should be triple-wrapped in polythene and the pack filled out with plastic foam pieces to enable it to float. The pack should be stowed on deck in a waterproof valise as close to the liferaft as possible. Since water is the most essential element of the body's metabolism under survival conditions, it will be useful to have several nine litre containers filled and handy for quick release on board.

Rationing

If all else fails and you find yourself adrift on the open sea, water, shelter and food – in that order – will be your main ingredients for survival. Food and water must be rationed and do not eat or drink anything in the first 24 hours. To start with, allow just a quarter litre of water per person per day unless you can be sure of catching rainwater. Any exertion, especially in the tropics, causes a loss of water through perspiration. Everything must be done to reduce this loss by resting in the shade and draping the body in clothes soaked in sea water. Avoid 'immersion foot' by removing footwear, drying the feet, loosely wrapping them in cloth and exercising the feet and toes.

It is important to remember that under survival conditions the intake of food, especially protein, must be modified in direct proportion to the availability of water. For example, one volume of protein requires two equivalent volumes of water for digestion and elimination of waste. A normally healthy active person requires some 3,000 calories per day but a non-active person in survival conditions could reduce his requirements to about 600 calories per day. If castaways are well nourished initially, there will be little cause for alarm if the calorie intake is low to start with. A healthy person is capable of living three or four weeks without food. Thirst can be reduced by sucking a button.

Obtaining sustenance from the sea could be a problem. Large parts of the oceans are biological deserts and the prospect of catching fish and other animals away from the convergence zones and continental shelves will be marginal. Fish will always follow dinghies. Brightly coloured fish, fish that 'puff up', fish with teeth like those of humans or with parrot-like mouths and fish covered with spikes or bristles should not be eaten as they likely to be poisonous. If there are sharks or swordfish about, throw wastes overboard at night.

A high standard of seamanship and an ability to improvise will compensate for many deficiencies, but when it comes to a serious emergency, there can be no excuse for not having the boat and its crew fully prepared.

Recommended Reading

Safety in Small Craft, by Guy Cole.
The Seaway Code: A Guide for Small Boat Users, published by the Department of Trade and Industry and the COI, 1974. From: HMSO.

Survival in the Desert

by Jack Jackson

The most important thing about desert survival is to avoid the need for it in the first place.

Know your vehicle's capabilities, do not overload it. Know how to maintain and repair it. Carry adequate spares and tools. Be fit yourselves and get sufficient sleep. Start your journey with 25 per cent more fuel and water than was calculated as necessary, to cover extra problems such as bad terrain, leaking containers and extra time spent over repairs or sitting out a bad sandstorm.

Know accurately where your next supplies of fuel and water are. Carry plastic sheet to make desert stills; carry space blankets. Carry more than one compass and know how to navigate properly. Use magnetic compasses away from vehicles and cameras. Do not leave the piste unless you really do know what you are doing. Travel only in the local winter months. Know how correct your odometer is for the wheels and tyres you are using. Make notes of distances, compass bearings and obvious landmarks as you go along, so you can retrace your route easily if you have to.

Observe correct check in and out procedures with local authorities. Preferably convoy with other vehicles. When lost, do not continue; stop, think and, if necessary, retrace your route.

Back-up Plans

If you are a large expedition, you should arrange a search and rescue plan with your back-up team before you start out. This would include the use and recognition of radio beacons and/or flares, for aircraft search. Many countries do not allow you to use radio communication.

For most expeditions, an air search is highly unlikely and high flying commercial passenger aircraft overhead are unlikely to notice you whatever you do. A search, if it does come, will be along the piste or markers; most often this will just be a case of other vehicles travelling through being asked by the local authorities to look out for you, when you fail to check in. Local drivers will not understand or appreciate coloured flares, so your best signal for outside help is fire; at night, if you hear a vehicle, cardboard boxes or wood are quickly and easily lit, but during the day you need lots of thick black smoke. The best fuel for this is a tyre. Bury most of it in sand to control the speed at which it burns (keep it well away and down wind from the vehicles or fuel) and start the exposed part burning with either petrol or diesel fuel with a rag wick. As the exposed part of the tyre burns away, you can uncover more from the sand to keep it going, or cover all of it with sand if you wish to put the fire out. Avoid inhaling the sulphurous fumes.

Headlights switched on and off at night can be used while the battery still has charge.

A Need to Survive

Once you are in a 'need to survive' situation, the important things are morale and water. Concentrate on getting your vehicles moving again, this will keep you occupied and help to keep up morale. To minimise water loss, do not do manual work during the day – work at night or in the early morning. Build shade and stay under it as much as possible, keep well covered with loose cotton clothing. 'Space blankets' with the reflective side out make the coolest shade. Keep warm and out of the wind at night.

Unless you are well off the piste with no chance of a search you should stay with the vehicle. If someone must walk out, pick one or two of the strongest, most determined persons to go. They must have a compass, torch, salt, anti-diarrhoea medicine, loose all-enveloping clothes, good footwear, good sunglasses and as much water as they can sensibly carry. In soft sand, a jerrycan of water can easily be hauled along on a rope from the waist; on mixed ground, tie the jerry to a sand ladder, one end of which is padded and tied to the waist. The person who walks out should follow the desert nomad pattern of walking in the evening till about 2300 hours, sleep until 0400 hours, walk again till 1000, then dig a shallow well in the sand and lie in it under the space blanket, reflective side out till the sun has lost its heat. If they have a full moon they can walk all night. In this way, fit men would make 60 to 70 kilometres on ten litres of water, less in soft sand.

Water

In a 'sit it out and survive' situation, with all manual labour kept to a minimum, food is relatively unimportant and dehydration staves off hunger, but water is *vital*. The average consumption of water in a hot, dry climate is eight litres a day. This can be lowered to four litres per day in a real emergency. Diarrhoea increases dehydration, so should be controlled by medicines where necessary. Salt intake should be kept up.

Water supply should be improved by making as many desert stills as possible. To make one, dig a hole about one-third of a metre deep and one metre circumference, place a clean saucepan or billy in the centre of the hole and cover the hole with a two-metre-square plastic sheet weighed down with stones, jerry cans or tools at the edges. Put one stone or similiar object in the centre to weigh it down directly over the billy can. Overnight, water vapour from the sand will evaporate and then condense on the underside of the plastic sheet, running down and dripping into the pan. All urine should be conserved and put into shallow containers around the central billy can. The water so collected should be boiled and sterilized before drinking.

If you have antifreeze in your radiator, then don't try to drink this, or use it at all, as it is highly poisonous. If you have not put antifreeze in the radiator, there is still likely to be some left in it from the previous use, or from the factory when the vehicle was first manufactured, so this water should be put into the desert still in the same way as the urine and the resulting condensate should be boiled or sterilized before drinking. Water from wells known to be bad can be made drinkable in the same way.

The minimum daily water requirements to maintain the body's water balance at rest, in the shade, are as follows:

Mean daily temperatures °C	*Litres of water* per 24 hours
35°	5.3
30°	2.4
25°	1.2
20° and below	1.0

It must be stressed that this is for survival. There will be gradual kidney malfunction and possible urinary tract infection, with women more at risk than men.

The will to live is essential. Once you give up, you will be finished.

If you find people in such a situation and do not have a doctor to handle them, feed them dilute salt water a teaspoonful at a time every few minutes for a couple of hours, before trying to take them on a long tough drive to a hospital. Sachets of salts for rehydration are available for your medical kit.

Survival – Jungles

by Robin Hanbury-Tenison

The key to survival in the tropics is comfort. If your boots fit, your clothes don't itch, your wounds don't fester, you have enough to eat, and you have the comforting presence of a local who is at home in the environment, then you are not likely to go far wrong.

Of course, jungle warfare is something else. The British, Americans, and, for all I know, several other armies have produced detailed manuals on how to survive under the most arduous conditions imaginable and with the minimum of resources. But most of us are extremely unlikely ever to find ourselves in such a situation. Even if you are unlucky enough to be caught in a guerilla war or survive an air crash in the jungle, I believe that the following advice will be as useful as trying to remember sophisticated techniques which probably require equipment you do not have to hand, anyway.

A positive will to survive is essential. The knowledge that others have travelled long distances and lived for days and even months without help or special knowledge gives confidence, while a calm appraisal of the circumstances can make them seem far less intimidating. The jungle need not be an uncomfortable place, although unfamiliarity may make it seem so. Morale is as important as ever and comfort, both physical and mental, a vital ingredient.

Clothing and Footwear

To start with, it is usually warm, but when you are wet, especially at night, you can become very cold very quickly. It is therefore important to be prepared and always try to keep a sleeping bag and a change of clothes dry. Excellent strong, lightweight plastic bags are now available in which these items should always be packed with the top folded over and tied. These can then be placed inside your rucksack or bag so that if dropped in a river or soaked by a sudden tropical downpour – and the effect is much the same – they, at least, will be dry. I usually have three such bags, one with dry clothes, one with camera equipment, notebooks etc., and one with food. Wet clothes should be worn. This is unpleasant for the first ten minutes in the morning but they will soon be soaking wet with sweat and dripping in any case and wearing them means you need carry only one change for the evening and sleeping in. It is well worth taking the time to rinse them out whenever you are in sunshine by a river so that you can dry them on hot rocks in half an hour or so. They can also be hung over the fire at night which makes them pleasanter to put on in the morning but also tends to make the stink of wood smoke.

Always wear loose clothes in the tropics. They may not be very becoming but constant wetting and drying will tend to shrink them and rubbing makes itches and scratches far worse. Cotton is excellent but should be of good quality so that the clothes do not rot and tear too easily.

For footwear, baseball boots or plimsolls are usually adequate but for long distances good leather boots will protect your feet much better from bruising and blisters. In leech country a shapeless cotton stocking worn between sock and shoe and tied with a drawstring below the knee, outside long trousers gives virtually complete protection. As far as I know, no one manufactures these yet, so they have to be made up specially, but they are well worth it.

Upsets and Dangers

Hygiene is important in the tropics. Small cuts can turn nasty very quickly and sometimes will not heal for a long time. The best protection is to make an effort to wash all over at least once a day if possible, at the same time looking out for any sore places, cleaning and treating them at once. On the other hand, where food and drink are concerned, it is usually not practical or polite to attempt to maintain perfectionist standards. Almost no traveller in the tropics can avoid receiving hospitality and few would wish to do so. It is often best therefore to accept that a mild stomach upset is likely – and be prepared (*see section on Health, page 342*).

In real life and death conditions, there are only two essentials for survival, a knife or machete and a compass, provided you are not injured, when the best thing to do is crawl, if possible, to water and wait for help. Other important items I would put in order of priority as follows: a map; a waterproof cover, cape or large bag; means of making fire, lifeboat matches or a lighter with spare flints, gas or petrol; a billy can; tea or coffee, sugar and dried milk. There are few tropical terrains which cannot be crossed with these, given time and determination.

Man can survive a long time without food, so try to keep this simple, basic and light. Water is less of a problem in the jungle, except in limestone mountains, but a metal water container should be carried and filled whenever possible. Rivers, streams and even puddles are unlikely to be dangerously contaminated, while rattans and lianas often contain water as do some other plants whose leaves may form catchments, such as pitcher plants. It is easy to drink from these, though best to filter the liquid through cloth and avoid the 'gunge' at the bottom.

Hunting and trapping are unlikely to be worth the effort to the inexperienced, although it is surprising how much can be found in streams and caught with hands. Prawns, turtles, frogs and even fish can be captured with patience and almost all are edible – and even tasty if you're hungry enough. Fruits, even if ripe and being eaten by other animals, are less safe, while some edible-looking plants and fungi can be very poisonous and should be avoided. Don't try for the honey of wild bees unless you know what you are doing as stings can be dangerous and those of hornets even fatal.

As regards shelter, there is a clear distinction between South America and the rest of the tropical world. In the South American interior, almost everyone uses a hammock. Excellent waterproof hammocks are supplied to the Brazilian and US armies and may be obtainable commercially. Otherwise, a waterproof sheet may be stretched across a line tied between the same two trees from which the hammock is slung. Elsewhere, however, hammocks are rarely used and will tend to be a nuisance under normal conditions. Lightweight canvas stretchers through which poles may be inserted before being tied apart on a raised platform make excellent beds and once again a waterproof sheet provides shelter. Plenty of nylon cord is always useful.

Fight It or Like It

The jungle can be a frightening place at first. Loud noises, quantities of unfamiliar creepy-crawlies, flying biting things and the sometimes oppressive heat can all conspire to get you down. But it can also be a very pleasant place if you decide to like it rather than fight it – and it is very seldom dangerous. Snakebite, for example, is extremely rare. During the fifteen months of the Royal Geographical Society's Mulu Expedition, in Borneo, no one was bitten, although we saw and avoided or caught and photographed many and even ate some! Most things, such as thorns, ants and sandflies are more irritating than painful and taking care to treat rather than scratch will usually prevent trouble.

Above all the jungle is a fascinating place – the richest environment on earth. The best help for morale is to be interested in what is going on around you and the best guide is usually a local resident who is as at home there as most of us are in cities. Fortunately, in most parts of the world where jungles survive there are still such people. By accepting their advice, recognising their expertise, and asking them to travel with you, you may help to reinforce their self-respect in the face of often overwhelming forces which try to make them adopt a so-called 'modern' way of life. At the same time, you will appreciate the jungle far more yourself – and have a far better chance of surviving in it.

Keeping Track

Photographic Gadgetry

by Bob Gibbons

There are three types of automatic camera. They all work differently and any one may be the most appropriate for a given type of photography. The amount of light reaching the film (the exposure) is a product of two things – the length of time the shutter is open (the shutter speed) and the size of the hole letting the light through (the aperture, expressed as an f/number). An automatic can therefore work in three ways: either you decide the shutter speed in advance and the camera then automatically sets the correct aperture as required (shutter-priority auto); or you decide on the aperture you want and the camera sets the corresponding correct shutter speed (aperture priority); or the camera sets both aperture and shutter speed and you do nothing (programmed shutter, rarely found on SLR cameras).

A few cameras allow you the choice of some or all of these methods at the flick of a switch (e.g. the Canon A1 and some Minoltas). So why the differences, and what does it matter? The reason it matters is because much of the skill in photography lies in gauging the most appropriate shutter speed and exposure combination for each shot, to make the best of a situation.

A skilled photographer may know, for example, that a shutter speed of at least as short as 1/250th second may be necessary to render a group of New Guinea dancers sharp – if he has a shutter-priority auto, he merely sets it on 1/250 and the aperture looks after itself. But if he has an aperture-priority auto, what aperture does he set it on to ensure that the shutter speed is fast enough? Of course, he can adjust the aperture until a speed of 1/250th is indicated, but the speed of handling of the automatic is lost – and what if the light changes?

Conversely, someone taking portraits of people may want a large aperture of, say, f/5.6 to throw a confused background out of focus; obviously an aperture-priority auto is preferable here. I have recently changed from a shutter-priority auto (Canon AE1) to an aperture-priority auto (Olympus OM2), for reasons other than their type of automation, and am inclined to think that shutter-priority is to be preferred for those situations where automatic exposure is at a premium, i.e. in action shots and changing situations.

One advantage of aperture-priority autos, however, is that they still work on auto with fixed aperture lenses, e.g. mirror lenses, older-type lenses, ellows, etc. which shutter-priority ameras cannot normally do. Prog- ammed shutters are fine for complete eginners, or those with little interest ı photography as an art – but not therwise.

₹ange of Lenses

f you have decided to buy an SLR nd you have any money left, you are kely to consider buying an additional ens or two to widen your photo- raphic capabilities and the choice ere is even greater than when buying he camera. Cameras normally come vith a 'standard' lens, of about 50mm ocal length, which covers an angle of pproximately 45° and views things in oughly the same perspective as the aked eye. It is possible, however, to uy a body only, without a standard ens, and you may feel, after reading n, that you would be better off with- ut a standard lens at all. But first we eed to consider what lenses are avail- ble and what they do.

Wide-angled lenses have a focal ength of less than 50mm (most com- nonly in the range 24–35mm) and ake in a correspondingly wider view han the standard lens. They are use- ul in confined situations, especially nside; for some views, if used arefully; for giving a greater depth of ield and freedom from camera shake han a standard lens; and if you turn hem round and mount them back to ront (with an adaptor) they are excel- ent for extreme close-ups.

Telephoto lenses have a longer focal ength than 50mm and have a narrow- r angle of view, i.e., they bring hings in closer. Common focal engths include 135mm, 200mm, 00mm and 500mm; a 500mm will give, in effect, a 10× magnification over a standard lens, i.e. an object taken at 20m with a 500mm lens will be the same size on the film as when taken from 2m with a standard lens. They are the antithesis of wide angle lenses and become progressively more difficult to use as the focal length increases, giving rise to a smaller depth of field and higher likelihood of camera shake. They are essential for wildlife photography, candid photo- graphy, and some special effects, while the shorter telephotos (e.g. 135mm) can be of great value in land- scape photography and portraiture. 135mm lenses are still the most popu- lar telephoto, and they are small, portable and cheap, yet 'long' enough to alter the camera's perspective and bring more distant objects closer.

Beyond 200mm tends to be the province of the specialist wildlife, sports or candid photographer – these longer lenses are heavy and bulky and you should carefully consider whether you will use one before wasting the space. I spent four weeks in the Himalayas recently with some Austra- lians, and one of them carried a 500mm lens throughout a 200 mile trek, using it once – to photograph the moon! An interesting alternative to the normal type of telephoto is the mirror lens, whose design has im- proved greatly in the last few years. These lenses use mirrors in part re- placement for lenses, thus 'folding' the light path. The resultant lens is short and light, but has several dis- advantages including the lack of any aperture control (they are fixed at one aperture, often f/8) and the tendency to render out-of-focus highlights as distracting rings. They are easy to use, however, and frequently focus closer than ordinary long telephoto lenses.

Macro lenses are imprecisely defined, but their principal characteristic is that they focus much closer than ordinary lenses. The most commonly available ones are 50–100mm in focal length, and because they also focus to infinity, can replace non-macro lenses of comparable focal length, including the standard lens. Zoom lenses (see below) are not fully comparable since they rarely focus as close as a true macro lens and the quality is well short of the superb close-up definition achieved by most macro lenses. The drawbacks include greater cost, generally larger size, and smaller maximum aperture than comparable non-macro lenses, but for anyone who does a reasonable amount of close-up work, especially the natural history photographer, they are invaluable, and I have used a 50mm macro in place of a standard lens for the last five years.

Zoom lenses may be wide angle, telephoto, or both at once, but they share the characteristic that the focal length (and therefore the angle of view) is variable within a defined range. Typical ranges include wide angle to standard (e.g. 28–50mm), wide angle through standard to telephoto (e.g. 35–70mm) as well as telephoto (e.g. 75–150mm).

Zoom lens design has advanced enormously in recent years and their quality and size rival that of comparable prime (fixed focal length) lenses. A zoom lens that includes 50mm amongst its focal lengths is becoming a serious alternative to the standard lens, as it has been for a long time on cine cameras. The disadvantages include increased weight when on the camera (they may be lighter than the two or three lenses they would replace in total, but each prime lens would be lighter when on the camera individually), and somewhat reduced definition and contrast, but they are improving all the time. In general one would not detect the difference in results from a good zoom and a prime lens. Many also have a 'macro' facility allowing reasonable close-ups which can be useful, but handholding a 15cm long lens for close-ups is not easy, and the result rarely stands up to close scrutiny. If buying a zoom lens, beware of the one that tries to do too much, avoid large bulky ones and don't buy a very cheap one unless you are convinced of its quality at all focal lengths and normal working apertures.

Convertors

Rear teleconvertors are clever pieces of optical equipment that fit between the camera body and the lens, and they double or treble the focal length of that lens. A standard 50mm lens with a 2× convertor thus becomes a 100mm lens. They are small and light and offer an obvious advantage to the traveller wanting a cheap, light alternative to extra lenses, their disadvantages are that they reduce the light reaching the film by two to three stops; their quality may be suspect especially in the 3× models; and they may emphasise failings in the lens they are used with. If you buy a good quality 2×, with multi-coating (e.g. Komura, Vivitar or Tamron) and avoid using it with wide angle lenses or extreme zooms, you should be satisfied. They have the added advantage that, in effect, they allow you to focus twice as close, because they double the focal length while keeping the same minimum focusing distance – a butterfly taken at 50cm with a 100mm lens is twice as large on the film as that taken with a 50mm lens.

A Traveller's Guide to Photography

by Rick Strange

Many people feel that they can walk into a camera store, buy a camera and walk out as a fully fledged photographer. Despite the fact that many modern cameras make the whole business of taking pictures remarkably easy, this really applies only to the technical side. It is still the person who holds the camera, frames the picture and pushes the button who makes a picture good or bad, saleable or non-saleable. After all, any camera, no matter how technically sophisticated, is only a tool and as good as the person who is using it.

It is essential for the photographer to get to know his equipment. He must practise with it for several weeks before he leaves, so that when it comes to the crunch he will know exactly what to do, instead of having to sit down with the instruction manual while the fantastic shot he was about to take vanishes for ever. Practise all the technical things so that they become second nature: focusing, changing lenses, setting exposure, changing film, following focus, lighting, using flash, close-ups, holding the camera correctly, framing, cleaning and the general care of the equipment. As soon as all of this is second nature, it is possible to start being creative. It is astounding how picture quality seems to improve 100 per cent overnight, once a few simple rules are followed.

Guidelines

Before we come to the makings of a good photograph, here are three other guidelines which will improve any picture:

1. Whatever the subject is and wherever the picture is taken, it is important that camera shake is never permitted to spoil what might otherwise be a good shot. Hold the camera firmly with both hands, brace your arms against the side of your body or chest, and, when actually shooting, squeeze the shutter as if it were the trigger of a rifle. Never jab or stab it. Perform the whole operation in slow motion and keep the camera up to your eye for at least a second after your have pushed the shutter. As well as bracing your arms, it is often a very good idea to brace your legs and even lean against any solid object which may be close at hand, like a tree or wall. All this in effect turns your body into a tripod and ensures that no body movement will be transmitted to the camera. When shooting in low light conditions which necessitate a slow shutter speed, hold your breath when you push the shutter. This and the bracing positions already mentioned should reduce camera shake to nil.
2. Being prepared for the unexpected is even more important

when you are travelling than in other conditions. You never know exactly what is going to be round the next corner so it is of vital importance that the camera is ready for action all the time. Never put off reloading when the end of the film has been reached. Do it at once and mark the used film so that the pictures on it can be correctly identified. Of course, in adverse weather conditions the camera should not be left lying around so that it might be damaged, but should be ready to go, in its case, which must be near to hand.

3. Seeing – and not just looking – is really a complete art on its own. It might sound ridiculous, but it is surprising how few people really see! Without looking tell yourself the colour of the tie the man next to you is wearing. What is the colour of the wallpaper in your office or sitting room? Things that you look at, touch or experience every day are registered by your brain, but only when you have trained yourself to observe are they consciously registered. Things that are so obvious that you do not notice them can ruin a photograph or, on the other hand, make one that you had not realised was there. Telephone wires running through the middle of a picture can ruin it, but most people don't even notice them when they push the shutter, because they have not 'seen' them. When viewing a picture you have taken, how often have you said 'Oh, I didn't notice that was in the picture'? Teach yourself to *see*. Start consciously observing, by talking to yourself about what your eyes are looking at.

Get the Picture

Of the three basic rules of photography – focus, exposure and composition – focus is the easiest, but remarkably often neglected. In the heat of the moment the simple tracking in or out of the focus ring on the lens is forgotten. This will soon become second nature if it is practised. Just remember that what you see through the viewfinder is what the film will reproduce. Always make sure that the subject you are photographing is as sharp as it can be in the viewfinder.

Exposure is not quite so easy. Many modern SLR cameras have built-in exposure meters which read an average light as it falls on the whole subject contained in the viewfinder. It is very easy to let a bright sky affect the light reading so that the rest of the picture is underexposed. Many countries with a hot climate have white painted houses. In a village scene, if an average light reading is taken, everything except the white houses will be underexposed. Conversely, if a large dark object is part of the picture and the reading is taken off this, then everything else will be overexposed.

An exposure meter is only a simple computer and not a magic instrument for producing perfect pictures. The information it gives must be interpreted with an intelligent appreciation of the situation. The basic rule to follow is that the correct light reading is the one off the main subject of the picture. Thus in a village scene, the exposure reading should be taken from the people, not from the houses or the sky. A local character may be your subject (rather than the white wall he is leaning against): move in close and get your light reading from his face – don't let the brightness of the wall affect the reading.

If the subject is too far away for you to take a reading, use something near to you which is lighted in the same way and has the same tonal values. Several modern makes of camera have spot reading light meters, which means that the light is read off a very small area in the middle of the frame. This is probably the most accurate type of meter, but again make sure that you take the reading off the subject.

When there are many different light values in a picture (e.g. bright sunlight and dark shadow), the best thing to do is to take a reading off both the light and the dark and then use an exposure which falls halfway between the two. If, however, you find yourself really in trouble because there are so many shades of light and dark and all the various degrees in between, find a nice section of a well-lit neutral colour (preferably medium grey) and take your readings from this. The tarmac road ten metres in front of you often gives a very good grey reading.

If you are really not sure what the exposure should be, try taking three pictures of the same subject, one at what you think is the right exposure, one at an f/stop above and another at an f/stop below. This way you can be sure that the picture is 'in the can'. After all, it is much cheaper to use more film and make sure of getting your picture than to have to go all the way back for another shot.

Composition is without a doubt the most difficult of the three basic rules, either to define or to teach. Generally it is something which is inborn or almost instinctive – people with a natural composition ability often become artists of one sort or another – but it can be learnt with practice. Although it is impossible to discuss composition very fully in an article of this length, here are a few practical suggestions which should help the photographer to produce pictures of a saleable quality.

The basic rule of composition is known as the Rule of Thirds. All this means is that if you divide any picture into thirds both horizontally and vertically, the points at which the thirds intersect are the optimum subject positions, with the lower right intersection point being the prime position.

Less technical, but just as important, is the policy of keeping your photographs simple. Don't try to say too much with one picture. After you have selected your subject concentrate on it and don't let it become cluttered up with uneccessary objects. You can use the additional lenses you are carrying for selective composition. Don't just use the telephoto lens for distant subjects: use it for close subjects, cutting out the uninteresting foreground. Make sure there are no trees 'growing' out of the tops of people's heads etc. – remember to see and not just look.

Tell a Story

Use your picture to tell a story about the subject. Always start off with an orientation shot which places the subject in its environment – in other words, a long shot. Move in closer to show the subject in more detail and finally get in really close to show extreme detail.

Always try to fill the viewfinder of your camera with the subject. Then you won't have to rehearse that all too common story, 'See those two black dots in the distance? Well, that's the Land Rover and our tent when we were halfway across the Sahara.' It might well be a beautiful shot of the desert, but if the subject is the expedition camp, then fill the frame with the expedition camp.

Wildlife photography has its own special requirements. A four-wheel-drive vehicle with high clearance, plenty of windows and a roof hatch can be invaluable for getting close to, and getting unusual shots of, some animals. Use backlighting or side-lighting if necessary and experiment with different angles – even shooting from under a vehicle or halfway up a tree. It is always best to use a slow approach, stopping often to give the animals time to get used to your presence. Rushing into things may cause the animals to retreat or charge you: either way you lose your picture. The cardinal rule in animal photography is patience.

In many parts of the world you will encounter people who expect to be paid for being photographed (small amounts of money, not gifts, are what they're after) and others who are reluctant to be photographed at all. There are several ways around this. You might use a telephoto lens which can give you a good close-up despite your distance from the subject. You can wait until the subject is occupied and shoot without being noticed. Have the camera prepared, by focusing on something the same distance away as your subject, so that you can shoot without delay if an opportunity occurs. You can pan the camera towards the subject, click the shutter as your subject comes into view and keep panning afterwards, so that it won't be obvious that you've taken the shot. If you're skilled enough, you'll be able to get a good picture while holding the camera at waist level and looking elsewhere. If all else fails, shoot from a window or a moving vehicle.

Camera Checklist

by Rick Strange

Camera body (two if possible) – 35mm type with built-in exposure meter and interchangeable lens.
Normal macro lens for normal and close-up work.
28mm or 35mm wide angle lens.
135mm telephoto lens.
400mm telephoto lens (for bird and animal photography)
(All lenses to be fitted with UV filters to protect lens and dust caps front and back).
Lightweight tripod.
Set of jeweller's screwdrivers.
Small pair of jeweller's pliers.
Lens cleaning tissue and fluid.
Antistatic cloth.
Spare light meter.
Electronic flash and spare batteries and cables.
Spare batteries for light meters.
Strong camera case (aluminium).
Your estimate of film required (plus a reserve).

Buying Equipment for Photography Off the Beaten Track

by David Hodgson

You may have heard of Murphy's Law. It states that if something can go wrong, it will go wrong – at the worst possible moment. Even if you've never heard of the law, you will have experienced it in action on any trip. And especially if you have been involved in photography or filming on the trip. Cameras jam, films get lost or stolen, lenses mist over at the most inconvenient moment or jam on the body when being changed and you miss that essential shot. Twenty years of magazine photography in some of the least accessible parts of the world have convinced me that Murphy's Law is about as inevitable and universal as the Law of Gravity.

In this article I have Murphy's Law very much in mind. But I am also making two other assumptions. The first is that photography is of some importance to you; that you need, and want, to take first-class pictures for serious use rather than a collection of fuzzy snaps for suitable burial in some album. Secondly I assume that funds are limited and that every penny has to be well spent. Incidentally, all the money in the world will not protect you from the ravages of Murphy's Law. One of the best financed and most lavishly equipped trips I have ever been on started out with £25,000 worth of cameras and I finished up being thankful that I had a battered, secondhand Leica to take their most important pictures.

Choosing Your Equipment

The motto here is: buy tough for travelling rough. The most sophisticated camera in the world is worse than useless if the electronic shutter fails halfway up a mountain. The more things there are to go wrong, the more things will go wrong. Built-in light meters are very convenient, especially if you nip down to the local dealer's when a CdS battery fails. But if the battery goes in the wilds, you will never replace it and the meter will be useless. So, if you are buying especially for the trip, why spend money on a built-in meter? Better to put the additional money towards a sturdy shutter and wind-on mechanism and use a separate, selenium cell meter. This is the type where a cell converts the light directly to electrical energy. There is no additional power supply to fail. I would suggest a Weston Meter. You can safely buy them secondhand at very reasonable prices. They are tough and extremely accurate. If you do decide to use a camera with a TTL (through the lens) metering system, then take along spare cells and make sure they are protected against excessive damp. But wear braces and a belt. Take a Weston along too.

This brings me to a point about back-up systems. Never put together your equipment on the basis that things will go right, but always in the certain knowledge they will go wrong. Have an answer ready when they do. Two camera bodies are a wise investment, especially when you are going to be a long way from repairmen and replacements. You can shoot black and white with one and colour with the other, thus improving your chances of making the widest possible sale when you get home (*see Selling Travel Photographs on page 482*). But which bodies?

Unless you have some specialist purpose which requires large format photography, then 35mm cameras have all the advantages. They are light, easy to use, take 36 pictures on one roll of film and produce negatives of sufficiently high quality to stand considerable enlargement – provided the exposure and processing have been correctly carried out.

The single-lens reflex is probably the most popular camera here. It is a well-proven design which allows you to see exactly what you are shooting. This is very valuable when taking close-up pictures, using either a macro lens or extension tubes, or when using telephoto lenses for capturing distant scenes. If you intend to shoot a lot of extreme close-ups or use lenses longer than 200mm frequently, then I would advise a SLR. Nikon, Pentax, Canon, Leicaflex and Minolta are cameras which have all been tested under professional conditions and come through with flying colours. Nikon, Pentax, Olympus and Canon are probably the most widely used by magazine and newspaper photographers. One of my Nikons was once struck by a jet fighter coming in to land – and went on taking pictures. All four of these manufacturers make models which combine great toughness with lightness in a small handy format. The weight factor could make a great difference to transportation problems and should be considered by an expedition photographer who is going to have to carry his or her own gear across difficult terrain.

But do not dismiss that much less popular type of 35mm camera, the rangefinder focus model. Perhaps the best known name here is Leica. Nikon used to make an excellent rangefinder camera and so did Canon. These were the standard photojournalist's equipment for decades before the SLR pushed them down into the third division.

Rangefinder cameras have a lot going for them as an expedition camera. They are simpler than the SLRs and less to go wrong can mean fewer problems miles from anywhere. Because they are rather unpopular you can buy them cheaply secondhand. The lack of a mirror makes them quieter to use, which makes for easier candid photography and wildlife studies. The rangefinder focus is very positive and easy to use under low light levels. They are much less satisfactory, however, when being used with long lenses (above 200 mm) or for extreme close-ups. The need for either type of photography really makes the SLR the front runner.

If you are switching from SLR to a rangefinder model then be sure to practise before starting on serious photography. There is a tendency to confuse the overall sharpness of the image as seen through the rangefinder screen with total picture sharpness and forget to focus as a result! With an SLR, of course, this mistake cannot happen.

Before moving on to the subject of buying cameras secondhand, I should mention the Nikonos, a very specialist camera that can be worth its weight in usable pictures on really tough trips. The Nikonos is an underwater camera with a lens fully sealed behind a glass plate and the controls similarly protected by O-rings. You can use the Nikonos on land as well, in the wettest mud or the worst sandstorms and simply wash it out when the muck gets too solid! If there is any chance of your equipment ending up soaked or seriously muddied then the Nikonos could be the answer. There are, of couse, other ways of protecting standard gear.

Buying Secondhand Safely

Let us start with the camera body. Check for general signs of wear inside as well as out, although external appearance will tell you a lot about how the camera has been treated. Look at the edges of the leather trim. If these are lifted, it may indicate that the camera has been repaired (you have to remove the trim to reach the screws) and perhaps by a none too fastidious mechanic. Internally, look at the tops of the screws. If they have been turned over and show bright metal they have certainly been got at by a ham-fisted repairer. Look for bare patches on the internal blacking, which could cause flare problems. Run your fingers along the chrome film guides and over the metal rollers which draw the film guides which draw the film onto the take-up spool. Any roughness will damage your films, causing what are called 'tram line' scratches along the sensitive emulsion.

Check the shutter blinds visually. If metal, do they look battered? If fabric, do they look worn? Now check the shutter by ear. Run it through *all* the speeds, especially the slow speeds which get used far less frequently and may be sluggish as a result. Does the mechanism sound smooth or a bit unsteady? If you are going to shoot reversal colour film (for transparencies), accurate shutter speeds are essential. Have them checked on a meter. Most well set up dealers can provide this service quite cheaply. You will almost certainly find that the speeds are not the same as those indicated by the setting. For example, 1/1,000th second may be only 1/900th. This does not matter. All shutters show a variation. What is important is that you *know* the exact shutter speed – so that you can set it on the meter – and that you have a constant error.

Check the wind-on by ear and by feel. It should sound as smooth and positive as it is to the touch. If the camera has a built-in meter, check this against a separate meter.

Check the strap connectors. Often these are the weakest part of a camera. If they give, you may lose everything.

Now turn your attention to the lens. There are two ways SLR and rangefinder cameras with interchangeable lenses match body to lens mount. One is by a bayonet lock and the other by a screw thread. I prefer the bayonet method because it is so much faster. You can easily cross the thread when trying to change lenses in a hurry. If you are buying a secondhand camera with a screw thread fastening system, check that the thread has not been damaged by somebody crossthreading the lens in a hurry.

Move the lens from infinity to maximum close-up several times. Does the helical thread movement feel, and sound, smooth? Grit can easily get inside the longer lenses and damage the mounts. Grease, used to pack the threads, can dry and make the focusing stiff or uncertain. The outer condition of the lens mount, again provides a reliable clue to its previous usage. Look at the surface of the lens, holding it in such a way that any scratches will show up. If you intend to take the lens away on a trip soon after purchase, run at least one film through to check the quality – even of a first class lens. The best way of doing this is to set the camera up on a tripod exactly at right angles with a brick wall. Focus on the lines of the bricks and take a picture at each f/stop (changing the shutter speed to correct the exposure). After processing, examine the frames with a powerful magnifying glass. Notice any distortions (the straight lines of the bricks may appear to bend) and see which f/stop gives the best definition. All lenses work best at one or two stops, usually f/5.6 or f/8.

Additional Equipment

Some photographers set off on trips hung around with more equipment than the average dealer's display window. It is a waste of time, effort and money to take more than you need. Furthermore, too many gadgets get between you and the picture-making. Keep life as simple as possible. You may need specialist gear for particular tasks, but for general shooting, here is a basic shopping list.

Lens hoods for all lenses. I prefer the screw-on variety to the clip-on type. They are less likely to get knocked off and lost. *Ultraviolet filters* for all lenses – to cut down haze at high altitudes or when photographing at sea, and to protect the lenses. *Wide camera straps* are much more comfortable than the normal, narrow variety. A separate *light meter*, for reasons already given. *Lenses* for general purpose 35mm photography my favourite combination is a slightly wide angle lens (a 35mm focal length is ideal) together with a slightly long lens. My best buy here would be either a 90mm lens or a 135mm. Both are excellent for candid portraiture, getting details of buildings, statues, etc., and landscape photography. The wide angle lens enables you to work close, frame boldly and operate successfully in a crowd.

What you do not need are as follows: A *tripod* solid enough to provide firm support will be too heavy to carry unless you are fully motorised. Even then it is likely to prove more trouble than it is worth. A much better alternative is a clamp which enables you to fasten the camera to a suitable support. I make my own from a Mole wrench with a camera locking screw attached. Given the flexibility of this type of wrench you can almost always find something steady enough to provide a really stable mount for long exposures. I would certainly not rule out *flash guns* completely, but unless you are intending to shoot a great many flash pictures, you will probably find a bulb gun lighter to carry, cheaper to buy and rather more reliable. If you are going a long way off the beaten track, bear in mind that an electronic gun will get through batteries far faster than a bulb gun – and provide less light. *Camera cases* tend to get in the way when you are working fast. There are better methods of protection.

Specialist Equipment

For close-up work you will need either a close-up lens, extension tubes or bellows. Some modern standard lenses will focus to within a few inches and you may find this sufficient for all but the most precise record of work. Otherwise I advise a close-up lens or extension tubes in preference to bellows because they are so much easier to carry around.

Fast focus with long lenses can prove a problem. The best answer is probably the Novoflex follow-focus system where, instead of a helical screw and twist action focus, the lens is focused by pulling in, or releasing, a pistol-like trigger. For very long lenses (400mm and upwards) you will need the shoulder-pod support which is designed especially for use with this lens. Although bulky and cumbersome, Novoflex lenses are the best bet for action shots of fast moving subjects, e.g. for bird photography. I paint the barrel of my 400mm Novoflex bright yellow. It makes it look less like a large calibre army pistol and in some areas of the world a mistaken identification could prove most unfortunate for the photographer!

Motorised cameras are increasingly popular. But this is something else which can go wrong so I advise you to purchase with an eye to rugged rather than elegant construction and take one along only if it is going to be really essential. Among their main uses are rapid sequence photography, for high speed action work, and remote control pictures via a trigger line or radio control.

Shopping Summary

My own choice, based on personal experience in the rough, would be as follows:
Nikon with 35mm and 135mm lenses. Weston Meter. Rox carrying case. Hoods. UV filters. Mole wrench converted to camera clamp. Small screwdriver set (as used by watch makers) for tightening loose screws. One centimetre wide paint brush. Bulb gun with spare battery. Spare batteries for CdS meter if carried. Two bodies for choice. Best buy secondhand: the Nikon F2.

Alternatively: a secondhand Leica M2 with 35mm and 90mm lens or an Olympus with lenses similar to the Nikon. For a motorised camera: the Olympus on the grounds of lightness.

For very rugged work, take a Nikonos with a 35mm lens, but this needs a special flash gun.

I can't guarantee you'll beat Murphy's Law by taking my advice. But you'll be in there with a chance!

Camera Care and Protection

by Dave Saunders and Robert Holmes

You have spent as much as you can afford on good camera gear for your trip abroad. Naturally, you don't *expect* it to fail, but you are realistic enough to include an extra camera body – just in case. Camera repair shops tend to be in short supply in remote regions of the world and you don't want your pictures to turn into the fish that got away.

Even if the journey is short and conditions far from severe, equipment can easily let you down by getting lost, breaking when dropped or simply expiring after long, devoted service.

Minimising the frustrations of such technical hitches calls for attention to detail. Caring for your camera goes beyond dusting it with a brush from time to time. It begins long before you set out and ends with a final check and brush-up when you return home.

Checklist

It is worthwhile following a routine checklist to avoid on-the-spot panics. First decide exactly what equipment you are going to take. This will, of course, be controlled by what you can afford. It will inevitably be a compromise between the full range of camera bodies, lenses and accessories you might conceivably use and the amount of weight you can allocate for photographic gear.

Choose only those items you will need for the specific type of photograph you plan to take, accounting for any harsh conditions such as sand, salt water or humidity you are likely to meet. Coping with travelling can be taxing enough without the additional burden of unnecessary accessories.

Are you likely to need a macro lens? What is the longest focal length you should include? Rather than taking a 200mm *and* a 400mm lens, would it be wiser to save weight but forfeit image quality by taking a ×2 tele converter?

You may find two camera bodies, three lenses and a small flash gun are sufficient. A miniature camera in your pocket at all times and a Polaroid camera can also be very handy.

If you need to buy extra bits and pieces, check everything well before you leave. Run at least one test roll of film through the camera, using various shutter speeds and aperture settings. Change lenses, try out the shutter release cable, the self-timer and the motordrive. Make sure it is all clean and working smoothly. Then study the results for anomalies.

Protection

If your travels are going to take you very near salt water, mud, sand or snow, it may be worth investing in a Nikonos underwater camera or waterproof housing, rather than risk destroying your land camera. A camera is generally pretty sturdy, but water will harm it. If you drop the camera in the sea, you have signed its death warrant and may as well give it to the kids to play with and claim a new one on insurance.

You can defend land cameras against salt spray by wiping with lint cloth lightly soaked in WD40 or a similar light oil. If you need to use a land camera in a sand storm, carefully apply 'O' ring grease to joints, mounts, and hinges, using a cotton bud. Tape over parts not in use, such as sync socket and motordrive terminal.

Take spare plastic bags to help protect gear under adverse conditions. Also include spare 'O' rings for the Nikonos, 'O' ring grease, cotton buds, chamois leather, brush, Dust-Off spray and a small watchmaker's screwdriver for on-the-spot maintenance.

A skylight or ultraviolet filter cuts down haze, but is more important as a lens protector. A filter should remain on each lens all the time to protect the coated front element. Scratched filters are much cheaper to replace than lenses. A lens hood can also shield the lens as well as cut down flare on *contre jour* shots.

Bags

Now, where do you put all of this? I prefer to use a large, soft camera bag for most of my photographic gear. It can be taken as hand luggage on a plane and stowed under the seat. Purpose-made bags and pouches by *Camera Care Systems* and *Lowe Pro* are excellent for adventurous photographers who are likely to find themselves hanging off a cliff face or swinging from the crow's nest.

Expensive looking cases are obvious targets for light-fingered locals. Don't rely on locks to keep out the thieves. If necessary, use a steel cable and padlock. Give the case distinguishing marks such as bright paint or coloured tape. You will then be able to identify it quickly and thieves will tend to avoid anything too conspicuous.

A watertight aluminium case will be useful for photography by the sea or in a desert as it will keep out the damp and dust. The sun is reflected by the silver, so the camera and films don't get too hot and you can use the case to stand or sit on. However, they are more awkward to work from when you are constantly 'dipping in' for something.

If you are carrying the minimum of photographic equipment, you may be able to 'wear' your camera bag in the form of a loose-fitting jacket with plenty of pockets – even in the sleeves. This protects your gear and enables you to be more agile – an important consideration if a camera bag is likely to be a hindrance.

Once you know what you are taking, insure it for its replacement value. Some household insurance policies do not cover photographic gear abroad and should be extended. Alternatively, shop around several insurance companies for the best deal, but watch out for small-print exemption clauses which may exclude travelling in private aircraft, scuba diving or mountaineering.

Keep a separate record of model and serial numbers, as this will help the police when items are lost or stolen. Reporting the loss will help when your claim is being processed.

By the time you actually set off, the bulk of the work will be done, though special environments will call for special attention.

Warnings

Cameras should not be left in direct sunlight when temperatures are high, as the glue holding the lens elements in place may melt and be knocked out of place.

When changing lenses or films, find a sheltered area. If it is sandy or dusty, keep the whole camera in a plastic bag. Cut a hole for the lens and secure the bag around the mount with a stiff elastic band. This can make composing and framing the picture a little difficult, but may save the camera.

Extremely cold conditions will give as many problems as the heat. Store everything in hermetically sealed metal cases and take plenty of gaffer tape to seal all hinges, cracks and joints against fine snow. Put cameras in airtight plastic bags with silica gel packets *before* coming indoors. That way, the condensation will not form in the cameras. Where possible, try to keep film and cameras at a constant temperature.

Avoid touching frozen metal parts with your cheek or you will stick to it, and keep moving so that *you* don't freeze up!

Cleaning

Cleaning materials are essential for both the camera body and for lenses. Lenses should be cleaned daily to prevent a build-up of dirt, which will cause soft, muddy photographs through flare and loss of definition. If you are using a UV filter, the same cleaning rules will apply to the filter as to the lens.

I first remove the dust and loose dirt with a *pocket 'Dust-Off'* which emits a strong jet of inert gas. Be careful to hold the 'Dust-Off' upright otherwise you will get vapour coming out which will leave a deposit on the lens or filter. Next, I carefully remove any stubborn dirt with a small *blower brush* and finally use 'Dust-Off' once more. Don't forget to check the rear element of your lens too. When I get a fingerprint on the lens I carefully wipe it off with *lens tissues*. Only buy tissues from a camera store. Lens tissues from opticians often contain silicones which can damage the coating on the lens. Breathing on the lens first can help but be careful. In sub-zero tempertures, the resulting ice will be far worse than any fingerprints!

It's not just the lens that should be cleaned regularly. So should the camera body – inside and out. I clean the outside with a stiff *typewriter brush* which removes even the most stubborn dirt and gets into all the nooks and crannies. Any dirt that does escape into the camera I clean out with my blower brush, carefully avoiding the shutter which can be easily damaged. Using 'Dust-Off' for the interior can do more harm than good by blasting dust into the camera mechanism. Look out for the tiny pieces of film which occasionally break off and get into the film, ruining whole rolls with deep scratches. I learnt my lesson recently in Nepal. A single hair from my brush got stuck in the film path and although I couldn't see it through the viewfinder it appeared, in varying degrees of focus, in ten rolls of film before it finally dislodged itself. That will not happen again!

Film and Film Care

by Dave Saunders

Film emulsion is sensitive material. Mistreat it, and it will complain by fogging or assuming a strange colour cast. All film deteriorates with time, and you will accelerate this process with careless handling.

Different films have different properties and some will complain more vehemently than others when subjected to adverse conditions. In general, 'amateur' film is more tolerant than 'professional' film, which is manufactured to more exacting standards. Amateur film is more stable and will last longer before processing. It is therefore the better choice for long trips, especially in hot climates where the deterioration process is speeded up.

Colour Film

So how do you choose from the bewildering array of film types on the market?

For our purposes, there are three broad categories of colour film.

1. Daylight reversal (transparency) film can be used with electronic flash, blue flashbulbs and, of course, in daylight.
2. Tungsten reversal (transparency) for tungsten/artificial light.
3. Colour negative (for prints) used for all lighting conditions and corrected during printing.

Tungsten films can be corrected for daylight, and vice versa, by using filters.

Magazines, books and brochures prefer to reproduce from transparencies and many will not even consider colour prints. If necessary you can always have prints made from transparencies.

Kodachrome is usually first choice, and some publications and photo libraries insist on it. Kodachrome 25 is the sharpest and least grainy ordinary slide film available, but because it is slow (25ASA) you forfeit flexibility. In anything other than bright conditions you may find you have to shoot at full aperture, which gives very little depth of field, and/or a slow shutter speed, with the danger of camera shake. I start to feel nervous when using f/1.8 at 1/30th or 1/15th sec.

Kodachrome 64 has similar sharpness and grain to Kodachrome 25, though it is a little more contrasty. The extra 1½ stops provided by the faster film (64ASA) allows greater flexibility. To warm up skin tones and increase overall colour saturation, use 81 series filters with Kodachrome film. The density and strength of colour (saturation) will also increase if you slightly underexpose reversal film.

Ektachrome 64 has a more saturated colour than Kodachrome and is sharp with little grain. However, all Ektachrome films should be processed soon after exposure and are therefore not suitable for long journeys in remote areas. On the other hand, Kodachrome is more stable and should survive up to six months between being exposed and processed. Black and white film is even hardier and should last for a year.

Ektachrome 200 High Speed film is good for general use and allows the use of faster shutter speeds and/or smaller apertures. This enables you to use a longer focal length lens without the need for a tripod, have greater depth of field and shoot in dull lighting conditions. This film can be uprated by one or two stops, giving even greater versatility. Similarly, Ektachrome 400 can be pushed two stops, making it in effect 1600ASA, but this gives coarse grained results.

Agfacolour CT18 (50ASA) is called Agfachrome in America. It is a general purpose daylight film which has more grain and is less sharp than Ektachrome.

3M's 1000 ASA film is grainy, but impressively sharp considering its fast speed.

Slow films are generally impractical for travel photography unless you can guarantee bright conditions and/or long exposure.

When buying film, check if processing is included in the price. Kodachrome, for example, is process-paid only in certain countries. Also check the expiry date of the film, it should be stamped on the packet. If you have no choice but to buy an old film, you may get away with it. The expiry date has a built-in safety margin and out of date films are usually all right for some months after the date indicated.

Black and White

If possible, take black and white film as well as colour. Some colour converts into mono satisfactorily if there is enough contrast, but there is inevitably a loss of quality. Certain magazines stipulate that black and white prints must be derived from black and white originals.

Kodak Plux X (125ASA) and Ilford FP4 (125ASA) are good fine-grained black and white films for general use. Kodak Tri X (400ASA) and Ilford HP5 (400ASA) are suitable for dull lighting and push-processing. Again, the faster films are grainier.

It is best to take much more film than you anticipate using. You can always bring home unexposed film and use it later. When you are confronted by magnificent scenery or an interesting incident in the street, you don't want to have to scrimp on film. The chance may never come again.

Running out of film abroad may, at best, be inconvenient. Prices may be highly inflated or your preferred film type may not be available. Kodachrome 25, Kodachrome 64, Ektachrome and Agfacolour CT18 are fairly universal, however.

Protection

It is a good idea to include the film on your insurance policy for camera equipment. But this normally only covers you for the price of replacement film. If you want them covered for the potential selling price of the pictures, premiums are exorbitant.

X-rays can be a danger to unexposed film. Some people are happy to pack spare film in the centre of their suitcase. Others will let the camera bag go through the X-ray machine at the airport. I always insist (pleasantly) on a hand search. I do this even if the machine claims to be safe for films because the bag is likely to pass through several airports and several X-ray machines. This can have a cumulative effect on the emulsion and fog the film. The faster the film (higher ASA rating) the more sensitive it will be to X-rays. A hand search may take a little longer, but I haven't missed a plane yet.

Lead-lined bags are available, but the protection they offer is nullified if the power of the X-ray machine is turned up so that the security people can see what's inside.

Some Eastern bloc countries will not let you take a camera as hand luggage, but they should not complain about film. In some countries you may be asked to pay import duty on unexposed film. It might be worth removing them from their packages so they appear to be exposed (for which no duty is payable).

Heat and humidity cause film to lose speed and contrast and colour film may show a magenta or green cast. If fungus grows on the film, there is very little you can do about it. But there are certain precautions you can take.

Until you need it, leave film in its plastic container or foil wrapping as this helps protect it. Colour film, in particular, should be carefully stored away from heat, humidity and extremes of cold or dryness.

Try to keep film at a constant temperature. In hot climates store it at or below 13°C (56°F) if possible. When you want to use the film, return it to room temperature slowly to avoid condensation inside the cassette. If you have access to a fridge, store the film there and take it out two hours before loading it into the camera.

Without a fridge, an airtight ice chest with freezer sachets may provide a possible solution. Packets of silica gel in an airtight container absorb moisture in humid climates. And insulated chamois bags are available to protect film from extremes of temperature. Exceptionally cold film becomes brittle and can crack or snap.

Wind off all exposed film so there is no danger of mistaking it for unexposed film and reusing it.

As a final note, unless you are abroad for several months, it is safer and cheaper to keep exposed film with you and have it developed when you return home. If you do opt to send film by post, mark the package 'Film only – do not X-ray' and send it first class airmail. Some airmail post is X-rayed as a security measure, and it has been known for films to go missing, only to be sold later as unused film!

A Bag of Junk – Useful Extras in the Camera Bag

by Robert Holmes

A photographer's camera bag is not unlike a woman's handbag. To the owner, an invaluable collection of essential paraphernalia; to everyone else, a miscellaneous hoard of junk.

I am always fascinated by what other photographers carry around with them and you may find it enlightening for me to share the secrets of my 'bag of junk'. The list is long, but has evolved over several years of hard travel and there is nothing that I could comfortably leave out.

Aside from photographic equipment and cleaning materials, I always carry a basic tool kit for simple repairs and equipment maintenance. It includes a set of *jeweller's screwdrivers* including a small *Philips screwdriver* to tighten any screws that come loose. Periodically check the screws in both the camera body and lenses because the continual vibration you get from any method of transport can loosen screws surprisingly quickly. I once had a lens literally fall apart in a very remote part of Turkey because I failed to notice the first two screws fall out! A small pair of *jeweller's pliers* will help straighten out bent metal parts or tighten loose nuts.

Two universal accessories which no photographer should ever be without are a *Swiss army knife* and a roll of *gaffer tape*. The Swiss army knife can be used for all the purposes it was made for plus a multitude of photographic applications which are limited only by your imagination. Gaffer tape is a two-inch wide, tough, cloth-backed tape that can be used for anything from repairing torn trousers to holding a damaged camera together. A whole roll is pretty bulky, so I wind off as much as I think I will need around the spanner that I carry to tighten the legs of my tripod.

A *black felt-tip pen* that will write on any surface from film leaders to plastic bags and a *red felt-tip* to write processing instructions on blue and yellow Ektachrome cassettes supplement my ever-present *notebook*. However good you think your memory is, take notes. It's always surprising how people and places are forgotten or confused after a few weeks.

Within the last few years more and more *batteries* have found their way into my baggage. I never feel happy unless I have plenty of spares for cameras, motordrives, exposure meters and flash guns. What a headache modern technology is! I used to carry a couple of spare sets for my flash gun and that was that, but now I almost need a portable generator. When you buy batteries, get them from a store with a fast turnover. They must be fresh. Date them as soon as you buy them and use them in date order. Lithium cells have a long shelf life and work in a wide range of temperatures but they may not have enough power output to cope with some of today's all-singing, all-dancing picture machines. If in doubt, ask your dealer.

Down in the bottom of my bag are a few objects that apparently have no place in a photographer's armoury but are nevertheless irreplaceable when needed.

A *small flash light* has saved my bacon on several occasions particularly when there is not quite enough light left to read by and you still have to set your camera settings. It can also be useful to provide a source of light to focus on when the light is fading.

A tripod light enough to travel is also prone to vibration so I carry a *string bag* that I can fill with rocks and hang under the tripod to steady it. It will also prevent vibration in long telephoto lenses if I loop the handles of the bag over the lens, close to the camera body, to weight it down on the tripod.

Weather rarely does what you want it to and on a cloudy sunless day, a *compass* will help you find out which direction the sun should be shining from. It will also tell you where to expect sunrise and sunset, the most photogenic times of day.

I often shoot architectural subjects with extreme wide-angle lenses and without a small *spirit level* I would not be able to keep my verticals vertical. It also keeps my horizons horizontal!

The *metal mirror* in my bag is not because of any narcissistic tendencies. I occasionally use a camera on a tripod at its maximum height, and, although I can see through the viewfinder, I cannot quite see to set the shutter and aperture. I can hold the mirror above the camera and check all the setting without leaving the ground. It also comes in handy for directing sunlight on to small objects and flowers in the shade.

I always used to worry about leaving equipment cases in hotel rooms so now I carry a *bicycle lock* with me. The long, thick cable type with a combination lock is the best and you can secure your camera cases to radiators or pipes or even the bed. It may not deter the determined thief but it will prevent any casual thefts.

So there it is. My innermost secrets revealed. Some of these things could help you be a better photographer but all of them will help you be a more reliable one.

By the way, there are two more important additions to the bag. However well you think you know your equipment, when something goes wrong in the field, if you have your *camera manual* with you, at least you can check everything before writing the camera off. If you do have to write it off, keep the *international list of service agents* handy.

Beneath the Waves

by Dave Saunders

Anyone who has put on a mask and snorkel and floated over a coral garden or sunken boat will have a glimpse of the fascinating world beneath the surface of the ocean. But we are not built to exist for long underwater and nor are most cameras. It is an alien environment with a new set of rules for the photographer.

The nice thing about underwater photography is that you can approach it at any level. It is possible to take satisfactory pictures with an ordinary land camera through the 'window' of a glass bottom boat, or even in rock pools using a bucket or water-tight box with a glass base. If the sun is shining on the subject, the pictures will be bright and clear.

But be careful when you are near water, especially salt water. Ordinary land cameras are like cats – they just don't want to get involved with water. So if you want to take a camera underwater, you will need either a purpose-built underwater camera or a water-tight housing.

Purpose-built Cameras

The cheapest underwater camera is the Minolta Weathermatic A(110), nicknamed the Yellow Submarine. The camera is light, robust and has a built-in flash unit. The manufacturer claims it is waterproof to a depth of five metres, making it ideal for beginners who want to take holiday snapshots.

The Pocket Marine 110, developed by Sea and Sea Products, can be taken down to 40m. It has a built-in flash as well as a socket for an extension flash. Its great advantage is its automatic wind-on mechanism which saves awkward manoeuvres underwater. This makes the camera a little more expensive than the Yellow Submarine.

Both models are also useful in grubby weather conditions on land – in rain, snow or sandstorms – as they are well insulated.

The Nikonos is probably the underwater camera most used by scuba divers. It is not larger than an ordinary 35mm camera, it is easy to operate and can give good results. Based on the French Calypso design, it is continually being improved. The Nikonos IV-A has a fully automatic exposure system, optional motordrive and automatic flash gun. There is no rangefinder for focusing, so you have to estimate focusing distances. Being a non-reflex camera, with a direct vision viewfinder, you may have problems with parallax when close to the subject. An external sportsfinder frame can be fixed to the top of the camera making viewing easier. The latest model, the Nikonos V, has a choice of auto or manual exposure. A bright LCD display in the viewfinder tells you the shutter speed, warns of over or under exposure and has a flash-ready signal.

The standard lens is the W-Nikkor 35mm f/2.5. Also available are 15mm, 28mm and 80mm lenses. For detailed shots of coral and tame fish, there are special close-up lenses or extension tubes.

Underwater Housings

Rather than investing in a whole new camera system, an alternative approach is to use an underwater housing around your land camera. In shallow water of less than ten metres, flexible plastic housings provide a relatively cheap method of protection for your camera. Controls are operated through a rubber glove set into the case.

In deeper water the flexible design is inappropriate as pressure increases with depth and the housing would collapse. Ikelite housings are made for 110, 35mm reflex and non-reflex and roll film cameras. These are rigid and some models can safely be taken to a depth of 100m.

The housing has controls which link into the focusing and aperture rings, as well as shutter release and film advance mechanisms. Rubber 'O' ring seals produce a water-tight chamber which keeps the camera dry. To avoid flooding, the rings must be cleaned and lightly greased with silicone each time a film is changed. Metal or plexiglass housings are available for all top brand reflex cameras. Metal housings are very strong and durable, but are heavy to carry and need careful attention to prevent corrosion. Plexiglass housings are much lighter and cheaper, and are available for a wider range of cameras. However, the plastic type ages more quickly and will eventually leak.

How Light Behaves

Light is refracted or bent more in water than in air. Objects underwater appear to be larger and nearer than they really are. Your eye sees the same distortion as the lens, so, with a reflex camera, you simply focus through the lens and the subsequent picture will then be in focus. The subject may be one and a half metres away, but will appear closer to the eye and to the lens. However, if you then look at the focusing ring, it will set at about one metre.

Because of the way light refracts through water, the effective focal length of the lens is increased, making it more telephoto when a flat underwater porthole is used. So, in effect, a 35mm lens underwater is approximately equivalent to a 45mm lens on land. Likewise a 15mm lens is equivalent to a 20mm.

A dome-shaped porthole, on the other hand, enables light from all directions to pass through it at right angles. This eliminates the problem of refraction and the angle of view of the fitted lens is unchanged.

Lenses

Wide angle lenses are generally more useful underwater. Visibility is seldom as good as above water, especially if there are numerous suspended particles. For a clear image it is important to move in close so as to reduce the amount of water between the camera and the subject. To include a whole diver in the frame when using a 35mm lens on a Nikonos, you need to be about two metres away. A wider lens, say 15mm, means you can move in much closer to the subject and thus minimise the amount of obstructing material between the camera and the subject.

Generally camera-to-subject distance should not exceed a quarter of the visibility. If the visibility is only one and a half metres (as it often is in temperate seas or inland lakes), you should restrict yourself to only taking subjects up to 0.3m from the lens.

The Nikonos 15mm lens is very inexpensive, but cheaper lenses and lens converters are available. The most common are the Sea and Sea 21mm lens and the Subatec Subawinder which is an attachment lens clipping onto the standard Nikonos 28mm or 35mm lenses underwater. The attachment can be removed underwater, enabling you to revert to the normal lens when you no longer need the wide angle.

Flash

With high speed emulsions such as Ektrachrome 400 (slides) and Kodacolour 400 (prints), it is often possible to get away without using flash, especially near the surface where it is brighter. When the sun is shining through the surface layers of water, you can obtain good results without flash down to about two metres. However, the deeper you go below the surface layers of water, the more the light is filtered out by the water. At ten metres below the surface, all the red has been filtered out of the ambient light, and flash is needed to restore the absorbed colour.

In tropical waters, the guide number of the flash gun (which indicates its power) is usually reduced to about a third of the 'in air' number. It is much safer to bracket your exposures, as the expense of film is nothing compared to the trouble and expense of getting into the water.

Underwater flashguns are either custom-made, or normal land units in plastic housings. Custom-made guns generally have a good wide angle performance, whereas units in housings generally have a narrow angle.

Instead of using a flash gun mounted close to the camera, place it at arm's length away, or even further, to give a better modelling light to the subject. Having two flash guns is even better and will give much greater control over lighting. With the flashgun further from the camera, fewer particles between the camera and the subject will be illuminated. If the flashgun is near the camera, the particles will be illuminated and detract from the subject.

Aiming the flash can be tricky. Although your eye and the camera lens 'see' the subject to be, say, two metres away, it is actually further. As the flash must strike the subject directly in order to light it up, the unit must be aimed *behind* the apparent position of the subject.

Diving Problems

Test your equipment in the swimming pool before you take it into the sea. Plan the shots beforehand. It is always better to have a good idea of what you want *before* you go into the water so you can have the right lens on the camera to do the job.

Keeping yourself stable while trying to take a picture can be a problem. Underwater you should be neutrally buoyant, such that you can hang suspended in the water without moving up or down. By breathing in you should rise slowly, and by breathing out you should gently sink. Wearing an adjustable buoyancy life jacket (A.B.L.J.) will allow you to increase or decrease your buoyancy by letting air into or out of it.

Sometimes you may need to grab onto a piece of coral to steady yourself. A wetsuit will help protect you against stings and scratches. And as you will be moving around slowly when taking pictures, you will feel the cold earlier than if you were swimming around energetically, and you will appreciate the warmth the suit gives you.

Near the sandy sea bed it is easy to churn up the water and disturb the sand, making the water cloudy. The secret is to keep still as possible, and perhaps even remove your fins. Restricting rapid movements also avoids scaring the more timid fish away. Taking a plastic bag of bread down with you usually guarantees plenty of potential subjects for your photography.

A Good Subject?

Even with very simple equipment it is possible to record interesting effects simply by looking at what is naturally around you underwater. Rays of light burst through the water in a spectacular way and are especially photogenic when they surround a silhouette. And you can get impressive effects by catching reflections on the surface when you look up at the sky through the water.

The best pictures are usually simple and clear. Select something to photograph, such as an attractive piece of coral, then position yourself to show it off to best advantage without too many distractions in the picture.

With a little thought and planning beforehand, achieving good results underwater is quite straightforward, although you should not be deterred by a high failure rate at first.

The Trouble with Photography

by David Hodgson

I have only been in jail three times in my life and, in each case, the stay was mercifully short! This was just as well since the jails were all in Africa and not amongst the healthiest places to spend a holiday. The cause, I hasten to add, was photographic rather than anything more sinister. A question of pointing a lens in the wrong direction at the wrong time. As a magazine photojournalist with an editor and offices to please, I was probably less discreet with my photography than the average traveller would ever need to be. All the same, great difficulties can be created quite unintentionally and with the most innocent of motives.

First of all find out exactly what the restrictions are and then stick to them. In many areas of the world, frontier security problems can turn an innocent border post picture into an excursion into espionage. At best you are likely to find your camera and film confiscated and the worst can be a whole lot worse. Avoid photographing military installations, troop movements, airfields etc., unless you have a compelling reason for doing so. And I mean one which is worth doing time for! Some countries have a ban on photographing examples of civil engineering, scenes that make the country look primitive – i.e. all the most photogenic places – and industrial plants. In Yugoslavia, some years ago, I was arrested for taking shots inside a chemical plant – and this after being given permission to do so. One traveller in Pakistan – which is full of absurd photographic restrictions – was nearly arrested for taking a picture of a river which just happened to have a bridge in the background. Train and aeroplane spotters beware: certain Iron Curtain and Third World countries regard the photographic or written record keeping involved as an offence. A bribe sometimes secures a bending of the rules.

Watch out for religious or cultural prohibitions. These can result in mob violence against you, especially in the remoter parts of the world. If you want to take pictures in places where the natives are far from friendly, then be careful. Respect their dignity and right of privacy. I should also add that a quite different problem can arise when you are *too* popular as a camera operator. Everybody in the neighbourhood seems to want to get in on the act. This happens mainly when a camera is a rare sight and you are looked on as a piece of street theatre. My advice here is to go through the pretence of taking pictures. If necessary – and you have sufficient film stock – waste a few frames or even a whole roll. You never know – some of the pictures may be worthwhile and you will satisfy the crowd's curiosity. When all the fuss has died down you can carry on with picture-taking without arousing much interest. If you are staying in an area for some time and want really candid shots, then let everybody get completely used to seeing you with your camera. Reckon on spending several days simply being seen around. Your novelty value will disappear very quickly.

One good way of persuading reluctant subjects to pose and rewarding them when they do is to carry a Polaroid camera around. Take one shot and let them have it. Then shoot your main pictures. But a word of warning – you can get through a lot of expensive Polaroid film unless you save this tactic for an emergency.

Filming

by Chris Hawkesworth

The lightness and versatility of the modern super 8mm camera make it the mainstay of the amateur cameraman's movie equipment. Film cartridges or cassettes for these cameras are easy to store and carry about, and are packed in such a way as to prevent dust penetration or other contamination *before use*. You can plug a lightweight microphone into the site of the camera and this will record sound onto a magnetic strip like a thin recording tape down the length of the film on the side opposite the sprocket holes. This strip can be read by a suitable projector with a sound head in it. There are built-in volume controls and limits, so you need have no worries. And, after all, why film a street musician playing silently?

Film

A 'fast' film – with a high ASA rating – enables you to shoot in low light conditions; early mornings, late evenings or inside buildings. In the bright light, however, fast films do not have the exposure tolerance of slower films, so very dark shadows can appear black on the finished film.

Use the slowest film you can find for normal shooting, but keep a few faster cassettes up your sleeve. Don't forget to reset your light meter before and after changing cassettes. Choose a 'reversal' film, i.e. a film like a 35mm slide. Have the film processed and then put it straight on the projector and look at the result. One word of caution, though: if you only have one copy or original and want to edit it and strike copies off your original, run it *as little as possible* or it will scratch irreparably. And every copy will then faithfully reproduce each scratch and speck of dirt. For editing purposes, copy your original and cut that copy first. When satisfied, and only then, work on the original with the same cuts that you made in your cutting copy.

Do not make your shots too long. You know what your subject is, but a stranger viewing your film has to be able to take the scene in. Shoot an average length of 5–6 seconds, counting to yourself. A long, general shot would stand 10 seconds, cut-aways 2–4 seconds.

For frame speed, I recommend 24 or 25 shots per second (fps). Most super 8mm cameras will run at slower and faster speeds, 16, 18, 32 and 64 fps. 24/25 gives you the best possible flicker-free picture and will cover up some mistakes e.g. panning too fast. It is the slowest speed you can use for transfer on to video tape. The only penalty is cost: you need 50 per cent more film than you would have needed shooting at 16 fps. Use the faster speeds for slow motion action.

Care

Care pays countless dividends later. Between cassettes (or cartridges), brush the camera gate, lens and movement with an airbrush. Keep your film cool and dry. Load the film into the camera in subdued light; and change the cartridges as speedily as possible. Do not allow your film to be X-rayed during security checks. It might fog, especially after repeated X-rays, whatever the security people say. If travelling by air, carry your film as hand luggage, in an insulated bag that can be used for the exposed film as well.

Technique

Your camera should be fitted with a zoom lens. Always focus on the subject using the telephoto end of the zoom. When you pull back, everything will then be in focus. Do not be tempted to zoom in and out with every shot; think of your zoom lens as a variable frame and only zoom if you want to highlight something. If travelling to a dry country, purchase a neutral density filter that fits over the outside of the lens to protect it. If filming mountains, or from planes, take a few extra ND filters. Use these to cut down the light as well as the ultraviolet element – this helps to even out the exposure. Remember to take the filters off when it gets dark.

In poor light, if the subject is interesting enough, shoot it with the lens aperture wide open (focus accurately). It is surprising how much the film can register, even in candlelight.

Different shots like 'cut-aways' introduce variation to the film – faces, hands, wheels, eyes, feet, hooves, tongues, for example. Or different angles: stand on something, lie down on the floor, lie on the roof of the bus. Strap the camera to an object for a tracking shot, e.g. attach it to a cycle frame, then ride the cycle. Another useful idea is to take a skateboard type helmet, drill a hole and put a bolt through that fits the base of the camera. When rigged in the field, the camera can run while you still have your hands free to ride the bike, horse, camel, canoe, etc.

Try to keep the camera steady on the general wide-angle shots and telephoto shots with no action. You can use wall tops, fence posts, door jambs, parked cars – anything! A tripod will help, but is extra equipment to lug about with you.

In foreign parts, especially on long trips, take two cameras. Split your filming between them – one might go wrong and you may find out too late, but at least you will have half your trip on record. Take plenty of batteries, as they are often difficult to get hold of in the Third World, and those you can get are often of doubtful quality and lose their power very quickly.

Film as Story

Lecturers should take slides as well. A combination of film and slides goes down much better than just film or just slides.

Your film must tell the story. You arrive (film a sign), you depart (film another sign); time passes (film a clock); day follows night; travelling is between places. Make sure that your film contains all these pointers to time and place.

Video

by Victoria Southwell

The last few years have seen incredible changes in video technology, as cameras and recorders become more versatile, more mobile, better quality – and cheaper. And the pace shows no sign of letting up with new inventions appearing on the market almost every month. They are an established fact of entertainment in the home, and more and more people are realising their potential – not just for 'home movies', but for expedition records and scientific study.

Which Format?

The first decision to make when buying or renting a video system is which format to go for. There are three – Beta, Video 2000 or VHS (Video Home System). Note that you cannot interchange between formats.

Most people buy VHS as there are more brand options and generally more facilities. However, the Beta format has longer tapes, which run for three and three-quarter hours while Video 2000 machines are unique in that they have double-sided tapes with a total time of eight hours.

If very lightweight equipment is a prime requirement, your best buy would be the new VHS-C format, designed for portable use only. Small 30-minute tapes are used, but they can be inserted into a full-sized VHS machine using a cassette adaptor.

The choice of video camera and portable videocassette recorder (VCR) has to be a personal one. There is a wide range, with prices for cameras starting at around £350 and going up to £950 while portable VCR's cost in the region of £400 to £900. It is possible to hire a complete portable system from a TV rental shop.

The first all-in-one systems with both camera and recorder in one unit are hovering on the horizon. Sony is already selling Beta Movie, a single unit combined camera and recorder known as a camcorder. It costs around £1000. JVC have launched the smallest and lightest video movie recorder ever, the GR-C1 VHS Video Movie. It weighs a mere 1.9kg, has a power consumption of 7.6 watts and a minimum battery life of 45 minutes. It costs around £800.

Both Beta Movie and Video Movie are camcorders that use the same VHS-C cassette as is used for the two-part portable systems already on sale. Kodak have recently produced an 8mm Kodavision system, but it costs more than the VHS Video Movie and uses a tape and cassette that are incompatible with any existing system.

Video vs Film

'Why use video instead of film?' After the initial outlay, video is cheaper to use. Film stock costs as much per minute as video costs per hour and video tape is re-usable.

'But can you edit it?' Yes, ideally you need two VCRs to edit a tape; one to play the original and the other to copy it in the right order. Unlike film, it is almost impossible to cut bits of videotape and join them back up to make an edited programme. Video heads are extremely small and brittle and would probably break off as soon as a tape join went over them, so editing has to be done electronically. JVC's Video Information Centre in London's Piccadilly offers two day courses in video movie-making and they also have editing facilities for hire.

Playback Overseas

It may not always be possible to play back your video cassette on a video system overseas. There are three different ways the picture signal is coded by the broadcaster and countries vary in their broadcast systems. For example, Britain uses PAL 1 (phase alternating lines), whereas the United States uses NTSC, and France, SECAM. In a NTSC country, a British cassette would not play at all; in another PAL country you get a picture but no sound and in a SECAM country you would only get a black and white picture with no sound. However, JVC have recently launched a 'globetrotters' colour monitor, the TM-90 PSN, which can be used with any component putting out a video signal, and can play back PAL/NTSC video discs. It weighs 9.6kg and costs around £350.

Foreign Customs

Foreign customs authorities are still extremely suspicious about the 'importation' of video equipment. Basically, how do they know you won't sell it and avoid duty? You are strongly advised to contact the embassy of the country you will be visiting to get advice. You may have to pay a large deposit as security when entering the country and be sure to take a receipt as proof of purchase to present to customs on your return.

Movie-Making

It is quite easy to acquire some skill in video photography fairly quickly because you can get instant playback and even check what you are doing while the camera is still working. Playback and monitoring are the great advantages in video movie-making. You quickly learn from and correct your mistakes!

Amateur video cameras are extremely simple to operate, so that even the beginner can concentrate on what he is filming rather than having to concern himself with technical matters. The only way to become competent is through practice; learn to feel confident in handling and operating the equipment.

Having mastered the controls, your next aim must be to gain skills in camera technique. There are three basic camera movements. *Panning* – moving the camera in a slow, smooth horizontal plane to take in a panorama. Always hold the opening and finishing shots for a few seconds. *Tilting* – moving the camera in a vertical plane. And *Zooming* – moving in and out on a subject. Don't zoom too often, a common amateur mistake.

Always hold the camera steady; if you are going to hand hold it, use a shoulder or breast rest. Look out for pieces of furniture, architecture or trees where you can rest it. Practice also swinging your body smoothly, keeping your feet still, and turning at the waist for panning shots.

Some cameras have a fade button, which means that if you come to the end of a scene, you can fade out the shot to black. You can also end a scene, for example, by letting the subject go out of focus. When you cut to the next scene, start the camera running and bring the subject into focus. Later, at the editing stage, you could make this a clean cut. Try to end each scene naturally and be aware of continuity. If Scene 1 ends with someone moving from left to right, then an observer in Scene 2 should echo the same movement with his head.

Video cameras don't like recording high degrees of contrast, they perform best in evenly lit conditions. Try not to pan from light areas to dark or you could get a phenomenon known as *comet-tailing*. This happens most often with cheaper cameras at wide aperture when light spills onto your next shot. If you photographed a car driving at night with its headlights on and then quickly cut to another night scene, the headlights from the first shot could dwell on the next.

Equipment and Tape Care

Looking after your equipment will help preserve its life and protect the delicate recording heads on the VCR. A few golden rules are listed below:

1. Keep your camera and tapes away from direct heat sources such as fires and car rear shelves. Heat from the sun can warp the camera body.
2. Water and other liquids will ruin cassettes and are death to the fragile components of a camera and VCR. Equally sand will ruin equipment.
3. All equipment, including tapes, is precision made and very susceptible to jarring. Avoid shocks and vibrations. Try to carry your equipment with you when travelling by air; never place it on a hard

shelf – pack it in foam padding or place it on a seat when travelling by car.

4. *Never* point a camera lens into the sun or a strong light source or you will burn the tubes.

5. Use a skylight filter to protect the lens. When not in use, always cap the lens, close the diaphragm and, if you've got a filter disc set it to the closed position.

6. Find out from the manufacturers what conditions your camera will operate in. Avoid humidity problems. When changes in temperature occur, condensation can form inside the cassette. If this happens, allow several hours for the tape to dry.

7. Store cassettes upright like books and keep them in the slipper cases. Store them *away from* magnetic sources like loudspeakers. Never take a tape on the tube, for example – you could erase it by sitting over the electric motor.

8. When you have finished with a recording, wind the cassette back to the start of the tape to avoid stretching or risk the tape becoming slack in the cassette.

9. Take plenty of batteries on an overseas trip, they never seem to last as long as you think. Remember extremes of temperature soak up battery power. Not only can zooming look amateurish, but it uses up a lot of power. Take a battery charger that can cope with the different current of the countries you'll be visiting. Finally, it is possible to buy or rent solar panels which generate twelve volts; you can charge your batteries from these when in a remote spot with sunshine but no electricity.

Selling Travel Photographs

by John Douglas

A two-man canoe expedition up the Amazon . . . a one-man trek through Afghanistan . . . a full-scale assault on Everest involving a party of sixty . . . a student group studying the fauna and flora of a remote Pacific island.

Question: What two features do these travellers have in common?
Answer: They will all be short of money and they'll all be taking at least one camera.

The object of this article is to draw attention to the fact that these two features are not unrelated. Too few expeditions or independent travellers, whether they be on the grand scale or simply a student adventure, are aware that the camera can make a substantial contribution to much-needed funds. When it is pointed out that a single picture may realise, say, £100, the hard-pressed traveller begins to see that he may be neglecting a very substantial source of revenue. While it is true that income from photography may not be received until some considerable time after arriving home, it can be used to pay off debts – or perhaps to finance the next excursion.

If photography is to pay, then advance planning is essential. Too often planning is no more than quick decisions regarding types of camera and the amount of film to be taken. Of course, these *are* essential questions and something might first be said about their relevance to potential markets.

Unless sponsorship and technical assistance are received, a movie camera is not worth taking. The production of a worthwhile expedition film or travelogue is such an expensive, specialised and time-consuming matter that it is best forgotten. In order to satisfy television and other markets, a film must approach near-professional standards with all that that implies in editing, cutting, dubbing, titling and so on, to say nothing of filming techniques. Of course, if a film unit from, for example, a regional TV network can be persuaded to send along a crew, then some of the profit, as well as a fine record of the traveller's achievements may accrue. But for the average trip this is unlikely to say the least. By all means take along a good 8mm movie camera but don't think of it as a source of income.

Format and Colour

With still photography, the position is quite different. It *is* worthwhile investing in, or having on loan, a good range of equipment. It will probably be advisable to take perhaps three cameras, two 35mm SLRs and a large format camera with an interchangeable back. If the latter is not available, then contrary to advice sometimes given, 35mm format is quite satisfactory for most markets except some calendar, postcard and advertising outlets.

A common planning argument is the old black and white versus colour controversy. It is *not* true that mono reproduction from colour is unacceptable. Expertly processed, some 70 to 80 per cent of colour will reproduce satisfactorily in black and white. However, conversion is more expensive and difficult than starting in the right medium and there are far more markets for mono than for colour. Although prices paid for black and white will only be some 50 to 60 per cent of those for colour, it is the larger market that makes it essential to take both sorts of film. A good plan is to take one-third fast black and white film and two-thirds colour reversal film. For formats larger than 35mm, take colour only. The reason for this imbalance is that it is easier to improve a sub-standard black and white during processing. To all intents and purposes, the quality of a colour picture is fixed once the shutter closes.

It is advisable to keep to one type of film with which you are familiar. Different colour films may reproduce with contrasting colour quality and spoil the effect of, say, an article illustrated with a sequence of colour pictures. Colour prints will not sell.

Outlets

Before leaving, the travel photographer should contact possible outlets for his work. Magazines generally pay well for illustrations, especially if accompanied by an article. Such UK markets as *The Traveller, The Geographical* magazine, the colour supplements of the Sunday newspapers or *Amateur Photographer* can be approached and, although they may not be able to give a firm *yes*, their advice can be helpful. Specialist journals, assuming they are illustrated, may be approached if the trip is relevant, but it should be remembered that the smaller circulation of such journals yields a lower rate of payment. It can be worth advertising the journey in the hope of obtaining lucrative photographic commissions, but beware of copyright snags if the film is provided free.

Overseas magazines such as the

American *National Geographic*, often pay exceptionally high rates but the market is tight. Much nearer home, local and national newspapers may take some pictures while the traveller is still abroad. If the picture editor is approached, he may accept some black and white pictures if they can be sent back through a UK agent. If the expedition is regionally based, local papers will usually be quite enthusiastic, but it is important to agree a reasonable fee beforehand, otherwise a payment of, say, £2 will hardly cover the costs involved. Local papers may also agree to take an illustrated story on the return home but, again, it is important to ensure that adequate payment will be made for the pictures published.

It is not the purpose of this article to discuss techniques of photography but the photographer working with an expedition is well advised to seek guidance, before he leaves home, from others who have worked in the area. There can be problems of climate, customs and the like of which it is as well to be aware before starting out.

Finally, one potentially contentious point *must* be settled before the first picture is taken. This is the matter of copyright ownership and the income received from the sale of photographs. In law, copyright is vested in the owner of the film and *not* in the photographer. This can cause headaches if the traveller has had film given to him by a third party.

Universal Appeal

Once the trip has started, the travel photographer will be looking for, perhaps, two sorts of photograph. Firstly, of course, there will be those which illustrate his travels, the changing scene, human and physical. But secondly, and so easily neglected, are those pictures which have a universal appeal irrespective of their location. Such shots as sunsets, children at play, brilliant displays of flowers, and so on always have a market. It is important, too, not to miss opportunities that are offered en route to the main location in which the travel photographer is to operate. Don't pack away your film while travelling to your destination. Have the camera ready on the journey.

Not unnaturally, the question 'what sells?' will be asked. There is no simple answer except to say that at some time or other almost any technically good photograph may have a market. (Throughout, it is assumed that the photographer is able to produce high quality pictures. There is never a market for the out-of-focus, under-exposed disaster!) Statements like 'the photograph that sells best is the one that no one else has' may not seem very helpful, yet this is the truth. It is no use building a collection which simply adds to an already saturated market. For example, a traveller passing through Agra will certainly visit the Taj Mahal – and photograph the splendid building. Yet the chances of selling such a photograph on the open market are dismal. It's all been done before, from every angle, in every light and mood. Perhaps a picture of the monument illuminated by a thunderstorm might be unusual enough to find a buyer but the best that can reasonably be hoped for is that the photographer will hit on a new angle or perhaps a human interest picture with the Taj as background.

On the other hand, a picture of village craftsmen at work might sell well, as will anything around which a story can be woven. Landscapes have a limited market but, given exceptional conditions of light, then a good scenic picture might reap high rewards in the calendar or advertising markets. The golden rule is to know the markets well enough to foresee needs. Sometimes the least obvious subjects are suddenly in demand.

Such was the case, for example, in 1976 during the raid on Entebbe Airport by Israeli forces. My own agency, Geoslides, was able to supply television with photographs of the old section of the airport and of the Kampala hospital just when they were needed. Yet who would expect a market for such subjects? Perhaps this is just another reason for carrying plenty of film. My own experience on my travels is that I am constantly looking around for subjects. Certainly it is no use sitting back waiting for something to appear in the viewfinder. It is wise not to ignore the obvious, everyday scenes. As I was preparing this article, Geoslides were asked for a photograph of a hailstorm in our Natal collection. Bad weather photographs sell well, so you should not always wait for brilliant sunshine.

Record Keeping and Processing

One most important but easily overlooked point is the matter of record keeping. In the conditions experienced by many travellers, this will not be easy, yet it cannot be emphasized too strongly that meticulous care must be taken to ensure that every picture is fully documented. It is true that certain photographs may be identified at a later date, for example, macrophotography of plants, but no shot should be taken without some recording of at least its subject and location. It is usually best to number the films in advance and to have an identification tag on the camera which will indicate the film being exposed. A notebook can also be prepared before the traveller leaves.

With the advertising market in mind, it is helpful to make sure that good photographs are taken which include the traveller's equipment. Less obviously, there is a market for photographs of proprietary brands of food, magazines, newspapers, items of clothing and equipment and so on in exotic and unusual settings.

If the traveller is to be away for a long time, it can be important to get some of the exposed film back home. There are dangers in this procedure because of the uncertainty of postal services, but provided some care is taken – perhaps with arrangements made through embassies – then there are advantages. Apart from the obvious problem of keeping exposed film in sub-optimum conditions, some preparatory work can be carried out by the traveller's agent. Of course, if the film is sent home, it is essential that labelling and recording are foolproof.

Serious Selling

Once the travel photographer has returned home, the serious business of selling begins. Topicality is a selling point, so there is no excuse for taking even a few days off, no matter how exhausted you may feel. Processing the film is clearly the first task, followed by cataloguing and the production of sample black and white enlargements. No one is going to buy if the goods are badly presented, so it is worth making sure that a portfolio of high quality mono enlargements and colour transparencies is prepared with a really professional appearance.

The first market to tackle will be the local newspapers. Following up the advances made before you set out is very important, no matter how lukewarm the original response. It often *looks* more professional if there are both a writer and a photographer to produce a magazine article, but it should be made clear to editors that a separate fee is expected for text and illustrations. This is invariably better than a lump sum or space-payment.

A direct source of income from photography can be slide shows for which the audience is charged. These are relatively easy to organize but must be prepared with slides of maps and an accompanying tape or live commentary. Incidentally, do not mix vertical and horizontal frames. It gives an untidy appearance to the show even when the screen actually accommodates the verticals. The bigger the screen the better. If these shows are to have a wide audience, it may be necessary to put the organization into the hands of an agent.

A photographic exhibition can provide helpful publicity but it will probably raise little or no income in itself. Branch librarians are usually helpful in accommodating exhibitions and if these showings precede some other event like a lecture or slide show, they can be indirect money spinners. For an exhibition, great care should be taken in making the display as professional as possible. Again, the bigger the enlargements, the better. As far as photography is concerned 'big is beautiful!' It is worth investing in a few really giant blow-ups.

Depending on the standing of the photographer, it can be a good plan to show some prints to the publicity department of the camera company or franchise agent whose equipment has been used, especially if you have made exclusive use of one company's products. The same may apply to the makers of the film that has been used.

If the traveller has not been too far off the beaten track throughout his travels, then travel firms may take photographs with which to illustrate brochures and posters. However, as with the calendar and postcard market, it must be pointed out that this is a specialist field, requiring not only particular sorts of photographs but pictures of a very high technical quality. This also applies to photographs used for advertising, although the suggestions made earlier regarding pictures of proprietary brands leaves this door slightly wider than usual.

Whenever an original transparency or negative is sent to or left with a publisher or agent, a signature must be obtained for it, a value placed on it should it be lost or damaged (anything up to £300 per original) and a record kept of its location.

Using an Agency

Lastly, when the catalogue is complete, the travel photographer will wish to put the whole of his saleable photograph collection on the market. Now a decision must be reached on the thorny issue of whether or not to use an agency. Of course, direct sales would mean an almost 100 per cent profit, while the agency sales will probably net only 50 per cent of the reproduction rights fee. But, as so often happens, it is the enlargement of the market, the professional expertise and marketing facilities of the agency which are attractive. It is worth making enquiries of a number of agencies (see the *Writers' and Artists' Yearbook*) and finding a company which offers the sort of terms and assistance that satisfy the travel photographer's requirements. It is usually preferable to deal with a company which does not expect to hold the collection but simply calls for pictures when needed. This allows much greater freedom to the copyright owner as well as being a check on what is happening in the market. Some agencies offer additional services to associate photographers in the way of help with the placing of literary as well as photographic material and in the organization of lecture services.

It may well be better to contact an agency before leaving. For a small consultancy fee, a good agency may be able to advise on the sort of pictures which sell well and on the level of reproduction fees which should be charged. There is nothing more annoying than selling rights for £25 and then finding that the market would have stood £50. Many amateurs sell their pictures for too low a fee and others assume that there is a set price irrespective of the use to which the photographic material is put. In fact, the market for photographic reproduction rights is something of a jungle and it may be better to gain professional advice rather than get lost. The same applies to locating markets. It is almost impossible for the inexperienced amateur to identify likely markets for his work. There are thousands of possible outlets and a small fortune could be lost in trying to locate a buyer for a particular picture, no matter how high its quality.

An ambitious and skilled travel photographer should expect to make a substantial profit from his photography, providing an effort is made along the lines indicated. In the case of a specialized and well-publicized trip it is not unknown for the whole of the cost of mounting the venture to be recouped from the sale of pictures. There are some simple points to remember. Don't treat the camera as a toy. Don't give the job of photographer to a non-specialist. Don't put all those transparencies and negatives in the back of a drawer when you get home. As a money spinner, the camera may be the most important piece of equipment the traveller carries.

Travel Writing

by Carol Wright

One airline public relations officer has termed travel writers 'professional holidaymakers'. Indeed, this is the enviable image the world has of the job. To the uninitiated, it is all lying on a palm-shaded beach with rum punch in one hand, a novel in the other. Most of my friends assume I'm on vacation when I go away and their 'have a good time' wishes enrage me. My own image, tempered by reality, is of lugging cases, heavy with handouts and brochures, not souvenirs, round unlovely airports in inevitable delays. If I am in a resort area, more time is spent 'counting the screws in the loos' or seeing yet more bedrooms and conference halls in new hotels. Of course, it rains on the one free morning allocated to beach lounging and I have seen press trip itineraries where a free morning was defined as not starting the tour before 8.30am.

One often see resorts out of season – when the paying public don't go. 'You should have been here last week' will be the title of my autobiography; the words are used so often by tourism officials greeting me in monsoon, gales, snow or hurricane. I have toured the Sahara in snow and spent a Hawaiian beach barbecue wrapped in garbage bags against the lash of the Pacific storm.

In the end, you get back jetlagged and are expected to be bright and breezy and take up office and home work without sympathy from those who stayed at home. To be a travel writer requires a special temperament, itchy feet and a knowledge of how to be ahead of the travelling crowd. Social life is wrecked; travel life is often the loneliness of room-serviced evenings and hours on planes next to non-English-speaking passengers.

Getting Started

Having delivered the bad news, travel writing is one of the most exciting jobs around; hard work, but once having made it into that élite circle, it offers the inestimable advantage of being able to see the world at someone else's expense. Getting in involves more than a talent for writing. It is a chicken-and-egg situation. It is difficult to sell stories until you have travelled somewhere and difficult to get travel facilities until you have had some travel stories published. It is as well to use holiday trips where possible as a springboard and when something has been sold to a magazine, hoard that cutting and show it to travel companies.

Anyone who has ever been on holiday thinks they can become a travel writer. I see so many manuscripts submitted to me as travel editor of a national magazine that prove this wrong. Diary-style and school-like 'what I did on my holiday' efforts are all too common. A subtle blend of a lively and different approach to a well-known place coupled with detail of what it means in terms of food, accommodation, and sightseeing to a reader is needed, as well as a paragraph showing ways of getting to a place and how much it will cost; something editors set great store by. This is the one place where advertisers can be mentioned – and it is advertisers who in the end dictate how much space is allocated to travel features. This space is dismally small in the UK; but in the US, many papers have complete travel supplements every week.

It is unlikely that the aspiring writer will easily get a travel editor's job. The most usual way is by transferring from another in-house job within a paper. And old travel writers die hard, the life style is too attractive to give up lightly. The freelance field is wide, competitive and adaptable to the travelling life. Earnings are low and one must work extremely hard to make a living. The advantages are a freedom to sell to the best available market, avoidance of office politics, and having to get editor's approval of where you go.

Good ideas and constant hard sell are essential. Time spent away travelling must be balanced with keeping one's name and ideas in editors' eyes and thoughts. The market must be studied continually and openings examined. A subscription to a magazine like the UK *Press Gazette* is worthwhile for news of new magazines, editorial changes etc. When attempting to get work in overseas publications, a file of good cuttings and a short biographical note is a help. English language papers abroad often accept travel pieces about the UK from British-based journalists since they then don't have to send their journalists to Britain.

Few, if any, publications will offer any expenses for travelling, although some do occasionally if a lot of research is involved. Editors expect travel writers to get to the places to be covered on their own. The *New York Times* refuses articles where free facilities have been accepted. At this point, the travel writer must establish his integrity and independence of line, not always easy when the travel trade is extremely hospitable – not to say generous – with travelling help.

Free Facilities

Travel companies rarely hound writers for coverage after a trip unless they feel they have literally been taken for a ride by someone not intending to write anything. But travel writers who want to remain such get careful about what trips they select. Some airlines still try and bind travel writers seeking long-haul tickets with a signed contract agreeing to publish articles by a certain date. The British Guild of Travel Writers advises members never to sign these and it is doubtful if these 'contracts' have any legal binding power.

Most hospitality is in the form of travel trips. These are getting so many and overlapping that many have to be filled with also-rans or friends of the travel editor. The true travel freelance, as he becomes more established, should ignore all of these except occasional well-run tours or those to places it would be very difficult to get to on his own. The material he can pick up independently while travelling outweighs the time wasted at endless formal banquets and in bars talking with colleagues on these trips.

In considering outlets for his work, there is the 'grey' area of sponsored magazines and press releases. Airlines, tourist boards, trains and hotel chains back magazines which sell their travel image and are usually lucrative forms of writing, although again one's complete freedom is at risk. Brochure writing for tour companies also pays well but the British Guild of Travel Writers is against such writing where the author's name appears in the copy. Anonymous writing is all right and often gives a fresh approach to a stereotyped copy.

A double-edged problem is the press release or feature travel story sent out by tourist offices and others. To enhance veracity and prestige, 'name' travel writers are often hired to write these and again a bias is inevitable. At the same time, other freelancer's markets are at risk since these features often flood provincial papers, house magazines and other publications which will use them and save the cost of commissioning another writer.

Whereas cookery and other writers often appear in advertisement praising some product, the Guild would dismiss any member appearing in a travel ad. On the other hand, it is virtually impossible to stop tour operators selecting quotations from published articles and using them in their brochures – which can again give the appearance of bias.

Specialization

Apart from these dubious outlets as far as integrity is concerned, the travel writer has a wide choice of outlet types. Specialization is a good idea and gets one's name established faster. One can concentrate on being the expert on a single country or an aspect of travel such as camping, skiing, cruising, trains, aviation, conventions or incentive travel and get close to publications specializing in these areas. As well as 'straight' travel destination pieces, the good freelance, to get more in fees than time and out of pocket expenses involved in a trip would warrant from one piece, will look for spinoff ideas perhaps local fashion, food, wine, architecture, economics or politics particularly in areas where newspapers do not have their own correspondents.

Photojournalism is a growing section of travel writing. It is initially costly setting up with good cameras, film and processing, but rewards can be good and a library built over the years can have recurring value and even possibly be sold as a complete unit. Photos can also be sold through specialised agents who will take a percentage of the fee negotiated. It's worthwhile getting updated lists of library contents circulated to picture editors and brochure compilers. Colour magazines and supplements like photo features on strange countries and their peoples. Broadcasting, with more and more radio stations coming on stream, is another source of income for those who can paint lively word pictures on the air, can cope with phone-in programmes on travel information and are prepared to learn to use and to drag round the world the heavy tape recorders used professionally.

Finance

The running costs of a successful travel writer can be heavy. Insurance, inoculations, visa fees and air port taxes, replacing suitcases frequently, all mount up with the added need of a wardrobe that can go skiing, on safari, trekking, cruising; everything from dining in *QE2*'s top grill room with millionaires to sleeping on the jungle floor. Fees are pathetically low and often need to be prized out of publishers. Wiring on spec. is wasteful unless at the very beginning and commissions should always be made in writing if possible. Nagging for fees unpaid is tricky if you want to keep in with that paper. But papers need pressure put on them; the bigger they are, the more reluctant they are to pay quickly compared with smaller and trade publications. A freelance is almost investing for the future when writing an article; payment can be literally years ahead.

Writers' Association

Agents are less use for selling most travel features; editors prefer personal contact and exchange of ideas with their writers. But for books, a good agent is worth their ten to fifteen per cent in fees making sure no rip-offs occur in the contract and for making sure payments come through. Membership of the Society of Authors is useful for those wanting to spend most of their time writing books.

I see a declining future for the traditional type of guide book. They are being challenged by the video and taped touring cassettes. But currently there is a boom in personal travel accounts where writing that takes the reader along a journey, and angle and personality are as important as the place covered. Reliable, readable clean copy will eventually earn the reward of editors coming to a writer with commissions. Belonging to a travel writers' association will advance the writer little but such an organization is useful for home contacts, having your name circulated widely on a membership list, as a general meeting ground for what's going on and maintaining standards of travel writing. Collective clout is sometimes useful in dealing with problematical publishers. Membership, contrary to what many hopefuls think, is not a passport to eternal free jet-set living. In the USA, the Society of American Travel Writers is a large body with an associate membership of high fee-paying Public Relations Officers in the travel industry and others who hold an impressive annual convention. The British Guild of Travel Writers (for information, contact the Secretary, 31 Riverside Court, Caversham, Reading, Berks (Tel: (0734) 481384)) with around 100 members excludes all but established full-time travel writers with income derived primarily from travel writing. Fees are kept low and used to cover guild expenses.

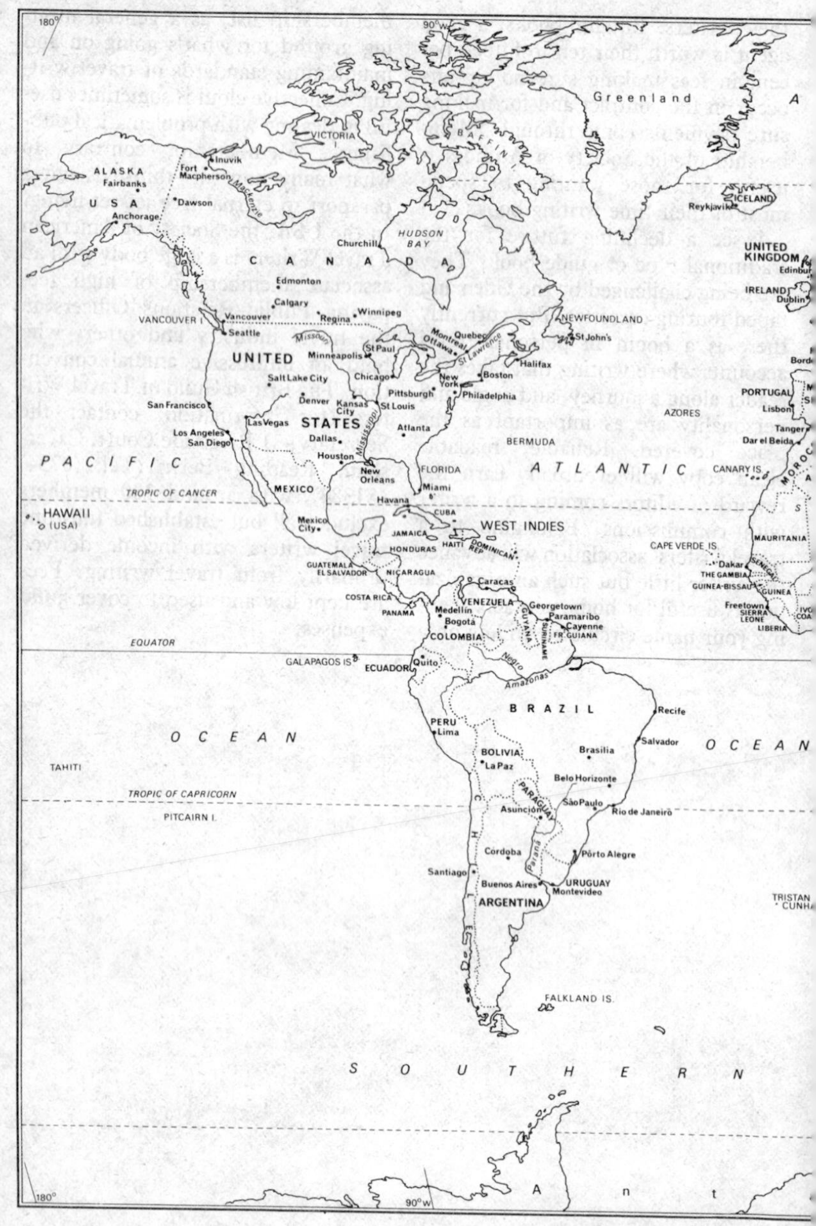
Greenland
ICELAND
Reykjavik
UNITED KINGDOM
IRELAND
Dublin
ALASKA
Fairbanks
USA
Anchorage
Dawson
Inuvik
Fort Macpherson
Mackenzie
VICTORIA I
BAFFIN I
HUDSON BAY
Churchill
CANADA
Edmonton
Calgary
Regina
Winnipeg
VANCOUVER I
Vancouver
Seattle
NEWFOUNDLAND
St John's
Quebec
Montreal
Ottawa
St Lawrence
Halifax
Boston
New York
Philadelphia
Pittsburgh
St Paul
Minneapolis
Missouri
Chicago
UNITED STATES
Salt Lake City
Denver
Kansas City
St Louis
San Francisco
Las Vegas
Los Angeles
San Diego
Dallas
Houston
Atlanta
Mississippi
New Orleans
FLORIDA
Miami
BERMUDA
AZORES
PORTUGAL
Lisbon
Tanger
Dar el Beida
CANARY IS.
PACIFIC
ATLANTIC
TROPIC OF CANCER
HAWAII (USA)
MEXICO
Mexico City
Havana
CUBA
WEST INDIES
JAMAICA
HAITI
DOMINICAN REP
HONDURAS
GUATEMALA
EL SALVADOR
NICARAGUA
COSTA RICA
PANAMA
CAPE VERDE IS.
MAURITANIA
Dakar
THE GAMBIA
GUINEA-BISSAU
GUINEA
Freetown
SIERRA LEONE
LIBERIA
Caracas
VENEZUELA
Georgetown
Paramaribo
Cayenne
GUYANA
SURINAME
FR. GUIANA
Medellin
Bogotá
COLOMBIA
EQUATOR
GALAPAGOS IS.
ECUADOR
Quito
Negro
Amazonas
BRAZIL
Recife
Salvador
PERU
Lima
OCEAN
BOLIVIA
La Paz
Brasilia
TAHITI
TROPIC OF CAPRICORN
Belo Horizonte
PARAGUAY
Asunción
São Paulo
Rio de Janeirō
PITCAIRN I.
Cordoba
Pôrto Alegre
Santiago
Buenos Aires
URUGUAY
Montevideo
ARGENTINA
CHILE
TRISTAN DA CUNHA
FALKLAND IS.
SOUTHERN
Ant
180°
90° W

OCEAN
Siberia
USSR
Yenisey
Ob
Lena
Irtysh
Amur
Volga
Yakutsk
FINLAND
Helsinki
Leningrad
Sverdlovsk
Moscow
Kuybyshev
Novosibirsk
Irkutsk
POLAND
Warsaw
Kiev
Volgograd
Vienna
ROMANIA
Belgrade
BULGARIA
BLACK SEA
Istanbul
Tbilisi
CASPIAN SEA
TURKEY
Ankara
Athens
GREECE
Tehran
IRAN
Kabul
AFGHANISTAN
Tashkent
Alma Ata
XINJIANG
MONGOLIA
Haerbin
Vladivostok
Shenyang
Beijing
CHINA
Seoul
KOREA
JAPAN
Tokyo
Huanghe
Xi'an
IRAQ
SYRIA
ISRAEL
JORDAN
Jerusalem
Baghdad
Cairo
EGYPT
Nile
SAUDI ARABIA
Riyadh
OMAN
YEMEN ARAB REP.
YEMEN PEOPLE'S DEM. REP.
PAKISTAN
Indus
TIBET
NEPAL
Kathmandu
Delhi
INDIA
Wuhan
Yangtze
Chongqing
Shanghai
Taipei
TAIWAN
Guangzhou
Hong Kong
Dacca
BANGLADESH
BURMA
Hanoi
LAOS
Bombay
Rangoon
THAILAND
Bangkok
VIETNAM
CHINA SEA
Manila
PHILIPPINES
ARABIAN SEA
Madras
ANDAMAN IS.
KAMPUCHEA
Ho Chi Minh City (Saigon)
SRI LANKA
Colombo
NICOBAR IS.
MARIANA IS.
CAROLINE IS.
LIBYA
CHAD
SUDAN
Addis Ababa
ETHIOPIA
SOMALIA
CENTRAL AFRICAN REP.
UGANDA
KENYA
Nairobi
Mogadishu
MALAYSIA
Kuala Lumpur
Singapore
SUMATRA
NEW GUINEA
SOLOMON IS.
CONGO
ZAÏRE
Kinshasa
SEYCHELLES
TANZANIA
Dar es Salaam
Jakarta
INDONESIA
JAVA
Luanda
ANGOLA
COMORO IS.
MALAWI
Darwin
ZAMBIA
Lusaka
Zambezi
MOÇAMBIQUE
Moçambique
INDIAN
Salisbury
ZIMBABWE
S.W. AFRICA
MADAGASCAR (MALAGASY REP.)
MAURITIUS
RÉUNION
BOTSWANA
Alice Springs
Pretoria
Maputo
AUSTRALIA
Brisbane
SOUTH AFRICA
Durban
LESOTHO
OCEAN
Perth
Kalgoorlie
Canberra
Sydney
Melbourne
TASMANIA
Hobart
Auckland
Wellington
Christchurch
NEW ZEALAND
OCEAN
90°E
180°

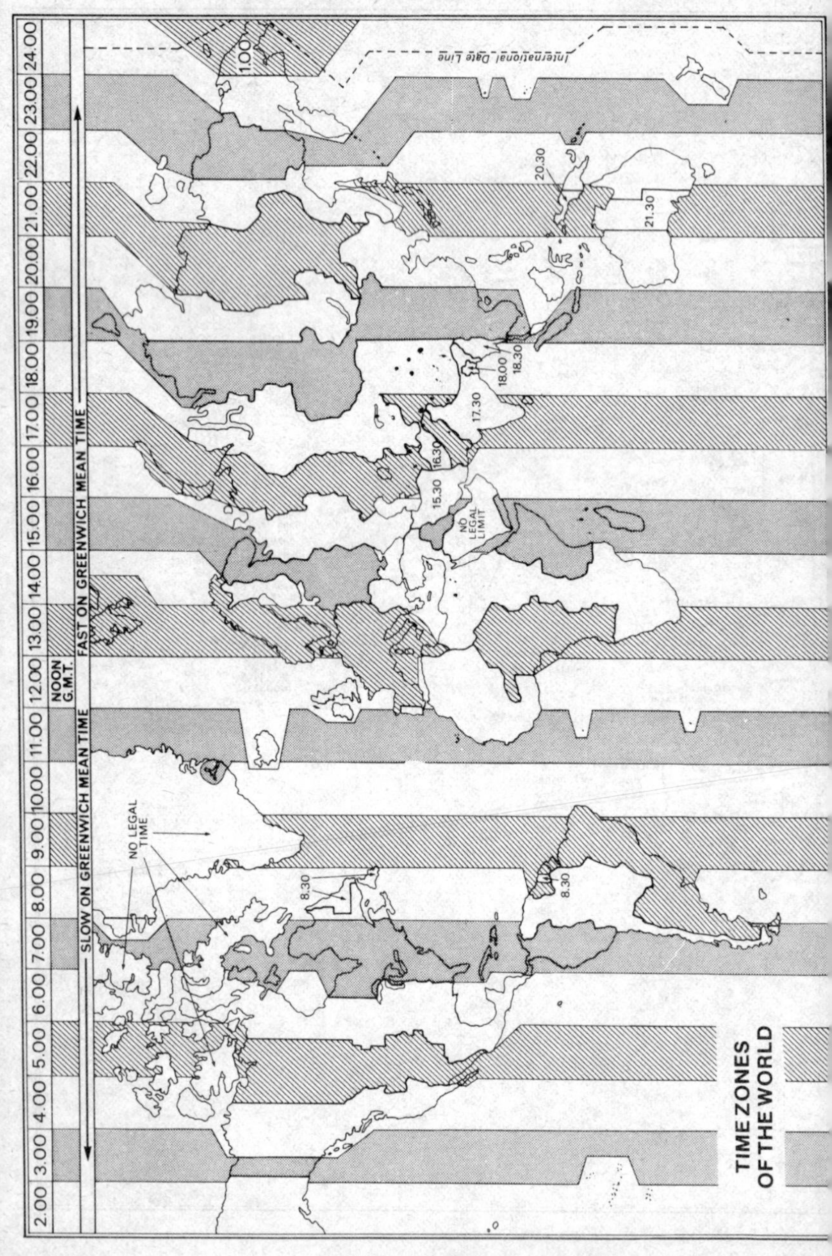

TIME ZONES OF THE WORLD
2.00
3.00
4.00
5.00
6.00
7.00
8.00
9.00
10.00
11.00
12.00
NOON G.M.T.
13.00
14.00
15.00
16.00
17.00
18.00
19.00
20.00
21.00
22.00
23.00
24.00
SLOW ON GREENWICH MEAN TIME
FAST ON GREENWICH MEAN TIME
International Date Line
NO LEGAL TIME
8.30
8.30
NO LEGAL LIMIT
15.30
16.30
17.30
18.00
18.30
20.30
21.30
1.00

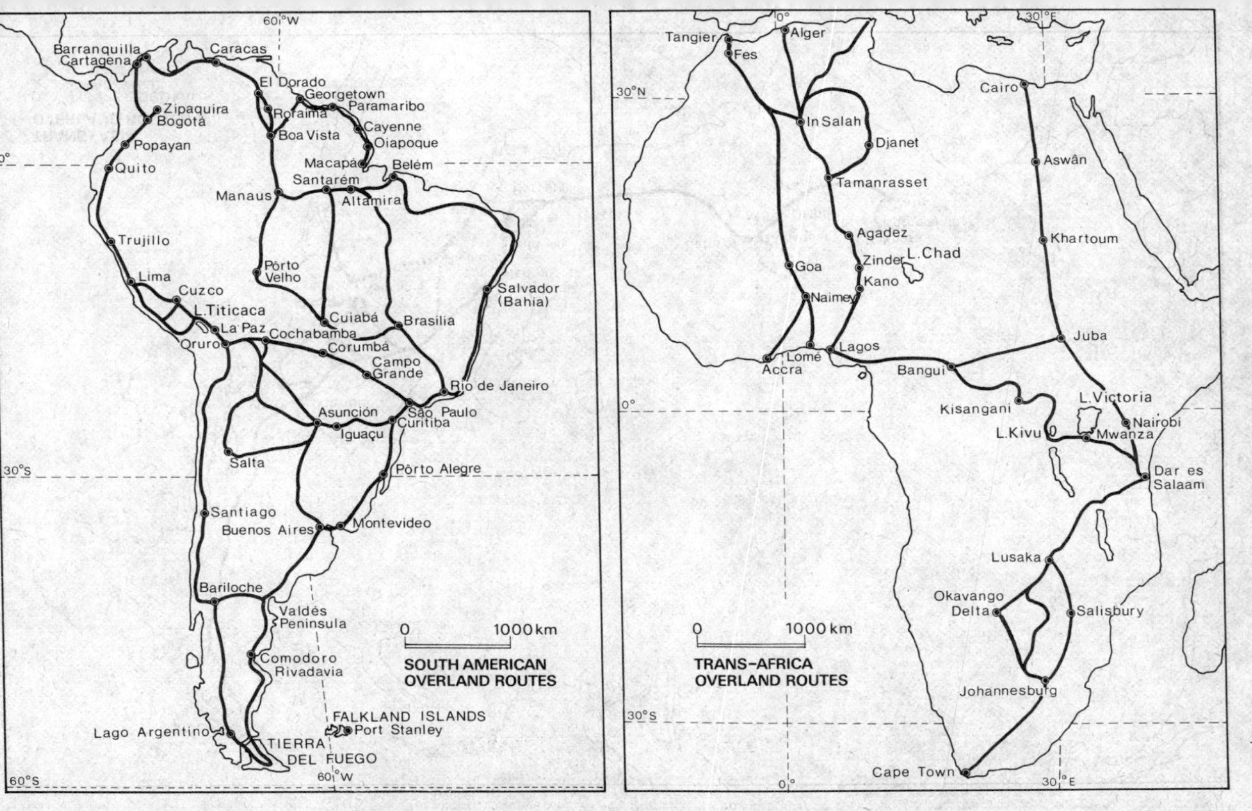
60°W
Barranquilla
Cartagena
Caracas
El Dorado
Georgetown
Paramaribo
Roraima
Zipaquira
Bogotá
Boa Vista
Cayenne
Oiapoque
Popayan
0°
Quito
Macapá
Belém
Santarém
Manaus
Altamira
Trujillo
Pôrto
Velho
Lima
Cuzco
Salvador
(Bahia)
L. Titicaca
Cuiabá
Brasilia
La Paz
Cochabamba
Oruro
Corumbá
Campo
Grande
Rio de Janeiro
Asunción
São Paulo
Curitiba
Iguaçu
Salta
30°S
Pôrto Alegre
Santiago
Buenos Aires
Montevideo
Bariloche
Valdés
Peninsula
0
1000 km
Comodoro
Rivadavia
SOUTH AMERICAN
OVERLAND ROUTES
FALKLAND ISLANDS
Port Stanley
Lago Argentino
TIERRA
DEL FUEGO
60°S
60°W
0°
30°E
Tangier
Alger
Fes
30°N
Cairo
In Salah
Djanet
Aswân
Tamanrasset
Agadez
Khartoum
Zinder
L. Chad
Goa
Kano
Naimey
Juba
Lagos
Lomé
Accra
Bangui
L. Victoria
0°
Kisangani
Nairobi
L. Kivu
Mwanza
Dar es
Salaam
Lusaka
Okavango
Delta
Salisbury
0
1000 km
TRANS-AFRICA
OVERLAND ROUTES
Johannesburg
30°S
Cape Town
0°
30°E

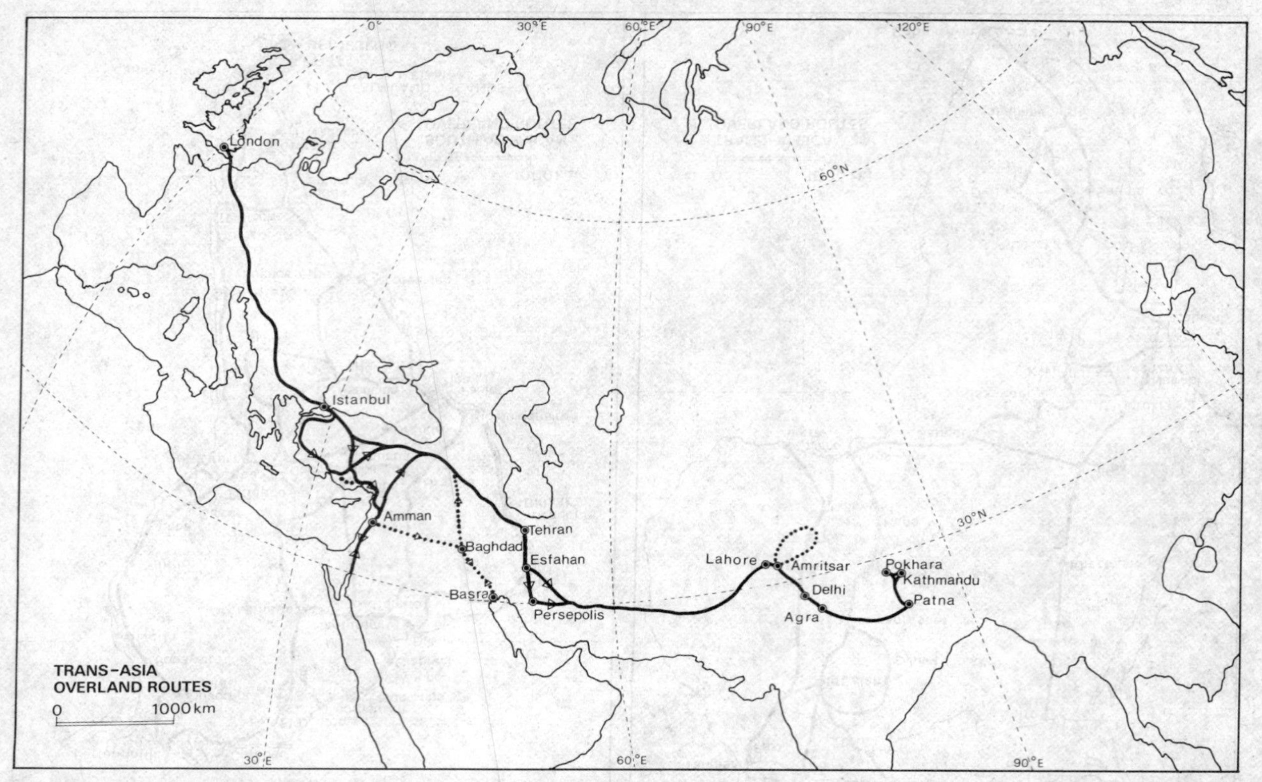
0°
30°E
60°E
90°E
120°E
60°N
30°N
London
Istanbul
Amman
Baghdad
Basra
Tehran
Esfahan
Persepolis
Lahore
Amritsar
Delhi
Agra
Pokhara
Kathmandu
Patna
TRANS-ASIA
OVERLAND ROUTES
0
1000 km
30°E
60°E
90°E

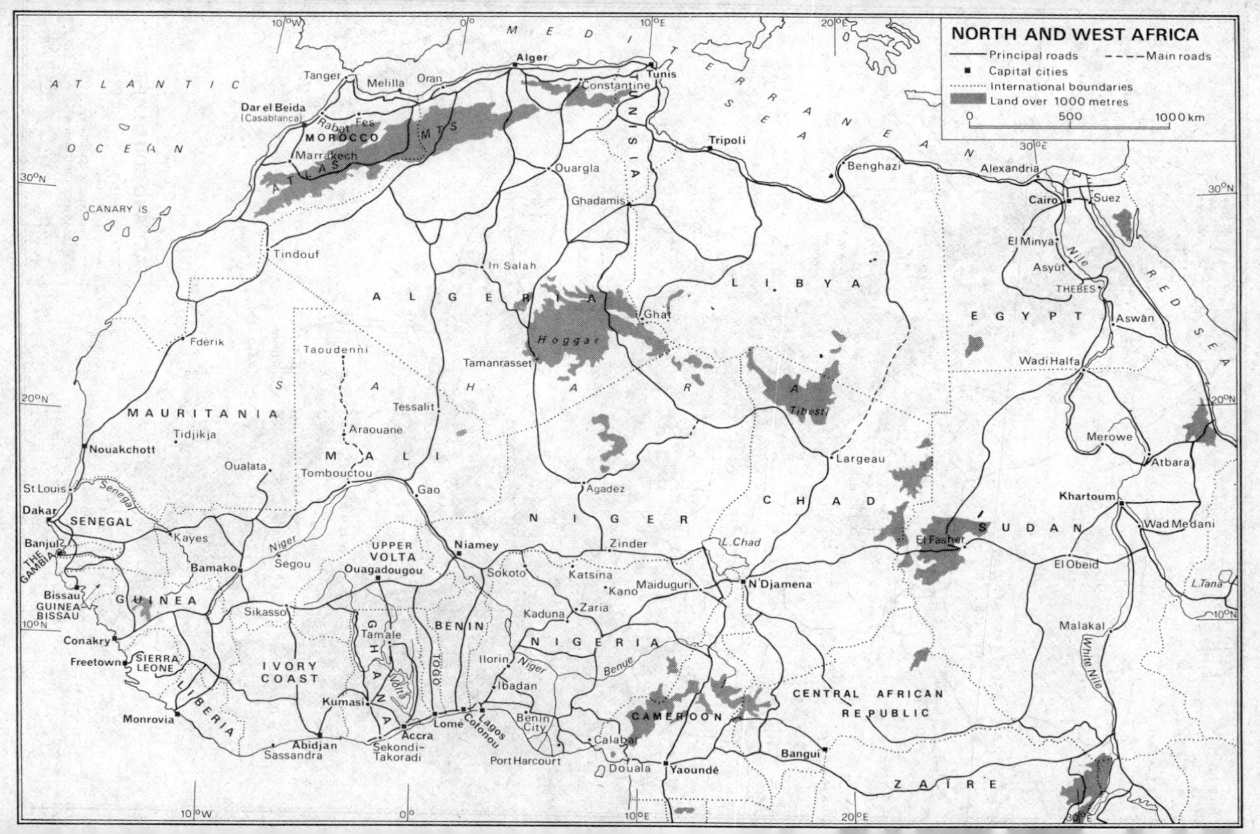
NORTH AND WEST AFRICA
Principal roads
Main roads
Capital cities
International boundaries
Land over 1000 metres
0
500
1000 km
MEDITERRANEAN
ATLANTIC
OCEAN
RED SEA
CANARY IS.
MOROCCO
ALGERIA
TUNISIA
LIBYA
EGYPT
SUDAN
CHAD
NIGER
MALI
MAURITANIA
SENEGAL
THE GAMBIA
GUINEA-BISSAU
GUINEA
SIERRA LEONE
LIBERIA
IVORY COAST
UPPER VOLTA
GHANA
TOGO
BENIN
NIGERIA
CAMEROON
CENTRAL AFRICAN REPUBLIC
ZAIRE
SAHARA
ATLAS MTS
Hoggar
Tibesti
Tanger
Dar el Beida (Casablanca)
Rabat
Fes
Melilla
Oran
Alger
Constantine
Tunis
Tripoli
Benghazi
Alexandria
Cairo
Suez
El Minya
Asyût
THEBES
Aswân
Wadi Halfa
Merowe
Atbara
Khartoum
Wad Medani
El Obeid
Malakal
White Nile
Nile
L. Tana
El Fasher
Marrakech
Tindouf
In Salah
Ouargla
Ghadamis
Ghat
Tamanrasset
Agadez
Largeau
N'Djamena
L. Chad
Zinder
Maiduguri
Kano
Katsina
Zaria
Kaduna
Sokoto
Niamey
Gao
Tessalit
Araouane
Taoudenni
Tombouctou
Oualata
Tidjikja
Fderik
Nouakchott
St Louis
Dakar
Banjul
Bissau
Conakry
Freetown
Monrovia
Kayes
Bamako
Segou
Niger
Senegal
Sikasso
Ouagadougou
Tamale
Volta
Kumasi
Abidjan
Sassandra
Sekondi-Takoradi
Accra
Lome
Cotonou
Lagos
Ibadan
Ilorin
Benin City
Port Harcourt
Benue
Calabar
Douala
Yaoundé
Bangui
30°N
20°N
10°N
10°W
0°
10°E
20°E
30°E

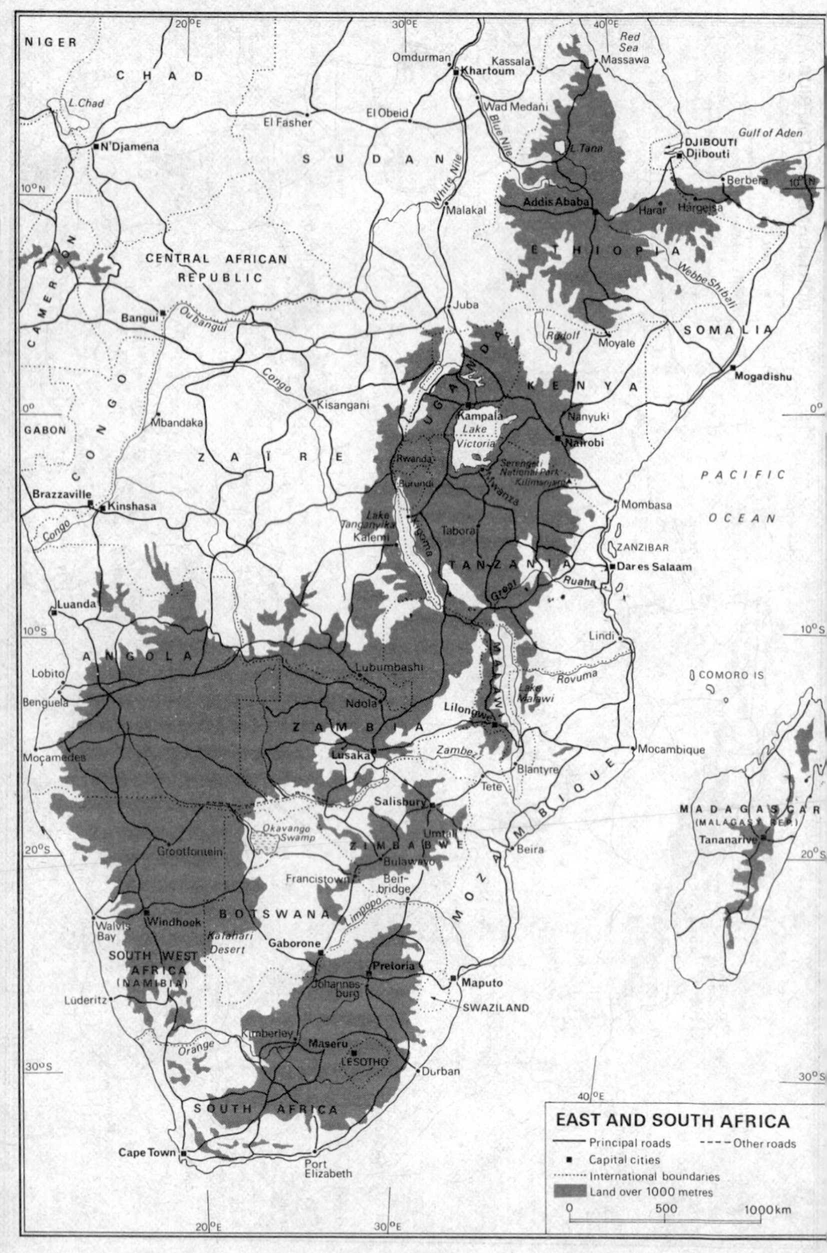

EAST AND SOUTH AFRICA
Principal roads
Other roads
Capital cities
International boundaries
Land over 1000 metres
0
500
1000km
NIGER
CHAD
SUDAN
ETHIOPIA
SOMALIA
DJIBOUTI
CENTRAL AFRICAN REPUBLIC
CAMEROON
CONGO
GABON
ZAÏRE
UGANDA
KENYA
TANZANIA
ANGOLA
ZAMBIA
MALAWI
MOZAMBIQUE
ZIMBABWE
BOTSWANA
SOUTH WEST AFRICA (NAMIBIA)
SOUTH AFRICA
LESOTHO
SWAZILAND
MADAGASCAR (MALAGASY REP.)
COMORO IS
ZANZIBAR
PACIFIC OCEAN
Red Sea
Gulf of Aden
Khartoum
Omdurman
Kassala
Massawa
Wad Medani
El Obeid
El Fasher
N'Djamena
L. Chad
Djibouti
Berbera
Harar
Hargeisa
Addis Ababa
L. Tana
Blue Nile
White Nile
Malakal
Webbe Shibeli
Juba
L. Rudolf
Moyale
Mogadishu
Bangui
Oubangui
Congo
Kisangani
Mbandaka
Kampala
Lake Victoria
Nanyuki
Nairobi
Serengeti National Park
Kilimanjaro
Mwanza
Rwanda
Burundi
Brazzaville
Kinshasa
Mombasa
Lake Tanganyika
Kalemi
Kigoma
Tabora
Dar es Salaam
Ruaha
Great
Luanda
Lindi
Lobito
Benguela
Lubumbashi
Ndola
Rovuma
Lake Malawi
Lilongwe
Moçamedes
Lusaka
Zambezi
Blantyre
Mocambique
Tete
Salisbury
Umtali
Okavango Swamp
Beira
Tananarive
Grootfontein
Bulawayo
Francistown
Beitbridge
Limpopo
Walvis Bay
Windhoek
Kalahari Desert
Gaborone
Pretoria
Johannesburg
Maputo
Luderitz
Kimberley
Maseru
Orange
Durban
Cape Town
Port Elizabeth
20°E
30°E
40°E
10°N
0°
10°S
20°S
30°S

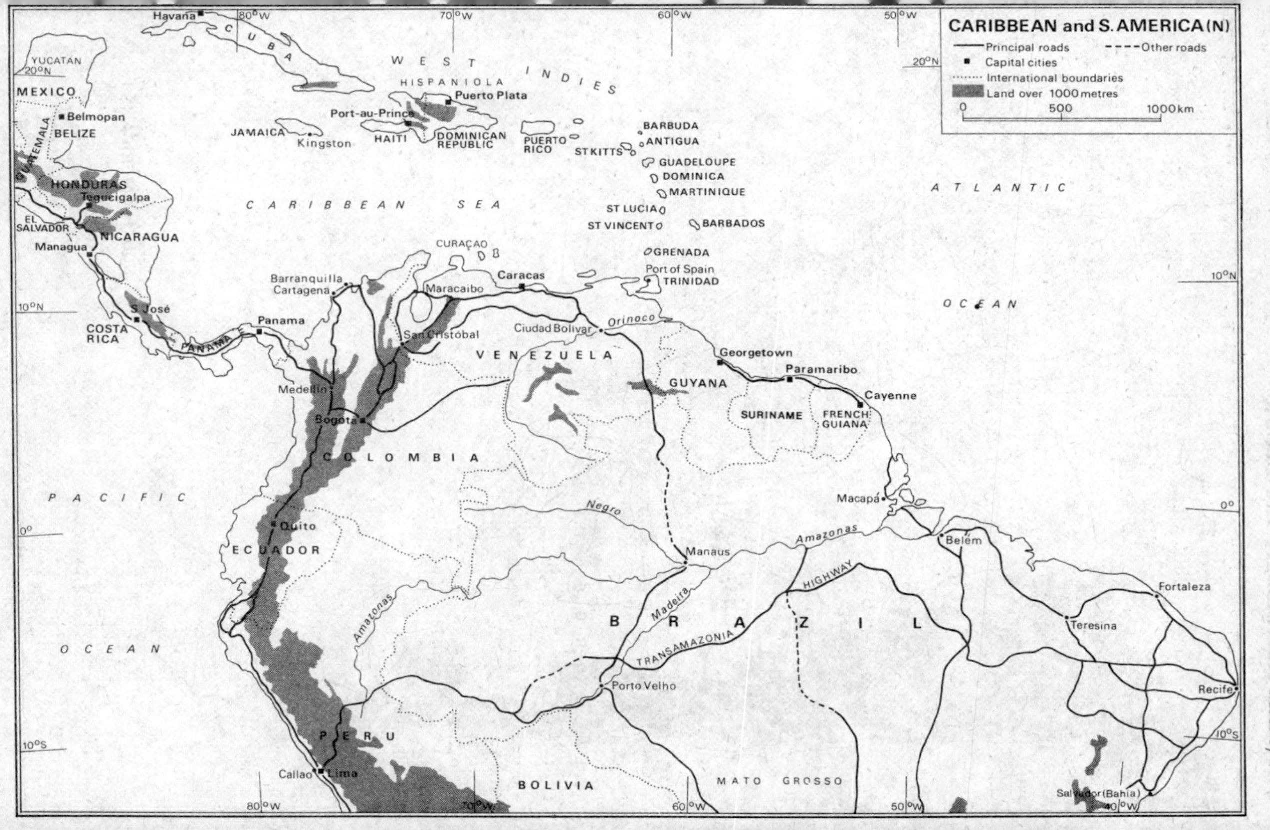
CARIBBEAN and S. AMERICA (N)
Principal roads
Other roads
Capital cities
International boundaries
Land over 1000 metres
0
500
1000km
CUBA
Havana
WEST INDIES
HISPANIOLA
Puerto Plata
Port-au-Prince
JAMAICA
Kingston
HAITI
DOMINICAN REPUBLIC
PUERTO RICO
ST KITTS
BARBUDA
ANTIGUA
GUADELOUPE
DOMINICA
MARTINIQUE
ST LUCIA
ST VINCENT
BARBADOS
GRENADA
Port of Spain
TRINIDAD
CURAÇAO
YUCATAN
MEXICO
Belmopan
BELIZE
GUATEMALA
HONDURAS
Tegucigalpa
EL SALVADOR
NICARAGUA
Managua
S. José
COSTA RICA
PANAMA
Panama
CARIBBEAN SEA
ATLANTIC
OCEAN
PACIFIC
OCEAN
Barranquilla
Cartagena
Maracaibo
Caracas
San Cristobal
Ciudad Bolivar
Orinoco
VENEZUELA
Georgetown
Paramaribo
Cayenne
GUYANA
SURINAME
FRENCH GUIANA
Medellin
Bogota
COLOMBIA
Negro
Macapá
Quito
ECUADOR
Manaus
Amazonas
Belém
HIGHWAY
Madeira
Fortaleza
Teresina
BRAZIL
TRANSAMAZONIA
Porto Velho
Recife
PERU
Callao
Lima
BOLIVIA
MATO GROSSO
Salvador (Bahia)
80°W
70°W
60°W
50°W
40°W
20°N
10°N
0°
10°S

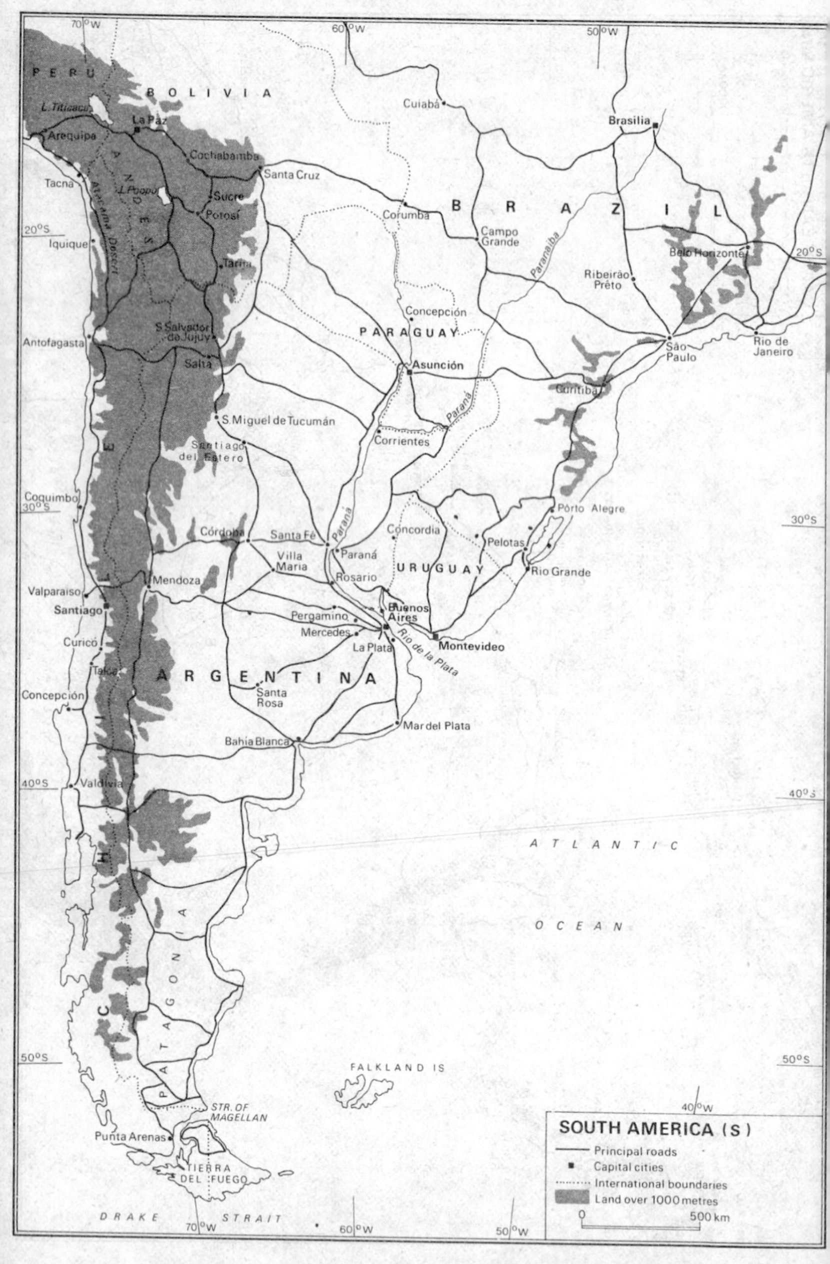
SOUTH AMERICA (S)
Principal roads
Capital cities
International boundaries
Land over 1000 metres
0
500 km
PERU
BOLIVIA
BRAZIL
PARAGUAY
URUGUAY
ARGENTINA
PATAGONIA
CHILE
ANDES
Atacama Desert
ATLANTIC
OCEAN
FALKLAND IS
STR. OF MAGELLAN
TIERRA DEL FUEGO
DRAKE STRAIT
L. Titicaca
L. Poopó
La Paz
Arequipa
Cochabamba
Santa Cruz
Tacna
Sucre
Potosí
Iquique
Tarija
Antofagasta
S. Salvador de Jujuy
Salta
S. Miguel de Tucumán
Santiago del Estero
Coquimbo
Córdoba
Santa Fé
Paraná
Villa Maria
Rosario
Mendoza
Valparaiso
Santiago
Pergamino
Mercedes
Buenos Aires
La Plata
Montevideo
Rio de la Plata
Curicó
Talca
Concepción
Santa Rosa
Mar del Plata
Bahía Blanca
Valdivia
Punta Arenas
Cuiabá
Brasília
Corumba
Campo Grande
Paranaiba
Belo Horizonte
Ribeirão Prêto
Concepción
Asunción
Corrientes
São Paulo
Rio de Janeiro
Curitiba
Paraná
Concordia
Pôrto Alegre
Pelotas
Rio Grande
70°W
60°W
50°W
40°W
20°S
30°S
40°S
50°S

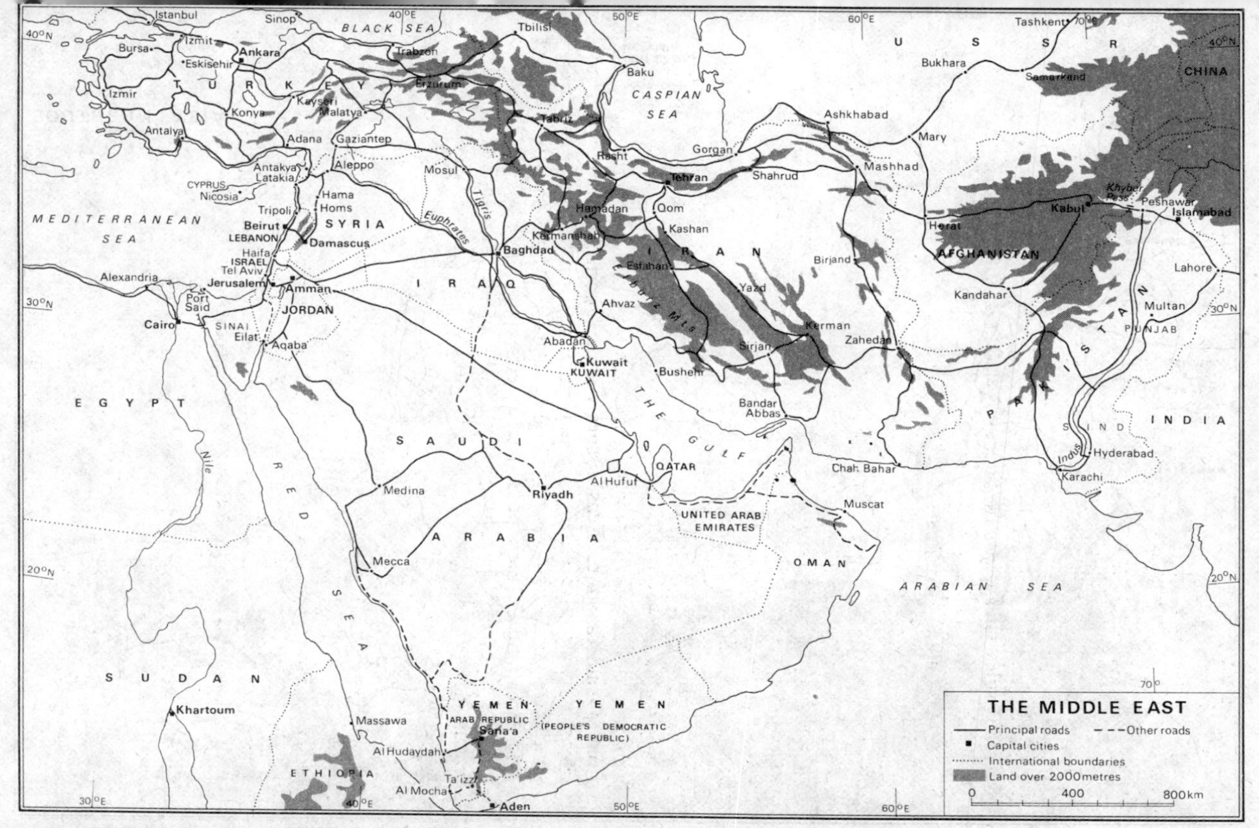
THE MIDDLE EAST
Principal roads
Other roads
Capital cities
International boundaries
Land over 2000metres
0 400 800km
U S S R
CHINA
AFGHANISTAN
PAKISTAN
INDIA
IRAN
IRAQ
TURKEY
SYRIA
LEBANON
ISRAEL
JORDAN
KUWAIT
QATAR
UNITED ARAB EMIRATES
OMAN
SAUDI ARABIA
YEMEN ARAB REPUBLIC
YEMEN (PEOPLE'S DEMOCRATIC REPUBLIC)
EGYPT
SUDAN
ETHIOPIA
CYPRUS
SINAI
PUNJAB
SIND
BLACK SEA
CASPIAN SEA
MEDITERRANEAN SEA
RED SEA
THE GULF
ARABIAN SEA
Tigris
Euphrates
Nile
Indus
Elburz Mts
Khyber Pass
Tashkent
Samarkand
Bukhara
Mary
Ashkhabad
Mashhad
Herat
Kandahar
Kabul
Peshawar
Islamabad
Lahore
Multan
Hyderabad
Karachi
Zahedan
Birjand
Kerman
Chah Bahar
Muscat
Bandar Abbas
Sirjan
Yazd
Shahrud
Gorgan
Tehran
Qom
Kashan
Esfahan
Bushehr
Ahvaz
Hamadan
Kermanshah
Rasht
Baku
Tbilisi
Tabriz
Baghdad
Abadan
Kuwait
Al Hufuf
Riyadh
Erzurum
Trabzon
Mosul
Medina
Mecca
Sana'a
Aden
Ta'izz
Al Mocha
Al Hudaydah
Massawa
Khartoum
Sinop
Ankara
Kayseri
Malatya
Gaziantep
Aleppo
Hama
Homs
Damascus
Amman
Aqaba
Eilat
Jerusalem
Tel Aviv
Haifa
Beirut
Tripoli
Latakia
Antakya
Adana
Konya
Eskisehir
Izmit
Istanbul
Bursa
Izmir
Antalya
Nicosia
Port Said
Cairo
Alexandria
40°N
30°N
20°N
30°E
40°E
50°E
60°E
70°E

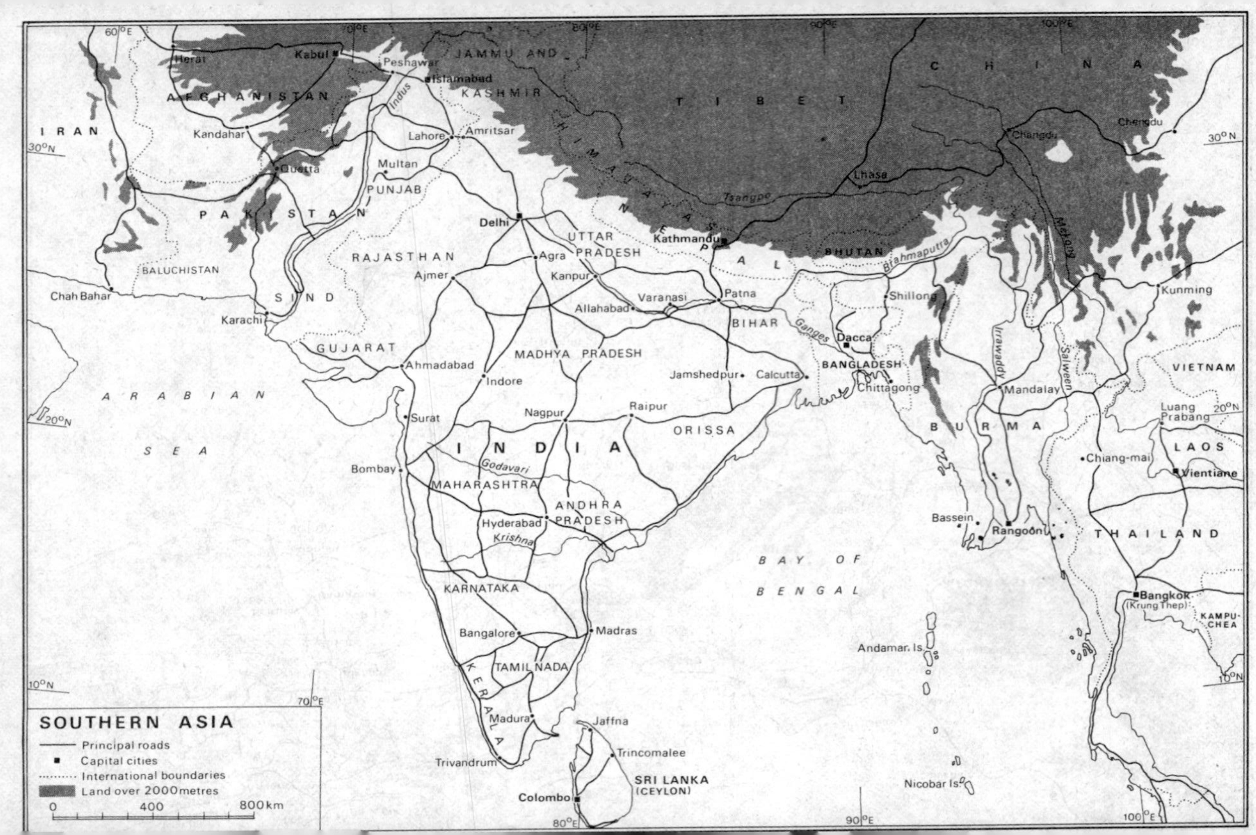
SOUTHERN ASIA
Principal roads
Capital cities
International boundaries
Land over 2000metres
0
400
800km
IRAN
AFGHANISTAN
Herat
Kandahar
Kabul
Quetta
Peshawar
Islamabad
BALUCHISTAN
PAKISTAN
Chah Bahar
Karachi
SIND
Indus
Multan
PUNJAB
Lahore
Amritsar
JAMMU AND KASHMIR
HIMALAYAS
TIBET
CHINA
Lhasa
Tsangpo
Chengdu
Changdu
Mekong
Kunming
NEPAL
Kathmandu
BHUTAN
Brahmaputra
Shillong
BANGLADESH
Dacca
Chittagong
Ganges
Delhi
UTTAR PRADESH
Agra
Kanpur
Allahabad
Varanasi
Patna
BIHAR
RAJASTHAN
Ajmer
GUJARAT
Ahmadabad
Surat
Bombay
MADHYA PRADESH
Indore
Jamshedpur
Calcutta
ORISSA
Raipur
Nagpur
INDIA
MAHARASHTRA
Godavari
ANDHRA PRADESH
Hyderabad
Krishna
KARNATAKA
Bangalore
Madras
TAMIL NADA
Madura
KERALA
Trivandrum
Jaffna
Trincomalee
SRI LANKA (CEYLON)
Colombo
ARABIAN SEA
BAY OF BENGAL
Andaman Is.
Nicobar Is.
BURMA
Irrawaddy
Mandalay
Salween
Bassein
Rangoon
VIETNAM
LAOS
Luang Prabang
Vientiane
Chiang-mai
THAILAND
Bangkok (Krung Thep)
KAMPU-CHEA
30°N
20°N
10°N
60°E
70°E
80°E
90°E
100°E

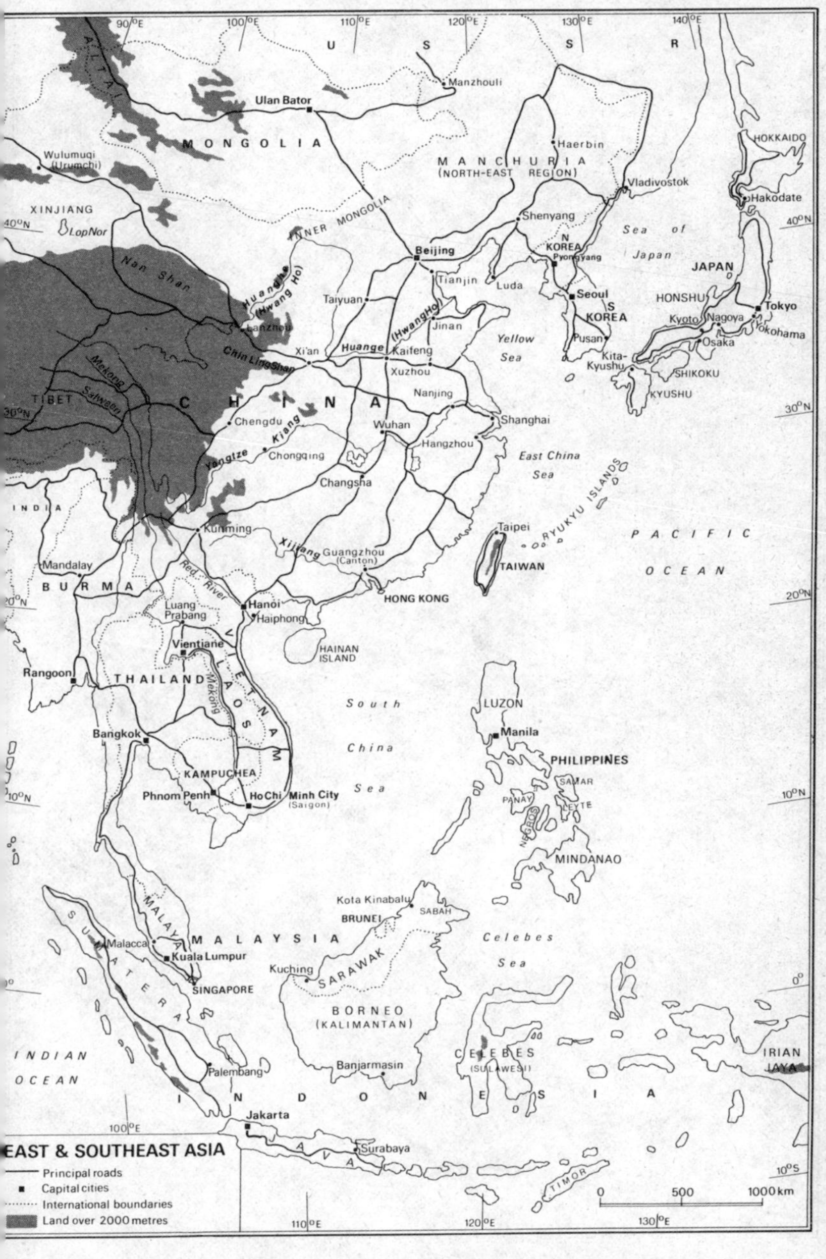
EAST & SOUTHEAST ASIA
Principal roads
Capital cities
International boundaries
Land over 2000 metres
0
500
1000 km
U S S R
MONGOLIA
Ulan Bator
Manzhouli
Wulumuqi (Urumchi)
XINJIANG
Lop Nor
ALTAI
INNER MONGOLIA
MANCHURIA (NORTH-EAST REGION)
Haerbin
Vladivostok
Shenyang
Beijing
Tianjin
Luda
N KOREA
Pyongyang
Seoul
S KOREA
Pusan
Nan Shan
Huanghe (Hwang Ho)
Taiyuan
Lanzhou
Chin Ling Shan
Xi'an
Huange
Kaifeng
(Hwang Ho)
Jinan
Xuzhou
Nanjing
Shanghai
Hangzhou
Wuhan
Chengdu
Chongqing
Yangtze Kiang
Changsha
TIBET
Mekong
Salween
CHINA
INDIA
Kunming
Xijiang
Guangzhou (Canton)
HONG KONG
Red River
Mandalay
BURMA
Hanoi
Haiphong
Luang Prabang
Vientiane
HAINAN ISLAND
Rangoon
THAILAND
LAOS
VIETNAM
Mekong
Bangkok
KAMPUCHEA
Phnom Penh
Ho Chi Minh City (Saigon)
MALAYA
MALAYSIA
Malacca
Kuala Lumpur
SINGAPORE
SUMATERA
Palembang
INDIAN OCEAN
INDONESIA
Jakarta
JAVA
Surabaya
TIMOR
Kota Kinabalu
SABAH
BRUNEI
SARAWAK
Kuching
BORNEO (KALIMANTAN)
Banjarmasin
CELEBES (SULAWESI)
Celebes Sea
IRIAN JAYA
South China Sea
LUZON
Manila
PHILIPPINES
SAMAR
PANAY
LEYTE
NEGROS
MINDANAO
Taipei
TAIWAN
RYUKYU ISLANDS
PACIFIC OCEAN
East China Sea
Yellow Sea
Sea of Japan
JAPAN
HOKKAIDO
Hakodate
HONSHU
Tokyo
Yokohama
Kyoto
Nagoya
Osaka
Kita-Kyushu
SHIKOKU
KYUSHU
90°E
100°E
110°E
120°E
130°E
140°E
40°N
30°N
20°N
10°N
0°
10°S

Rules and Regulations

DIRECTORY

British Government Representatives Overseas

Afghanistan	Karte Parwan, Kabul	30511/3
Algeria	Résidence Cassiopée, Bâtiment B, 7 Chemin des Glycines, Algiers (BP 43, Alger Gare)	605601/411/038/831
Angola	Rua Diogo Cao (CP 1244), Luanda	
Australia	Commonwealth Avenue, Canberra, ACT 2600	730422
or	Gold Fields House, Sydney Cove, Sydney, NSW 2000	27-7521
	There are also consulates in Melbourne, Brisbane, Perth and Adelaide	
Bahrain	PO Box 114, Government Road, North Manama, Bahrain	254002 (7 lines)
Bangladesh	DIT Building Annexe, Dilkhusha (PO Box 90), Dacca-2	243251-3, 244216-8 246867
Bolivia	Avenida Acre 2732-2754, La Paz (Casilla 694, La Paz)	51400/29404
Botswana	P Bag 23, Gaborone	2483/5
Brazil	Setor de Embaixadas Sul, Quadra 801 Conjunto K, Brasilia	225 2710/2625 2985/2745
or	Praia do Flamengo 284-2° andar Rio de Janeiro GB (Caixa Postal 669-ZC-00, Rio)	225-7252
or	Avenida Paulista 1938-17° andar, 01310, São Paulo (Caixa Postal 846), São Paulo SP	287-7722
Brunei	Room 45, 5th Floor, Hong Kong Bank Chambers, Djalan Chevalier, Bandar Seri Begawan, Brunei	26001/2
Burma	80 Strand Road, Rangoon (PO Box 638, Rangoon)	15700
Cameroon	Le Concorde, Av. Winston Churchill, Yaoundé (BP 547, Yaoundé)	220545
Chile	La Conceptión, 177 Providencia, Santiago (Casilla 72-D, Santiago)	239166
China	11 Kuang Hua Lu, Chien Kou Men Wai, Beijing	521961/4
Colombia	Calle 38, 13-35 Pisos 9-11, Bogotá (Apartado Aereo 4508, Bogotá)	698100
Costa Rica	Paseo Colon, 3203, Apartado 10056, San José	21-55-88
Cuba	Edificio Bolivar, Capdevila, 101-103, e Morro y Prado, Havana	61-5681
Dominican Rep.	Avenida Independencia No. 506, Santo Domingo	
Ecuador	(opp. Hotel Quito), Gonzalez Suarez, 111 Quito (Casilla 314, Quito)	230070/3

Egypt	Ahmed Raghab Street, Garden City, Cairo	20850/9
El Salvador	11a Avenida Norte (Bis), No. 611, Colonia Duenãs, San Salvador (Apartado (cc) 2350, San Salvador)	219106/220590, 223945
Ethiopia	Papassinos Bldg, Ras Desta Damtew Ave, Addis Ababa (PO Box 858, Addis Ababa)	15166/151252/3
Fiji	Civic Centre, Stinson Parade, Suva (PO Box 1355, Suva)	311033
Gabon	Bâtiment Sogame, Blvd de l'Indépendance, Libreville (BP 476, Libreville)	72-29-85
Gambia	48 Atlantic Road, Fajara, Banjul	Serrekunda 2133/2134/2578/2672
Ghana	Barclays Bank Bldg, High St, Accra (PO Box 296, Accra)	64123/34
Guatemala	Edificio Maya, Via 5, No 4-50, 8° Piso, Zona 4, Guatemala City	61329/64375
Guyana	44 Main Street, Georgetown (PO Box 625, Georgetown)	65881/4
Honduras	Apartado 290, Av. República de Chile, Tegucigalpa	22-31-91
Hong Kong	9th Floor, Gammon House, 12 Harcourt Rd, Hong Kong (PO Box 528, Hong Kong)	5-229541
Iceland	Laufasvegur 49, Reykjavik	15883/4
India	Chanakyapuri, New Delhi 21, 110021	690371
or	1 Ho Chi Minh Sarani, PO Box 9073, Calcutta, 700016	44-5171
or	PO Box 815, Mercantile Bank Bldgs, Mahatma Gandhi Road, Bombay, 400023	274874
or	PO Box 3710, 150A Anna Salai, Madras, 2-600002	83136
Indonesia	Djalan Thamrim 75, Djakarta	341091/8
Iran	Avenue Ferdowsi, Tehran (PO Box No 1513, Tehran)	375011 (10 lines)
Iraq	Sharia Salah, Ud-Din, Karkh, Baghdad	
Israel	192 Hayarkon St, Tel Aviv 63405	(03) 249171-8
Ivory Coast	5th Floor, Immeuble Shell, Av. Lamblin, Abidjan (BP 2581, Abidjan)	22-66-15/32-27-76/32-4980
Jamaica	Trafalgar Road, Kingston 10 (PO Box 575, Kingston)	926-9050
Japan	1 Ichibancho, Chiyoda-ku, Tokyo 102	(03) 265-5511
or	Hong Kong and Shanghai Bank Bldg, 45 Awajimachi, 4-chome, Higashi-ku, Osaka 541	(06) 231-3355/7
Jordan	Third Circle, Jebel Amman, Amman	37374-5
Kenya	13th Floor, Bruce House, Standard St, Nairobi (PO Box 30133, Nairobi)	335944
Korea	4 Chung-Dong, Sudaemoon-Ku, Seoul	75-7341/3
Kuwait	Arabian Gulf St, PO Box 300 Safat, Kuwait	439221/2
Laos	Rue Pandit J. Nehru, Vientiane (PO Box 224, Vientiane)	2333, 2374
Lebanon	Avenue de Paris, Ras Beirut, Beirut	36 41 08
Lesotho	PO Box 521, Maseru	3961

Liberia	PO Box 120, Mamba Point, Monrovia	221055/107/491
Madagascar	5 Rue Robert Ducrocq, Antananarivo (BP 167, Antananarivo)	251-51
Malawi	Lingadzi House, Lilongwe 3 (PO Box 300 42, Lilongwe)	31544
Malaysia	13th Floor, Wisma Damansara, Jalan Semantan, Kuala Lumpur (PO Box 1030, Kuala Lumpur)	941533
Mauritius	Cerné House, Chaussée, Port Louis (PO Box 586, Port Louis)	20201
Mexico	Lerma 71, Col Cuauhtémoc, Mexico City 5, DF (PO Box 96 Bis, Mexico City)	5114880/5143327
Mongolia	30 Enkh Taivny Gudamzh, Ulan Bator (PO Box 703, Ulan Bator)	51033
Morocco	17 Blvd. de la Tour, Rabat	20905/6
Mozambique	A. Vladimir I Lenine 310, Maputo (Caixa Postal 55, Maputo)	26011/2
Nepal	Lainchaur, Kathmandu (PO Box 106, Kathmandu)	11081, 11588/9
New Zealand	Reserve Bank of New Zealand Bldg, 9th Floor, The Terrace, Wellington 1. (PO Box 369, Wellington)	726-049
or	9th Floor, Norwich Union Bldg, 179 Queen Street, Auckland (P Bag, Auckland 1)	32-973
or	PO Box 1762, Christchurch	519-652
Nigeria	11 Eleke Crescent, Victoria Island, Lagos (PMB 12136, Lagos)	51630/1/2
or	Finance Corporation Building, Lebabon St, Ibadan (PMB 5010, Ibadan)	21551
or	United Bank for Africa Bldg, Hospital Road, Kaduna (PMB 2096, Kaduna)	22573/5
Oman	Muscat (PO Box 300, Muscat)	722411
Pakistan	Diplomatic Enclave, Ramma 5 Islamabad (PO Box 1122, Islamabad)	22131/5
or	York Place, Runnymede Lane, Port Trust Estate, Clifton, Karachi-6	53 20 41/46
Panama	Via España 120, Panama City (Apartado 889, Panama City)	23-0451
Papua New Guinea	United Church Bldg, 3rd Floor, Douglas St, Port Moresby (PO Box 739, Port Moresby)	212500
Paraguay	Calle Presidente Franco 706, Asunción (PO Box 404, Asunción)	49-146/44-472
Peru	Edificio Pacifico-Washington, Plaza Washington, Avenida Arequipa (sextra cuadra, Lima (PO Box 854, Lima)	283830
Philippines	Electra House, 115-117 Esteban St, Legaspi Village, Makati, Metro Manila (PO Box 1970 MCC, Manila)	8910-51/8
Qatar	PO Box 3, Doha	321991/4
Rwanda	PO Box 320, Kigali	5905
Saudi Arabia	Jeddah Towers, Citibank Bldg, Jeddah (PO Box 393, Jeddah)	27306/27122
Sénégal	20 Rue du Docteur Guillet, Dakar (BP 6025, Dakar)	27051
Seychelles	Victoria House, 3rd Floor, Victoria (PO Box 161, Victoria)	23055/6

Sierra Leone	Standard Bank of Sierra Leone Bldg, Lightfoot Boston St, Freetown	23961-5
Singapore	Tanglin Circus, Singapore 10 (Tanglin PO Box 19, Singapore)	639333
Solomon Islands	PO Box 676, Honiara	705706
Somalia	Waddada Xasan Geeddii Abtoow 7/8, Mogadishu (PO Box 1036, Mogadishu)	22088/9, 34072/3
South Africa	6 Hill St, Arcadia, Pretoria 0002	74-3121
or	5th Floor, Nedbank Mall, 145/7, Commissioner St, Johannesburg 2000 (PO Box 10101, Jo'burg)	218161
or	11th Floor, African Eagle Centre, 2 St. Georges St, Cape Town 8000 (PO Box 1346, Cape Town)	41-1466/8
or	7th Floor, Barclays Bank Bldg, Field St, Durban 4001	313131 (5 lines)
Sri Lanka	Galle Road, Kollupitiya, Colombo 3 (PO Box 1433, Colombo)	27611/17
Sudan	New Aboulela Bldg, Barlaman Ave, Khartoum	70760/6-9
Suriname	c/o VSH United Bldg, Vant Hogechuyasstraat, Paramaribo (PO Box 1300, Paramaribo)	72870
Swaziland	Allister Miller St, Mbabane (P Bag, Mbabane)	42581/6
Syria	Quartier Malki, 11 Mohammed Kurd Ali St, Immeuble Kotob, Damascus	712561
Tanzania	Permanent House, corner Azikiwe St/ Independence Ave, Dar es Salaam (PO Box 9112, Dar es Salaam)	29601
Thailand	Wireless Road, Bangkok	2527161/0
Tonga	PO Box 56, Nuku'alofa	21-020
Trinidad & Tobago	Furness House, Independence Square, Port-of-Spain	62-52861
Tunisia	5 Place de la Victoire, Tunis	245100/324/ 649/244805
Turkey	Sehit Ersan Caddesi, 46a Canyaka, Ankara	274310/5
or	Tepebasi, Beyoglu, Istanbul	4475459/498874
Uganda	10/12 Parliament Ave, Kampala	57301/4
USSR	Naberezhnaya Morisa Teresa 14, Moscow 72	2411033/4 Outside office hours 231-8511/2 231-2331
United Arab Emirates	PO Box 248, Abu Dhabi	43033/4/5
Uruguay	Calle Marco Bruto 1073, Montevideo	791033
Venezuela	Avenida La Estancia No 10, Ciudad Commercial, Tamanaco, Caracas, (Apartado 1246, Caracas)	91-12-55/91-14-77
Vietnam	16 Pho Ly Thuong Kiet, Hanoi	52349/52510
Yemen Arab Rep	13 Al Qasr al Jumhuri, Sana'a (PO Box 1287, Sana'a)	5428
South Yemen	28 Ho Chi Minh St, Khormaksar, Aden	24801-4
Zaïre	9 Avenue de l'Equateur, 5th Floor, Kinshasa (BP 8049, Kinshasa)	23483/6, 22666
Zambia	Independence Ave, Lusaka (PO Box 50050, Lusaka)	216770
Zimbabwe	Stanley House, Stanley Ave, Harare (PO Box 4490, Harare)	793781

United States Embassies Worldwide

Telephone numbers are preceded by direct-dial country and city codes where available.

Afghanistan	Wazir Akbar Khan Mina, Kabul	24230-9
Algeria	4 Chemin Cheich Bachir Brahimi, Algiers	601425
Argentina	4300 Colombia, Buenos Aires	54-1-774 7611
Australia	Moonah Place, Canberra	61-62-73 3711
Austria	IX Boltzmanngasse 16 A-1091, Vienna	43-222-31-55-11
Bahamas	Mosmar Building, Queen St, Nassau	609-322-4753
Bahrain	Shalkh Isa Road, Manama	973-714151
Bangladesh	Adamjee Court, Motijheel, Dacca	244220
Barbados	PO Box 302, Bridgetown	63574-7
Belgium	27 Blvd du Régent, Brussels	32-2-513-3830
Benin	Rue Caporal Anani Bernard, Cotonou	31-26-92
Bolivia	Banco Popular Del Peru Bldg, La Paz	591-2-350251
Botswana	Box 90, Gaborone	53982
Brazil	Avenida das Nocoes, Brasilia	55-61-223-0120
Bulgaria	1 Stamboliiski Blvd, Sofia	88-48-01
Burma	581 Merchant St, Rangoon	82055
Burundi	Chaussée Prince Louis Rwagasore, Bujumbura	34-54
Cameroon	Rue Nachtigal, Yaoundé	221633
Canada	100 Wellington St, Ottawa	613-238-5335
Cape Verde	Rua Hoji Ya Yenna 81, Praia	553
Central African Republic	Ave. President Dacko, Bangui	61-02-00
Chile	1343 Agustinas, Santiago	56-2-710133
China	Guang Hau Lu 17, Beijing	52-2033
Colombia	Calle 37, Bogotá	57-285-1300
Congo	Ave. Amilcar Cabral, Brazzaville	81-20-70
Costa Rica	Avenida 3 & Calle 1, San José	506-22-55-66
Cyprus	Therissos & Dositheos Sts, Nicosia	357-21-65151
Czechoslovakia	Trziste 15-12548, Prague	53-66-41
Denmark	Dag Hammarskjold Alle 24, Copenhagen	45-1-42-31-44
Djibouti	Villa Plateau du Serpent Blvd, Djibouti	35-38-49
Dominican Rep.	Calles Cesar Nicolas Penson & Leopoldo Navarro, Santo Domingo	682-2171
Ecuador	120 Avenida Patria, Quito	593-2-548-000
Egypt	5 Sharia Latin America, Cairo	28219
El Salvador	25 Avenida Norte, San Salvador	503-26-7100
Ethiopia	Entoto St, Addis Ababa	110666
Fiji	31 Loftus St, Suva	679-23031
Finland	Itainen Puistotie 14A, Helsinki	358-0-171931
France	2 Av. Gabriel, Paris	33-1-296-1202
Gabon	Blvd de la Mer, Libreville	72-20-03
Gambia	16 Buckle St, Banjul	526-7
German Dem. Rep.	Neustaedtische Kirchstrasse 4-5, Berlin	37-2-2202741

Fed. Rep. Germany	Delchmannsaue, Bonn	49-228-339-3390
Ghana	Liberia and Kinbu Roads, Accra	66811
Greece	91 Vasilissis Sophias Blvd, Athens	30-1-712951
Guatemala	7-01 Avenida de la Reforma, Guatemala	31-15-41
Guinea	Second Blvd & Ninth Ave, Conakry	415-40
Guinea-Bissau	Avenida Domingos Ramos, Bissau	28-16
Guyana	31 Main St, Georgetown	592-02-54900
Haiti	Harry Truman Blvd, Port-au-Prince	509-1-20200
Honduras	Avenido La Paz, Tegucigalpa	504-22-3121
Hungary	V Szabadsag Ter 12, Budapest	329-375
Iceland	Laufasvegur 21, Reykjavik	28100
India	Shanti Path, Chanakyapuri 21, New Delhi	690351
Indonesia	Medan Merdeka Selatan 5, Jakarta	62-21-340001-9
Ireland	42 Elgin St, Ballsbridge, Dublin	353-1-688777
Israel	71 Hayarkon St, Tel Aviv	972-3-654338
Italy	Via Veneto 119/A, Rome	39-6-06-4674
Ivory Coast	5 Rue Jesse Owens, Abidjan	32-09-79
Jamaica	2 Oxford Road, Kingston	809-92-94850
Japan	10-5 Akasaka 1-chome, Minato-ku, Tokyo	81-3-583-7141
Jordan	King Faisal St, Amman	38930
Kenya	Wabera St, Nairobi	254-2-334141
Korea	Sejong-Ro, Seoul	82-272-2601
Kuwait	Box 77, Kuwait	965-424151
Laos	Rue Bartholomie, Vientiane	3126
Lebanon	Corniche & Rue Ain Mreisseh, Beirut	361-800
Lesotho	Box MS 333, Maseru	22666
Liberia	111 United Nations Drive, Monrovia	231-22991
Libya	Shari Mohammad Thabit, Tripoli	34021
Luxembourg	22 Blvd Emmanuel Servals, Luxembourg	352-40123
Madagascar	14 Rue Rainitovo Antsohavala, Antananarivo	212-57
Malawi	Box 30016, Lilongwe	730-166
Malaysia	AIA Bldg, Jalan Ampang, Kuala Lumpur	60-3-26321
Mali	Rue Testard & Rue Mohamed V, Bamako	225834
Malta	Saint Anne St, Floriana, Valletta	623653
Mauritania	BP 222, Nouakchott	52660
Mauritius	John Kennedy St, Port Louis	2-3218
Mexico	Paseo de la Reforma 305, Mexico City	905-553-3333
Morocco	2 Av. de Marrakesh, Rabat	30361
Mozambique	35 Rua da Mesquita, Maputo	26051
Nepal	Pani Pokhari, Kathmandu	11199
Netherlands	Lange Vorhout 102, The Hague	31-70-62-49-11
New Zealand	29 Fitzherbert Terrace, Thorndon, Wellington	64-4-722-068
Nicaragua	Km 4½ Carretera Sur, Managua	505-2-23061
Niger	BP 11201, Niamey	72-26-61
Nigeria	2 Eleke Crescent, Lagos	610097

Norway	Drammensveien 18, Oslo	47-2-56-68-80
Oman	Box 966, Muscat	745-231
Pakistan	AID/UN Bldg, Islamabad	24071
Panama	Avenida Balboa & Calle 38, Panama	507-27-1777
Papua New Guinea	Armit St, Port Moresby	675-121-211455
Paraguay	1776 Mariscal Lopez Ave, Asunción	595-21-201-041
Peru	Avdas España & Inca Garcilaso de la Vega, Lima	51-14-286000
Philippines	1201 Roxas Blvd, Manila	63-2-598-011
Poland	Aleje Ujazdowskie 29/31, Warsaw	283041-9
Portugal	Avenida Duque de Loule 39, Lisbon	351-19-570102
Qatar	Fariq Bin Oman, Doha	870701
Romania	Strade Tudor Arghezi 7-9, Bucharest	40-0-12-4-40
Rwanda	Blvd de la Révolution, Kigali	5601
Saudi Arabia	Palestine Road, Ruwais, Jeddah	966-21-6670080
Sénégal	Avenue Jean XXIII, Dakar	21-42-96
Seychelles	Box 148, Victoria	23921
Sierra Leone	Walpole & Siaka Stevens Sts, Freetown	26481
Singapore	30 Hill St, Singapore	65-30251
Somalia	Corso Primo Luglio, Mogadishu	28011
South Africa	225 Pretorius St, Pretoria	27-12028-4266
Spain	Serrano 75, Madrid	34-1-276-3400
Sri Lanka	44 Galle Road, Colombo	21271
Sudan	Gamhouria Ave, Khartoum	74611
Suriname	Dr Sophie Redmondstraat 13, Paramaribo	73024
Swaziland	Warner St, Mbabane	22281
Sweden	Stradvagen 101, Stockholm	46-8-63-05-20
Switzerland	Jubilaeumstrasse 93, Bern	41-31-437011
Syria	Abu Rumaneh, Al Mansur St, Damascus	332315
Tanzania	City Drive, Dar es Salaam	68894
Thailand	95 Wireless Road, Bangkok	66-2-252-5040
Togo	Rue Pelletier Ceventou & Rue Vouban, Lomé	29-91
Trinidad & Tobago	15 Queen's Park West, Port-of-Spain	62-26371
Tunisia	144 Av. de la Liberté, Tunis	282-566
Turkey	110 Ataturk Blvd, Ankara	90-41-26-54-70
USSR	Ulitsa Chaykovskogo 19, Moscow	252-24-51
United Arab Emirates	Corniche Road, Abu Dhabi	971-2-361534
United Kingdom	24 Grosvenor Square, London W1	44-1-499-9000
Upper Volta (Burkina Faso)	BP 35, Ouagadougou	35442
Uruguay	Calle Lauro Muller 1776, Montevideo	40-90-51
Venezuela	Avdas Francisco de Miranda & Principal de la Floresta, Caracas	58-2-284-7111
Yemen Arab Rep.	Box 1088, Sana'a	72790
Yugoslavia	Kneza Milosa 50, Belgrade	38-11-645655
Zaïre	310 Av. des Aviateurs, Kinshasa	25881

Zambia	Box 1617, Lusaka	214911
Zimbabwe	78 Enterprise Rd, Highlands, Harare	791588

Australian Government Representation Worldwide

Algeria	60 Blvd Colonel Bougara, El-Biar, Algiers
Argentina	Avenida Santa Fé 846, Piso Swiss Air Bldg, Buenos Aires
Austria	Mattiellistrasse 2-4, A-1040, Vienna
Bangladesh	184 Gulshan Avenue, Gulshan
Bahrain	2nd Floor, Bahrain Chamber of Commerce Bldg, King Faisal Road, Manama
Belgium	5th, 6th, and 7th Floors, 52 Avenue des Arts, 1040 Brussels
Brazil	SHIS Q19, Conjunto 16, Casa 1, Brasilia DF (Caixa Postal 11-1256)
or	Rua Voluntarious Da Patria, 45/5 Andar, 5th Fllor, Botfogo-RJ, 22270 Rio de Janeiro, RJ
Britain	Australia House, The Strand, London WC2B 4LA
Burma	88 Strand Road, Rangoon
Canada	13th Floor, National Bldg, 130 Slater St, Ottawa K1P 5H6
Chile	420 Gertrudis Echenique, Las Condes, Santiago (PO Box 33, Correo 10)
China	15 Donzhimenwai St, San Li Tun, Beijing
Cyprus	2nd Floor, 4 Annis Kominis St, Nicosia
Denmark	Kristianagrade 21, DK-2100 Copenhagen
Egypt	1097 Corniche el Nil, Garden City, Cairo
Fiji	7th and 8th Floors, Dominion House, Thomson St, Suva (PO Box 214, Suva)
France	4 Rue Jean Rey, 75724 Paris
German Dem. Rep.	1110 Berlin-Niederschoenhausen, Grabbealle 34-40, Berlin (Postfach 650149, 1 Berlin 65)
Fed. Rep. of Germany	Godesburger Allee 107, 5300 Bonn 2, Bonn
Ghana	Milne Close, off Dr Amilcar Cabral Rd, Airport Residential Area, Accra (PO Box 2445, Accra)
Greece	15 Messogeion St, Ambelokipi, Athens (PO Box 3070, Ambelokipi)
Hong Kong	10th Floor, Connaught Centre, Connaught Rd, Hong Kong
India	No. 1/50-G Shanti Path, Chanakyapuri, New Delhi (PO Box 5210, New Delhi)
or	16th Floor, Maker Towers, E Block, Colaba, Bombay (PO Box 9937, Bombay)
Indonesia	Jalan Thamrin 15, Gambir, Jakarta
or	Jalan Raya, Sanur 146, Den Pasar, Bali (PO Box 279, Den Pasar)
Iran	123 Shalid Khalis Al-Islam Buli Avenue, Abassabad, Tehran
Iraq	Masbah 141/377, Baghdad
Ireland	Fitzwilton House, Wilton Terrace, Dublin 2
Israel	185 Hayarkon St, Tel Aviv
Italy	Via Alessandria 215, Rome 00198
Jamaica	4th Floor, National Life Bldg, 64 Knutsford Blvd, Kingston 5 (PO Box 560, Kingston)
Japan	No. 1-14 Mita 2-Chome, Minato-Ku, Tokyo
Jordan	Between 4th and 5th Circles, Wadi Sir Road, Jabel Amman, Amman (PO Box 35201, Amman)
Kenya	Development House, Moi Ave, Nairobi (PO Box 30360, Nairobi)

Kiribati	Tarawa (PO Box 77, Bairiki)
Korea	5th Floor, Kukong-Shell Building, 58-1, Shinmoonro, 1-Ka, Chongro-Ku, Seoul (KPO Box 562 Kang-Uha-Moon)
Kuwait	7th Floor, Al-Rashed Building, Fahd Al-Salem St, Kuwait (PO Box 25657, Safat, Kuwait)
Laos	Rue J. Nehru, Quartier Phone Xay, Vientiane (BP 292, Vientiane)
Lebanon	Farra Building, 463 Bliss St, Ras, Beirut
Malaysia	6 Jalan Yap Kwan Seng, Kuala Lumpur
Malta	6th Floor, Gaiety Lane, Sliema
Mexico	Paseo de la Reforma 195, 5° Piso, Mexico 5, DF, Mexico City
Nauru	Civic Centre, Nauru
Netherlands	Koninginnegracht 23/24, 2514AB The Hague
New Caledonia	8th Floor, 18 Rue du Maréchal Foch, Noumea (BP 22, Noumea)
New Zealand	72-78 Hobson St, Thorndon, Wellington (PO Box 12145, Wellington)
Nigeria	Plot 738, 16 Adeola Hopewell Rd, Victoria Island, Lagos (PO Box 2427, Lagos)
Pakistan	Plot 17, Sector G4/4, Diplomatic Enclave No. 2, Islamabad (PO Box 1046, Islamabad)
Papua New Guinea	Waigani, Hohola, Port Moresby (PO Box 9129, Port Moresby)
Peru	6th Floor, Edificio Plaza, Natalio Sanchez 220, Lima (Casilla 2977, Lima)
Phillippines	China Banking Corporation Bld, Paseo de Roxas (cnr Villar St), Makati, Rizal (PO Box 1274, Rizal)
Poland	3/5 Ulica Estonska, Saska Kepa, Warsaw
Portugal	Avenida de Liberdade 244-40, Lisbon 2
Saudi Arabia	Off Hamra Road, nr Medina Road, Jeddah (PO Box 4876, Jeddah)
Singapore	25 Napier Road, Singapore 10 (Tanglin PO Box 470, Singapore 10)
Solomon Islands	Hong Kong and Shanghai Bank Bldg, Mendana Ave, Honiara (PO Box 589, Honiara)
South Africa	302 Standard Bank Chambers, Church Square, Pretoria
or	10th Floor, 1001 Colonial Mutual Building, 106 Adderly St, Cape Town (PO Box 4749, Cape Town)
Spain	Paseo de la Castellano 143, Madrid 16
Sri Lanka	3 Cambridge Place, Colombo 7 (PO Box 742, Colombo)
Sweden	Sergels Torg 12, Stockholm (Box 7003, S-103 86 Stockholm)
Switzerland	29 Alpenstrasse, Berne
or	56-58 Rue de Moillebeau, Petit Saconnex 1211, Geneva 19
Syria	128A Farabi St, Mezzeh, Damascus (PO Box 3882, Damascus)
Tanzania	7th and 8th Floors, NLC Investment Bldg, Independence Ave, Dar es Salaam (PO Box 2969, Dar es Salaam)
Thailand	37 South Sathorn Road, Bangkok 12
Tonga	Salote Road, Nuku'alofa
Turkey	83 Nenehatun Caddesi, Gazi Osman, Pasa, Ankara
USSR	13 Kropotkinsky Pereulok, Moscow
United Arab Emirates	Sayed Mohammed Glass Tower Bldg, 14th Floor, Tourist Club Area, nr Tourist Club Gates, Abu Dhabi (PO Box 559, Abu Dhabi)
United States	1601 Massachusetts Ave, Washington DC 20036
or	International Building, 636 Fifth Ave, New York, NY 10020
	There are also consulates in Chicago, Honolulu, Houston, Los Angeles, and San Francisco
Vanuatu	Melitco House, Vila (PO Box 111, Vila)

Venezuela	Centro Plaza, 18th Floor, Torre A, Avenida Francisco de Miranda, Caracas
Vietnam	66 Ly Thuong Kiet, Hanoi
Western Samoa	Fea Gai Ma Leata Building, Beach Road, Tamaligi, Apia (PO Box 704, Apia)
Yugoslavia	13 Cjika Ljubina, 11000 Belgrade 6
Zambia	3rd Floor, Memaco House, Sapele Road (off Southend Road, Cairo Road) Lusaka (PO Box 35395, Lusaka)
Zimbabwe	3rd Floor, Throgmorton House, Cnr Samora Machel Ave and Julius Nyerere Way, Harare (PO Box 4541, Harare)

Canadian Government Representatives Abroad

Algeria	27 bis Rue d'Anjou, Hydra, Algiers (PO Box 225, Gare Alger, Algiers)	60 66 11
Argentina	Brunetta Bldg, Suipacha and Santa Fé, Buenos Aires (Casilla de Correo 1598, Buenos Aires)	32 90 81/8
Australia	Commonwealth Ave, Canberra, ACT 2600	(062) 73 3844
or	17th Floor, Prince's Gate East Tower, 151 Flinders St, Melbourne, Vic. 3000	63 8431
or	8th Floor, AMP Centre, 50 Bridge St, Sydney, NSW 2000	(02) 231 6522
Bangladesh	House CWN16/A, Road 48, Gulshan, Dacca (GPO Box 569, Dacca)	300181-5
Bolivia	Alborada Bldg, Office 508, 1420 J. De La Riva St, La Paz (Casilla 20408, La Paz)	3705224
Brazil	Ave des Nacoes, Number 16, Setor das Embaixadas Sul, Brasilia (Caixa Postal 07-0961, 70000 Brasilia, DF)	(61) 223 7515
or	Edificio Metropole, Ave Presidente Wilson 165, 6 Andar, Rio de Janeiro (Caixa Postal 2164-ZC-00, Rio de Janeiro)	240 9912
or	Edificio Top Center, Ave Paulista 854, 5th Floor, São Paulo (Caixa Postal 22002, São Paulo)	287 2122/2234/2213/2601, 285 3217/3240
Cameroon	Immeuble Soppo Priso, Rue Conrad Adenauer, Yaoundé (PO Box 572, Yaoundé)	22 22 03, 22 29 22, 22 19 36
Chile	Ahumada 11, 10th Floor, Santiago (Casilla 427, Santiago)	62256/7/8/9
China	10 San Li Tun Road, Chao Yang District, Beijing	521475/571/724/741/684
Colombia	Calle 76, No 11-52, 4th Floor, Bogotá (Apartado Aereo 53531, Bogotá)	235 5066
Costa Rica	6th Floor, Cronos Bldg, Calle 3 y Ave Central, San José (Apartado Postal 10303, San José)	23 04 46
Cuba	Calle 300, No 518 Esquina a7a, Miramar, Havana (PO Box 499 (HVA), Ottawa, KIN 8T7, Canada)	26421/2/3
Dominican Rep.	Mahatma Gandhi 200, Corner Juan Sanchez, Ramirez, Santo Domingo 1	(809) 689 0002
Ecuador	Edificio Belmonte, 146 Corea y Amazonas, 6th Floor, Quito (Sucursal 11CCI)	
Egypt	6 Sharia Mohamed Fahmi el Sayed, Garden City, Cairo (Post: Kasr el Doubara PO, Cairo)	23110
Ethiopia	African Solidarity Insurance Bldg, Unity Square, Addis Ababa (PO Box 1130, Addis Ababa)	44 83 35/6
Gabon	PO Box 4037, Libreville	72-41-54/56/69

Ghana	E 115/3 Independence Ave, Accra (PO Box 1639, Accra)	28555/02
Guatemala	Galerias España, 6th Floor, 7 Avenida 11–59, Zone 9, Guatemala City (PO Box 400, Guatemala, CA)	64955/6/7, 65839, 63049
Guyana	High and Young Streets, Georgetown (PO Box 660, Georgetown)	72081/5
Haiti	Edifice Banque Nova Scotia, Route de Delmas, Port-au-Prince (CP 826, Port-au-Prince)	2-2358, 2-4231, 2-4919
Hong Kong	14/15 Flrs, Asian House, 1 Hennessy Road, Hong Kong (PO Box 20264, Hong Kong)	5-282222/3/4/5/6/7, 5-282422/3
Iceland	Skulagata 20, Reykjavik	25355, 15337
India	7/8 Shanti Path, Chanakyapuri, New Delhi 110021 (PO Box 5207, New Delhi)	61 9461
Indonesia	5th Floor, WISMA Metropolitan, Djl Djendral Sudirman, Jakarta (PO Box 52/JKT, Jakarta)	584030-9 (day), 584031 (night)
Iran	57 Darya-e-Noor Ave, Takht-e-Tavoos, Tehran (PO Box 1610, Tehran) *Currently no ambassador. Consular services c/o Royal Danish Embassy, Tehran, immigration enquiries c/o Canadian Embassy, Kuwait.*	623177/548/549/ 192/629/202 622310/975
Iraq	47/1/7 Al Mansour, Baghdad (PO Box 323, Central Post Office, Baghdad)	552 1459/1932/3
Israel	220 Hayarkon St, Tel Aviv (PO Box 6410, Tel Aviv)	22 2822/3/4/5/6
Ivory Coast	Immeuble 'Le Général', 4ème et 5ème étages, Av Botreau-Roussel, Abidjan (01 CP 4104, Abidjan 01)	32 20 09
Jamaica	Royal Bank Bldg, 30–36 Knutsford Blvd, Kingston 5 (PO Box 1500, Kingston 10)	926 1500/ 1/2/3/4/5/6/7
Japan	3-38 Akasaka 7-chome, Minato-ku, Tokyo 107	408 2101-8
Kenya	Comcraft House, Hailé Sélassie Ave, Nairobi (PO Box 30481, Nairobi)	334 033/4/5/6
Korea	10th Floor, Kolon Bldg, 45 Mugyo-Dong, Jung-Ku, Seoul (PO Box 6299, Seoul 100)	776 4062/8
Kuwait	28 Quraish St, Nuzha District, Kuwait City (PO Box 25281, Safat, Kuwait City)	511451, 555754, 555934
Lebanon	Immeuble Sabbagh, Rue Hamra, Beirut (CP 2300, Beirut)	350 660/1/2/3/4/5
Malaysia	American International Assurance Bldg, Ampang Road, Kuala Lumpur (PO Box 990, Kuala Lumpur)	89722/3/4
Mexico	Melchor Ocampo 463-7, Mexico 5, DF	533 06 10
or	Hotel el Mirador Plaza, La Quebrada 74, Acapulco, Gro	3 72 91
or	Ave Vallarta No 1373, Guadalajara, Jalisco (PO Box 32-6, Jalisco)	(36) 25 9932
Morocco	13 bis Rue Jafaar As-Sadik, Rabat-Agdal (CP709, Rabat-Agdal)	71-375/6/7
New Zealand	ICI Bldg, Molesworth St, Wellington (PO Box 12-049, Wellington North)	739 577
Nigeria	Niger House, Tinubu St, Lagos (PO Box 851, Lagos)	660 130/153/177/ 201/211
Pakistan	Diplomatic Enclave, Sector G-5, Islamabad (GPO Box 1042, Islamabad)	21101/4/9, 21302/6, 21318

Paraguay	AZARA 532, Asunción (Casilla de Correo 173, Asunción)	43506/7
Peru	132 Calle Libertad, Miraflores, Lima (Casilla 1212, Lima)	46 38 90
Philippines	4th Floor, PAL Bldg, Ayala Ave, Makati, Rizal, Manila (PO Box 971, Commercial Centre, Makati, Rizal)	87 65 36, 87 78 46
Saudi Arabia	6th Floor, Office Tower, Commercial and Residential Centre, King Abdul Aziz St, Jeddah (PO Box 5050, Jeddah)	643 4900/4597/8/ 4587, 642 9798
Sénégal	45 Av. de la République, Dakar (PO Box 3373, Dakar)	210290
Singapore	Faber House, 7th, 8th & 9th Floors, 230 Orchard Road, Singapore 0923 (PO Box 845, Singapore 9016)	737 1322
South Africa	Nedbank Plaza, Cnr Church and Beatrix Streets, Arcadia, Pretoria 0083 (PO Box 26006, Arcadia, Pretoria 0007)	28 7062; at night 28-33
Sri Lanka	6 Gregory's Rd, Cinnamon Gardens, Colombo 7 (PO Box 1006, Colombo)	95841-3
Tanzania	Pan Africa Insurance Bldg, Independence Ave, Dar es Salaam (PO Box 1022, Dar es Salaam)	20651
Thailand	Boonmitr Bldg, 11th Floor, 138 Silom Road, Bangkok 5 (PO Box 2090, Bangkok)	234 1561-8
Tunisia	2 Place Vergile, Notre-Dame de Tunis, Tunis (CP 31, Belvédère, Tunis)	286 577
Turkey	Nenehatun Caddesi 75, Gaziosmanpasa, Ankara	27 58 03/4/5
USSR	23 Starokonyushenny Pereulok, Moscow	241 9155/ 3067/5070
Upper Volta (Burkina Faso)	PO Box 548, Ouagadougou	320 93
Venezuela	Ave La Estancia No 10, 16 piso Cuidad Commercial Tamanaco, Caracas (Apartado del Este No 62302, Caracas)	91 32 77
Zaïre	Edifice Shell, coin Av. Wangata et Blvd du 30-juin, Kinshasa (PO Box 8341, Kinshasa)	227 06, 243 46
Zambia	Barclays Bank, North End Branch, Cairo Road, Lusaka (PO Box 1313, Lusaka)	75187/8
Zimbabwe	45 Bainef Avenue, Harare (PO Box 1430, Harare)	

New Zealand Government Offices Worldwide

Australia		Commonwealth Avenue, Canberra, ACT 2600	(062) 73 3611 *Telex:* 71-62019 *Cable:* KAURI
Austria		Hollandstrasse 2/XII, Vienna	(0222) 26 44 81/82 *Telex:* 47-136582 *Cable:* WEKA
	or	PO Box 1471, A-1011, Vienna	
Bahrain		1st Floor, Manama Centre Building, Government Road, Manama	259-890 *Telex:* 490-8748 *Cable:* TEROTO
	or	PO Box 5881, Manama	
Canada		Suite 801, Metropolitan House, 99 Bank St, Ottawa Ont K1P 6G3	(613) 238-5991 *Telex:* 210-534282 *Cable:* MATAI

Chile	Avenida Isidora Goyenechea 3516, Las Condes, Santiago *or* Casilla 112, Correo Las Condes, Santiago	(02) 48-7071 *Telex:* 34-40066 *Cable:* INAKA
China	Ritan Dongerjie No. 1, Chao Yang District, Beijing	522731/2/3/4 *Telex:* 22124 *Cable:* RATA CN
Cook Islands	1st Floor, Philatelic Bureau Building, Takuvaine Road, Avarua, Rarotonga *or* PO Box 21, Rarotonga	(682) 2065 ext. 341/2/3 *Telex:* 722-62009 *Cable:* KAKAHO RG
Fiji	Ratu Sukuna House, cnr Victoria Parade & MacArthur Street, Suva *or* PO Box 1378, Suva	311422 *Telex:* 701-2161 *Cable:* NIKAU
France	7 ter, Rue Leonard da Vinci, Paris 75116	(01) 500 24 11 *Telex:* 42-611929 *Cable:* KOWHAI
Fed. Rep. of Germany	Bonn-Center HI 902, Bundeskanzlerplatz, 5300 Bonn	(0228) 21 40 21/2 *Telex:* 41-886322 *Cable:* MATANGA
Greece	An. Tsoha 15-17, Ambelokipi, Athens TT618	(01) 6410311/2/3 *Telex:* 601-216630 *Cable:* RAUPO
Hong Kong	3414 Connaught Centre, Connaught Road, Hong Kong *or* GPO Box 2790, Hong Kong	(5) 255-044 *Telex:* 802-73932 *Cable:* KAKA
Indonesia	Jalan Diponegoro No 41, Menteng, Jakarta *or* PO Box 2439 JKT, Jakarta	(021) 357 924/5, 359 796/7 *Telex:* 73-46109 *Cable:* TUI
Iran	Ave. Mirzai Shirazi, Afshin St No. 29, Tehran *or* PO Box 128, Tehran	625061/083 *Telex:* 88-212078 *Cable:* RAHUI
Iraq	2D/19 Zuwiya, Jadriyah (nr Baghdad University), Baghdad *or* PO Box 2350, Alwiyah, Baghdad	(01) 7768176/7/8 *Telex:* 491-2433 *Cable:* MAKOMAKA
Italy	Via Zara 28, Rome 00198	(06) 844 8663/59/73/96 *Telex:* 43-610682 *Cable:* RANGIORA
Japan	20-40 Kamiyama-cho, Shibuya-ku, Tokyo 150	(03) 460 8711/44 *Telex:* 72-22462 *Cable:* TITOKI
Korea	Publishers' Association Bldg, No 105-2 Sagan-dong, Chongr-ku, Seoul *or* CPO Box 1059, Seoul	(02) 720-7794/5 725-3707/720-4255 *Telex:* K27367 *Cable:* TAKAPU
Malaysia	193 Jalan Pekeliling, Kuala Lumpur 16-01 *or* PO Box 2003, Kuala Lumpur 01-02	(03) 486-422 *Telex:* 30284 *Cable:* ARAWA
Mexico	Homero No. 229, 8/0 Piso, Mexico DF, 11570 Mexico	511-7905 *Telex:* 1763154 *Cable:* KEA ME
Netherlands	Lange Voorhout 18, 2514 EE The Hague	(070) 46 93 24 *Telex:* 44-31557 *Cable:* TAUPATA
New Caledonia	4 Blvd Vauban, Noumea *or* PO Box 2219, Noumea	27 25 43 *Telex:* 036NM *Cable:* KERERU

Niue	Tapeu, Alofi *or* PO Box 78, Niue	22 *Cable:* KAHIKA
Papua New Guinea	6th Floor, Australian High Commission Bldg, Waigani, Port Moresby *or* PO Box 1144, Boroko, Port Moresby	(675) 259444 *Telex:* 703-22191 *Cable:* MAIRE
Peru	Avenida Salaverry 3006, San Isidro, Lima 27 *or* Casilla 5587, Lima 100	62-1890/40 *Telex:* 20254PU *Cable:* KOROMIKO
Philippines	10th Floor, Bankmer Bldg, 6756 Ayala Ave, Makati, Metro Manila *or* PO Box 2208 MCC, Makati Metro Manila	8180916 *Telex:* 756-63509/ 754-45284 *Cable:* MAMAKU PN
Singapore	13 Nassim Road, Singapore 1025	2359 966 *Telex:* 87-21244 *Cable:* TAINUI
Solomon Islands	Soltel House, Mendana Ave, Honiara *or* PO Box 697, Honiara	502-503 *Telex:* 778-66322 *Cable:* KOKAKO
Switzerland	28 Chemin du Petit-Saconnex, CH-1209 Geneva *or* PO Box 84, CH-1211 Geneva 19	(022) 34 95 30 *Telex:* 45-22820 *Cable:* KONINI
Tahiti	Air New Zealand Ltd, Vaima Center, Papeete *or* BP 73, Papeete	20170 *Telex:* none *Cable:* ENZEDAIR
Thailand	93 Wireless Rd, Bangkok 5 *or* PO Box 2719, Bangkok 5	(02) 251-8165 *Telex:* 86-81165 *Cable:* MANUKA
Tokelau	Savalalo St, Apia, Western Samoa *or* PO Box 865, Apia	20-822/3 *Telex:* 779222 *Cable:* TOKALANI
Tonga	Tungi Arcade, Taufa'ahau Road, Nuku'alofa *or* PO Box 830, Nuku'alofa	21122 *Telex:* 777-662216 *Cable:* KOTUKU
USSR	44 Ulitsa Vorovskovo, Moscow, 121069	290 34 85/12 77/57 04 *Telex:* 64-413187 *Cable:* RIMU
United Kingdom	New Zealand House, The Haymarket, London SW1Y 4TQ	01-930 8422 *Telex:* 24368 *Cable:* DEPUTY LONDON SW1
United States	37 Observatory Circle, NW Washington DC 20008	(202) 328, 4800 *Telex:* 230-89526/64272 *Cable:* TOTARA
Western Samoa	Beach Road, Apia *or* PO Box 208, Apia	21-711/714 *Telex:* 779222 *Cable:* TAWA

Embassies, High Commissions and Consulates in Britain

Consulates are closed on English Public holidays and on the national holidays observed in their own countries. Visa/consular offices have been listed for preference.

Algeria	6 Hyde Park Gate, London SW7 1QQ	221 7800/4
Antigua	Eastern Caribbean High Commission, 10 Kensington Court, London W8	937 9522
Argentina	Brazilian Embassy, Argentine Interest Section, 111 Cadogan Gardens, London SW3 2RQ	730 7173
Australia	Australia House, Strand, London WC2B 4LA	438 8194
Austria	18 Belgrave Mews West, London SW1X 8HU	235 2731
Bahamas	39 Pall Mall, London SW1 5JG	930 6967/8
Bahrain	98 Gloucester Road, London SW7 4AU	370 5132/3
Bangladesh	28 Queen's Gate, London SW7 5JA	584 0081/4
Barbados	6 Upper Belgrave Street, London SW1X 8AZ	235 8686/9
Belgium	103 Eaton Square, London SW1W 9AB	235 5422
Belize	15 Thayer Street, London W1	486 7073
Benin	125 High St, Edgware, Middx. HA8 7HS	951 1234
Bolivia	106 Eaton Square, London SW1W 9AD	235 4255
Botswana	162 Buckingham Palace Road, London SW1W 9TJ	730 5216/9
Brazil	Consular Section, 6 Deanery Street, London W1Y 5LH	499 7441
Bulgaria	186-188 Queen's Gate, London SW7 5HL	584 9400
Burma	19a Charles Street, Berkeley Square, London W1X 8ER	499 8841
Cameroon	84 Holland Park, London W11 3SB	727 0771/3
Canada	Visa and Immigration, 38 Grosvenor Street, London W1X 0AA	409 2071
Chile	12 Devonshire Street, London W1N 2DS	580 6392
China	13 Weymouth Mews, London W1N 3FQ	636 5726
Colombia	Suite 10, 140 Park Lane, London W1Y 3DF	493 4565
Costa Rica	Cromwell Mansions, 225 Cromwell Road, London SW5	373 0197
Cuba	15 Grape Street, London WC2H 8DR	240 2488
Cyprus	93 Park Street, London W1Y 4ET	499 8272
Czechoslovakia	28 Kensington Palace Gardens, London W8 4QY	727 9431
Denmark	55 Sloane Street, London SW1X 9SR	235 1255
Dominica	1 Collingham Gdns, London SW5 0HW	370 5194
Dominican Rep.	Flat 2, 103 Lexham Gdns, London W8 6JN	370 3231
Eastern Caribbean Sts.	10 Kensington Court, London W8 5DL	937 9522
Ecuador	3 Hans Crescent, Knightsbridge, London SW1X 0LS	584 1367
Egypt	19 Kensington Palace Gdn Mews, London W8 4QL	229 8818
El Salvador	Flat 9, Welbeck House, 62 Welbeck Street, London W1M 7HB	486 8182/3
Ethiopia	17 Prince's Gate, London SW7 1PZ	589 7212/5
Fiji	34 Hyde Park Gate, London SW7 5BN	584 3661
Finland	38 Chesham Place, London SW1X 8HW	235 9531
France	College House, Wright's Lane, London W8	937 1202
Gabon	48 Kensington Court, London W8 5DB	937 5285/9

Gambia	57 Kensington Court, London W8 5DG	937 6316
Federal Rep. Germany	23 Belgrave Square, London SW1X 8PZ	235 5033
German Dem. Rep.	33 Belgrave Mews South, London SW1X 8QB	235 4465
Ghana	38 Queen's Gate, London SW7 5HR	584 6311
Greece	1A Holland Park, London W11 3TP	727 8040
Grenada	1 Collingham Gardens, London SW5 0HW	373 7808/9
Guyana	3 Palace Court, Bayswater Rd, London W2 4LP	229 7684/8
Haiti	33 Abbots House, St Mary Abbots Terrace, London W14 8NU	602 3194
Honduras	47 Manchester Street, London W1M 5PB	486 3380
Hong Kong	6 Grafton Street, London W1X 3LB	499 9821
Hungary	35 Eaton Place, London SW1X 8BY	235 4048
Iceland	1 Eaton Terrace, London SW1W 8EY	730 5131
India	India House, Aldwych, London WC2B 4NA	836 8484
Indonesia	38 Grosvenor Square, London W1X 9AD	499 7661
Iran	50 Kensington Gdns, London W8 5DD	937 5225/8
Iraq	21 Queen's Gate, London SW7 5JG	584 7141
Rep. Ireland	17 Grosvenor Place, London SW1X 7HR	235 2171
Israel	15 Old Court Place, Kensington, London W8 4QB	937 8050
Italy	38 Eaton Place, London SW1	235 9371
Ivory Coast	2 Upper Belgrave Street, London SW1X 8BJ	235 6991
Jamaica	50 St James's Street, London SW1A 1JT	499 8600
Japan	43/46 Grosvenor Street, London W1X 0BA	493 6030
Jordan	66 Upper Phillimore Gdns, London W8 7HB	937 3685
Kenya	45 Portland Place, London W1N 4AS	636 2371/5
Korea Rep.	4 Palace Gate, London W8 5NF	581 0247
Kuwait	45 Queen's Gate, London SW7	589 4533
Laos	5 Palace Green, Kensington, London W8 4QA	937 9519
Lebanon	15 Palace Gardens Mews, London W8 4RB	727 6696
Lesotho	10 Collingham Road, London SW5 0NR	373 8581/4
Liberia	21 Prince's Gate, London SW7 1QB	589 9405
Luxembourg	27 Wilton Crescent, London SW1X 8SD	235 6961
Malawi	33 Grosvenor Street, London W1X 0HS	491 4172/7
Malaysia	45 Belgrave Square, London SW1X 8QT	235 8033
Malta	16 Kensington Square, London W8 5HH	938 1712/6
Mauritius	32/33 Elvaston Place, Gloucester Road, London SW7	581 0294-8
Mexico	8 Halkin Street, London SW1X 7DW	235 6393-6
Mongolia	7 Kensington Court, London W8 5DL	937 0150
Morocco	49 Queen's Gate Gardens, London SW7 5NE	581 5001/4
Nepal	12a Kensington Palace Gdns, London W8 4QU	229 1594/6231
Netherlands	38 Hyde Park Gate, London SW7 5DP	581 5040
New Zealand	New Zealand House, Haymarket, London SW1Y 4QT	930 8422
Nicaragua	8 Gloucester Road, London SW7 4PP	584 4365
Nigeria	56 Fleet Street, London EC4Y 1JV	353 3776/7/8/9
Norway	25 Belgrave Square, London SW1X 8QD	235 7151
Oman	44 Montpelier Square, London SW7 5DN	584 6782

Pakistan	35 Lowndes Square, London SW1X 9JN	235 2044
Panama	24 Tudor Street, London EC4Y 0AY	353 4792
Papua New Guinea	14 Waterloo Place, London SW1R 4AR	930 0922/7
Paraguay	Braemar Lodge, Cornwall Gardens, London SW7 4AQ	937 1235
Peru	52 Sloane Street, London SW1X 9SP	235 1917
Philippines	1 Cumberland House, Kensington High Street, London W8	937 3646
Poland	73 New Cavendish St., London W1N 7RB	636 4533
Portugal	Silver City House, 62 Brompton Road, London SW3 1BJ	235 6216
Qatar	115 Queen's Gate, London SW7 5LP	581 8611
Romania	4 Palace Green, London W8 4QD	937 9666/8
Saudi Arabia	30 Belgrave Square, London SW1X 8QB	235 0831
Sénégal	11 Phillimore Gdns, London W8 7QG	937 0925/6
Seychelles	50 Conduit Street, 4th Floor, PO Box 4PE, London W1A 4PE	439 9699
Sierra Leone	33 Portland Place, London W1N 3AG	636 6483-6
Singapore	5 Chesham Street, London SW1X 8ND	235 9067
Somalia	60 Portland Place, London W1N 3DG	580 7140, 7148
South Africa	South Africa House, Trafalgar Square, London WC2N 5DP	839 2211
Soviet Union	5 Kensington Palace Gdns, London W8 4QS	229 3215
Spain	20 Draycott Place, London SW3 2RZ	581 5921
Sri Lanka	13 Hyde Park Gardens, London W2 2LX	262 1841-7
Sudan	3 Cleveland Row, St. James's, London SW1A 1DD	839 8080
Swaziland	58 Pont Street, London SW1X 0AE	581 4976/7/8
Sweden	11 Montagu Place, London W1H 2AL	724 2101
Switzerland	16/18 Montagu Place, London W1H 2BQ	723 0701
Syria	8 Belgrave Square, London SW1X 8PH	245 9012
Tanzania	43 Hertford Street, London W1Y 7TF	499 8951-4
Thailand	29/30 Queen's Gate, London SW7 5JB	589 0173
Togo	20 Wellington Court, 116 Knightsbridge, London SW1	584 1948
Tonga	New Zealand House, 12th Floor, Haymarket, London SW1Y 4TE	839 3287
Trinidad & Tobago	42 Belgrave Square, London SW1X 8NT	245 9351
Tunisia	29 Prince's Gate, London SW7 1QG	584 8117
Turkey	Rutland Lodge, Rutland Gardens, Knightsbridge, London SW7 1BW	589 0949
Uganda	Uganda House, 58/59 Trafalgar Square, London WC2N 5DX	839 5783
United Arab Emirates	48 Prince's Gate, London SW7 2QA	589 3434
United States	5 Upper Grosvenor Street, London W1A 2JB	499 9000
Upper Volta (Burkina Faso)	150 Buckingham Palace Road, London SW1W 95A	730 8141
Uruguay	48 Lennox Gardens, London SW1X 0DL	589 8835-6
Venezuela	71a Park Mansions, Knightsbridge, London SW1X 7QU	589 9916
Vietnam	12-14 Victoria Road, London W8	937 1912/8564
Yemen Arab Republic	41 South Street, London W1Y 5PD	629 9905-8

Yemen People's Dem. Republic	57 Cromwell Road, London SW7 2ED	584 6607/9
Yugoslavia	7 Lexham Gardens, London W8 5JU	370 6105
Zaïre	26 Chesham Place, London SW1X 8HH	235 6137/8/9
Zambia	2 Palace Gate, London W8 5NG	
Zimbabwe	Zimbabwe House, 429 Strand, London WC2R 0SA	836 7755

Embassies, High Commissions and Consulates in the United States

Afghanistan	2100 M St, NW, Washington DC 20037	(202) 234 3770
Algeria	2118 Kalorama Road, NW, Washington DC 20008	(202) 328 5300
Argentina	1600 New Hampshire Ave, NW, Washington DC 20009	(202) 387 0705
Australia	1601 Massachusetts Ave, NW, Washington DC 20036	(202) 797 3000
Austria	2343 Massachusetts Ave, NW, Washington DC 20008	(202) 483 4474
Bahamas	600 New Hampshire Ave, NW, Washington DC 20037	(202) 338 3940
Bahrain	2600 Virginia Ave, NW, Washington DC 20037	(202) 324 0741
Bangladesh	3421 Massachusetts Ave, NW, Washington DC 20007	(202) 327 6644
Barbados	2144 Wyoming Ave, NW, Washington DC 20008	(202) 387 7373
Belgium	3330 Garfield St, NW, Washington DC 20008	(202) 333 6900
Benin	2737 Cathedral Ave, NW, Washington DC 20008	(202) 232 6656
Bolivia	3012 Massachusetts Ave, NW, Washington DC 20008	(202) 483 4410
Botswana	4301 Connecticut Ave, NW, Washington DC 20008	(202) 244 4990
Brazil	3006 Massachusetts Ave, NW, Washington DC 20008	(202) 797 0100
Bulgaria	2100 16th St, NW, Washington DC 20009	(202) 387 7970
Burma	2300 S St, NW, Washington DC 20008	(202) 332 9044
Burundi	2717 Connecticut Ave, NW, Washington DC 20008	(202) 387 4477
Cameroon	2349 Massachusetts Ave, NW, Washington DC 20008	(202) 265 8790
Canada	1746 Massachusetts Ave, NW, Washington DC 20036	(202) 785 1400
Cape Verde	1120 Connecticut Ave, NW, Washington DC 20036	(202) 659 3148
Central African Republic	1618 22nd St, NW, Washington DC 20008	(202) 483 7800
Chad	1901 Spruce Drive, NW, Washington DC 20012	(202) 882 2999
Chile	1732 Massachusetts Ave, NW, Washington DC 20036	(202) 785 1746
China	2300 Connecticut Ave, NW, Washington DC 20008	(202) 328 2500
Colombia	2118 Leroy Place, NW, Washington DC 20008	(202) 387 5828
Congo	14 E. 65th St, New York, NY 10021	(212) 744 7840
Costa Rica	2112 S St, NW, Washington DC 20008	(202) 234 2945
Cuban Interests	2630 16th St, NW Washington DC 20009	(202) 797 8518
Cyprus	2211 R St, NW, Washington DC 20008	(202) 462 5772
Czechoslovakia	3900 Linnean Ave, NW, Washington DC 20008	(202) 363 6315
Denmark	3200 Whitehaven St, NW, Washington DC 20008	(202) 234 4300
Dominican Rep.	1715 22nd St, NW, Washington DC 20008	(202) 332 6280
Ecuador	2535 15th St, NW, Washington DC 20009	(202) 234 7200
Egypt	2310 Decatur Place, NW, Washington DC 20008	(202) 232 5400
El Salvador	2308 California St, NW, Washington DC 20008	(202) 265 3480

Equatorial Guinea	801 Second Ave, New York NY 10017	(212) 599 1523
Ethiopia	2134 Kalorama Road, NW, Washington DC 20008	(202) 234 2281
Fiji	1629 K St, NW, Washington DC 20006	(202) 296 3928
Finland	3216 New Mexico Ave, NW, Washington DC 20016	(202) 363 2430
France	2535 Belmont Road, NW, Washington DC 20008	(202) 328 2600
Gabon	2034 20th St, NW, Washington DC 20009	(202) 797 1000
Gambia	1785 Massachusetts Ave, Washington DC 20036	(202) 265 3532
German Dem. Republic	1717 Massachusetts Ave, NW, Washington DC 20036	(202) 232 3134
Fed. Rep. Of Germany	4645 Reservoir Road, NW, Washington DC 20007	(202) 298 4000
Ghana	2460 16th St, NW, Washington DC 20007	(202) 462 0761
Great Britain	3100 Massachusetts Ave, NW, Washington DC 20008	(202) 462 1340
Greece	2221 Massachusetts Ave, NW, Washington DC 20008	(202) 667 3168
Grenada	1424 16th St, NW, Washington DC 20036	(202) 347 3198
Guatemala	2220 R St, NW, Washington DC 20008	(202) 332 2865
Guinea	2112 Leroy Place, NW, Washington DC 20008	(202) 483 9420
Guinea-Bissau	211 E 43rd St, New York, NY 10017	(212) 661 3977
Guyana	2490 Tracy Place, NW, Washington DC 20008	(202) 265 6900
Haiti	2311 Massachusetts Ave, NW, Washington DC 20008	(202) 332 4090
Honduras	4301 Connecticut Ave, NW, Washington DC 20008	(202) 966 7700
Hungary	3910 Shoemaker St, NW, Washington DC 20008	(202) 862 6730
Iceland	2022 Connecticut Ave, NW, Washington DC 20008	(202) 265 6653
India	2107 Massachusetts Ave, NW, Washington DC 20008	(202) 265 5050
Indonesia	2020 Massachusetts Ave, NW, Washington DC 20036	(202) 293 1745
Iraq	1801 P St, NW, Washington DC 20036	(202) 483 7500
Ireland	2234 Massachusetts Ave, NW, Washington DC 20008	(202) 462 3939
Israel	3514 International Drive, NW, Washington DC 20008	(202) 364 5500
Italy	1601 Fuller St, NW, Washington DC 20009	(202) 328 5500
Ivory Coast	2424 Massachusetts Ave, NW, Washington DC 20008	(202) 483 2400
Jamaica	1850 K St, NW, Washington DC 20009	(202) 452 0660
Japan	2520 Massachusetts Ave, NW, Washington DC 20008	(202) 234 2266
Jordan	2319 Wyoming Ave, NW, Washington DC 20008	(202) 265 1606
Kenya	2249 R St, NW, Washington DC 20008	(202) 387 6101
Korea	2370 Massachusetts Ave, NW, Washington DC 20008	(202) 483 7383
Kuwait	2940 Tilden St, NW, Washington DC 20008	(202) 966 0702
Laos	2222 S St, NW, Washington DC 20008	(202) 462 8600
Lebanon	2560 28th St, NW, Washington DC 20008	(202) 332 0300
Lesotho	1601 Connecticut Ave, NW, Washington DC 20009	(202) 462 4190
Liberia	5201 16th St, NW, Washington DC 20011	(202) 723 0437
Libya	1118 22nd St, NW, Washington DC 20037	(202) 452 1290
Luxembourg	2200 Massachusetts Ave, NW, Washington DC 20008	(202) 265 4171
Madagascar	2374 Massachusetts Ave, NW, Washington DC 20008	(202) 265 5525
Malawi	1400 20th St, NW, Washington DC 20036	(202) 296 5530
Malaysia	2401 Massachusetts Ave, NW, Washington DC 20008	(202) 328 2700
Mali	2130 R St, NW, Washington DC 20008	(202) 332 2249
Malta	2017 Connecticut Ave, NW, Washington DC 20008	(202) 462 3611

Mauritania	2129 Leroy Place, NW, Washington DC 20008	(202) 232 5700
Mauritius	4310 Connecticut Ave, NW, Washington DC 20008	(202) 244 1491
Mexico	2829 16th St, NW, Washington DC 20009	(202) 234 6000
Morocco	1601 21st St, NW, Washington DC 20009	(202) 462 7979
Nepal	2131 Leroy Place, NW, Washington DC 20008	(202) 667 4550
Netherlands	4200 Linnean Ave, NW, Washington DC 20008	(202) 244 5300
New Zealand	37 Observatory Circle, Washington DC 20008	(202) 328 4800
Nicaragua	1627 New Hampshire Ave, Washington DC 20009	(202) 387 4371
Niger	2204 R St, NW, Washington DC 20008	(202) 483 4224
Nigeria	2201 M St, NW, Washington DC 20037	(202) 223 9300
Norway	2720 34th St, NW, Washington DC 20008	(202) 333 6000
Oman	2342 Massachusetts Ave, NW, Washington DC 20008	(202) 387 1980
Pakistan	2315 Massachusetts Ave, NW, Washington DC 20008	(202) 332 8330
Panama	2862 McGill Terrace, NW, Washington DC 20008	(202) 483 1407
Papua New Guinea	1140 19th St, NW, Washington DC 20036	(202) 659 0856
Papua New Guinea	1140 19th St, NW, Washington DC 20036	(202) 659 0856
Paraguay	2400 Massachusetts Ave, NW, Washington DC 20008	(202) 483 6960
Peru	1700 Massachusetts Ave, NW, Washington DC 20036	(202) 833 9860
Philippines	1617 Massachusetts Ave, NW, Washington DC 20036	(202) 483 1414
Poland	2640 16th St, NW, Washington DC 20009	(202) 234 3800
Portugal	2125 Kalorama Road, NW, Washington DC 20008	(202) 265 1643
Qatar	600 New Hampshire Ave, NW, Washington DC 20037	(202) 338 0111
Romania	1607 23rd St, NW, Washington DC 20008	(202) 232 4747
Rwanda	1714 New Hampshire Ave, NW, Washington DC 20009	(202) 232 2882
Saint Lucia	41 E 42nd St, New York, NY 10017	(212) 697 9360
Saudi Arabia	1520 18th St, NW, Washington DC 20036	(202) 483 2100
Sénégal	2112 Wyoming Ave, NW, Washington DC 20008	(202) 234 0540
Seychelles	820 Second Ave, New York, NY 10017	(212) 687 9766
Sierra Leone	1701 19th St, NW, Washington DC 20009	(202) 265 7700
Singapore	1824 R St, NW, Washington DC 20009	(202) 667 7555
Somali Dem. Rep.	600 New Hampshire Ave, NW, Washington DC 20037	(202) 234 3261
South Africa	3051 Massachusetts Ave, NW, Washington DC 20008	(202) 232 4400
Spain	2700 15th St, NW, Washington DC 20009	(202) 265 0190
Sri Lanka	2148 Wyoming Ave, NW, Washington DC 20008	(202) 483 4025
Sudan	600 New Hampshire Ave, NW, Washington DC 20037	(202) 338 8565
Swaziland	4301 Connecticut Ave, NW, Washington DC 20008	(202) 362 6683
Sweden	600 New Hampshire Ave, Washington DC 20037	(202) 298 3500
Switzerland	2900 Cathedral Ave, NW, Washington DC 20008	(202) 462 1811
Suriname	2600 Virginia Ave, NW, Washington DC 20037	(202) 338 6980
Syria	2215 Wyoming Ave, NW, Washington DC 20008	(202) 232 6313
Tanzania	2139 R St, NW, Washington DC 20008	(202) 232 0501
Thailand	2300 Kalorama Road, NW, Washington DC 20008	(202) 667 1446
Togo	2208 Massachusetts Ave, NW, Washington DC 20008	(202) 234 4212
Trinidad & Tobago	1708 Massachusetts Ave, NW, Washington DC 20036	(202) 467 6490

Tunisia	2408 Massachusetts Ave, NW, Washington DC 20008	(202) 234 6644
Turkey	1606 23rd St, NW, Washington DC 20008	(202) 667 6400
Uganda	5909 16th St, NW, Washington DC 20011	(202) 726 7100
USSR	1125 16th St, NW, Washington DC 20036	(202) 628 7551
United Arab Emirates	600 New Hampshire Ave, NW, Washington DC 20037	(202) 338 6500
Upper Volta (Burkina Faso)	2340 Massachusetts Ave, NW, Washington DC 20008	(202) 332 5577
Uruguay	1918 F St, NW, Washington DC 20006	(202) 331 1313
Venezuela	2445 Massachusetts Ave, NW, Washington DC 20008	(202) 797 3800
Western Samoa	211 E 43rd St, New York NY 10017	(212) 682 1482
Yemen Arab Rep.	600 New Hampshire Ave, NW, Washington DC 20037	(202) 965 4760
Yugoslavia	2410 California St, NW, Washington DC 20008	(202) 462 6566
Zaïre	1800 New Hampshire Ave, NW, Washington DC 20009	(202) 234 7690
Zambia	2419 Massachusetts Ave, NW, Washington DC 20008	(202) 265 9717

Embassies, High Commissions and Consulates in Australia

Argentina	1st Floor, Suite 102, M.L.C. Tower, Woden, ACT 2606	824855/824555
Austria	107 Endeavour St, Red Hill, Canberra	951376
Bangladesh	43 Hampton Circuit, Yarralumla, Canberra, ACT 2600	
Belgium	19 Arkana St, Yarralumla, Canberra, ACT 2600	732501/732502
Brazil	11th Floor, 'Canberra House', 40 Marcus Clarke St, Canberra City, ACT 2601	
Bulgaria	Double Bay, New South Wales, 2028	367581
Burma	85 Mugga Way, Red Hill, Canberra, ACT 2603	
Canada	Commonwealth Avenue, Canberra, ACT 2600	733844
Chile	93 Endeavour St, Red Hill, Canberra, ACT 2603	
China	14 Federal Highway, Watson, Canberra, ACT 2602	412448
Colombia	PO Box 391, Double Bay (NSW), Sydney 2028	
Cyprus	37 Endeavour St, Red Hill, ACT 2603, Canberra	952120/952520
Czechoslavakia	169 Military Rd, Doler Heights	
Denmark	24 Beagle St, Red Hill, ACT 2603, Canberra	
Dominican Rep.	331 King William St, Box 1017, GPO Adelaide, Australia 5001	518411
Ecuador	2 Glen St, Hawthorn No 3122, Victoria, Melbourne	8187168
Egypt	125 Monaro Crescent, Red Hill, ACT 2603, Canberra	
Fiji	9 Beagle St, Red Hill, PO Box E159, Canberra, ACT 2600	
Finland	10 Darwin Avenue, Yarralumla, Canberra, ACT 2600	
France	6 Darwin Avenue, Yarralumla, Canberra, ACT 2600	
Fed. Rep. Germany	119 Empire Circuit, Yarralumla, Canberra, ACT 2600	006162/733177
German Dem. Rep.	12 Beagle St, Red Hill, Canberra, ACT 2603	
Ghana	PO Box 338, Manuka, Canberra	6162 951152
Greece	1 Stonehaven Crescent, Red Hill, Canberra, ACT 2603	
Hungary	79 Hopetown Circuit, Yarralumla, Canberra, ACT 2600	

Iceland	2 Montalto Avenue, Toorak 3142	
India	3-5 Moonah Place, Yarralumla, Canberra, ACT 2600	733999/733774
Indonesia	Piccadilly Court, 3rd Floor, 222 TITT, PO Box 6, Sydney	
Iran	14 Torres St, Red Hill, Canberra, ACT	
Iraq	48 Culgoa Circuit, O'Malley, ACT 2606	861333/861755
Rep. Ireland	200 Arkana St, Yarralumla, Canberra, ACT 2600	733 022
Israel	6 Turrana St, Yarralumla, Canberra, ACT 2600	
Italy	12 Grey St, Deakin, ACT 2600	733333
Japan	112 Empire Circuit, Yarralumla, Canberra, ACT 2000	
Jordan	20 Roabuck St, Red Hill, Canberra, ACT 2603	
Korea	113 Empire Circuit, Yarralumla, Canberra, ACT 2600	733044/733956
Lebanon	73 Endeavour St, Red Hill, Canberra, ACT 2603	95 7378
Libya	Jamahiriya, 50 Culgoa Circuit, O'Malley, Canberra	
Malaysia	71 State Circle, Yarralumla, Canberra, ACT 2600	731543/4/5
Malta	261 La Perouse St, Red Hill, Canberra, ACT 2603	
Mauritius	16 National Circuit, Suite 6, Barton, Canberra, ACT 2600	
Mexico	14 Perth Avenue, Yarralumla, Canberra, ACT 2600	
Netherlands	120 Empire Circuit, Yarralumla, Canberra, ACT 2600	733111
New Zealand	Commonwealth Avenue, Canberra, ACT 2600	
Nigeria	27 State Circle, Deakin, ACT 2600	731028/732869
Norway	3 Zeehan St, Red Hill, Canberra, ACT 2603	
Pakistan	59 Franklin St, Forrest, PO Box 198, Manuka, Canberra, ACT 2603	9500 212223
Papua New Guinea	Forster Crescent, Yarralumla, Canberra, ACT 2600	733322
Paraguay	PO Box 481, Mascot 2.020, Sydney	
Peru	94 Captain Cook, Canberra, ACT 2603	951016
Philippines	1 Moonah Place, Yarralumla, Canberra	732535
Poland	7 Turrana St, Yarralumla, Canberra, ACT 2600	
Portugal	8 Astrolabe St, Red Hill, Canberra, ACT 2603	
Romania	115 Ginahgulla Rd, Belleview, Sydney	
Seychelles	127 Commercial Rd, South Yarra, Victoria 3141	
Singapore	81 Mugga Way, Red Hill, Canberra, ACT 2603	
South Africa	Rhodes Place, Yarralumla, Canberra, ACT 2600	732424/5/6/7
Soviet Union	78 Canberra Av, Griffith, ACT 2603	959033
Spain	15 Arkana St, Yarralumla, ACT, PO Box 256, Woden, Canberra	
Sri Lanka	35 Empire Circuit, Forrest, Canberra, ACT 2603	
Sweden	9 Turrana St, Yarralumla, Canberra, ACT 2600	
Switzerland	7 Melbourne Avenue, Forrest, ACT 2603	733977
Thailand	111 Empire Circuit, Yarralumla, Canberra, ACT 2600	
Turkey	60 Mugga Way, Red Hill, Canberra, ACT 2603	
Uganda	PO Box 276, Woden 2606, Canberra	62824422
United States	Yarralumla, Canberra, ACT 2600	733711
Uruguay	Adelaide House Suite 5, Woden, ACT 2606	
Venezuela	Suite 106 MLC Tower, Woden, Canberra, ACT	
Vietnam	31 Endeavour St, Red Hill, Canberra, ACT 2603	952426
Yugoslavia	11 Nuyats St, PO Box 161, Manuka, ACT 2603, Canberra	

Embassies, High Commissions and Consulates in Canada

Antigua	Suite 205, 60 St Clair Av. East, Toronto, Ontario M4T 1L9	
Argentina	130 Slater St, 6th Floor, Ottawa	
Australia	The National Building, 13th Floor, 130 Slater St, Ottawa KIP 5H6	
Austria	445 Wilbrod St, Ottawa, Ontario KIN 6M7	(613) 56 31 444
Bangladesh	85 Range Rd, Suite No 1007, Sandringham Apartments, Ottawa	
Barbados	Suite 700, 151 Slater St, Ottawa, Ontario KIP 5HE	
Belgium	The Sandringham, 6th Floor, 85 Range Rd, Ottawa	
Benin	58 Gleeb Av, Ottawa, KIS 2C3	
Bolivia	85 Monterrey Dr, Ottawa	202 4834410
Brazil	255 Albert St, Suite 900, Ottawa KIP 6A9	
Bulgaria	325 Stewart St, Ottawa, Ontario	232 3215
Burundi	136 Rue Retcal FE, Piece 210 A, Ottawa K2P OP8	
Cameroon	170 Clemond Av, KIS 2B4	361 522
Chile	56 Sparks ST, Suite 801, Ottawa, Ontario KIP 5A9	
China	415 St Andrews, Ottawa	2344 721
Colombia	140 Wellington St, Suite No 112, Victoria Building, Ottawa 4, Ontario	
Costa Rica	No 2902, 1155 Dorchester Blvd West, Montreal	866 8159/866 0442
Cuba	388 Rue Main, Ottawa KIS 1E3	563 0141
Czechoslavakia	1305 Avenue des Pins, West Montreal, QUE, H36 1B2	
Denmark	85 Range Rd, Apt. 702, Ottawa K1N 8J6	
Dominican Rep.	3435 Drumond St, Suite No 5, Montreal H3G 1XB	843 4540
Eastern Caribbean	112 Kent St, Suite 1701, Ottawa, Ontario K1P 5P2	
Ecuador	150 10th St, 4th Floor, Suite 407, Ottawa, Ontario K1P 534	238 5032
Egypt	454 Laurier Av, East Ottawa, Ontario	2344 931
El Salvador	'The Driveway Place', 350 Queen Elizabeth Driveway, Suite 101, Ontario	
Finland	222 Somerset St West, Suite 401, Ottawa, Ontario, K2P 2G3	
France	1 Dundas St West, Suite 2405, Box 8, Toronto ONT MSG 123	
The Gambia	363 St Francois Xavier St, Suite 230, Montreal, Quebec H2Y 3P9	
Fed. Rep. Germany	1 Waverley St, Ottawa, Ontario K1N 8VA	534 226
Ghana	85 Range Rd, Suite 810, Ottawa, Ontario	236 0871
Greece	80 Maclaren Av, Ottawa, Ontario K2P 0KG	
Guinea	Suite 208, Place DeVille, 112 10th St, Ottawa	238 1133
Guyana	151 Slater St, Suite 309, Ottawa, K1P 5H3	
Haiti	Suite 1308, Place DeVille, 112 10th St, Ottawa	238 1628
Honduras	151 Slater St, Suite 300 A, Ottawa, Ontario K1P 583	
Hungary	7 Delaware Av, Ottawa, Ontario K2 POZ2	
Iceland	5005 Jean Talon St West, 3rd Floor, Montreal, Quebec H4P 1W7	
India	325 Howe St, 1st Floor, Vancouver, BC	

Indonesia	225 Albert St, Suite 101, Kent Sq. Building CPO, Box 430, Terminal A, Ottawa, Ontario	236 7403
Iran	Suite 307, 85 Range Rd, Ottawa K1N 8J6	236 9108
Iraq	215 McCleod St, Ottawa K2P O28	236 9177/9178
Rep. Ireland	170 Metcalfe St, Ottawa K2P 1P3, Ontario	233 628 12
Israel	Laurier Av. West, Ottawa K1R 7T3	
Italy	275 Slater St, 11th Floor, Ottawa K1P 5H9	232 2401
Ivory Coast	9 Av. Malborough, Ottawa, Ontario K1N 86E	235 9910/236 9919
Jamaica	Sandringham Apt, Suite 202-204, 85 Range Rd, Ottawa, Ontario	
Japan	255 Sussex Drive, Ottawa, Ontario, K1N 9E6	
Jordan	100 Bronson Av, Suite 701, Ottawa, Ontario KIR 6G8	
Kenya	Gillin Building Suite 600, 141 Laurier Av, West Ottawa, Ontario KIP 5J3	
Korea	151 Slater St, Suite 608, Ottawa, Ontario KIP 5H3	232 1717/232 1716
Lebanon	640 Lion St, Ottawa, Ontario KIS 375	236 5825
Lesotho	350 Bucks St, Suite 910, Ottawa, Ontario KR758	236 9449
Madagascar	459 St Sulpice St, Montreal H2Y 2U8	844 4427
Malawi	112 Kent St, Suite 905, Ottawa, Ontario KIP 5P2	236 8931/2
Malaysia	60 Boteler St, Ottawa, Ontario KIN 8Y7	237 518
Mali	Avenue Goulburn, 50 Ottawa, Ontario KIN UCB	232 15 01
Mexico	130 Albert St, Suite 206, Ottawa, Ontario KIP 5G4	
Morocco	38 Range Rd, Ottawa	
Netherlands	3rd Floor 275 Slater St, Ottawa, ONT K1P 5H9	237 5030
New Zealand	Metropolitan House, Suite 801, 99 Bank St, Ottawa, ONT KIP 6G3	
Nicaragua	Place DeVille, Suite 2224 Tower A, 320 Queen St, Ottawa, ONT KIR 5A3	
Niger	38 Av. Blackburn, Ottawa, Ontario K1N 8A2	
Nigeria	295 Metcalfe St, Ottawa K2P 1R9	236 9521
Norway	Suite 932, Royal Bank Centre, 90 Sparks St, Ottawa, ONT KIP 5B4	
Pakistan	2100 Drumond St, Apt 505, Montreal H3G 1X1	845 2297
Peru	170 Laurier Av. West, Suite 1007, Ottawa, ONT KIP 5V5	238 1777/1779
Philippines	130 Albert St, 606-607 Ottawa, Ontario	233 1121
Poland	773 Daly St, Ottawa 2	
Portugal	645 Island Park Drive, Ottawa KIY OB8	
Rwanda	Suite 903, 350 Park St, Ottawa, KIR 759	238 1603
Saudi Arabia	Suite 901, 99 Bank St, Ottawa, KIP 5P9	237 0100
Sénégal	57 Malborough Av, Ottawa	
Somalia	Suite 918, 112 Kent St, Ottawa, KIP 5P2	563 4541
South Africa	15 Sussex Drive, Ottawa KIM IM8	744 0330
Soviet Union	285 Charlotte St, Ottawa K1N845	235 4341/236 1413
Spain	350 Spark St, SUIR802, Ottawa, Ontario KIR 758	
Sri Lanka	85 Range Rd, 'The Sandringham', Suites 102-104, Ottawa, Ontario, KIN 8J6	
Sweden	441 Maclaren St, Ottawa, Ontario K2P 2H3	
Switzerland	5 Malborough Avenue, Ottawa, Ontario K1N 8E6	

Tanzania	50 Range Rd, Ottawa, Canada, KIN 84	
Thailand	85 Range Rd, Suite 704, Ottawa, Ontario K1N 8J6	237 1517
Trinidad & Tobago	73 Albert St, Room 508, Ottawa, Ontario K1P 5R5	232 2418/2419
Tunisia	115 O'Conner St, Ottawa	
Turkey	197 Wurtenburg St, Ottawa, Ontario K1N 8L9	
Uganda	170 Laurier Av, West, Suite 601, Ottawa K1P 525	233 7797
United States	100 Wellington St, Ottawa K1P 5TI	238 5335
Upper Volta (Burkina Faso)	48 Range Rd, Ottawa K1N 814	
Uruguay	1010 Ovest, Rue Ste Catherine, Suite 347, Montreal, Quebec H3B 161	
Venezuela	Suite 2000, 320 Queen St, Ottawa K1R 5A3	235 5151
Yugoslavia	17 Blackburn Av, Ottawa, Ontario K1N 8A2	
Zaïre	18 Range Rd, Ottawa 2, Ontario KIN 8JE	236 7103
Zambia	130 Albert St, Suite 1610, Ottawa, Ontario	
Zimbabwe	112 Kent St, Suite 915 Place deVille, Tower B, Ottawa, Ontario K1P 5P2	

Embassies, High Commissions and Consulates in New Zealand

Argentina	IBM Center, 151-165 The Terrace, 5th Floor, PO Box 1033, Wellington	
Australia	72-78 Hobson St, Thorndon, Wellington	
Belgium	Williston St 1, PO Box 3841, Wellington	
Canada	PO Box 12-049 Wellington N, ICI Building, 3rd Floor, Molesworth St, Wellington	739 577
Chile	Robert Jones House, 12th Floor, Jervois Quay, Wellington	
China	No 226 Glenmore St, Wellington	721 384
Czechoslovakia	12 Anne St, Wadestown, PO Box 2843	
Denmark	18th Floor, Challenge House, 105-109 The Terrace, PO Box 10035, Wellington 1	
Ecuador	PO Box 2987, Wellington	
Fiji	Robert Jones House, Jervois Quay, Wellington N2	
France	1 Williston St, DBP 1695, Wellington	
Fed. Rep. Germany	90-92 Hobson St, Wellington	
Hong Kong	General Building, G/F Corner Shortland St & O'Connell St, Auckland	
India	Princes Towers, 10th Floor, 180 Molesworth St, Wellington	736 390/736 391
Israel	13th Level, Williams City Centre, Plymmet Steps, PO Box 2171, Wellington	
Italy	38 Grant Rd, PO Box 463, Wellington	735 339/735 955
Japan	7th Floor, Norwich Insurance House, 3-11 Hunter St, Wellington 1	
Kiribati	33 Great South Rd, Otahuhu, Auckland	
Korea	12th Floor, Williams Parking Centre Building, Corner of Boulcoutt St & Gilmer Terrace, Wellington N.2	739 073/074

Malaysia	163 Terrace, PO Box 9422, Wellington	738 185/7
Netherlands	Investment House, 10th Floor, Ballance and Featherstone St, Wellington	738 652
Norway	38-42 Waring Taylor St, PO Box 1392, Wellington	
Papua New Guinea	Princes Towers, 11th Floor, 180 Molesworth St, Thorndon, Wellington	85127 4849
Peru	3rd Floor 36/37 Victoria St, Wellington	725 171/725 172
Philippines	Level 30, Williams City Centre, Boulcott St, Gillmer Terrace, Wellington	729 848
Portugal	47-49 Fort St, Auckland	
Romania	100 Devans Bay Rd, Wellington	
Singapore	17 Kabul St, Khandallah, Wellington	
South Africa	Molesworth House, 101-103 Molesworth St, Wellington, PO Box 12045	737 413/4
Soviet Union	57 Messines Rd, Karori, Wellington	721 864
Sweden	PO Box 1800, Wellington 1	
Switzerland	22-24 Panama St, 7th Floor, Wellington 1	721 593
Thailand	2 Burnel Av, PO Box 2530, Wellington 1	735 5385
United States	29 Fitzherbert Terrace, Wellington	722 068
Yugoslavia	24 Hatton St, Wellington 5	

Country Travelling To:	VISA REQUIREMENTS					Restrictions and Requirements
	Australia	*Canada*	*New Zealand*	*UK*	*USA*	
Afghanistan	*	*	*	*	*	* No Tourist or transit visas at present. Only allowed in if business or with official-need authorization from foreign ministry in Kabul.
Algeria	Yes	Yes	Yes	No	Yes	If wish to stay more than 3mths need a *permit de sejour* obtainable from nearest 'Wilaya'.
American Samoa	No	No	No	No	No	Need visa if over 30 days.
Andorra	No	No	No	No	No	
Anguilla	No	No	No	No	No	
Antigua	No*	No*	No*	No*	No*	* Must have return ticket.
Anti & Barbuda	No	No	No	No	No	
Argentina	Yes	*	Yes	Yes	Yes	* Tourists don't require visas, others do.
Australia	—	Yes	No	Yes	Yes	
Austria	No*	No*	No*	No	No*	* Up to 3mths; UK up to 6mths.
Bahamas	No	No	No	No	No	
Bahrain	Yes	Yes	Yes	Yes	Yes	
Bangladesh	Yes	No*	Yes	Yes	Yes	* Yes, if stay exceeds 30 days.
Barbados	No	No	No	No	No	
Belgium	No	No	No	No	No	

Belize	No	No	No	No	No	
Bermuda	No*	No*	No*	No*	No*	* Must have a return ticket.
Benin	Yes	Yes	Yes	Yes	Yes	
Bolivia	Yes	No	Yes	No*	No*	* Tourists don't/Others do.
Botswana	No	No	No	No	No	
Brazil	Yes	No*	Yes	No*	Yes	* Need passport endorsed for Brazil (must not expire within 6mths from date of arrival in Brazil), a roundtrip ticket and funds to meet expenses.
British Virgin Is.	No	No	No	No	No	
Bulgaria	Yes	Yes	Yes	Yes	Yes	
Burma	Yes*	Yes*	Yes*	Yes*	Yes*	* Valid for seven days days only.
Burundi	No	No	No	No	No	
Cameroon	Yes*	Yes*	Yes*	Yes*	Yes*	* Must have return ticket.
Canada	No	—	No	No	No	
Cayman Is.	No	No	No	No	No	
Cent. African Rep.	Yes	Yes	Yes	Yes	Yes	
Chad	Yes	Yes	Yes	Yes	Yes	
Chile	No	No	No	No	No	
China	Yes	Yes	Yes	Yes	Yes	
Colombia	Yes	Yes	Yes	No*	Yes	* Must have valid passport and a return or continuation ticket.

Country Travelling To:	*Visa Requirements*					*Restrictions and Requirements*
	Australia	*Canada*	*New Zealand*	*UK*	*USA*	
Congo	Yes	Yes	Yes	Yes	Yes	
Cook Islands	No*	No*	No*	No*	No*	* Must have valid passport and a return ticket. Need visa after 31 days.
Costa Rica	Yes	No*	Yes	No	Yes	* Need visa after 30 days.
Cuba	Yes	Yes	Yes	Yes	Yes	
Cyprus	No	No	No	No	No	
Czechoslovakia	Yes	Yes	Yes	Yes	Yes	
Denmark	No*	No*	No*	No*	No*	* Need visa if stay over 3mths.
Djibouti	Yes*	Yes*	Yes*	Yes*	Yes*	* and return ticket.
Dominica Commonwealth	No	No	No	No	No	
Dominican Rep.	Yes	No*	Yes	No	No*	* Tourist card needed.
Eastern Caribbean	No	No	No	No	No	
Ecuador	No*	No*	No*	No*	No*	* Need visa if staying over 3mths.
Egypt	Yes*	Yes*	Yes*	Yes*	Yes*	* Visitors must register with the Ministry of the Interior at al-Mugama within 7 days of arrival in Egypt.
El Salvador	Yes*	Yes*	Yes*	Yes*	Yes*	* Valid for 90 days.
Equator Guinea	Yes	Yes	Yes	Yes	Yes	

Ethiopia	Yes	Yes	Yes	Yes	Yes	
Fiji	No	No	No	No	No	
Finland	No	No	No	No	No	
France	No*	No*	No*	No*	No*	* Up to 3mths.
Gabon	Yes	Yes	Yes	Yes	Yes	
Gambia	No*	No*	No*	No*	Yes	* Up to 3mths.
Fed. Rep. Germany	No*	No*	No*	No*	No*	* Up to 3mths.
Germany (DR)	Yes	Yes	Yes	Yes	Yes	
Ghana	No*	No*	No*	No*	No*	* Need an Entry Permit.
Gibraltar	No	No	No	No	No	
Greece	No	No	No	No	No	
Grenada	No*	†	No*	No*	No*	* Up to 3mths. † Not issuing visas at present – need a return ticket and sufficient funds for stay.
Guinea	Yes	Yes	Yes	Yes	Yes	
Guyana	Yes	Yes	Yes	Yes	Yes	
Haiti	Yes	Yes	Yes	No	No	
Hawaii	Yes	No	Yes	Yes	No	
Hong Kong	No[a]	No[a]	No[a]	No[b]	No[c]	[a] Up to 3mths. [b] Up to 6mths [c] Up to 1mth.

Country Travelling To:	*Visa Requirements*					*Restrictions and Requirements*
	Australia	*Canada*	*New Zealand*	*UK*	*USA*	
Honduras	Yes	Yes	Yes	No*	No†	* Up to 2mths † Up to 3mths.
Hungary	Yes	Yes	Yes	Yes	Yes	
Iceland	No*	No*	No*	No*	No*	* Need return ticket.
India	No*	No*	No*	Yes	Yes	* Must have valid passport.
Indonesia	*	*	*	*	*	* Depends on the reason for visiting. Each individual must find out if a visa is necessary for their particular trip.
Iran	Yes*	Yes*	Yes*	Yes*	Yes*	* Cannot stay in Iran. Can get a transit visa which lasts for 2 weeks and allows you to pass through into Pakistan.
Iraq	Yes*	Yes*	Yes*	Yes*	Yes*	* No entry if passport contains Israeli visa.
Ireland (Rep.)	No	No	No	No	No	
Israel	No	No	No	No	No	
Italy	No	No	No	No	No	
Ivory Coast	Yes*	Yes*	Yes*	Yes*	Yes*	* Valid for 3mths.
Jamaica	No†	No*	No†	No†	No*	† Up to 3mths. * Need proof of citizenship and return ticket for visit not exceeding 6mths.
Japan	Yes	No[a]	No[b]	No[c]	Yes	[a] Up to 90 days. [b] Up to 30 days. [c] Up to 3mths.

Jordan	Yes	Yes	Yes	Yes	Yes	
Kenya	Yes	No	No	No	Yes	
Kiribati	Yes	No	Yes	No	Yes	
Korea	No*	No*	No*	No†	No*	* Up to 15 days. † Up to 60 days.
Kuwait	Yes	Yes	Yes	Yes	Yes	
Laos	Yes	Yes	Yes	Yes	Yes	
Lebanon	*	*	*	*	*	* Not allowed to visit Lebanon without approval of Lebanese authority.
Lesotho	Yes	No	Yes	No	Yes	
Liberia	Yes	Yes	Yes	Yes	Yes	
Libya	Yes	Yes	Yes	Yes	Yes	
Luxembourg	No*	No*	No*	No*	No*	* Up to 3mths.
Macao	No	No	No	No	No	
Madagascar	Yes	Yes	Yes	Yes	Yes	
Malawi	No*	No*	No*	No*	No*	* Up to 6mths.
Malaysia	No	No	No	No	No*	* Up to 3mths.
Mali	Yes	Yes	Yes	Yes	Yes	
Malta	No	No	No	No	No	
Mauritiana	Yes	Yes	Yes	Yes	Yes	

Country Travelling To:	Visa Requirements					Restrictions and Requirements
	Australia	Canada	New Zealand	UK	USA	
Mauritius	No	No	No	No	No	
Mexico	No*	No*	No*	No*	No*	* Need to get tourist card which is free of charge.
Mongolia	Yes	Yes	Yes	Yes	Yes	
Morocco	No	No	No	No	No	
Nepal	Yes*	Yes*	Yes*	Yes*	Yes*	* Valid for 3mths.
Netherlands	No*	No*	No*	No*	No*	* Up to 3mths.
New Zealand	No	No†	—	No†	No*	† Up to 6mths. * Up to 3mths. All visitors need an onward ticket and sufficient funds.
Nicaragua	Yes	Yes	Yes	No*	Yes	* Return ticket.
Nigeria	No*	No*	No*	No*	Yes	* Need entry permit.
N. Ireland	Yes	No	Yes	No	No	
Norway	No	No	No	No	No	
Oman	*	*	*	*	*	* Not issuing visas at present. To go to Oman you need a sponsor in Oman to apply for a 'No objection Certificate' for you (allows you to travel for 3mths).
Pakistan	No*	No*	No*	No*	No†	* Up to 3mths. † Up to 1mth.
Panama	Yes	Yes	Yes	Yes	Yes	

Papua New Guinea	No*	No*	No*	No*	No*	* Up to 30 days but need a return ticket.
Paraguay	No*	No*	No*	No	No	* Passport needs to be fully endorsed for all countries.
Peru	Yes	No	Yes	No	No	
Philippines	No*	No*	No*	No*	No*	* For 21 days as long as have ticket of onward travel.
Poland	Yes*	Yes*	Yes*	Yes*	Yes*	* Valid for 90 days.
Portugal	No[a]	No[b]	Yes	No[c]	No[b]	[a] Up to 3mths. [b] Need visa for Azores [c] Up to 2mths.
Qatar	Yes	Yes	Yes	Yes	Yes	
Romania	Yes	Yes	Yes	Yes	Yes	
Rwanda	Yes	Yes	Yes	Yes	Yes	
Saudi Arabia	Yes	Yes	Yes	No*	Yes	* If passport issued before 1/1/83 and P.5 reads 'Holder has right of abode in the UK' or if passport issued after 1/1/83 and stamped on P.1 – British Citizen.
Sénégal	Yes*	Yes*	Yes*	Yes*	Yes*	* Plus return ticket.
Sierra Leone	Yes	Yes	Yes	Yes	Yes	
Seychelles	No	No	No	No	No	
Singapore	No	No	No	No	No	
Solomon Is.	No	No	No	No	No	
Somali Dem. Rep.	Yes	Yes	Yes	Yes	Yes	
South Africa	Yes	Yes	Yes	No	Yes	

Country Travelling To:	*Visa Requirements*					*Restrictions and Requirements*
	Australia	*Canada*	*New Zealand*	*UK*	*USA*	
Soviet Union	Yes	Yes	Yes	Yes	Yes	
Spain	Yes	No*	Yes	No*	No*	* Up to 90 days.
Sri Lanka	No*	No*	No*	No*	No*	* Up to 6mths.
Sudan	Yes	Yes	Yes	Yes	Yes	
Swaziland	No	No	No	No	No	
Sweden	No	No	No	No	No	
Switzerland	No	No	No	No	No	
Syria	Yes	Yes	Yes	Yes	Yes	
Tahiti	No†	No*	No†	No†	No*	† Up to 3mths. * Up to 1mth.
Tanzania	No*	No*	No*	No*	Yes	* Need visitors' pass.
Thailand	No*	No*	No*	No*	No*	* Up to 15 days. If leave by rail need visa.
Togo	Yes	Yes	Yes	Yes	Yes	
Tonga	No	No	No	No	Yes	
Trinidad & Tobago	No	No	No	No	No	
Tunisia	Yes*	No	Yes	No	No	* Delivered on arrival.
Turkey	No*	No*	No*	No*	No*	* Up to 3mths.
Turks & Caicos Is.	No	No	No	No	No	
Uganda	Yes	Yes	Yes	Yes	Yes	

United Arab Emirates	Yes	Yes	Yes	No	Yes	If passport issued before 1/1/83 and has on P.5 'Holder has right of abode in UK' or issued after 1/1/83 and and stamped on P.1 – British Citizen.
United Kingdom	Yes	No	Yes	—	No	
US Virgin Is.	Yes*	No	Yes*	Yes*	No	* also evidence to prove you will be leaving the country.
United States	Yes*	No	Yes*	Yes*	—	* also evidence to prove you will be leaving the country.
Upper Volta (Burkina Faso)	Yes	Yes	Yes	Yes	Yes	
Uruguay	Yes	No	Yes	No	No	
Vanuatu	No	No	No	No	No	
Venezuela	Yes	Yes	Yes	Yes	Yes	
Vietnam	Yes*	Yes*	Yes*	Yes*	Yes*	* but cannot get one as a single person – have to go in an organized group.
P's Dem. Rep. Yemen	Yes*	Yes*	Yes*	Yes*	Yes*	* Need to have booked accommodation before going and a return ticket. If passport has an Israel stamp cannot get a visa.
Yemen Arab Rep.	Yes	Yes	Yes	Yes	Yes	
Yugoslavia	Yes	Yes	Yes	No	Yes	
Zaïre	Yes	Yes	Yes	Yes	Yes	
Zambia	No	No	Yes	No	Yes	
Zimbabwe	No	No	No	No	No	

Nationalities Banned Entry

In the interests of space, we have left out the ban on *South Africans* and *Israelis* which are so wide-reaching that nationals of these countries should automatically check whether they are allowed entry. Roughly speaking, Israelis are barred from any Muslim country and South Africans from any predominantly black country, and the bar will also spread to other countries which have close ties.

NB: Travellers should also note that having a stamp in your passport from a barred country can also be enough to stop you entering. If you wish, for instance, to go to both Israel and some of the Arab countries, you should get a second passport.

Benin	Morocco, Iran, Iraq.
Burma	Taiwan.
Greece	Nationals of, and people who have visited since 'independence' on November 15, 1983, Turkish Cyprus.
Hungary	South Korea.
Iran	United States.
Israel	Communist and Arab countries.
Japan	Criminals!
Jordan	Iran, Lebanon.
Malaysia	China, Albania, Bulgaria, Cuba, Czechoslovakia, East Germany, Hungary, Laos, Kampuchea, Vietnam, North Africa, Poland, Romania, Russia, Taiwan, Yugoslavia.
Mexico	Written authorization needed from the Immigration Authority for the nationals of the following countries: Albania, Angola, Bangladesh, Bhutan, Chile, Cuba, Djibouti, Dominica, Fiji, Grenada, Iran, Kiribati, North Korea, Lebanon, Maldives, Micronesia, Nauru, Papua New Guinea, Solomon Islands, Western Samoa, St. Vincent and the Grenadines, St. Lucia, Seychelles, Taiwan, Tonga, Tuvalu, Vanuatu, People's Republic of Yemen, and Zimbabwe.
Paraguay	Russia, Cuba and all countries with a Communist government.
USSR	China, Iran.

Exit Visas

This list, for the sake of space, includes only those countries which do require some form of exit visa. In other countries it is levied as an airport departure tax (*see list on page 667*).

Albania	Exit visa required by own nationals.
Bahamas	Departure tax of B$5 for adults and B$2.50 for children of 2–12.
Belize	Departure tax of $10.
Benin	Exit visa required. Ask when applying for entry visa.
British Virgin Islands	Departure tax of US$5.
Bulgaria	Exit visa required by own nationals.
Burma	Exit visa required by travellers staying more than 30 days.
Cameroon	Exit visa required. Costs £3.67.
China	Exit visa required by own nationals.
Costa Rica	Exit visa required. Costs $10.
Czechoslovakia	Exit visa required by own nationals.

Djibouti	Normally contained in entry visa. Check.
Ethiopia	Exit visa required. Costs £3.00.
German Dem. Rep.	Exit visa required. Nationals must apply. It is usually given free to tourists with the entry visa. Check.
Hungary	Exit visa required by own nationals.
India	No visa required, but you must have your Registration Certificate endorsed before departure. This is done by the Superintendent of Police in all District Headquarters.
Iran	Exit visa required by own nationals.
Iraq	Exit visa required by own nationals.
Ivory Coast	Yes, can be obtained with entry visa from embassies.
North Korea	Exit visa required by own nationals.
Laos	Exit visa required by own nationals.
Liberia	Required, but free. Ask from embassies when obtaining entry visa.
Libya	Exit visa required by own nationals.
Mongolia	Exit visa required by own nationals.
Niger	Yes. Ask at embassy when applying for entry visa.
Poland	Exit visa required by own nationals.
Romania	Exit visa required by own nationals.
USSR	Exit visa required by own nationals.
Vietnam	Exit visa required by own nationals.
Yugoslavia	Yes, but contained with entry visa.

Restrictions on Working Around the World

Afghanistan	Not granting visas at present, so no work possible.
Algeria	Only possible if there is a contract between Algeria and your own country, when you can come in as part of the project.
American Samoa	Severe restrictions. Immigration approval is necessary first, and this is only granted for special needs and skills that cannot be satisfied locally.
Andorra	There is an annual allocation of work permits that must be applied for personally in Andorra – after the applicant has secured a position.
Antigua and Barbuda	Work permits required. You can only work if locals cannot perform the function. Must arrange the permit in advance.
Argentina	Need a work permit.
Australia	Must have a work permit – they are not easy to get hold of.
Austria	Work permits are required for *all* types of employment, but are never issued for part-time employment.
Bahamas	Need a work permit, but no expatriate may be offered employment in a post for which a suitably qualified Bahamian is available.
Bahrain	Employer must get permit in Bahrain and send it to the employee to be stamped by the Embassy in his own country.
Bangladesh	Can work for up to three months without a permit.
Barbados	Work permits are issued to employers not employees – you must apply for a job beforehand.
Belgium	The Belgian employer must apply for the permit.
Belize	Work permit required.
Bermuda	Must have a job and work permit before entering.
Benin	Need to have a contract with a company or the Benin Government before applying.

Bolivia	Only residents in Bolivia are allowed employment.
Botswana	Need work permit.
Brazil	Working visas are only issued on the presentation of a work contract, duly certified by the Brazilian Ministry of Labour.
British Virgin Islands	Work permit required.
Bulgaria	It is not possible to get a work permit.
Burma	Government approval required.
Cameroon	You need a work permit, which can be obtained in the Cameroons.
Canada	Work permit required.
Cayman Islands	You must be in possession of a work permit.
Chile	Must have a contract with a company before applying.
China	No work unless either a teacher or technician when one works under contract.
Colombia	Work visa needed.
Costa Rica	Need a signed contract with employer.
Cuba	It is not possible to work here.
Cyprus	Work permit needed – must be obtained by employer.
Czechoslovakia	Permission to work involves a complicated procedure – enquire at embassy before you go.
Denmark	Nationals of EEC countries do not need permits. Other countries require permits, but they are not being issued at present.
Djibouti	Not much work available.
Dominica	Need work permit obtained from country of origin.
Dominican Rep.	Work permit required.
Eastern Caribbean	Work permit offered only if a national cannot do the job.
Ecuador	Work permit required.
El Salvador	Work permit can be obtained for technical or specialized work.
Ethiopia	It is not possible to work here.
Fiji	Need a work permit before entering Fiji.
Finland	Work permit required.
France	Nationals of EEC countries do not need work permits. Others do.
Gabon	Work permit required.
The Gambia	Work permit required.
Fed. Rep. of Germany	Nationals of EEC countries do not need permits. Others do, but they are only issued once work has been found.
German Dem. Rep.	It is not possible to work here.
Ghana	Work permit required.
Gibraltar	All foreign nationals except the British need work permits.
Great Britain	Commonwealth nationals aged 17 to 27 can work for two years on a holiday visa. All others need a work permit.
Greece	Need a permit issued by the Greek Ministry of Labour.
Grenada	Work permit needed.
Guyana	Work permit needed.
Haiti	First need to get a *Permit de Séjour*, then your employers must apply for a work permit for you.
Hong Kong	You need a work permit if working in the private sector, but not if working for the Hong Kong Government.
Hungary	Work permit needed.

Iceland	Need a work permit prior to accepting employment – prospective employer should apply for the permit.
India	No permit is needed, but you cannot take the money earned out.
Indonesia	Apply for the work permit out there.
Ireland	Not required by Commonwealth citizens, but needed by all others.
Iran	Work permit required.
Iraq	Work permit may be arranged by Foreign companies working in Iraq. Otherwise it is impossible to work in the country.
Israel	Apply to the embassy in your home country.
Italy	Nationals of EEC countries may work without permits. All others need them.
Ivory Coast	You are not allowed to work here unless sent by a private company which will arrange your permit for you.
Jamaica	Work permit required.
Japan	Long-term commercial business visa is needed if working for your own company in Japan. Others require work permits.
Jordan	You can only get work through a local company or a foreign company's local offices.
Kenya	Prospective employer in Kenya must obtain a permit for you before you arrive.
Korea	Need a work permit from the Korean embassy in your normal country of residence.
Kuwait	Need a contract from Kuwait before the permit will be issued.
Liberia	Work permit required.
Luxembourg	EEC citizens may work without a permit. All other nationals require one.
Macao	Work permit required.
Malawi	Work permit required.
Malaysia	Work permit required. You need a sponsor in Malaysia who agrees to assure your maintenance and repatriation.
Malta	Permits only issued for specialized skills not found on the island.
Mauritius	Work permit required.
Mexico	No work allowed unless you are specifically requested by a Mexican company.
Morocco	Work permit required.
Netherlands	EEC citizens do not need work permits. All other nationalities do.
New Zealand	All nationalities except Australians need a work permit.
Norway	Work permit required.
Oman	Work permit required. Need a sponsor – either an Omani company or Omani national.
Paraguay	No permit needed.
Peru	Arrange everything in Peru.
Poland	Foreigners cannot work in Poland.
Portugal	Work permit required.
Qatar	Work permit must be obtained by employer.
Sénégal	Work permits can be obtained in Dakar.
Seychelles	Apply for a Gainful Occupation Permit from the Seychelles.
Singapore	Permission to work depends on your nationality. Check with the embassy in your home country.
South Africa	Not allowed to accept employment without special permission from the Director General, Internal Affairs.
Spain	Permit needed to work legally.

Sri Lanka	Cannot work without Government approval.
Swaziland	Work permit required.
Sweden	Work permit required.
Switzerland	Work permit required.
Tahiti	Work permit difficult to obtain. Employer must apply and ensure the employee's return to his country of origin.
Tanzania	Work permit required.
Tonga	Work permit required.
Trinidad and Tobago	Work permit required.
Tunisia	Work permit required.
Turkey	Working visa required.
United Arab Emirates	Work permit needed – apply on arrival.
US Virgin Islands	Work permit required.
United States	Work permit (Green Card) required.
Upper Volta	Can work for Government aid schemes or as a volunteer without a permit.
Uruguay	Work permit needed.
Zambia	Work permit only arranged on firm offer of employment by a Zambian employer.
Zimbabwe	Apply for a work permit through your prospective employer.

Passport Offices

Great Britain

London Passport Office
Clive House
70–78 Petty France
London SW1H 9HD
Tel: 01-213 3344/7272/6161/3434

Liverpool Passport Office
5th Floor
India Buildings
Water Street
Liverpool L2 0QZ
Tel: 051-237 3010

Newport Passport Office
Olympia House
Upper Dock Street
Newport
Gwent NPT 1XA
Tel: (0633) 56292

Peterborough Passport Office
55 Westfield Road
Cambs PE3 6GT
Tel: (0733) 895555

Glasgow Passport Office
1st Floor
Empire House
131 West Nile Street
Glasgow G1 2RY
Tel: 041-332 0271

Belfast Passport Office
Hampton House
47–53 High Street
Belfast BT1 2AS
Tel: (0232) 232371

United States

Passport Agency
Room E
123 John F Kennedy Bldg
Government Center
Boston
MA 02203
Tel: (617) 223 3831

Room 331
Federal Office Bldg
230 South Dearborn Street
Chicago
IL 60604
Tel: (312) 353 7155

Federal Bldg
335 Merchant Street
Honolulu
HI 96813
Tel: (808) 546 2130

Hawthorne Federal Bldg
Room 2W16
1500 Aviation Blvd
Lawndale
Los Angeles
CA 90261
Tel: (213) 536 6503

Room 804
International Trade Mart
2 Canal Street
New Orleans
LA 70130
Tel: (504) 589 6161

Room 270
Rockefeller Center
630 Fifth Avenue
New York
NY 10020
Tel: (212) 541 7710

Room 4426
Federal Bldg
600 Arch Street
Philadelphia
PA 19106
Tel: (215) 597 7480

Room 1405
Federal Bldg
450 Golden Gate Avenue
San Francisco
CA 94102
Tel: (415) 556 2630

Room 906
Federal Bldg
915 Second Avenue
Seattle
WA 98174
Tel: (206) 442 7945

Passport Office
1425 K Street NW
Washington
DC 20524
Tel: (202) 783 8170

Australia

22 West Row
Canberra City
ACT 2601
Tel: (062) 613810

Commonwealth Government Centre
Cnr Hunter and Phillip Streets,
Sydney
NSW 2000

Mercantile Mutual Building
456 Hunter Street
Newcastle
NSW 2300
Tel: (049) 263655

Commonwealth Government Centre
Cnr Latrobe and Spring Streets
Melbourne
Victoria 3000
Tel: (03) 662 1722

Sun Alliance Building
45 Grenfell Street
Adelaide
South Australia 5000
Tel: (08) 212 2466

Commonwealth Government Centre
295 Ann Street
Brisbane
Queensland 4000
Tel: (07) 225 0122

City Centre Towers
44 St. George's Terrace
Perth
Western Australia 6000
Tel: (09) 325 4944

Commonwealth Government Centre
188 Collins Street
Hobart
Tasmania 7000
Tel: (002) 204050

Arkaba House
Esplanade
Darwin
Northern Territories 5790
Tel: (089) 814566

Passport applications can also be submitted to any official Australian Post Office.

Canada

Dept of External Affairs
Ottawa
Ont K1A 0GJ
Tel: (613) 995 8481

220 4th Ave E
Calgary
Alberta T2G 4X3
Tel: (403) 231 5171

Suite 601
440 King St.
Fredericton
New Brunswick
E3B 5H8
Tel: (506) 452 3900

Suite 1210
Barrington Tower
Scotia Square
Halifax
Nova Scotia
B3J 1P3
Tel: (902) 426 2770

Mezzanine Floor
Commerce House
1080 Beaver Hall Hill
Montreal
Quebec H2Z 1SB
Tel: (514) 283 2152

4th Floor
354 Water St.
Box 2185
St. Johns
Newfoundland
A1C 6E6
Tel: (709) 772 4616

Suite 605
101 22nd St E
Saskatoon
Saskatchewan
S7K 0E1
Tel: (306) 665 5106

Suite 228
816 Government St
Victoria
British Columbia
V8W 1W8
Tel: (604) 388 0213

Suite 308
391 York Ave
Winnipeg
Manitoba
R3C 0P6
Tel: (204) 949 2190

New Zealand

Dept of Internal Affairs
Government Life Building
99 Queen Street
Auckland 1
Tel: (9) 31184

Dept of Internal Affairs
The Local Government Building
114/118 Lambton Quay
Wellington
Tel: (4) 738699

Dept of Internal Affairs
Government Life Building
Cathedral Square
Christchurch 1
Tel: (3) 790290

Visa Agencies

Intercontinental Visa Service

Los Angeles World Trade Center
350 South Figueroa Street
Los Angeles
CA 90071
USA
Tel: (213) 625 7175
Specialize in visas, passport photos and travel books.

Thomas Cook

45 Berkeley Street
London W1A 1EB
Tel: 01-499 4000
Passport Department can obtain visas for almost any destination for £5.00 per person.

Visas International

3169 Barbara Ct Ste F
Los Angeles
California 90068
USA
Tel: (213) 850 1192
Visa service and Intourist Representative (USSR Hotels).

Travcour (UK)

Tempo House
15 Falcon Road
London SW11
Tel: (01) 223 4772/6966
Specialises in hard-to-obtain visas.

Customs Regulations

United Kingdom

The following chart gives the legal limits of goods which can be brought per adult into Britain duty free. List A is for goods obtained duty free or from outside the EEC. List B is for goods on which duty or tax has been paid within the EEC.

A

Tobacco:
200 cigarettes
or
100 cigarillos
or
50 cigars
or
250 grammes of tobacco.

These quantities can be doubled if you are resident outside Europe.

Alcoholic Drinks:
1 litre of alcoholic drinks over 22% vol (38.8% proof)
or
2 litres of alcoholic drinks not over 22% vol **or** fortified **or** sparkling wine
plus
2 litres of still table wine.

Perfume:
50 grammes (60cc or 2fl oz).

Toilet Water:
250cc (9fl oz).

Other Goods:
Worth £28.

B

Tobacco:
300 cigarettes
or
150 cigarillos
or
75 cigars
or
400 grammes of tobacco.

Alcoholic Drinks:
1½ litres of alcoholic drinks over 22% vol (38.8% proof)
or
3 litres of alcoholic drinks not over 22% vol **or** fortified **or** sparkling wine
plus
4 litres of still table wine.

Perfume:
75 grammes (90cc or 3fl oz).

Toilet Water:
375cc (13fl oz).

Other Goods:
£120 worth.

The following goods are restricted or prohibited:

Controlled drugs.
Firearms (including fireworks).
Flick knives.
Counterfeit coins.
Horror and pornographic literature, films, videos, etc.
Radio transmitters (eg CB) capable of operating on certain frequencies.
Improperly cooked meat and poultry.
Plants, parts thereof and plant produce.
Most animals and birds – alive or dead; certain articles derived from animals including ivory, furskins, reptile leather goods.
Any live mammal – unless a British import licence (rabies) has previously been issued.

Old photographic material valued at £200 or more, portraits over 50 years old and valued at £2,000 or more, antiques and collectors, items valued at £8,000 or more, and certain archaeological material are all subject to export controls and formalities should be completed through the Customs and Excise Office before you leave.

Notes:

1. Persons under 17 are not entitled to tobacco and drinks allowances.
2. If you are visiting the UK for less than six months, you are also entitled to bring in all personal effects (except those mentioned above) which you intend to take with you when you leave.

United States

Everyone entering the United States will be asked to fill in a Customs declaration listing everything except clothes, jewellery, toilet articles, etc, owned by you and intended for your own use. The exceptions are duty free. If jewellery worth $300 or more is sold within three years, duty must then be paid or the article will become subject to seizure.

Alcoholic Drinks:
Adult nonresidents can bring in not more than 1 litre of any form of alcohol for personal use. The amount varies from state to state, and in the more restrictive states, only the legal quantity will be released to you.

If you are only in transit, you are permitted up to 4 litres of alcohol, as long as it accompanies you out of the country.

Liquor-filled candy, and absinthe are prohibited goods.

Tobacco:
Your personal exemption may include 200 cigarettes (one carton), 50 cigars, or 2 kilograms of smoking tobacco, or proportionate quantities of each. An additional 100 cigars may be brought in under your gift exemption.

Gift Exemption:
A nonresident may take in goods valued at up to $100 for use as gifts, provided he/she is to remain in the country for at least 72 hours. This allowance may only be claimed once every 6 months.

Other Goods:
You may bring in articles worth up to $25 for personal use, including tobacco, alcohol (see earlier sections) and 150ml of perfume.

Antiques are free of duty if produced 100 years prior to the date of entry.

A person emigrating may bring in professional equipment duty free.

If in transit, you may take dutiable goods worth up to $200 through the United States without payment.

Prohibited Items

Lottery tickets, narcotics and dangerous drugs, obscene publications, seditious and treasonable materials, hazardous articles (e.g. fireworks, dangerous toys, toxic or poisonous substances), products made by convicts or forced labour, switchblade knives, pirate copies of copyright books.

Firearms and ammunition intended for lawful hunting or sporting purposes are admissible, provided you take the firearms and unfired ammunition with you out of the country.

Cultural objects, such as ethnic artwork, will be allowed in only if accompanied by a valid export certificate from their country of origin.

Food:
Bakery items, all cured cheeses, professionally canned foods are permitted. Most plants, or plant products are prohibited or require an import permit. The importation of meat, or meat products is dependent on the animal disease condition in the country of origin.

Medicine:
A traveller requiring medicines containing habit-forming drugs or narcotics should always carry a doctor's letter or prescription; make sure that all medicines are properly identified; and do not carry more than might normally be used by one person.

Pets:
Cats and dogs must be free of diseases communicable to man. Vaccination against rabies is not required for dogs and cats arriving from rabies-free countries. There are controls and prohibitions on all livestock, and anyone wishing to import any should apply to the US Customs for further information.

Australia

Each passenger over the age of 18 is entitled to the following duty free admissions:

200 cigarettes
or
250 grams cigars
or
250 grams tobacco
plus
1 litre of alcoholic liquor (including wine and beer).

General Items:
Gifts, souvenirs, household articles unused or less than 12 months old are duty free to a value of A$200.

Goods to the value of a further A$160 are dutiable at 20 per cent.

You may also take in:

Personal items of the type normally carried on your person or in your personal baggage including jewellery or toilet requisites, but not electrical items.
Binoculars.
Portable typewriters.
Exposed film.
Photographic cameras.
Personal sporting requisites.
Bicycles and motorcycles.
Clothing (excepting fur apparel, unless it is valued at A$150 or less, or you have owned and worn it for 12 months or more).

In order to qualify for duty-free status, goods should be for your personal use, and not have been bought on behalf of someone else, and should have travelled with you.

Prohibited Articles

Drugs of dependence.
Firearms and weapons.

Wildlife – there is a strict control of all wildlife and wildlife products in and out of Australia. Travellers should be warned that articles of apparel, accessories, ornaments, trophies, etc., made from endangered species of fauna will be seized if imported into Australia. This includes animals such as alligators and crocodiles, elephants, rhinoceros, snakes, lizards, turtles, zebra, and the large cats.

Domestic pets – you cannot bring in cats or dogs, except from the United Kingdom and Ireland, Papua New Guinea, Fiji, New Zealand, Hawaii, and Norfolk Island. The animals must have been resident in one of these approved countries for at least six months. A permit is required in all cases. Other goods – most meat and meat products, dairy produce, plants and plant produce.

Canada

Visitors may bring in duty free all items of personal baggage including clothing, jewellery, etc. Sporting equipment, radios, television sets, musical instruments, typewriters, cameras, are all included in this category.

Alcoholic Beverages:

The age limit is 18 in some provinces, and 19 in others, and should be checked before travelling.

1.1 litres (40oz) of liquor or wine
or
24 × 336ml (12oz cans or bottles) of beer, or its equivalent of 8.2 litres (288fl oz).

A further 9 litres (two gallons) of alcoholic beverages may be imported (except to Prince Edward Island and the Northwest Territories) on payment of duty.

Tobacco:

Persons over 16 years of age may bring in:

50 cigars,
200 cigarettes,
0.9kg (2lb) of manufactured tobacco.

Gifts:

Gifts may be imported duty free provided each gift does not exceed $25 (Canadian) in value, and does not contain tobacco products, alcoholic beverages, or advertising material.

Prohibited and Restricted Goods

Animals:

Any pet animal or bird requires a Canadian import permit and a veterinary certificate of health from its country of origin.

Domestic dogs and cats may be imported only from rabies-free countries without quarantine or vaccination if: they are shipped directly from that country, they are accompanied by a vet's certificate, and that the country has been rabies-free for the six months prior to the animal's departure.

Endangered species – restrictions on the movement of endangered species stretch also to products made from them. A permit is required for many skins, trophies, etc, as well as live animals.

Foods:

Meat and meat products are only allowed in if canned and sterile; or commercially cooked and prepared; and the total weight accompanying the traveller does not exceed 10kg per person.

Processed cheese and cooked eggs are the only permissible dairy products.

Food, in general, can be imported duty free, provided the amount is only sufficient for two days' personal use by the importer.

Plants:

It is forbidden to import plants or plant produce without permission under the Plant Quarantine Act.

Firearms:

Handguns are not allowed entry to Canada. Firearms are restricted to those with a legitimate sporting or recreational use. A permit is not required for long guns.

All explosives, ammunition, pyrotechnic devices, etc, except the following, are forbidden entry to Canada: sporting and competitive ammunition for personal use, distress and life-saving devices such as flares.

New Zealand

Personal effects will be allowed to enter duty free, provided they are your own property, are intended for your own use, and are not imported for commercial purposes. Items such as clothing, footwear, articles of adornment, watches, brushes and toilet requisites can be included here. Jewellery can be included, but not unmounted precious or semi-precious stones, and fur apparel purchased overseas can only be included if you have owned and worn it for more than 12 months.

Tobacco:

Passengers over 17 years of age are allowed the following:

200 cigarettes
or
250 grams of tobacco
or
50 cigars
or
a mixture of all three, weighing not more than 250 grams.

Alcohol:

Passengers over 17 years of age are allowed the following:

4.5 litres of wine (this is equivalent to six 750-ml bottles)
and
one bottle containing not more than 1,125ml of spirits or liqueur.

All passengers are given a general concession on goods up to a combined value of NZ$200. Persons travelling together may not combine their allowances. Children may claim their allowances provided the goods are their own property and of a type a child would reasonably expect to own.

Visitors to New Zealand are also permitted to bring in such items as a camera, a pair of binoculars, a portable radio and camping equipment, on condition that the goods leave the country with them.

Prohibited or Restricted Items

Drugs:
The import of drugs is strictly forbidden and incurr heavy penalties. Should they be necessary for your health, carry a letter of authorization and carry the medication in its original, clearly marked bottle.

Firearms:
The importation of any weapon is strictly controlled and requires a Police permit. Flick knives, sword sticks, knuckledusters, and other such weapons are prohibited.

Flora and Fauna:
The entry of domestic dogs and cats is governed by the Agricultural Quarantine Service to whom you should apply for further details.

The following goods must be declared:

Food of any kind.
Plants or parts of plants (dead or alive).
Animals (dead or alive) and animal products.
Equipment used with animals.
Equipment such as camping gear, golf clubs and used bicycles.

Vehicles

All countries will let you bring in a vehicle, whether car, camper van or yacht, without paying duty, either on presentation of a *carnet de passages* or on an assurance that you will not sell the vehicle for a certain length of time.

You may have to have the vehicle steam-cleaned to help prevent the spread of diseases in the soil.

Customs Offices:

Australia

The Australian Customs Representative
Canberra House
Maltravers Street
off Arundel Street
Strand
London WC2R 3EF
Tel: (01) 438-8000

The Australian Customs Representative
636 Fifth Avenue
New York
NY 10020
USA
Tel: (212) 245-4078

Office of the Counsellor (Customs)
Australian Embassy
7th Floor
Sankaido Bldg
9–13 Akasaka
1-Chome
Minato-Ku
Tokyo
Japan

The Australian Customs Representative
c/o Australian Commission
Connaught Centre
Connaught Road
Hong Kong

The Australian Customs Representative
c/o Australian Trade Commissioner
Lorne Towers (9th Floor)
12 Lorne Street
PO Box 3601
Auckland

The Collector of Customs
Sydney
NSW 2000
Tel: (02) 2-0521

The Collector of Customs
Melbourne
Victoria 3000
Tel: (03) 62-0461

The Collector of Customs
Brisbane
QLD 4000
Tel: (08) 31-0361

The Collector of Customs
Port Adelaide
SA 5015
Tel: (08) 47-5911

The Collector of Customs
Perth
WA 6000
Tel: (09) 321-9761

The Collector of Customs
Hobart
TAS 7000
Tel: (002) 30-1201

The Collector of Customs
Darwin
NT 5790
Tel: (089) 81-4444

The Secretary
Department of Business and Consumer Affairs
Canberra
ACT 2600
Tel: (062) 73-0414

Canada

Revenue Canada
Customs and Excise
Public Relations Branch
Ottawa
Ontario
Canada K1A O15
Tel: (613) 593-6220
For customs information.

Canada Customs
2 St André Street
Quebec
Quebec G1K 7P6
Tel: (418) 694-4445

400 Carre Youville
Montreal
Quebec
H2Y 3N4
Tel: (514) 283-2953

360 Coventry Road
Ottawa
Ontario
K1K 2C6
Tel: (631) 993-0534 (8.00am to 4.30pm); (613) 998-3326 (after 4.30pm and weekends)

Manulife Centre, 10th Floor
55 Bloor Street West
Toronto
Ontario
M5W 1A3
Tel: (416) 966-8022 (8.00am to 4.30pm); (416) 676-3643 (evenings and weekends)

Federal Bldg
269 Main Street
Winnipeg
Manitoba
R3C 1B3
Tel: (204) 949-6004

204 Towne Square
1919 Rose Street
Regina
Saskatchewan
S4P 3P1
Tel: (306) 359-6212

220–4th Avenue SE, Ste 720
PO Box 2970
Calgary
Alberta
T2P 2M7
Tel: (403) 231-4610

1001 West Pender Street
Vancouver
British Columbia
V6E 2M8
Tel: (604) 666-1545/6

New Zealand

Customs Office
Box 29
Auckland
Tel: 773-520

Customs Office
Box 2098
Christchurch
Tel: 796-660

Customs Office
Private Bag
Dunedin
Tel: 799251

Customs Office
Box 940
Hamilton
Tel: 82-724

Customs Office
Box 1345
Palmerston North
Tel: 76-059

Customs Office
Private Bag
Wellington
Tel: 736 099

United Kingdom

For notices and forms ask at any Customs and Excise office or write to:

HM Customs and Excise

Kent House
Upper Ground
London SE1 9PS

Other Customs and Excise offices in major cities in the UK are:

27 King Street
Aberdeen AB9 2SH
Tel: (0224) 648 251

Customs House
Belfast BT1 3EU
Tel: (0232) 234 466

Customs House
Liverpool L3 1DX
Tel: 051-227 4343

19/29 Woburn Place
London WC1H 0JQ
Tel: 01-632 3333
For London City and South.

93–107 Shaftesbury Avenue
London W1V 7AE
Tel: 01-437 9800
For London North and North West

Customs House
Lower Thames Street
London EC3R 6EE
Tel: 01-626 1515

Customs House
Trafford Road
Salford M5 3DB
Tel: 061-872 4282

39 Quayside
Newcastle-on-Tyne
NE1 3ES
Tel: (0623) 610 981
For Northern England.

United States of America

Customs Office

United States Embassy
Grosvenor Square
London W1A 2JB
For detailed information about US Customs regulations the brochures 'US Customs Hints for Visitors', and 'Importing a Car' are available on request.

US Customs Service

PO Box 7118
Washington
DC 20044
USA
For complaints and suggestions write to above address. On request 'Customs Hints for Returning US Residents – Know Before You Go'.

Currency Restrictions

Many countries impose restrictions on the import or export of local and foreign currency. Often these take the form of ceilings, normally reasonably generous, so that the traveller should rarely be aware of their existence. However, it is worth checking every country you intend to visit.

The following is a list applicable at the time of going to press, of currency regulations which may impinge on the traveller. The list is not comprehensive, as those countries with no restrictions, or restrictions relating only to residents are not included.

KEY TO COLUMNS

(1) Import of local currency prohibited.
(2) Export of local currency prohibited.
(3) Foreign currency may be imported but must be declared.
(4) Foreign currency may be exported by non-residents up to the amount imported and declared.
(5) Other.

Country	(1)	(2)	(3)	(4)	(5)
Albania	yes	yes	yes		
Algeria	yes				Keep a record of all exchange deals if you wish to re-change your money on exit.
Angola		yes	yes		Sale of imported foreign currency to customs on arrival is obligatory.
Australia					The ceiling on local currency leaving the country is A$250 in notes and A$5 in coins. If you wish to transfer more than A$10,000 out of the country, it must be authorized in advance.
Austria					No limit on exporting foreign currency, or Austrian currency, but advance permission is needed to take out more than A$15,000
Bangladesh			yes (if more than $150)		It is possible to reconvert 25 per cent of currency changed. A full declaration must be made on leaving.
Belize				yes	Only UK £10 may be imported.
Bermuda				yes	

Country	(1)	(2)	(3)	(4)	(5)
Botswana				May export up to equivalent of P200 in foreign currency	
British Virgin Islands				yes	
Burma	yes	yes	yes	yes	Foreign currency must be surrendered to an authorized dealer within one month of arrival in Burma. Reasonable amounts may be reconverted on departure.
Central African Republic			yes	yes	
China	yes	yes		yes	
Cuba	yes	yes		yes	
Cyprus	yes beyond CYL (Cyprian Pound 10)	yes	yes (over US$50)		
Czechoslovakia	yes	yes			There is a minimum spending limit of 30DM (approx. £8) per day.
Denmark				yes (up to 50,000Dkr)	
Dominica		yes		yes (but no more than US$5,000 in cash)	
Dominican Rep.	yes		yes		No limit on foreign traveller's cheques or bank notes. Exchange may take place at authorized dealers only.
El Salvador				yes	Up to 200.00 *colones* may be taken out in local currency, and the same changed into US dollars for export.
Equatorial Guinea	yes				Local currency up to PTG (*Ukuele*) 3,000 may be exported.
Fiji					Approval is needed to export more than F$2,000.
Finland			yes	yes	Local currency may also be exported, provided you can prove you brought it in.
France				yes (up to 5,000F, unless you declared a higher amount on entry)	
Gambia					There is a limit of D75 (approx. UK£15) to the local currency you can bring out.
Germany, Dem. Rep.	yes	yes	yes	yes	Only local remembrance coins may be exported. There is a minimum expenditure requirement of £6 a day.

Country	(1)	(2)	(3)	(4)	(5)
Ghana			yes		Unused currencies may be re-exchanged on presentation of a form to show that they were obtained from an authorized dealer while in Ghana.
Gibraltar			yes	yes	There is no limit on sterling if travelling to the UK.
Greece					There is a limit of Dr3,000 being taken in or out of the country in local currency.
Grenada					Prior permission for the export of currency must be obtained through application to the Ministry of Finance in accordance with the Exchange Control Ordinance.
Guinea	yes	yes	yes	yes	
Guinea-Bissau	yes	yes	yes	yes	
Guyana			yes	yes	
Hungary					Only 100 *Forints* may be taken out in coins. There are no other restrictions.
Iceland			yes	yes	A maximum of Ikr3,100 may be taken out in notes of Ikr100 or less.
India		yes (except *rupee* traveller's cheques)	yes (if more than US $1,000)	yes	
Iraq				yes (but declaration form must be completed on departure)	There is a minimum expenditure requirement of £300, at a rate of £15 per day.
Israel					A maximum of IS20.00, and US$3,000 in foreign currency may be exported (only US $500 in banknotes).
Italy					A maximum of 200,000 lire may be moved in or out. There are no restrictions on other currencies.
Ivory Coast					Approval is needed to take out more than CFA50,000.
Jamaica	yes				Unused currency will be exchanged on departure, on presentation of receipts for all exchanges made during the stay. A maximum of J$200 or equivalent can be exported.
Kenya	yes		yes	yes	Must have at least £250 unless you have a ticket out of Kenya
Korea			yes	yes	Up to 50,000 *Won* in local currency may be taken from the country
Malta			yes	yes	Movement of local currency is limited to Lm50 coming in, and Lm25 leaving per person.
Mauritius					You may be asked how much you spent and to satisfy exchange control officials on leaving.

Country	(1)	(2)	(3)	(4)	(5)
Morocco	yes		yes	yes	Foreign currency over the value of MDH (*Dirham*) 5,000 must be declared.
Mozambique	yes	yes	yes	yes	
Nicaragua			yes (US$ only)	yes	There is a minimum amount for conversion of US$60 on arrival. A maximum of 5,000 *cordobas* may be exported in local currency.
Nigeria			yes	yes	A maximum of 50 *Naira* may be moved in or out of the country in local currency. An exchange declaration must be presented on departure.
Norway			yes	yes	A maximum of 2,000 *Kroner* cash may be taken out of the country.
Philippines			yes (if over US$ 3,000)		
Poland		yes	yes	yes	A minimum of US$15 must be spent for food and accommodation. Currency vouchers are obtainable from Polorbis Travel Ltd, London, or all Polish National Tourist Offices.
Portugal					You must exchange a minimum of 5,000 *escudos* per entry to the country, and 500 *escudos* a day, unless you have paid for food and accommodation in advance. You can export 5,000 *escudos* in local currency, and up to the equivalent of 30,000 *escudos* in foreign currency.
Romania	yes	yes			
South Africa			yes	yes	Up to R200 may be taken out in banknotes.
Spain			yes	yes	A maximum of 150,000 *pesos* per person can be brought in in local currency, and a maximum of 20,000 *pesos* taken out. A maximum equivalent to 80,000 *pesos* may be taken out in foreign currency, unless the excess is declared on entry.
Sri Lanka	yes	yes	yes	yes	The import of Indian and Pakistani currency is also prohibited. A minimum of US$15 a day must be changed into local currency. An exchange declaration must be endorsed on departure.
Sudan	yes	yes	yes		
Sweden					A maximum of 6,000SwKr can be exported.
Tanzania	yes		yes		There is a minimum expenditure rate per three days: one person – US$40; a family of three – US$100. Local currency cannot be exchanged on leaving, so only change as necessary.
Trinidad and Tobago			yes	yes	A maximum of TT$200.00 per person may be exported in local currency.
Tunisia	yes	yes			Re-exchange of local into foreign currency by non-resident visitors is possible up to 30 per cent of the total amount imported and exchanged, with a maximum of TUD (*Dinar*) 100.
Turkey					The equivalent of US$100 can be taken out in Turkish *Lira*.

Country	(1)	(2)	(3)	(4)	(5)
Uganda	yes		yes		
USSR	yes	yes	yes	yes	The restrictions apply to banknotes and coins.
Vanuatu	yes				No restriction on the import of English or Australian currency; other currencies subject to approval. Export of English and Australian currencies restricted if journey includes non-sterling countries. Local and other currency exports restricted.
Vietnam	yes	yes	yes	yes	
Zaïre	yes	yes	yes		Export of foreign currency permitted provided it is declared up to the amounts not exchanged into local currency.
Zambia					A maximum of ZMK20.00 can be taken out in local currency. Keep a record of all exchanges for reconversion.
Zimbabwe					A maximum of Z$20.00 can be taken out in local currency.

Publishers and Publications

Book and Map Retailers

United Kingdom

The main travel book and map retailers in Greater London are:

Army and Navy Stores Ltd

105 Victoria Street
London SW1
Tel: 01-834 1234

Australian Gift Shop

113 Strand
London WC2
Tel: 01-836 2292

Barkers of Kensington

The Bookshop
63 Kensington High Street
London W8
Tel: 01-937 5432

Belsize Bookshop

193 Haverstock H1
London NW3
Tel: 01-794 4006

Berger & Tims (Booksellers)

7 Bresseden Place
London SW1
Tel: 01-828 8322

Botes Bookshop

1 Brook Street
Kingston-upon-Thames
London
Tel: 01-546 6655

Bush Books

Gen Booksellers
144 Shepherds Bush Centre
Shepherds Bush Garden
London W12
Tel: 01-749 7652

Chapter Travel Ltd

Travel Books/Travel Agents
102 St. John's Wood Terrace
London NW8 6PL
Tel: 01-586 9451
Telex: 8952387

Chapter Travel stocks a very wide range of travel books and maps including the complete Ordnance Survey, Michelin and TCI series. Please send s.a.e. for book lists on individual countries. All credit cards are accepted.

Compendium Bookshop

234 Camden High Street
London NW1
Tel: 01-485 9844 & 267 1525

A useful source of travel books that are difficult to obtain elsewhere.

Cook, Hammond & Kell Ltd

22 Caxton Street
London SW1
Tel: 01-222 2466

Crouch End Bookshop

2 Topsfield Parade
London N8
Tel: 01-348 8966

Faculty Books

98 Ballard's Lane
London N3
Tel: 01-346 7767

Fielders (Books and Stationers)

54 Wimbledon High Road
London SW19
Tel: 01-946 5044

W. & G. Foyle Ltd
Travel Department
Ground Floor
113–117 Charing Cross Road
London WC2H 0EB

Geographia
63 Fleet Street
London EC4
Tel: 01-353 2707

The Good Book Shop
91 Great Russell Street
London WC1
Tel: 01-580 8466

Hatchette
4 Regent Place
London W1
Tel: 01-734 5259/5633

Harrods (Bookshop)
Knightsbridge
London SW1
Tel: 01-730 1234

Hatchards Ltd
187 Piccadilly
London W1
Tel: 01-439 9921

Highgate Bookshop
Highgate High Street
London N6
Tel: 01-340 5625

Highhill Bookshops Ltd
6 Hampstead High Street
London NW3
Tel: 01-435 2218

Houben, W. & A.
2a Church Court
Richmond
London
Tel: 01-940 1055

The Kensington Bookshop
140 Kensington Church Street
London W8
Tel: 01-727 0544

The Kilburn Bookshop
8 Kilburn Bridge
Kilburn High Road
London NW6
Tel: 01-328 7071

The London Map Centre
22–24 Caxton Street
London SW1
Tel: 01-222 2466

Is the main agent for Ordnance Survey maps and retailers for all major publishers. At the same address is the retail outlet for the cartographic printing side of the firm, known as Cook, Hammond & Kell Ltd.

London Tourist Board
26 Grosvenor Gardens
Victoria
London SW1
Tel: 01-730 0791

Mandarin Books Ltd
22 Notting Hill Gate
London W11
Tel: 01-229 P327

Map Marketing
92–104 Carnwath Road
London SW6 3HW
Tel: 01-736 0297

Have a range of over 400 maps which have been laminated and can be supplied framed or unframed. The range includes a selection of world maps, more than 50 individual country maps, over 300 section maps of the UK and over 100 specialized UK maps – postal codes, marketing, counties.

McCarta Ltd
122 King's Road
London WC1X 9DS
Tel: 01-278 8276

Are Book and Map Publishers, Distributors and Retailers. They are agents for Kummerly and Frey, IGN (French Official Survey), Touring Club Italiano, Gabelli, Geocart, Toubis and Storti. As retailers, they have an extensive list of guide books and maps, especially of Europe. Also have a large range of scientific publications related to geography and geology.

Modern Books Co
Gen Booksellers
15–21 Praed Street
London W2
Tel: 01-402 9176

Mowbrays Bookshop

A. R. Mowbray & Co Ltd
28 Margaret Street
London W1
Tel: 01-580 2812

Neal Street Shops

29 Neal Street
London WC2
Tel: 01-240 0136

(Have two other shops on Neal Street.)

New City Bookshop Ltd

7 Byward Street
London EC3
Tel: 01-626 3346

Owl Bookshop

211 Kentish Town Road
London NW5
Tel: 01-485 7793

The Pan Bookshop

158 Fulham Road
London SW10
Tel: 01-373 4997

Penguin Bookshop

Unit 10
The Market
Covent Garden
London WC2
Tel: 01-379 7650

Arthur Probsthain

41 Great Russell Street
London WC1B 3PH
Tel: 01-636 1096

Oriental bookseller and publisher. Extensive specialized lists – topic or region – available.

Regent Bookshop

73 Parkway
London NW1
Tel: 01-485 9822

John Sandoe (Books) Ltd

10 Blacklands Terrace
London SW3
Tel: 01-589 9473

Snowden Smith Books

41 Godfrey Street
London SW3 3SX
Tel: 01-352 6756

Sells late 19th and- and early 20th-century books on travel and anthropology, including ethnology, tribal art, etc. Catalogues on request.

Edward Stanford Ltd

12–14 Long Acre
London WC2 9LP
Tel: 01-836 1321

Is the largest mapseller in London, carrying a wide range of maps, globes, charts and atlases, including Ordnance Survey and Directorate of Overseas Surveys maps. For anyone within reach of London planning to buy specific maps, Stanford's should be the first port of call.

Trailfinders Travel Centre

46–48 Earls Court Road
London W8 6EJ
Tel: 01-937 9631

Stocks quite a number of overland and budget guides and maps.

The Travel Bookshop

13 Blenheim Crescent
London W11
Tel: 01-229 5260
Owner: Sarah Anderson

Is London's first bookshop specializing in travel literature, opened in 1980 to provide a 'complete package for the traveller' including books on particular areas, current and old guide books, histories, cookery books and relevant fiction. Shop also stocks old and new maps and topographical prints.

Waterstone & Co Ltd (Booksellers)

62 Southampton Row
London WC1
Tel: 01-831 9019

and

121 Charing Cross Road
London WC2
Tel: 01-434 4291

and

99 Old Brompton Road
London SW7
Tel: 01-581 9091

Capt O. M. Watts Ltd

45 Albemarle Street
London W1X 4BJ
Tel: 01-493 4633
Telex: 298800

Sells a complete line of Admiralty Charts, tide tables and navigational instruments.

Whitcoulls New Zealand Bookshop

6 Royal Opera Arc
London SW1
Tel: 01-930 4587

Writers & Readers

144 Camden High Street
London NW1
Tel: 01-267 0511

YHA Bookshops

14 Southampton Street
London WC2E 7HY
Tel: 01-836 8541

Sell books, maps and guides for backpackers, hostellers, adventure sportsmen and budget travellers.

Travel Bookshops elsewhere in the UK:

Aberdeen Flight Shop

34 Bridge Street
Aberdeen
Scotland
Tel: 574 387

Austicks Polytechnic Bookshop

25 Cookridge Street
Leeds LS1 3AN
Tel: 445335

Best travel bookshop in Yorkshire. A large map selection including large-scale ordnance survey mapping.

Bauermeister Booksellers

19 George IV Bridge 1
Edinburgh
Tel: 031-226 5561

B. H. Blackwell Ltd

50 Broad Street
Oxford
Tel: 249 111

and

Hythe Bridge Street
Oxford
Tel: 244 944

Book and Candle Bell

1 Market Place
Woodstock
Oxford
Tel: Woodstock 812 391

Bookland & Co Ltd

12 Bridge Street
Chester
Tel: 43723

Books and maps.

Browns of Hull

24–28 George Street
Hull HU1 3AP
Tel: Hull 24513

Easons & Son Ltd

Gloucester Place 1
Dublin, Ireland
Tel: 788 644

Wm. George's Sons Ltd

89 Park Street
Bristol BS1 5PW
Tel: (0272) 276 602

Godfrey Ltd

32 Stonegate
York
Tel: 24531

Grass Roots Books

1 Newton Street
Piccadilly
Manchester M1 1HW
Tel: 061-236 3112

Is a co-operatively run radical bookshop with a wide range of books including an extensive section on cheap travel.

Fred Hanna Ltd

New and Secondhand Booksellers
29 Nassau Street 2
Dublin, Ireland
Tel: 77 12 55

and

Campus Bookshop
Belfield 4
Dublin, Ireland
Tel: 69 13 84

W. Hartley Seed

152–160 West Street
Sheffield
Yorks S1 3ST

Good selection of books and maps.

Heffer

20 Trinity Street
Cambridge CB2 3BG
Tel: (0223) 358 351

Very good selection of travel books.

Heffers Map Shop

3rd Floor
19 Sydney Street
Cambridge CB2 3HL

Are leading mapsellers in the region.

Himalayan Shop

97 Canongate 8
Edinburgh
Scotland
Tel: 031-556 9514

Hodges, Figgis & Co Ltd
The Booksellers

56 Dawson Street
Dublin, Ireland
Tel: 774 754

Hudsons Bookshops

116 New Street
Birmingham B2 4JJ
Tel: 021-643 8311

Jura Bookshop

44 Don Street
Jersey
Tel: 36809

The London Street Bookshop

35–39 London Street
Reading RG1 4PU

The Map Shop
(A. T. Atkinson & Partner)

15 High Street
Upton-upon-Severn
Worcestershire WR8 0HJ
Tel: (06846) 3146

Agents for Ordnance Survey, large-scale maps and guides for Europe and other areas worldwide in stock or obtained to order. Send for free catalogue stating area of interest.

Menzies

107 Princes Street 2
Edinburgh
Scotland
Tel: 031-226 6214

The Paperback Centre Ltd

20 Suffolk Street
Dublin, Ireland
Tel: 77 42 10

and

Stillorgan Shopping Centre
Dublin, Ireland
Tel: 88 42 10

Parker & Son Ltd

27 Broad Street
Oxford
Tel: (0865) 54156

Leading mapsellers with large travel-guide department. Ask for Stuart Kemp.

Peters Bookservice

28 Thorpe Street
Birmingham
Tel: 021-622 4380

Dick Phillips

Whitehall House
Nenthead
Alston
Cumbria CA9 3PS
Tel: (0498) 81440

Specializes in books and maps on Iceland and Faroe. He stocks maps at scales of between 1:750,000 and 1:25,000 (general maps) and thematic or specialized maps held in stock or usually obtainable by special order.

William Porteus & Co

19 Royal Exchange Place
Glasgow 1
Tel: 041-221 8623

Nigel Press Associates Ltd

Edenbridge
Kent TN8 6HS
Tel: (0732) 865 023

Offers a free service to bona fide *expeditions for the supply of map-like satellite images, of which they have a large archive covering most parts of the world. These Landsat satellite images can be produced at scales between 1:1,000,000 and 1:200,000 and are useful for navigation or research.*

RAC Motoring Services Ltd

Publications Manager
PO Box 100
RAC House
Lansdowne Road
Croydon
Surrey CR9 6HN

Sell guides, handbooks, phrase books and maps for motorists and other travellers in the UK and on the Continent, also touring aids.

Rallymaps of West Wellow

PO Box 11
Romsey
Hampshire SO5 8XX
Tel: (0794) 515 444 (24hr)
Mike Lillington

Mail order specialists for Ordnance Survey, geological, Michelin and IGN maps. Walking, climbing, books, map cases and sundries. Catalogue 25p.

Sherratt & Hughes Bookshop

17 St. Anne's Square
Manchester M2 7DP

Are leading map and guide retailers.

John Smith & Son (Glasgow) Ltd

57–61 St. Vincent Street
Glasgow G2 5TB
Tel: 041-221 7472

Ordnance Survey agents for West of Scotland. Foreign maps. Michelin maps.

James Thin Booksellers

53 Southbridge
Edinburgh 1
Tel: 031-556 6743

Watt & Grant Bookshop

247 Union Street
Aberdeen
Scotland
Tel: 24344

W. H. Willshaw Ltd

16 John Dalton Street
Manchester M2 6HS
Tel: 061-834 8734

Mainly booksellers but also sell maps.

Whitemans Bookshop

7 Orange Grove
Bath BA1 1LP
Tel: (0225) 64029

Have a whole room of books and maps devoted to travel, including a large range of Ordnance Survey maps and all other major UK maps to street plans: a range of foreign maps covering countries all over the world; atlases; walking guides; natural history guides; 'where to stay' guides and a wide range of books of interest to travellers, mostly of a practical nature, some of which cover unusual countries. Also undertake to order any obtainable map or book (at no extra charge) and operate a worldwide mail order service.

The USA:

Book-on-File

Box 195
Union City
New Jersey 07087-0195
USA

Will locate virtually any out-of-print book, from its title alone, no matter how old or long out of print, fiction or non-fiction, all authors and subjects.

The Complete Traveler

199 Madison Avenue
Corner 35th Street
New York
NY 10016
USA
Tel: (212) 685 9007, 679 4339

Books, maps, guides.

Dawsons Book Shop

535 North Larchmont Blvd
Los Angeles
CA 90004
USA
Tel: (213) 469 2186
Hours: 9am–5pm, Mon–Sat

Handles rare and unusual books at moderate prices, on a range of subjects.

Forsyth Travel Library Inc

PO Box 2975
9154 West 57th Street
Shawnee Mission
KS 66201-1357
USA
Tel: (913) 384 3440

Sells maps and travel books, including maps of the USA and Canada, Thomas Cook publications, rail passes, and many other guides, maps and travel books relating to all destinations. Free catalogue on request. Overseas inquiries should enclose four international reply coupons.

Gourmet Guides

1767 Stockton Street
San Francisco
CA 94133
USA
Tel: (415) 391 5903
Owner: Jean Bullock

Is a retail bookshop specializing in travel books and maps (and cookbooks – hence the name), including Fodor, Frommer, Fielding and others; many maps of Asia, the USA, Africa, and Latin America that are extremely difficult to find elsewhere. Owner imports some of these and is the only US source, stocking 'everything I can get hold of in the travel field'. Mail order. Lists of stock covering particular areas made up and available from time to time.

Hammond Map and Travel Center

57 West 43rd Street
New York
NY 10036
USA

Sells world, road and travel maps, political maps and weather charts.

Hippocrene Books, Inc

171 Madison Avenue
New York
NY 10016
USA

Are specialists in travel literature with Nagel Encyclopedia Guides, Lonely Planet titles and other travel books, Ravenstein Maps, Geographia Maps, Carta Maps, Century Travellers Series and J. A. Editions.

Intercontinental Visa Service

Los Angeles World Trade Center
350 South Figueroa Street
Los Angeles
CA 90071
USA
Tel: (213) 625 7175

Specializes in visas, passport photos and travel books.

The Map Centre, Inc

2611 University Ave
San Diego
California 92104-2894
USA
Tel: (619) 291 3830

Stocks over 5,000 maps and charts; is an agent for defence mapping and National Ocean Survey, nautical and aeronautical maps, plus publications of interest to boat owners, including tide tables, coastal pilots and navigational guides and globes. Motto is: If you can't find it on our maps . . . it's lost.

Pacific Travellers Supply

529 State Street
Santa Barbara
CA 93101
USA
Tel: (805) 963 44 38

Sells a complete selection of guidebooks, specializing in obscure and hard-to-find titles. Have fifty thousand maps representing the entire world. Feature several lines of convertible packs, luggage, and travel accessories.

The Travel Suppliers

194 E. Yorba Linda Blvd
Placentia
CA 92670
USA
Tel: (714) 528 2502

Maps, travel guides and accessories.

Wide World Bookshop

401 NE 45th
Seattle
WA 98105
USA
Tel: (206) 634 3453
Proprietors: Joan E. Marsden
Thomas W. Markosky

Sells a selection of unusual travel books, many of them imported maps and globes, language tapes and 'other trivia'. Catalogue.

Travel Book and Map Retailers elsewhere:

Australia

All Maps

Head Office:
431 Pacific Highway
Artarmon
Sydney
NSW
Australia

Branch Office:
132 Parramatta Road
Granville
Sydney
NSW
Australia

Gregory's Publishing Co

1 Unwins Bridge Road
St. Peters
Sydney
NSW 2044
Australia
Tel: (02) 517 1011

Sells road maps, guides, street directories and auto service manuals.

Austria

Okista

Türkenstr. 4
A-1090 Vienna
Austria

Mainly student travel books.

Belgium

La Route de Jade

Librairie du Voyageur
Rue de Stassart 116 (Place Stephanie)
B1050 Brussels
Belgium
Tel: (02) 512 96 54

Is a travel bookshop selling books, maps and guides on all aspects of travel in five continents. The exclusive distributor of ONC maps in Belgium.

Canada

Gulliver's Travel Bookshop

609 Black Street W6
Toronto
Canada
Tel: 537 7700

Oxbow Books

Box 244 Clarkson
Mississauga
Ontario L5J 3Y1
Canada

Sell out-of-print books on travel, exploration, geography, mountaineering, caving.

France

L'Asiathèque

6 Rue Christine
75006 Paris
France
Tel: 325 34 57

Offers books on the Far East and South-East Asia.

L'Astrolabe

La Librairie
46 Rue de Provence
75009 Paris
France
Tel: 285 42 95

Is the most important map seller in France, carrying Ordnance Survey maps of the UK, national surveys of Ireland, Norway, Denmark, Czechoslovakia, Guatemala, Peru, Bolivia, Pakistan, India, etc. Topographic maps, nautical charts, geological, astronomical and aeronautical charts and maps. Also stocks about 15,000 travel books and guides, old and new, in French and English and some in Spanish and German. Some scientific manuals, other personal accounts of travels. One of the few bookshops in Europe that can be of real help to somebody planning a serious expedition, by placing all the relevant literature and large-scale maps at the organizers' disposal. A new Natural History department, for travellers with an interest in ornithology, hergetology and geology.

Blondel La Rougery

7 Rue St. Lazare
75009 Paris
France
Tel: (1) 878 95 54

Maps.

Editions du Buot

30 Rue du Rendez-vous
75012 Paris
France
Tel: (1) 343 59 03

Maps.

La Grande Porte

4 Rue Dal Pozzo
06000 Nice
France
Tel: 87 71 24

Specializes in books on short- and long-distance travel with works also on seafaring and mountaineering, antiquarian books and postcards. Items also bought.

Librairie E.P.A.

Automobile -moto -train -aviation
83 Rue de Rennes
75006 Paris
France
Tel: 548 15 14

and

92 Rue St. Lazare
75009 Paris
France
Tel: 281 37 62

Librairie Gibert Jeune

Second Floor
5 Place St. Michel
75005 Paris
France

Has a wide choice of route maps and tourist guides.

Librairie Globe

2 Rue de Buci
75006 Paris
Tel: 326 54 99

Books on the USSR.

Librairie Maisonneuve Adrien

11 Rue St. Sulpice
75005 Paris
France
Tel: 326 86 35

Books on America and the Orient.

Librairie Orientale

51 Rue Monsieur le Prince
75006 Paris
France
Tel: 326 88 65

Books on the Orient and the Far East.

Librairie Ulysse

Pays et Voyages 14 h a 20 h.
35 Rue St. Louis en l'Isle
75004 Paris
France
Tel: 325 17 35

Sells geographical, travel and guide books and maps.

Le Tour du Monde

9 Rue de la Pompe
75116 Paris
France
Tel: 288 73 59 & 288 58 06

Sells travel books and guides, old and new, in or out of print on all aspects of foreign countries.

Germany, Federal Republic

Därr Expeditionsservice GmbH

Hauptstrasse 26
D-8011 Kirchheim-Heimstetten
Germany, Federal Republic
Tel: (089) 903 8015
Klaus and Erika Darr

This establishment has an exceptionally extensive range of maps, guides and other travel handbooks, covering the world but with a concentration of material about Africa, Asia, South America, and other expedition destinations, including Antarctica. Catalogue £1.00.

Geografische Buchhandlung (Geo Buch)

Rosental 6
D-8000 Munich 2
Germany, Federal Republic

Has a comprehensive range of travel books and maps.

Gleumes & Co

Gosso – Buchhandlung – Verlag
Hohenstaufenting 47–51
5 Koln 1
Germany, Federal Republic
Tel: (0221) 211 1550/215 650

Specializes in maps and travel guides.

Globetrott Shop

Karlsgraben 29
D-5100 Aachen
Germany, Federal Republic.

Publishes and sells handbooks for globetrotters and overlanders. (See also Equipment, Camping, Outdoor, etc., page 624.)

Dr Götze

Hermannstr. 5–7
2000 Hamburg 1
Germany, Federal Republic
Tel: (040) 322 477

Specializes in maps, guide books and tourist books.

Buchhandlung Kiepert KG

Hardenbergstr. 4–5
D-1000 Berlin 12
Germany, Federal Republic

Has a good selection of travel books, old and new and maps.

Schropp

Potsdamer Strasse 100
1000 Berlin 30
Germany, Federal Republic
Tel: 261 34 56

Maps, guidebooks, atlases.

Italy

Libreria Alpina

Via Coronedi-Berti 4
I-40137 Bologna
Italy
Tel: (051) 34 57 15

Specializes in books on mountains and mountaineering worldwide, in all languages. Catalogue.

Netherlands

Pied à Terre

Singel 393
1012 WN Amsterdam
Netherlands

Maps and guide books for walking, cycling and mountaineering. Travel books for globetrotters: Himalayas, Africa, Asia and South America.

van Wijngaarden

Overtoon 136
Amsterdam 1054NH
Netherlands
Tel: (020) 121 901

Is an established bookshop in the centre of Amsterdam, selling exclusively travel guides and maps – for hikers, cyclists, motorists, tourists, cityplans, maps of the surrounding regions and of the countries of Africa, South America, etc. Also Michelin, Baedeker, Frommer Guides, compasses. Agent of ONC and TPC maps.

Switzerland

Atlas Reisbuchladen

Schauplatzgasse 31
CH-3011 Bern
Switzerland
Tel: (031) 22 90 44

Sells travel books, guides, maps. Is the distributor for many map agencies from all parts of the world.

Buchhandlung Bider

Hochhaus Heuwaage
4010 Basel
Switzerland
Tel: (061) 23 00 69

Travel books and maps.

Librairie du Voyageur – Artou

9 Rue de Rive
CH-1204 Geneva
Switzerland
Tel: (022) 21 45 44

Large selection of travel books and maps; also old travel books, trekking and climbing guides.

Travel Book Shop

Gisela Treichler
Seilergraben 11
CH-8001
Postfach 216
CH-8025 Zurich
Switzerland
Tel: (01) 252 38 83

Is a highly thought of shop selling travel literature – maps, books, guides, timetables, vehicle manuals – of all kinds, and run by a well-travelled lady who is on hand to give advice and travel tips to customers.

Periodicals

Numbers at right indicate number of issues per year.

ABC TRAVEL GUIDES

ABC AIR ASIA	12
ABC AIR CARGO GUIDE	12
ABC AIR/RAIL EUROPE	12
ABC AIR TRAVEL ATLAS	2
ABC GUIDE TO INTERNATIONAL TRAVEL	4
ABC GUIDE TO PARTY BOOKING	1
ABC RAIL GUIDE	12
ABC SHIPPING GUIDE	12
ABC WORLD AIRWAYS GUIDE	12
VIDEOTEX TRAVEL DIRECTORY	2

ABC HISTORIC GUIDES

HISTORIC HOUSES, CASTLES AND GARDENS	Annual
MUSEUMS AND GALLERIES	Annual

ABC Travel Guides Ltd
World Timetable Centre
Dunstable
Beds. LU5 4HB

Air Cargo Guide

Schedules, transfer connections, international and domestic rates. Plus free annual supplement containing charges collect and COD facilities, conditions of acceptance, aircraft hold dimensions and other information.

Air/Rail Europe

Pocket guide to air and rail travel throughout Europe, plus through-flights with centres in the Middle East and North Africa and with New York and Washington. Also aircraft types, airline codes, etc.

Air Travel Atlas

Maps showing scheduled air routes, trunk routes and regional routes: also lists of city and country codes and airline designators.

Guide to International Travel

General information on visas, inoculations, etc., and country-by-country summary of essential travel data – currency, passport regulations, customs, taxes, working/banking hours and more.

Rail Guide

Routes, timetables and fares from London to main stations in UK. Connecting local transport, selected Continental and UK shipping services.

Shipping Guide

Detailed information on passenger shipping services throughout the world, schedules and fares for trans-ocean lines, shipping services and car ferries within each continent, and cargo/passenger lines: index of operators, ports, ships, etc. European car ferries section including North Africa and Middle East. Guide to cruises.

World Airways Guide

Timetables for all airlines, details of through-flights and main transfer connections, fares, airport/city terminal information. Free Hotel Guide to selected worldwide hotels inserted annually.

AFRICA GUIDE	1
ASIA AND PACIFIC	1
LATIN AMERICA AND THE CARIBBEAN	1
MIDDLE EAST REVIEW	1

World of Information
21 Gold Street
Saffron Walden
Essex CB10 1EJ
Political and economic guides, completely rewritten annually, aimed at travellers, especially business travellers, rather than academics.

AFRICA SOUTH OF THE SAHARA	1
FAR EAST AND AUSTRALASIA	1

MIDDLE EAST AND NORTH AFRICA 1
Europa Publications Ltd
18 Bedford Square
London WC1B 3JN
Background information, especially on political and economic aspects.

AMATEUR PHOTOGRAPHER 52
Surrey House
1 Throwley Way
Sutton
Surrey SM1 4QQ
Features, book reviews, product comparisons, the work of individual photographers and copious advertising.

AMERICAN IN BRITAIN 6
ARAB IN BRITAIN 4
Dominion Press Ltd
Dominion House
101 Southwark Street
London SE1 0JH

BUSINESS TRAVELLER 10
Perry Publications
49 Old Bond Street
London W1X 3AF
Tel: 01-629 4688
Features, air-fare cost-cutting information that will show quickly and clearly how to save dramatically on your air-travel costs.

CARIBBEAN DATELINE 4
PO Box 23276
L'Enfant Plaza
Washington
DC 20024, USA
Reports on news, trends and opportunities for the investor in the Caribbean and Central America, including separate periodic reports on the main countries.

CULTURAL SURVIVAL 4
11 Divinity Drive
Cambridge
Mass 02138
USA
Tel: (617) 495 2562
Cultural Survival was founded in 1972 to work with indigenous peoples and ethnic minorities in the Third World. The organisation's projects, research and publications are designed to help indigenous peoples survive, both physically and culturally, the rapid changes which contact with expanding industrial society brings by educating the public, influencing development theory and policy, and stimulating debate among academics, planners and indigenous peoples.

DESCENT
Cleeve House
Theale, nr Wedmore
Somerset BS28 4SL
Descent is the major English-language magazine covering the sport of caving. It provides full news coverage of discoveries and exploration in British caves as well as reports on the world's major expeditions. In addition it publishes extensive articles on the latest equipment and techniques, plus fine cave photographs.

DISCOUNT TRAVELLER
Pierwest UK Ltd
117 Praed Street
London W2 1RN
Features, news and advice on how to keep some style if you can't afford the QEII.

ECONOMY TRAVELLER 6
Box 547
Menlo Park
CA 94026-0547
USA
Comprehensive examination of major travel questions, with company-by-company, dollars and cents comparisons of competitive travel services based on 'own, original, independent, professional' research. Feature length articles on places, issues.

EXECUTIVE TRAVEL 12
Business Magazines International Ltd
Travelpoint House
21 Fleet Street
London EC4Y 1AP
Tel: 01-353 1042
Telex: 24438 TVLPNT
For frequent travellers looking for the best deals and facilities available for their business and leisure transportation and accommodation requirements.
News and features about who offers what plus temperature guides and contact numbers. Available on subscription at £11 per year or £5.50 introductory rate to WEXAS International subscribers.

EXPATRIATE, THE 12
Centre for Legal and Business Information
Rectory Road
Great Waldingfield
Sudbury
Suffolk CO10 0TL
Tel: Sudbury (0787) 78607
Investment, pensions information, selection of job advertisements, health, keeping in touch, tax, useful reading, reports on particular countries. Free sample on request.

EXPEDITION CLUB AUSTRIA CLUB-NACHRICHTEN

Postfach 1457
1010 Vienna
Austria
Newsletter with readers' reports on travels, news of events past and forthcoming, and classified advertisements. (*See Associations – Exploration, page 606.*)

EXPLORERS' JOURNAL 4

Official quarterly of the Explorers Club
The Explorers' Club
46 East 70th Street
New York
NY 10021
USA
Established 1904. Articles on scientific discoveries, expeditions, ornithology, personalities and many other branches of exploration. Reviews. Embraces space exploration.
Subscriptions: one year $15.00; two years $27.00; three years $40.00; outside US add $5.00; single copies $3.75.
(*See Associations – Exploration, page 606.*)

FORD'S FREIGHTER TRAVEL GUIDE 2
FORD'S INTERNATIONAL CRUISE GUIDE 4

Ford's Travel Guides
PO Box 505
22151 Clarendon Street
Woodland Hills
CA 91365
USA

Freighter Travel Guide
Established in 1952. Includes listings of travel agents, ports, freighter and cargo passenger services, steamship lines.
Price $7.50

International Cruise Guide
Current listings for worldwide passenger cruises including itinerary prices, calendar of cruise departure by port.
Price $8.95

FREIGHTER TRAVEL NEWS 12

Freighter Travel Club of America
1745 Scotch Ave, SE
PO Box 12693
Salem
OR 97309
USA
News, letters, reports on freighter cruises. Subscription rates $12 per year.

GEO 12

Gruner & Jahr AG & Co
Editorial Office:
Warburgstrasse 45
D-2000 Hamburg 36
West Germany
Subscriptions:
Postfach 111629
D-2000 Hamburg 11
West Germany
Travel and places in the style of the National Geographic magazine.

GEO 12

PO Box 2551
Boulder
CO 80322
USA
Concerned with place and a strong sense of where we are.

THE GEOGRAPHICAL MAGAZINE 12

1 Kensington Gore
London SW7 2AR
Articles, notes, news, reviews, classified advertisements.
(*See Associations – Exploration, etc., page 606.*)

GLOBE 6

Newsletter for the Globetrotters Club
The Globetrotters Club
BCM/Roving
London WC1N 3XX
Travel information. Articles on individual experiences, news of 'members on the move', tips, mutual-aid column for members.
(*See Associations – Exploration, etc., page 606.*)

GREAT EXPEDITIONS 6

PO Box 64699
Station G
Vancouver, BC V6R 4GT
Canada
Tel: (604) 734 3938
For people who want to travel and explore, offers trips, a free classified ads service, discounts on books, an information exchange, articles and travel notes. Magazine is US$18 annually (6 copies) in North America, US$24 elsewhere. Write for free brochure on trips and magazine.

THE HIDEAWAY REPORT 12

Harper Associates, Inc
PO Box 300
Fairfax Station
Virginia 22039
USA
A connoisseur's guide to peaceful and unspoiled places.

HOME AND AWAY 12

62 Tritton Road
London SE21 8DE
Magazine with advertisements, overseas job information, offers of services, features on areas and topics of interest to expatriates.

HOW TO PROTECT YOURSELF AGAINST MALARIA

IAMAT
736 Center Street
Lewiston
NY 14092
USA
Details about the disease, high-risk areas and much more.

HOW TO TRAVEL INEXPENSIVELY

Nomadic Books
PO Box 454
Athens
GA 30603
USA
A newsletter and catalogue of hard-to-find travel information.

INTERNATIONAL LIVING 12

2201 St. Paul Street
Baltimore
MD 21218
USA
For the jet-set! For people who want to live abroad . . . at the upper end of the expense scale.

INTERNATIONAL INVESTMENT LETTER 12

PO Box 9666
Arlington
VA 22209
USA
The letter regularly reports on major world markets, provides insights into the world's economic outlook, discusses unusual tactics for improving your investment return and analyses new investment programs. Also covers foreign bank accounts, real estate, retirement, stocks, bonds and CDs. Gives specific buy-and-sell advice. Subscription US$147.

INTERNATIONAL TRAVEL NEWS 12

Martin Publications, Inc
2120 28th Street
Sacramento
CA 94818
USA
New source for the business and/or pleasure traveller who often goes abroad. Contributions mostly from readers. Free sample copy on request. Subscription price: US$11 (year); US$13 (year) outside USA.

MAGIC INK TRAVEL CLUB NEWSLETTER Irregularly

Magic Ink Travel Club
22 Dane Road
Margate
Kent CT9 2AA
Tips, updates on travel, reprints of features and news articles, latest information on the travel guides published by the club.

MESSAGE POST 3

PO Box 190-TH
Philomath
OR 97370
USA
Newsletter about portable dwelling and long-period camping. Emphasizes low-cost shelters and simple amenities easily improvized anywhere. Plans, product reports, book reviews, gatherings, contacts. Price: $3.00 per year.

MILITARY TRAVEL NEWS 6
TRAVEL NEWS 6

PO Box 9
Oakton
VA 22124
USA
Newsletters providing current low-cost travel information on the USA, Caribbean, Europe, Far East and elsewhere.
***Military Travel News** is aimed at the US military member, on active duty or retired, and dependants.*
***Travel News** features travel bargains for all.*

MOBILITY INTERNATIONAL NEWS

62 Union Street
London SE1 1TD
Tel: (01) 403 5688
News of projects, organizations and other items of interest especially to the handicapped.

NATIONAL GEOGRAPHIC MAGAZINE 12
NATIONAL GEOGRAPHIC TRAVELER 4

National Geographic Society
Washington DC
USA
The National Geographic Magazine is a long-established magazine familiar to many. Noted for the quality of its photography, articles cover travel and expeditions and many other fields. The National Geographic Traveler concentrates on the US, Canada and Mexico.

NOMAD Infrequently

BCM-Nomad
London WC1V 6XX

or

Box 431
Grand Central Post Office
New York
NY 10017
USA
Newsletter aimed at people on the move and written by peripatetic publisher, with many readers' reports. Current issues are sent to any address on receipt of US$1.00 and for $2.00 a press card is also included. Press card is for people to use 'for what they can get away with'.
Ed: This is not recommended as a practice.

OFF BEAT 4

Marie Mattson Reports
1250 Vallejo Street
San Francisco
CA 94109
USA
Newsletter offering practical advice on visiting. We suggest that readers include international reply coupons when contacting overseas organizations.

VENICE-SIMPLON ORIENT EXPRESS MAGAZINE

Travel Publications International Ltd
55–56 St. Martin's Lane
London WC2N 4EA

OUTSIDE MAGAZINE 12

1165 N Clark Street
Chicago
IL 60610
USA
Tel: 312-951-0990
Outside Magazine is edited for the active adult. It is a contemporary lifestyle magazine that features sports, fitness, photography, adventure travel and portraits of men and women adventurers. Also regularly reviewed: wildlife outdoor clothing, product news, destinations/travel options, environmental and political issues.

PASSPORT 12

20 North Wacker Drive
Chicago
IL 60606
USA
Newsletter for discriminating and intellectually curious international travellers. Forthcoming cultural events worldwide, hotel and restaurants to seek out or avoid.

RADAR PUBLICATIONS

The Royal Association for Disability and Rehabilitation
25 Mortimer Street
London W1N 8AB
Tel: 01-637 5400
RADAR publishes guides on travel for the physically handicapped, as well as a list of publications useful to the disabled traveller, and where they can get hold of them.

RESIDENT ABROAD 12

F.T. Business Publishing Ltd
Greystoke Place
Fetter Lane
London EC4A 1ND
Magazine for expatriates

ST. JAMES GUIDES

A–Z WORLDWIDE HOTEL GUIDE 2
CAR FERRY GUIDE 1
HOLIDAY GUIDE – SUMMER 1
HOLIDAY GUIDE – WINTER 1
TRAVEL DIRECTORY 2

St. James Guides
5/11 Worship Street
London EC2A 2AY

A–Z Worldwide Hotel Guide

Produced for the UK travel agent and business traveller. Includes over 30,000 hotels.

Car Ferry Guide

Handbook for travel agents covering UK domestic, ex-UK and European services and other facts, e.g., on Motorail services and inclusive motoring.

Holiday Guides

Information on over 1,400 worldwide resorts – which operator goes where, which hotels they use, prices, airports of departure, coach holidays, special interest tours.

Travel Directory

Tour Operators, travel agents and organizers, airlines, shipping lines, car and coach hire, tourist offices and travel trade services, international hotels.

SAFARIPOSTEN – Denmark

Topas Globetrotterklub
Safari House
Lounsvej 29
DK-9640 Farsoe
Denmark
Tel: (08) 63 84 00
Telex: 60965 GLOBE DK
Annual expedition publication in Danish. There is also a bi-monthly newsletter of the name 'Blobetrotterklub Nyhedsbrev' and a bi-monthly newsletter in English called 'The Globetrotter's Newsletter'.

THE SOUTH AMERICAN EXPLORER 4

Official journal of the South American Explorers Club
South American Explorers Club
Casilla 3714
Lima 100
Peru
Subscriptions: 2239 E Colfax Avenue 205
Denver
CO 80206
USA
Subscription: $15.00. Accounts of scientific studies, adventure, and sports activities in South America written by Club members. Also, sections on news, Club activities, book reviews, letters, tips and notes. *(See Associations: Exploration, Adventure and Travel, page 606.)*

STANDBY

12 Fouberts Place
London W1V 1HH
*Over 1,000 pages of travel information published, and updated constantly on Prestel. Page *321#*

THOMAS COOK AIRPORT LINES 4
THOMAS COOK OVERSEAS TIMETABLE 6
THOMAS COOK TIMETABLE 12

Thomas Cook Ltd
PO Box 36
Peterborough PE3 6SB

Thomas Cook Airport Lines
Quarterly booklet timetable containing bus, coach and rail services to and from nearly 120 European Airports, with index maps. Annual subscription: £7.00, including p+p.

Thomas Cook Overseas Timetable
Detailed maps of railway systems, scenic routes, train departure times and fares: passport and visa requirements, city centre maps and even climatic conditions. Started 1981. £5.45 or £6.00 including p+p.

Thomas Cook Timetable
Comprehensive timetable of all trains known to run in the civilized world, and of local shipping services. £3.85 of £4.75 including p+p.

TRAVEL AFRICA 4
TRAVEL ASIA PACIFIC 6

Business Magazines International Ltd
Travelpoint House
21 Fleet Street
London EC4Y 1AP
Tel: 01-353 1402

Travel Africa
Europe's only specialist quarterly focusing on news and features about travel to and within the African Continent. Travel Africa knows no political boundaries covering all territories of interest to tourists and business travellers from Cairo to The Cape. Package-tour programmes, hotel facilities, safaris, air and surface transportation are all given prominence. The Indian Ocean islands of the Seychelles and Mauritius are also occasionally included in this colour quarterly. Available on subscription at £4.00 per annum in the UK and $16 elsewhere from the publishers at the above address.

Travel Asia Pacific
A specialist magazine, focusing on the latest developments within the Far East and Pacific regions for tourists and business travellers alike. Reviews all the latest package tour programmes, new hotels, air routes, rail, bus and car rental services to and within the region. Subscription: £4.00 per annum (including postage) UK; and $16 elsewhere from the publishers above.

TRAVELER'S DIRECTORY 1

Compiled by Tom Linn
6244 Baynton Street
Philadelphia
PA 19144
USA
For the 'budget-minded' traveller, an international register of people willing to offer a home of hospitality to travellers. The Directory is available only to people listed in it. Listings cost $25.00, this fee includes a quarterly Newsletter containing budget-minded travel information.

TRAVEL INFORMATION MANUAL (TIM)

A joint publication of Several IARA Airlines
PO Box 7627
1187 ZJ, Schiphol Airport
Netherlands
Gives full information on most recent passport, visa and health requirements, airport tax, customs, currency regulations. Aimed mainly at the travel industry.
TIMATIC (the automated TIM) is a joint venture between SITA and TIM. It provides real time access via airlines' reservation terminals (STRs) to

the TIM data base (visa, health, etc.). TIMATIC is available (and up to date) 24 hours a day. Note: SITA is a cooperative organization between airlines to meet their telecommunication needs.

THE TRAVELLER 4

WEXAS International
45 Brompton Road
Knightsbridge
London SW3 1DE
Established in 1970 as Expedition, Photofeatures on travels and expeditions. Letters, latest news on travel, expeditions and overland, book reviews, photography and medical advice. Articles on anything from the philosophy of travel to travel writing or Third World politics by experts. A lively, informative, entertaining magazine, with excellent photographic standards.

TRAVELORE REPORT 12

International Letter for People who Vacation and Travel
225 South Fifteenth Street
Philadelphia
PA 19102
USA
Monthly newsletter containing tips, features on exceptional values and discounts for travellers – destinations, accommodation, fares, dining, timely alerts.

TRAVEL SMART 12
TRAVEL SMART FOR BUSINESS 12

Communications House
40 Beechdale Road
Dobbs Ferry
NY 10522
USA

Travel Smart

Newsletter for sophisticated travellers who expect honest value for their money. Also discount-cruises, supercharters, hotels, car rentals, etc., for members, $29.00 per year.

Travel Smart for Business

High-level inside information for people responsible for business travel, designed to save money by maintaining efficiency. $96.00 per year.

TRAVELTIPS 6

163–07 Depot Road
Flushing
NY 11358
USA
First person accounts of freighter and passenger ship travel to all parts of the world. Cruise guide, budget travel news, tips on trips.

TROPICAL FRONTIERS

PO Box 1316
Eagle Pass
TX 78853
USA
Newsletter with news, events and travel data on 'the world's most exotic islands'.

TROPICAL ISLAND LIVING

PO Box 7263
Arlington
VA 22207
USA
Information, news on tropical islands.

TROTTER 5–6

c/o Ludmilla Tüting
Deutsche Zentrale für Globetrotter EV
Mittenwalder Str 7
D-1000 Berlin 161
Germany, Federal Republic
News and articles from outside Europe only. Tips, readers' reports, reports on the behaviour and misbehaviour of travellers, background information on 'developing countries', classified ads. For club members only, though non-members may advertise or obtain information on payment of fee.
(See Help and Advice: Exploration, etc., page 606.)

UNITED STATES TRAVEL & TOURISM NEWS

22 Sackville Street
London W1X 2EA

WORLD HOTEL DIRECTORY

Longman Group Ltd
Fourth Avenue
Harlow
Essex CM19 5AA
Part of the Financial Times International Year Books series published in the autumn.

WORLD VISION OF EUROPE RESOURCE DIRECTORY

146 Queen Victoria Street
London EC4V 4BX
The aim of the Directory is to draw attention to existing important information available to individuals/agencies involved in development work in Third World countries. Consists of eight areas of interest: development, relief/disasters/refugees, health, water/sanitation, agriculture, technology, logistics and recruitment/orientation. Practical guide and reference document for voluntary agencies, field staff and for individuals who are contemplating work overseas.

Book List

compiled by Sarah Anderson and Melissa Shales

This list, as in the last edition, is necessarily selective. Where we know that any book is still available, we have given prices – these are correct at the time of going to press, although they could change during the life of this book. Virtually all books on the list are currently available, we have only included out-of-print books where we feel them to be classics. These should be available from libraries.

We have split the list into two sections – a continent and country list of guide books and travel writing, and a list of 'how to' books on the more general aspects of travel. Books are in alphabetical order by title. Many categories have been removed to simplify the list, so that, for instance, all books on South America are now to be found under that heading, rather than in separate categories for Backpacking, etc. Europe has been included for the first time, in keeping with the rest of the handbook.

Travel 'literature' has been added as we feel that the discerning traveller will obviously benefit greatly from reading other people's impressions of places that he/she is going to visit. The many reprints of older classics currently on the market have not been included due to pressure of space, but are also well worth reading.

Continent and Country Guides

AFRICA

Africa – the Nile Route

by Kim Naylor
Pub. Lascelles £3.95
One of the few guides available which includes the Sudan.

Africa – an Overlander's Guide

by P. Cleggett
Pub. Bradt £1.95

Africa on a Shoestring

by Geoff Crowther
Pub. Lonely Planet £6.95
Revised and updated edition of this, by now, classic guide to Africa.

Alexandria. A History and Guide Pharos and Pharillon

by E. M. Forster
Pub. Michael Haag £5.95/£3.95
A series of short essays which capture the feeling of Alexandria. And an evocation of Alexandria.

Algeria and the Sahara. A Handbook for Desert Travellers

by Valerie and Jon Stevens
Pub. Constable £4.95
Guidebook including a detailed survey of the principal motor routes, a review of attitudes to be found towards tourists among Algerians and many travel tips.

Atlas Mountains; Morocco

by R. Collomb
Pub. West Col Productions, Reading £6.75
Practical trekking and touring guide.

Backpacker's Africa

by Hilary Bradt
Pub. Bradt £4.95

Berlitz Guides

Egypt
Kenya
Morocco
South Africa
Tunisia Each £2.45

Blue Guide Egypt

Pub. E. Benn £10.95
A new comprehensive guide.

The Blue Nile
The White Nile

by Alan Moorhead
Pub. Penguin £5.95
Starting with Burton and Speke, the author traces the sources of both the White and Blue Nile.

Cruising the Sahara

by Gerard Morgan-Grenville
Pub. David and Charles £2.25
Although published in 1974, this book is still relevant, offering detailed references on all aspects of desert planning and travel.

Dollarwise Guide to Egypt

by Nancy McGrath
Pub. Arthur Frommer £4.95
A guide to hotels, restaurants, nightspots and tours with an emphasis on the medium priced.

Egypt

Guide Poche Univers
Pub. Editions Marcus, Paris £8.90
Compact, comprehensive guidebook

Egypt Travel Guide

by Hans Strelocke
Pub. Polyglott-Verlag £1.95

Field Guide to the Birds of East Africa
Field Guide to the Birds of West Africa

by J. G. Williams/Sersale
Pub. Collins Each £7.95

Field Guide to the National Parks of East Africa

by J. G. Williams
Pub. Collins £7.95

The Gambia – A Holiday Guide

by Michael Tomkinson
From Luzac £3.95

Guide to East Africa

by Nina Casimati
Pub. Travelaid £4.95
Kenya, Tanzania and the Seychelles

Guide to Lesotho

by David Ambrose
From Lascelles £3.75
Comprehensive guide with a good map.

The Innocent Anthropologist.
Notes from a Mud Hut.

by Nigel Barley
Pub. British Museums £9.95
Funny, thoughtful account of life as an anthropologist in the Cameroons.

In Search of the Sahara

by Quentin Crewe
Pub. Michael Joseph £12.95
Quentin Crewe and pals roaming the Sahara

Journey to the Jade Sea

by John Hillaby
Pub. Paladin £1.95
An account of a 1,100-mile walk through Africa

Madagascar Today
Morocco Today
Tunisia Today
Zaïre Today

Pub. Editions Jeune Afrique Each £7.50
Awkward format, but informative guides.

Morocco. Pocket Travel Guide

From Lascelles £2.50
Chapters on each major city.

Morocco That Was

by Walter Harris
Pub. Eland Books £4.95

Nagel Guides

Algeria
Egypt
Morocco
From G. Cave £8.50–£17
Encyclopedic guides, sometimes out of date, but full of information.

North of South

by Shiva Naipaul
Pub. Penguin £2.95
Travels through Kenya, Tanzania and Zambia. Written in a scathing yet revealing way.

Penguin Guide to Ancient Egypt

by W. J. Murnane
Pub. Penguin £6.95
A wonderful guide.

The Sahara Handbook

by Simon and Jan Glen
Pub. Lascelles New edn
Classic guide to the Sahara and all desert travel. Essential reading.

Travelaid Guide to Egypt

Pub. Michael Haag £6.50
An accurate, informative guide

Travellers Guide to Egypt
Travellers Guide to Kenya and N. Tanzania
Travellers Guide to Southern Africa

Pub. Thornton Cox Each £3.50
Game parks, sights to see, places to stay and eat. Background on history, culture, society.

Travellers Guide Central and Southern Africa
Travellers Guide East Africa
Travellers Guide North Africa
Travellers Guide West Africa

Pub. IC Communications Each £6.95
Rather dry, but have places not included in other guides.

Vanishing Africa

by Mirella Ricciardi
Pub. Collins £15.00
Stunning photographic celebration of the Maasai.

Voices of Marrakesh

by E. Canetti
Pub. M. Boyars £3.95
Nobel prize winner's impressions

With Love . . . Siri and Ebba

by Siri Fraser and Ebbe Pederson
From Nicholas Saunders, 2 Neals Yard, London WC2
Letters home from two young girls travelling to Africa.

A Year in Marrakesh

by Peter Mayne
Pub. Eland Books £3.95
Written in 1953, a real evocation of Marrakesh

AMERICA, CENTRAL AND SOUTH

American Express Mexico

Pub. Mitchell Beazley £4.95

Apa Guides

Jamaica
Mexico
From Harrap Each £8.50
Lavishly illustrated, but packed with information.

Backpacking in Chile and Argentina
Backpacking in Mexico and Central America
Backpacking in Peru and Bolivia
Backpacking in Venezuela, Colombia and Ecuador

by G. and H. Bradt
Pub. Bradt £3.50–£5.95
Firsthand information about regulations, food, accommodation, transport, wildlife, parks, security, culture: with drawings, photos, entertaining asides and anecdotes.

Berlitz Guides

Bahamas
Bermuda
French West Indies
Jamaica
Mexico City
Puerto Rico
Rio de Janeiro
Southern Caribbean
Virgin Islands Each £2.45

Bermuda Today and Yesterday 1503–1980s

by Terry Tucker
Pub. Hale £7.95

The Budget Traveller's Latin America

Pub. CIEE, USA £2.95/$4.95
Comprehensive guide with information on low-cost transport to and within nineteen countries. Entry requirements, money, health, history, places of interest, etc.

Caribbean Island Hopping

by Frank Bellamy
Pub. Cadogan Books £5.95
Itineraries, prices, ways of getting there

Caribbean Today

by L. Doucet
Pub. Editions Jeune Afrique £7.50

Climbing and Hiking in Ecuador

by Rob Rachowiecki
Pub. Bradt £6.50
Up 30 peaks, and hikes through highlands, jungle and along the coast with background advice and information of value to all travellers.

Eight Feet in the Andes

by Dervla Murphy
Pub. John Murray £9.95
Woman, child and donkey walk 1,300 miles from Cajamarca to Cuzco.

Far Away and Long Ago. A Childhood in Argentina

by W. H. Hudson
Pub. Eland £3.95
Very evocative

Fisher Annotated Travel Guides

Bahamas
Bermuda
Caribbean
Mexico
Pub. Fisher, NY £3.95–£4.95
Clearly laid out guides with notes in the margin in red.

Fodor

Bermuda
Brazil
Budget Caribbean
Caribbean
Mexico
Mexico City and Acapulco
South America
Pub. Fodor £5.50–£9.95

Frommer

Mexico and Gutemala on $20
Mexico City and Acapulco
South America on $25
Pub. Frommer

Galapagos Guide

by A. White and Epler
From Bradt £5.50
About the only guide to these islands.

Grand Bahama

by P. J. H. Barratt
Pub. Macmillan £4.50
Strange mix of fact and legend; climate and geology, piracy and bootlegging, the growth of industry and tourism. Good reading.

In Patagonia

by Bruce Chatwin
Pub. Picador £2.50
Already a classic – an account of the author's journey through Patagonia.

Latin American Travel Guide including the Pan-American Highway Guide

Ed. Ernst Jahn
Pub. Comsco Publishing, NY
Prepared in cooperation with the Pan-American Union and the American Automobile Association. Facts and figures, not a guide to the tourist attractions.

Mexico: a Travel Survival Kit

by D. Richmond
Pub. Lonely Planet £3.95

Monuments of the Incas

by John Hemming and Edward Ranney
Pub. Hutchinson £30
Stunning black and white photographic portrait and fascinating text. Beautiful, interesting and useful.

Nagel Guides

Bolivia
Brazil
Central America
Mexico
Peru
From G. Cave £14–£17
Comprehensive encyclopedic guides

Old Patagonian Express

by Paul Theroux
Pub. Penguin £2.25
The author's account of a journey to the very tip of South America – all the way by train.

One Man's Mexico
by J. Lincoln
Pub. Century £4.95
A reprint from 1967

Penguin Travel Guides
Caribbean
Mexico
South America
Pub. Penguin £6.95–£7.95

South America on a Shoestring
by Geoff Crowther
Pub. Lonely Planet £6.95
Greatly expanded version of this budget guide to South America.

South America Overland
by I. Finlay
Pub. Deutsch £9.95

The South American Handbook
Pub. Trade and Travel £13.50
Annually revised. Winner of prizes and called 'the best guidebook to anywhere by anyone'.

South American River Trips vol. I
by G. N. Bradt
Pub. Bradt £3.95

South American River Trips vol. II
by T. and M. Jordan
Pub. Bradt £4.95

South American Survival
by Maurice Taylor
Pub. Wilton House Gentry £6.95
Full details on routes (including Amazonas), regional differences, statistics, sketch maps of countries, regions and towns.

Student Guide to Latin America
by Marjorie A. Cohen
Pub. E. P. Dutton, NY $2.95
Written for the Council on International Educational Exchange

Trails of Cordilleras Blanca and Huayhuash of Peru
by J. Bartle
Pub. Bradt £4.95

Travels with My Father
A South American Journey
by Daniel and Feliks Topolski
Pub. Elm Tree Books £9.95
Father and son set out on six-month overland trip through South America.

Yuraq Janka, Cordilleras Blanca and Rosko
by J. F. Ricker
Pub. Bradt £11.50
Brand new guide book and map.

AMERICA, NORTH

Alaska Travel Survival Kit
by Jim DuFresne
Pub. Lonely Planet £3.95
Lonely Planet continue their excellent series by going to more and more out of the way places.

America on Five Valium a Day
by Linda Blandford
Pub. Methuen £7.95
Compilation of witty articles written home to The Guardian.

American Express Guides
California
New York
Pub. Mitchell Beazley Each £4.95
Useful pocket-sized books

Apa Guides
Florida
Hawaii
From Harrap Each £8.95

Backpacking in North America
by H. and G. Bradt
Pub. Bradt £3.95

Berlitz Guides
California
Florida
Hawaii
Montreal
New York
From Cassell Each £2.45

Blue Guides
Boston
New York
Pub. E. Benn Each £7.95
Comprehensive new guides in this reliable series.

Blue Highways

by William Least Heat Moon
Pub. Secker and Warburg £8.95
Marvellous account of travels around backwoods America. Potential classic.

Canada: A Travel Survival Kit

by Mark Lightbody
Pub. Lonely Planet £4.95

Companion Guide to New York

by Michael Leapman
Pub. Collins £6.95
A true companion to this exciting city.

Fodor Guides

Canada
USA
Budget America
Budget Canada
Budget Hawaii
Cape Cod
Far West
Grand Canyon
New England
Pacific North Coast
South
Alaska
California
Colorado
Florida
Hawaii
Texas
Boston
Chicago
Dallas
Houston
Los Angeles
New Orleans
San Diego
San Francisco
Washington, DC
New York City
Pub. Fodor £5.95–£9.95

Frommer Guides

Dollarwise Canada
Dollarwise California
Dollarwise Florida
Dollarwise New England
Dollarwise SE and New Orleans
Hawaii on $25
New York on $25
Washington DC on $25
Boston Pocket Guide
Hawaii Pocket Guide
Las Vegas Pocket Guide
Los Angeles Pocket Guide
New Orleans Pocket Guide
New York Pocket Guide
Philadelphia and Atlantic City Pocket Guide
San Francisco Pocket Guide
Washington DC Pocket Guide
Pub. Frommer £2.95–£6.50

The Hawaiian Islands

by Carole Chester
Pub. Batsford £9.95

The Hip Pocket Guide to New York

by T. Page
Pub. Harper and Row £2.95
An excellent small guide

Michelin Green Guides

Canada
New England
New York City
Pub. Michelin Each £3.60
Excellent as ever.

Moneywise Guide to California

by Vicki Leon
Pub. Travelaid £5.95
Fun to read and full of practical advice.

Nagel Guides

Canada
New York
USA
From G. Cave £7–£18.50

Old Glory

by Jonathan Raban
Pub. Flamingo £2.95
A journey down the Mississippi

Penguin Guides

Canada
Hawaii
USA
USA for Business Travellers
Pub. Penguin £6.50–£7.50

Travel Brief USA

by Nigel Buxton
Pub. Sunday Telegraph £2.95

USA West. A Travel Guide to Hawaii, the Pacific States and SW.

Pub. Lonely Planet New edn.

Vagabonding in the USA

by Ed Buryn
From Lascelles £6.50

West Coast USA

by I. Van Dam
Pub. John Murray £5.95

ARCTIC AND ANTARCTIC

Antarctica

The Last Horizon
by John Béchervaise
Pub. Cassell £8.95
An account of Antarctica's unique wildlife, explorations past and present and ecological future by winner of the Queen's Polar Medal.

Antarctica. Wilderness at Risk

by B. Brewster
Pub. Reed £5.95

An African in Greenland

by Tété-Michel Kpomassie
Pub. Secker and Warburg £8.95
Run-away boy from Togo goes to live with the Eskimoes.

The Arctic Highway

by John Douglas
From Geoslides or Stackpole Books, USA
A full description of north Norway's famous road to the Arctic.

The Last Kings of Thule

by Jean Malaurie
Pub. Cape £17.50
Wonderfully sensitive portrait of traditional Eskimo life.

South

by Ernest Shackleton
Pub. Century £4.95
First published in 1919, this is the story of Shackleton's last expedition 1914–17.

Portrait of Antarctica

Pub. George Philip £9.95
Composite view of life over the last 40 years on the frozen continent by five enthusiasts.

South Pole Odyssey

by E. Wilson
Pub. Blandford £3.95
Selection from Edward Wilson's diary.

ASIA – GENERAL

All Asia Guide

Pub. Far Eastern Economic Review £6.50
Classic middle depth guide. 682pp of travel advice for businessmen and travellers from Afghanistan to Japan.

Apa Guides

Bali
Burma
Java
Korea
Malaysia
Nepal
Philippines
Singapore
Sri Lanka
From Harrap Each £8.95

Berlitz

Hong Kong
Singapore
Sri Lanka
Thailand Each £2.45

Fodor

Beijing, Guangzhou and Shanghai
Budget Japan
China
Hong Kong and Macao
India, Nepal and Sri Lanka
Israel
Japan
Korea
South East Asia
Tokyo and vicinity
Turkey
From Hodder and Stoughton £5.50–£9.95

Nagel Guides

Ceylon
China
Gulf Emirates
Iran
Israel
India
Philippines
Thailand
Turkey
From G. Cave £9–£25

Santhana

One Man's Road to the East
by Borna Babek
Pub. Bodley Head £6.50
Adventure and mysticism. A fine example of travelling against the odds.

Student Guide to Asia/Budget Traveler's Asia

Ed. David Jenkins for the Australian Union of Students
Pub. E. P. Dutton, NY $4.95/£3.50
Useful guide to 26 countries for students or other low-budget travellers.

Traveller's Survival Kit to the East

by Susan Griffith
Pub. Vacation Work £2.95

ASIA – WEST

Among the Believers

by V. S. Naipaul
Pub. Penguin £2.95

Arabia Through the Looking Glass

by Jonathan Raban
Pub. Fontana £2.95

Arabian Sands
Marsh Arabs

by Wilfred Thesiger
Pub. Penguin £2.25 and £2.95

Blue Guide Istanbul

by John Freely
Pub. E. Benn £8.95
By the same author as the famous but elusive Strolling Through Istanbul.

Business Guide to

Egypt
Kuwait
Oman
Saudi Arabia

Pub. World of Information/Longmans £2.95

The Companion Guide to Turkey

by John Freely
Pub. Collins £8.50
Reliable, comprehensive guide from Istanbul to the border.

Frommer

Israel on $25 and $30 a Day
From Lascelles £5.75

The Gulf Handbook

Eds Peter Kilner and Jonathan Wallace
Pub. Trade and Travel Publications £7.00
More modest offering from the publishers of The South American Handbook.

Insight Guide to Jordan

by Christine Osborne
Pub. Longmans £8.75

Iran Today

by J. Hureau

Iraq – Land of Two Rivers

by Gavin Young
Pub. Collins £15
Starting in Baghdad and central Iraq, this book moves south to Basra and the obscure lagoons and reed-beds of the Marsh Arabs and north to Kurdistan.

Israel and the Occupied Territories

by Gack and Wobcke
Pub. Lonely Planet New edn
Information on visiting the natural, modern and historic sites and attractions.

Israel Travellers Guide

Pub. Thornton Cox £3.50

Mecca and Medinah Today

by Kaidi, Bamante and Tidjani
Pub. Editions Jeune Afrique £7.50

MEED Guides

Bahrain
Jordan
Oman
Qatar
Saudi Arabia
UAE

From Noonan Hurst £7.95–£9.95

Touring Lebanon

by Philip Ward
Pub. Oleander £6
Not currently the easiest place to go . . .

Traveller's Guide to the Middle East

Pub. International Communications £4.95
Guide for the businessman or tourist including country-by-country information on how to get there, accommodation, local customs, transport, etc.

Turkey: A Travel Survival Kit

Pub. Lonely Planet NYP

West Asia on a Shoestring

by Tony Wheeler
Pub. Lonely Planet £3.95
Previously known as Across Asia on the Cheap.

ASIA – INDIAN SUBCONTINENT

Bangladesh. A Traveller's Guide

by Don Yeo
Pub. Lascelles £3.50
Only guide to this new republic.

Calcutta

by G. Moorhouse
Pub. Penguin £2.95
Riveting account of the city.

Everest: the Unclimbed Ridge

by Chris Bonington and Charles Clarke
Pub. Hodder and Stoughton £12.95
Account of the tragic 1982 expedition in which Peter Boardman and Joe Tasker lost their lives.

First Across the Roof of the World

by Graeme Dingle and Peter Hillary
Pub. Hodder and Stoughton £9.95
3,000-mile-walk from Darjeeling to K2 – the first traverse of the Himalayas.

Full Tilt

by Dervla Murphy
Pub. Century £4.95
Ireland to India on a bicycle.

A Guide to Trekking in Nepal

by S. Bezruchka
Pub. Cordee £5.95
Detailed descriptions of many routes and advice on organizing a trek.

A Handbook for Travellers in India, Pakistan, Nepal, Sri Lanka and Bangladesh

ed Prof L. F. Rushbrook Williams
Pub. John Murray £25
Periodically revised. First published in 1859.

Handguide to the Birds of the Indian Subcontinent

by M. Woodcock
Pub. Collins £3.50

The Himalayan Kingdoms: Nepal, Bhutan and Sikkim

by Bob Gibbons and Bob Ashford
Pub. Batsford £9.95

Heart of the Jungle

by K. K. Gurung
Pub. Andre Deutsch £9.95
Naturalist and manager of Tiger Tops discusses the Chitwan Valley.

India. A Practical Guide

by John Leak
Pub. Lascelles £3.95
If you can't find the Travel Survival Kit – grab this.

India. A Travel Survival Kit

by G. Crowther, P. Raj and Tony Wheeler
Pub. Lonely Planet £6.95
An excellent book. Winner of the Thomas Cook best guide book award

India File

by Trevor Fishlock
Pub. John Murray £9.95

An Insight and Guide to Pakistan

by Christine Osborne
Pub. Longmans £12.95

Into India

by John Keay
Pub. John Murray £4.95
An area-by-area coverage of modern India and Indian life.

A Journey in Ladakh

by Andrew Harvey
Pub. Chatto £8.50

Kashmir, Ladakh and Zanskar

by R. and M. Schettler
Pub. Lonely Planet £2.50

Kathmandu and the Kingdom of Nepal

by Prakash Raj
Pub. Lonely Planet £3.95

Maldives – Via Sri Lanka

Pub. Lascelles £2.95
The only guide to these increasingly popular islands.

Pakistan: A Travel Survival Kit

by Santiago
Pub. Lonely Planet £2.50

Pakistan. A Travellers Guide

by Adamson and Shaw
From Lascelles £6.95
An excellent comprehensive guide.

Plant Hunting in Nepal

by R. Lancaster
Pub. Croom Helm £6.95
Useful self-explanatory book.

A Short Walk in the Hindu Kush Slowly Down the Ganges

by Eric Newby
Pub. Picador Each £2.50
Two highly entertaining journeys.

Sri Lanka. A Travel Survival Kit

by Tony Wheeler
Pub. Lonely Planet £2.95

Travel Guide to North India

by Paige Palmer
Pub. Bradt £3.25

Trekkers Guide to the Himalaya and Karakoram

by Hugh Swift
Pub. Hodder and Stoughton £6.95
Excellent comprehensive guide.

Trekking in the Himalayas

by Stan Armington
Pub. Lonely Planet £2.95

Where Men and Mountains Meet

by John Keay
Pub. Century £4.95

ASIA – SOUTH EAST

Bali and Lombok. A Travel Survival Kit

by Mary Covernton and Tony Wheeler
Pub. Lonely Planet £3.95

Burma. A Travel Survival Kit

by Tony Wheeler
Pub. Lonely Planet £2.95
From Rangoon to Mandalay with sidetrips to Pagan and the Inkle Lakes.

A Dragon Apparent

by Norman Lewis
Pub. Eland £3.95
Travels in Cambodia, Laos and Vietnam. Written in 1951, it makes for poignant reading.

Golden Earth

by Norman Lewis
Pub. Eland £4.95
About Burma.

Great Railway Bazaar

by Paul Theroux
Pub. Penguin £1.95
A train journey through South East Asia: a modern classic.

Indonesia Handbook

by Bill Dalton
Pub. Moon Pubs £8.50
First-ever comprehensive guide (with detailed maps) to the islands of Micronesia, Polynesia and Melanesia with Papua New Guinea also. Indispensable.

Island Hopping through the Indonesian Archipelago

by Maurice Taylor
Pub. Wilton House Gentry £5.40
A guide to cheap, leisurely travel through Thailand, Malaysia, Indonesia. Good town plans and detailed advice.

The Land of the Great Sophy

by Roger Stevens
Pub. Methuen £8.50
Historical and archaeological guide.

Malaysia, Singapore and Brunei. A Travel Survival Kit

by G. Crowther and T. Wheeler
Pub. Lonely Planet £3.95

Philippines. A Travel Survival Kit

by Jens Peters
Pub. Lonely Planet £4.95

South East Asia Handbook

by Stefan Loose and Renate Ramb
Pub. Stefan Loose Publications US$16
Detailed guide to travel in Thailand, Singapore, Indonesia, Brunei, Malaysia and Burma.

South East Asia on a Shoestring

by Tony Wheeler
Pub. Lonely Planet £4.95
Guide for the budget traveller, with practical advice and some background information on eight SE Asian countries.

Thailand. A Travel Survival Kit

by J. Cumming
Pub. Lonely Planet £2.50

Thailand

by Gladys Nicol
Pub. Batsford £7.50
A description of Thai history and art from Bangkok to the rain forests.

ASIA – FAR EAST

China

by Sarah Allan and Cherry Barnett
Pub. Cassell £6.95
Gives a historical background to the major cities of China and general practical advice to the traveller.

China Companion

by Evelyn Garside
Pub. Deutsch £4.95
A guide to 100 cities, resorts, and places of interest in the people's republic. The author lived for some years in Beijing.

China Off the Beaten Track

by Brian Schwartz
Pub. Collins £5.95
Excellent guide to independent travel in China.

China Guidebook

by A. J. Keijzer and I. M. Kaplan
Dist. A. and C. Black £4.95
Authoritative guide to over 30 cities and 250 tourist sites.

China Today
Japan Today

Pub. Editions Jeunes Afrique Each £7.50

The Chinese. A Portrait

by David Bonavia
Pub. Penguin £1.95

Eastern Approaches

by Fitzroy MacLean
Pub. Macmillan £5.95
Originally published in 1949, this is a very exciting narrative of a journey through Russia and Central Asia.

Escape With Me!

by Osbert Sitwell
Pub. OUP £4.50
Oriental sketch-book of Grand Tour of the Orient in the 1930s.

Forbidden Journey

by Ella Maillart
Pub. Century £4.95
First published in 1937, Ella Maillart travelled with Peter Fleming.

From Heaven Lake

by Vikram Seth
Pub. Chatto £8.95
Seth hitch-hiked through Tibet to Nepal, an extraordinary journey. Winner of the 1983 Thomas Cook Travel Book Award.

Hong Kong, Macau and Canton

by C. Clewlow
Pub. Lonely Planet £3.95
Updated edition of the guide with all the latest information on high-speed Hong Kong and easy-going Macau.

Hong Kong, Macau and Taiwan

by Nina Nelson
Pub. Batsford £9.95

Japan. A Travel Survival Kit

by Ian McQueen
Pub. Lonely Planet £4.95
One of the less good guides in this series.

Japan. A Traveller's Companion

by Lesley Namioka
Pub. Vanguard Press, NY $8.95
Explains Japan for the visitor – including explanation of bath customs!

Korea and Taiwan. A Travel Survival Kit

by Geoff Crowther
Pub. Lonely Planet £3.95

Low City, High City

by Edward Seidensticker
Pub. Allen Lane £16.95
Tokyo from Edo to Earthquake. A fascinating portrait of the city.

North East Asia. A Travel Survival Kit

Pub. Lonely Planet NYP

On Your Own in China

by G. Earnshaw
Pub. Century £4.95
An up-to-date guide for the adventurous traveller.

Slow Boats to China

by Gavin Young
Pub. Penguin £2.95
The author travelled from Greece to China by a variety of different boats.

Traveller's Guide to the People's Republic of China

by Ruth L. Malloy
Pub. Wm Morrow, NY £6.50
Comprehensive English–Chinese phrasebook, descriptions of 90 cities and special sections for business people.

A Visitor's Guide to China

by Elizabeth Morrell
Pub. Michael Joseph £8.95

AUSTRALIA AND PACIFIC

Across the South Pacific

by Finlay and Sheppard
Pub. Angus and Robertson £9.95

Across the Top

by Malcolm Douglas and David Oldmeadow
From Lascelles £2.95

Australia. A Travel Survival Kit

by Tony Wheeler
Pub. Lonely Planet £6.95
Revised and expanded edition by a master guide writer.

Australia

by Vicki Peterson
Pub. Cassell £5.95
The author travelled 25,000km to research this book; an excellent overall guide.

Borneo

by John Mackinnon
Pub. Time-Life £7.50

Bushwalking in Papua New Guinea

by R. W. Nolan
Pub. Lonely Planet £3.95

Fodor Australia, New Zealand and South Pacific

From Hodder and Stoughton £9.95

Frommer

Australia on $20
New Zealand on $20 and $25
From Lascelles c. £5.75 each

Guide to the Outdoors

by Jeff Carter
From Lascelles £7.50
Practical, simple authoritative book by a man who has spent most of the last 25 years travelling and living outdoors in every corner of Australia.

How to Get Lost and Found In:

Australia
Cook Islands
Fiji
New Zealand
Tahiti
From Lascelles Each £4.95

In Papua New Guinea

by Christina Dodwell
Pub. Oxford Illustrated Press £7.95
One of the few up-to-date books on Papua New Guinea.

New Zealand. A Travel Survival Kit

by Tony Wheeler
Pub. Lonely Planet £2.95
Totally revised edition.

Outback

by Thomas Keneally
Pub. Hodder and Stoughton £12.95
Fabulous evocation by Booker Prize-winning author. Magnificent photographs.

Pacific Island Year Book

by Stuart Inder
Pub. Pacific Publications, Sydney

Papua New Guinea Handbook

by July Taylor
Pub. Pacific Publications, Sydney £8.50
Description of the country area by area.

Papua New Guinea. A Travel Survival Kit

by Tony Wheeler
Pub. Lonely Planet £2.95
Interesting and amusing guide with plenty of information on history, accommodation, sights and customs.

South Pacific Handbook

by Bill Dalton
Pub. Moon $8.50
Vocabs, diagrams, maps, town plans, archaeological sites, etc.

he South Seas Dream

· John Dyson
ıb. Heinemann £10
əautifully written account of time spent searching r paradise in the modern South Seas.

ahiti

· John Bounds
·om Lascelles £3.95

racks

Robyn Davidson
ıb. Granada £1.95
nazing account of a journey across the Australian sert on camels.

ramping in New Zealand

· Jim Dufresne
ıb. Lonely Planet £3.95
rimarily for the backpacker and crowd dodger. escribes 20 walks.

UROPE

he Aegean

· H. M. Denham
ıb. John Murray £25
sea-guide with information on cruising, the coast d islands.

lbania. A Travel Guide

Philip Ward
ıb. Oleander £5.95
teresting, up-to-date, but sledgehammer politics.

lpine Pass Route

· J. Hurdle
ıb. West Col. £3.95

merican Express Guides

Florence and Tuscany
Greece
Paris
Rome
South of France
Spain
Venice
ıb. Mitchell Beazley Each £4.95
andy, informative pocket guides.

mong the Russians

· Colin Thubron
ıb. Heinemann £8.95
iew of everyday life behind the Iron Curtain based conversation with the local populace.

Backpacker's Greece

by Marc S. Dubin
Pub. Bradt £4.95

Baedeker Guides

Austria
France
Germany
Greece
Holland/Belgium/Luxembourg
Italy
Portugal
Scandinavia
Spain
Yugoslavia Each £6.95
And city guides:
Amsterdam
Athens
Paris
Rome
Pub. A.A. Each £3.95

Berlitz

Forty-five guides covering countries, areas and cities.
From Cassell Each £2.45

The Big Red Train Ride

by Eric Newby
Pub. Penguin £2.25
A journey on the Trans-Siberian railway.

Black Lamb and Grey Falcon

by Rebecca West
Pub. Macmillan £6.95
A masterful mixture of travel, politics, anecdote, etc., on Yugoslavia.

Blue Guides

Athens and environs
Belgium and Luxembourg
Crete
Cyprus
Florence
Greece
Holland
N Italy
S Italy
Loire Valley
Malta
Moscow and Leningrad
Paris and environs
Portugal
Rome and environs
Sicily
Spain
Venice
Pub. E. Benn £3.95–£7.95

Companion Guides
Florence
Greek Islands
Mainland Greece
Rome
South of France
Venice
Yugoslavia
by various authors
Pub. Collins £5.95–£6.95

Complete Guide to the Soviet Union
by V. and J. Louis
Pub. Michael Joseph £6.95
The authors live in Moscow.

Corsica Mountains
by R. G. Collomb
Pub. West Col. £5.25

Fat Man on a Bicycle
by Tom Vernon
Pub. Fontana £1.95
A trip through France.

Fodor Guides
14 European countries Each £8.95
4 area guides Each £9.95
7 Budget guides Each £5.95
7 City guides Each £5.50

French Leave
by Richard Binns
Pub. Chiltern House £5.95
Third edition of this extremely popular guide.

Frommer Guides
Greece on $20
Scandinavia on $25
Spain, Morocco, and Canaries on $25
Europe on $25 £5.95–£7.95
Dollarwise France
Dollarwise Germany
Dollarwise Italy
Dollarwise Portugal £5.25–£6.50
City guides:
Amsterdam
Athens
Lisbon
Paris
Rome Each £2.95
From Lascelles

High Level: the Alps from End to End
by David Brett
Pub. Gollancz £10.95
Vivid account of 600-mile solitary walk through the Alps with a wealth of information for anyone going there.

Hitch-Hiker's Guide to Europe
by Ken Walsh
Pub. Pan £2.95

100 Hikes in the Alps
by I. Spring and H. Edwards
Pub. Cordee £5.50

Let's Go
Europe
France
Greece
Italy
Spain, Portugal and Morocco
Pub. Harvard Student Agencies £6.95–£7.95
From Columbus Books

Michelin Green Guides
10 European countries
19 French regions
Pub. Michelin Each £3.60
The classic guide that you cannot go wrong with.

Nagel Guides
24 European titles
From G. Cave £2–£21

Naples '44
by Norman Lewis
Pub. Eland £3.95
'A wonderful book' – Richard West. Spectator

Moscow – A Traveller's Companion
Ed Laurence Kelly
Pub. Constable £9.95/£5.95
Selection of writings on the city from all nationalities and periods of history.

Next Time You Go To Russia
by C. A. Ward
Pub. John Murray £5.75
A guide to historic landmarks in art museums.

Pauper's Paris
by M. Turner
Pub. Pan £2.50
Superb budget guide, packed full of useful tips.

Penguin Travel Guide Europe
Pub. Penguin £8.95

Picos de Europa. Northern Spain
by R. G. Collomb
Pub. West Col. £7.50

Pyrenees, Andorra, Cerdagne. A guide to the mountains for walkers and climbers
by A. Battagel
Pub. West Col. £6

Pyrenees. High Level Route
by G. Veron
Pub. West Col. £7.50

Romanian Journey
by A. Mackenzie
Pub. Hale £8.50

Rough Guides
Greece
Portugal
Spain
by Mark Ellingham
Pub. RKP Each £3.95
Excellent new series, a combination of practical information and scholarly fact. Many other titles in the pipeline.

Roumeli
by Patrick Leigh Fermor
Pub. Penguin £2.95
Beautifully written book of travels in Northern Greece.

Shell Guide to France
Pub. Michael Joseph £7.95

South From Granada
by Gerald Brenan
Pub. CUP £4.95
A classic book on Spain.

Spain
by Jan Morris
Pub. Penguin £1.75

Stranger in Spain
Traveller in Italy
Traveller in Rome
Traveller in South Italy
by H. V. Morton
Pub. Methuen £5.95–£6.95

A Time of Gifts
by Patrick Leigh Fermor
Pub. Penguin £1.95
A journey on foot from England to Hungary.

Trans-Siberia by Rail and a Month in Japan
by Barbara Lamplugh
Pub. Lascelles £1.95

Travellers Guides
Balearics
Corfu
Crete
Elba
Malta
Rhodes
Sardinia
Sicily
Pub. Cape £3.50–£5.95

Travellers Guides
Majorca
Portugal
South of France
Pub. Thornton Cox £1.95–£3.50

Travellers Survival Kit Europe
by K. Brown
Pub. Vacation Work £3.95
Too short to be terribly useful.

Venice
by James Morris
Pub. Faber £3.95
Superbly written, revealing account of Venice.

Venice for Pleasure
by J. G. Links
Pub. Bodley Head £5.95
A guide, based on walks.

Visitors Guide to the Dordogne
by N. Lands
Pub. Moorland £3.95

General

AIR TRAVEL

A Book of Air Journeys

by Ludovic Kennedy
Pub. Fontana £3.95
Anthology of writings on air travel from balloon flights to space missions.

Access Travel: Airports

From: Consumer Information Center, Dept 619-F, Pueblo, CO 81009, USA

Airport Information

Pub. British Airport Publications Free
How to get there, what to expect on arrival, how to get help and information, and where to stay – for all seven airports managed by the British Airports Authority.

Airport International

by Brian Moynahan
Pub. Pan £1.75
The inside story on airports and commercial aircraft operations. Revealing.

Care In the Air
Flight Plan

Pub. Airline Users' Committee Free
The first of these booklets has advice specifically for the handicapped while the second covers all aspects of air travel.

A Consumer Guide to Air Travel

by Frank Barratt
Pub. *Daily Telegraph* £3.95
Information and advice on air fares to passengers' rights.

The Flier's Handbook

The Traveller's Complete Guide to Airports, Aircraft and Air Travel.
ed Helen Varley
Pub. Pan £5.95
Covers planning, economics, security, airport vehicles, runways, guide to airports and air travel.

Hickman's World Air Travel Guide

Eds R. H. and M. E. Hickman
Pub. Elm Tree £3.95
Information on hundreds of countries, airlines, and airports as well as other aspects of travel, such as booking, visas and baggage.

The Jet Lag Book

by Don Kowet
Pub. Crown, USA $4.95
Good general book on how to avoid the miseries of long-haul flying from cramp upwards.

Jet Stress

by Judith Goeltz
Pub. International Institute of Natural Health Sciences, USA $14.95
One of the most comprehensive books available on jet lag, written by former stewardess.

Overcoming Jet Lag

by Dr Charles Ehret and Lynne Waller Scanlon
Pub. Berkeley Books $4.95
Dietary programme devised for the US Army rapid deployment force to counteract the most vicious effects of jet lag. Seems to work, but requires iron willpower.

Planetalk: The Consumer's Air Travel Guide

by Richard C. Levi and Sheryl Levi
Pub. Ace, USA $2.95
Covers complaints, how to book and understand ticketing, how to get the best fares, how to stay well while travelling, how to handle baggage, etc.

ATLASES

Bartholomew Junior Atlas of the World

Pub. Bartholomew £1.99
A colourful and clear pictorial atlas for children of all ages.

Bartholomew's World Atlas

Pub. Bartholomew £14.95
Classic atlas used as standard in many schools. Contains sections on cartography and map projections.

Philip's World Atlas

Pub. G. Philip £5.50
Smaller size atlas with good coverage and a higher than usual proportion of maps in the total number of pages.

Rand McNally Cosmopolitan World Atlas

Pub. Rand McNally £17.50

State of the World Atlas

by Kidron and Segal
Pub. Heinemann/Pan £9.50

The Times Atlas of the World

Pub. Times Books £40
512pp with index of 210,000 names. Widely acknowledged to be the best modern atlas.

The Times Concise Atlas of the World

Pub. Times Books £18.50
Maps reduced in size from those in the comprehensive edition, but still superbly drawn and put together.

The Times Atlas of the Oceans

Pub. Times Books £30.00
272pp and over 400 maps covering history, trade, resources and environment, as well as geography of the oceans. Excellent.

CYCLING

Bike Touring

by Raymond Bridge
Pub. Sierra Club Books £5.95
Comprehensive guide, information from what to buy to where to go.

Bikepacking for Beginners

by Robin Adshead
Pub. Oxford Illustrated Press £3.75

The CTC Book of Cycling

by John Whatmore
Pub. David and Charles £9.95
The first half is devoted to practical information and the second to actual routes around Britain.

Cycle Touring in Britain and the Rest of Europe

by Peter Knottley
Pub. Constable £4.95

Cycling in Europe

by N. Crane
Pub. Haynes £7.95

Fat Man on a Bicycle

by Tom Vernon
Pub. Fontana £1.95
Hilariously funny account of a journey from Muswell Hill to La Grande-Motte.

Full Tilt
Wheels Within Wheels

by Dervla Murphy
Pub. Century/Penguin £4.95/£1.95

Into the Remote Places

by Ian Hibbell
Pub. Robson Books £8.95

Journey to the Source of the Nile

by Nick Sanders
Pub. Nick Sanders Ltd £8.50
Cycle ride through the desert by the holder of the fastest time round the world on a bicycle.

The New Cyclist

by Tony Osman
Pub. Collins £4.95
A beginner's guide.

Richard's Bicycle Book

by Richard Ballantine
Pub. Pan £2.95
A manual of bicycle maintenance and enjoyment.

Round the World on a Wheel

by John Foster Fraser
Pub. Chatto £7.95
Record of a 19,000-mile bicycle journey around the world in 1896.

Two Wheel Trek

by Neil Clough
Pub. Arrow Books £1.75
Manchester to the Cape of Good Hope by bicycle.

TRAVEL FOR THE DISABLED

AA Guide for the Disabled

Pub. AA 95p (free to AA members)
Information about accommodation throughout the UK.

Access to the World

by Louise Weiss
Pub. Facts on File
Shortlisted for the Thomas Cook Guidebook Award.

Access Guides

From RADAR, 25 Mortimer Street, London W1N 8AB
Access to British towns and areas and cities abroad. Full publications list available.

Air Travel for the Handicapped

Consumer information free from TWA

Directory of Directories

From Rehabilitation International, NY
Lists 275 handbooks for the handicapped person covering hotels, restaurants, theatres, churches, transport and travel facilities in all countries. Claimed to be the most complete listing available.

Disabled Traveller's International Phrasebook

by Ian McNeil
From Disability Press, 60 Greenhayes Ave, Banstead, Surrey

Holidays for the Physically Handicapped

Pub. RADAR £1
Accommodation in the UK and a section on overseas holidays.

A List of Guidebooks for Handicapped Travellers

Pub. The President's Committee on Employment of the Handicapped, 1111 20th Street, NW, Washington, DC 20036, USA
Free pamphlet.

Motoring and Mobility for Disabled People

by Ann Darnbrough and Derek Kincade
Pub. RADAR £1

Travel Tips for the Handicapped

From US Travel Service, Dept of Commerce, Washington, DC 20230, USA

The Wheelchair Traveller

by Douglass R. Annand
From the author, Ball Hill Road, Milford, NH 03055, USA $7.95

EXPEDITIONS

Desert Expeditions

by Tom Sheppard
Pub. Expedition Advisory Centre £5

Expedition Catering

by Nigel Gifford
Pub. Expedition Advisory Centre £3

Expedition Equipment Manual

by Tony Lack
Pub. Expedition Advisory Centre £3

The Expedition Planner's Handbook and Directory

Pub. Expedition Advisory Centre £7.50

Joining an Expedition

by Nigel Winser £1

Notes for Overland Expeditions

by Shane Winser £1

Polar Notes

by Geoff Renner
Pub. Expedition Advisory Centre £5

The Expedition Handbook

ed Tony Land
Pub. Butterworth
From: Expedition Advisory Centre £7.50
Initial considerations, planning details, expedition field studies, appendices including addresses. Tips on fund-raising activities, getting reduced air fares, etc.

Expeditions and Exploration

by Nigel Gifford
Pub. Macmillan £14.65
An essential source book for both novice and professional expedition planners.

Expedition Medicine

A Planning Guide
by Robin Illingworth
Pub. Blackwell £1.25

The Expedition Organizer's Guide

by John Blashford-Snell and Richard Snailham
Pub. Daily Telegraph
Includes sections on planning, information, research and organization, personnel, finance, stores and vehicles, leadership and winding up an expedition.

Explorers Source Book

Ed Al Perrin
Pub. Harpers and Row, NY New edn
Advice, addresses, etc., on training, equipment, books and maps, governing bodies: by type of activity. Comprehensive and extremely useful.

Practical Advice for Expeditions in Tropical Rain Forest Regions

by Roger Chapman
Pub. Expedition Advisory Centre £5

MEDICINE

A.M.A. First Aid Manual

Pub. American Medical Association, 535 N Dearborn Street, Chicago, Ill, USA

merican Red Cross First Aid Text Book

ub. The Country Life Press, Garden City, NY

ritish Airways Travel Health Guide

d Dr A. S. R. Peffers
ub. Johnston and Bacon/Cassell New edn
seful short paperback.

he Care of Babies and Young Children in the Tropics

rom: National Association for Maternal and hild Welfare, Tavistock House North, Tavistock Square, London WC1
ree booklet. Mostly about medical problems, their revention and treatment.

he Cruising Sailor's Medical Guide

y Nicholas C. Leone MD and Elizabeth C. hillips, RN
ub. David McKay Co Inc, NY $12.50
ssential lifesaving information in a clear, well-rganized fashion – injuries, illness, dangerous arine life, emergency procedures at sea, water ccidents.

mergency Dentistry

y Dr David Watt
ub. Clausen Publications
ntended for those who must treat the occasional ental patient. Useful.

xpedition Medicine

ee *Expedition* section on page 594.

Foreign Language Guide to Health Care

ub. The Blue Cross Association. Blue ross/Blue Shield, 622 Third Avenue, New ork, NY 10017, USA
ree booklet giving translations of phrases concern-ng health and medicine into French, German, talian and Spanish.

oreign Travel Immunization Guide

y Hans H. Neumann, MD
ub. Medical Economics Co, USA $2.95
ublished annually. Guide to the immunizations ecessary for each area and a discussion of some ommon traveller's ills.

Health Hints for the Tropics

Ed Harry Most, MD
Pub. National Institute of Health, USA 75¢
Excellent source for travellers, said to be the best small booklet available on the subject.

Health Information for International Travel

Pub. US Dept of Health, Education and Welfare Free
Published annually. General information on the prevalence of disease and the inoculation requirements of foreign countries. Publication number (CDC) 79-8280.

How to Stay Healthy While Travelling

A Guide for Today's World Traveller
by Bob Young
Pub. Ross Erikson $4.95
Preparations, immunizations, diet and nutrition, obtaining medical care abroad, travel for the elderly, health problems associated with foreign travel.

How to Survive Your Holiday

The Traveller's Guide to Health
by Dr C. Allan Birch
Pub. Wigmore House £3.95
Reliable guide to many of the potential health hazards encountered abroad.

Medical Care for Mountain Climbers

by Peter Steele
Pub. Heinemann £4.75

New Advanced First Aid

by A. W. Gardner and P. J. Roylance
Pub. John Wright £4.95

Pocket Holiday Doctor

by Caroline Chapman and Caroline Lucas
Pub. Corgi £1.25
A sensible person's guide on how to cope with illness abroad.

Preservation of Personal Health in Warm Climates

Pub. Ross Institute of Tropical Hygiene

Pye's Surgical Handicraft

Ed J. Kyle
Pub. John Wright £15.00

The Ship Captain's Medical Guide

Pub. HMSO £25.00
Excellent handbook for anyone responsible for the health of others and reliant on his own resources.

Stay Healthy in Asia

Pub. Volunteers in Asia, Stanford, CA, USA
Guide for young American volunteers working in Asian communities over extended periods with suggestions on preventing, identifying and treating problems and locating doctors and hospitals.

Traveler's Guide to US Certified Doctors Abroad

Pub. Marquis Who's Who, Inc, USA $9.95
List of over 3,500 English-speaking doctors in 120 countries.

Traveling Healthy

Complete Guide to Medical Services in 23 Countries
by Sheilah M. Hillman and Robert S. Hillman, MD
Pub. Penguin, NY $7.95
Medical facilities and services in most of Europe plus emergency language, first-aid, self-help and Pharmocopeia and Drug Index.

The Traveller's Health Guide

by Dr Anthony C. Turner
Pub. Lascelles £1.95
Paperback by the Senior Overseas Medical Officer of British Airways Medical Services and Hon Associate Physician and Lecturer at the Hospital for Tropical Diseases, London. Invaluable for visitors to Africa, Asia or Latin America. Special sections on overlanding and cold climate comfort.

A Word or Two Before You Go

by Broughton Waddy, MD, and Ralph Townley
Pub. W. W. Norton and Co, NY $3.95
Excellent guide to the medical aspects of travel: all the diseases, likely and unlikely emergencies, etc.

OVERLANDING

Africa Overland

A Trek from Cape Town to Cairo
by Iain Finlay and Trish Sheppard
Pub. Angus and Robertson £5.95
Account of family of four travelling on foot, by bus, train and hitchhiking on their way south. With summaries of historic places visited, prices and places to stay.

The Asian Highway

The Complete Overland Guide from Europe to Australia
by Jack Jackson and Ellen Crampton
Pub. Angus and Robertson
A useful manual for any overlander, giving th benefit of Jack's experience of camping, customs driving, preparations and bureaucracy.

Jupiter's Travels

by Ted Simon
Pub. Penguin £1.95
A 63,000-mile motorbike journey around the world

Overland

by Peter Fraenkel
Pub. David and Charles £4.95
Indispensable money-saving guide to planning, pre paration, equipment, vehicle modification, etc. (bu not routes), by author with 160,000km of overlan experience in Africa, Asia and Europe.

Overland and Beyond

Advice for Overland Travellers
by Theresa and Jonathan Hewat
Pub. Lascelles £2.50
Planning equipment and the other essentials o overland travel, based on author's three-year tri around the world in a VW Camper.

Trans-African Motoring
Trans-Asia Motoring
Trans-Australia Motoring

by Colin McElduff
Pub. RAC, London
Useful books with a wealth of information for th overland travellers – from routes to regulations.

Wanderlust

Overland through Asia and Africa
by Dan Spitzer
Pub. Richard Marek Publishers, NY

World Understanding on Two Wheels

An Introduction to Overland Travel
by Paul R. Pratt
From: Lascelles £2.50
Based on the author's journey by motorcycle throug more than 60 countries.

PHOTOGRAPHY

Creative Techniques in Travel Photography

by John Douglas
Pub. Batsford £9.95
Covers all aspects of travel photography from plan ning to selling the finished product.

How to Take Better Travel Photos

by Lisl Dennis
Pub. Fisher, USA $7.95
What to do before you leave, equipment and how to carry it, lenses, faces/adventure/landscape/special events, problems, showing photos, turning professional. Readable and copiously illustrated.

The Photographer's Handbook

by John Hedgcoe
Pub. Ebury Press £10.95
Use of equipment, procedures, glossary, special projects.

Practical Wildlife Photography

by Ken Preston-Mafham
Pub. Focal Press £11.95
Not for the beginner, but very good for the experienced photographer with a serious interest in wildlife and plant photography.

Travel Photography

Pub. Time-Life
From Heinemann £10.25

The Underwater Photographer's Handbook

by Peter Rowlands
Pub. Macdonald £9.95
Clearly presented informative book on technical aspects and guide to world-wide diving sites.

RAILWAYS

Eurail Guide

How to Travel Europe and All the World by Train
by Martin L. Salzman and Kathryn S. Muilman
From Trade and Travel £5.95

The Great Railway Adventure

by Christopher Portway
Pub. Oxford Illustrated Press £7.95
Documentation of one man's experiences, travelling the world by train.

Fodor's Railways of the World

Ed Robert Fisher
Pub. David McKay
Timetables to menus – details of trains throughout the world.

SURVIVAL

Desert Travel and Research

by J. L. Cloudsley-Thompson
Pub. Institute of Biology, London
See also Africa – Guidebooks – for many useful books on travel in the Sahara (page 577).

Don't Die in the Bundu

by Col. D. H. Grainger
Pub. Howard Timmins, RSA

Desert Survival
Jungle Survival
Sea Survival
Snow Survival
Survival Against the Elements

From: Survival Aids Ltd, Morland, Penrith, Cumbria
All have useful information on first-aid, possible sources of injury, illness or danger.

Outdoor Survival Handbook

by David Platten
Pub. David and Charles £4.50
For trekkers and campers.

Stay Alive in the Desert

by K. E. M. Melville
Pub. Lascelles £2.50
Deals with the hazards of desert driving, including advice on equipping the vehicle, procedure if stuck or stranded, precautions when driving, against ill health, and hygiene.

Survival

Pub. Department of the Air Force, USA
Air Force Manual 64–5.

Survival Cards

Pub. Survival Cards, Box 805, Bloomington, IN 47401, USA $2.50
Ten small plastic cards giving 300 techniques – solar still, snares, signals, snakebite, hypothermia, amputation, etc. – for temperate, desert, arctic and tropical conditions.

Survival in Cold Water

The Physiology and Treatment of Immersion, Hypothermia and Drowning
by W. R. Keatinge
Pub. Blackwell Scientific Publications.

TRAVEL TIPS

Area Handbooks

Compiled by US State Department
From: Superintendent of Documents, US Government Printing Office $5–$10
Detailed information on history, politics, economics, population, health of many countries. Request by country.

The Art and Adventure of Travelling Cheaply

by Rick Berg
Pub. And/Or Press, USA $4.95
Very useful readable guide to attitude, philosophy and method in travel by all means, especially for the person who travels for Travel's sake.

Background Notes on Countries of the World

Compiled by US State Department
From: Superintendent of Documents, US Government Printing Office 35¢–75¢
Synopsis of countries' history, geography, climate, economy, current exchange rate, etc. Approximately 75 countries updated each year.

Charter Flight Directory

by Jens Jurgen
Pub. Travel Information Bureau, NY
Revised annually. Tips on air fares, ways of obtaining stopovers, getting airlines to pay for accommodation, etc. Also good address list.

The Complete Handbook for Travellers

by Hal Gieseking
A Wallaby Book
Pub. Pocket Books, NY $8.95
Useful guide to airlines, hotels, rental cars and other aspects of travel, written by the editor of The Travel Advisor *newsletter. Much of the information concerns travel within the USA.*

The Complete Traveller

Everything You Need to Know About Travel at Home and Abroad
by Joan Bakewell
Pub. Hamlyn £1.50
Extensive book full of snippets of information aimed mainly at the conventional traveller.

Consumer's Guide to Federal Publications

From: Superintendent of Documents, US Government Printing Office
Free catalogue listing government travel publications.

500 Inside Tips for the Long Haul Traveller

by Richard Harrington
Pub. WEXAS £2.25

Fools Paradise

by Brian Moynahan
Pub. Pan £1.75
Horrifically informative account of the tourist industry and the rip-offs inherent therein.

A Guide to Solo Travel Abroad

by Eleanor Adams Baxal
Pub. Berkshire Travel Press, USA $5.50
Pros and cons, some personal experiences of solo travel, projecting expenses, dealing with the opposite sex, etc.

Holiday Insurance

Pub. British Insurance Association, Aldermary House, Queen Street London EC4P 4JD
Free leaflet (enclose sae).

International Youth Hostel Federation Handbook

Pub. IYHF
Guide to youth hostelling principles and regulations with lists of all youth hostels with notes on their amenities, location, costs, etc.

MsAdventures

Worldwide Travelguide for Independent Women
by Gail Rubin Sereny
Pub. Chronicle Books, USA $5.95
Light reading, hard facts, a good guide for the lone woman traveller.

Notes on Commonwealth Countries

Pub. Royal Commonwealth Society
Detailed guides including information on cost of living, health and educational facilities, housing availability and rent and other useful information for potential residents.

Notice To Travellers

Pub. Bank of England
Free leaflet giving countries with special currency restrictions, sources of best rates of exchange, etc.

1,001 Sources for Free Travel Information

by Jens Jurgen
Pub. Travel Information Bureau, PO Box 105, King's Park, NY 11754, USA
Information on around 200 countries.

Penguin International Travel Handbook

by Peter and Magda Hall
Pub. Penguin £2.95
Advice and country-by-country guide.

Super Traveler

The Complete Handbook of Essential Facts, Regulations, Rights and Remedies for Trouble-free International Travel
by Saul Miller
Pub. Holt, Rinehart and Winston $6.95
For the American travelling abroad.

Survival Kit

Pub. CIEE, USA
Details of many intra-European charter flights and cheap accommodation in 33 countries.

Thomas Cook A–Z of Travel

by Edmund Swinglehurst and Janice Anderson
Pub. Constable £6.50

Time Off

A Psychological Guide to Vacations
by Stephen Shapiro PhD and Alan Tuckman, MD
Pub. Anchor Press/Doubleday, USA
Mental preparation to help avoid pre-holiday frenzy and post-holiday blues.

Traveler's Picture Dictionary

Pub. AJS International, USA
Pocket-sized, indexed, picture dictionary with sections on personal needs, drinks, food, clothes, medical aid, services.

The Traveling Woman

by Dena Kaye
Pub. Doubleday, NY $11.95
Practical information on food, clothing, accessories, packing and the pitfalls, pleasures and precautions involved in travel, alone or in camping.

Travel Guidebooks in Review

Ed Jan O. Heise
Pub. University of Michigan International Center
Guide to about 100 books on travel, written to provide a comprehensive overview' of the field.

The Travel Survival Guide

by Carol Wright
Pub. David and Charles £6.95
Easy to read, practical advice.

Travel Tips

by Edythe Syvertsen
Pub. Tempo/Grosset and Dunlop $1.95
By the editor of the New York Post. *Brief paperback on travelling by all means and in different environments.*

The Tropical Traveller

Hints, Ideas, Advice for Enterprising Travellers to Hot Countries
by John Hatt
Pub. Pan £2.50
An invaluable and very funny book for the independent traveller.

Trouble-Free Travel

What to Know Before You Go
by Marty Leshner
Pub. Franklin Watts, NY $7.95
Choosing means, luggage, staying healthy and sane, etc.

Whole World Handbook

A Student Guide to Work, Study and Travel Abroad
by Marjorie Cohen and Margaret Sherman
Pub. CIEE/Frommer, USA
An excellent compendium on student travel, including background reading, reports from students on travel and study abroad.

YMCA and YWCA Directories

Pub. YMCA
List own addresses in over 70 countries, plus other useful addresses of doctors, lawyers, consultates, priests, etc.

VEHICLES

Buying a Car Overseas

Pub. US Environmental Protection Agency
From: US Customs Service Offices
Free brochure, revised periodically.

The Four-Wheel Drive Book

by Jack Jackson
Pub. Gentry Books £10.95
Comprehensive view of four-wheel-drive vehicles and their uses with excellent sections on overlanding and expeditions.

A Guide to Land Rover Expeditions

Pub. Land Rover Ltd.
Free booklet with information on the vehicle, hints on cross-country driving and some general information on travel.

Importing a Car

Pub. US Customs Service
Free brochure, revised periodically.

Petersen's Complete Book of Four-Wheel Drive

Ed Spence Murray
Pub. Petersen Publishing Co, USA
Combines history of the military Jeep with practical tips for modern four-wheel-drives. Includes reports on sixteen vehicles submitted to comparison tests.

WEATHER

The Climate Advisor

by Gilbert Schwartz
Pub. Climate Guide Publications, USA
Non-technical reference guide to climate and weather in North America, with climate charts for over 350 locations.

The World Weather Guide

by E. A. Pearce and C. G. Smith
Pub. Hutchinson £7.95
Excellent reference with climate charts around the entire world and short sections on altitude and geography of each country.

WORKING ABROAD

Accepting a Job Abroad

A Practical Guide
by M. Tideswell
Pub. British Institute of Management Foundation
Useful guide for potential expatriates with good list of sources of information.

Berlitz Business Travel Guide

From Cassell £2.45
Covers 31 countries in W and E Europe.

International Herald Tribune Guide to Business Travel and Entertainment. Europe.

Pub. Thames and Hudson £7.95

International Directory of Voluntary Work

Pub. Vacation Work £4.50

Living Costs Overseas

A Guide for Businessmen
Pub. *Financial Times*
Up-to-date, but very expensive, information on living costs in 66 of the world's major business centres.

Summer Jobs Abroad

Pub. Vacation Work £4.95
Covers both short- and long-term employment. Invaluable.

Work Your Way Around the World

by Susan Griffith
Pub. Vacation Work £4.95
Covers both short- and long-term employment. Invaluable.

Working Abroad

Daily Telegraph Guide to Working and Living Overseas
by Godfrey Golzen and Margaret Stewart
Pub. Kogan Page c. £7
Factual profiles of living and working conditions in 39 countries and much other advice and information.

Working Abroad

The Expatriate's Guide
by David Young
Pub. *Financial Times* £9.95
Comprehensive guide to all aspects of expatriate employment.

Book and Map Publishers

John Bartholomew & Son Ltd

12 Duncan Street
Edinburgh EH9 1TA
Tel: 031-667 9341
Publish tourist, road, topographic/general maps and atlases. Free catalogue from Marketing Department.

Bradt Enterprises

41 Nortoft Road
Chalfont St. Peter
Bucks SL9 0LA
Tel: 02407 3478
and
95 Harvey Street
Cambridge
MA 02140
USA
Publishers of backpacking books.

Department of Defense and Mapping Agency

Hydrographic/Topographic Centre
Washington
DC 20315
USA
Publish charts of oceans and coasts of all areas of the world; and pilot charts. Supply maps or photocopies of maps on request provided that the exact area is specified.

Diadem Books Ltd

c/o Cordee
3a DeMontfort Street
Leicester
Tel: (0533) 708212
Publish books on climbing, mountain travel, walking, caving, skiing and other outdoor adventure sports.

Freytag Berndt u. Artaria KG

Kartographische Anstalt
Schottenfeldgasse 62
Vienna VII
Austria
Are large general map publishers.

Geographia Ltd

63 Fleet Street
London EC4Y 1PE
Tel: 01-353 2701/2
and
17–21 Conway Street
London W1P 6JD
Publish a wide range of maps and atlases.

Harian Publications

1 Vernon Avenue
Floral Park
NY 11001
USA
Publishers of retirement, shipping and other travel guides. Books are sent surface rate. Air mail according to weight. All orders prepaid plus postage.

Hydrographic Department

MOD (Navy)
Taunton
Somerset TA1 2DN
Tel: (0823) 87900
Telex: 46724
Publishes world series of Admiralty Charts and hydrographic publications. Available from appointed Admiralty Chart Agencies.

Institut Géographique National

Direction Générale
136 bis, Rue Grenelle
75700 Paris
France
Tel: 550 34 95
Mail Order Sales for Individuals:
107 Rue la Boetie
75008 Paris
France
Tel: 225 87 90
Mail Order Sales for Wholesalers:
IGN
Camp des Landes Villefranche sur Cher
41200 Romoratin
France
Tel: 549 85 442
Telex: 750535F IGN VIL
Publish and sell maps of France and very many of the former French possessions.

Kummerly und Frey Ltd

Hallerstrasse 6–10
CH-3001 Bern
Switzerland
Publish charts and political, topographic, road and other maps.

Roger Lascelles

Cartographic and Travel Publisher
47 York Road
Brentford
Middlesex TW8 0QP
Tel: 01-847 0935
Travel and cartographic publishers. Publish a catalogue every January and July. An extensive selection of guides, maps, town plans and travel books on Africa, America, Asia, Australia, and Europe.

Lonely Planet Publications

PO Box 88
South Yarra
Victoria 3141
Australia
Tel: (03) 429 5100
Publish low-cost travel guides to Australasia, Latin America, and Asia.

Rand McNally & Co

PO Box 2600
Chicago
IL 60680
USA
Retail:
10 East 53rd Street
New York
NY 10022
Rand McNally Map Store:
23 E Madison
Chicago
IL 60602
Rand McNally Map Store:
595 Market Street
San Francisco
CA 94105
Publish maps, atlases, guides and globes.

Michelin Guides

46 Rue de Breteuil
75341 Paris
France
Tel: 539 25 00
Publish maps and the famous Red and Green Guides.

National Geographic Society

17th and M Streets
Washington
DC 20036
USA
Publish mainly topographical maps to accompany the National Geographic Magazine, also sell wall, relief and archaeological maps, atlases and globes. Publish National Geographic Traveler (quarterly).

NOAA Distribution Branch, N/CG33 National Ocean Service

Riverdale
Maryland 20737
USA
The National Ocean Service (NOS) publishes and distributes aeronautical charts of the US. Charts of foreign areas are published by the Defense Mapping Agency Aerospace Center (DMAAC) and are sold by the NOS.

Ordnance Survey

Romsey Road
Maybush
Southampton SO9 4DH
Tel: (0703) 775555
The official civilian mapping agency for the UK.

Ordnance Survey Overseas Surveys Directorate (TISS)

Romsey Road
Maybush
Southampton SO9 4DH
Are the official UK publishers of maps of former (and current) British Possessions. Edward Stanford Ltd (q.v.) are the agents for the sale of OSD maps.

Passport Publications

20 N Wacker Drive
Chicago
IL 60606
USA
Tel: (312) 332 3571
Publish 'Passport' newsletter and other travel booklets and guides.

George Philip & Son Ltd

12 Long Acre
London WC2E 9LP
Tel: 01-836 1915
Publish a wide range of topographical and thematic maps, globes, atlases and charts.

Regenbogen-Verlag

Schmidgasse 3
CH-8001
Postfach 240
CH-8025 Zurich
Switzerland
and
c/o Los Amigos del Libro
Casilla Postal 450
Cochabamba
Bolivia
Publish books for the independent traveller making his own way.

Royal Geographical Society

Publications Department
1 Kensington Gore
London SW7 2AR
Tel: 01-589 5466
Sells maps originally published in the Geographical Journal and maps published separately by the Society; and expedition pamphlets, G.J. reprints and other papers on geography, expeditions and related subjects. Lists available on request.

Ludmilla Tüting

Mittenwalder Str. 7
D-1000 Berlin 61
Germany, Federal Republic
Tel: (030) 691 6885
Publishes and sells handbooks for globetrotters and overlanders.

US Department of the Interior Geological Survey

National Cartographic Information Center (NCIC)
507 National Center
Reston
VA 22092
USA
Information about maps and related data for US areas.

Vacation Work Publications

9 Park End Street
Oxford
Oxon. OX1 1HJ
Tel: (0865) 241 978
Publishes books on employment and budget travel abroad.

Book and Map Distributors

BAS Overseas Publications

BAS House
48–50 Sheen Lane
London SW14 8LP
Tel: 01-876 2131 and 878 7527/8
General sales agent for a wide range of British, American and European timetables, hotel directories, etc.

Bookpeople

2929 Fifth Street
Berkeley
CA 94710
USA

Bradt Enterprises

41 Nortoft Road
Chalfont St. Peter
Bucks SL9 0LA
Tel: (02407) 3478
and
95 Harvey Street
Cambridge
MA 02140
USA
Main importers into the USA and Europe of South America maps and books.

Cordee

3a De Montfort Street
Leicester LE1 7HD
Tel: (0533) 543 579
Distributors/Publishers on mountaineering, outdoor recreation, and travel books.

David and Charles Ltd

North Pomfret
VT
USA
Are distributors for David and Charles and several other British publishers in the US of overland and travel books.

French and European Publications

610 Fifth Avenue
New York
NY 10020
USA
Import Michelin Guides and maps and other tourist publications from France and Spain to the USA.

Golden Press Pty Ltd

2–12 Tennyson Road
Gladesville
NSW 2111
Australia
Tel: (02) 89 0421
and in Melbourne, Adelaide, Brisbane, Perth, Launceston and Hobart
Are wholesale distributors for Gregory's Street Directories, Guides and Sheet Maps.

Michelin Tyre PLC

81 Fulham Road
London SW3 6RD
Tel: 01-589 1460
Distributors of Michelin Maps, Red Hotel & Restaurant Guides and Green Tourist Guides – available from leading bookshops.

Neue Bucher AG

Gotthardstrasse 49
8027 Zurich
Switzerland
Tel: Zurich 202 7474
Handles books published by Regenbogen-Verlag.

Roger Lascelles

47 York Road
Brentford
Middx TW8 0QP
One of Britain's main distributors of travel books, guides, maps.

Writer's Digest Books

9933 Alliance Road
Cincinatti
OH 45242
USA
Is the distributor for Vacation Work Publications (UK), publishers of books on employment and budget travel in foreign countries. Also publishes books on travel writing and on finding jobs in the US.

Expedition Reports

The Royal Geographical Society

1 Kensington Gore
London SW7 2AR
Tel: 01-581 2057
Reports may be consulted in the Map Room, Monday to Friday 10am–5pm. The collection includes reports approved by the RGS, YET and MEF. (*See Associations: Exploration, Adventure and Travel on page 608.*)

Scientific Exploration Society

Home Farm
Mildenhall
nr Marlborough
Wilts

Training, Help and Advice

Associations: Exploration, Adventure and Travel

The Adirondack Mountain Club

172 Ridge Street
Glenfalls
NY 12801
Tel: (518) 793 7737
Founded in 1922, the ADK is a non-profit membership organization. Works to retain the wilderness and magic of New York's Adirondack and Catskill parks. Assists in construction and maintenance of trails and campsites, shelters and permanent facilities on private land acquired for that purpose. Hiking, skiing, snowshoeing, canoeing and mountaineering. Winter mountaineering schools, canoe and wilderness skills workshops, rock climbing schools and other programmes. Publish a series of fold-outs full of useful information: Taking a Hike? Leading a Hike?, Wilderness Tips, Coping with Trail Bugs, Hypothermia & Frostbite, For the Winter Mountaineer, For the Summer Backpacker. Several types of membership available. For details write to above adress.

Amicale des Sahariens

4 Rue de Coetlogon
75066 Paris
France

Arbeit Tourismus und Entwicklung

Missionsstrasse 21
CH–4003 Basel
Switzerland
Critical non-profit organization.

Brathay Exploration Group

Brathay Hall
Ambleside
Cumbria CA22 OHP
Tel: (09663) 3402
Organizes annual scientific, trekking and training expeditions to the Lake District, Scottish Highlands and worldwide. Gives administration and financial support. Write to Expeditionary Co-ordinator for details and application forms.

British Schools Exploring Society

at The Royal Geographical Society
1 Kensington Gore
London SW7 2AR
Tel: 01–584 0710
Organises one major expedition a year for 16–19 year olds.

Deutsche Zentrale für Globetrotter

c/o Ludmilla Tüting
Mittenwalder Str. 7
D–1000 Berlin 61
Germany, Federal Republic
A small informal association of globetrotters mainly from German-speaking Europe, linked by an interest in low cost travel and the desire to study the cultures of other countries at first hand. Founded in 1974, it has some 1,500 members. Membership is open to those who can prove that they have travelled on their own in countries outside Europe for at least three months. The club operates from a private address. Members meet regularly at different places in Germany. Non-members are also offered information and contacts, but must enclose a s.a.e. with enquiry. (For newsletter Trotter, see Periodicals, page 570).

Expedition Advisory Centre

at The Royal Geographical Society
1 Kensington Gore
London SW7 2AR
Tel: 01–581 2057
Centre for information and advice for expeditions. (See Travel and Expedition Advisers, Consultants and Agencies on page 618.)

Expedition Club-Austria

PO Box 1457
A–1011 Vienna
Austria
Was established in 1978 to hold meetings, publish a newsletter, organize camps, film evenings and other

events, and to act as a centre for the exchange of information for anyone interested in long distance travel but particularly between experienced expeditioners and would-be travellers. The Club also produces information sheets on relevant countries.

The Explorers Club

46 East 70th Street
New York
NY 10021
USA
Tel: (212) 628 83 83 Telex: 968528
Was founded in 1904 as an institution of serious purpose designed for and dedicated to the search for new knowledge of the earth and outer space. It serves as a focal point and catalyst in the identification and stimulation of institutional exploration, independent investigators and students. The Club has over 3000 members who continue to contribute actively to the constructive role of the explorer. The classes of membership are: Member, Fellow, Student, Corporate, each class being divided into Resident (living within 50 miles of the Headquarters) and Non-Resident. The Club has financed over 140 expeditions and awarded its flag to over 300 expeditions.
The James B. Ford Memorial Library *contains over 25,000 items, including maps, charts, archives and photographs, and is probably the largest private collection in North America wholly devoted to exploration. The Club publishes the quarterly* Explorers Journal *(see Periodicals, page 570). Lectures, seminars and special events and an Annual Dinner are held. There is an annual presentation of honours and awards.*
Formally constituted groups are located as follows: Southern Florida (Coral Gabels), Central Florida (Winter Park), Greater Peidmont (Southern Pines, NC), Great Lakes (Ann Arbor, MI), New England (Boston, MA), Northern California (Belvedere, CA), Southern California (Encino, CA), Pacific Northwest (Chehalis, WA), Philadelphia, Rocky Mountain (Boulder, CO), Texas (Dallas), Washington Group (Bethesda, MD), Britain (London), & Australia (Sydney).

Fédération Française de la Randonée Pedestre

Comité National des Sentiers de Grande Randonnée

8 Avenue Marceau
75008 Paris
France
Tel: 723 62 32

Globetrotters Club

BCM/Roving
London WC1N 3XX
A small informal association of travellers from all over the world, linked by an interest in low cost travel and the desire to study the cultures of other lands at first hand. Members share their personal experiences and detailed knowledge of local conditions. The club is small and personal and concentrates on attracting as new members only those 'non-tourists' with a genuine empathy for the people in other lands. Members may advertise in the club's newsletter Globe *(see Periodicals, page 570) and films and talks are held in London, California, Ontario and New York.*

Gruppe Neues Reisen

Höwarthstr. 4
D–8000 München
Germany, Federal Republic.
Tel: (089) 368 298
A non-profit club with critical views about tourism. Newsletter – Reisebriefe.

Guilde du Raid

11 Rue du Vaugirard
75006 Paris
France
Tel: 326 9752
Promotes adventure in remote parts of the world. It organizes meetings, conferences, lectures, film evenings and permanent exhibitions, and a small number of organized tour/treks. Since 1971 it has made annual grants under the heading of Nationale de l'Aventure *to responsible but adventurous expeditions having definite goals, usually those mounted by individuals or small groups. Other grants and donations in money or kind are available through the* Guilde, *as are also the advice of experts, access to documents, discounts and benefits from associated bodies, and help with the safe-keeping and sale of expedition reports and photos.*

JOLT

Journey of a Lifetime
16 Roxeth Hill
Harrow on the Hill
Middlesex HA2 0JT
Tel: 01-864 2461
The Jolt Trust provides journeys, expeditions and holidays abroad in order to advance the education of young persons between the ages of 15 and 19 years who are resident in city areas and who would benefit by reason of their disability, poverty or other social or economic circumstances.

The National Geographic Society

17th and M Streets, NW
Washington
DC 20036
USA
The Society's aim is to pursue and promlgate geographical knowledge and to promote research and exploration. The Society occasionally sponsors significant expeditions. (*See Periodicals, page 570.*)

Ocean Voyages

1709 Bridgeway
Sausalito
California 94965
USA
Tel: 415–3324681

A unique organization which provides exotic sailing experiences all over the world. Challenging trips for veteran sailors, good learning experiences for novices. Can arrange research expeditions. (See Associations: Sporting, page 610 and Travel: Passenger Shipping Agents and Advisory Services, page 708.)

Operation Raleigh

PO Box 370
The Warehouse
52 St Katharine's Way
London E1 9LB

Operation Raleigh is a four-year, round-the-world expedition (1984–88) involving 4,000 young people in valuable scientific, community and conservation projects, in over 50 countries. It follows the successful Operation Drake (1978–80) and is again under the patronage of HRH The Prince of Wales.

The expedition will traverse some of the most challenging and fascinating territories around the world. The 1,600 ton flagship 'Sir Walter Raleigh' generously sponsored by Hull City Council, will be fully equipped to carry out maritime research projects and will act as operational headquarters and communications centre for the duration of the expedition. Of the selected Venturers, 1,500 will come from the UK, and 1,500 from the USA.

Applications forms – for youngsters aged between 16–23, are available in the last quarter of every year from all branches of the Trustee Savings Bank. Forms for Directing Staff are available from the above address. Please send s.a.e.

The 153 Club

Hon. Sec. – Rod Davis
97 Thornlaw Road
West Norwood
London SE 27
Tel: 01–761 0696

Is a club for 'friends of the Sahara' who have travelled within the confines of the Michelin Map 153. The club publishes a newsletter. The annual subscription is currently £1.53!

Royal Geographical Society

1 Kensington Gore
London SW7 2AR
Tel: 01–589 5466

A focal point for geographers and explorers. It directly organizes and finances its own scientific expeditions and gives financial support, the loan of instruments, approval and advice to some 50+ expeditions each year. The Society honours outstanding geographers and explorers with a series of annual medals and awards.

The RGS maintains the largest private map collection in Europe, with over half a million sheets. It has a drawing office with a staff of expert cartographers and a library with over 1,000,000 books and periodicals on geography, travel and exploration. There is also an archive of historical records and expedition reports.

There are regular lectures, children's lectures, discussions, symposia and academic meetings in the Society's 760-seat lecture hall. Most of the leading names in exploration, mountaineering and geography have addressed the Society. The RGS publishes the Geographical Journal three times a year and a newsletter entitled 1 Kensington Gore, four times a year. There is a Young Member's Committee. Anyone with a geographical interest can apply for a Fellowship of the RGS. An applicant must be proposed and seconded by existing Fellows.

Royal Scottish Geographical Society

10 Randolph Crescent
off Queensbury Street
Edinburgh EG3 7TU
Tel: 031–225 3330

Also has centres in Aberdeen, Dundee, Dunfermline and Glasgow. It offers the following classes of Membership: Ordinary, Life, Student Associate, Junior, School Corporate, Country Areas, and Overseas. The Society houses a library, a map collection and over 200 periodicals. It arranges tours, excursions and lectures, and sells map reproductions and publications.

Scientific Exploration Society

Home Farm
Mildenhall
Nr. Marlborough
Wiltshire

Was formed in 1969 by a group of explorers, many of whom had been together on expeditions, with the aim of making their association more permanent so that personnel and useful equipment would not be dispersed but instead kept together for future undertakings. The Society exists to organize expeditions and to help others – universities, schools, services and individuals – to organize their own. It maintains close links with commerce, industry, educational establishments, the services and other kindred scientific and exploration organizations. The Society has 500 members, many of them expert explorers. All are eligible to take part in expeditions. Fully sponsored expeditions generally appoint their Leader, Secretary and Treasurer and many of their personnel from among the Society's membership. Other expeditions can be given the approval and support of the SES by the Council and may then borrow equipment, receive advice and use the SES name in their publicity. Though the Society

'approves and supports' expeditions it rarely gives cash to any project.
Members have to be proposed and seconded by existing members, and then elected by the Council. Expeditions organized by the Society include Zaïre River Expedition, 1974–5, Operation Drake 1978–80, and Operation Raleigh 1984–88.

Sea & Cruise Club

32 Berkeley Street
London W1X 5FA
Tel: 01–629 7391
A Club which aims to expand passenger shipping facilities. (See, Travel: Passenger Shipping Agents and Advisory Services on page 708.)

Seaworthy Women

2210 Wilshire Blvd.
Suite 254
Santa Monica
CA 90403
USA
Tel: (213) 659 69 67
Seaworthy Women is preparing for a five-year voyage round the world, departing from Los Angeles, California in March, 1985. They are making the cruise on a sailboat, a Bristol 34', and would like women to join them for two or three weeks for port-hopping and perhaps for some of the longer passages. Women desiring information should write to the above address and enclose a cheque made out to Seaworthy Women for $5.00. They will be sent an application form, scheduling information and costs. The $5.00 fee covers periodic mailings with advance information on dates and ports throughout the voyage and the appropriate people to contact to make arrangements for sailing with them.

South American Explorers' Club

Casilla 3714
Lima 100
Peru
Tel: 314480
and
2239 E. Colfax Ave. 205
Denver
CO 80206
USA
Tel: 303–320 0388
Exists to promote travel and sporting aspects of exploration; and to record, co-ordinate and publicise academic research on a wide variety of natural and social sciences. Membership is open to all. It publishes a magazine The South American Explorer, *(see Periodicals on page 570). The Club House, with reading rooms, maps and guidebooks is open most days and people are welcome to visit. The address is: Avenida Portugal 146, Brena District, Lima, Peru, near the US Embassy.*

Topas Globetrotterklub

Safarihuset
Lounsvej
DK–9640 Farsoe
Denmark
Tel: (08) 63 84 00 Telex: 60965 GLOBE DK
Established in 1973 and organizes cultural long range expeditions in Africa, Asia and Northern Scandinavia. Has 2,500 members, publishes a bi-monthly expedition newsletter and an annual publication, Safariposten *in Denmark. Own club house in Jutland with accommodation, travel library and lectures for members, bi-monthly meetings. Affiliated with International Globetrotters Club in Brussels and Malaga.*

International Globetrotters Club
(address same as above)

International travel club for overlanders and other travellers off the beaten track. Organizes overland expeditions in Africa, Asia and Northern Scandinavia, yacht cruises and exploratory projects, such as the river Niger from Tombouktou to the Atlantic in specially constructed craft. Publishes a bi-monthly newsletter, the Globetrotters *newsletter, in English. Main office and expedition base is in Denmark, information offices in Brussels and Malaga (see below).*

International Globetrotters Club

(The Globetrotters)
Rue Montserrat 3
B–1000 Brussels
Tel: (02) 511 84 61 Telex: 61543 SEVSEA B
Information office for the International Globetrotters Club of Denmark.

International Globetrotters Club

(The Globetrotters)
Club Internacional de Viajeros
Avenia de los Boliches 88
Los Boliches
Fuengi Rola
Malaga
Spain
Tel: (952) 47 13 45 and 47 13 50
Telex: 77686 Attn. Globetrotters
Information office for the International Globetrotters Club of Denmark, covering English and Scandinavian speaking members in Southern Europe.

Travel Wise Club

444 Robson Street
Vancouver
British Columbia
Canada
A club for those low-budget travellers with aims similar to those of the Globetrotters Club.

WEXAS International

45 Brompton Road Knightsbridge
London SW3 1DE
Tel: 01–589 3315/0500
WEXAS (for World Expeditionary Association) was founded in 1970 to provide an information and travel service for expeditions. Membership has since become open to anyone, and currently has thousands of members spread over 91 countries, for the majority of whom WEXAS is predominately a travel club. WEXAS's appeal derives from its worldwide programme of discount flights and holidays at special low rates. The Expeditions Committee of the Royal Geographical Society each year selects promising UK based expeditions to receive WEXAS grants. Members of WEXAS receive the Traveller magazine (see Periodicals, page 570), and are also eligible to receive other WEXAS publications and gifts.

Young Explorers Trust

(The Association of British Youth Exploration Societies)
at The Royal Geographical Society
1 Kensington Gore
London SW7 2AR
Tel: 01–589 9724
Exists to promote youth exploration and to provide a forum within which societies and individuals can exchange information and act together for their mutual benefit. It does not organize its own expeditions or make travel bookings. The Trust is a registered charity. Membership is open to groups or societies wishing to take part in the Trust's activities and to contribute to the Trusts's aims. Present members include all major national and regional bodies active in the field of youth expeditions as well as school and university groups.
Information is available on a wide range of topics and on a variety of foreign locations. The Trust has recently taken on a team of volunteer regional co-ordinators to assist with the flow of information and to provide a local focus for members as well as being the 'first link' for the 'unattached' youngster, enabling them to join in adventurous activities.
YETMAG, *a quarterly magazine which goes out free to all members, carries news, papers and speeches, preliminary expedition reports and other information.*

Associations – Sporting

The Adirondack Mountain Club

172 Ridge Street
Glenfalls
NY 12801
USA
Tel: (518) 793 7737
Hiking, skiing, snowshoeing, canoeing, and mountaineering. (See Associations: Exploration, Adventure and Travel, page 606.)

Alpine Club

74 South Audley Street
London W1Y 5FF
Tel: 01–499 1542
The Alpine Club is an association of experienced mountaineers, interested in the Alps and the greater Ranges (Himalayas, Andes, etc.). New recruits are welcome but are expected to have a reasonable amount of experience on joining. The Alpine Club Library is open to the public, and is used mainly by people planning treks and expeditions.

Cyclists Touring Club

69 Meadrow
Godalming
Surrey GU7 3HS
Tel: Godalming 7217

The International Long River Canoeist Club

c/o Peter Salisbury
238 Birmingham Road
Redditch
Worcs. B97 6EL
The International Long River Canoeist Club is the only United Kingdom association that can offer details of thousands of rivers around the World, from the Aa in France to the Zambezi in Zambia, from The Alsek in Canada/Alaska to the Zaïre in Zaïre. Members in 26 countries ready to offer help and advice.

National Handicapped Sports and Recreation Association

Capitol Hill Station
PO Box 18664
Denver
CO 80218
USA

Ski Club of Great Britain

118 Eaton Square
London SW1W 9AF
Tel: 01–245 1033 Telex: 291608 SKIDOM G
Prestel *36080
Offer members: unbiased advice on resorts, travel and equipment; snow reports; Club flights and special discounts; Reps in the Alps and UK; British Ski Tests; unique skiing parties for all standards and ages; artificial slope courses for intermediate and advanced skiers; insurance; Ski Survey magazine and a busy programme of lectures, filmshows and parties at our Club House in central London.

Transcyclist International

CPO Box 2064
Tokyo
Japan

Trancyclist UK
Stuart Lucas
12 Kincaidston Drive
Ayr
Scotland

Transcyclist USA
Dr Peter Frank
PO Box 513
Wayne
PA 19087
USA
The organization aims to establish a global frame of cross-national and cross-continental channels to allow for and encourage co-ordination and co-operation in unusual motorcycle and sporting ventures. Runs projects of unlimited travel and unspecified nature for the ambitious individual tourer, at home or overseas, with own machine or use of the TC 'Machine Loan Program'. Also two types of touring rallies – Blitz Rally (two day; Weekend), One Week Rally. Membership.

Associations – Mutual Aid

Central Bureau for Educational Visits & Exchanges

Seymour Mews House
Seymour Mews (off Wigmore Street)
London W1
Tel: 01-486 5101
Also has offices in Edinburgh and Belfast. Details of jobs, study opportunities, youth organizations and holidays in some 60 countries.

The Centre for International Briefing

The Castle
Farnham
Surrey GU9 0AG
Tel: (0252) 721194
Runs short residential courses for people about to go overseas, offering them the chance to meet a variety of specialist speakers, others going to the same country, nationals and returned expatriates from that country, and the use of the excellent library and resource centre as incidentals.

Commonwealth Youth Exchange Council

Executive Secretary
18 Fleet Street
London EC4Y 1AA
Tel: 01-353 3901
Promotes contact between groups of young people of the Commonwealth by funding visits by groups from Britain to an overseas Commonwealth country and vice versa.

Foyer International d'Acceuil de Paris

30 Rue Canabis
74014 Paris
France
Tel: 707 25 69
Holds all-discussion 'forums' for the exchange of information between travellers.

Globetrotters Club

BCM/Roving
London WC1N 3XX
A small informal association of travellers from all over the world, linked by an interest in low cost travel and the desire to study the cultures of other lands at first hand. Members share their personal experiences and detailed knowledge of local conditions.
(See Associations – Exploration, Adventure and Travel on page 606, for Deutsche Zentrale für Globetrotter, Globetrotters Club, Topas Globetrotterklub, International Globetrotters Club.)

Magic Ink Travel Club/Guides

The Capital Press Inc, Magic Ink
Bath Road
Margate
Kent CT9 1SN
Tel: (0843) 294 706
Part of Disabilities Unlimited, an organization that aims to bring together people with and without disabilities to form residential and working collectives, communes and cooperatives and to create job opportunities for those with disabilities. The Club and Guides produce the overland guide books previously published by BIT Information and Help Service which are so heavily dependent on feedback from travellers. The Guides are the only travel guides to be regularly up-dated. There is a newsletter called Magic Ink. *(See Periodicals, page 570.)*

Travelmates

496 Newcastle Street
West Perth
Western Australia 6005
Hostels and share-houses and share-a-car-service. *(See Associations – Hitchhiking, page 613 and Hostelling, page 719.)*

Travel Wise Club

444 Robson Street
Vancouver
British Columbia
Canada
A club for those low-budget travellers with aims similar to those of the Globetrotters Club. (See Associations – Adventure, Exploration and Travel.)

Women's Corona Society

501/2 Eland House
Stag Place
London SW1E 5DH
Tel: 01-828 1652/3
The Society exists to promote knowledge and understanding of the peoples and cultures of the world. (*See Travel and Expedition Advisers, Consultancies and Agencies, page 618.*)

Women Outdoors, Inc

Curtis Hall
474 Boston Avenue
Medford
MA 02155
USA
Tel: 617-381 3278
'Women Outdoors' was incorporated in 1980 to provide a clearing-house for women whose vocation or avocation lay in the outdoors. Members receive the Women's Outdoor Magazine *published quarterly. Aims are to build a network in which women can get in touch with other women who share similar interests, a clearing-house for information and women who want partners for trips.*

Associations – Disabled

The Across Trust

Crown House
Morden
Surrey
Tel: 01-540 38 97
Operates large luxury fully-equipped ambulances called 'Jumbulances' which take severely disabled people on organized group pilgrimages and holidays across Europe.

Disabled Living Foundation

346 Kensington High Street
London W14 8NS
Tel: 01-602 2941

DIVE (Disabled International Visits and Exchanges)

c/o The Central Bureau for Educational Visits and Exchanges
Seymour Mews House
Seymour Mews
London W1H 9PE
Tel: 01-486 5101
A national voluntary body set up to develop international travel and exchange opportunities for disabled people and professionals and volunteers working with them. DIVE offers advice on many aspects of international travel including contacts abroad, accommodation and sources of grant aid.

The Les Evans Holiday Fund for Sick and Handicapped Children

The Secretary
12a High Street
Brentwood
Essex
or
Mr Les Evans
5 Pentire Close
Upminster
Essex
Tel: Upminster 28103
Holidays arranged for children who are sick or severely handicapped. Caters for children aged 8–1[illegible] who are accompanied by fully qualified medical staff. Destinations have included the Mediterranean and Florida.

National Handicapped Sports and Recreation Association

See Associations – Sporting on page 610.

Mobility International

62 Union Street
London SE1 1TD
Tel: 01-403 5688
Exists to encourage the integration of handicapped people with the non-handicapped, by arranging international projects with a wide appeal, varying from youth festivals to more professional conferences and seminars. Handicap is not the common denominator; rather people attend because of their interest in the topic or emphasis of the particular project.

Project Phoenix Trust

68 Rochfords
Coffee Hall
Milton Keynes MK6 5DJ
A non-profit making organization the Trustees of which organize and run visits overseas of mixed ability groups of adults who a) would like a holiday which has a focal point, such as art, history, etc., b) would need some physical help in order to make such a visit possible, c) would be prepared to provide physical help to others to make the visit viable, d) may need some financial assistance in order to take part. These tours involve a lot of activity and are probably best suited to energetic and strong disabled people.

RADAR

Royal Association for Disability and Rehabilitation
25 Mortimer Street
London W1N 8AB
Tel: 01-637 5400

A registered Charity to help disabled people, by identifying the problems they encounter and then taking the necessary action to reduce or eliminate these problems. RADAR finds suitable accommodation and facilities for holidays for the disabled. Publishes a guide entitled Holidays for the Physically Handicapped *which is updated each year, and a monthly* Bulletin *and a quarterly journal called* Contact. *They also publish excellent comprehensive lists of publications and useful addresses for the disabled holiday maker. Holidays Officer – Deborah McGhie.*

Rehabilitation Inter USA

1123 Broadway
New York
NY 10010
USA
Disability Society with information on disabled travel in North America.

Society for the Advancement of Travel for the Handicapped (SATH)

International Head Office
Suite 1110
26 Court Street
Brooklyn
NY 11242
USA
Tel: (212) 858 54 83 Telex: 125656 TRAVMKTINT NYK
Is a 'non-profit educational forum for the exchange of knowledge and the gaining of new skills in how to facilitate travel for the handicapped, the elderly and the retired'. Information is available on tour operators, hotels and other travel related services; (s.a.e. requested with written enquiries). Membership is open to all who share SATH's concerns.

Associations – Hitchhiking

FRANCE

Allostop

The collective name for the associations Allauto, Provoya and Stop-Voyages. Allostop puts you in contact with drivers with a view to sharing petrol costs. Enrol sufficiently in advance. The sum of 130 F (which constitutes an annual subscription fee and which cannot be refunded) allows you to an unlimited number of journeys in a year starting from the date of enrolment. If you wish to make only one journey, the subscription is 35 F.
The main offices are:

Alsace

Allostop-Provoya
5 Rue de Général Zimmer
67000 Strasbourg
Tel: (88) 37 13 13
Open from 15.00 hrs to 18.30 hrs from Monday to Friday and from 10.00 hrs to 12.00 hrs on Saturday.

Aquitaine

Stop-Voyages
59 Rue des Ayres
33000 Bordeaux
Tel: (56) 81 24 59
Open from 15.00 hrs to 19.00 hrs from Monday to Friday.

Auvergne

Allostop-Provoya
chez Fréquence 101
22 Avenue des Etat-Unis
63000 Clermont-Ferrand
Tel: (73) 36 72 33
Open from 16.30 hrs to 19.30 hrs from Monday to Friday and from 10.00 hrs to 12.00 hrs on Saturday.

Bretagne

Allostop-Provoya
Au C.I.J. Bretagne
Maison du Champs de Mars
35043 Rennes
Tel: (99) 30 98 87
Open from 15.00 hrs to 18.00 hrs on Monday to Friday and from 9.00 hrs to 12.00 hrs on Saturday.

Languedoc

Allostop-Provoya
9 Rue du Plan de l'Olivier
34000 Montpellier
Tel: (67) 66 02 29
Open from 15.00 hrs to 18.00 hrs on Monday to Friday and 10.00 hrs to 12.30 hrs on Saturday.

Midi-Pyrénées

Allostop-Provoya
au C.R.I.J.
2 Rue Malbec
31000 Toulouse
Tel: (61) 22 68 13
Open from 15.30 hrs to 18.30 hrs from Tuesday to Friday and 10.30 hrs to 12.30 hrs on Saturday.

Nord-Pas-de-Calais

Allostop-Provoya
a l'Office du Tourisme
Palais Rihour
59800 Lille
Tel: (20) 57 96 69
Open from 15.00 hrs to 18.00 hrs on Monday to Friday and 10.30 hrs to 12.30 hrs on Saturday.

Pays de la Loire

Allostop-Provoya
au C.R.I.J.
10 rue Lafayette
44000 Nantes
Tel: (40) 89 04 85
Open from 15.30 hrs to 18.30 hrs from Tuesday to Friday and from 10.00 hrs to 12.00 hrs on Saturday.

Provence – Alpes de Sud–Côte d'Azur

Allostop-Provoya
3 Rue du Petit-St-Jean
13100 Aix-en-Provence
Tel: (42) 38 37 51
Open from 15.00 hrs to 18.30 hrs on Monday, Tuesday, Thursday and Friday. From 9.30 hrs to 11.00 hrs and 17.00 hrs to 19.00 hrs on Wednesday and 10.00 hrs to 13.00 hrs on Saturday.

Allostop-Provoya
M.J.X. Picaud
23 Avenue Raymond Picaud
06400 Cannes
Tel: (93) 38 60 88
Open from 14.00 hrs to 18.00 hrs on Tuesday to Friday and 10.00 hrs to 12.00 hrs on Saturday.

Paris

Allostop-Provoya
84 passage Brady
75010 Paris
Tel: (1) 246 00 66
Open from 9.00 hrs to 19.30 hrs on Monday to Friday and from 9.00 hrs to 13.00 hrs and 14.00 hrs to 18.00 hrs on Saturday.

Rhône-Alpes

Allostop-Provoya
9 Rue Barginet
Quartier Saint-Bruno
38000 Grenoble
Tel: (76) 96 72 99
Open from 15.00 hrs to 18.30 hrs on Monday to Friday and from 10.00 hrs to 12.30 hrs on Saturday.

Allostop-Provoya
8 Rue de la Bombarde
69005 Lyon
Tel: (7) 842 38 29
Open from 15.00 hrs to 19.00 hrs from Monday to Friday and 10.00 hrs to 13.00 hrs on Saturday.

BELGIUM

The Allostop card can be used for Taxi-stop in Belgium. Taxi-stop offices are:
Infor-Jeunes
27 Rue du Marche-aux-Herbes
1000 Brussels
Tel: (02) 511 69 30

Taxi-stop
24 Rue de France
Charleroi
Tel: (071) 31 63 42

Taxi-stop
34 Rue des Dominicains
Liège
Tel: (041) 32 38 70

Taxi-stop
31 Rue de Bruxelles
1300 Wavre
Tel: (010) 22 75 75

AUSTRALIA
Travelmates

496 Newcastle Street
West Perth
Western Australia 6005
Tel: (09) 328 66 85
Share a Car Service – A unique service operated from their office arranges for people to share cars on Interstate Trips departing Perth. They introduce the owner/drivers to intending passengers who are about to embark to the Northern Territory or to the Eastern States. Usual arrangement is to share part of the petrol cost and assist with driving. No bookings . . . simply standby operation; it is only suited to backpackers.
Average part share cost for passengers:
Adel. $45 Melb. $55 Syd. $65 Bris. $75 Darwin $75 Office fee $10.
(*See also Hostelling, page 719.*)

POLAND

There is an official hitchhiking scheme run by the National Tourist Office. Drivers get points for helping you. Ask before going.

Associations – Specialist

Action d'Urgence International

10 Rue Félix-Ziem
75018 Paris
France
Tel: 264 74 19
AUI runs training courses for people interested in helping rescue operations in times of natural disasters. Branches in France, Great Britain, Morocco, India, Dominican Republic and Guadeloupe.

Archaeology Abroad

31–34 Gordon Square
London WC1H 0PY
Archaeology Abroad provides information about opportunities for archaeological field work and excavations outside Britain. Archaeologists, students of archaeology and specialists who wish to be considered for archaeological work abroad are enrolled and information is provided on request to organizers of excavations who wish to recruit personnel.

Others interested in archaeology, and preferably with some experience of excavation, are also eligible for membership. The organization is not an employment agency.
A comprehensive insurance scheme, appropriate for excavation work, has been compiled with Sun Alliance Insurance group and is available to members and others travelling abroad on excavations. Messrs W. F. & R. K. Swan (Hellenic) Ltd have for a number of years generously made several free places available on their Hellenic cruises to student members of Archaeology Abroad.
An annual Bulletin (March) and two Newssheets (Spring and Autumn) are available to members by subscription, and these list all projects overseas on which information is received. The organization is small and is entirely dependent on subscriptions from individual members and corporate bodies. For further details write to The Secretary at the above address enclosing an s.a.e.

Christians Abroad

15 Tufton Street
London SW1P 3QQ
Tel: 01-222 2165
Arranges introductions for people going overseas to the local church in the host country and to people who know that country. Produces a series of information sheets about work abroad, mainly in the 'South' through volunteer, mission and government agencies.

Expats International

62 Tritton Street
London SE21 8DE
Tel: 01-670 4411

PO Box 302
Williamsburg
VA 23185
USA
Exists to help people going or living abroad, especially with property and financial matters. (See Periodical, Home and Away, page 570.)

Friends of the Earth

377 City Road
London EC1V 1NA
A campaigning organization, promoting policies which protect the natural environment. Their campaigns are pursued worldwide.

International Opportunities

Box 19107
Washington
DC 20036
USA
Information about overseas jobs. Directory: International Opportunities $3.00 (add $1.00 for overseas mail).

Survival International

29 Craven Street
London WC2N 5NT
Survival International is an international charity established in 1969. It now has National and Local Groups in many other countries. S.I. has the following objectives:

* *To help tribal peoples to exercise their right to survival and self-determination.*
* *To ensure that the interests of tribal peoples are properly represented in all decisions affecting their future.*
* *To secure for tribal peoples the ownership and use of adequate land and other resources and seek recognition of their rights over their traditional lands.*

Survival International publishes a quarterly newsletter, an annual review and special documents; organizes public meetings and exhibitions; lobbies governments, companies and international human rights organizations; issues Urgent Action Bulletins etc. Write for details.

World Wildlife Fund – United Kingdom

Panda House
11–13 Ockford Road
Godalming
Surrey GU7 1QU
Tel: 04868–20551 Telex: 859602

Headquarters
WWF – International
Avenue du Mont-Blanc
CH-1196
Gland
Switzerland
An International organization which raises money for the conservation of wildlife, natural habitats and natural resources throughout the world. Founded in 1961 with headquarters in Switzerland, since when it has opened national organizations in 24 countries. Between them these organizations have spent over £40 million on more than 6,000 projects in 135 countries. WWF makes sure that its projects have a sound scientific base by referring them to its sister scientific body, the International Union for the Conservation of Nature and Natural Resources (IUNC).

Third World Aid and Volunteer Programmes

Action Aid

PO Box 69
208 Upper St
London N1 1R2
Tel: 274 467
Aims to promote relief of poverty and distress worldwide. Has a volunteer programme which sends volunteers overseas.

British Council

10 Spring Gardens
London SW1A 2BN
Tel: 01-930 8466
Permanent appointments and contracts for teachers, especially of English as a foreign language and some educational advisors. Arranges for English students to study abroad.

British Red Cross Society

9 Grosvenor Crescent
London SW1X 7EJ
Tel: 01-235 5454
Objectives are to furnish aid in times of war and to help the sick and the poor worldwide. Help is also given to refugees and people in need in times of famine etc.
There is a permanent rota of volunteers, almost entirely medical, although they occasionally take volunteers with other skills.

British Volunteer Programme

22 Coleman Fields
London N1 7AG
Tel: 01-226 6616
Comprising four volunteer organizations (CIIR, IVS, UNA and VSO) all sending long-term volunteers overseas.

Catholic Institute for International Relations (CIIR)

22 Coleman Fields
London
Tel: 354 0883
Has a Health Programme in Yemen which takes medically qualified volunteers. Other volunteers are sent to Central America, Peru, Honduras, Zimbabwe, Ecuador and various other countries depending on their needs at the time. Volunteers are usually skilled e.g. teachers.

International Voluntary Service (IVS)

Ceresole House
53 Regents Rd
Leicester LE1 6YL
Tel: (0533) 541862
Has three programmes for Volunteers:
(1) Long-Term Service
A minimum of 2 years. Must be over 21. The work is in South Africa and the volunteers must be skilled or qualified and have had previous work experience e.g. engineer, agriculturalist, horticulturalist.
(2) Work Camp Programme
This is a short-term programme of 2–3 weeks. A particular project is undertaken, e.g. manual work, social work. The idea being to do a job that wouldn't otherwise get done. The work is in Europe, UK, Turkey, USA and Canada.
(3) Work Exchange Camp
Usually for 6 weeks in the Third World but volunteers must have had a year's involvement with IVS and previous work camp experience. The work involves manual projects which teach the volunteer what life is like in the Third World. Volunters are sent from the Third World to the UK to gain a similar experience.

United Nations Association (UNA)

Whitehall Court
London
Tel: 01-930 0679
Volunteers are sent overseas to help development. Volunteers must be skilled and prepared to work for a minimum of 2 years. The fare to the country is paid by UNA and the volunteer also receives a basic wage.

US Peace Corps

Washington
DC 20526
Places volunteers into positions in 60 developing countries. Volunteers with all kinds of backgrounds are accepted, though naturally those with specific skills, being more in demand, are easier to place.

Voluntary Services Overseas (VSO)

9 Belgrave Sq
London
Tel: 01-235 5191
Volunteers are selected from people with skills and qualifications e.g. Teaching, Nursing, Agriculturalists, Social Workers, Carpenters to work in the Third World. Volunteers must be over 20 and prepared to work for 2 years minimum. VSO pay the volunteer's airfare and a small wage is paid by the host country.

Christians Abroad

15 Tufton St
London SW1P 3QQ
Tel: 01-222 2165
Have three main objectives:
(1) To provide information and help to volunteers about the countries where their skills could be used to the greatest advantage.
(2) To provide teachers with contracts with overseas employers.
(3) If volunteers are going abroad they provide them with useful contacts in that country.

Christian Aid

PO Box No 1
London SW9 8BH
Tel: 01-733 5500

Aim to combat hunger and poverty throughout the world. Occasionally send volunteers overseas.

Crown Agents for Overseas Governments and Administration

4 Millbank
London SW1
Tel: 01-222 7730
Mostly appointments for overseas governments and public authorities in professional and sub-professional posts.

Overseas Development Administration

Abercrombie House
Eaglesham Rd
East Kilbride T75 8EA
Tel: (03552) 41199
Mainly government appointments overseas, covering a wide variety of posts including accountancy, engineering, economics, forestry, law, statistics as well as medical posts.

Oxfam

274 Banbury Rd
Oxford OX2 7DZ
Tel: (0865) 56777
Primary object is to relieve poverty, distress and suffering in any part of the world. Volunteers are sent overseas, but they must be people with specialist skills and qualifications. The main requirement is that the person recruited should have professional qualifications adaptable to the cultural context overseas, as well as the personal skills needed for a specific assignment.
There is not a demand for unqualified or unskilled staff.

Save the Children Fund

17 Grove Lane
Camberwell
London SE5 8RD
Tel: 01-703 5400
World's largest international children's charity.
Take on paid staff and only those who are fully qualified. Mainly send doctors, nurses and child-care workers overseas.

Voluntary Missionary Movement

Shenley Lane
London Coleny
Herts AL2 8AR
Tel: (0727) 24853
Volunteers must be skilled or qualified and over 21. Work is available for professions such as doctors, midwives, teachers, mechanics, civil engineers and physiotherapists. Volunteers are required to work a minimum of two years and during this time live very close to the native people.

Awards and Grants

Bourses ELF Aquitaine

Direction des Relations Publiques et de la Communication
7 Rue Nelaton
75739 Paris Cedex 15
France
Tel: 571 72 73
Grants to young people working in the field of international relations between France and the country visited.

La Guilde Européene du Raid

11 Rue du Vaugirard
75006 Paris
France
Tel: 326 97 52
The Guilde Européen du Raid finance expeditions of adventure, investigating and learning about different places, cultures and ideas, be it by foot, bicycle, plane or car. Have a useful library of files of information submitted by previous grantholders.
(See Associations: Exploration, Adventure and Travel on page 606.)

Mount Everest Foundation

Hon. Secretary: Simon Brown
212 Greys Road
Henley on Thames RG9 1QX
Tel: (0491) 576677
Bass Charington Awards and Barclays Bank Awards. Sponsor British and New Zealand expeditions only, proposing mountain exploration or research in high mountain regions. For applications grant forms write to above address or to the Royal Geographical Society, by August 31 or December 31. Give an average of 30 grants a year from £300 to £1,300.

The Rolex Awards for Enterprise

The Secretariat
PO Box 178
1211 Geneva 26
Switzerland
The Rolex Awards provide financial assistance for persons who have manifested the spirit of enterprise in order to bring to fruition projects which are off the beaten track and come within three broad fields of human endeavour: Applied Sciences and Invention,

Exploration and Discovery, the Environment. The Rolex Awards enjoy world renown. To enter: Send for official application form from the 'Rolex Awards for Enterprise Secretariat' at the above address. Project description must be in English.

The Royal Geographical Society

1 Kensington Gore
London SW7 2AR
Tel: 01-589 5466
See Associations: Exploration, Adventure and Travel, page 606.

Touring Club Royal de Belgique

Rue de la Loi 44
B 1040 Brussels
Belgium
Tel: (02) 233 22 11
Makes grants known as Les Bourses de Voyage Jeunesse *to Belgians aged between 16 and 25, for extensive travel. As well as the sizeable grant, successful applicants also receive vehicle accessories, travel tickets and various coupons.*

WEXAS International

45 Brompton Road
Knightsbridge
London SW3 1DE
Tel: 01-589 3315/0500
Promising UK based expeditions receive WEXAS grants.
Apply to the Royal Geographical Society for details. (See Associations: Exploration, Adventure, and Travel, page 606.)

Winston Churchill Memorial Trust

15 Queens Gate Terrace
London SW7 5PR
Tel: 01-584 9315
The Winston Churchill Memorial Trust awards about 100 travelling Fellowship grants annually to enable UK citizens, irrespective of their age or educational achievements, to carry out study projects overseas in approximately 10 categories of interest or occupation which are varied annually. Grants are not normally given for formal or academic studies.

Young Explorers Trust

Royal Geographical Society
1 Kensington Gore
London SW7 2AR
Tel: 01-589 9724
Gives grants to school and pre-University expeditions. (See Associations: Exploration, Adventure and Travel, page 606.)

Travel and Expedition Advisers, Consultancies and Agencies

Bolivian Adventure Tours SRL

PO Box 8412
La Paz
Bolivia
Tel: 792731 and 331003
Is a company offering two kinds of service for those interested in exploring the country, equipment for the extremely varied terrain, including camping gear, specially adapted vehicles, cartographic and photographic data; and information, advice, guides and transport for the various kinds of expedition to which Bolivia lends itself, from alpine climbing to jungle trekking.

Dick Philips

Whitehall House
Nenthead
Alston
Cumbria CA9 3PS
Long-established specialist in travel in those parts of Iceland beyond the interests of the mainstream travel trade.

Direction des Français a l'étranger et des Etrangers en France

21 bis Rue La Perouse
75016 Paris
France
Tel: 502 14 23
A government office responsible to the Ministry of Foreign Affairs which handles aid to French citizens in distress abroad, repatriation, legal aid, protection of the interests of the French citizens resident abroad and so on.

Expedition Advisory Centre

1 Kensington Gore
London SW7 2AR
Tel: 01-581 2057
The Expedition Advisory Centre provides an information and training service for those planning an expedition. It was founded by the Royal Geographical Society and the Young Explorers' Trust and is financed by The British Land Company plc as a sponsorship project.
In addition to organizing a variety of seminars and publications including The Expedition Planners' Handbook and Directory, *the Advisory Centre maintains a database for expedition planners. This includes a register of planned expeditions, lists of expedition consultants and suppliers, information for leaders on individual countries and a register of personnel who have offered their services to expeditions. Write with a s.a.e. to the Information Officer for further details.*

Geo-Travel

4 Christian Fields
London SW16 3JZ
Tel: 01-764 6292
In addition to acting as consultants to state tourist boards providing advice on the development of tourism in the Third World, expert advice is available on a consultancy basis for single travellers, groups and expeditions to polar areas, Asia (excl. USSR), Africa and Scandinavia.

OTU

137 Boulevard St. Michel
75005 Paris
France
Tel: 329 12 88
Issue international student identity cards on production of a student travel card issued by an educational institution.

Rainbow Ridge Consultants

Box 1021F
Honokaa
HL 96727
USA
Are specialists in the Far East and can provide contacts for travellers.

Royal Commonwealth Society

Northumberland Avenue
London WC2N 5BJ
The Royal Commonwealth Society provides a series of notes which contain handy concise information for people offered a contract job overseas. They average 16–18 pages and are revised approximately every three years. Subjects covered include country and people, cost of living and expenditure indicators, retail prices, health and educational facilities, exchange controls and remittances, cars and car prices, housing availability and rents, utilities and household goods, income tax rates, personal security, communications, leisure, background reading, useful addresses, etc.
They cost £4.00 each for addresses in the UK (£6.00 each overseas). All orders must be prepaid in UK Sterling cheque draft or money order drawn on or payable through UK bank.

K. & J. Slavin (Quest 80s) Ltd

Collow Abbey
East Torrington
Lincoln LN3 5SE
Tel: (0673) 858 274
Directors: Kenneth and Julie Slavin
Are expedition consultants offering complete logistical support services to individual and commercial clients on projects throughout the world. They are advisers to Land Rover Ltd in the expeditionary field and have a special franchise for the direct export of expedition-equipped Land Rovers and Range Rovers.

Women's Corona Society

501/2 Eland House
Stag Place
London SW1E 5DH
Tel: 01-828 1652/3
The Society exists to promote knowledge and understanding of the peoples and cultures of the world, to maintain services in pursuit of that aim, and to give help, advice and friendship to any woman who is going abroad on her own or accompanying her husband, to live temporarily in another country. Runs short practical courses at a nominal cost and arranges contacts where possible with members in the country concerned and recently returned. Up-to-date advice on all aspects of living abroad.

Courses: Sailing and Training Vessels

Mariners International Club

c/o Pat Billings, Membership Secretary
National Maritime Museum
Greenwich
London SW10 9NF
Tel: 01-440 9927 Telex: 8954958 SHATER G Ref 207
M.I.C., an association for the promotion of traditional sail and related skills, serves as an international forum for tall ship and windjammer activities. It publishes a quarterly magazine, Windjammer, *which lists current sailing opportunities on tall ships in many different parts of the world and gives news of tall ships and related activities.*

Ocean Voyages Inc

1709 Bridgeway
Sausalito
California 94965
USA
Tel: (415) 332 4681 Telex: 470-56L SAIL UI
The largest organization offering worldwide adventure sailing programmes. (Publish a 48-page brochure detailing these offerings). In addition to scheduled programmes, which offer active sail training for groups of four, six or larger, they can custom design yacht charters, arrange vessels for filming purposes, or for scientific research expeditions.

Ocean Youth Club

Central Office: The Bus Station
South Street
Gosport
Hants PO12 1EP
Tel: (07055) 28421-2
Adventure Training. Cruises on 72 foot yachts for young people aged 12–21.

Courses: Outdoor and Survival Training

Adirondack Mountain Club Inc.

See Associations: Exploration, Adventure & Travel, page 606.

Bremex

London Borough of Brent
Youth & Community Service
65 Forty Avenue
Wembley
Middx HA9 8JR
Tel: 01-904 5811
'Bremex' – The Brent Mountain Expedition Training Scheme – enables young people, including teachers, leaders and their aides to gain the specialized 'know-how' required to plan and enjoy adventurous expeditions. The Mountain Skills Courses cover a wide range of varied interests, and operate on five levels, from basic to post-advanced.

British Mountaineering Council

Crawford House
Precinct Centre
Booth Street East
Manchester M13 9RZ
Tel: 061-273 5839
The BMC offers a variety of courses in rock climbing, snow and ice climbing, mountaincraft, and Alpine climbing for most age groups. Cost from £45.00. Apply to C. Dodd at the above address.

The Drake Fellowship

10 Trinity Square
London EC3P 3AX
Tel: 01-488 8637/8
The Drake Fellowship aims to motivate young people between the ages of 15 and 25 who are unemployed by the use of challenging outdoor pursuits, in order that they eventually seek, gain and retain full-time employment and make a positive contribution to their community. The Fellowship is a registered charity with centres of activity in London, Bristol and Merseyside.

The National Centre for Mountain Activities

Plas y Brenin
Capel Curig
Nr Betws y Coed
North Wales LL24 0ET
Tel: (06904) 280
A very broad training programme including rock climbing, skiing, canoeing, orienteering for all levels of ability, introductory courses, advanced training and leadership courses, and assessment courses at the highest levels.

Outward Bound Trust

12 Upper Belgrave Street
London SW1X 8BA
Tel: 01-235 4286/7/8
Administers five fully equipped residential centres in Wales, Scotland, and Cumbria. Activities include sound basic training in sailing, climbing, canoeing, navigation and expeditions with accent on high achievement, safety and teamwork.

Survi-Camps

PO Box 2
Cowes
Isle of Wight PO31 8LH
Tel: (0983) 298 919
Want to help people to cope with crisis of misadventure effectively, safely and decisively. Have designed a series of training courses to suit a whole range of people from novices to highly experienced personnel. Their associated firm, Survi-Kits, *has designed a range of survival equipment. Their philosophy – 'Equip people properly and they stand a very good chance of surviving disaster. Train them properly and they will be able to fend for themselves in most circumstances.'*

The Survival School

Survival Aids Ltd
Moorland
Penrith
Cumbria
Run week long survival courses every fortnight which include instruction in shelter building, day and night navigation, food procurement and preparation, water purifying, fire lighting, etc. Two full time ex-military instructors. People who complete the basic course can apply for an advanced course. Also run 2 day weekend courses. Details on request. *(See Equipment: Survival, page 629.)*

Courses: Language

BBC Publications

144–152 Bermondsey Street
London SE1 3TH
Language courses for beginners to advanced (include French, Greek, German, and Russian). Also the Get by in ... *short introductory courses providing an opportunity for holiday makers and other travellers to learn some elementary spoken language for everyday use on a trip to the country – in Arabic, French, German, Greek, Italian, Portuguese, and Spanish.*

The Berlitz Schools of Languages Ltd

Wells House
79 Wells Street
London W1A 3Bz
Tel: 01-580 6482

Schools in many provincial towns. Have native tutors to teach almost any language under the sun. Courses range from leisurely group tuition (up to eight students in a group) to the Total Immersion course. Private tuition can be arranged at times and schedules to suit the student, or given in the form of a crash course of six hours a day, five days a week. In-company tuition can be given to groups of up to 12 people in the same company, or executive crash courses can be arranged for groups of 3 to 4 people. For all courses held worldwide, multi-media equipment can be bought to enable the student to extend his studies to the home.

National Institute of Adult Continuing Education

19B De Montfort Street
Leicester LE1 7GE
Publishes, twice a year, a booklet Residential Short Courses, *which gives details of languages courses of all kinds of levels of ability. Booklet price 95p (inc. p&p).*

Courses: Photographic

New York Institute of Photography

16–20 High Road
Wood Green
London N22 6BX
Tel: 01-888 1242
Photographic Studies.

The Royal Photographic Society

The Octagon
Milson Street
Bath
Tel: (0225) 62841
Offers a series of weekend workshops for both amateurs and professionals, aiming to provide background knowledge as well as specialist information. Of special interest to travellers may be the courses on Nature and Travel Photography.

Lecture Agencies

B–S Lectures

11a St. Annes Drive
Fence
Burnley
Lancashire BB12 9DY
Tel: (Nelson (0282)) 64844/694163)
The Agency caters mainly for the leaders of major expeditions who wish to present lectures. The lectures should be illustrated with good quality colour slides and/or colour film (16mm), and the presenters should be experienced speakers.

Robert Holland-Ford Associates

103 Lydyett Lane
Barnton
Northwich
Cheshire CW8 4JT
Tel: (0606) 76960
Concert/Lecture Agents and Promoters.

The Scottish Lecture Agency

36 Castle Street
Edinburgh
EH2 3BN
Tel: 031-226 6692/3/4
Lectures on a wide range of subjects including mountaineering, natural history, sailing, travel and underwater exploration.

Picture Libraries

Atlas Photo

23 Rue du Montparnasse
75006 Paris
France
Tel: (1) 544 19 92 Telex: 210 311F code 656
Pictures of all countries of the world, portraits, landscapes, industry, nature and towns.

British Association of Picture Libraries and Agencies

PO Box 4
Andoversford
Nr. Cheltenham
Glos GL54 4JS
Tel: (024 289) 373
Has good catalogue designed for picture researchers, but also useful for anyone looking for the right agency to place their pictures.

Bruce Coleman Colour Picture Library

17 Windsor Street
Uxbridge
Middlesex UB8 1AB

381 Fifth Avenue
New York
NY 10016
USA
Established in 1960, represents a number of well-known photographers, including Chris Bonington, specializes in wildlife, geography, anthropology, archaeology, science. Literature available on the agency's requirements and terms of business on receipt of s.a.e.

Chrisfilm and Video Ltd

The Mill
Glasshouses
Pateley Bridge
Harrogate
North Yorkshire HG3 5QH

Distributors of 16mm films and video cassettes (for hire or purchase) on canoeing, climbing, caving, skiing, sailing, pot-holing. Catalogue available by sending 50p to above address.

Documentation Française

Photothèque

8 Avenue de l'Opéra
75001 Paris
Tel: 296 14 22

Geoslides Photographic Library

4 Christian Fields
London SW16 3JZ
Tel: 01-746 6292
Collects photos taken by travellers, especially in Africa, Asia, the Arctic, sub-Arctic and Antartica; sells reproduction rights to publishers in a wide field, especially educational and publish free leaflets (send s.a.e.). Services for Freelance Photographers, services for Teachers, Lecturers, and Resource Centres and services for Publishers.

Robert Harding Picture Library Ltd

17A Newman Street
London W1P 3HD
Tel: 01-637 8969
Represents many expedition photographers, collects 35mm or 5.7cm square transparencies of exceptional quality on geographical, anthropological, botanical and zoological subjects and sells reproduction rights in photos of remote areas.

Jacana

30 Rue St. Marc
75002 Paris
France
Tel: 296 99 14
Zoology, botany, geology.

Roloc Color Slides

326 South Pickett Street
Alexandria
Virginia 22304
USA
Tel: (703) 751 8668
Middle East, Latin America and the Caribbean, Africa and the Pacific. Travellers can purchase these to complement or complete their own collection. Catalogues are available – for countries other than the USA and these cost 10 cents each.

Shell Film Library

25 The Burroughs
Hendon
London NW4 4AT

Equipment

Equipment:

Equipment: Living, Camping, Outdoor

Alles für Tramper

Bundesallee 88
D-1000 Berlin 41
Germany, Federal Republic
Tel: (030) 8518069

Basic Designs

Box 479
Muir Beach
CA 94965

Make the H20 Sun Shower, a solar-heated portable shower consisting of a heavy duty vinyl bag which holds 11½ litres of water and heats the water to between 32 and 49°C depending on exposure and the heat of the day. The pack measures 10×33cm and weighs only 340g.

L. L. Bean Inc.

Freeport
ME 04033
USA
Tel: (207) 865 3111

Operates a mail order service and has a salesroom which is open 24 hours a day, 365 days a year. Firm sells outdoor garments and accessories, boots and other footwear, canoes, compasses, axes, knives, binoculars, thermometers, stoves, tents, sleeping bags, packs and frames, skis and snowshoes, camp ware, travel bags, lamps, blankets.

Ets Becker (Igloo)

94 Routes Nationale 10
Coigieres
78310 Maurepad
France
Tel: (3) 051 5781

Berghaus

34 Dean Street
Newcastle upon Tyne
NE1 1PG
Tel: (0632) 23561

One of Britain's leading suppliers of high quality packs and clothing for hiking and climbing. Outfitters of many expeditions.

Blacks Camping and Leisure Ltd

Gailey
Stafford
ST19 5PP
Tel: (0902) 790 721

Head office of the firm formerly known as variously as Blacks of Greenock and Blacks Outdoor Centres. Blacks have tents and camping equipment for hire. Supply lightweight, patrol, frame, mountain, and touring tents; camp furniture, kitchen kits, stoves and lamps; clothing and accessories and convertible, specialist and summer-weight sleeping bags. There are five retail outlets in London and others in Birmingham, Bristol, Cardiff, Dundee, Edinburgh, Exeter, Glasgow, Hull, Leeds, Leicester, Liverpool, Manchester, Newcastle, Norwich, Nottingham, Plymouth, Reading, Sheffield, and Stoke.

Blue Puma

960 Samoa Blvd
Arcata
CA 95521
USA

Sleeping bags, kayaking and rafting clothing, foul weather clothing.

Camping Gaz International

Camping Gaz (GB) Ltd
126–130 St Leonards Road
Windsor
Berkshire
Tel: Windsor 55011

The best source of information on the availability of Camping Gaz throughout the world. Camping Gaz cartridges and cylinders, stoves, heaters, lanterns, portable refrigerators, coolboxes, stainless steel vacuum flasks and the Globetrotter *stove, which is very small and light, are available throughout the UK. Worldwide availability list for cartridges and cylinder refills available on request.*

Camping Surplus

53 Rue J Valles
75011 Paris
France

Sell airline carry-on bags.

Caravan Backpacking

1 Newfield Drive
Menston
Ilkley
W. Yorks
LS29 6JQ
Tel: (0943) 74870

Manufacture sleeping bags, lightweight tents, and rucksacks.

The Complete Traveler

199 Madison Avenue
New York
NY 10016
USA
Tel: (212) 679 4339

Copper Wood Travel Comforts

Southwater Industrial Estate
Southwater
Horsham
Sussex
Tel: (0403) 731 124

Co-Pilot Instruments

St James' House
121 Church Street
Shirley
Southampton
SO1 5LW
Tel: (0703) 788 147

For left-hand-drive vision in a right-hand-drive car. The CO-PILOT continental overtaking mirror lets you see for yourself when it is safe to pull out. By post £16.45 from above address.

Dana

PO Box 161723
Sacramento
CA 95816
USA

Sells globes, magnifying lamps, books and atlases and other accessories.

Direct Adventure Supplies

17 Pages Walk
London SE1
Tel: 01-231 3391

Offer a Mail Order service with a discount off a comprehensive range of outdoor equipment.

Early Winters Ltd

110 Prefontaine pl. S
Seattle
WA 98104
USA

Makers of backpacking and outdoor gear, including the Thousand Mile Socks which are guaranteed not to wear out before 1 year or 1,000 miles/1,600km of walking (whichever comes last), and manufacturers of a full line of gore-tex tents and raingear. Free colour catalogue.

Franzuz Company, Inc

352 Park Avenue South
New York
NY 10010
USA
Tel: 212-889 5850

Make voltage converters and adaptor plugs to fit electronic/portable appliances anywhere in the world.

Field and Trek (Equipment) Ltd

Mail Order
3 Wates Way
Brentwood
Essex
CM15 9TB
Tel: (0277) 221529

Field and Trek (Equipment) Ltd
Retail Shop
23–25 Kings Road
Brentwood
Essex
CM14 4ER
Tel: (0277) 222230

Field and Trek's illustrated catalogue offers products which are reduced in price by approximately 15 per cent off normal retail on most leading makes of expedition equipment, including tents, rucksacks, boots, waterproof clothing, sleeping bags and mountaineering gear. They allow a further six per cent discount on orders over £175 ex. VAT. Large mail order department. Expeditions entitled to special bulk purchase prices. Please ask for a quotation on expedition letter-head. Contract price list is free of charge. Illustrated retail catalogue and price list is available for £1.25.

Globetrotter Ausrustungen

Wandsbeker Chausee 41
D-2000 Hamburg 76
Germany, Federal Republic
Tel: (040) 250 44 03

Equipment for travellers; books, maps. Catalogue.

Hazel Constance

Gear for Outdoors
13 The Chase
Coulsdon
Surrey
CR3 2EJ
Tel: 01-660 7294

New bags for old! Damaged or worn sleeping bags may be worth saving. The filling from good quality bags can be used in a new shell. Top quality work. Some specialist clothing made to order. Send s.a.e. or phone for details. These sleeping bags have been used in places as far apart as Corsica, Yosemite and Everest Base Camp. This can help keep down the cost of equipment.

Hof and Turecek GmbH

Expeditions Service
A-1150 Vienna
Austria
Rustengasse 7
Tel: (0222) 85 71 01

Sells emergency and survival equipment, water purifiers, cooking appliances, camping gear, inc. tents, expedition food, lamps, navigational devices, books, maps, clothing, motoring equipment and spares, backpacking equipment, tools and bows and arrows. This shop is closely connected with the Expedition Club Austria. Dispatch of goods all over the world. Please order equipment catalogue free of charge.

Karrimor International Ltd

Avenue Parade
Accrington
Lancashire
BB5 6PR
Tel: (0254) 385911

Karrimor International is particularly known for the excellence of quality of its range of rucksacks, cycle luggage, adventure luggage and camera bags; all of which they manufacture themselves. They also act as UK distributors for Asolo/Karrimor Footwear, Trangia stoves, Ajungilak sleeping bags, Salewa winter hardware, Trak, Kneissl and Rolletto skis and a range of small travel accessories.

Koolatron Corporation

27 Catharine Avenue
Brantford
Ontario
Canada
N3T 1X5

Manufacture a line of 12-volt portable and build-in electronic coolers which hold up to 20kg of food, 110 or 220-volt adaptors ABS Case Ltd. Distributorships available. Export pricing from $88 to $181.

Lyon Ladders

Vicarage Lane
Dent
Sedbergh
Cumbria
Tel: (05875) 370

Distributors of the Petzel headlamp, a head torch consisting of a light unit and battery mounted on an elastic head cradle. The torch beam is adjustable from a narrow spot to a wide flood light. Requires one 4½V flat style battery. It weighs 6oz, and comes in a virtually unbreakable plastic case with a 3 year guarantee.

Manuel

16 Rue la Boétie
75008 Paris
France
Tel: 265 47 26

30 Avenue de la Grande Armée
75017 Paris
France
Tel: 380 09 30

Sport et Climat
223 Blvd St Germain
75007 Paris
Tel: 548 80 99

These three stores specialize in garments for tropical countries from head to foot.

North by Northeast

181 Conant Street
Pawtucket RIO2862
USA

A. B. Optimus Ltd

Sanders Lodge Estate
Rushden
Northants
NN10 9BQ
Tel: (0933) 57412

Are manufacturers of the well known Optimus Pressure Stoves, Lanterns and Cookers as well as LPG cooking and heating appliances.

Parks Products

3611 Cahuenga
Hollywood
CA 90068
USA
Tel: (213) 876 5454

Make voltage converters and adaptor plugs to fit electronic/portable appliances anywhere in the world.

Personal Alarms Ltd

28a Alma Vale Road
Clifton
Bristol
BS8 2HY

Handbags, suitcases, holdalls, brief cases, vanity cases and similar articles can be protected by The Light Lightalarm, *a new battery powered anti-pilfering alarm, available, excluding PP3 battery, at £9.95 (inc VAT), plus 50p post and packing, from the above address. It is set off by exposure to light – i.e. the opening of a suitcase.*

Phoenix Mountaineering Ltd

Coquetdale Trading Estate
Amble
Morpeth
Northumberland
NE65 0PE
Tel: (0665) 710 934

Manufacturers of lightweight tents, specialists in outdoor clothing, sleeping bags, and Alpine Climbing Helmets.

Pindisports

14–18 Holborn
London EC1
Tel: 01-242 3278

Provided some equipment for the 1972 Everest South West Face Expedition and the 1970 Annapurna South Face Expedition and are suppliers to the John Ridgway School of Adventure at Ardmore, Sutherland. They supply equipment for hill-walking, rockclimbing, big-wall climbing, alpinism, expeditions, shelter and survival; also guidebooks and magazines.

Ritec (Europe) Ltd

PO Box 465
St Helier
Jersey
Channel Islands

Clear-Shield – anti-stick surface treatment for motor vehicle windscreens, windows and headlamps. Repels water, dirt, salt, sand, ice, snow and insects. Makes cleaning much easier. Improves visibility and appearance.

Rohan

Long Preston
Nr. Skipton
N. Yorks
BD23 4PG
Tel: (07294) 263

Make specialist clothing for hot and cold climates. Send s.a.e. for Clothing System Catalogue.

Safariquip

20 Mill Brow
Marple Bridge
Stockport
SK6 5LL
Tel: 061-449 8148

Specialists in all kinds of equipment. Give customers special assistance and offer objective and unbiased advice. Catalogue carries an expanded section on useful and often hard-to-come-by equipment. Have special 84 inch wide seamfree terylene mosquito netting for sale off the roll so that customers can make up their own nets. Offer a wide range of lamps and stoves, and vehicle accessories, offer a design and build service for vehicle equipment. Compasses. Also help people wishing to buy or sell second-hand expedition equipment.

Sierra West

6 East Yanonali Street
Santa Barbara
CA 93101
USA
Tel: (805) 963 87 27

Sierra West is a manufacturer of high quality rainwear, outerwear, tents and backpacking accessories. For further information, please write and request a free colour catalogue.

Tatteljee Products

Nieuwendammerdijk 304
1023 BT
Amsterdam
Netherlands

Hand-made specialist outdoor products, and 'button-beds'. Available in UK through Field and Trek.

Technidraught

3 Rayleigh Road
Basingstoke
Hampshire
RG21 1TJ
Tel: (0256) 28186

Design and draughting specializing in maps and diagrams in black and white or colour suitable for publication, slides and exhibitions.

Tent and Tarpaulin Manufacturing Co.

Main Showrooms
256/258 Brixton Road
London
SW9 6AQ
Tel: 01-733 3665

Enquiries and Mail Order
101/3 Brixton Hill
London
SW2 1AA
Tel: 01-674 0121

Suppliers to commercial and private expeditions of all kinds of tent from the marquee to the two-man, of camp beds, air beds, stoves, mosquito nets, sand ladders, jerry cans (water and petrol), wire ropes and slings, towing chains, all types of ropes and tarpaulins. They also repair tents.

Tilley International plc

Dunmurry
Belfast BT17 9JA
Northern Ireland
Tel: (0232) 617 121
Lamp manufacturer

Transglobe

Weyerstr. 33
D-5000 Koln 1
Germany, Federal Republic
Tel: (0221) 239 398

Travel-Pac

Box 1213
Thousand Oaks
CA 91360
USA

Make travel belts of polyurethane-coated lightweight nylon for safeguarding traveller's cheques, money, passports, etc.

Travel Tips Ltd

PO Box 1051
1040 Speers Road
Oakeville
Ont. L6J 5E9
Canada
Tel: (416) 844 7372

and

Austin House, Inc
1051 Clinton St
Buffalo
NY 14206
USA
Tel: (716) 893 73 72

They specialize in travel accessories such as money belts, miniature packs, locks, hangers, converters, adaptor plugs, transformers, etc.

Traveler's Checklist

Cornwall Bridge Road
Sharon
CT 06069
USA
Tel: (203) 364 0144

International mail order company sells hard-to-find travel accessories, including electrical devices, security, health and grooming aids, money convertors, and other travel items.

Traveler's Service

681 Ellis Street
San Francisco
CA 94109
USA

Sell water filters, money bags, 'talking cards' with translations of useful phrases into three foreign languages.

Traveller International Products Ltd

51 Hays Mews
London
W1X 5DB
Tel: 01-499 2774

With the Traveller 'Travel Plug' Adaptor, there is no need to change plugs when changing countries. The plug retails at £4.45 to £4.95. Available from leading retail outlets or from your local travel agent.

Vango (Scotland) Ltd

6 Gareloch Road
Industrial Estate
Port Glasgow
PA14 5BE
Tel: (0475) 44122

Supply a lot of specialist climbing, camping and skiing equipment. Do not sell direct to the public but will refer public to nearest stockist. Contact above address. Most camping and outdoor shops sell their products and they are well established and respected.

Versandhaus Süd-West

Magirstrasse 35
D-7900 Ulm
Germany, Federal Republic
Tel: (0731) 1701
Telex: 712 640 VSW

Is a mail order house for mountaineers, backpackers, camping, trekking, survival, etc.

Wilderness Way International

PO Box 334
Northridge
CA 91324
USA

Make the collapsible two gallon/nine litre Water Sack which weighs 3½oz/100gm and consists of two bags, the inner being the larger so that it can never expand to its full size and is therefore less subject to stress. A handy item for backpackers and motorists.

YHA Services Ltd
14 Southampton Street
Covent Garden
London
WC2E 7HY
Tel: 01-836 8541
Telex: 269330

YHA Shops
166 Deansgate
Manchester
M3 3FE
Tel: 061-834 7119

90–98 Corporation Street
(Bull Street Subway)
Birmingham
B4 6XS
Tel: 021-236 7799

6–7 Bridge Street
Cambridge
CB2 1UA
Tel: (0223) 353956

131 Woodville Road
Cardiff
CF2 4DZ
Tel: (0222) 399 178

Supply lightweight tents, sleeping bags, rucksacks, and equipment for overland travel, mountaineering and caving, also weatherproof clothing and a good selection of boots.

Equipment: Cold Weather

Blacks Camping International
2121 Carling Ave
PO Box 6276
Ottowa
Ontario
Canada
K2A 1T4

L6 Carlton Street
Toronto
Ontario

3525 Queen Mary Road
Montreal

Makes excellent down gear. Catalogue.

Polywarm Products Ltd
Cambuslang Road
Rutherglen
Glasgow
G73 1RS
Telex:779968

Manufacture a selection of lightweight and compact specialist sleeping bags suitable for the mountaineer and hiker, including conventional and mummy-shaped bags, made of washable manmade fibres and stitched by a special process that prevents the filling from moving. The sleeping bags are all guaranteed for 12 months.

John Posey Co
PO Box 337
Jenks
OK 74037
USA

Make Coldguard, *a cream to be rubbed on the skin before exposure to cold. It acts like an extra pair of mittens/socks.*

Thinsulate® Thermal Insulation
3M
3M Center, Building 220-7W
St Paul
MN 55114
USA
Tel: (1) 800 328 1689 toll free

3M Canada Inc
PO Box 5757
Terminal A
London
Ontario
Canada N6A 4T1
Tel: (519) 451 2500

Thinsulate is the name of a new insulating material which is claimed to have twice the insulation value of anything else including down and to lose very little of its insulating power because its fibres absorb only about 1 per cent of their weight in water. This washable material is now being used in such products as Mountain Equipment, The North Face, Pacific/Ascente, REI, etc.

Wintergear
Unit 10
Cibyn Industrial Estate
Caernarfon
Gwynedd
LL55 2BD
Tel: Caernarfon (0286) 2270

Make Bivi bags and lightweight tents.

Note: Coldweather clothing, sleeping bags, etc. are also usually available in all well established outdoor and camping shops.

* All good outdoor equipment suppliers stock Cold Weather gear. (*See Equipment: Living, Camping Outdoor, page 624*).

Equipment: Survival

Aéro Shopping France
2 Rue Meissonier
75017 Paris
France
Tel: 763 81 47

Aeronautical equipment.

Globetrotter Ausrüstungen

Denart & Lechhart GmbH
Wandsbeker Chaussee 41
2000 Hamburg 76
Germany, Federal Republic
Tel: (040) 250 44 03

Sells books, maps and equipment, including survival and trekking equipment.

E. Lacroix

18 Rue Malher
75004 Paris
France
Tel: 887 53 20

Signalling and rescue devices, flares, preventive devices against avalanches, dryness, hail, and miscellaneous safety devices such as luminous alarm signals and the ballasted petard intended to frighten sharks and other tropical fish to protect fishermen.

Survival Cards

PO Box 805
Bloomington
IN 47401
USA

Supplies Survival Cards measuring 7.5×12.5cm and made from plastic, which are crammed with survival information, including edible plant classification, emergency shelter construction, first aid, Morse Code, climbing techniques and knot tying.

Pacrep

146 Hekili St
Kailua
Hawaii 96734

Distribute a large bag of thin, strong, very light material with inflatable collars at the top which will completely conceal a 'castaway' at sea and serve as a shark screen. The bag can also be used as a sleeping bag, pup tent, lean-to, stretcher or solar still.

Radio-Telecommunications

141 High Street
Blackpool
Lancs
Tel: (0253) 21200/22110

Manufacture the Strobe Beacon, a battery driven unit (using two HP2 sized cells), which gives off an intermittent flash of very bright white light to aid location by rescue teams. Many times brighter than torch beam, with multi-directional flash. Also has a built-in beam torch for map reading.

Survival Aids Ltd

Morland
Penrith
Cumbria
CA10 3AZ
Tel: (09314) 307

Produces a comprehensive Survival Equipment Catalogue and quarterly Survival News. *Firm supplies all sorts of equipment including survival kits, flares, emergency rations, compasses, knives, medical kits and clothing.* (*See Equipment: Medical, page 631 and Courses: Outdoor and Survival Training, page 620.*)

Survi-Camps and Survi-Kits

(*See Courses: Outdoor and Survival Training, page 620.*)

Equipment: Water Purifiers

Advanced Filtration Technology

2424 Bates Avenue
Concord
CA 94520
USA

Portable Water Filter and Super Straw.

Dantex Services Ltd

La Motte Chambers
St Helier
Jersey
Channel Islands
Tel: (534) 767 77
Telex: 4192231

Personal-size Water Purifier – small enough to fit in pocket or briefcase. Filters and purifies water from all sources except sea water. Safe and effective.

Johnson-Progress Ltd

Carpenters Road
Stratford
London
E15 2DS
Tel: 01-534 7431
Telex: 896156

Make Millbank Bags for filtering water.

Katadyn Products Inc

Industriestr. 27
Sh-8304 Wallisellen
Switzerland
Tel: (01) 830 36 77

Sharp Associates
PO Box 2169
Santa Fe
NM 87504
USA

Norman-Luthy (UK)
37 Town End
Wilsford
nr. Grantham,
Lincs.
NG32 3NX
Tel: (0400) 30285

Katadyn-France SA
24 Blvd. du Château
F-94500 Champigny s/Marne
Tel: (1) 880 37 70

Ets. Beckman N.V.
Dr Van de Perrelei 27
B-2200 Borgerhout
Belgium
Tel: (03) 235 31 32

Deutsche Katadyn GmbH
Schäufeleinstr. 20
D-8000 Munich 21
Germany, Federal Republic
Tel: (089) 57 20 53

Make portable water filters which clear and decontaminate water.

Kirby-Warick Ltd

Mildenhall
Bury St Edmunds
Suffolk
1P28 7AX
Tel: (0638) 716 321

Make puritabs (in two sizes) which are effervescent water-purifying tablets.

Portacel Ltd

Cannon Lane
Tonbridge
Kent
TN9 1PR
Tel: (0732) 364 411
Telex: 95467

Manufacture a portable aluminium gravity-fed water filter which removes all bacteria and water-borne diseases from the water and produces water that is safe to drink. It is not suitable for use in muddy or brackish water, and generally is only suitable for water that had been treated at a central water treatment works.

Sachs Motor Services Ltd

The Maltings
Tamworth Road
Ashby-de-la-Zouch
Leicestershire
LE6 5PS
Tel: (0530) 414 313

Sell the Filtron Camp 3000, the world's smallest water purification plant, which purifies any water in which bathing is possible to drinking standard.

Safariquip

(*See Equipment: Living, Camping, Outdoor, page 624.*)

Equipment: Medical

John Bell and Croyden

50 Wigmore Street
London W1
Tel: 01-935 5555

Chemists in London who specialize in making up travel and expedition supplies.

May & Baker Ltd

Dagenham
Essex
RM10 7XS
Tel: 01-592 3060

May & Baker are one of the largest pharmaceutical manufacturers in the UK. They have several remedies for the minor everyday accidents that occur at home or abroad. Avomine *tablets that take away the misery of travel sickness and have a long-lasting effect of up to 24 hrs.* Anthical *cream which provides relief from sunburn, prickly heat, jelly fish stings and other skin allergies.* Brulidine, *an antiseptic cream effective against a wide range of bacteria likely to infect a cut or a wound.* Anthisan *which will soothe away the pain and itching of insect bites and ease the swelling.* Brolene *drops of eye ointment to prevent or treat eye problems and infections caused by too much sun, seawater, harsh winds, dust and sand. May & Baker's leaflet* Your Guide to Holiday Health Care *is available by sending a s.a.e. to May & Baker Holiday Leaflet, CMS, 19–21 Great Portland Street, London W1.*

Survival Aids

Morland
Penrith
Cumbria
CA10 3AZ
Tel: (09314) 307

The firm supplies medical kits for general or special requirements and a large range of packed, lightweight expedition rations. (*See Equipment: Survival, page 629.*)

Tender Corp After Bite

Box 42
Littleton
NH 03561
USA

America's leading treatment for the relief of pain and irritation due to insect bites or strings. Convenient pen-like applicators or individually wrapped towelettes. For sample send (US) $3.00.

Wyeth Laboratories

PO Box 8299
Philadelphia
PA 19101
USA

Huntercombe Lane South
Taplow
Maidenhead
Berks
Tel: (062) 86 4377

Manufacturer of antivenoms against poisonous snakes of the United States. The serum is sold in a freeze dried condition, making it ideally suited for expeditions (no need for refrigeration), and in small quantities.

Equipment: Optical

Heron Optical Co

23–25 Kings Road
Brentwood
Essex
CM14 4ER
Tel: (0277) 222 230

Mail Order:
3 Wates Way
Brentwood
Essex CM15 9TB
Tel: (0277) 233 122

Stock all leading makes of binoculars, telescopes. Associate company of Field and Trek (Equipment) Ltd. (q.v.), (see Equipment: Living, Camping, Outdoor, page 624.)

Newbold & Bulford

Enbeco House
Carlton Park
Saxmundham
Suffolk
LP17 2NL
Tel: (0728) 2933

Supply Sunto compasses and binoculars.'

Olympus Optical Co (UK) Ltd

2–8 Honduras Street
London
EC1Y 0TX
Tel: 01-253 2772

Equipment: Photographic

Agfa-Gevaert Ltd

27 Great West Road
Brentford
Middlesex
TW8 9AX
Tel: 01-560 2131

Camera Care Systems

30 Alexandra Road
Clevedon
Avon
BS21 7QH
Tel: (0272) 87 1791

Manufacture protective casings for photographic equipment and offer a guaranteed camera repair service.

Canon UK Ltd

Brent Trading Centre
North Circular Road
Neasden
London
NW10 0JF
Tel: 01-459 1266

Delta Colour Ltd

Wheatfield House
Church Road
Paddock Wood
Kent TN12 6EX

Supply self-adhesive mounting board, exhibition display systems, photography and full colour and b/w printing and processing services.

D W Viewpacks Ltd

8 Peverel Drive
Granby
Milton Keynes
MK1 1NL
Tel: (0908) 642 323/642 373

Manufacturers of slide/photographic storage systems and lightboxes.

Fuji PhotoFilm (UK) Ltd

99 Baker St
London W1
Tel: 01-487 5711

Nicholas Hunter Slide Storage Systems

PO Box 22
Oxford
Oxon
OX1 2JP

Ilford UK Ltd

14 Tottenham Street
London W1
Tel: 01-636 7890

Keith Johnson Photographics

11 Great Marlborough St
London W1
Tel: 01-439 8811

Major suppliers for all photographic accessories.

Kodak Ltd

PO Box 66
Kodak House
Station Road
Hemel Hempstead
Herts.
HP1 1JU
Tel: (0442) 166 22
Enquires to: Ext. 48

Supply a limited number of films on trade terms to expeditions having the support of the Royal Geographical Society or a similar authority, provided that purchases are made in bulk, that one order is placed at a minimum value of £100 and that delivery at a UK address (excluding docks and airports) is accepted.

Minolta UK Ltd

1–3 Tanners Drive
Blakelands
Milton Keynes
MK14 5BU
Tel: (0908) 615 141

Nikon UK Ltd

20 Fulham Broadway
London SW6
Tel: 01-381 1551

Olympus Optical Co (UK) Ltd

2–8 Honduras St
London EC1
Tel: 01-253 2772

Pentax Ltd

Pentax House
South Hill Avenue
South Harrow
Middlesex
Tel: 01-864 4422

Photo Poste (Odeon Photo)

110 Blvd St Germain
75006 Paris
France
Tel: 329 4050

Is a photographic developing and printing service that will process photos or films sent from anywhere in the world, and send the results on anywhere. They will undertake a variety of processes; will give advice on film handling and photographic technique; will retain negatives safely until your journey is over; and charge reasonable prices for these services.

Photo Science Ltd

Charfleets Road
Canvey Island
Essex
SS8 0PH

Manufacturers/distributors of negatives/slide storage systems and photographic equipment.

TAMRAC

7032 Valjean Ave
Van Nuys
CA 91401
USA

Make the TeleZoom Pak (Model 517) and a full line of instant access foam padded weathproof cases for 35mm systems.

Kodak Processing Laboratories Worldwide

Kodak Ltd.

Australia:

PO Box 4742
Melbourne
Victoria 3001

Austria:

Albert Schweitzer-Gasse 4
A-1148 Vienna

Belgium:

Steenstraat 20
1800 Koningslo-Vilvoorde
Belgium

Canada:

9977 McLaughlin Road
Brampton
Ontario
L6X 2M4

Denmark:

Roskildevej 16
2620 Albertslund.

Finland:

Postilokero 758
00101 Helsinki 10

France:

Rond-Point George Eastman
93270 Sevran

Germany, Federal Rep.:

Postfach 369
7000 Stuttgart 60

Greece:

PO Box 1235
GR100 10 Athens

Italy:

Casella Postale 11057
20100 Milan.

Japan:

Far East Laboratories Ltd
Namiki Bldg
No. 2–10 Ginza 3-chome
Chuo-ku
Tokyo

Mexico:

Administration de Correos 68
Mexico 22 D.F.
Mexico 04870

Netherlands:

Treubstraat 11
2288EG Rijswijk Z.H.

New Zealand:

PO Box 3003
Wellington

Norway:

Trollasveien 6
1410 Kolbotn

Spain:

Apartado de Correos 130
Colmenar Viejo
Madrid.

South Africa:

102 Davies St
Doornfontein
Johannesburg 2094

Sweden:

S-162 85 Vallingby

Switzerland:

Case Postale
CH-1001 Lausanne

United Kingdom:

Head Office
Kodak House
Station Road
Hemel Hempstead
Hertfordshire

246 High Holborn
London
WC1V 7EA

Box 14
Hemel Hempstead
Hertfordshire
HP2 7EH

USA:

1065 Kapiolani Blvd
Honolulu
Hawaii 96814

Kodak Park
Rochester
NY 14650

Medical Requirements and Advice

Medical Requirements and Advice

Vaccination Chart

Abbreviations: C = Cholera. YF = Yellow Fever. T = Typhoid. M = Malaria. R = Recommended by DHSS.

Country	C	YF	T	M
Afghanistan	R	No	R	R
Albania	No	No	R	No
Algeria	R	No	R	R
Angola	R	R	R	R
Argentina	No	No	R	R
Australia	No	No	No	No
Austria	No	No	No	No
Azores	No	No	R	No
Bahamas	No	No	R	No
Bahrain	R	No	R	No
Bangladesh	R	No	R	R
Barbados	No	No	R	No
Belgium	No	No	No	No
Belize	No	No	R	R
Benin	R	Yes[1]	R	R
Bermuda	No	No	No	No
Bhutan	R	No	R	R
Bolivia	No	Yes*	R	R
Botswana	R	No	R	R
Brazil	No	R	R	R
Brunei	R	No	R	No
Bulgaria	No	No	R	No
Burma	R	No	R	R
Burundi	R	R	R	R
Cameroon	R	Yes[1]	R	R
Canada	No	No	No	No
Cape Verde Islands	No	No	R	R
Cayman Islands	No	No	R	No
Central African Rep.	R	Yes[1]	R	R
Chad	R	R	R	R
Chile	No	No	R	No
China	No	No	R	R
Colombia	No	R	R	R
Comoros	No	No	R	R
Congo	R	Yes[2]	R	R
Cook Islands	No	No	R	No
Costa Rica	No	No	R	R
Cuba	No	No	R	No
Cyprus	No	No	R	No
Czechoslovakia	No	No	No	No
Denmark	No	No	No	No
Djibouti	R	No	R	R
Dominica	No	No	R	No

Country	C	YF	T	M
Dominican Rep.	No	No	R	R
Ecuador	No	R	R	R
Egypt	R	No	R	R
El Salvador	No	No	R	R
Ethiopia	R	R	R	R
Falkland Islands	No	No	R	No
Fiji	No	No	R	No
Finland	No	No	No	No
France	No	No	R+	No
French Guyana	No	Yes[2]	R	R
French Polynesia	No	No	R	No
French West Indies	No	No	R	No
Gabon	R	R	R	R
Gambia	R	Yes[1]	R	R
Germany, Dem. Rep.	No	No	No	No
Germany, Fed. Rep.	No	No	No	No
Ghana	R	R	R	R
Gibraltar	No	No	R	No
Greece	No	No	R	No
Greenland	No	No	No	No
Grenada	No	No	R	No
Guam	No	No	R	No
Guatemala	No	No	R	R
Guinea	R	R	R	R
Guinea-Bissau	R	R	R	R
Guinea, Equatorial	R	R	R	R
Guyana	No	R	R	R
Haiti	No	No	R	R
Honduras	No	No	R	R
Hong Kong	No	No	R	No
Hungary	No	No	No	No
Iceland	No	No	No	No
India	R	No	R	R
Indonesia	R	No	R	R
Iran	R	No	R	R
Iraq	R	No	R	R
Ireland	No	No	No	No
Israel	R	No	R	No
Italy	No	No	R	No
Ivory Coast	R	Yes[1]	R	R
Jamaica	No	No	R	No
Japan	No	No	R	No
Jordan	R	No	R	R
Kampuchea	R	No	R	R
Kenya	R	R	R	R
Kiribati	No	No	R	No
Korea (North)	R	No	R	No
Korea (South)	R	No	R	R

Country	C	YF	T	M
Kuwait	R	No	R	No
Laos	R	No	R	R
Lebanon	R	No	R	No
Lesotho	R	No	R	No
Liberia	R	R	R	R
Libya	R	No	R	R
Luxembourg	No	No	No	No
Macao	No	No	R	No
Madagascar	R	No	R	R
Madeira	No	No	R	No
Malawi	R	No	R	R
Malaysia	R	No	R	R
Maldives	R	No	R	R
Mali	R	Yes[2]	R	R
Malta	No	No	R	No
Mauritania	R	Yes[2]	R	R
Mauritius	No	No	R	R
Mexico	No	No	R	R
Monaco	No	No	R	No
Mongolia	No	No	R	No
Montserrat	No	No	R	No
Morocco	R	No	R	R
Mozambique	Yes[1]	No	R	R
Namibia	R	No	R	R
Nauru	No	No	R	No
Nepal	R	No	R	R
Netherlands	No	No	No	No
Neth. Antilles	No	No	R	No
New Caledonia	No	No	R	No
New Zealand	No	No	No	No
Nicaragua	No	No	R	R
Niger	R	Yes[1]	R	R
Nigeria	R	Yes[1]	R	R
Norway	No	No	No	No
Oman	R	No	R	R
Pakistan	R	No	R	R
Panama	No	R	R	R
Panama Canal Zone	No	No	R	R
Papua New Guinea	R	No	R	R
Paraguay	No	No	R	R
Peru	No	R	R	R
Philippines	R	No	R	R
Poland	No	No	No	No
Portugal	No	No	R	No
Puerto Rico	No	No	R	No
Qatar	R	No	R	R
Reunion	No	No	R	No
Romania	No	No	R	No
Rwanda	R	R	R	R
Saint Helena	No	No	R	No
Saint Lucia	No	No	R	No
Saint Vincent and Grenadines	No	No	R	No
Samoa	No	No	R	No
São and Tome Principe	R	Yes[2]	R	R
Saudi Arabia	R	No	R	R
Senegal	R	Yes[1]	R	R
Seychelles	No	No	R	No
Sierra Leone	R	R[3]	R	R
Singapore	R	No	R	No
Solomon Is	No	No	R	R
Somalia	R	R	R	R
South Africa	R	No	R	R
Spain	No	No	R	No
Sri Lanka	R	No	R	R
Sudan	R	R[3]	R	R
Suriname	No	R	R	R
Swaziland	R	No	R	R
Sweden	No	No	No	No
Switzerland	No	No	No	No
Syria	R	No	R	R
Taiwan	R	No	R	No
Tanzania	R	R	R	R
Thailand	R	No	R	R
Togo	R	R	R	R
Trinidad & Tobago	No	No	R	No
Tunisia	R	No	R	No
Turkey	R	No	R	R
Tuvalu	No	No	R	No
Uganda	R	Yes[1]	R	R
United Arab Emirates	R	No	R	R
USA	No	No	No	No
USSR	No	No	R	No
Upper Volta (Burkina Faso)	R	Yes[1]	R	R
Uruguay	No	No	R	No
Vanuatu Rep.	No	No	R	R
Venezuela	No	R	R	R
Vietnam	R	No	R	R
Virgin Is	No	No	R	No
West Indies Associated States	No	No	R	No
Yemen People's Dem. Rep. (South)	R	No	R	R
Yemen Arab Rep. (North)	R	No	R	R
Yugoslavia	No	No	R	No
Zaïre	R	R	R	R
Zambia	R	R	R	R
Zimbabwe	R	No	R	R

1. Vaccinations which are an essential requirement for entry to the country concerned and for which you will require a certificate.
2. Except travellers arriving from a non-infected area and staying less than two weeks.
3. A certificate may be required on leaving the country.

*(Bolivia) – Yellow Fever required if going to Santa Sierra de la Cruz.
+(France) – Typhoid recommended only if going to the Mediterranean coastal area.

Note: Yellow Fever vaccinations do not apply for children under one year old.

Infectious Hepatitis: Travellers to places where sanitation is primitive should consider protection against infectious hepatitis. Seek advice from your doctor.

Tetanus: Travellers to areas should be actively immunized against tetanus if they have not previously been so. Seek advice from your doctor.

Vaccination Centres and Information

BELGIUM

In Belgium vaccinations may be given by a GP, in which case the yellow card must be countersigned by an authorized centre; or by one of the following vaccination centres, when no further endorsement is required:

Ministère de la Santé Publique et de la Famille

Inspection d'Hygiène – Service de vaccination
Quartier Vesale
B 1010 Brussels
Belgium

Ministère des Affaires Etrangères et du Commerce Extérieur

Centre Médical
Rue Bréderode 9
1000 Brussels
Belgium

FRANCE

In France vaccinations may be performed by a GP, in which case his signature must be endorsed by one of the following:

Direction de l'Action Sociale, de l'Hygiene et de la Santé

Service des Vaccinations
3bis Rue Mabillon
75270 Paris Cedex 06
France
Tel: 329 21 90

Institut Pasteur

25 Rue du Docteur Roux
75724 Paris Cedex 15
France
Tel: 306 19 19

Other vaccination centres in France:

Aérogare de Roissy

Tel: 862 22 63
Hours: 9am–12 noon and 2–6pm

Aérogare d'Orly

Paris
Tel: 853-2 34
Hours: 9am–12 noon and 2–9pm

Aérogare du Bourget

Tel: 208 98 90
Hours: 9–11am and 2.30–5pm

Air France

25 Blvd de Vaugirard
75015 Paris
Tel: (1) 320 13 50
Hours: Mon. To Fri. 9am to 4.30pm
Sun. 9am to 12.00 and 2.00pm to 4.30pm
Smallpox, yellow fever, cholera, typhoid, polio, meningitis, rabies.

Centre Médical d'Air France

1 Square Max Hymans
75014 Paris
Tel: (1) 323 94 64
Hours: 9am to 4.30pm Monday to Saturday
Note on Saturday closed between
12 noon and 2pm.

Centre UTA Vaccinations

50 Rue Arago
92 800 Puteaux
Hours: 9am to 4.30pm cholera, smallpox.
Yellow fever by appointment.

Hôpital de l'Institut Pasteur

211 Rue de Vaugirard
F 75015 Paris
Tel: 567 35 09
Hours: 9am to 5pm. All vaccinations including rabies.

Institut Arthur Vernes

36 Rue d'Assas
75006 Paris
Tel: 544 38 94

INDIA

International Inoculation Centre

New Delhi Municipal Committee Office
Town Hall
Parliament Street
New Delhi
Vaccination services in respect of cholera, typhoid and yellow fever are available to international travellers betwen 10am to 4pm on all working days.

SWITZERLAND

In Switzerland vaccinations are performed by GPs, at clinics or at vaccination centres, with the exception of yellow fever vaccination which can be obtained only at:

L'Institut d'Hygiène

2 Quai du Cheval Blanc
1227 Carouge/Geneva
Tel: (022) 43 80 75

Other vaccination centres in Switzerland are:

Schweizerisches Tropeninstitut Basel

Socinstrasse 75
4051 Basel
Tel: (061) 23 38 96
One can also obtain information on vaccinations here.

Ospedale S. Giovanni

Pronto socorso
65000 Bellinzona
Tel: (092) 25 03 33.
By appointment Thursdays 10–11am.

Inselspital Medinzinische Poliklinik

Freibrugstr. 3
3010 Bern
Tel: (031) 64 25 25.
By appointment.

Service du médecin cantonal

Département de la santé publique
Route des Cliniques 17
1700 Fribourg
Tel: (037) 21 14 44.
By appointment.

Institut d'Hygiène

Service du médecin cantonal
Quai Cheval-Blanc 2
1211 Geneva
Tel: (022) 43 80 75.
Tuesday and Friday 8.30–9.00am without appointment.

Policlinique médicale universitaire

Rue César-Roux 19
1005 Lausanne
Tel: (021) 20 90 48

Kantonsspital Spitalzentrum

1 Stock
Personalartz
6004 Luzern
Tel: (041) 25 11 25.
By appointment.

Institut for med. Mikrobiologie

Frohbergstr. 3
9000 St. Gallen
Tel: (071) 26 35 55

Swissair

Arztlicher Dienst Schulgebaude A
8058 Zürich Flughafen
Tel: (01) 812 68 39

Impfzentrum

Gloriastr. 30
8006 Zürich
Tel: (01) 257 26 06/257 26 26
Hours: Monday 16.30–19.00 hrs, Wednesday 13.00–16.00 hrs, Thursday 16.30–19.00 hrs, Friday 9.00–11.00 hrs, without appointment.

UK

In the UK, vaccination against diseases other than yellow fever can be carried out by the traveller's own doctor, or, exceptionally and by arrangement, at a hospital. A list of yellow fever vaccination centres, together with details of health precautions for the traveller, is given in the booklet *Notice to Travellers: Health protection*, prepared by the Health Departments of England, Wales and Northern Ireland and the Central Office of Information. This is available from the Department of Health and Social Security in London, the Welsh Office in Cardiff, the Department of Health and Social Services in Belfast, the Scottish Home and Health Department in Edinburgh, or from local offices of these departments. *Other places where the traveller can be given vaccinations or information about vaccinations are:*

British Airways Immunization

75 Regent Street
London W1R 7HG
Tel: 01-439 9584/5
Open Monday to Friday 8.30–16.30 hrs.

Central Public Health Laboratories

Colindale Avenue
London NW9
Tel: 01-205 7041
Gamma globulin for immunization against hepatitis, and rabies vaccine are supplied to general practitioner if appropriate. Vaccines for foreign travel are not supplied by the NHS and must be paid for.

Health Control Unit

Terminal 3 Arrivals
Heathrow Airport
Hounslow
Middx. TW6 1NB
Tel: 01-759 7209
Can give at any time up-to-date information on compulsory and recommended immunizations for different countries.

Hospital for Tropical Diseases

3 St Pancras Way
London NW1 0PE
Tel: 01-387 4411

Liverpool School of Tropical Medicine

Pembroke Place
Liverpool L3 5QA
Tel: Liverpool 7089393

London School of Hygiene and Tropical Medicine

Keppel Street
(Gower Street)
London WC1E 7HT
Tel: 01-636 86 36
Provide advice for intending travellers.

Thomas Cook Vaccination Centre

45 Berkeley Street
London W1A 1EB
Tel: 01-499 4000
Vaccinations and certificates given on the spot, also all vaccination information. Saturday mornings appointment necessary.

West London Designated Vaccinating Centre

53 Great Cumberland Place
London W1H 7HL
Tel: 01-262 6456
Hours: 9am to 5pm from Monday to Friday. No appointment necessary.

USA

Convenience Care Centers

World Trade Center
350 South Figueroa Street
Los Angeles
California 90071
People who need vaccinations prior to their overseas trips can have them taken care of here.

US Department of Health and Human Services

Public Health Service
Centers for Disease Control
Center for Prevention Services
Division of Quarantine
Atlanta
Georgia 30333
Publish a booklet annually, 'Health Information for International Travel' ($4.25) *available from Superintendent of Documents, US Govt. Printing Office, Washington DC 20402.*

The USHPS

330 Independence Avenue SW
Washington
DC 20201

Medical Care Abroad

American Diabetes Association

2 Park Ave
New York
NY 10016
USA
Offers a reprint of travel tips and a list of diabetes organizations throughout the world.

Comité Français pour la Santé

9 Rue Newton
75116 Paris
France
Tel: (1) 723 72 07
Publishes a booklet giving practical advice on health for travellers: Vous allez partir en voyage ... Miniguide santé du voyageur.

Caisse Primaire d'Assurance Maladie de Paris

Direction des Relations Internationales
173/175 rue de Bercy
75586 Paris Cedex 12
Tel: 346 12 53
The office to which French travellers should apply with any queries or claims about reimbursement of medical expenses incurred abroad.

Elvia Compagnie d'Assurances et d'Assistance

51 Rue de Ponthieu – entrée D1
75381 Paris Cedex 08
France
Tel: (1) 562 84 84 Telex: 290 963 F
One of the two most reliable companies in France offering assistance to the international traveller, instead of reimbursement afterwards. (See Europ Assistance below.)

Europ Assistance

23/25 Rue Chaptal
75445 Paris
France
Tel: 285 85 85
Provides a 24-hour service and a worldwide network of representatives, enabling the company to supply immediately a doctor, medic, medically-equipped aircraft or other assistance as needed. One of the two most reliable companies in France offering assistance to the international traveller, instead of reimbursement of expenses afterwards.

Europ Assistance Ltd

252 High Street
Croydon
Surrey
Tel: 01-680 1234
Provides a worldwide medical emergency service. Specialists in ambulance repatriation. Contracts incorporate medical expenses incurance. The Oper-

ational Headquarters is fully manned by experienced multi-lingual co-ordinators, 24 hours a day every day.

Exeter Hospital Aid Society

176 Fore Street
Exeter
Devon EX4 3AY
Offers a 'worldwide provident scheme' which can be useful to people whose medical expenses are not covered by their employer.

The Flying Doctors' Society of Africa

London House (AMREF)
68 Upper Richmond Road
London SW15 2PR
Tel: 01-874 0098
Provides financial backing for the East African Flying Doctor Service (part of the African Medical and Research Foundation). Members are guaranteed free air transport if injured or taken seriously ill while on safari in East Africa. Temporary membership is available for tourists or visitors to East Africa and confers the same benefits. (Cost: £5.00 for one month, £12.00 for one year.)

Hôpital St. Louis

40 Rue Bichat
75010 Paris
France
Tel: 205 83 10
Specializes in tropical and venereal diseases. Tests on returned travellers can be performed here at low costs.

IAMAT

International Association for Medical Assistance to Travellers.
736 Center Street
Lewiston
NY 14092
USA

St Vincent's Hospital
Victoria Parade
Melbourne 3065
Australia

123 Edward Street
Suite 725
Toronto
Ontario
Canada M5G 1E2

188 Nicklin Road
Guelph
Ontario
Canada N1H 7L5
A non-profit organization dedicated to the gathering and dissemination of health and sanitary information worldwide for the benefit of travellers and to assist them to find qualified medical care when travelling outside their country of residence. To this end IAMAT publishes a series of charts and a directory of English-speaking doctors who have been trained in Europe or North America, who are on call to IAMAT members 24 hours a day and who have agreed to a set fee schedule.
IAMAT membership is free to any travellers. They are supported by voluntary contributions from travellers.

Medic Alert Foundation

Turlock
California 95380
USA
Tel: (209) 668 3333
The Medic Alert Foundation emblem, worn as a bracelet or necklace, is engraved with the wearer's special condition (Blood group, a heart condition, an allergy to antibiotics), and a 24 hour emergency telephone number. The phone number (209) 634 4917 USA, which may be called collect from any location in the world, gives access to vital information filed for use in an emergency situation.

Medical Passport Foundation, Inc

PO Box 820
Deland
Florida 32720
USA
Tel: (904) 734 0639
Provides information and advice for those with pre-existing health problems. Provides the Medical Passport, and the Emergency Mini-Medical Passport which contain your medical history in portable form for on-the-spot medical identification of your medical record to any physician wherever you are. Contains emergency data and much more, which has saved lives as it has warned of certain allergic states, other current disorders such as diabetes, the caution required in the case of antibiotics. Adds to your peace of mind when travelling or at home.

Mondial Assistance

8 Place de la Concorde
75008 Paris
France
Tel: 266 39 42
Medical insurance and emergency service.

Ross Institute of Tropical Hygiene

Keppel Street
(Gower Street)
London WC1E 7HT
Provides advice for those travelling to tropical countries. Details of publications may be obtained from the publications secretary.

The Hospital for Tropical Diseases

3 St. Pancras Way
London NW1 0PE
Tel: 01-387 4411
Returned travellers suspecting disease may be refer-

red here by their general practitioners. (See Vaccination Centres, page 638.)

St John Ambulance Headquarters

1 Grosvenor Crescent
London SW1X 7EF
Tel: 01-235 5231
During office hours 01-235 5238 at other times.
Provides doctors and nurses and lay members with specialized aeromedical training to escort sick and injured persons by air to or from any part of the world. It owns special ambulances equipped to travel to and from the Continent with patients when air travel is not possible. Published definitive First Aid Manual *in association with The Red Cross.*

Trans-care International Ltd

193–195 High Street
Acton
London W3 9DD
Tel: 01-993 6151 (20 lines) Telex: 934525
Selected to be the official medical assistance organization to the British Olympic team in Los Angeles, Trans-care provides worldwide medical assistance services day and night.
Air ambulances, doctors, SRNs are always available. Response to all medical emergencies is immediate.

Note: For Medical Equipment see Equipment: Medical, page 631. For Medical Insurance, see Insurance, page 756.

Hospitals or clinics either run by English speaking doctors or which have interpreters

Argentina	British Hospital, Perdrial 74, 1280 Buenos Aires. Tel: 23-1081.
Andorra	Clinica Verge de Meritxell, Escaldes Centre Hospitalari, Andorra la Vella.
Austria	Contact the Osterreichische Arztekammer, Weihburggasse 10–12, 1010 Vienna. Tel: 01043/222/52 69 44 52 68 79.
Bermuda	King Edward VII Memorial Hospital; St Brendon's Hospital.
Burma	Kandawgyi Clinic for diplomats and foreigners.
Burundi	Bujumbura.
Chile	Santiago and a few major cities offer informal interpreting services but in general the personnel have a basic working knowledge of English.
China	Doctors may speak English in the large cities. Very unlikely elsewhere.
Colombia	Clinica Shio, Bogotá. Clinica Marly, Bogotá. Clinica Santa Fe, Bogotá. Clinica San Juan de Dios, Cali.
Czechoslavakia	Fakulini Poliklinika, Prague 2 Karlovo namesti 42. Free medical care for British subjects.
Dominican Republic	Clinca Gomez Patino, Avenue Independencia, Santo Domingo. Centro Medico Nacional, Ave Maximo Gomez, Santo Domingo. Clinica Yunen, Ave Bolivar, Santo Domingo.
Finland	Helsinki University Central Hospital, Meilahti, Haarrmanink 3.
Guyana	Georgetown Hospital, New Market St, Cummingsburg, Georgetown. St Joseph's Mercy Hospital, 129–136 Parade Street, Kingston, Georgetown. Medical Arts Centre, 265 Thomas St, Cummingsburg, Georgetown. Woodlands Hospital, 110–111 Carmichael St, Cummingsburg. Davis Memorial Hospital, 121 Durban St, Lodge. Prashad's Hospital, 258 Thomas and Middle Streets, Cummingsburg.
Iceland	Borgarspitalinn, Reykjavik. Landspitalinn, Reykjavik. Landakotsspitali, vid Tungotu, Reykjavik. Sjukrahusid, Akureyre. Sjukrahusid, Isafirdi. Sjukrahusid, Vestmannaeyjum.
Iraq	98% of the Medical Practitioners speak English.
Ivory Coast	Chu Cocody Chu Treichville

Jordan	Al-Ahli Hospital. Italian Hospital. Al-Khalidy Hospital. Al-Muasher Hospital. Shmeisani Maternity Hospital.
Korea	Seoul National University Hospital, 7601-1. Severance Hospital, 322-0161/79. Korea National Medical Centre, 265-91030/5. Songshim Hospital, 267-8111/9. Ewha Woman's Hospital, 762-5061/9. Korea University Hospital 762-5110/30. Korea General Hospital, 725-8021. Songmo Hospital, 771-76. Paik Foundation Hospital, 265-6121/9. Sunchonhyang Hospital, 794-7191/8. Kyonghee University Hospital, 966-1701/5.
Liberia	J. F. Kennedy Medical Centre, Government Hospital, Monrovia. St Joseph's Catholic Hospital (private), Monrovia. Phebbe Hospital, Dr Kasser's Clinic, Cooper's Clinic; ELWA Hospital.
Malta	St Luke's, Mangia. Tel: 21251, 607860; Craig Hospital, Gozo. Tel: 556851.
Mexico	American British Cowdray Hospital, Sur 136, Esq Observatorio, Mexico City.
Peru	Clinica Anglo Americana, Av. Salazar, (San Isidro). Tel: 403570. Clinica International, Washington 1475, (Lima). Tel: 288060. Clinica San Borja, Av. Del Aire 333, (San Borja). Tel: 413141.
Portugal	British Hospital, 49 Rue Saraiva de Carvalho, Lisbon.
El Salvador	Policlinica Salvaforena, SA, 25 Avenida Norte, San Salvador. Tel: 25 0588, 25 0565. Centro de emergencias, SA, Colonia la Esperanza, 2a Diagonal, San Salvador. Tel: 25 7153; 25 3583; 25 4651; 25 1871; 25 9303.
Tahiti	Dr Charles Fichier, Padfai Clinique, BP 545, Boulevard Podare, Papeete. Tel: 30202. Dr Charles Bronstein, Ardella Clinique, Rue Cardella, Papeete. Tel: 28190.
Turkey	American Hospital, Guzelbahce Sokak, Nisantasi. Tel: 14 86 030. French Hospital, Paster, Taskisla Pangalti, Tel: 14 84 756. French Hospital, La Paix, Buyukdere Caddesi, Sisli. Tel: 14 81 832. German Hospital, Siracevizler Caddesi 100, Tel: 14 35 500. Italian Hospital, Defterdar Yokusu, Tophane, Tel: 14 99 751.
Uruguay	British Hospital, Av. Italia 2402, Montevideo.

Travel by: Air, Road, Water and Sea

Air

Airlines of the World: Headquarter addresses

Letter codes, headquarter addresses and telephone numbers of many scheduled airlines. A list which may be useful for travellers with an unusual itinerary or enquiry or with a complaint about airline service.

Aer Lingus Teoranta – Irish International (EI)
Dublin Airport
Dublin
Ireland
Tel: 370011

Aeroflot (SU)
Leningradsky Prospekt 37
Moscow 125 167
USSR
Tel: 155 54 94

Aerolineas Argentinas (AR)
Paseo Colón 185
Buenos Aires
Argentina
Tel: 308551

Aeromexico (AM)
Paseo de la Reforma 445 – 1st Floor
Mexico City
Mexico 06500
Tel: 286-44-22

Aeroperu (PL)
Cailloma 818 (P12)
Lima
Peru
Tel: 27 6200

Air Afrique (RK)
3 Av. J. Anoma Ol
Box 1595
Abidjan,
Ivory Coast
Tel: 22-60-63

Air Algérie (AH)
Compagnie Nationale de Transports Aériens (Air Algérie)
1 Place Maurice Audin
Algiers
Dem Rep of Algeria
Tel: 63 92 34/5/6, 64 24 28

Air Burundi (PB)
PO Box 2460
Bujumbura
Burundi

Air BVI Ltd (BL)
Box 85
Roadtown
Tortola
British Virgin Islands
Tel: 5-2346

Air Cal (OC)
3636 Birch St
Newport Beach
CA 92660
USA
Tel: (714) 7000

Air Canada (AC)
Place Air Canada
5000 Dorchester Blvd. West
Montreal
Quebec
Canada
Tel: (514) 879 7000

Air Europe
Europe House
East Park
Crawley
West Sussex
RH10 6AS
Tel: (0293) 519 100

Air Florida (QH)
Executive Offices
3900 NW 79th Ave
Miami
FLA 33156
USA
Tel: (305) 592 8550

Air France (AF)
1 Square Max Hymans
75757 Paris
Cedex 15
France
Tel: 323 81 81

Air India (AI)
Air India Building
Nariman Point
Bombay 400021
India
Tel: 234142

Air Inter – Lignes Aériennes Intérieures (IT)
1 Avenue du Maréchal Devaux
F 91550 Paray Vieille Poste
France
Tel: 675 12 12

Air Jamaica (JM)
72–76 Harbour Street
Kingston
Jamaica
Tel. 922-3460
6 Bruton Street
London
W1X 8AX
Tel: 01-493 4455

Air Lanka (UL)
14 Sir Baron Jayatilaka Mawatha
PO Box 670
Colombo-1
Sri Lanka
Tel: 27731, 28331

Air Liberia (NL)
PO Box 2076
Monrovia
Liberia
Tel: 22144

Air Malawi (QM)
PO Box 84
Blantyre
Malawi
Tel: Blantyre 633 111

Air Mali (MY)
BP 2
Bamako
Rep of Mali
Tel: 233-36, 235-36

Air Malta (KM)
New Offices/Luqa Airport
Malta
Tel. (01) 356-824330

Air Mauritius (MK)
First Floor
Rogers House
5 President John Kennedy St
Port Louis
Mauritius
Tel: 086801

Fourth Floor
Heathcote House
20 Savile Row
London W1X 1AE
Tel: 01-734 7864/5

Air Midwest (ZV)
Hangar 20-W
Mid-Continental Airport
Wichita
KS 67209 USA
Tel: (316) 942 8137

Air Nauru (ON)
Yaren Republic of Nauru
Nauru Island
Central Pacific
Tel: 3310, 3311

Air New Zealand Ltd (TE)
International (TE)
Domestic (NZ)
Private Bag
Air New Zealand House
1 Queen Street
Auckland 1
New Zealand
Tel. 797 515

Air Niger (AW)
Immeuble Sonara (Boite Postale 865)
Naimey
Niger
Tel: 72-3899

Air Pacific (FJ)
Air Pacific Centre
263–269 Grantham Road
Raiwaqa
Suva
Fiji Is.
Tel: 386 444

Air Panama Internacional (OP)
Avenida Justo Arosemena y Calle 34
Panama City
Panama Republic
Tel. 25-0213, 25-8389

Air Polynesie (VT)
BP 314
Quai Bir Hakeim Papeete
Tahiti
French Polynesia
Tel: 25 580

Air UK (UK)
Berkeley House
51–53 High Street
Redhill
Surrey
RH1 1RX
Tel: (91) 65941
Manager General Services.

Air Zaïre (QC)
4 Avenue du Port
BP 8552
Kinshasa
Zaïre
Tel: 24986

Air Zimbabwe (RH)
PO Box AP1
Harare Airport
Harare
Zimbabwe
Tel: 52601

Alaska Airlines Inc (AS)
PO Box 68900
Seattle
EA 98168
USA
Tel: (206) 433 3200

ALIA – The Royal Jordanian Airlines (RJ)
PO Box 302
Amman
Jordan
Tel: 677736

Alitalia (AZ)
Palazzo Alitalia
Piazzale Giulio Pastore
Rome 00144
Italy
Tel: 54441

All Nippon Airways Co Ltd (NH)
27th Floor
Kasumigaseki Bldg., 3-2-5
Kasumigaseki
Chiyoda-ku
Tokyo
Japan
Tel: (580) 4711

ALM – Antillean Airlines (LM)
Hato Airport
Curaçao
Neth. Antilles
Tel: 47060

Aloha Airlines, Inc (AQ)
PO Box 30028
Honolulu
Hawaii
Tel: (808) 836-4201

American Airlines, Inc (AA)
PO Box 61616
Dallas/Fort Worth Airport
Texas 75261
USA
Tel: (214) 355 1234

Ansett Airlines of Australia (AN)
501 Swanston Street
Melbourne
Victoria 3000
Australia
Tel: 343-1211

Ariana Afghan Airlines (FG)
Jadde Maiwand
(PO Box 76)
Kabul
Afghanistan
Tel: 25541, 26541

Aspen Airways Inc (AP)
Hangar No. 5
Stapleton International Airport
Denver
CO 80207
USA
Tel: (303) 398 3744

Austrian Airlines (OS)
Fontanastrasse 1
PO Box 50
A-1107 Vienna
Austria
Tel: 68 35 11

Avensa – Aerovias Venezolanas SA (VE)
Ave. Vedantea-Esq Platanol
Edf. Banco de la Contruction de Oriente
Apartado 943
Caracas
Venezuela
Tel: 562 3022

Aviaco – Aviación y Comercio SA (AO)
Maudes 51
Edificio Minister
Madrid 3
Spain
Tel: 254 36 00

Avianca – Aerovias Nacionales de Colombia SA (AV)
Av. Eldorado 93-30
Bogotá
Colombia
Tel: 63 96 28, 63 95 11

Aviateca – Empresa Guatemalteca de Aviatión Aviateca (GU)
Avenida Hincapie Aeropuerto La Aurora
Guatemala City
Guatemala
Tel: 63227/8

Bahamasair (UP)
PO Box N-4881
Nassau
Bahamas
Tel: (809) 327-8451

Balkan Bulgarian Airlines (LZ)
Sofia Airport
Sofia
Bulgaria
Tel: 66 16 90

Bangladesh Biman (BG)
Bangladesh Biman Bldg.
Motijheel
Dacca
Bangladesh
Tel: 255911

Braathens SAFE Airtransport (BU)
Ruselokkveien 26
Oslo 2
Norway
Tel: (02) 41 10 20

British Airways (BA)
PO Box 10
Heathrow Airport
Hounslow
Middx
TW6 2JA
Tel: 01- 759 5511 (Main Switchboard)
370 5411 (Fares and Reservations)
370 4255 (Business Travel Enquiries)
759 2525 (Flight Enquiries)
(0293) 36321 (Charters – Concorde and Subsonic)
Customer Relations W49
West London Terminal
PO Box 115
Cromwell Road
London
SW7 4ED
Tel: 01-370 8881

British Caledonian Airways (BR)
Caledonian House
Crawley
Sussex
RH10 2XA
Tel: (02930) 27890

British Midland Airways (BD)
Donington Hall
Castle Donington
Derby
DE7 2SB
Tel: (0332) 810552 (Reservations)
(0332) 810742 (Administration)

British West Indian Airways – BWIA (BW)
International Airport
Piarco
Trinidad

Brit Air (Brittany Air) (DB)
Morlaix Airport
BP 156
29 20 4 Morlaix
France
Tel: (98) 62 10 22
Room 743
North Roof Office Block
Terminal Bldg.
Gatwick Airport
Gatwick
West Sussex
Tel: (0293) 50 20 44

Brymon Airways (BC)
Plymouth City Airport
Plymouth
Devon
Tel: (0752) 707023

Cameroon Airlines (UY)
BP 4092
United Republic of Cameroon
Tel: 42 25 25

Caribbean Airways (IQ)
Grantly Adams Airport
Christchurch
Barbados
West Indies
Tel: 86031

Cathay Pacific Airways (CX)
Swire House
9 Connaught Road C
Hong Kong
Tel: 5-250011

Cayman Airways Ltd (KX)
PO Box 11
George Town
Grand Cayman
BWI
Tel: 9-2673

China Airlines Ltd (CI)
131 Nanking East Road
Taipei
Taiwan
Tel: 7722626-50

Comair – Commercial Airways (Pty) Ltd (MN)
PO Box 7015
Banaero Park
1622 South Africa
Tel: 973 2911

Continental Airlines Inc (CO)
2929 Allen Parkway
PO Box 4607
Houston
TX 77210-4607
USA
Tel: (713) 630-5000

CP Air (CP)
1 Grant McConachie Way
Vancouver International Airport
BC V7B 1V1
Canada
Tel: (604) 270-5211

Cruzeiro do Sul SA Servicios Aereos (SC)
128 Avenida Rio Branco 128
PO Box 190
Rio de Janeiro
Brazil
Tel: 224 0522

Cubana – Empresa Consolidada Cubana de Aviación (CU)
Calle 23 No. 64
Havana
Cuba
Tel: 528 7249, 528 7069

Cyprus Airways Ltd (CY)
21 Athanasiou Dhiakou St
Nicosia
Cyprus
Tel: 43054

Danair A/S (DX)
Kastruplund Gade 13
DK-2770 Kastrup
Copenhagen
Denmark
Tel: (01) 51 50 55

Dan-Air Services Ltd (DA)
Newman House
Victoria Road
Horely
Surrey
Tel: 01-680 1011
J. Varrier – Associate Director, Scheduled Services

Delta Air Lines, Inc (DL)
Hartsfield Atlanta Airport
Atlanta
GA 30320
USA
Tel: (404) 346 6011

Deta – Linhas Aereas de Moçambique, LAM (TM)
Maputo International Airport
PO Box 2060
Maputo
Mozambique
Tel: 73-20-38

Dominicana de Aviación (DO)
Calle Leopoldo Navarro No. 61
Edificio San Rafael
Apartado de Correos No. 1415
Santo Domingo
Republic of Dominica
Tel: (809) 687-7111

Douglas Airways Pty Ltd (DZ)
PO Box 1179
Boroko
Papua New Guinea
Tel: 253 499

Eastern Air Lines, Inc (EA)
Miami International Airport
Miami
FL 33148 USA
Tel: (305) 873 2211

East–West Airlines Ltd (EW)
323 Castlereagh Street
Sydney NSW
Australia
Tel. (02) 20940

Egyptair (MS)
Almaza Airport
Heliopolis
Cairo
Egypt
Tel: 64255/9

El Al Israel Airlines (LY)
Ben Gurion Airport
Tel Aviv
Israel
Tel: (03) 976111

Ecuatoriana (EU)
Torres de la Almagro
Avenida Colon y Reina Victoria
Quito
Ecuador
Tel: 54900

Ethiopian Airlines (ET)
PO Box 1755
Addis Ababa
Ethiopia
Tel: 18 22 22

Faucett – Compania de Aviación SA (CF)
Jiron Union No. 926
Lima
Peru
Tel: 275 000

Fiji Air (PC)
Fiji Trading Co Bldg
PO Box 1259
Victoria Parade
Suva
Fiji
Tel: Suva 22 666-7

Finnair (AY)
Mannerheimintie 102
00250 Helsinki 25
Finland
Tel: 90/410411

Frontier Airlines, Inc (FL)
8250 Smith Road
Denver
CO 80207 USA
Tel: (303) 329 5151

Garuda Indonesian Airways (GA)
Jalan Ir H Djuanda 15
Djakarta
Indonesia
Tel: 370709

Ghana Airways (GH)
Ghana House
PO Box 1636
Accra
Ghana
Tel: 64851

GB Airways (GT)
Cloister Building
Gibraltar
Tel: 79200

Great Lakes Aviation Ltd (GX)
RR3
Box 115A
Spencer
Iowa 51301
USA
Tel: (712) 262 7734

Gulf Air (GF)
PO Box 138
Bahrain
Arabian Gulf
Tel: 322200

Guyana Airways Corporation (GY)
32 Main Street
PO Box 10223
Georgetown
Guyana
Tel: (02) 67201-4, 59490-4

Hawaiian Airlines (HA)
Honolulu International Airport
PO Box 30008
Honolulu
HI 96820
USA
Tel: (808) 525-5511

Iberia – Lineas Aereas de España (IB)
130 Calle Velazquez
Madrid 6
Spain
Tel: 2619100, 2619500

Icelandair (FI)
Reykjavik Airport
Reykjavik
Iceland
Tel: 1-27800

Indian Airlines (IC)
Airlines House
113 Gurdwara Rakabganj Road
New Delhi-110001
India

Iran Air (IR)
Mehrabad Airport
Tehran
PO Box 2600
Islamic Republic of Iran
Tel: 9111

Iraqi Airways (IA)
Saddam Hussain International Airport
Baghdad
Iraq
Tel: 887 2400

Japan AirLines – JAL (JL)
Daini Tekko Building
1-8-2 Marunouchi
Chiyoda-Ku
Tokyo
Japan
Tel: (03) 457 111 (International flights)
(03) 457 1181, 456 2111 (Domestic).

Jamahiriya Libyan Arab Airlines (LN)
PO Box 2555
Tripoli
Socialist People's Libyan Arab Jamahiriya
Tel: 602083/5, 602092/

JAT (See Yugoslav Airlines)

Karair oy (KR)
Mannerheimintie 102
SF-00250 Helsinki 25
Finland

Kenya Airways (KQ)
PO Box 19002
Nairobi
Kenya
Tel: 822171

KLM Royal Dutch Airlines (KL)
55 Amsterdamseweg
PO Box 7700
1117 ZL Schiphol Airport
Netherlands
Tel: (020) 499123

Kodiak Western Alaska Airlines Inc (KO)
PO Box 2457
Kodiak
Alaska 99615
USA
Tel: 486-3271

Korean Airlines (KE)
KAL Bldg
PO Box 868
Namdaemun-ro
118-2-ga
Chung-gu
Seoul
Republic of Korea
(CPO Box 864)
Tel. 771-66

Kuwait Airways Corporation (KU)
PO Box 394
International Airport
Kuwait
Tel: 711166/70

LAB (See Lloyd Aereo Boliviano)

LACSA – Lineas Aereas Costarricenses SA (LR)
La Uruca
San José
Costa Rica
Tel: 32-35-55

LADECO – Línea Aérea del Cobre (UC)
Aeroport Arturo Merino Benítez
Avda. Bulnes 147
PO Box 13740
Santiago
Chile
Tel: 86400

LAN-Chile Línea Aérea Nacional de Chile (LA)
Avenida Aguirre Cerda 5300
Los Cerillos Airport
Maipu
Santiago
Chile
Cas 147D
Tel: 573615

LAP – Líneas Aéreas Paraguayas (PZ)
Olivia 455
Asunción
Paraguay
Tel: 91-040/1/2

LIAT (1974) Ltd (LI)
PO Box 819
Coolidge Airport
Antigua
West Indies
Tel: (809) 462-0700

Lloyd Aereo Boliviano – LAB (LB)
Casilla 132
Cochabamba
Bolivia
Tel: 5911, 5912, 5913

Loftleidir Icelandic Airlines, Inc (LL)
Reykjavik Airport
Reykjavik
Iceland
Tel: 20-200

LOT – Polish Airlines (LO)
9 Warynskiego
Warsaw
Poland
Tel: 21-70-21, 28-10-09

Lufthansa – German Airlines (LH)
2/6 Von Gablenzstrasse
D-5000 Cologne 21
German Fed Rep
Tel: (0221) 8261

Luxair – Société Luxembourgeoise de Navigation Aérienne SA (LG)
L-2987
Luxembourg
Tel: 47981

Malaysian Airline System – MAS (MH)
PO Box 10513
Kuala Lumpur
Malaysia
Tel: 208844/203355/768555

Malev – Hungarian Airlines (MA)
1051 Budapest
Roosevelt Ter 2
Hungary
Tel: 189-033, 172 911

Mexicana – Compania Mexicana de Aviación, SA (MX)
Balderas 36
Mexico City 1
DF Mexico
Tel: 585-24-22

Middle East Airlines (ME)
PO Box 206
Beirut International Airport
Beirut
Lebanon
Tel: 272 220/316 316

Beirut: Customer Relations Manager (Address as above); London:
Fernand Saada, Vice-President (UK and Ireland)
MEA
80 Piccadilly
London
W1V 0DR
Tel: 01-493 6321

Mount Cook Airlines (NM)
47 Riccarton Road
Private Bag
Christchurch
New Zealand
Tel: 482-099

Iew York Air Inc (NY)
Iangar No. 5
.a Guardia Airport
'lushing
Iew York 15530
ISA
'el: (212) 895-5372

Iigeria Airways Ltd (WT)
.irways House
MB 1024
keja
.agos
Iigeria
'el: 900476

LM Cityhopper BV (HN)
O Box 7700
17 ZL Schiphol Airport (East)
msterdam
etherlands
'el: (020) 49 2227

ordair Ltd (ND)
320 Blvd Graham
ille Mont-Royal
uebec
anada
3P 3C8
el: (514) 340 8100
ranch Office:
O Box 4000
Iontreal International Airport
orval
uebec
anada
I4Y 1B8
el: (514) 367 7700

orcanair (NK)
Iangar No. 3 Mobile 3
askatoon
askatchewan
anada
7L 5X4
el: (306) 653 3702

Iorthwest Orient Airlines Inc (NW)
Iinneapolis/St Paul International Airport
t Paul
Iinnesota 55111
ISA
el: (612) 726 2111

lympic Airways (OA)
6 Syngrou Avenue
1741 Athens
reece
el: (01) 9292-111

zark Air Lines, Inc (OZ)
ambert Field
t Louis
IO 63415
ISA
el: (314) 895-6600

Pacific Southwestern Airlines
3225 North Harbor Drive
San Diego
CA 92112
USA

Pacific Western Airlines Ltd (PW)
Ste. 2800-700-2nd Street SW
Calgary,
Alberta
Canada
T2P 2W2
Tel: (413) 294-2000

Pakistan International Airlines – PIA (PK)
Avenue Centre
264 R.A. Lines
Stretchen Road
Karachi
Pakistan
Tel: 511061 Ext. 629

Pan American World Airways, Inc (PA)
Pan Am Building
200 Park Avenue
New York
NY 10017
USA
Tel. (212) 880 1234

In UK:
Consumer Action Representative
Pan Am
Terminal Three
Heathrow Airport
Hounslow
Middx.
Tel: 01-759 2595

PEOPLExpress Airlines Inc
Newark International Airport
North Terminal
Newark
New Jersey 07114
USA
Tel: (201) 961-2931

UK:
North Roof Office Block
Gatwick Airport
London
Gatwick
West Sussex
RH6 0BX

Philippine Airlines (PR)
6780 Ayala Avenue
PAL Building
Makati, Rizal
Philippines
Tel: 88-10-61

Piedmont Aviation, Inc (PI)
PO Box 2720
Smith Reynolds Airport
Winston-Salem
North Carolina 27156
USA
Tel. (919) 767-5100

Polynesian Airlines Ltd (PH)
Air Centre
Beach Road
Apia
Western Samoa
(PO Box 599)
Tel: Apia 21261

Prinair – Puerto Rico International Airlines, Inc (PQ)
International Airport
Isla Verde
Puerto Rico
00913
Tel: 791-2505

Qantas Airways Ltd (QF)
Qantas House
International Square
(Box 489 G.P.O.)
Sydney
NSW 2000
Australia
Tel: 236 3636

Quebecair Inc (QB)
PO Box 490
Dorval Airport,
Dorval
Quebec
Canada
H4Y 1B5
Tel: (514) 631-9802

Reeve Aleutian Airways, Inc (RV)
Passenger Service
W. 4700 Internal Airport Road
Anchorage
Alaska 99502
USA
Tel: (902) 243 1112

Republic Airlines Inc (RI)
7500 Airline Drive
Minneapolis
MN 55450
USA
Tel: (612) 726 7411

Royal Air Maroc (AT)
Aeroport Anfa
Casablanca
Morocco
Tel: 364184
Mr. El Alami, Public Relations

Royal Dutch Airlines (See KLM)

Royal Jordanian Airlines (See ALIA)

Sabena Belgian World Airlines (SN)
35 Rue Cardinal Mercier
B-100 Brussels
Belgium
Tel: (02) 511 90 60

SAHSA – Servicio Aereo de Honduras, S (SH)
PO Box 129
Tegucigalpa DC
Honduras
Tel: 22-0490, 22-4656, 22-8634

SAS – Scandinavian Airlines System (SK)
Ulvsundavagen 193
S-161 87 Stockholm-Bromma
Sweden
Tel: 780 10 00

SATA – Sociedad Acoriana de Transport Aereos (SP)
Av Infante D. Henrique 55
Ponta Delgada
Azores
Tel. 22311/5

Saudi Arabian Airlines (SV)
Saudia Building
PO Box 620
Jeddah
Saudi Arabia
Tel: 25222 (ten lines)

Singapore Airlines Ltd (SQ)
25 Airline House
Airline Road
Singapore 1781
Tel: 5423333

Solomon Islands Airways Ltd (IE)
PO Box 23
Honiara
Solomon Islands
Tel: 595

South African Airways (SA)
Airway Towers
39 Wolmarans Street
Braamfontein
Johannesburg
Rep of South Africa
Tel: 713-3167

Southwest Airlines, Inc
PO Box 37611
Dallas
TX 75235
USA
Tel: (512) 696-1221

Sudan Airways (SD)
PO Box 235
Ganhouria Avenue
Khartoum
Sudan
Tel: 70325
In UK:
Regional Manager UK and Europe
Sudan Airways
12 Grosvenor Street
London
W1X 9FB
Tel: 01-629 3385

Suriname Airways Ltd (PY)
PO Box 2029
Zorg en Hoop Airfield
Paramaribo
Suriname
Tel: 73939

Swissair – Swiss Air Transport Co Ltd (SR)
PO Box 8058
Zürich
Switzerland
Tel: 812 12 12

Syrian Arab Airlines (RB)
PO Box 417
Damascus
Syria
Tel: 220700/01, 231838

TAAG – Angola Airlines (DT)
PO Box 79
Rua Luis de Camoes
123-6 Andar
Luanda
Angola
Tel: 23523

Taca International Airlines, SA (TA)
Edificio Caribe 20
San Salvador
El Salvador
Tel: 23-2244

Talair Pty Ltd (GV)
PO Box 108
Goroka E.H.P.
Papua New Guinea
Tel: 721355

TAN Airlines – Transportes Aereos Nacionales, SA (TX)
Tegucigalpa
Honduras
Tel: 286 74/5

TAP Air Portugal (TP)
Edificio 25
Aeroporto (Apartado 5194)
Lisbon-5
Portugal
Tel: 899121

Tarom – Romanian Air Transport (RO)
Otopeni Airport
Bucharest
Socialist Rep of Romania
Tel: 794910, 333137

Thai Airways International (TG)
89 Vibhavadi Rangsit Road
Bangkok
Thailand
Tel: 5110121

THY – Turkish Airlines (TK)
Cumhuriyet Caddesi 199-201
Harbiye
Istanbul
Turkey
Tel: 462050, 462061

Transamerica Airlines (TV)
Oakland International Airport
PO Box 2504
Airport Station
Oakland
California 94614
USA
Tel: (415) 577-6000

Trans-Australia Airlines (TN)
50 Franklin Street
PO Box 2806 AA
Melbourne
Vic 3000
Australia
Tel: 345 1333

In UK:
49 Old Bond Street
London
W1V 4DO
Tel: 01-493 2557

Transbrasil S/A Linhas Aereas (TR)
Aeroporto de Congonhas Hangar
São Paulo
Brazil
Tel: 240-7411

Trans-Provincial Airlines Ltd (CD)
Box 280
Prince Rupert BC
Canada
Tel: 627-1341

Trinidad and Tobago Air Services (See BWIA)

Tunis Air (TU)
113 Ave. de la Liberté
Tunis
Tunisia
Tel: 288 100

TWA – Trans World Airlines, Inc (TW)
605 Third Avenue
New York
NY 10016
USA
Tel: (212) 557-3000

Uganda Airlines Corp (QU)
Kimathi Road
PO Box 5740
Kampala
Uganda
Tel: 32990

United Airlines (UA)
PO Box 66100
Chicago
IL 60666
USA
Tel. (312) 569 3000

United Air Services pty Ltd (UE)
PO Box 31184
Braamfontein 2017
Johannesburg
Rep of South Africa
Tel. 39-5681

US Air, Inc (AL)
Washington National Airport
Washington DC 20001
USA
Tel: (703) 892-7000

UTA – Union de Transports Aériens (UT)
50 rue Arago
92806 Puteaux
France
Tel: 776 4133
UTA Direction Générale

Varig – Brazilian Airlines (RG) 042
365 Av. Almirante Sylvio Noronha
Rio de Janeiro G.B. 20 000
Brazil ZC-00
Tel: 222 5141

VASP – Viacao Aerea São Paulo (VP)
Edificio VASP
04695 São Paulo
Brazil
Tel: (011) 533-7011

VIASA – Venezolana Internacional de Aviación SA (VA)
Torre Viasa
Av. Sur 25
Plaza Morelos, Los Caobos
Caracas
Venezuela
Tel: 572 9522

Virgin Atlantic
2 Woodstock Street
London W1
Tel: 409 2882

Western Airlines, Inc (WA)
Los Angeles Airport
6060 Avion Drive
PO Box 92005
World Way Postal Center
Los Angeles
CA 90009
USA
Tel. (213) 646-2345

Wien Air Alaska, Inc (WC)
18000 Pacific Highway 50
Seattle
WA 98188
USA
Tel: (206) 433 5294
and 4100 International
4100 International Airport
Anchorage
AK 99502
USA
Tel: (907) 243-2400

Windward Island Airways International NV (WM)
V-113160
PO Box 288
Philipsburg
St Maarten
Netherland Antilles
Tel: 4210

Yugoslav Airlines – JAT (JU)
Sava Centar
Milentija Popovica 9
Objekt B/111 Juzni Ulaz
11070 Belgrade
Yugoslavia
Tel: 683-164

Zambia Airways (QZ)
Ndeke House
Haile Selassie Avenue
Box 30272
Lusaka
Zambia
Tel: 213674

In UK:
K. S. Kongwa
Zambia Airways
163 Piccadilly
London
W1V 9DE
Tel: 01-491 7521

US Offices of Foreign International Airlines

Aeroflot, 1101, 16th Street, NW, Washington, DC 20036
Aeromexico, 8400 NW 52nd St, Miami, FL 33166
Aeroperu, 327 SE First St, Miami, FL 33131
Air Canada, 25th Floor, 116 6A Ave of the Americas, New York, NY 10036
Air Afrique, 1350 Ave of the Americas, New York, NY 10022
Air France, 666 Fifth Ave, New York, NY 10019
Air India, 345 Park Ave, New York, NY 10022
Air Pacific, Suite 108, 32133 West Lindero Canyon Road, Westlake Village, CA 91363.
ALIA – Royal Jordanian, 535 Fifth Ave, New York, NY 10017
Alitalia, 666 Fifth Ave, New York, NY 10019
Ariana Afghan Airlines, 535 Fifth Ave, Suite 1609, New York, NY 10017
British Airways, 245 Park Ave, New York, NY 10017
BWIA, 610 Fifth Ave, New York, NY 10020
China Airlines, 1648 K St, NW, Washington, DC 20006
Dominicana de Aviación, 1270 Ave of the Americas, New York, NY 10020
Egyptair, 720 Fifth Ave, New York, NY 10019
El Al Israel Airlines, 850 Third Ave, New York, NY 10022
Ethiopian Airlines, 200 E 42nd St, New York, NY 10017
Finnair, 10 E 40th St, New York, NY 10016
Faucett, 7720 NW 36th St, Suite 28, Miami FL 33166
Guyana Airways, 6555 NW 36th St, Suite 205-7, Miami, Florida
JAL Co, 655 Fifth Ave, New York, NY 10022
Kenya Airways, 424 Madison Ave, 6th Floor, New York, NY 10017
KLM, 437 Madison Ave, New York, NY 10017
LAB Airlines, 310 Madison Ave, Ste. 1316, NY 10017
LADECO, 2680 One Biscayne Tower, Miami, Florida
Icelandic Airlines, 630 Fifth Ave, New York, NY 10020
LOT-Polish Airlines, 500 5th Ave, New York, NY 10010
Lufthansa, 680 Fifth Ave, New York, NY 10019
MAS, Suite 2044, 420 Lexington Ave, New York, NY 10170
Malev, 630 Fifth Ave, New York, NY 10020
Middle East Airlines, 680 Fifth Ave, New York, NY 10019
Olympic Airways, 647 Fifth Ave, New York, NY 10022
Pakistan International, Suite 1027, 17th St NW, Washington, DC20036
Philippine Airlines, 212 Stockton St, San Francisco, CA 94108
Prinair, International Airport, Isla Verde, PR 00913
Qantas, 360 Post St, San Francisco, CA 94108
Republic Airlines, 7500 Airline Dr, Minneapolis, MN 55450
Royal Air Maroc, 680 Fifth Ave, New York, NY 10019
SAS, 138-02 Queen Blvd, Jamaica, NY 11435
Saudi Arabian, 747 Third Ave, New York, NY 10017
Singapore Airlines, 8370 Wilshire Blvd, Beverly Hills, Los Angeles, CA 90211-2381
South African Airways, 605 Fifth Ave, New York, NY 10017
Swissair, 608 Fifth Ave, New York, NY 10020
Taca International, PO Box 20047, New Orleans, LA 70141
TAN, PO Box 222, Miami Int. Airport, Miami, FL 33148
Thai Airways, Suite 230, 630 Fifth Ave, New York, NY 10111
UTA, 9841 Airport Blvd, Suite 1000, Los Angeles, CA 90045
Zambia Airways, Suite 812, 370 Lexington Ave, New York, NY 10017

London Area Airline Offices (not Headquarters)

Airline	*Address*	*Telephone numbers* *Fares*	*Reservations*	*Admin. & Enqs.*
Aer Lingus	223 Regent Street, London W1		437 8000	
Aeroflot	69/72 Piccadilly London W1V 9HH	492 1756	493 7436	493 7436/9
Aeromexico	Morley House, 320 Regent Street, London W1R 5AD	637 4108	637 4108	637 4107
Air Afrique	117 Piccadilly, London W1	493 4881	629 6114	493 4881
Air Algérie	10 Baker Street, London W1		487 5709	487 5903
Air Canada	140 Regent Street, London W1	759 2636	759 2636	759 2636
Air France	158 New Bond Street, London W1Y 0AY	499 9511	499 9511	499 9511
Air India	17 New Bond Street, London W1Y 0AY		491 7979	493 4050
Air Jamaica	6 Bruton Street, London W1		493 4455	
Air Lanka	1 Little Argyl Street London W1	439 0181	439 0291	
Air Malta	24 Pall Mall, London SW1	839 5872	930 2612	937 7181
ALIA Jordanian	177 Regent Street, London W1		734 2557	437 9465
Alitalia	205 Holland Park Ave, London W11 4XB		602 7111	759 2510
American Airlines	7 Albermarle Street, London W1	629 8817	629 8817	629 8817
Ariana Afghan Airlines	164 Piccadilly, London W1	493 1411	493 1411	493 1411
Austrian Airlines	50 Conduit Street, London W1		439 0741	
Avianca	2 Hanover Street, London W1	408 1889	408 1889	408 1889
BWIA	20 Regent Street, London SW1Y 4PH	839 7155	734 3796	839 7155
Balkan Bulgarian	322 Regent Street, London W1R 5AB		637 7637	637 7638
Bangladesh Biman	25 Sackville Street, London W1	439 0362	439 0362	439 0362
British Airways	PO Box 10, Heathrow Aiport, Hounslow Middlesex TW6 2JA	370 4255	370 4255	759 2525
British Caledonian	215 Piccadilly, London W1V 0PS		668 4222	434 1501/2
British Midland	Heathrow Airport, Hounslow, Middlesex		581 0864	745 7321

Airline	Address	Telephone numbers Fares	Reservations	Admin. & Enqs.
CP Air	62 Trafalgar Square, London WC2		930 5664	930 5664
Caribbean Airways	6 Bruton Street, London W1		493 6251	491 3817
Cathay Pacific Airways	123 Pall Mall, London SW1	930 444	930 7878	930 7878
Cyprus Airways	29 Hampstead Road, London NW1		388 5411	388 5424
Czechoslovak Airlines	17 Old Bond Street, London W1	499 6444	499 6442	499 6445
DanAir	36 New Broad Street, London EC2			638 1747
Delta Airlines	140 Regent Street, London W1	688 0935	668 0935 688 9135	668 0935
Eastern Airlines	49 Old Bond Street, London W1	409 3376	409 3376	491 7879
Egypt Air	296 Regent Street, London W1		580 5477	580 5477
El Al	185 Regent Street, London W1	437 8237	437 9255	439 2564
Ethiopian Airlines	85 Jermyn Street, London W1	930 9152	930 9152	930 9152
Finnair	130 Jermyn Street, London SW1Y 4UJ	930 3941	930 3941	930 3571
Ghana Airways	12 Old Bond Street, London W1X 4BL	499 0201	499 0201	
Gulf Air	73 Piccadilly, London W1	409 1951	409 1951	409 0191
Iberia	29 Glasshouse Street, London W1		437 5622 439 7539	437 9822
Icelandair	73 Grosvenor Street, London W1X 9DD	499 9971	499 9971	499 9971
Iranair	73 Piccadilly, London W1		409 0971	491 3565
Iraqi Airways	4 Lower Regent Street, London SW1Y 4PE	930 1155	930 1155	930 1155
Japan Airlines	Hanover Court, 5 Hanover Street, London W1R 0DR	629 9244	408 1000	629 9244
KLM	Time and Life Bldg, New Bond Street, London W1Y 0AD	560 6155	568 9144	568 9144
Kenya Airways	16 Conduit Street, London W1	409 0185	409 0277	409 3121
Korean Airlines	66 Haymarket, London SW1	930 6513	930 6513	930 6513
Kuwait Airlines	52 Piccadilly, London W1	409 3191	499 7681	409 3191
LAN Chile	32 St. James's Street, London SW1			839 3893
Libyan Arab Airlines	88 Piccadilly, London W1	499 0381	491 7851	499 1016

Airline	*Address*	*Fares*	*Telephone numbers* *Reservations*	*Admin. & Enqs.*
Lloyd Aereo Boliviano	4th Floor, 27 Cockspur Street, London SW1	930 1442	930 1442	930 1442
Loftleidir Icelandic	73 Grosvenor Street, London W1	499 9971	499 9971	499 9971
Lufthansa	23–26 Piccadilly, London W1	408 0322	408 0442	408 0322
Malaysian Airline System	25/27 St. George Street, Hanover Square, London W1R 9RE		491 4542	499 6286
Malev Hungarian	10 Vigo Street, London W1	439 0577	439 0577	439 0577
Middle East Airlines	80 Piccadilly, London W1	493 6321	493 5681	493 6321
New Zealand Air	15 Charles Street II, London SW1		930 1088	930 4951
Nigeria Airways	12 Conduit Street, London W1	629 3717	629 3717	493 9726
Northwest Orient	Reservations: 37 Sackville Street, London W1 Sales Office: 49 Albermarle Street, London W1	409 3422	439 0171	
Olympic Airways	141 New Bond Street, London W1Y 0BB		493 1233	493 7262
Pakistan International	45 Piccadilly, London W1	741 8066	734 5544	759 2544
Pan Am	193 Piccadilly, London W1	409 0688	409 0688	409 0688
People Express Airlines	North Roof Office Block, Gatwick Airport, London Gatwick, Sussex RH6 0BX			
Philippine Airlines	Centrepoint, 103 New Oxford Street, London WC1A 1QD	379 6855	379 6855	379 6855
Polish Airlines/Lot	313 Regent Street, London W1	580 5037	580 5037	580 5037
Qantas	169 Regent Street, London W1	995 4811	995 7722	955 1361
Royal Air Maroc	174 Regent Street, London W1	439 8854	439 4361	439 8854
Royal Brunei Airlines	Brunei House, 35 Norfolk Square, London W2		402 6049	402 6904
Sabena	36 Piccadilly, London W1	437 6960	437 6950	437 6950
Saudia/Saudi Arabian	171 Regent Street, London W1	995 7755	995 7777	995 7755

Airline	Address	Fares	Telephone numbers Reservations	Admin. & Enqs.
SAS	52 Conduit Street, London W1	437 7086	734 4040	734 6777
Singapore Airlines	143–147 Regent Street, London W1R 7LB	439 8111	995 5411	439 8111
South African Airways	251–259 Regent Street, London W1R 7AD	437 0932	734 9841	437 9621
Sudan Airways	12 Grosvenor Street, London W1X 9FB	629 3385	499 8101	499 068718
Swiss Air	Swiss Centre, 10 Wardour Street, London W1X 3FA	734 6737	439 4144	439 4144
Syrian Arab Airlines	27 Albermarle Street, London W1X 3FA	493 2851	493 2851	499 4707
Tap Air Portugal	38 Gillingham Street, London SW1	828 2092	828 0262	828 2092
Thai International	41 Albemarle Street, London W1	499 9113	499 9113	499 7953
Turkish Airlines THY	11 Hanover Street, London W1	499 9240	499 9247/8	499 9247/8
Trans Australia	49 Old Bond Street, London W1X 4DU	995 1344	995 1344	493 2557
TWA	Reservations: 200 Piccadilly, London W1		636 4090	636 4090
	Administration: 214 Oxford Street, London W1	636 5411		
Tunis Air	24 Sackville Street, London W1	734 7644	734 7644	734 7644
United Airlines	20 Savile Row, London W1	734 9281	734 9281	734 9281
UTA	177 Piccadilly, London 1	493 4881	629 6114	493 4881
Varig Brazilian	16 Hanover Street, London W1		629 5824	629 9406
VIASA Venezuelan	19 Grosvenor Street, London W1	629 1223	629 1223	629 1223
Virgin Atlantic	2 Woodstock Street, London W1	409 2882	409 2429	409 2882
Yugoslav Airlines	201 Regent Street, London W1	734 3614	734 0320	734 6252
Zambia Airlines	163 Piccadilly, London W1	491 7521	492 0658	491 7521

* Please note that this is not a complete list of airlines with London offices, but contains only the larger ones. For all other airlines, please refer to the list of Airlines of the World on page 646.

Airline Two-Letter Codes

Letters are often used in timetables, brochures and tickets to identify airlines. These are the codes for the main airlines, in alphabetical order.

Code	Airline
AA	American Airlines, Inc
AC	Air Canada
AF	Air France
AH	Air Algérie
AI	Air India
AL	US Air/Allegheny Commuter Airlines
AM	Aeromexico
AN	Ansett Airlines of Australia
AO	Aviaco
AP	Aspen Airways, Inc
AR	Aerolineas Argentinas
AS	Alaska Airlines
AT	Royal Air Maroc
AV	Avianca
AY	Finnair
AZ	Alitalia
BA	British Airways
BD	British Midland Airways
BL	Air BVI Ltd
BM	Aero Trasporti Italiani
BN	Braniff Inc
BP	Air Botswana Pty Ltd
BR	British Caledonian Airways
BT	Airlines of Northern Australia
BU	Braathens SAFE Airtransport
BW	BWIA International
CD	Trans-Provincial Airlines Ltd
CF	Faucett
CI	China Airlines
CO	Continental Airlines, Inc.
CP	CP Air
CU	Cubana Airlines
CX	Cathay Pacific Airways
CY	Cyprus Airways
DA	Dan-Air Services
DJ	Air Djibouti
DL	Delta Air Lines
DO	Dominicana De Aviación
DS	Air Sénégal
DT	TAAG-Angola Airlines
DW	DLT Deutsche Regionale Luftverkehrsgesellschaft m.b.H. German Domestic Airlines
DX	Danair
DZ	Douglas Airways
EA	Eastern Air Lines
EI	Aer Lingus (Irish)
ET	Ethiopian Airlines
EU	Empresa Ecuatoriana de Aviación
EW	East-West Airlines
FG	Ariana Afghan Airlines
FI	Flugfelag-Icelandair
FJ	Air Pacific
FL	Frontier Airlines
GA	Garuda Indonesian Airways
GB	Airborne Express
GF	Gulf Air
GH	Ghana Airways

Code	Airline
GJ	Ansett Airlines of South Australia
GL	Greenlandair
GN	Air Gabon
GT	Gibraltar Airways
GU	Aviateca
GV	Talair
GY	Guyana Airways Corp.
HA	Hawaiian Airlines
HB	Air Melanesie
HN	NLM – Dutch Airlines
IA	Iraqi Airways
IB	Iberia
IC	Indian Airlines
IE	Solomon Islands Airways
IF	Interflug
IG	Alisarda
II	Imperial Airways
IJ	Touraine Air Transport
IP	Airlines of Tasmania
IQ	Caribbean Airways
IR	Iranair
IS	Eagle Air
IT	Air Inter
IY	Yemen Airways
IZ	Arkia-Israeli Airlines
JL	Japan Air Lines
JM	Air Jamaica
JU	Yugoslav Airlines – JAT
KE	Korean Airlines
KL	KLM – Royal Dutch Airlines
KM	Air Malta
KO	Kodiak Western Alaska Airlines
KQ	Kenya Airways
KR	Karair
KU	Kuwait Airways
KX	Cayman Airways
LA	Lan Chile
LB	Lloyd Aero Boliviano
LG	Luxair – Luxembourg Airlines
LH	Lufthansa German Airlines
LI	Liat
LJ	Sierra Leone Airways
LL	Bell Air
LM	ALM – Antillean Airlines
LN	Libyan Airlines
LO	LOT – Polish Airlines
LR	LACSA
LV	LAV – Linea Aeropostal Venezolana
LX	Crossair
LY	El Al Israel Airlines
LZ	Bulgarian Airlines – Balkan
MA	Malev – Hungarian Airlines
MD	Air Madagascar
ME	Middle East Airlines/Airliban
MH	Malaysian Airline System
MK	Air Mauritius
MN	Commercial Airways
MR	Air Mauritaine
MS	Egyptair

Code	Airline
MX	Mexicana de Aviación
MY	Air Mali
NC	Newair
ND	Nordair
NE	Executive Airlink
NF	Air Vanuatu
NH	All Nippon Airways
NI	American International Airways
NL	Air Liberia
NM	Mt Cook Airlines
NU	Southwest Airlines
NW	Northwest Orient Airlines
NY	New York Air
NZ	Air New Zealand – Domestic
OA	Olympic Airways
OD	Emerald Airlines, Inc
OG	Air Guadeloupe
OH	Comair
OK	CSA-Czechoslovak Airlines
OM	Air Mongol – MIAT
ON	Air Nauru
OP	Air Panama Internacional
OS	Austrian Airlines
OZ	Ozark Air Lines, Inc
PA	Pan American World Airways
PB	Air Burundi
PC	Fiji Air
PD	Pem Air Ltd
PE	People Express Airlines
PH	Polynesian Airlines
PI	Piedmont Aviation
PK	Pakistan International Airlines
PL	Aeroperu
PR	Philippine Airlines
PV	Eastern Provincial Airways
PW	Pacific Western Airlines
PY	Suriname Airways
PZ	LAP – Lineas Aereas Paraguayas
QB	Quebecair, Inc
QF	Qantas Airways
QL	Lesotho Airways
QM	Air Malawi
QU	Uganda Airlines
QZ	Zambia Airways
RA	Royal Nepal Airlines
RB	Syrian Arab Airlines
RG	Varig, SA
RH	Air Zimbabwe
RI	Eastern Airlines of Australia
RJ	ALIA – Royal Jordanian Airlines
RK	Air Afrique
RN	Royal Air Inter
RO	Tarom – Romanian Air Transport
RV	Reeve Aleutian Airways
SA	South African Airways
SC	Cruziero Do Sul SA
SD	Sudan Airways
SH	SAHSA – Servicio Aereo De Honduras SA
SK	SAS – Scandinavian Airlines System
SN	Sabena – Belgian World Airlines
SP	SATA
SQ	Singapore Airlines
SR	Swissair
SU	Aeroflot Soviet Airlines
SV	Saudi Arabian Airlines
TA	Taca International Airlines
TC	Air Tanzania Corp
TE	Air New Zealand – International
TK	THY – Turkish Airlines
TM	Deta – LAM, Linhas Aereas De Mozambique
TN	Trans-Australia Airlines
TP	TAP Air Portugal
TS	Transports Aeriens du Benin TAB
TU	Tunis Air
TW	TWA – Trans World Airlines, Inc
TX	TAN Airlines
TY	Air Calédonie
TZ	Sansa
UA	United Airlines
UB	Burma Airways Corp.
UC	Ladeco
UE	United Air Services
UI	Flugfelag Nordurlands
UK	Air UK
UL	Air Lanka
UN	East Coast Airways
UP	Bahamasair
UT	UTA
UY	Cameroon Airlines
UZ	Air Resorts Airlines
VA	VIASA
VH	Air Volta
VP	VASP
VT	Air Polynésie
VU	Air Ivoire
WA	Western Airlines
WC	Wien Air Alaska, Inc
WM	Windward Island Airways International
WT	Nigeria Airways
WY	Oman Aviation Services
XY	Munz Northern Airlines, Inc
XZ	Air Tasmania
YK	Cyprus/Turkish Airlines
ZV	Air Midwest
ZP	Virgin Air

Airport/City Codes

For a job well done, you'll surely want to ADD (Addis Ababa) a TIP (Tripoli) to the payment. When things go wrong, such as when someone tries to ROB (Monrovia) you or to put the wrong TAB (Tobago) on your luggage, you'll certainly get MAD (Madrid). To ensure that LAX (Los Angeles) luggage handling does not MAR (Maracaibo) your trip, it's a good idea to familiarize yourself with the relevant airport/city code. A selection of these codes are given below, in alphabetical order of city. Have a good flight and may your luggage go with you.

A

ABR Aberdeen, SD, USA
ABJ Abidjan, Ivory Coast
AUH Abu Dhabi, Utd. Arab Emirates
ACA Acapulco, Mexico
ADD Addis Ababa, Ethiopia
ADE Aden, Dem. Rep. Yemen
AGA Agadir, Morocco
ALG Algiers, Algeria
ALY Alexandria, Egypt
AMS Amsterdam, Netherlands
ANC Anchorage, AK, USA
AXA Anguilla, Leeward Is.
ESB Ankara, Turkey
ANU Antigua, Leeward Is.
AUA Aruba, Neth. Antilles
ASU Asunción, Paraguay
ATH Athens, Greece
AIY Atlantic City, NJ, USA
ATL Atlanta, GA, USA
AKL Auckland, New Zealand

B

BGW Baghdad-Saddam Intl., Iraq
BAH Bahrain, Bahrain
BKK Bangkok, Thailand
BJL Banjul, Gambia
BGI Barbados, Barbados
BBQ Barbuda, Leeward Is.
BCN Barcelona, Spain
BSL Basel, Switzerland
BTR Baton Rouge, LA, USA
BEY Beirut, Lebanon
BFS Belfast, N. Ireland
BEG Belgrade, Yugoslavia
BEN Benghazi, Libya
TXL Berlin, West-Tegel Apt, Germany Fed. Rep.
BER Berlin West, Germany Fed. Rep.
BDA Bermuda, Atlantic Ocean
BDI Bird Island, Seychelles
BOG Bogotá, Colombia
BOI Boise, ID, USA
BOM Bombay, India
BOS Boston, MA, USA
BSB Brasilia, Brazil
BNE Brisbane, QL, Australia
BRU Brussels, Belgium
BUH Bucharest, Romania
BUD Budapest, Hungary
EZE Buenos Aires, Argentina Airport
BUF Buffalo, NY, USA

C

CAI Cairo, Egypt
CCU Calcutta, India
YYC Calgary, Alberta, Canada
CAP Cap Haitien, Haiti
CCS Caracas, Venezuela
ORD Chicago, IL, USA
CUU Chihuahua, Mexico
CVG Cincinnati, OH, USA
BKL Cleveland, OH, USA – Lakefront Airport
CLE Cleveland, OH, USA – Hopkins Airport
CGN Cologne/Bonn APT, Germany Fed. Rep.
CMB Colombo, Sri Lanka
CMH Columbus, OH, USA
CPH Copenhagen, Denmark
CUR Curaçao, Neth. Antilles

D

DKR Dakar, Senegal
DFW Dallas/Ft. Worth, TX, USA
DAM Damascus, Syria
DAR Dar es Salaam, Tanzania
DEL Delhi, India
DEN Denver, CO, USA
DSM Des Moines, IA, USA
DET Detroit City Airport, MI, USA
DTT Detroit, MI, USA
DTW Detroit – Metropol APT, MI, USA
HLP Djakarta, Indonesia
DXB Dubai, Utd. Arab Emirates
DUS Düsseldorf, West Fed. Rep.

E

EDI Edinburgh, UK
YEG Edmonton, Alberta, Canada
ELP El Paso, TX, USA
EBB Entebbe, Uganda

F

FAI Fairbanks, AK, USA
FDF Ft. de France, Martinique
FRA Frankfurt, Germany Fed. Rep.
FLL Ft. Lauderdale, FL, USA

G

YQX	Gander, Nfld., Canada
GVA	Geneva, Switzerland
GIB	Gibraltar
PIK	Glasgow, Scotland – Prestwick Airport
GEO	Georgetown, Guyana
GET	Grand Turk, Turks & Caicos Is.
GHC	Great Harbour Cay, Bahamas
GND	Grenada, Windward Is
GDC	Guadalajara, Mexico
GUM	Guam Island, Guam
GAO	Guatanamo, Cuba
GUA	Guatemala City, Guatemala

H

YHZ	Halifax, NS, Canada
HAM	Hamburg, Germany Fed. Rep.
YHM	Hamilton, Ontario, Canada
HAJ	Hanover, Germany Fed. Rep.
HRE	Harare, Zimbabwe
MDT	Harrisburg, PA, USA
BDL	Hartford Bradley Int., MA, USA
HAV	Havana, Cuba
HEL	Helsinki, Finland
HMO	Hermosillo, Mexico
ITO	Hilo, Hawaii, HI, USA
HNL	Honolulu, Int., HI, USA
HOU	Houston, Hobby Airport, TX, USA
IAH	Houston – Intercont. APT, TX, USA

I

IND	Indianapolis, IN, USA
INN	Innsbruck, Austria
ISB	Islamabad, Pakistan
IST	Istanbul, Turkey

J

JED	Jeddah, Saudi Arabia
JRS	Jerusalem
JNB	Johannesburg, South Africa
JNU	Juneau, AK, USA

K

KBL	Kabul, Afghanistan
MCI	Kansas City, MO, USA
KHI	Karachi, Pakistan
KRT	Khartoum, Sudan
KIN	Kingston, Jamaica
FIH	Kinshasa, Zaïre
ADQ	Kodiak, AK, USA, Kodiak Airport
KUL	Kuala Lumpur, Malaysia
KWI	Kuwait, Kuwait

L

LOS	Lagos, Nigeria
LPB	La Paz, Bolivia
LAS	Las Vegas, NV, USA
LED	Leningrad, USSR
LIM	Lima, Peru
LIS	Lisbon, Portugal
LGW	London, UK – Gatwick Airport
LHR	London, UK – Heathrow Airport
YXU	London, Ontario, Canada
LAX	Los Angeles, CA, USA
LUN	Lusaka, Zambia

M

MAA	Madras, India
MAD	Madrid, Spain
AGP	Malaga, Spain
MLA	Malta, Malta
MAO	Manaus, Brazil
MAN	Manchester, UK
MDL	Mandalay, Burma
MAR	Maracaibo, Venezuela
MRS	Marseille, France
YXH	Medicine Hat, Alberta, Canada
MEL	Melbourne, Australia
MEM	Memphis, TN, USA
MEX	Mexico City, Mexico
MIA	Miami, FL, USA
MGC	Michigan City, IN, USA
MXP	Milan, Italy – Malpenso Airport
MKE	Milwaukee, WI, USA
MSP	Minneapolis/St. Paul, MN, USA
ROB	Monrovia, Liberia
MBJ	Montego Bay, Jamaica
MUD	Montevideo, Uruguay
YIL	Montreal, Quebec, Canada
MNI	Montserrat, Leeward Is.
SVO	Moscow, USSR – Sheremetyevo Airport
MUC	Munich, Germany Fed. Rep.

N

NAN	Nadi, Fiji
NBO	Nairobi, Kenya
NAP	Naples, Italy
BNA	Nashville, TN, USA
NAS	Nassau, Bahamas
EWR	New York – Newark Airport, NY, USA
MSY	New Orleans, LA, USA
NPT	Newport, RI, USA
JFK	New York, NY, USA – J F Kennedy Airport
LGA	New York, NY, USA – La Guardia Airport
NYC	New York, NY, USA
NCE	Nice, France
OME	Nome, AK, USA
NUE	Nuremberg, Germany

O

OKA Okinawa – Naha Airport, Japan
OKC Oklahoma City, OK, USA
OSA Osaka, Japan
OSL Oslo, Norway
YOW Ottawa, Ontario, Canada

P

PPG Pago Pago, American Samoa
PTY Panama City, Panama
PPT Papeete, Tahiti
CDG Paris, France – Charles de Gaulle Airport
ORY Paris, France – Orly Airport
PER Perth, WA, Australia
PHL Philadelphia, PA, USA
PHX Phoenix, AZ, USA
PSA Pisa, Italy
PIT Pittsburgh, PA, USA
PTP Pointe-à-Pitre, Guadeloupe
PAP Port-au-Prince, Haiti
PDX Portland, OR, USA
POS Port of Spain, Trinidad
PRG Prague, Czechoslovakia
YPA Prince Albert, SA, Canada
YXS Prince George, BC, Canada
YPR Prince Rupert, BC, Canada

Q

YQB Quebec City, QU, Canada
UIO Quito, Ecuador

R

RBA Rabat, Morocco
RGN Rangoon, Burma
REK Reykjavik, Iceland
GIG Rio de Janeiro, Brazil
FCO Rome, Italy – Leonardo da Vinci Airport

S

YYT St. Johns, Nfld., Canada
SKB St. Kitts, Leeward Is.
SLC Salt Lake City, UT, USA
SFO San Francisco, CA, USA
SJO San José, Costa Rica
SIG San Juan, Puerto Rico – Isla Grande Airport
SJU San Juan, Puerto Rico – Isla Verde Airport
SAL San Salvador, El Salvador
SCL Santiago, Chile
SDQ Santo Domingo, Dominican Rep
CHG São Paulo, Brazil – Congonhas Airport
CGH São Paulo, Brazil – Viracopos Airport
YXE Saskatoon, SA, Canada
SEA Seattle, WA, USA – HM Jackson Airport
SEL Seoul, Korean Republic
SHA Shanghai, P R China
SNN Shannon, Ireland Rep.
SIN Singapore, Singapore
SOF Sofia, Bulgaria
ARN Stockholm, Sweden – Arlanda Airport
STR Stuttgart, West Germany
SYD Sydney, NSW, Australia

T

TPE Taipei, Taiwan
TPA Tampa, FL, USA
THR Tehran, Iran
TLV Tel Aviv, Israel
TCI Tenerife, Canary Is
TAB Tobago, Trinidad & Tobago
HND Tokyo, Japan – Hanedo Airport
NRT Tokyo, Japan – Narita Airport
YYZ Toronto, Ontario, Canada
TIP Tripoli, Libya
TUN Tunis, Tunisia
TRN Turin, Italy

V

YVR Vancouver, BC, Canada
YYJ Victoria, BC, Canada
VIE Vienna, Austria

W

WAW Warsaw, Poland
DCA Washington, DC, USA – National Airport
IAD Washington, DC, USA – Dulles Airport
YWG Winnipeg, MN, Canada

Z

ZAG Zagreb, Yugoslavia
ZRH Zurich, Switzerland

Airport Taxes

Please note that the prices in brackets are the equivalent to the local currency in British pounds at the time of going to press but are subject to currency fluctuations. They cannot be accurate but are offered as a guideline.

Country	Tax
Afghanistan	None
Algeria	None
America Samoa	None
Andorra	None
Anti & Barbuda	£4
Argentina	None
Australia	A.$20 (£12.90)
Austria	None
Bahamas	US $5 per adult. $2.50 per child.
Bahrain	None
Bangladesh	*Taka* 100.000 (£2.87)
Barbados	Barb. $16 (£5.75)
Belgium	None
Belize	US $4
Bermuda	US $5
Benin	None
Bolivia	US $14
Botswana	None
Brazil	None
British Virgin Is.	US $5
Bulgaria	None
Burma	K.15.00 (£1.30)
Burundi	1000 Bur. Francs (£6.12)
Cameroons	None
Canada	£5–£7
Cayman Is.	US $5
Cent. African Republic	4200 AF (£7.23)
Chad	4200 AF (£7.23)
Chile	US $5
China	None
Colombia	US $15
Congo	None
Costa Rica	US $10
Cyprus	£1.50C (£1.89)
Czechoslavakia	None
Denmark	None
Djibouti	None
Dominica	ECD 8.00 (£5.63)
Dominican Republic	DOP $10.00 (£7.19)
East Carribean	EC $5–10 (£3.52–£7.04)
Ecuador	US £5
Egypt	None
El Salvador	SAC 25.00 (£7.02)
Equatorial Guinea	None
Ethiopia	None
Fiji	F$5.00 (£3.40)
Finland	None
France	None
Gabon	None
The Gambia	£4
Fed. Rep. of Germany	None
Germany (DR)	None
Ghana	None unless ticket issued in Ghana then it is GHC 25 ($0.51)
Gibraltar	£1.00
Great Britain	None
Greece	None
Grenada	ECD 5.00 (£1.33)
Guinea	GS 200.0 (£6.09)
Guyana	GYD 50 (£9.57)
Haiti	US $10
Hawaii	None
Hong Kong	HK $100 (£9.18) per adult. HK $50 (£4.59) per child
Honduras	10% on international tickets
Hungary	None
Iceland	None
India	IR 50 (£3.26) Subcontinent. IR 100 (£6.52) Others.
Indonesia	4,000 Rup. (£2.80)
Ireland	None
Iran	None
Iraq	None
Israel	US $10
Italy	None
Ivory Coast	None
Jamaica	J. $20 (£3.62)
Japan	2,000 Yen (£6.16)
Jordan	3 JD (£5.76)
Kenya	Sh. 100 (£5.09)
Korea	*Won* 3,500 (£3.14)
Kuwait	None
Lebanon	LEL 20 (£2.48)
Lesotho	LSM 2.00 (£1.13)
Liberia	US $10
Libya	None
Luxembourg	None
Macao	None unless from Hong Kong then it is HK$8 (£0.73)
Madagascar	FMG 1500 (£2.08)
Malawi	MWK 10.00 (£5.26)
Malayasia	RGT 15 (£4.64)
Mali	MFR 5,000 (£4.16)
Malta	None
Mauritania	None
Mauritius	£6
Mexico	MEP 600.00 (£2.34)
Morocco	None
Nepal	None
Netherlands	None
New Zealand	US $2
Nicaragua	US $10
Niger	None
Nigeria	None
N. Ireland	None
Norway	None
Oman	*Rial* 4 (£8.16)
Pakistan	PAR 100.00 (£5.22)

Panama	BAL 10.00 (£7.19)	Tonga	TOP 5.00 (£3.25)
Papua New Guinea	NGK 10.00 (£6.66)	Trinidad & Tobago	TT $20 (£6.00)
Paraguay	None	Tunisia	£0.40
Peru	US $10	Turkey	None
Philippines	PHP 100 (£5.20)	Uganda	UGS 1000.00 (£2.46)
Poland	None		
Portugal	ESP 1000 (£5.11)	United Arab Emirates	None
Qatar	None	US Virgin Is.	None
Rwanda	AKZ 200 (£1.45)	United States	£2.00
Saudi Arabia	None	Upper Volta (Burkina Faso)	CFA 3,500 (£6.03)
Sénégal	CFA 1000 (£1.72)		
Sierra Leone	SLE 10.00 (£2.89)	Uruguay	US $2.50
Seychelles	None	Vanuatu	VUV 600 (£4.76)
Singapore	S$12 (£4.08)	Venezuela	VBO 47.00 (£2.19)
Solomon Is.	SBD 5.00 (£2.49)	Vietnam	US $5.00
Som. Dem. Rep.	SOM 50.00 (£2.04)	People's Dem. Rep. of Yemen	DYD 1.450 (£1.76)
South Africa	None		
Soviet Union	None	Yemen Arab Rep.	YEM 50 (£6.85) International flights. YEM 10 (£1.37) Domestic.
Spain	None		
Sri Lanka	Rs 100 (£2.87)		
Sudan	SUL £10 (£5.34)		
Swaziland	None		
Sweden	None	Yugoslavia	YUD 150 (£0.78)
Switzerland	None	Zaïre	None
Syria	None	Zambia	ZMK 10.00 (£4.25) International. ZMK 4.00 (£1.70) Domestic.
Tahiti	None		
Tanzania	£2.00		
Thailand	120 *Baht* (£3.76)		
Togo	None	Zimbabwe	None

International Flight Distances

London (Heathrow) to	Direct Flight Distance (Most direct aircraft & route) (km)	(miles)	London (Heathrow) to	Direct Flight Distance (Most direct aircraft & route) (km)	(miles)
Amsterdam	370	231	Milan	974	609
Ankara	2,824	1,765	Montreal	5,186	3,241
Athens	2,400	1,500	Moscow	2,491	1,557
Auckland	18,246	11,404	Munich	944	590
Beirut	3,459	2,162	Nairobi	6,795	4,247
Belgrade	1,704	1,065	Naples	1,618	1,011
Berlin	950	594	New York	5,504	3,440
Bombay	7,165	4,478	Nice	1,035	647
Brussels	347	217	Oslo	1,198	749
Buenos Aires	11,064	6,915	Palma	1,333	833
Cairo	3,501	2,188	Paris	344	215
Calcutta	7,933	4,958	Perth	14,413	9,008
Copenhagen	978	611	Prague	1,040	650
Dublin	446	279	Rangoon	8,930	5,581
Frankfurt	650	406	Rio de Janeiro	9,194	5,746
Geneva	749	468	Rome	1,451	907
Helsinki	1,835	1,147	San Francisco	8,562	5,351
Hong Kong	9,582	5,989	Singapore	10,806	6,754
Johannesburg	9,014	5,634	Stockholm	1,437	898
Kano, Nigeria	4,429	2,768	Sydney	16,909	10,568
Karachi	6,296	3,935	Tokyo	9,528	5,955
Lisbon	1,552	972	Toronto	5,672	3,545
Madrid	1,238	774	Vancouver	7,531	4,707
Malta	2,088	1,305	Washington	5,864	3,665
Mauritius	9,720	6,075	Zurich	784	490

Travel: Consumer Advice and Complaints

Association of British Travel Agents (ABTA)
55 Newman Street
London W1
Tel: 01-637 2444

Professional body of the British travel industry, with a bond to protect travellers against financial collapse.

Air Transport Association of America
1709 New York Avenue NW
Washington
DC 20006
USA

Of all the ATA activities, safety is foremost. Other objectives include the improvement of passenger and cargo traffic procedures, economic and technical research, and action on legislation affecting the industry.

Air Transport Users' Committee
129 Kingsway
London
WC2B 6NN
Tel: 01-242 3882

Small committee, funded by CAA, but acting independently, to investigate complaints.

American Society of Travel Agents
Consumer Affairs Department
4400 MacArthur Blvd NW
Washington
DC 20007
USA

Can be asked to vouch for, or establish the authenticity of travel agents, or to help with tour problems. Mediates disputes between consumers and travel related suppliers as well as providing 'reliability' checks on the travel industry.

Aviation Consumer Action Project
PO Box 19029
Washington
DC 20036
USA

Was created by Ralph Nader and promotes commercial air safety and passenger rights protection. Those with related concerns may contact the office to discover how to go about 'constructive complaining' to resolve problems.

Civil Aviation Authority
CAA House
45 Kingsway
London WC2
Tel: 01-379 7311

Overall controller of the British airline industry.

Civil Aeronautics Board
Office of Congressional, Community and Consumer Affairs
1825 Connecticut Avenue NW
Washington
DC 20428
USA
Tel: Consumer Office: (202) 673 6047
Congressional Office: (202) 673 5961

Represents the Board of Congress, local and state governments, airline offices, civic organizations and the national and local news media. Maintains two-way communication between Board and Congress on legislative, policy and constituent service issues and on matters which affect the air service to communities. The OCCA is also responsible for informing, assisting and protecting consumers in their dealings with the air transportation industry and informally resolving possible violations of the Federal Aviation Act and other regulations.

Federal Aviation Administration
Community and Consumer Liaison Division
APA-400
800 Independence Avenue SW
Washington
DC 20591
USA

Deals with complaints about air safety.

International Airline Passengers' Association (IAPA)
2nd Floor
Francis House
Francis Street
London
SW1P 1DF
Tel: 01-828 5841
Telex: 8813743 IAPA G
8952930 IAPA G

and

PO Box 660074
Dallas
TX 75266-0074
USA
Tel: (214) 438 8100 (Texas) or toll free
(800) 527 5888 (USA)
Telex: 792962 IAPA IRVG

Consumer information and assistance; representation; publications and lost luggage tracking. World's oldest and largest group of frequent air travellers. Offer optional insurance (see Insurance, page 756). Members also receive preferred rates at Hertz, Avis and National/Europcar locations and 2,000 hotels/motels worldwide.

International Air Transport Association (IATA)
26 Chemin de Joinville
PO Box 160
1216 Cointrin-Geneva
Switzerland
and

West London Terminal
Cromwell Road
London
SW7 4ED
Tel: 01-370 8267/4255

Professional body of the world's travel industry offering consumer protection to travellers with member organizations.

Air Taxi/Ambulance Operators

All members of ATOA are certified by the Civil Aviation Authority and subjected to monitoring checks by that body. They comply with the Association's Code of Practice.

Air Foyle Ltd
Luton Airport
Halcyon House
Luton
Beds.
LU2 9LU
Tel: (0582) 419 792

Air Foyle is available 24 hours a day, 7 days a week to fly anytime, anywhere.

All Seasons Aviation Ltd
Straverton Airport
Cheltenham
Glos.
Tel: (03843) 77841

Offers a fully approved ambulance service for stretcher cases.

BCA (Aviation) Ltd
Expedier House
Portsmouth Road
Hindhead
Surrey
GU26 6TJ
Tel: (042873) 7740/4720

Air taxi and air ambulance work.

Cabair Air Taxis Ltd
Elstree Aerodrome
Herts.
WD6 3AW
Tel: 01-953 4411

24 hour air taxi service

Continental Flight Services Ltd
Southampton Airport
Hants.
SO9 1FQ
Tel: (0703) 610 261

Provide a 24-hour, 7 days a week service for executive air taxi and light freight cargo to destinations in UK and Europe.

Crest Aviation
Biggin Hill Airport
Biggin Hill
Westerham
Kent
Tel: (09594) 75000

Specializes in the ad hoc charter of passengers and freight. Suited to long range freight movement.

Fairflight Ltd
Biggin Hill Airport
Biggin Hill
Kent
TN16 3BN
Tel: (09594) 7651

Air taxi and air ambulance.

Falcon Jet Centre Ltd
No. 2 Maintenance Area
London Heathrow Airport
Hounslow
Middlesex
Tel: 01-897 6021

Air ambulance services.

Gatwick Air Taxis Ltd
Broadwater House
Chailey
Sussex
BN8 4JE
Tel: (082) 572 3888

Efficient and economical 24 hour air taxi and air ambulance service.

Glos Air (Charter) Ltd
Bournemouth (Hurn) Airport
Christchurch
Dorset
BH23 6DQ
Tel: (0202) 578 601

Provides fast economical travel for up to seven passengers in each of their aircraft throughou Europe, Scandinavia and North Africa.

Jointair Ltd
Executive Jet Centre
London Heathrow Airport
Hounslow
Middlesex
TW6 3AE
Tel: 01-759 9933

Executive air taxi ad hoc and contract service for passenger, cargo, courier and air ambulance. Economic and efficient over short distances the Learjets are particularly suited to long range flights to the Middle East, North and West Africa where the high altitude and speed capability shows even greater economy.

Mountleigh Air Services Ltd
Leeds/Bradford Airport
Yeadon
Leeds
LS19 7TZ
Tel: Rawdon (0532) 501 242

Specialize in pressurized air taxi and ambulance work throughout Europe and North Africa.

Northern Executive Aviation Ltd
Hangar 522
Manchester International Airport
Wilmslow
Cheshire SL9 4LL
Tel: (061) 436 6666/489 3115

One of Britain's leading air taxi companies. Multi-purpose fleet carries out passenger and/or freight flights to and from destinations throughout Europe, the Middle East, Africa, the Far East, Australia, USA, and Canada. Ambulance operations. 24 hours 7 days a week.

Omega Air Travel Ltd
Building 509
Biggin Hill Airport
Westerham
Kent
Tel: Biggin Hill (09594) 71901

Fly to Scandinavia, Europe, and North Africa. Air ambulance service.

Shell Aircraft Ltd
Shell Centre
York Road
London
SE1 7NA
Tel: 01-934 1234

Operating base: Heathrow and London.

Thurston Aviation Ltd
London Stanstead Airport
Stanstead
Essex
CM24 8QW
Tel: (0279) 815 027

One of the most experienced companies in the air taxi field. A 24 hour service operated from London Stanstead Airport serving most of Europe, North Africa and the Middle East.

Trans-Care International Ltd
(Associate Member)
193/195 High Street
Acton
London
W3 9DD
Tel: 01-993 6151

Aircraft Services

Air Transport Operators Association
Clembro House
Weydown Road
Haslemere
Surrey
GU27 2HR
Tel: (0428) 52788

The ATOA, formed in 1967, is a non-profit making business association, and includes most of the major air-taxi companies and a number of third level airlines in its membership. They carry some half-million passengers and several million kilogrammes of freight each year throughout the UK, Europe, the Middle East and North Africa. Many members operate air ambulance flights.

Air and General Finance Ltd
13 Essex House
George Street
Croydon
Surrey
CR0 1PH
Tel: 01-688 9382

Financial services are provided for all aspects of the Aviation Industry. A leading company in the provision of finance for aircraft aquisition, Air and General Finance specializes in the field of commercial, transport and business aircraft.

Air & General Services Ltd
13 Essex House
George Street
Croydon
Surrey
CR0 1PH
Tel: 01-688 9382

Suppliers of aircraft, and will purchase used equipment and act as brokers for the sale and purchase of all aircraft types.

Roebuck Air Services
Roebuck House
Somerset Way
Iver
Bucks.
Tel: (02812) 2245

Provide road and air ambulance service to the general public and any business hours with employees abroad 24 hours a day, 7 days a week.

Road

Motoring Organizations Worldwide

Andorra
Automobil Club d'Andorre
Babotcamp 4
Lavella
Tel: 20890

Algeria
Fédération Algérienne du Sport Automobile et du Karting-99
bd Salah-Bouakouir
Alger

Touring Club d'Algérie
1 Rue Al-Idrissi
Algiers
B.P. – Alger Gare
Tel. 64 08 37/53 58 10/63 30 08

Argentina
Automovil Club Argentino
1850 Avenida del Libertador
Buenos Aires 1461
Tel. 802 6061/802 7061

Touring Club Argentino
Esmeralda 605
Buenos Aires
Tel: 392 7994/392 8170

Australia
Australian Automobile Association (AAA)
212 Northbourne Ave
Canberra
ACT 2601

Automobile Association of the Northern Territory
78–81 Smith Street
Darwin NT 5790
Tel: 81 3837

The Secretary
National Roads & Motorists Association
NRMA House
151 Clarence Street
Sydney
NSW 2000

RAC of Australia
89 Macquarie Street
Sydney
NSW

RAC of Queensland
CNR Ann & Boundary Streets
Brisbane
Qld.

RAC of South Australia
41 Hindmarsh Square
Adelaide
SA

RAC of Tasmania
Cnr Patrick & Murray Streets
Hobart
Tasmania

RAC of Victoria
123 Queen Street
Melbourne
Victoria

RAC of Western Australia
228 Adelaide Terrace
Perth
WA

Austria
Österreichischer Automobil – Motorrad – und Touring Club (OAMTC)
Postfach 252
Vienna 1015
Tel: 0222/72 990

Bahamas
Bahamas Automobile Club
West Avenue
Centreville
Nassau
Tel: 325 0514

Bangladesh
Automobile Association of Bangladesh
3/B Outer Circular Road
Moghbazar
Dacca 17
Tel: 243482/402241

Barbados
Barbados Automobile Association
Room 406
Plantations Building
Broad Street
Bridgetown B.W.

Belgium
Royal Auto-Club de Belgique
53 Rue d'Arlon
B-1040
Brussels

Touring Club Royal de Belgique
44 Rue de la Loi
Brussels

Bolivia
Automóvil Club Boliviano
Avenida 6 de Agosto
2993 San Jorge
Casilla 602
La Paz
Tel. 351/667/325/325 136

Brazil
Automóvil Club de Brasil
Rua do Passeto 90
Rio de Janeiro
Tel. 252 4055, 1470 (official)

Touring Club do Brasil
Praca Maua
Rio de Janeiro
Tel. 263 5583/254 2020

Brunei
Persatuan Automobile Brunei
(Automobile Association of Brunei – AAB)
Weight and Measure Section
State Secretariat
Brunei
Tel. Bureau du Président 4659

Bulgaria
Union des Automobilistes Bulgares
6 Rue Sueta Sofia
B.P. 257
Sofia
Tel: 87 88 01/02 8800 02

Burundi
Club Automobile Burundi
B.P. 544
Bujumbuba

Canada
Alberta Motor Association
11230–110 Street
Edmonton
Alberta

Canadian Automobile Association
1175 Courtwood Cresent
Ottawa
Ontario
Tel. 237 2150

Canadian Automobile Sports Clubs, Inc
5385 Younge Street
Suite 28
PO Box 97
Willowdale
Ontario
M2N 5S7

Hamilton Automobile Club
393 Main Street East
Box 2090
Hamilton
Ontario

Manitoba Motor League
870 Empress Street
Box 1400
Winnipeg
Manitoba

Maritime Automobile Association
Haymarket Square Shopping Centre
Saint John
New Brunswick

Ontario Motor League
2 Carlton Street
Suite 619
Toronto
Ont

Quebec Automobile Club
2600 Laurier Blvd
Quebec
PQ

The Secretary
Saskatchewan Motor Club Ltd
200 Albert Street North
Regina
Saskatchewan

The British Columbia Automobile Association
PO Box 9900
Vancouver
BC

Touring Club Montreal
1425 Rue de la Montagne
Montreal
PQ

Chile
Automovil Club de Chile
195 Avenida Pedro de Valdivia
Santiago
Casilla 16695 correo 9
Santiago
Tel: (2) 74 95 16/25 80 40

Colombia
Touring y Automovil Club de Colombia
Av. Caracas No 46-64/72
Bogotá
Tel: 232 7580

Costa Rica
Automobile-Touring Club de Costa Rica
Apartado 4646
San José
Tel: 3570

Cuba
Automovil y Aero Club de Cuba
Malecon 217
Bajos
Havana

Cyprus
Cyprus Automobile Association
PO Box 2279
30 Homer Avenue
Nicosia
Tel: 52 521

Czechoslovakia
Ustredni Automotoklub CSSR
O Pletalova 29
Prague
CZ 116 31
Tel: 223 592/220 140

Denmark
Foreneda Danske Motorejere
Blegdamsvej 124
2100 Copenhagen 0
Tel: 38 21 12

Ecuador
Automovil Club del Ecuador
Av 10 de Agosto y Callejon Negrete
Quito
Tel. 37779

Automovil Club de Ecuador (Aneta)
Av Eloy Alfaro 218 y Berlin
Casilla 2830
Quito

Egypt
Automobile et Touring Club d'Egypte
10 Rue Kasr-El-Nil
Cairo
Tel: 7431 76

El Salvador
Automovil Club de El Salvador
Alemeda Roosevelt y 41 Ave Sur 2173
San Salvador
Tel: 23-8077

Automovil Club de El Salvador (ACES)
PO Box 1177
San Salvador

Ethiopia
Automobile Club Eritreo
Via Giustino de Jacobis 4-6-8
BP 1187
Asmara

Finland
Automobile and Touring Club of Finland
10 Kansakoulukatu
Helsinki 00100
Tel: 694 00 22

France
Association Française des Automobilistes
9 Rue Allatole-de-la-Forge
Paris 75017
Tel: 227 82 00

Touring Club de France
6–8 Rue Firmin-Gillet
Paris Cedex 75737
Tel: 532 22 15

Gabon
Fédération Gabonaise de Sport Automobile
Siège B.P. 695
Libreville

Représentant en Paris:
M.M. Desert
72 Rue Ampère
75017
Paris.

Ghana
The Automobile Association of Ghana
Fanum House
1 Valley View
Labadi Road
Christianborg
Accra
Tel: 75983/74229

Germany
Allemeiner Deutscher Automobile Club E.V.
8 Am Westpark 8000
München 70
Tel: 89/76 76 1

Automobilclub von Deutschland
Lyoner Strasse 16
Postfach 71 0166
D-6000 Frankfurt

Deutscher Touring Automobil Club
Amalienburgstrasse 23
8000 München 60
Tel: 89/8 11 40 48

Great Britain
The Automobile Association
Fanum House
Basingstoke
Hampshire
RG21 2EA
Tel: 20123

The Camping Club of Great Britain and Ireland Ltd
11 Lower Grosvenor Place
London
SW1W 0E4
Tel: 828 1012/7

The Caravan Club
East Grinstead House
East Grinstead
West Sussex
RH19 1UA
Tel: 26944

The Royal Automobile Club
PO Box 100
RAC House
Landsdowne Road
Croydon
CR9 2JA

The Royal Scottish Automobile Club
11 Blythswood Square
Glasgow
G2 4AG
Tel: 221 3850

Greece
Automobile et Touring Club de Grèce
2 Rue Messogion
Athen 610
Tel: 779 16 15

Touring Club Hellenique
No 12 Rue Polytechniou
Athens 103
Tel: 521 08 72

Guatemala
Club de Automovilismo y Turismo de Guatemala (Catgua)
Guatemala CA
15 Calle (A) 1251
Case postale 1337
Zona 1
Tel. 64882/64883

Hong Kong
Hong Kong Automobile Association
Marsh Road
Wanchai Reclamation
PO Box 20045
Hennessy Road Post Office
Wanchai
Tel. 5-743394/725832/728504/737474

Hungary
Magyar Autoklub
Remer Floris u 4/a
1277 Budapest PF1
Tel: 152 040

Iceland
Icelandic Automobile Association
Noatun 17
Reykjavik
Tel: (91) 299 99

India
Automobile Association of Eastern India
13 Promothesh Barua Sarani
Calcutta 700019
West Bengal
Tel: 47-9012/5133, 48-2835

Automobile Association of Southern India
38A Mount Road PB 729
Madras 6

Automobile Association of Upper India
Connaught Place
New Delhi 110001, 14 F
Tel: 40409, 44312, 42063

Federation of Indian Automobile Associations (FIAA)
76 Vir Nariman Road
1st Floor Churchgate Reclamation
Bombay 400020
Tel: 291085 (2 lines)

Western India Automobile Association
76 Vir Nariman Road
Churchgate Reclamation
Bombay 400020

Indonesia
Ikatan Motor Indonesia (IMI)
Gedung KONI
Pusat Senayan
Djakarta
Kotakpos 609
Tel: 581 1102

Iran
Touring and Automobile Club of Islamic Republic of Iran
37 Avenue Martyre
Dr. Fayaz-Bakhche
Tehran 11146
B.P. 1294 Tehran
Tel: 679 142-7

Iraq
Iraq Automobile and Touring Club
Al Mansour
Baghdad
Tel: 35862

Israel
Automobile and Touring Club of Israel
19 Petah Tikvah Road
PO Box 36144
Tel Aviv 61360
Tel: 622961/2

Italy
Automobile Club d'Italia
8 Via Marsala
Rome 00815
Tel: 4998

Federazione Italiana del Campeggio e del Caravania
Uscita 19 'Prato-Calezano'
Autostrada del sole
Via V. Emanuele 11
Florence 50041
Tel: 055-882391/882392/882393

Touring Club Italiano
10 Corso Italia
Milan
Tel: (2) 809 871

Ivory Coast
Fédération Ivorienne du Sport Automobile et des Engines Assimilées (FISA)
OI BP 3883

Jamaica
Jamaica Automobile Association (JAA)
14 Ruthven Road
Kingston 10
Tel: (92) 91 200/1

Jamaica Motoring Club
BP 49
Kingston 1

Jamaica Touring Club
PO Box 49
Kingston 10

Japan
Japan Automobile Federation
Shiba-Koen
3–5–8 Minato-ku
Tokyo 105
Tel: 436 2811

Touring Club of Japan
Daini-Maijima Bldg. 5F
1–9 Yotsuya
Shinjuku-ku
Tokyo 160
Tel: (03) 335 1692/355 1661

Jordan
Royal Automobile Club of Jordan
PO Box 920
Amman
Tel: 22467

Kenya
Automobile Association of Kenya
Nyaku House
Hurlingham
PO Box 40.037
Nairobi
Tel: 720 882

Korea South
Korea Automobile Association
1 PO Box 2008
Seoul

Kuwait
Automobile Association of Kuwait and the Gulf
PO Box 2100
Airport Road
Khaldiah
Tel: (965) 83 21 92/83 24 08/83 23 88

Kuwait Automobil and Touring Club
PO Box 2100
Airport Road
Khaldiyah

Kuwait International Touring and Automobile Club
Khaldiah
Airport Road
PO Box 2100
Kuwait
Tel. 812 539/815192/818406

Lebanon
Automobile et Touring Club du Liban
Avenue Sami Solh Kalot
PO Box 3545
Beirut
Tel. 221698/221699/229222

Libya
Automobile and Touring Club of Libya
Al Fath Blvd
Maiden-Chazala
PO Box 3566
Tripoli

Liechtenstein
Automobile Club des Furstenturs Liechtenstein
Bannholzstrasse 10
9490 Vaduz

Luxembourg
Automobile Club du Grand Duché de Luxembourg
13 Route de Long W9
Bertrange
Helfenterbruck 8080
Tel: (352) 31 10 31

Malaysia
Automobile Association of Malaysia
30 Djalan Datuk Sulaiman
Taman Tun Dr. Ismail
Kuala Lumpur
Selangor

Malawi – see Zimbabwe

Malta
Malta Automobile Federation
48 St. Publuis Street
Saint Paul's Bay

Mauritius
Automobile Association of Mauritius
Labama Bldg.
35 Rue Sir William Newton
Port Louis
Tel: 21104

Mexico
Asociacion Mexicana Automovilistica (AMA) AC
Orizaba 7, Colonia Roma
Apartado 24-486
Mexico 7, DF
Tel: 511 10 84

Asociacion Mexicana Automovilistica
Av Shapultepec 276
Mexico

Asociacion Nacional Automovilistica
Miguel E Schultz 140
Mexico 4, DF

Morocco
Royal Automobile Club Marocain
3 Rue Lemercier
BP 94
Casablanca
Tel: (212) 250030/253504

Touring Club du Maroc
3 Avenue de l'Armée-Royale
Casablanca
Tel: (212) 279 288

Nepal
Automobile Association of Nepal
Traffic Police
Ramshah Path of Opp. Sinadnar
Kathmandu
Tel: 11093-15662

Netherlands
Koninklijke Nederlandse Toeristen Bond
ANWB
Wassenaarseweg 220
BP 93200
The Hague
Tel: (70) 26 44 26

New Zealand

Automobile Association Southland, Inc
PO Box 61
Invercargill
Tel: 89 003

Automobile Association (Otago), Inc
PO Box 174
Dunedin
Tel: 775 945

Automobile Association Nelson, Inc
204 Hardy Street
Nelson
Tel: 88 339

Automobile Association of Marlborough, Inc
PO Box 104
Blenheim
Tel: 83 399

The Automobile Association
(Wairarapa), Inc
Chapel Street
Masterton
Tel: 85 006

Automobile Association South Canterbury, Inc
37 Sophia Street
Timaru
Tel: 84 189

Automobile Association (Taranaki), Inc
46 Brougham Street
New Plymouth
Tel 75 646

Automobile Association (Wanganui), Inc
PO Box 4002
Wanganui
Tel: 54 549

Automobile Association (Central), Inc
AA House
166 Willis Street
Wellington 1

Automobile Association (South Taranaki), Inc
PO Box 118
Hawera
Tel: 5095

Automobile Association (Canterbury), Inc
210 Hereford Street
PO Box 994
Christchurch
Tel: 791 280

Automobile Association (Auckland), Inc
PO Box 5
Auckland
Tel: 774 660

Motorsport Association New Zealand (MANZ)
PO Box 3793
Wellington
9 Tinakori Road
Thorndon

The New Zealand Automobile Association, Inc
PO Box 1794
Wellington
Tel: (4) 735 484

Pioneer Amateur Sports Club
Club House
188 Oxford Terrace
Christchurch

Nigeria
Automobile Club of Nigeria
24 Mercy Eneli Surulere Nigeria
Lagos
Tel: 96 05 14/96 14 78

Norway
Norge Automobil Forbund
Stopgt 2
Oslo 1
Tel: (02) 42 94 00

Oman
Oman Automobile Association
PO Box 4503
Ruwi-Muscat

Pakistan
Automobile Association of West Pakistan
14B Shah Jamal
PO Box 76
Lahore

Karachi Automobile Association (KAA)
Standard Insurance House
1 Chundrigar Road
Karachi 0226
Tel: 23 21 73

Panama
Touring Automovil Club de Panama
Av Tivoli 8
Panama City

Papua New Guinea
Automobile Association of Papua New Guinea
GPO Box 5999
Boroko
Tel: 257 717

Paraguay
Touring Automovil Club Paraguayo
25 de Mayo y Brasil
Casilla de Correo 1204
Asunción
Tel: 26 075

Peru
Touring y Automovil Club de Peru
Cesar Vallejo 699
Lima 14
Casilla 2219
Lima 100
Tel: 403270/225957

Philippines
Philippines Motor Association
689 Aurora Blvd.
Quezon City
PO Box 999
Manila
Tel: 78 01 91

Poland
Polskie Towarzystwo-Turystyczno-Krajoz-
nawcze (PTTK)
UL Senatorskall
B.P. 13
Warsaw 00.075

Polski Zwiazek Motorway
UL Kazimierzowska 66
Warsaw 02.518
Tel: (22) 49 93 61

Portugal
Automóvel Club de Portugal
Apartado 2595
Rua Rosa Araujo 24 et 26
Lisbon 1200
Tel: (19) 56 39 31/77 54 75

Qatar
Automobile Touring Club of Qatar
Beda Road
PO Box 18
Doha
Tel: 413 265/415 718

Rwanda
Auto Moto Club of Rwanda
PO Box 822
Kigali

Romania
Automobil Clubul Român
N. 27 Rue N. Beloinais
Bucharest 70 166
B.P. 3107
Tel: 59 52 70/59 50 80

San Marino
Ente di Stato per il Turismo Sport e Spettacolo
Palazzo del Turismo
Republique de Saint-Marin
Tel: (1) 992 102/3/4/5

Sénégal
Automobile Club du Sénégal
Immeuble Chambre de Commerce
Place de l'Indépendance
B.P. 295
Dakar
Tel: 266 04/08

Touring Club du Sénégal
Bldg. Air Afrique
Place de l'Indépendance
B.P. 4049
Dakar
Tel: 348 21

Secretariat d'Etat au Tourisme
3e étage
Immeuble Kebe Extension
BP 4049
Av. Jean Jaurès x Peytavin
Dakar
Tel: 22 22 26

Singapore
Automobile Association of Singapore
AA House
336 River Valley Road
PO Box 85
Killiney Road
Singapore 9
Tel: 372 444

South Africa
Automobile Association of South Africa
Corbett Place
66 de Korte Street
PO Box 596
Braamfontein
Johannesburg 2001
Tel: 28 1400

The Automobile Association of South Africa
7 Martin Hammerschlag Way
Foreshore
PO Box 70
Cape Town

Spain
Real Automovil Club de España
3 Jose Abascal 10
Madrid
Tel: (1) 447 32 00

Sri Lanka
Automobile Association of Sri Lanka
Box 338
Colombo

Ceylon Motor Sports Club
4 Hunupitiya Road
PO Box 196
Colombo 2
Tel: 26 558

Sweden
Motormännens Riksföbund
Box 5855
32 Sturegatan
Stockholm 10248
Tel: (8) 67 05 80

Svenska Turistföreningen
Box 25
Vasagaten 48
Stockholm 10120
Tel: (8) 22 72 00

Switzerland
Automobile-Club de Suisse
Wasserwerkgasse 39
3000 Berne 13

Touring Club Suisse
9 Rue Pierre Fatio
Geneva
1211 Geneva 3
Tel: (22) 37 12 12

Office National Suisse du Tourisme
Case Postale 8027
Bellariastrasse 38
Zürich
Tel: (1) 202 37 37

Zelt Club Zürich
Psfach 8627
Im Studli 9
Gruningen

Syria
Touring Club of Syria
Rue Baron
Imm Jésuites
B.P. 28
Alep
Tel: 15 210/45 847/12 230

Touring Club of Syria
Rue Salhie
Place Youssef El-Azme
B.P. 3364
Damascus

Tanzania
The Automobile Association of Tanzania
PO Box 3004
Cargen House
Maktaba Street
Dar es Salaam
Tel: 21965

Thailand
Royal Automobile Association of Thailand
151 Rachadapisek Road
Bang Khen
Bangkok 10900
Tel: (662) 511 22 30, 511 22 31

Trinidad and Tobago
Trinidad and Tobago Automobile Association
14 Woodford Street
Port of Spain
Tel: 62 27 194

Trinidad
Trinidad Automobile Association
Room 2
94 Frederick Street
Trinidad

Tunisia
National Automobile Club de Tunisie
29 Avenue Habib Bourguiba
Tunis

Touring Club de Tunisia
15 Rue d'Allemagne
Tunis
Tel: (1) 24 31 82

Turkey
Turkiye Turing ve Otomobil Kurumu
364 Sisli Meydani
Istanbul
Tel: 46 70 90

United Arab Emirates
Automobile and Touring Club for UAE
PO Box 1183
Sharjah

United States of America
American Automobile Association
8111 Gatehouse Road
Falls Church
VA 22042

American Automobile Touring Alliance
888 Worcester Street
Wellesley
Massachusetts 02181
Tel: (617) 237 5200

Uruguay
Automovil Club del Uruguay
Av Agraciada 1532
Casilla Correo 387
Montevideo
Tel: 98 47 10/13 (Club)
91 15 51, 91 12 51/2/3 (Rescue Service)

Centro Automovilista del Uruguay
Boulevard Artigas 1773
Montevideo
Tel. 42091/2, 461 31, 45016, 412528/9

Touring Club Uruguayo
Ave Uruguay 2009-2015
Montevideo
Tel. 4 48 75, 4 61 93, 4 78 09

USSR
Federacia Automobilnogo Sporta SSSR
(Federation Automobile of the USSR)
BP 395
Moscow D-362
Tel. 4918 661

Intourist
Dept. of International Organizations
16 Marx Prospect
Moscow 103009
Tel: 203 69 62

Vatican City
Commission pour la Pastorale des Migrations et du Tourisme
Palais Saint-Calixte
Tel: (6) 698 7131

Venezuela
Touring y Automovil Club de Venezuela
Centro Integral
Santa Rosa de Lima
Locales 11, 12, 13 y 14
Apt. de Correos 68102
Caracas
Tel: 91 63 73

Vietnam
Automobile Club de Vietnam
17 Duong Ho Xuan Huong
Saigon
Tel: 23273

Yugoslavia
Auto-Moto Savez Jugoslavise
Ruzveltova 18
B.P. 66
Beograd 11001
Tel: (11) 401 699

Zaïre
Office National du Tourisme
Coins Blvd. du Bojuin et Avenue de Ritona
B.P. 9502
Kinshasa
Tel: 2 24 17, 2 58 28

Zaïre Automobile Federation
Bldg. Forescom 118
Avenue du Port
BP 2491
Kinshasa

Zimbabwe
Automobile Association of Zimbabwe
57 Samora Machel Avenue
PO Box 585
Harare C1
Tel: 70 70 21 (Agent for Malawi)

Main Car Rental Companies

Avis-Rent-a-Car
World Headquarters
Avis Rent a Car System, Inc
900 Old Country Road
Garden City
New York
NY 11530
USA

Avis House
Station Road
Bracknell
Berks.
RG12 1HZ
Tel: (0344) 426644

4420 Côte de Liesse Road
Montreal
Quebec
H4N 2V5
Canada

140 Pacific Highway
N. Sydney
NSW 2060
Australia

Avis in one of the world's largest car rental companies, operating in over 100 countries.

Budget-Rent-a-Car International Inc
International House
85 Great North Road
Hatfield
Hertfordshire
AL9 5EF
Tel: (07072) 60321

One of the top three car and van rental companies in the world, with 2,300 offices in 85 countries.

Europcar International
B.P. 23
92223 Bagneaux
Cedex
France

Central Reservation – UK and Worldwide
Bushey House
High Street
Bushey
Herts.
WD2 1RE

735 Main Street
Johnson City
New York
NY 13790
USA

Hertz-Rent-a-Car
Headquarters
Hertz System Inc
660 Madison Avenue
New York
NY 10021
USA
Tel: (212) 980 2121

Radnor House
1272 London Road
Norbury
London
SW16 4XW
Tel: 01-679 1777

Hertz-Rent-a-Car is the world's largest vehicle rental and leasing company, operating a network of 43,000 locations in 119 countries.

InterRent International
Head Office
InterRent Autovermeitung GmbH
International System Division
Tangstedeter Landstrasse 81
2000 Hamburg 62
Germany, Federal Rep.

InterRent/Swan National Ltd
305/307 Chiswick High Road
London
W4 4HH
Tel: 01-995 9242

Dollar Rent a Car Systems, Inc
World Headquarters
6141 W. Century Blvd.
PO Box 45048
Los Angeles
CA 90045
USA
Tel: (213) 776 8100

World Travel Headquarters Pty Ltd
Kindersley House
33–35 Bligh Street
Sydney 2000,
NSW
Australia

Vehicles – Accessories/Spares/ Outfitting

ABC Equipment
The Green
Clayton
Doncaster
DN5 7DD
Tel: (0977) 43103
Telex: 547291

Are suppliers of all Land Rover and Range Rover spares, specializing in export. Will ship to all parts of the world at short notice. Special arrangements for expedition requirements.

Auto Accessories
66 Avenue de la Grande Armée
75017 Paris
France
Tel: 380 13 86

All car accessories, sand ladders, jerry cans, air filters.

Brownchurch (Land Rovers) Ltd
Hare Row
off Cambridge Heath Road
London
E29 BY
Tel: 01-729 3606
Telex: 299397 BRNCH

Cover all Land Rover needs for trips anywhere, including the fitting of jerry cans and holders, sand ladders, sump and light guards, crash bars, winches, water purifying plants, roofracks (custom-made if necessary), overdrive units. They also supply new vehicles and offer a service, maintenance and spares service for Land and Range Rovers.

Dick Cepek Inc
5302 Tweedy Blvd
South Gate
CA 90280
USA
Tel: (213) 566 5171

Leading 4WD tyre specialists. Also has warehouse full of camping and off-road accessories. Free catalogue for addresses in the US and Canada. Others send $2.00 for air mail postage.

S.E.E. A. Framery
8 Route Nationale
94440 Santeny
France
Tel: (1) 386 06 64

Jeep, Dodge, G.M.C. parts and spares

Four Wheel Drives
304 Middlesborough Road
Blackburn South
Vic. 3130
Australia
Tel. (03) 89 0509

Manual winches and Land Rover spares.

Michelin Tyre plc
81 Fulham Road
London
SW3 6RD
Tel: 01-589 1460

Tyres, maps, guides

RAC Motoring Services Ltd
PO Box 100
RAC House
Lansdowne Road
Croydon
Surrey
CR9 2JA

Sells a range of maps, atlases, guides and touring aids, including headlamp deflector sets, emergency windscreens, holdalls and even Linguaphone records.

Société Schneebeli-Chabaud
8 Rue Proudhon
93210 La Plaine Saint-Denis
France

Vehicle air-conditioning and heating systems.

Tyre Services (Aust.) Pty Ltd
971 Ipswich Road
Moorooka
Brisbane
Qld. 4105
Australia
Tel: (07) 392 27 66

PO Box 4
Moorooka
Qld. 4105

Branches at:
Sunshine Coast (071) 435 288
Mackay (079) 513 277
Townsville (077) 794 299
Cairns (070) 519 375

Queensland's largest off-road equipment specialists.

Safariquip
See Equipment: Living, Camping and Outdoors page 624.

Vehicles: Purchase, Hire & Conversion

Caravaning and Camping-Cars & Motor-Homes
7 Rue Aude
92210 Saint-Cloud
France
Tel: (1) 771 91 71

Have camping vehicles and motor homes for sale and hire and will undertake conversions.

Cross Country Vehicles
Unit 22
Bridge Street Mill
Witney
Oxon
Tel: (0993) 76622

Sell and convert vehicles, prepare them for safari use. Range Rover and Land Rover specialists – new and used vehicles – and any other 4WD vehicle too. They offer service, special preparation, conversion parts (new and reconditioned, mail order). Mail order list free application.

Dunsfold Land Rovers Ltd
Alfold Road
Dunsfold
Surrey
Tel: (048 649) 567

Offers free advice to those contemplating overland travel; expedition hardware, air conditioning, left-hand drive conversions, comprehensive stores, re-building to owner's specifications; and sales of new and second hand Land Rovers.

Garage Boursault
11 Rue Boursault
75017 Paris
France
Tel: 293 65 65

Specializes in preparation and fitting out of Land Rovers and Range Rovers.

Harvey Hudson
Woodford
London
E18 1AS
Tel: 01-989 66 44

Land Rover specialists, suppliers of new and used vehicles to expeditions.

Land Rover Ltd
Direct Sales Department
Lode Lane
Solihull
West Midlands
B92 8NW
Tel: 021-743 42 42

Manufacturers of Land Rovers and Range Rovers. Purchase must be through authorized dealers.

Manchester Garages Ltd
Oxford Road
Manchester
M13 0JD
Tel: 061-224 7301

Service/Sales/Parts.

Mobile Holiday Hire
1a Grosvenor Road
Hanwell
London W7

149 Broadway
West Ealing
London W13
Tel: 01-567 6155 and 579 4146

Supply cars, mini-buses, motor caravans and vans for holiday transport

Scotty's
PO Box 21609
Concord
CA 94521
USA

Parts, sales and service. Land Rover, Leyland.

STRAKIT
Bonville
Gellainville
2860 Chartres
Tel: (37) 28 54 82

Prepares vehicles for expeditions and overland travel and sells accessories.

V.A.G. (UK) Ltd
Yeomans Drive
Blakelands
Milton Keynes
MK14 5AN

Autorent Manager
V.A.G. (UK) Ltd
95 Baker Street
London
W1M 1FB

Have a rental programme called 'Autorent'. Involved with the whole range of Volkswagen and Audi passenger cars. The conversion companies they approve are: Richard Holdsworth Conversions Ltd., Auto-Sleepers Ltd., Auto Homes (UK) Ltd., and Devon Conversions Ltd.

Vehicles: Shipment

Hermann Ludwig GmbH & Co
Head Office:
Billstrasse 180
D-2000 Hamburg 28
Germany, Federal Republic
Tel: (040) 78 10 01

PO Box 10 02 40
D-2000 Hamburg 1
Germany, Federal Republic

Eagle House
161–189 City Road
London
EC1V 1LB
Tel: 01-251 0601

53 Park Place
Suite 1101
New York
NY 10007
USA
Tel: (212) 608 4140

Uni-Ocean Forwarding Co. Ltd.
Samwon Bldg. Annex
2nd Floor,
Suite 205
12-1 Bukchang-Dong
Chung-Ku
Seoul
Korea
Tel: 778-0131/5

Agents for Hermann Ludwig GmbH.

V. B. Perkins & Co Pty
Box 1019
Darwin
NT 5794
Australia

Operate a roll-on/roll-off vehicle shipping service between Singapore and Darwin.

R. G. Shaw Shipping Ltd
11–13 Southwark Street
London SE1
Tel: 01-638 3566

Agents for many lines throughout the world, handling cargo (not passenger-accompanied).

Malay States Shipping Co. Pte. Ltd
Shipbrokers and Shipping Agents
79 Robinson Road
26-00, CPF Bldg.
Singapore 0106
Republic of Singapore
Tel: 2203266
Telex: RS24057 AB: MASSCO

Branches at Kuala Lumpur, Port Kelang, Penang, Pasir Gudang. Agents for B.P. Shipping Ltd. Yangming Marine Transport Corp. (Yang Ming Line), V. B. Perkins & Co Pty. Ltd., Taiwan Navigation Co. Ltd.

P. T. Helu-Trans
Cik's Building, 3rd Floor
84–86 Jalan Cikini Raya
Jakarta Pusat
Indonesia
Tel: 32 46 79, 32 51 75

Agents for Hermann Ludwig GmbH.

100 Albert Road
South Melbourne 3205
Vic.
Australia
Tel: (03) 690 21 00

Handle all kind of transportation worldwide. Deal especially with the shipment of passenger cars by air or sea all over the world. The most frequent shipments are to Canada, the East and West coast of the US, Central America, Australia, New Zealand, West Africa, The Middle East, and to the Far East (Japan, Taiwan, the Philippines).

Kuehne & Nagel, Inc
Suite 7751
One World Trade Center
New York
NY 10048
U.S.A.

One of the largest shipping agents in the US, with offices in all major ports.

Driving Requirements Worldwide

Countries	*Any Bond Required*	*Special Permits*	*Special Motor Insurance*	*Fuel Rationing*
Afghanistan	No	International	No	No
Algeria	Need to get Algerian insurance for the car	International	Algerian Insurance	No
American Samoa	No	Valid driving licence	Need minimum liability – Rental cars have it	No
Andorra	No	No	Green Card insurance	No
Antigua	No	Driving permit obtained at Police Station by showing valid driving licence	No	No
Anti & Barbuda	No	Drivers Permit obtained from Police Stations. Cost £2	No	No
Argentina	No	Valid International licence	No	No
Australia	Need 'Triptych' or a '*carnet de passage en Douane*' will cover up to 12 months	No	No	No
Austria	No	No	Must have third-party insurance	No

Bahamas	Yes, if vehicle to be in country for 6 months or less	No, up to 3 months. After this need a Bahamian drivers licence	Insurance against injury or death is compulsory	No
Bahrain	20% from price of car – give to Customs	Internat. acceptable after Police clearance		
Bangladesh	*Carnet de passage*	Valid International Driving Licence	No	No
Barbados	Need to apply to the Controller of Customs, Bridgetown	Visitors Driving Permit	No	No
Belgium	No	Valid National Driving Licence	No	No
Belize	No	No	No	No
Bermuda	Cars older than 6 mnths cannot be imported	Bermuda Driving Licence req. after 30 days residence	Third Party automobile liability	No
Benin		International		
Bolivia	Proof that you will be taking the car out again	Internat. if issued by member of Federacion Inter-Am de Touring y Automovil clubs	No	No
Botswana	Vehicle should be correctly registered and licensed in home country	Need to be over 18 – can drive on valid driving licence up to 6 months	Third Party Risk	No
Brazil	No	International Licence	Third Party	No fuel on Sundays or after 8.00pm every day

Countries	*Any Bond Required*	*Special Permits*	*Special Motor Insurance*	*Fuel Rationing*
British Virgin Islands	No	BVI Temporary Licence	No	No
Bulgaria	No	Valid Drivers Licence	Green Card Insurance	No
Burma	Entry by overland route not allowed	No	No	No
Cameroon	*Carnet de passage*	International Driving Licence	No	No (can be difficult to obtain)
Canada	No	No	No	No
Cayman Islands	Duty at 27.5% charged but refunded if re-exported within 12 mnths	International Driving Licence	Third Party	No
Central African Republic	Need a *Carnet*	International		Fuel Shortages
Chad	*Carnet*	International	Green Card or Land All Risk	Fuel expensive
Chile	No	International Licence	No	No
China	No foreign vehicles allowed except trade vehicles			
Colombia	*Carnets de passage en Douane*	International Driving Licence	No	No
Congo		International		

Costa Rica	No	Valid Drivers Licence	Third Party Insurance	No
Cuba	NB No cars allowed in	Foreign or International		
Cyprus	No	Valid Drivers Licence	Special Insurance obtained at port	No
Czechoslovakia	No	No	Green Card	No
Denmark	No	Valid Drivers Licence	No	No
Djibouti	No	No	No	No
Dominica	Yes	Special Driving Licence obtained from Police HQ	Third Party	No
Dominican Republic	No	No	No	No
Eastern Caribbean	No	Temporary local licence	No	No
Ecuador	No	No	No	No
Egypt	Diesel operated vehicles not allowed in. *Carnet de passage* (not vehicles over 5 yrs old)	International Licence	Compulsory insurance obtained at port on arrival	No
El Salvador	No	Valid licence and proof of ownership and registration in another country to obtain permit allowing car to remain for 60 days	No	No
Ethiopia	Get given new number plates on entry!	Foreign can be used for 1 month. Thereafter, can use International	No	Fuel shortages

Countries	*Any Bond Required*	*Special Permits*	*Special Motor Insurance*	*Fuel Rationing*
Fiji	Yes – refundable on exit	International Drivers Licence	Comprehensive or Third Party	No
Finland	No	Valid drivers licence & sign attached showing nationality	Third Party	No
France	No	Valid drivers licence	Third Party	No
Gabon	No	International	No	No
The Gambia	No	International Driving Licence. Gambia Driving Licence.	Fully insured	No
Federal Republic Germany	No	Valid Drivers Licence	Full advised – 3rd Party obligatory	No
Germany (D.R.)	No	Valid Drivers Licence	Green Card	No
Ghana	No NB At the moment there's some trouble at the border – overland travel is difficult	International – must be endorsed by Police Licensing officer	No	Yes – obtainable in small quantities
Gibraltar	No	Valid Drivers Licence	Minimum Third Party Insurance	No
Great Britain	No	National – up to 6 months Internat – up to 1 year	No	No
Greece	No	No	Green Card	No

Grenada	75% of value of vehicle given to Customs	International	No	No
Guinea		International		
Guyana	No	Need permission from Chief Licensing Officer, Licence Revenue Division, Smith & Princes Street, Georgetown.	Third Party	No
Haiti	Yes – very expensive NB Advised to hire car rather than take one.	Foreign or International	No	No
Hong Kong	No	Valid driving licence – after 12 mnths must apply for HK driving licence	No	No
Honduras		Foreign or International		
Hungary	Registration No. must be put on Entry Visa	Valid Driving Licence	Green Card/Third Party	
Iceland	Prohibited to take in more than 200 litres of fuel in tank	International Drivers Licence	Green Card	No
India	*Carnet de passage*. Also reassure Customs that you will be taking car back	International	Third Party	No
Indonesia	*Carnet de passage*. Must have booked onward passage for vehicle before entry	International	Internat. certificate of insurance, endorsed for Indonesia	No

Countries	*Any Bond Required*	*Special Permits*	*Special Motor Insurance*	*Fuel Rationing*
Ireland (Republic)	No	No	No	No
Iran	*Carnet de passage.* If you don't have this you have to be escorted and pay for it	International – 2 photos may be required	No – must carry car documents	No
Iraq	No bond but vehicles only allowed in for 2 months	Valid international automobile certificate	Third Party	
Israel	No	International Drivers Licence	Third Party	No
Italy	No	International Drivers Licence	International Green Card	No
Ivory Coast	No	The Pine-Leaf Licence & International Licence	Green Card/Third Party	No
Jamaica	Import Licence	Valid Licence	Must be Insured	Petrol stations closed on Wednesday and Sunday
Japan	*Carnet de passage.* Tax has to be paid – customs clearance. NB Not advised to take car.	International	No	No
Jordan	No	International Licence	No	No

Kenya	*Carnet de passage* compulsory	Valid drivers licence for up to 90 days – should have it endorsed at local Police Station	Third Party	No
Korea	Can only enter through Pusan via Pukwan Ferry. Can drive for 30 days and then lengthen another 30 days.	Must be over 25, have valid passport and international licence to drive hired cars	No	No
Kuwait	Triptyque required for cars imported for personal use.	International Drivers Licence – should be endorsed by traffic authorities.	Preferable to have cars insured with local insurance firm: Fee W50,000 (US $62) for 1 month – reimbursed when leave	No
Laos	No	International	No	No
Lebanon	*Carnet de passage*	International	Get insurance from Lebanese border	No
Lesotho		International		
Liberia	No	Valid Drivers Licence	No	No
Libya	*Carnet de passage*	International		
Luxembourg	Vehicles imported temp & in brand new condition need Customs Documents	Valid Drivers Licence	International Insurance. Green Card.	No
Macao	Not poss to bring cars in	No self-drive hire cars so cannot drive		

Countries	*Any Bond Required*	*Special Permits*	*Special Motor Insurance*	*Fuel Rationing*
Madagascar		International		
Malawi	*Carnet de passage*. (Valid for 4 months and issued at border)	No	No	No (Available 0600 hrs – 1800 hrs)
Malaysia	Free import on cond it leaves within 90 days International Circ	International or Foreign licence endorsed by Min. of Rd Transport	Third Party	No
Mali	No	No	No	Fuel obtained in big towns
Malta	No if imported by *bona fide* tourists for up to 3 months	No	Third Party	Petrol Stations closed Sundays
Mauritania	*Carnet*	International		
Mauritius	Import Licence reqd	Brit Licence or Internat Licence endorsed by Traffic section of Police Dept	At least Third Party	No
Mexico	No. Must produce proof of ownership or rental	No	No	No
Mongolia	No	International Licence	No	No
Morocco	No	No	Green Insurance Card	No
Nepal	*Carnet de passage* Fill in form at Customs	International	No	Available in Kathmandu

Netherlands	No	No	Green Card	No
New Zealand	Customs Duty and Sales Tax	International Driving Licence	Third Party	No
Nicaragua	No, up to 30 days – extension requires Customs deposit	No, up to 30 days – after need Nic Licence	No	No
Niger	No	International Permit	Insure in case of fire	No
Nigeria	Proof that car will be leaving the country to show at Customs	International – 2 photos required	No	No
Norway	No	No	Third Party	No
Norway	No	Valid Driving Licence	Fully comprehensive	No
Oman	No	Valid driving Licence	Fully Comprehensive Insurance	No
Pakistan	No	International – 2 photos required	No	No
Panama	Proof of ownership needed. No problem if taking car out again	International	Green Card	No
Papua New Guinea	45% cash deposit on vehicle + 2½% value of vehicle not refundable	Current Australian or International	No	No
Paraguay	No	International Licence	Green Card	No

Countries	*Any Bond Required*	*Special Permits*	*Special Motor Insurance*	*Fuel Rationing*
Peru	No	CDP, AIT, FIA issued by Touring & Automobile Clubs of the World	No	No
Philippines	No	International	No	No
Poland	No	No	Green Card	Have to buy fuel/petrol coupons in own country or on border
Portugal	Yes, if indefinite import is considered	If memb of Ints Rd Conv do not need special licence – others need internat licence	Normal insurance + *Carnet de passage en Douane*	No
Qatar	No	Temp 90 day licence and must pass on oral high-way code test	Third Party	No
Romania	No	International Driving Licence	Green Card	No
Rwanda	*Carnet*	International		
Saudi Arabia		Internat or foreign up to 3 months. Women not permitted to drive	Advised to have Third Party	No
Sénégal	Motor Ass Pass	Valid Internat Licence + Customs Pass	International Insurance	No
Sierra Leone		International		

Seychelles	Duty of up to 120% depending on cc & country of origin	Valid Licence	No	No
Singapore	45% of vehicle (market) value	International	No	No
Solomon Islands		International		
Somali Democratic Republic	NB Tourist visa not issued at moment so does not apply			
South Africa	Valid triptyque or carnet is req or cash bond of 115% of vehicle's value must be lodged with Customs	Valid Licence printed in English	S.A. 3rd Party Ins	No fuel on Sundays
Soviet Union	No	Valid Licence in accord with Int Convent on Rd Traffic	Green Card	No
Spain	No	British or Inter Licence	Green Card. Third Party Bail Bond advised	No
Sri Lanka	Valid *Carnet de passage*/Triptyque	Valid Licence – need endorsement on lic by comm of Motor Traffic	Third Party	No
Sudan	Register with the Customs	International	No	Authorities supply Petrol – enough to get you through. Difficult to obtain unless Black Market
Swaziland	No	No	No	No

Countries	*Any Bond Required*	*Special Permits*	*Special Motor Insurance*	*Fuel Rationing*
Sweden	No	No	No	No
Switzerland	No	No	Ins of home country	No
Syria	No	International	No	No
Tahiti	No	International Licence	No	No
Tanzania	*Carnet de passage*	Inter Licence – must report to driving lic issuing auth on arrival	Third party	No
Thailand	No	International Driving Licence	No	No
Togo		International		
Tonga	No	Local licence required issued by Police Dept	No	No
Trinidad & Tobago	Equiv to Cust Duty 45% CIF value + market valuation. 45% manual and 52% automatic	International	Comprehensive Third Party	No
Tunisia	No	No	Green Card	No
Turkey		No	Green Card, Inter or Turkish Third Party	No
Uganda	No	International Driving Licence	No	No

United Arab Emirates	No	International Licence	Third Party	No
US Virgin Islands	No	$2.00 special permit	No	No
United States	No	British or Inter Licence	No	No
Upper Volta (Burkina Faso)	No	No	International Motor Insurance	No
Uruguay	No	Inter Licence, permit for driving for 90 days	No	No
Vanuatu		No if British or French (90 days). Others – international		
Venezuela	Ownership papers. Declare not going to sell it to Consul in country before – need Declaration Papers	International	Third Party	No
Vietnam	Check with Customs when you enter	International Licence Local licence	No	No
People's Democratic Republic of Yemen	NB Not allowed to take cars or drive (Taxis available)			
Yemen Arab Republic	Legalized documents from Embassy before you go	No	No	No
Yugoslavia	No	International	Green Card	No

Countries	*Any Bond Required*	*Special Permits*	*Special Motor Insurance*	*Fuel Rationing*
Zaïre	*Carnet de passage*	International	No	No
Zambia	No	No except at National Parks – entry fee at Gate	Temp 3rd Party valid for Zambia obtainable at Border	No
Zimbabwe	No	No	No	No

International Road Signs

▲ Warning signs ● Regulative signs ■ Informative signs

Colours may vary from country to country, but are usually red and black on a white background.

WARNING SIGNS

Right bend · Double bend · Dangerous bend · Danger! Train

Cross roads · Intersection w/minor road · Merging traffic · Road narrows · Uneven road · Slippery road · Other dangers

Round-about · Give way · Dangerous descent · Road work · Tunnel · Opening bridge · Animals

Level crossing with barrier · Level crossing without barrier · Pedestrians · Children · Two-way traffic · Falling rocks · Traffic signals ahead

INFORMATIVE SIGNS

Motorway exit · Priority road · End of priority road · One-way traffic · Hospital · First-aid station · Mechanical help

REGULATIVE SIGNS

Road closed · No entry · No right turn · Direction obligatory

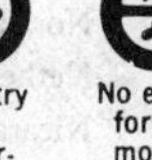

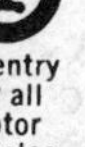

No U-turns · No entry for motorcars · No entry for motor-cycles · No entry for all motor vehicles · No entry for bicycles · No entry for pedestrians · Priority to oncoming vehicles

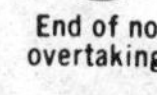

No overtaking · End of no overtaking · Maximum load · Axle weight limit · Width limit · Height limit · No parking

Maximum speed limit · End of speed limit · End of all restrictions · Halt sign · Customs · No stopping · Use of horns prohibited

International Vehicle Licence Plates

A	Austria
ADN	South Yemen
AL	Albania
AND	Andorra
AUS	Australia
B	Belgium
BDS	Barbados
BG	Bulgaria
BH	Belize
BR	Brazil
BRN	Bahrain
BRU	Brunei
BS	Bahamas
BUR	Burma
C	Cuba
CDN	Canada
CH	Switzerland
CI	Ivory Coast
CL	Sri Lanka
CO	Colombia
CR	Costa Rica
CS	Czechoslovakia
CY	Cyprus
D	German Federal Republic
DDR	German Democratic Republic
DK	Denmark
DOM	Dominican Republic
DY	Benin
DZ	Algeria
E	Spain
EAK	Kenya
EAT	Tanzania
EAU	Uganda
EAZ	Zanzibar
EC	Ecuador
EIR	Ireland
ET	Egypt
F	France
FJI	Fiji
FL	Liechtenstein
G	Gabon
GB	Great Britain
GBA	Alderney
GBG	Guernsey
GBJ	Jersey
GBM	Isle of Man
GBZ	Gibraltar
GH	Ghana
GLA	Guatemala
GR	Greece
GUY	Guyana
H	Hungary
HK	Hong Kong
HKJ	Jordan
I	Italy
IL	Israel
IND	India
IR	Iran
IRQ	Iraq
IS	Iceland
J	Japan
JA	Jamaica
K	Kampuchea
L	Luxembourg
LAO	Lao People's Dem Republic
LAR	Libya
LB	Liberia
LS	Lesotho
M	Malta
MA	Morocco
MAL	Malaysia
MC	Monaco
MEX	Mexico
MS	Mauritius
MW	Malawi
N	Norway
NA	Netherlands Antilles
NIC	Nicaragua
NIG	Niger
NL	Netherlands
NZ	New Zealand
P	Portugal
PA	Panama
PAK	Pakistan
PE	Peru
PI	Philippines
PL	Poland
PY	Paraguay

R Romania
RA Argentina
RB Botswana
RC Taiwan
RCA Central African Republic
RCB Congo
RCH Chile
RH Haiti
RI Indonesia
RIM Mauritania
RL Lebanon
RM Madagascar
RMM Mali
RNR Zambia
ROK Korea
RSM San Marino
RSR Zimbabwe
RU Burundi
RWA Rwanda
S Sweden
SD Swaziland
SDV Vatican City
SF Finland
SGP Singapore
SME Suriname
SN Sénégal
SU USSR
SWA South West Africa (Namibia)
SY Seychelles
SYR Syria
T Thailand
TG Togo
TN Tunisia
TR Turkey
TT Trinidad & Tobago
U Uruguay
USA USA
VN Vietnam
WAG Gambia
WAL Sierra Leone
WAN Nigeria
WD Dominica
WG Grenada
WL St. Lucia
WS Western Samoa
WV St. Vincent
YU Yugoslavia
YV Venezuela
Z Zambia
ZA South Africa
ZR Zaïre

Metric Tyre Pressure Conversion Chart

Pounds per sq in	*Kilograms per sq cm*	*Atmospheres*	*KiloPascals (kPa)*
14	0.98	0.95	96.6
16	1.12	1.08	110.4
18	1.26	1.22	124.2
20	1.40	1.36	138.0
22	1.54	1.49	151.8
24	1.68	1.63	165.6
26	1.83	1.76	179.4
28	1.96	1.90	193.2
30	2.10	2.04	207.0
32	2.24	2.16	220.8
36	2.52	2.44	248.4
40	2.80	2.72	276.0
50	3.50	3.40	345.0
55	3.85	3.74	379.5
60	4.20	4.08	414.0
65	4.55	4.42	448.5

Litre to Gallon Conversion

To Convert:	Multiply by
Gallons to Litres	4.546
Litres to Gallons	0.22

Measures of Capacity

2 pints =	1 Quart =	1.136 Litres
4 Quarts =	1 Gallon =	4.546 Litres
	5 Gallons =	22.73 Litres

Water

Passenger Cruise and Passenger/Cargo Freighter Lines

Alaska Marine Highway System
Pouch R
Juneau
Alaska 98811

American President Lines
Passenger Department
1950 Franklin Street
Oakland
California 94612
USA

Cargo passenger service from the US to the Orient and back. Usually keep to set schedule and itinerary. Vagabond Cruises – from the US to a port, or ports in the Orient and/or Southeast/west Asia area. Itineraries are indefinite and no specific ports-of-call or number of ports can be projected in advance. Voyages vary in length from one to three months. Find yourself in foreign ports rarely visited by other tourists.

American Cruise Lines Inc
Marine Park
Haddam
Conn 06438
USA

Cruises.

Bahamas Cruise Lines, Inc
4600 West Kennedy Blvd
Tampa
Florida 33609
USA

Cruises.

Black Sea Shipping Co
1 Potemkinstev Square
Odessa 270025
USSR

UK Agent – CTC Lines
1–3 Lower Regent Street
London
SW1Y 4NN
Tel: 01-930 5833

Passenger Cruise and Passenger/Cargo Freighter Lines, from Soviet Union to Bulgaria, Turkey, Greece, Cyprus, Syria, Lebanon and Egypt. Subject to alteration. From Soviet Union to Europe.

Black Star Line Ltd
FW Hartmann and Co. Inc
17 Battery Place
5th Floor
New York
NY 10004
USA
Tel: (212) 425 6100

From Canada and US Atlantic and Gulf Ports to West Africa.

Blue Funnel Line
India Blgs
Liverpool
L2 0RB
Tel: 051-236 5630

Golden Bear Travel
Pier 27
San Francisco
California 94111
USA
Tel: (415) 391 7759

Cruises.

Blue Star Line
Three Embarcadero Center
Suite 2260
San Francisco
CA 94111

34–35 Leadenhall Street
London
EC3A 1AR

Cargo/Passenger services from Great Britain to Canada (West Coast) and the US.

Botel Cruises
Corneldo's Travel
Bathhouse
52–60 Holborn Viaduct
London
EC1A 2FD

Cruises.

Carnival Cruise Lines, Inc
3915 Biscayne Blvd
Miami
Florida 33137
USA
Tel: (305) 576 9260

UK Agent – Equity Tours (UK) Ltd
77/79 Great Eastern Street
London
EC2A 3HU
Tel: 01-235 1656

Cruises.

Columbus Line
Reederei GmbH (Hamburg Sud)
Ost-West Strasse 59
2000 Hamburg 11
Germany, Federal Rep.

Cargo Passenger service from Europe to the South Pacific Islands, Papua New Guinea, Australia, Singapore and back to Europe

Commodore Cruise Line Ltd
1007 North America Way
Miami
Florida 33132
USA

Cruises to the Caribbean and South America.

Compagnie Générale Maritime
Sotramar Voyages
12 Rue Godot de Mauroy
75009 Paris
France

Freighter services to the French West Indies, South Atlantic, Madagascar, the Pacific, South America, Canada and the US. UK Agent, P & S Travel (See Shipping Agents and Advisers, page 708).

Compagnie Maritime Zaïroise
BP 9496
6th Floor
UZB Centre
Place de la Poste
Kinshasa
Zaïre

Cargo/Passenger services from Europe to the Canary Islands and West Africa.

Costa Line Cruises
Suite 21
Duke Street House
415–417 Oxford Street
London
W1R 1FH
Tel: 01-409 0118

Linea 'C'-Costa Schiffsreisen Gmbh
Schillerstrasse 18–20
D-6000 Frankfurt Main 1
Germany, Federal Republic
Tel: (0611) 283 649

Cruises.

CTC Lines
1 Lower Regent Street
London
SW1X 4NN
Tel: 01-930 5833

Love Holidays Inc (US Agent)
5330 Corbin Ave.
Suite 115
Tarzana
California
USA
Tel: (213) 345 7741

Cruises.

Cunard Line Ltd
South Western House
Canute Road
Southampton
SO9 1ZA
Tel: (0703) 29933

8 Berkeley Street
London
W1X 6NR
Tel: 01-491 3930

555 Fifth Avenue
New York
NY 10017
(212) 880 7500

Cruises.

Curnow Shipping Ltd
The Shipyard
Porthleven
Helston
Cornwall
TR1 3JA
Tel: (03265) 63434

Passenger ships from Great Britain to South Africa.

Delta Steamship Lines Inc
One Market Plaza
Steuart Street Tower
Suite 2700
San Francisco
CA 94106
USA
Tel: (415) 777 8300

(UK Agent) Mundy Travel Ltd
River House
119/121 Minories
London
EC3 1DR
Tel: 01-480 5823

Cargo/Passenger services from the US to South America, and back. From the US to West Africa and back. From Canada to the US, Mexico, South America, the US and back to Canada.

The Delta Queen Steamboat Co
511 Main Street
Cincinatti
Ohio 45202
USA
Tel: (800) 543 1949

Abbeygate Travel Ltd
Apex House
Oundle Road
Peterborough
PE2 9NN
Tel: (0733) 644 52

Cruises.

DEURGO Inh. Carl E. Press
Deichstrasse 11
D-2000 Hamburg 11
Germany, Federal Republic
Tel: (040) 76007-0

Steamship, Passenger and Cargo Freighter Lines. Ship all sorts of automobiles and are the head office for all the various European TASP offices.

Epirotiki Lines
Head Office: Aktki Miaouli 87
Piraeus
Greece

Epirotiki Lines
127–131 Regent Street
London
W1R 7HA
Tel: 01-734 0805, 734 1487

Epirotiki Lines Inc
551 Fifth Ave
New York
NY 10017
USA
Tel: (212) 599 1750

Cruises.

Far Eastern Shipping Co.
International Cruise Center Inc
226 Seventh Street
Garden City
NY 11530
USA

UK Agent – CTC Lines

Cargo Passenger Service from the Soviet Union to Japan and Hong Kong.

Far East Travel Centre
14 Golden Square
London
W1A 4XE

Six to eight sailings a year from Singapore to Fremantle.

Fred Olsen
11 Conduit Street
London W1R 0LS
Tel: 01-409 2019 Reservations.

Bergen Line
505 Fifth Ave
New York
NY 10017
USA
Tel: (212) 986 2711

Cruises and Cargo/Passenger service from Great Britain to Madeira and the Canary Islands.

Geest Line
Geest Industries Ltd
White House Chambers
Spalding
Lincs.
PE11 2AL
Tel: (0775) 6111

Cargo/Passenger service from Great Britain to the West Indies. Service is very popular so early application is advised – bookings can be made through P & S Travel (see Shipping Advisers and Agents page 708).

General Steamship Corporation Ltd
400 California Street
San Francisco
CA 94104
USA
Tel: (415) 772 9304

Handle all lines and specialize in freighter cruises.

Hamburg South American Line
Hamburg Sud
Reiseagentur GmbH
Ost-West Strasse 59
2000 Hamburg 11
Postfach 11 15 40
Germany, Federal Republic.

Wainwright Bros & Co. Ltd
20 Moorfields High Walk
London
EC2Y 9DN
Tel: 01-628 2373

Columbus Line Inc
One World Trade Center
Suite 3247
New York
NY 10048
USA
Tel: (212) 432 9350

Cargo/Passenger service from Europe to South America and back again.

Hellenic Lines Ltd
61–65 Filonos Street
Piraeus
Greece
Tel: 417 1541, 412 5965

Holland America Cruises
300 Elliot Avenue West
Seattle
WA 98119
USA
Tel: (206) 281 3535

Wilhelminakade 88
3000 AL Rotterdam
Netherlands
Tel: (10) 3922214

Cruises.

Home Line Cruises Inc
One World Trade Center
Suite 3969
New York
NY 10048
USA
Tel: (212) 432 1414

Cruises.

Ivaran Lines
United States Navigation Inc
One Edgewater Plaza
Staten Island
New York
NY 10305
USA
Tel: (212) 442 9300

Cargo/Passenger service from the US to South America and back.

Lauro Lines
Lauro Bldg
Via Crestoforo Colombo 45
80133 Naples
Italy
Tel: 311 229

1st Floor
84–86 Roseberry Avenue
London
EC1R 4QS
Tel: 01-837 2157/8

One Biscayne Tower
Miami
Florida 33131
USA
Tel: (305) 374 4120

Cargo/Passenger services – Mediterranean to the Caribbean, Central America and back. Also to South America.

Linblad Travel Inc
8 Wright Street
PO Box 912
West Port
Connecticut 06881
USA
Tel: (203) 226 8531

Cruises.

Lykes Lines
Passenger Dept.
300 Poydras Street
New Orleans
Louisiana 70130
USA
Tel: (504) 523 6611

Box 1139
Houston
Texas 77001
USA

320 California Street
San Francisco
CA 94104
USA

Freighter cruises from the US Gulf to the West Coast of South America, the Far East, Southern and Eastern Africa, the Mediterranean, UK and North Europe. From US Pacific Coast Port to Japan and Korea.

Nauru Pacific Line (Aust Pty) Ltd
80 Collins Street
Melbourne
Victoria 3000
Australia
Tel: (03) 653 5709

Nauru Air and Shipping Agency
China Basin Bldg
185 Berry Street
San Francisco
CA 94107
USA
Tel: (415) 543 1737

Reiseorganisation der NAVIS
Billhorner Kanalstrausse 60
D-2000 Hamburg 28
Postfach 10 48 48
D-2000 Hamburg 1
Germany Federal Republic
Tel: (040) 789 48-1

Ships to North and South America.

Nigerian National Shipping Line Ltd
Development House
PO Box No. 326
21 Wharf Road
Apapa
Lagos
Nigeria

Ibex House
42–47 Minories
London
EC3N 1DY
Tel: 01-480 5694

Cargo/Passenger service from Great Britain to West Africa.

Norwegian Caribbean Lines
One Biscayne Tower
Miami
Florida 33131
USA
Tel: (305) 358 6680

Clareville House
26–27 Oxendon Street
London
SW1Y 4EL
Tel: 01-930 5925

Cruises.

Ocean Cruise Lines
6–10 Frederick Close
Stanhope Place
London
W2 2HD

Cruises.

Egdon Oldendorff
PO Box 2135
Funfhausen 1
2400 Lübeck
Germany, Federal Republic
Tel: (451) 71264

Norton, Lilley and Co., Inc
Operations Dept.
245 Monticello Arcade
Norfolk
VA 23510
USA
Tel: (804) 622 7035

Cargo/Passenger services, different routes from Europe to the US.

Orient Eclipse Cruises, Inc
1080 Fifth Ave
New York
NY 10028
USA
Tel: (212) 831 5059

Cruises.

Pan-Islamic Steamship Co. Ltd
Writer's Chambers
Dunolly Road
PO Box 4855
Karachi 2
Pakistan
Tel: 228 691

Cargo/Passenger service Pakistan – Arabian Gulf.

Paul Mundy Ltd
Quadrant Arcade
Regent Street
London W1R 6EJ
Tel: 01-734 4404

Cruises.

Paquet Cruises
5 Blvd. Malesherbes
Paris 8
France
Tel: 266 57 59

1007 North American Way
Miami 33132
USA
Tel: (305) 347 8100

UK Agents – see Costa Lines Cruises
Equity Tours (UK) Ltd

Cruises.

P&O Cruises
Beaufort House
St Botolph Street
London
EC3A 7DX
Tel: 01-283 8080, Reservations 377 2551

P&O Booking Centre
Level 5
Kindersley House
33 Bligh Street
Sydney
N.S.W. 2000
Australia
Tel: 237 0333

2029 Century Park East
Los Angeles
CA 90067
USA
Tel: (213) 553 1770

Cruises and a Round-the-World Service on the Sea Princess.

Polish Ocean Lines (American Lines Division)
Slaska 49A
81–310 Gdynia
Poland
Tel: 20 31 01

Asia and Australia Lines Division
Pulaskiego 8
81–368 Gdynia
Poland
Tel: 20 76 71

Africa and Mediterranean Lines Division
Durga 76
80–831 Gdansk
Poland
Tel: 31 48 51

European and West Africa Lines Division
Hryniewieckiego 8
70–606 Szczecin
Poland
Tel: 46041

Gdynia America Shipping Lines (London) Ltd
238 City Road
London
EC1V 2QL
Tel: 01-251 3389

For Canada and the USA
McLean Kennedy Ltd
410 St. Nicholas Street
Passenger Dept
Montreal H2Y 2P5
Tel: (541) 849 6111

Modern cargo/passenger vessels. Trips from Europe to Canada, USA, South America, East, West and North Africa, Singapore, Thailand, Hong Kong, Japan, South Africa, New Zealand, Australia, the Middle East and India.

Princess Cruises
2029 Century Park East
Los Angeles
California 90067
USA
Tel: (213) 553 1770

Princess Cruises – P&O Cruises Ltd
P&O Bldg.
2 Castlereagh Street
Sydney 2000
NSW
Australia
Tel: 231 66 55

409 Granville Street
Vancouver BC
Canada
V6C 1T2
Tel: (604) 682 3811

UK address same as for P&O Cruises.

Fly/cruise to the Mexican Riviera, Panama Canal, Alaska and the Caribbean.

Prudential Lines, Inc
Room 3701
One World Trade Center
New York
NY 10048
USA
Tel: (212) 524 8212/8217

Cargo/Passenger from the US to the Mediterranean and back.

Royal Carribean Cruises
903 South America Way
Miami
FL 33132
USA
Tel: (305) 379 2601, Reservations 379 4731

35 Piccadilly
London
W1V 9PB
Tel: 01-434 1991

Cruises year round from Miami throughout the Caribbean, the Bahamas, Bermuda, and Mexico's Yucatan.

Royal Viking Line
One Embarcadero Center
San Francisco
California 94111
USA
Tel: (415) 398 8000

15th Floor
630 Fifth Ave
New York
NY 10020
USA
Tel: (212) 757 0921

Royal Viking Line (UK)
Nuttfield House
Fifth Floor
41/46 Piccadilly
London
W1V 9AJ
Tel: 01-743 0773

Cruises around South Africa, in the Mediterranean, to Europe, Canada, the South Pacific, Hong Kong, Alaska.

St Helena Shipping Co. Ltd
Curnow Shipping Ltd
The Shipyard
Prothleven
Helston
Cornwall
TR13 3JA
Tel: (03265) 63434

From Great Britain to the Canary Islands, St Helena, Ascension Island, St. Helena, South Africa.

Schools Abroad
Cruises Dept.
Grosvenor House
Bolnore Road
Haywards Heath
West Sussex
RH16 4BX
Tel: (0444) 414 122

Cruises.

Scheepvaart Maatschappij Suriname N.V.
44 Waterkant
PO Box 1824
Paramaribo
Suriname
Tel: 72447

Hansen & Tideman Inc
310 Sanlin Bldg.
442 Canal Street
New Orleans
LA 70130
USA
Tel: (504) 586 8755

Cargo/Passenger service – Suriname, Brazil, Caribbean, Mexico, US, Suriname. Ship may call, subject to cargo requirements, at one or two Caribbean Islands before Paramaribo. Also Suriname, Europe, Suriname.

Shipping Corporation of India Ltd
Shipping House
245 Madame Cama Road
Bombay 40041
India
Tel: 202 6666

24 St Mary Axe
London
EC3A 8DE
Tel: 01-283 4425/7

Cargo/Passenger services – India, Malaysia, Singapore. India: mainland to the Andaman Islands (intending passengers, other than Indian residents, must obtain permission from the Ministry of Home Affairs before travelling).

Sitmar Cruises
10100 Santa Monica Blvd
Los Angeles
California 90067
USA
Tel: (213) 553 1666

Prudential Bldgs
39 Martin Place
Sydney
N.S.W. 200
Australia
Tel: 239 9000

7 Rolls Bldgs
Fetter Lane
London
EC4A 1BA
Tel: 01-405 9266

Cruises to the Mexican Riviera, the Caribbean, through the Panama Canal and to Canada and Alaska.

Society Expedition Cruises
723 Broadway East
Seattle
Washington
DC 98102
USA
Tel: (206) 324 9400

Special Expeditions Inc
133 East 55th Street
New York
NY 10022
USA
Tel: (212) 888 7980

Eileen Houlder
22 Petersham Mews
London
SW7 5NR
Tel: 01-584 9042

Cruises.

Sun Line Cruises
1 Rockefeller Plaza
New York 10020
USA
Tel: (212) 397 6400

Fly cruises to the Caribbean, Panama Canal, Yucatan, the Greek Islands and Turkey.

United States Lines
27 Commerce Drive
Cranford
New Jersey
USA
Tel: (201) 272 9600

Cargo/Passenger service from the US to South and East Africa, the US to South America and back.

Windjammer Barefoot Cruises
PO Box 120
Miami Beach
FL 33119
USA
Tel: (305) 373 2090

Cruises.

World Explorer Cruises
Three Embarcadero Center
San Francisco
CA 94111
USA
Tel: (415) 391 92 62

Cruises.

Passenger Shipping Agents and Advisory Services

Ask Mr Foster Travel
740 Polhemus Road
San Mateo
CA 94402
USA
Tel: (415) 349 6216
Maggi Horn
Offers expert advice on freighter travel.

Freighter Cruise Service
Suite 103
5929 Monkland Avenue
Montreal
Quebec
Canada H4A 197
Tel: (514) 481 0447
Agents for all freighter and all steamship companies.

Can also arrange any type of trip by air and land. Reservations should be made well in advance. Handle cruises to South America, the Orient, Yugoslavia and the Mediterranean, South and East Africa, the Middle and Far East, Australia, New Zealand and the South Seas, Hong Kong and Japan

Freighter Travel Club of America
1745 Scoth Ave, S.E.
PO Box 12693
Salem
OR 97309
USA

Offer members answers to specific questions regarding freighter travel, steamship lines, travel agencies, etc. Publish a monthly newsletter Freighter Travel News *which is full of first-hand stories about freighter travel, tips on where to go, what to do while there, where to eat and stay. They do not sell tickets or book passages, nor are they connected in any way with travel agents.*

Freighter World Cruises, Inc
180 So. Lade 335F
Pasadena
CA 91101
USA
Tel: (818) 449 3106

Offers bi-weekly listings of space available from US to worldwide ports. One year's subscription costs US $28.00

Halsey Marine Ltd
22 Boston Place
Dorset Square
London
NW1 6HZ
Tel: 01-724 1303

Leading privately owned international yacht charter specialists. Yachts available as far afield as French Polynesia, the Malaysian coast. Also supply yachts and other vessels for commercial purposes.

Ocean Voyages
1709 Bridgeway
Sausalito
California 94965
USA
Tel: (415) 332 4681

A unique organization which provides exotic sailing experiences all over the world. Offers challenging trips for veteran sailors, good learning experiences for novices – and great vacations for all. Can arrange special charters for friends who want to travel together, research expeditions, conferences for business corporations. Island hopping and exploring, long ocean passages, leisurely cruising, deep sea diving, a one-week trip, an eight-week trip or anything in between.

P & S Travel Ltd
3 Cathedral Place
London EC4M 7DX
Tel: 01 248 6747

Information relating to various shipping lines. Agents for shipping lines (Geest, Polish Ocean Lines, South African Marine Corporation (UK) Ltd., Compagnie Général Maritime). Emphasis on freighter travel.

Pearl's Freighter Trips
175 Great Neck Road
Suite 406W
Great Neck
NY 11021
USA
Tel: (516) 487 8351 and (212) 895 7645
Mrs Pearl Hoffman

Helps plan and book worldwide freighter trips. No charge for the service, but please enclose s.a.e. US money order or other compensations for costs of reply. Preference shown to those taking round trips. Can only control space from the States and no connecting voyages from Europe.

Sea & Cruise Club
32 Berkeley Street
London
W1X 5FA
Tel: 01-629 7391

The aims of the club are to provide expert information and booking facilities for worldwide passenger shipping, to act as a voice for members in order to improve and expand passenger shipping facilities, to negotiate, on behalf of its members, beneficial rates on cruises and other travel arrangements, to provide shipowners, ship designers and cruise operators with an understanding of the needs of the sea traveller. Annual Membership: £5.75 (Single) £10.00 (Family)

Stewart Moffat Travel
Zimpel's Centreway
160 St George's Terrace
Perth 6000
Australia
Tel: 321 2424

General Sales Agents for the Blue Funnel Line vessel Princess Mashuri which operates South Pacific Cruises out of Sydney and Asian Cruises out of Singapore. Also general Sales Agents for the Pearl Cruises vessel Pearl of Scandinavia which operates exclusively in Asian waters.

Operators of Car Ferries from the UK

Brittany Ferries
Millbay Docks
Plymouth
PL1 3EW
Tel: (0725) 21321

The Brittany Centre
Wharf Road
Portsmouth
PO2 7RU
Tel: (0705) 827701

DFDS Seaways
Latham House
16 Minories
London
EC3N 1AD
Tel: 01-265 0821

Tyne Commission Quay
North Shields
Tyne & Wear
NE29 6EE
Tel: (0632) 575655

Olau-Line (UK) Ltd
Sheerness
Kent
ME12 1SN
Tel: (0795) 667535

P&O Ferries Channel Services
Arundel Towers
Portland Terrace
Southampton
SO9 4AE
Tel: 01-623 1505 London Reservations
(0703) 34141 General Enquiries.

DFDS Prins Ferries
Latham House
16 Minories
London
EC3N 1AD
Tel: 01-481 3211

Sally The Viking Line
81 Piccadilly
London W1
Tel: 01-409 0536

Fred Olsen Lines
11 Conduit Street
London
W1R 0LS
Tel: 01-409 2019

Hoverspeed
International Hoverport
Ramsgate
Kent
CT12 5HS
Tel: (0843) 55555 General Reservations
01-554 7061 London Reservations.

Norfolk Line Ltd
Atlas House
Southgates Road
Great Yarmouth
Norfolk
NR30 3LN
Tel: (0493) 56133

Humberside North Sea Ferries Ltd
King George Dock
Hedon Road
Hull
Humberside
HU9 5QA
Tel: (0482) 795141

Sealink UK Ltd
163/203 Eversholt Street
London
NW1 1BG
Tel: 01-387 1234

and at principal rail stations, British Rail offices and agencies.

Smyril Line
Orkney and Shetland Services
PO Box 5
P&O Ferry Terminal
Aberdeen
AB9 8DL
Tel: (0224) 572615

DFDS Tor Line
See DFDS Seaways

Townsend Thoresen
Enterprise House
Channel View Road
Dover
CT17 9TJ
Tel: (0304) 203388 Reservations.

127 Regent Street
London
W1R 8LB
Tel: 01-734 4431

Car Ferry House
Canute Road
Southampton
SO9 5GP
Tel: (0703) 34488

Ferry operators elsewhere in the world are too numerous to list here. We recommend that you consult a copy of the ABC Shipping Guide (see Periodicals, page 570) for detailed information.

Railways

Representatives of Association of Foreign Railways in the UK:

Austrian Railways
c/o Austrian National Tourist Office
30 St George Street
London
W1R 9FA
Tel: 01-629 0461

Belgian Maritime Transport Authority
22–25A Sackville Street
London
W1X 1DE
Tel: 01-437 8405

Belgian National Railways
22–25A Sackville Street
London
W1X 1DE
Tel: 01-734 1491

Danish State Railways
c/o DFDS Danish Seaways
Latham House
16 Minories
London
EC3N 1AD
Tel: 01-481 3211

French Railways – SNCF
French Railways House
179 Piccadilly
London
W1V 0BA
Tel: 01-493 9731

German Federal Railway – DB
10 Old Bond Street
London
W1X 4EN
Tel: 01-499 3095

Luxembourg National Railways – CFL
c/o Luxembourg National Tourist and Trade Office
36/37 Piccadilly
London
W1V 9PA
Tel: 01-434 2800

Netherlands Railways
4 New Burlington Street
London
W1X 1FE
Tel: 01-734 3301

Norwegian State Railways – NSB
Travel Bureau
21/24 Cockspur Street
London
SW1Y 5DA
Tel: 01-930 6666

Swiss Federal Railways
Swiss Centre
1 New Coventry Street
London
W1V 8EE
Tel: 01-734 1921

Low Cost Travel

Australia

Aussiepass

Allows unlimited travel on the entire Ansett Pioneer express system for 15 to 60 days.

Austrailpass

Must be purchased in the UK or Ireland. Allows unlimited first class travel (or economy class if first class is not available) over all rail systems – interstate, country, suburban (except the metropolitan area of Adelaide) in Australia. Different rates are available for 14 and 21 days, 1, 2, and 3 months.

Eaglepass

Offers unlimited travel over the Greyhound Express Coach network. Contact Greyhound Australia Pty. Ltd., Exchange Travel, 66/70 Parker Road, Hastings, East Sussex. Tel: (0424) 443 888.

Europe

Eurail Pass

Available from Britrail Offices and:
Europe by Eurail Inc.
Box 20100
Colombus
OH 43220
USA
Tel: (614) 889 9100

Unlimited travel for one month in nineteen countries in Europe and North Africa (excluding Great Britain and Northern Ireland, although it is valid in the Republic of Ireland).

India

Indrail Pass

Rail Pass available to visitors and Indians who live outside their country, valid for 7, 21, 30, 60 or 90 days, and permitting unlimited travel on Indian railways.

New Zealand

Kiwi Coach Pass

Unlimited kilometres of first class coach travel throughout New Zealand on the scheduled services operated by the following motor coach companies; Mount Cook Line, Railways & Road Services, Newmans. Available for 7, 10, 15, or 25 days. Contact New Zealand Tourist Board, or Mount Cook Line Office.

Travel Pass

A railpass, roadpass, seapass – offers unlimited travel on New Zealand railways, coaches, ferries at very reasonable cost. Passes for 15 or 22 consecutive days (can be extended up to 6 additional days). Available from any New Zealand Railway ticket office, Govt. Tourist Bureau, accredited Travel Agent or Trade Commissioners Office.

United Kingdom

Britrail Pass

Unlimited travel throughout England, Wales and Scotland (including passage on Britrail's Sealink Ships to the Isle of Wight), and are issued for either first class or economy class travel for periods of 7, 14, or 21 days or for one month with children from 5 to 13 years travelling half fare.

Britrail Youth Pass

For 14- to 25-year-olds, unlimited economy class travel.

Britrail Senior Citizens Pass

Anyone 65 or over can travel first class at economy rates.

For information on all British Rail Services contact any major British Rail Station in the UK, or the following addresses in the US:

Britrail International
510 West Sixth Street
Los Angeles
CA 90014
USA

Britrail Travel International
333 North Michigan Ave
Chicago
IL 60601
USA

Inter Rail Point

YMCA
Special programmes
2nd Floor, Crown House
550 Mauldeth Road
Manchester
M21 2RX
Tel: 061-881 5321

Offers budget priced accommodation, together with programmed activities such as sight-seeing tours, international evenings and sports events. Run during the summer for young people travelling throughout Europe on the Interrail ticket issued by the European network.

Transalpino

15 Greycoat Place
London SW1
Tel: 01-222 9521

Transalpino is the world's largest youth rail organization. Offering large discounts off rail/sea/rail services to more than 2000 European destinations. Tickets valid for 2 months and can be purchased by anyone under 26.

Greyhound Lines International

14/16 Cockspur Street
London SW1
Tel: 01-839 5591

For information on Low Cost travel passes in the US and Canada. Also office for Ansett Pioneer.

USA

Ameripass

Entitles purchaser to travel over Greyhound's entire route system and routes of participating connecting bus lines while pass is valid. Stop-overs permitted. (For Greyhound address see below.)

See the U.S.A. Pass

Unlimited mileage pass available to all foreign visitors on both Greyhound and Trailways (the two largest companies).

Must be purchased in advance at a travel agent.

U.S.A. Rail Pass

One of the best travel bargains in the U.S., the pass entitles you to unlimited, nationwide 'coach' (tourist class train) travel.

Greyhound International

For Office in UK see Low Cost Travel, United Kingdom.

Day to Day

Day to Day

Foreign Tourist Boards in Great Britain

Where there is no tourist office listed, please contact the relevant embassy or consulate (*see page 520*).

Albania	c/o Albturist, Regent Holidays, 13 Small St, Bristol	(0272) 211711
Algeria	6 Hyde Park Gate, London SW7	584 5152
Andorra	63 Westover Rd, London SW18 2RF	874 4806
Angola	34 Percy Street, London W1P 9FQ	637 1945
Antigua & Barbuda	Antigua House, 15 Thayer St, London W1M 5DL	486 7073/5
Australia	4th Floor, Heathcoat House, 20 Savile Row, London W1X 1AE	434 4371
Austria	30 St George St, London W1R 9FA	629 0461
Bahamas	23 Old Bond St, London W1X 4PQ	629 5238
Barbados	6 Upper Belgrave St, London SW1X 8AZ	235 2449
Belgium	38 Dover St, London W1X 3RB	499 5379
Belize	West India Committee, 48 Albemarle St, London W1X 4AR	629 6355
Bermuda	9-10 Savile Row, London W1X 2BL	734 9822
Brazil	15 Berkeley Street, London W1	499 0877
British Virgin Islands	48 Albemarle St, London W1X 4AR	629 6355
Bulgaria	18 Prince's St, London W1R 7RE	499 6988
Canada	Canada House, Trafalgar Square, London SW1Y 5BJ	629 9492
Cayman Islands	Hambleton House, 176 Curzon St, London W1Y 7FE	493 5161
China	4 Glentworth St, London NW1	935 9427
Cyprus	213 Regent St, London W1R 8DA	734 9822
Czechoslovakia	17–19 Old Bond St, London	629 6058
Denmark	Sceptre House, 169/173 Regent St, London W1R 8PY	734 2637
Eastern Caribbean	15b Thayer St, London W1M 5LS	486 9119
Egypt	168 Piccadilly, London W1Y 9DE	493 5282
Finland	66 Haymarket, London SW1Y 4RF	839 4048
France	178 Piccadilly, London W1V 0AL	491 7622
East Germany	c/o Berolina Travel Ltd, 20 Conduit St, London W1R 9TD	629 1664
West Germany	61 Conduit St, London W1R 0EN	734 2600
Gibraltar	Arundel Great Court, 179 The Strand, London WC2R 1EH	836 0777/8

Greece	195/7 Regent St, London W1R 8DL	734 5997
Hong Kong	125 Pall Mall, London SW1Y 5EA	930 4775
Hungary	c/o Danube Travel, 6 Conduit St, London W1	493 0263
Iceland	c/o Icelandair, 73 Grosvenor St, London W1X 9DD	499 9971
India	7 Cork St, London W1X 2AB	437 3677
Iraq	c/o Iraqui Airways, 4 Lower Regent St, London SW1	930 1155
Israel	18 Great Marlborough St, London W1V 1AF	434 3651
Italy	1 Prince's St, London W1A 7RA	408 1254
Jamaica	Jamaica House, 50 St James's St, London SW1A 1JT	493 3647 499 1707/8
Japan	167 Regent St, London W1R 7FD	734 9638
Jordan	217 Regent St, London W1	437 9465
Kenya	13 New Burlington St, London W1X 1FF	839 4477/8
Korea	Vogue House, 1 Hanover Square, London W1R 9RD	408 1591
Luxembourg	36/37 Piccadilly, London W1V 9PA	343 2800
Macao	13 Dover St, London W1X 3PH	629 6828
Malawi	52 High Holburn, London WC1	409 2031
Malaysia	17 Curzon St, London W1Y 7FE	499 7388
Malta	16 Kensington Square, London W8 5HH	938 1712/6
Mauritius	23 Ramillies Place, London W1A 3BF	439 4461
Mexico	7 Cork St, London W1X 1PB	734 1058
Morocco	174 Regent St, London W1R 6HB	437 0073/4
Netherlands	143 New Bond St, London W1Y 0QS	499 9367
New Zealand	New Zealand House, 80 Haymarket, London SW1Y 4QT	930 8422
Norway	20 Pall Mall, London SW1Y 5NE	839 6255
Philippines	199 Piccadilly, London W1	439 3481
Poland	c/o Polorbis Travel Ltd, 82 Mortimer St, London W1N	637 4971
Portugal	New Bond Street House, 1/5 New Bond St, London W1Y 0NP	493 3873
Romania	77/81 Gloucester Place, London W1H 3PG	935 8590
Seychelles	50 Conduit St, London W1A 4PE	439 9699
Singapore	33 Heddon St, London W1	437 0033
South Africa	Regency House, 1-4 Warwick St, London W1R 5WB	439 9661
Spain	57/58 St James's St, London SW1A 1LD	499 0901
Sri Lanka	52 High Holborn, London WC1V 6RL	405 1194
Sudan	308 Regent St, London W1R 5AL	631 1785
Sweden	3 Cork St, London W1X 1HA	437 5816
Switzerland	Swiss Centre, 1 New Coventry St, London W1V 8EE	734 1921
Tanzania	77 South Audley St, London W1Y 5TA	499 7727
Thailand	9 Stafford St, London W1X 3FE	499 7670
Trinidad & Tobago	20 Lower Regent St, London SW1Y 4PH	839 7155
Tunisia	7a Stafford St, London W1	499 2234
Turkey	1st Floor, 170/173 Piccadilly, London W1V 9DD	734 8681/2
Turks & Caicos Islands	West India Committee, 48 Albemarle St, London W1X 4AR	629 6355

USSR	292 Regent St, London W1R 6QL	631 1252
USA	22 Sackville St, London W1	439 7744
US Virgin Islands	25 Bedford Square, London WC1B 3HG	637 8481
Yugoslavia	143 Regent St, London W1	
Zambia	163 Piccadilly, London W1V 9DE	493 1188, 493 0848

Foreign Tourist Offices in the United States

Australia	1270 Ave of the Americas, New York, NY 10020	489 7550
Austria	545 5th Ave, New York, NY 10017	697 1651
Bermuda	Rockefeller Center, 630 5th Ave, New York, NY 10111	397 7700
Brazil	551 5th Ave, New York, NY 10017	682 1055
Britain	680 5th Ave, New York, NY 10019	581 4700
British Virgin Islands	370 Lexington Ave, New York, NY 10017	696 0400
Caribbean	20 E 46th St, New York, NY 10017	682 0435
Chile	1 World Trade Center, Suite 5121, New York, Ny 10048	
China	159 Lexington Ave, New York	725 4950
Colombia	140 E 57th St, New York, NY 10022	688 0151
Dominican Rep.	485 Madison Ave, New York, NY 10022	826 0750
Eastern Caribbean	220 E 42nd St, New York, NY 10017	986 9370
Ecuador	167 W 72nd St, New York NY 10023	873 0600
Egypt	630 5th Ave, New York, NY 10111	246 6960
El Salvador	PO Box 818, Radio City Station, 200 W 58th St, New York, NY 10019	
French Polynesia	200 E 42nd St, New York, NY 10017	
France	610 5th Ave, New York, NY 10020 *Also covers the French West Indies.*	757 1125
Galapagos Islands	888 7th Ave, New York, NY 10019	
Gambia	19 E 47th St, New York, NY 10003	759 2323
West Germany	747 3rd Ave, New York, NY 10017	308 3300
Ghana	445 Park Ave, Suite 903, New York, NY 10022	688 8350
Haiti	1270 Avenue of the Americas, New York, NY 10020	757 3517
Honduras	501 5th Ave, New York, NY 10017	869 0766
Hong Kong	548 5th Ave, New York, NY 10036	947 5008
Hungary	630 5th Ave, New York	582 7412
Iceland	75 Rockefeller Plaza, New York, NY 10019	582 2802
India	30 Rockefeller Plaza, New York, NY 10020	586 4901
Indonesia	5 E 68th St, New York, NY 10021	
Iraq	14 E 79th St, New York, NY 10021	
Israel	350 5th Ave, New York, NY 10118	560 0650

Ivory Coast	c/o Air Afrique, 1350 Ave of the Americas, New York, NY 10019	
Jamaica	2 Dag Hammarskjold Plaza, New York	688 7650
Japan	45 Rockefeller Plaza, New York, NY 10020	757 5640
Kenya	15 E 21st St, New York, NY 10022	486 1300
Korea	460 Park Ave, New York, NY 10016	688 7543
Lebanon	405 Park Ave, New York, NY 10022	421 2201
Mexico	630 5th Ave, New York, NY 10020	265 4696
Morocco	521 5th Ave, New York, NY 10175	557 2520
New Zealand	630 5th Ave, New York, NY 10020	586 0060
Panama	630 5th Ave, New York, NY 10020	246 5841
Philippines	556 5th Ave, New York, NY 10036	575 7915
St Lucia	41 E 42nd St, New York, NY 10017	867 2950
St Maarten Saba & St Eustatius	25 W 39th St, New York	840 6655
St Vincent & the Grenadines	220 E 40th St, New York	986 9370
Sénégal	200 Park Ave, New York, NY 10003	682 4695
South Africa	610 5th Ave, New York, NY 10020	245 3720
Spain	665 5th Ave, New York, NY 10022	759 8822
Sri Lanka	609 5th Ave, New York	935 0369
Suriname	1 Rockefeller Plaza, Suite 1408, New York, NY 10020	581 3063
Switzerland	608 5th Ave, New York, NY 10020	757 5944
Tanzania	201 E 42nd St, New York, NY 10017	986 7124
Thailand	5 World Trade Center, New York, NY 10048	432 0433
Tunisia	630 5th Ave, Suite 863, New York, NY 10020	582 3670
Turkey	821 United Nations Plaza, New York, NY 10017	687 2194
Uganda	801 2nd Ave, New York	
USSR	45 E 49th St, New York, NY 10017	371 6953
Uruguay	301 E 47th St, Apt 21-0, New York, NY 10017	
Venezuela	450 Park Ave, New York, NY 1101	355 1101
Zambia	150 E 58th St, New York, NY 10022	758 9450
Zimbabwe	535 5th Ave, New York, NY 10017	

Foreign Tourist Offices in New Zealand

Australia	15th Floor, Quay Tower, 29 Customs St, Auckland 1. (PO Box 1646, Auckland)
Great Britain	PO Box 3655, Wellington
Fiji	47 High St, Auckland
Hong Kong	General Buildings, G/F Corner Shortland St and O'Connell St, Auckland. (PO Box 1313, Auckland)
Ireland	c/o Rodney Walsh Ltd, 87 Queen St, Auckland
Malaysia	Malaysian Airline System, Suite 8, 5th Floor, Air New Zealand House, 1 Queen St, Auckland 1
Singapore	c/o Rodney Walsh Ltd, 87 Queen St, Auckland

Foreign Tourist Offices in Australia

Austria	19th Floor, 1 York St, Sydney, NSW 2000	27 85 81
Canada	8th Floor, AMP Centre, 50 Bridge St, Sydney NSW 2000	
Denmark	60 Market St, PO Box 4531, Melbourne, Victoria 3001	
West Germany	c/o Lufthansa German Airlines, Lufthansa House, 12th Floor, 143 Macquarie St, Sydney NSW 2000	
Greece	51-57 Pitt St, Sydney NSW 2000	
Hong Kong	Bligh House, 4-6 Bligh St, Sydney NSW 2000	
India	Carlton Centre, Elizabeth St, Sydney NSW 2000	232 1600
Jordan	(Alia GSA) Metralco Services Pty Ltd, 4th Floor, 15 Young St, Sydney NSW 2000	
or	(Alia GSA), 167 St Georges Terrace, Perth 6000	
Macao	Suite 604, 135 Macquarie St, Sydney NSW 2000	
or	GPO Box M973, Perth, Western Australia 6001	
Malaysia	12th Floor, R & W House, 92 Pitt St, Sydney NSW 2000	232 3751
Mexico	24 Burton St, Darlinghurst, Sydney NSW 2000	
South Africa	AMEV-UDC House, 115 Pitt St, Sydney NSW 2001	231 6166
Singapore	8th Floor, Gold Fields House, 1 Alfred St, Sydney Cove NSW 2000	
Sri Lanka	FP Leonard Advertising Pty Ltd, 1st Floor, 110 Bathurst St, Sydney 2000	
Switzerland	203-233 New South Head Rd, PO Box 82, Edgecliff, Sydney NSW 2027	
American Samoa	327 Pacific Highway, North Sydney NSW 2060	
Thailand	12th Floor, Royal Exchange Building, Corner Bridge and Pitt Streets, Sydney NSW 2000	27 75 49

Foreign Tourist Boards in Canada

Antigua & Barbuda	Suite 205, 60 St Clair Ave East, Toronto, Ontario M4T 1L9
Australia	120 Eglington Ave East, Suite 220, Toronto, Ontario M4P 1E2
Austria	2 Bloor St East, Suite 3330, Toronto, Ontario M4W 1A8
or	Suite 1220–1223, 736 Granville St, Vancouver, BC
or	1010 Ouest Rue Sherbrooke, Montreal, Quebec
Barbados	615 Dorchester Blvd West, Suite 960, Montreal, Quebec H3B 1P5
or	Suite 1508, Box 11, 20 Queen St West, Toronto, Ontario M5H 3R3
Bermuda	Suite 510, 1075 Bay St, Toronto, Ontario M5S 2B1
British Virgin Islands	Mr W. Draper, 801 York Mills Road, Suite 201, Don Mills, Ontario M3B 1X7
Cayman Islands	234 Eglington Ave. East, Suite 600, Toronto, Ontario

Denmark	PO Box 115, Station 'N', Toronto, Ontario M8V 3S4
Eastern Caribbean	Suite 205, 60 St Clair Ave East, Toronto, Ontario M4T 1L9
France	1 Dandas St West, Suite 2405, Box 8, Toronto, Ontario M5G 123
West Germany	2 Fundy, PO Box 417, Place Bonaventure, Montreal PQ, H5A 1B8
Greece	1233 Rue de la Montagne, Montreal QC, H3G 1Z2
Israel	102 Bloor St West, Toronto, Ontario M5S 1M8
Jamaica	2221 Yonge St, Suite 507, Toronto, Ontario M4S 2B4
Jordan	181 University Ave, Suite 1716, Box 28, Toronto, Ontario M5H 3M7
or	1801 McGill College Ave, Suite 1160, Montreal, Quebec H3A 2N4
Kenya	Gillin Building 600, 141 Laurier Ave. West, Ottawa, Ontario
Macao	Suite 601, 700 Bay St, Toronto, Ontario M5G 1Z6
or	475 Main St, Vancouver, British Columbia V6A 2T7
Mexico	1 Place Ville Marie, Suite 2409, Montreal 113, Quebec
or	1008 Pacific Centre, Toronto Dominion Bank Tower, Vancouver 1 British Columbia
Morocco	2 Carlton St, Suite 1803, Toronto, Ontario M5B 1K2
Peru	Mr Raziel Zisman, 344 Bloor St West, Suite 303, Toronto, Ontario
Portugal	Suite 1150, 1801 McGill College Ave, Montreal, Quebec H3A 2N4
South Africa	Suite 1001, 20 Eglington Ave West, Toronto, Ontario M4R 1K8
Spain	60 Bloor St West, Suit 201, Toronto, Ontario M4W 3B8
Switzerland	PO Box 215, Commerce Court, Toronto, Ontario M5L 1E8
Trinidad & Tobago	York Centre, 145 King St West, and University Ave, Toronto, Ontario M5H 1J8
USSR	2020 University St, Suite 434, Montreal, Quebec H3A 2A5
US Virgin Islands	11 Adelaide St West, Suite 406, Toronto, Ontario M5H 1L9

Hostelling Associations

American Youth Hostels
National Administrative Offices
1332 1 Street NW
Suite 800
Washington
DC 20005
USA
Tel: (202) 783 6161

Maintain 300 hostels in the United States, sponsor inexpensive educational and recreational outdoor travel programmes for all ages, such as bicycling, hiking, canoeing, skiing, and motor trips.

Australia Youth Hostels Association Inc.
60 Mary Street
Surry Hill
NSW 2010
Australia

Canadian Hostelling Association
333 River Road
Tower A, 3rd Floor
Vanier City
Ontario
Canada K1L 8H9
Tel: (613) 746 3844
Telex: 053-3660

Offers inexpensive accommodation, provides facilities for school groups, embraces a wide range of challenging outdoor recreational activities, caters for all ages, backgrounds and tastes. The CHA counts more than 32,000 members and over 70 hostels nationwide.

Fédération Unie des Auberges de Jeunesse
National Office (admin. and enquiries)
6 Rue Mesnil
75116 Paris
France
Tel: 261 84 03

International Youth Hostel Federation
Midland Bank Chambers
Howardsgate
Welwyn Garden City
Hertfordshire
Tel: (96) 32487

Polish Association of Youth Hostels
Chocimska 28
Warsaw
Poland

Travelmates
496 Newcastle Street
West Perth
Western Australia 6005

Accommodation is structured for young (18–35) travellers mostly from overseas, arriving with a pack on their back. No bookings . . . simply first come first served. No wardens, curfews and/or other hassles. The Hostels and Share Houses operate on a communal self-help . . . do-it-yourself . . . basis with cleaning duties etc. being part of the tariff. Individual rooms are not provided. Bedrooms in Share-Houses have two beds to suit pairs or couples. Hostels are dormitory style with 3–6 beds per room depending on size. Kitchens, toilets, hot showers are accessible 24 hours a day. Hostels $4.50 daily, Share Houses $26.00 weekly. (Australian dollars). *See Hitchhiking, page 613.*

Young Men's Christian Association – YMCA
King George's House
Stockwell Road
London
Tel: 01-274 7861

and

Crown House
550 Mauldeth Road West
Manchester M21 2RX
Tel:061-881 5321/2/3

The YMCA has hostels worldwide. For information and addresses, contact the above.

Youth Hostel Association (South America)
Av. Corrientes 1373
1 piso
Buenos Aires
Argentina

For information on Youth Hostels throughout South America.

Young Women's Christian Association – YWCA
9/11 Lockyer Street
Plymouth
Tel: (0752) 660321

and

Alexandra Residential Club
Water Lane
Clifton
York
Tel: (0904) 29468

The YWCA has hostels worldwide. For information and addresses contact the above.

Accommodation: Home Exchange, Time-sharing

Association of British Time-share Agents
ABITA
Deerhurst House
Epping Road
Roydon
Harlow
Essex

Domus Publications Ltd
246/248 Great Portland Street
London W1
Tel: 01-387 7878

Publish two very useful Home Exchange/Timesharing magazines:
Homes & Travel Abroad – *covers all aspects of buying and setting up a home abroad. General features cover travel to countries near and far, all types of holidays and hints for travellers.*
Holiday Time-sharing – *explains everything there is to know about timesharing. It also features travel articles, the best ways of getting to a country and handy hints for travellers.*

Experiment in International Living
Upper Wyche
Malvern
Worcs. WR14 4EN
Tel: (05741) 5280

For those interested in finding out more about the Japanese and their life style, The Experiment in International Living (UK office) can arrange for you to stay with a Japanese family in many parts of Japan, as a 'paying guest', at very reasonable costs.

The Great Exchange Ltd
Roxburghe House
273 Regent Street
London W1R 7PB
Tel: 01-629 0235

and

PO Box 12028
Glendale
Los Angeles
CA91214-0347
USA

For a small fee, Great Exchange will register your home in the Greater London area and arrange swops with suitable partners in New York, Florida or California.

Hapimag
Comser International
Orantecq House
Fairview Road
Timperly
Cheshire
Tel: 061-904 9750

Holiday Service
Ringstr. 26
8608 Memmelsdorf
Germany, Federal Republic

A company in Germany is currently offering a 'Swop Your Home' programme of more than 5,000 home swoppers in 53 countries. The list of potential home swoppers offered by the company includes about 3,000 offers from the US. Colour photos of the accommodation offered are available. Full details from above address.

Homefinders
New Roman House
10 East Road
London N1 6AU
Tel: 01-253 4628

Publish the magazine Time-sharing Homes, *full of useful information.*

Home Interchange Ltd
8 Hillside High Street
Farningham
Kent DA4 0DD

Homesitters
Moat Farm
Buckland
Nr. Aylesbury
Bucks HP22 5HY
Tel: Aylesbury 631 289

One way to prevent burglary when on holiday is to employ a professional 'Homesitter' to live in your house while you are away. The 'Homesitters' are carefully selected and screeened, and they abide by strict rules. They work closely with Crime Prevention Officers.

Intervac – International Home Exchange Service
Mrs Hazel Nayar, BA
6 Siddals Lane
Allestree
Derby DE3 2DY
Tel: (0332) 558 931

Intervac Home Exchange has been established 30 years, and now has more than 6,500 members in 40 countries. A Directory and two Supplements are published each year, and any number of exchanges may be arranged for one annual fee. International hospitality and let/rent arrangements are also possible.

Interval International
Suite One
6 Porchester Terrace
London W2
Tel: 01-402 3986

and

Interval International
World Headquarters
7000 SW 62nd Avenue
Suite 306
Miami
Florida 33143
USA

Interservice Home Exchange
Box 87
Glen Echo
Maryland 20812
USA

RCL – Resort Condominiums International
Headquarters
9333 North Meridien Street
PO Box 80229
Indianapolis
Indiana 46280
USA

and

RCI, (UK) Ltd
308 Regent Street
London W1
Tel: 01-637 8047

Operates the world's largest exchange programme for Time-share owners.

Traveler's Home Exchange Club, Inc
PO Box 825
Parker
Colorado 80134
USA

Hotel Reservation Numbers in UK

International hotel groups and representatives.

Ambassador	(01) 434 1488
Apart Hotel International	(01) 434 1936
Best Western	(01) 940 9766
CP Hotels International	(01) 930 8852
Ciga Hotel	(01) 930 4147
Hilton Hotels	(01) 493 8000
Holiday Inns International	(01) 723 1277
Hotel Representatives, Inc	(01) 583 3050
Hyatt	(01) 734 3873
Inter-Continental	(01) 409 3131
Loews Overseas Reservations	(01) 487 4005
Keytel International	(01) 402 8182
Mandarin International	(01) 583 3411
Marriott Hotels & Resorts	(01) 493 0281 (individual) (01) 434 2299 (group)
Meridien Hotels	(01) 491 3516
Penta Hotels	(01) 897 6363
Ramada Hotels International	(01) 235 5264
Sheraton	(01) 636 6411
Southern Sun Hotel Groups	(01) 636 7087
Steigenberger Reservations Service	(01) 486 5754
Tom Eden Associates	(01) 734 4267
Trust House Forte	(01) 567 3444
Western International Hotels	(01) 408 0636

Worldwide Currencies

Country	*Unit*	*1 Unit = 100 (unless otherwise stated)*
Afghanistan	Afghani	Puls
Albania	Lek	Quintar
Algeria	Dinar	Centimes
Angola	Kwanza	Lweis
Antigua	CFD	Cents
Argentina	New Peso	Centavos
Australia	Dollar	Cents
Austria	Schilling	Groschen
Bahamas	Dollar	Cents
Bahrain	Dinar	1000 Fils
Bangladesh	Taka	Poisha
Barbados	Dollar	Cents
Belgium	Franc	Centimes
Belize	Dollar	Cents
Benin	CFA Franc	—
Bermuda	Dollar	Cents
Bhutan	Indian Rupee	—
Bolivia	Peso	Centavos
Botswana	Pula	Thebe
Brazil	Cruzeiro	Centavos
British Virgin Islands	US Dollar	Cents
Brunei	Dollar	Cents
Bulgaria	Lev	Stotinki
Burma	Kyat	Pyas
Burundi	Franc	Centimes
Cameroon	CFA Franc	—

Country	*Unit*	*1 Unit = 100 (unless otherwise stated)*
Canada	Dollar	Cents
Cape Verde Islands	Escudo	Centavos
Cayman Islands	Cayman Islands Dollar	Cents
Central African Rep.	CFA Franc	Centimes
Chad	CFA Franc	Cents
Chile	Peso	10 Centesimos
China	Yuan	Fen
Colombia	Peso	Centavos
Comoro Arch.	CFA Franc	—
Congo	CFA Franc	—
Cook Islands	New Zealand Dollar	Cents
Costa Rica	Colon	Centavos
Cuba	Peso	Centavos
Cyprus	Pound	1000 Mils
Czechoslovakia	Koruna	Halers
Denmark	Krone	Ore
Djibouti	Djib. Franc	Centimes
Dominica	East Caribbean Dollar	Cents
Dominican Republic	Peso	Centavos
Ecuador	Sucre	Centavos
Egypt	Pound	Piastres
El Salvador	Colon	Centavos
Equatorial Guinea	Ukulele	Centimos
Ethiopia	Birr	Cents
Falkland Islands	Falkland Islands Pound	—
Fiji	Dollar	Cents
Finland	Marka	Penni
France	Franc	Centimes
Gabon	CFA Franc	—
Gambia	Dalasi	Batut
Fed. Rep. German	Mark	Pfennig
German Dem. Rep.	Mark	Pfennig
Ghana	Cedi	Pesawas
Gibraltar	Pound	Pence
Greece	Drachma	Lepta
Grenada	East Caribbean Dollar	Cents
Guatemala	Quetzal	Centavos
Guinea	Sily	Couris
Guinea-Bissau	Peso da Guinea-Bissau (GWE)	Centavos
Guyana	Dollar	Cents
Haiti	Gourde	Centimes
Honduras	Lempira	Centavos
Hong Kong	Dollar	Cents
Hungary	Forint	Fillers

Country	*Unit*	*1 Unit = 100 (unless otherwise stated)*
Iceland	Krona	Aur
India	Rupee	Paisa
Indonesia	Rupiah	Sen
Iran	Rial	Dinars
Iraq	Dinar	1000 Fils
Ireland	Pound	Pence
Israel	Shekel	10 Agorot
Italy	Lira	—
Ivory Coast	CFA Franc	—
Jamaica	Dollar	Cents
Japan	Yen	—
Jordan	Dinar	1000 Fils
Kampuchea	Riel	Centimes
Kenya	Shilling	Cents
Kiribati	Australian Dollar	Cents
Korea, North	Won	Jun
Korea, South	Won	Chon
Kuwait	Dinar	1000 Fils
Laos	Kip Pot Po	Centimes
Lebanon	Livra	—
Lesotho	Malote	Licente
Liberia	Dollar	Cents
Libya	Dina	1000 Dirham
Liechtenstein	Swiss Franc	Centimes
Luxembourg	Franc	Centimes
Macao	Pataca	Avos
Madagascar	Franc	Centimes
Malawi	Kwacha	Tambala
Malaysia	Ringit	Sen
Maldive Islands	Maldivian Rupee	Laree
Mali	Franc	Centimes
Malta	Pound	Cents
Mauritania	Ouguiya	5 Khoums
Mauritius	Rupee	Cents
Mexico	Peso	Centavos
Micronesia	US Dollar	Cents
Montserrat	East Caribbean Dollar	Cents
Morocco	Dirham	Centimes
Mozambique	Metical	Centavos
Nauru	Australian Dollar	Cents
Nepal	Rupee	Pice
Netherlands	Guilder	Cents
Netherlands Antilles	Guilder or Florin	Cents
New Caledonia	Franc	Centimes

Country	*Unit*	*1 Unit = 100 (unless otherwise stated)*
New Zealand	Dollar	Cents
Nicaragua	Cordoba	Centavos
Niger	CFA Franc	—
Nigeria	Naira	Kobos
Norway	Krone	Ore
Oman	Rials Omani	1000 Baizas
Pakistan	Rupee	Paisa
Panama	Balboa	Cents
Papua New Guinea	Kina	Toea
Paraguay	Guarani	Centimos
Peru	Sol	Centavos
Philippines	Peso	Centavos
Poland	Zloty	Groszy
Portugal	Escudo	Centavos
Puerto Rico & US Virgin Islands	US Dollar	Cents
Qatar	Ryal	Centimes
Réunion	Franc	Centimes
Romania	Leu	Bani
Rwanda	Rwandese Franc	Centimes
St Kitts-Nevisi	EC Dollar	Cents
St Lucia	EC Dollar	Cents
St Vincent & the Grenadines	EC Dollar	Cents
American Samoa	US Dollar	Cents
Western Samoa	Tala	Sene
São Tomé & Principe	Dobra	—
Saudi Arabia	Ryal	Hallalah
Sénégal	CFA Franc	—
Seychelles	Rupee	Cents
Sierra Leone	Leone	Cents
Singapore	Dollar	Cents
Solomon Islands	Dollar	Cents
Somalia	Shilling	Cents
South Africa	Rand	Cents
Spain	Peseta	Centimos
Sri Lanka	Rupee	Cents
Sudan	Pound	Piastres (1 Piastre = 100 Milliemes)
Suriname	Guilder or Florin	Cents
Swaziland	Lilangeni	Cents
Sweden	Krona	Ore
Switzerland	Franc	Centimes
Syria	Pound	Piastres
Taiwan	New Taiwan Dollar	Cents
Tanzania	Shilling	Cents

Country	*Unit*	*1 Unit = 100 (unless otherwise stated)*
Thailand	Baht	Satang
Togo	CFA Franc	—
Tonga	Pa'anga	Seniti
Trinidad & Tobago	Dollar	Cents
Tunisia	Dinar	1000 Millimes
Turkey	Lira	Kurus
Turks & Caicos Islands	US Dollar	Cents
Tuvalu	Australia Dollar	Cents
Uganda	Shilling	Cents
USSR	Rouble	Kopeks
United Arab Emirates	UAE Dirham	Fils
United Kingdom	Pound	Pence
USA	Dollar	Cents
Upper Volta	CFA Franc	—
Uruguay	Peso	Centimos
Vanuatu	Franc	Centimes
Venezuela	Bolivar	Centimos
Vietnam	Dông	10 Hào
North Yemen	Riyal	Fils
South Yemen	Dinar	1000 Fils
Yugoslavia	New Dinar	Paras
Zaïre	Zaïre	Makutas
Zambia	Kwacha	Ngwee
Zimbabwe	Dollar	Cents

CFA = Communauté Financière Africaine.

Banking Hours

Algeria	7.45–11.50, 14.15–17.00 Mon.–Fri. in winter; 7.15–11.00, 15.00–17.30 Mon.–Fri. in summer.
American Samoa	9.00–15.00 Mon.–Fri.
Andorra	9.00–13.00, 15.00–18.00 Mon–Fri.; 9.00–13.00 Sat.
Antigua and Barbuda	9.00–13.00 Mon.–Thurs.; 9.00–13.00, 15.00–17.00 Fri.
Argentina	10.00–16.00 Mon.–Fri.
Australia	10.00–15.00 Mon.–Thurs.; 10.00–17.00 Fri.
Austria	8.00–12.30, 13.30–15.00 Mon., Tues., Wed., Fri.; 8.00–12.30, 13.30–17.30 Thurs.
Bahamas	Nassau and Freeport: 9.30–15.00 Mon.–Thurs.; 9.30–1700 Fri. Opening times vary considerably in the Family Islands.
Bahrain	7.30–12.00 Sat.–Wed.; 7.30–11.00 Thurs.
Bangladesh	9.00–13.00 Sat.–Thurs. (Closed Fri.)

Barbados	8.00–13.00 Mon.–Thurs.; 8.00–13.00, 15.00–17.00 Fri. Barclays Bank and Bank of Nova Scotia: 8.00–15.00 Mon.–Thurs.; 8.00–13.00, 15.00–17.00 Fri.
Belgium	9.00–12.00, 14.00–16.00 Mon.–Fri.
Belize	8.00–12.00, 13.00–16.00 Mon.–Fri.; 8.00–12.30 Sat.
Bermuda	9.30–15.00 Mon.–Thurs.; 9.30–15.00, 16.30–17.30 Fri.
Benin	8.00–11.30, 14.30–15.30 Mon.–Fri.
Bolivia	7.30/9.00–16.00 Mon.–Fri.
Botswana	8.15–12.45 Mon.–Fri.; 8.15–10.45 Sat.
Brazil	10.00–16.00 Mon.–Fri.
British Virgin Islands	9.00–14.00 Mon.–Thurs.; 9.00–14.00, 16.00–17.30 Fri.
Burma	10.00–13.00 Mon.–Fri.
Brunei	9.00–12.00, 14.00–15.15 Mon.–Fri. West: 8.00–13.30 Mon.–Fri.
Burundi	7.00–12.00 Mon.–Fri.
Cameroon	East: 8.00–11.30, 14.30–15.30 Mon.–Fri. West: 8.00–13.30 Mon.–Fri.
Canada	10.00–15.00 Mon.–Fri.
Cayman Islands	9.30–14.30 Mon.–Thurs.; 9.30–16.30 Fri.
Central African Rep	7.00–13.00 Mon.–Fri.
Chad	7.00–12.00 Mon.–Sat.
Chile	9.00–14.00 Mon.–Fri.
China	8.00–12.00, 14.00–18.00 Mon.–Sat.
Colombia	9.00–15.00 Mon.–Fri.
Congo	7.00–12.00 Mon.–Sat.
Costa Rica	9.00–15.00 Mon.–Fri.
Cuba	8.00–12.00, 14.15–15.15 Mon.–Fri.; 8.00–12.00 Sat.
Czechoslovakia	8.00–14.00 Mon.–Fri.
Denmark	Copenhagen: 9.30–16.00 Mon., Wed., Fri., 9.30–18.00. Banks in the provinces usually close from 12.00–14.00.
Djibouti	8.00/9.00–12.00, 15.00–20.00 Mon.–Fri.
Dominica	9.00–12.30, 14.00–15.00 Mon.–Fri.
Dominican Rep.	8.30–1.30 Mon.–Fri. *Bureaux de Change* are open from 8.00–17.00 Mon.–Fri. and 8.00–12.00 Sat.
Eastern Caribbean	9.00–12.00 Mon.–Thurs.; 9.00–14.00, 15.00–17.30 Fri.
Ecuador	9.00–12.00, 14.30–16.00 Mon.–Fri.
Egypt	9.30–12.30 Mon.–Thurs.; 10.30–12.30 Sat. Close Fri.
El Salvador	9.00–13.00, 13.45–15.30 Mon.–Fri.
Ethiopia	9.00–17.00 Mon.–Fri. with 3 hour lunch closing.
Fiji	9.00–15.00 Mon.–Fri.
Finland	9.30–16.00 Mon.–Fri.
France	9.00–12.00, 14.00–16.00. Closed Sun. and either Sat. or Mon.
French Guiana	7.30–11.30, 14.15–16.30 Mon.–Fri. Sat. morning.
French West Indies	8.00–12.00, 14.30–16.00 Mon.–Fri.
Gabon	7.00–12.00 Mon.–Fri.
The Gambia	8.00–12.00, 14.00–17.00 Mon.–Fri.
Fed. Rep. of Germany	9.00–15.00 Mon.–Fri.
German Dem. Rep.	9.00–17.00 Mon.–Fri.; 9.00–13.00 Sat.

Ghana	8.30–12.00, 14.00–17.30, closed Wed. and Sat. afternoons.
Gibraltar	9.00–15.30 Mon.–Thurs.; 9.00–3.30, 17.00–18.00 Fri.
Great Britain	9.30–15.30 Mon.–Fri. Barclays open Sat. morning.
Greece	8.00–14.00 Mon.–Fri. The Credit Bank Exchange Centre, Syntapma Square, Athens, remains open 7 days a week from 7.45–14.00, 16.30–20.00.
Guatemala	8.30–12.00, 14.00–16.00 Mon.–Fri.
Guinea	Mon.–Sat. mornings only.
Guyana	8.00–12.00 Mon.–Fri., 8.00–11.00 Sat. Bank at Timerhi International Airport remains open from 8.00–14.00.
Haiti	9.00–13.00 Mon.–Fri.
Honduras	8.00–12.00, 14.00–16.00 Mon.–Fri.; 8.30–12.00 Sat.
Hong Kong	10.00–15.00 Mon.–Fri., 9.30–12.00 Sat.
Hungary	8.00–16.00 Mon.–Fri.
Iceland	9.15–16.00 Mon., Tues., Wed., Fri.; 9.15–16.00, 17.00–18.00 Thurs.
India	10.30–14.30 Mon.–Fri.; 10.30–12.30 Sat.
Indonesia	10.00–15.00 Mon.–Fri.; 9.00–12.00 Sat.
Iran	8.00–13.00, 16.00–18.00 Sat.–Thurs.
Iraq	Summer: 8.30–12.30 Sat.–Wed.; 8.30–11.30 Thurs. Winter: 9.00–13.00 Sat.–Wed.; 9.00–12.00 Thurs.
Israel	8.30–12.30, 16.00–17.30 Mon., Tues., Thurs.; 8.30–12.30 Wed.; 8.30–12.00 Sat.
Italy	8.30–13.00 Mon.–Fri.
Ivory Coast	8.00–11.30, 14.30–16.30 Mon.–Fri.
Jamaica	9.00–14.00 Mon.–Thurs.; 9.00–12.00, 14.30–17.00 Fri.
Japan	9.00–15.00 Mon.–Fri.; 9.00–12.00 Sat.
Jordan	8.00–14.00 Sat.–Thurs.
Kampuchea	8.30–15.30 Mon.–Fri.; 8.30–12.00 Sat.
Kenya	9.00–13.00 Mon.–Fri.; 9.00–12.30 on the first and last Sat. of each month.
Korea	10.00–17.00 Mon.–Fri.; 10.00–14.00 Sat.
Kuwait	8.00–12.00 Sat.–Thurs.
Lebanon	8.30–12.30 Mon.–Fri.; 8.30–12.00 Sat.
Liberia	8.00–12.00 Mon.–Thurs.: 8.00–14.00 Fri.
Libya	Winter: mornings. Summer: mornings and 16.00–17.00.
Luxembourg	8.00–12.00, 13.30–16.30 Mon.–Fri.
Macao	9.00–16.00/17.00 Mon.–Fri.; 9.00–13.00 Sat.
Madagascar	8.00–11.00, 14.00–16.00 Mon.–Fri.
Malawi	Mon.–Sat. mornings, Commercial Bank 16.30–18.00 Fri.
Malaysia	10.00–15.00 Mon.–Fri.; 9.30–11.30 Sat.
Mali	7.30–14.30 Mon.–Fri.; 7.30–12.00 Sat.
Malta	8.30–12.00, 16.00–19.00 Mon.–Fri.
Mauritania	8.00–11.15, 14.30–16.30 Mon.–Fri.
Mauritius	10.00–14.00 Mon.–Fri.; 10.00–12.00 Sat.
Mexico	9.00–13.00 Mon.–Fri.
Micronesia	9.30–14.30 Mon.–Fri.
Morocco	8.30–11.30, 15.00–17.30 Mon.–Fri.
Nepal	10.00–15.00 Sat.–Thurs.; 10.00–12.00 Fri., closed Sat.
Netherlands Antilles	8.30–11.00, 14.00–16.00 Mon.–Fri.

New Caledonia	7.00–10.30, 13.30–15.30 Mon.–Fri.; 7.30–11.00 Sat.
New Zealand	10.00–16.00 Mon.–Fri.
Nicaragua	9.00–12.00, 14.00–16.00 Mon.–Fri.
Niger	Mornings only.
Nigeria	8.30–12.30, 14.00–17.00 Mon.–Fri.
Norway	8.00–15.45 Mon.–Fri.
Oman	8.00–13.00, 14.00–19.00 Sat.–Thurs.
Pakistan	9.00–13.00 Mon.–Thurs.; 9.00–10.30 Sat. in rural areas; 9.00–11.30 Sat. in main cities.
Panama	8.00–13.00 Mon.–Fri.
Papua New Guinea	9.00–14.00 Mon.–Fri.; 8.30–11.30 Sat.
Paraguay	7.30–11.00 Mon.–Fri.
Peru	8.30–12.45 Mon.–Fri. (Varies according to the season)
Philippines	9.00–18.00 Mon.–Fri.; 9.00–12.30 Sat.
Poland	9.00–12.00 Mon.–Fri.
Portugal	8.30–11.45, 13.00–14.45 Mon.–Fri. In Lisbon, certain central branches are also open from 18.00–23.00. The bank at the Vilamoura Shopping Centre on the Algarve opens daily from 9.00–21.00
Qatar	7.30–11.30 Sat.–Thurs.
American Samoa	9.00–14.00 Mon.–Thurs.; 9.00–17.00 Fri.
Western Samoa	9.30–15.00 Mon.–Fri.; 9.30–11.30 Sat.
Saudi Arabia	7.00/8.00–14.30 Sat.–Thurs.
Sénégal	8.00–12.00, 14.00–18.00 Mon.–Fri.
Seychelles	8.30–13.00 Mon.–Fri.; 8.30–12.30 Sat.
Sierra Leone	8.00–13.00 Mon.–Fri.; 9.30–11.30 Sat.
Singapore	10.00–15.00 Mon.–Fri.; 9.30–11.30 Sat.
Somalia	8.00–11.30 Sat.–Thurs.
South Africa	9.00–15.30 Mon., Tues., Thurs.; 9.15–13.00 Wed.; 8.30–11.00 Sat.
Spain	9.30–14.30 Mon.–Fri.
Sri Lanka	9.00–13.00 Mon.; 9.00–13.30 Tues.–Fri. Closed Sat. and Sun.
Sudan	8.30–12.00 Sat.–Thurs.
Suriname	7.30–13.00 Mon.–Fri.; 7.30–11.00 Sat.
Swaziland	8.30–13.00 Mon.–Fri.; 9.00–11.00 Sat.
Sweden	9.30–15.00 Mon.–Fri.
Switzerland	8.00–16.30 Mon.–Fri.
Syria	8.00–14.30 Closed Fri.
Tahiti	7.45–15.30 Mon.–Fri.
Taiwan	9.00–15.30 Mon.–Fri.; 9.00–12.00 Sat.
Tanzania	8.00–12.00, 14.00–17.00 Mon.–Sat.
Thailand	8.30–15.30 Mon.–Fri.
Togo	7.30–11.30, 14.30–15.30 Mon.–Fri.
Tonga	9.30–15.30 Mon.–Fri.
Trinidad & Tobago	9.00–14.00 Mon.–Thurs.; 9.00–13.00, 15.00–17.00 Fri.
Tunisia	8.30–13.00, 15.00–17.00 Mon.–Fri.
Turkey	8.30–12.00, 13.30–17.00 Mon.–Fri.
Uganda	8.30–12.30 Mon.–Fri.; 8.00–11.00 Sat.
USSR	USSR State Bank for Exchange 9.00–12.30 Mon.–Fri.; 9.00–11.00 Sat.

United Arab Emirates	8.00–12.00 Sat.–Wed.; 8.00–11.00 Thurs.
US Virgin Islands	9.00–15.00 Mon.–Fri.
United States	9.30–18.00 Mon.–Sat. with late opening on one or two evening. Some states permit Sun. opening.
Upper Volta (Burkina Faso)	7.30–12.30, 15.00–17.30 Mon.–Fri.
Uruguay	Summer: 12.00–16.00 Mon.–Fri. Winter: 13.00–17.00 Mon.–Fri.
Venezuela	8.30–11.30, 14.30–17.30 Mon.–Fri.
Vietnam	8.00–11.30, 14.00–16.00 Mon.–Fri.; 8.00–11.00 Sat.
Windward Islands	8.00–12.00 Mon.–Fri., late opening Fri.
Zaïre	8.00–11.30 Mon.–Fri.
Zambia	8.15–12.45 Mon., Tues., Wed., Fri.; 8.15–12.00 Thurs.; 8.15–11.00 Sat.
Zimbabwe	8.30–14.00 Mon., Tues., Thurs., Fri.; 8.30–12.00 Wed.; 8.30–11.00 Sat.

Shopping Hours

Afghanistan	8.00–18.00 Sat.–Thurs. Closed Thurs. afternoon or all day Fri.
American Samoa	8.30–16.30 Mon.–Fri.; 8.30–12.00 Sat.
Andorra	8.00–20.00. Varied midday closing.
Antigua & Barbuda	8.30–16.00 Mon.–Fri.; 9.00–12.00 Sat.
Argentina	Generally 9.00–19.00 Mon.–Fri. Govt. offices are open 12.00–19.00 Mon.–Fri.
Australia	Generally 9.00–17.30 Mon.–Fri.; 9.00–12.00 Sat. Corner stores open later, but all shops close on Sunday. Late night shopping on Thurs. or Fri.
Austria	8.00–18.00 with one or two hour breaks at midday Mon.–Fri., Sat. 8.00–12.00 noon.
Bahamas	9.00–17.00 Mon.–Sat.
Bahrain	8.00–12.00, 15.30–18.30 Sat.–Thurs. Closed Fri.
Bangladesh	10.00–20.00 Mon.–Fri.; 9.00–14.00 Sat.
Barbados	8.00–16.00 Mon.–Fri.; 8.00–12.00 Sat.
Belgium	9.00–18.00 daily
Belize	8.00–12.00, 13.00–16.00 Mon.–Fri.; 8.00–12.30 Sat.
Benin	8.00–11.30, 14.30–15.30 Mon.–Fri.
Bermuda	Generally 9.00–17.00 Mon.–Sat.
Bolivia	8.00–12.00, 13.00–18.30 Mon.–Sat.
Botswana	8.00–13.00, 14.15–17.30 Mon.–Fri.; 8.00–13.00 Sat.
Brazil	9.00–19.30 Mon.–Fri., 8.00–13.00 Sat.
British Virgin Islands	9.00–17.00 Mon.-Fri.
Burma	9.30–16.30 Mon.–Fri.
Burundi	7.00–12.00, 14.00–17.00 Mon.–Fri.
Canada	Open until 17.30/18.00. Thurs. and Fri. open till 21.00. Small neighbourhood stores remain open late and on Sundays.
Cayman Islands	9.00–17.00 Mon.–Sat.
Central African Rep.	8.00–12.00, 16.00–19.00 Mon.–Sat.
Chad	7.00/8.00–18.30/19.00, Tues.–Sat. with long lunch closing.

Chile	9.00–18.00 every day.
China	8.00–12.00, 14.00–18.00 daily.
Colombia	9.00–16.30 Mon.–Sat., 2 hour lunch closing.
Congo	8.00–18.30 Tues.–Sun., 2 hour lunch closing.
Costa Rica	9.00–18.00 Mon.–Sat.
Cuba	12.30–19.30 Mon.–Sat.
Cyprus	Usually 8.00/9.00–12.00, 15.00–18.00/19.00 Mon.–Sat.
Czechoslovakia	9.00–12.00, 14.00–18.00 or 9.00–18.00. Some major shops open till 20.00 on Thurs. and Sat. till noon.
Denmark	9.00–17.30 Mon.–Thurs.; 9.00–19.00/20.00 Fri.; 9.00–12.00/13.00/14.00 Sat.
Djibouti	8.00/9.00–12.00, 15.00–20.00 Mon.–Sat.
Dominica	9.00–12.30, 14.00–15.00 Mon.–Fri.
Dominican Rep.	8.30–12.00, 14.00–18.00 Mon.–Sat.
Eastern Caribbean	8.30–12.00, 13.00–16.00 Mon.–Sat. Half day Thurs.
Ecuador	8.30–18.30 Mon.–Fri., 2 hour lunch closing.
Egypt	Usually 9.00–20.00 in summer, and 10.00–19.00 in winter.
El Salvador	9.00–12.00, 14.00–18.00 Mon.–Fri., 8.00–12.00 Sat.
Ethiopia	8.00–20.00 Mon.–Fri., 2 or 3 hour lunch closing.
Fiji	8.00–17.00 Mon.–Fri.; late night Fri.
Finland	8.00–20.00 Mon.–Fri.; 8.00–18.00 Sat.
France	Food shops: 7.00–18.30/19.30 Mon.–Sat. Others: 9.00–18.30/19.30. Many close for all or half of Monday. Some food shops open on Sunday morning. In small towns many shops close between 12.00 and 14.00 for lunch.
French West Indies	8.00–12.00, 15.00–18.00 Mon.–Sat.
Gabon	8.00–18.30 Tues.–Sat., long lunch closing. Closed Mon.
Gambia	8.00–18.00 Mon.–Fri., 2 or 3 hour lunch closing; 8.00–12.00 Sat.
Fed. Rep. Germany	9.00–18.00 Mon.–Fri.; 8.00–13.00 Sat.
German Dem. Rep.	9.00–17.00 Mon.–Fri.; 9.00–13.00 Sat.
Ghana	9.00–15.30 Mon.–Thurs.; 9.00–15.30, 17.00–18.00 Fri. Closed Sat.
Great Britain	9.30–17.30 Mon.–Sat.; late night Thurs. or Fri.; half day on Wed. or Thurs. in small towns.
Greece	8.00–14.30, Mon., Wed., Sat.; 8.00–13.30, 17.00–20.00, Tues., Thurs., Fri.
Guinea	7.30–16.30, 2 hour lunch closing.
Guyana	8.00–16.00 Mon.–Fri. with lunchtime closing. Open Sat. mornings.
Honduras	8.00–18.00 Mon.–Fri., lunchtime closing. Open Sat. mornings.
Hong Kong	Central District – 10.00–18.00. Elsewhere – 10.00–21.00. Most shops remain open on Sunday.
Hungary	10.00–18.00 Mon.–Fri.; open till 20.00 on Thurs.; 9.00–13.00 Sat.
Iceland	9.00–18.00 Mon.–Thurs., 9.00–22.00 Fri., open Sat. morning.
India	Most government offices open 10.00–13.00 and 14.00–17.00 Mon.–Sat., except on the 2nd Sat. of the month.
Indonesia	During the 28 days following Ramadan, government and many other offices work a shorter business day, generally 8.00–12.00. Businesses otherwise open by 7.30.
Iran	Government offices generally open from 8.00–16.30 Sat.–Wed., private firms and shops generally close on Fri., open Sat.–Thurs. in the earlier part of the day and evening (summer) or all day (winter).
Iraq	9.00–13.00, 16.00–20.00 Sat.–Thurs. Everything closes on Friday.

Israel	8.00–13.00, 16.00–19.00 Sunday–Fri. (NB Arab shops are closed on Fri., and Christian ones on Sunday)
Italy	8.30/9.00–12.30/13.00, 15.30/14.00–19.30/20.00 Mon.–Sat. In Northern Italy the lunchbreak is shorter and shops close earlier.
Ivory Coast	8.00–12.00, 14.30–16.30 Mon.–Fri. Closed 17.30 Sat.
Jamaica	8.30–16.30, half day closing Wed. in Kingston.
Japan	9.00–17.00 or 10.00–18.00, Mon.–Fri.; 9.00–12.00 Sat. Closed Sun. Some stores also close one other day in the week.
Jordan	8.00–13.00, 16.00–18.00 Sat.–Thurs.
Kenya	8.00–18.00 Mon.–Sat. A few shops open Sun. 8.00–13.00.
Korea	Dept Stores: 10.30–19.30. Small shops: 8.00–22.00 Mon.-Fri. with half day on Sat.
Kuwait	8.30–12.30, 16.30–21.00. Some close Thurs. evening. Closed Fri.
Lebanon	Hours vary. Open late in winter.
Leeward Islands	8.00–16.00 Mon.–Sat. Closed Thurs. afternoon.
Liberia	8.00–18.00 Mon.–Sat., close for lunch.
Libya	Closed Fri.
Luxembourg	8.00–12.00, 14.00–18.00 Tues.–Sat. Closed Mon. morning. Only the largest supermarkets remain open at lunchtime.
Macao	9.00–22.00 Mon.–Sat. (Some stores close earlier, depending on the location.)
Madagascar	8.00–12.00, 14.00–18.00 Mon.–Fri.
Malawi	8.00–16.00 Mon.–Fri.
Malaysia	9.30–19.00 Daily. Supermarkets and Dept. Stores open from 10.00–22.00.
Mali	9.00–12.00, 15.00–18.00 Mon.–Fri. Open Sat. morning.
Malta	8.30–12.00, 16.00–19.00 Mon.–Sat.
Mauritius	8.00–19.00 Mon.–Sat.
Mexico	9.00–19.00 generally Mon., Tue., Thurs. and Fri.
Morocco	8.30–12.00, 14.00–18.30 Mon.–Sat.
Netherlands Antilles	8.00–12.00, 14.00–18.00 Mon.–Sat.
New Zealand	Normally 9.00–17.00 Mon.–Fri. One late night per week, usually Fri. in each town. Food and ice cream shops known as dairies generally open 9.00–19.00 Sat. and Sun. sometimes too.
Nicaragua	9.00–12.00, 14.00–16.00 Mon.–Sat.
Niger	8.00–12.00, 15.00–18.30 Mon.–Fri., 8.00–12.00 Sat.
Nigeria	8.30–12.30, 14.00–17.00 Mon.–Fri. Usually closed Sat. and Sun.
Norway	9.00–17.00 Mon.–Sat.
Oman	8.00–13.00 Sat.–Thurs.
Pakistan	9.30–13.00 Mon.–Thurs.; 9.00–10.30 Sat. in rural areas; 9.00–11.30 in main cities.
Panama	8.00–18.00 Mon.–Sat., long lunch closing.
Paraguay	7.00–11.30, 15.00–18.30 Mon.–Fri.; 7.00–11.30 Sat.
Peru	Some offices open for a continuous working day with short lunch closing, others for two shifts per day with a 2 or 3 hour lunch break. Summer (Jan.–Mar.) generally shorter hours than in winter. Shops 10.00/10.45–19.00/19.50
Philippines	Business and government normally 8.00/8.30–17.00 with a two hour lunch until 14.30/15.30. Closed Sat. and Sun.
Poland	7.00–19.00 Food stores; 11.00–19.00 other shops.
Portugal	9.00–13.00, 15.00–19.00 Mon.–Fri.; 9.00–13.00 Sat.

Qatar	7.30–12.30, 14.30/15.30–18.00 Sun.–Thurs.
Réunion	8.00–12.00, 14.00–18.00.
Saudi Arabia	Government offices 8.00–16.00 in winter (23rd Sept.–21st May), 7.00–15.00 in summer, Sat.–Wed. 1 hour lunch closing. During Ramadan, 8.00–14.00. Government offices open to the public morning only. Businesses normally 8.30–13.30, 16.30–20.30 Sat.–Thurs.
Sénégal	8.00–12.00, 14.30–18.00 Dec.–May. Longer lunch and open later June–Nov.
Seychelles	8.00–12.00, 13.00–16.00/17.00 Mon.–Fri.
Singapore	Shops in the city: 10.00–18.00 Dept. Stores: 10.00–22.00. Most shops are open 7 days a week.
South Africa	8.30–17.00 Mon.–Fri., 8.30–12.45/13.00 Sat. Most shops are closed on Sun. Many businesses shut for lunch.
Spain	9.00/10.00–13.00/13.30, 15.00/15.30–19.30/20.00. There are general stores in most towns that are open all day from 10.00–20.00
Sri Lanka	8.30–4.30 Mon.–Fri.; 8.30–13.00 Sat.
Sudan	8.00–13.00, 17.00–20.00 Sat.–Thurs.
Suriname	7.00–13.00, 16.00–18.00 Mon.–Sat.
Swaziland	8.00–17.00 Mon.–Fri.; 8.30–14.00 Sat.
Sweden	9.30–17.30 Mon.–Fri.; 9.30–14.00 Sat.
Switzerland	8.00–12.00, 14.00–18.00. Close at 16.00 on Sat. Often close all day Mon.
Syria	8.00–13.30, 16.30–21.00 Sat.–Thurs.
Tahiti	7.30–11.30, 13.30–17.30 Mon.–Fri., 7.30–11.30 Sat.
Tanzania	8.00–12.00, 14.00–17.00 Mon.–Sat.
Thailand	Usually open until 19.00 or 20.00. No standard hours.
Togo	8.00–18.00 Mon.–Fri., 2 hour lunch closing. Open Sat. morning.
Tonga	8.30–12.30, 13.30–16.40 Mon.–Fri.; 8.30–12.00 Sat. Closed Sun.
Trinidad & Tobago	8.00–16.00 Mon.–Fri. and Sat. morning. Supermarkets closed Thurs. afternoon.
Tunisia	8.30–13.00, 15.00–17.00 Mon.–Fri.; Sat. 9.00–14.00.
Turkey	9.00–13.00, 14.00–19.00 Mon.–Sat. Small shops may stay open late and not close for the lunch hour.
US Virgin Islands	9.00–17.00 Mon.–Sat.
United Arab Emirates	8.00–12.00, 16.00–19.00. Closed Fri.
USSR	Food stores: 8.00–20.00, some till 22.00. Other shops: 11.00–20.00. Some big dept stores: 8.00–21.00. Only food stores open on Sundays – till 19.00.
Upper Volta	7.30–12.30, 15.00–17.30 Mon.–Fri.
Uruguay	9.00–12.00, 14.00–19.00 Mon.–Fri. (Many stores stay open at lunchtime.) 9.00–12.30 Sat.
Venezuela	9.00–13.00, 14.00–16.30 Mon.–Fri.
Windward Islands	Usually 8.00–12.00 and 12.00–13.00 or 13.30–16.00. Some closing Wed. or Thurs. afternoon.
Zimbabwe	8.00–17.00, often with an hour for lunch. Closed Sat. afternoon and Sun. Selected pharmacies have day-and-night services in all main centres.

Clothing Sizes

LADIES

Dresses, Coats, Skirts/Jr Sizes						*Misses Sizes*					
American	7	9	11	13	15	8	10	12	14	16	18
British	9	11	13	15	17	10	12	14	16	18	20
Continental	34	36	38	40	42	38	40	42	44	46	48

Blouses, Sweaters						
American	10	12	14	16	18	20
British	32	34	36	38	40	42
Continental	38	40	42	44	46	48

Shoes											
American	4½	5	5½	6	6½	7	7½	8	8½	9	9½
British	3	3½	4	4½	5	5½	6	6½	7	7½	8
Continental	35½	36	36½	37	37½	38	38½	39	39½	40	40½

CHILDREN

American	3	4	5	6	6X
British	18	20	22	24	26
Continental	98	104	110	116	122

(*For older children, sizes usually correspond with their ages.*)

Shoes									
American	8	9	10	11	12	13	1	2	3
British	7	8	9	10	11	12	13	1	2
Continental	24	25	27	28	29	30	32	33	34

MEN

Suits									
American	34	35	36	37	38	39	40	41	42
British	34	35	36	37	38	39	40	41	42
Continental	44	46	48	49½	51	52½	54	55½	57

Shirts								
American	14½	15	15½	16	16½	17	17½	18
British	14½	15	15½	16	16½	17	17½	18
Continental	37	38	39	41	42	43	44	45

Public Holidays

(*Dates of some Religious Holidays may change from one year to another according to Lunar Calendar*).

Algeria Jan 1; May 1; June 19; July 5; Nov 1 (approx. Use lunar months). Europeans observe Christian holidays.

Andorra Sept 8: National Holiday of Meritxell.

Antigua Jan 1; Easter; May 31; Whitsun; Nov 1.

Antigua and Barbuda Dec 25; Jan 1; May 1; Aug 1; Nov 1.

Argentina Jan 1, Labour Day; May 25, Revolution (1810) Day; June 20, Flag Day; July 9, Independence (1816) Day; Aug 17, Death of General José de San Martin; Oct 12, Discovery of America (Columbus Day); and Dec 25, Christmas. On a number of other days, government offices, banks, insurance companies, and courts are closed, but closing is optional for business and commerce. These include: Jan 1, New Year's Day; Jan 6, Epiphany; and several days with variable dates – Carnival Monday and Tuesday before Ash Wednesday, Holy Thursday and Good Friday before Easter, and

Corpus Christi; Aug 15, Assumption of the Virgin Mary; Nov 1, All Saints' Day and Dec 8, Feast of the Immaculate Conception. In addition, there are local patriotic or religious holidays, which may be observed by part or all of the community in various cities or provinces.

Australia Jan 1; Australia Day (last Monday in Jan); Good Friday, Easter Sunday, Easter Monday + Bank Holiday; April 25, ANZAC Day; the Queen's Birthday; Dec 25 and 26. Holidays vary from State to State and only ANZAC Day and Australia Day are National Holidays.

Austria Jan 1; Jan 6; Easter Monday; May 1; Ascension Day; Whit Monday; Corpus Christi; Aug 15; Assumption Day; Oct 26, National Day; Nov 1, All Saints' Day; Dec 8, Immaculate Conception; Dec 25; Dec 26.

Bahamas Jan 1; Good Friday; Easter Monday; Labour Day (early June); Whit Monday; July 10, Independence Day; Emancipation Day (early Aug); Oct 12, Discovery Day; Dec 25; Dec 26. Those holidays which fall on a Sunday are normally observed on the following day. Offices and stores are generally closed throughout the country on public holidays.

Bangladesh Dec–Jan, Eid-e-Miladunnabi; Feb 21, Shaheed Dibash; Feb, Maghi Purnima; Feb–Mar, Shivaratri; Mar 26, Independence Day; Apr, Bengali New Year's Day; May, Tagore's birthday; May, Nazrul's birthday; May, Shab-e-Barat; July, Eid-ul-Fitr; Sept, Eid-ul-Azha; Oct, Durga Puja; Oct, Muharram; Dec 16, Victory Day; Dec 25.

Barbados Jan 1; Good Friday; Easter Monday; Whit Monday; First Monday in July, Aug and Sept; Independence Day; Nov 30; Dec 25; Dec 26.

Belgium Jan 1; Easter Monday; May 1; Ascension Day; Pentecost Monday; July 21, National Holiday; Aug 15, Assumption Day; Nov 1, All Saints' Day; Nov 11, Armistice Day; Nov 15, King's Birthday (only for administrative and public offices, schools etc); 25 Dec; 26 Dec.

Belize Jan 1; Mar 9; May 1; May 24; Sept 10; Sept 24, National Day; Oct 12; Nov 19; Dec 25; Dec 26. Good Friday, Holy Saturday and Easter Monday. Those holidays which fall on a Sunday are normally observed on the following day.

Bermuda Jan 1; Good Friday; Bermuda Day; Queen's Birthday; Cup Match; Somer's Day; Labour Day; Remembrance Day; Dec 25; Dec 26.

Bolivia Jan 1; Feb 3; Carnival Week (preceding Lent); Holy Week (3 days preceding Easter; May 1, Labour day; May 2, Lake Titicaca (reed and canoe regatta); Corpus Christi; 23 June, St John's Day; 29 June; St Peter & Paul Tiquina; July 15–16, La Paz Day, July 21, Martyrs' Day; Aug 6–7, Independence Festival; Sept 8; Oct 12; Nov 1, All Saints' Day; Nov 17–18; Dec 8, Immaculate Conception; Dec 25.

Botswana Jan 1; Jan 2; Easter; May 31, Ascension Day; July 16, President's Day; July 17; Sept 30, Botswana Day; Oct 1; Oct 2; Dec 25; Dec 26.

Brazil Jan 1; Carnival (3 days preceding Lent); Easter; Apr 21, Tiradentes Day; May 1, Labour Day; Sept 7, Independence Day; Nov 2, All Souls' Day; Nov 15, Proclamation of the Republic; Dec 25.

Burma Jan 4, Independence Day; Feb 12, Union Day; Mar 2, Peasants' Day; Mar 27, Armed Forces Day; mid-Apr, Thingyan Water Festival; May 1, Worker's Day; early May, Buddah's Day; July, Full moon of Wazo; Oct, Thadingyut Festival; Nov, Tazaundaing Festival of Lights; Dec 25.

Burundi Jan 1; Ascension; May 1; July 1; Aug 15; Sept 18; Nov 1; Dec 25.

Canada Jan 1; Easter; May 20; July 1; Sept 2; Oct 14; Nov 11; Dec 25; Dec 26.

Cayman Islands Jan 1; Ash Wednesday; Easter; May 20, Discovery Day; Queen's Birthday; July 1, Constitution Day; Nov 11, Monday after Remembrance Sunday; Dec 25; Dec 26.

Chile May 1; May 21; Sept 18.

China New Year's Day; Spring Festival – Lunar New Year (3 days); May 1; Oct 1 + 2.

Colombia Jan 1; Jan 6; Mar 19; Easter; May 1; Ascension Day; Corpus Christi; June 29; July 20; Aug 7; Oct 12; Nov 1; Nov 11; Dec 8; Dec 25.

Costa Rica Jan 1; St Joseph's Day; Easter; Apr 11, National Heroes Day; May 1, Labour Day; Corpus Christi; June 29, Sts Peter & Paul; July 25; Aug 2, Our Lady of Angels; Sept 15, Independence Day; Oct 12, Day of the Race; Dec 8, Immaculate Conception; Dec 25; Dec 29–31, Civic Holiday.

Czechoslovakia	Jan 1; Easter Monday; May 1; May 9, Liberation Day; Dec 25; Dec 26.
Denmark	Jan 1; Easter; Apr 16, National Day (School Holiday), Queen Margrethe II's Birthday; Great Prayer Day; Ascension Day; Whit Monday; June 5, Constitution Day; Dec 25; Dec 26.
Djibouti	June 27.
Dominica	Jan 1; Jan 2; Shrove Tuesday and Monday preceding; Easter; Whit Monday; May 1; 1st Monday in Aug; Nov 1–3; Dec 25; Dec 26.
Dominican Republic	Jan 1; Jan 6; Jan 21; Jan 26, Duarte Day; Feb 27, Independence Day; Easter; May 1, Labour Day; Corpus Christi, Aug 16, Restoration Day; Sept 24, Patron Saint Day; Dec 25.
Eastern Caribbean States	Jan 1; Easter; 1st Monday in May, Labour Day; Whit Monday; August Monday – National Day of each island.
Finland	Jan 1; Easter; May 1; May 26; June 9; June 23; Nov 3; Dec 6; Dec 25; Dec 26.
France	Jan 1; Easter; May 1; May 8; Ascension Day; Whitsun; July 14; Assumption; Nov 1, All Saints' Day; Nov 11, Remembrance Day; Dec 25.
The Gambia	Feb 1; Feb 18; Easter; May 1; Aug 15; Dec 25; Dec 26; Id-El Fizr; Id-El-Kabir; Mawlud-El-Nabi.
Germany–East (Dem. Rep.)	Jan 1; May 1; Oct 7; Whit Monday.
Germany–West (Fed. Rep.)	Jan 1; Jan 6, Epiphany; Easter; May 1, Labour Day; Ascension Day; Whit Monday; Corpus Christi; June 17, Day of Unity; Aug 15, Ascension of the Virgin Mary; Day of Prayer and Repentance; Dec 25; Dec 26.
Gibraltar	Jan 1; Mar 12, Commonwealth Day; Easter; May 1; last Monday in May; Queen's Birthday; last Monday in Aug; Dec 25; Dec 26.
Greece	Jan 1; Jan 6, Epiphany; Shrove Monday; Mar 25; Easter; May 1, Labour Day; June 11, Day of the Holy Spirit; Aug 15, Assumption of the Virgin Mary; Oct 28, Ochi Day; Dec 25; Dec 26.
Guyana	Jan 1; Feb 23, Republic Anniversary; Easter; May 1, Labour Day; First Monday in July, Caribbean Day; First Monday in Aug, Freedom Day; Dec 25; Dec 26. You-Man-Nabi; Phagwah; Deepavali; Eid-ul-Azha – dates to be decided annually.
Hong Kong	The first weekday in Jan; Lunar New Year's Day; the second and third day of Lunar New Year; Ching Ming Festival; Easter; Tuen Ng (Dragon Boat) Festival; the Queen's Birthday; Saturday preceding the last Monday in July; last Monday in Aug, Liberation Day; day following the Chinese Mid-Autumn Festival; Chung Yeung Festival; Dec 25; Dec 26.
Hungary	Jan 1; Apr 4, Liberation Day; Easter; May 1; Aug 20, Constitution Day; Nov 7, Anniversary of the Great October Socialist Revolution; Dec 25; Dec 26.
Iceland	Jan 1; Easter; Apr 18, First Day of Summer; May 1; Ascension Day; Whit Monday; June 17, National Day; Dec 24, 25, 26, 31.
India	Jan 1; Jan 26, Republic Day; Aug 15, Independence Day; Oct 2, Mahatma Gandhi's Birthday; Dec 25. Also thirty-two other religious or special occasions which are observed either with national or regional holidays. Government offices are normally closed on these days.
Indonesia	Jan 1; Easter; Mar 13, Hari Maulud Nabi (Muslim Festival); Ascension Day; Waicak Day (celebrating Buddha's birth); June 9, Galunggan in Bali (a New Year Feast lasting ten days); Sekaten (birth of Mohammed); Aug 17, Independence Day; Sept 25–26, Idul Fitri (Muslim festival); Dec 25. Dates for certain holidays change with the lunar calendar. In addition to the holidays listed, business visitors should note the Islamic month of fasting, Ramadan.
Iraq	Jan 1; Jan 6; Feb 8; Mar 21; May 1; July 14; July 17. In addition there are various religious holidays, including Ramadan.
Israel	All business activity ceases on Saturdays and religious holidays, the dates of which vary from one year to another: Passover, first day; Passover, last day; Israel Independence Day; Shavout (Feast of Weeks); Pentecost; Rosh Hashana (New Year); Yom Kippur (Day of Atonement); First Day of Tabernacles; Last Day of Tabernacles; Hanukkah.

Italy	On Italian National Holidays, offices, shops and schools are closed: Jan 1; Easter; Apr 25, Liberation Day; May 1, Labour Day; Aug 15, Assumption of the Blessed Virgin Mary; Nov 1, All Saints' Day; Dec 8, Immaculate Conception of the Blessed Virgin Mary; Dec 25; Dec 26.
Ivory Coast	Jan 1; Easter; May 1, Labour Day; Ascension Day; Whit Monday; Aug 15, Assumption of the Virgin Mary; Nov 1, All Saints' Day; Dec 7, National Day; Dec 25; Dates for Ramadan and Tabaski (Feast of the Mutton-Muslim) vary from one year to another.
Jamaica	Jan 1; Ash Wednesday; Easter; May 23, Labour Day; First Monday in Aug, Independence Day; Third Monday in Oct, National Heroes' Day; Dec 25; Dec 26.
Japan	Jan 1; Jan 2, 3, 4, Bank Holidays (all commercial firms closed); Jan 15, Adults' Day; Feb 11, National Foundation Day; Vernal Equinox Day (variable date); Apr 29, the Emperor's birthday; May 1; May 3, Consitution Memorial Day; May 5, Children's Day; Sept 15, Respect of the Aged Day; Autumnal Equinox Day (variable date); Oct 10, Physical Culture Day; Nov 3, Culture Day; Nov 23, Labour Thanksgiving Day; Dec 28, New Year's holiday begins (lasts five to ten days). Also 'Golden Week' in late spring when some firms remain closed. Some manufacturers close for a week during the summer.
Jordan	Jan 1; Mar 22; May 1; May 10; May 25; July 1–4; Aug 11; Sept 6–10; Nov 14; Dec 5; Dec 25.
Kenya	Jan 1; Easter; May 1; June 1, Madaraka day; Oct 20, Kenyatta Day; Dec 12, Independence Day; Dec 25; Dec 26; Idd-ul-Fitr (an Islamic feast at the end of Ramadan).
Korea	Jan 1–3; Mar 1, Independence Day; Apr 5, Arbor Day; May 5, Children's Day; Early May, Buddha's birthday; Early June, Memorial Day; July 17, Constitution Day; Aug 15, Liberation Day; Korean Thanksgiving Day; Oct 1, Armed Forces Day; Oct 3, National Foundation Day; Oct 9, Hangul Day; Oct 24, United Nations Day; Dec 25.
Kuwait	Religious holidays vary from one year to another. The only fixed holidays in Kuwait are New Year's Day and Kuwait National Day (Feb 25). October to May or June is generally considered the best period for foreign business visitors; business slackens off in the summer.
Liberia	Jan 1; Feb 11, Armed Forces Day; Mar 15, J. J. Robert's birthday; Second Wednesday in March, Decoration Day; Apr 12, National Redemption Day; Second Friday in April, Fast & Prayer Day; May 14, National Unification Day; May 25, African Liberation Day; July 26, Independence Day; Aug 24, National Flag Day; 1st Thursday in Nov, Thanksgiving Day; Nov 29, William V. S. Tubman's birthday; Dec 25.
Luxembourg	Jan 1; Easter; May 1; Ascension Day; Whit Monday; June 23, National Day; Aug 15, Assumption Day; Nov 1, All Saints' Day; Dec 25; Dec 26. In addition to these Public Holidays, there are various Bank Holidays throughout the year.
Macao	Jan 1; Feb, Chinese New Year; Apr, Ching Ming Festival; Easter; Apr 25, Anniversary of Portuguese Revolution; May 1; Jun 10, Camoens Day and Portuguese Communities; June, Corpus Christi, Dragon Boat Festival, Feast of St John the Baptist; Aug 15, Assumption of Our Lady; Sept, Mid-Autumn Festival; Oct 5, Republic Day; Oct 22, Festival of Ancestors; Nov 1–2, All Saints' Day–All Souls' Day; Dec 1, Restoration of Independence; Dec 8, Feast of Immaculate Conception; Dec 22, Winter Solstice; Dec 24–25, Christmas.
Malaysia	Jan 1 (for Kuala Lumpur); Feb 1, City Day (for Kuala Lumpur); Feb 2–3, Chinese New Year; May 1; Labour Day; May 15, Wesak Day; June 6, Birthsay of Dymm Sri Paduka Baginda Yang diPertuan Agong; Hari Raya Puasa (dates vary); Aug 31, National Day; Sept 26, Awal Muharram; Oct 23, Deepavali; Dec 5, Birthday of Prophet Muhammad; Dec 25.
Mali	Jan 1; Jan 20, Festival of the Army; May 1, Labour Day; May 25, Africa Day; Sept 22, National Day; Nov 19.
Malta	Jan 1; Mar 31; Easter; May 1; Aug 15; Dec 13; Dec 25.
Mauritius	Jan 1; Jan 2; Jan 19; Feb 2; Feb 29; Mar 12; Apr 2; May 1; June 30; Aug 30; Oct 24; Nov 1; Dec 25.
Mexico	Jan 1; Feb 5; Feb 24; Mar 21; Easter; May 1; May 5; Sept 1; Sept 16; Oct 12; Nov 20; Dec 25.
Morocco	Mar 3; Nov 6; Religious holidays vary from one year to another.

Netherlands	Jan 1; Easter; Ascension Day; Whit Monday; Dec 25; Dec 26. Queen's Day, April 30 and Liberation Day, May 5 are public holidays for the Civil Service, but shops and offices etc. need not necessarily be closed.
New Zealand	Jan 1; Feb 6, New Zealand Day; Easter; Apr 25, ANZAC Day; the Queen's Birthday (generally observed in early June); Oct, Labour Day; Dec 25; Dec 26. Also a holiday for the provincial anniversary in each provincial district i.e. Jan 29, Auckland; Dec 16, Canterbury; Nov 1, Hawkes Bay; Nov 1, Marlborough; Feb 1, Nelson; Feb 6, Northland; Mar 23, Otago; Mar 23, Southland; Mar 31, Taranaki; Jan 22, Wellington.
Nicaragua	Jan 1; Easter; May 1; July 19; Sept 14; Sept 15; Dec 24; Dec 25.
Niger	Apr 15, National Armed Forces Day; Aug 3, Proclamation of Independence; Dec 18; Proclamation of the Republic.
Norway	May 17.
Oman	Nov 18 and Nov 19, National Day.
Paraguay	Jan 1; Feb 3, San Blas Patron Saint; Mar 1, Hero's Day; Easter; May 1, Labour Day; May 14 and 15, Independence Day; June 12, Chaco Peace; Corpus Christi; Aug 15, Assumption Day; Aug 25, Constitution Day; Sept 29, Battle of Boqueron (Chaco War); Oct 12, Colombus Day; Nov 1, All Saints' Day; Dec 8, Immaculate Conception; Dec 25.
Peru	Jan 1; Easter; May 1, Labour Day; June 24, Countryman's Day/Day of the Peasant; June 29, St Peter and St Paul; July 28–29, Independence Days; Aug 30, St Rose of Lima; Oct 8, Combat of Angamos; Nov 1, All Saints' Day; Dec 8, Immaculate Conception; Dec 25. Banks closed June 30 and Dec 31.
Philippines	Jan 1; Easter; May 1, Labour Day; June 12, Independence Day; July 4, Philippine-American Day; Nov 30, National Heroes' Day; Dec 25; Dec 30, Rizal Day. Additional holidays such as Bataan Day and General Elections Day may be called by the President of the Republic.
Poland	Jan 1; Easter; May 1, Labour Day; Corpus Christi; July 22, National Day; Nov 1, All Saints' Day; Dec 25; Dec 26.
Portugal	Jan 1; Shrove Tuesday; Easter; Apr 25; May 1; Corpus Christi; June 10; Aug 15; Oct 5; Nov 1; Dec 1; Dec 8; Dec 25. There are also various local holidays in towns and villages throughout the country. Details from local tourist offices. Carnival is also an important event in Portugal and takes place during the four days preceding Lent.
Qatar	Feb 22, Anniversary of the Accession of HH The Emir, Sheikh Khalifa Bin Hamad Al-Thani; Sept 3, Independence Day. Eid Al-Fitr, Eid Al-Adha and Hijri New Year change dates annually as they follow the lunar calendar.
El Salvador	Jan 1; Easter; May 1; Aug 1–6, August Festivities; Sept 15; Nov 2; Dec 25. Banks closed June 29 and 30.
Samoa (American)	All United States holidays and Apr 17, Flag Day.
Saudi Arabia	During the month of Ramadan (which varies from one year to another according to the lunar calendar), all Muslims refrain from eating, drinking and smoking from sunrise to sunset. Business hours are shortened. Non-Muslims must also observe the fast while in public.
Sénégal	All Christian Holidays; All Muslim holidays, which vary yearly; Apr 4; Ascension Day; May Day; Assumption Day.
Seychelles	Jan 1; Jan 2; Easter; May 1, Labour Day; Assumption Day; June 5, Liberation Day; June 29, Independence Day; Corpus Christi; Aug 15, Assumption of Mary; Nov 1, All Saints' Day; Dec 8, Feast of the Immaculate Conception; Dec 25; Sept; La Fete La Digue/Annual Regatta; Nov, Annual Fishing Competition.
Singapore	Jan 1; May 1, Labour Day; May 17, Vesak Day; Aug 9, National Day; Oct 29, Hari Raya Punsa; Dec 25. Holidays with variable dates are Hari Raya Haji, Chinese New Year, Good Friday and Deepavali. When a holiday falls on a Sunday, the next day is taken as a public holiday.
South Africa	Jan 1; Apr 6, Founder's Day; Easter; Family Day; Ascension Day; May 31, Republic Day; Oct 10, Kruger Day; Dec 16, Day of the Vow; Dec 25; Dec 26, Day of Goodwill.
Spain	Jan 6; Mar 19; Easter; May 1; June 21; July 25; Aug 15; Oct 12; Nov 18; Dec 8; Dec 25.

Sweden	Jan 1; Jan 6, Epiphany; Easter; May 1, Labour Day; Ascension Day; Whit Monday; Midsummer's Day; All Saint's Day; Dec 25; Dec 26.
Switzerland	Jan 1; Easter; Ascension Day; Whit Monday; Dec 25; Dec 26. Certain Cantons: Jan 2; May 1; Corpus Christi; Aug 1, National Day.
Tahiti	Jan 1; Easter; May 1, Labour Day; May 8, Victory Day; Ascension Day; Pentecost; Whit Monday; July 14, National Day; Aug 15, Assumption; Nov 1, All Saints' Day; Nov 11, Armistice Day; Dec 25.
Tanzania	Jan 12, Revolution of Zanzibar; Feb 5, Chama Chamapinduzi (CCM) Day; Apr 26, Union Day; May 1; July 7, Saba-Saba Farmers' Day; Dec 9, Independence and Republic Day; Dec 25. Muslim Holidays vary according to lunar calendar.
Thailand	Jan 1; Apr 13, The Songkran Festival (Buddhist New Year); May 5, Coronation Day Anniversary; May, Visakhja Puja (Buddhist Festival); June/July, Buddhist Lent Begins; Aug 12, Queen's Birthday; Oct 23, Chulalongkorn Day; Dec 5, King's Birthday; Dec 31.
Tonga	Jan 1; Easter; Apr 25, ANZAC Day; May 4, Birthday of HRH Crown Prince Tupouto'a; May 13–21, Red Cross Week; Early June, Opening of Parliament; June 4, Emancipation Day; July 4, Birthday of HM King Taufa'ahua Tupou IV and Coronation Day; Early July, Heilala Festival; Late Aug to early Sept, Royal Agricultural Shows; Nov 4, Consitution Day; Early Dec, Music Festival; Dec 4, King Tupou I Day; Dec 25; Dec 26.
Trinidad and Tobago	Jan 1; Easter; Whit Monday; Corpus Christi; Labour Day; First Monday in Aug, Discovery Day; Aug 31, Independence Day; Sept 24, Republic Day; Eid-Ul-Fitr (Muslim Festival); Divali (Hindu Festival); Dec 25; Dec 26.
Tunisia	Jan 1; Jan 18; Mar 20; Easter; May 1; June 1–2; Aug 3; Aug 13; Sept 3; Oct 15.
Turkey	Jan 1; Apr 23, National Independence Children's Day; May 19, Youth and Sports Day; Aug 30, Victory Day (Anniversary of the Declaration of the Turkish Republic).
Turks and Caicos	Jan 1; Easter; June 6, James McCartney Memorial Day; Aug 1, Emancipation Day; Oct 12, International Human Rights Day; Dec 25; Dec 26.
United Arab Emirates	Jan 1; 12 Rabia Al Awal, Prophet's Birthday; 27 Rajab, Ascension Day; 1 Shawwal, Id Al-Fitr; Aug 6, Accession Day of HH Sheikh Zayed, President of UAE; 10 Dhul Hiffa, Id Al Adha; 1 Muharram, Muslim New Year; Dec 2, National Day.
USSR	Jan 1; Mar 8, International Women's Day; May 1–2, International Labour Day; May 9, Victory Day; Oct 7, Constitution Day; Nov 7–8, October Revolution.
Upper Volta	Jan 1; May 1; Catholic and Muslim Festivals.
Uruguay	Jan 1; Jan 6; Apr 19, Day of 33 Orientals; May 1; May 18, Battle of Las Piedras; June 19, Birth of Artigas; July 18, Constitution Day; Aug 25, Independence Day; Oct 12, Columbus Day; Nov 2, All Souls' Day; Dec 25. Carnival Week (Feb or Mar) and Tourist Week (Mar or Apr) have variable dates.
Virgin Islands (British)	Jan 1; Feb 23, Commemoration of visit by HM The Queen ; Easter; Commonwealth Day; Queen's Birthday; July 1, Territory Day; First Monday, Tuesday and Wednesday in Aug; Oct 21, St Ursula's Day; Nov 14, Prince of Wales' Birthday; Dec 25; Dec 26.
Virgin Islands (United States)	Jan 1; Jan 6; Jan 15, Martin Luther King's Birthday; Feb 13, Abraham Lincoln's Birthday; Feb 20, George Washington's Birthday; Mar 17, St Patrick's Day; 31 Mar, Transfer Day; Easter; mid-Apr, Rolex Regatta; Apr 23–30, Carnival Calypso Tent on St Thomas; Apr 30–May 5, Carnival Week St Thomas; May 4, Children's Parade; May 5, Adult's Parade; May 31, Memorial Day; June 18, Organic Act Day; July 3, Danish West Indies Emancipation Day; July 4, Independence Day; July 25, Hurricane Supplication Day; Sept 3, Labour Day; Oct 8, Columbus Day and Puerto Rico/Virgin Islands Friendship Day; Oct 19, Hurricane Thanksgiving Day; Nov 1, Liberty Day; Mid-Nov, Virgin Islands Charterboat League Show; Nov 11, Veterans' Day; Nov 22, National Thanksgiving Day; Dec 25; Dec 26; Dec 27, Opening of Crucian Christmas Fiesta.
Yugoslavia	Jan 1; Jan 2; May 1–2; July 4; Nov 29–30.
Zaïre	Jan 1; Jan 4; May 1; May 20; June 24; June 30; Aug 1; Oct 14; Oct 27; Nov 17; Nov 24; Dec 25.
Zambia	Jan 1; Mar 17; Apr 20–21; May 1; May 25; July 2–3; Aug 6; Oct 24–26; Dec 25; Dec 26.

Worldwide Voltage Guide

In general, all references to 110V apply to the range from 100V to 160V. References to 220V apply to the range from 200V to 260V. Where 110/220V is indicated, voltage varies within country, depending on location.

An adapter kit may be necessary to provide prongs of various types that will fit into outlets which do not accept plugs from the traveller's own country. A converter is also necessary where the voltage differs from that of the traveller's electrical appliances. Plugging an electrical appliance manufactured to 110V into a 220V outlet without using a converter may destroy the appliance and blow fuses elsewhere in the building.

Aden	220V
Afghanistan	220V
Algeria	110/220V
Angola	220V
Anguilla	220V
Antigua	110/220V
†Argentina	220V
Aruba	110V
†Australia	220V
Austria	220V
Azores	110/220V
Bahamas	110/220V
Bahrain	220V
Bangladesh	220V
Barbados	110/220V
Belgium	110/220V
Belize	110/220V
Benin	220V
Bermuda	110/220V
Bhutan	220V
Bolivia	110/220V
Bonaire	110/220V
Botswana	220V
†Brazil	110/220V
Brit. Virgin I.	110/220V
Bulgaria	110/220V
Burma	220V
Burundi	220V
Cameroon	110/220V
Canada	110/220V
Canary I.	110/220V
Cayman I.	110V
Cen. African Rep.	220V
Chad	220V
***Channel I. (Brit.)**	220V
†Chile	220V
China	220V
Colombia	110V
Costa Rica	110/220V
Cuba	110V
Curaçao	110V
***Cyprus**	220V
Czechoslovakia	110/220V
Denmark	220V
Dominica	220V
Dominican Rep.	110/220V
Ecuador	110/220V
Egypt	110/220V
El Salvador	110V
Ethiopia	110/220V
Fiji	220V
Finland	220V
France	110/220V
French Guiana	110/220V
Gabon	220V
Gambia	220V
†Germany	110/220V
Ghana	220V
Gibraltar	220V
***Great Britain**	220V
†Greece	110/220V
Greenland	220V
Grenada	220V
Grenadines	220V
Guadeloupe	110/220V
Guatemala	110/220V
Guinea	220V
Guyana	110/220V
Haiti	110/220V
Honduras	110/220V
***Hong Kong**	220V
Hungary	220V
Iceland	220V
†India	220V
Indonesia	110/220V
Iran	220V
Iraq	220V
Ireland	220V
Isle of Man	220V
Israel	220V
Italy	110/220V
Ivory Coast	220V
Jamaica	110/220V
Japan	110V
Jordan	220V
Kampuchea	110/220V
Kenya	220V
Korea, South	220V
Kuwait	220V
Lao People's Dem. Rep. (Laos)	110/220V
Lebanon	110/220V
Lesotho	220V
Liberia	110/220V
Libya	110/220V
Liechtenstein	220V
Luxembourg	110/220V
Macao	110/220V
Madagascar	220V
†Madeira	220V
Majorca	110V
Malawi	220V
Malaysia	110/220V
Mali	110/220V
Malta	220V
Martinique	110/220V
Mauritania	220V
Mexico	110/220V

Monaco	110/220V
Montserrat	220V
Morocco	110/220V
Mozambique	220V
Nepal	220V
Netherlands	110/220V
Neth. Antilles	110/220V
Nevis	220V
New Caledonia	220V
New Zealand	220V
Nicaragua	110/220V
Niger	220V
***Nigeria**	220V
Norway	220V
Oman	220V
Pakistan	220V
Panama	110V
Papua New Guinea	220V
†Paraguay	220V
Peru	220V
Philippines	110/220V
Poland	110/220V
Portugal	110/220V
Puerto Rico	110V
Qatar	220V
Romania	110/220V
Rwanda	220V
St. Barthélemy	220V
St. Eustatius	110/220V
St. Kitts	220V
St. Lucia	220V
St. Maarten	110/220V
St. Vincent	220V
Saudi Arabia	110/220V
Sénégal	110V
Seychelles	220V
Sierra Leone	220V
***Singapore**	110/220V
Somalia	110/220V
South Africa	220V
Spain	110/220V
Sri Lanka	220V
Sudan	220V
Suriname	110/220V
Swaziland	220V
†Sweden	110/220V
Switzerland	110/220V
Syria	110/220V
Tahiti	110/220V
Taiwan	110/220V
Tanzania	220V
Togo	110/220V
Tonga	220V
Trinidad and Tobago	110/220V
Tunisia	110/220V
Turkey	110/220V
Turks & Caicos I.	110V
Uganda	220V
Upper Volta (Burkina Faso)	220V
Uruguay	220V
United Arab Emirates	220V
USA	110V
USSR	110/220V
US Virgin I.	110V
Vanuatu	220V
Venezuela	110/220V
Vietnam	110/220V
Yemen	220V
Yugoslavia	220V
Zaïre	220V
Zambia	220V
***Zimbabwe**	220V

**Denotes countries in which plugs with 3 square pins are used (in whole or part).*
†Countries using DC in certain areas.

English language newspapers/magazines published abroad

(*Those countries where English is spoken widely have not, in the main, been included, as information is easy to obtain.*)

Argentina
Buenos Aires Herald (weekly newspaper) $A7.00
Azopardo 455, 1107 Bs. As.
The Review of the River Plate (on financial matters)

Antigua
Nation's Voice – twice a month
Worker's Voice – once a week
Standard – once a week
Outlet – once a week

Bahamas
Nassau Guardian – daily
Nassau Tribune – daily
Freeport News – daily

Bangladesh
Bangladesh Observer – daily
Bangladesh Times – daily
New Nation – daily
Holiday – weekly
Bangladesh Today – weekly
Tide – weekly

Barbados
The Advocate – News – daily
The Nation – Mon–Fri
Junior Nation – Mon–Fri
The Sunday Sun
The Bajan – monthly

Belize
Sunday Times – 40¢, weekly
Reporter – 40¢, weekly
Amandala – 40¢, weekly
The Voice – 40¢, weekly
The Beacon – 40¢, weekly
Disweek – 40¢, weekly
The Tribune – 40¢, weekly

Bermuda
Royal Gazette – 30¢, daily
Mid Ocean News – 40¢, Fri
Bermuda Sun – 45¢, Fri
Numerous magazines

Botswana
Botswana Daily News – Free
Botswana Guardian – 10 *thebe*, Fri

Burma
The Working People's Daily
The Guardian Daily

Cayman Islands
Cayman Compass – $0.25
Horizon magazine – Free, bi-monthly
Nor'Wester – $3.00, bi-monthly
Tourist Weekly – Free
Looking – Free, monthly

China
China daily
China Reconstructs – monthly
China Pictorial – monthly
Peking Review – weekly

Costa Rica
Tico Times – US$40.00 (annual fee), weekly

Czechoslovakia
Czechoslavakia Life – 5 Czech crowns, monthly
Welcome to Czechoslovakia – US$1.20, quarterly

Commonwealth of Dominica
Dominica Chronicle – weekly

Dominican Republic
Santo Domingo News – Free, weekly

Fiji
Fiji Times – daily
Fiji Sun – daily

The Gambia
Gambia News Bulletin – twice a week
The Senegambia Sun – daily

Guyana
Guyana Chronicle – 25¢, daily
Guyana Chronicle – 50¢, Sunday issue

Hong Kong
South China Morning Post – daily incl. Sunday, HK$1.50
Hong Kong Standard – daily incl. Sunday HK £1.50

Hungary
Daily News – 10p
Hungarian Week – 10p

Iceland
News from Iceland – monthly

Iraq
Baghdad Times – daily, 100 fils (20 pence)

Israel
Jerusalem Post – daily

Jamaica
The Daily Gleaner – daily, J$0.60
The Star – daily, J$0.40

Jordan
Jordan Times – 100 *fils*, daily
Jerusalem Star – 150 *fils*, weekly

Kenya
The Standard – Ksh 2, daily
Nation – Ksh 2, daily
Kenya Times – Ksh 2, daily
The Weekly Review – Ksh 7.50

Korea
Korea Herald – 11 pence, daily excl. Mon.
Korea Times – 11 pence, daily excl. Mon.
Korea News Review – weekly

Liberia
The Observer
The New Liberian
The Scope
The Express
The Mirror
The Bong Crier
Afro Media magazine

Malaysia
New Straits Times
New Sunday Times
Malay Mail
Sunday Mail
The Star
The National Echo
Sarawak Tribune
Sarawak Vanguard
Malaysia Focus
Sabah Times
Daily Express
Sarawak Herald

Malta
The Times – 5¢, daily
Weekend Chronicle – 5¢, weekly

Mexico
The News – daily
(American newspapers from 'Sanborns')

Oman
Oman Daily Observer – daily
Times of Oman – weekly
Akhbar Oman – weekly

Paraguay
Guarani News – Gs 250, monthly

Peru
Lima Times

Qatar
Daily Gulf Times – 1 *Qatari Riyal*
Weekly Gulf Times – 2 *Qatari Riyals*

Samoa
Samoa News – 40¢, Fridays
News Bulletin – Free, Mon–Fri
Samoa Journal – 40¢, Thursdays

Seychelles
The Nation – R1 (1 Seychelles rupee)

Singapore
Straits Times – 7 days

Sri Lanka
National dailies published in English, Sinhala and Tamil languages

Swaziland
Times of Swaziland – 17 cents, daily
Swazi Observer – 17 cents, daily

Tahiti
Tahiti Sun Press

Tanzania
Daily News

Trinidad and Tobago
Trinidad Guardian – 50¢ TT, daily
Express – 50¢ TT, daily

Turkey
Daily News – 50 TL
Middle East Review – 200 TL, monthly
Outlook – weekly

Turks and Caicos Islands
Turks and Caicos Current magazine – bi-monthly

United Arab Emirates
Gulf News – daily
Khaleej Times – daily
Emirate News – daily
Gulf Mirror – daily
Gulf Commercial Magazine – weekly
Recorder – weekly

Main American Express Travel Service Offices Worldwide

American Express Services can be used by cardholders as a poste restante *address (letters and telegrams only – no parcels) and for emergency cheque encashment. American Express Traveller's Cheques can be bought or exchanged here and a refund service helps you to keep travelling when you lose your Traveller's Cheques. A Bureau de Change–Foreign Exchange Service is also available so you can exchange your Traveller's Cheques or foreign currency to local money.*

Algeria
Tipaza
Altour(R)
Ghemoua Place
Blida
Tel: 46 14 50/51

American Samoa
Pago Pago
Samoan Holiday and Travel Centre(R)
Lumana Building
Tel: 633 5336

Andorra
Andorra la Vella
Viatges Relax(R)
Carrer Roc Dels Escolls 12
Tel: 22044, 22055, 22639

Antigua
St John's
V. E. B. Nicholson & Son Travel Service Ltd(R)
Long and Thames Streets
Tel: (809) 462 2095

Argentina
Buenos Aires
City Service Travel Agency(R)
Florida 890, 4th Floor
Tel: 312 8416

Aruba
Oranjestad
S. E. L. Maduro & Sons (Aruba) Inc(R)
Rockefellestraat 1
Netherland Antilles
Tel: 23888, 26039

Australia
Adelaide, South Australia
American Express
13 Grenfell Street
Tel: (08) 212 7099

Brisbane. Queensland
American Express
60 Queen St
Tel: (07) 229 2022

Canberra, Australia Capital Territory
American Express Centrepoint
City Walk & Petrie Plaza
Tel: (062) 491691, 491560; 477750

Darwin, Northern Territory
Travelers World Pty. Ltd(R)
18 Knuckey St
Tel: (089) 814699

Melbourne, Victoria
American Express
105 Elizabeth St
Tel: (03) 6024666

Perth, Western Australia
American Express
Shop 30, Carousel Shopping Centre
1358 Albany Highway
Tel: (09) 458 8988

Sydney, New South Wales
American Express
Pittwater Rd, Dee Why.
Tel: (02) 981 1771

Austria
Innsbruck, Tyrol
American Express
Brixnerstrasse 3
Tel: (5222) 22491, 27386

Klagenfurt
Reiseburo Springer & Sohne(R)
Leutschacher strasse 17
Tel: (4222) 33520

Linz
American Express
Buergerstrasse 14
Tel: (732) 669013

Salzberg
American Express
5 Mozartplatz
Tel: (6222) 42501

Vienna
American Express
Kaerntnerstrasse 21/23
Tel: (222) 520544

Bahamas
Freeport, Grand Bahama
Mundytours(R)
Kipling Building C
2nd Floor
Tel: (809) 352 4444, 3526641

Nassau
Playtours(R)
Shirley St
Tel: (809) 32 22931/7

Bahrain
Manama
Kanoo Travel Agency(R)
Al Khalifa Rd
Tel: 254081

Bangladesh
Dacca
Vantage International Ltd(R)
Hotel Sonargaon
Kawran Bazar
Tel: 233183, 230802, 282111-2

Barbados
Bridgetown
Barbados International Travel Services(R)
Independence Square
Tel: (809) 42-61622

Speightstown, St Peter
Barbados International Travel Services(R)
Queen St
Tel: 24182

Belgium
Antwerp
American Express
Frankrijklei 21
Tel: (031) 325920

Brussels
American Express
2 Place Louise
Tel: (02) 512 17 40

Brussels-Evere
American Express
Avenue des Loisirs 2, Bte 2
Tel: (02) 241 8762

Belize
Belize City
Belize Global Travel Service Ltd(R)
Albert St 41
Tel: 7185, 7363/4

Bermuda
Hamilton
L. P. Gutteridge Ltd(R)
Harold Hayes Frith Building
Bermudiana Rd
Tel: (809) 295 4545

Bolivia
La Paz
Magri Tourismo Ltda(R)
Av. 16 de Julio 1490, 5th Fl
Tel: 341201, 340762, 323954

Borneo
Bandar Seri Begawan, Brunei State
Travel Centre (Borneo) Limited(R)
1st Floor Mile
1/4 Jalan Tutong
Tel: 24739, 25236

Brazil
Brasilia, D.F.
Kontik-Franstur SA(R)
Setor Commercial Sul
Edif Central, 10 Andar S/1007
Tel: 224 8922, 224 9636

Iguassu Falls, Parana
Inter Express Ltda(R)
Rua Jorge Schmmelpfeng 600
Sala 106–108
Tel: (0455) 74-1988, 74-2319

Rio De Janeiro
Kontik-Franstur SA(R)
Avenida Atlantica 2316-A
Copacabana
Tel: (021) 235-1396

Salvador, Bahia
Kontik-Franstur SA(R)
Praca da Inglaterra 2
Tel: (071) 242-0433

Saõ Paulo
Kontik-Franstur SA(R)
Rua Marconi 71
2nd Floor
Tel: (011) 259 4211

British Virgin Islands
Roadtown, Tortola
Travel Plan Ltd/Romney Associates Consultants(R)
Waterfront Plaza
Tel: 84942872

Bulgaria
Sofia
Balkantourist(R)
No 1 Vitosha Blvd

Cameroon
Douala
Camvoyages(R)
15 Ave. de la Liberté
Tel: 42 25 44, 42, 31 88

Canada
Brandon, Manitoba
Clement Travel Services Ltd(R)
907 Rosser Avenue
Tel: (204) 727 0119

Calgary, Alberta
American Express
185 Scotia Fashion Centre(R)
225 Seventh Avenue SW
Tel: (403) 261 5982

Charlotte Town, Prince Edward Island
Linkletter Travel(R)
157 Pownall St
Tel: (902) 892 4148

Edmonton, Alberta
American Express
10303 Jasper Avenue
Principal Plaza
Mezzanine
Tel: (403) 421 0608

Montreal, Quebec
American Express
2000 Peel Building
1141 De Maisonneuve West
Tel: (514) 284 3300

Niagara Falls, Ontario
Matthews Travel International Inc(R)
4732 Valley Way
Tel: (416)354 5649, 356 5649

Ottawa, Ontario
American Express
Manulife Tower
220 Laurier Ave West
Tel: (613) 563 0231

Quebec City, Quebec
Voyages Québec Monde (1981) Inc(R)
225 Est, Boulevard Charest
Tel: (418) 529 2547

Regina, Saskatchewan
Reidy Travel Ltd(R)
1923 Hamilton St
Tel: (306) 569 2444

Saint John, New Brunswick
Waddell-Leore Travel Agency Ltd(R)
86 Germain St
Tel: (506) 652 3620

St John's, Newfoundland
Cook's Travel World(R)
327 Freshwater Rd
Tel: (709) 753 8111

Sydney, Nova Scotia
J. A. Young & Son(R)
181 Charlotte St
Tel: (902) 539 4800

Toronto, Ontario
American Express
50 Bloor St West
Tel: (416) 967 3411

Vancouver, British Columbia
American Express
701 W. Georgia St
Tel: (604) 669 2813

Winnipeg, Manitoba
Mackie Travel Service(R)
285 Garry St
Tel: (204) 949 0388

Chile
Santiago
Turismo Cocha(R)
Augustinas 1173
Tel: 83341, 82164, 60518

Colombia
Barranquilla
Tierra Mar Aire Ltda(R)
Carrera 45
Calle 34 Esquinal
Local 2
Tel: 317183, 410541

Bogotá
Tierra Mar Aire Ltda(R)
Calle 92-15-63
Tel: 573642, 573682

Cali
Tierra Mar Aire Ltda(R)
Carrera 3 No 8–13
Tel: 731333

Cartagena
Tierra Mar Aire Ltda
Cr. 4-7-196 Boc Agrande
Tel: 43628, 43646

Medellin
Tierra Mar Aire Ltda
Calle 49A, 46-32
Tel: 420820

Santa Marta
Tierra Mar Aire Ltda
Carrera 4, 14-35
Tel: 3497, 4190

Costa Rica
San José
Tam Travel Agency(R)
Avenidas Central-Primera, 2F1
Tel: 33 00 44

Curaçao
Willemstad
Maduro Travel(R)
Winkelcentrum Colon
Roodeweg 43
Tel: 599 9 26300

Cyprus
Larnaca
A. L. Mantovani & Sons Ltd(R)
6 Gregor Afxentiou St
Tel: (411) 52024/5

Limassol
A. L. Mantovani & Sons Ltd
130 Spyro Araouza St
Tel: (51) 62045/6

Nicosia
A. L. Mantovani & Sons Ltd(R)
35-37 Evagoras Avenue
Tel: (21) 43777/9

Czechoslovakia
Prague
Cedok, Foreign Travel Div(R)
Na Prikope 18
Tel: 22 42 51/9

Denmark
Copenhagen
American Express
Amagertorv 18 (Stroget)
Tel: (01) 122301

Dominican Republic
Santa Domingo
Vimenca Travel Agency
Abraham Lincoln 306
Tel: 532 2233, 532 2318

Ecuador
Guayaquil
Ecuadorian Tours Cia Ltda(R)
9 de Octobre 1500 y Antepara
Tel: 397111, 394984

Quito
Ecuadorian Tours, SA(R)
Amazonas 339
Tel: 543722, 239777

Egypt
Aswan
American Express
Old Cataract Hotel

Cairo
American Express
15 Sharia Kasr il Nil
Tel: 750892, 743460

American Express (Financial Services)
Cairo Airport
Tel: 963276 Ext. 2946

American Express
Nile Hilton Hotel
Tel: 743383

Luxor
American Express
New Winter Palace Hotel
Tel: 2245

El Salvador
San Salvador
El Salvador Travel Service(R)
Centro Comercial La Mascota
Tel: 23 0177

Fiji Islands
Nadi
The Travel Company Ltd(R)
Nadi International Airport
Tel: 72325

Suva
The Travel Company Ltd(R)
189 Victoria Place
Tel: 22345

Finland
Hanko (Hango)
Travek Travelbureau(R)
Bulevardi 10
Tel: (911) 86821

Helsinki
Travek Travelbureau Ltd(R)
Etelaranta 16
Tel: 90 171900

Turku
Travek Travelbureau Ltd(R)
Humalistonkatu 3
Tel: (921) 337111

France
Cannes
American Express
8 Rue Des Belges
Tel: (1693) 381587

Le Havre
American Express
57 Quai Georges V
Tel: (35) 425911, 412312

Lourdes
Office Catholique de Voyages (Ocat)(R)
14 Chausse du Bourg
Tel: 94 20 84, 94 34 94

Lyon
American Express
Rue Childebert
Tel: (07) 837 40 69

Nice
American Express
11 Promenade des Anglais
Tel: (093) 872982

Paris 09
American Express
11 Rue Scribe
Tel: (01) 266 0999

Paris 17
American Express
83 bis, Rue de Courcelles
Tel: (01) 766 0300

Rouen
American Express
1/3 Place Jacques Lelieur
Tel: (35) 981980, 981144, 884724

St Jean de Luz
Socoa-Voyages(R)
31 Boulevard Thiers
Tel: 26 06 27

Gabon
Libreville
Eurafrique Voyages(R)
Rue de la Grande Poste
Tel: 723707, 723909, 720189

Germany
Berlin 15
American Express
11 Kurfuerstendamn
Tel: (030) 882 7575

Bremen
American Express
Am Wall 138
Tel: (0421) 314171

Dusseldorf
American Express
Heinrich Heine-Allee No. 14
Tel: (0211) 80222

Frankfurt/Main
American Express
5 Steinweg
Tel: (0611) 21051

Hamburg
Bruhns Reisen(R)
Kirchenallee 34
Tel: (040) 2801101

Heidelberg
American Express
Friedrich-Ebert-Anlage 16
Tel: (06221) 29001

Munich
American Express
Promenadplatz 6
Tel: (089) 21990

Stuttgart
American Express
Lautenschlagerstrasse 3
Tel: (0711) 20890

Ghana
Accra
Scantravel (Ghana) Ltd(R)
High St
Tel: 63134, 64204

Takorada
Scantravel (Ghana) Ltd(R)
Atlantic Hotel
Tel: 2201, 3300, 3301, 3302

Tema
Scantravel (Ghana) Ltd(R)
Meridian Hotel
Tel: 2878/80 Ext. 241

Gibraltar
Gibraltar
Sterling Travel Ltd(R)
18/20 John Mackintosh Square
Tel: 71787, 71788

Greece
Athens
American Express
2 Hermou St
Constitution Sq
Tel: (01) 324 4975

Corfu
Corfu Tourist Center Ltd(R)
Acadimias St 11
Tel: (661) 33975, 24055/6

Heraklion, Crete
Creta Travel Bureau SA(R)
25th August St 27-29
Tel: (081) 222763, 222764, 222765

Rhodes
Georgiadis Tourism & Shipping(R)
Vass. Sophias St No 41
Tel: (0241) 27300, 27493

Salonica
American Express
International AE
Venizelou St 10
Tel: (031) 225 302

Grenada, West Indies
St Georges
Grenada International Travel Services(R)
Church St
Tel: (809) 444 2945

Guadeloupe, French West Indies
Pointe-a-Pitre
Petrelluzzi Travel Agency(R)
2 Rue Henry IV
Tel 824-341, 821, 399

Guatemala
Guatemala City
Clark Tours(R)
7A Ave 6-53 Zona 4
Edif El Triangulo 2nd Fl
Tel: (501-2) 310213/16

Guyana
Georgetown
Guyana Stores Ltd(R)
19 Water St
Tel: 68171, 66181, 68401

Haiti
Port-au-Prince
Agence Citadelle(R)
35 Place du Marron Inconnu
Tel: 25900

Honduras
La Ceiba
Agencia de Viajes Trans Mundo S de RL(R)
8 A Calle Entre Ave
San Isidor and Ave Republica
Tel: 42 2820, 42 2840

San Pedro Sula, Cortes
Agencia de Viajes Trans Mundo S de RL(R)
6 Ave SO No 15
Tel: 541140, 544188

Tegucigalpa
Trans Mundo Tours(R)
5A Calle No 315
Entre 3Y4 Aves
Tel: 22 2193, 22 8835, 22 890

Hong Kong
Hong Kong, Kowloon
American Express
Golden Crown Court
66-70 Nathan Rd
Tel: (3) 7210179

Hong Kong, Kowloon
American Express
Yu To Sang Building
Mezzanine
37 Queens Rd Central
Tel: (5) 210211

Hungary
Budapest
Ibusz, Bureau No 3(R)
Petrofi Ter 3
Tel: 184-848, 185-707, 184-865

Siofok
Ibusz Travel
Petrofi Setany 38
Tel: (3684) 11106

Iceland
Reykjavik
Utsyn Travel Agency
17 Austurstraeti
Tel: (01) 20100

India
Bombay
American Express
276 Dr Dadabhai Naoroji Road
Majithia Chambers
Tel: 266361

Calcutta
American Express
21 Old Court House St
Tel: 236281, 232133, 230225, 230551

Madras
Binny Ltd
65 Armenian St
Tel: 30181, 26978, 29815

New Delhi
American Express
Wenger House
Connaught Place
Tel: 344119

Srinagar, Kashmir
Kai Travels Private Ltd
Tara Bhavan Place-Blvd 2
Tel: 4180, 5373, 4366, 3545, 6535

Indonesia
Denpasar, Bali
P. T. Pacto, Ltd(R)
Jalan Sanur Beach
Tel: 4446, 6670, 8247/8

Jakarta, Pusat
P. T. Pacto, Ltd
Pacto Limited
24 Jl Cikini Raya
Tel: 320309, 324011, 324075, 344837

Ireland
Cork
Casey Travel Ltd
60 South Mall
Tel: 021 201213/4

Dublin
American Express
116 Grafton St
Tel: (01) 772874

Galway
John Ryan (Travel) Ltd(R)
27 William St
Tel: (091) 64631, 62335

Limerick
Riordans Travel Ltd(R)
2 Sarsfield St
Tel: (061) 44666, 49441, 44226, 44234

Israel
Haifa
Meditrad Ltd
2 Khayat Square
Tel: (04) 642266

Jerusalem, New City
Meditrad Ltd
27 King George St
Tel: (03) 294654

Tel Aviv
Meditrad Ltd
16 Ben Yehuda St
Tel: (03) 294654

Italy
Bologna
Renotur, Centro Turistico Internazionale
Piazza XX Settembre 6
Tel: (051) 264643, 264724

Cagliari, Sardinia
Sartourist Travel Office
Piazza Deffenu 14
Tel: (070) 652971/3, 664385, 664374

Catania, Sicily
La Duca Viaggi
Via Etnea 65
Tel: (095) 316155, 316711, 316113

Florence
Universalturismo SPA
Via Degli Speziali 7/R
Tel: (055) 217241

Genoa
Aviomar SNC
Via Ettore Vernazza 48
Tel: (010) 595551/3, 540882, 591553/4

Milan
American Express
19 Via Vittor Pisani
Tel: (02) 6709060/69

Naples
Airontour SAS
Vis S. Brigida 68
Tel: (081) 360377, 310411, 310399

Rome
American Express
Piazza di Spagna 38
Tel: (06) 67641

Turin
Malan Viaggi SPA
Via Accademia Delle Scienze 1
Tel: (011) 51 38 41/8

Venice
American Express
1471 San Moise (San Marco)
Tel: (041) 700844

Verona
Vertours SRL
Galleria Pellicciai 13
Tel: (045) 594988

Ivory Coast
Abidjan
Socopao Voyages
2000 Av Chardy
Immeuble Alpha, 01
Tel: 323554

Jamaica
Kingston
Martins Jamaica
New Kingston Complex
85 Knutsford Blvd
Tel: 926 1351, 926 1260-2

Mandeville
Martins Jamaica
Willowgate Shopping Center
Tel: 962 2203

Montego Bay
Martins Jamaica
Mutual Life Bldg
32 Market St
Tel: 952 4350

Ocho Rios
Martins Jamaica
Mutual Life Bldg
2 Graham St
Tel: 974 2594/6

Port Antonio
Martins Jamaica
City Centre Shopping Plaza
Tel: 9932625

Japan
Naha City, Okinawa
Okinawa Tourist Service
2 21 8 Maejima
Tel: 795 220

Okinawa City
Okinawa Tourist Service
241 Aza-Yamazato

Osaka
American Express
Umeda Mitsui Bldg, Kita-ku
5-10 Sonezaki 2-chome
Tel: (06) 315 0781

Tokyo
American Express
Ginza 4-Star Bldg 4-1
Ginza 4-chome, Chuo-ku
Tel:(03) 564 4361

Jordan
Amman
International Traders
King Hussein St
Tel: 62356 661014/5

Aqaba
International Traders
Municipality Square
Tel: 37575316

Kenya
Mombasa
Etco (Mombasa) Ltd
Nkrumah Rd
Tel: (011) 312461, (011) 311994

Nairobi
Express Kenya Ltd
Baricho Rd 1
Tel: 334722/28

Korea
Seoul
Sejong Travel Service Co Ltd
New Korea Bldg, 192-11
Eulchi-ro 1-ka Chunga-ku
Tel: 7781471-4, 7785711-5

Kuwait
Kuwait, Safet
Al-Kazemi Travel Agencies
Fahed Al Salem St
Tel: 450655/9

La Réunion (Ile de)
St Denis
Bourbon Voyages
14 Rue Rontaunay
Tel: 216818

Lesotho
Maseru
Manica Freight Services
Kingsway
Tel: (0501) 22554

Liechtenstein
Vaduz
Reisa Travel Agency
Heiligkreuz 19
Tel:(075) 23734

Malagasy Republic
Tananarive
Madagascar Airtours
Madagascar Hilton Hotel
Tel: 24192

Malawi
Blantyre
Manica Travel Services
Victoria Av
Tel: 634533

Lilongwe
Manica Travel Services
Centre House, Capital City
Lilongwe 3
Tel: 730133, 730421

Limbe, Blantyre
Manica Travel Services
Churchill Rd
Tel: 652322

Mzuzu
Manica Travel Services
Viphya Drive
Tel: 332638, 332677

Malaysia
Kota Kinabula, Sabah
Discovery Tours (Sabah) Sdn. Bhd.
122 Wisma Sabah Complex
First Floor
Tel: 57735, 53787

Kuala Lumpur
Mayflower Acme Tours, Sdn Bhd
18 Jalan Segambut Pusat
Kuala Lumpur 12-01
Tel: (03) 486 739

Kuching, Sarawak
Sarawak Travel Agencies
4 Holiday Inn Arcade
Tel: 23708

Penang
Mayflower Acme Tours, Sdn Bhd
Unit 2, 3rd Fl. Green Hall Bldg
8 Green Hall
Tel: 04 23724

Maldives
Malé
Treasure Island Enterprise Ltd
H-8 Marine Drive
Tel: 485, 532

Malta
Valletta
A. & V. Von Brockdorff Ltd
14 Zachary St
Tel: 624312, 621167, 623825

Martinique, French West Indies
Fort de France
Roger Albert Voyages
7 Rue Victor Hugo
Tel: 71 44 44, 71 71 71

Mauritius
Port Louis
MTTB Ltd
Corner Sir William Newton and Royal Roads
Tel: (08) 2041/44841/2

Mexico
Acapulco
American Express
Costera Miguel Aleman 709-1
Tel: 41095, 41520

Cozumel
Barbachano (Clubs, SA)
Hotel Cozumel Caribe
Quintana Roo
Tel: 20100

Mexico City
American Express
Hamburgo 75
Mexico 6 DF
Tel: (905) 533 0380

Monterrey
American Express
Calle Padre Mier 1424 Pte
Esq Bravo Sur
Nuevo Leon
Tel: (83) 441240, 430460

Puerto Vallarta, Jalisco
Miller Travel Service
100 Paseo de la Garzas
Tel: 21197, 21297, 21397

Monaco
Monte Carlo
American Express
35 Blvd Princesse Charlotte
Tel: (093) 309652

Morocco
Casablanca
Voyages Schwarts SA
112 Av du Prince
Moulay Abdullah
Tel: 731 33, 780 54

Marrakesh
Voyages Schwartz SA
Immeuble Moutaouskil 1
Rue Mauritania
Tel: 333 21

Tangier
Voyages Schwartz SA
54 Boulevard Pasteur
Tel: 334 59, 334 71

Namibia
Swakopmund
Woker Freight Services
Standard Bank Building
Moltke St
Tel (0641) 4950 5211

Windhoek
Woker Freight Services
145 Kaiser St
Tel: (061) 37946

Nepal
Kathmandu
Yeti Travels Pvt Ltd
Hotel Mayalu, Ground Floor
Jamal Tole, Durbar Marg
Tel:13596, 11234

Netherlands
Amsterdam
American Express
Damrak 66
Tel: (020) 262042

Enschede
American Express
Boulevard 1945-70
Tel: (053) 324120

Rotterdam
American Express
92 Meent
Tel: (010) 330300

The Hague
American Express
Venestraat 20
Tel: (070) 469515

New Caledonia
Noumea
Center Voyages
27 Bis Av du Maréchal Foch
Tel: 272278, 284737

New Zealand
Auckland
American Express
95 Queen St
Tel: (09) 798243

Christchurch
American Express
226 High St
Tel: 66772

Nigeria
Lagos
Mandilas Travel Ltd
96/102 Broad St
Tel: (01) 662756, 663220

Norway
Bergen
Wing Travel Bureau of Scandinavia Ltd
Strandgt 5
Tel: (05) 321080

Oslo
Winge Travel Bureau of Scandinavia
Karl Johans Gate 33, Oslo 1
Tel: (02) 429150

Stavanger
Winge Travel Bureau of Scandinavia
14 Kirkegaten
Tel: 045 30020

Tromso
Winge Travel Bureau of Scandinavia
Frederick Langes Gt 19/21
Tel: (083) 85035

Trondheim
Winge Travel Bureau of Scandinavia
Olav Tryggvassons Gt 30
Tel: (07) 533000

Oman
Mina-al-Fahal
Zubair Travel & Service Bureau
BBME Building
Tel: 607739

Muscat
Zubair Travel & Service Bureau
Muscat Intercontinental Hotel
Airport Highway
Qurum
Tel: 601224

Muscat-Ruwi
Zubair Travel & Service Bureau
Bank of Oman
Bahrain & Kuwait Building
Mazin Bin Ghadooba St
Tel: 701487/9

Salalah, Dhofar
Zubair Travel & Service Bureau
POB 8809
Tel: 461145, 462855

Pakistan
Islamabad
American Express
Elahi Chambers
I & T Centre
Ramna 6/1
Tel: 29422/5, 28865

Karachi
American Express
Standard Insurance House
1.1 Chunrigar Rd
Tel: 226435/38

Lahore
American Express
112 Rafi Mansion
Shahrah-E-Quaid-E-Azam
Tel: 312435

Rawalpindi
American Express
Ground Floor
Rahim Plaza
Muree Rd
Tel: 65766/65, 65128

Papua New Guinea
Port Moresby
Coral Sea Travel Services (New Guinea)
PNGBC Building
Musgrove & Douglas Sts

Paraguay
Asunción
Inter-Express, SRL
Yegros 690
Inter-Express Bldg
Tel: 90 111 115

People's Republic of China
Beijing (Peking)
American Express
Room 1527
Peking Hotel
East Chang An Av
Tel: 552231. Ext 1527

Peru
Arequipa
Lima Tours, SA
Santa Catalina 120
Tel: 22 4210, 22 41143

Cuzco
Lima Tours, SA
Av Solnte. 567
Tel: 2809

Iquitos
Explorama Tours
Jr Putumayo 150
Tel: 234968, 235471, 235063

Lima
Lima Tours, SA
Belen 1040
Tel: 276624

Philippines
Angeles City
American Express
710 Friendship Highway
Riverside Subdivision
Tel: (055) 5391, 4053

Makati
American Express
7 West Drive Arcade
Makati Ave Corner Passay Rd
Tel: 88 58 18, 88 59 61, 88 58 93

Manila
American Express
Ground Floor
Philamlife Bldg
UN Ave, Ermita
Tel: 509601/05, 599386

Poland
Gdansk
Orbis
22 Heweliusza St
Tel: 322081

Krakow
Orbis
Al Puszkina 1
Tel: (094) 224746, 224632

Poznan
Orbis
Plac Gen. H. Dabrowskiego 1
Tel: 330941

Warsaw
Orbis Travel
Marszalkowska 142
Tel: (022) 267501

Zakopane
Orbis
Krupowki St 22
Tel: 4151

Portugal
Faro, Algarve
Star Travel Service
Rue Conselheiro Bivar 36
Tel: 25125/7

Funchal, Madeira
Star Travel Service
Avenida Arraiga 23
Tel: 32001

Lisbon
Star Travel Service
Avenida Sidonio Pais 4-A
Tel: (01) 599871, 539841/50

Oporto
Star Travel Service
Avenida Dos Aliados 202
Tel: (02) 23637/8

Praia da Vitoria, Azores
Star Travel
Rua Serpa Pinto 74
Terceira Island
Tel: 52623, 52166

Qatar
Doha
Darwish Travel Bureau
Clock Tower Square
Tel: 418666

Qatar Tour
Volkswagen Bldg
Tel: 423465, 423453

Rumania
Bucharest
National Tourist Office, Carpati
Boulevard Magheru Nr. 7
Tel: 145160

Saudi Arabia
Al Khobar
Kanoo Travel Agency
King Khalid St
Tel: 864-0039, 864-1647, 864 1992

Damman
Kanoo Travel Agency
King Faisal St
Tel: (83) 22499, 23084

Dhahran
International Travel Agency
Dhahran International Hotel
Airport PO
Tel: 891 8555, Ext 420/422 and 434

Jeddah
Ace Travel
Hassan Bin Thabet St
Tel: 6533102, 6533106

Riyadh
Ace Travel
Green Glove Bldg
Olaya Main Rd
Central Prov.
Tel: 4648810

Sénégal
Dakar
Socopao Voyages
51 Ave Albert Sarraut
Tel: 222416, 222576

Seychelles
Victoria, Mahé
Travel Services Ltd
Victoria House
State House Ave
Tel: 22414

Sierra Leone
Freetown
A. Yazbeck & Sons Agencies
22 Siaka Stevens ST
Tel: 22374, 24423, 22063

Singapore
Singapore
American Express
Holiday Inn Bldg, 4th Fl
Scotts Road, 04-07/08
Tel: 7375988

South Africa
Cape Town, Cape Province
American Express
Union Castle Bldg, 1st Fl
55 St Georges St
Tel: (021) 413451

Durban, Natal
American Express
320 West St, Suite 617
Tel: (031) 326211

Johannesburg, Transvaal
American Express
Merbrook House
123 Commissioner St
Tel: (011) 374000

American Express
Unitas Bldg, 2nd Fl
42 Marshall St
Tel: (011) 833 1441

Killarney
Freight Services Travel Ltd
Shop 76, Killarney Mall
60 Riviera Road
Tel: (011) 41 6010

Kimberley, Cape Province
American Express
Nedbank Bldg, 3rd Fl, Room 31
Cnr. Chapel & Currue Sts
Tel: (0531) 2 8164/5

Pretoria, Transvaal
American Express
Shop 22/23 Koedoe Arcade
Pretorius St
Tel: (012) 269182

Spain
Barcelona
American Express
Paseo de Gracia 101
Chaflan Rosellon
Tel: 03 218 6712, 217 1750

Granada
Viajes Bonal, SA
Avenida Calvo Sotelo 19
Tel: (58) 276312, 276316

Ibiza
Viajes Iberia, SA
Avenida de España 70
Tel: (71) 302014, 300650

Lanzarote
Viajes CYRASA
Centro Atlantico, Local Nr 60A
Carretera de las Playas
Tel: (28) 825 851/2

Las Palmas, Gran Canaria
Viajes CYRASA
Triana 114
Tel: (928) 364100, 364300

Madrid
American Express
Plaza de las Cortes 2
Tel: (01) 2221180, 4296875

Mahon, Menorca
Viajes Iberia, SA
General Goded 35
Tel: (71) 362845, 362908

Malaga, Andalucia
Viajes Alhambra
Plaza de las Flores S/N
Tel: (952) 219080, 219090, 228101/2

Palma de Mallorca
Viajes Iberia SA
Passeig des Born 14
Tel: (71) 226743, 236747

Puerto de la Cruz, Teneriffe
Viajes Iberia SA
Avenida Generismo Franco, S/N
Tel: (922) 38 1350, 38 1358

Puerto Pollensa, Mallorca
Viajes Iberia, SA
Juan XX111, 3
Tel: (71) 530 262

Santiago de Compostela
Viajes Amado, SA
Avenida Figueroa 6
Tel: (81) 593641, 593402

Sri Lanka
Colombo
Mackinnons Travel Ltd
Mackinnons Bldg, York St
4 Leydian Bastian Rd
Tel: 22641, 29563, 29881, 20456

St. Lucia
Castries
Carib Travel Agency
5 Jeremie St
Tel: (809) 455 2151

St. Maarten
Philipsburg
S. E. L. Maduro & Sons (WI) Inc
Emmaplein
Tel: 3407, 3408, 3410

Sudan
Khartoum
Contomichalos Travel & Tourism
Al Barlman St
Tel: 70929, 70601

Suriname
Paramaribo
Travel Bureau C. Kersten & Co, NV
Hotel Krasnapolsky
Domineestraat 39
Tel: 74448, 77148

Swaziland
Manzini
Musgrove and Watson
Shop No 1B Encozini Bldg
Lot 527 Ngwane St
Tel: 52237

Mbabane
Musgrove and Watson
Mbabane House
Allister Miller St
Tel: 42298

Sweden
Goteborg
Resespecialisterna Resebureau AB
Ostra Hamngaten 39
Tel: (031) 174020

Stockholm
Resespecialisterna Resebureau AB
Sturegaten 8
S-11435 Stockholm
Tel: (8) 238300

Switzerland
Berne
American Express
Marktgasse 37
Tel: (031) 22 94 01

Geneva
American Express
7 Rue du Mont Blanc
Tel: (022) 31 7600

Lausanne
American Express
14 Avenue Mon-Repos
Tel: (021) 207425

Locarno
Danzas Ltd
Piazza Stazione 2
Tel: (091) 33 66 73

Montreux
Montreux-Voyages
Avenue de Alpes 43
Tel: (021) 624121, 614661

Zurich
American Express
Bahnofstrasse 20
Tel: (01) 211 83 70

Syria
Damascus
Chami Travel
Rue Fardous
Mouradi Bldg
Tel: 111652, 119553

Tahiti
Papeete
Tahiti Tours
Rue Jeanne d'Arc
Tel: 27870

Taiwan (Republic of China)
Taipei
American Express
No 137 Nanking E. Rd
Sec 2
Tel: 5313174/76, 5639341/46

Thailand
Bangkok
S. E. A. Tours Co Ltd
965 Rama 1 Rd
Siam Center Room 414
Tel: 251 4862/9

Togo
Lomé
Société Togolaise Maritime et Portuaire (STMP)
2 Rue du Commerce
Tel: 6190

Trinidad & Tobago
Port-of-Spain
Hub Travel Ltd
68-72 Maraval Rd
Tel: (62) 54085, 53011

Tobago
Hub Travel Ltd
Milford Rd
Scarborough
Tel: 639 8778

Tunisia
Tunis
Carthage Tours
59 Av Bourguiba
Tel: 254 304/326/605/908/391

Turkey
Ankara
Turk Ekspres
Sehit Adem Yavuz Sokak 14/5
Kizilay
Tel: (041) 253282, 170576

Antalya
Pamfilya Travel Agency
30 Agusto Caddesi
No 57B & C
Tel: (311) 11698, 12745, 21988

Istanbul
Turk Ekspres
Cumhuriyet Caddesi 91, Kat 6
Elmadag
Tel: (011) 10274/5

Izmir
Egetur Travel Agency
Nato Arkasi
Talatpasa Bulvari 2B
Tel: (051) 21725/7, 217921

United Arab Emirates (UAE)
Abu Dhabi
United Travel Agency
Bin Yas St/Umm Anar St
Tel: (2) 821310

Dubai
Kanoo Travel Agency
Khalid Bin Walid St
Tel: (4) 434614, 421100

Sharjah
Kanoo Travel Agency
Al Ouroob St
Tel: (6) 356058

UK
Channel Isles
St. Brelade
Marshalls Travel
1 Quennevais Precinct
Jersey, CI
Tel: (0534) 41278, 45561

England
London
American Express
6 Haymarket
Tel: (01) 930 4411

American Express
78 Brompton Rd
Knightsbridge
Tel: (01) 584 6182

American Express
Travel Financial Services at British Airways
421 Oxford St

Wimbledon Travel Ltd
85 High St
Wimbledon Village
Tel: (01) 947 6281/3, 946 6813

Isle of Man
Douglas
Palace Travel
Palace Bldgs
Central Promenade
Tel: (0624) 3721

Northern Ireland
Belfast
Hamilton Travel
23/31 Waring St
Tel: (0232) 230231

Scotland
Aberdeen
American Express
Glencraig House
193 Union St
Tel: (0224) 52734

Edinburgh
American Express
139 Prince's St
Tel: (031) 225 7881

Wales
Cardiff, South Glamorgan
Worldwide Travel Ltd
33 Oxford House
The Hayes
Tel: (0222) 440413

United States
California
San Francisco
American Express
237 Post St
Tel: (415) 981 5533

New York
American Express
American Express Plaza Lobby
Tel: (212) 323 4590

American Express
New York Hilton Hotel
1335 Av of the Americas
Tel: (212) 664 7798/8001/8080

American Express
374 Park Av
Tel: (212) 421 8240

New York (Queens)
American Express
JFK Int'l Airport Main Lobby
International Arrivals Bldg
Tel: (212) 656 5673

Washington DC, District of Columbia
American Express
1150 Connecticut Av NW
Tel: (202) 457 1300

Uruguay
Montevideo
Turisport Limitada
Mercedes 942
Tel: 914823, 906300

USSR
Moscow
American Express
21-A Sadovo-Kudrinskaya St
Tel: (95) 254 4495/4305/4505/2111

Venezuela
Caracas
Turismo Consolidado Turisol CA
CCCT-Nivel C-2, Local 53F-07
Chuao
Tel: 927922

Maracaibo
Turismo Consolidado Turisol CA
Av. 4 Res. La Guajira Locales 2 and 3
Zulia
Tel: 79501, 70611

Virgin Is. (US)
Christiansted, St. Croix
Southerland Tours
Kings Alley
Tel: (809) 773 0340

St. Thomas
Tropic Tours
International Plaza
Tel: (809) 774 1855, (800) 524 4334

Western Samoa
Apia
Retzlaffs Tours & Travel
Beach Rd
Tel: 21724/5

Yugoslavia
Belgrade
Atlas, Yugoslav Travel Agency
Mose Pijade 11
Tel: (011) 341-471, 332-522

Dubrovnik
Atlas, Yugoslav Travel Agency
Pile 1
Tel: (050) 27 333

Sarajevo
Atlas, Yugoslav Travel Agency
Ulica JNA 81
Tel: (071) 532 521

Zadar
Atlas, Yugoslav Travel Agency
Branimirova Obala 12
Tel: (057) 23339

Zambia
Lusaka
Eagle Travel Ltd
Permanent House, Cairo Rd
Tel: 214916, 214735

Ndola
Eagle Travel Ltd
PO Box 70650
Tel: 216857, 217540

Zimbabwe
Bulawayo
Musgrove & Watson (Pvt) Ltd
79 Fife St
Tel: (19) 62521

Gweru
Musgrove & Watson
Electricity House
Sixth St
Tel: (154) 3316

Harare
Musgrove & Watson Travel
Hardwicke House
Samora Machel Ave
Tel: 703421, 708441

Mutare
Musgrove & Watson
Corner Main St & Second Ave
Tel: (120) 64112

Insurance

Automobile Association
Fanum House
Leicester Square
London W1
Tel: (01) 954 7373 or (01) 954 7511
Has a reasonably priced scheme to cover overland travel abroad.

Assist-Card
745 Fifth Avenue
New York
NY 10022
Tel: (212) 752 2788
Outside New York 1-800-221-4564
An organization to help with travel crises such as loss of passport, illness, theft, legal trouble. Cardholders may telephone the office (collect) in 28 European countries and both North and South American countries, where a multilingual staff is on call 24 hours a day, 5 days – $30.00, 10 days – $50.00, 16 days – $60.00, 22 days – $70.00, 30 days – $80.00, 45 days – $100.00, 60 days – $120.00, 90 days – $180.00.

Baggot Evans & Co Ltd
99 Church Road
London SE19 2PR
Tel: (01) 771 9691 and 761 1335
Can arrange insurance on motor vehicles of most types in the UK throughout the whole of Europe including the USSR. Other countries in Near Middle and Far East as well as Africa are available by special arrangement for which a full itinerary should be sent. They can obtain cover for sea transits of vehicles to countries other than those mentioned and for goods and equipment to all ports of the world. They also offer personal accident, sickness and baggage insurance.

Campbell Irvine Ltd
48 Earls Court Road
Kensington
London W8 6EJ
Tel: (01) 937 6981
Specialize in unusual insurance and can offer travellers insurance against medical expenses, repatriation, personal accident, cancellation and curtailment and personal liability, also baggage and money cover subject to certain restrictions. Vehicle insurance can be arranged and usually takes the form of Third Party insurance (for countries where British insurers have adequate representation); accidental damage, fire and theft insurance (worldwide, including sea transit risks). Carnet Indemnity insurance is available in order that travellers can obtain carnet de passages *documents from the Automobile Association.*

Centre de Documentation et d'Information de l'Assurance
2 Rue de la Chassée d'Antin
75009 Paris
France
Tel: 824 96 12
Will give advice to travellers on insurance problems.

R. L. Davison & Co Ltd
Lloyd's Insurance Brokers
5 Stone House
London EC3A 7AX
Tel: (01) 377 9876
Offer Carnet *Indemnity insurance for travellers in Asia and elsewhere.*

International Airline Passengers Association (IAPA)
PO Box 113
London SW1P 1DF
Tel: (01) 828 5841
Maximum cover offered £760,000. Basic membership costs £20 per year.

International Airline Passengers Association
PO Box 660074
Dallas
TX. 75266-0074
USA
Tel: 214/438 8100 (Texas)
or toll-free 800/527 5888 (USA)
Telex: 792962 IAPA IRVG
World's oldest and largest group of frequent air travellers. Offer optional insurance coverages including up to $1.5 million Lloyd's London travel accident protection. Members also receive preferred rates at Hertz, Avis and National/Europcar locations and 2,000 hotel/motels worldwide; consumer information and assistance; representation; publications; and lost luggage tracking.

Kemper Group
Long Grove
IL 60049
USA
Offer a 12 month travel accident policy which gives the same cover and at the same premium as the insurance offered at airport terminals for only 21 days cover. The policy, which must be ordered a week in advance, covers approved charter flights.

Midland Bank Insurance Services
Midland Bank PLC
Head Office
Poultry
London EC2P 2BX
Tel: (01) 606 9911 Ext 3215
Telex: 8811822
Midland Bank Insurance Services, in conjunction with Bishopsgate Insurance, have brought out a new package of travel insurance for customers. Cover offered – up to £1,000 cancellation, unlimited medical expenses, up to £500 hospital benefit, personal accident (death £5,000, other capital benefit £15,000), up to £1,000 on baggage, £300 on money, personal liability up to £500,000, a 24 hour advisory service for emergencies and free cover for children under 2 years of age. Also certain optional extensions.

Medisure
Norman Frizzell Motor & General
Frizzell House
County Gates
Poole BH13 6BH
Tel: (0202) 292 333
Medisure is a new medical insurance scheme which pays for National Health Service emergency hospital treatment for overseas visitors not covered by reciprocal agreements. Available exclusively from the three post offices at Heathrow Airport, Medisure

provides medical insurance for up to £50,000 per person with cover available for a maximum period of six months. No age restrictions and the cost is £9.00 for 31 days cover plus £7.00 for each additional month. Advice is obtainable 24 hours a day on an emergency telephone line.

Pinon Assureur
3 Rue de Liège
75009 Paris
France
Tel: 878 02 98 and 878 95 530
Is one of the rare insurance companies that will insure cameras and photographic equipment. Premiums amount to about 3 per cent of the value of the items insured and the firm will insure for a minimum premium of 200 Francs.

Getting in Touch With Home

A Country by Country Guide

Afghanistan
Air mail post to UK: About 7 days.
Telegrams: May be sent from Central Post Office, Kabul (closes 21.00 hours).
Telex: Public terminal at PTT Office, Jade Ibn Sina (next to Kabul Hotel).
Telephoning the UK: International operator service, reasonably efficient; shortage of lines may cause delay.

Algeria
Air mail post to UK: 3–4 days.
Telegrams: May be sent from any post office (8.00–19.00). Main post office in Algiers at 5 Blvd Mohamed Khemisti offers 24 hour service.
Telex: At main post office Algiers; also public facilities at Aurassi and Aletti Hotels.
Telephoning the UK: IDD to UK, also international operator service 24 hours, but subject to delays.

Argentina
Air mail post to UK: About 7 days.
Telegrams: May be sent from General Post Office (Correo Central), corner of Samrieto and L N Alem.
Telex: ENTEL (state-owned telephone and telegraph company) has two booths in Buenos Aires; also from General Post Office.
Telephoning the UK: IDD; also 24 hour international operator service.

Andorra
Air mail Post to UK: 4–5 days.
Telegrams: Services available throughout.
Telex: Services available throughout.
Telephoning the UK: Normal code dial system.

Antigua
Air mail post to UK: 3–4 days.
Telegrams: May be sent from Cable & Wireless, High Street, St. John's or from your hotel.
Telex: From Cable & Wireless, St. John's.
Telephoning the UK: Through hotel operator or via Cable & Wireless.

Australia
Air mail post to UK: About 7 days.
Telegrams: May be sent from local Post Offices and by telephone.
Telex: Telecom operates Public Telex Bureaux at all capital city Chief Telegraph Offices and at the following Telecom country offices: Canberra, Newcastle, Dubbo, Wollongong, Ballarat, Townsville, Rockhampton, Mt Gambier, Darwin, Alice Springs, Launceston.
Telephoning the UK: IDD; also operator-connected calls.

Austria
Air mail post to UK: 3–5 days.
Telegrams: From Post Offices (Mon–Fri 08.00–12.00, 14.00–18.00. Sat 08.00–10.00 in selected offices. Main and station post offices in larger cities open round the clock, including Saturdays, Sundays and public holidays).
Telex: From Post Offices.
Telephoning the UK: From Post Offices or international call boxes.

Bahamas
Air mail post to UK: 3–5 days.
Telegrams: May be sent through BATELCO, offices in Nassau and Freeport.
Telex: Through BATELCO.
Telephoning the UK: International operator service.

Bahrain
Air mail post to UK: 3–4 days.
Telegrams: Ordinary, letter telegrams may be sent 24 hours a day from Cable & Wireless, Mercury House, Al-Khalifa Road, Manama.
Telex: Public call offices at Cable & Wireless open 24 hours.
Telephoning the UK: IDD.

Bangladesh
Air mail post to UK: 3–4 days.
Telegrams: From telegraph and post offices; major hotels.
Telex: Links with almost every country in the world. Hotel Intercontinental in Dacca has a public telex service. Telex facilities also available from Chittagong, Khulna.
Telephoning the UK: IDD.

Barbados
Air mail post to UK: 4–7 days.
Telegrams: Via Cable & Wireless (WI) Ltd, Wildey, St. Michael.
Telex: Via Cable & Wireless.
Telephoning the UK: IDD.

Belgium
Air mail post to UK: 3–4 days.
Telegrams: In main Towns telegraph offices (usually found in the stations or close at hand) are open day and night.
Telex: Extensive facilities available throughout.
Telephoning the UK: IDD.

Belize
Air mail post to UK: 4–8 days.
Telegrams: Via Cable & Wireless, Belize City; BTA National Telephone System.
Telex: International Telex services available via Cable & Wireless and BTA National Telephone System.
Telephoning the UK: International operator service.

Bermuda
Air mail post to UK: 5–7 days.
Telegrams: From all post offices.
Telex: Via Cable & Wireless.
Telephoning the UK: IDD.

Bolivia
Air mail post to UK: About 4 days.
Telegrams: From West Coast of America Telegraph Co Ltd, main office at Edificio Electra, Calle Mercado 1150, La Paz; and sub-offices at Hotels La Paz, Sheraton, Libertador, Crillon, El Dorado, Gloria. Ordinary, urgent and letter telegrams.
Telex: Public telex facilities also available at West Coast of America Telegraph offices.
Telephoning the UK: International operator service.

Botswana
Air mail post to UK: 7 days.
Telegrams: May be sent via post offices.
Telex: Via post offices.
Telephoning the UK: International operator service.

Brazil
Air mail post to UK: 4–6 days.
Telegrams: From EMBRATEL (Empresa Brasileira de Telecomunicacoes SA) offices in Rio de Janeiro and São Paulo.
Telex: International Telex facilities available at EMBRATEL offices.
Telephoning the UK: IDD.

Burma
Air mail post to UK: Slow – 7–10 days; air letter forms quicker and more reliable than normal air letters.
Telegrams: From Posts and Telecommunications Corporation, 125 Phayres Street, Rangoon.
Telex: Telex facilities in Tourist Burma office and hotels in Rangoon.
Telephoning the UK: International operator service.

Burundi
Air mail post to UK: 3–4 days.
Telegrams: From any post office.
Telex: Available from post offices.

Cameroon
Air mail post to UK: 7 days.
Telegrams: Telegraph office does not operate at night, and messages are apt to be delayed.
Telex: Facilities available from the main telegraph office in Yaoundé and also larger hotels in Yaoundé and Douala.
Telephoning the UK: International operator service.

Canada
Air mail post to UK: 4–8 days.
Telegrams: Cannot be sent through the post offices in Canada. Telegrams or 'Telepost' messages should be telephoned or delivered to CN/CP Telecommunications – address and telephone number can be found in the local telephone directory. In Newfoundland and Labrador telegrams are sent through Terra Nova Tel.
Telex: Telex facilities easily located in all major Canadian cities.
Telephoning the UK: IDD.

Cayman Islands
Air mail post to UK: About 5 days.
Telegrams: Public Telegraph operates daily from 07.30–18.00 hours Cayman time. Telecommunications provided by Cable & Wireless (West Indies) Ltd.
Telex: Available at Cable & Wireless office; many hotels and apartments have their own telex.
Telephoning the UK: IDD.

Chile
Air mail post to UK: 3–4 days.
Telegrams: From Transradio Chilena at Bandera 168, Santiago, and at Esmeralda 932, Valparaiso; ordinary and letter telegrams.
Telex: Facilities at Transradio Chilena, Bandera 168, and at ITT Communicaciones Mundiales SA, Agustinas 1054, Santiago.
Telephoning the UK: International operator service.

China
Air mail post to UK: 4–6 days.
Telegrams: From Administration of Telecommunications at 11 Sichanganjian Street, Beijing, and at Nanking Road East 30, Shanghai, or any telegraph office. Ordinary, urgent or letter telegrams.
Telex: Telex facilities available at Administration of Telecommunications offices.
Telephoning the UK: International operator service from Beijing.

Colombia
Air mail post to UK: 5 days.
Telegrams: From any chief telegraph office in main towns. Ordinary and urgent telegrams.

Telex: International telex facilities available at hotels Tequendama and Hilton, Bogotá, at Telecom (Empresa Nacional de Telecommunicaciones) offices and chief telegraph office in main towns.
Telephoning the UK: IDD.

Costa Rica
Air mail post to UK: 6–8 days.
Telegrams: May be sent from Radiografica Costarricense.
Telex: From Radiografica Costarricense.
Telephoning the UK: IDD.

Czechoslovakia
Air mail post to UK: about 7 days.
Telegrams: Facilities available at all main post offices.
Telex: Telex for tourists not available.
Telephoning the UK: IDD.

Cyprus
Air mail post to UK: 3 days.
Telegrams: From any telegraphic office, including Electra House, Museum Street, Nicosia. 24 hour service. Ordinary and urgent telegrams.
Telex: No public telex offices, but larger hotels have telex facilities.
Telephoning the UK: IDD.

Denmark
Air mail post to UK: 3 days.
Telegrams: May be sent from main post offices.
Telex: Facilities available from your hotel or main post offices in major towns.
Telephonong the UK: IDD.

Djibouti
Air mail post to UK: About 3 days.
Telegrams: May be sent from main post offices.
Telex: Available from any post office.
Telephoning the UK: International telephone calls (by satellite) are possible 24 hours a day.

Dominica
Air mail post to UK: About 7 days.
Telegrams: Available from All America Cables and Radio ITT, Julio Verne 21, Santo Domingo; RCA Global Communications, El Conde 203, Santo Domingo.
Telex: Facilities available from All America Cables and Radio ITT and RCA Global Communications.
Telephoning the UK: International operator service.

Eastern Caribbean States
Air mail post to UK: About 7 days.
Telegrams: Services available from General Post Office in capital.
Telex: General Post office.
Telephoning the UK: International operator service.

Ecuador
Air mail post to UK: 6–7 days.
Telegrams: From chief telegraph office in main towns. In Quito 24 hour service. Also from Hotel Quito and Hotel Colón up to 20.00 hours. Ordinary and urgent telegrams.
Telex: Public booths at Hotels Quito, Colón and Humboldt, Quito; Hotels Humboldt, Continental, Gran Hotel, Palace, Guayaquil; also at IETEL (Instituto Ecuatoriano de Telecomunicaciones) offices.
Telephoning the UK: International operator service; sometimes long delays in securing connection.

Egypt
Air mail post to UK: Minimum 5 days.
Telegrams: From telegraph offices. Ordinary telegrams.
Telex: Public telex facilities at major hotels for guests only; other telex services in Cairo at: 19 El Alfi Street (24 hours); 26 July Street, Zamalek; 85 Abdel Khalek Sarwat Street, Attaba; El Tazaran Street, Nasr City; Transit Hall, Cairo Airport.
Telephoning the UK: International operator service; calls should be booked in advance.

Ethiopia
Air mail post to UK: 4 days.
Telegrams: From Telecommunications Authority, Adoua Square, Addis Ababa, and telegraphic offices. Ordinary, urgent and letter telegrams.
Telex: Facilities available at Telecommunications Board, Churchill Road, Addis Ababa, and at Heroes Square, Asmara.
Telephoning the UK: Link available from Addis 15.00–20.00 East African time.

Fiji
Air mail post to UK: 5 days.
Telegrams: Overseas telegrams accepted at all telegraph offices. Ordinary and deferred (LT) telegrams.
Telex: International telex facilities available at Fiji International Telecommunications Ltd (FINTEL), Victoria Parade, Suva, or at major hotels.
Telephoning the UK: International operator service.

Finland
Air mail post to UK: About 7 days.
Telegrams: Can be left with the nearest post office or hotel desk.
Telex: Facilities available at Post Offices.
Telephoning the UK: IDD.

France
Air mail post to UK: 2 days.
Telegrams: Facilities available throughout.
Telex: Extensive facilities available.

Gambia
Air mail post to UK: 3 days.
Telegrams: From Cable & Wireless, Mercury House, Telegraph Road, Banjul. Ordinary telegrams.
Telex: Public telex booth at the GPO, Russell Street, Banjul, and at Cable and Wireless, Banjul.
Telephoning the UK: 24 hour international operator service.

German Democratic Republic
Air mail post to UK: 2 days.
Telegrams: May be sent from main post offices.
Telex: From post offices but dependent on place in GDR.
Telephoning the UK: IDD.

Federal Republic of Germany
Air mail post to UK: About 3 days.
Telegrams: May be sent from post offices.
Telex:
Telephoning the UK: IDD.

Ghana
Air mail post to UK: 5 days.
Telegrams: From External Telecommunication Service of Posts and Telecommunications Corporation, Extelcom House, High St, Accra, and Stewart Avenue, Kumasi. Ordinary, urgent and letter telegrams.
Telex: Public call facilities at External Telecommunication Service offices.
Telephoning the UK: Operator connected calls may be made 08.15–18.15 hours, weekdays only. Often difficult and delays sometimes of 2–3 days.

Gibraltar
Air mail post to UK: 2–6 days.
Telegrams: Via Cable & Wireless in Gibraltar.
Telex: Via Cable and Wireless.
Telephoning the UK: Automatic almost everywhere in the world.

Greece
Air mail post to UK: 4–5 days.
Telegrams: May be sent from OYE (Telecommunication Centre).
Telex: Facilities available from OTE.
Telephoning the UK: IDD.

Guyana
Air mail post to UK: 7–10 days.
Telegrams: Can be sent 24 hours a day from Bank of Guyana Building, Avenue of the Republic, and Church Street, Georgetown. Ordinary and night letter telegrams.
Telex: Public call offices at the Bank of Guyana Building.
Telephone: International operator service at all times.

Hong Kong
Air mail to UK: 3–5 days.
Telegrams: From telegraphic offices. Ordinary, letter and social telegrams.
Telex: Public telex facilities available at Mercury House, 3 Connaught Road, Central, Hong Kong Island, and at Ocean Terminal, Kowloon and from Kai Tak Airport.
Telephoning the UK: IDD, and 24 hour international operator service.

Hungary
Air mail post to UK: About 4 days.
Telegrams: May be sent from hotel desks.
Telephoning the UK: IDD.

Iceland
Air mail post to UK: All items automatically sent by air – 7–10 days.
Telegrams: From Chief Telegraphic Office, Reykjavik.
Telex: There are no public telex facilities.
Telephone: International operator service 24 hours a day.

India
Air mail post to UK: 6–7 days.
Telegrams: From any telegraphic office. Express, letter and urgent.
Telex: International telex facilities available 24 hours a day at large hotels, and at telegraph/telex offices in major cities.
Telephoning the UK: IDD from Bombay and New Delhi only, between 18.30 and 06.30 GMT.

Indonesia
Air mail post to UK: 7–10 days.
Telegrams: From any telegraphic office; in Djakarta facilities available 24 hours.
Telex: Public telex facilities operated from Directorate General for Posts and Communications, Djl. Medan Merdeka Selatan 12 (24 hours); also in some major hotels; and at the chief telegraphic offices in Semarang, Jogjakarta, Surabaya and Denpasar.
Telephoning the UK: International operator service 24 hours, seven days a week.

Iran
Air mail post to UK: 4–5 days.
Telegrams: Must be despatched from Chief Telegraph Office, Meidane Sepah, Tehran, which is open all night. Ordinary, letter and urgent telegrams.
Telex: Public facilities at Chief Telegraph Office and at some hotels.
Telephoning the UK: International operator service.

Iraq
Air mail post to UK: 5–10 days.
Telegrams: Telegraph office attached to central post office in Rashid Street, Baghdad, also at Basrah, Kerkuk and Musul.
graphic offices.
Telex: Facilities available at the PTT in Rashid Street, Baghdad, and at a number of hotels.
Telephoning the UK: IDD in the cities of Baghdad, Basrak, Musul and Kerkak.

Israel
Air mail post to UK: 4–7 days.
Telegrams: From telegraphic offices. Ordinary.
Telex: Facilities available to guests in most deluxe hotels in Jerusalem and Tel Aviv. Public telex booths at 23 Rehov Yafo, Jerusalem; 7 Rehov Mikve Yisrael, Tel Aviv.
Telephoning the UK: IDD 19.00–07.00 weekdays; 15.00–07.00 Sunday at cheaper rate.

Ivory Coast
Air mail post to UK: About 10 days.
Telegrams: May be sent from the post offices.
Telex: Facilities in the post offices.
Telephoning the UK: International operator service.

Jamaica
Air mail post to UK: About 10–14 days.
Telegrams: Telegram service available from any post office (inland).
Telex: Telex service available from Jamaica International Telecommunication Limited, Jamintel Centre, 15 North Street, Kingston.

Japan
Air mail post to UK: 4–6 days.
Telegrams: May be sent from the main hotels, from offices of Kokusai Denshin Denwa Co Ltd and of Nippon Denshin Denwa Kosha and from larger post offices in major cities. Ordinary, letter, and express telegrams.
Telex: Telex booths are available at main post offices and main offices of Kokusai Denshin Denwa Co Ltd and Nippon Denshin Denwa Kosha.
Telephoning the UK: IDD.

Jordan
Air mail post to UK: About 5 days.
Telegrams: Overseas service reasonably good. May be sent from the Central Telegraph Office; Post Office, 1st Circle, Jebel Amman; or any post office.
Telex: Public telex facilities are available at the Central Telegraph Office and in a number of hotels.
Telephoning the UK: IDD.

Kenya
Air mail post to UK: 3–4 days.
Telegrams: Overseas telegrams can be sent from all post and telegraphic offices. Nairobi GPO open 24 hours. Ordinary, letter and urgent telegrams.
Telex: Facilities available at Nairobi GPO. New Stanley and Hilton Hotels have facilities for their guests, otherwise no public call booths.
Telephoning the UK: International operator service.

Korea
Air mail post to UK: 7–10 days.
Telegrams: May be sent by dialling 115 and delivering message in English or by visiting a telegraph office of the Korea International Telecommunication Office (KIT) near Capitol Building and delivering message in written English.
Telex: Telex facilities available in main hotels; also from the Post Office in Seoul and office of Korea International Telecommunications Services.
Telephoning the UK: IDD.

Kuwait
Air mail post to UK: 5 days.
Telegrams: Telegrams sent from Chief Telegraph Office 6 hours after being handed in at the Post Office.
Telex: Facilities available at main hotels or from main Post Office (24 hours).
Telephoning the UK: IDD.

Liberia
Air mail to UK: 3–7 days.
Telegrams: Facilities provided by the Liberian Telecommunications Corporation and French Cables, Monrovia.
Telex: Services provided by the Liberian Telecommunications Corporation.

Luxembourg
Air mail to UK: about 3 days.
Telegrams: Telegram facilities available at the Main Post Office in Luxembourg City: Bureau de Postes, 8a Avenue Monterey (open 07.00–20.45 Mon–Sat); Luxembourg Railway Station Main Post Office, 9 Place de la Gare (open 24 hours, 7 days a week).
Telex: Facilities available from post offices named above. Also Luxembourg Airports Post Office, inside main airport terminal, 1st floor.
Telephoning the UK: IDD.

Macao
Air mail post to UK: About 3 days.
Telegrams: May be sent from hotels and from the General Post Office in Leal Senado Square.
Telex: Facilities from the General Post Office.
Telephoning the UK: Most hotels have direct dial telephones but otherwise through operators or from the General Post Office.

Malaysia
Air mail post to UK: 4–7 days.
Telegrams: May be sent by phone 24 hours a day by dialling 104, or at any Telegraph office and most post offices. Ordinary, urgent, letter and greetings telegrams.
Telex: Public facilities available 24 hours at Telegraph Office, Djalan Raja Chulan, Kuala Lumpur, and most hotels.
Telephoning the UK: IDD.

Malta
Air mail post to UK: 3 days.
Telegrams: From TELEMALTA offices and most hotels.
Telex: Facilities from TELEMALTA and most hotels.
Telephoning the UK: IDD.

Mexico
Air mail post to UK: About 7 days.
Telegrams: Telegraphic system maintained by Telegrafos Nacionalies, and telegrams to be handed in to their offices. In Mexico City the main office for international telegrams is at Balderas y Colón, Mexico 1, DF.
Telex: International telex facilities available at a number of locations in Mexico City; hotels reluctant to despatch messages for guests but willing to receive them.
Telephoning the UK: IDD or through operator.

Morocco
Air mail post to UK: At least 5 days.
Telegrams: From all telegraph offices. Ordinary and urgent telegrams.
Telex: International telex facilities available at Hotels Hilton and Tour Hassan, Rabat; Hotels El Mansour and Marhaba, Casablanca.
Telephoning the UK: IDD. Calls may be made at any time, but delays might be experienced.

New Zealand
Air mail post to UK: About 7 days.
Telegrams: From all post offices 09.00–17.00 hours, and telephoned through at any time. Ordinary, letter, and urgent telegrams.
Telex: All major hotels, banks, Government offices and some commercial practices have telex facilities.
Telephoning the UK: IDD.

Niger
Air mail post to UK: Varies.
Telegrams: From Chief Telegraph Office, Niamey, and at all other telegraph offices. Ordinary, urgent, and letter telegrams.
Telex: Public facilities available at Chief Telegraph Office, Niamey.
Telephoning the UK: Good quality direct telephone line to Paris from Niamey, which links with UK. Service available at 08.30, 12.30, 15.30 and 18.00 hours daily in Niamey. Calls should be made by asking exchange for L'Inter Radio.

Oman
Air mail post to UK: About 1 week.
Telegrams: May be sent from post offices.
Telex: Facilities available from post offices.

Pakistan
Air mail post to UK: 4 days.
Telegrams: Post offices, telegraph offices and hotels. The Central Telegraph Office, 1.1. Chundrigar Road, Karachi, provides 24 hour service.
Telex: The Central Telegraph Office provides telex facilities 24 hours.
Telephoning the UK: International operator service.

Paraguay
Air mail post to UK: 7–10 days.
Telegrams: May be sent from post offices, banks and hotels.
Telex: Facilities available from post offices, banks and hotels.
Telephoning the UK: Via operator – no direct dialling.

Peru
Air mail post to UK: About 10 days.
Telegrams: From ENTEL PERU telegraph offices. Ordinary and night telegrams.
Telex: Telex machines with international connections installed at hotels Bolivar, Crillon and Sheraton in Lima.
Telephoning the UK: International operator service at all times.

Philippines
Air mail post to UK: 10 days, often more.
Telegrams: From Eastern Telecommunications Philippines Incorporated offices. Ordinary and urgent telegrams.
Telex: Public telex booths operated by Eastern Telecommunications Philippines, Inc, Globe-Mackay Cable and Radio Corporation, and RCA Communications, Inc.
Telephoning the UK: International operator service 24 hours.

Portugal
Air mail post to UK: About 3 days.
Telegrams: Facilities available from all post offices.
Telex: From post offices.
Telephoning the UK: IDD.

Qatar
Telegrams: For telegraph service dial 130.
Telex: Facilities available from Qatar National Telephone Service (QNTS).
Telephoning the UK: IDD.

El Salvador
Air mail post to UK: 7–10 days.
Telephoning the UK: IDD.

Samoa
Air mail post to UK: About 10 days (US mail system).
Telegrams: Available from post office.
Telex: Facilities at post office.
Telephoning the UK: IDD.

Sénégal
Air mail post to UK: About 7 days.
Telegrams: Available at most major post offices.
Telex: Facilities for private subscribers.

Seychelles
Air mail post to UK: About 7 days.
Telegrams: Via Cable & Wireless.
Telex: Via Cables and Wireless.
Telephoning the UK: IDD.

Sierra Leone
Air mail post to UK: 5 days.

Telegrams: From Mercury House, 7 Wallace Johnson Street, Freetown. Ordinary, urgent and letter telegrams.
Telex: Facilities available at Mercury House.
Telephoning the UK: International operator calls between 11.00 and midnight local time any day of the week.

Singapore
Air mail post to UK: Usually 5 days, but can take 10–14.
Telegrams: From telegraph offices. Ordinary, urgent, letter, and social telegrams.
Telex: Public telex facilities available at Central Telegraph Office, 35 Robinson Road.
Telephoning the UK: IDD; operator service 24 hours.

South Africa
Air mail post to UK: 3–7 days.
Telegrams: Telegraph service available in every town however small.
Telex: Public call facilities available in Cape Town, Durban, Johannesburg and Pretoria post offices. Most hotels and offices have telex.
Telephoning the UK: IDD available from all centres.

Spain
Air mail post to UK: 4–5 days.
Telegrams: May be sent from main post offices.
Telex: Facilities from main post offices.
Telephoning the UK: IDD.

Sri Lanka
Air mail post to UK: 4–7 days.
Telegrams: From all post offices. Ordinary, letter and urgent telegrams.
Telex: Public telephone booth at OTS Building, Duke Street, Colombo.
Telephoning the UK: International operator service 24 hours.

Swaziland
Air mail post to UK: About 6 days.
Telegrams: May be sent from most post offices.
Telex: Facilities from most post offices.
Telephoning the UK: IDD or through exchange no. 90.

Sweden
Air mail post to UK: About 6 days.
Telegrams: Telephone the telegram in by dialling 0021 or send by post.
Telex: Public telexes not available.
Telephoning the UK: IDD.

Switzerland
Air mail post to UK: 2–4 days.
Telegrams: May be sent from post offices and hotels.
Telex: Some hotels have telex facilities.
Telephoning the UK: IDD.

Tahiti
Telegrams: Facilities can be found at the Office des postes et telecommunications, Boulevard Pomare, Papeete, Tahiti.
Telex: Services from the Office des postes et telecommunications.
Telephoning the UK: Dial 19 and give name and number of person receiving call.

Tanzania
Air mail post to UK: About 7 days.
Telegrams: From post office. Ordinary, urgent, letter, and greetings telegrams.
Telex: Public telex at post office in Mkwepu Street, Dar es Salaam, and in some hotels.
Telephoning the UK: International operator service 24 hours.

Thailand
Air mail post to UK: 5 days.
Telegrams: From GPO Building, New Road, Bangkok, or any telegraph office. Ordinary, urgent, letter telegrams.
Telex: Public call office facilities at the GPO, New Road, Bangkok.
Telephoning the UK: International operator service, by contacting Long Distance Telephone Office behind GPO in New Road (Tel: 32054 or 37056).

Tonga
Telegrams: Via Cable & Wireless, Salote Road. Tel: 21-499.
Telex: Via Cable & Wireless. Private booths available.
Telephoning the UK: Dial 913 for International operator.

Trinidad and Tobago
Air mailpost to UK: About 6 days.
Telegrams: Via Trinidad and Tobago External Telecommunications Company Ltd (TEXTEL) located at 1 Edward Street, Port of Spain, Trinidad.
Telex: TEXTEL provide a telex agency service for the receipt of telex messages on behalf of customers who do not have their own installations.
Telephoning the UK: IDD.

Tunisia
Air mail post to UK: About 5 days.
Telegrams: From Central Post Office in Rue Charles de Gaulle, Tunis (24 hours), and other telegraph offices.
Telephoning the UK: IDD; International operator service 24 hours.

Turkey
Air mail post to UK: 3 days.
Telegrams: From telegraph and post offices. Ordinary and urgent telegrams.
Telex: Public call office at main post office, Ulus, Ankara and at main post office, Telegraf Gisesi, Sirkeci, Istanbul (24 hours).
Telephoning the UK: International operator service.

Turks and Caicos Islands
Air mail to UK: 5–10 days
Telegrams: Via Cable and Wireless.
Telex: Via Cable & Wireless.
Telephoning the UK: Through operator.

United Arab Emirates
Air mail post to UK: 5 days.
Telegrams: Phone and send telegrams from Emirtel offices in each town. Emirtel is the Federal telephone company.
Telephoning the UK: IDD.

USSR
Air mail post to UK: Over 10 days.
Telegrams: Usually reach UK within a few hours. May be sent from hotels. Ordinary, urgent and letter telegrams.
Telex: Telex installed in offices of Commercial Department of British Embassy (Kutuzovsky Prospekt 7/4).
Telephoning the UK: International calls booked through hotel service bureau or by visiting Central Post Office, 7 Gorky Street. Operator service. Be prepared to give STD code number.

USA
Air mail post to UK: 5–6 days but varies. More from West Coast.
Telegrams: From all post and telegraph offices. Full and night letter telegrams.
Telex: Western Union international telex facilities throughout USA.
Telephoning the UK: IDD from biggest cities; 24 hour operator service otherwise.

Upper Volta (Burkina Faso)
Air mail post to UK: 5–6 days.
Telegrams: Address them to la poste centrale.
Telephoning the UK: Via operator.

Uruguay
Air mail post to UK: About 7 days.
Telegrams: Public booths in main banking and commercial offices.
Telex: Facilities in main banking and commercial offices.
Telephoning the UK: Via the operator.

Venezuela
Air mail post to UK: 3–7 days.
Telegrams: Usual telegram services from public telegraph offices, ordinary, and night letter telegrams.
Telex: Public telex facilities provided by CANTV.
Telephoning the UK: IDD.

British Virgin Islands
Air mail post to UK: 5–10 days.
Telegrams: Via Cable & Wireless.
Telex: Via Cable & Wireless.
Telephoning the UK: Through operator.

United States Virgin Islands
Air mail post to UK: About 6 days.
Telegrams: Extensive facilities available.
Telex: Full facilities available.
Telephoning the UK: Through operator.

Yemen Arab Republic (North)
Air mail post to UK: 3–4 days.
Telegrams: From any telegraph office. Ordinary, urgent, and letter telegrams.
Telex: Telex booths at Cable & Wireless offices in Sana'a, Hodeida and Taiz.
Telephoning the UK: Telephone link available 08.00–20.30 local time.

Yugoslavia
Air mail post to UK: 4–5 days.
Telegrams: Facilities at post offices.
Telex: Via post offices.
Telephoning the UK: IDD.

Zaïre
Air mail post to UK: 4–10 days.
Telegrams: From Chief Telegraph Offices. Ordinary and urgent telegrams.
Telex: Facilities only available at Kinshasa and Lubumbashi Chief Telegraph Offices; also at Intercontinental Hotel.
Telephoning the UK: International operator service.

Zambia
Air mail post to UK: 5–7 days.
Telegrams: From telegraph offices. Urgent will be accepted at Lusaka Central Telegraph Office up to 21.00 Mon.–Sat.
Telex: Public telex facilities at Lusaka GPO; also main hotels.
Telephoning the UK: International operator service.

Zimbabwe
Air mail post to UK: About 5 days.
Telegrams: Facilities found in all major cities and tourist centres.
Telex: From all major cities and tourist centres.

International Direct Dialling

(Reproduced by courtesy of British Telecom)

Countries in alphabetical order to which international direct dialling is available. Country codes ar the same worldwide.

Country	*Country Code*	*Time Difference (+ or − GMT)*
Algeria	213	Nil
Andorra	33 078	+1
Anguilla (LI)	1 809 4972	−4
Antigua (LI)	1 809 46	−4
Antilles Neth.	599	−4
Argentina	54	−3
Australia	61	+8 to +10
Austria	43	+1
Bahamas	1 809	−5
Bahrain	973	+3
Barbados	1 809 42	−4
Belgium	32	+1
Benin	229	+1
Bermuda	1 809 29	−4
Botswana	267	+2
Brazil	55	−3
British Virgin Is	1 809 49	−4
Brunei	673	+8
Burma	95	+6½
Cameroon	237	+1
Canada	1	−3½ to −9
Cayman Islands	1 809 94	−5
Chile	56	−4
Colombia	57	−5
Costa Rica	506	−6
Cuba (Havana only)	53	−5
Cyprus	357	+2
Czechoslovakia	42	+1
Denmark	45	+1
Djibouti	253	+3
Dominica (WI)	1 809 449	−4
Dominican Rep	1 809	−5
Egypt	20	+2
El Salvador	503	−6
Ethiopia	251	+3
Faroe Islands	45 42	+1
Fiji	679	+12
Finland	358	+2
France	33	+1
French Polynesia	689	−10
Gabon	241	+1
Gambia	220	Nil
Germany, Dem. Rep.	37	+1
Germany, Fed. Rep.	49	+1
Gibraltar	350	+1
Greece	30	+2
Grenada (WI)	1 809 444	−4
Guatemala	502	−6
Guyana	592	−3
Honduras	504	−5
Hong Kong	852	+8
Hungary	36	+1
Iceland	354	Nil
India	91	+5½
Indonesia	62	+7 to +9
Iran	98	+3½
Iraq	964	+3
Israel	972	+2
Italy	39	+1
Ivory Coast	225	Nil
Jamaica	1 809	−5
Japan	81	+9
Jordan	962	+2
Kenya	254	+3
Kuwait	965	+3
Lebanon	961	+2
Lesotho	266	+2
Libya	218	+2
Liechtenstein	41 75	+1
Luxembourg	352	+1
Macao	853	+8
Madeira	351 91	Nil
Malawi	265	+2
Malaysia	60	+7½ to 8
Maldive Islands	960	+5
Malta	356	+1
Mauritius	230	+4
Mexico	52	−6 to −8
Monaco	33 93	+1
Montserrat (LI)	1 809 491	−4
Morocco	212	Nil
Nauru	674	+12
Nepal	977	+5½
Netherlands	31	+1
New Caledonia	687	+11
New Zealand	64	+12
Nicaragua	505	−6
Nigeria	234	+1
Norway	47	+1
Oman	968	+4
Pakistan	92	+5
Panama	507	−5
Papua New Guinea	675	+10
Philippines	63	+8
Poland	48	+1
Portugal	351	Nil
Qatar	974	+3
Romania	40	+2
St Christopher & Nevis (LI)	1 809 469	−4
St Lucia (WI)	1 809 45	−4
St Vincent and Bequia (WI)	1 809 45	−4

Country	*Country Code*	*Time Difference (+ or − GMT)*
Samoa USA	684	−11
Samoa Western	685	−11
San Marino	39 541	+1
Saudi Arabia	966	+3
Sénégal	221	Nil
Seychelles	248	+4
Sierra Leone	232	Nil
Singapore	65	+7
Solomon Islands	677	+11
South Africa	27	+2
South West Africa/Namibia	264	+2
South Korea	82	+9
Spain	34	+1
Sri Lanka	94	+5½
Swaziland	268	+2
Sweden	46	+1
Switzerland	41	+1
Taiwan	886	+8
Tanzania	255	+3
Thailand	66	+7
Tonga	676	+13
Trinidad & Tobago	1 809	−4
Tunisia	216	+1
Turkey	90	+3
Turks and Caicos I	1 809 946	−5
Uganda	256	+3
United Arab Emirates –		
Abu Dhabi	971 2	+4
Dubai	971 4	+4
Ajman	971 6	+4
Sharjar	971 6	+4
Ras Al Khaimah	971 77	+4
Fujairah	971 70	+4
United Kingdom		
Uruguay	598	−3
USA (except Alaska and Hawaii)	1	−5 to −9
USA Alaska	1 907	−9½ to −11½
USA Hawaii	1 808	−10
USSR (Moscow)	7	+3 to +12
Vatican City	39 66982	+1
Venezuela	58	−4
Yemen Arab Rep.	967	+3
Yugoslavia	38	+1
Zambia	260	+2
Zimbabwe	263	+2

(WI) – Winward Isles
(LI) – Leeward Isles

International Access code
The International Access Code, to be dialled before the country code, varies from country to country. Contact local Operator for relevant number. UK International Access Code – 010.

Charge Bands, Standard and Cheap Rates
These vary worldwide due to time differences. For further information on charge bands dialling from UK contact British Telecom for their booklet *International Telephone Guide*. IDD cheap rate, available to most countries from the UK, is from 8 pm to 8 am Monday to Friday, all day Saturday and Sunday. For charge bands and cheap and standard rates elsewhere contact local Operator.

Note: Countries are being added to the direct dialling system every year. If you would prefer to dial direct, ask the Operator if the country wanted is now in the IDD system.

Climate

Climate

Worldwide Weather Guide

The information given below details temperature and humidity at important cities throughout the world.
Temperature – Average daily maximum and minimum temperatures are shade temperatures. Maximum temperatures usually occur in early afternoon, and minimum temperatures just before sunrise.
Humidity – Measured as a daily figure at one or more fixed hours daily. It is normally lowest in the early afternoon and highest just before sunrise. High humidity combined with high temperatures increases discomfort.
Precipitation – Includes all forms of moisture falling on the earth, mainly rain and snow. Average monthly.

		J	F	M	A	M	J	J	A	S	O	N	D
Accra													
Temperature F	Max	87	88	88	88	87	84	81	80	81	85	87	88
	Min	73	75	76	76	75	74	73	71	73	74	75	75
Temperature C	Max	31	31	31	31	31	29	38	38	38	29	31	31
	Min	23	24	24	24	24	23	23	22	23	23	24	24
Humidity %	am	95	96	95	96	96	97	97	97	96	97	97	97
	pm	61	61	63	65	68	74	76	77	72	71	66	64
Precipitation	mm	15	33	56	81	142	178	46	15	36	64	36	23
Amsterdam – De Bilt													
Temperature F	Max	40	42	49	56	64	70	72	71	67	57	48	42
	Min	31	31	34	40	46	51	55	55	50	44	38	33
Temperature C	Max	4	5	10	13	18	21	22	22	19	14	9	5
	Min	−1	−1	1	4	8	11	13	13	10	7	3	1
Humidity %	am	90	90	86	79	75	75	79	82	86	90	92	91
	pm	82	76	65	61	59	59	64	65	67	72	81	85
Precipitation	mm	68	53	44	49	52	58	77	87	72	72	70	64
Athens													
Temperature F	Max	55	57	60	68	77	86	92	92	84	75	66	58
	Min	44	44	46	52	61	68	73	73	67	60	53	47
Temperature C	Max	13	14	16	20	25	30	33	33	29	24	19	15
	Min	6	7	8	11	16	20	23	23	19	15	12	8
Humidity %	am	77	74	71	65	60	50	47	48	58	70	78	78
	pm	62	57	54	48	47	39	34	34	42	52	61	63
Precipitation	mm	62	37	37	23	23	14	6	7	15	51	56	71
Auckland													
Temperature F	Max	73	73	71	67	62	58	56	58	60	63	66	70
	Min	60	60	59	56	51	48	46	46	49	52	54	57
Temperature C	Max	23	23	22	19	17	14	13	14	16	17	19	21
	Min	16	16	15	13	11	9	8	8	9	11	12	14
Humidity %	am	71	72	74	78	80	83	84	80	76	74	71	70
	pm	62	61	65	69	70	73	74	70	68	66	64	64
Precipitation	mm	79	84	81	97	127	137	145	117	102	102	89	79

		J	F	M	A	M	J	J	A	S	O	N	D
Bahrain													
Temperature F	Max	68	70	75	84	92	96	99	100	96	90	82	71
	Min	57	59	63	70	78	82	85	85	81	75	69	60
Temperature C	Max	20	21	24	29	33	36	37	38	36	32	28	22
	Min	14	15	17	21	26	28	29	29	27	24	21	16
Humidity %	am	85	83	80	75	71	69	69	74	75	80	80	85
	pm	71	70	70	66	63	64	67	65	64	66	70	77
Precipitation	mm	8	18	13	8	0	0	0	0	0	0	18	18
Bangkok													
Temperature F	Max	89	91	93	95	93	91	90	90	89	88	87	87
	Min	68	72	75	77	77	76	76	76	76	75	72	68
Temperature C	Max	32	33	34	35	34	33	32	32	32	31	31	31
	Min	20	22	24	25	25	24	24	24	24	25	22	20
Humidity %	am	91	92	92	90	91	90	91	92	94	93	92	91
	pm	53	55	56	58	64	67	66	66	70	70	65	56
Precipitation	mm	8	20	36	58	198	160	160	175	305	206	66	5
Beirut													
Temperature F	Max	62	63	66	72	78	83	87	89	86	81	73	65
	Min	51	51	54	58	64	69	73	74	73	69	61	55
Temperature C	Max	17	17	19	22	26	28	31	32	30	27	23	18
	Min	11	11	12	14	18	21	23	23	23	21	16	12
Humidity %	am	72	72	72	72	69	67	66	65	64	65	67	70
	pm	70	70	69	67	64	61	58	57	57	62	61	69
Precipitation	mm	191	157	94	56	18	3	0	0	5	51	132	185
Berlin													
Temperature F	Max	35	37	46	56	66	72	75	74	68	56	45	38
	Min	26	26	31	39	47	53	57	56	50	42	36	29
Temperature C	Max	2	3	8	13	19	22	24	23	20	13	7	3
	Min	−3	−3	0	4	8	12	14	13	10	6	2	−1
Humidity %	am	89	89	88	84	80	80	84	88	92	93	92	91
	pm	82	78	67	60	57	58	61	61	65	73	83	86
Precipitation	mm	46	40	33	42	49	65	73	69	48	49	46	43
Bombay													
Temperature F	Max	83	83	86	89	91	89	85	85	85	89	89	97
	Min	67	67	72	76	80	79	77	76	76	76	73	79
Temperature C	Max	28	28	30	32	33	32	29	29	29	32	32	31
	Min	12	12	17	20	23	21	22	22	22	21	18	13
Humidity %	am	70	71	73	75	74	79	83	83	85	81	73	70
	pm	61	62	65	67	68	77	83	81	78	71	64	62
Precipitation	mm	2.5	2.5	2.5	0	18	485	617	340	264	64	13	2.5
Brussels													
Temperature F	Max	40	44	51	58	65	72	73	72	69	60	48	42
	Min	30	32	36	41	46	52	54	54	51	45	38	32
Temperature C	Max	4	7	10	14	18	22	23	22	21	15	9	6
	Min	−1	0	2	5	8	11	12	12	11	7	3	0
Humidity %	am	92	92	91	91	90	87	91	93	94	93	93	92
	pm	86	81	74	71	65	65	68	69	69	77	85	86
Precipitation	mm	66	61	53	60	55	76	95	80	63	83	75	88
Buenos Aires													
Temperature F	Max	85	83	79	72	64	57	57	60	64	69	76	82
	Min	63	63	60	53	47	41	42	43	46	50	56	61
Temperature C	Max	29	28	26	22	18	14	14	16	18	21	24	28
	Min	17	17	16	12	8	5	6	6	8	10	13	16

		J	F	M	A	M	J	J	A	S	O	N	D
Buenos Aires cont'd													
Humidity %	am	81	83	87	88	90	91	92	90	86	83	79	79
	pm	61	63	69	71	74	78	79	74	68	65	60	62
Precipitation	mm	79	71	109	89	76	61	56	61	79	86	84	99
Cairo													
Temperature F	Max	65	69	75	83	91	95	96	95	90	86	78	68
	Min	47	48	52	57	63	68	70	71	68	65	58	50
Temperature C	Max	18	21	24	28	33	35	36	35	32	30	26	20
	Min	8	9	11	14	17	20	20	22	20	18	14	10
Humidity %	am	69	64	63	55	50	55	65	69	68	67	68	70
	pm	40	33	27	21	18	20	24	28	31	31	38	41
Precipitation	mm	5	5	5	3	3	0	0	0	0	0	3	5
Calcutta													
Temperature F	Max	80	84	93	97	96	92	89	89	90	89	84	79
	Min	55	59	69	75	77	79	79	78	78	74	64	55
Temperature C	Max	27	29	34	36	36	33	32	32	32	32	29	26
	Min	13	15	21	24	25	26	26	26	26	24	18	13
Humidity %	am	85	82	79	76	77	82	86	88	86	85	79	80
	pm	52	45	46	56	62	75	80	82	81	72	63	55
Precipitation	mm	10	31	36	43	140	297	325	328	252	114	20	5
Christchurch													
Temperature F	Max	70	69	66	62	56	51	50	52	57	62	66	69
	Min	53	53	50	45	40	36	35	36	40	44	47	51
Temperature C	Max	21	21	19	17	13	11	10	11	14	17	19	21
	Min	12	12	10	7	4	2	2	2	4	7	8	11
Humidity %	am	65	71	75	82	85	87	87	81	72	63	64	67
	pm	59	60	69	71	69	72	76	66	69	60	64	60
Precipitation	mm	56	43	48	48	66	66	69	48	46	60	64	60
Colombo													
Temperature F	Max	86	87	88	88	87	85	85	85	85	85	85	85
	Min	72	72	74	76	78	77	77	77	77	75	73	72
Temperature C	Max	30	31	31	31	31	29	29	29	29	29	29	29
	Min	22	22	23	24	25	26	25	25	25	24	23	22
Humidity %	am	73	71	71	74	78	80	79	78	76	77	77	74
	pm			67	66	66	70	76	78	77	76	75	76
75	69												
Precipitation	mm	89	69	147	231	371	224	135	109	160	348	315	147
Copenhagen													
Temperature F	Max	36	36	41	51	61	67	71	70	64	54	45	40
	Min	28	28	31	38	46	52	57	56	51	44	38	34
Temperature C	Max	2	2	5	10	16	19	22	21	18	12	7	4
	Min	−2	−3	−1	3	8	11	14	14	11	7	3	1
Humidity %	am	88	86	85	79	70	70	74	78	83	86	88	89
	pm	85	83	78	68	59	60	62	64	69	76	83	87
Precipitation	mm	49	39	32	38	43	47	71	66	62	59	48	49
Delhi													
Temperature F	Max	70	75	87	97	105	102	96	93	93	93	84	73
	Min	44	49	58	68	79	83	81	79	75	65	52	46
Temperature C	Max	21	24	31	36	41	39	36	34	34	34	29	23
	Min	7	9	14	20	26	28	27	26	24	18	11	8
Humidity %	am	72	67	49	35	35	53	75	80	72	56	51	69
	pm	41	35	23	19	20	36	59	64	51	32	31	42
Precipitation	mm	23	18	13	8	13	74	180	173	117	10	3	10

		J	F	M	A	M	J	J	A	S	O	N	D
Djakarta													
Temperature F	Max	84	84	86	87	87	87	87	87	88	87	86	85
	Min	74	74	74	75	75	74	73	73	74	74	74	74
Temperature C	Max	29	29	30	31	31	31	31	31	31	31	30	29
	Min	23	23	23	24	24	23	23	23	23	23	23	23
Humidity %	am	95	95	94	94	94	93	92	90	90	90	92	92
	pm	75	75	73	71	69	67	64	61	62	64	68	71
Precipitation	mm	300	300	211	147	114	97	64	43	66	112	142	203
Frankfurt													
Temperature F	Max	38	41	51	60	69	74	77	76	69	58	47	39
	Min	29	30	35	42	49	55	58	57	52	44	38	32
Temperature C	Max	3	5	11	16	20	23	25	24	21	14	8	4
	Min	−1	−2	2	6	9	13	15	14	11	7	3	0
Humidity %	am	86	86	84	79	78	78	81	85	89	91	89	88
	pm	77	70	57	51	50	52	53	54	60	68	77	81
Precipitation	mm	58	44	38	44	55	73	70	76	57	52	55	54
Haifa													
Temperature F	Max	65	67	71	77	83	85	88	90	88	85	78	68
	Min	49	50	53	58	65	71	75	76	74	68	60	53
Temperature C	Max	18	19	22	25	28	29	31	32	31	29	26	20
	Min	9	10	12	14	18	22	24	24	23	20	16	12
Humidity %	am	66	65	62	60	62	67	70	70	67	66	61	66
	pm	56	56	56	57	59	66	68	69	66	66	56	56
Precipitation	mm	175	109	41	25	5	0	0	0	3	25	94	185
Hamilton, Bermuda													
Temperature F	Max	68	68	68	71	76	81	85	86	84	79	74	70
	Min	58	57	57	59	64	69	73	74	72	69	63	60
Temperature C	Max	20	20	20	22	24	27	29	30	29	26	23	21
	Min	14	14	14	15	18	21	23	23	22	21	17	16
Humidity %	am	78	76	77	78	81	82	81	79	81	79	76	77
	pm	70	69	69	70	75	74	73	69	73	72	70	70
Precipitation	mm	112	119	122	104	117	112	114	137	132	147	127	119
Harare													
Temperature F	Max	78	78	78	78	74	70	70	74	79	83	81	79
	Min	60	60	58	55	49	44	44	47	53	58	60	60
Temperature C	Max	26	26	26	26	23	21	21	23	26	28	27	26
	Min	16	16	14	13	9	7	7	8	12	14	16	16
Humidity %	am	74	77	75	68	60	58	56	50	43	43	56	67
	pm	57	53	52	44	37	36	33	28	26	26	43	57
Precipitation	mm	196	178	117	28	13	3	0	3	5	28	97	163
Hong Kong													
Temperature F	Max	64	63	67	75	82	85	87	87	85	81	74	68
	Min	56	55	60	67	74	78	78	78	77	73	65	59
Temperature C	Max	18	17	19	24	28	29	31	31	29	27	23	20
	Min	13	13	16	19	23	26	26	26	25	23	18	15
Humidity %	am	77	82	84	87	87	86	87	87	83	75	73	74
	pm	66	73	74	77	78	77	77	77	72	63	60	63
Precipitation	mm	33	46	74	137	292	394	381	367	257	114	43	31
Istanbul													
Temperature F	Max	46	47	51	60	69	77	82	82	76	68	59	51
	Min	37	36	38	45	53	60	65	66	61	55	48	41
Temperature C	Max	8	9	11	16	21	25	28	28	24	20	15	11
	Min	3	2	3	7	12	16	18	19	16	13	9	5

		J	F	M	A	M	J	J	A	S	O	N	D
Istanbul cont'd													
Humidity %	am	82	82	81	81	82	79	79	79	81	83	82	82
	pm	75	72	67	62	61	58	56	55	59	64	71	74
Precipitation	mm	109	92	72	46	38	34	34	30	58	81	103	119
Jeddah													
Temperature F	Max	84	84	85	91	95	97	99	99	96	95	91	86
	Min	66	65	67	70	74	75	79	80	77	73	71	67
Temperature C	Max	29	29	29	33	35	36	37	37	36	35	33	30
	Min	19	18	19	21	23	24	26	27	25	23	22	19
Humidity %	am	58	52	52	52	51	56	55	59	65	60	55	55
	pm	54	52	52	56	55	55	50	51	61	61	59	54
Precipitation	mm	5	0	0	0	0	0	0	0	0	0	25	31
Johannesburg													
Temperature F	Max	78	77	75	72	66	62	63	68	73	77	77	78
	Min	58	58	55	50	43	39	39	43	48	53	55	57
Temperature C	Max	26	25	24	22	19	17	17	20	23	25	25	26
	Min	14	14	13	10	6	4	4	6	9	12	13	14
Humidity %	am	75	78	79	74	70	70	69	64	59	64	67	70
	pm	50	53	50	44	36	33	32	29	30	37	45	47
Precipitation	mm	114	109	89	38	25	8	8	8	23	56	107	125
Kathmandu													
Temperature F	Max	65	67	77	83	86	85	84	83	83	80	74	67
	Min	35	39	45	53	61	67	68	68	66	56	45	37
Temperature C	Max	18	19	25	28	30	29	29	28	28	27	23	19
	Min	2	4	7	12	16	19	20	20	19	13	7	3
Humidity %	am	89	90	73	68	72	79	86	87	86	88	90	89
	pm	70	68	53	54	61	72	82	84	83	81	78	73
Precipitation	mm	15	41	23	58	122	246	373	345	155	38	8	3
Kuala Lumpur													
Temperature F	Max	90	92	92	91	91	91	90	90	90	89	89	89
	Min	72	72	73	74	73	72	73	73	73	73	73	72
Temperature C	Max	32	33	33	33	33	33	32	32	32	32	32	32
	Min	22	22	23	23	23	22	23	23	23	23	23	22
Humidity %	am	97	97	97	97	97	96	95	96	96	96	97	97
	pm	60	60	58	63	66	63	63	62	64	65	66	61
Precipitation	mm	158	201	259	292	224	130	99	163	218	249	259	191
Lagos													
Temperature F	Max	88	89	89	89	87	85	83	82	83	85	88	88
	Min	74	77	78	77	76	74	74	73	74	74	75	75
Temperature C	Max	31	32	32	32	31	29	28	28	28	29	31	31
	Min	23	25	26	25	24	23	23	23	23	23	24	24
Humidity %	am	84	83	82	81	83	87	87	85	86	86	85	86
	pm	65	69	72	72	76	80	80	76	77	76	72	68
Precipitation	mm	28	46	102	150	269	460	279	64	140	206	69	25
Lima													
Temperature F	Max	82	83	83	80	74	68	67	66	68	71	74	78
	Min	66	67	66	63	60	58	57	56	57	58	60	62
Temperature C	Max	28	28	28	27	23	20	19	19	20	22	23	26
	Min	19	19	19	17	16	14	14	13	14	14	16	17
Humidity %	am	93	92	92	93	95	95	94	95	94	94	93	93
	pm	69	66	64	66	76	80	77	78	76	72	71	70
Precipitation	mm	3	0	0	0	5	5	8	8	8	3	3	0

		J	F	M	A	M	J	J	A	S	O	N	D
Lisbon													
Temperature F	Max	57	59	63	67	71	77	81	82	79	72	63	58
	Min	46	47	50	53	55	60	63	63	62	58	52	47
Temperature C	Max	14	15	17	20	21	25	27	28	26	22	17	15
	Min	8	8	10	12	13	15	17	17	17	14	11	9
Humidity %	am	85	80	78	69	68	65	62	64	70	75	81	84
	pm	71	64	64	56	57	54	48	49	54	59	68	72
Precipitation	mm	111	76	109	54	44	16	3	4	33	62	93	103
London (UK)													
Temperature F	Max	43	44	50	56	62	69	71	71	65	58	50	45
	Min	36	36	38	42	47	53	56	56	52	46	42	38
Temperature C	Max	6	7	10	13	17	20	22	21	19	14	10	7
	Min	2	2	3	6	8	12	14	13	11	8	5	4
Humidity %	am	86	85	81	71	70	70	71	76	80	85	85	87
	pm	77	72	64	56	57	58	59	62	65	70	78	81
Precipitation	mm	54	40	37	37	46	45	57	59	49	57	64	48
Madrid													
Temperature F	Max	47	52	59	65	70	80	87	85	77	65	55	48
	Min	35	36	41	45	50	58	63	63	57	48	42	36
Temperature C	Max	9	11	15	18	21	27	31	30	25	19	13	9
	Min	2	2	5	7	10	15	17	17	14	10	5	2
Humidity %	am	86	83	80	74	72	66	58	62	72	81	84	86
	pm	71	62	56	49	49	41	33	35	46	58	65	70
Precipitation	mm	39	34	43	48	47	27	11	15	32	53	47	48
Manila													
Temperature F	Max	86	88	91	93	93	91	88	87	88	88	87	86
	Min	69	69	71	73	75	75	75	75	75	74	72	70
Temperature C	Max	30	31	33	34	34	33	31	31	31	31	31	30
	Min	21	21	22	23	24	24	24	24	24	23	22	21
Humidity %	am	89	88	85	85	88	91	91	92	93	92	91	90
	pm	63	59	55	55	61	68	74	73	73	71	69	67
Precipitation	mm	23	13	18	33	130	254	432	422	356	193	145	66
Melbourne													
Temperature F	Max	78	78	75	68	62	57	56	59	63	67	71	75
	Min	57	57	55	51	47	44	42	43	46	48	51	54
Temperature C	Max	26	26	24	20	17	14	13	15	17	19	22	24
	Min	14	14	13	11	8	7	6	6	8	9	11	12
Humidity %	am	58	62	64	72	79	83	82	76	68	61	60	59
	pm	48	50	51	56	62	67	65	60	55	52	52	51
Precipitation	mm	48	46	56	58	53	53	48	48	58	66	58	58
Mexico City													
Temperature F	Max	66	69	75	77	78	76	73	73	74	70	68	66
	Min	42	43	47	51	54	55	53	54	53	50	46	43
Temperature C	Max	19	21	24	25	26	24	23	23	23	21	20	19
	Min	6	6	8	11	12	13	12	12	12	10	8	6
Humidity %	am	79	72	68	66	69	82	84	85	86	83	82	81
	pm	34	28	26	29	29	48	50	50	54	47	41	37
Precipitation	mm	13	5	10	20	53	119	170	152	130	51	18	8
Miami													
Temperature F	Max	74	75	78	80	84	86	88	88	87	83	78	76
	Min	61	61	64	67	71	74	76	76	75	72	66	62
Temperature C	Max	23	24	26	27	29	30	31	31	31	28	26	24
	Min	16	16	18	19	22	23	24	24	24	22	19	17

		J	F	M	A	M	J	J	A	S	O	N	D
Miami cont'd													
Humidity %	am	81	82	77	73	75	75	75	76	79	80	77	82
	pm	66	63	62	64	67	69	68	68	70	69	64	65
Precipitation	mm	71	53	64	81	173	178	155	160	203	234	71	51
Moscow													
Temperature F	Max	15	22	32	50	66	70	73	72	61	48	35	24
	Min	3	8	18	34	46	51	55	53	45	37	26	15
Temperature C	Max	−9	−6	0	10	19	21	23	22	16	9	2	−5
	Min	−16	−14	−8	1	8	11	13	12	7	3	−3	−10
Humidity %	am	82	82	82	73	58	62	68	74	78	81	87	85
	pm	77	66	64	54	43	47	54	55	59	67	79	83
Precipitation	mm	39	38	36	37	53	58	88	71	58	45	47	54
Nairobi													
Temperature F	Max	77	79	77	75	72	70	69	70	75	76	74	74
	Min	54	55	57	58	56	53	51	52	52	55	56	55
Temperature C	Max	25	26	25	24	22	21	21	21	24	24	23	23
	Min	12	13	14	14	13	12	11	11	11	13	13	13
Humidity %	am	74	74	81	88	88	89	86	86	82	82	86	81
	pm	44	40	45	56	62	60	58	56	45	43	53	53
Precipitation	mm	38	64	125	211	158	46	15	23	31	53	109	86
Nassau													
Temperature F	Max	77	77	79	81	84	87	88	89	88	85	81	79
	Min	65	64	66	69	71	74	75	76	75	73	70	67
Temperature C	Max	25	25	26	27	29	31	31	32	31	29	27	26
	Min	18	18	19	21	22	23	24	24	24	23	21	19
Humidity %	am	84	82	81	79	79	81	80	82	84	83	83	84
	pm	64	62	64	65	65	68	69	70	73	71	68	66
Precipitation	mm	36	38	36	64	117	163	147	135	175	165	71	33
New York													
Temperature F	Max	37	38	45	57	68	77	82	80	79	69	51	41
	Min	24	24	30	42	53	60	66	66	60	49	37	29
Temperature C	Max	3	3	7	14	20	25	28	27	26	21	11	5
	Min	−4	−4	−1	6	12	16	19	19	16	9	3	−2
Humidity %	am	72	70	70	68	70	74	77	79	79	76	75	73
	pm	60	58	55	53	54	58	58	60	61	57	60	61
Precipitation	mm	94	97	91	81	81	84	107	109	86	89	76	91
Oslo													
Temperature F	Max	28	30	39	50	61	68	72	70	60	48	38	32
	Min	19	19	25	34	43	50	55	53	46	38	31	25
Temperature C	Max	−2	−1	4	10	16	20	22	21	16	9	3	0
	Min	−7	−7	−4	1	6	10	13	12	8	3	−1	−4
Humidity %	am	86	84	80	75	68	69	74	79	85	88	88	87
	pm	82	74	64	57	52	55	59	61	66	72	83	85
Precipitation	mm	49	35	26	43	44	70	82	95	81	74	68	63
Ottawa													
Temperature F	Max	21	22	33	51	66	76	81	77	68	54	39	24
	Min	3	3	16	31	44	54	58	55	48	37	26	9
Temperature C	Max	−6	−6	1	11	19	24	27	25	20	12	4	−4
	Min	−16	−16	−9	−1	7	12	14	13	9	3	−3	−13
Humidity %	am	83	88	84	76	77	80	80	84	90	86	84	83
	pm	76	73	66	58	55	56	53	54	59	63	68	75
Precipitation	mm	74	56	71	69	64	89	86	66	81	74	76	66

		J	F	M	A	M	J	J	A	S	O	N	D
Papeete													
Temperature F	Max	89	89	89	89	87	86	86	86	86	87	88	88
	Min	72	72	72	72	70	69	68	68	69	70	71	72
Temperature C	Max	32	32	32	32	31	30	30	30	30	31	31	31
	Min	22	22	22	22	21	21	20	20	21	21	22	22
Humidity %	am	82	82	84	85	84	85	83	83	81	79	80	81
	pm	77	77	78	78	78	79	77	78	76	76	77	78
Precipitation	mm	252	244	429	142	102	76	53	43	53	89	150	249
Paris													
Temperature F	Max	42	45	55	61	69	75	80	79	73	61	50	43
	Min	30	31	37	42	49	55	59	58	53	45	38	33
Temperature C	Max	5	7	13	16	20	24	27	26	23	16	10	6
	Min	−1	0	3	6	9	13	15	14	12	7	4	0
Humidity %	am	89	87	87	84	83	82	79	85	89	92	91	90
	pm	80	72	60	56	56	55	50	54	60	69	78	80
Precipitation	mm	52	46	53	56	69	85	56	89	93	77	80	57
Port-of-Spain													
Temperature F	Max	87	88	89	90	90	89	88	88	89	89	89	88
	Min	69	68	68	69	71	71	71	71	71	71	71	69
Temperature C	Max	31	31	32	32	32	32	31	31	32	32	32	31
	Min	21	20	20	21	22	22	22	22	22	22	22	21
Humidity %	am	89	87	85	83	84	87	88	87	87	87	89	89
	pm	68	65	63	61	63	69	71	73	73	74	76	71
Precipitation	mm	69	41	46	53	94	193	218	246	193	170	183	125
Prague													
Temperature F	Max	49	53	64	73	82	88	91	89	84	71	57	50
	Min	7	10	18	29	36	44	49	47	38	29	24	14
Temperature C	Max	10	11	18	23	28	31	33	32	29	22	14	10
	Min	−13	−12	−8	−2	2	7	9	8	4	−2	−5	−10
Humidity %	am	84	83	82	77	75	74	77	81	84	87	87	87
	pm	73	67	55	47	45	46	49	48	51	60	73	78
Precipitation	mm	18	18	18	27	48	54	68	55	31	33	20	21
Rangoon													
Temperature F	Max	89	92	96	97	92	86	85	86	86	88	88	88
	Min	65	67	71	76	77	76	76	76	76	76	73	67
Temperature C	Max	32	33	36	36	33	30	29	29	30	31	31	31
	Min	18	19	22	24	25	24	24	24	24	24	23	19
Humidity %	am	71	72	74	71	80	87	89	89	87	83	79	75
	pm	52	52	54	64	76	75	88	88	86	77	72	61
Precipitation	mm	3	5	8	51	307	480	582	528	394	180	69	10
Rio de Janeiro													
Temperature F	Max	84	85	83	80	77	76	75	76	75	77	79	82
	Min	73	73	72	69	66	64	63	64	65	66	68	71
Temperature C	Max	29	29	28	27	25	24	24	24	24	25	26	28
	Min	23	23	22	21	19	18	17	18	18	19	20	22
Humidity %	am	82	84	87	87	87	87	86	84	84	83	82	82
	pm	70	71	74	73	70	69	68	66	72	72	72	72
Precipitation	mm	125	122	130	107	79	53	41	43	66	79	104	137
Rome													
Temperature F	Max	52	55	59	66	74	82	87	86	79	71	61	55
	Min	40	42	45	50	56	63	67	67	62	55	49	44
Temperature C	Max	11	13	15	19	23	28	30	30	26	22	16	13
	Min	5	5	7	10	13	17	20	20	17	13	9	6

		J	F	M	A	M	J	J	A	S	O	N	D
Rome cont'd													
Humidity %	am	85	86	83	83	77	74	70	73	83	86	87	85
	pm	68	64	56	54	54	48	42	43	50	59	66	70
Precipitation	mm	71	62	57	51	46	37	15	21	63	99	129	93
San Francisco													
Temperature F	Max	55	59	61	62	63	66	65	65	69	68	63	57
	Min	45	47	48	49	51	52	53	53	55	54	51	47
Temperature C	Max	13	15	16	17	17	19	18	18	21	20	17	14
	Min	7	8	9	9	11	11	12	12	13	12	11	8
Humidity %	am	85	84	83	83	85	88	91	92	88	85	83	83
	pm	69	66	61	61	62	64	69	70	60	58	60	68
Precipitation	mm	119	97	79	38	18	3	0	0	8	25	64	112
Singapore													
Temperature F	Max	86	88	88	88	89	88	88	87	87	87	87	87
	Min	73	73	75	75	75	75	75	75	75	74	74	74
Temperature C	Max	30	31	31	31	34	31	31	31	31	31	31	31
	Min	23	23	24	24	24	24	24	24	24	23	23	23
Humidity %	am	82	77	76	77	79	79	79	78	79	78	79	82
	pm	78	71	70	74	73	73	72	72	72	72	75	78
Precipitation	mm	252	173	193	188	173	173	170	196	178	208	254	257
Stockholm													
Temperature F	Max	30	30	37	47	58	67	71	68	60	49	40	35
	Min	23	22	26	34	43	51	57	56	49	41	34	29
Temperature C	Max	−1	−1	3	8	14	19	22	20	15	9	5	2
	Min	15	15	14	1	6	11	14	13	9	5	1	−2
Humidity %	am	85	83	82	76	66	68	74	81	87	88	89	88
	pm	83	77	68	60	53	55	59	64	69	76	85	86
Precipitation	mm	43	30	25	31	34	45	61	76	60	48	53	48
Sydney													
Temperature F	Max	78	78	76	71	66	61	60	63	67	71	74	77
	Min	65	65	63	58	52	48	46	48	51	56	60	63
Temperature C	Max	26	26	24	22	19	16	16	17	19	22	23	25
	Min	18	18	17	14	11	9	8	9	11	13	16	17
Humidity %	am	68	71	73	76	77	77	76	72	67	65	65	66
	pm	64	65	65	64	63	62	60	56	55	57	60	62
Precipitation	mm	89	102	127	135	127	117	117	76	74	71	74	74
Tehran													
Temperature F	Max	45	50	59	71	82	93	99	97	90	76	63	51
	Min	27	32	39	49	58	66	72	71	64	53	43	33
Temperature C	Max	7	10	15	22	28	34	37	36	32	24	17	11
	Min	−3	0	4	9	14	19	22	22	18	12	6	1
Humidity %	am	77	73	61	54	55	50	51	47	49	53	63	76
	pm	75	59	39	40	47	49	41	46	49	54	66	75
Precipitation	mm	46	38	46	36	13	3	3	3	3	8	20	31
Tokyo													
Temperature F	Max	47	48	54	63	71	76	83	86	79	69	60	52
	Min	29	31	36	46	54	63	70	72	66	55	43	33
Temperature C	Max	8	9	12	17	22	24	28	30	26	21	16	11
	Min	−2	−1	2	8	12	17	21	22	19	13	6	1
Humidity %	am	73	71	75	81	85	89	91	92	91	88	83	77
	pm	48	48	53	59	62	68	69	66	68	64	58	51
Precipitation	mm	48	74	107	135	147	165	142	152	234	208	97	56

		J	F	M	A	M	J	J	A	S	O	N	D
Vancouver													
Temperature F	Max	41	44	50	58	64	69	74	73	65	57	48	43
	Min	32	34	37	40	46	52	54	54	49	44	39	35
Temperature C	Max	5	7	10	14	18	21	23	23	18	14	9	6
	Min	0	1	3	4	8	11	12	12	9	7	4	2
Humidity %	am	93	91	91	89	88	87	89	90	92	92	91	91
	pm	85	78	70	67	63	65	62	62	72	80	84	88
Precipitation	mm	218	147	127	84	71	64	31	43	91	147	211	224
Vienna													
Temperature F	Max	34	38	47	58	67	73	76	75	68	56	45	37
	Min	25	28	30	42	50	56	60	59	53	44	37	30
Temperature C	Max	1	3	8	15	19	23	25	24	20	14	7	3
	Min	−4	−3	−1	6	10	14	15	15	11	7	3	−1
Humidity %	am	81	80	78	72	74	74	74	78	83	86	84	84
	pm	72	66	57	49	52	55	54	54	56	64	74	76
Precipitation	mm	39	44	44	45	70	67	84	72	42	56	52	45
Warsaw													
Temperature F	Max	32	32	42	53	67	73	75	73	66	55	42	35
	Min	22	21	28	37	48	54	58	56	49	41	33	28
Temperature C	Max	0	1	6	13	19	23	24	23	19	14	6	3
	Min	−7	−6	−2	3	8	12	14	13	9	5	1	−2
Humidity %	am	83	82	83	83	79	82	84	88	90	89	90	86
	pm	74	71	64	59	55	60	63	63	63	67	78	78
Precipitation	mm	27	24	25	43	57	88	105	93	58	50	43	43
Zurich													
Temperature F	Max	36	41	51	59	67	73	76	75	69	57	45	37
	Min	26	28	34	40	47	53	56	56	51	43	35	29
Temperature C	Max	2	5	10	15	19	23	25	24	20	14	7	3
	Min	−3	−2	1	4	8	12	14	13	11	6	2	−2
Humidity %	am	88	88	86	81	80	80	81	85	90	92	90	89
	pm	74	65	55	51	52	52	52	53	57	64	73	76
Precipitation	mm	74	69	64	76	101	129	136	124	102	77	73	64

Guide to Rainy Seasons

Within each region, the places mentioned in the table are arranged in order of decreasing latitude north of the equator, increasing latitude south of the equator. This is a reminder that at any given time of the year opposite seasons are to be found north and south of the equator. December to February, for example, bring winter to the northern hemisphere, summer to the southern hemisphere. In the belt stretching about up to 10° north and south of the equator, the equatorial climate tends to prevail: the seasons are almost indistinguishable from each other and rain, broadly speaking, is more evenly spread throughout the year than elsewhere. But a lot depends on altitude and other features of geographical location; proximity to the sea or to mountains, and the nature of prevailing winds and currents.

The places listed are not necessarily typical of other places within the same region or country. And they represent only a minute sample globally. Total annual rainfall should always be taken into account, since the rainy season in one place may be less wet than the dry season in another. At best, this table is a rough guide only.

+ represents a month having more than 1/12 of the annual total rainfall.
– represents a month having less than 1/12 of the annual total rainfall.
• indicates the month(s) with the highest average rainfall of the year.

	Total annual rainfall, cm	J	F	M	A	M	J	J	A	S	O	N	D	Latitude
Asia														
Istanbul, Turkey	80.5	+	+	+	–	–	–	–	–	–	+	+	•	41° 0′N
Beijing, China	134.1	–	–	–	–	–	+	•	•	+	–	–	–	39° 50′N
Seoul, Korea	125.0	–	–	–	–	–	+	•	•	+	–	–	–	37° 31′N
Tokyo, Japan	156.5	–	–	–	+	+	+	+	+	•	+	–	–	35° 45′N
Tehran, Iran	24.6	•	+	•	+	–	–	–	–	–	–	–	+	35° 44′N
Osaka, Japan	133.6	–	–	–	+	+	•	+	+	+	+	–	–	34° 40′N
Kabul, Afghanistan	34.0	–	+	•	•	–	–	–	–	–	–	–	–	34° 28′N
Beirut, Lebanon	89.7	•	+	+	–	–	–	–	–	–	–	+	•	33° 53′N
Damascus, Syria	22.4	•	•	–	–	–	–	–	–	–	–	+	+	33° 30′N
Baghdad, Iraq	15.0	+	+	•	+	–	–	–	–	–	–	+	+	33° 20′N
Nagasaki, Japan	191.8	–	–	–	+	+	•	+	+	+	–	–	–	32° 47′N
Amman, Jordan	27.9	•	•	+	–	–	–	–	–	–	–	+	+	32° 0′N
Jerusalem, Israel	53.3	•	•	+	–	–	–	–	–	–	–	+	+	31° 47′N
Shanghai, China	113.5	–	–	–	–	–	•	+	+	+	–	–	–	31° 15′N
Hankow (Wuhan), China	125.7	–	–	–	+	+	•	+	–	–	–	–	–	30° 32′N
Kuwait City, Kuwait	12.7	+	+	•	–	–	–	–	–	–	–	+	•	29° 30′N
Delhi, India	64.0	–	–	–	–	–	+	•	•	+	–	–	–	28° 38′N
Kathmandu, Nepal	142.7	–	–	–	–	+	+	•	•	+	–	–	–	27° 45′N
Agra, India	68.1	–	–	–	–	–	+	•	•	+	–	–	–	27° 17′N
Cherrapunji, India	1,079.8	–	–	–	–	+	•	•	+	+	–	–	–	25° 17′N
Taipei, Taiwan	212.9	–	–	+	–	+	+	+	•	+	–	–	–	25° 2′N
Karachi, Pakistan	18.3	–	–	–	–	–	–	•	+	–	–	–	–	24° 53′N
Riyadh, Saudi Arabia	9.1	–	+	+	•	+	–	–	–	–	–	–	–	24° 41′N
Guangzhou, China	164.3	–	–	–	+	+	•	+	+	–	–	–	–	23° 10′N
Calcutta, India	160.0	–	–	–	–	+	+	•	•	+	–	–	–	22° 36′N
Hong Kong	216.1	–	–	–	–	+	•	•	•	+	–	–	–	22° 11′N
Mandalay, Burma	82.8	–	–	–	–	•	•	+	+	+	+	–	–	22° 0′N
Jeddah, Saudi Arabia	8.1	–	–	–	–	–	–	–	–	–	–	•	•	21° 29′N

	Total annual rainfall, cm	J	F	M	A	M	J	J	A	S	O	N	D	Latitude
Hanoi, Vietnam	168.1	–	–	–	–	+	+	+	●	+	–	–	–	21° 5′N
Bombay, India	181.4	–	–	–	–	–	●	●	+	+	–	–	–	18° 55′N
Hyderabad, India	75.2	–	–	–	–	–	+	+	+	●	+	–	–	17° 10′N
Rangoon, Burma	261.6	–	–	–	–	+	+	●	+	+	–	–	–	16° 45′N
Manila, Philippines	208.5	–	–	–	–	–	+	●	●	+	+	–	–	14° 40′N
Bangkok, Thailand	139.7	–	–	–	–	+	+	+	+	●	+	–	–	13° 45′N
Madras, India	127.0	–	–	–	–	–	–	–	+	+	●	●	+	13° 8′N
Mangalore, India	329.2	–	–	–	–	–	●	●	+	–	–	–	–	12° 55′N
Aden (Perim Is.), Yemen People's Dem Rep (South)	4.8	+	–	+	–	–	–	–	+	●	–	–	–	12° 50′N
Colombo, Sri Lanka	236.5	–	–	–	+	●	+	–	–	–	●	●	–	6° 56′N
Sandakan, Malaysia	314.2	●	+	–	–	–	–	–	–	–	–	+	+	5° 53′N
Kuala Lumpur, Malaysia	244.1	–	–	+	●	+	–	–	–	+	+	+	–	3° 9′N
Singapore	241.3	●	–	–	–	–	–	–	–	–	+	●	●	1° 17′N
Djakarta, Indonesia	179.8	●	●	+	–	–	–	–	–	–	–	–	+	6° 9′S
Africa														
Algiers, Algeria	76.5	+	+	+	–	–	–	–	–	–	+	●	●	36° 42′N
Tangier, Morocco	90.2	+	+	+	+	–	–	–	–	–	+	●	+	35° 50′N
Tripoli, Libya	38.9	+	+	–	–	–	–	–	–	–	+	+	●	32° 49′N
Marrakech, Morocco	23.9	+	+	●	+	–	–	–	–	–	+	+	+	31° 40′N
Cairo, Egypt	3.6	+	+	+	–	–	–	–	–	–	–	–	+	30° 1′N
Tombouctou, Mali	24.4	–	–	–	–	–	+	●	●	+	–	–	–	16° 50′N
Khartoum, Sudan	17.0	–	–	–	–	–	–	+	●	+	–	–	–	15° 31′N
Dakar, Sénégal	55.4	–	–	–	–	–	–	+	●	+	–	–	–	14° 34′N
Zungeru, Nigeria	115.3	–	–	–	–	+	+	+	+	●	–	–	–	9° 45′N
Harar, Ethiopia	89.7	–	–	+	+	+	+	+	●	+	–	–	–	9° 20′N
Addis Ababa, Ethiopia	123.7	–	–	–	–	–	+	●	●	+	–	–	–	9° 2′N
Freetown, Sierra Leone	343.4	–	–	–	–	–	+	●	●	+	+	–	–	8° 30′N
Lagos, Nigeria	183.6	–	–	–	–	+	●	+	–	–	+	–	–	6° 25′N
Cotonou, Benin	132.6	–	–	+	+	●	●	–	–	–	+	–	–	6° 20′N
Monrovia, Liberia	513.8	–	–	–	–	+	●	●	–	+	+	–	–	6° 18′N
Accra, Ghana	72.4	–	–	+	+	+	●	–	–	–	+	–	–	5° 35′N
Mongalla, Sudan	94.5	–	–	–	+	+	+	●	+	+	+	–	–	5° 8′N
Libreville, Gabon	251.0	+	+	+	+	+	–	–	–	–	+	●	+	0° 25′N
Entebbe, Uganda	150.6	–	–	+	●	+	–	–	–	–	–	+	–	0° 3′N
Nairobi, Kenya	95.8	–	–	+	●	+	–	–	–	–	–	+	+	1° 20′S
Mombasa, Kenya	120.1	–	–	–	+	●	+	–	–	–	–	–	–	4° 0′S
Kinshasa, Zaïre	135.4	+	+	+	+	+	–	–	–	–	+	●	+	4° 20′S
Kananga, Zaïre	158.2	+	+	+	+	–	–	–	–	–	+	●	●	5° 55′S
Lilongwe, Malawi	78.7	●	●	+	–	–	–	–	–	–	–	–	+	14° 0′S
Lusaka, Zambia	83.3	●	+	+	–	–	–	–	–	–	–	+	+	15° 25′S
Harare, Zimbabwe	82.8	●	+	+	–	–	–	–	–	–	–	+	+	17° 50′S

	Total annual rainfall, cm	J	F	M	A	M	J	J	A	S	O	N	D	Latitu
Tamatave, Madagascar	325.6	+	+	•	+	–	+	+	–	–	–	–	–	18° 2′S
Beira, Mozambique	152.2	•	+	+	–	–	–	–	–	–	+	+	+	19° 50′
Johannesburg, South Africa	70.9	+	+	+	–	–	–	–	–	–	–	+	•	26° 10′
Maputo, Mozambique	75.9	•	+	+	–	–	–	–	–	–	–	+	+	26° 35′
Cape Town, South Africa	50.8	–	–	–	+	+	+	•	+	+	–	–	–	33° 55′
Sub-Arctic														
Reykjavik, Iceland	77.2	+	–	–	–	–	–	–	–	+	•	+	+	64° 10′
Australasia and Pacific														
Honolulu, HI, USA	64.3	•	+	+	–	–	–	–	–	–	–	+	•	21° 25′
Tulagi, Solomon Is.	313.4	+	•	+	–	–	–	–	–	–	–	–	+	8° 0′S
Port Moresby, Papua New Guinea	101.1	+	•	+	+	–	–	–	–	–	–	–	+	9° 24′
Manihiki, Cook Is.	248.2	•	+	–	–	–	–	–	–	–	+	+	+	10° 24′
Thursday Is., Australia	171.5	•	+	+	+	–	–	–	–	–	–	–	+	10° 30′
Darwin, Australia	149.1	•	+	+	–	–	–	–	–	–	–	+	+	12° 20′
Apia, Western Samoa	285.2	•	+	+	+	–	–	–	–	–	–	+	+	13° 50′
Cairns, Australia	225.3	+	+	•	+	–	–	–	–	–	–	–	+	16° 55′
Tahiti, French Polynesia	162.8	•	•	+	+	–	–	–	–	–	–	+	•	17° 45′
Suva, Fiji	297.4	+	+	•	–	–	–	–	–	–	–	–	+	18° 0′S
Perth, Australia	90.7	–	–	–	–	+	•	•	+	+	+	–	–	31° 57′
Sydney, Australia	118.1	–	+	+	•	+	+	+	–	–	–	–	–	33° 53′
Auckland, New Zealand	124.7	–	–	–	–	+	+	•	+	–	–	–	–	36° 52′
Melbourne, Australia	65.3	–	–	+	+	–	–	–	–	+	•	+	+	37° 40′
Wellington, New Zealand	120.4	–	–	–	–	+	+	•	+	–	+	–	–	41° 19′
Christchurch, New Zealand	63.8	+	–	–	–	+	+	•	–	–	–	–	+	43° 33′
Central America and Caribbean														
Monterey, Mexico	58.2	–	–	–	–	–	+	+	+	•	+	–	–	25° 40′
Mazatlán, Mexico	84.8	–	–	–	–	–	–	+	+	•	–	–	–	23° 10′
Havana, Cuba	122.4	–	–	–	–	+	+	+	+	+	•	–	–	23° 8′N
Mérida, Mexico	92.7	–	–	–	–	+	•	+	+	+	+	–	–	20° 50′
Mexico City, Mexico	74.9	–	–	–	–	–	+	•	+	+	–	–	–	19° 20′
Port-au-Prince, Haiti	135.4	–	–	–	+	•	–	–	+	+	+	–	–	18° 40′
Santo Domingo, Dominican Rep	141.7	–	–	–	–	+	+	+	+	•	+	+	–	18° 30′
Kingston, Jamaica	80.0	–	–	–	–	+	+	–	+	+	•	+	–	18° 0′N
Acapulco, Mexico	154.2	–	–	–	–	–	•	+	+	+	+	–	–	16° 51′
Salina Cruz, Mexico	102.6	–	–	–	–	–	–	+	+	•	–	–	–	16° 10′
Dominica, Leeward Is.	197.9	–	–	–	–	–	+	•	+	+	+	+	–	15° 20′
Guatemala City, Guatemala	131.6	–	–	–	–	+	•	+	+	+	+	–	–	14° 40′
Tegucigalpa, Honduras	162.1	–	–	–	–	–	•	+	–	+	+	–	–	14° 10′
San José, Costa Rica	179.8	–	–	–	–	+	+	+	+	•	•	–	–	10° 0′N
Balboa Heights, Panama	177.0	–	–	–	–	+	+	+	+	+	•	•	–	9° 0′N

	Total annual rainfall, cm	J	F	M	A	M	J	J	A	S	O	N	D	Latitude
South America														
Caracas, Venezuela	83.3	–	–	–	–	+	•	•	•	•	•	+	–	10° 30′N
Ciudad Bolivar, Venezuela	101.6	–	–	–	–	+	+	•	+	+	–	+	–	8° 5′N
Georgetown, Guyana	225.3	+	–	–	–	+	•	+	–	–	–	–	+	6° 50′N
Bogotá, Colombia	105.9	–	–	+	+	+	–	–	–	–	•	+	–	4° 34′N
Quito, Ecuador	112.3	+	+	+	•	+	–	–	–	–	–	–	–	0° 15′S
Belém, Brazil	243.8	+	•	•	+	+	–	–	–	–	–	–	–	1° 20′S
Guayaquil, Ecuador	97.3	•	•	•	+	–	–	–	–	–	–	–	–	2° 15′S
Manaus, Brazil	181.1	+	+	•	–	–	–	–	–	–	–	+	+	3° 0′S
Recife, Brazil	161.0	–	–	+	+	+	•	+	+	–	–	–	–	8° 0′S
Lima, Peru	4.8	–	–	–	–	+	+	+	•	•	–	–	–	12° 0′S
Salvador (Bahía), Brazil	190.0	–	–	–	•	•	+	+	–	–	–	–	–	13° 0′S
Cuiabá, Brazil	139.5	+	+	•	–	–	–	–	–	–	+	+	+	15° 30′S
Concepción, Bolivia	114.3	•	+	+	–	–	–	–	–	–	–	•	+	15° 50′S
La Paz, Bolivia	57.4	•	+	+	–	–	–	–	–	–	–	+	+	16° 20′S
Rio de Janeiro, Brazil	108.2	+	+	+	+	–	–	–	–	–	–	+	•	23° 0′S
São Paulo, Brazil	142.8	+	+	+	+	–	–	–	–	–	–	+	•	23° 40′S
Asunción, Paraguay	131.6	+	+	–	+	+	–	–	–	–	+	+	•	25° 21′S
Tucumán, Argentina	97.0	•	+	+	–	–	–	–	–	–	–	+	+	26° 50′S
Santiago, Chile	36.1	–	–	–	–	+	•	+	+	–	–	–	–	33° 24′S
Buenos, Aires, Argentina	95.0	–	–	+	+	–	–	–	–	–	+	+	•	34° 30′S
Montevideo, Uruguay	95.0	–	–	•	•	+	+	–	–	–	–	–	–	34° 50′S
Valdivia, Chile	260.1	–	–	–	+	+	•	+	+	–	–	–	–	39° 50′S

Sea Temperatures at 40 Resorts and Cities (in degrees Centigrade)

	J	F	M	A	M	J	J	A	S	O	N	D
Acapulco Mexico	24	24	24	25	26	27	28	28	28	27	26	25
Agadir Morocco	17	17	18	18	19	19	22	22	22	22	21	18
Algiers Algeria	15	14	15	15	17	20	23	24	23	21	18	16
Athens Greece	14	14	14	15	18	22	24	24	23	21	19	16
Bangkok Thailand	26	27	27	28	28	28	28	28	28	27	27	27
Barcelona Spain	13	12	13	14	16	19	22	24	22	21	16	14
Cairo Egypt	15	15	18	21	24	26	27	27	26	24	21	17

	J	F	M	A	M	J	J	A	S	O	N	D
Copenhagen Denmark	3	2	3	5	9	14	16	16	14	12	8	5
Corfu Greece	14	14	14	16	18	21	23	24	23	21	18	16
Dubrovnik Yugoslavia	13	13	13	15	17	22	23	24	22	19	16	14
Faro Portugal	15	15	15	16	17	18	19	20	20	19	17	16
Hong Kong	18	18	21	24	25	27	28	28	27	26	24	21
Honolulu Hawaii, USA	24	24	24	25	26	26	27	27	27	27	26	25
Istanbul Turkey	8	8	8	11	15	20	22	23	21	19	15	11
Kingston Jamaica	26	26	26	27	27	28	29	29	28	28	27	27
Las Palmas Canary Islands	19	18	18	18	19	20	21	22	23	23	21	20
Lisbon Portugal	14	14	14	15	16	17	18	19	19	18	16	15
Los Angeles USA	14	14	15	15	16	18	19	20	19	18	17	15
Malaga Spain	15	14	14	15	17	18	21	22	21	19	17	16
Malta	15	14	15	15	18	21	24	25	24	22	19	17
Miami USA	22	23	24	25	28	30	31	32	30	28	25	23
Mombasa Kenya	27	28	28	28	28	27	25	25	27	27	27	27
Naples Italy	14	13	14	15	18	21	24	25	23	21	18	16
Nassau Bahamas	23	23	23	24	25	27	28	28	28	27	26	24
New Orleans USA	13	14	17	21	26	28	30	30	28	23	18	14
New York USA	3	2	4	8	13	18	22	23	21	17	11	6
Nice France	13	12	13	14	16	20	22	23	21	19	16	14
Palma Majorca	14	13	14	15	17	21	24	25	24	21	18	15
Rio de Janeiro Brazil	25	25	26	25	24	23	22	22	22	22	23	24
Rome Italy	14	13	13	14	17	21	23	24	23	20	18	15
San Francisco USA	11	11	12	12	13	14	15	15	16	15	13	11
Stockholm Sweden	3	1	1	2	5	10	15	15	13	10	7	4
Sydney Australia	23	24	23	20	18	18	16	17	18	19	19	21
Tahiti Fr. Polynesia	27	27	27	28	28	27	26	26	26	26	27	27

	J	F	M	A	M	J	J	A	S	O	N	D
Tel Aviv Israel	16	16	17	18	21	24	25	27	27	24	21	18
Tenerife Canary Islands	19	18	18	18	19	20	21	22	23	23	21	20
Tunis Tunisia	15	14	14	15	17	20	23	25	24	22	19	16
Vancouver Canada	8	7	8	9	11	13	14	14	13	12	11	10
Venice Italy	9	8	10	13	17	21	23	24	21	18	14	11
Wellington New Zealand	17	18	18	17	14	14	13	13	12	14	14	17

Altitudes of Selected Cities (in metres)

City	Metres
Amsterdam, Netherlands	5
Asunción, Paraguay	77
Athens, Greece	0
Auckland, New Zealand	0
Bangkok, Thailand	12
Beirut, Lebanon	8
Bogotá, Colombia	2,590
Bridgetown, Barbados	0
Brussels, Belgium	58
Buenos Aires, Argentina	14
Calcutta, India	26
Cape Town, South Africa	8
Caracas, Venezuela	964
Casablanca, Morocco	49
Cayenne, French Guiana	8
Copenhagen, Denmark	8
Curaçao, Netherlands Antilles	0
Damascus, Syria	213
Dublin, Ireland	9
Frankfurt, West Germany	91
Geneva, Switzerland	377
Glasgow, Scotland	59
Guatemala City, Guatemala	1,478
Havana, Cuba	9
Helsinki, Finland	8
Hong Kong	8
Istanbul, Turkey	9
Jerusalem, Israel	762
Juneau, Alaska	0
Kabul, Afghanistan	2,219
Karachi, Pakistan	15
Kingston, Jamaica	8
La Paz, Bolivia	3,720
Lima, Peru	153
Lisbon, Portugal	87
Madrid, Spain	655
Manila, Philippines	8
Mexico City, Mexico	2,240
Montevideo, Uruguay	9
Moscow, USSR	191
Oslo, Norway	12
Panama City, Panama	12
Port-au-Prince, Haiti	8
Port-of-Spain, Trinidad	8
Quito, Ecuador	2,819
Rabat, Morocco	0
Rangoon, Burma	17
Rio de Janeiro, Brazil	9
Rome, Italy	14
St. George's, Grenada	0
St. John's, Antigua	0
Santiago, Chile	550
Singapore	8
Stockholm, Sweden	11
Suva, Fiji	0
Sydney, Australia	8
Tegucigalpa, Honduras	975
Tehran, Iran	1,220
Tokyo, Japan	9
Vienna, Austria	168

Weather Information

London Weather Centre
284–286 High Holborn
London
WC1V 7HX
Tel: 01-836 4311 Public Enquiries
430 5709 Climatological Enquiries
430 5511 General Enquiries.

Can answer all regional weather enquiries.

Meterological Office
(Overseas Enquiry Bureau)
Bracknell
Berkshire
Tel: (0344) 420242 Ext. 2267

National Meterological Center
5200 Auth Road
Camp Springs
MD 20233
USA

Is the head office. Regional and local offices can also give weather information.

International Time Comparison

Hours ahead (+) or behind (−) Greenwich Mean Time (GMT)

Afghanistan	+ 4½
Algeria	GMT
summer until late Oct.	+ 1
Angola	+ 1
Argentina	− 3
Australia	
New South Wales	+11
Queensland	+10
South Australia	+10½
Tasmania	+11
Victoria	+11
Western Australia	+ 8
summer until late Oct:	
NSW, Qld, Tas, Vic	+10
SA	+ 9½
WA	+ 8
Bahrain	+ 3
Bangladesh	+ 6
Belize	− 6
Benin	+ 1
Bhutan	+ 6
Bolivia	− 4
Botswana	+ 2
Brazil	
Fernando de Noronha	− 2
East, all coast and Brasilia	− 3
West	− 4
Territory of Acre	− 5
Brunei	+ 8
Bulgaria	+ 2
Burma	+ 6½
Burundi	+ 2
Cameroon	+ 1
Canada	
Atlantic Time	− 4
Central Time	− 6
Eastern Time	− 5
Mountain Time	− 7
Newfoundland	− 3½
Pacific Time	− 8
Yukon Territory	− 8
summer until late Oct:	
Atlantic Time	− 3
Central Time	− 5
Eastern Time	− 4
Mountain Time	− 6
Newfoundland	− 2½
Pacific Time	− 7
Yukon Territory	− 7
Cape Verde Is	− 1
Cayman Is	− 5
Central African Rep	+ 1
Chad	+ 1
Chile	− 3
mid-March until mid-Oct	− 4
China	+ 8
Colombia	− 5
Comoro Arch.	+ 3
Congo	+ 1
Cook Is	− 9½
summer until late Oct	−10

Costa Rica	− 6
Cuba	− 5
summer until mid-Oct	− 4
Djibouti	+ 3
Dominican Rep	− 4
Ecuador	− 5
Egypt	+ 2
El Salvador	− 6
Equatorial Guinea	+ 1
Ethiopia	+ 3
Falkland Is	− 4
Port Stanley	− 3
Fiji	+12
French Guiana	− 3
French Polynesia	−10
Gabon	+ 1
Gambia	GMT
Ghana	GMT
Guatemala	− 6
Guinea	GMT
Guinea-Bissau	GMT
Guyana	− 3
Haiti	− 5
Honduras	− 6
Hong Kong	+ 8
Iceland	GMT
India	+ 5½
Indonesia	
Central Zone (Kalimantan, Sulawesi, Timor)	+ 8
East Zone (Molucca Is, Irian Jaya)	+ 9
West Zone (Java, Sumatra, Bali)	+ 7
Iran	+ 3½
Iraq	+ 3
Israel	+ 2
Ivory Coast	GMT
Jamaica	− 5
summer until late Oct	− 4
Japan	+ 9
Jordan	+ 2
Kampuchea	+ 7
Kenya	+ 3
Kiribati Rep	+12
Korea, North	+ 9
Korea, South	+ 9
Kuwait	+ 3
Lao People's Dem Rep (Laos)	+ 7
Lebanon	+ 2
Lesotho	+ 2
Liberia	GMT
Libya	+ 2
Macao	+ 8
Madagascar	+3
Malawi	+2
Malaysia	
Peninsular Malaysia	+ 7½
Sabah, Sarawak	+ 8
Maldive Is	+ 5
Mali	GMT
Mauritania	GMT
Mauritius	+ 4
Mexico	
General Mexico Time	− 6
Lower California & N. Pacific Coast	− 7
Baja California Norte	− 8
summer until late Oct: Baja California Norte	− 7
Micronesia	
Caroline Is except Kusaie, Pingelap & Truk	+10
Guam and Mariana Is	+10
Kusaie, Pingelap	+12
Marshall Is (Kwajelein −12)	+12
Truk	+11
Morocco	GMT
Mozambique	+ 2
Nauru	+12
Nepal	+ 5
New Caledonia	+11
New Zealand	+13
summer until late Oct	+12
Nicaragua	− 6
Niger	+ 1
Nigeria	+ 1
Oman	+ 4
Pakistan	+ 5
Panama	− 5
Papua New Guinea	+10
Paraguay	− 3
Peru	− 5
Philippines	+ 8
Qatar	+ 3
Réunion	+ 4
Rwanda	+ 2
Samoa, American & Western	−11
São Tomé & Principe	GMT
Saudi Arabia	+ 3

Sénégal	GMT
Seychelles	+ 4
Sierra Leone	GMT
Singapore	+ 7½
Solomon Is	+11
Somalia	+ 3
South Africa	+ 2
Sri Lanka	+ 5½
Sudan	+ 2
Suriname	− 3½
Swaziland	+ 2
Syria	+ 2
Taiwan	+ 8
Tanzania	+ 3
Thailand	+ 7
Togo	GMT
Tonga	+13
Trinidad & Tobago	− 4
Tunisia	+ 1
Turkey	+ 3
Turks & Caicos Is	− 5
summer until late Oct	− 4
Tuvalu Is	+12
Uganda	+ 3
United Arab Emirates	+ 4
UK	GMT
mid-March until late Oct	+ 1
USA	
Central Time	− 6
Eastern Time	− 5
Hawaiian Is	−10
Mountain Time	− 7
Pacific Time	− 8
Alaska, Ketchikan to 58°N	− 8
58°N–141°W	− 9
141°W–162°W	−10
162°W–Western Tip	−11
summer until late Oct:	
Central Time	− 5
Eastern Time	− 4
Hawaiian Is	−10
Mountain Time	− 6
Pacific Time	− 7
Alaska, Ketchikan to 58°N	− 7
58°N–141°W	− 8
141°W–162°W	− 9
162°W–Western Tip	−10
USSR (Moscow)	+ 3
Upper Volta (Burkina Faso)	GMT
Uruguay	− 3
Vanuatu Rep	+11
Venezuela	− 4
Vietnam	+ 7
Yemen Arab Rep (North)	+ 3
Yemen People's Dem Rep (South)	+ 3
Zaïre	
Kasai, Katanga, Kivu, Orientale	+ 2
Kinshasa, Mbandaka	+ 1
Zambia	+ 2
Zimbabwe	+ 2

Communication

Vocabularies

English

1 Good morning
2 Good day
3 Good evening
4 Good night
5 Goodbye
6 Yes/No
7 Please
8 Thank you
9 I, you, he, she
10 Do you speak English?
11 I do not understand
12 Do you understand?
13 What is your name?
14 How are you?
15 Very well
16 How far?
17 How much is it?
18 Too much
19 You are welcome
20 Excuse me
21 I am sorry
22 What is this?
23 Where?
24 When?
25 Which way?
26 Do you have?
27 I want
28 Airport
29 Automobile
30 Bank
31 Barber
32 Beauty salon/parlour
33 Bed
34 Breakfast
35 Bus
36 Change/Money
37 Check/Bill
38 Church
39 Dentist
40 Dinner
41 Doctor
42 Exchange
43 Flat tyre/puncture
44 Gasoline/petrol
45 Hospital
46 Hotel
47 Information
48 Lavatory/Toilet
49 Lunch
50 Maybe
51 Men/Gentlemen
52 Occupied
53 Pharmacy
54 Post office
55 Registered letter
56 Room (Hotel)
57 Shop/Store
58 Sick
59 Sleep
60 Soap
61 Stamp (postage)
62 Station (railroad)
63 Suitcase
64 Telephone
65 Ticket (travel)
66 Time (of day)
67 Today
68 Tomorrow
69 Towel

70 Train
71 Waiter
72 Water (drinking)
73 Women/Ladies
74 Food
75 Milk
76 Cheese
77 Yogurt
78 Eggs
79 Meat
80 Tomato
81 Sugar
82 Good
83 Bad
84 Broken

French

1 Bonjour
2 Bonjour
3 Bon soir
4 Bonne nuit
5 Au revoir
6 Oui/Non
7 S'il vous plaît
8 Merci
9 Je, tu, il, elle
10 Parlez-vous anglais?
11 Je ne comprends pas
12 Comprenez-vous?
13 Comment vous appelez-vous?
14 Comment ça va?
15 Très bien
16 A quelle distance?
17 Combien?
18 Trop cher
19 De rien
20 Pardon
21 Je regrette
22 Qu'est-ce que c'est?
23 Où?
24 Quand?
25 Quelle direction?
26 Avez-vous?
27 Je veux
28 L'aéroport
29 Voiture
30 Banque
31 Friseur
32 Le salon de beauté
33 Le lit
34 Le petit déjeuner
35 L'autobus
36 La monnaie
37 Le compte
38 L'église
39 Le dentiste
40 dîner
41 Le médecin
42 Le bureau de change
43 Le pneu crevé
44 l'essence
45 L'hôpital
46 L'hôtel
47 Les renseignements
48 La toilette
49 Le déjeuner
50 Peut-être
51 Les hommes
52 Occupé
53 La pharmacie
54 Le bureau de poste
55 La lettre recommandée
56 La chambre
57 Le magasin
58 Malade
59 Dormir
60 Savon
61 Timbre
62 La gare
63 La valise
64 Téléphone
65 Le billet
66 L'heure
67 Aujourd'hui
68 Demain
69 La serviette
70 Le train
71 Garçon
72 L'eau
73 Dames
74 Le nourriture

75 Le lait
76 Le fromage
77 Le yaourt
78 Les oeux
79 La viande
80 Le tomate
81 Le sucre
82 Bon/bonne
83 Mauvais
84 Cassé

German

1 Guten Morgen
2 Guten Tag
3 Guten Abend
4 Gute Nacht
5 Auf Wiedersehen
6 Ja/Nein
7 Bitte
8 Danke
9 Ich, sie, er, sie
10 Sprechen Sie Englisch?
11 Das verstehe ich nicht
12 Verstehen Sie?
13 Wie Heißen Sie?
14 Wie geht's?
15 Gut
16 Wie weit?
17 Wieviel ist es?
18 Zuviel
19 Herzlich willkommen
20 Entschuldigen Sie!
21 Entschuldigung
22 Was ist das?
23 Wo?
24 Wann?
25 In welcher richtung
26 Haben Sie?
27 Ich möchte
28 Der Flughafen
29 Das Auto
30 Die Bank
31 Friseur
32 Der Schönheitssalon
33 Ein Bett
34 Das Frühstück
35 Der Bus
36 Das Geld
37 Die Rechnung
38 Die Kirche
39 Der Zahnarzt
40 Das Essen
41 Der Arzt
42 Wehsel
43 Platten
44 Das Benzin
45 Das Krankenhaus
46 Das Hotel
47 Die Auskunft
48 Die Toilette
49 Das Mittagessen
50 Vielleicht
51 Herren
52 Beschäftigt
53 Die Grogerie
54 Das Postamt
55 Eingeschriebener Brief
56 Das Zimmer
57 Das Geschäft
58 Krank
59 Schlafen
60 Die Seife
61 Eine Briefmarke
62 Der Bahnhof
63 Der Koffer
64 Das Telefon
65 Die Fahrkarte
66 Die Zeit
67 heute
68 morgen
69 Das Handtuch
70 Der Zug
71 Herr Ober
72 Das Wasser
73 Damen
74 Das Essen
75 Die Milch
76 Der Käse
77 Der Joghurt
78 Eier
79 Fleisch

80 Tomaten
81 Zucker
82 Gut
83 Schlecht
84 Kaputt

Italian

1 Buon giorno
2 Buon giorno
3 Buona sera
4 Buona notte
5 Ciao (familiar): Arrivederci (final)
6 Sì/No
7 Per favore
8 Grazie
9 Io, Tu, Lui, Lei
10 Parla inglese?
11 Non capisco
12 Capisci?
13 Come si chiama?
14 come sta?
15 Benissimo
16 Quanto dista
17 Quant'é
18 Troppo caro
19 Prego
20 Mi scusi
21 Mi dispiace
22 Che cosa questo
23 Dove
24 Quando
25 Qualevia
26 Avete?
27 Vorrei
28 Aeroporto
29 Macchina
30 Banca
31 Barbiere
32 Instituto di bellezza
33 Il letto
34 Prima colazione
35 Autobus
36 Il demaro
37 Il conto
38 La chiesa
39 Il dentista
40 Cena
41 medico
42 Cambio
43 Forata
44 Benzina
45 L'ospedale
46 Albergo
47 Informazioni
48 Gabinetti
49 Pranzo
50 Forse
51 Uomini/Signori
52 Occupato
53 Farmacia
54 Ufficio postale
55 Raccomandata
56 Camera
57 Il negozio
58 Sento male
59 Domire
60 Sapone
61 Francobollo
62 Stazione
63 Una valigia
64 Telefono
65 Biglietto
66 Il tempo
67 Oggi
68 Domani
69 Un asciugamano
70 Treno
71 Cameriere
72 Acqua minerale
73 Signore/donne
74 Il cibo
75 Latte
76 Formaggio
77 Yogurt
78 Uova
79 Carne
80 Pomodoro
81 Zucchero
82 Buono
83 Cattivo
84 Rotto

Spanish

1 Buenos dias
2 Buenos dias
3 Buenas noches
4 Buenas noches
5 Adios
6 Si/No
7 Por favor
8 Gracias
9 Yo, tu usted, ello, ella
10 ¿Habla usted Ingles?
11 No entiendo
12 ¿Entiende?
13 ¿Como se llama?
14 ¿Como esta?
15 Muy bien
16 ¿Hasta donde?
17 ¿Cuanto vale?
18 Demasiado
19 De nada
20 Perdoname
21 Lo siento
22 ¿Que es esto?
23 ¿Donde?
24 ¿Cuando?
25 ¿Por donde?
26 Tiene Vd?
27 Quiero
28 El aeropuerto
29 El coche
30 El banco
31 El barbero
32 Salon de belleza
33 La cama
34 Desayuno
35 El autobus
36 Cambio
37 La cuenta
38 La iglesia
39 La dentista
40 La cena
41 El medico
42 Cambio
43 Neumatico pinchado
44 La gasolina
45 El hospital
46 El hotel
47 Informacion
48 Lavabo/los servicios
49 Almuerzo
50 Quizas
51 Hombres (caballeros)
52 Occupado
53 Farmacia
54 El correro
55 Carta certificada
56 Habitacion
57 Tienda
58 Enfermo
59 Sueno
60 Jabon
61 El sello
62 La estacion
63 La maleta
64 Telefono
65 La billeta
66 La hora
67 Hoy
68 Mañana
69 Una servilleta
70 El tren
71 Camarero
72 Agua
73 Damas
74 La comida
75 El leche
76 Queso
77 Yogur
78 Huevos
79 Carne
80 Tomate
81 Azucar
82 Bueno
83 Mal
83 Roto
84 Broken

Greek

1 Kalimera
2 Kalimerasas

3 Kalispera
4 Kalinihta
5 Adio
6 Ne/Ohi
7 Parakolo
8 Efharisto
9 Egho, essi, aftos, afti
10 Milate Anglika?
11 Den karalaveno
12 Me katal avenete?
13 Thos-te moo?
14 Pos oste?
15 Poli kala
16 Posso makria
17 Posso ine
18 Ine pavapoli
19 Parakalo
20 Me sinhorite
21 Lipame poli
22 Tiine afto
23 Pou ine
24 Pote
25 Poss boro nah paho sto
26 Ehete
27 Thelo tha ithela
28 Aerodromio
29 Ahftokeeneelo
30 Trapeza
31 Kommotirio
32 Institouto Kallonis
33 Dhomahteeo
34 Proghevma
35 Leeforio
36 Lefta
37 Logháriasmos
38 Eklissia
39 Odhondoyeeahtro
40 Dhipno
41 Ghiatro
42 Trapeza
43 Lastiho
44 Venzini
45 Nossokomio
46 Sto ksehnoahokheeo
47 Pleerofoneeon
48 Tovaleta
49 Messimeriano faghito
50 Issos
51 Kirios
52 Katilimeno
53 Farmatio
54 Tahidhromio
55 Thelo na sklo afto to ghrama sistimeno
56 Thomatio
57 Magazi
58 Arostos
59 Kimitho
60 Ena sapooni
61 Ena grammatossimo
62 Strathmos
63 Valitsa
64 Tilefoniko
65 Issitiria
66 Khrono
67 Simera
68 Avrio
69 Petseta
70 Treno
71 Servitoros
72 Nero
73 Kirion
74 Fai
75 Gala
76 Tiri
77 Ghiaourti
78 Avgo
79 Greas
80 Domata
81 Zahari
82 Kala
83 Kakos
84 Spazmeno

Russian

1 Dobroye utro
2 Dobray den'
3 Dobray vyetchar
4 Dobray nochi
5 Dasvidanya
6 Da/Net
7 Pozhalsta

8 Spasiba
9 Ya, Vy, On, Ana'
10 Vui govorite po-angliiski?
11 Ne panimayou
12 Ve panimayeche
13 Kak vash zavout?
14 Kak dela?
15 Ochen harosho
16 Daleko?
17 Skol'ko stoit
18 Dorogoy
19 Pozhalsta
20 Izvinite
21 Minye zhal
22 Chto eto?
23 Gde
24 Kogda
25 Kuda
26 U vas yest?
27 Ya khotel bi
28 Aeroport
29 Avtomobil
30 Bank
31 Parikmakher
32 Parikmakherskaya
33 Kravach
34 Zavtrak
35 Avtobus
36 Dzengi
37 Afisha
38 Tser'kov
39 Zubnoyvrach
40 Obed
41 Doktor/vrach
42 Veksel
43 Proboi
44 Benzyn/Diesel
45 Balnitsa
46 Gostinitsa
47 Informatsiya
48 Toalet
49 Uzhin
50 Modzet bytch
51 Mudzshchine
52 Zanyato
53 Aptye
54 Pochta
55 Zakaznoye pismo
56 Komnata
57 Magazin
58 Bol'noi
59 Son
60 Mylo
61 Marku
62 Vokzal
63 Chemodan
64 Telefon
65 Bilet
66 Chasay
67 Sevodnya
68 Zavtra
69 Polotentse
70 Poezd
71 Djevouschha
72 Voda
73 Dzenshchtine
74 Eda
75 Moloka
76 Syr
77 Kefir
78 Yaytsa
79 Myaso
80 Pomidori
81 Saharu
82 Harasho
83 Ploho
84 Izlomannyi

Turkish

1 Gun aydin
2 Lyi gunler
3 Lyi geceler
4 Lyi geceler
5 Allahaismarladik
6 Evet/Hayir
7 Lutfen
8 Tesekkur ederim
9 Ben, sen, O
10 Temei angrighe bolo cho?
11 Anlamiyorum
12 Anliyormusum?

13 Isminez nedir?
14 Naislsinez?
15 Cok iyiyim
16 Nerede?
17 Ne kadar?
18 Cok pahali
19 Hos geldin
20 Pardon
21 Ozur dilerim
22 Bu ne dir?
23 Neresi?
24 Ne zaman?
25 Nereye?
26 Sizde varmidir?
27 Ben islerim
28 Hava limani
29 Araba
30 Banka
31 Berber
32 Guzellik salon
33 Yatak
34 Sahab kahvaltiis
35 Otobus
36 Para
37 Hesap
38 Kilise
39 Disci
40 Aksam yemegi
41 Doktor
42 Exchange
43 Igneile delme
44 Benzin
45 Hastahene
46 Otel
47 Malvmat
48 Tuvalet
49 Ogle yemegi
50 Belki
51 Kibar simfindan kimse
52 Mesgul
53 Eczacilik
54 Posta yazihane
55 Taahhutlu
56 Oda
57 Dukkan
58 Hasta
59 Uyku
60 Sabun
61 Posta pulu
62 Istasyon
63 Dagaj
64 Telefon
65 Bilet
66 Saat
67 Bugun
68 Yarin
69 Havlu
70 Tren
71 Garson
72 Su
73 Kadin
74 Yemek
75 Sut
76 Peynir
77 Yogurt
78 Ymurta
79 Et
80 Domates
81 Seter
82 Iya
83 Fena
84 Kirildi

Arabic

1 Sabah al-khair
2 Illah Bilkhayr
3 Masaa al Khayr
4 Tisbah 'ala khair
5 Fi aman illah
6 Naan/Laa
7 Mindfudluk
8 Ashkurak
9 Ana/Inta/Huwa/Hiya
10 Takallam ingleesi?
11 Ma ta arif
12 Tuf ham?
13 Shismak?
14 Shlonak?
15 Taib katheer
16 Cham masaafah?
17 Cham floos?

18 Waajid floos
19 Ahlan wa sahlan
20 Saamah
21 Anna mistassif
22 Shinoo haatha?
23 Wayn?
24 Mata?
25 Ay tariig?
26 Andak?
27 Ariid
28 Matar
29 Sayyaara
30 Bank
31 Hallaa
32 Bahu
33 Margad
34 El futoor
35 Bas
36 Floos
37 Hisab
38 Keneesa
39 Hakiim-issnaan
40 El-'asha
41 Tabiib
42 Baddal
43 Fuxt
44 Gaz
45 Mistashfa
46 Iukanda
47 Maluumaat
48 Bayt mayy
49 El-ghada
50 Yimkin
51 Asheb
52 Yihtau
53 Farmasiyy
54 Markaz maklab
55 Guraf
56 Daar
57 Makhzan
58 Mariidh
59 Naam
60 Saabunn
61 Taabi
62 Mahattah
63 Santa
64 Tilifon
65 Tazkara
66 Wagt
67 Al yom
68 Baachir
69 Manṣaf
70 Treen
71 Gersoon
72 Maay
73 Sawahib or Sahibat
74 Akil
75 Haliib
76 Jibin
77 Laban khamus
78 Bayl
79 Laham
80 Tamaat
81 Shakarr
82 Zahn
83 Mu zayn
84 Kharaab

Urdu (Hindi)

1 Namaste
2 Salam
3 Salam
4 Namaste
5 Khuda Hafiz
6 Haan/Nahee
7 Mahirbani
8 Shukryia
9 Mein, aap
10 Tum angrezi bol sakte ho?
11 Mujay samajh nahee ati
12 Apka sarnajh lagti hai
13 Apka naam kiya hai?
14 Ap khaiseh ho?
15 Bahut achchha hun
16 Kitneh dour?
17 Kitneh?
18 Bohuut mungha?
19 Koee baat na heea
20 Maaf korna
21 Maaf kiihayeh
22 Ye kiya hai?

23 Kahan?
24 Kub?
25 Consa rasta?
26 Ab ka pas hai?
27 Mujeh chahiyeh
28 Erodrom
29 Car
30 Beyk
31 Nai
32 Saundar -ya prasaadhan kee duka
33 Chaar pai
34 Naastaa
35 Bas
36 Pesai
37 Hysab
38 Gyrja
39 Dato kaa daaktaar
40 Khana
41 Daktar
42 Bidulna
43 Chhed
44 Petrol
45 Huspital
46 Hotel
47 Malumat
48 Paxana
49 Dopahar kaa khaanaa
50 Hu sukta hai
51 Saheb
52 Bharaa haa
53 Davaa khaanaa
54 Whad
55 Rajistar karnaa citthii
56 Camrah
57 Dukaan
58 Bimar
59 Sona
60 Sabwn
61 Tyket
62 Station
63 Sutkes
64 Telifun
65 Tyket
66 Wagt
67 Aaje
68 Kull
69 Tewlia
70 Gari
71 Bairaa
72 Pani
73 Begem
74 Khana
75 Dood
76 Paneer
77 Dahee
78 Andai
79 Goasht
80 Tamatar
81 Khand
82 Atcha
83 Bura
84 Toot gayer

Malay

1 Salamat pagi
2 Tabek
3 Tabek
4 Malam
5 Salamat jalan
6 Ya or Ada/Tidak
7 Silakan
8 Terema Kasi
9 Saya, owa, dia, dia
10 Buleh chacup bemasa ingris?
11 Tabuleh herti
12 Buleh herti?
13 Apa nama?
14 Apa kavar?
15 Banyak baik
16 Berapa jalan?
17 Berapa harga?
18 Sangat banyak
19 Tidak apa
20 Ampunkan saya
21 Saya sangat susa hati
22 Apa ini?/itu?
23 Mana?
24 Bila?
25 Apa jalan?

26 Ada
27 Saya mamu
28 Tempat kapal terrabang
29 Kreta
30 Kantor bangk
31 Jantan kedeh
32 Tukang chukur
33 Tempat tidur
34 Makan pagi
35 Bus
36 Wong/Duit
37 Kira Kira
38 Masjid (ingris)
39 Tukang gigi
40 Makan Malam
41 Tukang orang obat
42 Kedeh dapat wong
43 Tyre petcha
44 Miniak
45 Rumah sakit
46 Rumah makanan or hotel
47 I want to ask . . .
Saya mahu tanya . . .
48 Jamban
49 Tiffin
50 Barangkali
51 Jantan
52 Orang ada sina
53 Kedeh obat
54 Tampat kirim surat
55 Surat daftar
56 Bilek
57 Kedeh
58 Sakit
59 Tidur
60 Sabun
61 Stamp
62 Syation kreta api
63 Barang barang
64 Telephone
65 Ticket or surat
66 Wakth
67 Ini hari
68 Besok
69 Kain tangan
70 Kreta api
71 Boy/waiter
72 Ayer
73 Perumpuan
74 Makan
75 Sush
76 Keju
77 Yogat
78 Telor
79 Daging
80 Buah tomato
81 Gula
82 Baik
83 Jahat (people)
Busuk (fruit)
84 Petcha

Swahili

1 Habari za asubuhi
2 Jambo
3 Habari za jioni
4 Hala salama
5 Kwa heri
6 Ndio/Hapana (hata)
7 Tafadhali
8 Ahsante sana
9 Mimi, wewe
10 Unasema Kiingereza?
11 Sielewi
12 Unaelewa?
13 Jina lako nami?
14 Habari yako?/Habari gani?
15 Nzvrisana
16 Ni umnbli gani?
17 Pesa ngapi (money)
Bei gani (what price)
18 Ghali sana
19 Izuri
20 Aisei (attracting attention)
Samahani (asking apology)
21 Samahani (general apology)
Pole (sympathy)
22 Hiki ni Kitu gani?
23 Wapi?
24 Lini?
25 Njia gani?
26 (wewe) una . . .
Kuna . . . (is there . . ?)

7 (Mimi) naomba (polite)
(Mimi) nataka

8 Stesheni ndege

9 Gari (any vehicle)
Motokaa

0 Nyumba ya kuwekea

1 kinyozi

2 uzuri sebule kubwa

3 Kitanda

4 Chmshakinywa

5 Kifupi chaonnibus

6 Pesa

7 Hati ya fedha

8 Kanisa

9 Daktari wa meno

0 Taz

1 Daktari

2 Badalisha

3 Choma

4 Mafuta ya motafaa

5 Hospitali

6 Hoteli

7 Habari

8 Kivao

9 Chakula cha adhuhuri

0 Labda

1 Mw ungwana

2 Twaa

3 Duka la mw uza dawa

4 Posta

5 Barua ya regista

6 Chumba

7 Duka

8 Ninaumura (I am sick)
Ugonjura (sickness)

9 Iala

0 Sabuni

1 Tikiti ya posta

2 Stesheni ya gari la moshi

3 Kasha jepesi la kuchukulia nguo

4 Simu ya kupelekea asuti mbali

5 Cheti

6 Wakati/saa

7 Leo

8 Kesho

9 Kitambaa

0 Fundisha

71 Mtumishi

72 maji (ya kunywa)

73 Akina bibi

74 Chakula

75 Maziuara

76 Chizi

77 Maziura ya mgando

78 Nyama

79 Nyma

80 Nyanya

81 Sukari

82 Nzuri/Nzuri sana

83 Baya

84 Vunjika

Numbers 1–20

French

Un
deux
trois
quatre
cinq
six
sept
huit
neuf
dix
onze
douze
treize
quatorze
quinze
seize
dix-sept
dix-huit
dix-neuf
vingt

German

ein
zwei
drei
vier
funf
sechs
sieben
acht
neun
zehn
elf
zwolf

dreizehn
vierzehn
funfzehn
sechzehn
siebzehn
achtzehn
neunzehn
swanzig

Italian

uno
due
tre
quattro
cinque
sei
sette
otto
nove
dieci
undici
dodici
tredici
quattordici
quindici
sedici
diciassette
diciotto
diciannove
venti

Spanish

uno
dos
tres
cuatro
cinco
seis
siete
ocho
nueve
diez
once
doce
trece
catorce
quince
dieciseis
diecisiete
dieciocho
diecinueve
veinte

Arabic

wahed
ithnain
thalatha
arba's
khamsa
sitta
sab'a
thamia
tis'a
'ashra
ahad'ashar
ithna'ashar
thalathat'ashar
'arba'at'ashar
sittat'ashar
saba'at'ashar
thamaniat'ashar
tis'at'ashar
'ishreen

Greek

ena
theeo
treea
tessera
pende
exee
epta
okto
enea
theka
endeka
thotheka
thekatreea
thekatessera
thekapende
thekaexee
thekaepta
thekaokto
thekaenea
eekossee

Malay

satu
dva
tiga
empat
lima
enam
tujuh
lapan
sembilan
se pulah
sebelas
tiga belas
lima belas
tujuh belas
sembilan belas
dva belas
empat belas
enam belas
lapan belas
dva belas
puluh

Russian

udeen'
dva

tree
chyety'rye
pyat
shest
syem
vo'syem
dye'vyat
dye'syat
udeen'atsut
dvyenat'sut
treenat'sut
chetyr'natsut
pyatnat'sut
shestnat'sut
syemnat'sut
vosyemnat'sut
dyevyatnat'sut
dvat'sut

Swahili

mjoa
mbili
tatu
nne
tano
sita
saba
nane
tisa
kumi
kumi na moja
kumi na mbili
kumi na tatu
kumi na nne
kumi na tano
kumi na sita
kumi na saba
kumi na nane
ishirini

Turkish

bir
iki
uc
dort
bes
alti
yedi
sekiz
dokuz
on
on bir
on iki
on uc
on dort
on bes
on alti
on yedi
on sekiz
on dokuz
yirmi

Urdu (Hindi)

ek
do
tin
char
panca
chhe
sat
ath
nan
das
gyarah
barah
terah
chaudah
panarah
solah
satrah
atharah
unnis
bis

The Arabic Alphabet

Arabic letter	Symbol used in the phonetic transcription	Arabic letter	Symbol used in the phonetic transcription
أ	a	ض	dh*
ب	b	ط	t*
ت	t	ظ	dh*
ث	th	ع	
ج	j	غ	gh
ح	h*	ف	f
خ	kh	ق	g
د	d	ك	k
ذ	dh	ل	l
ر	r	م	m
ز	z	ن	n
س	s	ه	h
ش	sh	و	w, oo or ou
ص	s*	ى	y, ee or ai

Letters marked with the asterisk * are difficult to describe with reference to English, but are here given their nearest equivalent. There is however a difference in pronunciation between the letters ة and ح ، س and ص ظ ، ض and ذ and ط and ت although they are transcribed ح and ة = h, ص and س = s, and ض ، ظ and ذ = dh. Short vowels are not normally represented in the Arabic script, so بن (bn) represents bun (coffee beans). Certain letters have different forms, depending on whether they occur at the end of a word (final) or elsewhere (non-final). The non-final forms are shorter.

The Greek Alphabet

Greek		English equivalent	Phonetic pronunciation	Greek		English equivalent	Phonetic pronunciation
Α	α	a	as in bar	Ξ	ξ	x	like ks in thanks
Β	β	v		Ο	ο	o	as in bone
Γ	γ	g	as in go*	Π	π	p	
Δ	δ	d	like th in this	Ρ	ρ	r	
Ε	ε	e	as in get	Σ	σ, ς	s	as in kiss
Ζ	ζ	z		Τ	τ	t	
Η	η	i	like ee in meet	Υ	υ	i	like ee in meet
Θ	θ	th	as in thin	Φ	φ	f	
Ι	ι	i	like ee in meet	Χ	χ	ch	as in Scottish loch
Κ	κ	k		Ψ	ψ	ps	as in tipsy
Λ	λ	l		Ω	ω	o	as in bone
Μ	μ	m		ΟΥ	ου	ou	as in soup
Ν	ν	n					

* except before i- and e-sounds, when it's pronounced like y in yes

The Russian Alphabet

Russian		Character	English equivalent	Phonetic pronunciation	Phonetics used
А	а	*А а*	a	(*ah*) as in p*ar*tner	ah
Б	б	*Б б*	b	(*beh*) like *b* in *b*ump	b
В	в	*В в*	v	(*veh*) like *v* in *v*ine	v
Г	г	*Г г*	g	(*geh*) like *g* in *g*one	g, gh
Д	д	*Д д*	d	(*deh*) like *d* in *d*uck	d
Е	е	*Е е*	e	(*yen*) like *ye* in *ye*s	e
Ё	ё	*Ё ё*	—	(*yaw*) as in *yaw*n	—
Ж	ж	*Ж ж*	zh	(*zheh*) as *s* in lei*s*ure	zh
З	з	*З з*	z	(*zeh*) like *z* in *z*ero	z
И	и	*И и*	i	(*ee*) as *ee* in s*ee*	ee
Й	й	*Й й*	—	combination with vowel	—
К	к	*К к*	k	(*kah*) like *k* in *k*iss	k
Л	л	*Л л*	l	(*el*) as *l* in *l*ook	l
М	м	*М м*	m	(*em*) as *m* in *m*oon	m
Н	н	*Н н*	n	(*en*) as *n* in *n*ot	n
О	о	*О о*	o	(*o*) like *o* in j*o*b	o
П	п	*П п*	p	(*peh*) like *p* in *p*ie	p
Р	р	*Р р*	r	(*reh*) like *r* in ar*r*est	r
С	с	*С с*	s	(*ess*) like *s* in ma*s*s	s
Т	т	*Т т*	t	(*teh*) like *t* in *t*ask	t
У	у	*У у*	u	(*oo*) like *oo* in n*oo*n	oo
Ф	ф	*Ф ф*	f	(*ef*) as *f* in *f*at	f
Х	х	*Х х*	kh	(*khah*) as *kh* in *kh*aki	kh
Ц	ц	*Ц ц*	ts	(*tseh*) as *ts* in si*ts*	ts
Ч	ч	*Ч ч*	ch	(*cheh*) as *ch* in *ch*ill	ch
Ш	ш	*Ш ш*	sh	(*shah*) like *sh* in *sh*op	sh
Щ	щ	*Щ щ*	shsh	(*shshah*)	shsh
Ъ	ъ	*ъ*	—	HARDMARK	
Ы	ы	*ы*	—	(*very*) as *i* in m*i*tt	y
Ь	ь	*ь*	—	SOFTMARK	—
Э	э	*Э э*	e	(*eh*) like *e* in s*e*nd	e
Ю	ю	*Ю ю*	yoo	(*yoo*) as in *you*	yoo
Я	я	*Я я*	yah	(*yah*) unaccented *ya*	yah, ya

The Morse Code

The principal methods used for transmission of messages of the Morse Code are sound, flashing light, telegraphy, and line telegraphy.

Construction of the Morse Code

Symbols of the Morse Code are expressed by an arrangement of dots and dashes, as shown below. A dot is used as the unit of duration. A dash is equal to three units (or dots). The space between each dot or dash is one unit; between special characters three units; and between words seven units.

Alphabet

A	. –	N	– .
B	– . . .	O	– – –
C	– . – .	P	. – – .
D	– . .	Q	– – . –
E	.	R	. – .
F	. . – .	S	. . .
G	– – .	T	–
H	. . . .	U	. . –
I	. .	V	. . . –
J	. – – –	W	. – –
K	– . –	X	– . . –
L	. – . .	Y	– . – –
M	– –	Z	– – . .

Numerals

1	. – – – –	6	– . . . .
2	. . – – –	7	– – . . .
3	. . . – –	8	– – – . .
4	. . . . –	9	– – – – .
5	. . . . .	0	– – – – –

Special Characters

The bar over two or more letters indicates that they are to be transmitted as a single character.

$\overline{AA}$	. – . –	Unknown station call.
$\overline{AR}$	. – . – .	End of transmission sign is used when no receipt is required.
$\overline{BT}$	– . . . –	Long break. Precedes and follows the text portion of the message.
EEEEEEEE	. . . .	Error. A succession of eight or more Es means 'Erase the portion of the message just transmitted; the correct portion will follow': or if followed by AR means, 'Cancel this message'.
$\overline{IMI}$	. . – – . .	Repeat. Made by the recipient, to the originator. If made alone means 'Repeat all of your last transmission'. If the sign is followed by the letters AA (all after), AB (all before), WA (word after) or WB (word before), followed by a word, then it means 'Repeat only that portion of the message so indicated'. It is used by the originator to precede the second transmission of the whole, or a portion of the message.
K	– . –	'Invitation to transmit' or 'This is the end of my transmission to you and a response is necessary'.
R	. – .	Received; means 'I have received your last transmission'.
AAA	. – . – . –	Period. A full stop in plain language.

INTERNATIONAL SEARCH AND RESCUE SIGNS

Require map and compass	□
Require fuel and oil	L
All is well	LL
Vehicle damaged	L⅂
Require medical attention	—
Require medical supplies	=

Cannot proceed	X
Require food and water	F
Require an engineer	W
Yes	Y
No	N
Do not understand	⅃L
Require light and radio	—|—
Require firearms and ammunition	⩔
Proceeding in this direction	↑
Indicate direction to be taken	K
Require clothing	≡
Safe to land (in this direction)	←
Do not land here	✱
Shall try to continue	<|

Metric Data Conversion Table

Imperial units to Metric (SI) units

Quantity	*Imperial unit*	*SI equivalent* *Accurate*	*Rough approximation*
Length	inch	0.0254m	4 in = 10cm
	foot	0.3048m	10ft = 3m
	yard	0.9144m	10yds = 9m
	mile	1.6093km	10 miles = 16km
Area	sq inch	645.16mm^2 (sq millimetres)	
	sq foot	0.0929m^2	100sq ft = 9.3m^2
	sq yard	0.836m^2	100sq yd = 84m^2
	sq mile	2.58999km^2	10sq miles = 26km^2
	acre	0.40469ha (hectare) 4046.9m^2	10 acres = 4ha 1 acre = 4,000m^2
Volume	cu inch	1.6387×10^{-5}m^3	1cu in = 16cm^3
	cu foot	0.0283m^3	1cu ft = 28 litres 1,000cu ft = 28m^3
	UK gallon	0.004546m^3	1 UK gal = 4.5 litres 1,000 UK gal = 4.5m^3
Mass	ounce	0.0284kg	1oz = 28gm
	pound	0.4536kg	10lb = 4.5kg
Pressure	pound per sq inch	6894.8N/m^2 (newtons per sq metre)	1lb/sq in = 7,000N/m^2 10lb/sq in = 7N/cm^2
Density	pound per cu foot	16.018kg/m^3	1lb/cu ft = 16kg/m^3
Temperature	degree Fahrenheit (°F)	0.555 degree Celsius (C)	
Temperature scale	t°F	5/9(t°F × 32)C (e.g. 70°F = 21.1C 80°F = 26.7C 90°F = 32.2C)	
Power	horsepower	0.7457kw	10hp = 7.5kw
Force	pound force	4.4482N	10lbf = 44.5N

Metric (SI) units to Imperial units

Quantity	*SI unit*	*Imperial equivalent* *Accurate*	*Rough approximation*
Length	centimetre (cm)	0.394in	10cm = 4in
	metre (m)	3.281ft 1.094yds	10m = 33ft
	kilometre (km)	0.621 miles	100km = 62 miles
Area	square metre (m^2)	10.764 sq ft	$10m^2$ = 12sq yds
	hectare ($10,000m^2$)	2.471 acres	1ha = 2.5 acres = 12,000sq yds
	square kilometre (km^2)	0.386sq miles	$100km^2$ = 40sq miles
Volume	cu metre (m^3)	35.315cu ft	$1m^3$ = 35cu ft $1m^3$ = 1.3cu yds
	litre (1)	0.22 UK gal	100 litres = 3.5cu ft = 22 UK gal
Mass	kilogramme (kg)	2.205lb	10kg = 22lb
	gramme (g)	0.035oz	100g = 3.5oz
Pressure	newtons per sq metre (N/m^2)	1.4504×10^{-4}lb/sq in	$1N/m^2 = 1.5 \times 10^{-4}$ lb/in^2 or 16/sq in
Density	kilogramme per cu metre (kg/m^3)	0.062lb/cu ft	$100kg/m^3$ = 6lb/cu ft
	gramme per cu cm (g/cm^3)	0.036lb/cu in	$30g/cm^3$ = 6lb/cu ft
Temperature	degree Celsius (C)	1.8° Fahrenheit (°F)	
Temperature scale	tC	= (9/5tC + 32)°F (e.g. 20C = 68°F 30C = 86°F 40C = 104°F)	
Power	kilowatts	1.341hp	1kw = 1.3hp
Force	newton	0.22481lbf	IN = 0.22lbf

Other Conversion Data

	unit	*equivalent*
Velocity	knot	0.8684 miles per hour
	mile per hour	1.1515 knots
Volume	UK gallon	0.8333 US gallons
	US gallon	1.2 UK gallons

* *See page 701 for Metric Tyre Pressure Conversion and page 702 for Liquid Conversion Charts.*

Index